Collins

POCKET

Spanish
Dictionary

HarperCollins Publishers
Westerhill Road
Bishopbriggs
Glasgow
G64 2QT

Seventh Edition 2013

10 9 8 7 6 5 4

© HarperCollins Publishers 2013, 2010, 2007, 2002, 1995

ISBN 978-0-00-748548-2

Collins® is a registered trademark of HarperCollins Publishers Limited

www.collins.co.uk

A catalogue record for this book is available from the British Library

Typeset by Aptara in India and Davidsons Publishing Solutions, Glasgow

Printed in China by RR Donnelly APS

Acknowledgements

We would like to thank those authors and publishers who kindly gave permission for copyright material to be used in the Collins Corpus. We would also like to thank Times Newspapers Ltd for providing valuable data.

ÍNDICE

CONTENTS

PROJECT MANAGEMENT
Carol McCann

CONTRIBUTORS
Teresa Álvarez García
Gaëlle Amiot-Cadey
Cordelia Lilly
Val McNulty
Complexli

COMPUTING
Thomas Callan

FOR THE PUBLISHER
Lucy Cooper
Kerry Ferguson
Ruth O'Donovan
Elaine Higgleton

SERIES EDITOR
Rob Scriven

INTRODUCCIÓN

Estamos muy satisfechos de que hayas decidido comprar este diccionario y esperamos que lo disfrutes y que te sirva de gran ayuda ya sea en el colegio, en el trabajo, en tus vacaciones o en casa.

Esta introducción pretende darte algunas indicaciones para ayurdarte a sacar el mayor provecho de este diccionario; no sólo de su extenso vocabulario, sino de toda la información que te proporciona cada entrada. Esta te ayudará a leer y comprender – y también a comunicarte y a expresarte – en inglés moderno. Este diccionario comienza con una lista de abreviaturas utilizadas en el texto y con una ilustración de los sonidos representados por los símbolos fonéticos.

EL MANEJO DE TU DICCIONARIO

La amplia información que te ofrece este diccionario aparece presentada en distintas tipografías, con caracteres de diversos tamaños y con distintos símbolos, abreviaturas y paréntesis. Los apartados siguientes explican las reglas y símbolos utilizados.

ENTRADAS

Las palabras que consultas en el diccionario – las entradas – aparecen ordenades alfabéticamente y en color para una identificación más rápida. La palabra que aparece en la parte superior de cada página es la primera entrada (si aparece en la página izquierda) y la última entrada (si aparece en la página derecha) de la página en cuestión. La información sobre el uso o la forma de determinadas entradas aparece entre paréntesis, detrás de la transcripción fonética, y generalmente en forma abreviada y en cursiva

(p. ej.: (*fam*), (*Com*)). En algunos casos se ha considerado oportuno agrupar palabras de una misma familia (**nación, nacionalismo; accept, acceptance**) bajo una misma entrada que aparece en color.

Las expresiones de uso corriente en las que aparece una entrada se dan en negrita (p. ej.: **hurry:** [...] **to be in a ~**).

SÍMBOLOS FONÉTICOS
La transcripción fonética de cada entrada inglesa (que indica su pronunciación) aparece entre corchetes, inmediatamente después de la entrada (p. ej. **knife** [naif]). En las páginas xv-xviii encontrarás una lista de los símbolos fonéticos utilizados en este diccionario.

TRADUCCIONES
Las traducciones de las entradas aparecen en caracteres normales, y en los casos en los que existen significados o usos diferentes, éstos aparecen separados mediante un punto y coma. A menudo encontrarás también otras palabras en cursiva y entre paréntesis antes de las traducciones. Estas sugieren contextos en los que la entrada podría aparecer (p. ej.: **alto** (*persona*) o (*sonido*)) o proporcionan sinónimos (p. ej.: **mismo** (*semejante*)).

PALABRAS CLAVE
Particular relevancia reciben ciertas palabras inglesas y españolas que han sido consideradas palabras 'clave' en cada lengua. Estas pueden, por ejemplo, ser de utilización muy corriente o tener distintos usos (**de, haber; get, that**). La combinación de triángulos y números te permitirá

distinguir las diferentes categorías gramaticales y los diferentes significados. Las indicaciones en cursiva y entre paréntesis proporcionan además importante información adicional.

FALSOS AMIGOS

Las palabras que se prestan a confusión al traducir han sido identificadas. En tales entradas existen unas notas que te ayudaran a evitar errores.

INFORMACIÓN GRAMATICAL

Las categorías gramaticales aparecen en forma abreviada y en cursiva después de la transcripción fonética de cada entrada (*vt*, *adv*, *conj*). También se indican la forma femenina y los plurales irregulares de los sustantivos del inglés (**child, -ren**).

INTRODUCTION

We are delighted that you have decided to buy this Spanish dictionary and hope you will enjoy and benefit from using it at school, at home, on holiday or at work.

This introduction gives you a few tips on how to get the most out of your dictionary – not simply from its comprehensive wordlist but also from the information provided in each entry. This will help you to read and understand modern Spanish, as well as communicate and express yourself in the language. This dictionary begins by listing the abbreviations used in the text and illustrating the sounds shown by the phonetic symbols.

USING YOUR DICTIONARY

A wealth of information is presented in the dictionary, using various typefaces, sizes of type, symbols, abbreviations and brackets. The various conventions and symbols used are explained in the following sections.

HEADWORDS

The words you look up in a dictionary – 'headwords' – are listed alphabetically. They are printed in **colour** for rapid identification. The headwords appearing at the top of each page indicate the first (if it appears on a left-hand page) and last word (if it appears on a right-hand page) dealt with on the page in question.

Information about the usage or form of certain headwords is given in brackets after the phonetic spelling. This usually appears in abbreviated form and in italics (e.g. (*fam*), (*Com*)).

Where appropriate, words related to headwords are grouped in the same entry (**nación, nacionalismo; accept, acceptance**) and are also in colour. Common expressions in which the headword appears are shown in a different bold roman type (e.g. **cola:** [...] **hacer ~**).

PHONETIC SPELLINGS

The phonetic spelling of each headword (indicating its pronunciation) is given in square brackets immediately after the headword (e.g. **cohete** [ko^{1}ete]). A list of these symbols is given on pages xv–xviii.

TRANSLATIONS

Headword translations are given in ordinary type and, where more than one meaning or usage exists, these are separated by a semi-colon. You will often find other words in italics in brackets before the translations. These offer suggested contexts in which the headword might appear (e.g. **fare** (*on trains, buses*)) or provide synonyms (e.g. **litter** (*rubbish*) o (*young animals*)). The gender of the Spanish translation also appears in italics immediately following the key element of the translation, except where this is a regular masculine singular noun ending in 'o', or a regular feminine noun ending in 'a'.

KEY WORDS

Special status is given to certain Spanish and English words which are considered as 'key' words in each language. They may, for example, occur very frequently or have several types of usage (e.g. **de, haber; get, that**). A combination of triangles and numbers helps you to distinguish different parts of speech and different meanings. Further helpful information is provided in brackets and italics.

FALSE FRIENDS
Words which can be easily confused have been identified in the dictionary. Notes at such entries will help you to avoid these common translation pitfalls.

GRAMMATICAL INFORMATION
Parts of speech are given in abbreviated form in italics after the phonetic spellings of headwords (e.g. *vt*, *adv*, *conj*). Genders of Spanish nouns are indicated as follows: *nm* for a masculine and *nf* for a feminine noun. Feminine and irregular plural forms of nouns are also shown (**irlandés, esa; luz** (*pl* **luces**)).

ABREVIATURAS

ABBREVIATIONS

abreviatura	*ab(b)r*	abbreviation
adjetivo, locución adjetiva	*adj*	adjective, adjectival phrase
administración	*Admin*	administration
adverbio, locución adverbial	*adv*	adverb, adverbial phrase
agricultura	*Agr*	agriculture
anatomía	*Anat*	anatomy
Argentina	*Arg*	Argentina
arquitectura	*Arq, Arch*	architecture
Australia	*Aust*	Australia
el automóvil	*Aut(o)*	the motor car and motoring
aviación, viajes aéreos	*Aviac, Aviat*	flying, air travel
biología	*Bio(l)*	biology
botánica, flores	*Bot*	botany
inglés británico	BRIT	British English
Centroamérica	CAM	Central America
química	*Chem*	chemistry
comercio, finanzas, banca	*Com(m)*	commerce, finance, banking
informática	*Comput*	computing
conjunción	*conj*	conjunction
construcción	*Constr*	building
compuesto	*cpd*	compound element
Cono Sur	CS	Southern Cone
cocina	*Culin*	cookery
economía	*Econ*	economics
eletricidad, electrónica	*Elec*	electricity, electronics
enseñanza, sistema escolar y universitario	*Escol*	schooling, schools and universities
España	ESP	Spain
especialmente	*esp*	especially
exclamación, interjección	*excl*	exclamation, interjection
femenino	*f*	feminine
lengua familiar (! vulgar)	*fam(!)*	colloquial usage (! particularly offensive)
ferrocarril	*Ferro*	railways
uso figurado	*fig*	figurative use
fotografía	*Foto*	photography
(verbo inglés) del cual la partícula es inseparable	*fus*	(phrasal verb) where the particle is inseparable
generalmente	*gen*	generally
geografía, geología	*Geo*	geography, geology

ABREVIATURAS

ABBREVIATIONS

geometría	*Geom*	geometry
historia	*Hist*	history
uso familiar	*inf(!)*	colloquial usage
(! vulgar)		(! particularly offensive)
infinitivo	*infin*	infinitive
informática	*Inform*	computing
invariable	*inv*	invariable
irregular	*irreg*	irregular
lo jurídico	*Jur*	law
América Latina	*LAm*	Latin America
gramática, lingüística	*Ling*	grammar, linguistics
masculino	*m*	masculine
matemáticas	*Mat(h)*	mathematics
masculino/femenino	*m/f*	masculine/feminine
medicina	*Med*	medicine
México	MÉX, MEX	Mexico
lo militar, ejército	*Mil*	military matters
música	*Mús, Mus*	music
substantivo, nombre	*n*	noun
navegación, náutica	*Náut, Naut*	sailing, navigation
sustantivo numérico	*num*	numeral noun
Nueva Zelanda	*NZ*	New Zealand
complemento	*obj*	(grammatical) object
	o.s.	oneself
peyorativo	*pey, pej*	derogatory, pejorative
fotografía	*Phot*	photography
fisiología	*Physiol*	physiology
plural	*pl*	plural
política	*Pol*	politics
participio de pasado	*pp*	past participle
preposición	*prep*	preposition
pronombre	*pron*	pronoun
psicología, psiquiatría	*Psico, Psych*	psychology, psychiatry
tiempo pasado	*pt*	past tense
química	*Quím*	chemistry
ferrocarril	*Rail*	railways
religión	*Rel*	religion
Río de la Plata	RPL	River Plate
	sb	somebody
Cono Sur	SC	Southern Cone
enseñanza, sistema escolar	*Scol*	schooling, schools
y universitario		and universities
singular	*sg*	singular

ABREVIATURAS

España	*SP*
sujeto	*su(b)j*
subjuntivo	*subjun*
tauromaquia	*Taur*
también	*tb*
técnica, tecnología	*Tec(h)*
telecomunicaciones	*Telec, Tel*
imprenta, tipografía	*Tip, Typ*
televisión	*TV*
universidad	*Univ*
inglés norteamericano	*US*
verbo	*vb*
verbo intransitivo	*vi*
verbo pronominal	*vr*
verbo transitivo	*vt*
zoología	*Zool*
marca registrada	®
indica un equivalente cultural	≈

ABBREVIATIONS

Spain	
something	
(grammatical) subject	
subjunctive	
bullfighting	
also	
technical term, technology	
telecommunications	
typography, printing	
television	
university	
American English	
verb	
intransitive verb	
reflexive verb	
transitive verb	
zoology	
registered trademark	
introduces a cultural equivalent	

SPANISH PRONUNCIATION

VOWELS

a	[a]	pata	not as long as *a* in far. When followed by a consonant in the same syllable (i.e. in a closed syllable), as in *a*mante, the *a* is short, as in b*a*t
e	[e]	me	like *e* in they. In a closed syllable, as in g*e*nte, the *e* is short as in p*e*t
i	[i]	pino	as in m*ea*n or mach*i*ne
o	[o]	lo	as in l*o*cal. In a closed syllable, as in c*o*ntrol, the *o* is short as in c*o*t
u	[u]	lunes	as in r*u*le. It is silent after q, and in gue, gui, unless marked güe, güi e.g. antigüedad, when it is pronounced like *w* in w*o*lf

SEMIVOWELS

i, y	[j]	bien hielo yunta	pronounced like *y* in yes
u	[w]	huevo fuento antigüedad	unstressed *u* between consonant and vowel is pronounced like *w* in well. See notes on *u* above.

DIPHTHONGS

ai, ay	[ai]	baile	as *i* in ride
au	[au]	auto	as *ou* in shout
ei, ey	[ei]	buey	as *ey* in grey
eu	[eu]	deuda	both elements pronounced independently [e] + [u]
oi, oy	[oi]	hoy	as *oy* in toy

CONSONANTS

b	[b, β]	boda bomba labor	see notes on v below
c	[k]	caja	*c* before *a, o, u* is pronounced as in cat
ce, ci	[θe, θi]	cero cielo	*c* before *e* or *i* is pronounced as in thin
ch	[tʃ]	chiste	*ch* is pronounced as *ch* in chair
d	[d, ð]	danés ciudad	at the beginning of a phrase or after *l* or *n*, d is pronounced as in English. In any other position it is pronounced like *th* in the

g	[g, ɣ]	**g**afas	**g** before *a*, *o* or *u* is pronounced as in
		pa**g**a	**g**ap, if at the beginning of a phrase
			or after *n*. In other positions the sound
			is softened
ge, gi	[xe, xi]	**ge**nte	**g** before *e* or *i* is pronounced similar
		girar	to *ch* in Scottish lo**ch**
h		**h**aber	*h* is always silent in Spanish
j	[x]	**j**ugar	*j* is pronounced similar to *ch* in Scottish
			lo**ch**
ll	[ʎ]	ta**ll**e	*ll* is pronounced like the *y* in *y*et or the *lli*
			in mi**lli**on
ñ	[ʃ]	ni**ñ**o	*ñ* is pronounced like the *ni* in o**ni**on
q	[k]	**q**ue	*q* is pronounced as *k* in *k*ing
r, rr	[r, rr]	qui**t**ar	*r* is always pronounced in Spanish,
		ga**rr**a	unlike the silent *r* in dance*r*. *rr* is trilled,
			like a Scottish *r*
s	[s]	quizá**s**	*s* is usually pronounced as in pa**ss**,
		i**s**la	but before *b*, *d*, *g*, *l*, *m* or *n* it is
			pronounced as in ro**s**e
v	[b, β]	**v**ía	*v* is pronounced something like *b*.
			At the beginning of a phrase or after
			m or *n* it is pronounced as *b* in *b*oy.
			In any other position the sound is
			softened
z	[θ]	tena**z**	*z* is pronounced as *th* in *th*in

f, k, l, m, n, p, t and x are pronounced as in English.

STRESS
The rules of stress in Spanish are as follows:

(a)   when a word ends in a vowel or in *n* or *s*, the second last syllable is stressed:
      pat**a**ta, pat**a**tas; c**o**me, c**o**men
(b)   when a word ends in a consonant other than *n* or *s*, the stress falls on the last syllable:
      par**e**d, habl**a**r
(c)   when the rules set out in (a) and (b) are not applied, an acute accent appears over the stressed vowel:
      com**ú**n, geograf**í**a, ingl**é**s

In the phonetic transcription, the symbol [¹] precedes the syllable on which the stress falls.

LA PRONUNCIACIÓN INGLESA

VOCALES

	Ejemplo inglés	Explicación
[ɑ:]	father	Entre *a* de p*a*dre y *o* de n*o*che
[ʌ]	but, come	*a* muy breve
[æ]	man, cat	Con los labios en la posición de *e* en p*e*na y luego se pronuncia el sonido *a* parecido a la *a* de c*a*rro
[ə]	father, ago	Vocal neutra parecida a una *e* u *o* casi muda
[ə:]	bird, heard	Entre *e* abierta y *o* cerrada, sonido alargado
[ɛ]	get, bed	Como en p*e*rro
[ɪ]	it, big	Más breve que en s*í*
[i:]	tea, see	Como en f*i*no
[ɔ]	hot, wash	Como en t*o*rre
[ɔ:]	saw, all	Como en p*o*r
[u]	put, book	Sonido breve, más cerrado que b*u*rro
[u:]	too, you	Sonido largo, como en *u*no

DIPTONGOS

	Ejemplo inglés	Explicación
[aɪ]	fly, high	Como en fr*ai*le
[au]	how, house	Como en p*au*sa
[ɛə]	there, bear	Casi como en v*ea*, pero el sonido *a* se mezcla con el indistinto [ə]
[eɪ]	day, obey	*e* cerrada seguida por una *i* débil
[ɪə]	here, hear	Como en man*ía*, mezclándose el sonido *a* con el indistinto [ə]
[əu]	go, note	[ə] seguido por una breve *u*
[əɪ]	boy, oil	Como en v*oy*
[uə]	poor, sure	*u* bastante larga más el sonido indistinto [ə]

CONSONANTES

	Ejemplo inglés	Explicación
[b]	big, lobby	Como en tumban
[d]	mended	Como en conde, andar
[g]	go, get, big	Como en grande, gol
[dʒ]	gin, judge	Como en la ll andaluza y en Generalitat (catalán)
[ŋ]	sing	Como en vínculo
[h]	house, he	Como la jota hispanoamericana
[j]	young, yes	Como en ya
[k]	come, mock	Como en caña, Escocia
[r]	red, tread	Se pronuncia con la punta de la lengua hacia atrás y sin hacerla vibrar
[s]	sand, yes	Como en casa, sesión
[z]	rose, zebra	Como en desde, mismo
[ʃ]	she, machine	Como en chambre (francés), roxo (portugués)
[tʃ]	chin, rich	Como en chocolate
[v]	valley	Como f, pero se retiran los dientes superiores vibrándolos contra el labio inferior
[w]	water, which	Como la u de huevo, puede
[ʒ]	vision	Como en journal (francés)
[θ]	think, myth	Como en receta, zapato
[ð]	this, the	Como en hablado, verdad

f, l, m, n, p, t y x iguales que en español.

El signo [*] indica que la r final escrita apenas se pronuncia en inglés británico cuando la palabra siguiente empieza con vocal.
El signo [¹] indica la sílaba acentuada.

LOS NÚMEROS

NUMBERS

un, uno(a)	1	one
dos	2	two
tres	3	three
cuatro	4	four
cinco	5	five
seis	6	six
siete	7	seven
ocho	8	eight
nueve	9	nine
diez	10	ten
once	11	eleven
doce	12	twelve
trece	13	thirteen
catorce	14	fourteen
quince	15	fifteen
dieciséis	16	sixteen
diecisiete	17	seventeen
dieciocho	18	eighteen
diecinueve	19	nineteen
veinte	20	twenty
veintiuno	21	twenty-one
veintidós	22	twenty-two
treinta	30	thirty
cuarenta	40	forty
cincuenta	50	fifty
sesenta	60	sixty
setenta	70	seventy
ochenta	80	eighty
noventa	90	ninety
cien, ciento	100	a hundred, one hundred
ciento uno(a)	101	a hundred and one
doscientos(as)	200	two hundred
trescientos(as)	300	three hundred
cuatrocientos(as)	400	four hundred
quiniento(as)	500	five hundred
seiscientos(as)	600	six hundred
setecientos(as)	700	seven hundred
ochocientos(as)	800	eight hundred
novecientos(as)	900	nine hundred
mil	1000	a thousand
cinco mil	5000	five thousand
un millón	1000000	a million

LOS NÚMEROS

NUMBERS

primer, primero(a), 1º, 1er, (1ª, 1era) — first, 1st
segundo(a), 2º (2ª) — second, 2nd
tercer, tercero(a), 3º (3ª) — third, 3rd
cuarto(a), 4º (4ª) — fourth, 4th
quinto(a), 5º (5ª) — fifth, 5th
sexto(a), 6º (6ª) — sixth, 6th
séptimo(a) — seventh
octavo(a) — eighth
noveno(a) — ninth
décimo(a) — tenth
undécimo(a) — eleventh
duodécimo(a) — twelfth
decimotercio(a) — thirteenth
decimocuarto(a) — fourteenth
decimoquinto(a) — fifteenth
decimosexto(a) — sixteenth
decimoséptimo(a) — seventeenth
decimoctavo(a) — eighteenth
decimonoveno(a) — nineteenth
vigésimo(a) — twentieth
trigésimo(a) — thirtieth
centésimo(a) — hundredth
milésimo(a) — thousandth

NÚMEROS QUEBRADOS ETC

FRACTIONS ETC

un medio — a half
un tercio — a third
un cuarto — a quarter
un quinto — a fifth
cero coma cinco, 0,5 — (nought) point five, 0.5
tres coma cuatro, 3,4 — three point four, 3.4
diez por cien(to) — ten per cent
cien por cien — a hundred per cent

EJEMPLOS

EXAMPLES

va a llegar el 7 (de mayo) — he's arriving on the 7th (of May)
vive en el número 7 — he lives at number 7
el capítulo/la página 7 — chapter/page 7
llegó séptimo — he came in 7th

N.B. In Spanish the ordinal numbers from 1 to 10 are commonly used; from 11 to 20 rather less; above 21 they are rarely written and almost never heard in speech.

LA HORA

¿qué hora es?

es/son

medianoche, las doce (de la noche)
la una (de la madrugada)

la una y cinco
la una y diez
la una y cuarto *or* quince

la una y veinticinco

la una y media *or* treinta
las dos menos veinticinco, la una treinta y cinco
las dos menos veinte, la una cuarenta
las dos menos cuarto, la una cuarenta y cinco
las dos menos diez, la una cincuenta
mediodía, las doce (de la tarde)

la una (de la tarde)

las siete (de la tarde)

¿a qué hora?

a medianoche
a las siete

en veinte minutos
hace quince minutos

THE TIME

what time is it?

it's o it is

midnight, twelve p.m.
one o'clock (in the morning), one (a.m.)

five past one
ten past one
a quarter past one, one fifteen

twenty-five past one, one twenty-five

half-past one, one thirty
twenty-five to two, one thirty-five
twenty to two, one forty
a quarter to two, one forty-five
ten to two, one fifty
twelve o'clock, midday, noon

one o'clock (in the afternoon), one (p.m.)

seven o'clock (in the evening), seven (p.m.)

(at) what time?

at midnight
at seven o'clock

in twenty minutes
fifteen minutes ago

SPANISH VERB TABLES

1 Gerund **2** Imperative **3** Present **4** Preterite **5** Future **6** Present subjunctive **7** Imperfect subjunctive **8** Past participle **9** Imperfect

Etc indicates that the irregular root is used for all persons of the tense, e.g. **oír: 6** oiga, oigas, oigamos, oigáis, oigan

1a HABLAR 1 hablando **2** habla, hablad **3** hablo, hablas, habla, hablamos, habláis, hablan **4** hablé, hablaste, habló, hablamos, hablasteis, hablaron **5** hablaré, hablarás, hablará, hablaremos, hablaréis, hablarán **6** hable, hables, hable, hablemos, habléis, hablen **7** hablara, hablaras, hablara, habláramos, hablarais, hablaran **8** hablado **9** hablaba, hablabas, hablaba, hablábamos, hablabais, hablaban

1b cambiar 2 cambia **3** cambio *etc* **6** cambie *etc*

1c enviar 2 envía **3** envío, envías, envía, envíen **6** envíe, envíes, envíe, envíen

1d evacuar 2 evacua **3** evacuo *etc* **6** evacue *etc*

1e situar 2 sitúa **3** sitúo, sitúas, sitúa, sitúen **6** sitúe, sitúes, sitúe, sitúen

1f cruzar 4 crucé **6** cruce *etc*

1g picar 4 piqué **6** pique *etc*

1h pagar 4 pagué **6** pague *etc*

1i averiguar 4 averigüé **6** averigüe *etc*

1j cerrar 2 cierra **3** cierro, cierras, cierra, cierran **6** cierre, cierres, cierre, cierren

1k errar 2 yerra **3** yerro, yerras, yerra, yerran **6** yerre, yerres, yerre, yerren

1l contar 2 cuenta **3** cuento, cuentas, cuenta, cuentan **6** cuente, cuentes, cuente, cuenten

1m degollar 2 degüella **3** degüello, degüellas, degüella, degüellan **6** degüelle, degüelles, degüelle, degüellen

1n jugar 2 juega **3** juego, juegas, juega, juegan **6** juegue, juegues, juegue, jueguen

1o ESTAR 2 está **3** estoy, estás, está, están **4** estuve, estuviste, estuvo, estuvimos, estuvisteis, estuvieron **6** esté, estés, esté, estén **7** estuviera *etc*

1p andar 4 anduve *etc* **7** anduviera *etc*

1q dar 3 doy **4** di, diste, dio, dimos, disteis, dieron **7** diera *etc*

2a COMER 1 comiendo **2** come, comed **3** como, comes, come, comemos, coméis, comen **4** comí, comiste, comió, comimos, comisteis, comieron **5** comeré, comerás, comerá, comeremos, comeréis, comerán **6** coma, comas, coma, comamos, comáis, coman **7** comiera, comieras, comiera, comiéramos, comierais, comieran **8** comido **9** comía, comías, comía, comíamos, comíais, comían

2b vencer 3 venzo **6** venza *etc*

2c coger 3 cojo **6** coja *etc*

2d parecer 3 parezco **6** parezca *etc*

2e leer 1 leyendo **4** leyó, leyeron **7** leyera *etc*

2f tañer 1 tañendo **4** tañó, tañeron

2g perder 2 pierde **3** pierdo, pierdes, pierde, pierden **6** pierda, pierdas, pierda, pierdan

2h mover 2 mueve 3 muevo, mueves, mueve, mueven 6 mueva, muevas, mueva, muevan

2i oler 2 huele 3 huelo, hueles, huele, huelen 6 huela, huelas, huela, huelan

2j HABER 3 he, has, ha, hemos, han 4 hube, hubiste, hubo, hubimos, hubisteis, hubieron 5 habré *etc* 6 haya *etc* 7 hubiera *etc*

2k tener 2 ten 3 tengo, tienes, tiene, tienen 4 tuve, tuviste, tuvo, tuvimos, tuvisteis, tuvieron 5 tendré *etc* 6 tenga *etc* 7 tuviera *etc*

2l caber 3 quepo 4 cupe, cupiste, cupo, cupimos, cupisteis, cupieron 5 cabré *etc* 6 quepa *etc* 7 cupiera *etc*

2m saber 3 sé 4 supe, supiste, supo, supimos, supisteis, supieron 5 sabré *etc* 6 sepa *etc* 7 supiera *etc*

2n caer 1 cayendo 3 caigo 4 cayó, cayeron 6 caiga *etc* 7 cayera *etc*

2o traer 1 trayendo 3 traigo 4 traje, trajiste, trajo, trajimos, trajisteis, trajeron 6 traiga *etc* 7 trajera *etc*

2p valer 2 vale 3 valgo 5 valdré *etc* 6 valga *etc*

2q poner 2 pon 3 pongo 4 puse, pusiste, puso, pusimos, pusisteis, pusieron 5 pondré *etc* 6 ponga *etc* 7 pusiera *etc* 8 puesto

2r hacer 2 haz 3 hago 4 hice, hiciste, hizo, hicimos, hicisteis, hicieron 5 haré *etc* 6 haga *etc* 7 hiciera *etc* 8 hecho

2s poder 1 pudiendo 2 puede 3 puedo, puedes, puede, pueden 4 pude, pudiste, pudo, pudimos, pudisteis, pudieron 5 podré *etc* 6 pueda, puedas, pueda, puedan 7 pudiera *etc*

2t querer 2 quiere 3 quiero, quieres, quiere, quieren 4 quise, quisiste, quiso, quisimos, quisisteis, quisieron 5 querré *etc* 6 quiera, quieras, quiera, quieran 7 quisiera *etc*

2u ver 3 veo 6 vea *etc* 8 visto 9 veía *etc*

2v SER 2 sé 3 soy, eres, es, somos, sois, son 4 fui, fuiste, fue, fuimos, fuisteis, fueron 6 sea *etc* 7 fuera *etc* 9 era, eras, era, éramos, erais, eran

2w placer 3 plazco 6 plazca *etc*

2x yacer 3 yace or yaz 3 yazco or yazgo 6 yazca or yazga *etc*

2y roer 1 royendo 3 roo or roigo or royo 6 roa or roiga *etc* 7 royó, royeron, 6 roa or roiga *etc* 7 royera *etc*

3a VIVIR 1 viviendo 2 vive, vivid 3 vivo, vives, vive, vivimos, vivís, viven 4 viví, viviste, vivió, vivimos, vivisteis, vivieron 5 viviré, vivirás, vivirá, viviremos, viviréis, vivirán 6 viva, vivas, viva, vivamos, viváis, vivan 7 viviera, vivieras, viviera, viviéramos, vivierais, vivieran 8 vivido 9 vivía, vivías, vivía, vivíamos, vivías, vivían

3b esparcir 3 esparzo 6 esparza *etc*

3c dirigir 3 dirijo 6 dirija *etc*

3d distinguir 3 distingo 6 distinga *etc*

3e delinquir 3 delinco 6 delinca *etc*

3f lucir 3 luzco 6 luzca *etc*

3g instruir 1 instruyendo 2 instruye 3 instruyo, instruyes, instruye, instruyen 4 instruyó, instruyeron 6 instruya *etc* 7 instruyera *etc*

3h gruñir 1 gruñendo 4 gruñó, gruñeron

3i sentir 1 sintiendo **2** siente **3** siento, sientes, siente, sienten **4** sintió, sintieron **6** sienta, sientas, sienta, sintamos, sintáis, sientan **7** sintiera *etc*

3j dormir 1 durmiendo **2** duerme **3** duermo, duermes, duerme, duermen **4** durmió, durmieron **6** duerma, duermas, duerma, durmamos, durmáis, duerman **7** durmiera *etc*

3k pedir 1 pidiendo **2** pide **3** pido, pides, pide, piden **4** pidió, pidieron **6** pida *etc* **7** pidiera *etc*

3l reír 2 ríe **3** río, ríes, ríe, ríen **4** reí,rieron **6** ría, rías, ría, riamos, riáis, rían **7** riera *etc*

3m erguir 1 irguiendo **2** yergue **3** yergo, yergues, yergue, yerguen **4** irguió, irguieron **7** irguiera *etc*

3n reducir 3 reduzco **5** reduje *etc*

6 reduzca *etc* **7** redujera *etc*

3o decir 2 di **3** digo **4** dije, dijiste, dijo, dijimos, dijisteis, dijeron **5** diré *etc* **6** diga *etc* **7** dijera *etc* **8** dicho

3p oír 1 oyendo **2** oye **3** oigo, oyes, oye, oyen **4** oyó, oyeron *etc* **7** oyera *etc*

3q salir 2 sal **3** salgo **5** saldré *etc* **6** salga *etc*

3r venir 2 ven **3** vengo, vienes, viene, vienen **4** vine, viniste, vino, vinimos, vinisteis, vinieron **5** vendré *etc* **6** venga *etc* **7** viniera *etc*

3s ir 1 yendo **2** ve **3** voy, vas, va, vamos, vais, van **4** fui, fuiste, fue, fuimos, fuisteis, fueron **6** vaya, vayas, vaya, vayamos, vayáis, vayan **7** fuera *etc* **9** iba, ibas, iba, íbamos, ibais, iban

VERBOS IRREGULARES EN INGLÉS

PRESENTE	PASADO	PARTICIPIO	PRESENTE	PASADO	PARTICIPIO
arise	arose	arisen	draw	drew	drawn
awake	awoke	awoken	dream	dreamed,	dreamed,
be (am, is,	was, were	been		dreamt	dreamt
are; being)			drink	drank	drunk
bear	bore	born(e)	drive	drove	driven
beat	beat	beaten	dwell	dwelt	dwelt
become	became	become	eat	ate	eaten
begin	began	begun	fall	fell	fallen
bend	bent	bent	feed	fed	fed
bet	bet,	bet,	feel	felt	felt
	betted	betted	fight	fought	fought
bid (at auction,	bid	bid	find	found	found
cards)			flee	fled	fled
bid (say)	bade	bidden	fling	flung	flung
bind	bound	bound	fly	flew	flown
bite	bit	bitten	forbid	forbad(e)	forbidden
bleed	bled	bled	forecast	forecast	forecast
blow	blew	blown	forget	forgot	forgotten
break	broke	broken	forgive	forgave	forgiven
breed	bred	bred	forsake	forsook	forsaken
bring	brought	brought	freeze	froze	frozen
build	built	built	get	got	got,
burn	burnt,	burnt,			(us) gotten
	burned	burned	give	gave	given
burst	burst	burst	go (goes)	went	gone
buy	bought	bought	grind	ground	ground
can	could	(been able)	grow	grew	grown
cast	cast	cast	hang (suspend)	hung	hung
catch	caught	caught	hang (execute)	hanged	hanged
choose	chose	chosen	have	had	had
cling	clung	clung	hear	heard	heard
come	came	come	hide	hid	hidden
cost (be	cost	cost	hit	hit	hit
valued at)			hold	held	held
cost (work	costed	costed	hurt	hurt	hurt
out price of)			keep	kept	kept
creep	crept	crept	kneel	knelt,	knelt,
cut	cut	cut		kneeled	kneeled
deal	dealt	dealt	know	knew	known
dig	dug	dug	lay	laid	laid
do (does)	did	done	lead	led	led

PRESENTE	PASADO	PARTICIPIO	PRESENTE	PASADO	PARTICIPIO
lean	leant, leaned	leant, leaned	shear	sheared	shorn, sheared
leap	leapt, leaped	leapt, leaped	shed	shed	shed
learn	learnt, learned	learnt, learned	shine	shone	shone
			shoot	shot	shot
leave	left	left	show	showed	shown
lend	lent	lent	shrink	shrank	shrunk
let	let	let	shut	shut	shut
lie (lying)	lay	lain	sing	sang	sung
light	lit, lighted	lit, lighted	sink	sank	sunk
			sit	sat	sat
lose	lost	lost	slay	slew	slain
make	made	made	sleep	slept	slept
may	might	–	slide	slid	slid
mean	meant	meant	sling	slung	slung
meet	met	met	slit	slit	slit
mistake	mistook	mistaken	smell	smelt, smelled	smelt, smelled
mow	mowed	mown, mowed	sow	sowed	sown, sowed
must	(had to)	(had to)	speak	spoke	spoken
pay	paid	paid	speed	sped, speeded	sped, speeded
put	put	put			
quit	quit, quitted	quit, quitted	spell	spelt, spelled	spelt, spelled
read	read	read	spend	spent	spent
rid	rid	rid	spill	spilt, spilled	spilt, spilled
ride	rode	ridden			
ring	rang	rung	spin	spun	spun
rise	rose	risen	spit	spat	spat
run	ran	run	spoil	spoiled, spoilt	spoiled, spoilt
saw	sawed	sawed, sawn	spread	spread	spread
say	said	said	spring	sprang	sprung
see	saw	seen	stand	stood	stood
seek	sought	sought	steal	stole	stolen
sell	sold	sold	stick	stuck	stuck
send	sent	sent	sting	stung	stung
set	set	set	stink	stank	stunk
sew	sewed	sewn	stride	strode	stridden
shake	shook	shaken	strike	struck	struck

PRESENTE	PASADO	PARTICIPIO	PRESENTE	PASADO	PARTICIPIO
strive	strove	striven	tread	trod	trodden
swear	swore	sworn	wake	woke,	woken,
sweep	swept	swept		waked	waked
swell	swelled	swollen,	wear	wore	worn
		swelled	weave (on	wove	woven
swim	swam	swum	loom)		
swing	swung	swung	weave (wind)	weaved	weaved
take	took	taken	wed	wedded,	wedded,
teach	taught	taught		wed	wed
tear	tore	torn	weep	wept	wept
tell	told	told	win	won	won
think	thought	thought	wind	wound	wound
throw	threw	thrown	wring	wrung	wrung
thrust	thrust	thrust	write	wrote	written

pencil; **a mano** by hand; **cocina a gas** gas stove

7 (*razón*): **a dos euros el kilo** at two euros a kilo; **a más de 50 km por hora** at more than 50 km per hour

8 (*dativo*): **se lo di a él** I gave it to him; **se lo compré a él** I bought it from him

9 (*complemento directo*): **vi al policía** I saw the policeman

10 (*tras ciertos verbos*): **voy a verle** I'm going to see him; **empezó a trabajar** he started working *o* to work

11 (*+ infin*): **al verle, le reconocí inmediatamente** when I saw him I recognized him at once; **el camino a recorrer** the distance we *etc* have to travel; **¡a callar!** keep quiet!; **¡a comer!** let's eat!

---

abad, esa [aˈβað, ˈðesa] *nm/f* abbot/abbess; **abadía** *nf* abbey

abajo [aˈβaxo] *adv* (*situación*) (down) below, underneath; (*en edificio*) downstairs; (*dirección*) down, downwards; **el piso de ~** the downstairs flat; **la parte de ~** the lower part; **¡~ el gobierno!** down with the government!; **cuesta/río ~** downhill/downstream; **de arriba ~** from top to bottom; **el ~ firmante** the undersigned; **más ~** lower *o* further down

abalanzarse [aβalanˈθarse] /1f/ *vr*: **~ sobre** *o* **contra** to throw o.s. at

abanderado, -a [aβandeˈraðo, a] *nm/f* (*portaestandarte*) standard bearer; (*de un movimiento*) champion, leader; (*LAM: linier*) linesman, assistant referee

abandonado, -a [aβandoˈnaðo, a] *adj* derelict; (*desatendido*) abandoned; (*desierto*) deserted; (*descuidado*) neglected

abandonar [aβandoˈnar] /1a/ *vt* to leave; (*persona*) to abandon, desert; (*cosa*) to abandon, leave behind; (*descuidar*) to neglect; (*renunciar a*) to give up; (*Inform*) to quit; **abandonarse**

---

a [a] *prep* **1** (*dirección*) to; **fueron a Madrid/Grecia** they went to Madrid/Greece; **me voy a casa** I'm going home

2 (*distancia*): **está a 15 km de aquí** it's 15 km from here

3 (*posición*): **estar a la mesa** to be at table; **al lado de** next to, beside; *V tb* **puerta**

4 (*tiempo*): **a las 10/a medianoche** at 10/midnight; **a la mañana siguiente** the following morning; **a los pocos días** after a few days; **estamos a 9 de julio** it's the 9th of July; **a los 24 años** at the age of 24; **al año/a la semana** a year/week later

5 (*manera*): **a la francesa** the French way; **a caballo** on horseback; **a oscuras** in the dark

6 (*medio, instrumento*): **a lápiz** in

vr: **~se a** to abandon o.s. to; **abandono** *nm* (*acto*) desertion, abandonment; (*estado*) abandon, neglect; (*renuncia*) withdrawal, retirement; **ganar por abandono** to win by default

abanico [aβa'niko] *nm* fan; (*Naut*) derrick

abarcar [aβar'kar] /1g/ *vt* to include, embrace; (*LAM*) to monopolize

abarrotado, -a [aβarro'taðo, a] *adj* packed

abarrotar [aβarro'tar] /1a/ *vt* (*local, estadio, teatro*) to fill, pack

abarrote [aβa'rrote] *nm* packing; **abarrotes** *nmpl* (*LAM*) groceries; **tienda de ~s** (*LAM*) grocery store

abarrotero, -a [aβarro'tero, a] *nm/f* (*LAM*) grocer

abastecer [aβaste'θer] /2d/ *vt*: **~ (de)** to supply (with); **abastecimiento** *nm* supply

abasto [a'βasto] *nm* supply; **no dar ~ a algo** not to be able to cope with sth

abatible [aβa'tiβle] *adj*: **asiento ~** tip-up seat; (*Auto*) reclining seat

abatido, -a [aβa'tiðo, a] *adj* dejected, downcast

abatir [aβa'tir] /3a/ *vt* (*muro*) to demolish; (*pájaro*) to shoot *o* bring down; (*fig*) to depress

abdicar [aβði'kar] /1g/ *vi* to abdicate

abdomen [aβ'ðomen] *nm* abdomen

abdominal [aβðomi'nal] *nm*: **~es** abdominals; (*Deporte: tb*: **ejercicios ~es**) sit-ups

abecedario [aβeθe'ðarjo] *nm* alphabet

abedul [aβe'ðul] *nm* birch

abeja [a'βexa] *nf* bee

abejorro [aβe'xorro] *nm* bumblebee

abertura [aβer'tura] *nf* = **apertura**

abeto [a'βeto] *nm* fir

abierto, -a [a'βjerto, a] *pp de* **abrir** ▷ *adj* open

abismal [aβis'mal] *adj* (*fig*) vast, enormous

abismo [a'βismo] *nm* abyss

ablandar [aβlan'dar] /1a/ *vt* to soften ▷ **ablandarse** *vr* to get softer

abocado, -a [aβo'kaðo, a] *adj*: **verse ~ al desastre** to be heading for disaster

abochornar [aβotʃor'nar] /1a/ *vt* to embarrass; **abochornarse** *vr* to get flustered; (*Bot*) to wilt; **~se de** to get embarrassed about

abofetear [aβofete'ar] /1a/ *vt* to slap (in the face)

abogado, -a [aβo'ɣaðo, a] *nm/f* lawyer; (*notario*) solicitor; (*en tribunal*) barrister, advocate, attorney (*US*); **~ defensor** defence lawyer (*BRIT*), defense attorney (*US*)

abogar [aβo'ɣar] /1h/ *vi*: **~ por** to plead for; (*fig*) to advocate

abolir [aβo'lir] *vt* to abolish; (*cancelar*) to cancel

abolladura [aβoʎa'ðura] *nf* dent

abollar [aβo'ʎar] /1a/ *vt* to dent

abombarse [aβom'barse] /1a/ (*LAM*) *vr* to go bad

abominable [aβomi'naβle] *adj* abominable

abonado, -a [aβo'naðo, a] *adj* (*deuda*) paid(-up) ▷ *nm/f* subscriber

abonar [aβo'nar] /1a/ *vt* (*deuda*) to settle; (*terreno*) to fertilize; (*idea*) to endorse; **abonarse** *vr* to subscribe; **abono** *nm* payment; fertilizer; subscription

abordar [aβor'ðar] /1a/ *vt* (*barco*) to board; (*asunto*) to broach

aborigen [aβo'rixen] *nmf* aborigine

aborrecer [aβorre'θer] /2d/ *vt* to hate, loathe

abortar [aβor'tar] /1a/ *vi* (*malparir*) to have a miscarriage; (*deliberadamente*) to have an abortion; **aborto** *nm* miscarriage; abortion

abovedado, -a [aβoβe'ðaðo, a] *adj* vaulted, domed

abrasar [aβra'sar] /1a/ *vt* to burn (up); (*Agr*) to dry up, parch

abrazar [aβra'θar] /1f/ *vt* to embrace, hug

abrazo [a'βraθo] *nm* embrace, hug; **un ~** (*en carta*) with best wishes

abrebotellas [aβreβo'teʎas] *nm inv* bottle opener

abrecartas [aβre'kartas] *nm inv* letter opener

abrelatas [aβre'latas] *nm inv* tin (BRIT) o can (US) opener

abreviatura [aβreβja'tura] *nf* abbreviation

abridor [aβri'ðor] *nm* bottle opener; (*de latas*) tin (BRIT) o can (US) opener

abrigado, a [aβriɣa'ðor, a] *adj* (LAM) warm

abrigar [aβri'ɣar] /1h/ *vt* (*proteger*) to shelter; (*ropa*) to keep warm; (*fig*) to cherish

abrigo [a'βriɣo] *nm* (*prenda*) coat, overcoat; (*lugar protegido*) shelter

abril [a'βril] *nm* April; V tb **julio**

abrillantador [aβriʎanta'ðor] *nm* polish

abrillantar [aβriʎan'tar] /1a/ *vt* (*pulir*) to polish

abrir [a'βrir] /3a/ *vt* to open (up) ▷ *vi* to open; **abrirse** *vr* to open (up); (*extenderse*) to open out; (*cielo*) to clear; **~se paso** to find o force a way through

abrochar [aβro'tʃar] /1a/ *vt* (*con botones*) to button (up); (*zapato, con broche*) to do up

abrupto, -a [a'βrupto, a] *adj* abrupt; (*empinado*) steep

absoluto, -a [aβso'luto, a] *adj* absolute; **en ~** *adv* not at all

absolver [aβsol'βer] /2h/ *vt* to absolve; (*Jur*) to pardon; (: *acusado*) to acquit

absorbente [aβsor'βente] *adj* absorbent; (*interesante*) absorbing

absorber [aβsor'βer] /2a/ *vt* to absorb; (*embeber*) to soak up

absorción [aβsor'θjon] *nf* absorption; (*Com*) takeover

abstemio, -a [aβs'temjo, a] *adj* teetotal

abstención [aβsten'θjon] *nf* abstention

abstenerse [aβste'nerse] /2k/ *vr*: **~ (de)** to abstain o refrain (from)

abstinencia [aβsti'nenθja] *nf* abstinence; (*ayuno*) fasting

abstracto, -a [aβs'strakto, a] *adj* abstract

abstraer [aβstra'er] /2o/ *vt* to abstract; **abstraerse** *vr* to be o become absorbed

abstraído, -a [aβstra'iðo, a] *adj* absent-minded

absuelto [aβ'swelto] *pp de* **absolver**

absurdo, -a [aβ'surðo, a] *adj* absurd

abuchear [aβutʃe'ar] /1a/ *vt* to boo

abuela [a'βwela] *nf* grandmother

abuelo [a'βwelo] *nm* grandfather; **abuelos** *nmpl* grandparents

abultado, -a [aβul'taðo, a] *adj* bulky

abultar [aβul'tar] /1a/ *vi* to be bulky

abundancia [aβun'danθja] *nf*: **una ~ de** plenty of; **abundante** *adj* abundant, plentiful

abundar [aβun'dar] /1a/ *vi* to abound, be plentiful

aburrido, -a [aβu'rriðo, a] *adj* (*hastiado*) bored; (*que aburre*) boring; **aburrimiento** *nm* boredom, tedium

aburrir [aβu'rrir] /3a/ *vt* to bore; **aburrirse** *vr* to be bored, get bored

abusado, -a [aβu'saðo, a] *adj* (LAM fam: *astuto*) sharp, cunning ▷ *excl*: **¡~!** (*inv*) look out!, careful!

abusar [aβu'sar] /1a/ *vi* to go too far; **~ de** to abuse

abusivo, -a [aβu'siβo, a] *adj* (*precio*) exorbitant

abuso [a'βuso] *nm* abuse

acá [a'ka] *adv* (*lugar*) here

acabado, -a [aka'βaðo, a] *adj* finished, complete; (*perfecto*) perfect; (*agotado*) worn out; (*fig*) masterly ▷ *nm* finish

acabar [aka'βar] /1a/ *vt* (*llevar a su fin*) to finish, complete; (*consumir*) to use up; (*rematar*) to finish off ▷ *vi* to finish, end; **acabarse** *vr* to finish, stop; (*terminarse*) to be over; (*agotarse*) to run out; **~ con** to put an end to;

~ de llegar to have just arrived; **~ haciendo** o **por hacer algo** to end up (by) doing sth; **¡se acabó!** (*¡basta!*) that's enough!; (*se terminó*) it's all over!

acabose [aka'βose] nm: **esto es el ~** this is the last straw

academia [aka'ðemja] nf academy; **~ de idiomas** language school; V tb **colegio**; **académico, -a** adj academic

acalorado, -a [akalo'raðo, a] adj (*discusión*) heated

acampar [akam'par] /1a/ vi to camp

acantilado [akanti'laðo] nm cliff

acaparar [akapa'rar] /1a/ vt to monopolize; (*acumular*) to hoard

acariciar [akari'θjar] /1b/ vt to caress; (*esperanza*) to cherish

acarrear [akarre'ar] /1a/ vt to transport; (*fig*) to cause, result in

acaso [a'kaso] adv perhaps, maybe; **(por) si ~** (just) in case

acatar [aka'tar] /1a/ vt to respect; (*ley*) to obey, observe

acatarrarse [akata'rrarse] /1a/ vr to catch a cold

acceder [akθe'ðer] /2a/ vi to accede, agree; **~ a** (*petición etc*) to agree to; (*tener acceso a*) to have access to; (*Inform*) to access

accesible [akθe'siβle] adj accessible

acceso [ak'θeso] nm access, entry; (*camino*) access road; (*Med*) attack, fit

accesorio, -a [akθe'sorjo, a] adj accessory ▷ nm accessory

accidentado, -a [akθiðen'taðo, a] adj uneven; (*montañoso*) hilly; (*azaroso*) eventful ▷ nm/f accident victim

accidental [akθiðen'tal] adj accidental

accidente [akθi'ðente] nm accident; **accidentes** nmpl (*de terreno*) unevenness sg; **~ laboral** o **de trabajo/de tráfico** industrial/road o traffic accident

acción [ak'θjon] nf action; (*acto*) action, act; (*Com*) share; (*Jur*) action, lawsuit; **accionar** /1a/ vt to work, operate; (*ejecutar*) to activate

accionista [akθjo'nista] nmf shareholder

acebo [a'θeβo] nm holly; (*árbol*) holly tree

acechar [aθe'tʃar] /1a/ vt to spy on; (*aguardar*) to lie in wait for; **acecho** nm: **estar al acecho (de)** to lie in wait (for)

aceite [a'θeite] nm oil; **~ de girasol/oliva** olive/sunflower oil; **aceitera** nf oilcan; **aceitoso, -a** adj oily

aceituna [aθei'tuna] nf olive; **~ rellena** stuffed olive

acelerador [aθelera'ðor] nm accelerator

acelerar [aθele'rar] /1a/ vt to accelerate

acelga [a'θelɣa] nf chard, beet

acento [a'θento] nm accent; (*acentuación*) stress

acentuar [aθen'twar] /1e/ vt to accent; to stress; (*fig*) to accentuate

acepción [aθep'θjon] nf meaning

aceptable [aθep'taβle] adj acceptable

aceptación [aθepta'θjon] nf acceptance; (*aprobación*) approval

aceptar [aθep'tar] /1a/ vt to accept; (*aprobar*) to approve; **~ hacer algo** to agree to do sth

acequia [a'θekja] nf irrigation ditch

acera [a'θera] nf pavement (BRIT), sidewalk (US)

acerca [a'θerka]: **~ de** prep about, concerning

acercar [aθer'kar] /1g/ vt to bring o move nearer; **acercarse** vr to approach, come near

acero [a'θero] nm steel

acérrimo, -a [a'θerrimo, a] adj (*partidario*) staunch; (*enemigo*) bitter

acertado, -a [aθer'taðo, a] adj correct; (*apropiado*) apt; (*sensato*) sensible

acertar [aθer'tar] /1j/ vt (*blanco*) to hit; (*solución*) to get right; (*adivinar*) to guess ▷ vi to get it right, be right; **~ a** to manage to; **~ con** to happen o hit on

acertijo [aθer'tixo] *nm* riddle, puzzle

achacar [atʃa'kar] /1g/ *vt* to attribute

achacoso, -a [atʃa'koso, a] *adj* sickly

achicar [atʃi'kar] /1g/ *vt* to reduce; (*Naut*) to bale out

achicharrar [atʃitʃa'rrar] /1a/ *vt* to scorch, burn

achichincle [atʃi'tʃinkle] *nmf* (*LAm fam*) minion

achicoria [atʃi'korja] *nf* chicory

achuras [a'tʃuras] *nf* (*LAm Culin*) offal

acicate [aθi'kate] *nm* spur

acidez [aθi'ðeθ] *nf* acidity

ácido, -a ['aθiðo, a] *adj* sour, acid ▷ *nm* acid

acierto *etc* [a'θjerto] *vb* V **acertar** ▷ *nm* success; (*buen paso*) wise move; (*solución*) solution; (*habilidad*) skill, ability

acitronar [aθitro'nar] /1a/ (*LAm*) *vt* (*fam*) to brown

aclamar [akla'mar] /1a/ *vt* to acclaim; (*aplaudir*) to applaud

aclaración [aklara'θjon] *nf* clarification, explanation

aclarar [akla'rar] /1a/ *vt* to clarify, explain; (*ropa*) to rinse ▷ *vi* to clear up; **aclararse** *vr* (*explicarse*) to understand; **~se la garganta** to clear one's throat

aclimatación [aklimata'θjon] *nf* acclimatization

aclimatar [aklima'tar] /1a/ *vt* to acclimatize; **aclimatarse** *vr* to become o get acclimatized

acné [ak'ne] *nm* acne

acobardar [akoβar'ðar] /1a/ *vt* to daunt, intimidate

acogedor, a [akoxe'ðor, a] *adj* welcoming; (*hospitalario*) hospitable

acoger [ako'xer] /2c/ *vt* to welcome; (*abrigar*) to shelter

acogida [ako'xiða] *nf* reception; refuge

acomedido, -a [akome'ðiðo, a] (*LAm*) *adj* helpful, obliging

acometer [akome'ter] /2a/ *vt* to attack; (*emprender*) to undertake; **acometida** *nf* attack, assault

acomodado, -a [akomo'ðaðo, a] *adj* (*persona*) well-to-do

acomodador, a [akomoða'ðor, a] *nm/f* usher(ette)

acomodar [akomo'ðar] /1a/ *vt* to adjust; (*alojar*) to accommodate; **acomodarse** *vr* to conform; (*instalarse*) to install o.s.; (*adaptarse*) to adapt o.s.; **~se (a)** to adapt (to)

acompañar [akompa'nar] /1a/ *vt* to accompany; (*documentos*) to enclose

acondicionar [akondiθjo'nar] /1a/ *vt* to get ready, prepare; (*pelo*) to condition

aconsejar [akonse'xar] /1a/ *vt* to advise, counsel; **~ a algn hacer o que haga algo** to advise sb to do sth

acontecer [akonte'θer] /2d/ *vi* to happen, occur; **acontecimiento** *nm* event

acopio [a'kopjo] *nm* store, stock

acoplar [ako'plar] /1a/ *vt* to fit; (*Elec*) to connect; (*vagones*) to couple

acorazado, -a [akora'θaðo, a] *adj* armour-plated, armoured ▷ *nm* battleship

acordar [akor'ðar] /1l/ *vt* (*resolver*) to agree, resolve; (*recordar*) to remind; **acordarse** *vr* to agree; **~ hacer algo** to agree to do sth; **~se (de algo)** to remember (sth); **acorde** *adj* (*Mus*) harmonious ▷ *nm* chord; **acorde con** (*medidas etc*) in keeping with

acordeón [akorðe'on] *nm* accordion

acordonado, -a [akorðo'naðo, a] *adj* (*calle*) cordoned-off

acorralar [akorra'lar] /1a/ *vt* to round up, corral

acortar [akor'tar] /1a/ *vt* to shorten; (*duración*) to cut short; (*cantidad*) to reduce; **acortarse** *vr* to become shorter

acosar [ako'sar] /1a/ *vt* to pursue relentlessly; (*fig*) to hound, pester; **acoso** *nm* harassment; **acoso escolar** bullying; **acoso sexual** sexual harassment

acostar [akos'tar] /1l/ *vt* (*en cama*) to put to bed; (*en suelo*) to lay down;

acostarse vr to go to bed; to lie down; **~se con algn** to sleep with sb

acostumbrado, -a [akostum'braðo, a] adj usual; **estar ~ a (hacer) algo** to be used to (doing) sth

acostumbrar [akostum'brar] /1a/ vt: **~ a algn a algo** to get sb used to sth ▷ vi: **~ (a hacer algo)** to be in the habit (of doing sth); **acostumbrarse** vr: **~se a** to get used to

acotación [akota'θjon] nf marginal note; (Geo) elevation mark; (de límite) boundary mark; (Teat) stage direction

acotamiento [akota'mjento] (LAM) nm hard shoulder (BRIT), berm (US)

acre ['akre] adj (olor) acrid; (fig) biting ▷ nm acre

acreditar [akreði'tar] /1a/ vt (garantizar) to vouch for, guarantee; (autorizar) to authorize; (dar prueba de) to prove; (Com: abonar) to credit; (embajador) to accredit

acreedor, a [akree'ðor, a] nm/f creditor

acribillar [akriβi'ʎar] /1a/ vt: **~ a balazos** to riddle with bullets

acróbata [a'kroβata] nmf acrobat

acta ['akta] nf certificate; (de comisión) minutes pl, record; **~ de nacimiento/ de matrimonio** birth/marriage certificate; **~ notarial** affidavit

actitud [akti'tuð] nf attitude; (postura) posture

activar [akti'βar] /1a/ vt to activate; (acelerar) to speed up

actividad [aktiβi'ðað] nf activity

activo, -a [ak'tiβo, a] adj active; (vivo) lively ▷ nm (Com) assets pl

acto ['akto] nm act, action; (ceremonia) ceremony; (Teat) act; **en el ~** immediately

actor [ak'tor] nm actor; (Jur) plaintiff ▷ adj: **parte ~a** prosecution

actriz [ak'triθ] nf actress

actuación [aktwa'θjon] nf action; (comportamiento) conduct, behaviour;

(Jur) proceedings pl; (desempeño) performance

actual [ak'twal] adj present(-day), current; **actualidad** nf present; **en la actualidad** at present; (hoy día) nowadays; **actualizar** /1f/ vt to update, modernize; **actualmente** adv at present; (hoy día) nowadays

> No confundir actual con la palabra inglesa actual.
> No confundir actualmente con la palabra inglesa actually.

actuar [ak'twar] /1e/ vi (obrar) to work, operate; (actor) to act, perform ▷ vt to work, operate; **~ de** to act as

acuarela [akwa'rela] nf watercolour

acuario [a'kwarjo] nm aquarium; **A~** (Astro) Aquarius

acuático, -a [a'kwatiko, a] adj aquatic

acudir [aku'ðir] /3a/ vi to attend, turn up; (ir) to go; **~ a** to turn to; **~ en ayuda de** to go to the aid of; **~ a una cita** to keep an appointment

acuerdo [a'kwerðo] vb V **acordar** ▷ nm agreement; **¡de ~!** agreed!; **de ~ con** (persona) in agreement with; (acción, documento) in accordance with; **estar de ~** (persona) to agree

acumular [akumu'lar] /1a/ vt to accumulate, collect

acuñar [aku'ɲar] /1a/ vt (moneda) to mint; (frase) to coin

acupuntura [akupun'tura] nf acupuncture

acurrucarse [akurru'karse] /1g/ vr to crouch; (ovillarse) to curl up

acusación [akusa'θjon] nf accusation

acusar [aku'sar] /1a/ vt to accuse; (revelar) to reveal; (denunciar) to denounce

acuse [a'kuse] nm: **~ de recibo** acknowledgement of receipt

acústico, -a [a'kustiko, a] adj acoustic ▷ nf acoustics pl

adaptación [aðapta'θjon] nf adaptation

adaptador [aðapta'ðor] *nm* (*Elec*) adapter; **~ universal** universal adapter

adaptar [aðap'tar] /1a/ *vt* to adapt; (*acomodar*) to fit

adecuado, -a [aðe'kwaðo, a] *adj* (*apto*) suitable; (*oportuno*) appropriate

a. de J.C. *abr* (= *antes de Jesucristo*) B.C.

adelantado, -a [aðelan'taðo, a] *adj* advanced; (*reloj*) fast; **pagar por ~** to pay in advance

adelantamiento [aðelanta'mjento] *nm* (*Auto*) overtaking

adelantar [aðelan'tar] /1a/ *vt* to move forward; (*avanzar*) to advance; (*acelerar*) to speed up; (*Auto*) to overtake ▷ *vi* (*ir delante*) to go ahead; (*progresar*) to improve; **adelantarse** *vr* to move forward

adelante [aðe'lante] *adv* forward(s), ahead ▷ *excl* come in!; **de hoy en ~** from now on; **más ~** later on; (*más allá*) further on

adelanto [aðe'lanto] *nm* advance; (*mejora*) improvement; (*progreso*) progress

adelgazar [aðelɣa'θar] /1f/ *vt* to thin (down) ▷ *vi* to get thin; (*con régimen*) to slim down, lose weight

ademán [aðe'man] *nm* gesture; **ademanes** *nmpl* manners

además [aðe'mas] *adv* besides; (*por otra parte*) moreover; (*también*) also; **~ de** besides, in addition to

adentrarse [aðen'trarse] /1a/ *vr*: **~ en** to go into, get inside; (*penetrar*) to penetrate (into)

adentro [a'ðentro] *adv* inside, in; **mar ~** out at sea; **tierra ~** inland

adepto, -a [a'ðepto, a] *nm/f* supporter

aderezar [aðere'θar] /1f/ *vt* (*ensalada*) to dress; (*comida*) to season; **aderezo** *nm* dressing; seasoning

adeudar [aðeu'ðar] /1a/ *vt* to owe

adherirse [aðe'rirse] /3i/ *vr*: **~ a** to adhere to; (*partido*) to join

adhesión [aðe'sjon] *nf* adhesion; (*fig*) adherence

adicción [aðik'θjon] *nf* addiction

adición [aði'θjon] *nf* addition

adicto, -a [a'ðikto, a] *adj*: **~ a** addicted to; (*dedicado*) devoted to ▷ *nm/f* supporter, follower; (*toxicómano etc*) addict

adiestrar [aðjes'trar] /1a/ *vt* to train, teach; (*conducir*) to guide, lead

adinerado, -a [aðine'raðo, a] *adj* wealthy

adiós [a'ðjos] *excl* (*para despedirse*) goodbye!, cheerio!; (*al pasar*) hello!

aditivo [aði'tiβo] *nm* additive

adivinanza [aðiβi'nanθa] *nf* riddle

adivinar [aðiβi'nar] /1a/ *vt* to prophesy; (*conjeturar*) to guess; **adivino, -a** *nm/f* fortune-teller

adj *abr* (= *adjunto*) encl

adjetivo [aðxe'tiβo] *nm* adjective

adjudicar [aðxuði'kar] /1g/ *vt* to award; **adjudicarse** *vr*: **~se algo** to appropriate sth

adjuntar [aðxun'tar] /1a/ *vt* to attach, enclose; **adjunto, -a** *adj* attached, enclosed ▷ *nm/f* assistant

administración [aðministra'θjon] *nf* administration; (*dirección*) management; **administrador, a** *nm/f* administrator; manager(ess)

administrar [aðminis'trar] /1a/ *vt* to administer; **administrativo, -a** *adj* administrative

admirable [aðmi'raβle] *adj* admirable

admiración [aðmira'θjon] *nf* admiration; (*asombro*) wonder; (*Ling*) exclamation mark

admirar [aðmi'rar] /1a/ *vt* to admire; (*extrañar*) to surprise

admisible [aðmi'siβle] *adj* admissible

admisión [aðmi'sjon] *nf* admission; (*reconocimiento*) acceptance

admitir [aðmi'tir] /3a/ *vt* to admit; (*aceptar*) to accept

adobar [aðo'βar] /1a/ *vt* (*cocinar*) to season

adobe [a'ðoβe] *nm* adobe, sun-dried brick

adolecer [aðole'θer] /2d/ *vi*: ~ **de** to suffer from

adolescente [aðoles'θente] *nmf* adolescent, teenager

adonde *conj* (to) where

adónde [a'ðonde] *adv* = **dónde**

adopción [aðop'θjon] *nf* adoption

adoptar [aðop'tar] /1a/ *vt* to adopt

adoptivo, -a [aðop'tiβo, a] *adj* (*padres*) adoptive; (*hijo*) adopted

adoquín [aðo'kin] *nm* paving stone

adorar [aðo'rar] /1a/ *vt* to adore

adornar [aðor'nar] /1a/ *vt* to adorn

adorno [a'ðorno] *nm* (*objeto*) ornament; (*decoración*) decoration

adosado, -a [aðo'saðo, a] *adj* (*casa*) semidetached

adosar [aðo'sar] /1a/ (*LAm*) *vt* (*adjuntar*) to attach, enclose (*with a letter*)

adquiera *etc vb* V **adquirir**

adquirir [aðki'rir] /3i/ *vt* to acquire, obtain

adquisición [aðkisi'θjon] *nf* acquisition

adrede [a'ðreðe] *adv* on purpose

ADSL *nm abr* ADSL

aduana [a'ðwana] *nf* customs *pl*

aduanero, -a [aðwa'nero, a] *adj* customs *cpd* ▷ *nm/f* customs officer

adueñarse [aðwe'narse] /1a/ *vr*: ~ **de** to take possession of

adular [aðu'lar] /1a/ *vt* to flatter

adulterar [aðulte'rar] /1a/ *vt* to adulterate

adulterio [aðul'terjo] *nm* adultery

adúltero, -a [a'ðultero, a] *adj* adulterous ▷ *nm/f* adulterer/ adulteress

adulto, -a [a'ðulto, a] *adj, nm/f* adult

adverbio [að'βerβjo] *nm* adverb

adversario, -a [aðβer'sarjo, a] *nm/f* adversary

adversidad [aðβersi'ðað] *nf* adversity; (*contratiempo*) setback

adverso, -a [að'βerso, a] *adj* adverse

advertencia [aðβer'tenθja] *nf* warning; (*prefacio*) preface, foreword

advertir [aðβer'tir] /3i/ *vt* to notice; (*avisar*): ~ **a algn de** to warn sb about o of

Adviento [að'βjento] *nm* Advent

advierta *etc vb* V **advertir**

aéreo, -a [a'ereo, a] *adj* aerial

aerobic [ae'roβik] *nm*, (*LAm*)

aerobics [ae'roβiks] *nmpl* aerobics *sg*

aerodeslizador [aeroðesliθa'ðor] *nm* hovercraft

aeromozo, -a [aero'moθo, a] *nm/f* (*LAm*) air steward(ess)

aeronáutica [aero'nautika] *nf* aeronautics *sg*

aeronave [aero'naβe] *nm* spaceship

aeroplano [aero'plano] *nm* aeroplane

aeropuerto [aero'pwerto] *nm* airport

aerosol [aero'sol] *nm* aerosol

afamado, -a [afa'maðo, a] *adj* famous

afán [a'fan] *nm* hard work; (*deseo*) desire

afanador, a [afana'ðor, a] (*LAm*) *nm/f* (*de limpieza*) cleaner

afanar [afa'nar] /1a/ *vt* to harass; (*fam*) to pinch; **afanarse** *vr*: ~**se por** to strive to

afear [afe'ar] /1a/ *vt* to disfigure

afección [afek'θjon] *nf* (*Med*) disease

afectado, -a [afek'taðo, a] *adj* affected

afectar [afek'tar] /1a/ *vt* to affect

afectísimo, -a [afek'tisimo, a] *adj* affectionate; **suyo** ~ yours truly

afectivo, -a [afek'tiβo, a] *adj* (*problema etc*) emotional

afecto [a'fekto] *nm* affection; **tenerle** ~ **a algn** to be fond of sb

afectuoso, -a [afek'twoso, a] *adj* affectionate

afeitar [afei'tar] /1a/ *vt* to shave; **afeitarse** *vr* to shave

afeminado, -a [afemi'naðo, a] *adj* effeminate

Afganistán [afɣanis'tan] *nm* Afghanistan

afianzar [afjan'θar] /1f/ *vt* to strengthen, secure; **afianzarse** *vr* to become established

afiche [a'fitʃe] *nm* (LAM) poster

afición [afi'θjon] *nf*: ~ **a** fondness o liking for; **la** ~ the fans *pl*; **pinto por** ~ I paint as a hobby; **aficionado, -a** *adj* keen, enthusiastic; (*no profesional*) amateur ▷ *nm/f* enthusiast, fan; amateur; **ser aficionado a algo** to be very keen on o fond of sth

aficionar [afiθjo'nar] /1a/ *vt*: ~ **a algn a algo** to make sb like sth; **aficionarse** *vr*: ~**se a algo** to grow fond of sth

afilado, -a [afi'laðo, a] *adj* sharp

afilar [afi'lar] /1a/ *vt* to sharpen

afiliarse [afi'ljarse] /1b/ *vr* to affiliate

afín [a'fin] *adj* (*parecido*) similar; (*conexo*) related

afinar [afi'nar] /1a/ *vt* (*Tec*) to refine; (*Mus*) to tune ▷ *vi* (*tocar*) to play in tune; (*cantar*) to sing in tune

afincarse [afin'karse] /1g/ *vr* to settle

afinidad [afini'ðað] *nf* affinity; (*parentesco*) relationship; **por** ~ by marriage

afirmación [afirma'θjon] *nf* affirmation

afirmar [afir'mar] /1a/ *vt* to affirm, state; **afirmativo, -a** *adj* affirmative

afligir [afli'xir] /3c/ *vt* to afflict; (*apenar*) to distress

aflojar [aflo'xar] /1a/ *vt* to slacken; (*desatar*) to loosen, undo; (*relajar*) to relax ▷ *vi* to drop; (*bajar*) to go down; **aflojarse** *vr* to relax

afluente [aflu'ente] *adj* flowing ▷ *nm* (*Geo*) tributary

afmo., -a. *abr* (= *afectísimo/a suyo/a*) Yours

afónico, -a [a'foniko, a] *adj*: **estar** ~ to have a sore throat; to have lost one's voice

aforo [a'foro] *nm* (*de teatro etc*) capacity

afortunado, -a [afortu'naðo, a] *adj* fortunate, lucky

África ['afrika] *nf* Africa; ~ **del Sur** South Africa; **africano, -a** *adj*, *nm/f* African

afrontar [afron'tar] /1a/ *vt* to confront; (*poner cara a cara*) to bring face to face

afrutado, -a [afru'taðo, a] *adj* fruity

after ['after] *nm*, **afterhours** ['afterauars] *nm inv* after-hours club

afuera [a'fwera] *adv* out, outside; **afueras** *nfpl* outskirts

agachar [aɣa'tʃar] /1a/ *vt* to bend, bow; **agacharse** *vr* to stoop, bend

agalla [a'ɣaʎa] *nf* (*Zool*) gill; **tener ~s** (*fam*) to have guts

agarradera [aɣarra'ðera] *nf* (LAM), **agarradero** [aɣarra'ðero] *nm* handle

agarrado, -a [aɣa'rraðo, a] *adj* mean, stingy

agarrar [aɣa'rrar] /1a/ *vt* to grasp, grab; (LAM: *tomar*) to take, catch; (*recoger*) to pick up ▷ *vi* (*planta*) to take root; **agarrarse** *vr* to hold on (tightly)

agencia [a'xenθja] *nf* agency; ~ **de créditos/publicidad/viajes** credit/advertising/travel agency; ~ **inmobiliaria** estate agent's (office) (BRIT), real estate office (US)

agenciar [axen'θjar] /1b/ *vt* to bring about; **agenciarse** *vr* to look after o.s.; ~**se algo** to get hold of sth

agenda [a'xenda] *nf* diary; ~ **electrónica** PDA

> No confundir *agenda* con la palabra inglesa *agenda*.

agente [a'xente] *nmf* agent; (*tb*: ~ **de policía**) policeman/policewoman; ~ **de seguros** insurance broker; ~ **de tránsito** (LAM) traffic cop; ~ **inmobiliario** estate agent (BRIT), realtor (US)

ágil ['axil] *adj* agile, nimble; **agilidad** *nf* agility, nimbleness

agilizar [axili'θar] /1f/ *vt* (*trámites*) to speed up

agiotista [axjo'tista] (*LAM*) *nmf* (*usurero*) usurer

agitación [axita'θjon] *nf* (*de mano etc*) shaking, waving; (*de líquido etc*) stirring; agitation

agitado, -a [axi'aðo, a] *adj* hectic; (*viaje*) bumpy

agitar [axi'tar] /1a/ *vt* to wave, shake; (*líquido*) to stir; (*fig*) to stir up, excite; **agitarse** *vr* to get excited; (*inquietarse*) to get worried o upset

aglomeración [aɣlomera'θjon] *nf*: **~ de tráfico/gente** traffic jam/mass of people

agnóstico, -a [aɣ'nostiko, a] *adj*, *nm/f* agnostic

agobiar [aɣo'βjar] /1b/ *vt* to weigh down; (*oprimir*) to oppress; (*cargar*) to burden

agolparse [aɣol'parse] /1a/ *vr* to crowd together

agonía [aɣo'nia] *nf* death throes *pl*; (*fig*) agony, anguish

agonizante [aɣoni'θante] *adj* dying

agonizar [aɣoni'θar] /1f/ *vi* to be dying

agosto [a'ɣosto] *nm* August

agotado, -a [aɣo'taðo, a] *adj* (*persona*) exhausted; (*acabado*) finished; (*Com*) sold out; (: *libros*) out of print; **agotador, a** *adj* exhausting

agotamiento [aɣota'mjento] *nm* exhaustion

agotar [aɣo'tar] /1a/ *vt* to exhaust; (*consumir*) to drain; (*recursos*) to use up, deplete; **agotarse** *vr* to be exhausted; (*acabarse*) to run out; (*libro*) to go out of print

agraciado, -a [aɣra'θjaðo, a] *adj* (*atractivo*) attractive; (*en sorteo etc*) lucky

agradable [aɣra'ðaβle] *adj* pleasant, nice

agradar [aɣra'ðar] /1a/ *vt*, *vi* to please; **él me agrada** I like him

agradecer [aɣraðe'θer] /2d/ *vt* to thank; (*favor etc*) to be grateful for; **agradecido, -a** *adj* grateful;

¡muy agradecido! thanks a lot!; **agradecimiento** *nm* thanks *pl*; gratitude

agradezca *etc* [aɣra'ðeθka] *vb* V **agradecer**

agrado [a'ɣraðo] *nm*: **ser de tu** *etc* **~** to be to your *etc* liking

agrandar [aɣran'dar] /1a/ *vt* to enlarge; (*fig*) to exaggerate; **agrandarse** *vr* to get bigger

agrario, -a [a'ɣrarjo, a] *adj* agrarian, land *cpd*; (*política*) agricultural, farming *cpd*

agravante [aɣra'βante] *adj* aggravating ▷ *nm* o *f*: **con el** o **la ~ de que ...** with the further difficulty that ...

agravar [aɣra'βar] /1a/ *vt* (*pesar sobre*) to make heavier; (*irritar*) to aggravate; **agravarse** *vr* to worsen, get worse

agraviar [aɣra'βjar] /1b/ *vt* to offend; (*ser injusto con*) to wrong

agredir [aɣre'ðir] /3a/ *vt* to attack

agregado [aɣre'ɣaðo] *nm* aggregate; (*persona*) attaché; **A~** ≈ teacher (*who is not head of department*)

agregar [aɣre'ɣar] /1h/ *vt* to gather; (*añadir*) to add; (*persona*) to appoint

agresión [aɣre'sjon] *nf* aggression

agresivo, -a [aɣre'siβo, a] *adj* aggressive

agriar [a'ɣrjar] *vt* to (turn) sour

agrícola [a'ɣrikola] *adj* farming *cpd*, agricultural

agricultor, a [aɣrikul'tor, a] *nm/f* farmer

agricultura [aɣrikul'tura] *nf* agriculture, farming

agridulce [aɣri'ðulθe] *adj* bittersweet; (*Culin*) sweet and sour

agrietarse [aɣrje'tarse] /1a/ *vr* to crack; (*la piel*) to chap

agrio, -a ['aɣrjo, a] *adj* bitter

agrupación [aɣrupa'θjon] *nf* group; (*acto*) grouping

agrupar [aɣru'par] /1a/ *vt* to group

agua ['aɣwa] *nf* water; (*Naut*) wake; (*Arq*) slope of a roof;

a

aguas *nfpl* (*Med*) water *sg*, urine *sg*; (*Naut*) waters; **~s abajo/ arriba** downstream/upstream; **~ bendita/destilada/potable** holy/distilled/drinking water; **~ caliente** hot water; **~ corriente** running water; **~ de colonia** eau de cologne; **~ mineral (con/sin gas)** (fizzy/non-fizzy) mineral water; **~ oxigenada** hydrogen peroxide; **~s jurisdiccionales** territorial waters

aguacate [aɣwaˈkate] *nm* avocado (pear)

aguacero [aɣwaˈθero] *nm* (heavy) shower, downpour

aguado, -a [aˈɣwaðo, a] *adj* watery, watered down

aguafiestas [aɣwaˈfjestas] *nm inv, nf inv* spoilsport

aguamiel [aɣwaˈmjel] (*LAM*) *nf* fermented maguey *o* agave juice

aguanieve [aɣwaˈnjeβe] *nf* sleet

aguantar [aɣwanˈtar] /1a/ *vt* to bear, put up with; (*sostener*) to hold up ▷ *vi* to last; **aguantarse** *vr* to restrain o.s.; **aguante** *nm* (*paciencia*) patience; (*resistencia*) endurance

aguar [aˈɣwar] /1i/ *vt* to water down

aguardar [aɣwarˈðar] /1a/ *vt* to wait for

aguardiente [aɣwarˈðjente] *nm* brandy, liquor

aguarrás [aɣwaˈrras] *nm* turpentine

aguaviva [aɣwaˈbiβa] (*RPL*) *nf* jellyfish

agudeza [aɣuˈðeθa] *nf* sharpness; (*ingenio*) wit

agudo, -a [aˈɣuðo, a] *adj* sharp; (*voz*) high-pitched, piercing; (*dolor, enfermedad*) acute

agüero [aˈɣwero] *nm*: **buen/mal ~** good/bad omen

aguijón [aɣiˈxon] *nm* sting; (*fig*) spur

águila [ˈaɣila] *nf* eagle; (*fig*) genius

aguileño, -a [aɣiˈleɲo, a] *adj* (*nariz*) aquiline; (*rostro*) sharp-featured

aguinaldo [aɣiˈnaldo] *nm* Christmas box

aguja [aˈɣuxa] *nf* needle; (*de reloj*) hand; (*Arq*) spire; (*Tec*) firing-pin; **agujas** *nfpl* (*Zool*) ribs; (*Ferro*) points

agujerear [aɣuxereˈar] /1a/ *vt* to make holes in

agujero [aɣuˈxero] *nm* hole

agujetas [aɣuˈxetas] *nfpl* stitch *sg*; (*rigidez*) stiffness *sg*

ahí [aˈi] *adv* there; (*allá*) over there; **de ~ que** so that, with the result that; **~ llega** here he comes; **por ~** that way; **200 o por ~** 200 or so

ahijado, -a [aiˈxaðo, a] *nm/f* godson/ daughter

ahogar [aoˈɣar] /1h/ *vt* to drown; (*asfixiar*) to suffocate, smother; (*fuego*) to put out; **ahogarse** *vr* (*en agua*) to drown; (*por asfixia*) to suffocate

ahogo [aˈoɣo] *nm* breathlessness; (*económico*) financial difficulty

ahondar [aonˈdar] /1a/ *vt* to deepen, make deeper; (*fig*) to study thoroughly ▷ *vi*: **~ en** to study thoroughly

ahora [aˈora] *adv* now; (*hace poco*) a moment ago, just now; (*dentro de poco*) in a moment; **~ voy** I'm coming; **~ mismo** right now; **~ bien** now then; **por ~** for the present

ahorcar [aorˈkar] /1g/ *vt* to hang

ahorita [aoˈrita] *adv* (*esp LAM fam*: *en este momento*) right now; (*hace poco*) just now; (*dentro de poco*) in a minute

ahorrar [aoˈrrar] /1a/ *vt* (*dinero*) to save; (*esfuerzos*) to save, avoid; **ahorro** *nm* (*acto*) saving; **ahorros** *nmpl* (*dinero*) savings

ahuecar [aweˈkar] /1g/ *vt* to hollow (out); (*voz*) to deepen; **ahuecarse** *vr* to give o.s. airs

ahumar [auˈmar] /1a/ *vt* to smoke, cure; (*llenar de humo*) to fill with smoke ▷ *vi* to smoke; **ahumarse** *vr* to fill with smoke

ahuyentar [aujenˈtar] /1a/ *vt* to drive off, frighten off; (*fig*) to dispel

aire [ˈaire] *nm* air; (*viento*) wind; (*corriente*) draught; (*Mus*) tune; **al ~ libre** in the open air; **~ aclimatizado**

o **acondicionado** air conditioning;
airear /1a/ *vt* to air; **airearse** *vr* to get
some fresh air; **airoso, -a** *adj* windy;
draughty; *(fig)* graceful

aislado, -a [ais'laðo, a] *adj* isolated;
(incomunicado) cut off; *(Elec)* insulated

aislar [ais'lar] /1a/ *vt* to isolate; *(Elec)*
to insulate

ajardinado, -a [axarði'naðo, a] *adj*
landscaped

ajedrez [axe'ðreθ] *nm* chess

ajeno, -a [a'xeno, a] *adj (que pertenece
a otro)* somebody else's; **~ a** foreign to

ajetreado, -a [axetre'aðo, a] *adj* busy

ajetreo [axe'treo] *nm* bustle

ají [a'xi] *nm* chil(l)i, red pepper; *(salsa)*
chil(l)i sauce

ajillo [a'xiʎo] *nm*: **gambas al ~** garlic
prawns

ajo ['axo] *nm* garlic

ajuar [a'xwar] *nm* household
furnishings *pl*; *(de novia)* trousseau; *(de
niño)* layette

ajustado, -a [axus'taðo, a] *adj*
(tornillo) tight; *(cálculo)* right; *(ropa)*
tight(-fitting); *(resultado)* close

ajustar [axus'tar] /1a/ *vt (adaptar)* to
adjust; *(encajar)* to fit; *(Tec)* to engage;
(Tip) to make up; *(apretar)* to tighten;
(concertar) to agree (on); *(reconciliar)* to
reconcile; *(cuenta, deudas)* to settle ▷ *vi*
to fit; **ajustarse** *vr*: **~se a** *(precio etc)*
to be in keeping with, fit in with; **~ las
cuentas a algn** to get even with sb

ajuste [a'xuste] *nm* adjustment;
(Costura) fitting; *(acuerdo)*
compromise; *(de cuenta)* settlement

al [al] = **a + el**; *V* **a**

ala ['ala] *nf* wing; *(de sombrero)*
brim; *(futbolista)* winger; **~ delta**
hang-glider

alabanza [ala'βanθa] *nf* praise

alabar [ala'βar] /1a/ *vt* to praise

alacena [ala'θena] *nf* cupboard
(BRIT), closet (US)

alacrán [ala'kran] *nm* scorpion

alambrada [alam'braða] *nm* wire
fence; *(red)* wire netting

alambre [a'lambre] *nm* wire; **~ de
púas** barbed wire

alameda [ala'meða] *nf (plantío)*
poplar grove; *(lugar de paseo)* avenue,
boulevard

álamo ['alamo] *nm* poplar

alarde [a'larðe] *nm* show, display;
hacer ~ de to boast of

alargador [alarɣa'ðor] *nm* extension
cable *o* lead

alargar [alar'ɣar] /1h/ *vt* to lengthen,
extend; *(paso)* to hasten; *(brazo)*
to stretch out; *(cuerda)* to pay out;
(conversación) to spin out; **alargarse** *vr*
to get longer

alarma [a'larma] *nf* alarm; **~ de
incendios** fire alarm; **alarmante** *adj*
alarming; **alarmar** /1a/ *vt* to alarm;
alarmarse *vr* to get alarmed

alba ['alβa] *nf* dawn

albahaca [al'βaka] *nf (Bot)* basil

Albania [al'βanja] *nf* Albania

albañil [alβa'ɲil] *nm* bricklayer;
(cantero) mason

albarán [alβa'ran] *nm (Com)* delivery
note, invoice

albaricoque [alβari'koke] *nm* apricot

albedrío [alβe'ðrio] *nm*: **libre ~** free will

alberca [al'βerka] *nf* reservoir; *(LAM)*
swimming pool

albergar [alβer'ɣar] /1h/ *vt* to shelter

albergue [al'βerɣe] *vb V* **albergar**
▷ *nm* shelter, refuge; **~ juvenil** youth
hostel

albóndiga [al'βondiɣa] *nf* meatball

albornoz [alβor'noθ] *nm (de los
árabes)* burnous; *(para el baño)*
bathrobe

alborotar [alβoro'tar] /1a/ *vi* to
make a row ▷ *vt* to agitate, stir up;
alborotarse *vr* to get excited; *(mar)* to
get rough; **alboroto** *nm* row, uproar

álbum ['alβum] *(pl* **álbums** *o*
álbumes) *nm* album; **~ de recortes**
scrapbook

albur [al'βur] *(LAM) nm (juego de
palabras)* pun; *(doble sentido)* double
entendre

alcachofa [alka'tʃofa] nf (globe) artichoke

alcalde, -esa [al'kalde, alkal'desa] nm/f mayor(ess)

alcaldía [alkal'dia] nf mayoralty; (lugar) mayor's office

alcance [al'kanθe] vb V **alcanzar** ▷ nm (Mil, Radio) range; (fig) scope; (Com) adverse balance; **estar al/ fuera del ~ de algn** to be within/ beyond sb's reach

alcancía [alkan'θia] (LAM) nf (para ahorrar) money box; (para colectas) collection box

alcantarilla [alkanta'riʎa] nf (de aguas cloacales) sewer; (en la calle) gutter

alcanzar [alkan'θar] /1f/ vt (algo: con la mano, el pie) to reach; (alguien: en el camino etc) to catch up (with); (autobús) to catch; (bala) to hit, strike ▷ vi (ser suficiente) to be enough; **~ a hacer** to manage to do

alcaparra [alka'parra] nf (Bot) caper

alcayata [alka'jata] nf hook

alcázar [al'kaθar] nm fortress; (Naut) quarter-deck

alcoba [al'koβa] nf bedroom

alcohol [al'kol] nm alcohol; **~ metílico** methylated spirits pl (BRIT), wood alcohol (US); **alcohólico, -a** adj, nm/f alcoholic; **alcoholímetro** nm Breathalyser®, drunkometer (US); **alcoholismo** nm alcoholism

alcornoque [alkor'noke] nm cork tree; (fam) idiot

aldea [al'dea] nf village; **aldeano, -a** adj village cpd ▷ nm/f villager

aleación [alea'θjon] nf alloy

aleatorio, -a [alea'torjo, a] adj random

aleccionar [alekθjo'nar] /1a/ vt to instruct; (adiestrar) to train

alegar [ale'ɣar] /1h/ vt (dificultad etc) to plead; (Jur) to allege ▷ vi (LAM) to argue

alegoría [aleɣo'ria] nf allegory

alegrar [ale'ɣrar] /1a/ vt (causar alegría) to cheer (up); (fuego) to poke; (fiesta) to liven up; **alegrarse** vr (fam) to get merry o tight; **~se de** to be glad about

alegre [a'leɣre] adj happy, cheerful; (fam) merry, tight; (chiste) risqué, blue; **alegría** nf happiness; merriment

alejar [ale'xar] /1a/ vt to move away, remove; (fig) to estrange; **alejarse** vr to move away

alemán, -ana [ale'man, ana] adj, nm/f German ▷ nm (lengua) German

Alemania [ale'manja] nf Germany

alentador, a [alenta'ðor, a] adj encouraging

alentar [alen'tar] /1j/ vt to encourage

alergia [a'lerxja] nf allergy

alero [a'lero] nm (de tejado) eaves pl; (Auto) mudguard

alerta [a'lerta] adj inv, nm alert

aleta [a'leta] nf (de pez) fin; (de ave) wing; (de foca, Deporte) flipper; (de coche) mudguard

aletear [alete'ar] /1a/ vi to flutter

alevín [ale'βin] nm fry, young fish

alevosía [aleβo'sia] nf treachery

alfabeto [alfa'βeto] nm alphabet

alfalfa [al'falfa] nf alfalfa, lucerne

alfarería [alfare'ria] nf pottery; (tienda) pottery shop; **alfarero, -a** nm/f potter

alféizar [al'feiθar] nm window-sill

alférez [al'fereθ] nm (Mil) second lieutenant; (Naut) ensign

alfil [al'fil] nm (Ajedrez) bishop

alfiler [alfi'ler] nm pin; (broche) clip

alfombra [al'fombra] nf carpet; (más pequeña) rug; **alfombrilla** nf rug, mat; (Inform) mouse mat o pad

alforja [al'forxa] nf saddlebag

algas ['alɣas] nfpl seaweed sg

álgebra ['alxeβra] nf algebra

algo ['alɣo] pron something; (en frases interrogativas) anything ▷ adv somewhat, rather; **¿~ más?** anything else?; (en tienda) is that all?; **por ~ será** there must be some reason for it

algodón [alɣo'ðon] nm cotton; (planta) cotton plant; **~ de azúcar**

candy floss (BRIT), cotton candy (US); **~ hidrófilo** cotton wool (BRIT), absorbent cotton (US)

alguien ['alɣjen] pron someone, somebody; (en frases interrogativas) anyone, anybody

alguno, -a [al'ɣuno, a] adj some; (después de n): **no tiene talento ~** he has no talent, he doesn't have any talent ▷ pron (alguien) someone, somebody; **algún que otro libro** some book or other; **algún día iré** I'll go one o some day; **sin interés ~** without the slightest interest; **~ que otro** an occasional one; **~s piensan** some (people) think

alhaja [a'laxa] nf jewel; (tesoro) precious object, treasure

alhelí [ale'li] nm wallflower, stock

aliado, -a [a'ljaðo, a] adj allied

alianza [a'ljanθa] nf alliance; (anillo) wedding ring

aliar [a'ljar] /1c/ vt to ally; **aliarse** vr to form an alliance

alias ['aljas] adv alias

alicatado [alika'taðo] (ESP) nm tiling

alicate [ali'kate] nm, **alicates** [ali'kates] nmpl pliers pl

aliciente [ali'θjente] nm incentive; (atracción) attraction

alienación [aljena'θjon] nf alienation

aliento [a'ljento] nm breath; (respiración) breathing; **sin ~** breathless

aligerar [alixe'rar] /1a/ vt to lighten; (reducir) to shorten; (aliviar) to alleviate; (mitigar) to ease; (paso) to quicken

alijo [a'lixo] nm (Naut: descarga) unloading

alimaña [ali'maɲa] nf pest

alimentación [alimenta'θjon] nf (comida) food; (acción) feeding; (tienda) grocer's (shop)

alimentar [alimen'tar] /1a/ vt to feed; (nutrir) to nourish; **alimentarse** vr: **~se (de)** to feed (on)

alimenticio, -a [alimen'tiθjo, a] adj food cpd; (nutritivo) nourishing, nutritious

alimento [ali'mento] nm food; (nutrición) nourishment

alineación [alinea'θjon] nf alignment; (Deporte) line-up

alinear [aline'ar] /1a/ vt to align; (Deporte) to select, pick; **alinearse**

aliñar [ali'ɲar] /1a/ vt (Culin) to dress; **aliño** nm (Culin) dressing

alioli [ali'oli] nm garlic mayonnaise

alisar [ali'sar] /1a/ vt to smooth

alistar [ali'star] /1a/ vt to recruit; **alistarse** vr to enlist; (inscribirse) to enrol

aliviar [ali'βjar] /1b/ vt (carga) to lighten; (persona) to relieve; (dolor) to relieve, alleviate

alivio [a'liβjo] nm alleviation, relief

aljibe [al'xiβe] nm cistern

allá [a'ʎa] adv (lugar) there; (por ahí) over there; (tiempo) then; **~ abajo** down there; **más ~** further on; **más ~ de** beyond; **¡~ tú!** that's your problem!

allanamiento [aʎana'mjento] nm (LAM Policía) raid, search; **~ de morada** breaking and entering

allanar [aʎa'nar] /1a/ vt to flatten, level (out); (igualar) to smooth (out); (fig) to subdue; (Jur) to burgle, break into

allegado, -a [aʎe'ɣaðo, a] adj near, close ▷ nm/f relation

allí [a'ʎi] adv there; **~ mismo** right there; **por ~** over there; (por ese camino) that way

alma ['alma] nf soul; (persona) person

almacén [alma'θen] nm (depósito) warehouse, store; (Mil) magazine; (LAM) grocer's shop, food store, grocery store (US); **(grandes) almacenes** nmpl department store sg; **almacenaje** nm storage

almacenar [almaθe'nar] /1a/ vt to store, put in storage; (proveerse) to stock up with

almanaque [alma'nake] nm almanac

almeja [al'mexa] *nf* clam

almendra [al'mendra] *nf* almond;
almendro *nm* almond tree

almíbar [al'miβar] *nm* syrup

almidón [almi'ðon] *nm* starch

almirante [almi'rante] *nm* admiral

almohada [almo'aða] *nf* pillow;
(*funda*) pillowcase; **almohadilla** *nf*
cushion; (*Tec*) pad; (*LAM*) pincushion

almohadón [almoa'ðon] *nm* large
pillow

almorranas [almo'rranas] *nfpl* piles,
haemorrhoids (*BRIT*), hemorrhoids
(*US*)

almorzar [almor'θar] /1f, 1l/ *vt*: **~
una tortilla** to have an omelette for
lunch ▷ *vi* to (have) lunch

almuerzo [al'mwerθo] *vb* V
almorzar ▷ *nm* lunch

alocado, -a [alo'kaðo, a] *adj* crazy

alojamiento [aloxa'mjento] *nm*
lodging(s) (*pl*); (*viviendas*) housing

alojar [alo'xar] /1a/ *vt* to lodge;
alojarse *vr*: **~se en** to stay at; (*bala*)
to lodge in

alondra [a'londra] *nf* lark, skylark

alpargata [alpar'ɣata] *nf* rope-soled
shoe, espadrille

Alpes ['alpes] *nmpl*: **los ~** the Alps

alpinismo [alpi'nismo] *nm*
mountaineering, climbing; **alpinista**
nmf mountaineer, climber

alpiste [al'piste] *nm* birdseed

alquilar [alki'lar] /1a/ *vt* (*propietario*,
inmuebles) to let, rent (out); (*coche*) to
hire out; (*TV*) to rent (out); (*alquilador*,
inmuebles, *TV*) to rent; (*coche*) to hire;
"se alquila casa" "house to let (*BRIT*)
o for rent (*US*)"

alquiler [alki'ler] *nm* renting, letting;
hiring; (*arriendo*) rent; hire charge; **de
~** for hire; **~ de automóviles** car hire

alquimia [al'kimja] *nf* alchemy

alquitrán [alki'tran] *nm* tar

alrededor [alreðe'ðor] *adv*
around, about; **alrededores** *nmpl*
surroundings; **~ de** around, about;
mirar a su ~ to look (round) about one

alta ['alta] *nf* (certificate of) discharge

altar [al'tar] *nm* altar

altavoz [alta'βoθ] *nm* loudspeaker;
(*amplificador*) amplifier

alteración [altera'θjon] *nf*
alteration; (*alboroto*) disturbance

alterar [alte'rar] /1a/ *vt* to alter;
to disturb; **alterarse** *vr* (*persona*) to
get upset

altercado [alter'kaðo] *nm* argument

alternar [alter'nar] /1a/ *vt* to
alternate ▷ *vi* to alternate; (*turnar*) to
take turns; **alternarse** *vr* to alternate;
(*turnar*) to take turns; **~ con** to mix
with; **alternativo, -a** *adj* alternative;
(*alterno*) alternating ▷ *nf* alternative;
(*elección*) choice; **alterno, -a** *adj*
alternate; (*Elec*) alternating

Alteza [al'teθa] *nf* (*tratamiento*)
Highness

altibajos [alti'βaxos] *nmpl* ups and
downs

altiplanicie [altipla'niθje] *nf*,
altiplano [alti'plano] *nm* high
plateau

altisonante [altiso'nante] *adj* high-
flown, high-sounding

altitud [alti'tuð] *nf* height; (*Aviat*,
Geo) altitude

altivo, -a [al'tiβo, a] *adj* haughty,
arrogant

alto, -a ['alto, a] *adj* high; (*persona*)
tall; (*sonido*) high, sharp; (*noble*) high,
lofty ▷ *nm* halt; (*Mus*) alto; (*Geo*)
hill ▷ *adv* (*estar*) high; (*hablar*) loud,
loudly ▷ *excl* halt!; **la pared tiene dos
metros de ~** the wall is two metres
high; **en alta mar** on the high seas;
en voz alta in a loud voice; **las altas
horas de la noche** the small (*BRIT*)
o wee (*US*) hours; **en lo ~ de** at the
top of; **pasar por ~** to overlook;
altoparlante *nm* (*LAM*) loudspeaker

altura [al'tura] *nf* height; (*Naut*)
depth; (*Geo*) latitude; **la pared tiene
1.80 de ~** the wall is 1 metre 80 (cm)
high; **a estas ~s** at this stage; **a esta
~ del año** at this time of the year

alubia [aˈluβja] nf bean; (judía verde) French bean; (judía blanca) cannellini bean

alucinación [aluθinaˈθjon] nf hallucination

alucinar [aluθiˈnar] /1a/ vi to hallucinate ▷ vt to deceive; (fascinar) to fascinate

alud [aˈluð] nm avalanche; (fig) flood

aludir [aluˈðir] /3a/ vi: **~ a** to allude to; **darse por aludido** to take the hint

alumbrado [alumˈbraðo] nm lighting

alumbrar [alumˈbrar] /1a/ vt to light (up) ▷ vi (Med) to give birth

aluminio [aluˈminjo] nm aluminium (BRIT), aluminum (US)

alumno, -a [aˈlumno, a] nm/f pupil, student

alusión [aluˈsjon] nf allusion

alusivo, -a [aluˈsiβo, a] adj allusive

aluvión [aluˈβjon] nm (Geo) alluvium; (fig) flood

alverja [alˈβerxa] (LAM) nf pea

alza [ˈalθa] nf rise; (Mil) sight

alzamiento [alθaˈmjento] nm (rebelión) rising

alzar [alˈθar] /1f/ vt to lift (up); (precio, muro) to raise; (cuello de abrigo) to turn up; (Agr) to gather in; (Tip) to gather; **alzarse** vr to get up, rise; (rebelarse) to revolt; (Com) to go fraudulently bankrupt; (Jur) to appeal

ama [ˈama] nf lady of the house; (dueña) owner; (institutriz) governess; (madre adoptiva) foster mother; **~ de casa** housewife; **~ de llaves** housekeeper

amabilidad [amaβiliˈðað] nf kindness; (simpatía) niceness; **amable** adj kind; nice; **es usted muy amable** that's very kind of you

amaestrado, -a [amaesˈtraðo, a] adj (en circo etc) performing

amaestrar [amaesˈtrar] /1a/ vt to train

amago [aˈmaɣo] nm threat; (gesto) threatening gesture; (Med) symptom

amainar [amaiˈnar] /1a/ vi (viento) to die down

amamantar [amamanˈtar] /1a/ vt to suckle, nurse

amanecer [amaneˈθer] /2d/ vi to dawn ▷ nm dawn; **~ afiebrado** to wake up with a fever

amanerado, -a [amaneˈraðo, a] adj affected

amante [aˈmante] adj: **~ de** fond of ▷ nmf lover

amapola [amaˈpola] nf poppy

amar [aˈmar] /1a/ vt to love

amargado, -a [amarˈɣaðo, a] adj bitter

amargar [amarˈɣar] /1h/ vt to make bitter; (fig) to embitter; **amargarse** vr to become embittered

amargo, -a [aˈmarɣo, a] adj bitter

amarillento, -a [amariˈʎento, a] adj yellowish; (tez) sallow

amarillo, -a [amaˈriʎo, a] adj, nm yellow

amarra [aˈmarra] nf (Naut) mooring line; **amarras** nfpl: **soltar ~s** (Naut) to set sail

amarrado, -a [amaˈrraðo, a] (LAM) adj (fam) mean, stingy

amarrar [amaˈrrar] /1a/ vt to moor; (sujetar) to tie up

amasar [amaˈsar] /1a/ vt (masa) to knead; (mezclar) to mix, prepare; (confeccionar) to concoct

amateur [ˈamatur] nmf amateur

amazona [amaˈθona] nf horsewoman; **Amazonas** nm: **el (río) Amazonas** the Amazon

ámbar [ˈambar] nm amber

ambición [ambiˈθjon] nf ambition; **ambicionar** /1a/ vt to aspire to; **ambicioso, -a** adj ambitious

ambidextro, -a [ambiˈðekstro, a] adj ambidextrous

ambientación [ambjentaˈθjon] nf (Cine, Lit etc) setting; (Radio etc) sound effects pl

ambiente [amˈbjente] nm atmosphere; (medio) environment

ambigüedad [ambiɣwe'ðað] nf ambiguity; **ambiguo, -a** adj ambiguous

ámbito ['ambito] nm (campo) field; (fig) scope

ambos, -as ['ambos, as] adj pl, pron pl both

ambulancia [ambu'lanθja] nf ambulance

ambulante [ambu'lante] adj travelling, itinerant

ambulatorio [ambula'torio] nm state health-service clinic

amén [a'men] excl amen; **~ de** besides

amenaza [ame'naθa] nf threat; **amenazar** /1f/ vt to threaten ▷ vi: **amenazar con hacer** to threaten to do

ameno, -a [a'meno, a] adj pleasant

América [a'merika] nf America; **~ del Norte/del Sur** North/South America; **~ Central/Latina** Central/Latin America; **americano, -a** adj, nm/f American; Latin o South American

ametralladora [ametraʎa'ðora] nf machine gun

amigable [ami'ɣaβle] adj friendly

amígdala [a'miɣðala] nf tonsil; **amigdalitis** nf tonsillitis

amigo, -a [a'miɣo, a] adj friendly ▷ nm/f friend; (amante) lover; **ser ~ de** to like, be fond of

aminorar [amino'rar] /1a/ vt to diminish; (reducir) to reduce; **~ la marcha** to slow down

amistad [amis'tað] nf friendship; **amistades** nfpl (amigos) friends; **amistoso, -a** adj friendly

amnesia [am'nesja] nf amnesia

amnistía [amnis'tia] nf amnesty

amo ['amo] nm owner; (jefe) boss

amolar [amo'lar] /1l/ vt to annoy; (MÉX fam) to ruin, damage

amoldar [amol'dar] /1a/ vt to mould; (adaptar) to adapt

amonestación [amonesta'θjon] nf warning; **amonestaciones** nfpl marriage banns

amonestar [amones'tar] /1a/ vt to warn; (Rel) to publish the banns of

amontonar [amonto'nar] /1a/ vt to collect, pile up; **amontonarse** vr to crowd together; (acumularse) to pile up

amor [a'mor] nm love; (amante) lover; **hacer el ~** to make love; **~ propio** self-respect

amoratado, -a [amora'taðo, a] adj purple

amordazar [amorða'θar] /1f/ vt to muzzle; (fig) to gag

amorfo, -a [a'morfo, a] adj amorphous, shapeless

amoroso, -a [amo'roso, a] adj affectionate, loving

amortiguador [amortiɣwa'ðor] nm shock absorber; (parachoques) bumper; **amortiguadores** nmpl (Auto) suspension sg

amortiguar [amorti'ɣwar] /1i/ vt to deaden; (ruido) to muffle; (color) to soften

amotinar [amoti'nar] /1a/ vt to stir up, incite (to riot); **amotinarse** vr to mutiny

amparar [ampa'rar] /1a/ vt to protect; **ampararse** vr to seek protection; (de la lluvia etc) to shelter; **amparo** nm help, protection; **al amparo de** under the protection of

amperio [am'perjo] nm ampère, amp

ampliación [amplja'θjon] nf enlargement; (extensión) extension

ampliar [am'pljar] /1c/ vt to enlarge; to extend

amplificador [amplifika'ðor] nm amplifier

amplificar [amplifi'kar] /1g/ vt to amplify

amplio, -a ['ampljo, a] adj spacious; (falda etc) full; (extenso) extensive; (ancho) wide; **amplitud** nf spaciousness; extent; (fig) amplitude

ampolla [am'poʎa] nf blister; (Med) ampoule

amputar [ampu'tar] /1a/ vt to cut off, amputate

amueblar [amwe'βlar] /1a/ vt to furnish

anales [a'nales] nmpl annals

analfabetismo [analfaβe'tismo] nm illiteracy; **analfabeto, -a** adj, nm/f illiterate

analgésico [anal'xesiko] nm painkiller, analgesic

análisis [a'nalisis] nm inv analysis

analista [ana'lista] nmf (gen) analyst

analizar [anali'θar] /1f/ vt to analyse

analógico, -a [ana'loxiko, a] adj (Inform) analog; (reloj) analogue (BRIT), analog (US)

análogo, -a [a'naloɣo, a] adj analogous, similar

ananá [ana'na] nm pineapple

anarquía [anar'kia] nf anarchy; **anarquista** nmf anarchist

anatomía [anato'mia] nf anatomy

anca ['anka] nf rump, haunch; **ancas** nfpl (fam) behind sg

ancho, -a ['antʃo, a] adj wide; (falda) full; (fig) liberal ▷ nm width; (Ferro) gauge; **le viene muy ~ el cargo** (fig) the job is too much for him; **ponerse ~** to get conceited; **quedarse tan ~** to go on as if nothing had happened; **estar a sus anchas** to be at one's ease

anchoa [an'tʃoa] nf anchovy

anchura [an'tʃura] nf width; (amplitud) wideness

anciano, -a [an'θjano, a] adj old, aged ▷ nm/f old man/woman ▷ nm elder

ancla ['ankla] nf anchor

Andalucía [andalu'θia] nf Andalusia; **andaluz, a** adj, nm/f Andalusian

andamiaje [anda'mjaxe], **andamio** [an'damjo] nm scaffold(ing)

andar [an'dar] /1p/ vt to go, cover, travel ▷ vi to go, walk, travel; (funcionar) to go, work; (estar) to be ▷ nm walk, gait, pace; **andarse** vr (irse) to go away o off; **~ a pie/a caballo/en bicicleta** to go on foot/ on horseback/by bicycle; **¡anda!**

(sorpresa) go on!; **anda en** o **por los 40** he's about 40; **~ haciendo algo** to be doing sth

andén [an'den] nm (Ferro) platform; (Naut) quayside; (LAM: acera) pavement (BRIT), sidewalk (US)

Andes ['andes] nmpl: **los ~** the Andes

andinismo [andin'ismo] nm (LAM) mountaineering, climbing

Andorra [an'dorra] nf Andorra

andrajoso, -a [andra'xoso, a] adj ragged

anduve [an'duβe] vb V **andar**

anécdota [a'nekðota] nf anecdote, story

anegar [ane'ɣar] /1h/ vt to flood; (ahogar) to drown

anemia [a'nemja] nf anaemia

anestesia [anes'tesja] nf anaesthetic; **~ general/local** general/local anaesthetic

anexar [anek'sar] /1a/ vt to annex; (documento) to attach; **anexión** [anek'sjon] nm annexation; **anexo, -a** adj attached ▷ nm annexe

anfibio, -a [an'fiβjo, a] adj amphibious ▷ nm amphibian

anfiteatro [anfite'atro] nm amphitheatre; (Teat) dress circle

anfitrión, -ona [anfi'trjon, ona] nm/f host(ess)

ánfora ['anfora] nf (cántaro) amphora; (LAM Pol) ballot box

ángel ['anxel] nm angel; **~ de la guarda** guardian angel

angina [an'xina] nf (Med) inflammation of the throat; **~ de pecho** angina; **tener ~s** to have tonsillitis, have a sore throat

anglicano, -a [angli'kano, a] adj, nm/f Anglican

anglosajón, -ona [anglosa'xon, 'xona] adj Anglo-Saxon

anguila [an'gila] nf eel

angula [an'gula] nf elver, baby eel

ángulo ['angulo] nm angle; (esquina) corner; (curva) bend

angustia [an'gustja] nf anguish

anhelar [ane'lar] /1a/ *vt* to be eager for; (*desear*) to long for, desire ▷ *vi* to pant, gasp; **anhelo** *nm* eagerness; desire

anidar [ani'ðar] /1a/ *vi* to nest

anillo [a'niʎo] *nm* ring; **~ de boda** wedding ring; **~ de compromiso** engagement ring

animación [anima'θjon] *nf* liveliness; (*vitalidad*) life; (*actividad*) bustle

animado, -a [ani'maðo, a] *adj* lively; (*vivaz*) animated; **animador, a** *nm/f* (TV) host(ess), compère ▷ *nf* (*Deporte*) cheerleader

animal [ani'mal] *adj* animal; (*fig*) stupid ▷ *nm* animal; (*fig*) fool; (*bestia*) brute

animar [ani'mar] /1a/ *vt* (Bio) to animate, give life to; (*fig*) to liven up, brighten up, cheer up; (*estimular*) to stimulate; **animarse** *vr* to cheer up, feel encouraged; (*decidirse*) to make up one's mind

ánimo ['animo] *nm* (*alma*) soul; (*mente*) mind; (*valentía*) courage ▷ *excl* cheer up!

animoso, -a [ani'moso, a] *adj* brave; (*vivo*) lively

aniquilar [aniki'lar] /1a/ *vt* to annihilate, destroy

anís [a'nis] *nm* aniseed; (*licor*) anisette

aniversario [aniβer'sarjo] *nm* anniversary

anoche [a'notʃe] *adv* last night; **antes de ~** the night before last

anochecer [anotʃe'θer] /2d/ *vi* to get dark ▷ *nm* nightfall, dark; **al ~** at nightfall

anodino, -a [ano'ðino, a] *adj* dull, anodyne

anomalía [anoma'lia] *nf* anomaly

anonadado, -a [anona'ðaðo, a] *adj*: **estar ~** to be stunned

anonimato [anoni'mato] *nm* anonymity

anónimo, -a [a'nonimo, a] *adj* anonymous; (*Com*) limited ▷ *nm*

(*carta*) anonymous letter; (*: maliciosa*) poison-pen letter

anormal [anor'mal] *adj* abnormal

anotación [anota'θjon] *nf* note; annotation

anotar [ano'tar] /1a/ *vt* to note down; (*comentar*) to annotate

ansia ['ansja] *nf* anxiety; (*añoranza*) yearning; **ansiar** /1b/ *vt* to long for

ansiedad [ansje'ðað] *nf* anxiety

ansioso, -a [an'sjoso, a] *adj* anxious; (*anhelante*) eager; **~ de** *o* **por algo** greedy for sth

antaño [an'taɲo] *adv* in years gone by, long ago

Antártico [an'tartiko] *nm*: **el (océano) ~** the Antarctic (Ocean)

ante ['ante] *prep* before, in the presence of; (*encarado con*) faced with ▷ *nm* (*piel*) suede; **~ todo** above all

anteanoche [antea'notʃe] *adv* the night before last

anteayer [antea'jer] *adv* the day before yesterday

antebrazo [ante'βraθo] *nm* forearm

antecedente [anteθe'ðente] *adj* previous ▷ *nm* antecedent; **antecedentes** *nmpl* (*profesionales*) background *sg*; **~s penales** criminal record

anteceder [anteθe'ðer] /2a/ *vt* to precede, go before

antecesor, a [anteθe'sor, a] *nm/f* predecessor

antelación [antela'θjon] *nf*: **con ~** in advance

antemano [ante'mano]: **de ~** *adv* beforehand, in advance

antena [an'tena] *nf* antenna; (*de televisión etc*) aerial; **~ parabólica** satellite dish

antenoche [ante'notʃe] (*LAM*) *adv* the night before last

anteojo [ante'oxo] *nm* eyeglass; **anteojos** *nmpl* (*esp LAM*) glasses, spectacles

antepasados [antepa'saðos] *nmpl* ancestors

anteponer [antepo'ner] /2q/ vt to place in front; (fig) to prefer

anterior [ante'rjor] adj preceding, previous; **anterioridad** nf: **con anterioridad a** prior to, before

antes ['antes] adv (con anterioridad) before ▷ prep: **~ de** before ▷ conj: **~ (de) que** before; **~ bien** (but) rather; **dos días ~** two days before o previously; **no quiso venir ~** she didn't want to come any earlier; **tomo el avión ~ que el barco** I take the plane rather than the boat; **~ de** o **nada** (en el tiempo) first of all; (indicando preferencia) above all; **~ que yo** before me; **lo ~ posible** as soon as possible; **cuanto ~ mejor** the sooner the better

antibalas [anti'βalas] adj inv: **chaleco ~** bulletproof jacket

antibiótico [anti'βjotiko] nm antibiotic

anticaspa [anti'kaspa] adj inv anti-dandruff cpd

anticipación [antiθipa'θjon] nf anticipation; **con 10 minutos de ~** 10 minutes early

anticipado, -a [antiθi'paðo, a] adj (in) advance; **por ~** in advance

anticipar [antiθi'par] /1a/ vt to anticipate; (adelantar) to bring forward; (Com) to advance; **anticiparse** vr: **~se a su época** to be ahead of one's time

anticipo [anti'θipo] nm (Com) advance

anticonceptivo, -a [antikonθep'tiβo, a] adj, nm contraceptive

anticongelante [antikonxe'lante] nm antifreeze

anticuado, -a [anti'kwaðo, a] adj out-of-date, old-fashioned; (desusado) obsolete

anticuario [anti'kwarjo] nm antique dealer

anticuerpo [anti'kwerpo] nm (Med) antibody

antidepresivo [antiðepre'siβo] nm antidepressant

antidoping [anti'ðopin] adj inv: **control ~** drugs test

antídoto [an'tiðoto] nm antidote

antiestético, -a [anties'tetiko, a] adj unsightly

antifaz [anti'faθ] nm mask; (velo) veil

antiglobalización [antiglobaliθa'θjon] nf anti-globalization; **antiglobalizador, a** adj anti-globalization cpd

antiguamente [antiɣwa'mente] adv formerly; (hace mucho tiempo) long ago

antigüedad [antiɣwe'ðað] nf antiquity; (artículo) antique; (rango) seniority

antiguo, -a [an'tiɣwo, a] adj old, ancient; (que fue) former

Antillas [an'tiʎas] nfpl: **las ~** the West Indies

antílope [an'tilope] nm antelope

antinatural [antinatu'ral] adj unnatural

antipatía [antipa'tia] nf antipathy, dislike; **antipático, -a** adj disagreeable, unpleasant

antirrobo [anti'rroβo] adj inv (alarma etc) anti-theft

antisemita [antise'mita] adj anti-Semitic ▷ nmf anti-Semite

antiséptico, -a [anti'septiko, a] adj antiseptic ▷ nm antiseptic

antisistema [antisis'tema] adj inv anticapitalist

antivirus [anti'birus] nm inv (Inform) antivirus program

antojarse [anto'xarse] /1a/ vr (desear): **se me antoja comprarlo** I have a mind to buy it; (pensar): **se me antoja que ...** I have a feeling that ...

antojo [an'toxo] nm caprice, whim; (rosa) birthmark; (lunar) mole

antología [antolo'xia] nf anthology

antorcha [an'tortʃa] nf torch

antro ['antro] nm cavern

antropología [antropoloˈxia] *nf*
anthropology

anual [aˈnwal] *adj* annual

anuario [aˈnwarjo] *nm* yearbook

anublado, -a *adj* overcast

anulación [anulaˈθjon] *nf* (*de un
matrimonio*) annulment; (*cancelación*)
cancellation

anular [anuˈlar] /1a/ *vt* (*contrato*) to
annul, cancel; (*suscripción*) to cancel;
(*ley*) to repeal ▷ *nm* ring finger

anunciar [anunˈθjar] /1b/ *vt* to
announce; (*proclamar*) to proclaim;
(*Com*) to advertise

anuncio [aˈnunθjo] *nm*
announcement; (*señal*) sign; (*Com*)
advertisement; (*cartel*) poster

anzuelo [anˈθwelo] *nm* hook; (*para
pescar*) fish hook

añadidura [aɲaðiˈðura] *nf* addition,
extra; **por ~** besides, in addition

añadir [aɲaˈðir] /3a/ *vt* to add

añejo, -a [aˈɲexo, a] *adj* old; (*vino*)
mature

añicos [aˈɲikos] *nmpl*: **hacer ~** to
smash, shatter

año [ˈaɲo] *nm* year; **¡Feliz A~ Nuevo!**
Happy New Year!; **tener 15 ~s** to be
15 (years old); **los ~s 80** the eighties;
~ bisiesto/escolar/fiscal/sabático
leap/school/tax/sabbatical year; **el ~
que viene** next year

añoranza [aɲoˈranθa] *nf* nostalgia;
(*anhelo*) longing

apa [ˈapa] *excl* (*LAm*) goodness me!,
good gracious!

apabullar [apaβuˈʎar] /1a/ *vt* to crush

apacible [apaˈθiβle] *adj* gentle, mild

apaciguar [apaθiˈɣwar] /1i/ *vt* to
pacify, calm (down)

apadrinar [apaðriˈnar] /1a/ *vt* to
sponsor, support; (*Rel: niño*) to be
godfather to

apagado, -a [apaˈɣaðo, a] *adj* (*volcán*)
extinct; (*color*) dull; (*voz*) quiet; (*sonido*)
muted, muffled; (*persona: apático*)
listless; **estar ~** (*fuego, luz*) to be out;
(*radio, TV etc*) to be off

apagar [apaˈɣar] /1h/ *vt* to put out;
(*sonido*) to silence, muffle; (*sed*) to
quench; (*Elec, Radio, TV*) to turn off;
(*Inform*) to toggle off

apagón [apaˈɣon] *nm* blackout,
power cut

apalabrar [apalaˈβrar] /1a/ *vt* to
agree to; (*obrero*) to engage

apalear [apaleˈar] /1a/ *vt* to beat,
thrash

apantallar [apantaˈʎar] /1a/ *vt* (*LAm*)
to impress

apañar [apaˈɲar] /1a/ *vt* to pick up;
(*asir*) to take hold of, grasp; (*reparar*)
to mend, patch up; **apañarse** *vr* to
manage, get along

apapachar [apapaˈtʃar] /1a/ *vt* (*LAm
fam*) to cuddle, hug

aparador [aparaˈðor] *nm* sideboard;
(*LAm: escaparate*) shop window

aparato [apaˈrato] *nm* apparatus;
(*máquina*) machine; (*doméstico*)
appliance; (*boato*) ostentation; **al ~**
(*Telec*) speaking; **~ digestivo** digestive
system; **aparatoso, -a** *adj* showy,
ostentatious

aparcamiento [aparkaˈmjento] *nm*
car park (*BRIT*), parking lot (*US*)

aparcar [aparˈkar] /1g/ *vt, vi* to park

aparear [apareˈar] /1a/ *vt* (*objetos*)
to pair, match; (*animales*) to mate;
aparearse *vr* to form a pair; to mate

aparecer [apareˈθer] /2d/ *vi* to
appear; **aparecerse** *vr* to appear

aparejador, a [aparexaˈðor, a] *nm/f*
(*Arq*) quantity surveyor

aparejo [apaˈrexo] *nm* harness;
(*Naut*) rigging; (*de poleas*) block and
tackle

aparentar [aparenˈtar] /1a/ *vt* (*edad*)
to look; (*fingir*): **~ tristeza** to pretend
to be sad

aparente [apaˈrente] *adj* apparent;
(*adecuado*) suitable

aparezca *etc vb V* **aparecer**

aparición [apariˈθjon] *nf*
appearance; (*de libro*) publication; (*de
fantasma*) apparition

apariencia [apa'rjenθja] nf
(outward) appearance; **en ~**
outwardly, seemingly

apartado, -a [apar'taðo, a] adj
separate; (lejano) remote ▷ nm
(tipográfico) paragraph; **~ de correos**
(ESP), **~ postal** (LAM) post office box

apartamento [aparta'mento] nm
apartment, flat (BRIT)

apartar [apar'tar] /1a/ vt to separate;
(quitar) to remove; **apartarse** vr to
separate, part; (irse) to move away;
(mantenerse aparte) to keep away

aparte [a'parte] adv (separadamente)
separately; (además) besides ▷ nm
aside; (tipográfico) new paragraph

aparthotel [aparto'tel] nm serviced
apartments

apasionado, -a [apasjo'naðo, a] adj
passionate

apasionar [apasjo'nar] /1a/ vt to
excite; **apasionarse** vr to get excited;
le apasiona el fútbol she's crazy
about football

apatía [apa'tia] nf apathy

apático, -a [a'patiko, a] adj apathetic

Apdo. nm abr (= Apartado (de Correos))
P.O. Box

apeadero [apea'ðero] nm halt,
stopping place

apearse [ape'arse] /1a/ vr (jinete) to
dismount; (bajarse) to get down o out;
(de coche) to get out

apechugar [apetʃu'ɣar] /1h/ vi: **~
con algo** to face up to sth

apegarse [ape'ɣarse] /1h/ vr: **~ a**
to become attached to; **apego** nm
attachment, devotion

apelar [ape'lar] /1a/ vi to appeal; **~ a**
(fig) to resort to

apellidar [apeʎi'ðar] /1a/ vt to call,
name; **apellidarse** vr: **se apellida
Pérez** her (sur)name's Pérez

apellido [ape'ʎiðo] nm surname

apenar [ape'nar] /1a/ vt to grieve,
trouble; (LAM: avergonzar) to
embarrass; **apenarse** vr to grieve;
(LAM: avergonzarse) to be embarrassed

apenas [a'penas] adv scarcely, hardly
▷ conj as soon as, no sooner

apéndice [a'pendiθe] nm appendix;
apendicitis nf appendicitis

aperitivo [aperi'tiβo] nm (bebida)
aperitif; (comida) appetizer

apertura [aper'tura] nf opening; (Pol)
liberalization

apestar [apes'tar] /1a/ vt to infect
▷ vi: **~ (a)** to stink (of)

apetecer [apete'θer] /2d/ vt: **¿te
apetece una tortilla?** do you fancy an
omelette?; **apetecible** adj desirable;
(comida) appetizing

apetito [ape'tito] nm appetite;
apetitoso, -a adj appetizing; (fig)
tempting

apiadarse [apja'ðarse] /1a/ vr: **~ de**
to take pity on

ápice ['apiθe] nm whit, iota

apilar [api'lar] /1a/ vt to pile o heap up

apiñar [api'nar] /1a/ vt to crowd;
apiñarse vr to crowd o press together

apio ['apjo] nm celery

apisonadora [apisona'ðora] nf
steamroller

aplacar [apla'kar] /1g/ vt to placate

aplastante [aplas'tante] adj
overwhelming; (lógica) compelling

aplastar [aplas'tar] /1a/ vt to squash
(flat); (fig) to crush

aplaudir [aplau'ðir] /3a/ vt to
applaud

aplauso [a'plauso] nm applause; (fig)
approval, acclaim

aplazamiento [aplaθa'mjento] nm
postponement

aplazar [apla'θar] /1f/ vt to postpone,
defer

aplicación [aplika'θjon] nf
application; (para móvil, internet) app;
(esfuerzo) effort

aplicado, -a [apli'kaðo, a] adj
diligent, hard-working

aplicar [apli'kar] /1g/ vt (ejecutar) to
apply; **aplicarse** vr to apply o.s.

aplique etc [a'plike] vb V **aplicar** ▷ nm
wall light o lamp

aplomo [a'plomo] *nm* aplomb, self-assurance

apodar [apo'ðar] /1a/ *vt* to nickname

apoderado [apoðe'raðo] *nm* agent, representative

apoderar [apoðe'rar] /1a/ *vt* to authorize; **apoderarse** *vr*: **~se de** to take possession of

apodo [a'poðo] *nm* nickname

apogeo [apo'xeo] *nm* peak, summit

apoquinar [apoki'nar] /1a/ *vt* (*fam*) to cough up, fork out

aporrear [aporre'ar] /1a/ *vt* to beat (up)

aportar [apor'tar] /1a/ *vt* to contribute ▷ *vi* to reach port; **aportarse** *vr* (LAM: *llegar*) to arrive, come

aposta [a'posta] *adv* deliberately, on purpose

apostar [apos'tar] /1a, 1l/ *vt* to bet, stake; (*tropas etc*) to station, post ▷ *vi* to bet

apóstol [a'postol] *nm* apostle

apóstrofo [a'postrofo] *nm* apostrophe

apoyar [apo'jar] /1a/ *vt* to lean, rest; (*fig*) to support, back; **apoyarse** *vr*: **~se en** to lean on; **apoyo** *nm* support, backing

apreciable [apre'θjaβle] *adj* considerable; (*fig*) esteemed

apreciar [apre'θjar] /1b/ *vt* to evaluate, assess; (*Com*) to appreciate, value; (*persona*) to respect; (*tamaño*) to gauge, assess; (*detalles*) to notice

aprecio [a'preθjo] *nm* valuation, estimate; (*fig*) appreciation

aprehender [apreen'der] /2a/ *vt* to apprehend, detain

apremio [a'premjo] *nm* urgency

aprender [apren'der] /2a/ *vt, vi* to learn; **aprenderse** *vr*: **~se algo de memoria** to learn sth (off) by heart

aprendiz, a [apren'diθ, a] *nm/f* apprentice; (*principiante*) learner; **aprendizaje** *nm* apprenticeship

aprensión [apren'sjon] *nm* apprehension, fear; **aprensivo, -a** *adj* apprehensive

apresar [apre'sar] /1a/ *vt* to seize; (*capturar*) to capture

apresurado, -a [apresu'raðo, a] *adj* hurried, hasty

apresurar [apresu'rar] /1a/ *vt* to hurry, accelerate; **apresurarse** *vr* to hurry, make haste

apretado, -a [apre'taðo, a] *adj* tight; (*escritura*) cramped

apretar [apre'tar] /1j/ *vt* to squeeze; (*Tec*) to tighten; (*presionar*) to press together, pack ▷ *vi* to be too tight

apretón [apre'ton] *nm* squeeze; **~ de manos** handshake

aprieto [a'prjeto] *nm* squeeze; (*dificultad*) difficulty; **estar en un ~** to be in a fix

aprisa [a'prisa] *adv* quickly, hurriedly

aprisionar [aprisjo'nar] /1a/ *vt* to imprison

aprobación [aproβa'θjon] *nf* approval

aprobar [apro'βar] /1l/ *vt* to approve (of); (*examen, materia*) to pass ▷ *vi* to pass

apropiado, -a [apro'pjaðo, a] *adj* appropriate, suitable

apropiarse [apro'pjarse] /1b/ *vr*: **~ de** to appropriate

aprovechado, -a [aproβe'tʃaðo, a] *adj* industrious, hardworking; (*económico*) thrifty; (*pey*) unscrupulous

aprovechar [aproβe'tʃar] /1a/ *vt* to use; (*explotar*) to exploit; (*experiencia*) to profit from; (*oferta, oportunidad*) to take advantage of ▷ *vi* to progress, improve; **aprovecharse** *vr*: **~se de** to make use of; (*pey*) to take advantage of; **¡que aproveche!** enjoy your meal!

aproximación [aproksima'θjon] *nf* approximation; (*de lotería*) consolation prize

aproximadamente [aproksimaða'mente] *adv* approximately

aproximar [aproksi'mar] /1a/ vt to bring nearer; **aproximarse** vr to come near, approach

apruebe etc vb V **aprobar**

aptitud [apti'tuð] nf aptitude

apto, -a ['apto, a] adj: **~ (para)** suitable (for)

apuesto, -a [a'pwesto, a] adj neat, elegant ▷ nf bet, wager

apuntar [apun'tar] /1a/ vt (con arma) to aim at; (con dedo) to point at o to; (anotar) to note (down); (Teat) to prompt; **apuntarse** vr (Deporte: tanto, victoria) to score; (Escol) to enrol

▌ No confundir apuntar con la palabra inglesa appoint.

apunte [a'punte] nm note

apuñalar [apuɲa'lar] /1a/ vt to stab

apurado, -a [apu'raðo, a] adj needy; (difícil) difficult; (peligroso) dangerous; (LAM: con prisa) hurried, rushed

apurar [apu'rar] /1a/ vt (agotar) to drain; (recursos) to use up; (molestar) to annoy; **apurarse** vr (preocuparse) to worry; (esp LAM: darse prisa) to hurry

apuro [a'puro] nm (aprieto) fix, jam; (escasez) want, hardship; (vergüenza) embarrassment; (LAM: prisa) haste, urgency

aquejado, -a [ake'xaðo, a] adj: **~ de** (Med) afflicted by

aquel, aquella, aquellos, -as [a'kel, a'keʎa, a'keʎos, -as] adj that, those pl ▷ pron that (one), those (ones) pl

aquél, aquélla, aquéllos, -as [a'kel, a'keʎa, a'keʎos, -as] pron that (one), those (ones) pl

aquello [a'keʎo] pron that, that business

aquí [a'ki] adv (lugar) here; (tiempo) now; **~ arriba** up here; **~ mismo** right here; **~ yace** here lies; **de ~ a siete días** a week from now

ara ['ara] nf: **en ~s de** for the sake of

árabe ['araβe] adj Arab ▷ nmf Arab ▷ nm (Ling) Arabic

Arabia [a'raβja] nf Arabia; **~ Saudí** o **Saudita** Saudi Arabia

arado [a'raðo] nm plough

Aragón [ara'ɣon] nm Aragon; **aragonés, -esa** adj, nm/f Aragonese

arancel [aran'θel] nm tariff, duty

arandela [aran'dela] nf (Tec) washer

araña [a'raɲa] nf (Zool) spider; (lámpara) chandelier

arañar [ara'ɲar] /1a/ vt to scratch

arañazo [ara'ɲaθo] nm scratch

arbitrar [arβi'trar] /1a/ vt to arbitrate in; (Deporte) to referee ▷ vi to arbitrate

arbitrario, -a [arβi'trarjo, a] adj arbitrary

árbitro ['arβitro] nm arbitrator; (Deporte) referee; (Tenis) umpire

árbol ['arβol] nm (Bot) tree; (Naut) mast; (Tec) axle, shaft; **~ de Navidad** Christmas tree

arboleda [arβo'leða] nf grove, plantation

arbusto [ar'βusto] nm bush, shrub

arca ['arka] nf chest, box

arcada [ar'kaða] nf arcade; (de puente) arch, span; **arcadas** nfpl (náuseas) retching sg

arcaico, -a [ar'kaiko, a] adj archaic

arce ['arθe] nm maple tree

arcén [ar'θen] nm (de autopista) hard shoulder; (de carretera) verge

archipiélago [artʃi'pjelaɣo] nm archipelago

archivador [artʃiβa'ðor] nm filing cabinet

archivar [artʃi'βar] /1a/ vt to file (away); **archivo** nm archive(s) (pl); (Inform) file; **archivo adjunto** (Inform) attachment; **archivo de seguridad** (Inform) backup file

arcilla [ar'θiʎa] nf clay

arco ['arko] nm (Mat) arc; (Mil, Mus) bow; **~ iris** rainbow

arder [ar'ðer] /2a/ vt, vi to burn; **estar que arde** (persona) to fume

ardid [ar'ðið] nm ploy, trick

ardiente [ar'ðjente] adj ardent

ardilla [ar'ðiʎa] nf squirrel

ardor [ar'ðor] nm (calor) heat; (fig) ardour; **~ de estómago** heartburn

arduo, -a ['arðwo, a] *adj* arduous

área ['area] *nf* area; (*Deporte*) penalty area

arena [a'rena] *nf* sand; (*de una lucha*) arena; **arenal** *nm* (*terreno arenoso*) sandy area

arenisca [are'niska] *nf* sandstone; (*cascajo*) grit

arenoso, -a [are'noso, a] *adj* sandy

arenque [a'renke] *nm* herring

arete [a'rete] *nm* (*LAM*) earring

Argel [ar'xel] *n* Algiers

Argelia [ar'xelja] *nf* Algeria; **argelino, -a** *adj, nm/f* Algerian

Argentina [arxen'tina] *nf*: **(la) ~** Argentina

argentino, -a [arxen'tino, a] *adj* Argentinian; (*de plata*) silvery ▷ *nm/f* Argentinian

argolla [ar'ɣoʎa] *nf* (large) ring

argot [ar'ɣo] *nm* slang

argucia [ar'ɣuθja] *nf* subtlety, sophistry

argumentar [arɣumen'tar] /1a/ *vt, vi* to argue

argumento [arɣu'mento] *nm* argument; (*razonamiento*) reasoning; (*de novela etc*) plot; (*Cine, TV*) storyline

aria ['arja] *nf* aria

aridez [ari'ðeθ] *nf* aridity, dryness

árido, -a ['ariðo, a] *adj* arid, dry

Aries ['arjes] *nm* Aries

arisco, -a [a'risko, a] *adj* surly; (*insociable*) unsociable

aristócrata [aris'tokrata] *nmf* aristocrat

arma ['arma] *nf* arm; **armas** *nfpl* arms; **~ blanca** blade, knife; **~ de doble filo** double-edged sword; **~ de fuego** firearm; **~s de destrucción masiva** weapons of mass destruction

armada [ar'maða] *nf* armada; (*flota*) fleet

armadillo [arma'ðiʎo] *nm* armadillo

armado, -a [ar'maðo, a] *adj* armed; (*Tec*) reinforced

armadura [arma'ðura] *nf* (*Mil*) armour; (*Tec*) framework; (*Zool*) skeleton; (*Física*) armature

armamento [arma'mento] *nm* armament; (*Naut*) fitting-out

armar [ar'mar] /1a/ *vt* (*soldado*) to arm; (*máquina*) to assemble; (*navío*) to fit out; **~la, ~ un lío** to start a row, kick up a fuss

armario [ar'marjo] *nm* wardrobe; (*de cocina, baño*) cupboard; **~ empotrado** built-in cupboard

armatoste [arma'toste] *nm* (*mueble*) monstrosity; (*máquina*) contraption

armazón [arma'θon] *nm o* body, chassis; (*de mueble etc*) frame; (*Arq*) skeleton

armiño [ar'miɲo] *nm* stoat; (*piel*) ermine

armisticio [armis'tiθjo] *nm* armistice

armonía [armo'nia] *nf* harmony

armónica [ar'monika] *nf* harmonica

armonizar [armoni'θar] /1f/ *vt* to harmonize; (*diferencias*) to reconcile

aro ['aro] *nm* ring; (*tejo*) quoit; (*LAM: pendiente*) earring

aroma [a'roma] *nm* aroma; **aromaterapia** *nf* aromatherapy; **aromático, -a** *adj* aromatic

arpa ['arpa] *nf* harp

arpía [ar'pia] *nf* shrew

arpón [ar'pon] *nm* harpoon

arqueología [arkeolo'xia] *nf* archaeology; **arqueólogo, -a** *nm/f* archaeologist

arquetipo [arke'tipo] *nm* archetype

arquitecto, -a *nm/f* architect; **arquitectura** *nf* architecture

arrabal [arra'βal] *nm* suburb; (*LAM*) slum; **arrabales** *nmpl* (*afueras*) outskirts

arraigar [arrai'ɣar] /1h/ *vi* to take root

arrancar [arran'kar] /1g/ *vt* (*sacar*) to extract, pull out; (*arrebatar*) to snatch (away); (*Inform*) to boot; (*fig*) to extract ▷ *vi* (*Auto, máquina*) to start; (*ponerse en marcha*) to get going; **~ de** to stem from

arranque *etc* [a'rranke] *vb* V **arrancar** ▷ *nm* sudden start; (*Auto*) start; (*fig*) fit, outburst

arrasar [arra'sar] /1a/ vt (aplanar) to level, flatten; (destruir) to demolish

arrastrar [arras'trar] /1a/ vt to drag (along); (fig) to drag down, degrade; (agua, viento) to carry away ▷ vi to drag, trail on the ground; **arrastrarse** vr to crawl; (fig) to grovel; **llevar algo arrastrado** to drag sth along

arrear [arre'ar] /1a/ vt to drive on, urge on ▷ vi to hurry along

arrebatar [arreβa'tar] /1a/ vt to snatch (away), seize; (fig) to captivate

arrebato [arre'βato] nm fit of rage, fury; (éxtasis) rapture

arrecife [arre'θife] nm reef

arreglado, -a [arre'ɣlaðo, a] adj (ordenado) neat, orderly; (moderado) moderate, reasonable

arreglar [arre'ɣlar] /1a/ vt (poner orden) to tidy up; (algo roto) to fix, repair; (problema) to solve; **arreglarse** vr to reach an understanding; **arreglárselas** (fam) to get by, manage

arreglo [a'rreɣlo] nm settlement; (orden) order; (acuerdo) agreement; (Mus) arrangement, setting

arremangar [arreman'gar] /1h/ vt to roll up, turn up; **arremangarse** vr to roll up one's sleeves

arremeter [arreme'ter] /2a/ vi: ~ **contra algn** to attack sb

arrendamiento [arrenda'mjento] nm letting; (el alquilar) hiring; (contrato) lease; (alquiler) rent; **arrendar** /1j/ vt to let; to lease; to rent; **arrendatario, -a** nm/f tenant

arreos [a'rreos] nmpl (de caballo) harness sg, trappings

arrepentimiento [arrepenti'mjento] nm regret, repentance

arrepentirse [arrepen'tirse] /3i/ vr to repent; ~ **de (haber hecho) algo** to regret (doing) sth

arresto [a'rresto] nm arrest; (Mil) detention; (audacia) boldness, daring; ~ **domiciliario** house arrest

arriar [a'rrjar] /1c/ vt (velas) to haul down; (bandera) to lower, strike; (un cable) to pay out

○ **PALABRA CLAVE**

arriba [a'rriβa] adv **1** (posición) above; **desde arriba** from above; **arriba del todo** at the very top, right on top; **Juan está arriba** Juan is upstairs; **lo arriba mencionado** the aforementioned

2 (dirección): **calle arriba** up the street

3: **de arriba abajo** from top to bottom; **mirar a algn de arriba abajo** to look sb up and down

4: **para arriba: de 50 euros para arriba** from 50 euros up(wards)

▷ adj: **de arriba: el piso de arriba** the upstairs flat (BRIT) o apartment; **la parte de arriba** the top o upper part

▷ prep: **arriba de** (LAM: por encima de) above; **arriba de 200 dólares** more than 200 dollars

▷ excl: **¡arriba!** up!; **¡manos arriba!** hands up!; **¡arriba España!** long live Spain!

arribar [arri'βar] /1a/ vi to put into port; (llegar) to arrive

arriesgado, -a [arrjes'ɣaðo, a] adj (peligroso) risky; (audaz) bold, daring

arriesgar [arrjes'ɣar] /1h/ vt to risk; (poner en peligro) to endanger; **arriesgarse** vr to take a risk

arrimar [arri'mar] /1a/ vt (acercar) to bring close; (poner de lado) to set aside; **arrimarse** vr to come close o closer; ~**se a** to lean on

arrinconar [arrinko'nar] /1a/ vt (colocar) to put in a corner; (enemigo) to corner; (fig) to put to one side; (abandonar) to push aside

arroba [a'rroβa] nf (en dirección electrónica) at sign, @

arrodillarse [arroði'ʎarse] /1a/ vr to kneel (down)

arrogante [arro'ɣante] *adj* arrogant
arrojar [arro'xar] /1a/ *vt* to throw, hurl; (*humo*) to emit, give out; (*Com*) to yield, produce; **arrojarse** *vr* to throw o hurl o.s.
arrojo [a'rroxo] *nm* daring
arrollador, a [arroʎa'ðor, a] *adj* overwhelming
arrollar [arro'ʎar] /1a/ *vt* (*Auto*) to run over; (*Deporte*) to crush
arropar [arro'par] /1a/ *vt* to cover (up), wrap up; **arroparse** *vr* to wrap o.s. up
arroyo [a'rrojo] *nm* stream; (*de la calle*) gutter
arroz [a'rroθ] *nm* rice; **~ con leche** rice pudding
arruga [a'rruɣa] *nf* (*de cara*) wrinkle; (*de vestido*) crease; **arrugar** /1h/ *vt* to wrinkle; to crease; **arrugarse** *vr* to get creased
arruinar [arrwi'nar] /1a/ *vt* to ruin, wreck; **arruinarse** *vr* to be ruined
arsenal [arse'nal] *nm* naval dockyard; (*Mil*) arsenal
arte ['arte] *nm* (*gen m en sg, f en pl*) art; (*maña*) skill, guile; **artes** *nfpl* arts; **Bellas A~s** Fine Art *sg*
artefacto [arte'fakto] *nm* appliance
arteria [ar'terja] *nf* artery
artesanía [artesa'nia] *nf* craftsmanship; (*artículos*) handicrafts *pl*; **artesano, -a** *nm/f* artisan, craftsman/woman
ártico, -a ['artiko, a] *adj* Arctic ▷ *nm*: **el (océano) Á~** the Arctic (Ocean)
articulación [artikula'θjon] *nf* articulation; (*Med, Tec*) joint
artículo [ar'tikulo] *nm* article; (*cosa*) thing, article; **artículos** *nmpl* goods; **~s de escritorio** stationery
artífice [ar'tifiθe] *nmf* (*fig*) architect
artificial [artifi'θjal] *adj* artificial
artillería [artiʎe'ria] *nf* artillery
artilugio [arti'luxjo] *nm* gadget
artimaña [arti'maɲa] *nf* trap, snare; (*astucia*) cunning

artista [ar'tista] *nmf* (*pintor*) artist, painter; (*Teat*) artist, artiste; **~ de cine** film actor/actress; **artístico, -a** *adj* artistic
artritis [ar'tritis] *nf* arthritis
arveja [ar'βexa] *nf* (*LAM*) pea
arzobispo [arθo'βispo] *nm* archbishop
as [as] *nm* ace
asa ['asa] *nf* handle; (*fig*) lever
asado [a'saðo] *nm* roast (meat); (*LAM: barbacoa*) barbecue

○ **ASADO**
○
○ Traditional Latin American
○ barbecues, especially in the River
○ Plate area, are celebrated in the
○ open air around a large grill which is
○ used to grill mainly beef and various
○ kinds of spicy pork sausage. They
○ are usually very common during
○ the summer and can go on for
○ several days.

asador [asa'ðor] *nm* spit
asadura, asaduras [asa'ðura(s)] *nf, nfpl* entrails *pl*, offal *sg*
asalariado, -a [asala'rjaðo, a] *adj* paid, salaried ▷ *nm/f* wage earner
asaltar [asal'tar] /1a/ *vt* to attack, assault; (*fig*) to assail; **asalto** *nm* attack, assault; (*Deporte*) round
asamblea [asam'blea] *nf* assembly; (*reunión*) meeting
asar [a'sar] /1a/ *vt* to roast
ascendencia [asθen'denθja] *nf* ancestry; (*LAM: influencia*) ascendancy; **de ~ francesa** of French origin
ascender [asθen'der] /2g/ *vi* (*subir*) to ascend, rise; (*ser promovido*) to gain promotion ▷ *vt* to promote; **~ a** to amount to; **ascendiente** *nm* influence ▷ *nmf* ancestor
ascensión [asθen'sjon] *nf* ascent; **la A~** the Ascension
ascenso [as'θenso] *nm* ascent; (*promoción*) promotion

ascensor [asθen'sor] *nm* lift (BRIT), elevator (US)

asco ['asko] *nm*: **el ajo me da ~** I hate *o* loathe garlic; **estar hecho un ~** to be filthy; **¡qué ~!** how revolting *o* disgusting!

ascua ['askwa] *nf* ember

aseado, -a [ase'aðo, a] *adj* clean; (*arreglado*) tidy; (*pulcro*) smart

asear [ase'ar] /1a/ *vt* (*lavar*) to wash; (*ordenar*) to tidy (up)

asediar [ase'ðjar] /1b/ *vt* (Mil) to besiege, lay siege to; (*fig*) to chase, pester; **asedio** *nm* siege; (Com) run

asegurado, a [aseɣu'raðo, a] *adj* insured

asegurador, -a [aseɣura'ðor, a] *nm/f* insurer

asegurar [aseɣu'rar] /1a/ *vt* (*consolidar*) to secure, fasten; (*dar garantía de*) to guarantee; (*preservar*) to safeguard; (*afirmar, dar por cierto*) to assure, affirm; (*tranquilizar*) to reassure; (*hacer un seguro*) to insure; **asegurarse** *vr* to assure o.s., make sure

asemejarse [aseme'xarse] /1a/ *vr* to be alike; **~ a** to be like, resemble

asentado, -a [asen'taðo, a] *adj* established, settled

asentar [asen'tar] /1j/ *vt* (*sentar*) to seat, sit down; (*poner*) to place, establish; (*alisar*) to level, smooth down *o* out; (*anotar*) to note down ▷ *vi* to be suitable, suit

asentir [asen'tir] /3i/ *vi* to assent, agree; **~ con la cabeza** to nod (one's head)

aseo [a'seo] *nm* cleanliness; **aseos** *nmpl* toilet *sg* (BRIT), cloakroom *sg* (BRIT), restroom *sg* (US)

aséptico, -a [a'septiko, a] *adj* germ-free, free from infection

asequible [ase'kiβle] *adj* (*precio*) reasonable; (*meta*) attainable; (*persona*) approachable

asesinar [asesi'nar] /1a/ *vt* to murder; (Pol) to assassinate; **asesinato** *nm* murder; assassination

asesino, -a [ase'sino, a] *nm/f* murderer, killer; (Pol) assassin

asesor, a [ase'sor, a] *nm/f* adviser, consultant; **asesorar** /1a/ *vt* (Jur) to advise, give legal advice to; (Com) to act as consultant to; **asesorarse** *vr*: **asesorarse con** *o* **de** to take advice from, consult; **asesoría** *nf* (*cargo*) consultancy; (*oficina*) consultant's office

asestar [ases'tar] /1a/ *vt* (*golpe*) to deal

asfalto [as'falto] *nm* asphalt

asfixia [as'fiksja] *nf* asphyxia, suffocation; **asfixiar** /1b/ *vt* to asphyxiate, suffocate; **asfixiarse** *vr* to be asphyxiated, suffocate

así [a'si] *adv* (*de esta manera*) in this way, like this, thus; (*aunque*) although; (*tan pronto como*) as soon as; **~ que** so; **~ como** as well as; **~ y todo** even so; **¿no es ~?** isn't it?, didn't you? *etc*; **~ de grande** this big

Asia ['asja] *nf* Asia; **asiático, -a** *adj, nm/f* Asian, Asiatic

asiduo, -a [a'siðwo, a] *adj* assiduous; (*frecuente*) frequent ▷ *nm/f* regular (customer)

asiento [a'sjento] *nm* (*mueble*) seat, chair; (*de coche, en tribunal etc*) seat; (*localidad*) seat, place; (*fundamento*) site; **~ delantero/trasero** front/back seat

asignación [asiɣna'θjon] *nf* (*atribución*) assignment; (*reparto*) allocation; (*sueldo*) salary; (Com) allowance; **~ (semanal)** (weekly) pocket money

asignar [asiɣ'nar] /1a/ *vt* to assign, allocate

asignatura [asiɣna'tura] *nf* subject; (*curso*) course

asilo [a'silo] *nm* (*refugio*) asylum, refuge; (*establecimiento*) home, institution; **~ político** political asylum

asimilar [asimi'lar] /1a/ *vt* to assimilate

asimismo [asi'mismo] *adv* in the same way, likewise

asistencia [asis'tenθja] *nf* audience; (*Med*) attendance; (*ayuda*) assistance; **~ en carretera** roadside assistance; **asistente, -a** *nm/f* assistant; **los asistentes** those present; **asistente social** social worker

asistido, -a [asis'tiðo, a] *adj*: **~ por ordenador** computer-assisted

asistir [asis'tir] /3a/ *vt* to assist, help ▷ *vi*: **~ a** to attend, be present at

asma ['asma] *nf* asthma

asno ['asno] *nm* donkey; (*fig*) ass

asociación [asoθja'θjon] *nf* association; (*Com*) partnership; **asociado, -a** *adj* associate ▷ *nm/f* associate; (*Com*) partner

asociar [aso'θjar] /1b/ *vt* to associate

asomar [aso'mar] /1a/ *vt* to show, stick out ▷ *vi* to appear; **asomarse** *vr* to appear, show up; **~ la cabeza por la ventana** to put one's head out of the window

asombrar [asom'brar] /1a/ *vt* to amaze, astonish; **asombrarse** *vr*: **~se (de)** (*sorprenderse*) to be amazed (at); (*asustarse*) to be frightened (at); **asombro** *nm* amazement, astonishment; (*susto*) fright; **asombroso, -a** *adj* amazing

asomo [a'somo] *nm* hint, sign

aspa ['aspa] *nf* (*cruz*) cross; (*de molino*) sail; **en ~** X-shaped

aspaviento [aspa'βjento] *nm* exaggerated display of feeling; (*fam*) fuss

aspecto [as'pekto] *nm* (*apariencia*) look, appearance; (*fig*) aspect

áspero, -a ['aspero, a] *adj* (*al tacto*) rough; (*al gusto*) sharp, sour; (*voz*) harsh

aspersión [asper'sjon] *nf* sprinkling

aspiración [aspira'θjon] *nf* breath, inhalation; (*Mus*) short pause; **aspiraciones** *nfpl* (*ambiciones*) aspirations

aspirador [aspira'ðor] *nm* = **aspiradora**

aspiradora [aspira'ðora] *nf* vacuum cleaner, Hoover®

aspirante [aspi'rante] *nmf* (*candidato*) candidate; (*Deporte*) contender

aspirar [aspi'rar] /1a/ *vt* to breathe in ▷ *vi*: **~ a** to aspire to

aspirina [aspi'rina] *nf* aspirin

asqueroso, -a [aske'roso, a] *adj* disgusting, sickening

asta ['asta] *nf* lance; (*arpón*) spear; (*mango*) shaft, handle; (*Zool*) horn; **a media ~** at half mast

asterisco [aste'risko] *nm* asterisk

astilla [as'tiʎa] *nf* splinter; (*pedacito*) chip; **astillas** *nfpl* (*leña*) firewood *sg*

astillero [asti'ʎero] *nm* shipyard

astro ['astro] *nm* star

astrología [astrolo'xia] *nf* astrology; **astrólogo, -a** *nm/f* astrologer

astronauta [astro'nauta] *nmf* astronaut

astronomía [astrono'mia] *nf* astronomy

astucia [as'tuθja] *nf* astuteness; (*destreza*) clever trick

asturiano, -a [astu'rjano, a] *adj*, *nm/f* Asturian

astuto, -a [as'tuto, a] *adj* astute; (*taimado*) cunning

asumir [asu'mir] /3a/ *vt* to assume

asunción [asun'θjon] *nf* assumption; (*Rel*): **A~** Assumption

asunto [a'sunto] *nm* (*tema*) matter, subject; (*negocio*) business

asustar [asus'tar] /1a/ *vt* to frighten; **asustarse** *vr* to be/become frightened

atacar [ata'kar] /1g/ *vt* to attack

atadura [ata'ðura] *nf* bond, tie

atajar [ata'xar] /1a/ *vt* (*enfermedad, mal*) to stop ▷ *vi* (*persona*) to take a short cut

atajo [a'taxo] *nm* short cut

atañer [ata'ɲer] *vi*: **~ a** to concern

ataque *etc* [a'take] *vb* V **atacar** ▷ *nm* attack; **~ cardíaco** heart attack

atar [a'tar] /1a/ *vt* to tie, tie up

atarantado, -a [ataran'taðo, a] *adj*
(LAM: *aturdido*) dazed

atardecer [atarðe'θer] /2d/ *vi* to get
dark ▷ *nm* evening; (*crepúsculo*) dusk

atareado, -a [atare'aðo, a] *adj* busy

atascar [atas'kar] /1g/ *vt* to clog
up; (*obstruir*) to jam; (*fig*) to hinder;
atascarse *vr* to stall; (*cañería*) to get
blocked up; **atasco** *nm* obstruction;
(*Auto*) traffic jam

ataúd [ata'uð] *nm* coffin

ataviar [ata'βjar] /1c/ *vt* to deck,
array

atemorizar [atemori'θar] /1f/ *vt* to
frighten, scare

Atenas [a'tenas] *nf* Athens

atención [aten'θjon] *nf* attention;
(*bondad*) kindness ▷ *excl* (be) careful!,
look out!; **en ~ a esto** in view of this

atender [aten'der] /2g/ *vt* to attend
to, look after; (*Telec*) to answer ▷ *vi* to
pay attention

atenerse [ate'nerse] /2k/ *vr*: **~ a** to
abide by, adhere to

atentado [aten'taðo] *nm* crime,
illegal act; (*asalto*) assault; (*tb*: **~
terrorista**) terrorist attack; **~ contra
la vida de algn** attempt on sb's life; **~
suicida** suicide bombing

atentamente [atenta'mente] *adv*:
Le saluda ~ Yours faithfully

atentar [aten'tar] /1a/ *vi*: **~ o
contra** to commit an outrage against

atento, -a [a'tento, a] *adj* attentive,
observant; (*cortés*) polite, thoughtful;
estar ~ a (*explicación*) to pay
attention to

atenuar [ate'nwar] /1e/ *vt* (*disminuir*)
to lessen, minimize

ateo, -a [a'teo, a] *adj* atheistic ▷ *nm/f*
atheist

aterrador, a [aterra'ðor, a] *adj*
frightening

aterrizaje [aterri'θaxe] *nm* landing;
~ forzoso emergency o forced landing

aterrizar [aterri'θar] /1f/ *vi* to land

aterrorizar [aterrori'θar] /1f/ *vt*
to terrify

atesorar [ateso'rar] /1a/ *vt* to hoard

atestar [ates'tar] /1a, 1j/ *vt* to pack,
stuff; (*Jur*) to attest, testify to

atestiguar [atesti'ɣwar] /1i/ *vt* to
testify to, bear witness to

atiborrar [atiβo'rrar] /1a/ *vt* to fill,
stuff; **atiborrarse** *vr* to stuff o.s.

ático ['atiko] *nm* (*desván*) attic; **~ de
lujo** penthouse flat

atinado, -a [ati'naðo, a] *adj* correct;
(*sensato*) wise, sensible

atinar [ati'nar] /1a/ *vi* (*acertar*) to be
right; **~ al blanco** to hit the target;
(*fig*) to be right

atizar [ati'θar] /1f/ *vt* to poke; (*horno
etc*) to stoke; (*fig*) to stir up, rouse

atlántico, -a [at'lantiko, a] *adj*
Atlantic ▷ *nm*: **el (océano) A~** the
Atlantic (Ocean)

atlas ['atlas] *nm inv* atlas

atleta [at'leta] *nmf* athlete; **atlético,
-a** *adj* athletic; **atletismo** *nm*
athletics *sg*

atmósfera [at'mosfera] *nf*
atmosphere

atolladero [atoʎa'ðero] *nm*: **estar
en un ~** to be in a jam

atómico, -a [a'tomiko, a] *adj* atomic

átomo ['atomo] *nm* atom

atónito, -a [a'tonito, a] *adj*
astonished, amazed

atontado, -a [aton'taðo, a] *adj*
stunned; (*bobo*) silly, daft

atormentar [atormen'tar] /1a/ *vt* to
torture; (*molestar*) to torment; (*acosar*)
to plague, harass

atornillar [atorni'ʎar] /1a/ *vt* to
screw on o down

atosigar [atosi'ɣar] /1h/ *vt* to harass,
pester

atracador, a [atraka'ðor, a] *nm/f*
robber

atracar [atra'kar] /1g/ *vt* (*Naut*) to
moor; (*robar*) to hold up, rob ▷ *vi* to
moor; **atracarse** *vr*: **~se (de)** to stuff
o.s. (with)

atracción [atrak'θjon] *nf* attraction

atraco [a'trako] *nm* holdup, robbery

atracón [atra'kon] *nm*: **darse** *o* **pegarse un ~ (de)** *(fam)* to stuff o.s. (with)

atractivo, -a [atrak'tiβo, a] *adj* attractive ▷ *nm* appeal

atraer [atra'er] /20/ *vt* to attract

atragantarse [atraɣan'tarse] /1a/ *vr*: **~ (con algo)** to choke (on sth); **se me ha atragantado el chico ese/el inglés** I can't stand that boy/English

atrancar [atran'kar] /1g/ *vt* (*con tranca, barra*) to bar, bolt

atrapar [atra'par] /1a/ *vt* to trap; (*resfriado etc*) to catch

atrás [a'tras] *adv* (*movimiento*) back(wards); (*lugar*) behind; (*tiempo*) previously; **ir hacia ~** to go back(wards); to go to the rear; **estar ~** to be behind *o* at the back

atrasado, -a [atra'saðo, a] *adj* slow; (*pago*) overdue, late; (*país*) backward

atrasar [atra'sar] /1a/ *vi* to be slow; **atrasarse** *vr* to stay behind, lag behind; (*tren*) to be *o* run late; (*llegar tarde*) to be late; **atraso** *nm* slowness; lateness, delay; (*de país*) backwardness; **atrasos** *nmpl* (*Com*) arrears

atravesar [atraβe'sar] /1j/ *vt* (*cruzar*) to cross (over); (*traspasar*) to pierce; (*período*) to go through; (*poner al través*) to lay *o* put across; **atravesarse** *vr* to come in between; (*intervenir*) to interfere

atraviese *etc* [atra'βjese] *vb V* **atravesar**

atreverse [atre'βerse] /2a/ *vr* to dare; (*insolentarse*) to be insolent; **atrevido, -a** *adj* daring; insolent; **atrevimiento** *nm* daring; insolence

atribución [atriβu'θjon] *nf* attribution; **atribuciones** *nfpl* (*Pol*) powers, functions; (*Admin*) responsibilities

atribuir [atriβu'ir] /3g/ *vt* to attribute; (*funciones*) to confer

atributo [atri'βuto] *nm* attribute

atril [a'tril] *nm* (*para libro*) lectern; (*Mus*) music stand

atropellar [atrope'ʎar] /1a/ *vt* (*derribar*) to knock over *o* down; (*empujar*) to push (aside); (*Auto*) to run over *o* down; (*agraviar*) to insult; **atropello** *nm* (*Auto*) accident; (*empujón*) push; (*agravio*) wrong; (*atrocidad*) outrage

atroz [a'troθ] *adj* atrocious, awful

A.T.S. *nm abr, nf abr* (= *Ayudante Técnico Sanitario*) nurse

atuendo [a'twendo] *nm* attire

atún [a'tun] *nm* tuna, tunny

aturdir [atur'ðir] /3a/ *vt* to stun; (*ruido*) to deafen; (*fig*) to dumbfound, bewilder

audacia [au'ðaθja] *nf* boldness, audacity; **audaz** *adj* bold, audacious

audición [auði'θjon] *nf* hearing; (*Teat*) audition

audiencia [au'ðjenθja] *nf* audience; (*Jur*) high court

audífono [au'ðifono] *nm* (*para sordos*) hearing aid

auditor [auði'tor] *nm* (*Jur*) judge advocate; (*Com*) auditor

auditorio [auði'torjo] *nm* audience; (*sala*) auditorium

auge ['auxe] *nm* boom; (*clímax*) climax

augurar [auɣu'rar] /1a/ *vt* to predict; (*presagiar*) to portend

augurio [au'ɣurjo] *nm* omen

aula ['aula] *nf* classroom; (*en universidad etc*) lecture room

aullar [au'ʎar] /1a/ *vi* to howl, yell

aullido [au'ʎiðo] *nm* howl, yell

aumentar [aumen'tar] /1a/ *vt* to increase; (*precios*) to put up; (*producción*) to step up; (*con microscopio, anteojos*) to magnify ▷ *vi* to increase, be on the increase; **aumento** *nm* increase; rise

aun [a'un] *adv* even; **~ así** even so; **~ más** even *o* yet more

aún [a'un] *adv* still, yet; **~ está aquí** he's still here; **~ no lo sabemos** we don't know yet; **¿no ha venido ~?** hasn't she come yet?

aunque [a'unke] *conj* though, although, even though

aúpa [a'upa] *excl* come on!

auricular [auriku'lar] *nm (Telec)*
earpiece; **auriculares** *nmpl (cascos)*
headphones
aurora [au'rora] *nf* dawn
ausencia [au'senθja] *nf* absence
ausentarse [ausen'tarse] /1a/ *vr* to
go away; *(por poco tiempo)* to go out
ausente [au'sente] *adj* absent
austero, -a [aus'tero, a] *adj* austere
austral [aus'tral] *adj* southern ▷ *nm*
monetary unit of Argentina (1985-1991)
Australia [aus'tralja] *nf* Australia;
australiano, -a *adj, nm/f* Australian
Austria ['austrja] *nf* Austria
austriaco, -a, austríaco, -a
[aus'triako, a] *adj* Austrian ▷ *nm/f*
Austrian
auténtico, -a [au'tentiko, a] *adj*
authentic
auto ['auto] *nm (Jur)* edict, decree;
(: *orden*) writ; **autos** *nmpl (Jur)*
proceedings; (: *acta*) court record *sg*
autoadhesivo, -a [autoaðe'siβo,
a] *adj* self-adhesive; *(sobre)* self-sealing
autobiografía [autoβjoɣra'fia] *nf*
autobiography
autobomba [auto'bomba] *nm (RPL)*
fire engine
autobronceador, a
[autoβronθea'ðor, a] *adj* (self-)tanning
autobús [auto'βus] *nm* bus; **~ de
línea** long-distance coach
autocar [auto'kar] *nm* coach (BRIT),
(passenger) bus (US); **~ de línea**
intercity coach or bus
autóctono, -a [au'toktono, a] *adj*
native, indigenous
autodefensa [autoðe'fensa] *nf*
self-defence
autodidacta [autoði'ðakta] *adj*
self-taught
autoescuela [autoes'kwela] *nf* (ESP)
driving school
autógrafo [au'toɣrafo] *nm* autograph
autómata [au'tomata] *nm*
automaton
automático, -a [auto'matiko, a] *adj*
automatic ▷ *nm* press stud

automóvil [auto'moβil] *nm*
(motor) car (BRIT), automobile (US);
automovilismo *nm (actividad)*
motoring; *(Deporte)* motor racing;
automovilista *nmf* motorist, driver
autonomía [autono'mia] *nf*
autonomy; **autónomo, -a,** (ESP)
autonómico *adj* autonomous
autopista [auto'pista] *nf* motorway
(BRIT), freeway (US); **~ de cuota** (LAM)
o **peaje** (ESP) toll (BRIT) o turnpike
(US) road
autopsia [au'topsja] *nf* post-
mortem, autopsy
autor, a [au'tor, a] *nm/f* author
autoridad [autori'ðað] *nf* authority;
autoritario, -a *adj* authoritarian
autorización [autoriθa'θjon] *nf*
authorization; **autorizado, -a** *adj*
authorized; *(aprobado)* approved
autorizar [autori'θar] /1f/ *vt* to
authorize; to approve
autoservicio [autoser'βiθjo] *nm*
(tienda) self-service shop o store;
(restaurante) self-service restaurant
autostop [auto'stop] *nm* hitch-
hiking; **hacer ~** to hitch-hike;
autostopista *nmf* hitch-hiker
autovía [auto'βia] *nf* ≈ dual
carriageway (BRIT), ≈ divided highway
(US)
auxiliar [auksi'ljar] /1b/ *vt* to
help ▷ *nmf* assistant; **auxilio** *nm*
assistance, help; **primeros auxilios**
first aid *sg*
Av *abr* (= *Avenida*) Av(e)
aval [a'βal] *nm* guarantee; *(persona)*
guarantor
avalancha [aβa'lantʃa] *nf* avalanche
avance [a'βanθe] *nm* advance; *(pago)*
advance payment; *(Cine)* trailer
avanzar [aβan'θar] /1f/ *vt, vi* to
advance
avaricia [aβa'riθja] *nf* avarice, greed;
avaricioso, -a *adj* avaricious, greedy
avaro, -a [a'βaro, a] *adj* miserly, mean
▷ *nm/f* miser
Avda *abr* (= *Avenida*) Av(e)

AVE ['aβe] nm abr (= Alta Velocidad Española) ≈ bullet train

ave ['aβe] nf bird; **~ de rapiña** bird of prey

avecinarse [aβeθi'narse] /1a/ vr (tormenta, fig) be on the way

avellana [aβe'ʎana] nf hazelnut; **avellano** nm hazel tree

avemaría [aβema'ria] nm Hail Mary, Ave Maria

avena [a'βena] nf oats pl

avenida [aβe'niða] nf (calle) avenue

aventajar [aβenta'xar] /1a/ vt (sobrepasar) to surpass, outstrip

aventón [aβen'ton] nm (LAM) push; **pedir ~** to hitch a lift, hitch a ride (US)

aventura [aβen'tura] nf adventure; **aventurero, -a** adj adventurous

avergonzar [aβerɣon'θar] /1f, 1l/ vt to shame; (desconcertar) to embarrass; **avergonzarse** vr to be ashamed; to be embarrassed

avería [aβe'ria] nf (Tec) breakdown, fault

averiado, -a [aβe'rjaðo, a] adj broken-down; **"~"** "out of order"

averiar [aβe'rjar] /1c/ vt to break; **averiarse** vr to break down

averiguar [aβeri'ɣwar] /1i/ vt to investigate; (descubrir) to find out, ascertain

avestruz [aβes'truθ] nm ostrich

aviación [aβja'θjon] nf aviation; (fuerzas aéreas) air force

aviador, a [aβja'ðor, a] nm/f aviator, airman/woman

ávido, -a ['aβiðo, a] adj avid, eager

avinagrado, -a [aβina'ɣraðo, a] adj sour, acid

avión [a'βjon] nm aeroplane; (ave) martin; **~ de reacción** jet (plane)

avioneta [aβjo'neta] nf light aircraft

avisar [aβi'sar] /1a/ vt (advertir) to warn, notify; (informar) to tell; (aconsejar) to advise, counsel; **aviso** nm warning; (noticia) notice

avispa [a'βispa] nf wasp

avispado, -a [aβis'paðo, a] adj sharp, clever

avivar [aβi'βar] /1a/ vt to strengthen, intensify

axila [ak'sila] nf armpit

ay [ai] excl (dolor) ow!, ouch!; (aflicción) oh!, oh dear!; **¡ay de mí!** poor me!

ayer [a'jer] adv, nm yesterday; **antes de ~** the day before yesterday; **~ por la tarde** yesterday afternoon/evening; **~ mismo** only yesterday

ayote [a'jote] nm (LAM) pumpkin

ayuda [a'juða] nf help, assistance ▷ nm page; **ayudante, -a** nm/f assistant, helper; (Escol) assistant; (Mil) adjutant

ayudar [aju'ðar] /1a/ vt to help, assist

ayunar [aju'nar] /1a/ vi to fast; **ayunas** nfpl: **estar en ayunas** to be fasting; **ayuno** nm fast; fasting

ayuntamiento [ajunta'mjento] nm (consejo) town/city council; (edificio) town/city hall

azafata [aθa'fata] nf air hostess (BRIT) o stewardess

azafrán [aθa'fran] nm saffron

azahar [aθa'ar] nm orange/lemon blossom

azar [a'θar] nm (casualidad) chance, fate; (desgracia) misfortune, accident; **por ~** by chance; **al ~** at random

Azores [a'θores] nfpl: **las (Islas) ~** the Azores

azotar [aθo'tar] /1a/ vt to whip, beat; (pegar) to spank; **azote** nm (látigo) whip; (latigazo) lash, stroke; (en las nalgas) spank; (calamidad) calamity

azotea [aθo'tea] nf (flat) roof

azteca [aθ'teka] adj, nmf Aztec

azúcar [a'θukar] nm sugar; **azucarado, -a** adj sugary, sweet

azucarero, -a [aθuka'rero, a] adj sugar cpd ▷ nm sugar bowl

azucena [aθu'θena] nf white lily

azufre [a'θufre] nm sulphur

azul [a'θul] adj, nm blue; **~ celeste/ marino** sky/navy blue

azulejo [aθu'lexo] nm tile

azuzar [aθu'θar] /1f/ vt to incite, egg on

B.A. *abr* (= *Buenos Aires*) B.A.

baba ['baβa] *nf* spittle, saliva; **babear** /1a/ *vi* to drool, slaver

babero [ba'βero] *nm* bib

babor [ba'βor] *nm* port (side)

babosada [baβo'saða] *nf*: **decir ~s** (*LAM fam*) to talk rubbish; **baboso, -a** *adj* (*LAM*) silly

baca ['baka] *nf* (*Auto*) luggage *o* roof rack

bacalao [baka'lao] *nm* cod(fish)

bache ['batʃe] *nm* pothole, rut; (*fig*) bad patch

bachillerato [batʃiʎe'rato] *nm* two-year advanced secondary school course

bacinica [baθi'nika] *nf* potty

bacteria [bak'terja] *nf* bacterium, germ

Bahama [ba'ama]: **las (Islas) ~, las ~s** *nfpl* the Bahamas

bahía [ba'ia] *nf* bay

bailar [bai'lar] /1a/ *vt*, *vi* to dance; **bailarín, -ina** *nm/f* dancer; (*de ballet*) ballet dancer; **baile** *nm* dance; (*formal*) ball

baja ['baxa] *nf* drop, fall; (*Mil*) casualty; **dar de ~** (*soldado*) to discharge; (*empleado*) to dismiss

bajada [ba'xaða] *nf* descent; (*camino*) slope; (*de aguas*) ebb

bajar [ba'xar] /1a/ *vi* to go *o* come down; (*temperatura, precios*) to drop, fall ▷ *vt* (*cabeza*) to bow; (*escalera*) to go *o* come down; (*precio, voz*) to lower; (*llevar abajo*) to take down; **bajarse** *vr* (*de vehículo*) to get out; (*de autobús*) to get off; **~ de** (*coche*) to get out of; (*autobús*) to get off; **~se algo de Internet** to download sth from the internet

bajío [ba'xio] *nm* (*LAM*) lowlands *pl*

bajo, -a ['baxo, a] *adj* (*mueble, número, precio*) low; (*piso*) ground *cpd*; (*de estatura*) small, short; (*color*) pale; (*sonido*) faint, soft, low; (*voz, tono*) deep; (*metal*) base; (*humilde*) low, humble ▷ *adv* (*hablar*) softly, quietly; (*volar*) low ▷ *prep* under, below, underneath ▷ *nm* (*Mus*) bass; **~ la lluvia** in the rain

bajón [ba'xon] *nm* fall, drop

bakalao [baka'lao] *nm* (*Mus*) rave music

bala ['bala] *nf* bullet

balacear [balaθe'ar] /1a/ *vt* (*LAM, CAM*) to shoot

balance [ba'lanθe] *nm* (*Com*) balance; (: *libro*) balance sheet; (: *cuenta general*) stocktaking

balancear [balanθe'ar] /1a/ *vt* to balance ▷ *vi* to swing (to and fro); (*vacilar*) to hesitate; **balancearse** *vr* to swing (to and fro); (*vacilar*) to hesitate

balanza [ba'lanθa] *nf* scales *pl*, balance; **~ comercial** balance of trade; **~ de pagos/de poder(es)** balance of payments/of power

balaustrada [balaus'traða] *nf* balustrade; (*pasamanos*) banister

balazo [ba'laθo] *nm* (*tiro*) shot; (*herida*) bullet wound

balbucear [balβuθe'ar] /1a/ vi, vt to stammer, stutter

balcón [bal'kon] nm balcony

balde ['balde] nm bucket, pail; **de ~** (for) free, for nothing; **en ~** in vain

baldosa [bal'dosa] nf (azulejo) floor tile; (grande) flagstone; **baldosín** nm tile

Baleares [bale'ares] nfpl: **las (Islas) ~** the Balearic Islands

balero [ba'lero] nm (LAM: juguete) cup-and-ball toy

baliza [ba'liθa] nf (Aviat) beacon; (Naut) buoy

ballena [ba'ʎena] nf whale

ballet [ba'le] (pl **ballets**) [ba'le] nm ballet

balneario, -a [balne'arjo, a] adj ▷ nm spa; (LAM: en la costa) seaside resort

balón [ba'lon] nm ball

baloncesto [balon'θesto] nm basketball

balonmano [balon'mano] nm handball

balonred [balon'reð] nm netball

balsa ['balsa] nf raft; (Bot) balsa wood

bálsamo ['balsamo] nm balsam, balm

baluarte [ba'lwarte] nm bastion, bulwark

bambú [bam'bu] nm bamboo

banana [ba'nana] nf (LAM) banana; **banano** nm (LAM) banana tree; (fruta) banana

banca ['banka] nf (Com) banking

bancario, -a [ban'karjo, a] adj banking cpd, bank cpd

bancarrota [banka'rrota] nf bankruptcy; **declararse** o **hacer ~** to go bankrupt

banco ['banko] nm bench; (Escol) desk; (Com) bank; (Geo) stratum; **~ de crédito/de ahorros** credit/savings bank; **~ de arena** sandbank; **~ de datos** (Inform) data bank

banda ['banda] nf band; (pandilla) gang; (Naut) side, edge; **la B~ Oriental** Uruguay; **~ sonora** soundtrack

bandada [ban'daða] nf (de pájaros) flock; (de peces) shoal

bandazo [ban'daθo] nm: **dar ~s** to veer from side to side

bandeja [ban'dexa] nf tray; **~ de entrada/salida** in-tray/out-tray

bandera [ban'dera] nf flag

banderilla [bande'riʎa] nf banderilla

bandido [ban'diðo] nm bandit

bando ['bando] nm (edicto) edict, proclamation; (facción) faction; **los ~s** (Rel) the banns

bandolera [bando'lera] nf: **llevar en ~** to wear across one's chest

banquero [ban'kero] nm banker

banqueta [ban'keta] nf stool; (LAM: acera) pavement (BRIT), sidewalk (US)

banquete [ban'kete] nm banquet; (para convidados) formal dinner; **~ de boda** wedding reception

banquillo [ban'kiʎo] nm (Jur) dock, prisoner's bench; (banco) bench; (para los pies) footstool

banquina [ban'kina] nf (RPL) hard shoulder (BRIT), berm (US)

bañadera [baɲa'ðera] nf (LAM) bath(tub)

bañador [baɲa'ðor] nm swimming costume (BRIT), bathing suit (US)

bañar [ba'ɲar] /1a/ vt to bath, bathe; (objeto) to dip; (de barniz) to coat; **bañarse** vr (en el mar) to bathe, swim; (en la bañera) to have a bath

bañera [ba'ɲera] nf (ESP) bath(tub)

bañero, -a [ba'ɲero, a] nm/f lifeguard

bañista [ba'ɲista] nmf bather

baño ['baɲo] nm (en bañera) bath; (en río, mar) dip, swim; (cuarto) bathroom; (bañera) bath(tub); (capa) coating; **darse** o **tomar un ~** (en bañera) to have o take a bath; (en mar, piscina) to have a swim; **~ María** bain-marie

bar [bar] nm bar

barahúnda [bara'unda] nf uproar, hubbub

baraja [ba'raxa] nf pack (of cards); **barajar** /1a/ vt (naipes) to shuffle; (fig) to jumble up

baranda [ba'randa], **barandilla** [baran'diʎa] nf rail, railing

barata [ba'rata] nf (LAM) (bargain) sale

baratillo [bara'tiʎo] nm (tienda) junk shop; (subasta) bargain sale; (conjunto de cosas) second-hand goods pl

barato, -a [ba'rato, a] adj cheap ▷ adv cheap, cheaply

barba ['barβa] nf (mentón) chin; (pelo) beard

barbacoa [barβa'koa] nf (parrilla) barbecue; (carne) barbecued meat

barbaridad [barβari'ðað] nf barbarity; (acto) barbarism; (atrocidad) outrage; **una ~ de** (fam) loads of; **¡qué ~!** (fam) how awful!

barbarie [bar'βarje] nm barbarism; (crueldad) barbarity

bárbaro, -a ['barβaro, a] adj barbarous, cruel; (grosero) rough, uncouth ▷ nm/f barbarian ▷ adv: **lo pasamos ~** (fam) we had a great time; **¡qué ~!** (fam) how marvellous!; **un éxito ~** (fam) a terrific success; **es un tipo ~** (fam) he's a great bloke

barbero [bar'βero] nm barber, hairdresser

barbilla [bar'βiʎa] nf chin, tip of the chin

barbudo, -a [bar'βuðo, a] adj bearded

barca ['barka] nf (small) boat; **barcaza** nf barge

Barcelona [barθe'lona] nf Barcelona

barco ['barko] nm boat; (buque) ship; **~ de carga** cargo boat; **~ de vela** sailing ship

barda ['barða] nf (LAM: de madera) fence

baremo [ba'remo] nm scale

barítono [ba'ritono] nm baritone

barman ['barman] nm barman

barniz [bar'niθ] nm varnish; (en la loza) glaze; (fig) veneer; **barnizar** /1f/ vt to varnish; (loza) to glaze

barómetro [ba'rometro] nm barometer

barquillo [bar'kiʎo] nm cone, cornet

barra ['barra] nf bar, rod; (de un bar, café) bar; (de pan) French loaf; (palanca) lever; **~ de carmín** o **de labios** lipstick; **~ libre** free bar

barraca [ba'rraka] nf hut, cabin

barranco [ba'rranko] nm ravine; (fig) difficulty

barrena [ba'rrena] nf drill

barrer [ba'rrer] /2a/ vt to sweep; (quitar) to sweep away

barrera [ba'rrera] nf barrier

barriada [ba'rrjaða] nf quarter, district

barricada [barri'kaða] nf barricade

barrida [ba'rriða] nm sweep, sweeping

barriga [ba'rriɣa] nf belly; (panza) paunch; **barrigón, -ona, barrigudo, -a** adj potbellied

barril [ba'rril] nm barrel, cask

barrio ['barrjo] nm (vecindad) area, neighborhood (US); (en las afueras) suburb; **~ chino** red-light district

barro ['barro] nm (lodo) mud; (objetos) earthenware; (Med) pimple

barroco, -a [ba'rroko, a] adj, nm Baroque

barrote [ba'rrote] nm (de ventana etc) bar

bartola [bar'tola] nf: **tirarse a la ~** to take it easy, be lazy

bártulos ['bartulos] nmpl things, belongings

barullo [ba'ruʎo] nm row, uproar

basar [ba'sar] /1a/ vt to base; **basarse** vr: **~se en** to be based on

báscula ['baskula] nf (platform) scales pl

base ['base] nf base; **a ~ de** on the basis of; (mediante) by means of; **~ de datos** database

básico, -a ['basiko, a] adj basic

basílica [ba'silika] nf basilica

básquetbol ['basketbol] nm (LAM) basketball

 PALABRA CLAVE

bastante [bas'tante] adj **1** (suficiente) enough; **bastante dinero** enough o sufficient money; **bastantes libros** enough books

2 (*valor intensivo*): **bastante gente** quite a lot of people; **tener bastante calor** to be rather hot

▶ *adv*: **bastante bueno/malo** quite good/rather bad; **bastante rico** pretty rich; **(lo) bastante inteligente (como) para hacer algo** clever enough o sufficiently clever to do sth

bastar [bas'tar] /1a/ *vi* to be enough o sufficient; **bastarse** *vr* to be self-sufficient; **~ para** to be enough to; **¡basta!** (that's) enough!

bastardo, -a [bas'tarðo, a] *adj, nm/f* bastard

bastidor [basti'ðor] *nm* frame; (*de coche*) chassis; (*Teat*) wing; **entre ~es** behind the scenes

basto, -a ['basto, a] *adj* coarse, rough ▷ *nmpl*: **~s** (*Naipes*) one of the suits in the Spanish card deck

bastón [bas'ton] *nm* stick, staff; (*para pasear*) walking stick

bastoncillo [baston'θiʎo] *nm* cotton bud

basura [ba'sura] *nf* rubbish, refuse (*BRIT*), garbage (*US*) ▷ *adj*: **comida/ televisión ~** junk food/TV

basurero [basu'rero] *nm* (*hombre*) dustman (*BRIT*), garbage collector o man (*US*); (*lugar*) rubbish dump; (*cubo*) (rubbish) bin (*BRIT*), trash can (*US*)

bata ['bata] *nf* (*gen*) dressing gown; (*cubretodo*) smock, overall; (*Med, Tec etc*) lab(oratory) coat

batalla [ba'taʎa] *nf* battle; **de ~** for everyday use; **~ campal** pitched battle

batallón [bata'ʎon] *nm* battalion

batata [ba'tata] *nf* sweet potato

batería [bate'ria] *nf* battery; (*Mus*) drums *pl*; **~ de cocina** kitchen utensils *pl*

batido, -a [ba'tiðo, a] *adj* (*camino*) beaten, well-trodden ▷ *nm* (*Culin*) batter; **~ (de leche)** milk shake

batidora [bati'ðora] *nf* beater, mixer; **~ eléctrica** food mixer, blender

batir [ba'tir] /3a/ *vt* to beat, strike; (*vencer*) to beat, defeat; (*revolver*) to beat, mix; **batirse** *vr* to fight; **~ palmas** to clap, applaud

batuta [ba'tuta] *nf* baton; **llevar la ~** (*fig*) to be the boss

baúl [ba'ul] *nm* trunk; (*LAM Auto*) boot (*BRIT*), trunk (*US*)

bautismo [bau'tismo] *nm* baptism, christening

bautizar [bauti'θar] /1f/ *vt* to baptize, christen; (*fam: diluir*) to water down; **bautizo** *nm* baptism, christening

bayeta [ba'jeta] *nf* floor cloth

baza ['baθa] *nf* trick; **meter ~** to butt in

bazar [ba'θar] *nm* bazaar

bazofia [ba'θofja] *nf* trash

be [be] *nf* name of the letter B; **be chica/ grande** (*LAM*) V/B; **be larga** (*LAM*) B

beato, -a [be'ato, a] *adj* blessed; (*piadoso*) pious

bebé [be'βe] (*pl* **bebés**) *nm* baby

bebedero [beβe'ðero] *nm* (*para animales*) drinking trough

bebedor, a [beβe'ðor, a] *adj* hard-drinking

beber [be'βer] /2a/ *vt, vi* to drink

bebido, -a [be'βiðo, a] *adj* drunk ▷ *nf* drink

beca ['beka] *nf* grant, scholarship; **becario, -a** [be'karjo, a] *nm/f* scholarship holder, grant holder; (*en prácticas laborales*) intern

bedel [be'ðel] *nm* porter, janitor; (*Univ*) porter

béisbol ['beisβol] *nm* baseball

Belén [be'len] *nm* Bethlehem; **belén** (*de Navidad*) nativity scene, crib

belga ['belɣa] *adj, nmf* Belgian

Bélgica ['belxika] *nf* Belgium

bélico, -a ['beliko, a] *adj* (*actitud*) warlike

belleza [be'ʎeθa] *nf* beauty

bello, -a ['beʎo, a] *adj* beautiful, lovely; **Bellas Artes** Fine Art *sg*

bellota [be'ʎota] *nf* acorn

bemol [be'mol] *nm* (*Mus*) flat; **esto tiene ~es** (*fam*) this is a tough one

bencina [ben'sina] *nf* (*LAM: gasolina*) petrol (*BRIT*), gas (*US*)

bendecir [bende'θir] /3o/ *vt* to bless

bendición [bendi'θjon] *nf* blessing

bendito, -a [ben'dito, a] *pp de* **bendecir** ▷ *adj* holy; (*afortunado*) lucky; (*feliz*) happy; (*sencillo*) simple ▷ *nm/f* simple soul

beneficencia [benefi'θenθja] *nf* charity

beneficiario, -a [benefi'θjarjo, a] *nm/f* beneficiary

beneficio [bene'fiθjo] *nm* (*bien*) benefit, advantage; (*Com*) profit, gain; **a ~ de** for the benefit of; **beneficioso, -a** *adj* beneficial

benéfico, -a [be'nefiko, a] *adj* charitable

beneplácito [bene'plaθito] *nm* approval, consent

benévolo, -a [be'neβolo, a] *adj* benevolent, kind

benigno, -a [be'niɣno, a] *adj* kind; (*suave*) mild; (*Med: tumor*) benign, non-malignant

berberecho [berβe'retʃo] *nm* cockle

berenjena [beren'xena] *nf* aubergine (*BRIT*), eggplant (*US*)

Berlín [ber'lin] *nm* Berlin

berlinesa [berli'nesa] *nf* (*LAM*) doughnut, donut (*US*)

bermudas [ber'muðas] *nfpl* Bermuda shorts

berrido [be'rriðo] *nm* bellow(ing)

berrinche [be'rrintʃe] *nm* (*fam*) temper, tantrum

berro ['berro] *nm* watercress

berza ['berθa] *nf* cabbage

besamel [besa'mel] *nf* (*Culin*) white sauce, bechamel sauce

besar [be'sar] /1a/ *vt* to kiss; (*fig: tocar*) to graze; **besarse** *vr* to kiss (one another); **beso** *nm* kiss

bestia ['bestja] *nf* beast, animal; (*fig*) idiot; **~ de carga** beast of burden;

bestial *adj* bestial; (*fam*) terrific; **bestialidad** *nf* bestiality; (*fam*) stupidity

besugo [be'suɣo] *nm* sea bream; (*fam*) idiot

besuquear [besuke'ar] /1a/ *vt* to cover with kisses; **besuquearse** *vr* to kiss and cuddle

betabel [beta'bel] *nm* (*LAM*) beetroot (*BRIT*), beet (*US*)

betún [be'tun] *nm* shoe polish; (*Química*) bitumen

biberón [biβe'ron] *nm* feeding bottle

Biblia ['biβlja] *nf* Bible

bibliografía [biβljoɣra'fia] *nf* bibliography

biblioteca [biβljo'teka] *nf* library; (*estantes*) bookshelves *pl*; **~ de consulta** reference library; **bibliotecario, -a** *nm/f* librarian

bicarbonato [bikarβo'nato] *nm* bicarbonate

bicho ['bitʃo] *nm* (*animal*) small animal; (*sabandija*) bug, insect; (*Taur*) bull

bici ['biθi] *nf* (*fam*) bike

bicicleta [biθi'kleta] *nf* bicycle, cycle; **ir en ~** to cycle

bidé [bi'ðe] *nm* bidet

bidón [bi'ðon] *nm* (*grande*) drum; (*pequeño*) can

PALABRA CLAVE

bien [bjen] *nm* **1** (*bienestar*) good; **te lo digo por tu bien** I'm telling you for your own good; **el bien y el mal** good and evil

2 (*posesión*): **bienes** goods; **bienes de consumo/equipo** consumer/capital goods; **bienes inmuebles** *o* **raíces/ bienes muebles** real estate *sg*/ personal property *sg*

▷ *adv* **1** (*de manera satisfactoria, correcta etc*) well; **trabaja/come bien** she works/eats well; **contestó bien** he answered correctly; **me siento bien** I feel fine; **no me siento bien** I don't feel very well; **se está bien aquí** it's nice here

2: **hiciste bien en llamarme** you were right to call me

3 (*valor intensivo*) very; **un cuarto bien caliente** a nice warm room; **bien se ve que ...** it's quite clear that ...

4: **estar bien: estoy muy bien aquí** I feel very happy here; **está bien que vengan** it's all right for them to come; **¡está bien! lo haré** oh all right, I'll do it

5 (*de buena gana*): **yo bien que iría pero ...** I'd gladly go but ...

▸ *excl*: **¡bien!** (*aprobación*) OK!; **¡muy bien!** well done!

▸ *adj inv*: **gente bien** posh people

▸ *conj* **1**: **bien ... bien: bien en coche bien en tren** either by car or by train

2: **no bien** (*esp LAM*): **no bien llegue te llamaré** as soon as I arrive I'll call you

3: **si bien** even though; V tb **más**

bienal [bje'nal] *adj* biennial
bienestar [bjenes'tar] *nm* well-being
bienvenido, -a [bjembe'niðo, a] *excl* welcome! ▸ *nf* welcome; **dar la bienvenida a algn** to welcome sb
bife ['bife] *nm* (*LAM*) steak
bifurcación [bifurka'θjon] *nf* fork
bígamo, -a ['biɣamo, a] *adj* bigamous ▸ *nm/f* bigamist
bigote [bi'ɣote] *nm* moustache; **bigotudo, -a** *adj* with a big moustache
bikini [bi'kini] *nm* bikini; (*Culin*) toasted cheese and ham sandwich
bilingüe [bi'lingwe] *adj* bilingual
billar [bi'ʎar] *nm* billiards *sg*; **billares** *nmpl* (*lugar*) billiard hall; (*galería de atracciones*) amusement arcade; **~ americano** pool
billete [bi'ʎete] *nm* ticket; (*de banco*) banknote (*BRIT*), bill (*US*); (*carta*) note; **~ de ida** o **sencillo** single (*BRIT*) o one-way (*US*) ticket; **~ de ida y vuelta** return (*BRIT*) o round-trip (*US*) ticket; **~ electrónico** e-ticket; **sacar (un) ~**

to get a ticket; **un ~ de cinco libras** a five-pound note
billetera [biʎe'tera] *nm* wallet
billón [bi'ʎon] *nm* billion
bimensual [bimen'swal] *adj* twice monthly
bingo ['bingo] *nm* bingo
biocarburante [biokarβu'rante], **biocombustible** [biokombus'tiβle] *nm* biofuel
biodegradable [bioðeɣra'ðaβle] *adj* biodegradable
biografía [bjoɣra'fia] *nf* biography
biología [biolo'xia] *nf* biology; **biológico, -a** *adj* biological; (*cultivo, producto*) organic; **biólogo, -a** *nm/f* biologist
biombo ['bjombo] *nm* (folding) screen
bioterrorismo [bioterro'rismo] *nm* bioterrorism
biquini [bi'kini] *nm* = **bikini**
birlar [bir'lar] /1a/ *vt* (*fam*) to pinch
Birmania [bir'manja] *nf* Burma
birome [bi'rome] *nf* (*LAM*) ballpoint (pen)
birria ['birrja] *nf* (*fam*): **ser una ~** (*película, libro*) to be rubbish
bis [bis] *excl* encore!
bisabuelo, -a [bisa'βwelo, a] *nm/f* great-grandfather/mother
bisagra [bi'saɣra] *nf* hinge
bisiesto [bi'sjesto] *adj*: **año ~** leap year
bisnieto, -a [bis'njeto, a] *nm/f* great-grandson/daughter
bisonte [bi'sonte] *nm* bison
bistec [bis'tek], **bisté** [bis'te] *nm* steak
bisturí [bistu'ri] *nm* scalpel
bisutería [bisute'ria] *nf* imitation o costume jewellery
bit [bit] *nm* (*Inform*) bit
bizco, -a ['biθko, a] *adj* cross-eyed
bizcocho [biθ'kotʃo] *nm* (*Culin*) sponge cake
blanco, -a ['blanko, a] *adj* white ▸ *nm/f* white man/woman, white ▸ *nm* (*color*) white; (*en texto*) blank;

(*Mil*, *fig*) target; **en ~** blank; **noche en ~** sleepless night; **estar sin blanca** to be broke

blandir [blan'dir] *vt* to brandish

blando, -a ['blando, a] *adj* soft; (*tierno*) tender, gentle; (*carácter*) mild; (*fam*) cowardly

blanqueador [blankea'ðor] *nm* (*LAM*) bleach

blanquear [blanke'ar] /1a/ *vt* to whiten; (*fachada*) to whitewash; (*paño*) to bleach; (*dinero*) to launder ▷ *vi* to turn white

blanquillo [blan'kiʎo] *nm* (*LAM*, *CAM*) egg

blasfemar [blasfe'mar] /1a/ *vi* to blaspheme; (*fig*) to curse

bledo ['bleðo] *nm*: **(no) me importa un ~** I couldn't care less

blindado, -a [blin'daðo, a] *adj* (*Mil*) armour-plated; (*antibalas*) bulletproof; **coche** *o* (*LAM*) **carro ~** armoured car

bloc [blok] (*pl* **blocs**) *nm* writing pad

blof [blof] *nm* (*LAM*) bluff; **blofear** /1a/ *vi* (*LAM*) to bluff

blog [bloɣ] (*pl* **blogs**) *nm* blog

bloguero, -a [blo'ɣero, a] *nm/f* blogger

bloque ['bloke] *nm* block; (*Pol*) bloc

bloquear [bloke'ar] /1a/ *vt* to blockade; **bloqueo** *nm* blockade; (*Com*) freezing, blocking; **bloqueo mental** mental block

blusa ['blusa] *nf* blouse

bobada [bo'βaða] *nf* foolish action (*o* statement); **decir ~s** to talk nonsense

bobina [bo'βina] *nf* (*Tec*) bobbin; (*Foto*) spool; (*Elec*) coil

bobo, -a ['boβo, a] *adj* (*tonto*) daft, silly; (*cándido*) naïve ▷ *nm/f* fool, idiot ▷ *nm* (*Teat*) clown, funny man

boca ['boka] *nf* mouth; (*de crustáceo*) pincer; (*de cañón*) muzzle; (*entrada*) mouth, entrance; **bocas** *nfpl* (*de río*) mouth *sg*; **~ abajo/arriba** face down/up; **se me hace la ~ agua** my mouth is watering; **~ de incendios** hydrant; **~ del estómago** pit of the stomach;

~ de metro tube (*BRIT*) *o* subway (*US*) entrance

bocacalle [boka'kaʎe] *nf* side street; **la primera ~** the first turning *o* street

bocadillo [boka'ðiʎo] *nm* sandwich

bocado [bo'kaðo] *nm* mouthful, bite; (*de caballo*) bridle

bocajarro [boka'xarro]: **a ~** *adv* (*Mil*) at point-blank range

bocanada [boka'naða] *nf* (*de vino*) mouthful, swallow; (*de aire*) gust, puff

bocata [bo'kata] *nm* (*fam*) sandwich

bocazas [bo'kaθas] *nm inv*, *nf inv* (*fam*) bigmouth

boceto [bo'θeto] *nm* sketch, outline

bochorno [bo'tʃorno] *nm* (*vergüenza*) embarrassment; (*calor*): **hace ~** it's very muggy

bocina [bo'θina] *nf* (*Mus*) trumpet; (*Auto*) horn; (*para hablar*) megaphone

boda ['boða] *nf* (*tb*: **~s**) wedding, marriage; (*fiesta*) wedding reception; **~s de plata/de oro** silver/golden wedding *sg*

bodega [bo'ðeɣa] *nf* (*de vino*) (wine) cellar; (*depósito*) storeroom; (*de barco*) hold

bodegón [boðe'ɣon] *nm* (*Arte*) still life

bofetada [bofe'taða] *nf* slap (in the face)

boga ['boɣa] *nf*: **en ~** in vogue

Bogotá [boɣo'ta] *n* Bogota

bohemio, -a [bo'emjo, a] *adj*, *nm/f* Bohemian

bohío [bo'io] *nm* (*LAM*) shack, hut

boicot [boi'ko(t)] (*pl* **boicots**) *nm* boycott; **boicotear** /1a/ *vt* to boycott

bóiler ['boiler] *nm* (*LAM*) boiler

boina ['boina] *nf* beret

bola ['bola] *nf* ball; (*canica*) marble; (*Naipes*) (grand) slam; (*betún*) shoe polish; (*mentira*) tale, story; **bolas** *nfpl* (*LAM*) bolas; **~ de billar** billiard ball; **~ de nieve** snowball

boleadoras [bolea'ðoras] *nfpl* bolas *sg*

bolear [bole'ar] /1a/ *vt* (*LAM*: *zapatos*) to polish, shine

bolera [bo'lera] nf skittle o bowling alley

bolero, -a [bo'lero, a] nm bolero ▷ nm/f (LAM: limpiabotas) shoeshine boy/girl

boleta [bo'leta] nf (LAM: permiso) pass, permit; (de rifa) ticket; (recibo) receipt; (para votar) ballot; **~ de calificaciones** report card

boletería [bolete'ria] nf (LAM) ticket office

boletín [bole'tin] nm bulletin; (periódico) journal, review; **~ de noticias** news bulletin

boleto [bo'leto] nm (esp LAM) ticket; **~ de apuestas** betting slip; **~ de ida y vuelta** (LAM) round-trip ticket; **~ electrónico** (LAM) e-ticket; **~ redondo** (LAM) round-trip ticket

boli ['boli] nm Biro®

bolígrafo [bo'liɣrafo] nm ball-point pen, Biro®

bolilla [bo'liʎa] nf (LAM) topic

bolillo [bo'liʎo] nm (LAM) (bread) roll

bolita [bo'lita] nf (LAM) marble

bolívar [bo'liβar] nm monetary unit of Venezuela

Bolivia [bo'liβja] nf Bolivia; **boliviano, -a** adj, nm/f Bolivian

bollería [boʎe'ria] nf cakes pl and pastries pl

bollo ['boʎo] nm (de pan) roll; (chichón) bump, lump; (abolladura) dent

bolo ['bolo] nm skittle; (píldora) (large) pill; **(juego de) ~s** skittles sg

bolsa ['bolsa] nf (saco) bag; (LAM) pocket; (de mujer) handbag; (Anat) cavity, sac; (Com) stock exchange; (Minería) pocket; **~ de agua caliente** hot water bottle; **~ de aire** air pocket; **~ de dormir** (LAM) sleeping bag; **~ de papel** paper bag; **~ de plástico** plastic (o carrier) bag; **~ de la compra** shopping bag

bolsillo [bol'siʎo] nm pocket; (cartera) purse; **de ~** pocket

bolso ['bolso] nm (bolsa) bag; (de mujer) handbag

bomba ['bomba] nf (Mil) bomb; (Tec) pump ▷ adj (fam): **noticia ~** bombshell ▷ adv (fam): **pasarlo ~** to have a great time; **~ atómica/de humo/de retardo** atomic/smoke/time bomb

bombacha [bom'batʃa] nf (LAM) panties pl

bombardear [bombarðe'ar] /1a/ vt to bombard; (Mil) to bomb; **bombardeo** nm bombardment; bombing

bombazo [bom'baθo] nm (LAM: explosión) explosion; (fam: notición) bombshell; (éxito) smash hit

bombear [bombe'ar] /1a/ vt (agua) to pump (out o up)

bombero [bom'bero] nm fireman

bombilla [bom'biʎa] (ESP), **bombita** [bom'bita] (LAM) nf (light) bulb

bombo ['bombo] nm (Mus) bass drum; (Tec) drum

bombón [bom'bon] nm chocolate; (LAM: de caramelo) marshmallow

bombona [bom'bona] nf: **~ de butano** gas cylinder

bonachón, -ona [bona'tʃon, ona] adj good-natured

bonanza [bo'nanθa] nf (Naut) fair weather; (fig) bonanza; (Minería) rich pocket o vein

bondad [bon'dað] nf goodness, kindness; **tenga la ~ de** (please) be good enough to

bonito, -a [bo'nito, a] adj pretty; (agradable) nice ▷ nm (atún) tuna (fish)

bono ['bono] nm voucher; (Finanzas) bond

bonobús [bono'βus] nm (ESP) bus pass

Bono Loto, bonoloto [bono'loto] nm o f (ESP) state-run weekly lottery; V tb **lotería**

boquerón [boke'ron] nm (pez) (kind of) anchovy; (agujero) large hole

boquete [bo'kete] nm gap, hole

boquiabierto, -a [bokia'βjerto, a] adj open-mouthed (in astonishment); **quedarse ~** to be amazed o flabbergasted

boquilla [bo'kiʎa] nf (de riego) nozzle; (de cigarro) cigarette holder; (Mus) mouthpiece

borbotón [borβo'ton] nm: **salir a borbotones** to gush out

borda ['borða] nf (Naut) gunwale, rail; **echar o tirar algo por la ~** to throw sth overboard

bordado [bor'ðaðo] nm embroidery

bordar [bor'ðar] /1a/ vt to embroider

borde ['borðe] nm edge, border; (de camino etc) side; (en la costura) hem; **al ~ de** (fig) on the verge o brink of ⊳ adj: **ser ~** (ESP fam) to be rude; **bordear** /1a/ vt to border

bordillo [bor'ðiʎo] nm kerb (BRIT), curb (US)

bordo ['borðo] nm (Naut) side; **a ~** on board

borlote [bor'lote] nm (LAM) row, uproar

borrachera [borra'tʃera] nf (ebriedad) drunkenness; (orgía) spree, binge

borracho, -a [bo'rratʃo, a] adj drunk ⊳ nm/f (que bebe mucho) drunkard, drunk; (temporalmente) drunk, drunk man/woman

borrador [borra'ðor] nm (escritura) first draft, rough sketch; (goma) rubber (BRIT), eraser

borrar [bo'rrar] /1a/ vt to erase, rub out

borrasca [bo'rraska] nf storm

borrego, -a [bo'rreɣo, a] nm/f lamb; (oveja) sheep; (fig) simpleton ⊳ nm (LAM fam) false rumour

borrico, -a [bo'rriko, a] nm donkey; (fig) stupid man ⊳ nf she-donkey; (fig) stupid woman

borrón [bo'rron] nm (mancha) stain

borroso, -a [bo'rroso, a] adj vague, unclear; (escritura) illegible

bosque ['boske] nm wood; (grande) forest

bostezar [boste'θar] /1f/ vi to yawn; **bostezo** nm yawn

bota ['bota] nf (calzado) boot; (de vino) leather wine bottle; **~s de agua o goma** Wellingtons

botánico, -a [bo'taniko, a] adj botanical ⊳ nm/f botanist

botar [bo'tar] /1a/ vt to throw, hurl; (Naut) to launch; (esp LAM fam) to throw out ⊳ vi to bounce

bote ['bote] nm (salto) bounce; (golpe) thrust; (vasija) tin, can; (embarcación) boat; (LAM pey: cárcel) jail; **de ~ en ~** packed, jammed full; **~ salvavidas** lifeboat; **~ de la basura** (LAM) dustbin (BRIT), trash can (US)

botella [bo'teʎa] nf bottle; **botellín** nm small bottle; **botellón** nm (ESP fam) outdoor drinking session (involving groups of young people)

botijo [bo'tixo] nm (earthenware) jug

botín [bo'tin] nm (calzado) half boot; (polaina) spat; (Mil) booty

botiquín [boti'kin] nm (armario) medicine chest; (portátil) first-aid kit

botón [bo'ton] nm button; (Bot) bud

botones [bo'tones] nm inv bellboy, bellhop (US)

bóveda ['boβeða] nf (Arq) vault

boxeador [boksea'ðor] nm boxer

boxeo [bok'seo] nm boxing

boya ['boja] nf (Naut) buoy; (flotador) float

boyante [bo'jante] adj prosperous

bozal [bo'θal] nm (de caballo) halter; (de perro) muzzle

braga ['braɣa] nf (de bebé) nappy, diaper (US); **bragas** nfpl (de mujer) panties

bragueta [bra'ɣeta] nf fly (BRIT), flies pl (BRIT), zipper (US)

braille [breil] nm braille

brasa ['brasa] nf live o hot coal

brasero [bra'sero] nm brazier

brasier [bra'sjer] nm (LAM) bra

Brasil [bra'sil] nm: **(el) ~** Brazil; **brasileño, -a** adj, nm/f Brazilian

brassier [bra'sjer] nm (LAM) V **brasier**

bravo, -a ['braβo, a] adj (valiente) brave; (feroz) ferocious; (salvaje) wild; (mar etc) rough, stormy ⊳ excl bravo!; **bravura** nf bravery; ferocity

braza ['braθa] nf fathom; **nadar a la ~** to swim (the) breast-stroke

brazalete [braθa'lete] *nm* (*pulsera*) bracelet; (*banda*) armband

brazo ['braθo] *nm* arm; (*Zool*) foreleg; (*Bot*) limb, branch; **cogidos** *etc* **del ~** arm in arm

brebaje [bre'βaxe] *nm* potion

brecha ['bretʃa] *nf* (*hoyo, vacío*) gap, opening; (*Mil, fig*) breach

brega ['breγa] *nf* (*lucha*) struggle; (*trabajo*) hard work

breva ['breβa] *nf* (*Bot*) early fig

breve ['breβe] *adj* short, brief; **en ~** (*pronto*) shortly ▷ *nf* (*Mus*) breve; **brevedad** *nf* brevity, shortness

bribón, -ona [bri'βon, ona] *adj* idle, lazy ▷ *nm/f* (*pícaro*) rascal, rogue

bricolaje [briko'laxe] *nm* do-it-yourself, DIY

brida ['briða] *nf* bridle, rein; (*Tec*) clamp

bridge [britʃ] *nm* bridge

brigada [bri'γaða] *nf* (*unidad*) brigade; (*trabajadores*) squad, gang ▷ *nm* ≈ sergeant major

brillante [bri'ʎante] *adj* brilliant ▷ *nm* diamond

brillar [bri'ʎar] /1a/ *vi* to shine; (*joyas*) to sparkle

brillo ['briʎo] *nm* shine; (*brillantez*) brilliance; (*fig*) splendour; **sacar ~ a** to polish

brincar [brin'kar] /1g/ *vi* to skip about, hop about, jump about

brinco ['brinko] *nm* jump, leap

brindar [brin'dar] /1a/ *vi*: **~ a** *o* **por** to drink (a toast) to ▷ *vt* to offer, present

brindis ['brindis] *nm inv* toast

brío ['brio] *nm* spirit, dash

brisa ['brisa] *nf* breeze

británico, -a [bri'taniko, a] *adj* British ▷ *nm/f* Briton, British person

brizna ['briθna] *nf* (*de hierba*) blade; (*de tabaco*) leaf

broca ['broka] *nf* (*Tec*) drill bit

brocha ['brotʃa] *nf* (*large*) paintbrush; **~ de afeitar** shaving brush

broche ['brotʃe] *nm* brooch

broma ['broma] *nf* joke; **en ~** in fun, as a joke; **~ pesada** practical joke; **bromear** /1a/ *vi* to joke

bromista [bro'mista] *adj* fond of joking ▷ *nmf* joker, wag

bronca ['bronka] *nf* row; **echar una ~ a algn** to tell sb off

bronce ['bronθe] *nm* bronze; **bronceado, -a** *adj* bronze *cpd*; (*por el sol*) tanned ▷ *nm* (sun)tan; (*Tec*) bronzing

bronceador [bronθea'ðor] *nm* suntan lotion

broncearse [bronθe'arse] /1a/ *vr* to get a suntan

bronquios ['bronkjos] *nmpl* bronchial tubes

bronquitis [bron'kitis] *nf inv* bronchitis

brotar [bro'tar] /1a/ *vi* (*Bot*) to sprout; (*aguas*) to gush (forth); (*Med*) to break out

brote ['brote] *nm* (*Bot*) shoot; (*Med, fig*) outbreak

bruces ['bruθes]: **de ~** *adv*, **caer** *o* **dar de ~** to fall headlong, fall flat

bruja ['bruxa] *nf* witch; **brujería** *nf* witchcraft

brujo ['bruxo] *nm* wizard, magician

brújula ['bruxula] *nf* compass

bruma ['bruma] *nf* mist

brusco, -a ['brusko, a] *adj* (*súbito*) sudden; (*áspero*) brusque

Bruselas [bru'selas] *nf* Brussels

brutal [bru'tal] *adj* brutal; **brutalidad** *nf* brutality

bruto, -a ['bruto, a] *adj* (*idiota*) stupid; (*bestial*) brutish; (*peso*) gross; **en ~** raw, unworked

Bs.As. *abr* = **Buenos Aires**

bucal [bu'kal] *adj* oral; **por vía ~** orally

bucear [buθe'ar] /1a/ *vi* to dive ▷ *vt* to explore; **buceo** *nm* diving

bucle ['bukle] *nm* curl

budismo [bu'ðismo] *nm* Buddhism

buen [bwen] *adj* V **bueno**

buenamente [bwena'mente] *adv* (*fácilmente*) easily; (*voluntariamente*) willingly

buenaventura [bwenaβen'tura]
nf (*suerte*) good luck; (*adivinación*)
fortune

buenmozo [bwen'moθo] *adj* (*LAM*)
handsome

 PALABRA CLAVE

bueno, -a, *antes de nmsg* **buen**
['bweno, a] *adj* **1** (*excelente etc*) good;
es un libro bueno, es un buen libro
it's a good book; **hace bueno, hace
buen tiempo** the weather is fine, it is
fine; **el bueno de Paco** good old Paco;
fue muy bueno conmigo he was very
nice *o* kind to me
2 (*apropiado*): **ser bueno para** to be
good for; **creo que vamos por buen
camino** I think we're on the right track
3 (*irónico*): **le di un buen rapapolvo**
I gave him a good *o* real ticking off;
¡buen conductor estás hecho!
some driver *o* a fine driver you are!;
¡estaría bueno que ...! a fine thing it
would be if ...!
4 (*atractivo, sabroso*): **está bueno este
bizcocho** this sponge is delicious;
Julio está muy bueno (*fam*) Julio's
gorgeous
5 (*saludos*): **¡buen día!** (*LAM*), **¡buenos
días!** (good) morning!; **¡buenas
(tardes)!** good afternoon!; (*más tarde*)
good evening!; **¡buenas noches!**
good night!
6 (*otras locuciones*): **estar de buenas**
to be in a good mood; **por las buenas
o por las malas** by hook or by crook;
de buenas a primeras all of a sudden
▷ *excl*: **¡bueno!** all right!; **bueno, ¿y
qué?** well, so what?

Buenos Aires [bweno'saires] *nm*
Buenos Aires

buey [bwei] *nm* ox

búfalo ['bufalo] *nm* buffalo

bufanda [bu'fanda] *nf* scarf

bufete [bu'fete] *nm* (*despacho de
abogado*) lawyer's office

bufón [bu'fon] *nm* clown

buhardilla [buar'ðiʎa] *nf* attic

búho ['buo] *nm* owl; (*fig*) hermit, recluse

buitre ['bwitre] *nm* vulture

bujía [bu'xia] *nf* (*vela*) candle; (*Elec*)
candle (power); (*Auto*) spark plug

bula ['bula] *nf* (*papal*) bull

bulbo ['bulβo] *nm* (*Bot*) bulb

bulevar [bule'βar] *nm* boulevard

Bulgaria [bul'yarja] *nf* Bulgaria;
búlgaro, -a *adj, nm/f* Bulgarian

bulla ['buʎa] *nf* (*ruido*) uproar; (*de
gente*) crowd

bullicio [bu'ʎiθjo] *nm* (*ruido*) uproar;
(*movimiento*) bustle

bulto ['bulto] *nm* (*paquete*) package;
(*fardo*) bundle; (*tamaño*) size,
bulkiness; (*Med*) swelling, lump;
(*silueta*) vague shape

buñuelo [bu'ɲwelo] *nm* ≈ doughnut,
≈ donut (*US*); (*fruta de sartén*) fritter

buque ['buke] *nm* ship, vessel; **~ de
guerra** warship

burbuja [bur'βuxa] *nf* bubble

burdel [bur'ðel] *nm* brothel

burgués, -esa [bur'yes, esa] *adj*
middle-class, bourgeois; **burguesía**
nf middle class, bourgeoisie

burla ['burla] *nf* (*mofa*) gibe; (*broma*)
joke; (*engaño*) trick; **burlar** /1a/ *vt*
(*engañar*) to deceive ▷ *vi* to joke;
burlarse *vr* to joke; **burlarse de** to
make fun of

burlón, -ona [bur'lon, ona] *adj*
mocking

buró [bu'ro] *nm* bureau

burocracia [buro'kraθja] *nf*
bureaucracy

burrada [bu'rraða] *nf*: **decir ~s** to
talk nonsense; **hacer ~s** to act stupid;
una ~ (*ESP*: *mucho*) a (hell of a) lot

burro, -a ['burro, a] *nm/f* (*Zool*)
donkey; (*fig*) ass, idiot

bursátil [bur'satil] *adj* stock-
exchange *cpd*

bus [bus] *nm* bus

busca ['buska] *nf* search, hunt ▷ *nm*
bleeper; **en ~ de** in search of

buscador [buska'ðor] nm (Internet) search engine
buscar [bus'kar] /1g/ vt to look for; (Inform) to search ▷ vi to look, search, seek; **se busca secretaria** secretary wanted
busque etc ['buske] vb V **buscar**
búsqueda ['buskeða] nf = **busca**
busto ['busto] nm (Anat, Arte) bust
butaca [bu'taka] nf armchair; (de cine, teatro) stall, seat
butano [bu'tano] nm butane (gas)
buzo ['buθo] nm diver
buzón [bu'θon] nm (gen) letter box; (en la calle) pillar box (BRIT)

C. abr (= centígrado) C.; (= compañía) Co
C/ abr (= calle) St
cabal [ka'βal] adj (exacto) exact; (correcto) right, proper; (acabado) finished, complete; **cabales** nmpl: **estar en sus ~es** to be in one's right mind
cabalgar [kaβal'ɣar] /1h/ vt, vi to ride
cabalgata [kaβal'ɣata] nf procession
caballa [ka'βaʎa] nf mackerel
caballería [kaβaʎe'ria] nf mount; (Mil) cavalry
caballero [kaβa'ʎero] nm gentleman; (de la orden de caballería) knight; (trato directo) sir
caballete [kaβa'ʎete] nm (Arte) easel; (Tec) trestle
caballito [kaβa'ʎito] nm (caballo pequeño) small horse, pony; **caballitos** nmpl merry-go-round sg
caballo [ka'βaʎo] nm horse; (Ajedrez) knight; (Naipes) ≈ queen; **ir en ~** to ride; **~ de carreras** racehorse; **~ de vapor** o **de fuerza** horsepower

cabaña [ka'βaɲa] nf (casita) hut, cabin

cabecear [kaβeθe'ar] /1a/ vt, vi to nod

cabecera [kaβe'θera] nf head; (Imprenta) headline

cabecilla [kaβe'θiʎa] nm ringleader

cabellera [kaβe'ʎera] nf (head of) hair; (de cometa) tail

cabello [ka'βeʎo] nm (tb: **~s**) hair sg; **~ de ángel** confectionery and pastry filling made of pumpkin and syrup

caber [ka'βer] /2l/ vi (entrar) to fit, go; **caben tres más** there's room for three more

cabestrillo [kaβes'triʎo] nm sling

cabeza [ka'βeθa] nf head; (Pol) chief, leader; **~ de ajo** bulb of garlic; **~ de familia** head of the household; **~ rapada** skinhead; **cabezada** nf (golpe) butt; **dar una cabezada** to nod off; **cabezón, -ona** adj with a big head; (vino) heady; (obstinado) pig-headed

cabida [ka'βiða] nf space

cabina [ka'βina] nf cabin; (de avión) cockpit; (de camión) cab; **~ telefónica** (tele)phone box (BRIT) o booth

cabizbajo, -a [kaβiθ'βaxo, a] adj crestfallen, dejected

cable ['kaβle] nm cable

cabo ['kaβo] nm (de objeto) end, extremity; (Mil) corporal; (Naut) rope, cable; (Geo) cape; **al ~ de tres días** after three days; **llevar a ~** to carry out

cabra ['kaβra] nf goat

cabré etc [ka'βre] vb V **caber**

cabrear [kaβre'ar] /1a/ vt to annoy; **cabrearse** vr (enfadarse) to fly off the handle

cabrito [ka'βrito] nm kid

cabrón [ka'βron] nm cuckold; (fam!) bastard (!)

caca ['kaka] nf pooh

cacahuete [kaka'wete] nm (ESP) peanut

cacao [ka'kao] nm cocoa; (Bot) cacao

cacarear [kakare'ar] /1a/ vi (persona) to boast; (gallo) to crow

cacarizo, -a [kaka'riθo, a] adj (LAM) pockmarked

cacería [kaθe'ria] nf hunt

cacerola [kaθe'rola] nf pan, saucepan

cachalote [katʃa'lote] nm sperm whale

cacharro [ka'tʃarro] nm (cerámica) piece of pottery; **cacharros** nmpl pots and pans

cachear [katʃe'ar] /1a/ vt to search, frisk

cachemir [katʃe'mir] nm cashmere

cachetada [katʃe'taða] nf (LAM fam: bofetada) slap

cachete [ka'tʃete] nm (Anat) cheek; (bofetada) slap (in the face)

cachivache [katʃi'βatʃe] nm piece of junk; **cachivaches** nmpl junk sg

cacho ['katʃo] nm (small) bit; (LAM: cuerno) horn

cachondeo [katʃon'deo] nm (ESP fam) farce, joke

cachondo, -a [ka'tʃondo, a] adj (Zool) on heat; (caliente) randy, sexy; (gracioso) funny

cachorro, -a [ka'tʃorro, a] nm/f (de perro) pup, puppy; (de león) cub

cachucha [ka'tʃutʃa] nf (MÉX fam) cap

cacique [ka'θike] nm chief, local ruler; (Pol) local party boss

cacto ['kakto] nm, **cactus** ['kaktus] nm inv cactus

cada ['kaða] adj inv each; (antes de número) every; **~ día** each day, every day; **~ dos días** every other day; **~ uno/a** each one, every one; **~ vez más/menos** more and more/less and less; **~ vez que ...** whenever, every time (that) ...; **uno de ~ diez** one out of every ten

cadáver [ka'ðaβer] nm (dead) body, corpse

cadena [ka'ðena] nf chain; (TV) channel; **trabajo en ~** assembly line work; **~ montañosa** mountain range; **~ perpetua** (Jur) life imprisonment; **~ de caracteres** (Inform) character string

cadera [ka'ðera] nf hip

cadete [ka'ðete] nm cadet

caducar [kaðu'kar] /1g/ vi to expire; **caduco, -a** adj (idea etc) outdated, outmoded; **de hoja caduca** deciduous

caer [ka'er] /2n/ vi to fall; **caerse** vr to fall (down); **dejar ~** to drop; **su cumpleaños cae en viernes** her birthday falls on a Friday

café [ka'fe] (pl **cafés**) nm (bebida, planta) coffee; (lugar) café ▷ adj (color) brown; **~ con leche** white coffee; **~ solo, ~ negro** (LAM) (small) black coffee

cafetera [kafe'tera] nf V **cafetero**

cafetería [kafete'ria] nf cafe

cafetero, -a [kafe'tero, a] adj coffee cpd ▷ nf coffee pot; **ser muy ~** to be a coffee addict

cagar [ka'ɣar] /1h/ (fam!) vt to bungle, mess up ▷ vi to have a shit (!)

caído, -a [ka'iðo, a] adj fallen ▷ nf fall; (declive) slope; (disminución) fall, drop

caiga etc ['kaiɣa] vb V **caer**

caimán [kai'man] nm alligator

caja ['kaxa] nf box; (para reloj) case; (de ascensor) shaft; (Com) cash box; (donde se hacen los pagos) cashdesk; (en supermercado) checkout, till; **~ de ahorros** savings bank; **~ de cambios** gearbox; **~ de fusibles** fuse box; **~ fuerte** o **de caudales** safe, strongbox

cajero, -a [ka'xero, a] nm/f cashier ▷ nm: **~ automático** cash dispenser

cajetilla [kaxe'tiʎa] nf (de cigarrillos) packet

cajón [ka'xon] nm big box; (de mueble) drawer

cajuela [kax'wela] nf (MÉX: Auto) boot (BRIT), trunk (US)

cal [kal] nf lime

cala ['kala] nf (Geo) cove, inlet; (de barco) hold

calabacín [kalaβa'θin] nm (Bot) baby marrow; (: más pequeño) courgette (BRIT), zucchini (US)

calabacita [kalaβa'θita] (LAM) nf courgette (BRIT), zucchini (US)

calabaza [kala'βaθa] nf (Bot) pumpkin

calabozo [kala'βoθo] nm (cárcel) prison; (celda) cell

calado, -a [ka'laðo, a] adj (prenda) lace cpd ▷ nm (Naut) draught ▷ nf (de cigarrillo) puff; **estar ~ (hasta los huesos)** to be soaked (to the skin)

calamar [kala'mar] nm squid

calambre [ka'lambre] nm (Elec) shock

calar [ka'lar] /1a/ vt to soak, drench; (penetrar) to pierce, penetrate; (comprender) to see through; (vela, red) to lower; **calarse** vr (Auto) to stall; **~se las gafas** to stick one's glasses on

calavera [kala'βera] nf skull

calcar [kal'kar] /1g/ vt (reproducir) to trace; (imitar) to copy

calcetín [kalθe'tin] nm sock

calcio ['kalθjo] nm calcium

calcomanía [kalkoma'nia] nf transfer

calculador, a [kalkula'ðor, a] adj calculating ▷ nf calculator

calcular [kalku'lar] /1a/ vt (Mat) to calculate, compute; **~ que ...** to reckon that ...

cálculo ['kalkulo] nm calculation

caldera [kal'dera] nf boiler

calderilla [kalde'riʎa] nf (moneda) small change

caldo ['kaldo] nm stock; (consomé) consommé

calefacción [kalefak'θjon] nf heating; **~ central** central heating

calefón [kale'fon] nm (RPL) boiler

calendario [kalen'darjo] nm calendar

calentador [kalenta'ðor] nm heater

calentamiento [kalenta'mjento] nm (Deporte) warm-up; **~ global** global warming

calentar [kalen'tar] /1j/ vt to heat (up); **calentarse** vr to heat up, warm up; (fig: discusión etc) to get heated

calentón, -ona [kalen'ton, ona] (RPL fam) adj (sexualmente) horny, randy (BRIT)

calentura [kalen'tura] nf (Med) fever, (high) temperature

calesita [kale'sita] nf (LAM) merry-go-round, carousel

calibre [ka'liβre] nm (de cañón) calibre, bore; (diámetro) diameter; (fig) calibre

calidad [kali'ðað] nf quality; **de ~** quality cpd; **en ~ de** in the capacity of

cálido, -a ['kaliðo, a] adj hot; (fig) warm

caliente [ka'ljente] vb V calentar ▷ adj hot; (fig) fiery; (disputa) heated; (fam: cachondo) randy

calificación [kalifika'θjon] nf qualification; (de alumno) grade, mark

calificado, -a [kalifi'kaðo, a] adj (LAM: competente) qualified; (obrero) skilled

calificar [kalifi'kar] /1g/ vt to qualify; (alumno) to grade, mark; **~ de** to describe as

calima [ka'lima] nf (cerca del mar) mist

cáliz ['kaliθ] nm chalice

caliza [ka'liθa] nf limestone

callado, -a [ka'ʎaðo, a] adj quiet

callar [ka'ʎar] /1a/ vt (asunto delicado) to keep quiet about, say nothing about; (persona, oposición) to silence ▷ vi to keep quiet, be silent; (dejar de hablar) to stop talking; **callarse** vr to keep quiet, be silent; **¡calla!** be quiet!

calle ['kaʎe] nf street; (Deporte) lane; **~ arriba/abajo** up/down the street; **~ de sentido único** one-way street; **~ mayor** (ESP) high (BRIT) o main (US) street; **~ peatonal** pedestrianized o pedestrian street; **~ principal** (LAM) high (BRIT) o main (US) street; **poner a algn (de patitas) en la ~** to kick sb out; **callejear** /1a/ vi to wander (about) the streets; **callejero, -a** adj street cpd ▷ nm street map; **callejón** nm alley, passage; **callejón sin salida** cul-de-sac; **callejuela** nf side-street, alley

callista [ka'ʎista] nmf chiropodist

callo ['kaʎo] nm callus; (en el pie) corn; **callos** nmpl (Culin) tripe sg

calma ['kalma] nf calm

calmante [kal'mante] nm sedative, tranquillizer

calmar [kal'mar] /1a/ vt to calm, calm down; (calmarse) vr (tempestad) to abate; (mente etc) to become calm

calor [ka'lor] nm heat; (calor agradable) warmth; **tener ~** to be o feel hot

caloría [kalo'ria] nf calorie

calumnia [ka'lumnja] nf slander

caluroso, -a [kalu'roso, a] adj hot; (sin exceso) warm; (fig) enthusiastic

calva ['kalβa] nf bald patch; (en bosque) clearing

calvario [kal'βarjo] nm stations pl of the cross

calvicie [kal'βiθje] nf baldness

calvo, -a ['kalβo, a] adj bald; (terreno) bare, barren; (tejido) threadbare

calza ['kalθa] nf wedge, chock

calzado, -a [kal'θaðo, a] adj shod ▷ nm footwear ▷ nf roadway, highway

calzador [kalθa'ðor] nm shoehorn

calzar [kal'θar] /1f/ vt (zapatos etc) to wear; (un mueble) to put a wedge under; **calzarse** vr: **~se los zapatos** to put on one's shoes; **¿qué (número) calza?** what size do you take?

calzón [kal'θon] nm (tb: **calzones**) shorts pl; (LAM: de hombre) pants pl; (: de mujer) panties pl

calzoncillos [kalθon'θiʎos] nmpl underpants

cama ['kama] nf bed; **~ individual/ de matrimonio** single/double bed; **hacer la ~** to make the bed

camaleón [kamale'on] nm chameleon

cámara ['kamara] nf chamber; (habitación) room; (sala) hall; (Cine) cine camera; (fotográfica) camera; **~ de aire** inner tube; **~ de comercio** chamber of commerce; **~ digital** digital camera; **~ de gas** gas chamber; **~ frigorífica** cold-storage room

camarada [kamaˈraða] nm comrade, companion

camarero, -a [kamaˈrero, a] nm waiter ▷ nf (en restaurante) waitress; (en casa, hotel) maid

camarógrafo, -a [kamaˈroɣrafo, a] nm/f (LAM) cameraman/camerawoman

camarón [kamaˈron] nm shrimp

camarote [kamaˈrote] nm cabin

cambiable [kamˈbjaβle] adj (variable) changeable, variable; (intercambiable) interchangeable

cambiante [kamˈbjante] adj variable

cambiar [kamˈbjar] /1b/ vt to change; (trocar) to exchange ▷ vi to change; **cambiarse** vr (mudarse) to move; (de ropa) to change; **~ de idea** u **opinión** to change one's mind; **~se de ropa** to change (one's clothes)

cambio [ˈkambjo] nm change; (trueque) exchange; (Com) rate of exchange; (oficina) bureau de change; (dinero menudo) small change; **a ~ de** in return o exchange for; **en ~** on the other hand; (en lugar de eso) instead; **~ climático** climate change; **~ de divisas** (Com) foreign exchange; **~ de velocidades** gear lever

camelar [kameˈlar] /1a/ vt (persuadir) to sweet-talk

camello [kameˈʎo] nm camel; (fam: traficante) pusher

camerino [kameˈrino] nm dressing room

camilla [kaˈmiʎa] nf (Med) stretcher

caminar [kamiˈnar] /1a/ vi (marchar) to walk, go ▷ vt (recorrer) to cover, travel

caminata [kamiˈnata] nf long walk; (por el campo) hike

camino [kaˈmino] nm way, road; (sendero) track; **a medio ~** halfway (there); **en el ~** on the way, en route; **~ de** on the way to; **~ particular** private road; **C~ de Santiago** Way of St James; see note **"Camino de Santiago"**

● **CAMINO DE SANTIAGO**
●
● The *Camino de Santiago* is
● a medieval pilgrim route
● stretching from the Pyrenees to
● Santiago de Compostela in north-
● west Spain, where tradition has
● it the body of the Apostle James is
● buried. Nowadays it is a popular
● tourist route as well as a religious
● one. The *concha* (cockleshell) is a
● symbol of the *Camino de Santiago*,
● because it is said that when St
● James' body was found it was
● covered in shells.

camión [kaˈmjon] nm lorry, truck (US); (LAM: autobús) bus; **~ cisterna** tanker; **~ de la basura** dustcart, refuse lorry; **~ de mudanzas** removal (BRIT) o moving (US) van; **camionero** nm lorry o truck (US) driver, trucker (esp US); **camioneta** [kamjoˈneta] nf van, small truck; **camionista** nmf (LAM) lorry o truck driver

camisa [kaˈmisa] nf shirt; (Bot) skin; **~ de fuerza** straitjacket

camiseta [kamiˈseta] nf tee-shirt; (ropa interior) vest; (de deportista) top

camisón [kamiˈson] nm nightdress, nightgown

camorra [kaˈmorra] nf: **buscar ~** to look for trouble

camote [kaˈmote] nm (LAM) sweet potato; (bulbo) tuber, bulb; (fam: enamoramiento) crush

campamento [kampaˈmento] nm camp

campana [kamˈpana] nf bell; **campanada** nf peal; **campanario** nm belfry

campanilla [kampaˈniʎa] nf small bell

campaña [kamˈpaɲa] nf (Mil, Pol) campaign; **~ electoral** election campaign

campechano, -a [kampeˈtʃano, a] adj (franco) open

campeón, -ona [kampe'on, ona] nm/f champion; **campeonato** nm championship

cámper ['kamper] nm o f (LAM) caravan (BRIT), trailer (US)

campera [kam'pera] nf (RPL) anorak

campesino, -a [kampe'sino, a] adj country cpd, rural; (gente) peasant cpd ▷ nm/f countryman/woman; (agricultor) farmer

campestre [kam'pestre] adj country cpd, rural

camping ['kampin] nm camping; (lugar) campsite; **ir de** o **hacer ~** to go camping

campista [kam'pista] nmf camper

campo ['kampo] nm (fuera de la ciudad) country, countryside; (Agr, Elec, Inform) field; (de fútbol) pitch; (de golf) course; (Mil) camp; **~ de batalla** battlefield; **~ de minas** minefield; **~ petrolífero** oilfield; **~ visual** field of vision; **~ de concentración/ de internación/de trabajo** concentration/internment/labour camp; **~ de deportes** sports ground, playing field

camuflaje [kamu'flaxe] nm camouflage

cana ['kana] nf V **cano**

Canadá [kana'ða] nm Canada; **canadiense** adj, nmf Canadian ▷ nf fur-lined jacket

canal [ka'nal] nm canal; (Geo) channel, strait; (de televisión) channel; (de tejado) gutter; **C~ de la Mancha** English Channel; **C~ de Panamá** Panama Canal

canaleta [kana'leta] nf (LAM: de tejado) gutter

canalizar [kanali'θar] /1f/ vt to channel

canalla [ka'naʎa] nf rabble, mob ▷ nm swine

canapé [kana'pe] (pl **canapés**) nm sofa, settee; (Culin) canapé

Canarias [ka'narjas] nfpl: **las (Islas) ~** the Canaries

canario, -a [ka'narjo, a] adj of o from the Canary Isles ▷ nm/f native o inhabitant of the Canary Isles ▷ nm (Zool) canary

canasta [ka'nasta] nf (round) basket

canasto [ka'nasto] nm large basket

cancela [kan'θela] nf (wrought-iron) gate

cancelación [kanθela'θjon] nf cancellation

cancelar [kanθe'lar] /1a/ vt to cancel; (una deuda) to write off

cáncer ['kanθer] nm (Med) cancer; **C~** (Astro) Cancer

cancha ['kantʃa] nf (de baloncesto, tenis etc) court; (LAM: de fútbol etc) pitch; **~ de tenis** (LAM) tennis court

canciller [kanθi'ʎer] nm chancellor

canción [kan'θjon] nf song; **~ de cuna** lullaby

candado [kan'daðo] nm padlock

candente [kan'dente] adj red-hot; (tema) burning

candidato, -a [kandi'ðato, a] nm/f candidate

cándido, -a ['kandiðo, a] adj simple; naive

No confundir cándido con la palabra inglesa candid.

candil [kan'dil] nm oil lamp; **candilejas** nfpl (Teat) footlights

canela [ka'nela] nf cinnamon

canelones [kane'lones] nmpl cannelloni

cangrejo [kan'grexo] nm crab

canguro [kan'guro] nm kangaroo; **hacer de ~** to baby-sit

caníbal [ka'niβal] adj, nmf cannibal

canica [ka'nika] nf marble

canijo, -a [ka'nixo, a] adj frail, sickly

canilla [ka'niʎa] nf (LAM) tap (BRIT), faucet (US)

canjear [kanxe'ar] /1a/ vt to exchange

cano, -a ['kano, a] adj grey-haired, white-haired ▷ nf (tb: **canas**) white o grey hair; **tener canas** to be going grey

canoa [ka'noa] nf canoe

canon ['kanon] nm canon; (pensión) rent; (Com) tax

canonizar [kanoni'θar] /1f/ vt to canonize

canoso, -a [ka'noso, a] adj grey-haired

cansado, -a [kan'saðo, a] adj tired, weary; (tedioso) tedious, boring

cansancio [kan'sanθjo] nm tiredness, fatigue

cansar [kan'sar] /1a/ vt (fatigar) to tire, tire out; (aburrir) to bore; (fastidiar) to bother; **cansarse** vr to tire, get tired; (aburrirse) to get bored

cantábrico, -a [kan'taβriko, a] adj Cantabrian

cantante [kan'tante] adj singing ▷ nmf singer

cantar [kan'tar] /1a/ vt to sing ▷ vi to sing; (insecto) to chirp ▷ nm (acción) singing; (canción) song; (poema) poem

cántaro ['kantaro] nm pitcher, jug; **llover a ~s** to rain cats and dogs

cante ['kante] nm Andalusian folk song; **~ jondo** flamenco singing

cantera [kan'tera] nf quarry

cantero [kan'tero] nm (LAM: arriate) border

cantidad [kanti'ðað] nf quantity, amount; **~ de** lots of

cantimplora [kantim'plora] nf water bottle, canteen

cantina [kan'tina] nf canteen; (de estación) buffet; (esp LAM) bar

cantinero, -a [kanti'nero, a] nm/f (LAM) barman/barmaid, bartender (US)

canto ['kanto] nm singing; (canción) song; (borde) edge, rim; (de un cuchillo) back; **~ rodado** boulder

cantor, a [kan'tor, a] nm/f singer

canturrear [kanturre'ar] /1a/ vi to sing softly

canuto [ka'nuto] nm (tubo) small tube; (fam: porro) joint

caña ['kaɲa] nf (Bot: tallo) stem, stalk; (: carrizo) reed; (de cerveza) glass of beer; (Anat) shinbone; **~ de azúcar** sugar cane; **~ de pescar** fishing rod

cañada [ka'ɲaða] nf (entre dos montañas) gully, ravine; (camino) cattle track

cáñamo ['kaɲamo] nm hemp

cañería [kaɲe'ria] nf (tubo) pipe

caño ['kaɲo] nm (tubo) tube, pipe; (de aguas servidas) sewer; (Mus) pipe; (de fuente) jet

cañón [ka'ɲon] nm (Mil) cannon; (de fusil) barrel; (Geo) canyon, gorge

caoba [ka'oβa] nf mahogany

caos ['kaos] nm chaos

capa ['kapa] nf cloak, cape; (Geo) layer, stratum; **~ de ozono** ozone layer

capacidad [kapaθi'ðað] nf (medida) capacity; (aptitud) capacity, ability

capacitar [kapaθi'tar] /1a/ vt: **~ a algn para algo** to qualify sb for sth; **capacitarse** vr: **~se para algo** to qualify for sth

caparazón [kapara'θon] nm shell

capataz [kapa'taθ] nm foreman

capaz [ka'paθ] adj able, capable; (amplio) capacious, roomy

capellán [kape'ʎan] nm chaplain; (sacerdote) priest

capicúa [kapi'kua] adj inv (número, fecha) reversible

capilla [ka'piʎa] nf chapel

capital [kapi'tal] adj capital ▷ nm (Com) capital ▷ nf (de nación) capital (city); **~ social** equity o share capital

capitalismo [kapita'lismo] nm capitalism; **capitalista** adj, nmf capitalist

capitán [kapi'tan] nm captain

capítulo [ka'pitulo] nm chapter

capó [ka'po] nm (Auto) bonnet (BRIT), hood (US)

capón [ka'pon] nm (gallo) capon

capota [ka'pota] nf (de mujer) bonnet; (Auto) hood (BRIT), top (US)

capote [ka'pote] nm (abrigo: de militar) greatcoat; (: de torero) cloak

capricho [ka'pritʃo] nm whim, caprice; **caprichoso, -a** adj capricious

Capricornio [kapri'kornjo] *nm*
Capricorn

cápsula ['kapsula] *nf* capsule

captar [kap'tar] /1a/ *vt* (*comprender*)
to understand; (*Radio*) to pick up;
(*atención, apoyo*) to attract

captura [kap'tura] *nf* capture;
arrest; **capturar** /1a/ *vt* to capture;
(*Jur*) to arrest

capucha [ka'putʃa] *nf* hood, cowl

capuchón [kapu'tʃon] *nm* (*ESP: de
bolígrafo*) cap

capullo [ka'puʎo] *nm* (*Zool*) cocoon;
(*Bot*) bud; (*fam!*) idiot

caqui ['kaki] *nm* khaki

cara ['kara] *nf* (*Anat, de moneda*) face;
(*de disco*) side; (*fig*) boldness ▷ *prep*: **~ a**
facing; **de ~ a** opposite, facing; **dar la
~** to face the consequences; **¿~ o cruz?**
heads or tails?; **¡qué ~ más dura!**
what a nerve!

Caracas [ka'rakas] *nf* Caracas

caracol [kara'kol] *nm* (*Zool*) snail;
(*concha*) (sea)shell

carácter (*pl* **caracteres**) [ka'rakter,
karak'teres] *nm* character; **tener
buen/mal ~** to be good-natured/bad
tempered

característico, -a [karakte'ristiko,
a] *adj* characteristic ▷ *nf* characteristic

caracterizar [karakteri'θar] /1f/ *vt*
to characterize, typify

caradura [kara'ðura] *nmf*: **es un ~**
he's got a nerve

carajillo [kara'xiʎo] *nm* black coffee
with brandy

carajo [ka'raxo] *nm* (*fam!*): **¡~!** shit! (!)

caramba [ka'ramba] *excl* good
gracious!

caramelo [kara'melo] *nm* (*dulce*)
sweet; (*azúcar fundido*) caramel

caravana [kara'βana] *nf* caravan;
(*fig*) group; (*de autos*) tailback

carbón [kar'βon] *nm* coal; **papel ~**
carbon paper

carbono [kar'βono] *nm* carbon

carburador [karβura'ðor] *nm*
carburettor

carburante [karβu'rante] *nm* fuel

carcajada [karka'xaða] *nf* (*loud*)
laugh, guffaw

cárcel ['karθel] *nf* prison, jail; (*Tec*)
clamp

carcoma [kar'koma] *nf* woodworm

cardar [kar'ðar] /1a/ *vt* (*Tec*) to card,
comb; (*pelo*) to backcomb

cardenal [karðe'nal] *nm* (*Rel*)
cardinal; (*Med*) bruise

cardiaco, -a [kar'ðjako, a],
cardíaco, a [kar'ðiako, a] *adj*
cardiac; (*ataque*) heart *cpd*

cardinal [karði'nal] *adj* cardinal

cardo ['karðo] *nm* thistle

carecer [kare'θer] /2d/ *vi*: **~ de** to
lack, be in need of

carencia [ka'renθja] *nf* lack; (*escasez*)
shortage; (*Med*) deficiency

careta [ka'reta] *nf* mask

carga ['karɣa] *nf* (*peso, Elec*) load; (*de
barco*) cargo, freight; (*Mil*) charge;
(*obligación, responsabilidad*) duty,
obligation

cargado, -a [kar'ɣaðo, a] *adj* loaded;
(*Elec*) live; (*café, té*) strong; (*cielo*)
overcast

cargamento [karɣa'mento] *nm*
(*acción*) loading; (*mercancías*) load,
cargo

cargar [kar'ɣar] /1h/ *vt* (*barco, arma*)
to load; (*Elec*) to charge; (*Com: algo
en cuenta*) to charge, debit; (*Mil*) to
charge; (*Inform*) to load ▷ *vi* (*Auto*) to
load (up); **~ con** to pick up, carry away;
(*peso: fig*) to shoulder, bear; **cargarse**
vr (*fam: estropear*) to break; (: *matar*)
to bump off

cargo ['karɣo] *nm* (*puesto*) post, office;
(*responsabilidad*) duty, obligation; (*Jur*)
charge; **hacerse ~ de** to take charge
of o responsibility for

carguero [kar'ɣero] *nm* freighter,
cargo boat; (*avión*) freight plane

Caribe [ka'riβe] *nm*: **el ~** the
Caribbean; **del ~** Caribbean;
caribeño, -a *adj* Caribbean

caricatura [karika'tura] *nf* caricature

caricia [ka'riθja] nf caress
caridad [kari'ðað] nf charity
caries ['karjes] nf inv tooth decay
cariño [ka'riɲo] nm affection, love;
(*caricia*) caress; (*en carta*) love …;
tener ~ a to be fond of; **cariñoso, -a**
adj affectionate
carisma [ka'risma] nm charisma
caritativo, -a [karita'tiβo, a] adj
charitable
cariz [ka'riθ] nm: **tener** o **tomar
buen/mal ~** to look good/bad
carmín [kar'min] nm (tb: **~ de labios**)
lipstick
carnal [kar'nal] adj carnal; **primo ~**
first cousin
carnaval [karna'βal] nm carnival

○ **CARNAVAL**
○
○ The 3 days before *miércoles de ceniza*
○ (Ash Wednesday), when fasting
○ traditionally starts, are the time for
○ *carnaval*, an exuberant celebration
○ which dates back to pre-Christian
○ times. Although in decline during
○ the Franco years, the *carnaval* has
○ grown in popularity recently in
○ Spain, Cádiz and Tenerife being
○ particularly well-known for their
○ celebrations. *El martes de carnaval*
○ (Shrove Tuesday) is the biggest day,
○ with colourful street parades, fancy
○ dress, fireworks and a general party
○ atmosphere.

carne ['karne] nf flesh; (*Culin*) meat;
se me pone la ~ de gallina sólo verlo
I get the creeps just seeing it; **~ de
cerdo/de cordero/de ternera/de
vaca** pork/lamb/veal/beef; **~ molida**
(*LAM*), **~ picada** (*ESP*) mince (*BRIT*),
ground meat (*US*); **~ de gallina** (*fig*)
gooseflesh
carné [kar'ne] (pl **carnés**) (*ESP*) nm: **~ de
conducir** driving licence (*BRIT*), driver's
license (*US*); **~ de identidad** identity
card; **~ de socio** membership card

carnero [kar'nero] nm sheep, ram;
(*carne*) mutton
carnet [kar'ne] (pl **carnets**) nm (*ESP*)
= **carné**
carnicería [karniθe'ria] nf butcher's
(shop); (*fig: matanza*) carnage,
slaughter
carnicero, -a [karni'θero, a] adj
carnivorous ▷ nm/f (tb fig) butcher
▷ nm carnivore
carnívoro, -a [kar'niβoro, a] adj
carnivorous
caro, -a ['karo, a] adj dear; (*Com*) dear,
expensive ▷ adv dear, dearly
carpa ['karpa] nf (*pez*) carp; (*de circo*)
big top; (*LAM: de camping*) tent
carpeta [kar'peta] nf folder, file
carpintería [karpinte'ria] nf
carpentry, joinery; **carpintero** nm
carpenter
carraspear [karraspe'ar] /1a/ vi to
clear one's throat
carraspera [karras'pera] nf
hoarseness
carrera [ka'rrera] nf (*acción*)
run(ning); (*espacio recorrido*) run;
(*certamen*) race; (*trayecto*) course;
(*profesión*) career; **a la ~** at (full)
speed; **~ de obstáculos** (*Deporte*)
steeplechase
carrete [ka'rrete] nm reel, spool;
(*Tec*) coil
carretera [karre'tera] nf (main)
road, highway; **~ nacional** ≈ A road
(*BRIT*), ≈ state highway (*US*); **~ de
circunvalación** ring road
carretilla [karre'tiʎa] nf trolley; (*Agr*)
(wheel)barrow
carril [ka'rril] nm furrow; (*de autopista*)
lane; (*Ferro*) rail
carril bici [karil'βiθi] nm cycle lane,
bikeway (*US*)
carrito [ka'rrito] nm trolley
carro ['karro] nm cart, wagon; (*Mil*)
tank; (*LAM: coche*) car; **~ patrulla** (*LAM*)
patrol o panda (*BRIT*) car
carrocería [karroθe'ria] nf bodywork
no pl (*BRIT*)

carroña [kaˈrroɲa] nf carrion no pl

carroza [kaˈrroθa] nf (vehículo) coach

carrusel [karruˈsel] nm merry-go-round, roundabout (BRIT)

carta [ˈkarta] nf letter; (Culin) menu; (naipe) card; (mapa) map; (Jur) document; **~ certificada/urgente** registered/special delivery letter

cartabón [kartaˈβon] nm set square

cartearse [karteˈarse] /1a/ vr to correspond

cartel [karˈtel] nm (anuncio) poster, placard; (Escol) wall chart; (Com) cartel; **cartelera** nf hoarding, billboard; (en periódico etc) entertainments guide; **"en cartelera"** "showing"

cartera [karˈtera] nf (de bolsillo) wallet; (de colegial, cobrador) satchel; (de señora) handbag (BRIT), purse (US); (para documentos) briefcase; (Com) portfolio; **ocupa la ~ de Agricultura** he is Minister of Agriculture

carterista [karteˈrista] nmf pickpocket

cartero [karˈtero] nm postman

cartilla [karˈtiʎa] nf primer, first reading book; **~ de ahorros** savings book

cartón [karˈton] nm cardboard; **~ piedra** papier-mâché

cartucho [karˈtutʃo] nm (Mil) cartridge

cartulina [kartuˈlina] nf card

casa [ˈkasa] nf house; (hogar) home; (Com) firm, company; **~ consistorial** town hall; **~ de huéspedes** boarding house; **~ de socorro** first aid post; **~ independiente** detached house; **~ rodante** (cs) caravan (BRIT), trailer (US); **en ~** at home

casado, -a [kaˈsaðo, a] adj married ▷ nm/f married man/woman

casar [kaˈsar] /1a/ vt to marry; (Jur) to quash, annul; **casarse** vr to marry, get married

cascabel [kaskaˈβel] nm (small) bell

cascada [kasˈkaða] nf waterfall

cascanueces [kaskaˈnweθes] nm inv (a pair of) nutcrackers, nutcracker sg

cascar [kasˈkar] /1g/ vt to split; (nuez) to crack; **cascarse** vr to crack, split, break (open)

cáscara [ˈkaskara] nf (de huevo, fruta seca) shell; (de fruta) skin; (de limón) peel

casco [ˈkasko] nm (de bombero, soldado) helmet; (Naut: de barco) hull; (Zool: de caballo) hoof; (botella) empty bottle; (de ciudad): **el ~ antiguo** the old part; **el ~ urbano** the town centre; **los ~s azules** the UN peace-keeping force, the blue helmets

cascote [kasˈkote] nm piece of rubble; **cascotes** nmpl rubble sg

caserío [kaseˈrio] nm hamlet, group of houses; (casa) farmhouse

casero, -a [kaˈsero, a] adj (pan etc) home-made; (persona): **ser muy ~** to be home-loving ▷ nm/f (propietario) landlord/lady; **"comida casera"** "home cooking"

caseta [kaˈseta] nf hut; (para bañista) cubicle; (de feria) stall

casete [kaˈsete] nm o f cassette

casi [ˈkasi] adv almost; **~ nunca** hardly ever, almost never; **~ nada** next to nothing; **~ te caes** you almost o nearly fell

casilla [kaˈsiʎa] nf (casita) hut, cabin; (para cartas) pigeonhole; (Ajedrez) square; **~ postal** o **de Correo(s)** (LAM) P.O. Box; **casillero** nm (para cartas) pigeonholes pl

casino [kaˈsino] nm club; (de juego) casino

caso [ˈkaso] nm case; **en ~ de ...** in case of ...; **el ~ es que** the fact is that; **en ese ~** in that case; **en todo ~** in any case; **hacer ~ a** to pay attention to; **hacer** o **venir al ~** to be relevant

caspa [ˈkaspa] nf dandruff

cassette [kaˈset] nm o f = **casete**

castaña [kasˈtaɲa] nf V **castaño**

castaño, -a [kas'taɲo, a] *adj*
chestnut(-coloured), brown ▷ *nm*
chestnut tree ▷ *nf* chestnut
castañuelas [kasta'ɲwelas] *nfpl*
castanets
castellano, -a [kaste'ʎano, a] *adj*
Castilian ▷ *nm/f* Castilian ▷ *nm* (*Ling*)
Castilian, Spanish
castigar [kasti'ɣar] /1h/ *vt* to punish;
(*Deporte*) to penalize; **castigo** *nm*
punishment; (*Deporte*) penalty
Castilla [kas'tiʎa] *nf* Castile
castillo [kas'tiʎo] *nm* castle
castizo, -a [kas'tiθo, a] *adj* (*Ling*) pure
casto, -a ['kasto, a] *adj* chaste, pure
castor [kas'tor] *nm* beaver
castrar [kas'trar] /1a/ *vt* to castrate
casual [ka'swal] *adj* chance,
accidental; **casualidad** *nf*
chance, accident; (*combinación de
circunstancias*) coincidence; **da la
casualidad de que ...** it (just) so
happens that ...; **¡qué casualidad!**
what a coincidence!

No confundir *casual* con la palabra
inglesa *casual*.

cataclismo [kata'klismo] *nm*
cataclysm
catador [kata'ðor] *nm* taster
catalán, -ana [kata'lan, ana] *adj,
nm/f* Catalan ▷ *nm* (*Ling*) Catalan
catalizador [kataliθa'ðor] *nm*
catalyst; (*Auto*) catalytic converter
catalogar [katalo'ɣar] /1h/ *vt* to
catalogue; **~ (de)** (*fig*) to classify as
catálogo [ka'taloɣo] *nm* catalogue
Cataluña [kata'luɲa] *nf* Catalonia
catar [ka'tar] /1a/ *vt* to taste, sample
catarata [kata'rata] *nf* (*Geo*) (water)
fall; (*Med*) cataract
catarro [ka'tarro] *nm* catarrh;
(*constipado*) cold
catástrofe [ka'tastrofe] *nf*
catastrophe
catear [kate'ar] /1a/ *vt* (*fam: examen,
alumno*) to fail
cátedra ['kateðra] *nf* (*Univ*) chair,
professorship

catedral [kate'ðral] *nf* cathedral
catedrático, -a [kate'ðratiko, a]
nm/f professor
categoría [kateɣo'ria] *nf* category;
(*rango*) rank, standing; (*calidad*)
quality; **de ~** (*hotel*) top-class
cateto, -a [ka'teto, a] *nm/f* yokel
catolicismo [katoli'θismo] *nm*
Catholicism
católico, -a [ka'toliko, a] *adj, nm/f*
Catholic
catorce [ka'torθe] *num* fourteen
cauce ['kauθe] *nm* (*de río*) riverbed;
(*fig*) channel
caucho ['kautʃo] *nm* rubber
caudal [kau'ðal] *nm* (*de río*) volume,
flow; (*fortuna*) wealth; (*abundancia*)
abundance
caudillo [kau'ðiʎo] *nm* leader, chief
causa ['kausa] *nf* cause; (*razón*)
reason; (*Jur*) lawsuit, case; **a** *o* **por ~
de** because of; **causar** /1a/ *vt* to cause
cautela [kau'tela] *nf* caution,
cautiousness; **cauteloso, -a** *adj*
cautious, wary
cautivar [kauti'βar] /1a/ *vt* to
capture; (*fig*) to captivate
cautiverio [kauti'βerjo] *nm*,
cautividad [kautiβi'ðað] *nf*
captivity
cautivo, -a [kau'tiβo, a] *adj, nm/f*
captive
cauto, -a ['kauto, a] *adj* cautious,
careful
cava ['kaβa] *nm* champagne-type wine
cavar [ka'βar] /1a/ *vt* to dig
caverna [ka'βerna] *nf* cave, cavern
cavidad [kaβi'ðað] *nf* cavity
cavilar [kaβi'lar] /1a/ *vt* to ponder
cayendo *etc* [ka'jendo] *vb* V **caer**
caza ['kaθa] *nf* (*acción: gen*) hunting;
(*: con fusil*) shooting; (*una caza*) hunt,
chase; (*animales*) game ▷ *nm* (*Aviat*)
fighter; **ir de ~** to go hunting; **~
mayor** game hunting; **cazador, a**
nm/f hunter/huntress ▷ *nf* jacket;
cazar /1f/ *vt* to hunt; (*perseguir*) to
chase; (*prender*) to catch

cazo ['kaθo] nm saucepan

cazuela [ka'θwela] nf (vasija) pan; (guisado) casserole

CD nm abr (= compact disc) CD

CD-ROM [θeðe'rom] nm abr CD-ROM

CE nm abr (= Consejo de Europa) Council of Europe

cebada [θe'βaða] nf barley

cebar [θe'βar] /1a/ vt (animal) to fatten (up); (anzuelo) to bait; (Mil, Tec) to prime

cebo ['θeβo] nm (para animales) feed, food; (para peces, fig) bait; (de arma) charge

cebolla [θe'βoʎa] nf onion; **cebolleta** nf spring onion

cebra ['θeβra] nf zebra

cecear [θeθe'ar] /1a/ vi to lisp

ceder [θe'ðer] /2a/ vt to hand over; (renunciar a) to give up, part with ▷ vi (renunciar) to give in, yield; (disminuir) to diminish, decline; (romperse) to give way

cederom [θeðe'rom] nm CD-ROM

cedro ['θeðro] nm cedar

cédula ['θeðula] nf certificate, document; **~ de identidad** (LAM) identity card; **~ electoral** (LAM) ballot

cegar [θe'ɣar] /1h, 1j/ vt to blind; (tubería etc) to block up, stop up ▷ vi to go blind; **cegarse** vr: **~se (de)** to be blinded (by)

ceguera [θe'ɣera] nf blindness

ceja ['θexa] nf eyebrow

cejar [θe'xar] /1a/ vi (fig) to back down

celador, a [θela'ðor, a] nm/f (de edificio) watchman; (de museo etc) attendant

celda ['θelda] nf cell

celebración [θeleβra'θjon] nf celebration

celebrar [θele'βrar] /1a/ vt to celebrate; (alabar) to praise ▷ vi to be glad; **celebrarse** vr to occur, take place

célebre ['θeleβre] adj famous

celebridad [θeleβri'ðað] nf fame; (persona) celebrity

celeste [θe'leste] adj sky-blue

celestial [θeles'tjal] adj celestial, heavenly

celo¹ ['θelo] nm zeal; (Rel) fervour; **celos** nmpl jealousy sg; **dar ~s a algn** to make sb jealous; **tener ~s de algn** to be jealous of sb; **en ~** (animales) on heat

celo²® ['θelo] nm Sellotape®

celofán [θelo'fan] nm Cellophane®

celoso, -a [θe'loso, a] adj jealous; (trabajador) zealous

celta ['θelta] adj Celtic ▷ nmf Celt

célula ['θelula] nf cell

celulitis [θelu'litis] nf cellulite

cementerio [θemen'terjo] nm cemetery, graveyard

cemento [θe'mento] nm cement; (hormigón) concrete; (LAM: cola) glue

cena ['θena] nf evening meal, dinner; **cenar** /1a/ vt to have for dinner ▷ vi to have dinner

cenicero [θeni'θero] nm ashtray

ceniza [θe'niθa] nf ash, ashes pl

censo ['θenso] nm census; **~ electoral** electoral roll

censura [θen'sura] nf (Pol) censorship; **censurar** /1a/ vt (idea) to censure; (cortar: película) to censor

centella [θen'teʎa] nf spark

centenar [θente'nar] nm hundred

centenario, -a [θente'narjo, a] adj hundred-year-old ▷ nm centenary; **ser ~** to be one hundred years old

centeno [θen'teno] nm rye

centésimo, -a [θen'tesimo, a] adj hundredth

centígrado [θen'tiɣraðo] adj centigrade

centímetro [θen'timetro] nm centimetre (BRIT), centimeter (US)

céntimo ['θentimo] nm cent

centinela [θenti'nela] nm sentry, guard

centollo, -a [θen'toʎo, a] nm/f large (o spider) crab

central [θen'tral] adj central ▷ nf head office; (Tec) plant; (Telec) exchange; **~ eléctrica** power station; **~ nuclear** nuclear power station; **~ telefónica** telephone exchange

centralita [θentra'lita] *nf* switchboard

centralizar [θentrali'θar] /1f/ *vt* to centralize

centrar [θen'trar] /1a/ *vt* to centre

céntrico, -a ['θentriko, a] *adj* central

centrifugar [θentrifu'ɣar] /1h/ *vt* to spin-dry

centro ['θentro] *nm* centre; **~ comercial** shopping centre; **~ de atención al cliente** call centre; **~ de salud** health centre; **~ escolar** school; **~ juvenil** youth club; **~ social** community centre; **~ turístico** (*lugar muy visitado*) tourist centre; **~ urbano** urban area, city

centroamericano, -a [θentroameri'kano, a] *adj, nm/f* Central American

ceñido, -a [θe'niðo, a] *adj* tight

ceñir [θe'nir] *vt* (*rodear*) to encircle, surround; (*ajustar*) to fit (tightly)

ceño ['θeno] *nm* frown, scowl; **fruncir el ~** to frown, knit one's brow

cepillar [θepi'ʎar] /1a/ *vt* to brush; (*madera*) to plane (down)

cepillo [θe'piʎo] *nm* brush; (*para madera*) plane; **~ de dientes** toothbrush

cera ['θera] *nf* wax

cerámica [θe'ramika] *nf* pottery; (*arte*) ceramics *pl*

cerca ['θerka] *nf* fence ▷ *adv* near, nearby, close ▷ *prep*: **~ de** near, close to

cercanía [θerka'nia] *nf* closeness; **cercanías** *nfpl* outskirts, suburbs

cercano, -a [θer'kano, a] *adj* close, near

cercar [θer'kar] /1g/ *vt* to fence in; (*rodear*) to surround

cerco ['θerko] *nm* (*Agr*) enclosure; (*LAM*) fence; (*Mil*) siege

cerdo ['θerðo] *nm* pig; **carne de ~** pork

cereal [θere'al] *nm* cereal; **cereales** *nmpl* cereals, grain *sg*

cerebro [θe'reβro] *nm* brain; (*fig*) brains *pl*

ceremonia [θere'monja] *nf* ceremony; **ceremonioso, -a** *adj* ceremonious

cereza [θe'reθa] *nf* cherry

cerilla [θe'riʎa] *nf*, **cerillo** [se'riʎo] *nm* (*LAM*) match

cero ['θero] *nm* nothing, zero

cerquillo [θer'kiʎo] *nm* (*LAM*) fringe (*BRIT*), bangs *pl* (*US*)

cerrado, -a [θe'rraðo, a] *adj* closed, shut; (*con llave*) locked; (*tiempo*) cloudy, overcast; (*curva*) sharp; (*acento*) thick, broad

cerradura [θerra'ðura] *nf* (*acción*) closing; (*mecanismo*) lock

cerrajero, -a [θerra'xero, a] *nm/f* locksmith

cerrar [θe'rrar] /1j/ *vt* to close, shut; (*paso, carretera*) to close; (*grifo*) to turn off; (*trato, cuenta, negocio*) to close ▷ *vi* to close, shut; (*la noche*) to come down; **cerrarse** *vr* to close, shut; **~ con llave** to lock; **~ un trato** to strike a bargain

cerro ['θerro] *nm* hill

cerrojo [θe'rroxo] *nm* (*herramienta*) bolt; (*de puerta*) latch

certamen [θer'tamen] *nm* competition, contest

certero, -a [θer'tero, a] *adj* accurate

certeza [θer'teθa] *nf* certainty

certidumbre [θerti'ðumbre] *nf* = **certeza**

certificado, -a [θertifi'kaðo, a] *adj* certified; (*Correos*) registered ▷ *nm* certificate; **~ médico** medical certificate

certificar [θertifi'kar] /1g/ *vt* (*asegurar, atestar*) to certify

cervatillo [θerβa'tiʎo] *nm* fawn

cervecería [θerβeθe'ria] *nf* (*fábrica*) brewery; (*taberna*) public house, pub

cerveza [θer'βeθa] *nf* beer

cesar [θe'sar] /1a/ vi to cease, stop
▷ vt to remove from office
cesárea [θe'sarea] nf Caesarean
(section)
cese ['θese] nm (de trabajo) dismissal;
(de pago) suspension
césped ['θespeð] nm grass, lawn
cesta ['θesta] nf basket
cesto ['θesto] nm (large) basket,
hamper
cfr abr (= confróntese, compárese) cf
chabacano, -a [tʃaβa'kano, a] adj
vulgar, coarse
chabola [tʃa'βola] nf shack; **barriada**
or **barrio de ~s** shanty town
chacal [tʃa'kal] nm jackal
chacha ['tʃatʃa] nf (fam) maid
cháchara ['tʃatʃara] nf chatter; **estar
de ~** to chatter away
chacra ['tʃakra] nf (LAM) smallholding
chafa ['tʃafa] adj (LAM fam) useless, dud
chafar [tʃa'far] /1a/ vt (aplastar) to
crush; (arruinar) to ruin
chal [tʃal] nm shawl
chalado, -a [tʃa'laðo, a] adj (fam)
crazy
chalé [tʃa'le] (pl **chalés**) nm = **chalet**
chaleco [tʃa'leko] nm waistcoat,
vest (US); **~ salvavidas** life jacket;
~ de seguridad, ~ reflectante (Auto)
high-visibility vest
chalet (pl **chalets**) [tʃa'le, tʃa'les] nm
villa, ≈ detached house
chamaco, -a [tʃa'mako, a] nm/f
(LAM) kid
champán [tʃam'pan] nm champagne
champiñón [tʃampi'non] nm
mushroom
champú [tʃam'pu] (pl **champús** o
champúes) nm shampoo
chamuscar [tʃamus'kar] /1g/ vt to
scorch, singe
chance ['tʃanθe] nm o f (LAM) chance,
opportunity
chancho, -a ['tʃantʃo, a] nm/f
(LAM) pig
chanchullo [tʃan'tʃuʎo] nm (fam)
fiddle

chandal [tʃan'dal] nm tracksuit
chantaje [tʃan'taxe] nm blackmail
chapa ['tʃapa] nf (de metal) plate,
sheet; (de madera) board, panel; (LAM
Auto) number (BRIT) o license (US)
plate; **chapado, -a** adj: **chapado en
oro** gold-plated
chaparrón [tʃapa'rron] nm
downpour, cloudburst
chaperón [tʃape'ron] nm (LAM): **hacer
de ~** to play gooseberry; **chaperona**
nf (LAM): **hacer de chaperona** to play
gooseberry
chapulín [tʃapu'lin] nm (LAM)
grasshopper
chapurrar [tʃapurr'ar] /1a/,
chapurrear [tʃapurre'ar] /1a/ vt
(idioma) to speak badly
chapuza [tʃa'puθa] nf botched job
chapuzón [tʃapu'θon] nm: **darse un
~** to go for a dip
chaqueta [tʃa'keta] nf jacket
chaquetón nm (three-quarter-
length) coat
charca ['tʃarka] nf pond, pool
charco ['tʃarko] nm pool, puddle
charcutería [tʃarkute'ria] nf (tienda)
shop selling chiefly pork meat products;
(productos) cooked pork meats pl
charla ['tʃarla] nf talk, chat;
(conferencia) lecture; **charlar** /1a/ vi
to talk, chat; **charlatán, -ana** nm/f
chatterbox; (estafador) trickster
charol¹ [tʃa'rol] nm varnish; (cuero)
patent leather
charol² [tʃa'rol] nm, **charola**
[tʃa'rola] nf (LAM) tray
charro ['tʃarro] nm (vaquero) typical
Mexican
chasco ['tʃasko] nm (desengaño)
disappointment
chasis ['tʃasis] nm inv chassis
chasquido [tʃas'kiðo] nm (de lengua)
click; (de látigo) crack
chat [tʃat] nm (Internet) chat room
chatarra [tʃa'tarra] nf scrap (metal)
chatear [tʃate'ar] /1a/ vi (Internet)
to chat

chato, -a ['tʃato, a] *adj* flat; *(nariz)* snub

chaucha ['tʃautʃa] *(LAM)* *nf* runner *(BRIT)* o pole *(US)* bean

chaval, a [tʃa'βal, a] *nm/f* kid *(fam)*, lad/lass

chavo, -a ['tʃaβo, a] *nm/f (LAM fam)* guy/girl

checar [tʃe'kar] /1g/ *vt (LAM)*: **~ tarjeta** *(al entrar)* to clock in o on; *(al salir)* to clock off o out

checo, -a ['tʃeko, a] *adj, nm/f* Czech ▷ *nm (Ling)* Czech

checo(e)slovaco, -a [tʃeko(e)slo'βako, a] *adj, nm/f* Czech, Czechoslovak

Checo(e)slovaquia [tʃeko(e)slo'βakja] *nf* Czechoslovakia

cheque ['tʃeke] *nm* cheque *(BRIT)*, check *(US)*; **cobrar un ~** to cash a cheque; **~ abierto/en blanco/cruzado** open/blank/crossed cheque; **~ al portador** cheque payable to bearer; **~ de viajero** traveller's cheque

chequeo [tʃe'keo] *nm (Med)* check-up; *(Auto)* service

chequera [tʃe'kera] *nf (LAM)* chequebook *(BRIT)*, checkbook *(US)*

chévere ['tʃeβere] *adj (LAM)* great

chícharo ['tʃitʃaro] *nm (LAM)* pea

chichón [tʃi'tʃon] *nm* bump, lump

chicle ['tʃikle] *nm* chewing gum

chico, -a ['tʃiko, a] *adj* small, little ▷ *nm/f* child; *(muchacho)* boy; *(muchacha)* girl

chiflado, -a [tʃi'flaðo, a] *adj* crazy

chiflar [tʃi'flar] /1a/ *vt* to hiss, boo ▷ *vi (esp LAM)* to whistle

chilango, -a [tʃi'lango, a] *adj (LAM)* of o from Mexico City

Chile ['tʃile] *nm* Chile

chile ['tʃile] *nm* chilli pepper

chileno, -a *adj, nm/f* Chilean

chillar [tʃi'ʎar] /1a/ *vi (persona)* to yell, scream; *(animal salvaje)* to howl; *(cerdo)* to squeal

chillido [tʃi'ʎiðo] *nm (de persona)* yell, scream; *(de animal)* howl

chimenea [tʃime'nea] *nf* chimney; *(hogar)* fireplace

China ['tʃina] *nf:* **(la) ~** China

chinche ['tʃintʃe] *nf* bug; *(Tec)* drawing pin *(BRIT)*, thumbtack *(US)* ▷ *nmf* nuisance, pest

chincheta [tʃin'tʃeta] *nf* drawing pin *(BRIT)*, thumbtack *(US)*

chingado, -a [tʃin'gaðo, a] *adj (esp LAM fam!)* lousy; **hijo de la chingada** bastard *(!)*

chino, -a ['tʃino, a] *adj, nm/f* Chinese ▷ *nm (Ling)* Chinese

chipirón [tʃipi'ron] *nm* squid

Chipre ['tʃipre] *nf* Cyprus; **chipriota** *adj* Cypriot ▷ *nmf* Cypriot

chiquillo, -a [tʃi'kiʎo, a] *nm/f* kid *(fam)*

chirimoya [tʃiri'moja] *nf* custard apple

chiringuito [tʃirin'gito] *nm* small open-air bar

chiripa [tʃi'ripa] *nf* fluke

chirriar [tʃi'rrjar] /1b/ *vi* to creak, squeak

chirrido [tʃi'rriðo] *nm* creak(ing), squeak(ing)

chisme ['tʃisme] *nm (habladurías)* piece of gossip; *(fam: objeto)* thingummyjig

chismoso, -a [tʃis'moso, a] *adj* gossiping ▷ *nm/f* gossip

chispa ['tʃispa] *nf* spark; *(fig)* sparkle; *(ingenio)* wit; *(fam)* drunkenness

chispear [tʃispe'ar] /1a/ *vi (lloviznar)* to drizzle

chiste ['tʃiste] *nm* joke, funny story

chistoso, -a [tʃis'toso, a] *adj* funny, amusing

chivo, -a ['tʃiβo, a] *nm/f* (billy/nanny-) goat; **~ expiatorio** scapegoat

chocante [tʃo'kante] *adj* startling; *(extraño)* odd; *(ofensivo)* shocking

chocar [tʃo'kar] /1g/ *vi (coches etc)* to collide, crash ▷ *vt* to shock; *(sorprender)* to startle; **~ con** to collide with; *(fig)* to run into, run up against; **¡chócala!** *(fam)* put it there!

chochear [tʃotʃe'ar] /1a/ vi to dodder, be senile

chocho, -a ['tʃotʃo, a] adj doddering, senile; (fig) soft, doting

choclo ['tʃoklo] (LAM) nm (grano) sweetcorn; (mazorca) corn on the cob

chocolate [tʃoko'late] adj chocolate ▷ nm chocolate; **chocolatina** nf chocolate

chófer ['tʃofer] nm driver

chollo ['tʃoʎo] nm (fam) bargain, snip

choque ['tʃoke] vb V **chocar** ▷ nm (impacto) impact; (golpe) jolt; (Auto) crash; (fig) conflict; **~ frontal** head-on collision

chorizo [tʃo'riθo] nm hard pork sausage (type of salami)

chorrada [tʃo'rraða] nf (fam): **¡es una ~!** that's crap! (!); **decir ~s** to talk crap (!)

chorrear [tʃorre'ar] /1a/ vi to gush (out), spout (out); (gotear) to drip, trickle

chorro ['tʃorro] nm jet; (fig) stream

choza ['tʃoθa] nf hut, shack

chubasco [tʃu'βasko] nm squall

chubasquero [tʃuβas'kero] nm cagoule, raincoat

chuche ['tʃutʃe] nf (fam) sweetie (BRIT fam), candy (US)

chuchería [tʃutʃe'ria] nf trinket

chuleta [tʃu'leta] nf chop, cutlet

chulo, -a ['tʃulo, a] adj (encantador) charming; (fam: estupendo) great, fantastic ▷ nm (tb: **~ de putas**) pimp

chupaleta [tʃupa'leta] nf (LAM) lollipop

chupar [tʃu'par] /1a/ vt to suck; (absorber) to absorb; **chuparse** vr to grow thin

chupete [tʃu'pete] nm dummy (BRIT), pacifier (US)

chupetín [tʃupe'tin] nf (LAM) lollipop

chupito [tʃu'pito] nm (fam) shot

chupón [tʃu'pon] nm (piruleta) lollipop; (LAM: chupete) dummy (BRIT), pacifier (US)

churrería [tʃurre'ria] nf stall or shop which sells "churros"

churro ['tʃurro] nm (type of) fritter

chusma ['tʃusma] nf rabble, mob

chutar [tʃu'tar] /1a/ vi to shoot (at goal)

Cía abr (= compañía) Co.

cianuro [θja'nuro] nm cyanide

ciberacoso [θiβera'koso] nm cyberbullying

ciberataque [θiβera'take] nm cyber attack

cibercafé [θiβerka'fe] nm cybercafé

cibernauta [θiβer'nauta] nmf cybernaut

ciberterrorista [θiβerterro'rista] nmf cyberterrorist

cicatriz [θika'triθ] nf scar

cicatrizar [θikatri'θar] /1f/ vt to heal; **cicatrizarse** vr to heal (up), form a scar

ciclismo [θi'klismo] nm cycling

ciclista [θi'klista] adj cycle cpd ▷ nmf cyclist

ciclo ['θiklo] nm cycle

ciclón [θi'klon] nm cyclone

cicloturismo [θiklotu'rismo] nm touring by bicycle

ciego, -a ['θjeɣo, a] adj blind ▷ nm/f blind man/woman

cielo ['θjelo] nm sky; (Rel) heaven; **¡~s!** good heavens!

ciempiés [θjem'pjes] nm inv centipede

cien [θjen] num V **ciento**

ciencia ['θjenθja] nf science; **ciencias** nfpl science sg; **ciencia-ficción** nf science fiction

científico, -a [θjen'tifiko, a] adj scientific ▷ nm/f scientist

ciento ['θjento] num hundred; **pagar al 10 por ~** to pay at 10 per cent

cierre ['θjerre] vb V **cerrar** ▷ nm closing, shutting; (con llave) locking; **~ de cremallera** zip (fastener)

cierro etc vb V **cerrar**

cierto, -a ['θjerto, a] adj sure, certain; (un tal) a certain; (correcto) right, correct; **~ hombre** a certain man; **ciertas personas** certain o some people; **sí, es ~** yes, that's correct; **por ~** by the way

ciervo ['θjerβo] nm deer; (macho) stag

cifra ['θifra] nf number; (secreta) code; **cifrar** /1a/ vt to code, write in code

cigala [θi'ɣala] nf Norway lobster

cigarra [θi'ɣarra] nf cicada

cigarrillo [θiɣa'rriʎo] nm cigarette

cigarro [θi'ɣarro] nm cigarette; (puro) cigar

cigüeña [θi'ɣweɲa] nf stork

cilíndrico, -a [θi'lindriko, a] adj cylindrical

cilindro [θi'lindro] nm cylinder

cima ['θima] nf (de montaña) top, peak; (de árbol) top; (fig) height

cimentar [θimen'tar] /1j/ vt to lay the foundations of; (fig: fundar) to found

cimiento [θi'mjento] nm foundation

cincel [θin'θel] nm chisel

cinco ['θinko] num five

cincuenta [θin'kwenta] num fifty

cine ['θine] nm cinema; **cinematográfico, -a** adj cine-, film cpd

cínico, -a ['θiniko, a] adj cynical ▷ nm/f cynic

cinismo [θi'nismo] nm cynicism

cinta ['θinta] nf band, strip; (de tela) ribbon; (película) reel; (de máquina de escribir) ribbon; (magnetofónica) tape; **~ adhesiva** sticky tape; **~ aislante** insulating tape; **~ de vídeo** videotape; **~ métrica** tape measure

cintura [θin'tura] nf waist

cinturón [θintu'ron] nm belt; **~ de seguridad** safety belt

ciprés [θi'pres] nm cypress (tree)

circo ['θirko] nm circus

circuito [θir'kwito] nm circuit

circulación [θirkula'θjon] nf circulation; (Auto) traffic

circular [θirku'lar] /1a/ adj, nf circular ▷ vt to circulate ▷ vi (Auto) to drive;

"circule por la derecha" "keep (to the) right"

círculo ['θirkulo] nm circle; **~ vicioso** vicious circle

circunferencia [θirkunfe'renθja] nf circumference

circunstancia [θirkuns'tanθja] nf circumstance

cirio ['θirjo] nm (wax) candle

ciruela [θi'rwela] nf plum; **~ pasa** prune

cirugía [θiru'xia] nf surgery; **~ estética** o **plástica** plastic surgery

cirujano [θiru'xano] nm surgeon

cisne ['θisne] nm swan

cisterna [θis'terna] nf cistern, tank

cita ['θita] nf appointment, meeting; (de novios) date; (referencia) quotation

citación [θita'θjon] nf (Jur) summons sg

citar [θi'tar] /1a/ vt to make an appointment with; (Jur) to summons; (un autor, texto) to quote; **citarse** vr: **se ~on en el cine** they arranged to meet at the cinema

cítrico, -a ['θitriko, a] adj citric ▷ nm: **~s** citrus fruits

ciudad [θju'ðað] nf town; (capital de país etc) city; **ciudadano, -a** nm/f citizen

cívico, -a ['θiβiko, a] adj civic

civil [θi'βil] adj civil ▷ nm (guardia) policeman; **civilización** nf civilization; **civilizar** /1f/ vt to civilize

cizaña [θi'θaɲa] nf (fig) discord

cl abr (= centilitro) cl.

clamor [kla'mor] nm clamour, protest

clandestino, -a [klandes'tino, a] adj clandestine; (Pol) underground

clara ['klara] nf (de huevo) egg white

claraboya [klara'βoja] nf skylight

clarear [klare'ar] /1a/ vi (el día) to dawn; (el cielo) to clear up, brighten up; **clarearse** vr to be transparent

claridad [klari'ðað] nf (del día) brightness; (de estilo) clarity

clarificar [klarifi'kar] /1g/ vt to clarify

clarinete [klari'nete] *nm* clarinet

claro, -a ['klaro, a] *adj* clear; (*luminoso*) bright; (*color*) light; (*evidente*) clear, evident; (*poco espeso*) thin ▷ *nm* (*en bosque*) clearing ▷ *adv* clearly ▷ *excl*: **¡~ que sí!** of course!; **¡~ que no!** of course not!

clase ['klase] *nf* class; **~ alta/media/obrera** upper/middle/working class; **dar ~s** to teach; **~s particulares** private lessons *o* tuition *sg*

clásico, -a ['klasiko, a] *adj* classical

clasificación [klasifika'θjon] *nf* classification; (*Deporte*) league (table)

clasificar [klasifi'kar] /1g/ *vt* to classify

claustro ['klaustro] *nm* cloister

cláusula ['klausula] *nf* clause

clausura [klau'sura] *nf* closing, closure

clavar [kla'βar] /1a/ *vt* (*clavo*) to hammer in; (*cuchillo*) to stick, thrust

clave ['klaβe] *nf* key; (*Mus*) clef; **~ de acceso** password; **~ lada** (*LAM*) dialling (*BRIT*) *o* area (*US*) code

clavel [kla'βel] *nm* carnation

clavícula [kla'βikula] *nf* collar bone

clavija [kla'βixa] *nf* peg, pin; (*Elec*) plug

clavo ['klaβo] *nm* (*de metal*) nail; (*Bot*) clove

claxon ['klakson] (*pl* **claxons**) *nm* horn

clérigo ['kleriɣo] *nm* priest

clero ['klero] *nm* clergy

clicar [kli'kar] /1a/ *vi* (*Inform*) to click; **clica en el icono** click on the icon; **~ dos veces** to double-click

cliché [kli'tʃe] *nm* cliché; (*Foto*) negative

cliente, -a ['kljente, a] *nm/f* client, customer; **clientela** *nf* clientele, customers *pl*

clima ['klima] *nm* climate; **climatizado, -a** *adj* air-conditioned

clímax ['klimaks] *nm inv* climax

clínico, -a ['kliniko, a] *adj* clinical ▷ *nf* clinic; (*particular*) private hospital

clip [klip] (*pl* **clips**) *nm* paper clip

clítoris ['klitoris] *nm inv* clitoris

cloaca [klo'aka] *nf* sewer, drain

clonar [klo'nar] /1a/ *vt* to clone

cloro ['kloro] *nm* chlorine

club [klub] (*pl* **clubs** *o* **clubes**) *nm* club; **~ nocturno** night club

cm *abr* (= *centímetro*) cm

coágulo [ko'aɣulo] *nm* clot

coalición [koali'θjon] *nf* coalition

coartada [koar'taða] *nf* alibi

coartar [koar'tar] /1a/ *vt* to limit, restrict

coba ['koβa] *nf*: **dar ~ a algn** (*adular*) to suck up to sb

cobarde *adj* cowardly ▷ *nmf* coward; **cobardía** *nf* cowardice

cobaya [ko'βaja] *nf* guinea pig

cobertizo [koβer'tiθo] *nm* shelter

cobertura [koβer'tura] *nf* cover; (*Com*) coverage; **~ de dividendo** (*Com*) dividend cover; **no tengo ~** (*Telec*) I can't get a signal

cobija [ko'βixa] *nf* (*LAM*) blanket; **cobijar** /1a/ *vt* (*cubrir*) to cover; (*abrigar*) to shelter; **cobijo** *nm* shelter

cobra ['koβra] *nf* cobra

cobrador, a [koβra'ðor, a] *nm/f* (*de autobús*) conductor/conductress; (*de impuestos, gas*) collector

cobrar [ko'βrar] /1a/ *vt* (*cheque*) to cash; (*sueldo*) to collect, draw; (*objeto*) to recover; (*precio*) to charge; (*deuda*) to collect ▷ *vi* to be paid; **cóbrese al entregar** cash on delivery (COD) (*BRIT*), collect on delivery (COD) (*US*); **¿me cobra, por favor?** (*en tienda*) how much do I owe you?; (*en restaurante*) can I have the bill, please?

cobre ['koβre] *nm* copper; **cobres** *nmpl* (*Mus*) brass instruments

cobro ['koβro] *nm* (*de cheque*) cashing; **presentar al ~** to cash

cocaína [koka'ina] *nf* cocaine

cocción [kok'θjon] *nf* (*Culin*) cooking; (*el hervir*) boiling

cocer [ko'θer] /2b, 2h/ *vt, vi* to cook; (*en agua*) to boil; (*en horno*) to bake

coche ['kotʃe] nm (Auto) car, automobile (US); (de tren, de caballos) coach, carriage; (para niños) pram (BRIT); **ir en ~** to drive; **~ de bomberos** fire engine; **~ (comedor)** (Ferro) (dining) car; **~ de carreras** racing car; **~-escuela** learner car; **~ fúnebre** hearse; **coche-cama** nm (Ferro) sleeping car, sleeper

cochera [ko'tʃera] nf garage; (de autobuses, trenes) depot

coche-restaurante ['kotʃerestau'rante] (pl **coches-restaurante**) nm (Ferro) dining-car, diner

cochinillo [kotʃi'niʎo] nm suckling pig

cochino, -a [ko'tʃino, a] adj filthy, dirty ▷ nm/f pig

cocido [ko'θiðo] nm stew

cocina [ko'θina] nf kitchen; (aparato) cooker, stove; (actividad) cookery; **~ eléctrica** electric cooker; **~ de gas** gas cooker; **cocinar** /1a/ vt, vi to cook

cocinero, -a [koθi'nero, a] nm/f cook

coco ['koko] nm coconut

cocodrilo [koko'ðrilo] nm crocodile

cocotero [koko'tero] nm coconut palm

cóctel ['koktel] nm cocktail; **~ Molotov** Molotov cocktail, petrol bomb

codazo [ko'ðaθo] nm: **dar un ~ a algn** to nudge sb

codicia [ko'ðiθja] nf greed; **codiciar** /1b/ vt to covet

código ['koðiɣo] nm code; **~ de barras** bar code; **~ de (la) circulación** highway code; **~ de la zona** (LAM) dialling (BRIT) o area (US) code; **~ postal** postcode

codillo [ko'ðiʎo] nm (Zool) knee; (Tec) elbow (joint)

codo ['koðo] nm (Anat, de tubo) elbow; (Zool) knee

codorniz [koðor'niθ] nf quail

coexistir [koeksis'tir] /3a/ vi to coexist

cofradía [kofra'ðia] nf brotherhood, fraternity

cofre ['kofre] nm (de joyas) box; (de dinero) chest

coger [ko'xer] /2c/ vt (ESP) to take (hold of); (: objeto caído) to pick up; (: frutas) to pick, harvest; (: resfriado, ladrón, pelota) to catch ▷ vi: **~ por el buen camino** to take the right road; **cogerse** vr (el dedo) to catch; **~se a algo** to get hold of sth

cogollo [ko'ɣoʎo] nm (de lechuga) heart

cogote [ko'ɣote] nm back o nape of the neck

cohabitar [koaβi'tar] /1a/ vi to live together, cohabit

coherente [koe'rente] adj coherent

cohesión [koe'sjon] nm cohesion

cohete [ko'ete] nm rocket

cohibido, -a [koi'βiðo, a] adj (Psico) inhibited; (tímido) shy

coincidencia [koinθi'ðenθja] nf coincidence

coincidir [koinθi'ðir] /3a/ vi (en idea) to coincide, agree; (en lugar) to coincide

coito ['koito] nm intercourse, coitus

coja etc vb V **coger**

cojear [koxe'ar] /1a/ vi (persona) to limp, hobble; (mueble) to wobble, rock

cojera [ko'xera] nf limp

cojín [ko'xin] nm cushion

cojo, -a ['koxo, a] vb V **coger** ▷ adj (que no puede andar) lame, crippled; (mueble) wobbly ▷ nm/f lame person

cojón [ko'xon] nm (fam!): **¡cojones!** shit! (!); **cojonudo, -a** adj (fam) great, fantastic

col [kol] nf cabbage; **~es de Bruselas** Brussels sprouts

cola ['kola] nf tail; (de gente) queue; (lugar) end, last place; (para pegar) glue, gum; **hacer ~** to queue (up)

colaborador, a [kolaβora'ðor, a] nm/f collaborator

colaborar [kolaβo'rar] /1a/ vi to collaborate

colado, -a [ko'laðo, a] *adj* (*metal*) cast ▷ *nf*: **hacer la colada** to do the washing

colador [kola'ðor] *nm* (*de té*) strainer; (*para verduras etc*) colander

colapso [ko'lapso] *nm* collapse

colar [ko'lar] /1l/ *vt* (*líquido*) to strain off; (*metal*) to cast ▷ *vi* to ooze, seep (through); **colarse** *vr* to jump the queue; **~se en** to get into without paying; (*en una fiesta*) to gatecrash

colcha ['koltʃa] *nf* bedspread

colchón [kol'tʃon] *nm* mattress; **~ inflable** air bed, inflatable mattress

colchoneta [koltʃo'neta] *nf* (*en gimnasio*) mat; **~ hinchable** air bed, inflatable mattress

colección [kolek'θjon] *nf* collection; **coleccionar** /1a/ *vt* to collect; **coleccionista** *nmf* collector

colecta [ko'lekta] *nf* collection

colectivo, -a [kolek'tiβo, a] *adj* collective, joint ▷ *nm* (LAM: *autobús*) (small) bus

colega [ko'leɣa] *nmf* colleague; (ESP: *amigo*) mate

colegial, a [kole'xjal, a] *nm/f* schoolboy/girl

colegio [ko'lexjo] *nm* college; (*escuela*) school; (*de abogados etc*) association; **~ electoral** polling station; **~ mayor** (ESP) hall of residence; *see note* **"colegio"**

● COLEGIO

● A *colegio* is often a private primary
● or secondary school. In the state
● system it means a primary school
● although these are also called
● *escuela*. State secondary schools
● are called *institutos*. Extracurricular
● subjects, such as computing or
● foreign languages, are offered in
● private schools called *academias*.

cólera ['kolera] *nf* (*ira*) anger ▷ *nm* (Med) cholera

colesterol [koleste'rol] *nm* cholesterol

coleta [ko'leta] *nf* pigtail

colgante [kol'ɣante] *adj* hanging ▷ *nm* (*joya*) pendant

colgar [kol'ɣar] /1h, 1l/ *vt* to hang (up); (*ropa*) to hang out ▷ *vi* to hang; (*teléfono*) to hang up

cólico ['koliko] *nm* colic

coliflor [koli'flor] *nf* cauliflower

colilla [ko'liʎa] *nf* cigarette end, butt

colina [ko'lina] *nf* hill

colisión *nf* collision; **~ frontal** head-on crash

collar [ko'ʎar] *nm* necklace; (*de perro*) collar

colmar [kol'mar] /1a/ *vt* to fill to the brim; (*fig*) to fulfil, realize

colmena [kol'mena] *nf* beehive

colmillo [kol'miʎo] *nm* (*diente*) eye tooth; (*de elefante*) tusk; (*de perro*) fang

colmo ['kolmo] *nm*: **¡eso es ya el ~!** that's beyond a joke!

colocación [koloka'θjon] *nf* (*acto*) placing; (*empleo*) job, position

colocar [kolo'kar] /1g/ *vt* to place, put, position; (*poner en empleo*) to find a job for; **~ dinero** to invest money; **colocarse** *vr* (*conseguir trabajo*) to find a job

Colombia [ko'lombja] *nf* Colombia; **colombiano, -a** *adj, nm/f* Colombian

colonia [ko'lonja] *nf* colony; (*de casas*) housing estate; (*agua de colonia*) cologne; **~ proletaria** (LAM) shantytown

colonización [koloniθa'θjon] *nf* colonization; **colonizador, a** *adj* colonizing ▷ *nm/f* colonist, settler

colonizar [koloni'θar] /1f/ *vt* to colonize

coloquio [ko'lokjo] *nm* conversation; (*congreso*) conference

color [ko'lor] *nm* colour

colorado, -a [kolo'raðo, a] *adj* (*rojo*) red; (LAM: *chiste*) rude

colorante [kolo'rante] *nm* colouring (matter)

colorear [kolore'ar] /1a/ vt to colour

colorete [kolo'rete] nm blusher

colorido [kolo'riðo] nm colour(ing)

columna [ko'lumna] nf column; (pilar) pillar; (apoyo) support; **~ vertebral** spine, spinal column; (fig) backbone

columpiar [kolum'pjar] /1b/ vt to swing; **columpiarse** vr to swing; **columpio** nm swing

coma ['koma] nf comma ▷ nm (Med) coma

comadre [ko'maðre] nf (madrina) godmother; (chismosa) gossip; **comadrona** nf midwife

comal [ko'mal] nm (LAM) griddle

comandante [koman'dante] nm commandant

comarca [ko'marka] nf region

comba ['komba] nf (cuerda) skipping rope; **saltar a la ~** to skip

combate [kom'bate] nm fight

combatir [komba'tir] /3a/ vt to fight, combat

combinación [kombina'θjon] nf combination; (Química) compound; (prenda) slip

combinar [kombi'nar] /1a/ vt to combine

combustible [kombus'tiβle] nm fuel

comedia [ko'meðja] nf comedy; (Teat) play, drama; **comediante** nmf (comic) actor/actress

comedido, -a [kome'ðiðo, a] adj moderate

comedor [kome'ðor] nm (habitación) dining room; (cantina) canteen

comensal [komen'sal] nmf fellow guest/diner

comentar [komen'tar] /1a/ vt to comment on; **comentario** nm comment, remark; (Lit) commentary; **comentarios** nmpl gossip sg; **comentarista** nmf commentator

comenzar [komen'θar] /1f, 1j/ vt, vi to begin, start; **~ a hacer algo** to begin o start doing o to do sth

comer [ko'mer] /2a/ vt to eat; (Damas, Ajedrez) to take, capture ▷ vi to eat; (almorzar) to have lunch; **comerse** vr to eat up

comercial [komer'θjal] adj commercial; (relativo al negocio) business cpd; **comercializar** /1f/ vt (producto) to market; (pey) to commercialize

comerciante [komer'θjante] nmf trader, merchant

comerciar [komer'θjar] /1b/ vi to trade, do business

comercio [ko'merθjo] nm commerce, trade; (tienda) shop, store; (negocio) business; (grandes empresas) big business; (fig) dealings pl; **~ electrónico** e-commerce; **~ exterior** foreign trade

comestible [komes'tiβle] adj eatable, edible ▷ nm: **~s** food sg, foodstuffs

cometa [ko'meta] nm comet ▷ nf kite

cometer [kome'ter] /2a/ vt to commit

cometido [kome'tiðo] nm task, assignment

cómic ['komik] (pl **cómics**) nm comic

comicios [ko'miθjos] nmpl elections

cómico, -a ['komiko, a] adj comic(al) ▷ nm/f comedian

comida [ko'miða] nf (alimento) food; (almuerzo, cena) meal; (de mediodía) lunch; **~ basura** junk food; **~ chatarra** (LAM) junk food

comidilla [komi'ðiʎa] nf: **ser la ~ del barrio** o **pueblo** to be the talk of the town

comienzo [ko'mjenθo] vb V **comenzar** ▷ nm beginning, start

comillas [ko'miʎas] nfpl quotation marks

comilón, -ona [komi'lon, ona] adj greedy ▷ nf (fam) blow-out

comino [ko'mino] nm cumin (seed); **no me importa un ~** I don't give a damn!

comisaría [komisa'ria] nf police station; (Mil) commissariat

comisario [komiˈsarjo] nm (Mil etc) commissary; (Pol) commissar

comisión [komiˈsjon] nf commission

comité [komiˈte] (pl **comités**) nm committee

comitiva [komiˈtiβa] nf retinue

como ['komo] adv as; (tal como) like; (aproximadamente) about, approximately ▷ conj (ya que, puesto que) as, since; **¡~ no!** of course!; **~ no lo haga hoy** unless he does it today; **~ si** as if; **es tan alto ~ ancho** it is as high as it is wide

cómo ['komo] adv how?, why? ▷ excl what?, I beg your pardon? ▷ nm: **el ~ y el porqué** the whys and wherefores

cómoda ['komoða] nf chest of drawers

comodidad [komoðiˈðað] nf comfort

comodín [komoˈðin] nm joker

cómodo, -a ['komoðo, a] adj comfortable; (práctico, de fácil uso) convenient

compact [komˈpakt] (pl **compacts**) nm (tb: **~ disc**) compact disk

compacto, -a [komˈpakto, a] adj compact

compadecer [kompaðeˈθer] /2d/ vt to pity, be sorry for; **compadecerse** vr: **~se de** to pity, be sorry for

compadre [komˈpaðre] nm (padrino) godfather; (amigo) friend, pal

compañero, -a [kompaˈɲero, a] nm/f companion; (novio) boyfriend/ girlfriend; **~ de clase** classmate

compañía [kompaˈɲia] nf company; **hacer ~ a algn** to keep sb company

comparación [komparaˈθjon] nf comparison; **en ~ con** in comparison with

comparar [kompaˈrar] /1a/ vt to compare

comparecer [kompareˈθer] /2d/ vi to appear (in court)

comparsa [komˈparsa] nmf extra

compartim(i)ento [komparti'm(i)ento] nm (Ferro) compartment

compartir [komparˈtir] /3a/ vt to share; (dinero, comida etc) to divide (up), share (out)

compás [komˈpas] nm (Mus) beat, rhythm; (Mat) compasses pl; (Naut etc) compass

compasión [kompaˈsjon] nf compassion, pity

compasivo, -a [kompaˈsiβo, a] adj compassionate

compatible [kompaˈtiβle] adj compatible

compatriota [kompaˈtrjota] nmf compatriot, fellow countryman/ woman

compenetrarse [kompeneˈtrarse] /1a/ vr to be in tune

compensación [kompensaˈθjon] nf compensation

compensar [kompenˈsar] /1a/ vt to compensate

competencia [kompeˈtenθja] nf (incumbencia) domain, field; (Jur, habilidad) competence; (rivalidad) competition

competente [kompeˈtente] adj competent

competición [kompetiˈθjon] nf competition

competir [kompeˈtir] /3k/ vi to compete

compinche [komˈpintʃe] nmf (LAM fam) mate, buddy (US)

complacer [komplaˈθer] /2w/ vt to please; **complacerse** vr to be pleased

complaciente [komplaˈθjente] adj kind, obliging, helpful

complejo, -a [komˈplexo, a] adj, nm complex

complementario, -a [komplemenˈtarjo, a] adj complementary

completar [kompleˈtar] /1a/ vt to complete

completo, -a [komˈpleto, a] adj complete; (perfecto) perfect; (lleno) full ▷ nm full complement

complicado, -a [kompliˈkaðo, a] *adj* complicated; **estar ~ en** to be mixed up in

cómplice [ˈkompliθe] *nmf* accomplice

complot [komˈplo(t)] (*pl* **complots**) *nm* plot

componer [kompoˈner] /2q/ *vt* (*Mus, Lit, Imprenta*) to compose; (*algo roto*) to mend, repair; (*arreglar*) to arrange; **componerse** *vr*: **~se de** to consist of

comportamiento [komportaˈmjento] *nm* behaviour, conduct

comportarse [komporˈtarse] /1a/ *vr* to behave

composición [komposiˈθjon] *nf* composition

compositor, a [komposiˈtor, a] *nm/f* composer

compostura [komposˈtura] *nf* (*actitud*) composure

compra [ˈkompra] *nf* purchase; **hacer la ~/ir de ~s** to do the/go shopping; **comprador, a** *nm/f* buyer, purchaser; **comprar** /1a/ *vt* to buy, purchase

comprender [komprenˈder] /2a/ *vt* to understand; (*incluir*) to comprise, include

comprensión [komprenˈsjon] *nf* understanding; **comprensivo, -a** *adj* (*actitud*) understanding

compresa [komˈpresa] *nf* (*higiénica*) sanitary towel (*BRIT*) o napkin (*US*)

comprimido, -a [kompriˈmiðo, a] *adj* compressed ▷ *nm* (*Med*) pill, tablet

comprimir /3a/ *vt* to compress; (*Inform*) to compress, zip

comprobante [komproˈβante] *nm* proof; (*Com*) voucher; **~ de compra** proof of purchase

comprobar [komproˈβar] /1l/ *vt* to check; (*probar*) to prove; (*Tec*) to check, test

comprometer [kompromeˈter] /2a/ *vt* to compromise; (*exponer*) to endanger; **comprometerse** *vr* (*involucrarse*) to get involved

compromiso [komproˈmiso] *nm* (*obligación*) obligation; (*cometido*) commitment; (*convenio*) agreement; (*dificultad*) awkward situation

compuesto, -a [komˈpwesto, a] *adj*: **~ de** composed of, made up of ▷ *nm* compound

computador [komputaˈðor] *nm*, **computadora** [komputaˈðora] *nf* computer; **~ central** mainframe computer; **~ personal** personal computer

cómputo [ˈkomputo] *nm* calculation

comulgar [komulˈɣar] /1h/ *vi* to receive communion

común [koˈmun] *adj* common ▷ *nm*: **el ~** the community

comunicación [komunikaˈθjon] *nf* communication; (*informe*) report

comunicado [komuniˈkaðo] *nm* announcement; **~ de prensa** press release

comunicar [komuniˈkar] /1g/ *vt* to communicate ▷ *vi* to communicate; **comunicarse** *vr* to communicate; **está comunicando** (*Telec*) the line's engaged (*BRIT*) o busy (*US*); **comunicativo, -a** *adj* communicative

comunidad [komuniˈðað] *nf* community; **~ autónoma** (*ESP*) autonomous region; **~ de vecinos** residents' association; **C~ Económica Europea (CEE)** European Economic Community (EEC)

comunión [komuˈnjon] *nf* communion

comunismo [komuˈnismo] *nm* communism; **comunista** *adj, nmf* communist

PALABRA CLAVE

con [kon] *prep* **1** (*medio, compañía, modo*) with; **comer con cuchara** to eat with a spoon; **pasear con algn** to go for a walk with sb

2 (a pesar de): **con todo, merece nuestros respetos** all the same o even so, he deserves our respect
3 (para con): **es muy bueno para con los niños** he's very good with (the) children
4 (+ infin): **con llegar tan tarde se quedó sin comer** by arriving o because he arrived so late he missed out on eating
▶ conj: **con que: será suficiente con que le escribas** it will be enough if you write to her

concebir [konθe'βir] /3k/ vt to conceive ▷ vi to conceive
conceder [konθe'ðer] /2a/ vt to concede
concejal, a [konθe'xal, a] nm/f town councillor
concentración [konθentra'θjon] nf concentration
concentrar [konθen'trar] /1a/ vt to concentrate; **concentrarse** vr to concentrate
concepto [kon'θepto] nm concept
concernir [konθer'nir] vi to concern; **en lo que concierne a ...** with regard to ...; **en lo que a mí concierne** as far as I'm concerned
concertar [konθer'tar] /1j/ vt (entrevista) to arrange; (precio) to agree ▷ vi to harmonize, be in tune
concesión [konθe'sjon] nf concession
concesionario, -a [konθesjo'narjo, a] nm/f (Com) (licensed) dealer, agent
concha ['kontʃa] nf shell
conciencia [kon'θjenθja] nf conscience; **tener/tomar ~ de** to be/become aware of; **tener la ~ limpia** o **tranquila** to have a clear conscience
concienciar [konθjen'θjar] /1b/ vt to make aware; **concienciarse** vr to become aware
concienzudo, -a [konθjen'θuðo, a] adj conscientious

concierto [kon'θjerto] vb V **concertar** ▷ nm concert; (obra) concerto
conciliar [konθi'ljar] /1b/ vt to reconcile; **~ el sueño** to get to sleep
concilio [kon'θiljo] nm council
conciso, -a [kon'θiso, a] adj concise
concluir [konklu'ir] /3g/ vt to conclude ▷ **concluirse** vr to conclude
conclusión [konklu'sjon] nf conclusion
concordar [konkor'ðar] /1l/ vt to reconcile ▷ vi to agree, tally
concordia [kon'korðja] nf harmony
concretar [konkre'tar] /1a/ vt to make concrete, make more specific; **concretarse** vr to become more definite
concreto, -a [kon'kreto, a] adj, nm (LAM) concrete; **en ~** (en resumen) to sum up; (específicamente) specifically; **no hay nada en ~** there's nothing definite
concurrido, -a [konku'rriðo, a] adj (calle) busy; (local, reunión) crowded
concursante [konkur'sante] nm competitor
concurso [kon'kurso] nm (de público) crowd; (Escol, Deporte, competición) competition; (ayuda) help, cooperation
condal [kon'dal] adj: **la ciudad ~** Barcelona
conde ['konde] nm count
condecoración [kondekora'θjon] nf (Mil) medal
condena [kon'dena] nf sentence; **condenación** nf condemnation; (Rel) damnation; **condenar** /1a/ vt to condemn; (Jur) to convict; **condenarse** vr (Rel) to be damned
condesa [kon'desa] nf countess
condición [kondi'θjon] nf condition; **a ~ de que ...** on condition that ...; **condicional** adj conditional
condimento [kondi'mento] nm seasoning

condominio [kondo'minjo] nm
condominium

condón [kon'don] nm condom

conducir [kondu'θir] /3n/ vt to take,
convey; (Auto) to drive ▷ vi to drive;
(fig) to lead; **conducirse** vr to behave

conducta [kon'dukta] nf conduct,
behaviour

conducto [kon'dukto] nm pipe, tube;
(fig) channel

conductor, a [konduk'tor, a]
adj leading, guiding ▷ nm (Física)
conductor; (de vehículo) driver

conduje etc [kon'duxe] vb V **conducir**

conduzco etc vb V **conducir**

conectado, -a [konek'taðo, a] adj
(Inform) on-line

conectar [konek'tar] /1a/ vt to
connect (up); (enchufar) plug in

conejillo [kone'xiʎo] nm: **~ de Indias**
guinea pig

conejo [ko'nexo] nm rabbit

conexión [konek'sjon] nf connection

confección [konfek'θjon] nf
preparation; (industria) clothing
industry

confeccionar [konfekθjo'nar] /1a/
vt to make (up)

conferencia [konfe'renθja] nf
conference; (lección) lecture; (Telec)
call; **~ de prensa** press conference

conferir [konfe'rir] /3i/ vt to award

confesar [konfe'sar] /1j/ vt to
confess, admit

confesión [konfe'sjon] nf confession

confesionario [konfesjo'narjo] nm
confessional

confeti [kon'feti] nm confetti

confiado, -a [kon'fjaðo, a] adj
(crédulo) trusting; (seguro) confident

confianza [kon'fjanθa] nf trust;
(aliento, confidencia) confidence;
(familiaridad) intimacy, familiarity

confiar [kon'fjar] /1c/ vt to entrust
▷ vi to trust; **~ en algn** to trust sb;
~ en que ... to hope that ...

confidencial [konfiðen'θjal] adj
confidential

confidente [konfi'ðente] nmf
confidant/confidante; (policial)
informer

configurar [konfiɣu'rar] /1a/ vt to
shape, form

confín [kon'fin] nm limit; **confines**
nmpl confines, limits

confirmar [konfir'mar] /1a/ vt to
confirm

confiscar [konfis'kar] /1g/ vt to
confiscate

confite [kon'fite] nm sweet (BRIT),
candy (US); **confitería** nf (tienda)
confectioner's (shop)

confitura [konfi'tura] nf jam

conflictivo, -a [konflik'tiβo, a] adj
(asunto, propuesta) controversial; (país,
situación) troubled

conflicto [kon'flikto] nm conflict;
(fig) clash

confluir [konflu'ir] /3g/ vi (ríos etc) to
meet; (gente) to gather

conformar [konfor'mar] /1a/ vt
to shape, fashion ▷ vi to agree;
conformarse vr to conform;
(resignarse) to resign o.s.; **~se con**
algo to be happy with sth

conforme [kon'forme] adj
(correspondiente): **~ con** in line with; (de
acuerdo) agreed ▷ adv as ▷ excl agreed!
▷ prep: **~ a** in accordance with; **estar**
~s (con algo) to be in agreement
(with sth); **quedarse ~ (con algo)** to
be satisfied (with sth)

confortable [konfor'taβle] adj
comfortable

confortar [konfor'tar] /1a/ vt to
comfort

confrontar [konfron'tar] /1a/ vt to
confront; (dos personas) to bring face
to face; (cotejar) to compare

confundir [konfun'dir] /3a/ vt
(equivocar) to mistake, confuse;
(turbar) to confuse; **confundirse**
vr (turbarse) to get confused;
(equivocarse) to make a mistake;
(mezclarse) to mix

confusión [konfu'sjon] nf confusion

confuso, -a [kon'fuso, a] *adj* confused

congelado, -a [konxe'laðo, a] *adj* frozen ▷ *nmpl*: **~s** frozen food *sg* o foods; **congelador** *nm* freezer, deep freeze

congelar [konxe'lar] /1a/ *vt* to freeze; **congelarse** *vr* (*sangre, grasa*) to congeal

congeniar [konxe'njar] /1b/ *vi* to get on (*BRIT*) o along (*US*) (well)

congestión [konxes'tjon] *nf* congestion

congestionar [konxestjo'nar] /1a/ *vt* to congest

congraciarse [kongra'θjarse] /1b/ *vr* to ingratiate o.s.

congratular [kongratu'lar] /1a/ *vt* to congratulate

congregar [kongre'ɣar] /1h/ *vt* to gather together; **congregarse** *vr* to gather together

congresista [kongre'sista] *nmf* delegate, congressman/woman

congreso [kon'greso] *nm* congress

conjetura [konxe'tura] *nf* guess; **conjeturar** /1a/ *vt* to guess

conjugar [konxu'ɣar] /1h/ *vt* to combine, fit together; (*Ling*) to conjugate

conjunción [konxun'θjon] *nf* conjunction

conjunto, -a [kon'xunto, a] *adj* joint, united ▷ *nm* whole; (*Mus*) band; **en ~** as a whole

conmemoración [konmemora'θjon] *nf* commemoration

conmemorar [konmemo'rar] /1a/ *vt* to commemorate

conmigo [kon'miɣo] *pron* with me

conmoción [konmo'θjon] *nf* shock; (*fig*) upheaval; **~ cerebral** (*Med*) concussion

conmovedor, a [konmoβe'ðor, a] *adj* touching, moving; (*emocionante*) exciting

conmover [konmo'βer] /2h/ *vt* to shake, disturb; (*fig*) to move

conmutador [konmuta'ðor] *nm* switch; (*LAM*: *Telec*) switchboard; (: *central*) telephone exchange

cono ['kono] *nm* cone; **C~ Sur** Southern Cone

conocedor, a [kono'θe'ðor, a] *adj* expert, knowledgeable ▷ *nm/f* expert

conocer [kono'θer] /2d/ *vt* to know; (*por primera vez*) to meet, get to know; (*entender*) to know about; (*reconocer*) to recognize; **conocerse** *vr* (*una persona*) to know o.s.; (*dos personas*) to (get to) know each other; **~ a algn de vista** to know sb by sight

conocido, -a [kono'θiðo, a] *adj* (well-)known ▷ *nm/f* acquaintance

conocimiento [konoθi'mjento] *nm* knowledge; (*Med*) consciousness; **conocimientos** *nmpl* (*saber*) knowledge *sg*

conozco *etc* [ko'noθko] *vb V* **conocer**

conque ['konke] *conj* and so, so then

conquista [kon'kista] *nf* conquest; **conquistador, a** *adj* conquering ▷ *nm* conqueror; **conquistar** /1a/ *vt* to conquer

consagrar [konsa'ɣrar] /1a/ *vt* (*Rel*) to consecrate; (*fig*) to devote

consciente [kons'θjente] *adj* conscious

consecución [konseku'θjon] *nf* acquisition; (*de fin*) attainment

consecuencia [konse'kwenθja] *nf* consequence, outcome; (*firmeza*) consistency

consecuente [konse'kwente] *adj* consistent

consecutivo, -a [konseku'tiβo, a] *adj* consecutive

conseguir [konse'ɣir] /3d, 3k/ *vt* to get, obtain; (*sus fines*) to attain

consejero, -a [konse'xero, a] *nm/f* adviser, consultant; (*Pol*) minister (*in a regional government*)

consejo [kon'sexo] *nm* advice; (*Pol*) council; (*Com*) board; **~ de administración** board of directors;

~ de guerra court-martial; **~ de ministros** cabinet meeting

consenso [kon'senso] *nm* consensus

consentimiento [konsenti'mjento] *nm* consent

consentir [konsen'tir] /3i/ *vt* (*permitir, tolerar*) to consent to; (*mimar*) to pamper, spoil; (*aguantar*) to put up with ▷ *vi* to agree, consent; **~ que algn haga algo** to allow sb to do sth

conserje [kon'serxe] *nm* caretaker; (*portero*) porter

conserva [kon'serβa] *nf*: **en ~** (*alimentos*) tinned (BRIT), canned; **conservas** *nfpl* (*tb*: **~s alimenticias**) tinned (BRIT) o canned foods

conservación [konserβa'θjon] *nf* conservation; (*de alimentos, vida*) preservation

conservador, a [konserβa'ðor, a] *adj* (*Pol*) conservative ▷ *nm/f* conservative

conservante [konser'βante] *nm* preservative

conservar [konser'βar] /1a/ *vt* to conserve, keep; (*alimentos, vida*) to preserve; **conservarse** *vr* to survive

conservatorio [konserβa'torjo] *nm* (*Mus*) conservatoire, conservatory

considerable [konsiðe'raβle] *adj* considerable

consideración [konsiðera'θjon] *nf* consideration; (*estimación*) respect

considerado, -a [konsiðe'raðo, a] *adj* (*atento*) considerate; (*respetado*) respected

considerar [konsiðe'rar] /1a/ *vt* to consider

consigna [kon'siɣna] *nf* (*orden*) order, instruction; (*para equipajes*) left-luggage office (BRIT), checkroom (US)

consigo [kon'siɣo] *vb V* **conseguir** ▷ *pron* (*m*) with him; (*f*) with her; (*usted*) with you; (*reflexivo*) with o.s.

consiguiendo *etc* [konsi'ɣjendo] *vb V* **conseguir**

consiguiente [konsi'ɣjente] *adj* consequent; **por ~** and so, therefore, consequently

consistente [konsis'tente] *adj* consistent; (*sólido*) solid, firm; (*válido*) sound

consistir [konsis'tir] /3a/ *vi*: **~ en** (*componerse de*) to consist of

consola [kon'sola] *nf* (*mueble*) console table; **~ de juegos** games console

consolación [konsola'θjon] *nf* consolation

consolar [konso'lar] /1l/ *vt* to console

consolidar [konsoli'ðar] /1a/ *vt* to consolidate

consomé [konso'me] (*pl* **consomés**) *nm* consommé, clear soup

consonante [konso'nante] *adj* consonant, harmonious ▷ *nf* consonant

consorcio [kon'sorθjo] *nm* consortium

conspiración [konspira'θjon] *nf* conspiracy

conspirar [konspi'rar] /1a/ *vi* to conspire

constancia [kons'tanθja] *nf* constancy; **dejar ~ de algo** to put sth on record

constante [kons'tante] *adj*, *nf* constant

constar [kons'tar] /1a/ *vi* (*evidenciarse*) to be clear o evident; **~ de** to consist of

constipado, -a [konsti'paðo, a] *adj*: **estar ~** to have a cold ▷ *nm* cold

> No confundir *constipado* con la palabra inglesa *constipated*.

constitución [konstitu'θjon] *nf* constitution

constituir [konstitu'ir] /3g/ *vt* (*formar, componer*) to constitute, make up; (*fundar, erigir, ordenar*) to constitute, establish

construcción [konstruk'θjon] *nf* construction, building

constructor, a [konstruk'tor, a] *nm/f* builder

construir [konstruˈir] /3g/ vt to build, construct

construyendo etc [konstruˈjendo] vb V **construir**

consuelo [konˈswelo] nm consolation, solace

cónsul [ˈkonsul] nm consul; **consulado** nm consulate

consulta [konˈsulta] nf consultation; **horas de ~** (Med) surgery hours; **consultar** /1a/ vt to consult; **consultar algo con algn** to discuss sth with sb; **consultorio** nm (Med) surgery

consumición [konsumiˈθjon] nf consumption; (bebida) drink; (comida) food; **~ mínima** cover charge

consumidor, a [konsumiˈðor, a] nm/f consumer

consumir [konsuˈmir] /3a/ vt to consume; **consumirse** vr to be consumed; (persona) to waste away

consumismo [konsuˈmismo] nm consumerism

consumo [konˈsumo] nm consumption

contabilidad [kontaβiliˈðað] nf accounting, book-keeping; (profesión) accountancy; **contable** nmf accountant

contactar [kontakˈtar] /1a/ vi: **~ con algn** to contact sb

contacto [konˈtakto] nm contact; (Auto) ignition; **estar en ~ con** to be in touch with

contado, -a [konˈtaðo, a] adj: **~s** (escasos) numbered, scarce, few ▷ nm: **pagar al ~** to pay (in) cash

contador [kontaˈðor] nm (aparato) meter; (LAm: contable) accountant

contagiar [kontaˈxjar] /1b/ vt (enfermedad) to pass on, transmit; (persona) to infect; **contagiarse** vr to become infected

contagio [konˈtaxjo] nm infection; **contagioso, -a** adj infectious; (fig) catching

contaminación [kontaminaˈθjon] nf contamination; (del ambiente etc) pollution

contaminar [kontamiˈnar] /1a/ vt to contaminate; (aire, agua) to pollute

contante [konˈtante] adj: **dinero ~ (y sonante)** hard cash

contar [konˈtar] /1l/ vt (páginas, dinero) to count; (anécdota etc) to tell ▷ vi to count; **~ con** to rely on, count on

contemplar [kontemˈplar] /1a/ vt to contemplate; (mirar) to look at

contemporáneo, -a [kontempoˈraneo, a] adj, nm/f contemporary

contenedor [konteneˈðor] nm container

contener [konteˈner] /2k/ vt to contain, hold; (risa etc) to hold back, contain; **contenerse** vr to control o restrain o.s.

contenido, -a [konteˈniðo, a] adj (moderado) restrained; (risa etc) suppressed ▷ nm contents pl, content

contentar [kontenˈtar] /1a/ vt (satisfacer) to satisfy; (complacer) to please; **contentarse** vr to be satisfied

contento, -a [konˈtento, a] adj (alegre) pleased; (feliz) happy

contestación [kontestaˈθjon] nf answer, reply

contestador [kontestaˈðor] nm: **~ automático** answering machine

contestar [kontesˈtar] /1a/ vt to answer (back), reply; (Jur) to corroborate, confirm

> No confundir contestar con la palabra inglesa contest.

contexto [konˈteksto] nm context

contigo [konˈtiɣo] pron with you

contiguo, -a [konˈtiɣwo, a] adj adjacent, adjoining

continente [kontiˈnente] adj, nm continent

continuación [kontinwaˈθjon] nf continuation; **a ~** then, next

continuar [konti'nwar] /1e/ vt to continue, go on with ▷ vi to continue, go on; **~ hablando** to continue talking o to talk

continuidad [kontinwi'ðað] nf continuity

continuo, -a [kon'tinwo, a] adj (sin interrupción) continuous; (acción perseverante) continual

contorno [kon'torno] nm outline; (Geo) contour; **contornos** nmpl neighbourhood sg, surrounding area sg

contra ['kontra] prep against ▷ adv against ▷ nm con ▷ nf: **la C~ (nicaragüense)** the Contras pl

contraataque [kontraa'take] nm counterattack

contrabajo [kontra'βaxo] nm double bass

contrabandista [kontraβan'dista] nmf smuggler

contrabando [kontra'βando] nm (acción) smuggling; (mercancías) contraband

contracción [kontrak'θjon] nf contraction

contracorriente [kontrako'rrjente] nf cross-current

contradecir [kontraðe'θir] /3o/ vt to contradict

contradicción [kontraðik'θjon] nf contradiction

contradictorio, -a [kontraðik'torjo, a] adj contradictory

contraer [kontra'er] /2o/ vt to contract; (limitar) to restrict; **contraerse** vr to contract; (limitarse) to limit o.s.

contraluz [kontra'luθ] nm o f view against the light

contrapartida [kontrapar'tiða] nf: **como ~ (de)** in return (for)

contrapelo [kontra'pelo]: **a ~** adv the wrong way

contrapeso [kontra'peso] nm counterweight

contraportada [kontrapor'taða] nf (de revista) back cover

contraproducente [kontraproðu'θente] adj counterproductive

contrario, -a [kon'trarjo, a] adj contrary; (persona) opposed; (sentido, lado) opposite ▷ nm/f enemy, adversary; (Deporte) opponent; **al ~, por el ~** on the contrary; **de lo ~** otherwise

contrarreloj [kontrarre'lo(x)] nf (tb: **prueba ~**) time trial

contrarrestar [kontrarres'tar] /1a/ vt to counteract

contrasentido [kontrasen'tiðo] nm contradiction

contraseña [kontra'seɲa] nf (frase) password

contrastar [kontras'tar] /1a/ vt to verify ▷ vi to contrast

contraste [kon'traste] nm contrast

contratar [kontra'tar] /1a/ vt (firmar un acuerdo para) to contract for; (empleados, obreros) to hire, engage

contratiempo [kontra'tjempo] nm setback

contratista [kontra'tista] nmf contractor

contrato [kon'trato] nm contract

contraventana [kontraβen'tana] nf shutter

contribución [kontriβu'θjon] nf (municipal etc) tax; (ayuda) contribution

contribuir [kontriβu'ir] /3g/ vt, vi to contribute; (Com) to pay (in taxes)

contribuyente [kontriβu'jente] nmf (Com) taxpayer; (que ayuda) contributor

contrincante [kontrin'kante] nm opponent

control [kon'trol] nm control; (inspección) inspection, check; **~ de pasaportes** passport inspection; **controlador, a** nm/f controller; **controlador aéreo** air-traffic controller; **controlar** /1a/ vt to control; to inspect, check

contundente [kontun'dente] *adj* (*argumento*) convincing; **instrumento ~** blunt instrument

contusión [kontu'sjon] *nf* bruise

convalecencia [kombale'θenθja] *nf* convalescence

convalecer [kombale'θer] /2d/ *vi* to convalesce, get better

convalidar [kombali'ðar] /1a/ *vt* (*título*) to recognize

convencer [komben'θer] /2b/ *vt* to convince; (*persuadir*) to persuade

convención [komben'θjon] *nf* convention

conveniente [kombe'njente] *adj* suitable; (*útil*) useful

convenio [kom'benjo] *nm* agreement, treaty

convenir [kombe'nir] /3r/ *vi* (*estar de acuerdo*) to agree; (*ser conveniente*) to suit, be suitable

> No confundir *convenir* con la palabra inglesa *convene*.

convento [kom'bento] *nm* monastery; (*de monjas*) convent

convenza *etc* [kom'benθa] *vb V* **convencer**

converger [komber'xer] /2c/, **convergir** [komber'xir] /3c/ *vi* to converge

conversación [kombersa'θjon] *nf* conversation

conversar [komber'sar] /1a/ *vi* to talk, converse

conversión [komber'sjon] *nf* conversion

convertir [komber'tir] /3i/ *vt* to convert

convidar [kombi'ðar] /1a/ *vt* to invite; **~ a algn a una cerveza** to buy sb a beer

convincente [kombin'θente] *adj* convincing

convite [kom'bite] *nm* invitation; (*banquete*) banquet

convivencia [kombi'βenθja] *nf* coexistence, living together

convivir [kombi'βir] /3a/ *vi* to live together

convocar [kombo'kar] /1g/ *vt* to summon, call (together)

convocatoria [komboka'torja] *nf* summons *sg*; (*anuncio*) notice of meeting

cónyuge ['konyuxe] *nmf* spouse

coñac ['koɲa(k)] (*pl* **coñacs**) *nm* cognac, brandy

coño ['koɲo] (*fam!*) *excl* (*enfado*) shit (!); (*sorpresa*) bloody hell (!)

cool [kul] *adj* (*fam*) cool

cooperación [koopera'θjon] *nf* cooperation

cooperar [koope'rar] /1a/ *vi* to cooperate

coordinar [koorði'nar] /1a/ *vt* to coordinate

copa ['kopa] *nf* cup; (*vaso*) glass; (*de árbol*) top; (*de sombrero*) crown; **copas** *nfpl* (*Naipes*) one of the suits in the Spanish card deck; (**tomar una**) **~** (to have a) drink

copia ['kopja] *nf* copy; (*Inform*): **~ de respaldo** *o* **de seguridad** backup copy; **copiar** /1b/ *vt* to copy

copla ['kopla] *nf* verse; (*canción*) (popular) song

copo ['kopo] *nm*: **~s de maíz** cornflakes; **~ de nieve** snowflake

coqueta [ko'keta] *adj* flirtatious, coquettish; **coquetear** /1a/ *vi* to flirt

coraje [ko'raxe] *nm* courage; (*ánimo*) spirit; (*ira*) anger

coral [ko'ral] *adj* choral ▷ *nf* choir ▷ *nm* (*Zool*) coral

coraza [ko'raθa] *nf* (*armadura*) armour; (*blindaje*) armour-plating

corazón [kora'θon] *nm* heart

corazonada [koraθo'naða] *nf* impulse; (*presentimiento*) hunch

corbata [kor'βata] *nf* tie

corchete [kor'tʃete] *nm* catch, clasp

corcho ['kortʃo] *nm* cork; (*Pesca*) float

cordel [kor'ðel] *nm* cord, line

cordero [kor'ðero] *nm* lamb

cordial [kor'ðjal] *adj* cordial

cordillera [korði'ʎera] *nf* range (of mountains)

Córdoba ['korðoβa] nf Cordova
cordón [kor'ðon] nm (cuerda) cord, string; (de zapatos) lace; (Mil etc) cordon; **~ umbilical** umbilical cord
cordura [kor'ðura] nf: **con ~** (obrar, hablar) sensibly
corneta [kor'neta] nf bugle
cornisa [kor'nisa] nf cornice
coro ['koro] nm chorus; (conjunto de cantores) choir
corona [ko'rona] nf crown; (de flores) garland
coronel [koro'nel] nm colonel
coronilla [koro'niʎa] nf (Anat) crown (of the head)
corporal [korpo'ral] adj corporal, bodily
corpulento, -a [korpu'lento, a] adj (persona) heavily-built
corral [ko'rral] nm farmyard
correa [ko'rrea] nf strap; (cinturón) belt; (de perro) lead, leash; **~ del ventilador** (Auto) fan belt
corrección [korrek'θjon] nf correction; (reprensión) rebuke; **correccional** nm reformatory
correcto, -a [ko'rrekto, a] adj correct; (persona) well-mannered
corredizo, -a [korre'ðiθo, a] adj (puerta etc) sliding
corredor, a [korre'ðor, a] nm/f (Deporte) runner ⊳ nm (pasillo) corridor; (balcón corrido) gallery; (Com) agent, broker
corregir [korre'xir] /3c, 3k/ vt (error) to correct; **corregirse** vr to reform
correo [ko'rreo] nm post, mail; (persona) courier; **Correos** nmpl Post Office sg; **~ aéreo** airmail; **~ basura** (por Internet) spam; **~ electrónico** email, electronic mail; **~ web** webmail
correr [ko'rrer] /2a/ vt to run; (cortinas) to draw; (cerrojo) to shoot ⊳ vi to run; (líquido) to run, flow; **correrse** vr to slide, move; (colores) to run
correspondencia
[korrespon'denθja] nf correspondence; (Ferro) connection

corresponder [korrespon'der] /2a/ vi to correspond; (convenir) to be suitable; (pertenecer) to belong; (tocar) to concern; **corresponderse** vr (por escrito) to correspond; (amarse) to love one another
correspondiente
[korrespon'djente] adj corresponding
corresponsal [korrespon'sal] nmf (newspaper) correspondent
corrido, -a [ko'rriðo, a] adj (avergonzado) abashed ⊳ nf (de toros) bullfight; **un kilo ~** a good kilo
corriente [ko'rrjente] adj (agua) running; (dinero, cuenta etc) current; (común) ordinary, normal ⊳ nm current month; **~ eléctrica** electric current; **estar al ~ de** to be informed about
corrija etc [ko'rrixa] vb V **corregir**
corro ['korro] nm ring, circle (of people)
corromper [korrom'per] /2a/ vt (madera) to rot; (fig) to corrupt
corrosivo, -a [korro'siβo, a] adj corrosive
corrupción [korrup'θjon] nf rot, decay; (fig) corruption
corsé [kor'se] nm corset
cortacésped [korta'θespeð] nm lawn mower
cortado, -a [kor'taðo, a] adj (con cuchillo) cut; (leche) sour; (desconcertado) embarrassed; (tímido) shy ⊳ nm coffee with a little milk
cortafuegos [korta'fweɣos] nm inv (en el bosque) firebreak, fire lane (us); (Internet) firewall
cortalápices [korta'lapiθes] nm inv (pencil) sharpener
cortar [kor'tar] /1a/ vt to cut; (suministro) to cut off; (un pasaje) to cut out ⊳ vi to cut; **cortarse** vr (turbarse) to become embarrassed; (leche) to turn, curdle; **~se el pelo** to have one's hair cut
cortauñas [korta'uɲas] nm inv nail clippers pl

corte ['korte] *nm* cut, cutting; (*de tela*) piece, length ▷ *nf* (*real*) court; **~ y confección** dressmaking; **~ de corriente** *o* **luz** power cut; **las C~s** the Spanish Parliament *sg*

cortejo [kor'texo] *nm* entourage; **~ fúnebre** funeral procession

cortés [kor'tes] *adj* courteous, polite

cortesía [korte'sia] *nf* courtesy

corteza [kor'teθa] *nf* (*de árbol*) bark; (*de pan*) crust

cortijo [kor'tixo] *nm* (ESP) farm, farmhouse

cortina [kor'tina] *nf* curtain

corto, -a ['korto, a] *adj* (*breve*) short; (*tímido*) bashful; **~ de luces** not very bright; **~ de vista** short-sighted; **estar ~ de fondos** to be short of funds; **cortocircuito** *nm* short-circuit; **cortometraje** *nm* (*Cine*) short

cosa ['kosa] *nf* thing; **~ de** about; **eso es ~ mía** that's my business

coscorrón [kosko'rron] *nm* bump on the head

cosecha [ko'setʃa] *nf* (*Agr*) harvest; (*de vino*) vintage; **cosechar** /1a/ *vt* to harvest, gather (in)

coser [ko'ser] /2a/ *vt* to sew

cosmético, -a [kos'metiko, a] *adj*, *nm* cosmetic

cosquillas [kos'kiʎas] *nfpl*: **hacer ~** to tickle; **tener ~** to be ticklish

costa ['kosta] *nf* (*Geo*) coast; **C~ Brava** Costa Brava; **C~ Cantábrica** Cantabrian Coast; **C~ del Sol** Costa del Sol; **a toda ~** at any price

costado [kos'taðo] *nm* side

costanera [kosta'nera] *nf* (LAM) promenade, sea front

costar [kos'tar] /1l/ *vt* (*valer*) to cost; **me cuesta hablarle** I find it hard to talk to him

Costa Rica [kosta'rika] *nf* Costa Rica; **costarricense** *adj*, *nmf* Costa Rican

coste ['koste] *nm* V **costo**

costear [koste'ar] /1a/ *vt* to pay for

costero [kos'tero, a] *adj* coastal

costilla [kos'tiʎa] *nf* rib; (*Culin*) cutlet

costo ['kosto] *nm* cost, price; **~ de la vida** cost of living; **costoso, -a** *adj* costly, expensive

costra ['kostra] *nf* (*corteza*) crust; (*Med*) scab

costumbre [kos'tumbre] *nf* custom, habit; **como de ~** as usual

costura [kos'tura] *nf* sewing, needlework; (*zurcido*) seam

costurera [kostu'rera] *nf* dressmaker

costurero [kostu'rero] *nm* sewing box *o* case

cotidiano, -a [koti'ðjano, a] *adj* daily, day to day

cotilla [ko'tiʎa] *nf* gossip; **cotillear** /1a/ *vi* to gossip; **cotilleo** *nm* gossip(ing)

cotizar [koti'θar] /1f/ *vt* (*Com*) to quote, price; **cotizarse** *vr*: **~se a** to sell at, fetch; (*Bolsa*) to stand at, be quoted at

coto ['koto] *nm* (*terreno cercado*) enclosure; (*de caza*) reserve

cotorra [ko'torra] *nf* parrot

coyote [ko'jote] *nm* coyote, prairie wolf

coz [koθ] *nf* kick

crack [krak] *nm* (*droga*) crack

cráneo ['kraneo] *nm* skull, cranium

cráter ['krater] *nm* crater

crayón [kra'jon] *nm* (LAM: *lápiz*) (coloured) pencil; (*cera*) crayon

creación [krea'θjon] *nf* creation

creador, a [krea'ðor, a] *adj* creative ▷ *nm/f* creator

crear [kre'ar] /1a/ *vt* to create, make

creativo, -a [krea'tiβo, a] *adj* creative

crecer [kre'θer] /2d/ *vi* to grow; (*precio*) to rise

creces ['kreθes]: **con ~** *adv* amply, fully

crecido, -a [kre'θiðo, a] *adj* (*persona*, *planta*) full-grown; (*cantidad*) large

crecimiento [kreθi'mjento] *nm* growth; (*aumento*) increase

credencial [kreðen'θjal] *nf* (LAM: *tarjeta*) card; **credenciales**

nfpl credentials; **~ de socio** (LAM) membership card

crédito ['kreðito] *nm* credit

credo ['kreðo] *nm* creed

creencia [kre'enθja] *nf* belief

creer [kre'er] /2e/ *vt, vi* to think, believe; **creerse** *vr* to believe o.s. (to be); **~ en** to believe in; **creo que sí/ no** I think/don't think so; **¡ya lo creo!** I should think so!

creído, -a [kre'iðo, a] *adj* (*engreído*) conceited

crema ['krema] *nf* cream; **~ batida** (LAM) whipped cream; **~ pastelera** (confectioner's) custard

cremallera [krema'ʎera] *nf* zip (fastener) (BRIT), zipper (US)

crepe ['krepe] *nf* (ESP) pancake

cresta ['kresta] *nf* (Geo, Zool) crest

creyendo *etc* [kre'jendo] *vb* V **creer**

creyente [kre'jente] *nmf* believer

creyó *etc* [kre'jo] *vb* V **creer**

crezco *etc* [kre'jo] *vb* V **crecer**

cría ['kria] *vb* V **criar** ▷ *nf* (*de animales*) rearing, breeding; (*animal*) young; V tb **crío**

criadero [kria'ðero] *nm* (Zool) breeding place

criado, -a [kri'aðo, a] *nm* servant ▷ *nf* servant, maid

criador [kria'ðor] *nm* breeder

crianza [kri'anθa] *nf* rearing, breeding; (*fig*) breeding

criar [kri'ar] /1c/ *vt* (*educar*) to bring up; (*producir*) to grow, produce; (*animales*) to breed

criatura [kria'tura] *nf* creature; (*niño*) baby, (small) child

cribar [kri'βar] /1a/ *vt* to sieve

crimen ['krimen] *nm* crime

criminal [krimi'nal] *adj, nmf* criminal

crin [krin] *nf* (tb: **~es**) mane

crío, -a ['krio, a] *nm/f* (fam: chico) kid

crisis ['krisis] *nf inv* crisis; **~ nerviosa** nervous breakdown

crismas ['krismas] *nm inv* (ESP) Christmas card

cristal [kris'tal] *nm* crystal; (*de ventana*) glass, pane; (*lente*) lens; **cristalino, -a** *adj* crystalline; (*fig*) clear ▷ *nm* lens of the eye

cristianismo [kristja'nismo] *nm* Christianity

cristiano, -a [kris'tjano, a] *adj, nm/f* Christian

Cristo ['kristo] *nm* Christ; (*crucifijo*) crucifix

criterio [kri'terjo] *nm* criterion; (*juicio*) judgement

criticar [kriti'kar] /1g/ *vt* to criticize

crítico, -a ['kritiko, a] *adj* critical ▷ *nm* critic ▷ *nf* criticism

Croacia [kro'aθja] *nf* Croatia

croissan, croissant [krwa'san] *nm* croissant

cromo ['kromo] *nm* chrome

crónico, -a ['kroniko, a] *adj* chronic ▷ *nf* chronicle, account

cronómetro [kro'nometro] *nm* stopwatch

croqueta [kro'keta] *nf* croquette, rissole

cruce ['kruθe] *vb* V **cruzar** ▷ *nm* (*para peatones*) crossing; (*de carreteras*) crossroads

crucero [kru'θero] *nm* (*viaje*) cruise

crucificar [kruθifi'kar] /1g/ *vt* to crucify

crucifijo [kruθi'fixo] *nm* crucifix

crucigrama [kruθi'ɣrama] *nm* crossword (puzzle)

cruda ['kruða] *nf* (LAM fam) hangover

crudo, -a ['kruðo, a] *adj* raw; (*no maduro*) unripe; (*petróleo*) crude; (*rudo, cruel*) cruel ▷ *nm* crude (oil)

cruel [krwel] *adj* cruel; **crueldad** *nf* cruelty

crujiente [kru'xjente] *adj* (*galleta etc*) crunchy

crujir [kru'xir] /3a/ *vi* (*madera etc*) to creak; (*dedos*) to crack; (*dientes*) to grind; (*nieve, arena*) to crunch

cruz [kruθ] *nf* cross; (*de moneda*) tails *sg*; **~ gamada** swastika; **C~ Roja** Red Cross

cruzado, -a [kru'θaðo, a] adj crossed
▷ nm crusader ▷ nf crusade
cruzar [kru'θar] /1f/ vt to cross;
cruzarse vr (líneas etc) to cross;
(personas) to pass each other
cuaderno [kwa'ðerno] nm notebook;
(de escuela) exercise book; (Naut)
logbook
cuadra ['kwaðra] nf (caballeriza)
stable; (Lam) (city) block
cuadrado, -a [kwa'ðraðo, a] adj
square ▷ nm (Mat) square
cuadrar [kwa'ðrar] /1a/ vt to square
▷ vi: **~ con** to square with, tally with;
cuadrarse vr (soldado) to stand to
attention
cuadrilátero [kwaðri'latero]
nm (Deporte) boxing ring; (Mat)
quadrilateral
cuadrilla [kwa'ðriʎa] nf party, group
cuadro ['kwaðro] nm square; (Arte)
painting; (Teat) scene; (diagrama)
chart; (Deporte, Med) team; **tela a
~s** checked (Brit) o chequered (Us)
material
cuajar [kwa'xar] /1a/ vt (leche) to
curdle; (sangre) to congeal; (Culin) to
set; **cuajarse** vr to curdle; to congeal;
(llenarse) to fill up
cuajo ['kwaxo] nm: **de ~** (arrancar) by
the roots; (cortar) completely
cual [kwal] adv like, as ▷ pron: **el ~** etc
which; (persona, sujeto) who; (persona,
objeto) whom ▷ adj such as; **cada ~**
each one; **tal ~** just as it is
cuál [kwal] pron interrogativo which
(one)
cualesquier [kwales'kjer],
cualesquiera [kwales'kjera] adj pl,
pron pl de **cualquier**
cualidad [kwali'ðað] nf quality
cualquier [kwal'kjer], **cualquiera**
[kwal'kjera] adj any ▷ pron anybody;
~ día/libro any day/book; **un coche
~a servirá** any car will do; **no es un
hombre ~a** he isn't just anybody; **eso
~a lo sabe hacer** anybody can do
that; **es un ~a** he's a nobody

cuando ['kwando] adv when; (aún
si) if, even if ▷ conj (puesto que) since
▷ prep: **yo, ~ niño ...** when I was a
child o as a child I ...; **~ no sea así**
even if it is not so; **~ más** at (the)
most; **~ menos** at least; **~ no** if not,
otherwise; **de ~ en ~** from time
to time
cuándo ['kwando] adv when; **¿desde
~?** since when?
cuantía [kwan'tia] nf (importe: de
pérdidas, deuda, daños) extent

PALABRA CLAVE

cuanto, -a ['kwanto, a] adj **1** (todo):
tiene todo cuanto desea he's got
everything he wants; **le daremos
cuantos ejemplares necesite** we'll
give him as many copies as o all the
copies he needs; **cuantos hombres
la ven** all the men who see her
2: **unos cuantos: había unos
cuantos periodistas** there were
(quite) a few journalists
3 (+ más): **cuanto más vino bebas
peor te sentirás** the more wine you
drink the worse you'll feel
▶ pron: **tiene cuanto desea** he has
everything he wants; **tome cuanto/
cuantos quiera** take as much/many
as you want
▶ adv: **en cuanto: en cuanto
profesor** as a teacher; **en cuanto a
mí** as for me; V tb **antes**
▶ conj **1**: **cuanto más gana menos
gasta** the more he earns the less he
spends; **cuanto más joven se es
más se es confiado** the younger you
are the more trusting you are
2: **en cuanto: en cuanto llegue/
llegué** as soon as I arrive/arrived

cuánto, -a ['kwanto, a] adj
(exclamación) what a lot of;
(interrogativo: sg) how much?;
(: pl) how many? ▷ pron, adv how;
(interrogativo: sg) how much?; (: pl)

how many?; **¡cuánta gente!** what a lot of people!; **¿~ cuesta?** how much does it cost?; **¿a ~s estamos?** what's the date?

cuarenta [kwa'renta] *num* forty

cuarentena [kwaren'tena] *nf* quarantine

cuaresma [kwa'resma] *nf* Lent

cuarta ['kwarta] *nf* V **cuarto**

cuartel [kwar'tel] *nm* (*Mil*) barracks *pl*; **~ de bomberos** (*LAM*) fire station; **~ general** headquarters *pl*

cuarteto [kwar'teto] *nm* quartet

cuarto, -a ['kwarto, a] *adj* fourth ▷ *nm* (*Mat*) quarter, fourth; (*habitación*) room ▷ *nf* (*Mat*) quarter, fourth; (*palmo*) span; **~ de baño** bathroom; **~ de estar** living room; **~ de hora** quarter (of an) hour; **~ de kilo** quarter kilo; **~s de final** quarter finals

cuatro ['kwatro] *num* four

Cuba ['kuβa] *nf* Cuba

cuba ['kuβa] *nf* cask, barrel

cubalibre [kuβa'liβre] *nm* (white) rum and coke®

cubano, -a [ku'βano, a] *adj, nm/f* Cuban

cubata [ku'βata] *nm* = **cubalibre**

cubeta [ku'βeta] *nf* (*balde*) bucket, tub

cúbico, -a ['kuβiko, a] *adj* cubic

cubierto, -a [ku'βjerto, a] *pp de* **cubrir** ▷ *adj* covered ▷ *nm* cover; (*en la mesa*) place ▷ *nf* cover, covering; (*neumático*) tyre; (*Naut*) deck; **cubiertos** *nmpl* cutlery *sg*; **a ~** under cover

cubilete [kuβi'lete] *nm* (*en juegos*) cup

cubito [ku'βito] *nm*: **~ de hielo** ice cube

cubo ['kuβo] *nm* cube; (*balde*) bucket, tub; (*Tec*) drum; **~ de (la) basura** dustbin (*BRIT*), trash can (*US*)

cubrir [ku'βrir] /3a/ *vt* to cover; **cubrirse** *vr* (*cielo*) to become overcast

cucaracha [kuka'ratʃa] *nf* cockroach

cuchara [ku'tʃara] *nf* spoon; (*Tec*) scoop; **cucharada** *nf* spoonful; **cucharadita** *nf* teaspoonful

cucharilla [kutʃa'riʎa] *nf* teaspoon

cucharón [kutʃa'ron] *nm* ladle

cuchilla [ku'tʃiʎa] *nf* (large) knife; (*de arma blanca*) blade; **~ de afeitar** razor blade

cuchillo [ku'tʃiʎo] *nm* knife

cuchitril [kutʃi'tril] *nm* hovel

cuclillas [ku'kliʎas] *nfpl*: **en ~** squatting

cuco, -a ['kuko, a] *adj* pretty; (*astuto*) sharp ▷ *nm* cuckoo

cucurucho [kuku'rutʃo] *nm* cornet

cueca ['kweka] *nf* Chilean national dance

cuello ['kweʎo] *nm* (*Anat*) neck; (*de vestido, camisa*) collar

cuenca ['kwenka] *nf* (*Anat*) eye socket; (*Geo*) bowl, deep valley

cuenco ['kwenko] *nm* (earthenware) bowl

cuenta ['kwenta] *vb* V **contar** ▷ *nf* (*cálculo*) count, counting; (*en café, restaurante*) bill (*BRIT*), check (*US*); (*Com*) account; (*de collar*) bead; **a fin de ~s** in the end; **caer en la ~** to catch on; **darse ~ de** to realize; **tener en ~** to bear in mind; **echar ~s** to take stock; **~ atrás** countdown; **~ corriente/de ahorros/a plazo (fijo)** current/savings/deposit account; **~ de correo** (*Internet*) email account; **cuentakilómetros** *nm inv* ≈ milometer, clock; (*velocímetro*) speedometer

cuento ['kwento] *vb* V **contar** ▷ *nm* story; **~ chino** tall story; **~ de hadas** fairy tale *o* story

cuerda ['kwerða] *nf* rope; (*hilo*) string; (*de reloj*) spring; **~ floja** tightrope; **~s vocales** vocal cords; **dar ~ a un reloj** to wind up a clock

cuerdo, -a ['kwerðo, a] *adj* sane; (*prudente*) wise, sensible

cuerno ['kwerno] *nm* horn

cuero ['kwero] *nm* leather; **en ~s** stark naked; **~ cabelludo** scalp

cuerpo ['kwerpo] *nm* body

cuervo ['kwerβo] *nm* crow

cuesta ['kwesta] vb V **costar** ▷ nf slope; (en camino etc) hill; **~ arriba/ abajo** uphill/downhill; **a ~s** on one's back

cueste etc vb V **costar**

cuestión [kwes'tjon] nf matter, question, issue

cuete ['kwete] adj (LAM fam) drunk ▷ nm (cohete) rocket; (fam: embriaguez) drunkenness; (Culin) steak

cueva ['kweβa] nf cave

cuidado [kwi'ðaðo] nm care, carefulness; (preocupación) care, worry ▷ excl careful!, look out!; **eso me tiene sin ~** I'm not worried about that

cuidadoso, -a [kwiða'ðoso, a] adj careful; (preocupado) anxious

cuidar [kwi'ðar] /1a/ vt (Med) to care for; (ocuparse de) to take care of, look after ▷ vi: **~ de** to take care of, look after; **cuidarse** vr to look after o.s.; **~se de hacer algo** to take care to do sth

culata [ku'lata] nf (de fusil) butt

culebra [ku'leβra] nf snake

culebrón [kule'βron] nm (fam) soap (opera)

culo ['kulo] nm bottom, backside; (de vaso) bottom

culpa ['kulpa] nf fault; (Jur) guilt; **por ~ de** because of; **echar la ~ a algn** to blame sb for sth; **tener la ~ (de)** to be to blame (for); **culpable** adj guilty ▷ nmf culprit; **culpar** /1a/ vt to blame; (acusar) to accuse

cultivar [kulti'βar] /1a/ vt to cultivate

cultivo [kul'tiβo] nm (acto) cultivation; (plantas) crop

culto, -a ['kulto, a] adj (que tiene cultura) cultured, educated ▷ nm (homenaje) worship; (religión) cult

cultura [kul'tura] nf culture

culturismo [kultu'rismo] nm body-building

cumbia ['kumbja] nf popular Colombian dance

cumbre ['kumbre] nf summit, top

cumpleaños [kumple'aɲos] nm inv birthday

cumplido, -a [kum'pliðo, a] adj (abundante) plentiful; (cortés) courteous ▷ nm compliment; **visita de ~** courtesy call

cumplidor, a [kumpli'ðor, a] adj reliable

cumplimiento [kumpli'mjento] nm (de un deber) fulfilment; (acabamiento) completion

cumplir [kum'plir] /3a/ vt (orden) to carry out, obey; (promesa) to carry out, fulfil; (condena) to serve; **cumplirse** vr (plazo) to expire; **hoy cumple dieciocho años** he is eighteen today; **~ con** (deber) to carry out, fulfil

cuna ['kuna] nf cradle, cot

cundir [kun'dir] /3a/ vi (noticia, rumor, pánico) to spread; (rendir) to go a long way

cuneta [ku'neta] nf ditch

cuña ['kuɲa] nf wedge

cuñado, -a [ku'ɲaðo, a] nm/f brother-/sister-in-law

cuota ['kwota] nf (parte proporcional) share; (cotización) fee, dues pl

cupe etc ['kupe] vb V **caber**

cupiera etc [ku'pjera] vb V **caber**

cupo etc ['kupo] vb V **caber** ▷ nm quota

cupón [ku'pon] nm coupon

cúpula ['kupula] nf dome

cura ['kura] nf (curación) cure; (método curativo) treatment ▷ nm priest

curación [kura'θjon] nf cure; (acción) curing

curandero, -a [kuran'dero, a] nm/f healer; (pey) quack

curar [ku'rar] /1a/ vt (Med: herida) to treat, dress; (: enfermo) to cure; (Culin) to cure, salt; (cuero) to tan ▷ **curarse** vr to get well, recover

curiosear [kurjose'ar] /1a/ vt to glance at, look over ▷ vi to look round, wander round; (explorar) to poke about

curiosidad [kurjosi'ðað] nf curiosity

curioso, -a [ku'rjoso, a] *adj* curious ▷ *nm/f* bystander, onlooker

curita [ku'rita] *nf* (LAM) sticking plaster

currante [ku'rrante] *nmf* (fam) worker

currar [ku'rrar] /1a/ *vi* to work

currículo [ku'rrikulo], **currículum** [ku'rrikulum] *nm* curriculum vitae

cursi ['kursi] *adj* (fam) affected

cursillo [kur'siʎo] *nm* short course

cursiva [kur'siβa] *nf* italics *pl*

curso ['kurso] *nm* course; **en ~** (*año*) current; (*proceso*) going on, under way

cursor [kur'sor] *nm* (Inform) cursor

curul [ku'rul] *nm* (LAM: *escaño*) seat

custodia [kus'toðja] *nf* (*cuidado*) safekeeping; (Jur) custody

cutis ['kutis] *nm inv* skin, complexion

cutre ['kutre] *adj* (fam: *lugar*) grotty

cuyo, -a ['kujo, a] *pron* (*de quien*) whose; (*de que*) whose, of which; **en ~ caso** in which case

C.V. *abr* (= *caballos de vapor*) H.P.

d

D. *abr* (= *Don*) Esq

dado, -a ['daðo, a] *pp de* **dar** ▷ *nm* die; **dados** *nmpl* dice; **~ que** given that

daltónico, -a [dal'toniko, a] *adj* colour-blind

dama ['dama] *nf* (gen) lady; (Ajedrez) queen; **damas** *nfpl* draughts; **~ de honor** bridesmaid

damasco [da'masko] *nm* (LAM) apricot

danés, -esa [da'nes, esa] *adj* Danish ▷ *nm/f* Dane

dañar [da'ɲar] /1a/ *vt* (*objeto*) to damage; (*persona*) to hurt; **dañarse** *vr* (*objeto*) to get damaged

dañino, -a [da'ɲino, a] *adj* harmful

daño ['daɲo] *nm* (*a un objeto*) damage; (*a una persona*) harm, injury; **~s y perjuicios** (Jur) damages; **hacer ~ a** to damage; (*persona*) to hurt, injure; **hacerse ~** to hurt o.s.

dañoso, -a [da'ɲoso, a] *adj* harmful

○ **PALABRA CLAVE**

dar [dar] /1q/ vt **1** (gen) to give; (obra de teatro) to put on; (film) to show; (fiesta) to have; **dar algo a algn** to give sb sth o sth to sb; **dar de beber a algn** to give sb a drink; **dar de comer** to feed **2** (producir: intereses) to yield; (: fruta) to produce

3 (locuciones + n): **da gusto escucharle** it's a pleasure to listen to him; V tb **paseo**

4 (+ n: = perífrasis de verbo): **me da asco** it sickens me

5 (considerar): **dar algo por descontado/entendido** to take sth for granted/as read; **dar algo por concluido** to consider sth finished

6 (hora): **el reloj dio las seis** the clock struck six (o'clock)

7: **me da lo mismo** it's all the same to me; V tb **igual**; **más**

▶ vi **1**: **dar a** (habitación) to overlook, look on to; (accionar: botón etc) to press, hit

2: **dar con: dimos con él dos horas más tarde** we came across him two hours later; **al final di con la solución** I eventually came up with the answer

3: **dar en** (blanco, suelo) to hit; **el sol me da en la cara** the sun is shining (right) in my face

4: **dar de sí** (zapatos etc) to stretch, give

▶ **darse** vr **1**: **darse un baño** to have a bath; **darse un golpe** to hit o.s.

2: **darse por vencido** to give up

3 (ocurrir): **se han dado muchos casos** there have been a lot of cases

4: **darse a: se ha dado a la bebida** he's taken to drinking

5: **se me dan bien/mal las ciencias** I'm good/bad at science

6: **dárselas de: se las da de experto** he fancies himself o poses as an expert

dardo ['darðo] nm dart

dátil ['datil] nm date

dato ['dato] nm fact, piece of information; **~s personales** personal details

dcha. abr (= derecha) r

d. de C. abr (= después de Cristo) A.D. = **Anno Domini**

○ **PALABRA CLAVE**

de [de] prep (**de + el = del**) **1** (posesión, pertenencia) of; **la casa de Isabel/mis padres** Isabel's/my parents' house; **es de ellos/ella** it's theirs/hers

2 (origen, distancia, con números) from; **soy de Gijón** I'm from Gijón; **de 8 a 20** from 8 to 20; **salir del cine** to go out of o leave the cinema; **de 2 en 2** 2 by 2, 2 at a time

3 (valor descriptivo): **una copa de vino** a glass of wine; **la mesa de la cocina** the kitchen table; **un billete de 50 euros** a 50-euro note; **un niño de tres años** a three-year-old (child); **una máquina de coser** a sewing machine; **ir vestido de gris** to be dressed in grey; **la niña del vestido azul** the girl in the blue dress; **trabaja de profesora** she works as a teacher; **de lado** sideways; **de atrás/delante** rear/front

4 (hora, tiempo): **a las 8 de la mañana** at 8 o'clock in the morning; **de día/noche** by day/night; **de hoy en ocho días** a week from now; **de niño era gordo** as a child he was fat

5 (comparaciones): **más/menos de cien personas** more/less than a hundred people; **el más caro de la tienda** the most expensive in the shop; **menos/más de lo pensado** less/more than expected

6 (causa): **del calor** from the heat

7 (tema) about; **clases de inglés** English classes; **¿sabes algo de él?** do you know anything about him?; **un libro de física** a physics book

8 (adj + de + infin): **fácil de entender** easy to understand

9 (*oraciones pasivas*): **fue respetado de todos** he was loved by all **10** (*condicional + infin*) if; **de ser posible** if possible; **de no terminarlo hoy** if I *etc* don't finish it today

dé [de] *vb* V **dar**

debajo [de'βaxo] *adv* underneath; **~ de** below, under; **por ~ de** beneath

debate [de'βate] *nm* debate; **debatir** /3a/ *vt* to debate

deber [de'βer] /2a/ *nm* duty ▷ *vt* to owe ▷ *vi*: **debe (de)** it must, it should; **deberse** *vr*: **~se a** to be owing *o* due to; **deberes** *nmpl* (*Escol*) homework *sg*; **debo hacerlo** I must do it; **debe de ir** he should go

debido, -a [de'βiðo, a] *adj* proper, due; **~ a** due to, because of

débil [de'βil] *adj* weak; (*luz*) dim; **debilidad** *nf* weakness; dimness

debilitar [deβili'tar] /1a/ *vt* to weaken; **debilitarse** *vr* to grow weak

débito ['deβito] *nm* debit; **~ bancario** (*LAM*) direct debit (*BRIT*) *o* billing (*US*)

debutar [deβu'tar] /1a/ *vi* to make one's debut

década ['dekaða] *nf* decade

decadencia [deka'ðenθja] *nf* (*estado*) decadence; (*proceso*) decline, decay

decaído, -a [deka'iðo, a] *adj*: **estar ~** (*persona*) to be down

decano, -a [de'kano, a] *nm/f* (*Univ etc*) dean

decena [de'θena] *nf*: **una ~** ten (or so)

decente [de'θente] *adj* decent

decepción [deθep'θjon] *nf* disappointment

No confundir *decepción* con la palabra inglesa *deception*.

decepcionar [deθepθjo'nar] /1a/ *vt* to disappoint

decidir [deθi'ðir] /3a/ *vt* to decide ▷ *vi* to decide; **decidirse** *vr*: **~se a** to make up one's mind to

décimo, -a ['deθimo, a] *num* tenth ▷ *nf* tenth

decir [de'θir] /3o/ *vt* to say; (*contar*) to tell; (*hablar*) to speak ▷ *nm* saying; **decirse** *vr*: **se dice** it is said; **~ para** *o* **entre sí** to say to o.s.; **querer ~** to mean; **es ~** that is to say; **¡dígame!** (*en tienda etc*) can I help you?; (*Telec*) hello?

decisión [deθi'sjon] *nf* decision; (*firmeza*) decisiveness

decisivo, -a [deθi'siβo, a] *adj* decisive

declaración [deklara'θjon] *nf* (*manifestación*) statement; (*de amor*) declaration; **~ de ingresos** *o* **de la renta** income tax return

declarar [dekla'rar] /1a/ *vt* to declare ▷ *vi* to declare; (*Jur*) to testify; **declararse** *vr* to propose

decoración [dekora'θjon] *nf* decoration

decorado [deko'raðo] *nm* (*Cine, Teat*) scenery, set

decorar [deko'rar] /1a/ *vt* to decorate; **decorativo, -a** *adj* ornamental, decorative

decreto [de'kreto] *nm* decree

dedal [de'ðal] *nm* thimble

dedicación [deðika'θjon] *nf* dedication

dedicar [deði'kar] /1g/ *vt* (*libro*) to dedicate; (*tiempo, dinero*) to devote; (*palabras: decir, consagrar*) to dedicate, devote; **dedicatoria** *nf* (*de libro*) dedication

dedo ['deðo] *nm* finger; **~ (del pie)** toe; **~ pulgar** thumb; **~ índice** index finger; **~ mayor** *o* **cordial** middle finger; **~ anular** ring finger; **~ meñique** little finger

deducción [deðuk'θjon] *nf* deduction

deducir [deðu'θir] /3n/ *vt* (*concluir*) to deduce, infer; (*Com*) to deduct

defecto [de'fekto] *nm* defect, flaw; **defectuoso, -a** *adj* defective, faulty

defender [defen'der] /2g/ *vt* to defend; **defenderse** *vr*: **me defiendo en inglés** (*fig*) I can get by in English

defensa [de'fensa] *nf* defence ▷ *nm* (*Deporte*) defender, back; **defensivo, -a** *adj* defensive ▷ *nf*: **a la defensiva** on the defensive

defensor, -a [defen'sor, a] *adj* defending ▷ *nm/f* (*abogado defensor*) defending counsel; (*protector*) protector

deficiencia [defi'θjenθja] *nf* deficiency

deficiente [defi'θjente] *adj* (*defectuoso*) defective; **~ en** lacking o deficient in ▷ *nmf*: **ser un ~ mental** to be mentally handicapped

déficit ['defiθit] (*pl* **déficits**) *nm* deficit

definición [defini'θjon] *nf* definition

definir [defi'nir] /3a/ *vt* (*determinar*) to determine, establish; (*decidir*) to define; (*aclarar*) to clarify; **definitivo, -a** *adj* definitive; **en definitiva** definitively; (*en resumen*) in short

deformación [deforma'θjon] *nf* (*alteración*) deformation; (*Radio etc*) distortion

deformar [defor'mar] /1a/ *vt* (*gen*) to deform; **deformarse** *vr* to become deformed; **deforme** *adj* (*informe*) deformed; (*feo*) ugly; (*mal hecho*) misshapen

defraudar [defrau'ðar] /1a/ *vt* (*decepcionar*) to disappoint; (*estafar*) to defraud

defunción [defun'θjon] *nf* death, demise

degenerar [dexene'rar] /1a/ *vi* to degenerate

degollar /1m/

degradar [deɣra'ðar] /1a/ *vt* to debase, degrade; **degradarse** *vr* to demean o.s.

degustación [deɣusta'θjon] *nf* sampling, tasting

dejar [de'xar] /1a/ *vt* to leave; (*permitir*) to allow, let; (*abandonar*) to abandon, forsake; (*beneficios*) to produce, yield ▷ *vi*: **~ de** (*parar*) to stop; (*no hacer*) to fail to; **dejarse**:

~ a un lado to leave o set aside; **~ entrar/salir** to let in/out; **~ pasar** to let through

del [del] = **de + el**; ∨ **de**

delantal [delan'tal] *nm* apron

delante [de'lante] *adv* in front; (*enfrente*) opposite; (*adelante*) ahead ▷ *prep*: **~ de** in front of, before

delantero, -a [delan'tero, a] *adj* front; (*patas de animal*) fore ▷ *nm* (*Deporte*) forward, striker

delatar [dela'tar] /1a/ *vt* to inform on o against, betray; **delator, -a** *nm/f* informer

delegación [deleɣa'θjon] *nf* (*acción: delegados*) delegation; (*Com: oficina*) district office, branch; **~ de policía** (LAM) police station

delegado, -a [dele'ɣaðo, a] *nm/f* delegate; (*Com*) agent

delegar [dele'ɣar] /1h/ *vt* to delegate

deletrear [deletre'ar] /1a/ *vt* to spell (out)

delfín [del'fin] *nm* dolphin

delgado, -a [del'ɣaðo, a] *adj* thin; (*persona*) slim, thin; (*tela etc*) light, delicate

deliberar [deliβe'rar] /1a/ *vt* to debate, discuss

delicadeza [delika'ðeθa] *nf* delicacy; (*refinamiento, sutileza*) refinement

delicado, -a [deli'kaðo, a] *adj* delicate; (*sensible*) sensitive; (*sensible*) touchy

delicia [de'liθja] *nf* delight

delicioso, -a [deli'θjoso, a] *adj* (*gracioso*) delightful; (*exquisito*) delicious

delimitar [delimi'tar] /1a/ *vt* (*función, responsabilidades*) to define

delincuencia [delin'kwenθja] *nf*: **~ juvenil** juvenile delinquency; **delincuente** *nmf* delinquent; (*criminal*) criminal

delineante [deline'ante] *nmf* draughtsman/draughtswoman; (US) draftsman/draftswoman

delirante [deli'rante] *adj* delirious

delirar [deli'rar] /1a/ *vi* to be delirious, rave

delirio [de'lirjo] *nm* (Med) delirium; (*palabras insensatas*) ravings *pl*

delito [de'lito] *nm* (*gen*) crime; (*infracción*) offence

delta ['delta] *nm* delta

demacrado, -a [dema'kraðo, a] *adj*: **estar ~** to look pale and drawn, be wasted away

demanda [de'manda] *nf* (*pedido*, Com) demand; (*petición*) request; (Jur) action, lawsuit; **demandar** /1a/ *vt* (*gen*) to demand; (Jur) to sue, file a lawsuit against

demás [de'mas] *adj*: **los ~ niños** the other children, the remaining children ▷ *pron*: **los/las ~** the others, the rest (of them); **lo ~** the rest (of it)

demasía [dema'sia] *nf* (*exceso*) excess, surplus; **comer en ~** to eat to excess

demasiado, -a [dema'sjaðo, a] *adj*: **~ vino** too much wine ▷ *adv* (*antes de adj, adv*) too; **~s libros** too many books; **¡es ~!** it's too much!; **~ despacio** too slowly; **~s** too many

demencia [de'menθja] *nf* (*locura*) madness

democracia [demo'kraθja] *nf* democracy

demócrata [de'mokrata] *nmf* democrat; **democrático, -a** *adj* democratic

demoler [demo'ler] /2h/ *vt* to demolish; **demolición** *nf* demolition

demonio [de'monjo] *nm* devil, demon; **¡~s!** hell!, damn!; **¿cómo ~s?** how the hell?

demora [de'mora] *nf* delay

demos ['demos] *vb* V **dar**

demostración [demostra'θjon] *nf* demonstration; (*de cariño, fuerza*) show; (*de cólera, gimnasia*) display

demostrar [demos'trar] /1l/ *vt* (*probar*) to prove; (*mostrar*) to show; (*manifestar*) to demonstrate

den [den] *vb* V **dar**

denegar [dene'ɣar] /1h, 1j/ *vt* (*rechazar*) to refuse; (Jur) to reject

denominación [denomina'θjon] *nf* (*acto*) naming

● **DENOMINACIÓN**
●
● The *denominación de origen*, often
● abbreviated to *D.O.*, is a prestigious
● product classification given to
● designated regions by the awarding
● body, the *Consejo Regulador de la
● Denominación de Origen*, when their
● produce meets the required quality
● and production standards. It is
● often associated with *manchego*
● cheeses and many of the wines
● from the Rioja and Ribera de Duero
● regions.

---

densidad [densi'ðað] *nf* density; (*fig*) thickness

denso, -a ['denso, a] *adj* (*apretado*) solid; (*espeso, pastoso*) thick, dense; (*fig*) heavy

dentadura [denta'ðura] *nf* (set of) teeth *pl*; **~ postiza** false teeth *pl*

dentera [den'tera] *nf* (*grima*): **dar ~ a algn** to set sb's teeth on edge

dentífrico, -a [den'tifriko, a] *adj* dental ▷ *nm* toothpaste

dentista [den'tista] *nmf* dentist

dentro ['dentro] *adv* inside ▷ *prep*: **~ de** in, inside, within; **por ~** (on the) inside; **mirar por ~** to look inside; **~ de tres meses** within three months

denuncia [de'nunθja] *nf* (*delación*) denunciation; (*acusación*) accusation; (*de accidente*) report; **denunciar** /1b/ *vt* to report; (*delatar*) to inform on o against

departamento [departa'mento] *nm* (*sección*) department, section; (LAM: *piso*) flat (BRIT), apartment (US)

depender [depen'der] /2a/ *vi*: **~ de** to depend on; **depende** it (all) depends

dependienta [depen'djenta] *nf* saleswoman, shop assistant

dependiente [depen'djente] adj
dependent ▷ nm salesman, shop
assistant

depilar [depi'lar] /1a/ vt (con cera) to
wax; (cejas) to pluck

deportar [depor'tar] /1a/ vt to
deport

deporte [de'porte] nm sport; **hacer
~** to play sports; **deportista** adj
sports cpd ▷ nmf sportsman/woman;
deportivo, -a adj (club, periódico)
sports cpd ▷ nm sports car

depositar [deposi'tar] /1a/ vt (dinero)
to deposit; (mercaderías) to put away,
store; **depositarse** vr to settle

depósito [de'posito] nm (gen)
deposit; (de mercaderías) warehouse,
store; (de agua, gasolina etc) tank; **~ de
cadáveres** mortuary

depredador, a [depreða'ðor, a] adj
predatory ▷ nm predator

depresión [depre'sjon] nf
depression; **~ nerviosa** nervous
breakdown

deprimido, -a [depri'miðo, a] adj
depressed

deprimir [depri'mir] /3a/ vt to
depress; **deprimirse** vr (persona) to
become depressed

deprisa [de'prisa] adv quickly,
hurriedly

depurar [depu'rar] /1a/ vt to purify;
(purgar) to purge

derecha [de'retʃa] nf V **derecho**

derecho, -a [de'retʃo, a] adj right,
right-hand ▷ nm (privilegio) right;
(lado) right(-hand) side; (leyes) law
▷ nf right(-hand) side; (Pol) right
▷ adv straight, directly; **derechos**
nmpl (impuestos) taxes; (de autor)
royalties; **la(s) derecha(s)** (Pol) the
Right; **tener ~ a** to have a right to; **a
la derecha** on the right; (dirección)
to the right

deriva [de'riβa] nf: **ir** o **estar a la ~** to
drift, be adrift

derivado [deri'βaðo] nm (Industria,
Química) by-product

derivar [deri'βar] /1a/ vt to derive;
(desviar) to direct ▷ vi to derive, be
derived; (Naut) to drift; **derivarse** vr to
derive, be derived

derramamiento [derrama'mjento]
nm (dispersión) spilling; **~ de sangre**
bloodshed

derramar [derra'mar] /1a/ vt to
spill; (verter) to pour out; (esparcir) to
scatter; **derramarse** vr to pour out

derrame [de'rrame] nm (de
líquido) spilling; (de sangre)
shedding; (de tubo etc) overflow;
(pérdida) leakage; **~ cerebral** brain
haemorrhage

derredor [derre'ðor] adv: **al** o **en ~ de**
around, about

derretir [derre'tir] /3k/ vt (gen) to
melt; (nieve) to thaw; **derretirse** vr
to melt

derribar [derri'βar] /1a/ vt to knock
down; (construcción) to demolish;
(persona, gobierno, político) to bring
down

derrocar [derro'kar] /1g/ vt (gobierno)
to bring down, overthrow

derrochar [derro'tʃar] /1a/ vt to
squander; **derroche** nm (despilfarro)
waste, squandering

derrota [de'rrota] nf (Naut) course;
(Mil) defeat, rout; **derrotar** /1a/ vt
(gen) to defeat; **derrotero** nm (rumbo)
course

derrumbar [derrum'bar]
/1a/ vt (edificio) to knock down;
derrumbarse vr to collapse

des [des] vb V **dar**

desabrochar [desaβro'tʃar] /1a/ vt
(botones, broches) to undo, unfasten;
desabrocharse vr (ropa etc) to come
undone

desacato [desa'kato] nm (falta de
respeto) disrespect; (Jur) contempt

desacertado, -a [desaθer'taðo, a]
adj (equivocado) mistaken; (inoportuno)
unwise

desacierto [desa'θjerto] nm mistake,
error

desaconsejar [desakonse'xar] /1a/ vt: **~ algo a algn** to advise sb against sth

desacreditar [desakreði'tar] /1a/ vt (desprestigiar) to discredit, bring into disrepute; (denigrar) to run down

desacuerdo [desa'kwerðo] nm disagreement, discord

desafiar [desa'fjar] /1c/ vt (retar) to challenge; (enfrentarse a) to defy

desafilado, -a [desafi'laðo, a] adj blunt

desafinado, -a [desafi'naðo, a] adj: **estar ~** to be out of tune

desafinar [desafi'nar] /1a/ vi to be out of tune; **desafinarse** vr to go out of tune

desafío [desa'fio] nm (reto) challenge; (combate) duel; (resistencia) defiance

desafortunado, -a [desafortu'naðo, a] adj (desgraciado) unfortunate, unlucky

desagradable [desaɣra'ðaβle] adj (fastidioso, enojoso) unpleasant; (irritante) disagreeable

desagradar [desaɣra'ðar] /1a/ vi (disgustar) to displease; (molestar) to bother

desagradecido, -a [desaɣraðe'θiðo, a] adj ungrateful

desagrado [desa'ɣraðo] nm (disgusto) displeasure; (contrariedad) dissatisfaction

desagüe [de'saɣwe] nm (de un líquido) drainage; (cañería) drainpipe; (salida) outlet, drain

desahogar [desao'ɣar] /1h/ vt (aliviar) to ease, relieve; (ira) to vent; **desahogarse** vr (distenderse) to relax; (desfogarse) to let off steam (fam)

desahogo [desa'oɣo] nm (alivio) relief; (comodidad) comfort, ease

desahuciar [desau'θjar] /1b/ vt (enfermo) to give up hope for; (inquilino) to evict

desairar [desai'rar] /1a/ vt (menospreciar) to slight, snub

desalentador, -a [desalenta'ðor, a] adj discouraging

desaliño [desa'liɲo] nm slovenliness

desalmado, -a [desal'maðo, a] adj (cruel) cruel, heartless

desalojar [desalo'xar] /1a/ vt (expulsar, echar) to eject; (abandonar) to move out of ▷ vi to move out

desamor [desa'mor] nm (frialdad) indifference; (odio) dislike

desamparado, -a [desampa'raðo, a] adj (persona) helpless; (lugar: expuesto) exposed; (: desierto) deserted

desangrar [desan'grar] /1a/ vt to bleed; (fig: persona) to bleed dry; **desangrarse** vr to lose a lot of blood

desanimado, -a [desani'maðo, a] adj (persona) downhearted; (espectáculo, fiesta) dull

desanimar [desani'mar] /1a/ vt (desalentar) to discourage; (deprimir) to depress; **desanimarse** vr to lose heart

desapacible [desapa'θiβle] adj unpleasant

desaparecer [desapare'θer] /2d/ vi to disappear; (el sol, la luz) to vanish; **desaparecido, -a** adj missing; **desaparición** nf disappearance; (de especie etc) extinction

desapercibido, -a [desaperθi'βiðo, a] adj (desprevenido) unprepared; **pasar ~** to go unnoticed

desaprensivo, -a [desapren'siβo, a] adj unscrupulous

desaprobar [desapro'βar] /1l/ vt (reprobar) to disapprove of; (condenar) to condemn; (no consentir) to reject

desaprovechado, -a [desaproβe'tʃaðo, a] adj (oportunidad, tiempo) wasted; (estudiante) slack

desaprovechar [desaproβe'tʃar] /1a/ vt to waste

desarmador [desarma'ðor] nm (LAM) screwdriver

desarmar [desar'mar] /1a/ vt (Mil, fig) to disarm; (Tec) to take apart, dismantle; **desarme** nm disarmament

desarraigar [desarrai'ɣar] /1h/ vt to uproot; **desarraigo** nm uprooting

desarreglar [desarre'ɣlar] /1a/ vt (desordenar) to disarrange; (trastocar) to upset, disturb

desarrollar [desarro'ʎar] /1a/ vt (gen) to develop; **desarrollarse** vr to develop; (ocurrir) to take place; (film) to develop; **desarrollo** nm development

desarticular [desartiku'lar] /1a/ vt (huesos) to dislocate; (objeto) to take apart; (grupo terrorista etc) to break up

desasosegar [desasose'ɣar] /1h, 1j/ vt (inquietar) to disturb, make uneasy

desasosiego etc [desaso'sjeɣo] vb V **desasosegar** ▷ nm (intranquilidad) uneasiness, restlessness; (ansiedad) anxiety

desastre [de'sastre] nm disaster; **desastroso, -a** adj disastrous

desatar [desa'tar] /1a/ vt (nudo) to untie; (paquete) to undo; (separar) to detach; **desatarse** vr (zapatos) to come untied; (tormenta) to break up

desatascar [desatas'kar] /1g/ vt (cañería) to unblock, clear

desatender [desaten'der] /2g/ vt (no prestar atención a) to disregard; (abandonar) to neglect

desatino [desa'tino] nm (idiotez) foolishness, folly; (error) blunder

desatornillar [desatorni'ʎar] /1a/ vt to unscrew

desatrancar [desatran'kar] /1g/ vt (puerta) to unbolt; (cañería) to unblock

desautorizado, -a [desautori'θaðo, a] adj unauthorized

desautorizar [desautori'θar] /1f/ vt (oficial) to deprive of authority; (informe) to deny

desayunar [desaju'nar] /1a/ vi to have breakfast ▷ vt to have for breakfast; **desayuno** nm breakfast

desazón [desa'θon] nf anxiety

desbarajuste [desβara'xuste] nm confusion, disorder

desbaratar [desβara'tar] /1a/ vt (deshacer, destruir) to ruin

desbloquear [desβloke'ar] /1a/ vt (negociaciones, tráfico) to get going again; (Com: cuenta) to unfreeze

desbordar [desβor'ðar] /1a/ vt (sobrepasar) to go beyond; (exceder) to exceed ▷ **desbordarse** vr (líquido, río) to overflow; (entusiasmo) to erupt

descabellado, -a [deskaβe'ʎaðo, a] adj (disparatado) wild, crazy

descafeinado, -a [deskafei'naðo, a] adj decaffeinated ▷ nm decaffeinated coffee

descalabro [deska'laβro] nm blow; (desgracia) misfortune

descalificar [deskalifi'kar] /1g/ vt to disqualify; (desacreditar) to discredit

descalzar [deskal'θar] /1f/ vt (zapato) to take off; **descalzo, -a** adj barefoot(ed)

descambiar [deskam'bjar] /1b/ vt to exchange

descaminado, -a [deskami'naðo, a] adj (equivocado) on the wrong road; (fig) misguided

descampado [deskam'paðo] nm open space

descansado, -a [deskan'saðo, a] adj (gen) rested; (que tranquiliza) restful

descansar [deskan'sar] /1a/ vt (gen) to rest ▷ vi to rest, have a rest; (echarse) to lie down

descansillo [deskan'siʎo] nm (de escalera) landing

descanso [des'kanso] nm (reposo) rest; (alivio) relief; (pausa) break; (Deporte) interval, half time

descapotable [deskapo'taβle] nm (tb: **coche ~**) convertible

descarado, -a [deska'raðo, a] adj shameless; (insolente) cheeky

descarga [des'karɣa] nf (Arq, Elec, Mil) discharge; (Naut) unloading; (Inform) download; **descargable** adj downloadable; **descargar** /1h/ vt to unload; (golpe) to let fly; **descargarse** vr to unburden o.s.; **descargarse algo de Internet** to download sth from the internet

descaro [des'karo] nm nerve

descarriar [deska'rrjar] /1c/ vt
(descaminar) to misdirect; (fig) to lead
astray; **descarriarse** vr (perderse) to
lose one's way; (separarse) to stray;
(pervertirse) to err, go astray

descarrilamiento
[deskarrila'mjento] nm (de tren)
derailment

descarrilar [deskarri'lar] /1a/ vi to
be derailed

descartar [deskar'tar] /1a/ vt
(rechazar) to reject; (eliminar) to
rule out; **descartarse** vr (Naipes) to
discard; **~se de** to shirk

descendencia [desθen'denθja]
nf (origen) origin, descent; (hijos)
offspring

descender [desθen'der] /2g/ vt
(bajar: escalera) to go down ▷ vi to
descend; (temperatura, nivel) to fall,
drop; **~ de** to be descended from

descendiente [desθen'djente] nmf
descendant

descenso [des'θenso] nm descent; (de
temperatura) drop

descifrar [desθi'frar] /1a/ vt to
decipher; (mensaje) to decode

descolgar [deskol'ɣar] /1h, 1l/ vt
(bajar) to take down; (teléfono) to pick
up; **descolgarse** vr to let o.s. down

descolorido, -a [deskolo'riðo, a] adj
faded; (pálido) pale

descompasado, -a
[deskompa'saðo, a] adj (sin proporción)
out of all proportion; (excesivo)
excessive

descomponer [deskompo'ner]
/2q/ vt (desordenar) to disarrange,
disturb; (Tec) to put out of order;
descomponerse vr (corromperse) to
rot, decompose; (Tec) to break down

descomposición
[deskomposi'θjon] nf (de un
objeto) breakdown; (de fruta etc)
decomposition; **~ de vientre**
(Med) stomach upset, diarrhoea,
diarrhea (US)

descompostura [deskompos'tura]
nf breakdown, fault; (LAM: diarrea)
diarrhoea, diarrhea (US)

descompuesto, -a
[deskom'pwesto, a] adj (corrompido)
decomposed; (roto) broken (down)

desconcertado, -a
[deskonθer'taðo, a] adj disconcerted,
bewildered

desconcertar [deskonθer'tar] /1j/
vt (confundir) to baffle; (incomodar) to
upset, put out; **desconcertarse** vr
(turbarse) to be upset

desconchado, -a [deskon'tʃaðo, a]
adj (pintura) peeling

desconcierto etc [deskon'θjerto]
vb V **desconcertar** ▷ nm (gen)
disorder; (desorientación) uncertainty;
(inquietud) uneasiness

desconectar [deskonek'tar] /1a/ vt
to disconnect

desconfianza [deskon'fjanθa] nf
distrust

desconfiar [deskon'fjar] /1c/ vi to be
distrustful; **~ de** to mistrust, suspect

descongelar [deskonxe'lar] /1a/ vt
to defrost; (Com, Pol) to unfreeze

descongestionar [desconxestjo'nar]
/1a/ vt (cabeza, tráfico) to clear

desconocer [deskono'θer] /2d/ vt
(ignorar) not to know, be ignorant of

desconocido, -a [deskono'θiðo, a]
adj unknown ▷ nm/f stranger

desconocimiento
[deskonoθi'mjento] nm (falta de
conocimientos) ignorance

desconsiderado, -a
[deskonsiðe'raðo, a] adj
inconsiderate; (insensible) thoughtless

desconsuelo [deskon'swelo] nm
(tristeza) distress; (desesperación)
despair

descontado, -a [deskon'taðo, a]
adj: **dar por ~ (que)** to take it for
granted (that)

descontar [deskon'tar] /1l/ vt
(deducir) to take away, deduct; (rebajar)
to discount

descontento, -a [deskon'tento, a] *adj* dissatisfied ▷ *nm* dissatisfaction, discontent

descorchar [deskor'tʃar] /1a/ *vt* to uncork

descorrer [desko'rrer] /2a/ *vt* (*cortina, cerrojo*) to draw back

descortés [deskor'tes] *adj* (*mal educado*) discourteous; (*grosero*) rude

descoser [desko'ser] /2a/ *vt* to unstitch; **descoserse** *vr* to come apart (at the seams)

descosido, -a [desko'siðo, a] *adj* (*costura*) unstitched

descreído, -a [deskre'iðo, a] *adj* (*incrédulo*) incredulous; (*falto de fe*) unbelieving

descremado, -a [deskre'maðo, a] *adj* skimmed

describir [deskri'βir] /3a/ *vt* to describe; **descripción** *nf* description

descrito [des'krito] *pp de* **describir**

descuartizar [deskwarti'θar] /1f/ *vt* (*animal*) to carve up, cut up

descubierto, -a [desku'βjerto, a] *pp de* **descubrir** ▷ *adj* uncovered, bare; (*persona*) bare-headed ▷ *nm* (*bancario*) overdraft; **al ~** in the open

descubrimiento [deskuβri'mjento] *nm* (*hallazgo*) discovery; (*revelación*) revelation

descubrir [desku'βrir] /3a/ *vt* to discover, find; (*inaugurar*) to unveil; (*vislumbrar*) to detect; (*revelar*) to reveal, show; (*quitar la tapa de*) to uncover; **descubrirse** *vr* to reveal o.s.; (*quitarse sombrero*) to take off one's hat; (*confesar*) to confess

descuento [des'kwento] *vb V* **descontar** ▷ *nm* discount

descuidado, -a [deskwi'ðaðo, a] *adj* (*sin cuidado*) careless; (*desordenado*) untidy; (*olvidadizo*) forgetful; (*dejado*) neglected; (*desprevenido*) unprepared

descuidar [deskwi'ðar] /1a/ *vt* (*dejar*) to neglect; (*olvidar*) to overlook ▷ **descuidarse** *vr* (*distraerse*) to be careless; (*estar desaliñado*) to let o.s.

go; (*desprevenirse*) to drop one's guard; **¡descuida!** don't worry!; **descuido** *nm* (*dejadez*) carelessness; (*olvido*) negligence

PALABRA CLAVE

desde ['desðe] *prep* **1** (*lugar*) from; **desde Burgos hasta mi casa hay 30 km** it's 30 km from Burgos to my house
2 (*posición*): **hablaba desde el balcón** she was speaking from the balcony
3 (*tiempo, + adv, n*): **desde ahora** from now on; **desde entonces/la boda** since then/the wedding; **desde niño** since I *etc* was a child; **desde tres años atrás** since three years ago
4 (*tiempo, + vb*) since; for; **nos conocemos desde 1988/desde hace 20 años** we've known each other since 1988/for 20 years; **no le veo desde 2005/desde hace 5 años** I haven't seen him since 2005/for 5 years
5 (*gama*): **desde los más lujosos hasta los más económicos** from the most luxurious to the most reasonably priced
6: **desde luego (que no)** of course (not)
▷ *conj*: **desde que: desde que recuerdo** for as long as I can remember; **desde que llegó no ha salido** he hasn't been out since he arrived

desdén [des'ðen] *nm* scorn

desdeñar [desðe'ɲar] /1a/ *vt* (*despreciar*) to scorn

desdicha [des'ðitʃa] *nf* (*desgracia*) misfortune; (*infelicidad*) unhappiness; **desdichado, -a** *adj* (*sin suerte*) unlucky; (*infeliz*) unhappy

desear [dese'ar] /1a/ *vt* to want, desire, wish for

desechar [dese'tʃar] /1a/ *vt* (*basura*) to throw out o away; (*ideas*) to reject, discard

desecho [de'setʃo] nm (desprecio) contempt; **desechos** nmpl rubbish sg, waste sg

desembalar [desemba'lar] /1a/ vt to unpack

desembarazar [desembara'θar] /1f/ vt (desocupar) to clear; (desenredar) to free; **desembarazarse** vr: **~se de** to free o.s. of, get rid of

desembarcar [desembar'kar] /1g/ vt (mercancías etc) to unload ▷ vi to disembark

desembocadura [desemboka'ðura] nf (de río) mouth; (de calle) opening

desembocar [desembo'kar] /1g/ vi: **~ en** to flow into; (fig) to result in

desembolso [desem'bolso] nm payment

desembrollar [desembro'ʎar] /1a/ vt (madeja) to unravel; (asunto, malentendido) to sort out

desemejanza [deseme'xanθa] nf dissimilarity

desempaquetar [desempake'tar] /1a/ vt (regalo) to unwrap; (mercancía) to unpack

desempate [desem'pate] nm (Fútbol) replay, play-off; (Tenis) tie-break(er)

desempeñar [desempe'ɲar] /1a/ vt (cargo) to hold; (deber, función) to perform; (lo empeñado) to redeem; **~ un papel** (fig) to play (a role)

desempleado, -a [desemple'aðo, a] nm/f unemployed person; **desempleo** nm unemployment

desencadenar [desenkaðe'nar] /1a/ vt to unchain; (ira) to unleash; **desencadenarse** vr to break loose; (tormenta) to burst; (guerra) to break out

desencajar [desenka'xar] /1a/ vt (mandíbula) to dislocate; (mecanismo, pieza) to disconnect, disengage

desencanto [desen'kanto] nm disillusionment

desenchufar [desentʃu'far] /1a/ vt to unplug

desenfadado, -a [desenfa'ðaðo, a] adj (desenvuelto) uninhibited; (descarado) forward; **desenfado** nm (libertad) freedom; (comportamiento) free and easy manner; (descaro) forwardness

desenfocado, -a [desenfo'kaðo, a] adj (Foto) out of focus

desenfreno [desen'freno] nm wildness; (falta de control) lack of self-control

desenganchar [desengan'tʃar] /1a/ vt (gen) to unhook; (Ferro) to uncouple

desengañar [desenga'ɲar] /1a/ vt to disillusion; **desengañarse** vr to become disillusioned; **desengaño** nm disillusionment; (decepción) disappointment

desenlace etc [desen'laθe] nm outcome

desenmascarar [desenmaska'rar] /1a/ vt to unmask

desenredar [desenre'ðar] /1a/ vt (pelo) to untangle; (problema) to sort out

desenroscar [desenros'kar] /1g/ vt to unscrew

desentenderse [desenten'derse] /2g/ vr: **~ de** to pretend not to know about; (apartarse) to have nothing to do with

desenterrar [desente'rrar] /1j/ vt to exhume; (tesoro, fig) to unearth, dig up

desentonar [desento'nar] /1a/ vi (Mus) to sing (o play) out of tune; (color) to clash

desentrañar [desentra'ɲar] /1a/ vt (misterio) to unravel

desenvoltura [desembol'tura] nf ease

desenvolver [desembol'βer] /2h/ vt (paquete) to unwrap; (fig) to develop; **desenvolverse** vr (desarrollarse) to unfold, develop; (arreglárselas) to cope

deseo [de'seo] nm desire, wish; **deseoso, -a** adj: **estar deseoso de hacer** to be anxious to do

desequilibrado, -a [desekili'βraðo, a] adj unbalanced

desertar [deser'tar] /1a/ *vi* to desert

desértico, -a [de'sertiko, a] *adj*
desert *cpd*

desesperación [desespera'θjon] *nf*
desperation, despair; (*irritación*) fury

desesperar [desespe'rar] /1a/ *vt* to
drive to despair; (*exasperar*) to drive
to distraction ▷ *vi*: **~ de** to despair
of; **desesperarse** *vr* to despair,
lose hope

desestabilizar [desestaβili'θar] /1f/
vt to destabilize

desestimar [desesti'mar] /1a/ *vt*
(*menospreciar*) to have a low opinion
of; (*rechazar*) to reject

desfachatez [desfatʃa'teθ] *nf*
(*insolencia*) impudence; (*descaro*)
rudeness

desfalco [des'falko] *nm*
embezzlement

desfallecer [desfaʎe'θer] /2d/ *vi*
(*perder las fuerzas*) to become weak;
(*desvanecerse*) to faint

desfasado, -a [desfa'saðo, a] *adj*
(*anticuado*) old-fashioned; **desfase**
nm (*diferencia*) gap

desfavorable [desfaβo'raβle] *adj*
unfavourable

desfigurar [desfiɣu'rar] /1a/ *vt* (*cara*)
to disfigure; (*cuerpo*) to deform

desfiladero [desfila'ðero] *nm* gorge

desfilar [desfi'lar] /1a/ *vi* to parade;
desfile *nm* procession; **desfile de
modelos** fashion show

desgana [des'ɣana] *nf* (*falta de
apetito*) loss of appetite; (*renuencia*)
unwillingness; **desganado, -a** *adj*:
estar desganado (*sin apetito*) to have
no appetite; (*sin entusiasmo*) to have
lost interest

desgarrar [desɣa'rrar] /1a/ *vt* to tear
(up); (*fig*) to shatter; **desgarro** *nm* (*en
tela*) tear; (*aflicción*) grief

desgastar [desɣas'tar] /1a/ *vt*
(*deteriorar*) to wear away *o* down;
(*estropear*) to spoil; **desgastarse** *vr*
to get worn out; **desgaste** *nm* wear
(and tear)

desglosar [desɣlo'sar] /1a/ *vt* to
detach; (*factura*) to break down

desgracia [des'ɣraθja] *nf* misfortune;
(*accidente*) accident; (*vergüenza*)
disgrace; (*contratiempo*) setback; **por
~** unfortunately; **desgraciado, -a**
adj (*sin suerte*) unlucky, unfortunate;
(*miserable*) wretched; (*infeliz*)
miserable

desgravar [desɣra'βar] /1a/ *vt*
(*producto*) to reduce the tax *o* duty on

desguace [des'ɣwaθe] *nm* (*lugar*)
scrapyard

deshabitado, -a [desaβi'taðo, a] *adj*
uninhabited

deshacer [desa'θer] /2r/ *vt* (*casa*) to
break up; (*Tec*) to take apart; (*enemigo*)
to defeat; (*diluir*) to melt; (*contrato*) to
break; (*intriga*) to solve; **deshacerse**
vr (*disolverse*) to melt; (*despedazarse*)
to come apart *o* undone; **~se** to get rid
of; **~se en lágrimas** to burst into tears

deshecho, -a [de'setʃo, a] *adj*
undone; (*roto*) smashed; (*persona*)
weak; **estoy ~** I'm shattered

desheredar [desere'ðar] /1a/ *vt* to
disinherit

deshidratar [desiðra'tar] /1a/ *vt* to
dehydrate

deshielo [des'jelo] *nm* thaw

deshonesto, -a [deso'nesto, a] *adj*
indecent

deshonra [de'sonra] *nf* (*deshonor*)
dishonour; (*vergüenza*) shame

deshora [de'sora]: **a ~** *adv* at the
wrong time

deshuesadero [deswesa'ðero] *nm*
(*LAM*) junkyard

deshuesar [deswe'sar] /1a/ *vt* (*carne*)
to bone; (*fruta*) to stone

desierto, -a [de'sjerto, a] *adj* (*casa,
calle, negocio*) deserted ▷ *nm* desert

designar [desiɣ'nar] /1a/ *vt* (*nombrar*)
to designate; (*indicar*) to fix

desigual [desi'ɣwal] *adj* (*lucha*)
unequal; (*terreno*) uneven

desilusión [desilu'sjon] *nf*
disillusionment; (*decepción*)

disappointment; **desilusionar** /1a/ vt to disillusion; (decepcionar) to disappoint; **desilusionarse** vr to become disillusioned

desinfectar [desinfek'tar] /1a/ vt to disinfect

desinflar [desin'flar] /1a/ vt to deflate

desintegración [desinteɣra'θjon] nf disintegration

desinterés [desinte'res] nm (desgana) lack of interest; (altruismo) unselfishness

desintoxicar [desintoksi'kar] /1g/ vt to detoxify; **desintoxicarse** vr (drogadicto) to undergo detoxification

desistir [desis'tir] /3a/ vi (renunciar) to stop, desist

desleal [desle'al] adj (infiel) disloyal; (Com: competencia) unfair; **deslealtad** nf disloyalty

desligar [desli'ɣar] /1h/ vt (desatar) to untie, undo; (separar) to separate; **desligarse** vr (de un compromiso) to extricate o.s.

desliz [des'liθ] nm (fig) lapse; **deslizar** /1f/ vt to slip, slide

deslumbrar [deslum'brar] /1a/ vt to dazzle

desmadrarse [desma'ðrarse] /1a/ vr (fam: descontrolarse) to run wild; (: divertirse) to let one's hair down; **desmadre** nm (fam: desorganización) chaos; (: jaleo) commotion

desmán [des'man] nm (exceso) outrage; (abuso de poder) abuse

desmantelar [desmante'lar] /1a/ vt (deshacer) to dismantle; (casa) to strip

desmaquillador [desmaki*óðor] nm make-up remover

desmayar [desma'jar] /1a/ vi to lose heart; **desmayarse** vr (Med) to faint; **desmayo** nm (Med: acto) faint; (: estado) unconsciousness

desmemoriado, -a [desmemo'rjaðo, a] adj forgetful

desmentir [desmen'tir] /3i/ vt (contradecir) to contradict; (refutar) to deny

desmenuzar [desmenu'θar] /1f/ vt (deshacer) to crumble; (carne) to chop; (examinar) to examine closely

desmesurado, -a [desmesu'raðo, a] adj disproportionate

desmontable [desmon'taβle] adj (que se quita) detachable; (que se puede plegar etc) collapsible, folding

desmontar [desmon'tar] /1a/ vt (deshacer) to dismantle; (tierra) to level ▷ vi to dismount

desmoralizar [desmorali'θar] /1f/ vt to demoralize

desmoronar [desmoro'nar] /1a/ vt to wear away, erode; **desmoronarse** vr (edificio, dique) to collapse; (economía) to decline

desnatado, -a [desna'taðo, a] adj skimmed

desnivel [desni'βel] nm (de terreno) unevenness

desnudar [desnu'ðar] /1a/ vt (desvestir) to undress; (despojar) to strip; **desnudarse** vr (desvestirse) to get undressed; **desnudo, -a** adj naked ▷ nm nude; **desnudo de** devoid o bereft of

desnutrición [desnutri'θjon] nf malnutrition; **desnutrido, -a** adj undernourished

desobedecer [desoβeðe'θer] /2d/ vt, vi to disobey; **desobediencia** nf disobedience

desocupado, -a [desoku'paðo, a] adj at leisure; (desempleado) unemployed; (deshabitado) empty, vacant

desodorante [desoðo'rante] nm deodorant

desolación [desola'θjon] nf (de lugar) desolation; (fig) grief

desolar [deso'lar] /1a/ vt to ruin, lay waste

desorbitado, -a [desorβi'taðo, a] adj (excesivo: ambición) boundless; (: deseos) excessive; (: precio) exorbitant

desorden [de'sorðen] nm confusion; (político) disorder

desorganización
[desorɣaniθa'θjon] nf (de persona) disorganization; (en empresa, oficina) disorder, chaos

desorientar [desorjen'tar] /1a/ vt (extraviar) to mislead; (confundir, desconcertar) to confuse; **desorientarse** vr (perderse) to lose one's way

despabilado, -a [despaβi'laðo, a] adj (despierto) wide-awake; (fig) alert, sharp

despachar [despa'tʃar] /1a/ vt (negocio) to do, complete; (enviar) to send, dispatch; (vender) to sell, deal in; (billete) to issue; (mandar ir) to send away

despacho [des'patʃo] nm (oficina) office; (de paquetes) dispatch; (venta) sale (of goods); (comunicación) message; **~ de billetes** o (LAm) **boletos** booking office

despacio [des'paθjo] adv slowly

desparpajo [despar'paxo] nm self-confidence; (pey) nerve

desparramar [desparra'mar] /1a/ vt (esparcir) to scatter; (líquido) to spill

despecho [des'petʃo] nm spite

despectivo, -a [despek'tiβo, a] adj (despreciativo) derogatory; (Ling) pejorative

despedida [despe'ðiða] nf (adiós) farewell; (de obrero) sacking

despedir [despe'ðir] /3k/ vt (visita) to see off, show out; (empleado) to dismiss; (inquilino) to evict; (objeto) to hurl; (olor etc) to give out o off; **despedirse** vr: **~se de** to say goodbye to

despegar [despe'ɣar] /1h/ vt to unstick ▷ vi (avión) to take off; **despegarse** vr to come loose, come unstuck; **despego** nm detachment

despegue etc [des'peɣe] vb V **despegar** ▷ nm takeoff

despeinado, -a [despei'naðo, a] adj dishevelled, unkempt

despejado, -a [despe'xaðo, a] adj (lugar) clear, free; (cielo) clear; (persona) wide-awake, bright

despejar [despe'xar] /1a/ vt (gen) to clear; (misterio) to clarify, clear up ▷ vi (el tiempo) to clear; **despejarse** vr (tiempo, cielo) to clear (up); (misterio) to become clearer; (cabeza) to clear

despensa [des'pensa] nf larder

despeñar [despe'ɲar] /1a/ vt (arrojar) to fling down; **despeñarse** vr to fling o.s. down; (coche) to tumble over

desperdicio [desper'ðiθjo] nm (despilfarro) squandering; **desperdicios** nmpl (basura) rubbish sg, garbage sg (us); (residuos) waste sg

desperezarse [despere'θarse] /1f/ vr to stretch

desperfecto [desper'fekto] nm (deterioro) slight damage; (defecto) flaw, imperfection

despertador [desperta'ðor] nm alarm clock

despertar [desper'tar] /1j/ vt (persona) to wake up; (recuerdos) to revive; (sentimiento) to arouse ▷ vi to awaken, wake up; **despertarse** vr to awaken, wake up

despido etc [des'piðo] vb V **despedir** ▷ nm dismissal, sacking

despierto, -a [des'pjerto, a] pp de **despertar** ▷ adj awake; (fig) sharp, alert

despilfarro [despil'farro] nm (derroche) squandering; (lujo desmedido) extravagance

despistar [despis'tar] /1a/ vt to throw off the track o scent; (fig) to mislead, confuse; **despistarse** vr to take the wrong road; (fig) to become confused

despiste [des'piste] nm absent-mindedness; **un ~** a mistake o slip

desplazamiento [desplaθa'mjento] nm displacement

desplazar [despla'θar] /1f/ vt to move; (Física, Naut, Tec) to displace; (fig) to oust; (Inform) to scroll;

desplazarse vr (persona, vehículo) to travel

desplegar [desple'ɣar] /1h, 1j/ vt (tela, papel) to unfold, open out; (bandera) to unfurl

despliegue etc [des'pljeɣe] vb V **desplegar** ▷ nm display

desplomarse [desplo'marse] /1a/ vr (edificio, gobierno, persona) to collapse

desplumar [desplu'mar] /1a/ vt (ave) to pluck; (fam: estafar) to fleece

despoblado, -a [despo'βlaðo, a] adj (sin habitantes) uninhabited

despojar [despo'xar] /1a/ vt (a alguien: de sus bienes) to divest of, deprive of; (casa) to strip, leave bare; (de su cargo) to strip of

despojo [des'poxo] nm (acto) plundering; (objetos) plunder, loot; **despojos** nmpl (de ave, res) offal sg

desposado, -a [despo'saðo, a] adj, nm/f newly-wed

despreciar [despre'θjar] /1b/ vt (desdeñar) to despise, scorn; (afrentar) to slight; **desprecio** nm scorn, contempt; slight

desprender [despren'der] /2a/ vt (desatar) to unfasten; (olor) to give off; **desprenderse** vr (botón: caerse) to fall off; (broche) to come unfastened; (olor, perfume) to be given off; **~se de algo que ...** to draw from sth that ...

desprendimiento [desprendi'mjento] nm (gen) loosening; (generosidad) disinterestedness; (de tierra, rocas) landslide; **~ de retina** detachment of the retina

despreocupado, -a [despreoku'paðo, a] adj (sin preocupación) unworried; nonchalant; (negligente) careless

despreocuparse [despreoku'parse] /1a/ vr to be carefree, not to worry; **~ de** to have no interest in

desprestigiar [despresti'xjar] /1b/ vt (criticar) to run down; (desacreditar) to discredit

desprevenido, -a [despreβe'niðo, a] adj (no preparado) unprepared, unready

desproporcionado, -a [desproporθjo'naðo, a] adj disproportionate, out of proportion

desprovisto, -a [despro'βisto, a] adj: **~ de** devoid of

después [des'pwes] adv afterwards, later; (próximo paso) next; **poco ~** soon after; **un año ~** a year later; **~ se debatió el tema** next the matter was discussed; **~ de comer** after lunch; **~ de corregido el texto** after the text had been corrected; **~ de todo** after all

desquiciado, -a [deski'θjaðo, a] adj deranged

destacar [desta'kar] /1g/ vt to emphasize, point up; (Mil) to detach, detail ▷ vi (resaltarse) to stand out; (persona) to be outstanding o exceptional; **destacarse** vr to stand out; (persona) to be outstanding o exceptional

destajo [des'taxo] nm: **trabajar a ~** to do piecework

destapar [desta'par] /1a/ vt (botella) to open; (cacerola) to take the lid off; (descubrir) to uncover; **destaparse** vr (revelarse) to reveal one's true character

destartalado, -a [destarta'laðo, a] adj (desordenado) untidy; (ruinoso) tumbledown

destello [des'teʎo] nm (de estrella) twinkle; (de faro) signal light

destemplado, -a [destem'plaðo, a] adj (Mus) out of tune; (voz) harsh; (Med) out of sorts; (Meteorología) unpleasant, nasty

desteñir [deste'ɲir] vt, vi to fade; **desteñirse** vr to fade; **esta tela no destiñe** this fabric will not fade

desternillarse [desterni'ʎarse] /1a/ vr: **~ de risa** to split one's sides laughing

desterrar [deste'rrar] /1j/ vt (exilar) to exile; (fig) to banish, dismiss

destiempo [des'tjempo]: **a ~** *adv* at the wrong time

destierro *etc* [des'tjerro] *vb* V **desterrar** ▷ *nm* exile

destilar [desti'lar] /1a/ *vt* to distil; **destilería** *nf* distillery

destinar [desti'nar] /1a/ *vt* (*funcionario*) to appoint, assign; (*fondos*) to set aside

destinatario, -a [destina'tarjo, a] *nm/f* addressee

destino [des'tino] *nm* (*suerte*) destiny; (*de viajero*) destination; **con ~ a Londres** (*avión, barco*) (bound) for London; (*carta*) to London

destituir [destitu'ir] /3g/ *vt* to dismiss

destornillador [destorniʎa'ðor] *nm* screwdriver

destornillar [destorni'ʎar] /1a/ *vt* (*tornillo*) to unscrew; **destornillarse** *vr* to unscrew

destreza [des'treθa] *nf* (*habilidad*) skill; (*maña*) dexterity

destrozar [destro'θar] /1f/ *vt* (*romper*) to smash, break (up); (*estropear*) to ruin; (*nervios*) to shatter

destrozo [des'troθo] *nm* (*acción*) destruction; (*desastre*) smashing; **destrozos** *nmpl* (*pedazos*) pieces; (*daños*) havoc *sg*

destrucción [destruk'θjon] *nf* destruction

destruir [destru'ir] /3g/ *vt* to destroy

desuso [de'suso] *nm* disuse; **caer en ~** to fall into disuse, become obsolete

desvalijar [desβali'xar] /1a/ *vt* (*persona*) to rob; (*casa, tienda*) to burgle; (*coche*) to break into

desván [des'βan] *nm* attic

desvanecer [desβane'θer] /2d/ *vt* (*disipar*) to dispel; (*borrar*) to blur; **desvanecerse** *vr* (*humo etc*) to vanish, disappear; (*duda*) to be dispelled; (*color*) to fade; (*recuerdo, sonido*) to fade away; (*Med*) to pass out

desvariar [desβa'rjar] /1c/ *vi* (*enfermo*) to be delirious

desvelar [desβe'lar] /1a/ *vt* to keep awake; **desvelarse** *vr* (*no poder dormir*) to stay awake; (*vigilar*) to be vigilant *o* watchful

desventaja [desβen'taxa] *nf* disadvantage

desvergonzado, -a [desβerɣon'θaðo, a] *adj* shameless

desvestir [desβes'tir] /3k/ *vt* to undress; **desvestirse** *vr* to undress

desviación [desβja'θjon] *nf* deviation; (*Auto*) diversion, detour

desviar [des'βjar] /1c/ *vt* to turn aside; (*río*) to alter the course of; (*navío*) to divert, re-route; (*conversación*) to sidetrack; **desviarse** *vr* (*apartarse del camino*) to turn aside; (*: barco*) to go off course

desvío [des'βio] *vb* V **desviar** ▷ *nm* (*desviación*) detour, diversion; (*fig*) indifference

desvivirse [desβi'βirse] /3a/ *vr*: **~ por** to long for, crave for; **~ por los amigos** to do anything for one's friends

detallar [deta'ʎar] /1a/ *vt* to detail

detalle [de'taʎe] *nm* detail; (*fig*) gesture, token; **al ~** in detail; (*Com*) retail *cpd*

detallista [deta'ʎista] *nmf* retailer

detective [detek'tiβe] *nmf* detective; **~ privado** private detective

detención [deten'θjon] *nf* (*arresto*) arrest; (*prisión*) detention

detener [dete'ner] /2k/ *vt* (*gen*) to stop; (*Jur*) to arrest; (*objeto*) to keep; **detenerse** *vr* to stop; **~se en** (*demorarse*) to delay over, linger over

detenidamente [deteniða'mente] *adv* (*minuciosamente*) carefully; (*extensamente*) at great length

detenido, -a [dete'niðo, a] *adj* (*arrestado*) under arrest ▷ *nm/f* person under arrest, prisoner

detenimiento [deteni'mjento] *nm*: **con ~** thoroughly; (*observar, considerar*) carefully

detergente [deter'xente] nm detergent

deteriorar [deterjo'rar] /1a/ vt to spoil, damage; **deteriorarse** vr to deteriorate; **deterioro** nm deterioration

determinación [determina'θjon] nf (empeño) determination; (decisión) decision; **determinado, -a** adj (preciso) certain

determinar [determi'nar] /1a/ vt (plazo) to fix; (precio) to settle; **determinarse** vr to decide

detestar [detes'tar] /1a/ vt to detest

detractor, a [detrak'tor, a] nm/f detractor

detrás [de'tras] adv (tb: **por ~**) behind; (atrás) at the back ▷ prep: **~ de** behind

detrimento [detri'mento] nm: **en ~ de** to the detriment of

deuda [de'uða] nf debt; **~ exterior/ pública** foreign/national debt

devaluación [deβalwa'θjon] nf devaluation

devastar [deβas'tar] /1a/ vt (destruir) to devastate

deveras [de'βeras] nf inv (LAM): **un amigo de (a) ~** a true o real friend

devoción [deβo'θjon] nf devotion

devolución [deβolu'θjon] nf (reenvío) return, sending back; (reembolso) repayment; (Jur) devolution

devolver [deβol'βer] /2h/ vt to return; (lo extraviado, prestado) to give back; (carta al correo) to send back; (Com) to repay, refund; (fam: vomitar) to throw up ▷ vi (fam) to be sick

devorar [deβo'rar] /1a/ vt to devour

devoto, -a [de'βoto, a] adj devout ▷ nm/f admirer

devuelto [de'βwelto], **devuelva** etc [de'βwelβa] vb V **devolver**

di [di] vb V **dar; decir**

día ['dia] nm day; **~ libre** day off; **D~ de Reyes** Epiphany (6 January); **D~ de la Independencia** Independence Day; **¿qué ~ es?** what's the date?;

estar/poner al ~ to be/keep up to date; **el ~ de hoy/de mañana** today/ tomorrow; **al ~ siguiente** on the following day; **vivir al ~** to live from hand to mouth; **de ~** by day; **en pleno ~** in full daylight

diabetes [dja'betes] nf diabetes sg

diablo ['djaβlo] nm devil; **diablura** nf prank

diadema [dja'ðema] nf tiara

diafragma [dja'fraɣma] nm diaphragm

diagonal [djaɣo'nal] adj diagonal

diagrama [dja'ɣrama] nm diagram

dial [di'al] nm dial

dialecto [dja'lekto] nm dialect

dialogar [djalo'ɣar] /1h/ vi: **~ con** (Pol) to hold talks with

diálogo ['djaloɣo] nm dialogue

diamante [dja'mante] nm diamond

diana ['djana] nf (Mil) reveille; (de blanco) centre, bull's-eye

diapositiva [djaposi'tiβa] nf (Foto) slide, transparency

diario, -a ['djarjo, a] adj daily ▷ nm newspaper; **a ~** daily; **de** o **para ~** everyday

diarrea [dja'rrea] nf diarrhoea

dibujar [diβu'xar] /1a/ vt to draw, sketch; **dibujo** nm drawing; **dibujos animados** cartoons

diccionario [dikθjo'narjo] nm dictionary

dice etc vb V **decir**

dicho, -a ['ditʃo, a] pp de **decir** ▷ adj (susodicho) aforementioned ▷ nm saying

dichoso, -a [di'tʃoso, a] adj happy

diciembre [di'θjembre] nm December

dictado [dik'taðo] nm dictation

dictador [dikta'ðor] nm dictator; **dictadura** nf dictatorship

dictar [dik'tar] /1a/ vt (carta) to dictate; (Jur: sentencia) to pass; (decreto) to issue; (LAM: clase) to give

didáctico, -a [di'ðaktiko, a] adj educational

diecinueve [djeθinu'eβe] *num* nineteen

dieciocho [djeθi'otʃo] *num* eighteen

dieciséis [djeθi'seis] *num* sixteen

diecisiete [djeθi'sjete] *num* seventeen

diente ['djente] *nm* (*Anat, Tec*) tooth; (*Zool*) fang; (: *de elefante*) tusk; (*de ajo*) clove

diera *etc* ['djera] *vb* V **dar**

diesel ['disel] *adj*: **motor ~** diesel engine

diestro, -a ['djestro, a] *adj* (*derecho*) right; (*hábil*) skilful

dieta ['djeta] *nf* diet; **estar a ~** to be on a diet

diez [djeθ] *num* ten

diferencia [dife'renθja] *nf* difference; **a ~ de** unlike; **diferenciar** /1b/ *vt* to differentiate between ▷ *vi* to differ; **diferenciarse** *vr* to differ, be different; (*distinguirse*) to distinguish o.s.

diferente [dife'rente] *adj* different

diferido [dife'riðo] *nm*: **en ~** (*TV etc*) recorded

difícil [di'fiθil] *adj* difficult

dificultad [difikul'tað] *nf* difficulty; (*problema*) trouble

dificultar [difikul'tar] /1a/ *vt* (*complicar*) to complicate, make difficult; (*estorbar*) to obstruct

difundir [difun'dir] /3a/ *vt* (*calor, luz*) to diffuse; (*Radio*) to broadcast; **difundirse** *vr* to spread (out); **~ una noticia** to spread a piece of news

difunto, -a [di'funto, a] *adj* dead, deceased ▷ *nm/f* deceased (person)

difusión [difu'sjon] *nf* (*de programa*) broadcasting

diga *etc* ['diɣa] *vb* V **decir**

digerir [dixe'rir] /3i/ *vt* to digest; (*fig*) to absorb; **digestión** *nf* digestion; **digestivo, -a** *adj* digestive

digital [dixi'tal] *adj* digital

dignarse [diɣ'narse] /1a/ *vr* to deign to

dignidad [diɣni'ðað] *nf* dignity

digno, -a ['diɣno, a] *adj* worthy

digo *etc* *vb* V **decir**

dije *etc* *vb* V **decir**

dilatar [dila'tar] /1a/ *vt* to dilate; (*prolongar*) to prolong

dilema [di'lema] *nm* dilemma

diluir [dilu'ir] /3g/ *vt* to dilute

diluvio [di'luβjo] *nm* deluge, flood

dimensión [dimen'sjon] *nf* dimension

diminuto, -a [dimi'nuto, a] *adj* tiny, diminutive

dimitir [dimi'tir] /3a/ *vi* to resign

dimos ['dimos] *vb* V **dar**

Dinamarca [dina'marka] *nf* Denmark

dinámico, -a [di'namiko, a] *adj* dynamic

dinamita [dina'mita] *nf* dynamite

dinamo [di'namo], (*Lam*) **dínamo** ['dinamo] *nf* dynamo

dineral [dine'ral] *nm* fortune

dinero [di'nero] *nm* money; **~ efectivo** *o* **metálico** cash; **~ suelto** (loose) change

dio [djo] *vb* V **dar**

dios [djos] *nm* god; **D~** God; **¡D~ mío!** (oh) my God!; **¡por D~!** for God's sake!; **diosa** *nf* goddess

diploma [di'ploma] *nm* diploma

diplomacia [diplo'maθja] *nf* diplomacy; (*fig*) tact

diplomado, -a [diplo'maðo, a] *adj* qualified

diplomático, -a [diplo'matiko, a] *adj* diplomatic ▷ *nm/f* diplomat

diputación [diputa'θjon] *nf* (*tb*: **~ provincial**) ≈ county council

diputado, -a [dipu'taðo, a] *nm/f* delegate; (*Pol*) ≈ member of parliament (*brit*) ≈ representative (*us*)

dique ['dike] *nm* dyke

diré *etc* [di're] *vb* V **decir**

dirección [direk'θjon] *nf* direction; (*señas*) address; (*Auto*) steering; (*gerencia*) management; (*Pol*) leadership; **"~ única"** "one-way street"; **"~ prohibida"** "no entry"

direccional [direkθjo'nal] *nf* (LAM Auto) indicator

directa [di'rekta] *nf* (Auto) top gear

directivo, -a [direk'tiβo, a] *adj* (junta) managing ▷ *nf* (tb: **junta directiva**) board of directors

directo, -a [di'rekto, a] *adj* direct; (TV) live; **transmitir en ~** to broadcast live

director, a [direk'tor, a] *adj* leading ▷ *nm/f* director; (Escol) head (teacher) (BRIT), principal (US); (gerente) manager/manageress; (Prensa) editor; **~ de cine** film director; **~ general** general manager

directorio [direk'torjo] *nm* (LAM: telefónico) phone book

dirigente [diri'xente] *nmf* (Pol) leader

dirigir [diri'xir] /3c/ *vt* to direct; (carta) to address; (obra de teatro, film) to direct; (Mus) to conduct; (comercio) to manage; **dirigirse** *vr*: **~se a** to go towards, make one's way towards; (hablar con) to speak to

dirija *etc* [di'rixa] *vb* V **dirigir**

disciplina [disθi'plina] *nf* discipline

discípulo, -a [dis'θipulo, a] *nm/f* disciple

Discman® ['diskman] *nm* Discman®

disco ['disko] *nm* disc (BRIT), disk (US); (Deporte) discus; (Telec) dial; (Auto: semáforo) light; (Mus) record; **~ compacto** compact disc; **~ de larga duración** long-playing record (LP); **~ flexible o floppy** floppy disk; **~ de freno** brake disc; **~ rígido** hard disk

disconforme [diskon'forme] *adj* differing; **estar ~ (con)** to be in disagreement (with)

discordia [dis'korðja] *nf* discord

discoteca [disko'teka] *nf* disco(theque)

discreción [diskre'θjon] *nf* discretion; (reserva) prudence; **comer a ~** to eat as much as one wishes

discreto, -a [dis'kreto, a] *adj* discreet

discriminación [diskrimina'θjon] *nf* discrimination

disculpa [dis'kulpa] *nf* excuse; (pedir perdón) apology; **pedir ~s a/por** to apologize to/for; **disculpar** /1a/ *vt* to excuse, pardon; **disculparse** *vr* to excuse o.s.; to apologize

discurso [dis'kurso] *nm* speech

discusión [disku'sjon] *nf* (diálogo) discussion; (riña) argument

discutir [disku'tir] /3a/ *vt* (debatir) to discuss; (pelear) to argue about; (contradecir) to argue against ▷ *vi* to discuss; (disputar) to argue

disecar [dise'kar] /1g/ *vt* (para conservar: animal) to stuff; (: planta) to dry

diseñar [dise'nar] /1a/ *vt, vi* to design

diseño [di'seno] *nm* design

disfraz [dis'fraθ] *nm* (máscara) disguise; (excusa) pretext; **disfrazar** /1f/ *vt* to disguise; **disfrazarse** *vr*: **disfrazarse de** to disguise o.s. as

disfrutar [disfru'tar] /1a/ *vt* to enjoy ▷ *vi* to enjoy o.s.; **~ de** to enjoy, possess

disgustar [disɣus'tar] /1a/ *vt* (no gustar) to displease; (contrariar, enojar) to annoy, to upset; **disgustarse** *vr* to get upset; (dos personas) to fall out

> No confundir *disgustar* con la palabra inglesa *disgust*.

disgusto [dis'ɣusto] *nm* (contrariedad) annoyance; (tristeza) grief; (riña) quarrel

disimular [disimu'lar] /1a/ *vt* (ocultar) to hide, conceal ▷ *vi* to dissemble

diskette [dis'ket] *nm* (Inform) diskette, floppy disk

dislocar [dislo'kar] /1g/ *vt* to dislocate; **dislocarse** *vr* (articulación) to sprain, dislocate

disminución [disminu'θjon] *nf* decrease, reduction

disminuido, -a [disminu'iðo, a] *nm/f*: **~ mental/físico** mentally/physically-handicapped person

disminuir [disminu'ir] /3g/ *vt* to decrease, diminish

disolver [disol'βer] /2h/ vt (gen) to dissolve; **disolverse** vr to dissolve; (Com) to go into liquidation

dispar [dis'par] adj different

disparar [dispa'rar] /1a/ vt, vi to shoot, fire

disparate [dispa'rate] nm (tontería) foolish remark; (error) blunder; **decir ~s** to talk nonsense

disparo [dis'paro] nm shot

dispersar [disper'sar] /1a/ vt to disperse; **dispersarse** vr to scatter

disponer [dispo'ner] /2q/ vt (arreglar) to arrange; (ordenar) to put in order; (preparar) to prepare, get ready ▷ vi: **~ de** to have, own; **disponerse** vr: **~se para** to prepare to, prepare for

disponible [dispo'niβle] adj available

disposición [disposi'θjon] nf arrangement, disposition; (voluntad) willingness; (Inform) layout; **a su ~** at your service

dispositivo [disposi'tiβo] nm device, mechanism

dispuesto, -a [dis'pwesto, a] pp de **disponer** ▷ adj (arreglado) arranged; (preparado) disposed

disputar [dispu'tar] /1a/ vt (carrera) to compete in

disquete [dis'kete] nm (Inform) diskette, floppy disk

distancia [dis'tanθja] nf distance; **distanciar** /1b/ vt to space out; **distanciarse** vr to become estranged; **distante** adj distant

diste ['diste], **disteis** ['disteis] vb V **dar**

distinción [distin'θjon] nf distinction; (elegancia) elegance; (honor) honour

distinguido, -a [distin'giðo, a] adj distinguished

distinguir [distin'gir] /3d/ vt to distinguish; (escoger) to single out; **distinguirse** vr to be distinguished

distintivo [distin'tiβo] nm badge; (fig) characteristic

distinto, -a [dis'tinto, a] adj different; (claro) clear

distracción [distrak'θjon] nf distraction; (pasatiempo) hobby, pastime; (olvido) absent-mindedness, distraction

distraer [distra'er] /2o/ vt (atención) to distract; (divertir) to amuse; (fondos) to embezzle; **distraerse** vr (entretenerse) to amuse o.s.; (perder la concentración) to allow one's attention to wander

distraído, -a [distra'iðo, a] adj (gen) absent-minded; (entretenido) amusing

distribuidor, a [distriβui'ðor, a] nm/f distributor; (Com) dealer, agent

distribuir [distriβu'ir] /3g/ vt to distribute

distrito [dis'trito] nm (sector, territorio) region; (barrio) district; **~ postal** postal district; **D~ Federal** (LAM) Federal District

disturbio [dis'turβjo] nm disturbance; (desorden) riot

disuadir [diswa'ðir] /3a/ vt to dissuade

disuelto [di'swelto] pp de **disolver**

DIU nm abr (= dispositivo intrauterino) IUD

diurno, -a ['djurno, a] adj day cpd

divagar [diβa'ɣar] /1h/ vi (desviarse) to digress

diván [di'βan] nm divan

diversidad [diβersi'ðað] nf diversity, variety

diversión [diβer'sjon] nf (gen) entertainment; (actividad) hobby, pastime

diverso, -a [di'βerso, a] adj diverse ▷ nm: **~s** (Com) sundries; **~s libros** several books

divertido, -a [diβer'tiðo, a] adj (chiste) amusing; (fiesta etc) enjoyable

divertir [diβer'tir] /3i/ vt (entretener, recrear) to amuse; **divertirse** vr (pasarlo bien) to have a good time; (distraerse) to amuse o.s.

dividendo [diβi'ðendo] nm (Com: often pl) dividend, dividends

dividir [diβi'ðir] /3a/ vt (gen) to divide; (distribuir) to distribute, share out

divierta etc [di'βjerta] vb V **divertir**

divino, -a [di'βino, a] adj divine

divirtiendo etc [diβir'tjendo] vb V **divertir**

divisa [di'βisa] nf (emblema) emblem, badge; **divisas** nfpl foreign exchange sg

divisar [diβi'sar] /1a/ vt to make out, distinguish

división [diβi'sjon] nf division; (de partido) split; (de país) partition

divorciar [diβor'θjar] /1b/ vt to divorce; **divorciarse** vr to get divorced; **divorcio** nm divorce

divulgar [diβul'γar] /1h/ vt (desparramar) to spread; (hacer circular) to divulge

DNI nm abr (ESP) = **Documento Nacional de Identidad** see note

- **DNI**
-
- The Documento Nacional de Identidad
- is a Spanish ID card which must be
- carried at all times and produced on
- request for the police. It contains
- the holder's photo, fingerprints and
- personal details. It is also known as
- the DNI or carnet de identidad.

Dña. abr (= Doña) Mrs

do [do] nm (Mus) C

dobladillo [doβla'ðiλo] nm (de vestido) hem; (de pantalón: vuelta) turn-up (BRIT), cuff (US)

doblar [do'βlar] /1a/ vt to double; (papel) to fold; (caño) to bend; (la esquina) to turn, go round; (film) to dub ▷ vi to turn; (campana) to toll; **doblarse** vr (plegarse) to fold (up), crease; (encorvarse) to bend; **~ a la derecha/izquierda** to turn right/left

doble ['doβle] adj double; (de dos aspectos) dual; (fig) two-faced ▷ nm double ▷ nmf (Teat) double, stand-in;

dobles nmpl (Deporte) doubles sg; **con ~ sentido** with a double meaning

doce ['doθe] num twelve; **docena** nf dozen

docente [do'θente] adj: **personal ~** teaching staff; **centro ~** educational institution

dócil ['doθil] adj (pasivo) docile; (obediente) obedient

doctor, a [dok'tor, a] nm/f doctor

doctorado [dokto'raðo] nm doctorate

doctrina [dok'trina] nf doctrine, teaching

documentación [dokumenta'θjon] nf documentation; (de identidad etc) papers pl

documental [dokumen'tal] adj, nm documentary

documento [doku'mento] nm (certificado) document; **~ adjunto** (Inform) attachment; **D~ Nacional de Identidad** national identity card; V **DNI**

dólar ['dolar] nm dollar

doler [do'ler] /2h/ vt, vi to hurt; (fig) to grieve; **dolerse** vr (de su situación) to grieve, feel sorry; (de las desgracias ajenas) to sympathize; **me duele el brazo** my arm hurts

dolor [do'lor] nm pain; (fig) grief, sorrow; **~ de cabeza** headache; **~ de estómago** stomach ache

domar [do'mar] /1a/ vt to tame

domesticar [domesti'kar] /1g/ vt to tame

doméstico, -a [do'mestiko, a] adj (vida, servicio) home; (tareas) household; (animal) tame, pet

domicilio [domi'θiljo] nm home; **~ particular** private residence; **servicio a ~** delivery service; **sin ~ fijo** of no fixed abode

dominante [domi'nante] adj dominant; (persona) domineering

dominar [domi'nar] /1a/ vt to dominate; (idiomas) to be fluent in ▷ vi to dominate, prevail

d

domingo [do'miŋgo] nm Sunday;
D~ de Ramos Palm Sunday; **D~ de
Resurrección** Easter Sunday

dominio [do'minjo] nm (tierras)
domain; (autoridad) power, authority;
(de las pasiones) grip, hold; (de idioma)
command

don [don] nm (talento) gift; **D~ Juan
Gómez** Mr Juan Gómez, Juan Gómez
Esq. (BRIT); see note **"don"**

* **DON**
*
* Don or doña is a term used before
* someone's first name – eg Don
* Diego, Doña Inés – when showing
* respect or being polite to someone
* of a superior social standing or to
* an older person. It is becoming
* somewhat rare, but it does however
* continue to be used with names and
* surnames in official documents and
* in correspondence: eg Sr. D. Pedro
* Rodríguez Hernández, Sra. Dña Inés
* Rodríguez Hernández.

dona ['dona] nf (LAM) doughnut,
donut (US)

donar [do'nar] /1a/ vt to donate

donativo [dona'tiβo] nm donation

donde ['donde] adv where ▷ prep: **el
coche está allí ~ el farol** the car is
over there by the lamppost o where
the lamppost is; **en ~** where, in which

dónde ['donde] adv interrogativo
where?; **¿a ~ vas?** where are you going
(to)?; **¿de ~ vienes?** where have you
been?; **¿por ~?** where?, whereabouts?

dondequiera [donde'kjera] adv
anywhere ▷ conj: **~ que** wherever;
por ~ everywhere, all over the place

donut® [do'nut] nm (ESP) doughnut,
donut (US)

doña ['dona] nf: **~ Alicia** Alicia; **D~
Carmen Gómez** Mrs Carmen Gómez;
V tb **don**

dorado, -a [do'raðo, a] adj (color)
golden; (Tec) gilt

dormir [dor'mir] /3j/ vt: **~ la siesta**
to have an afternoon nap ▷ vi to sleep;
dormirse vr to fall asleep

dormitorio [dormi'torjo] nm
bedroom

dorsal [dor'sal] nm (Deporte) number

dorso ['dorso] nm (de mano) back; (de
hoja) other side

dos [dos] num two

dosis ['dosis] nf inv dose, dosage

dotado, -a [do'taðo, a] adj gifted; **~
de** endowed with

dotar [do'tar] /1a/ vt to endow; **dote**
nf dowry; **dotes** nfpl (talentos) gifts

doy [doj] vb V **dar**

drama ['drama] nm drama;
dramaturgo, -a nm/f dramatist,
playwright

drástico, -a ['drastiko, a] adj drastic

drenaje [dre'naxe] nm drainage

droga ['droɣa] nf drug; **drogadicto, -a**
nm/f drug addict

drogar [dro'ɣar] /1h/ vt to drug;
drogarse vr to take drugs

droguería [droɣe'ria] nf ≈ hardware
shop (BRIT) o store (US)

ducha ['dutʃa] nf (baño) shower; (Med)
douche

ducharse [du'tʃarse] /1a/ vr to take
a shower

duda ['duða] nf doubt; **no cabe ~**
there is no doubt about it; **dudar** /1a/
vt to doubt ▷ vi to doubt; **dudoso,
-a** adj (incierto) hesitant; (sospechoso)
doubtful

duela etc vb V **doler**

duelo ['dwelo] vb V **doler** ▷ nm
(combate) duel; (luto) mourning

duende ['dwende] nm imp, goblin

dueño, -a ['dweɲo, a] nm/f
(propietario) owner; (de pensión,
taberna) landlord/lady; (empresario)
employer

duerma etc ['dwerma] vb V **dormir**

dulce ['dulθe] adj sweet ▷ adv gently,
softly ▷ nm sweet

dulcería [dulθe'ria] nf (LAM)
confectioner's (shop)

dulzura [dul'θura] *nf* sweetness; (*ternura*) gentleness

dúo ['duo] *nm* duet

duplicar [dupli'kar] /1g/ *vt* (*hacer el doble de*) to duplicate

duque ['duke] *nm* duke; **duquesa** *nf* duchess

durable [du'raβle] *adj* durable

duración [dura'θjon] *nf* (*de película, disco etc*) length; (*de pila etc*) life; (*curso: de acontecimientos etc*) duration

duradero, -a [dura'ðero, a] *adj* (*tela*) hard-wearing; (*fe, paz*) lasting

durante [du'rante] *adv* during

durar [du'rar] /1a/ *vi* to last; (*recuerdo*) to remain

durazno [du'rasno] *nm* (*LAM: fruta*) peach; (: *árbol*) peach tree

durex ['dureks] *nm* (*LAM: tira adhesiva*) Sellotape® (*BRIT*), Scotch tape® (*US*)

dureza [du'reθa] *nf* (*cualidad*) hardness

duro, -a ['duro, a] *adj* hard; (*carácter*) tough ▷ *adv* hard ▷ *nm* (*moneda*) five peseta coin

DVD *nm abr* (= *disco de vídeo digital*) DVD

e

e

E *abr* (= *este*) E

e [e] *conj* and

ébano ['eβano] *nm* ebony

ebrio, -a ['eβrjo, a] *adj* drunk

ebullición [eβuʎi'θjon] *nf* boiling

echar [e'tʃar] /1a/ *vt* to throw; (*agua, vino*) to pour (out); (*empleado: despedir*) to fire, sack; (*hojas*) to sprout; (*cartas*) to post; (*humo*) to emit, give out ▷ *vi*: **~ a correr** to start running *o* to run, break into a run; **~ a llorar** to burst into tears; **echarse** *vr* to lie down; **~ llave a** to lock (up); **~ abajo** (*gobierno*) to overthrow; (*edificio*) to demolish; **~ mano a** to lay hands on; **~ una mano a algn** (*ayudar*) to give sb a hand; **~ de menos** to miss; **~ una mirada** to give a look; **~ sangre** to bleed; **~se atrás** to back out

eclesiástico, -a [ekle'sjastiko, a] *adj* ecclesiastical

eco ['eko] *nm* echo; **tener ~** to catch on

ecología [ekolo'xia] nf ecology; **ecológico, -a** adj (producto, método) environmentally-friendly; (agricultura) organic; **ecologista** adj environmental, conservation cpd ▷ nmf environmentalist

economía [ekono'mia] nf (sistema) economy; (carrera) economics

económico, -a [eko'nomiko, a] adj (barato) cheap, economical; (persona) thrifty; (Com: año etc) financial; (: situación) economic

economista [ekono'mista] nmf economist

Ecuador [ekwa'ðor] nm Ecuador

ecuador [ekwa'ðor] nm equator

ecuatoriano, -a [ekwato'rjano, a] adj, nm/f Ecuador(i)an

ecuestre [e'kwestre] adj equestrian

edad [e'ðað] nf age; **¿qué ~ tienes?** how old are you?; **tiene ocho años de ~** he is eight (years old); **ser de ~ mediana/avanzada** to be middle-aged/getting on; **la E~ Media** the Middle Ages

edición [eði'θjon] nf (acto) publication; (ejemplar) edition

edificar [eðifi'kar] /1g/ vt, vi to build

edificio [eði'fiθjo] nm building; (fig) edifice, structure

Edimburgo [eðim'burɣo] nm Edinburgh

editar [eði'tar] /1a/ vt (publicar) to publish; (preparar textos) to edit

editor, a [eði'tor, a] nm/f (que publica) publisher; (redactor) editor ▷ adj: **casa ~a** publishing company; **editorial** adj editorial ▷ nm leading article, editorial; (tb: **casa editorial**) publisher

edredón [eðre'ðon] nm; duvet

educación [eðuka'θjon] nf education; (crianza) upbringing; (modales) (good) manners pl

educado, -a [eðu'kaðo, a] adj well-mannered; **mal ~** ill-mannered

educar [eðu'kar] /1g/ vt to educate; (criar) to bring up; (voz) to train

efectivamente [efekti̯βa'mente] adv (como respuesta) exactly, precisely; (verdaderamente) really; (de hecho) in fact

efectivo, -a [efek'tiβo, a] adj effective; (real) actual, real ▷ nm: **pagar en ~** to pay (in) cash; **hacer ~ un cheque** to cash a cheque

efecto [e'fekto] nm effect, result; **efectos** nmpl (personales) effects; (bienes) goods; (Com) assets; **~ invernadero** greenhouse effect; **~s especiales** special effects; **~s secundarios** side effects; **~s sonoros** sound effects; **en ~** in fact; (respuesta) exactly, indeed

efectuar [efek'twar] /1e/ vt to carry out; (viaje) to make

eficacia [efi'kaθja] nf (de persona) efficiency; (de medicamento etc) effectiveness

eficaz [efi'kaθ] adj (persona) efficient; (acción) effective

eficiente [efi'θjente] adj efficient

egipcio, -a [e'xipθjo, a] adj, nm/f Egyptian

Egipto [e'xipto] nm Egypt

egoísmo [eɣo'ismo] nm egoism

egoísta [eɣo'ista] adj egoistical, selfish ▷ nmf egoist

Eire ['eire] nm Eire

ej. abr (= ejemplo) eg

eje ['exe] nm (Geo, Mat) axis; (de rueda) axle; (de máquina) shaft, spindle

ejecución [exeku'θjon] nf execution; (cumplimiento) fulfilment; (actuación) performance; (Jur: embargo de deudor) attachment

ejecutar [exeku'tar] /1a/ vt to execute, carry out; (matar) to execute; (cumplir) to fulfil; (Mus) to perform; (Jur: embargar) to attach, distrain

ejecutivo, -a [exeku'tiβo, a] adj executive; **el (poder) ~** the executive (power)

ejemplar [exem'plar] adj exemplary ▷ nm example; (Zool) specimen; (de libro) copy; (de periódico) number, issue

ejemplo [e'xemplo] nm example; **por ~** for example

ejercer [exer'θer] /2b/ vt to exercise; (influencia) to exert; (un oficio) to practise ▷ vi: **~ de** to practise as

ejercicio [exer'θiθjo] nm exercise; (período) tenure; **~ comercial** business year; **hacer ~** to take exercise

ejército [e'xerθito] nm army; **E~ del Aire/de Tierra** Air Force/Army; **entrar en el ~** to join the army, join up

ejote [e'xote] nm (LAM) green bean

⭕ **PALABRA CLAVE**

el [el] (fem **la**, neutro **lo**, pl **los, las**) artículo definido **1** the; **el libro/la mesa/los estudiantes/las flores** the book/table/students/flowers
2 (con n abstracto o propio, no se traduce): **el amor/la juventud** love/youth
3 (posesión, se traduce a menudo por adj posesivo): **romperse el brazo** to break one's arm; **levantó la mano** he put his hand up; **se puso el sombrero** she put her hat on
4 (valor descriptivo): **tener la boca grande/los ojos azules** to have a big mouth/blue eyes
5 (con días) on; **me iré el viernes** I'll leave on Friday; **los domingos suelo ir a nadar** on Sundays I generally go swimming
6 (lo + adj): **lo difícil/caro** what is difficult/expensive; (cuán): **no se da cuenta de lo pesado que es** he doesn't realize how boring he is
▶ pron demostrativo **1**: **mi libro y el de usted** my book and yours; **las de Pepe son mejores** Pepe's are better; **no la(s) blanca(s) sino la(s) gris(es)** not the white one(s) but the grey one(s)
2: **lo de: lo de ayer** what happened yesterday; **lo de las facturas** that business about the invoices
▶ pron relativo **1**: **el que** etc (indef): **el**

(los) que quiera(n) que se vaya(n) anyone who wants to can leave; **llévese el/la que más le guste** take the one you like best; (def): **el que compré ayer** the one I bought yesterday; **los que se van** those who leave
2: **lo que: lo que pienso yo/más me gusta** what I think/like most
▶ conj: **el que: el que lo diga** the fact that he says so; **el que sea tan vago me molesta** his being so lazy bothers me
▶ excl: **¡el susto que me diste!** what a fright you gave me!
▶ pron personal **1** (persona: m) him; (: f) her; (: pl) them; **lo/las veo** I can see him/them
2 (animal, cosa: sg) it; (: pl) them; **lo (o la) veo** I can see it; **los (o las) veo** I can see them
3: **lo** (como sustituto de frase): **no lo sabía** I didn't know; **ya lo entiendo** I understand now

él [el] pron (persona) he; (cosa) it; (después de prep: persona) him; (: cosa) it; **mis libros y los de él** my books and his

elaborar [elaβo'rar] /1a/ vt (producto) to make, manufacture; (preparar) to prepare; (madera, metal etc) to work; (proyecto etc) to work on o out

elástico, -a [e'lastiko, a] adj elastic; (flexible) flexible ▷ nm elastic; (gomita) elastic band

elección [elek'θjon] nf election; (selección) choice, selection; **elecciones generales** general election sg

electorado [elekto'raðo] nm electorate, voters pl

electricidad [elektriθi'ðað] nf electricity

electricista [elektri'θista] nmf electrician

eléctrico, -a [e'lektriko, a] adj electric

electro... [elektro] pref electro...;
electrocardiograma nm
electrocardiogram; **electrocutar**
/1a/ vt to electrocute; **electrodo**
nm electrode; **electrodomésticos**
nmpl (electrical) household
appliances

electrónico, -a [elek'troniko, a] adj
electronic ▷ nf electronics sg

electrotren [elektro'tren] nm
express electric train

elefante [ele'fante] nm elephant

elegancia [ele'ɣanθja] nf elegance,
grace; (estilo) stylishness

elegante [ele'ɣante] adj elegant,
graceful; (estiloso) stylish,
fashionable

elegir [ele'xir] /3c, 3k/ vt (escoger)
to choose, select; (optar) to opt for;
(presidente) to elect

elemental [elemen'tal] adj (claro,
obvio) elementary; (fundamental)
elemental, fundamental

elemento [ele'mento] nm element;
(fig) ingredient; **elementos** nmpl
elements, rudiments

elepé [ele'pe] nm LP

elevación [eleβa'θjon] nf elevation;
(acto) raising, lifting; (de precios) rise;
(Geo etc) height, altitude

elevado, -a [ele'βaðo, a] pp de **elevar**
▷ adj high

elevar [ele'βar] /1a/ vt to raise, lift
(up); (precio) to put up; **elevarse** vr
(edificio) to rise; (precios) to go up

eligiendo etc [eli'xjenðo], **elija** etc
[e'lixa] vb V **elegir**

eliminar [elimi'nar] /1a/ vt to
eliminate, remove

eliminatoria [elimina'torja] nf
heat, preliminary (round)

elite [e'lite], **élite** ['elite] nf elite

ella ['eʎa] pron (persona) she; (cosa) it;
(después de prep: persona) her; (: cosa)
it; **de ~** hers

ellas ['eʎas] pron V **ellos**

ello ['eʎo] pron neutro it; **es por ~
que ...** that's why ...

ellos, -as ['eʎos, as] pron personal pl
they; (después de prep) them; **de ~** theirs

elogiar [elo'xjar] /1b/ vt to praise;
elogio nm praise

elote [e'lote] nm (LAM) corn on the cob

eludir [elu'ðir] /3a/ vt to avoid

email ['imeil] nm email m; (dirección)
email address; **mandar un ~ a algn**
to email sb, send sb an email

embajada [emba'xaða] nf embassy

embajador, a [embaxa'ðor, a] nm/f
ambassador/ambassadress

embalar [emba'lar] /1a/ vt to parcel,
wrap (up); **embalarse** vr to go fast

embalse [em'balse] nm (presa) dam;
(lago) reservoir

embarazada [embara'θaða] adj f
pregnant ▷ nf pregnant woman
▪ No confundir embarazada con la
palabra inglesa embarrassed.

embarazo [emba'raθo] nm (de mujer)
pregnancy; (impedimento) obstacle,
obstruction; (timidez) embarrassment;
embarazoso, -a adj awkward;
(violento) embarrassing

embarcación [embarka'θjon] nf
(barco) boat, craft; (acto) embarkation

embarcadero [embarka'ðero] nm
pier, landing stage

embarcar [embar'kar] /1g/ vt
(cargamento) to ship, stow; (persona) to
embark, put on board; **embarcarse** vr
to embark, go on board

embargar [embar'ɣar] /1h/ vt (Jur) to
seize, impound

embargo [em'barɣo] nm (Jur) seizure;
(Com etc) embargo

embargue etc [em'barɣe] vb V
embargar

embarque etc [em'barke] vb V
embarcar ▷ nm shipment, loading

embellecer [embeʎe'θer] /2d/ vt to
embellish, beautify

embestida [embes'tiða] nf attack,
onslaught; (carga) charge

embestir [embes'tir] /3k/ vt to
attack, assault; to charge, attack ▷ vi
to attack

emblema [em'blema] nm emblem

embobado, -a [embo'βaðo, a] adj (atontado) stunned, bewildered

embolia [em'bolja] nf (Med) clot, embolism

émbolo ['embolo] nm (Auto) piston

emborrachar [emborra'tʃar] /1a/ vt to make drunk, intoxicate; **emborracharse** vr to get drunk

emboscada [embos'kaða] nf ambush

embotar [embo'tar] /1a/ vt to blunt, dull

embotellamiento [emboteʎa'mjento] nm (Auto) traffic jam

embotellar [embote'ʎar] /1a/ vt to bottle

embrague [em'braɣe] nm (tb: **pedal de ~**) clutch

embrión [em'brjon] nm embryo

embrollo [em'broʎo] nm (enredo) muddle, confusion; (aprieto) fix, jam

embrujado, -a [embru'xaðo, a] adj bewitched; **casa embrujada** haunted house

embrutecer [embrute'θer] /2d/ vt (atontar) to stupefy

embudo [em'buðo] nm funnel

embuste [em'buste] nm (mentira) lie; **embustero, -a** adj lying, deceitful ▷ nm/f (mentiroso) liar

embutido [embu'tiðo] nm (Culin) sausage; (Tec) inlay

emergencia [emer'xenθja] nf emergency; (surgimiento) emergence

emerger [emer'xer] /2c/ vi to emerge, appear

emigración [emiɣra'θjon] nf emigration; (de pájaros) migration

emigrar [emi'ɣrar] /1a/ vi (personas) to emigrate; (pájaros) to migrate

eminente [emi'nente] adj eminent, distinguished; (elevado) high

emisión [emi'sjon] nf (acto) emission; (Com etc) issue; (Radio, TV: acto) broadcasting; (: programa) broadcast, programme, program (us)

emisor, a [emi'sor, a] nm transmitter ▷ nf radio o broadcasting station

emitir [emi'tir] /3a/ vt (olor etc) to emit, give off; (moneda etc) to issue; (opinión) to express; (Radio) to broadcast

emoción [emo'θjon] nf emotion; (excitación) excitement; (sentimiento) feeling

emocionante [emoθjo'nante] adj (excitante) exciting, thrilling

emocionar [emoθjo'nar] /1a/ vt (excitar) to excite, thrill; (conmover) to move, touch; (impresionar) to impress

emoticón [emoti'kon], **emoticono** [emoti'kono] nm smiley

emotivo, -a [emo'tiβo, a] adj emotional

empacho [em'patʃo] nm (Med) indigestion; (fig) embarrassment

empalagoso, -a [empala'ɣoso, a] adj cloying; (fig) tiresome

empalmar [empal'mar] /1a/ vt to join, connect ▷ vi (dos caminos) to meet, join; **empalme** nm joint, connection; (de vías) junction; (de trenes) connection

empanada [empa'naða] nf pie, pasty

empañarse [empa'ɲarse] /1a/ vr (nublarse) to get misty, steam up

empapar [empa'par] /1a/ vt (mojar) to soak, saturate; (absorber) to soak up, absorb; **empaparse** vr: **~se de** to soak up

empapelar [empape'lar] /1a/ vt (paredes) to paper

empaquetar [empake'tar] /1a/ vt to pack, parcel up

empastar [empas'tar] /1a/ vt (embadurnar) to paste; (diente) to fill

empaste [em'paste] nm (de diente) filling

empatar [empa'tar] /1a/ vi to draw, tie; **~on a dos** they drew two-all; **empate** nm draw, tie

empecé [empe'θe] vb V **empezar**

empedernido, -a [empeðer'niðo, a] adj hard, heartless; (fijado) inveterate; **un fumador ~** a heavy smoker

empeine [em'peine] nm (de pie, zapato) instep

empeñado, -a [empe'ɲaðo, a] adj (persona) determined; (objeto) pawned

empeñar [empe'ɲar] /1a/ vt (objeto) to pawn, pledge; (persona) to compel; **empeñarse** vr (endeudarse) to get into debt; **~se en hacer** to be set on doing, be determined to do

empeño [em'peɲo] nm (determinación) determination; **casa de ~s** pawnshop

empeorar [empeo'rar] /1a/ vt to make worse, worsen ▷ vi to get worse, deteriorate

empezar [empe'θar] /1f, 1j/ vt, vi to begin, start

empiece etc [em'pjeθe] vb V **empezar**

empiezo etc [em'pjeθo] vb V **empezar**

emplasto [em'plasto] nm (Med) plaster

emplazar [empla'θar] /1f/ vt (ubicar) to site, place, locate; (Jur) to summons; (convocar) to summon

empleado, -a [emple'aðo, a] nm/f (gen) employee; (de banco etc) clerk

emplear [emple'ar] /1a/ vt (usar) to use, employ; (dar trabajo a) to employ; **emplearse** vr (conseguir trabajo) to be employed; (ocuparse) to occupy o.s.

empleo [em'pleo] nm (puesto) job; (puestos: colectivamente) employment; (uso) use, employment

empollar [empo'ʎar] /1a/ vt (fam) to swot (up); **empollón, -ona** nm/f (fam) swot

emporio [em'porjo] nm (LAM: gran almacén) department store

empotrado, -a [empo'traðo, a] adj (armario etc) built-in

emprender [empren'der] /2a/ vt (empezar) to begin, embark on; (acometer) to tackle, take on

empresa [em'presa] nf enterprise; (Com) firm, company; **empresariales** nfpl business studies; **empresario, -a** nm/f (Com) businessman/woman

empujar [empu'xar] /1a/ vt to push, shove

empujón [empu'xon] nm push, shove

empuñar [empu'ɲar] /1a/ vt (asir) to grasp, take (firm) hold of

PALABRA CLAVE

en [en] prep **1** (posición) in; (: sobre) on; **está en el cajón** it's in the drawer; **en Argentina/La Paz** in Argentina/La Paz; **en el colegio/la oficina** at school/the office; **está en el suelo/quinto piso** it's on the floor/the fifth floor

2 (dirección) into; **entró en el aula** she went into the classroom; **meter algo en el bolso** to put sth into one's bag

3 (tiempo) in; on; **en 1605/3 semanas/invierno** in 1605/3 weeks/winter; **en (el mes de) enero** in (the month of) January; **en aquella ocasión/época** on that occasion/at that time

4 (precio) for; **lo vendió en 20 dólares** he sold it for 20 dollars

5 (diferencia) by; **reducir/aumentar en una tercera parte/un 20 por ciento** to reduce/increase by a third/20 per cent

6 (manera, forma): **en avión/autobús** by plane/bus; **escrito en inglés** written in English

7 (después de vb que indica gastar etc) on; **han cobrado demasiado en dietas** they've charged too much to expenses; **se le va la mitad del sueldo en comida** half his salary goes on food

8 (tema, ocupación): **experto en la materia** expert on the subject; **trabaja en la construcción** he works in the building industry

9 (adj + en + infin): **lento en reaccionar** slow to react

enagua(s) [ena'ɣwa(s)] nf (pl) (esp LAM) petticoat sg, underskirt sg

enajenación [enaxena'θjon] *nf*: **~mental** mental derangement

enamorado, -a [enamo'raðo, a] *adj* in love ▷ *nm/f* lover; **estar ~ (de)** to be in love (with)

enamorar [enamo'rar] /1a/ *vt* to win the love of; **enamorarse** *vr*: **~se (de)** to fall in love (with)

enano, -a [e'nano, a] *adj* tiny ▷ *nm/f* person of small stature

encabezamiento [enkaβeθa'mjento] *nm* (*de carta*) heading; (*de periódico*) headline

encabezar [enkaβe'θar] /1f/ *vt* (*movimiento, revolución*) to lead, head; (*lista*) to head; (*carta*) to put a heading to

encadenar [enkaðe'nar] /1a/ *vt* to chain (together); (*poner grilletes a*) to shackle

encajar [enka'xar] /1a/ *vt* (*ajustar*): **~ en** to fit (into) ▷ *vi* to fit (well); (*fig: corresponder a*) to match

encaje [en'kaxe] *nm* (*labor*) lace

encallar [enka'ʎar] /1a/ *vi* (*Naut*) to run aground

encaminar [enkami'nar] /1a/ *vt* to direct, send

encantado, -a [enkan'taðo, a] *adj* (*hechizado*) bewitched; (*muy contento*) delighted; **¡~!** how do you do!, pleased to meet you

encantador, a [enkanta'ðor, a] *adj* charming, lovely ▷ *nm/f* magician, enchanter/enchantress

encantar [enkan'tar] /1a/ *vt* to charm, delight; (*hechizar*) to bewitch, cast a spell on; **me encanta eso** I love that; **encanto** *nm* (*magia*) spell, charm; (*fig*) charm, delight

encarcelar [enkarθe'lar] /1a/ *vt* to imprison, jail

encarecer [enkare'θer] /2d/ *vt* to put up the price of ▷ **encarecerse** *vr* to get dearer

encargado, -a [enkar'ɣaðo, a] *adj* in charge ▷ *nm/f* agent, representative; (*responsable*) person in charge

encargar [enkar'ɣar] /1h/ *vt* to entrust; (*recomendar*) to urge, recommend; **encargarse** *vr*: **~se de** to look after, take charge of; **~ algo a algn** to put sb in charge of sth

encargo [en'karɣo] *nm* (*pedido*) assignment, job; (*responsabilidad*) responsibility; (*Com*) order

encariñarse [enkari'narse] /1a/ *vr*: **~ con** to grow fond of, get attached to

encarnación [enkarna'θjon] *nf* incarnation, embodiment

encarrilar [enkarri'lar] /1a/ *vt* (*tren*) to put back on the rails; (*fig*) to correct, put on the right track

encasillar [enkasi'ʎar] /1a/ *vt* (*Teat*) to typecast; (*pey*) to pigeonhole

encendedor [enθende'ðor] *nm* lighter

encender [enθen'der] /2g/ *vt* (*con fuego*) to light; (*luz, radio*) to put on, switch on; (*avivar: pasiones etc*) to inflame; **encenderse** *vr* to catch fire; (*excitarse*) to get excited; (*de cólera*) to flare up; (*el rostro*) to blush

encendido, -a [enθen'diðo, a] *adj* alight; (*aparato*) (switched) on ▷ *nm* (*Auto*) ignition

encerado, -a [enθe'raðo, a] *adj* (*suelo*) waxed ▷ *nm* (*Escol*) blackboard

encerrar [enθe'rrar] /1j/ *vt* (*confinar*) to shut in o up; (*comprender, incluir*) to include, contain; **encerrarse** *vr* to shut o lock o.s. up o in

encharcado, -a [entʃar'kaðo, a] *adj* (*terreno*) flooded

encharcar [entʃar'kar] /1g/ *vt* to swamp, flood; **encharcarse** *vr* to become flooded

enchufado, -a [entʃu'faðo, a] *nm/f* (*fam*) well-connected person

enchufar [entʃu'far] /1a/ *vt* (*Elec*) to plug in; (*Tec*) to connect, fit together; **enchufe** *nm* (*Elec: clavija*) plug; (: *toma*) socket; (*de dos tubos*) joint, connection; (*fam: influencia*) contact, connection; (: *puesto*) cushy job

encía [en'θia] *nf* gum

encienda etc [en'θjenda] vb V
  encender

encierro etc [en'θjerro] vb V
  encerrar ▷ nm shutting in o up;
  (calabozo) prison

encima [en'θima] adv (sobre) above,
over; (además) besides; **~ de** (en) on,
on top of; (sobre) above, over; (además
de) besides, on top of; **por ~ de** over;
¿llevas dinero ~? have you (got) any
money on you?; **se me vino ~** it took
me by surprise

encina [en'θina] nf (holm) oak

encinta [en'θinta] adj f pregnant

enclenque [en'klenke] adj weak,
sickly

encoger [enko'xer] /2c/ vt (gen) to
shrink, contract; **encogerse** vr to
shrink, contract; (fig) to cringe; **~se de
hombros** to shrug one's shoulders

encomendar [enkomen'dar]
/1j/ vt to entrust, commend;
encomendarse vr: **~se a** to put one's
trust in

encomienda etc [enko'mjenda]
vb V **encomendar** ▷ nf (encargo)
charge, commission; (elogio) tribute;
(LAM) parcel, package; **~ postal** (LAM:
servicio) parcel post

encontrar [enkon'trar] /1l/ vt (hallar)
to find; (inesperadamente) to meet, run
into; **encontrarse** vr to meet (each
other); (situarse) to be (situated); **~se
con** to meet; **~se bien (de salud)**
to feel well

encrucijada [enkruθi'xaða] nf
crossroads sg

encuadernación
[enkwaðerna'θjon] nf binding

encuadrar [enkwa'ðrar] /1a/ vt
(retrato) to frame; (ajustar) to fit,
insert; (encerrar) to contain

encubrir [enku'βrir] /3a/ vt (ocultar)
to hide, conceal; (criminal) to harbour,
shelter

encuentro [en'kwentro] vb V
  encontrar ▷ nm (de personas)
meeting; (Auto etc) collision, crash;
(Deporte) match, game; (Mil)
encounter

encuerado, -a [enkwe'raðo, a] adj
(LAM) nude, naked

encuesta [en'kwesta] nf inquiry,
investigation; (sondeo) public opinion
poll

encumbrar [enkum'brar] /1a/ vt
(persona) to exalt

endeble [en'deβle] adj (argumento,
excusa, persona) weak

endemoniado, -a [endemo'njaðo,
a] adj possessed (of the devil);
(travieso) devilish

enderezar [endere'θar] /1f/ vt
(poner derecho) to straighten (out);
(: verticalmente) to set upright; (fig) to
straighten o sort out; (dirigir) to direct;
enderezarse vr (persona sentada) to
sit up straight

endeudarse [endeu'ðarse] /1a/ vr to
get into debt

endiablado, -a [endja'βlaðo, a]
adj devilish, diabolical; (humorístico)
mischievous

endilgar [endil'ɣar] /1h/ vt (fam):
~ algo a algn to lumber sb with sth

endiñar [endi'ɲar] /1a/ vt: **~ algo a
algn** to land sth on sb

endosar [endo'sar] /1a/ vt (cheque etc)
to endorse

endulzar [endul'θar] /1f/ vt to
sweeten; (suavizar) to soften

endurecer [endure'θer] /2d/ vt to
harden; **endurecerse** vr to harden,
grow hard

enema [e'nema] nm (Med) enema

enemigo, -a [ene'miɣo, a] adj
enemy, hostile ▷ nm/f enemy

enemistad [enemis'tað] nf enmity

enemistar [enemis'tar] /1a/ vt
to make enemies of, cause a rift
between; **enemistarse** vr to become
enemies; (amigos) to fall out

energía [ener'xia] nf (vigor)
energy, drive; (empuje) push; (Tec,
Elec) energy, power; **~ atómica/
eléctrica/eólica** atomic/electric/

wind power; **~ solar** solar energy o power

enérgico, -a [e'nerxiko, a] adj (gen) energetic; (voz, modales) forceful

energúmeno, -a [ener'ɣumeno, a] nm/f madman/woman

enero [e'nero] nm January

enfadado, -a [enfa'ðaðo, a] adj angry, annoyed

enfadar [enfa'ðar] /1a/ vt to anger, annoy; **enfadarse** vr to get angry o annoyed

enfado [en'faðo] nm (enojo) anger, annoyance; (disgusto) trouble, bother

énfasis ['enfasis] nm emphasis, stress

enfático, -a [en'fatiko, a] adj emphatic

enfermar [enfer'mar] /1a/ vt to make ill ▷ vi to fall ill, be taken ill

enfermedad [enferme'ðað] nf illness; **~ venérea** venereal disease

enfermera [enfer'mera] nf V **enfermero**

enfermería [enferme'ria] nf infirmary; (de colegio etc) sick bay

enfermero, -a [enfer'mero, a] nm (male) nurse ▷ nf nurse

enfermizo, -a [enfer'miθo, a] adj (persona) sickly, unhealthy; (fig) unhealthy

enfermo, -a [en'fermo, a] adj ill, sick ▷ nm/f invalid, sick person; (en hospital) patient; **caer o ponerse ~** to fall ill

enfocar [enfo'kar] /1g/ vt (foto etc) to focus; (problema etc) to consider, look at

enfoque etc [en'foke] vb V **enfocar** ▷ nm focus

enfrentar [enfren'tar] /1a/ vt (peligro) to face (up to), confront; (oponer) to bring face to face; **enfrentarse** vr (dos personas) to face o confront each other; (Deporte: dos equipos) to meet; **~se a o con** to face up to, confront

enfrente [en'frente] adv opposite; **~ de** opposite, facing; **la casa de ~** the house opposite, the house across the street

enfriamiento [enfria'mjento] nm chilling, refrigeration; (Med) cold, chill

enfriar [enfri'ar] /1c/ vt (alimentos) to cool, chill; (algo caliente) to cool down; **enfriarse** vr to cool down; (Med) to catch a chill; (amistad) to cool

enfurecer [enfure'θer] /2d/ vt to enrage, madden; **enfurecerse** vr to become furious, fly into a rage; (mar) to get rough

enganchar [engan'tʃar] /1a/ vt to hook; (dos vagones) to hitch up; (Tec) to couple, connect; (Mil) to recruit; **engancharse** vr (Mil) to enlist, join up

enganche [en'gantʃe] nm hook; (Tec) coupling, connection; (acto) hooking (up); (Mil) recruitment, enlistment; (Lam: depósito) deposit

engañar [enga'ɲar] /1a/ vt to deceive; (estafar) to cheat, swindle; **engañarse** vr (equivocarse) to be wrong; (asimismo) to deceive o kid o.s.

engaño [en'gaɲo] nm deceit; (estafa) trick, swindle; (error) mistake, misunderstanding; (ilusión) delusion; **engañoso, -a** adj (tramposo) crooked; (mentiroso) dishonest, deceitful; (aspecto) deceptive; (consejo) misleading

engatusar [engatu'sar] /1a/ vt (fam) to coax

engendro [en'xendro] nm (Bio) foetus; (fig) monstrosity

englobar [englo'βar] /1a/ vt to include, comprise

engordar [engor'ðar] /1a/ vt to fatten ▷ vi to get fat, put on weight

engorroso, -a [engo'rroso, a] adj bothersome, trying

engranaje [engra'naxe] nm (Auto) gear

engrasar [engra'sar] /1a/ vt (Tec: poner grasa) to grease; (: lubricar) to lubricate, oil; (manchar) to make greasy

engreído, -a [engre'iðo, a] *adj* vain, conceited

enhebrar [ene'βrar] /1a/ *vt* to thread

enhorabuena [enora'βwena] *excl* ¡~! congratulations! ▷ *nf*: **dar la ~ a** to congratulate

enigma [e'niɣma] *nm* enigma; (*problema*) puzzle; (*misterio*) mystery

enjambre [en'xambre] *nm* swarm

enjaular [enxau'lar] /1a/ *vt* to (put in a) cage; (*fam*) to jail, lock up

enjuagar [enxwa'ɣar] /1h/ *vt* (*ropa*) to rinse (out)

enjuague *etc* [en'xwaɣe] *vb* V **enjuagar** ▷ *nm* (*Med*) mouthwash; (*de ropa*) rinse, rinsing

enjugar [enxu'ɣar] /1h/ *vt* to wipe (off); (*lágrimas*) to dry; (*déficit*) to wipe out

enlace [en'laθe] *nm* link, connection; (*relación*) relationship; (*tb*: **~ matrimonial**) marriage; (*de trenes*) connection; **~ sindical** shop steward

enlatado, -a [enla'taðo, a] *adj* (*alimentos, productos*) tinned, canned

enlazar [enla'θar] /1f/ *vt* (*unir con lazos*) to bind together; (*atar*) to tie; (*conectar*) to link, connect; (*LAM*) to lasso

enloquecer [enloke'θer] /2d/ *vt* to drive mad ▷ *vi* to go mad

enmarañar [enmara'ɲar] /1a/ *vt* (*enredar*) to tangle up, entangle; (*complicar*) to complicate; (*confundir*) to confuse

enmarcar [enmar'kar] /1g/ *vt* (*cuadro*) to frame

enmascarar [enmaska'rar] /1a/ *vt* to mask; **enmascararse** *vr* to put on a mask

enmendar [enmen'dar] /1j/ *vt* to emend, correct; (*constitución etc*) to amend; (*comportamiento*) to reform; **enmendarse** *vr* to reform, mend one's ways; **enmienda** *nf* correction; amendment; reform

enmudecer [enmuðe'θer] /2d/ *vi* (*perder el habla*) to fall silent; (*guardar silencio*) to remain silent

ennoblecer [ennoβle'θer] /2d/ *vt* to ennoble

enojado, -a [eno'xaðo, a] *adj* (*LAM*) angry

enojar [eno'xar] /1a/ *vt* (*encolerizar*) to anger; (*disgustar*) to annoy, upset; **enojarse** *vr* to get angry; to get annoyed

enojo [e'noxo] *nm* (*cólera*) anger; (*irritación*) annoyance

enorme [e'norme] *adj* enormous, huge; (*fig*) monstrous

enredadera [enreða'ðera] *nf* (*Bot*) creeper, climbing plant

enredar [enre'ðar] /1a/ *vt* (*cables, hilos etc*) to tangle (up), entangle; (*situación*) to complicate, confuse; (*meter cizaña*) to sow discord among o between; (*implicar*) to embroil, implicate; **enredarse** *vr* to get entangled, get tangled (up); (*situación*) to get complicated; (*persona*) to get embroiled; (*LAM fam*) to meddle

enredo [en'reðo] *nm* (*maraña*) tangle; (*confusión*) mix-up, confusion; (*intriga*) intrigue

enriquecer [enrike'θer] /2d/ *vt* to make rich; (*fig*) to enrich; **enriquecerse** *vr* to get rich

enrojecer [enroxe'θer] /2d/ *vt* to redden ▷ *vi* (*persona*) to blush; **enrojecerse** *vr* to blush

enrollar [enro'ʎar] /1a/ *vt* to roll (up), wind (up)

ensalada [ensa'laða] *nf* salad

ensaladilla [ensala'ðiʎa] *nf* (*tb*: **~ rusa**) ≈ Russian salad

ensanchar [ensan'tʃar] /1a/ *vt* (*hacer más ancho*) to widen; (*agrandar*) to enlarge, expand; (*Costura*) to let out; **ensancharse** *vr* to get wider, expand

ensayar [ensa'jar] /1a/ *vt* to test, try (out); (*Teat*) to rehearse

ensayo [en'sajo] *nm* test, trial; (*Química*) experiment; (*Teat*) rehearsal; (*Deporte*) try; (*Escol, Lit*) essay

enseguida [ense'ɣuiða] *adv* at once, right away

ensenada [ense'naða] nf inlet, cove

enseñanza [ense'nanθa] nf
(educación) education; (acción)
teaching; (doctrina) teaching, doctrine;
~ primaria/secundaria/superior
primary/secondary/higher education

enseñar [ense'nar] /1a/ vt (educar) to
teach; (mostrar, señalar) to show

enseres [en'seres] nmpl belongings

ensuciar [ensu'θjar] /1b/ vt (manchar)
to dirty, soil; (fig) to defile; **ensuciarse**
vr to get dirty; (niño) to dirty one's
nappy

entablar [enta'βlar] /1a/ vt (recubrir)
to board (up); (Ajedrez, Damas) to set
up; (conversación) to strike up; (Jur) to
file ▷ vi to draw

ente ['ente] nm (organización) body,
organization; (fam: persona) odd
character

entender [enten'der] /2g/ vt
(comprender) to understand; (darse
cuenta) to realize ▷ vi to understand;
(creer) to think, believe ▷ nm: **a mi
~** in my opinion; **entenderse** vr
(comprenderse) to be understood;
(ponerse de acuerdo) to agree, reach an
agreement; **~ de** to know all about; **~
algo de** to know a little about; **~ en** to
deal with, have to do with; **~se mal** to
get on badly

entendido, -a [enten'diðo, a] adj
(comprendido) understood; (hábil)
skilled; (inteligente) knowledgeable
▷ nm/f (experto) expert ▷ excl agreed!;
entendimiento nm (comprensión)
understanding; (inteligencia) mind,
intellect; (juicio) judgement

enterado, -a [ente'raðo, a] adj well-
informed; **estar ~ de** to know about,
be aware of

enteramente [entera'mente] adv
entirely, completely

enterar [ente'rar] /1a/ vt (informar) to
inform, tell; **enterarse** vr to find out,
get to know

enterito [ente'rito] nm (LAM) boiler
suit (BRIT), overalls (US)

entero, -a [en'tero, a] adj (total) whole,
entire; (fig: recto) honest; (: firme) firm,
resolute ▷ nm (Com: punto) point

enterrar [ente'rrar] /1j/ vt to bury

entidad [enti'ðað] nf (empresa) firm,
company; (organismo) body; (sociedad)
society; (Filosofía) entity

entienda etc [en'tjenda] vb V
entender

entierro [en'tjerro] nm (acción) burial;
(funeral) funeral

entonación [entona'θjon] nf (Ling)
intonation

entonar [ento'nar] /1a/ vt (canción) to
intone; (colores) to tone; (Med) to tone
up ▷ vi to be in tune

entonces [en'tonθes] adv then, at
that time; **desde ~** since then; **en
aquel ~** at that time; **(pues) ~** and so

entornar [entor'nar] /1a/ vt (puerta,
ventana) to half close, leave ajar; (los
ojos) to screw up

entorno [en'torno] nm setting,
environment; **~ de redes** (Inform)
network environment

entorpecer [entorpe'θer] /2d/ vt
(entendimiento) to dull; (impedir) to
obstruct, hinder; (: tránsito) to slow
down, delay

entrado, -a [en'traðo, a] adj: **~ en
años** elderly; **(una vez) ~ el verano**
in the summer(time), when summer
comes ▷ nf (acción) entry, access;
(sitio) entrance, way in; (Com) receipts
pl, takings pl; (Culin) entrée; (Deporte)
innings sg; (Teat) house, audience;
(para el cine etc) ticket; (Inform) input;
entradas y salidas (Com) income and
expenditure; **entrada de aire** (Tec)
air intake o inlet; **de entrada** from
the outset

entramparse [entram'parse] /1a/ vr
to get into debt

entrante [en'trante] adj next,
coming; **entrantes** nmpl starters;
mes/año ~ next month/year

entraña [en'trana] nf (fig: centro)
heart, core; (raíz) root; **entrañas**

nfpl (Anat) entrails; *(fig)* heart *sg*;
entrañable *adj (amigo)* dear;
(recuerdo) fond; **entrañar** /1a/ *vt*
to entail

entrar [en'trar] /1a/ *vt (introducir)* to
bring in; *(Inform)* to input ▷ *vi (meterse)*
to go o come in, enter; *(comenzar)*:
~ diciendo to begin by saying; **me
entró sed/sueño** I started to feel
thirsty/sleepy; **no me entra** I can't
get the hang of it

entre ['entre] *prep (dos)* between; *(en
medio de)* among(st)

entreabrir [entrea'βrir] /3a/ *vt* to
half-open, open halfway

entrecejo [entre'θexo] *nm*: **fruncir
el ~** to frown

entredicho [entre'ðitʃo] *nm (Jur)*
injunction; **poner en ~** to cast doubt
on; **estar en ~** to be in doubt

entrega [en'treɣa] *nf (de mercancías)*
delivery; *(de novela etc)* instalment;
entregar /1h/ *vt (dar)* to hand (over),
deliver; **entregarse** *vr (rendirse)*
to surrender, give in, submit;
entregarse a *(dedicarse)* to devote
o.s. to

entremeses [entre'meses] *nmpl*
hors d'œuvres

entremeter [entreme'ter] /2a/ *vt*
to insert, put in; **entremeterse** *vr* to
meddle, interfere; **entremetido, -a**
adj meddling, interfering

entremezclar [entremeθ'klar] /1a/
vt to intermingle; **entremezclarse** *vr*
to intermingle

entrenador, a [entrena'ðor, a] *nm/f*
trainer, coach

entrenar [entre'nar] /1a/ *vt (Deporte)*
to train ▷ **entrenarse** *vr* to train

entrepierna [entre'pjerna] *nf* crotch

entresuelo [entre'swelo] *nm*
mezzanine

entretanto [entre'tanto] *adv*
meanwhile, meantime

entretecho [entre'tetʃo] *nm (LAM)* attic

entretejer [entrete'xer] /2a/ *vt* to
interweave

entretener [entrete'ner] /2k/ *vt*
(divertir) to entertain, amuse; *(detener)*
to hold up, delay; **entretenerse** *vr*
(divertirse) to amuse o.s.; *(retrasarse)*
to delay, linger; **entretenido,
-a** *adj* entertaining, amusing;
entretenimiento *nm* entertainment,
amusement

entrever [entre'βer] /2u/ *vt* to
glimpse, catch a glimpse of

entrevista [entre'βista] *nf* interview;
entrevistar /1a/ *vt* to interview;
entrevistarse *vr*: **entrevistarse con**
to have an interview with

entristecer [entriste'θer] /2d/ *vt*
to sadden, grieve; **entristecerse** *vr*
to grow sad

entrometerse [entrome'terse] /2a/
vr: **~ (en)** to interfere (in o with)

entumecer [entume'θer] /2d/ *vt* to
numb, benumb; **entumecerse** *vr (por
el frío)* to go o become numb

enturbiar [entur'βjar] /1b/ *vt (el
agua)* to make cloudy; *(fig)* to confuse;
enturbiarse *vr (oscurecerse)* to become
cloudy; *(fig)* to get confused, become
obscure

entusiasmar [entusjas'mar] /1a/ *vt*
to excite, fill with enthusiasm; *(gustar
mucho)* to delight; **entusiasmarse**
vr: **~se con** o **por** to get enthusiastic o
excited about

entusiasmo [entu'sjasmo] *nm*
enthusiasm; *(excitación)* excitement

entusiasta [entu'sjasta] *adj*
enthusiastic ▷ *nmf* enthusiast

enumerar [enume'rar] /1a/ *vt* to
enumerate

envainar [embai'nar] /1a/ *vt* to
sheathe

envalentonar [embalento'nar]
/1a/ *vt* to give courage to;
envalentonarse *vr (pey: jactarse)* to
boast, brag

envasar [emba'sar] /1a/ *vt*
(empaquetar) to pack, wrap; *(enfrascar)*
to bottle; *(enlatar)* to can; *(embolsar)*
to pocket

envase [em'base] nm packing, wrapping; bottling; canning; (recipiente) container; (paquete) package; (botella) bottle; (lata) tin (BRIT), can

envejecer [embexe'θer] /2d/ vt to make old, age ▷ vi (volverse viejo) to grow old; (parecer viejo) to age

envenenar [embene'nar] /1a/ vt to poison; (fig) to embitter

envergadura [emberɣa'ðura] nf (fig) scope

enviar [em'bjar] /1c/ vt to send; **~ un mensaje a algn** (por móvil) to text sb, send sb a text message

enviciar [embi'θjar] /1b/ vi (trabajo etc) to be addictive; **enviciarse** vr: **~se (con o en)** to get addicted (to)

envidia [em'biðja] nf envy; **tener ~ a** to envy, be jealous of; **envidiar** /1b/ vt to envy

envío [em'bio] nm (acción) sending; (de mercancías) consignment; (de dinero) remittance

enviudar [embju'ðar] /1d/ vi to be widowed

envoltorio [embol'torjo] nm package

envoltura [embol'tura] nf (cobertura) cover; (embalaje) wrapper, wrapping

envolver [embol'βer] /2h/ vt to wrap (up); (cubrir) to cover; (enemigo) to surround; (implicar) to involve, implicate

envuelto [em'bwelto] vb V **envolver**

enyesar [enje'sar] /1a/ vt (pared) to plaster; (Med) to put in plaster

enzarzarse [enθar'θarse] /1f/ vr: **~ en algo** to get mixed up in sth; (disputa) to get involved in sth

épico, -a ['epiko, a] adj epic ▷ nf epic (poetry)

epidemia [epi'ðemja] nf epidemic

epilepsia [epi'lepsja] nf epilepsy

episodio [epi'soðjo] nm episode

época ['epoka] nf period, time; (Historia) age, epoch; **hacer ~** to be epoch-making

equilibrar [ekili'βrar] /1a/ vt to balance; **equilibrio** nm balance, equilibrium; **mantener/perder el equilibrio** to keep/lose one's balance; **equilibrista** nmf (funámbulo) tightrope walker; (acróbata) acrobat

equipaje [eki'paxe] nm luggage (BRIT), baggage (US); (avíos) equipment, kit; **~ de mano** hand luggage; **hacer el ~** to pack

equipar [eki'par] /1a/ vt (proveer) to equip

equiparar [ekipa'rar] /1a/ vt (comparar): **~ con** to compare with; **equipararse** vr: **~se con** to be on a level with

equipo [e'kipo] nm (conjunto de cosas) equipment; (Deporte) team; (de obreros) shift; **~ de música** music centre

equis ['ekis] nf (the letter) X

equitación [ekita'θjon] nf (acto) riding

equivalente [ekiβa'lente] adj, nm equivalent

equivaler [ekiβa'ler] /2p/ vi: **~ a** to be equivalent o equal to

equivocación [ekiβoka'θjon] nf mistake, error

equivocado, -a [ekiβo'kaðo, a] adj wrong, mistaken

equivocarse [ekiβo'karse] /1g/ vr to be wrong, make a mistake; **~ de camino** to take the wrong road

era ['era] vb V **ser** ▷ nf era, age

erais ['erais], **éramos** ['eramos], **eran** ['eran] vb V **ser**

eras ['eras], **eres** ['eres] vb V **ser**

erección [erek'θjon] nf erection lift; (poner derecho) to straighten

erigir [eri'xir] /3c/ vt to erect, build; **erigirse** vr: **~se en** to set o.s. up as

erizo [e'riθo] nm hedgehog; **~ de mar** sea urchin

ermita [er'mita] nf hermitage; **ermitaño, -a** nm/f hermit

erosión [ero'sjon] nf erosion

erosionar [erosjo'nar] /1a/ vt to erode

erótico, -a [e'rotiko, a] *adj* erotic;
erotismo *nm* eroticism

errante [e'rrante] *adj* wandering,
errant

errar *vt*: ~ **el camino** to take the
wrong road; ~ **el tiro** to miss

erróneo, -a [e'rroneo, a] *adj*
(*equivocado*) wrong, mistaken

error [e'rror] *nm* error, mistake;
(*Inform*) bug; ~ **de imprenta** misprint

eructar [eruk'tar] /1a/ *vt* to belch,
burp

erudito, -a [eru'ðito, a] *adj* erudite,
learned

erupción [erup'θjon] *nf* eruption;
(*Med*) rash

es [es] *vb V* **ser**

esa ['esa], **esas** ['esas] *adj*
demostrativo, *pron V* **ese**

ésa ['esa], **ésas** *pron V* **ése**

esbelto, -a [es'βelto, a] *adj* slim,
slender

esbozo [es'βoθo] *nm* sketch, outline

escabeche [eska'βetʃe] *nm* brine; (*de
aceitunas etc*) pickle; **en** ~ pickled

escabullirse [eskaβu'ʎirse] /3a/ *vr*
to slip away; (*largarse*) to clear out

escafandra [eska'fandra] *nf* (*buzo*)
diving suit; (*escafandra espacial*)
spacesuit

escala [es'kala] *nf* (*proporción*,
Mus) scale; (*de mano*) ladder; (*Aviat*)
stopover; **hacer** ~ **en** (*gen*) to stop off
at *o* call in at; (*Aviat*) to stop over in

escalafón [eskala'fon] *nm* (*escala de
salarios*) salary scale, wage scale

escalar [eska'lar] /1a/ *vt* to climb,
scale

escalera [eska'lera] *nf* stairs *pl*,
staircase; (*escala*) ladder; (*Naipes*) run;
~ **mecánica** escalator; ~ **de caracol**
spiral staircase; ~ **de incendios** fire
escape

escalfar [eskal'far] /1a/ *vt* (*huevos*)
to poach

escalinata [eskali'nata] *nf* staircase

escalofriante [eskalo'frjante] *adj*
chilling

escalofrío [eskalo'frio] *nm* (*Med*)
chill; **escalofríos** *nmpl* (*fig*) shivers

escalón [eska'lon] *nm* step, stair; (*de
escalera*) rung

escalope [eska'lope] *nm* (*Culin*)
escalope

escama [es'kama] *nf* (*de pez, serpiente*)
scale; (*de jabón*) flake; (*fig*) resentment

escampar [eskam'par] /1a/ *vb
impersonal* to stop raining

escandalizar [eskandali'θar] /1f/ *vt*
to scandalize, shock; **escandalizarse**
vr to be shocked; (*ofenderse*) to be
offended

escándalo [es'kandalo] *nm* scandal;
(*alboroto, tumulto*) row, uproar;
escandaloso, -a *adj* scandalous,
shocking

escandinavo, -a [eskandi'naβo, a]
adj, *nm/f* Scandinavian

escanear [eskane'ar] /1a/ *vt* to scan

escaño [es'kaɲo] *nm* bench; (*Pol*) seat

escapar [eska'par] /1a/ *vi* (*gen*) to
escape, run away; (*Deporte*) to break
away; **escaparse** *vr* to escape, get
away; (*agua, gas, noticias*) to leak (out)

escaparate [eskapa'rate] *nm* shop
window; **ir de ~s** to go window
shopping

escape [es'kape] *nm* (*de agua, gas*)
leak; (*de motor*) exhaust

escarabajo [eskara'βaxo] *nm* beetle

escaramuza [eskara'muθa] *nf*
skirmish

escarbar [eskar'βar] /1a/ *vt* (*gallina*)
to scratch

escarceos [eskar'θeos] *nmpl*: **en sus
~ con la política** in his occasional
forays into politics; ~ **amorosos**
love affairs

escarcha [es'kartʃa] *nf* frost;
escarchado, -a *adj* (*Culin: fruta*)
crystallized

escarlatina [eskarla'tina] *nf* scarlet
fever

escarmentar [eskarmen'tar] /1j/
vt to punish severely ▷ *vi* to learn
one's lesson

escarmiento etc [eskar'mjento] vb
V **escarmentar** ▷ nm (ejemplo) lesson;
(castigo) punishment

escarola [eska'rola] nf endive

escarpado, -a [eskar'paðo, a] adj
(pendiente) sheer, steep; (rocas) craggy

escasear [eskase'ar] /1a/ vi to be
scarce

escasez [eska'seθ] nf (falta) shortage,
scarcity; (pobreza) poverty

escaso, -a [es'kaso, a] adj (poco)
scarce; (raro) rare; (ralo) thin, sparse;
(limitado) limited

escatimar [eskati'mar] /1a/ vt to
skimp (on), be sparing with

escayola [eska'jola] nf plaster

escena [es'θena] nf scene; **escenario**
nm (Teat) stage; (Cine) set; (fig) scene;
escenografía nf set o stage design

> No confundir escenario con la
palabra inglesa scenery.

escéptico, -a [es'θeptiko, a] adj
sceptical ▷ nm/f sceptic

esclarecer [esklare'θer] /2d/ vt
(misterio, problema) to shed light on

esclavitud [esklaβi'tuð] nf slavery

esclavizar [esklaβi'θar] /1f/ vt to
enslave

esclavo, -a [es'klaβo, a] nm/f slave

escoba [es'koβa] nf broom; **escobilla**
nf brush

escocer [esko'θer] /2b, 2h/ vi to
burn, sting; **escocerse** vr to chafe,
get chafed

escocés, -esa [esko'θes, esa] adj
Scottish ▷ nm/f Scotsman/woman,
Scot

Escocia [es'koθja] nf Scotland

escoger [esko'xer] /2c/ vt to choose,
pick, select; **escogido, -a** adj chosen,
selected

escolar [esko'lar] adj school cpd ▷ nmf
schoolboy/girl, pupil

escollo [es'koʎo] nm (fig) pitfall

escolta [es'kolta] nf escort; **escoltar**
/1a/ vt to escort

escombros [es'kombros] nmpl
(basura) rubbish sg; (restos) debris sg

esconder [eskon'der] /2a/ vt to
hide, conceal; **esconderse** vr to hide;
escondidas nfpl: **a escondidas**
secretly; **escondite** nm hiding place;
(juego) hide-and-seek; **escondrijo** nm
hiding place, hideout

escopeta [esko'peta] nf shotgun

escoria [es'korja] nf (desecho mineral)
slag; (fig) scum, dregs pl

Escorpio [es'korpjo] nm Scorpio

escorpión [eskor'pjon] nm scorpion

escotado, -a [esko'taðo, a] adj
low-cut

escote [es'kote] nm (de vestido) low
neck; **pagar a ~** to share the expenses

escotilla [esko'tiʎa] nf (Naut)
hatchway

escozor [esko'θor] nm (dolor)
sting(ing)

escribible [eskri'βiβle] adj writable

escribir [eskri'βir] /3a/ vt, vi to write;
~ a máquina to type; **¿cómo se
escribe?** how do you spell it?

escrito, -a [es'krito, a] pp de
escribir ▷ nm (documento) document;
(manuscrito) text, manuscript; **por ~**
in writing

escritor, a [eskri'tor, a] nm/f writer

escritorio [eskri'torjo] nm desk

escritura [eskri'tura] nf (acción)
writing; (caligrafía) (hand)writing; (Jur:
documento) deed

escrúpulo [es'krupulo] nm scruple;
(minuciosidad) scrupulousness;
escrupuloso, -a adj scrupulous

escrutinio [eskru'tinjo] nm (examen
atento) scrutiny; (Pol: recuento de votos)
count(ing)

escuadra [es'kwaðra] nf (Mil etc)
squad; (Naut) squadron; (de coches
etc) fleet; **escuadrilla** nf (de aviones)
squadron; (LAM: de obreros) gang

escuadrón [eskwa'ðron] nm
squadron

escuálido, -a [es'kwaliðo, a] adj
skinny, scraggy; (sucio) squalid

escuchar [esku'tʃar] /1a/ vt to listen
to ▷ vi to listen

escudo ['es'kuðo] *nm* shield

escuela [es'kwela] *nf* school; **~ de artes y oficios** (*ESP*) ≈ technical college; **~ de choferes** (*LAM*) driving school; **~ de manejo** (*LAM*) driving school

escueto, -a [es'kweto, a] *adj* plain; (*estilo*) simple

escuincle [es'kwinkle] *nm* (*LAM fam*) kid

esculpir [eskul'pir] /3a/ *vt* to sculpt; (*grabar*) to engrave; (*tallar*) to carve; **escultor, a** *nm/f* sculptor; **escultura** *nf* sculpture

escupidera [eskupi'ðera] *nf* spittoon

escupir [esku'pir] /3a/ *vt* to spit (out) ▷ *vi* to spit

escurreplatos [eskurre'platos] *nm inv* plate rack

escurridero [eskurri'ðero] *nm* (*LAM*) draining board (*BRIT*), drainboard (*US*)

escurridizo, -a [eskurri'ðiθo, a] *adj* slippery

escurridor [eskurri'ðor] *nm* colander

escurrir [esku'rrir] /3a/ *vt* (*ropa*) to wring out; (*verduras, platos*) to drain ▷ *vi* (*los líquidos*) to drip; **escurrirse** *vr* (*secarse*) to drain; (*resbalarse*) to slip, slide; (*escaparse*) to slip away

ese ['ese], **esa** ['esa], **esos** ['esos], **esas** ['esas] *adj demostrativo* that *sg*, those *pl* ▷ *pron* that (one) *sg*, those (ones) *pl*

ése ['ese], **ésa** ['esa], **ésos** ['esos], **ésas** ['esas] *pron* that (one) *sg*, those (ones) *pl*; **~ ... éste ...** the former ... the latter ...; **¡no me vengas con ésas!** don't give me any more of that nonsense!

esencia [e'senθja] *nf* essence; **esencial** *adj* essential

esfera [es'fera] *nf* sphere; (*de reloj*) face; **esférico, -a** *adj* spherical

esforzarse [esfor'θarse] /1f, 1l/ *vr* to exert o.s., make an effort

esfuerzo [es'fwerθo] *vb* V **esforzarse** ▷ *nm* effort

esfumarse [esfu'marse] /1a/ *vr* (*apoyo, esperanzas*) to fade away

esgrima [es'ɣrima] *nf* fencing

esguince [es'ɣinθe] *nm* (*Med*) sprain

eslabón [esla'ßon] *nm* link

eslip [ez'lip] *nm* pants *pl* (*BRIT*), briefs *pl*

eslovaco, -a [eslo'ßako, a] *adj, nm/f* Slovak, Slovakian ▷ *nm* (*Ling*) Slovak, Slovakian

Eslovaquia [eslo'ßakja] *nf* Slovakia

esmalte [es'malte] *nm* enamel; **~ de uñas** nail varnish *o* polish

esmeralda [esme'ralda] *nf* emerald

esmerarse [esme'rarse] /1a/ *vr* (*aplicarse*) to take great pains, exercise great care; (*afanarse*) to work hard

esmero [es'mero] *nm* (great) care

esnob [es'nob] *adj inv* (*persona*) snobbish ▷ *nmf* snob

eso ['eso] *pron* that, that thing *o* matter; **~ de su coche** that business about his car; **~ de ir al cine** all that about going to the cinema; **a ~ de las cinco** at about five o'clock; **en ~** thereupon, at that point; **~ es** that's it; **¡~ sí que es vida!** now this is really living!; **por ~ te lo dije** that's why I told you; **y ~ que llovía** in spite of the fact it was raining

esos ['esos] *adj demostrativo* V **ese**

ésos ['esos] *pron* V **ése**

espacial [espa'θjal] *adj* (*del espacio*) space *cpd*

espaciar [espa'θjar] /1b/ *vt* to space (out)

espacio [es'paθjo] *nm* space; (*Mus*) interval; (*Radio, TV*) programme, program (*US*); **el ~** space; **~ aéreo/exterior** air/outer space; **espacioso, -a** *adj* spacious, roomy

espada [es'paða] *nf* sword; **espadas** *nfpl* (*Naipes*) one of the suits in the Spanish card deck

espaguetis [espa'ɣetis] *nmpl* spaghetti *sg*

espalda [es'palda] *nf* (*gen*) back; **~s** *pl* (*hombros*) shoulders; **a ~s de algn**

behind sb's back; **estar de ~s** to have one's back turned; **tenderse de ~s** to lie (down) on one's back; **volver la ~ a algn** to cold-shoulder sb

espantajo [espan'taxo] *nm*, **espantapájaros** [espanta'paxaros] *nm inv* scarecrow

espantar [espan'tar] /1a/ *vt* (*asustar*) to frighten, scare; (*ahuyentar*) to frighten off; (*asombrar*) to horrify, appal; **espantarse** *vr* to get frightened *o* scared; to be appalled

espanto [es'panto] *nm* (*susto*) fright; (*terror*) terror; (*asombro*) astonishment; **espantoso, -a** *adj* frightening, terrifying; (*ruido*) dreadful

España [es'paɲa] *nf* Spain; **español, a** *adj* Spanish ▷ *nm/f* Spaniard ▷ *nm* (*Ling*) Spanish

esparadrapo [espara'ðrapo] *nm* surgical tape

esparcir [espar'θir] /3b/ *vt* to spread; (*derramar*) to scatter; **esparcirse** *vr* to spread (out); to scatter; (*divertirse*) to enjoy o.s.

espárrago [es'parraɣo] *nm* asparagus

esparto [es'parto] *nm* esparto (grass)

espasmo [es'pasmo] *nm* spasm

espátula [es'patula] *nf* spatula

especia [es'peθja] *nf* spice

especial [espe'θjal] *adj* special; **especialidad** *nf* speciality, specialty (*us*)

especie [es'peθje] *nf* (*Bio*) species; (*clase*) kind, sort; **pagar en ~** to pay in kind

especificar [espeθifi'kar] /1g/ *vt* to specify; **específico, -a** *adj* specific

espécimen [es'peθimen] (*pl* **especímenes**) *nm* specimen

espectáculo [espek'takulo] *nm* (*gen*) spectacle; (*Teat etc*) show

espectador, a [espekta'ðor, a] *nm/f* spectator

especular [espeku'lar] /1a/ *vt*, *vi* to speculate

espejismo [espe'xismo] *nm* mirage

espejo [es'pexo] *nm* mirror; **~ retrovisor** rear-view mirror

espeluznante [espeluθ'nante] *adj* horrifying, hair-raising

espera [es'pera] *nf* (*pausa, intervalo*) wait; (*Jur: plazo*) respite; **en ~ de** waiting for; (*con expectativa*) expecting

esperanza [espe'ranθa] *nf* (*confianza*) hope; (*expectativa*) expectation; **hay pocas ~s de que venga** there is little prospect of his coming; **~ de vida** life expectancy

esperar [espe'rar] /1a/ *vt* (*aguardar*) to wait for; (*tener expectativa de*) to expect; (*desear*) to hope for ▷ *vi* to wait; to expect; to hope; **hacer ~ a algn** to keep sb waiting; **~ un bebé** to be expecting (a baby)

esperma [es'perma] *nf* sperm

espeso, -a [es'peso, a] *adj* thick; **espesor** *nm* thickness

espía [es'pia] *nmf* spy; **espiar** /1c/ *vt* (*observar*) to spy on

espiga [es'piɣa] *nf* (*Bot: de trigo etc*) ear

espigón [espi'ɣon] *nm* (*Bot*) ear; (*Naut*) breakwater

espina [es'pina] *nf* thorn; (*de pez*) bone; **~ dorsal** (*Anat*) spine

espinaca [espi'naka] *nf* spinach

espinazo [espi'naθo] *nm* spine, backbone

espinilla [espi'niʎa] *nf* (*Anat: tibia*) shin(bone); (: *en la piel*) blackhead

espinoso, -a [espi'noso, a] *adj* (*planta*) thorny, prickly; (*asunto*) difficult

espionaje [espjo'naxe] *nm* spying, espionage

espiral [espi'ral] *adj*, *nf* spiral

espirar [espi'rar] /1a/ *vt* to breathe out, exhale

espiritista [espiri'tista] *adj*, *nmf* spiritualist

espíritu [es'piritu] *nm* spirit; **E~ Santo** Holy Ghost; **espiritual** *adj* spiritual

espléndido, -a [es'plendiðo, a] *adj* (*magnífico*) magnificent, splendid; (*generoso*) generous

esplendor [esplen'dor] *nm* splendour

espolvorear [espolβore'ar] /1a/ *vt* to dust, sprinkle

esponja [es'ponxa] *nf* sponge; (*fig*) sponger; **esponjoso, -a** *adj* spongy

espontaneidad [espontanei'ðað] *nf* spontaneity; **espontáneo, -a** *adj* spontaneous

esposa [es'posa] *nf* V **esposo**; **esposar** /1a/ *vt* to handcuff

esposo, -a [es'poso, a] *nm* husband ▷ *nf* wife; **esposas** *nfpl* handcuffs

espray [es'prai] *nm* spray

espuela [es'pwela] *nf* spur

espuma [es'puma] *nf* foam; (*de cerveza*) froth, head; (*de jabón*) lather; **~ de afeitar** shaving foam; **espumadera** *nf* skimmer; **espumoso, -a** *adj* frothy, foamy; (*vino*) sparkling

esqueleto [eske'leto] *nm* skeleton

esquema [es'kema] *nm* (*diagrama*) diagram; (*dibujo*) plan; (*Filosofía*) schema

esquí [es'ki] (*pl* **esquís**) *nm* (*objeto*) ski; (*deporte*) skiing; **~ acuático** water-skiing; **esquiar** /1c/ *vi* to ski

esquilar [eski'lar] /1a/ *vt* to shear

esquimal [eski'mal] *adj*, *nmf* Eskimo

esquina [es'kina] *nf* corner; **esquinazo** *nm*: **dar esquinazo a algn** to give sb the slip

esquirol [eski'rol] *nm* (*ESP*) strikebreaker, blackleg

esquivar [eski'βar] /1a/ *vt* to avoid

esta ['esta] *adj demostrativo*, *pron* V **este¹**

está [es'ta] *vb* V **estar**

ésta ['esta] *pron* V **éste**

estabilidad [estaβili'ðað] *nf* stability; **estable** *adj* stable

establecer [estaβle'θer] /2d/ *vt* to establish; **establecerse** *vr* to establish o.s.; (*echar raíces*) to settle (down); **establecimiento** *nm* establishment

establo [es'taβlo] *nm* (*Agr*) stall; (*para vacas*) cowshed; (*para caballos*) stable; (*esp LAM*) barn

estaca [es'taka] *nf* stake, post; (*de tienda de campaña*) peg

estacada [esta'kaða] *nf* (*cerca*) fence, fencing; (*palenque*) stockade

estación [esta'θjon] *nf* station; (*del año*) season; **~ de autobuses/ ferrocarril** bus/railway station; **~ balnearia (de turistas)** seaside resort; **~ de servicio** service station

estacionamiento [estaθjona'mjento] *nm* (*Auto*) parking; (*Mil*) stationing

estacionar [estaθjo'nar] /1a/ *vt* (*Auto*) to park; (*Mil*) to station

estada [es'taða], **estadía** [esta'ðia] *nf* (*LAM*) stay

estadio [es'taðjo] *nm* (*fase*) stage, phase; (*Deporte*) stadium

estadista [esta'ðista] *nm* (*Pol*) statesman; (*Estadística*) statistician

estadística [esta'ðistika] *nf* figure, statistic; (*ciencia*) statistics *sg*

estado [es'taðo] *nm* (*Pol: condición*) state; **~ civil** marital status; **~ de ánimo** state of mind; **~ de cuenta(s)** bank statement; **~ mayor** staff; **E~s Unidos (EE.UU.)** United States (of America) (USA); **estar en ~ (de buena esperanza)** to be pregnant

estadounidense [estaðouni'ðense] *adj* United States *cpd*, American ▷ *nmf* American

estafa [es'tafa] *nf* swindle, trick; **estafar** /1a/ *vt* to swindle, defraud

estáis *vb* V **estar**

estallar [esta'ʎar] /1a/ *vi* to burst; (*bomba*) to explode, go off; (*epidemia, guerra, rebelión*) to break out; **~ en llanto** to burst into tears; **estallido** *nm* explosion; (*fig*) outbreak

estampa [es'tampa] *nf* print, engraving; **estampado, -a** *adj* printed ▷ *nm* (*dibujo*) print; (*impresión*) printing; **estampar** /1a/ *vt* (*imprimir*) to print; (*marcar*) to stamp; (*metal*) to engrave; (*poner sello en*) to stamp; (*fig*) to stamp, imprint

estampida [estam'piða] *nf*
stampede
estampido [estam'piðo] *nm* bang,
report
estampilla [estam'piʎa] *nf* (LAM)
(postage) stamp
están [es'tan] *vb* V **estar**
estancado, -a [estan'kaðo, a] *adj*
stagnant
estancar [estan'kar] /1g/ *vt* (aguas)
to hold up, hold back; (Com) to
monopolize; (fig) to block, hold up;
estancarse *vr* to stagnate
estancia [es'tanθja] *nf* (permanencia)
stay; (sala) room; (LAM) farm, ranch;
estanciero *nm* (LAM) farmer, rancher
estanco, -a [es'tanko, a] *adj*
watertight ▷ *nm* tobacconist's (shop)

○ **ESTANCO**
○
○ Cigarettes, tobacco, postage
○ stamps and official forms are all sold
○ under state monopoly and usually
○ through a shop called an *estanco*.
○ Tobacco products are also sold in
○ *quioscos* and bars but are generally
○ more expensive. The number of
○ *estanco* licences is regulated by
○ the state.

estándar [es'tandar] *adj, nm*
standard
estandarte [estan'darte] *nm* banner,
standard
estanque [es'tanke] *nm* (lago) pool,
pond; (Agr) reservoir
estanquero, -a [estan'kero, a] *nm/f*
tobacconist
estante [es'tante] *nm* (armario) rack,
stand; (biblioteca) bookcase; (anaquel)
shelf; **estantería** *nf* shelving,
shelves *pl*

PALABRA CLAVE

estar [es'tar] /1o/ *vi* **1** (posición) to be;
está en la plaza it's in the square;
¿**está Juan?** is Juan in?; **estamos a 30
km de Junín** we're 30 km from Junín
2 (+ adj o adv: estado) to be; **estar
enfermo** to be ill; **está muy elegante**
he's looking very smart; ¿**cómo
estás?** how are you keeping?
3 (+ gerundio) to be; **estoy leyendo**
I'm reading
4 (uso pasivo): **está condenado a
muerte** he's been condemned to
death; **está envasado en …** it's
packed in …
5: **estar a**: ¿**a cuántos estamos?**
what's the date today?; **estamos a 9
de mayo** it's the 9th of May
6 (locuciones): ¿**estamos?** (¿de
acuerdo?) okay?; (¿listo?) ready?
7: **estar con**: **está con gripe** he's
got (the) flu
8: **estar de**: **estar de vacaciones/
viaje** to be on holiday/away o on a
trip; **está de camarero** he's working
as a waiter
9: **estar para**: **está para salir**
he's about to leave; **no estoy para
bromas** I'm not in the mood for jokes
10: **estar por** (propuesta etc) to be in
favour of; (persona etc) to support, side
with; **está por limpiar** it still has to
be cleaned
11: **estar sin**: **estar sin dinero** to have
no money; **está sin terminar** it isn't
finished yet
▶ **estarse** *vr*: **se estuvo en la cama
toda la tarde** he stayed in bed all
afternoon

estas ['estas] *adj demostrativo, pron*
V **este¹**
éstas ['estas] *pron* V **éste**
estatal [esta'tal] *adj* state *cpd*
estático, -a [es'tatiko, a] *adj* static
estatua [es'tatwa] *nf* statue
estatura [esta'tura] *nf* stature,
height
este¹ ['este] *nm* east
este² ['este], **esta** ['esta], **estos**
['estos], **estas** ['estas] *adj*

demostrativo this sg, these pl ▷ pron this (one) sg, these (ones) pl

esté [es'te] vb V **estar**

éste ['este], **ésta** ['esta], **éstos** ['estos], **éstas** ['estas] pron this (one) sg, these (ones) pl; **ése ... ~ ...** the former ... the latter ...

estén [es'ten] vb V **estar**

estepa [es'tepa] nf (Geo) steppe

estera [es'tera] nf matting

estéreo [es'tereo] adj inv, nm stereo; **estereotipo** nm stereotype

estéril [es'teril] adj sterile, barren; (fig) vain, futile; **esterilizar** /1f/ vt to sterilize

esterlina [ester'lina] adj: **libra ~** pound sterling

estés [es'tes] vb V **estar**

estético, -a [es'tetiko, a] adj aesthetic ▷ nf aesthetics sg

estiércol [es'tjerkol] nm dung, manure

estigma [es'tiɣma] nm stigma

estilo [es'tilo] nm style; (Tec) stylus; (Natación) stroke; **algo por el ~** something along those lines

estima [es'tima] nf esteem, respect

estimación [estima'θjon] nf (evaluación) estimation; (aprecio, afecto) esteem, regard

estimar [esti'mar] /1a/ vt (evaluar) to estimate; (valorar) to value; (apreciar) to esteem, respect; (pensar, considerar) to think, reckon

estimulante [estimu'lante] adj stimulating ▷ nm stimulant

estimular [estimu'lar] /1a/ vt to stimulate; (excitar) to excite

estímulo [es'timulo] nm stimulus; (ánimo) encouragement

estirar [esti'rar] /1a/ vt to stretch; (dinero, suma etc) to stretch out; **estirarse** vr to stretch

estirón [esti'ron] nm pull, tug; (crecimiento) spurt, sudden growth; **dar un ~** (niño) to shoot up

estirpe [es'tirpe] nf stock, lineage

estival [esti'βal] adj summer cpd

esto ['esto] pron this, this thing o matter; **~ de la boda** this business about the wedding

Estocolmo [esto'kolmo] nm Stockholm

estofado [esto'faðo] nm stew

estómago [es'tomaɣo] nm stomach; **tener ~** to be thick-skinned

estorbar [estor'βar] /1a/ vt to hinder, obstruct; (fig) to bother, disturb ▷ vi to be in the way; **estorbo** nm (molestia) bother, nuisance; (obstáculo) hindrance, obstacle

estornudar [estornu'ðar] /1a/ vi to sneeze

estos ['estos] adj demostrativo V **este¹**

éstos ['estos] pron V **éste**

estoy [es'toi] vb V **estar**

estrado [es'traðo] nm platform

estrafalario, -a [estrafa'larjo, a] adj odd, eccentric

estrago [es'traɣo] nm ruin, destruction; **hacer ~s en** to wreak havoc among

estragón [estra'ɣon] nm tarragon

estrambótico, -a [estram'botiko, a] adj odd, eccentric; (peinado, ropa) outlandish

estrangular [estrangu'lar] /1a/ vt (persona) to strangle; (Med) to strangulate

estratagema [estrata'xema] nf (Mil) stratagem; (astucia) cunning

estrategia [estra'texja] nf strategy; **estratégico, -a** adj strategic

estrato [es'trato] nm stratum, layer

estrechar [estre'tʃar] /1a/ vt (reducir) to narrow; (vestido) to take in; (persona) to hug, embrace; **estrecharse** vr (reducirse) to narrow, grow narrow; (2 personas) to embrace; **~ la mano** to shake hands

estrechez [estre'tʃeθ] nf narrowness; (de ropa) tightness; **estrecheces** nfpl financial difficulties

estrecho, -a [es'tretʃo, a] adj narrow; (apretado) tight; (íntimo) close,

intimate; (*miserable*) mean ▷ *nm* strait;
~ de miras narrow-minded

estrella [es'treʎa] *nf* star; **~ fugaz**
shooting star; **~ de mar** starfish

estrellar [estre'ʎar] /1a/ *vt* (*hacer
añicos*) to smash (to pieces); (*huevos*) to
fry; **estrellarse** *vr* to smash; (*chocarse*)
to crash; (*fracasar*) to fail

estremecer [estreme'θer] /2d/ *vt*
to shake; **estremecerse** *vr* to shake,
tremble

estrenar [estre'nar] /1a/ *vt* (*vestido*)
to wear for the first time; (*casa*) to
move into; (*película, obra de teatro*) to
première; **estrenarse** *vr* (*persona*) to
make one's début; **estreno** *nm* (*Cine
etc*) première

estreñido, -a [estre'niðo, a] *adj*
constipated

estreñimiento [estreni'mjento] *nm*
constipation

estrepitoso, -a [estrepi'toso, a] *adj*
noisy; (*fiesta*) rowdy

estrés [es'tres] *nm* stress

estría [es'tria] *nf* groove

estribar [estri'βar] /1a/ *vi*: **~ en** to
rest on

estribillo [estri'βiʎo] *nm* (*Lit*) refrain;
(*Mus*) chorus

estribo [es'triβo] *nm* (*de jinete*)
stirrup; (*de coche, tren*) step; (*de puente*)
support; (*Geo*) spur; **perder los ~s** to
fly off the handle

estribor [estri'βor] *nm* (*Naut*)
starboard

estricto, -a [es'trikto, a] *adj* (*riguroso*)
strict; (*severo*) severe

estridente [estri'ðente] *adj* (*color*)
loud; (*voz*) raucous

estropajo [estro'paxo] *nm* scourer

estropear [estrope'ar] /1a/ *vt* to
spoil; (*dañar*) to damage; **estropearse**
vr (*objeto*) to get damaged; (*la piel etc*)
to be ruined

estructura [estruk'tura] *nf* structure

estrujar [estru'xar] /1a/ *vt* (*apretar*)
to squeeze; (*aplastar*) to crush; (*fig*) to
drain, bleed

estuario [es'twarjo] *nm* estuary

estuche [es'tutʃe] *nm* box, case

estudiante [estu'ðjante] *nmf*
student; **estudiantil** *adj inv* student
cpd

estudiar [estu'ðjar] /1b/ *vt* to study

estudio [es'tuðjo] *nm* study; (*Cine,
Arte, Radio*) studio; **estudios** *nmpl*
studies; (*erudición*) learning *sg*;
estudioso, -a *adj* studious

estufa [es'tufa] *nf* heater, fire

estupefaciente [estupefa'θjente]
nm narcotic

estupefacto, -a [estupe'fakto, a]
adj speechless, thunderstruck

estupendo, -a [estu'pendo, a] *adj*
wonderful, terrific; (*fam*) great; **¡~!**
that's great!, fantastic!

estupidez [estupi'ðeθ] *nf* (*torpeza*)
stupidity; (*acto*) stupid thing (to do)

estúpido, -a [es'tupiðo, a] *adj*
stupid, silly

estuve *etc* [es'tuβe] *vb* V **estar**

ETA ['eta] *nf abr* (*Pol*: = *Euskadi Ta
Askatasuna*) ETA

etapa [e'tapa] *nf* (*de viaje*) stage;
(*Deporte*) leg; (*parada*) stopping place;
(*fig*) stage, phase

etarra [e'tarra] *nmf* member of ETA

etc. *abr* (= *etcétera*) etc

etcétera [et'θetera] *adv* etcetera

eternidad [eterni'ðað] *nf* eternity;
eterno, -a *adj* eternal, everlasting;
(*despectivo*) never-ending

ético, -a ['etiko, a] *adj* ethical ▷ *nf*
ethics

etiqueta [eti'keta] *nf* (*modales*)
etiquette; (*rótulo*) label, tag

Eucaristía [eukaris'tia] *nf* Eucharist

euforia [eu'forja] *nf* euphoria

euro ['euro] *nm* (*moneda*) euro

eurodiputado, -a [euroðipu'taðo,
a] *nm/f* Euro MP, MEP

Europa [eu'ropa] *nf* Europe; **europeo,
-a** *adj, nm/f* European

Euskadi [eus'kaði] *nm* the Basque
Provinces *pl*

euskera [eus'kera] *nm* (*Ling*) Basque

evacuación [eβakwa'θjon] *nf* evacuation

evacuar [eβa'kwar] /1d/ *vt* to evacuate

evadir [eβa'ðir] /3a/ *vt* to evade, avoid; **evadirse** *vr* to escape

evaluar [eβa'lwar] /1e/ *vt* to evaluate

evangelio [eβan'xeljo] *nm* gospel

evaporar [eβapo'rar] /1a/ *vt* to evaporate; **evaporarse** *vr* to vanish

evasión [eβa'sjon] *nf* escape, flight; *(fig)* evasion; **~ de capitales** flight of capital

evasivo, -a [eβa'siβo, a] *adj* evasive ▷ *nf (pretexto)* excuse; **contestar con evasivas** to avoid giving a straight answer

evento [e'βento] *nm* event

eventual [eβen'twal] *adj* possible, conditional (upon circumstances); *(trabajador)* casual, temporary

■ No confundir *eventual* con la palabra inglesa *eventual*.

evidencia [eβi'ðenθja] *nf* evidence, proof

evidente [eβi'ðente] *adj* obvious, clear, evident

evitar [eβi'tar] /1a/ *vt (evadir)* to avoid; *(impedir)* to prevent; **~ hacer algo** to avoid doing sth

evocar [eβo'kar] /1g/ *vt* to evoke, call forth

evolución [eβolu'θjon] *nf* *(desarrollo)* evolution, development; *(cambio)* change; *(Mil)* manoeuvre; **evolucionar** /1a/ *vi* to evolve; *(Mil, Aviat)* to manoeuvre

ex [eks] *adj* ex-; **el ex ministro** the former minister, the ex-minister

exactitud [eksakti'tuð] *nf* exactness; *(precisión)* accuracy; *(puntualidad)* punctuality; **exacto, -a** *adj* exact; accurate; punctual; **¡exacto!** exactly!

exageración [eksaxera'θjon] *nf* exaggeration

exagerar [eksaxe'rar] /1a/ *vt* to exaggerate

exaltar [eksal'tar] /1a/ *vt* to exalt, glorify; **exaltarse** *vr (excitarse)* to get excited o worked up

examen [ek'samen] *nm* examination; **~ de conducir** driving test; **~ de ingreso** entrance examination

examinar [eksami'nar] /1a/ *vt* to examine; **examinarse** *vr* to be examined, take an examination

excavadora [ekskaβa'ðora] *nf* digger

excavar [ekska'βar] /1a/ *vt* to excavate

excedencia [eksθe'ðenθja] *nf (Mil)* leave; **estar en ~** to be on leave; **pedir o solicitar la ~** to ask for leave

excedente [eksθe'ðente] *adj, nm* excess, surplus

exceder [eksθe'ðer] /2a/ *vt* to exceed, surpass; **excederse** *vr (extralimitarse)* to go too far

excelencia [eksθe'lenθja] *nf* excellence; **E~** Excellency; **excelente** *adj* excellent

excéntrico, -a [eks'θentriko, a] *adj, nm/f* eccentric

excepción [eksθep'θjon] *nf* exception; **a ~ de** with the exception of, except for; **excepcional** *adj* exceptional

excepto [eks'θepto] *adv* excepting, except (for)

exceptuar [eksθep'twar] /1e/ *vt* to except, exclude

excesivo, -a [eksθe'siβo, a] *adj* excessive

exceso [eks'θeso] *nm* excess; *(Com)* surplus; **~ de equipaje/peso** excess luggage/weight; **~ de velocidad** speeding

excitado, -a [eksθi'taðo, a] *adj* excited; *(emociones)* aroused

excitar [eksθi'tar] /1a/ *vt* to excite; *(incitar)* to urge; **excitarse** *vr* to get excited

exclamación [eksklama'θjon] *nf* exclamation

exclamar [ekskla'mar] /1a/ *vi* to exclaim

excluir [eksklu'ir] /3g/ *vt* to exclude; (*dejar fuera*) to shut out; (*solución*) to reject

exclusiva [eksklu'siβa] *nf* V **exclusivo**

exclusivo, -a [eksklu'siβo, a] *adj* exclusive; (*Prensa*) exclusive, scoop; (*Com*) sole right o agency; **derecho ~** sole o exclusive right

Excmo. *abr* (= *Excelentísimo*) *courtesy title*

excomulgar [ekskomul'ɣar] /1h/ *vt* (*Rel*) to excommunicate

excomunión [ekskomu'njon] *nf* excommunication

excursión [ekskur'sjon] *nf* excursion, outing; **excursionista** *nmf* (*turista*) sightseer

excusa [eks'kusa] *nf* excuse; (*disculpa*) apology; **excusar** /1a/ *vt* to excuse

exhaustivo, -a [eksaus'tiβo, a] *adj* (*análisis*) thorough; (*estudio*) exhaustive

exhausto, -a [ek'sausto, a] *adj* exhausted

exhibición [eksiβi'θjon] *nf* exhibition; (*demostración*) display, show

exhibir [eksi'βir] /3a/ *vt* to exhibit; to display, show

exigencia [eksi'xenθja] *nf* demand, requirement; **exigente** *adj* demanding

exigir [eksi'xir] /3c/ *vt* (*gen*) to demand, require; **~ el pago** to demand payment

exiliado, -a [eksi'ljaðo, a] *adj* exiled ▷ *nm/f* exile

exilio [ek'siljo] *nm* exile

eximir [eksi'mir] /3a/ *vt* to exempt

existencia [eksis'tenθja] *nf* existence; **existencias** *nfpl* stock *sg*

existir [eksis'tir] /3a/ *vi* to exist, be

éxito ['eksito] *nm* (*triunfo*) success; (*Mus, Teat*) hit; **tener ~** to be successful

No confundir *éxito* con la palabra inglesa *exit*.

exorbitante [eksorβi'tante] *adj* (*precio*) exorbitant; (*cantidad*) excessive

exótico, -a [ek'sotiko, a] *adj* exotic

expandir [ekspan'dir] /3a/ *vt* to expand

expansión [ekspan'sjon] *nf* expansion

expansivo, -a [ekspan'siβo, a] *adj*: **onda expansiva** shock wave

expatriarse [ekspa'trjarse] /1b/ *vr* to emigrate; (*Pol*) to go into exile

expectativa [ekspekta'tiβa] *nf* (*espera*) expectation; (*perspectiva*) prospect

expedición [ekspeði'θjon] *nf* (*excursión*) expedition

expediente [ekspe'ðjente] *nm* expedient; (*Jur: procedimiento*) action, proceedings *pl*; (*: papeles*) dossier, file, record

expedir [ekspe'ðir] /3k/ *vt* (*despachar*) to send, forward; (*pasaporte*) to issue

expensas [eks'pensas] *nfpl*: **a ~ de** at the expense of

experiencia [ekspe'rjenθja] *nf* experience

experimentado, -a [eksperimen'taðo, a] *adj* experienced

experimentar [eksperimen'tar] /1a/ *vt* (*en laboratorio*) to experiment with; (*probar*) to test, try out; (*notar, observar*) to experience; (*deterioro, pérdida*) to suffer; **experimento** *nm* experiment

experto, -a [eks'perto, a] *adj* expert ▷ *nm/f* expert

expirar [ekspi'rar] /1a/ *vi* to expire

explanada [ekspla'naða] *nf* (*paseo*) esplanade

explayarse [ekspla'jarse] /1a/ *vr* (*en discurso*) to speak at length; **~ con algn** to confide in sb

explicación [eksplika'θjon] *nf* explanation

explicar [ekspli'kar] /1g/ *vt* to explain; **explicarse** *vr* to explain (o.s.)

explícito, -a [eks'pliθito, a] *adj*
explicit

explique *etc* [eks'plike] *vb V* **explicar**

explorador, a [eksplora'ðor, a] *nm/f*
(*pionero*) explorer; (*Mil*) scout ▷ *nm*
(*Med*) probe; (*radar*) (radar) scanner

explorar [eksplo'rar] /1a/ *vt* to
explore; (*Med*) to probe; (*radar*) to scan

explosión [eksplo'sjon] *nf* explosion;
explosivo, -a *adj* explosive

explotación [eksplota'θjon] *nf*
exploitation; (*de planta etc*) running

explotar [eksplo'tar] /1a/ *vt* to
exploit; (*planta*) to run, operate ▷ *vi*
to explode

exponer [ekspo'ner] /2q/ *vt* to
expose; (*cuadro*) to display; (*vida*) to
risk; (*idea*) to explain; **exponerse** *vr*:
~se a (hacer) algo to run the risk of
(doing) sth

exportación [eksporta'θjon]
nf (*acción*) export; (*mercancías*)
exports *pl*

exportar [ekspor'tar] /1a/ *vt* to
export

exposición [eksposi'θjon] *nf* (*gen*)
exposure; (*de arte*) show, exhibition;
(*explicación*) explanation; (*narración*)
account, statement

expresamente [ekspresa'mente]
adv (*decir*) clearly; (*concretamente*)
expressly

expresar [ekspre'sar] /1a/ *vt* to
express; **expresión** *nf* expression

expresivo, -a [ekspre'siβo, a] *adj*
expressive; (*cariñoso*) affectionate

expreso, -a [eks'preso, a] *adj*
(*explícito*) express; (*claro*) specific,
clear; (*tren*) fast

express [eks'pres] *adv* (LAM): **enviar
algo ~** to send sth special delivery

exprimidor [eksprimi'ðor] *nm*
(lemon) squeezer

exprimir [ekspri'mir] /3a/ *vt* (*fruta*)
to squeeze; (*zumo*) to squeeze out

expuesto, -a [eks'pwesto, a] *pp de*
exponer ▷ *adj* exposed; (*cuadro etc*) on
show, on display

expulsar [ekspul'sar] /1a/ *vt* (*echar*)
to eject, throw out; (*alumno*) to expel;
(*despedir*) to sack, fire; (*Deporte*) to
send off; **expulsión** *nf* expulsion;
sending-off

exquisito, -a [ekski'sito, a] *adj*
exquisite; (*comida*) delicious

éxtasis ['ekstasis] *nm* ecstasy

extender [eksten'der] /2g/ *vt* to
extend; (*los brazos*) to stretch out,
hold out; (*mapa, tela*) to spread (out),
open (out); (*mantequilla*) to spread;
(*certificado*) to issue; (*cheque, recibo*)
to make out; (*documento*) to draw up;
extenderse *vr* to extend; (*persona:
en el suelo*) to stretch out; (*costumbre,
epidemia*) to spread; **extendido,
-a** *adj* (*abierto*) spread out, open;
(*brazos*) outstretched; (*costumbre etc*)
widespread

extensión [eksten'sjon] *nf* (*de
terreno, mar*) expanse, stretch; (*de
tiempo*) length, duration; (*Telec*)
extension; **en toda la ~ de la palabra**
in every sense of the word

extenso, -a [eks'tenso, a] *adj*
extensive

exterior [ekste'rjor] *adj* (*de
fuera*) external; (*afuera*) outside,
exterior; (*apariencia*) outward;
(*deuda, relaciones*) foreign ▷ *nm*
exterior, outside; (*aspecto*) outward
appearance; (*Deporte*) wing(er);
(*países extranjeros*) abroad; **al ~**
outwardly, on the outside

exterminar [ekstermi'nar] /1a/ *vt* to
exterminate

externo, -a [eks'terno, a] *adj*
(*exterior*) external, outside; (*superficial*)
outward ▷ *nm/f* day pupil

extinguir [ekstin'gir] /3d/ *vt* (*fuego*)
to extinguish, put out; (*raza, población*)
to wipe out; **extinguirse** *vr* (*fuego*) to
go out; (*Bio*) to die out, become extinct

extintor [ekstin'tor] *nm* (fire)
extinguisher

extirpar [ekstir'par] /1a/ *vt* (*Med*) to
remove (surgically)

extra ['ekstra] adj inv (tiempo) extra; (vino) vintage; (chocolate) good-quality ▷ nmf extra ▷ nm extra; (bono) bonus

extracción [ekstrak'θjon] nf extraction; (en lotería) draw

extracto [eks'trakto] nm extract

extradición [ekstraði'θjon] nf extradition

extraer [ekstra'er] /2o/ vt to extract, take out

extraescolar [ekstraesko'lar] adj: **actividad ~** extracurricular activity

extranjero, -a [ekstran'xero, a] adj foreign ▷ nm/f foreigner ▷ nm foreign countries pl; **en el ~** abroad

No confundir extranjero con la palabra inglesa stranger.

extrañar [ekstra'ɲar] /1a/ vt (sorprender) to find strange o odd; (echar de menos) to miss; **extrañarse** vr (sorprenderse) to be amazed, be surprised; **me extraña** I'm surprised

extraño, -a [eks'traɲo, a] adj (extranjero) foreign; (raro, sorprendente) strange, odd

extraordinario, -a [ekstraorði'narjo, a] adj extraordinary; (edición, número) special ▷ nm (de periódico) special edition; **horas extraordinarias** overtime sg

extrarradio [ekstra'rraðjo] nm suburbs pl

extravagante [ekstraβa'ɣante] adj (excéntrico) eccentric; (estrafalario) outlandish

extraviado, -a [ekstra'βjaðo, a] adj lost, missing

extraviar [ekstra'βjar] /1c/ vt to mislead, misdirect; (perder) to lose, misplace; **extraviarse** vr to lose one's way, get lost

extremar [ekstre'mar] /1a/ vt to carry to extremes

extremaunción [ekstremaun'θjon] nf extreme unction

extremidad [ekstremi'ðað] nf (punta) extremity; **extremidades** nfpl (Anat) extremities

extremo, -a [eks'tremo, a] adj extreme; (último) last ▷ nm end; (situación) extreme; **en último ~** as a last resort

extrovertido, -a [ekstroβer'tiðo, a] adj ▷ nm/f extrovert

exuberante [eksuβe'rante] adj exuberant; (fig) luxuriant, lush

eyacular [ejaku'lar] /1a/ vt, vi to ejaculate

f

fa [fa] *nm* (*Mus*) F

fabada [fa'βaða] *nf* bean and sausage stew

fábrica ['faβrika] *nf* factory; **marca de ~** trademark; **precio de ~** factory price

> No confundir *fábrica* con la palabra inglesa *fabric*.

fabricación [faβrika'θjon] *nf* (*manufactura*) manufacture; (*producción*) production; **de ~ casera** home-made; **~ en serie** mass production

fabricante [faβri'kante] *nmf* manufacturer

fabricar [faβri'kar] /1g/ *vt* (*manufacturar*) to manufacture, make; (*construir*) to build; (*cuento*) to fabricate, devise

fábula ['faβula] *nf* (*cuento*) fable; (*chisme*) rumour; (*mentira*) fib

fabuloso, -a [faβu'loso, a] *adj* fabulous, fantastic

facción [fak'θjon] *nf* (*Pol*) faction; **facciones** *nfpl* (*del rostro*) features

faceta [fa'θeta] *nf* facet

facha ['fatʃa] (*fam*) *nf* (*aspecto*) look; (*cara*) face

fachada [fa'tʃaða] *nf* (*Arq*) façade, front

fácil ['faθil] *adj* (*simple*) easy; (*probable*) likely

facilidad [faθili'ðað] *nf* (*capacidad*) ease; (*sencillez*) simplicity; (*de palabra*) fluency; **facilidades** *nfpl* facilities; **"~es de pago"** "credit facilities"

facilitar [faθili'tar] /1a/ *vt* (*hacer fácil*) to make easy; (*proporcionar*) to provide

factor [fak'tor] *nm* factor

factura [fak'tura] *nf* (*cuenta*) bill; **facturación** *nf*: **facturación de equipajes** luggage check-in; **facturar** /1a/ *vt* (*Com*) to invoice, charge for; (*Aviat*) to check in

facultad [fakul'tað] *nf* (*aptitud, Escol etc*) faculty; (*poder*) power

faena [fa'ena] *nf* (*trabajo*) work; (*quehacer*) task, job

faisán [fai'san] *nm* pheasant

faja ['faxa] *nf* (*para la cintura*) sash; (*de mujer*) corset; (*de tierra*) strip

fajo ['faxo] *nm* (*de papeles*) bundle; (*de billetes*) wad

falda ['falda] *nf* (*prenda de vestir*) skirt; **~ pantalón** culottes *pl*, split skirt

falla ['faʎa] *nf* (*defecto*) fault, flaw; **~ humana** (*LAM*) human error

fallar [fa'ʎar] /1a/ *vt* (*Jur*) to pronounce sentence on; (*Naipes*) to trump ▷ *vi* (*memoria*) to fail; (*plan*) to go wrong; (*motor*) to miss; **~ a algn** to let sb down

Fallas ['faʎas] *nfpl see note* **"Fallas"**

○ **FALLAS**
○
○ In the week of the 19th of March
○ (the feast of St Joseph, San José),
○ Valencia honours its patron
○ saint with a spectacular *fiesta*
○ called *las Fallas*. The *Fallas* are

- huge sculptures, made of wood,
- cardboard, paper and cloth,
- depicting famous politicians and
- other targets for ridicule, which are
- set alight and burned by the *falleros*,
- members of the competing local
- groups who have just spent months
- preparing them.

fallecer [faʎe'θer] /2d/ *vi* to pass away, die; **fallecimiento** *nm* decease, demise

fallido, -a [fa'ʎiðo, a] *adj* frustrated, unsuccessful

fallo ['faʎo] *nm* (*Jur*) verdict, ruling; (*fracaso*) failure; **~ cardíaco** heart failure; **~ humano** (ESP) human error

falsificar [falsifi'kar] /1g/ *vt* (*firma etc*) to forge; (*moneda*) to counterfeit

falso, -a ['falso, a] *adj* false; (*moneda etc*) fake; **en ~** falsely

falta ['falta] *nf* (*defecto*) fault, flaw; (*privación*) lack, want; (*ausencia*) absence; (*carencia*) shortage; (*equivocación*) mistake; (*Deporte*) foul; **echar en ~** to miss; **hacer ~ hacer algo** to be necessary to do sth; **me hace ~ una pluma** I need a pen; **~ de educación** bad manners *pl*; **~ de ortografía** spelling mistake

faltar [fal'tar] /1a/ *vi* (*escasear*) to be lacking, be wanting; (*ausentarse*) to be absent, be missing; **faltan dos horas para llegar** there are two hours to go till arrival; **~ (al respeto) a algn** to be disrespectful to sb; **¡no faltaba más!** (*no hay de qué*) don't mention it!

fama ['fama] *nf* (*renombre*) fame; (*reputación*) reputation

familia [fa'milja] *nf* family; **~ numerosa** large family; **~ política** in-laws *pl*

familiar [fami'ljar] *adj* (*relativo a la familia*) family *cpd*; (*conocido, informal*) familiar ▷ *nmf* relative, relation

famoso, -a [fa'moso, a] *adj* famous ▷ *nm/f* celebrity

fan [fan] (*pl* **fans**) *nm* fan

fanático, -a [fa'natiko, a] *adj* fanatical ▷ *nm/f* fanatic; (*Cine, Deporte etc*) fan

fanfarrón, -ona [fanfa'rron, ona] *adj* boastful

fango ['fango] *nm* mud

fantasía [fanta'sia] *nf* fantasy, imagination; **joyas de ~** imitation jewellery *sg*

fantasma [fan'tasma] *nm* (*espectro*) ghost, apparition; (*presumido*) show-off

fantástico, -a [fan'tastiko, a] *adj* fantastic

farmacéutico, -a [farma'θeutiko, a] *adj* pharmaceutical ▷ *nm/f* chemist (BRIT), pharmacist

farmacia [far'maθja] *nf* chemist's (shop) (BRIT), pharmacy; **~ de guardia** all-night chemist

fármaco ['farmako] *nm* drug

faro ['faro] *nm* (*Naut: torre*) lighthouse; (*Auto*) headlamp; **~s antiniebla** fog lamps; **~s delanteros/traseros** headlights/rear lights

farol [fa'rol] *nm* lantern, lamp

farola [fa'rola] *nf* street lamp (BRIT) o light (US)

farra ['farra] *nf* (LAM *fam*) party; **ir de ~** to go on a binge

farsa ['farsa] *nf* farce

farsante [far'sante] *nmf* fraud, fake

fascículo [fas'θikulo] *nm* part, instalment (BRIT), installment (US)

fascinar [fasθi'nar] /1a/ *vt* to fascinate

fascismo [fas'θismo] *nm* fascism; **fascista** *adj, nmf* fascist

fase ['fase] *nf* phase

fashion ['faʃon] *adj* (*fam*) trendy

fastidiar [fasti'ðjar] /1b/ *vt* (*disgustar*) to annoy, bother; (*estropear*) to spoil; **fastidiarse** *vr*: **¡que se fastidie!** (*fam*) he'll just have to put up with it!

fastidio [fas'tiðjo] *nm* (*disgusto*) annoyance; **fastidioso, -a** *adj* (*molesto*) annoying

fatal [fa'tal] *adj* (*gen*) fatal; (*desgraciado*) ill-fated; (*fam: malo,* *pésimo)* awful; **fatalidad** *nf (destino)* fate; *(mala suerte)* misfortune

fatiga [fa'tiɣa] *nf (cansancio)* fatigue, weariness

fatigar [fati'ɣar] /1h/ *vt* to tire, weary

fatigoso, -a [fati'ɣoso, a] *adj (que cansa)* tiring

fauna ['fauna] *nf* fauna

favor [fa'βor] *nm* favour (BRIT), favor (US); **haga el ~ de ...** would you be so good as to ..., kindly ...; **por ~** please; **a ~ de** in favo(u)r of; **favorable** *adj* favourable (BRIT), favorable (US)

favorecer [faβore'θer] /2d/ *vt* to favour (BRIT), favor (US); *(vestido etc)* to become, flatter; **este peinado le favorece** this hairstyle suits him

favorito, -a [faβo'rito, a] *adj, nm/f* favourite (BRIT), favorite (US)

fax [faks] *nm inv* fax; **mandar por ~** to fax

fe [fe] *nf (Rel)* faith; *(documento)* certificate; **actuar con buena/mala fe** to act in good/bad faith

febrero [fe'βrero] *nm* February

fecha ['fetʃa] *nf* date; **~ límite** *o* **tope** closing *o* last date; **~ de caducidad** *(de alimentos)* sell-by date; *(de contrato)* expiry date; **con ~ adelantada** postdated; **en ~ próxima** soon; **hasta la ~** to date, so far

fecundo, -a [fe'kundo, a] *adj (fértil)* fertile; *(fig)* prolific; *(productivo)* productive

federación [feðera'θjon] *nf* federation

felicidad [feliθi'ðað] *nf* happiness; **felicidades** *nfpl* best wishes, congratulations; *(en cumpleaños)* happy birthday

felicitación [feliθita'θjon] *nf (tarjeta)* greetings card

felicitar [feliθi'tar] /1a/ *vt* to congratulate

feliz [fe'liθ] *adj* happy

felpudo [fel'puðo] *nm* doormat

femenino, -a [feme'nino, a] *adj* ▷ *nm* feminine

feminista [femi'nista] *adj, nmf* feminist

fenomenal [fenome'nal] *adj* phenomenal

fenómeno [fe'nomeno] *nm* phenomenon; *(fig)* freak, accident ▷ *excl* great!, marvellous!

feo, -a ['feo, a] *adj (gen)* ugly; *(desagradable)* bad, nasty

féretro ['feretro] *nm (ataúd)* coffin; *(sarcófago)* bier

feria ['ferja] *nf (gen)* fair; *(descanso)* holiday, rest day; *(LAM: cambio)* small change; *(LAM: mercado)* village market

feriado, -a [fe'rjaðo, a] *(LAM) nm* (public) holiday

fermentar [fermen'tar] /1a/ *vi* to ferment

feroz [fe'roθ] *adj (cruel)* cruel; *(salvaje)* fierce

férreo, -a ['ferreo, a] *adj* iron *cpd*

ferretería [ferrete'ria] *nf (tienda)* ironmonger's (shop) (BRIT), hardware store; **ferretero** *nm* ironmonger

ferrocarril [ferroka'rril] *nm* railway

ferroviario, -a [ferrovja'rjo, a] *adj* rail *cpd*

ferry ['ferri] *(pl* **ferrys** *o* **ferries)** *nm* ferry

fértil ['fertil] *adj (productivo)* fertile; *(rico)* rich; **fertilidad** *nf (gen)* fertility; *(productividad)* fruitfulness

fervor [fer'βor] *nm* fervour (BRIT), fervor (US)

festejar [feste'xar] /1a/ *vt (celebrar)* to celebrate

festejo [fes'texo] *nm* celebration; **festejos** *nmpl (fiestas)* festivals

festín [fes'tin] *nm* feast, banquet

festival [festi'βal] *nm* festival

festividad [festiβi'ðað] *nf* festivity

festivo, -a [fes'tiβo, a] *adj (de fiesta)* festive; *(Cine, Lit)* humorous; **día ~** holiday

feto ['feto] *nm* foetus

fiable [fi'aβle] *adj (persona)* trustworthy; *(máquina)* reliable

fiambre ['fjambre] nm (Culin) cold meat (BRIT), cold cut (US)

fiambrera [fjam'brera] nf ≈ lunch box

fianza ['fjanθa] nf surety; (Jur): **libertad bajo ~** release on bail

fiar [fi'ar] /1c/ vt (salir garante de) to guarantee; (vender a crédito) to sell on credit; (secreto) to confide ▷ vi: **~ (de)** to trust (in); **fiarse** vr: **~se de** to trust (in), rely on; **~se de algn** to rely on sb

fibra ['fiβra] nf fibre (BRIT), fiber (US); **~ óptica** (Inform) optical fibre (BRIT) o fiber (US)

ficción [fik'θjon] nf fiction

ficha ['fitʃa] nf (Telec) token; (en juegos) counter, marker; (tarjeta) (index) card; **fichaje** nm signing(-up); **fichar** /1a/ vt (archivar) to file, index; (Deporte) to sign (up); **estar fichado** to have a record; **fichero** nm box file; (Inform) file

ficticio, -a [fik'tiθjo, a] adj (imaginario) fictitious; (falso) fabricated

fidelidad [fiðeli'ðað] nf (lealtad) fidelity, loyalty; **alta ~** high fidelity, hi-fi

fideos [fi'ðeos] nmpl noodles

fiebre ['fjeβre] nf (Med) fever; (fig) fever, excitement; **tener ~** to have a temperature; **~ aftosa** foot-and-mouth disease

fiel [fjel] adj (leal) faithful, loyal; (fiable) reliable; (exacto) accurate; **los fieles** nmpl the faithful

fieltro ['fjeltro] nm felt

fiera ['fjera] nf V **fiero**

fiero, -a ['fjero, a] adj (cruel) cruel; (feroz) fierce; (duro) harsh ▷ nf (animal feroz) wild animal o beast; (fig) dragon

fierro ['fjerro] nm (LAM) iron

fiesta ['fjesta] nf party; (de pueblo) festival; **(día de) ~** (public) holiday; **~ mayor** annual festival; **~ patria** (LAM) independence day

○ **FIESTA**
○
○ Fiestas can be official public holidays
○ (such as the Día de la Constitución), or
○ special holidays for each comunidad
○ autónoma, many of which are
○ religious feast days. All over Spain
○ there are also special local fiestas for
○ a patron saint or the Virgin Mary.
○ These often last several days and
○ can include religious processions,
○ carnival parades, bullfights,
○ dancing and feasts of typical local
○ produce.

figura [fi'ɣura] nf (gen) figure; (forma, imagen) shape, form; (Naipes) face card

figurar [fiɣu'rar] /1a/ vt (representar) to represent; (fingir) to feign ▷ vi to figure; **figurarse** vr (imaginarse) to imagine; (suponer) to suppose

fijador [fixa'ðor] nm (Foto etc) fixative; (de pelo) gel

fijar [fi'xar] /1a/ vt (gen) to fix; (estampilla) to affix, stick (on); **fijarse** vr: **~se en** to notice

fijo, -a ['fixo, a] adj (gen) fixed; (firme) firm; (permanente) permanent ▷ adv: **mirar ~** to stare; **teléfono ~** landline

fila ['fila] nf row; (Mil) rank; **~ india** single file; **ponerse en ~** to line up, get into line

filatelia [fila'telja] nf philately, stamp collecting

filete [fi'lete] nm (de carne) fillet steak; (pescado) fillet

filiación [filja'θjon] nf (Pol etc) affiliation

filial [fi'ljal] adj filial ▷ nf subsidiary

Filipinas [fili'pinas] nfpl: **las (Islas) ~** the Philippines; **filipino, -a** adj, nm/f Philippine

filmar [fil'mar] /1a/ vt to film, shoot

filo ['filo] nm (gen) edge; **sacar ~ a** to sharpen; **al ~ del medio día** at about midday; **de doble ~** double-edged

filología [filolo'xia] nf philology; **~ inglesa** (Univ) English Studies

filón [fi'lon] nm (Minería) vein, lode; (fig) gold mine

filosofía [filoso'fia] nf philosophy; **filósofo, -a** nm/f philosopher

filtrar [fil'trar] /1a/ vt, vi to filter, strain; **filtrarse** vr to filter; **filtro** nm (Tec, utensilio) filter

fin [fin] nm end; (objetivo) aim, purpose; **al ~ y al cabo** when all's said and done; **a ~ de** in order to; **por ~** finally; **en ~** in short; **~ de semana** weekend

final [fi'nal] adj final ▷ nm end, conclusion ▷ nf final; **al ~** in the end; **a ~es de** at the end of; **finalidad** nf (propósito) purpose, aim; **finalista** nmf finalist; **finalizar** /1f/ vt to end, finish ▷ vi to end, come to an end; (Inform) to log out o off

financiar [finan'θjar] /1b/ vt to finance; **financiero, -a** adj financial ▷ nm/f financier

finca ['finka] nf (casa de recreo) house in the country; (ESP: bien inmueble) property, land; (LAM: granja) farm

finde ['finde] nm abr (fam: = fin de semana) weekend

fingir [fin'xir] /3c/ vt (simular) to simulate, feign ▷ vi (aparentar) to pretend

finlandés, -esa [finlan'des, esa] adj Finnish ▷ nm/f Finn ▷ nm (Ling) Finnish

Finlandia [fin'landja] nf Finland

fino, -a ['fino, a] adj fine; (delgado) slender; (de buenas maneras) polite, refined; (jerez) fino, dry

firma ['firma] nf signature; (Com) firm, company

firmamento [firma'mento] nm firmament

firmar [fir'mar] /1a/ vt to sign

firme ['firme] adj firm; (estable) stable; (sólido) solid; (constante) steady; (decidido) resolute ▷ nm road (surface); **firmeza** nf firmness; (constancia) steadiness; (solidez) solidity

fiscal [fis'kal] adj fiscal ▷ nm (Jur) public prosecutor; **año ~** tax o fiscal year

fisgonear [fisɣone'ar] /1a/ vt to poke one's nose into ▷ vi to pry, spy

físico, -a ['fisiko, a] adj physical ▷ nm physique ▷ nm/f physicist ▷ nf physics sg

fisura [fi'sura] nf crack; (Med) fracture

flác(c)ido, -a ['flakθiðo, a] adj flabby

flaco, -a ['flako, a] adj (muy delgado) skinny, thin; (débil) weak, feeble

flagrante [fla'ɣrante] adj flagrant

flama ['flama] nf (LAM) flame; **flamable** adj (LAM) flammable

flamante [fla'mante] adj (fam) brilliant; (: nuevo) brand-new

flamenco, -a [fla'menko, a] adj (de Flandes) Flemish; (baile, música) flamenco ▷ nm (baile, música) flamenco; (Zool) flamingo

flamingo [fla'mingo] nm (LAM) flamingo

flan [flan] nm creme caramel

■ No confundir flan con la palabra inglesa flan.

flauta ['flauta] (Mus) nf flute

flecha ['fletʃa] nf arrow

flechazo [fle'tʃaθo] nm: **fue un ~** it was love at first sight

fleco ['fleko] nm fringe

flema ['flema] nm phlegm

flequillo [fle'kiʎo] nm (de pelo) fringe

flexible [flek'siβle] adj flexible

flexión [flek'sjon] nf press-up

flexo ['flekso] nm adjustable table lamp

flirtear [flirte'ar] /1a/ vi to flirt

flojera [flo'xera] nf (LAM): **me da ~** I can't be bothered

flojo, -a ['floxo, a] adj (gen) loose; (sin fuerzas) limp; (débil) weak

flor [flor] nf flower; **a ~ de** on the surface of; **flora** nf flora; **florecer** /2d/ vi (Bot) to flower, bloom; (fig) to flourish; **florería** nf (LAM) florist's (shop); **florero** nm vase; **floristería** nf florist's (shop)

flota ['flota] nf fleet

flotador [flota'ðor] nm (gen) float; (para nadar) rubber ring

flotar [flo'tar] /1a/ *vi* to float; **flote** *nm*: **a flote** afloat; **salir a flote** (*fig*) to get back on one's feet

fluidez [flui'ðeθ] *nf* fluidity; (*fig*) fluency

fluido, -a ['flwiðo, a] *adj* ▷ *nm* fluid

fluir [flu'ir] /3g/ *vi* to flow

flujo ['fluxo] *nm* flow; **~ y re~** ebb and flow

flúor ['fluor] *nm* fluoride

fluorescente [flwores'θente] *adj* fluorescent ▷ *nm* (*tb*: **tubo ~**) fluorescent tube

fluvial [flu'βi'al] *adj* (*navegación, cuenca*) fluvial, river *cpd*

fobia ['fobja] *nf* phobia; **~ a las alturas** fear of heights

foca ['foka] *nf* seal

foco ['foko] *nm* focus; (*Elec*) floodlight; (*Teat*) spotlight; (*LAm*) (light) bulb

fofo, -a ['fofo, a] *adj* soft, spongy; (*músculo*) flabby

fogata [fo'ɣata] *nf* bonfire

fogón [fo'ɣon] *nm* (*de cocina*) ring, burner

folio ['foljo] *nm* (*hoja*) sheet (of paper), page

follaje [fo'ʎaxe] *nm* foliage

folleto [fo'ʎeto] *nm* pamphlet

follón [fo'ʎon] *nm* (*fam: lío*) mess; (: *conmoción*) fuss; **armar un ~** to kick up a fuss

fomentar [fomen'tar] /1a/ *vt* (*Med*) to foment

fonda ['fonda] *nf* ≈ boarding house

fondo ['fondo] *nm* (*de caja etc*) bottom; (*de coche, sala*) back; (*Arte etc*) background; (*reserva*) fund; **fondos** *nmpl* (*Com*) funds, resources; **una investigación a ~** a thorough investigation; **en el ~** at bottom, deep down

fonobuzón [fonoβu'θon] *nm* voice mail

fontanería [fontane'ria] *nf* plumbing; **fontanero** *nm* plumber

footing ['futin] *nm* jogging; **hacer ~** to jog

forastero, -a [foras'tero, a] *nm/f* stranger

forcejear [forθexe'ar] /1a/ *vi* (*luchar*) to struggle

forense [fo'rense] *nmf* pathologist

forma ['forma] *nf* (*figura*) form, shape; (*Med*) fitness; (*método*) way, means; **estar en ~** to be fit; **las ~s** the conventions; **de ~ que ...** so that ...; **de todas ~s** in any case

formación [forma'θjon] *nf* (*gen*) formation; (*enseñanza*) training; **~ profesional** vocational training

formal [for'mal] *adj* (*gen*) formal; (*fig: persona*) serious; (: *de fiar*) reliable; **formalidad** *nf* formality; seriousness; **formalizar** /1f/ *vt* (*Jur*) to formalize; (*situación*) to put in order, regularize; **formalizarse** *vr* (*situación*) to be put in order, be regularized

formar [for'mar] /1a/ *vt* (*componer*) to form, shape; (*constituir*) to make up, constitute; (*Escol*) to train, educate; **formarse** *vr* (*Escol*) to be trained (*o* educated); (*cobrar forma*) to form, take form; (*desarrollarse*) to develop

formatear [formate'ar] /1a/ *vt* to format

formato [for'mato] *nm* format; **sin ~**

formidable [formi'ðaβle] *adj* (*temible*) formidable; (*asombroso*) tremendous

fórmula ['formula] *nf* formula

formulario [formu'larjo] *nm* form

fornido, -a [for'niðo, a] *adj* well-built

foro ['foro] *nm* forum

forrar [fo'rrar] /1a/ *vt* (*abrigo*) to line; (*libro*) to cover; **forro** *nm* (*de cuaderno*) cover; (*costura*) lining; (*de sillón*) upholstery; **forro polar** fleece

fortalecer [fortale'θer] /2d/ *vt* to strengthen

fortaleza [forta'leθa] *nf* (*Mil*) fortress, stronghold; (*fuerza*) strength; (*determinación*) resolution

fortuito, -a [for'twito, a] *adj* accidental

fortuna [for'tuna] *nf* (*suerte*) fortune, (good) luck; (*riqueza*) fortune, wealth

forzar [for'θar] /1f, 1l/ *vt* (*puerta*) to force (open); (*compeler*) to compel

forzoso, -a [for'θoso, a] *adj* necessary

fosa ['fosa] *nf* (*sepultura*) grave; (*en tierra*) pit; **~s nasales** nostrils

fósforo ['fosforo] *nm* (*Química*) phosphorus; (*cerilla*) match

fósil ['fosil] *nm* fossil

foso ['foso] *nm* ditch; (*Teat*) pit

foto ['foto] *nf* photo, snap(shot); **sacar una ~** to take a photo o picture; **~ (de) carné** passport(-size) photo

fotocopia [foto'kopja] *nf* photocopy; **fotocopiadora** *nf* photocopier; **fotocopiar** /1b/ *vt* to photocopy

fotografía [fotoɣra'fia] *nf* (*arte*) photography; (*una fotografía*) photograph; **fotografiar** /1c/ *vt* to photograph

fotógrafo, -a [fo'toɣrafo, a] *nm/f* photographer

fotomatón [fotoma'ton] *nm* photo booth

FP *nf abr* (*ESP*) = **Formación Profesional**

fracasar [fraka'sar] /1a/ *vi* (*gen*) to fail

fracaso [fra'kaso] *nm* failure

fracción [frak'θjon] *nf* fraction

fractura [frak'tura] *nf* fracture, break

fragancia [fra'ɣanθja] *nf* (*olor*) fragrance, perfume

frágil ['fraxil] *adj* (*débil*) fragile; (*Com*) breakable

fragmento [fraɣ'mento] *nm* fragment

fraile ['fraile] *nm* (*Rel*) friar; (: *monje*) monk

frambuesa [fram'bwesa] *nf* raspberry

francés, -esa [fran'θes, esa] *adj* French ▷ *nm/f* Frenchman/woman ▷ *nm* (*Ling*) French

Francia ['franθja] *nf* France

franco, -a ['franko, a] *adj* (*cándido*) frank, open; (*Com: exento*) free ▷ *nm* (*moneda*) franc

francotirador, a [frankotira'ðor, a] *nm/f* sniper

franela [fra'nela] *nf* flannel

franja ['franxa] *nf* fringe

franquear [franke'ar] /1a/ *vt* (*camino*) to clear; (*carta, paquete*) to frank, stamp; (*obstáculo*) to overcome

franqueo [fran'keo] *nm* postage

franqueza [fran'keθa] *nf* frankness

frasco ['frasko] *nm* bottle, flask

frase ['frase] *nf* sentence; **~ hecha** set phrase; (*pey*) stock phrase

fraterno, -a [fra'terno, a] *adj* brotherly, fraternal

fraude ['frauðe] *nm* (*cualidad*) dishonesty; (*acto*) fraud

frazada [fra'saða] *nf* (*LAM*) blanket

frecuencia [fre'kwenθja] *nf* frequency; **con ~** frequently, often

frecuentar [frekwen'tar] /1a/ *vt* to frequent

frecuente [fre'kwente] *adj* frequent

fregadero [freɣa'ðero] *nm* (kitchen) sink

fregar [fre'ɣar] /1h, 1j/ *vt* (*frotar*) to scrub; (*platos*) to wash (up); (*LAM fam: fastidiar*) to annoy; (: *malograr*) to screw up

freír [fre'ir] /3l/ *vt* to fry

frenar [fre'nar] /1a/ *vt* to brake; (*fig*) to check

frenazo [fre'naθo] *nm*: **dar un ~** to brake sharply

frenesí [frene'si] *nm* frenzy

freno ['freno] *nm* (*Tec, Auto*) brake; (*de cabalgadura*) bit; (*fig*) check; **~ de mano** handbrake

frente ['frente] *nm* (*Arq, Mil, Pol*) front; (*de objeto*) front part ▷ *nf* forehead, brow; **~ a** in front of; (*en situación opuesta a*) opposite; **chocar de ~** to crash head-on; **hacer ~ a** to face up to

fresa ['fresa] *nf* (*ESP*) strawberry

fresco, -a ['fresko, a] *adj* (*nuevo*) fresh; (*frío*) cool; (*fam: descarado*) cheeky ▷ *nm* (*aire*) fresh air; (*Arte*) fresco; (*LAM: bebida*) fruit juice o drink ▷ *nm/f* (*fam*): **ser un(a) ~/a** to have a nerve; **tomar**

el ~ to get some fresh air; **frescura** nf
freshness; (descaro) cheek, nerve

frialdad [frjal'dað] nf (gen) coldness;
(indiferencia) indifference

frigidez [frixi'ðeθ] nf frigidity

frigo ['friɣo] nm fridge

frigorífico [friɣo'rifiko] nm
refrigerator

frijol [fri'xol] nm kidney bean

frío, -a ['frio, a] vb V **freír** ▷ adj
cold; (indiferente) indifferent ▷ nm
cold(ness); indifference; **hace ~** it's
cold; **tener ~** to be cold

frito, -a ['frito, a] adj fried; **fritos** nmpl
fried food; **me trae ~ ese hombre** I'm
sick and tired of that man

frívolo, -a ['friβolo, a] adj frivolous

frontal [fron'tal] adj frontal ▷ nm:
choque ~ head-on collision

frontera [fron'tera] nf frontier;
fronterizo, -a adj frontier cpd;
(contiguo) bordering

frontón [fron'ton] nm (Deporte:
cancha) pelota court; (: juego) pelota

frotar [fro'tar] /1a/ vt to rub; **frotarse**
vr: **~se las manos** to rub one's hands

fructífero, -a [fruk'tifero, a] adj fruitful

fruncir [frun'θir] /3b/ vt to pucker;
(Costura) to gather; **~ el ceño** to knit
one's brow

frustrar [frus'trar] /1a/ vt to frustrate

fruta ['fruta] nf fruit; **frutería** nf fruit
shop; **frutero, -a** adj fruit cpd ▷ nm/f
fruiterer ▷ nm fruit dish o bowl

frutilla [fru'tiʎa] nf (LAM) strawberry

fruto ['fruto] nm fruit; (fig: resultado)
result; (: beneficio) benefit; **~s secos**
nuts and dried fruit

fucsia ['fuksja] nf fuchsia

fue [fwe] vb V **ser**; **ir**

fuego ['fweɣo] nm (gen) fire; **~ amigo**
friendly fire; **~s artificiales** o **de
artificio** fireworks; **a ~ lento** on a
low flame o gas; **¿tienes ~?** have you
(got) a light?

fuente ['fwente] nf fountain;
(manantial, fig) spring; (origen) source;
(plato) large dish

fuera ['fwera] vb V **ser**; **ir** ▷ adv
out(side); (en otra parte) away; (excepto,
salvo) except, save ▷ prep: **~ de**
outside; (fig) besides; **~ de sí** beside
o.s.; **por ~** (on the) outside

fuera-borda [fwera'βorða] nm inv
(barco) speedboat

fuerte ['fwerte] adj strong; (golpe)
hard; (ruido) loud; (comida) rich; (lluvia)
heavy; (dolor) intense ▷ adv strongly;
hard; loud(ly); **ser ~ en** to be good at

fuerza ['fwerθa] vb V **forzar** ▷ nf
(fortaleza) strength; (Tec, Elec) power;
(coacción) force; (Mil: tb: **~s**) forces pl; **~s
armadas (FF.AA.)** armed forces; **~s
aéreas** air force sg; **a ~ de** by (dint of);
cobrar ~s to recover one's strength;
tener ~s para to have the strength
to; **a la ~** forcibly, by force; **por ~** of
necessity; **~ de voluntad** willpower

fuga ['fuɣa] nf (huida) flight, escape;
(de gas etc) leak

fugarse [fu'ɣarse] /1h/ vr to flee, escape

fugaz [fu'ɣaθ] adj fleeting

fugitivo, -a [fuxi'tiβo, a] adj fugitive
▷ nm/f fugitive

fui etc [fwi] vb V **ser**; **ir**

fulano, -a [fu'lano, a] nm/f so-and-
so, what's-his-name

fulminante [fulmi'nante] adj (fig:
mirada) withering; (Med) sudden,
serious; (fam) terrific, tremendous;
(éxito, golpe) sudden; **ataque ~** stroke

fumador, a [fuma'ðor, a] nm/f
smoker

fumar [fu'mar] /1a/ vt, vi to smoke;
~ en pipa to smoke a pipe

función [fun'θjon] nf function; (de
puesto) duties pl; (Teat etc) show;
entrar en funciones to take up
one's duties

funcionar [funθjo'nar] /1a/ vi (gen)
to function; (máquina) to work; **"no
funciona"** "out of order"

funcionario, -a [funθjo'narjo, a]
nm/f civil servant

funda ['funda] nf (gen) cover; (de
almohada) pillowcase

fundación [funda'θjon] *nf*
foundation

fundamental [fundamen'tal] *adj*
fundamental, basic

fundamento [funda'mento] *nm*
(*base*) foundation

fundar [fun'dar] /1a/ *vt* to found;
fundarse *vr*: **~se en** to be founded on

fundición [fundi'θjon] *nf* (*acción*)
smelting; (*fábrica*) foundry

fundir [fun'dir] /3a/ *vt* (*gen*) to fuse;
(*metal*) to smelt, melt down; (*nieve etc*)
to melt; (*Com*) to merge; (*estatua*) to
cast; **fundirse** *vr* (*colores etc*) to merge,
blend; (*unirse*) to fuse together; (*Elec:
fusible, lámpara etc*) to blow; (*nieve
etc*) to melt

fúnebre ['funeßre] *adj* funeral *cpd*,
funereal

funeral [fune'ral] *nm* funeral;
funeraria *nf* undertaker's (BRIT),
mortician's (US)

funicular [funiku'lar] *nm* (*tren*)
funicular; (*teleférico*) cable car

furgón [fur'ɣon] *nm* wagon;
furgoneta *nf* (*Auto, Com*) (transit) van
(BRIT), pickup (truck) (US)

furia ['furja] *nf* (*ira*) fury; (*violencia*)
violence; **furioso, -a** *adj* (*iracundo*)
furious; (*violento*) violent

furtivo, -a [fur'tiβo, a] *adj* furtive
▷ *nm* poacher

fusible [fu'siβle] *nm* fuse

fusil [fu'sil] *nm* rifle; **fusilar** /1a/ *vt*
to shoot

fusión [fu'sjon] *nf* (*gen*) melting;
(*unión*) fusion; (*Com*) merger,
amalgamation

fútbol ['futβol] *nm* football (BRIT),
soccer (US); **~ americano** American
football (BRIT), football (US); **~ sala**
indoor football (BRIT) o soccer (US);
futbolín *nm* table football; **futbolista**
nmf footballer

futuro, -a [fu'turo, a] *adj* future
▷ *nm* future

g

gabardina [gaβar'ðina] *nf*
gabardine; (*prenda*) raincoat

gabinete [gaβi'nete] *nm* (*Pol*)
cabinet; (*estudio*) study; (*de abogados
etc*) office

gachas ['gatʃas] *nfpl* porridge *sg*

gafas ['gafas] *nfpl* glasses; **~ de sol**
sunglasses

gafe ['gafe] *nm* (*fam*) jinx

gaita ['gaita] *nf* bagpipes *pl*

gajes ['gaxes] *nmpl*: **los ~ del oficio**
occupational hazards

gajo ['gaxo] *nm* (*de naranja*) segment

gala ['gala] *nf* full dress; **galas** *nfpl*
finery *sg*; **estar de ~** to be in one's best
clothes; **hacer ~ de** to display

galápago [ga'lapaɣo] *nm* (*Zool*)
turtle, sea/freshwater turtle (US)

galardón [galar'ðon] *nm* award,
prize

galaxia [ga'laksja] *nf* galaxy

galera [ga'lera] *nf* (*nave*) galley; (*carro*)
wagon; (*Tip*) galley

galería [gale'ria] nf (gen) gallery; (balcón) veranda(h); (de casa) corridor; **~ comercial** shopping mall

Gales ['gales] nm: **(el País de) ~** Wales; **galés, -esa** adj Welsh ▷ nm/f Welshman/woman ▷ nm (Ling) Welsh

galgo, -a ['galɣo, a] nm/f greyhound

gallego, -a [ga'ʎeɣo, a] adj ▷ nm/f Galician

galleta [ga'ʎeta] nf biscuit (BRIT), cookie (US)

gallina [ga'ʎina] nf hen ▷ nm (fam) chicken; **gallinero** nm henhouse; (Teat) top gallery

gallo ['gaʎo] nm cock, rooster

galopar [galo'par] /1a/ vi to gallop

gama ['gama] nf (fig) range

gamba ['gamba] nf prawn (BRIT), shrimp (US)

gamberro, -a [gam'berro, a] nm/f hooligan, lout

gamuza [ga'muθa] nf chamois

gana ['gana] nf (deseo) desire, wish; (apetito) appetite; (voluntad) will; (añoranza) longing; **de buena ~** willingly; **de mala ~** reluctantly; **me da ~s de** I feel like, I want to; **tener ~s de** to feel like; **no me da la (real) ~** I (really) don't feel like it

ganadería [ganaðe'ria] nf (ganado) livestock; (ganado vacuno) cattle pl; (cría, comercio) cattle raising

ganadero, -a [gana'ðero, a] nm/f (hacendado) rancher

ganado [ga'naðo] nm livestock; **~ caballar/cabrío** horses pl/goats pl; **~ porcino/vacuno** pigs pl/cattle pl

ganador, -a [gana'ðor, a] adj winning ▷ nm/f winner

ganancia [ga'nanθja] nf (lo ganado) gain; (aumento) increase; (beneficio) profit; **ganancias** nfpl (ingresos) earnings; (beneficios) profit sg, winnings

ganar [ga'nar] /1a/ vt (obtener) to get, obtain; (sacar ventaja) to gain; (Com) to earn; (Deporte, premio) to win; (derrotar) to beat; (alcanzar) to reach ▷ vi (Deporte) to win; **ganarse** vr: **~se la vida** to earn one's living

ganchillo [gan'tʃiʎo] nm crochet

gancho [gan'tʃo] nm (gen) hook; (colgador) hanger

gandul, -a [gan'dul, a] adj, nm/f good-for-nothing, layabout

ganga ['ganga] nf bargain

gangrena [gan'grena] nf gangrene

ganso, -a ['ganso, a] nm/f (Zool) gander/goose; (fam) idiot

ganzúa [gan'θua] nf skeleton key

garabato [gara'βato] nm (escritura) scrawl, scribble

garaje [ga'raxe] nm garage; **garajista** nmf mechanic

garantía [garan'tia] nf guarantee

garantizar [garanti'θar] /1f/ vt to guarantee

garbanzo [gar'βanθo] nm chickpea

garfio ['garfjo] nm grappling iron

garganta [gar'ɣanta] nf (interna) throat; (externa, de botella) neck; **gargantilla** nf necklace

gárgara ['garɣara] nf gargling; **hacer ~s** to gargle

gargarear [garɣare'ar] /1a/ vi (LAM) to gargle

garita [ga'rita] nf cabin, hut; (Mil) sentry box

garra ['garra] nf (de gato, Tec) claw; (de ave) talon; (fam) hand, paw

garrafa [ga'rrafa] nf carafe, decanter

garrapata [garra'pata] nf tick

gas [gas] nm gas; **~es lacrimógenos** tear gas sg

gasa ['gasa] nf gauze

gaseoso, -a [gase'oso, a] adj gassy, fizzy ▷ nf lemonade, pop (fam)

gasoil [ga'soil], **gasóleo** [ga'soleo] nm diesel (oil)

gasolina [gaso'lina] nf petrol, gas(oline) (US); **gasolinera** nf petrol (BRIT) o gas (US) station

gastado, -a [gas'taðo, a] adj (dinero) spent; (ropa) worn out; (usado: frase etc) trite

g

gastar [gas'tar] /1a/ vt (dinero, tiempo) to spend; (consumir) to use (up); (desperdiciar) to waste; (llevar) to wear; **gastarse** vr to wear out; (estropearse) to waste; **~ en** to spend on; **~ bromas** to crack jokes; **¿qué número gastas?** what size (shoe) do you take?

gasto ['gasto] nm (desembolso) expenditure, spending; (consumo, uso) use; **gastos** nmpl (desembolsos) expenses; (cargos) charges, costs

gastronomía [gastrono'mia] nf gastronomy

gatear [gate'ar] /1a/ vi (andar a gatas) to go on all fours

gatillo [ga'tiʎo] nm (de arma de fuego) trigger; (de dentista) forceps

gato ['gato] nm cat; (Tec) jack; **andar a gatas** to go on all fours

gaucho, -a ['gautʃo, a] nm/f gaucho

gaviota [ga'βjota] nf seagull

gay [ge] adj, nm gay, homosexual

gazpacho [gaθ'patʃo] nm gazpacho

gel [xel] nm gel; **~ de baño/ducha** bath/shower gel

gelatina [xela'tina] nf jelly; (polvos etc) gelatine

gema ['xema] nf gem

gemelo, -a [xe'melo, a] adj, nm/f twin; **gemelos** nmpl (de camisa) cufflinks; **~s de campo** field glasses, binoculars

gemido [xe'miðo] nm (quejido) moan, groan; (lamento) howl

Géminis ['xeminis] nm Gemini

gemir [xe'mir] /3k/ vi (quejarse) to moan, groan; (viento) to howl

generación [xenera'θjon] nf generation

general [xene'ral] adj general ▷ nm general; **por lo** o **en ~** in general; **Generalitat** nf regional government of Catalonia; **generalizar** /1f/ vt to generalize; **generalizarse** vr to become generalized, spread

generar [xene'rar] /1a/ vt to generate

género ['xenero] nm (clase) kind, sort; (tipo) type; (Bio) genus; (Ling)

gender; (Com) material; **~ humano** human race

generosidad [xenerosi'ðað] nf generosity; **generoso, -a** adj generous

genial [xe'njal] adj inspired; (idea) brilliant; (estupendo) wonderful

genio ['xenjo] nm (carácter) nature, disposition; (humor) temper; (facultad creadora) genius; **de mal ~** bad-tempered

genital [xeni'tal] adj genital ▷ nm: **~es** genitals

gente ['xente] nf (personas) people pl; (parientes) relatives pl

gentil [xen'til] adj (elegante) graceful; (encantador) charming

> No confundir *gentil* con la palabra inglesa *gentle*.

genuino, -a [xe'nwino, a] adj genuine

geografía [xeoɣra'fia] nf geography

geología [xeolo'xia] nf geology

geometría [xeome'tria] nf geometry

gerente [xe'rente] nmf (supervisor) manager; (jefe) director

geriatría [xerja'tria] nf (Med) geriatrics sg

germen ['xermen] nm germ

gesticulación [xestikula'θjon] nf (ademán) gesticulation; (mueca) grimace

gesticular [xestiku'lar] /1a/ vi (con ademanes) to gesticulate; (con muecas) to make faces

gestión [xes'tjon] nf management; (diligencia, acción) negotiation

gesto ['xesto] nm (mueca) grimace; (ademán) gesture

Gibraltar [xiβral'tar] nm Gibraltar; **gibraltareño, -a** adj of o from Gibraltar, Gibraltarian ▷ nm/f Gibraltarian

gigante [xi'ɣante] adj, nmf giant; **gigantesco, -a** adj gigantic

gilipollas [xili'poʎas] (fam) adj inv daft ▷ nmf berk (BRIT), jerk (esp US)

gimnasia [xim'nasja] nf gymnastics pl; **gimnasio** nm gym(nasium); **gimnasta** nmf gymnast; **gimnástica** nf gymnastics sg

ginebra [xi'neβra] nf gin

ginecólogo, -a [xine'koloɣo, a] nm/f gyn(a)ecologist

gira ['xira] nf tour, trip

girar [xi'rar] /1a/ vt (dar la vuelta) to turn (around); (: rápidamente) to spin; (Com: giro postal) to draw; (comerciar: letra de cambio) to issue ▷ vi to turn (round); (rápido) to spin

girasol [xira'sol] nm sunflower

giratorio, -a [xira'torjo, a] adj revolving

giro ['xiro] nm (movimiento) turn, revolution; (Ling) expression; (Com) draft; **~ bancario** bank draft; **~ postal** money order

gis [xis] nm (LAM) chalk

gitano, -a [xi'tano, a] adj, nm/f gypsy

glacial [gla'θjal] adj icy, freezing

glaciar [gla'θjar] nm glacier

glándula ['glandula] nf gland

global [glo'βal] adj global; **globalización** nf globalization

globo ['gloβo] nm (esfera) globe, sphere; (aeróstato, juguete) balloon

glóbulo ['gloβulo] nm globule; (Anat) corpuscle

gloria ['glorja] nf glory

glorieta [glo'rjeta] nf (de jardín) bower, arbour, arbor (us); (Auto) roundabout (BRIT), traffic circle (US)

glorioso, -a [glo'rjoso, a] adj glorious

glotón, -ona [glo'ton, ona] adj gluttonous, greedy ▷ nm/f glutton

glucosa [glu'kosa] nf glucose

gobernador, -a [goβerna'ðor, a] adj governing ▷ nm/f governor; **gobernante** adj governing

gobernar [goβer'nar] /1j/ vt (dirigir) to guide, direct; (Pol) to rule, govern ▷ vi to govern; (Naut) to steer

gobierno [go'βjerno] vb V **gobernar** ▷ nm (Pol) government; (dirección) guidance, direction; (Naut) steering

goce etc ['goθe] vb V **gozar** ▷ nm enjoyment

gol [gol] nm goal

golf [golf] nm golf

golfo, -a ['golfo, a] nm/f (pilluelo) street urchin; (vagabundo) tramp; (gorrón) loafer; (gamberro) lout ▷ nm (Geo) gulf ▷ nf (fam!: prostituta) slut

golondrina [golon'drina] nf swallow

golosina [golo'sina] nf (dulce) sweet; **goloso, -a** adj sweet-toothed

golpe ['golpe] nm blow; (de puño) punch; (de mano) smack; (de remo) stroke; (fig: choque) clash; **no dar ~** to be bone idle; **de un ~** with one blow; **de ~** suddenly; **~ (de estado)** coup (d'état); **golpear** /1a/ vt, vi to strike, knock; (asestar) to beat; (de puño) to punch; (golpetear) to tap

goma ['goma] nf (caucho) rubber; (elástico) elastic; (tira) rubber o elastic (BRIT) band; **~ (de borrar)** eraser, rubber (BRIT); **~ espuma** foam rubber

gomina [go'mina] nf hair gel

gomita [go'mita] nf rubber o elastic (BRIT) band

gordo, -a ['gorðo, a] adj (gen) fat; (fam) enormous; **el (premio) ~** (en lotería) first prize

gorila [go'rila] nm gorilla

gorra ['gorra] nf cap; (de niño) bonnet; (militar) bearskin; **andar** o **ir** o **vivir de ~** to sponge; **entrar de ~** (fam) to gatecrash

gorrión [go'rrjon] nm sparrow

gorro ['gorro] nm cap; (de niño, mujer) bonnet

gorrón, -ona [go'rron, ona] nm/f scrounger; **gorronear** /1a/ vi (fam) to sponge, scrounge

gota ['gota] nf (gen) drop; (de sudor) bead; (Med) gout; **gotear** /1a/ vi to drip; (lloviznar) to drizzle; **gotera** nf leak

gozar [go'θar] /1f/ vi to enjoy o.s.; **~ de** (disfrutar) to enjoy; (poseer) to possess

GPS nm abr (= global positioning system) GPS

gr abr (= gramo(s)) g

grabación [graβa'θjon] nf recording

grabado [gra'βaðo] nm print, engraving

grabador, -a [graβa'ðor, a] nm/f engraver ▷ nf tape-recorder; **~ a de CD/DVD** CD/DVD writer

grabar [gra'βar] /1a/ vt to engrave; (discos, cintas) to record

gracia ['graθja] nf (encanto) grace, gracefulness; (humor) humour, wit; **¡muchas ~s!** thanks very much!; **~s a** thanks to; **tener ~** (chiste etc) to be funny; **no me hace ~** I am not too keen; **dar las ~s a algn por algo** to thank sb for sth; **gracioso, -a** adj (garboso) graceful; (chistoso) funny; (cómico) comical ▷ nm/f (Teat) comic character

grada ['graða] nf (de escalera) step; (de anfiteatro) tier, row; **gradas** nfpl (de estadio) terraces

grado ['graðo] nm degree; (de aceite, vino) grade; (grada) step; (Mil) rank; **de buen ~** willingly; **~ centí~/ Fahrenheit** degree centigrade/ Fahrenheit

graduación [graðwa'θjon] nf (del alcohol) proof, strength; (Escol) graduation; (Mil) rank

gradual [gra'ðwal] adj gradual

graduar [gra'ðwar] /1e/ vt (gen) to graduate; (Mil) to commission; **graduarse** vr to graduate; **~se la vista** to have one's eyes tested

gráfico, -a ['grafiko, a] adj graphic ▷ nm diagram ▷ nf graph; **gráficos** nmpl (tb Inform) graphics

grajo ['graxo] nm rook

gramático, -a [gra'matiko, a] nm/f (persona) grammarian ▷ nf grammar

gramo ['gramo] nm gramme (BRIT), gram (US)

gran [gran] adj V **grande**

grana ['grana] nf (color) scarlet

granada [gra'naða] nf pomegranate; (Mil) grenade

granate [gra'nate] adj inv maroon

Gran Bretaña [grambre'taŋa] nf Great Britain

grande ['grande], **gran** (antes de nmsg) adj (de tamaño) big, large; (alto) tall; (distinguido) great; (impresionante) grand ▷ nm grandee

granel [gra'nel] nm: **a ~** (Com) in bulk

granero [gra'nero] nm granary, barn

granito [gra'nito] nm (Agr) small grain; (roca) granite

granizado [grani'θaðo] nm iced drink

granizar [grani'θar] /1f/ vi to hail; **granizo** nm hail

granja ['granxa] nf (gen) farm; **granjero, -a** nm/f farmer

grano ['grano] nm grain; (semilla) seed; (Med) pimple, spot; **~ de café** coffee bean

granuja [gra'nuxa] nm rogue; (golfillo) urchin

grapa ['grapa] nf staple; (Tec) clamp; **grapadora** nf stapler

grasa ['grasa] nf V **graso**; **grasiento, -a** adj greasy; (de aceite) oily; **graso, -a** adj fatty; (aceitoso) greasy ▷ nf grease; (de cocina) fat, lard; (sebo) suet; (mugre) filth

gratinar [grati'nar] /1a/ vt to cook au gratin

gratis ['gratis] adv free

grato, -a ['grato, a] adj (agradable) pleasant, agreeable

gratuito, -a [gra'twito, a] adj (gratis) free; (sin razón) gratuitous

grave ['graβe] adj heavy; (fig, Med) grave, serious; **gravedad** nf gravity

Grecia ['greθja] nf Greece

gremio ['gremjo] nm trade, industry

griego, -a ['grjeɣo, a] adj ▷ nm/f Greek

grieta ['grjeta] nf crack

grifo ['grifo] nm tap (BRIT), faucet (US)

grillo ['griʎo] nm (Zool) cricket

gripa ['gripa] nf (LAM) flu, influenza

gripe ['gripe] nf flu, influenza; **~ A** swine flu; **~ aviar** bird flu

gris [gris] adj grey

gritar [gri'tar] /1a/ vt, vi to shout, yell; **grito** nm shout, yell; (de horror) scream

grosella [gro'seʎa] nf (red)currant

grosero, -a [gro'sero, a] adj (poco cortés) rude, bad-mannered; (ordinario) vulgar, crude

grosor [gro'sor] nm thickness

grúa ['grua] nf (Tec) crane; (de petróleo) derrick

grueso, -a ['grweso, a] adj thick; (persona) stout ▷ nm bulk; **el ~ de** the bulk of

grulla ['gruʎa] nf crane

grumo ['grumo] nm clot, lump

gruñido [gru'ɲiðo] nm grunt; (fig) grumble

gruñir [gru'ɲir] /3h/ vi (animal) to grunt, growl; (fam) to grumble

grupo ['grupo] nm group; (Tec) unit, set; **~ de presión** pressure group

gruta ['gruta] nf grotto

guacho, -a ['gwatʃo, a] nm/f (LAM) homeless child

guajolote [gwaxo'lote] nm (LAM) turkey

guante ['gwante] nm glove; **~s de goma** rubber gloves; **guantera** nf glove compartment

guapo, -a ['gwapo, a] adj good-looking; attractive; (elegante) smart

guarda ['gwarða] nmf (persona) warden, keeper ▷ nf (acto) guarding; (custodia) custody; **~ jurado** (armed) security guard; **guardabarros** nm inv mudguard (BRIT), fender (US); **guardabosques** nm inv gamekeeper; **guardacostas** nm inv coastguard vessel ▷ nmf guardian, protector; **guardaespaldas** nm inv, nf inv bodyguard; **guardameta** nm goalkeeper; **guardar** /1a/ vt (gen) to keep; (vigilar) to guard, watch over; (dinero: ahorrar) to save; **guardarse** vr (preservarse) to protect o.s.; **guardarse de algo** (evitar) to avoid sth; **guardar cama** to stay in bed; **guardarropa** nm (armario) wardrobe; (en establecimiento público) cloakroom

guardería [gwarðe'ria] nf nursery

guardia ['gwarðja] nf (Mil) guard; (cuidado) care, custody ▷ nmf guard; (policía) policeman/woman; **estar de ~** to be on guard; **montar ~** to mount guard; **la G~ Civil** the Civil Guard

guardián, -ana [gwar'ðjan, ana] nm/f (gen) guardian, keeper

guarida [gwa'riða] nf (de animal) den, lair; (refugio) refuge

guarnición [gwarni'θjon] nf (de vestimenta) trimming; (de piedra) mount; (Culin) garnish; (arneses) harness; (Mil) garrison

guarro, -a ['gwarro, a] nm/f pig

guasa ['gwasa] nf joke; **guasón, -ona** adj (bromista) joking ▷ nm/f wit; joker

Guatemala [gwate'mala] nf Guatemala

guay [gwai] adj (fam) super, great

güero, -a ['gwero, a] adj (LAM) blond(e)

guerra ['gerra] nf war; **~ civil/fría** civil/cold war; **dar ~** to be a nuisance; **guerrero, -a** adj fighting; (carácter) warlike ▷ nm/f warrior

guerrilla [ge'rriʎa] nf guerrilla warfare; (tropas) guerrilla band o group

guía ['gia] vb V **guiar** ▷ nmf (persona) guide ▷ nf (libro) guidebook; **~ telefónica** telephone directory; **~ del turista/del viajero** tourist/traveller's guide

guiar [gi'ar] /1c/ vt to guide, direct; (Auto) to steer; **guiarse** vr: **~se por** to be guided by

guinda ['ginda] nf morello cherry

guindilla [gin'diʎa] nf chil(l)i pepper

guiñar [gi'ɲar] /1a/ vi to wink

guión [gi'on] nm (Ling) hyphen, dash; (Cine) script; **guionista** nmf scriptwriter

guiri ['giri] nmf (fam, pey) foreigner

guirnalda [gir'nalda] nf garland

guisado [gi'saðo] nm stew

guisante [gi'sante] nm pea

guisar [gi'sar] /1a/ vt, vi to cook; **guiso** nm cooked dish

g

guitarra [giˈtarra] *nf* guitar
gula [ˈgula] *nf* gluttony, greed
gusano [guˈsano] *nm* worm; (*lombriz*) earthworm
gustar [gusˈtar] /1a/ *vt* to taste, sample ▷ *vi* to please, be pleasing; **~ de algo** to like o enjoy sth; **me gustan las uvas** I like grapes; **le gusta nadar** she likes o enjoys swimming
gusto [ˈgusto] *nm* (*sentido, sabor*) taste; (*placer*) pleasure; **tiene un ~ amargo** it has a bitter taste; **tener buen ~** to have good taste; **sentirse a ~** to feel at ease; **¡mucho** o **tanto ~ (en conocerle)!** how do you do?, pleased to meet you; **el ~ es mío** the pleasure is mine; **tomar ~ a** to take a liking to; **con ~** willingly, gladly

ha [a] *vb* V **haber**
haba [ˈaβa] *nf* bean
Habana [aˈβana] *nf*: **la ~** Havana
habano [aˈβano] *nm* Havana cigar
habéis *vb* V **haber**

 PALABRA CLAVE

haber [aˈβer] /2j/ *vb auxiliar* **1** (*tiempos compuestos*) to have; **había comido** I have/had eaten; **antes/después de haberlo visto** before seeing/after seeing o having seen it

2: **¡haberlo dicho antes!** you should have said so before!

3: **haber de: he de hacerlo** I must do it; **ha de llegar mañana** it should arrive tomorrow

▷ *vb impersonal* **1** (*existencia: sg*) there is; (: *pl*) there are; **hay un hermano/dos hermanos** there is one brother/there are two brothers; **¿cuánto hay de aquí a Sucre?** how far is it from here to Sucre?

2 (*obligación*): **hay que hacer algo** something must be done; **hay que apuntarlo para acordarse** you have to write it down to remember
3: **¡hay que ver!** well I never!
4: **¡no hay de qué!**, (*LAM*) **¡no hay por qué!** don't mention it!, not at all!
5: **¿qué hay?** (*¿qué pasa?*) what's up?, what's the matter?; (*¿qué tal?*) how's it going?
▶ **haberse** *vb impersonal*: **habérselas con algn** to have it out with sb
▶ *vt*: **he aquí unas sugerencias** here are some suggestions
▶ *nm* (*en cuenta*) credit side
▶ **haberes** *nmpl* assets; **¿cuánto tengo en el haber?** how much do I have in my account?; **tiene varias novelas en su haber** he has several novels to his credit

habichuela [aβiˈtʃwela] *nf* kidney bean
hábil [ˈaβil] *adj* (*listo*) clever, smart; (*capaz*) fit, capable; (*experto*) expert; **día ~** working day; **habilidad** *nf* skill, ability
habitación [aβitaˈθjon] *nf* (*cuarto*) room; (*Bio: morada*) habitat; **~ sencilla** *o* **individual** single room; **~ doble** *o* **de matrimonio** double room
habitante [aβiˈtante] *nmf* inhabitant
habitar [aβiˈtar] /1a/ *vt* (*residir en*) to inhabit; (*ocupar*) to occupy ▷ *vi* to live
hábito [ˈaβito] *nm* habit
habitual [aβiˈtwal] *adj* habitual
habituar [aβiˈtwar] /1e/ *vt* to accustom; **habituarse** *vr*: **~se a** to get used to
habla [ˈaβla] *nf* (*capacidad de hablar*) speech; (*idioma*) language; (*dialecto*) dialect; **perder el ~** to become speechless; **de ~ francesa** French-speaking; **estar al ~** to be in contact; (*Telec*) to be on the line; **¡González al ~!** (*Telec*) Gonzalez speaking!

hablador, a [aβlaˈðor, a] *adj* talkative
▷ *nm/f* chatterbox
habladuría [aβlaðuˈria] *nf* rumour; **habladurías** *nfpl* gossip *sg*
hablante [aˈβlante] *adj* speaking
▷ *nmf* speaker
hablar [aˈβlar] /1a/ *vt* to speak, talk
▷ *vi* to speak; **hablarse** *vr* to speak to each other; **~ con** to speak to; **de eso ni ~** no way, that's out of the question; **~ de** to speak of *o* about; **"se habla inglés"** "English spoken here"
habré *etc* [aˈβre] *vb V* **haber**
hacendado, -a [aθenˈdaðo, a] *nm/f* (*LAM*) rancher, farmer
hacendoso, -a [aθenˈdoso, a] *adj* industrious

PALABRA CLAVE

hacer [aˈθer] /2r/ *vt* **1** (*fabricar, producir, conseguir*) to make; **hacer una película/un ruido** to make a film/noise; **el guisado lo hice yo** I made *o* cooked the stew
2 (*ejecutar: trabajo etc*) to do; **hacer la colada** to do the washing; **hacer la comida** to do the cooking; **¿qué haces?** what are you doing?; **hacer el malo** *o* **el papel del malo** (*Teat*) to play the villain
3 (*estudios, algunos deportes*) to do; **hacer español/económicas** to do *o* study Spanish/economics; **hacer yoga/gimnasia** to do yoga/go to the gym
4 (*transformar, incidir en*): **esto lo hará más difícil** this will make it more difficult; **salir te hará sentir mejor** going out will make you feel better
5 (*cálculo*): **2 y 2 hacen 4** 2 and 2 make 4; **éste hace 100** this one makes 100
6 (*+ sub*): **esto hará que ganemos** this will make us win; **harás que no quiera venir** you'll stop him wanting to come
7 (*como sustituto de vb*) to do; **él bebió y yo hice lo mismo** he drank and I did likewise

8: **no hace más que criticar** all he does is criticize
▸ vb semi-auxiliar (+ infin: directo): **les hice venir** I made o had them come; **hacer trabajar a los demás** to get others to work
▸ vi **1**: **haz como que no lo sabes** act as if you don't know
2 (ser apropiado): **si os hace** if it's alright with you
3: **hacer de: hacer de Otelo** to play Othello
▸ vb impersonal **1**: **hace calor/frío** it's hot/cold; V tb **bueno; sol; tiempo**
2 (tiempo): **hace tres años** three years ago; **hace un mes que voy/ no voy** I've been going/I haven't been for a month
3: **¿cómo has hecho para llegar tan rápido?** how did you manage to get here so quickly?
▸ **hacerse** vr **1** (volverse) to become; **se hicieron amigos** they became friends
2 (acostumbrarse): **hacerse a** to get used to
3: **se hace con huevos y leche** it's made out of eggs and milk; **eso no se hace** that's not done
4 (obtener): **hacerse de** o **con algo** to get hold of sth
5 (fingirse): **hacerse el sordo/sueco** to turn a deaf ear/pretend not to notice

hacha ['atʃa] nf axe; (antorcha) torch
hachís [a'tʃis] nm hashish
hacia ['aθja] prep (en dirección de) towards; (cerca de) near; (actitud) towards; **~ adelante/atrás** forwards/backwards; **~ arriba/ abajo** up(wards)/down(wards); **~ mediodía** about noon
hacienda [a'θjenda] nf (propiedad) property; (finca) farm; (LAM) ranch; **~ pública** public finance; **(Ministerio de) H~** Exchequer (BRIT), Treasury Department (US)

hada ['aða] nf fairy
haga etc ['aɣa] vb V **hacer**
Haití [ai'ti] nm Haiti
halagar [ala'ɣar] /1h/ vt to flatter
halago [a'laɣo] nm flattery
halcón [al'kon] nm falcon, hawk
hallar [a'ʎar] /1a/ vt (gen) to find; (descubrir) to discover; (toparse con) to run into; **hallarse** vr to be (situated)
halterofilia [altero'filja] nf weightlifting
hamaca [a'maka] nf hammock
hambre ['ambre] nf hunger; (carencia) famine; (fig) longing; **tener ~** to be hungry; **¡me muero de ~!** I'm starving!; **hambriento, -a** adj hungry, starving
hamburguesa [ambur'ɣesa] nf hamburger; **hamburguesería** nf burger bar
hámster ['xamster] nm hamster
han [an] vb V **haber**
harapo [a'rapo] nm rag
haré etc [a're] vb V **hacer**
harina [a'rina] nf flour; **~ de maíz** cornflour (BRIT), cornstarch (US); **~ de trigo** wheat flour
hartar [ar'tar] /1a/ vt to satiate, glut; (fig) to tire, sicken; **hartarse** vr (de comida) to fill o.s., gorge o.s.; (cansarse): **~se de** to get fed up with; **harto, -a** adj (lleno) full; (cansado) fed up ▷ adv (bastante) enough; (muy) very; **estar harto de** to be fed up with
has [as] vb V **haber**
hasta ['asta] adv even ▷ prep (alcanzando a) as far as, up/down to; (de tiempo: a tal hora) till, until; (: antes de) before ▷ conj: **~ que** until; **~ luego** o **ahora/el sábado** see you soon/on Saturday; **~ pronto** see you soon
hay [ai] vb V **haber**
Haya ['aja] nf: **la ~** The Hague
haya etc ['aja] vb V **haber** ▷ nf beech tree
haz [aθ] vb V **hacer** ▷ nm (de luz) beam
hazaña [a'θaɲa] nf feat, exploit

hazmerreír [aθmerre'ir] *nm inv* laughing stock

he [e] *vb V* **haber**

hebilla [e'βiʎa] *nf* buckle, clasp

hebra ['eβra] *nf* thread; (*Bot: fibra*) fibre, grain

hebreo, -a [e'βreo, a] *adj, nm/f* Hebrew ⊳ *nm* (*Ling*) Hebrew

hechizar [etʃi'θar] /1f/ *vt* to cast a spell on, bewitch

hechizo [e'tʃiθo] *nm* witchcraft, magic; (*acto de magia*) spell, charm

hecho, -a ['etʃo, a] *pp de* **hacer** ⊳ *adj* (*carne*) done; (*Costura*) ready-to-wear ⊳ *nm* deed, act; (*dato*) fact; (*cuestión*) matter; (*suceso*) event ⊳ *excl* agreed!, done!; **¡bien ~!** well done!; **de ~** in fact, as a matter of fact; **el ~ es que ...** the fact is that ...

hechura [e'tʃura] *nf* (*forma*) form, shape; (*de persona*) build

hectárea [ek'tarea] *nf* hectare

helada [e'laða] *nf* frost

heladera [ela'ðera] *nf* (*LAM: refrigerador*) refrigerator

helado, -a [e'laðo, a] *adj* frozen; (*glacial*) icy; (*fig*) chilly, cold ⊳ *nm* ice-cream

helar [e'lar] /1j/ *vt* to freeze, ice (up); (*dejar atónito*) to amaze ⊳ *vi* to freeze; **helarse** *vr* to freeze

helecho [e'letʃo] *nm* fern

hélice ['eliθe] *nf* (*Tec*) propeller

helicóptero [eli'koptero] *nm* helicopter

hembra ['embra] *nf* (*Bot, Zool*) female; (*mujer*) woman; (*Tec*) nut

hemorragia [emo'rraxja] *nf* haemorrhage (*BRIT*), hemorrhage (*US*)

hemorroides [emo'rroiðes] *nfpl* haemorrhoids (*BRIT*), hemorrhoids (*US*)

hemos ['emos] *vb V* **haber**

heno ['eno] *nm* hay

heredar [ere'ðar] /1a/ *vt* to inherit; **heredero, -a** *nm/f* heir(ess)

hereje [e'rexe] *nmf* heretic

herencia [e'renθja] *nf* inheritance

herido, -a [e'riðo, a] *adj* injured, wounded ⊳ *nm/f* casualty ⊳ *nf* wound, injury

herir [e'rir] /3i/ *vt* to wound, injure; (*fig*) to offend

hermanación [ermana'θjon] *nf* (*de ciudades*) twinning

hermanado, -a [erma'naðo, a] *adj* (*ciudad*) twinned

hermanastro, -a [erma'nastro, a] *nm/f* stepbrother/sister

hermandad [erman'dað] *nf* brotherhood

hermano, -a [er'mano, a] *nm* brother ⊳ *nf* sister; **~ gemelo** twin brother; **~ político** brother-in-law; **hermana política** sister-in-law

hermético, -a [er'metiko, a] *adj* hermetic; (*fig*) watertight

hermoso, -a [er'moso, a] *adj* beautiful, lovely; (*estupendo*) splendid; (*guapo*) handsome; **hermosura** *nf* beauty

hernia ['ernja] *nf* hernia; **~ discal** slipped disc

héroe ['eroe] *nm* hero

heroína [ero'ina] *nf* (*mujer*) heroine; (*droga*) heroin

herradura [erra'ðura] *nf* horseshoe

herramienta [erra'mjenta] *nf* tool

herrero [e'rrero] *nm* blacksmith

hervidero [erβi'ðero] *nm* (*fig*) swarm; (*Pol etc*) hotbed

hervir [er'βir] /3i/ *vi* to boil; (*burbujear*) to bubble; **~ a fuego lento** to simmer; **hervor** *nm* boiling; (*fig*) ardour, fervour

heterosexual [eterosek'swal] *adj* heterosexual

hice *etc* ['iθe] *vb V* **hacer**

hidratante [iðra'tante] *adj*: **crema ~** moisturizing cream, moisturizer; **hidratar** /1a/ *vt* to moisturize; **hidrato** *nm* hydrate; **hidrato de carbono** carbohydrate

hidráulico, -a [i'ðrauliko, a] *adj* hydraulic

hidro... [iðro] *pref* hydro..., water-...;
hidrodeslizador *nm* hovercraft;
hidroeléctrico, -a *adj* hydroelectric;
hidrógeno *nm* hydrogen

hiedra ['jeðra] *nf* ivy

hiel [jel] *nf* gall, bile; (*fig*) bitterness

hielo ['jelo] *vb* V **helar** ▷ *nm* (*gen*) ice;
(*escarcha*) frost; (*fig*) coldness, reserve

hiena ['jena] *nf* hyena

hierba ['jerβa] *nf* (*pasto*) grass; (*Culin,
Med: planta*) herb; **mala ~** weed; (*fig*)
evil influence; **hierbabuena** *nf* mint

hierro ['jerro] *nm* (*metal*) iron; (*objeto*)
iron object

hígado ['iɣaðo] *nm* liver

higiene [i'xjene] *nf* hygiene;
higiénico, -a *adj* hygienic

higo ['iɣo] *nm* fig; **~ seco** dried fig;
higuera *nf* fig tree

hijastro, -a [i'xastro, a] *nm/f*
stepson/daughter

hijo, -a ['ixo, a] *nm/f* son/daughter,
child; (*uso vocativo*) dear; **hijos** *nmpl*
children, sons and daughters; **~/hija
político/a** son-/daughter-in-law; **~
adoptivo** adopted child; **~ de papá/
mamá** daddy's/mummy's boy; **~ de
puta** (*fam!*) bastard (!), son of a bitch
(!); **~ único** only child

hilera [i'lera] *nf* row, file

hilo ['ilo] *nm* thread; (*Bot*) fibre; (*de
metal*) wire; (*de agua*) trickle, thin
stream

hilvanar [ilβa'nar] /1a/ *vt* (*Costura*)
to tack (BRIT), baste (US); (*fig*) to do
hurriedly

himno ['imno] *nm* hymn; **~ nacional**
national anthem

hincapié [inka'pje] *nm*: **hacer ~ en**
to emphasize

hincar [in'kar] /1g/ *vt* to drive (in),
thrust (in)

hincha ['intʃa] *nmf* (*fam*) fan

hinchado, -a [in'tʃaðo, a] *adj* (*gen*)
swollen; (*persona*) pompous

hinchar [in'tʃar] /1a/ *vt* (*gen*) to swell;
(*inflar*) to blow up, inflate; (*fig*) to
exaggerate; **hincharse** *vr* (*inflarse*) to

swell up; (*fam: llenarse*) to stuff o.s.;
hinchazón *nf* (*Med*) swelling; (*altivez*)
arrogance

hinojo [i'noxo] *nm* fennel

hipermercado [ipermer'kaðo] *nm*
hypermarket, superstore

hípico, -a ['ipiko, a] *adj* horse *cpd*

hipnotismo [ipno'tismo] *nm*
hypnotism; **hipnotizar** /1f/ *vt* to
hypnotize

hipo ['ipo] *nm* hiccups *pl*

hipocresía [ipokre'sia] *nf* hypocrisy;
hipócrita *adj* hypocritical ▷ *nmf*
hypocrite

hipódromo [i'poðromo] *nm*
racetrack

hipopótamo [ipo'potamo] *nm*
hippopotamus

hipoteca [ipo'teka] *nf* mortgage

hipótesis [i'potesis] *nf inv* hypothesis

hispánico, -a [is'paniko, a] *adj*
Hispanic

hispano, -a [is'pano, a] *adj* Hispanic,
Spanish, Hispano- ▷ *nm/f* Spaniard;
Hispanoamérica *nf* Spanish o Latin
America; **hispanoamericano, -a** *adj*,
nm/f Spanish o Latin American

histeria [is'terja] *nf* hysteria

historia [is'torja] *nf* history; (*cuento*)
story, tale; **historias** *nfpl* (*chismes*)
gossip *sg*; **dejarse de ~s** to come to
the point; **pasar a la ~** to go down
in history; **historiador, a** *nm/f*
historian; **historial** *nm* (*profesional*)
curriculum vitae, C.V.; (*Med*) case
history; **histórico, -a** *adj* historical;
(*fig*) historic

historieta [isto'rjeta] *nf* tale,
anecdote; (*de dibujos*) comic strip

hito ['ito] *nm* (*fig*) landmark

hizo ['iθo] *vb* V **hacer**

hocico [o'θiko] *nm* snout

hockey ['xoki] *nm* hockey; **~ sobre
hielo** ice hockey

hogar [o'ɣar] *nm* fireplace, hearth;
(*casa*) home; (*vida familiar*) home life;
hogareño, -a *adj* home *cpd*; (*persona*)
home-loving

hoguera [o'ɣera] *nf* (*gen*) bonfire
hoja ['oxa] *nf* (*gen*) leaf; (*de flor*)
petal; (*de papel*) sheet; (*página*)
page; **~ de afeitar** razor blade; **~ de
cálculo electrónica** spreadsheet; **~
informativa** leaflet, handout; **~ de
solicitud** application form
hojalata [oxa'lata] *nf* tin(plate)
hojaldre [o'xaldre] *nm* (*Culin*) puff
pastry
hojear [oxe'ar] /1a/ *vt* to leaf through,
turn the pages of
hojuela [o'xwela] *nf* (*LAM*) flake
hola ['ola] *excl* hello!
Holanda [o'landa] *nf* Holland;
holandés, -esa *adj* Dutch ▷ *nm/f*
Dutchman/woman ▷ *nm* (*Ling*)
Dutch
holgado, -a [ol'ɣaðo, a] *adj* loose,
baggy; (*rico*) well-to-do
holgar [ol'ɣar] /1h, 1l/ *vi* (*descansar*) to
rest; (*sobrar*) to be superfluous
holgazán, -ana [olɣa'θan, ana] *adj*
idle, lazy ▷ *nm/f* loafer
hollín [o'ʎin] *nm* soot
hombre ['ombre] *nm* man; (*raza
humana*): **el ~** man(kind) ▷ *excl* (*para
énfasis*) man, old chap; **¡sí ~!** (*claro*)
of course!; **~ de negocios** businessman;
~-rana frogman; **~ de bien** *o* **pro**
honest man
hombrera [om'brera] *nf* shoulder
strap
hombro ['ombro] *nm* shoulder
homenaje [ome'naxe] *nm* (*gen*)
homage; (*tributo*) tribute
homicida [omi'θiða] *adj* homicidal
▷ *nmf* murderer; **homicidio** *nm*
murder, homicide
homologar [omolo'ɣar] /1h/ *vt* (*Com*)
to standardize
homólogo, -a [o'moloɣo, a] *nm/f*
counterpart, opposite number
homosexual [omosek'swal] *adj*, *nmf*
homosexual
honda ['onda] *nf* (*cs*) catapult
hondo, -a ['ondo, a] *adj* deep; **lo
~** the depth(s) (*pl*), the bottom;

hondonada *nf* hollow, depression;
(*cañón*) ravine
Honduras [on'duras] *nf* Honduras
hondureño, -a [ondu'reɲo, a] *adj*,
nm/f Honduran
honestidad [onesti'ðað] *nf* purity,
chastity; (*decencia*) decency; **honesto,
-a** *adj* chaste; decent, honest;
(*justo*) just
hongo ['oŋgo] *nm* (*Bot: gen*) fungus;
(*: comestible*) mushroom; (*: venenoso*)
toadstool
honor [o'nor] *nm* (*gen*) honour (*BRIT*),
honor (*US*); **en ~ a la verdad** to be
fair; **honorable** *adj* honourable (*BRIT*),
honorable (*US*)
honorario, -a [ono'rarjo, a] *adj*
honorary ▷ *nm*: **~s** fees
honra ['onra] *nf* (*gen*) honour (*BRIT*),
honor (*US*); (*renombre*) good name;
honradez *nf* honesty; (*de persona*)
integrity; **honrado, -a** *adj* honest,
upright; **honrar** /1a/ *vt* to honour
(*BRIT*) *o* honor (*US*)
hora ['ora] *nf* hour; (*tiempo*) time;
¿qué ~ es? what time is it?; **¿a qué
~?** at what time?; **media ~** half an
hour; **a la ~ de comer/de recreo** at
lunchtime/at playtime; **a primera
~** first thing (in the morning); **a
última ~** at the last moment; **a
altas ~s** in the small hours; **¡a
buena ~!** about time, too!; **pedir ~**
to make an appointment; **dar la ~**
to strike the hour; **~s de oficina/de
trabajo** office/working hours; **~s
de visita** visiting times; **~s extras** *o*
extraordinarias overtime *sg*; **~s pico**
(*LAM*) rush *o* peak hours; **~s punta**
rush hours
horario, -a [o'rarjo, a] *adj* hourly,
hour *cpd* ▷ *nm* timetable; **~ comercial**
business hours
horca ['orka] *nf* gallows *sg*
horcajadas [orka'xaðas]: **a ~** *adv*
astride
horchata [or'tʃata] *nf* cold drink made
from tiger nuts and water, tiger nut milk

horizontal [oriθon'tal] *adj* horizontal

horizonte [ori'θonte] *nm* horizon

horma ['orma] *nf* mould

hormiga [or'miɣa] *nf* ant; **hormigas** *nfpl* (*Med*) pins and needles

hormigón [ormi'ɣon] *nm* concrete; **~ armado/pretensado** reinforced/ prestressed concrete; **hormigonera** *nf* cement mixer

hormigueo [ormi'ɣeo] *nm* (*comezón*) itch

hormona [or'mona] *nf* hormone

hornillo [or'niʎo] *nm* (*cocina*) portable stove; **~ de gas** gas ring

horno ['orno] *nm* (*Culin*) oven; (*Tec*) furnace; **alto ~** blast furnace

horóscopo [o'roskopo] *nm* horoscope

horquilla [or'kiʎa] *nf* hairpin; (*Agr*) pitchfork

horrendo, -a [o'rrendo, a] *adj* horrendous, frightful

horrible [o'rriβle] *adj* horrible, dreadful

horripilante [orripi'lante] *adj* hair-raising, horrifying

horror [o'rror] *nm* horror, dread; (*atrocidad*) atrocity; **¡qué ~!** (*fam*) how awful!; **horrorizar** /1f/ *vt* to horrify, frighten; **horrorizarse** *vr* to be horrified; **horroroso, -a** *adj* horrifying, ghastly

hortaliza [orta'liθa] *nf* vegetable

hortelano, -a [orte'lano, a] *nm/f* (market) gardener

hortera [or'tera] *adj* (*fam*) tacky

hospedar [ospe'ðar] /1a/ *vt* to put up; **hospedarse** *vr*: **~se (con/en)** to stay *o* lodge (with/at)

hospital [ospi'tal] *nm* hospital

hospitalario, -a [ospita'larjo, a] *adj* (*acogedor*) hospitable; **hospitalidad** *nf* hospitality

hostal [os'tal] *nm* small hotel

hostelería [ostele'ria] *nf* hotel business *o* trade

hostia ['ostja] *nf* (*Rel*) host, consecrated wafer; (*fam: golpe*) whack, punch ▷ *excl*: **¡~(s)!** (*fam!*) damn!

hostil [os'til] *adj* hostile

hotdog [ot'dog] *nm* (*LAM*) hot dog

hotel [o'tel] *nm* hotel; *see note* **"hotel"**; **hotelero, -a** *adj* hotel *cpd* ▷ *nm/f* hotelier

○ **HOTEL**
○
○
● In Spain you can choose from
● the following categories of
● accommodation, in descending
● order of quality and price: hotel
● (from 5 stars to 1), *hostal*, *pensión*,
● *casa de huéspedes*, *fonda*. Quality
● can vary widely even within these
● categories. The State also runs
● luxury hotels called *paradores*,
● which are usually sited in places
● of particular historical interest
● and are often historic buildings
● themselves.

hoy [oi] *adv* (*este día*) today; (*en la actualidad*) now(adays) ▷ *nm* present time; **~ (en) día** now(adays)

hoyo ['ojo] *nm* hole, pit

hoz [oθ] *nf* sickle

hube *etc* ['uβe] *vb* V **haber**

hucha ['utʃa] *nf* money box

hueco, -a ['weko, a] *adj* (*vacío*) hollow, empty; (*resonante*) booming ▷ *nm* hollow, cavity

huelga ['welɣa] *vb* V **holgar** ▷ *nf* strike; **declararse en ~** to go on strike, come out on strike; **~ general** general strike; **~ de hambre** hunger strike

huelguista [wel'ɣista] *nmf* striker

huella ['weʎa] *nf* (*acto de pisar, pisada*) tread(ing); (*marca del paso*) footprint, footstep; (: *de animal, máquina*) track; **~ de carbono** carbon footprint; **~ dactilar** *o* **digital** fingerprint

huelo *etc* *vb* V **oler**

huérfano, -a ['werfano, a] *adj* orphan(ed) ▷ *nm/f* orphan

huerta ['werta] nf market garden (BRIT), truck farm (US); (de Murcia, Valencia) irrigated region

huerto ['werto] nm kitchen garden; (de árboles frutales) orchard

hueso ['weso] nm (Anat) bone; (de fruta) stone

huésped, a ['wespeð, a] nm/f guest

huevas ['weβas] nfpl roe sg

huevera [we'βera] nf eggcup

huevo ['weβo] nm egg; **~ duro/ escalfado/estrellado** o **frito/ pasado por agua** hard-boiled/ poached/fried/soft-boiled egg; **~s revueltos** scrambled eggs; **~ tibio** (LAM) soft-boiled egg

huida [u'iða] nf escape, flight

huir [u'ir] /3g/ vt (escapar) to flee, escape; (evadir) to avoid

hule ['ule] nm oilskin; (esp LAM) rubber

hulera [u'lera] nf (LAM) catapult

humanidad [umani'ðað] nf (género humano) man(kind); (cualidad) humanity

humanitario, -a [umani'tarjo, a] adj humanitarian

humano, -a [u'mano, a] adj (gen) human; (humanitario) humane ▷ nm human; **ser ~** human being

humareda [uma'reða] nf cloud of smoke

humedad [ume'ðað] nf (del clima) humidity; (de pared etc) dampness; **a prueba de ~** damp-proof; **humedecer** /2d/ vt to moisten, wet; **humedecerse** vr to get wet

húmedo, -a ['umeðo, a] adj (mojado) damp, wet; (tiempo etc) humid

humilde [u'milde] adj humble, modest

humillación [umiʎa'θjon] nf humiliation; **humillante** adj humiliating

humillar [umi'ʎar] /1a/ vt to humiliate

humo ['umo] nm (de fuego) smoke; (gas nocivo) fumes pl; (vapor) steam, vapour; **humos** nmpl (fig) conceit sg

humor [u'mor] nm (disposición) mood, temper; (lo que divierte) humour; **de buen/mal ~** in a good/bad mood; **humorista** nmf comic; **humorístico, -a** adj funny, humorous

hundimiento [undi'mjento] nm (gen) sinking; (colapso) collapse

hundir [un'dir] /3a/ vt to sink; (edificio, plan) to ruin, destroy; **hundirse** vr to sink, collapse

húngaro, -a ['ungaro, a] adj, nm/f Hungarian

Hungría [un'gria] nf Hungary

huracán [ura'kan] nm hurricane

huraño, -a [u'raɲo, a] adj (antisocial) unsociable

hurgar [ur'yar] /1h/ vt to poke, jab; (remover) to stir (up); **hurgarse** vr: **~se (las narices)** to pick one's nose

hurón [u'ron] nm (Zool) ferret

hurtadillas [urta'ðiʎas]: **a ~** adv stealthily, on the sly

hurtar [ur'tar] /1a/ vt to steal; **hurto** nm theft, stealing

husmear [usme'ar] /1a/ vt (oler) to sniff out, scent; (fam) to pry into

huyo etc vb V **huir**

iba etc ['iβa] vb V **ir**
ibérico, -a [i'βeriko, a] adj Iberian
iberoamericano, -a
[iβeroameri'kano, a] adj, nm/f Latin American
Ibiza [i'βiθa] nf Ibiza
iceberg [iθe'ber] nm iceberg
icono [i'kono] nm icon
ida ['iða] nf going, departure; **~ y vuelta** round trip, return
idea [i'ðea] nf idea; **no tengo la menor ~** I haven't a clue
ideal [iðe'al] adj, nm ideal; **idealista** nmf idealist; **idealizar** /1f/ vt to idealize
ídem ['iðem] pron ditto
idéntico, -a [i'ðentiko, a] adj identical
identidad [iðenti'ðað] nf identity
identificación [iðentifika'θjon] nf identification
identificar [iðentifi'kar] /1g/ vt to identify; **identificarse** vr: **~se con** to identify with

ideología [iðeolo'xia] nf ideology
idilio [i'ðiljo] nm love affair
idioma [i'ðjoma] nm language
> No confundir *idioma* con la palabra inglesa *idiom*.

idiota [i'ðjota] adj idiotic ▷ nmf idiot
ídolo ['iðolo] nm (tb fig) idol
idóneo, -a [i'ðoneo, a] adj suitable
iglesia [i'ɣlesja] nf church
ignorante [iɣno'rante] adj ignorant, uninformed ▷ nmf ignoramus
ignorar [iɣno'rar] /1a/ vt not to know, be ignorant of; (*no hacer caso a*) to ignore
igual [i'ɣwal] adj equal; (*similar*) like, similar; (*mismo*) (the) same; (*constante*) constant; (*temperatura*) even ▷ nmf, conj equal; **al ~ que** prep like, just like; **~ que** the same as; **me da o es ~** I don't care; **son ~es** they're the same
igualar [iɣwa'lar] /1a/ vt (*gen*) to equalize, make equal; (*terreno*) to make even; (*allanar, nivelar*) to level (off); **igualarse** vr (*platos de balanza*) to balance out
igualdad [iɣwal'dað] nf equality; (*similaridad*) sameness; (*uniformidad*) uniformity
igualmente [iɣwal'mente] adv equally; (*también*) also, likewise ▷ excl the same to you!
ilegal [ile'ɣal] adj illegal
ilegítimo, -a [ile'xitimo, a] adj illegitimate
ileso, -a [i'leso, a] adj unhurt
ilimitado, -a [ilimi'taðo, a] adj unlimited
iluminación [ilumina'θjon] nf illumination; (*alumbrado*) lighting
iluminar [ilumi'nar] /1a/ vt to illuminate, light (up); (*fig*) to enlighten
ilusión [ilu'sjon] nf illusion; (*quimera*) delusion; (*esperanza*) hope; **hacerse ilusiones** to build up one's hopes; **ilusionado, -a** adj excited; **ilusionar** /1a/ vi: **le ilusiona ir de vacaciones** he's looking forward to going on

holiday; **ilusionarse** vr (entusiasmarse) to get excited

iluso, -a [i'luso, a] adj easily deceived ▷ nm/f dreamer

ilustración [ilustra'θjon] nf illustration; (saber) learning, erudition; **la l~** the Enlightenment; **ilustrado, -a** adj illustrated; learned

ilustrar [ilus'trar] /1a/ vt to illustrate; (instruir) to instruct; (explicar) to explain, make clear

ilustre [i'lustre] adj famous, illustrious

imagen [i'maxen] nf (gen) image; (dibujo) picture

imaginación [imaxina'θjon] nf imagination

imaginar [imaxi'nar] /1a/ vt (gen) to imagine; (idear) to think up; (suponer) to suppose; **imaginarse** vr to imagine; **imaginario, -a** adj imaginary; **imaginativo, -a** adj imaginative

imán [i'man] nm magnet

imbécil [im'beθil] nmf imbecile, idiot

imitación [imita'θjon] nf imitation; **a ~ de** in imitation of

imitar [imi'tar] /1a/ vt to imitate; (parodiar, remedar) to mimic, ape

impaciente [impa'θjente] adj impatient; (nervioso) anxious

impacto [im'pakto] nm impact

impar [im'par] adj odd

imparcial [impar'θjal] adj impartial, fair

impecable [impe'kaβle] adj impeccable

impedimento [impeði'mento] nm impediment, obstacle

impedir [impe'ðir] /3k/ vt (obstruir) to impede, obstruct; (estorbar) to prevent; **~ a algn hacer** o **que algn haga algo** to prevent sb (from) doing sth

imperativo, -a [impera'tiβo, a] adj (urgente, Ling) imperative

imperdible [imper'ðiβle] nm safety pin

imperdonable [imperðo'naβle] adj unforgivable, inexcusable

imperfecto, -a [imper'fekto, a] adj imperfect

imperio [im'perjo] nm empire; (autoridad) rule, authority; (fig) pride, haughtiness

impermeable [imperme'aβle] adj waterproof ▷ nm raincoat, mac (BRIT)

impersonal [imperso'nal] adj impersonal

impertinente [imperti'nente] adj impertinent

ímpetu ['impetu] nm (impulso) impetus, impulse; (impetuosidad) impetuosity; (violencia) violence

implantar [implan'tar] /1a/ vt (costumbre) to introduce

implemento [imple'mento] nm (LAM) tool, implement

implicar [impli'kar] /1g/ vt to involve; (entrañar) to imply

implícito, -a [im'pliθito, a] adj (tácito) implicit; (sobreentendido) implied

imponente [impo'nente] adj (impresionante) impressive, imposing; (solemne) grand

imponer [impo'ner] /2q/ vt (gen) to impose; (exigir) to exact; **imponerse** vr to assert o.s.; (prevalecer) to prevail; **imponible** adj (Com) taxable

impopular [impopu'lar] adj unpopular

importación [importa'θjon] nf (acto) importing; (mercancías) imports pl

importancia [impor'tanθja] nf importance; (valor) value, significance; (extensión) size, magnitude; **no tiene ~** it's nothing; **importante** adj important; valuable, significant

importar [impor'tar] /1a/ vt (del extranjero) to import; (costar) to amount to ▷ vi to be important, matter; **me importa un rábano** or **un bledo** I couldn't care less; **¿le**

importa que fume? do you mind if I smoke?; **no importa** it doesn't matter

importe [im'porte] *nm* (*cantidad*) amount; (*valor*) value

imposible [impo'siβle] *adj* impossible; (*insoportable*) unbearable, intolerable

imposición [imposi'θjon] *nf* imposition; (*Com*) tax; (*inversión*) deposit

impostor, a [impos'tor, a] *nm/f* impostor

impotencia [impo'tenθja] *nf* impotence; **impotente** *adj* impotent

impreciso, -a [impre'θiso, a] *adj* imprecise, vague

impregnar [impreɣ'nar] /1a/ *vt* to impregnate; **impregnarse** *vr* to become impregnated

imprenta [im'prenta] *nf* (*acto*) printing; (*aparato*) press; (*casa*) printer's; (*letra*) print

imprescindible [impresθin'diβle] *adj* essential, vital

impresión [impre'sjon] *nf* impression; (*Imprenta*) printing; (*edición*) edition; (*Foto*) print; (*marca*) imprint; **~ digital** fingerprint

impresionante [impresjo'nante] *adj* impressive; (*tremendo*) tremendous; (*maravilloso*) great, marvellous

impresionar [impresjo'nar] /1a/ *vt* (*conmover*) to move; (*afectar*) to impress, strike; (*película fotográfica*) to expose; **impresionarse** *vr* to be impressed; (*conmoverse*) to be moved

impreso, -a [im'preso, a] *pp de* **imprimir** ▷ *adj* printed; **impresos** *nmpl* printed matter *sg*; **impresora** *nf* printer

imprevisto, -a [impre'βisto, a] *adj* unforeseen; (*inesperado*) unexpected

imprimir [impri'mir] /3a/ *vt* to stamp; (*textos*) to print; (*Inform*) to output, print out

improbable [impro'βaβle] *adj* improbable; (*inverosímil*) unlikely

impropio, -a [im'propjo, a] *adj* improper

improvisado, -a [improβi'saðo, a] *adj* improvised

improvisar [improβi'sar] /1a/ *vt* to improvise

improviso [impro'βiso] *adv*: **de ~** unexpectedly, suddenly

imprudencia [impru'ðenθja] *nf* imprudence; (*indiscreción*) indiscretion; (*descuido*) carelessness; **imprudente** *adj* unwise, imprudent; (*indiscreto*) indiscreet

impuesto, -a [im'pwesto, a] *adj* imposed ▷ *nm* tax; **~ de venta** sales tax; **~ sobre el valor añadido (IVA)** value added tax (VAT)

impulsar [impul'sar] /1a/ *vt* to drive; (*promover*) to promote, stimulate

impulsivo, -a [impul'siβo, a] *adj* impulsive; **impulso** *nm* impulse; (*fuerza, empuje*) thrust, drive; (*fig: sentimiento*) urge, impulse

impureza [impu're θa] *nf* impurity; **impuro, -a** *adj* impure

inaccesible [inakθe'siβle] *adj* inaccessible

inaceptable [inaθep'taβle] *adj* unacceptable

inactivo, -a [inak'tiβo, a] *adj* inactive

inadecuado, -a [inaðe'kwaðo, a] *adj* (*insuficiente*) inadequate; (*inapto*) unsuitable

inadvertido, -a [inaðβer'tiðo, a] *adj* (*no visto*) unnoticed

inaguantable [inaɣwan'taβle] *adj* unbearable

inalámbrico, -a [ina'lambriko, a] *adj* cordless, wireless

inanimado, -a [inani'maðo, a] *adj* inanimate

inaudito, -a [inau'ðito, a] *adj* unheard-of

inauguración [inauɣura'θjon] *nf* inauguration; (*de exposición*) opening

inaugurar [inauɣu'rar] /1a/ *vt* to inaugurate; (*exposición*) to open

inca ['inka] *nmf* Inca

incalculable [inkalkuˈlaβle] *adj* incalculable

incandescente [inkandesˈθente] *adj* incandescent

incansable [inkanˈsaβle] *adj* tireless, untiring

incapacidad [inkapaθiˈðað] *nf* incapacity; (*incompetencia*) incompetence; **~ física/mental** physical/mental disability

incapacitar [inkapaθiˈtar] /1a/ *vt* (*inhabilitar*) to incapacitate, handicap; (*descalificar*) to disqualify

incapaz [inkaˈpaθ] *adj* incapable

incautarse [inkauˈtarse] /1a/ *vr*: **~ de** to seize, confiscate

incauto, -a [inˈkauto, a] *adj* (*imprudente*) incautious, unwary

incendiar [inθenˈdjar] /1b/ *vt* to set fire to; (*fig*) to inflame; **incendiarse** *vr* to catch fire; **incendiario, -a** *adj* incendiary

incendio [inˈθendjo] *nm* fire

incentivo [inθenˈtiβo] *nm* incentive

incertidumbre [inθertiˈðumbre] *nf* (*inseguridad*) uncertainty; (*duda*) doubt

incesante [inθeˈsante] *adj* incessant

incesto [inˈθesto] *nm* incest

incidencia [inθiˈðenθja] *nf* (*Mat*) incidence

incidente [inθiˈðente] *nm* incident

incidir [inθiˈðir] /3a/ *vi*: **~ en** (*influir*) to influence; (*afectar*) to affect

incienso [inˈθjenso] *nm* incense

incierto, -a [inˈθjerto, a] *adj* uncertain

incineración [inθineraˈθjon] *nf* incineration; (*de cadáveres*) cremation

incinerar [inθineˈrar] /1a/ *vt* to burn; (*cadáveres*) to cremate

incisión [inθiˈsjon] *nf* incision

incisivo, -a [inθiˈsiβo, a] *adj* sharp, cutting; (*fig*) incisive

incitar [inθiˈtar] /1a/ *vt* to incite, rouse

inclemencia [inkleˈmenθja] *nf* (*severidad*) harshness, severity; (*del tiempo*) inclemency

inclinación [inklinaˈθjon] *nf* (*gen*) inclination; (*de tierras*) slope, incline; (*de cabeza*) nod, bow; (*fig*) leaning, bent

inclinar [inkliˈnar] /1a/ *vt* to incline; (*cabeza*) to nod, bow; **inclinarse** *vr* to lean, slope; to bow; (*encorvarse*) to stoop; **~se a** (*parecerse*) to take after, resemble; **~se ante** to bow down to; **me inclino a pensar que ...** I'm inclined to think that ...

incluir [inkluˈir] /3g/ *vt* to include; (*incorporar*) to incorporate; (*meter*) to enclose

inclusive [inkluˈsiβe] *adv* inclusive ▷ *prep* including

incluso, -a [inˈkluso, a] *adv* even

incógnita [inˈkoɣnita] *nf* (*Mat*) unknown quantity

incógnito [inˈkoɣnito] *nm*: **de ~** incognito

incoherente [inkoeˈrente] *adj* incoherent

incoloro, -a [inkoˈloro, a] *adj* colourless

incomodar [inkomoˈðar] /1a/ *vt* to inconvenience; (*molestar*) to bother, trouble; (*fastidiar*) to annoy

incomodidad [inkomoðiˈðað] *nf* inconvenience; (*fastidio, enojo*) annoyance; (*de vivienda*) discomfort

incómodo, -a [inˈkomoðo, a] *adj* (*inconfortable*) uncomfortable; (*molesto*) annoying; (*inconveniente*) inconvenient

incomparable [inkompaˈraβle] *adj* incomparable

incompatible [inkompaˈtiβle] *adj* incompatible

incompetente [inkompeˈtente] *adj* incompetent

incompleto, -a [inkomˈpleto, a] *adj* incomplete, unfinished

incomprensible [inkomprenˈsiβle] *adj* incomprehensible

incomunicado, -a [inkomuniˈkaðo, a] *adj* (*aislado*) cut off, isolated; (*confinado*) in solitary confinement

incondicional [inkondi'θjo'nal] *adj*
unconditional; (*apoyo*) wholehearted;
(*partidario*) staunch

inconfundible [inkonfun'diβle] *adj*
unmistakable

incongruente [inkon'grwente] *adj*
incongruous

inconsciente [inkons'θjente] *adj*
unconscious; thoughtless

inconsecuente [inkonse'kwente]
adj inconsistent

inconstante [inkons'tante] *adj*
inconstant

incontable [inkon'taβle] *adj*
countless, innumerable

inconveniencia [inkombe'njenθja]
nf unsuitability, inappropriateness;
(*falta de cortesía*) impoliteness;
inconveniente *adj* unsuitable;
impolite ▷ *nm* obstacle; (*desventaja*)
disadvantage; **el inconveniente es
que ...** the trouble is that ...

incordiar [inkor'ðjar] /1b/ *vt* (*fam*)
to hassle

incorporar [inkorpo'rar] /1a/ *vt* to
incorporate; **incorporarse** *vr* to sit up;
~se a to join

incorrecto, -a [inko'rrekto, a] *adj*
incorrect, wrong; (*comportamiento*)
bad-mannered

incorregible [inkorre'xiβle] *adj*
incorrigible

incrédulo, -a [in'kreðulo, a] *adj*
incredulous, unbelieving; sceptical

increíble [inkre'iβle] *adj* incredible

incremento [inkre'mento] *nm*
increment; (*aumento*) rise, increase

increpar [inkre'par] /1a/ *vt* to
reprimand

incruento, -a [in'krwento, a] *adj*
bloodless

incrustar [inkrus'tar] /1a/ *vt* to
incrust; (*piedras: en joya*) to inlay

incubar [inku'βar] /1a/ *vt* to incubate

inculcar [inkul'kar] /1g/ *vt* to inculcate

inculto, -a [in'kulto, a] *adj* (*persona*)
uneducated; (*grosero*) uncouth ▷ *nm/f*
ignoramus

incumplimiento
[inkumpli'mjento] *nm* non-
fulfilment; **~ de contrato** breach of
contract

incurrir [inku'rrir] /3a/ *vi*: **~ en** to
incur; (*crimen*) to commit

indagar [inda'ɣar] /1h/ *vt* to
investigate; to search; (*averiguar*) to
ascertain

indecente [inde'θente] *adj* indecent,
improper; (*lascivo*) obscene

indeciso, -a [inde'θiso, a] *adj* (*por
decidir*) undecided; (*vacilante*) hesitant

indefenso, -a [inde'fenso, a] *adj*
defenceless

indefinido, -a [indefi'niðo, a] *adj*
indefinite; (*vago*) vague, undefined

indemne [in'demne] *adj* (*objeto*)
undamaged; (*persona*) unharmed,
unhurt

indemnizar [indemni'θar] /1f/ *vt* to
indemnify; (*compensar*) to compensate

independencia [indepen'denθja] *nf*
independence

independiente [indepen'djente]
adj (*libre*) independent; (*autónomo*)
self-sufficient

indeterminado, -a
[indetermi'naðo, a] *adj* indefinite;
(*desconocido*) indeterminate

India ['indja] *nf*: **la ~** India

indicación [indika'θjon] *nf*
indication; (*señal*) sign; (*sugerencia*)
suggestion, hint

indicado, -a [indi'kaðo, a] *adj*
(*momento, método*) right; (*tratamiento*)
appropriate; (*solución*) likely

indicador [indika'ðor] *nm* indicator;
(*Tec*) gauge, meter

indicar [indi'kar] /1g/ *vt* (*mostrar*)
to indicate, show; (*termómetro etc*) to
read, register; (*señalar*) to point to

índice ['indiθe] *nm* index; (*catálogo*)
catalogue; (*Anat*) index finger,
forefinger; **~ de materias** table of
contents

indicio [in'diθjo] *nm* indication, sign;
(*en pesquisa etc*) clue

indiferencia [indife'renθja] nf
indifference; (apatía) apathy;
indiferente adj indifferent

indígena [in'dixena] adj indigenous,
native ▷ nmf native

indigestión [indixes'tjon] nf
indigestion

indigesto, -a [indi'xesto, a] adj
indigestible; (fig) turgid

indignación [indiɣna'θjon] nf
indignation

indignar [indiɣ'nar] /1a/ vt to anger,
make indignant; **indignarse** vr: **~se
por** to get indignant about

indigno, -a [in'diɣno, a] adj
(despreciable) low, contemptible;
(inmerecido) unworthy

indio, -a ['indjo, a] adj, nm/f Indian

indirecto, -a [indi'rekto, a] adj
indirect ▷ nf insinuation, innuendo;
(sugerencia) hint

indiscreción [indiskre'θjon] nf
(imprudencia) indiscretion; (irreflexión)
tactlessness; (acto) gaffe, faux pas

indiscreto, -a [indis'kreto, a] adj
indiscreet

indiscutible [indisku'tiβle] adj
indisputable, unquestionable

indispensable [indispen'saβle] adj
indispensable, essential

indispuesto, -a [indis'pwesto, a]
adj (enfermo) unwell, indisposed

indistinto, -a [indis'tinto, a] adj
indistinct; (vago) vague

individual [indiβi'ðwal] adj
individual; (habitación) single ▷ nm
(Deporte) singles sg

individuo, -a [indi'βiðwo, a] adj
▷ nm individual

índole ['indole] nf (naturaleza) nature;
(clase) sort, kind

inducir [indu'θir] /3n/ vt to induce;
(inferir) to infer; (persuadir) to persuade

indudable [indu'ðaβle] adj
undoubted; (incuestionable)
unquestionable

indultar [indul'tar] /1a/ vt (perdonar)
to pardon, reprieve; (librar de pago)

to exempt; **indulto** nm pardon;
exemption

industria [in'dustrja] nf industry;
(habilidad) skill; **industrial** adj
industrial ▷ nm industrialist

inédito, -a [i'neðito, a] adj (libro)
unpublished; (nuevo) new

ineficaz [inefi'kaθ] adj (inútil)
ineffective; (ineficiente) inefficient

ineludible [inelu'ðiβle] adj
inescapable, unavoidable

ineptitud [inepti'tuð] nf ineptitude,
incompetence; **inepto, -a** adj inept,
incompetent

inequívoco, -a [ine'kiβoko, a]
adj unequivocal; (inconfundible)
unmistakable

inercia [i'nerθja] nf inertia; (pasividad)
passivity

inerte [i'nerte] adj inert; (inmóvil)
motionless

inesperado, -a [inespe'raðo, a] adj
unexpected, unforeseen

inestable [ines'taβle] adj unstable

inevitable [ineβi'taβle] adj
inevitable

inexacto, -a [inek'sakto, a] adj
inaccurate; (falso) untrue

inexperto, -a [ineks'perto, a] adj
(novato) inexperienced

infalible [infa'liβle] adj infallible;
(plan) foolproof

infame [in'fame] adj infamous;
infamia nf infamy; (deshonra)
disgrace

infancia [in'fanθja] nf infancy,
childhood

infantería [infante'ria] nf infantry

infantil [infan'til] adj child's,
children's; (pueril, aniñado) infantile;
(cándido) childlike

infarto [in'farto] nm (tb: **~ de
miocardio**) heart attack; **~ cerebral**
stroke

infatigable [infati'ɣaβle] adj tireless,
untiring

infección [infek'θjon] nf infection;
infeccioso, -a adj infectious

infectar [infek'tar] /1a/ vt to infect;
infectarse vr

infeliz [infe'liθ] adj unhappy,
wretched ▷ nmf wretch

inferior [infe'rjor] adj inferior;
(situación) lower ▷ nmf inferior,
subordinate

inferir [infe'rir] /3i/ vt (deducir) to
infer, deduce; (causar) to cause

infidelidad [infiðeli'ðað] nf
infidelity, unfaithfulness

infiel [in'fjel] adj unfaithful, disloyal;
(falso) inaccurate ▷ nmf infidel,
unbeliever

infierno [in'fjerno] nm hell

ínfimo, -a ['infimo, a] adj (vil) vile,
mean; (más bajo) lowest

infinidad [infini'ðað] nf infinity;
(abundancia) great quantity

infinito, -a [infi'nito, a] adj ▷ nm
infinite

inflación [infla'θjon] nf (hinchazón)
swelling; (monetaria) inflation; (fig)
conceit

inflamable [infla'maβle] adj
flammable

inflamar [infla'mar] /1a/ vt (Med, fig)
to inflame; **inflamarse** vr to catch fire;
to become inflamed

inflar [in'flar] /1a/ vt (hinchar) to
inflate, blow up; (fig) to exaggerate;
inflarse vr to swell (up); (fig) to get
conceited

inflexible [inflek'siβle] adj inflexible;
(fig) unbending

influencia [in'flwenθja] nf influence

influir [influ'ir] /3g/ vt to influence

influjo [in'fluxo] nm influence

influya etc vb V **influir**

influyente [influ'jente] adj
influential

información [informa'θjon] nf
information; (noticias) news sg; (Jur)
inquiry; **I~** (oficina) information desk;
(Telec) Directory Enquiries (BRIT),
Directory Assistance (US); (mostrador)
Information Desk

informal [infor'mal] adj informal

informar [infor'mar] /1a/ vt (gen) to
inform; (revelar) to reveal; make known
▷ vi (Jur) to plead; (denunciar) to inform;
(dar cuenta de) to report on; **informarse**
vr to find out; **~se de** to inquire into

informática [infor'matika] nf V
informático

informático, -a [infor'matiko,
a] adj computer cpd ▷ nf (Tec)
information technology; computing;
(Escol) computer science o studies

informe [in'forme] adj shapeless
▷ nm report

infracción [infrak'θjon] nf
infraction, infringement

infravalorar [infraβalo'rar]
/1a/ vt to undervalue; (Finanzas) to
underestimate

infringir [infrin'xir] /3c/ vt to
infringe, contravene

infundado, -a [infun'daðo, a] adj
groundless, unfounded

infundir [infun'dir] /3a/ vt to
infuse, instil

infusión [infu'sjon] nf infusion; **~ de
manzanilla** camomile tea

ingeniería [inxenje'ria] nf
engineering; **~ genética** genetic
engineering; **ingeniero, -a** nm/f
engineer; **ingeniero de caminos**
civil engineer

ingenio [in'xenjo] nm (talento) talent;
(agudeza) wit; (habilidad) ingenuity,
inventiveness; **~ azucarero** sugar
refinery; **ingenioso, -a** adj ingenious,
clever; (divertido) witty

ingenuo, -a [in'xenwo, a] adj
ingenuous

ingerir [inxe'rir] /3i/ vt to ingest;
(tragar) to swallow; (consumir) to
consume

Inglaterra [ingla'terra] nf England

ingle ['ingle] nf groin

inglés, -esa [in'gles, esa] adj English
▷ nm/f Englishman/woman ▷ nm
(Ling) English

ingrato, -a [in'grato, a] adj
ungrateful

ingrediente [ingre'ðjente] *nm* ingredient

ingresar [ingre'sar] /1a/ *vt* (*dinero*) to deposit ▷ *vi* to come *o* go in; **~ en el hospital** to go into hospital

ingreso [in'greso] *nm* (*entrada*) entry; (: *en hospital etc*) admission; **ingresos** *nmpl* (*dinero*) income *sg*; (: *Com*) takings *pl*

inhabitable [inaβi'taβle] *adj* uninhabitable

inhalar [ina'lar] /1a/ *vt* to inhale

inhibir [ini'βir] /3a/ *vt* to inhibit

inhóspito, -a [i'nospito, a] *adj* (*región, paisaje*) inhospitable

inhumano, -a [inu'mano, a] *adj* inhuman

inicial [ini'θjal] *adj, nf* initial

iniciar [ini'θjar] /1b/ *vt* (*persona*) to initiate; (*empezar*) to begin, commence; (*conversación*) to start up

iniciativa [iniθja'tiβa] *nf* initiative; **~ privada** private enterprise

ininterrumpido, -a [ininterrum'piðo, a] *adj* uninterrupted

injertar [inxer'tar] /1a/ *vt* to graft; **injerto** *nm* graft

injuria [in'xurja] *nf* (*agravio, ofensa*) offence; (*insulto*) insult

> No confundir *injuria* con la palabra inglesa *injury*.

injusticia [inxus'tiθja] *nf* injustice

injusto, -a [in'xusto, a] *adj* unjust, unfair

inmadurez [inmaðu'reθ] *nf* immaturity

inmediaciones [inmeðja'θjones] *nfpl* neighbourhood *sg*, environs

inmediato, -a [inme'ðjato, a] *adj* immediate; (*contiguo*) adjoining; (*rápido*) prompt; (*próximo*) neighbouring, next; **de ~** immediately

inmejorable [inmexo'raβle] *adj* unsurpassable; (*precio*) unbeatable

inmenso, -a [in'menso, a] *adj* immense, huge

inmigración [inmiɣra'θjon] *nf* immigration

inmolar [inmo'lar] /1a/ *vt* to immolate, sacrifice

inmoral [inmo'ral] *adj* immoral

inmortal [inmor'tal] *adj* immortal; **inmortalizar** /1f/ *vt* to immortalize

inmóvil [in'moβil] *adj* immobile

inmueble [in'mweβle] *adj*: **bienes ~s** real estate *sg*, landed property *sg* ▷ *nm* property

inmundo, -a [in'mundo, a] *adj* filthy

inmune [in'mune] *adj*: **~ (a)** (*Med*) immune (to)

inmunidad [inmuni'ðað] *nf* immunity

inmutarse [inmu'tarse] /1a/ *vr* to turn pale; **no se inmutó** he didn't turn a hair; **siguió sin ~** he carried on unperturbed

innato, -a [in'nato, a] *adj* innate

innecesario, -a [inneθe'sarjo, a] *adj* unnecessary

innovación [innoβa'θjon] *nf* innovation

innovar [inno'βar] /1a/ *vt* to introduce

inocencia [ino'θenθja] *nf* innocence

inocentada [inoθen'taða] *nf* practical joke

inocente [ino'θente] *adj* (*ingenuo*) naive, innocent; (*no culpable*) innocent; (*sin malicia*) harmless ▷ *nmf* simpleton; **día de los (Santos) I~s** ≈ April Fools' Day

○ **DÍA DE LOS INOCENTES**
○
○ The 28th December, *el día de los*
○ *(Santos) Inocentes*, is when the
○ Church commemorates the story
○ of Herod's slaughter of the innocent
○ children of Judea in the time of
○ Christ. On this day Spaniards play
○ *inocentadas* (practical jokes) on each
○ other, much like our April Fools'
○ Day pranks, eg typically sticking a
○ *monigote* (cut-out paper figure) on

someone's back, or broadcasting
unlikely news stories.

inodoro [ino'ðoro] *nm* toilet (*BRIT*), lavatory (*BRIT*), washroom (*US*)

inofensivo, -a [inofen'siβo, a] *adj* inoffensive

inolvidable [inolβi'ðaβle] *adj* unforgettable

inoportuno, -a [inopor'tuno, a] *adj* untimely; (*molesto*) inconvenient

inoxidable [inoksi'ðaβle] *adj*: **acero ~** stainless steel

inquietar [inkje'tar] /1a/ *vt* to worry, trouble; **inquietarse** *vr* to worry, get upset; **inquieto, -a** *adj* anxious, worried; **inquietud** *nf* anxiety, worry

inquilino, -a [inki'lino, a] *nm/f* tenant

insaciable [insa'θjaβle] *adj* insatiable

inscribir [inskri'βir] /3a/ *vt* to inscribe; (*en lista*) to put; (*en censo*) to register

inscripción [inskrip'θjon] *nf* inscription; (*Escol etc*) enrolment; (*en censo*) registration

insecticida [insekti'θiða] *nm* insecticide

insecto [in'sekto] *nm* insect

inseguridad [inseɣuri'ðað] *nf* insecurity; **~ ciudadana** lack of safety in the streets

inseguro, -a [inse'ɣuro, a] *adj* insecure; (*inconstante*) unsteady; (*incierto*) uncertain

insensato, -a [insen'sato, a] *adj* foolish, stupid

insensible [insen'siβle] *adj* (*gen*) insensitive; (*movimiento*) imperceptible; (*sin sensación*) numb

insertar [inser'tar] /1a/ *vt* to insert

inservible [inser'βiβle] *adj* useless

insignia [in'siɣnja] *nf* (*señal distintiva*) badge; (*estandarte*) flag

insignificante [insiɣnifi'kante] *adj* insignificant

insinuar [insi'nwar] /1e/ *vt* to insinuate, imply

insípido, -a [in'sipiðo, a] *adj* insipid

insistir [insis'tir] /3a/ *vi* to insist; **~ en algo** to insist on sth; (*enfatizar*) to stress sth

insolación [insola'θjon] *nf* (*Med*) sunstroke

insolente [inso'lente] *adj* insolent

insólito, -a [in'solito, a] *adj* unusual

insoluble [inso'luβle] *adj* insoluble

insomnio [in'somnjo] *nm* insomnia

insonorizado, -a [insonori'θaðo, a] *adj* (*cuarto etc*) soundproof

insoportable [insopor'taβle] *adj* unbearable

inspección [inspek'θjon] *nf* inspection, check; **inspeccionar** /1a/ *vt* (*examinar*) to inspect, examine; (*controlar*) to check

inspector, a [inspek'tor, a] *nm/f* inspector

inspiración [inspira'θjon] *nf* inspiration

inspirar [inspi'rar] /1a/ *vt* to inspire; (*Med*) to inhale; **inspirarse** *vr*: **~se en** to be inspired by

instalación [instala'θjon] *nf* (*equipo*) fittings *pl*, equipment; **~ eléctrica** wiring

instalar [insta'lar] /1a/ *vt* (*establecer*) to instal; (*erguir*) to set up, erect; **instalarse** *vr* to establish o.s.; (*en una vivienda*) to move into

instancia [ins'tanθja] *nf* (*ruego*) request; (*Jur*) petition; **en última ~** as a last resort

instantáneo, -a [instan'taneo, a] *adj* instantaneous; **café ~** instant coffee

instante [ins'tante] *nm* instant, moment; **al ~** right now

instar [ins'tar] /1a/ *vt* to press, urge

instaurar [instau'rar] /1a/ *vt* (*costumbre*) to establish; (*normas, sistema*) to bring in, introduce; (*gobierno*) to install

instigar [insti'ɣar] /1h/ *vt* to instigate

instinto [ins'tinto] nm instinct; **por ~** instinctively

institución [institu'θjon] nf institution, establishment

instituir [institu'ir] /3g/ vt to establish; (fundar) to found; **instituto** nm (gen) institute; **Instituto Nacional de Enseñanza** (ESP) ≈ (state) secondary (BRIT) o high (US) school

institutriz [institu'triθ] nf governess

instrucción [instruk'θjon] nf instruction

instructor [instruk'tor] nm instructor

instruir [instru'ir] /3g/ vt (gen) to instruct; (enseñar) to teach, educate

instrumento [instru'mento] nm instrument; (herramienta) tool, implement

insubordinarse [insuβorði'narse] /1a/ vr to rebel

insuficiente [insufi'θjente] adj (gen) insufficient; (Escol: nota) unsatisfactory

insular [insu'lar] adj insular

insultar [insul'tar] /1a/ vt to insult; **insulto** nm insult

insuperable [insupe'raβle] adj (excelente) unsurpassable; (problema etc) insurmountable

insurrección [insurrek'θjon] nf insurrection, rebellion

intachable [inta'tʃaβle] adj irreproachable

intacto, -a [in'takto, a] adj intact

integral [inte'ɣral] adj integral; (completo) complete; **pan ~** wholemeal bread

integrar [inte'ɣrar] /1a/ vt to make up, compose; (Mat, fig) to integrate

integridad [inteɣri'ðað] nf wholeness; (carácter) integrity; **íntegro, -a** adj whole, entire; (honrado) honest

intelectual [intelek'twal] adj, nmf intellectual

inteligencia [inteli'xenθja] nf intelligence; (ingenio) ability; **inteligente** adj intelligent

intemperie [intem'perje] nf: **a la ~** outdoors, out in the open, exposed to the elements

intención [inten'θjon] nf intention, purpose; **con segundas intenciones** maliciously; **con ~** deliberately

intencionado, -a [intenθjo'naðo, a] adj deliberate; **mal ~** ill-disposed, hostile

intensidad [intensi'ðað] nf (gen) intensity; (Elec, Tec) strength; **llover con ~** to rain hard

intenso, -a [in'tenso, a] adj intense; (sentimiento) profound, deep

intentar [inten'tar] /1a/ vt (tratar) to try, attempt; **intento** nm attempt

interactivo, -a [interak'tiβo, a] adj interactive

intercalar [interka'lar] /1a/ vt to insert

intercambio [inter'kambjo] nm exchange; swap

interceder [interθe'ðer] /2a/ vi to intercede

interceptar [interθep'tar] /1a/ vt to intercept

interés [inte'res] nm interest; (parte) share, part; (pey) self-interest; **intereses creados** vested interests

interesado, -a [intere'saðo, a] adj interested; (prejuiciado) prejudiced; (pey) mercenary, self-seeking

interesante [intere'sante] adj interesting

interesar [intere'sar] /1a/ vt to interest, be of interest to ▷ vi to interest, be of interest; **interesarse** vr: **~se en** o **por** to take an interest in

interferir [interfe'rir] /3i/ vt to interfere with; (Telec) to jam ▷ vi to interfere

interfono [inter'fono] nm intercom, entry phone

interino, -a [inte'rino, a] adj temporary ▷ nm/f temporary holder of a post; (*Med*) locum; (*Escol*) supply teacher

interior [inte'rjor] *adj* inner, inside; (*Com*) domestic, internal ▷ *nm* interior, inside; (*fig*) soul, mind; **Ministerio del I~** ≈ Home Office (*BRIT*), ≈ Department of the Interior (*US*)

interjección [interxek'θjon] *nf* interjection

interlocutor, a [interloku'tor, a] *nm/f* speaker

intermedio, -a [inter'meðjo, a] *adj* intermediate ▷ *nm* interval

interminable [intermi'naβle] *adj* endless

intermitente [intermi'tente] *adj* intermittent ▷ *nm* (*Auto*) indicator

internacional [internaθjo'nal] *adj* international

internado [inter'naðo] *nm* boarding school

internar [inter'nar] /1a/ *vt* to intern; (*en un manicomio*) to commit; **internarse** *vr* (*penetrar*) to penetrate

internauta [inter'nauta] *nmf* web surfer, internet user

Internet [inter'net] *nm o f* internet, Internet

interno, -a [in'terno, a] *adj* internal, interior; (*Pol etc*) domestic ▷ *nm/f* (*alumno*) boarder

interponer [interpo'ner] /2q/ *vt* to interpose, put in; **interponerse** *vr* to intervene

interpretación [interpreta'θjon] *nf* interpretation

interpretar [interpre'tar] /1a/ *vt* to interpret; (*Teat, Mus*) to perform, play; **intérprete** *nmf* (*Ling*) interpreter, translator; (*Mus, Teat*) performer, artist(e)

interrogación [interroɣa'θjon] *nf* interrogation; (*Ling: tb*: **signo de ~**) question mark

interrogar [interro'ɣar] /1h/ *vt* to interrogate, question

interrumpir [interrum'pir] /3a/ *vt* to interrupt

interrupción [interrup'θjon] *nf* interruption

interruptor [interrup'tor] *nm* (*Elec*) switch

intersección [intersek'θjon] *nf* intersection

interurbano, -a [interur'βano, a] *adj* (*Telec*) long-distance

intervalo [inter'βalo] *nm* interval; (*descanso*) break

intervenir [interβe'nir] /3r/ *vt* (*controlar*) to control, supervise; (*Med*) to operate on ▷ *vi* (*participar*) to take part, participate; (*mediar*) to intervene

interventor, a [interβen'tor, a] *nm/f* inspector; (*Com*) auditor

intestino [intes'tino] *nm* intestine

intimar [inti'mar] /1a/ *vi* to become friendly

intimidad [intimi'ðað] *nf* intimacy; (*familiaridad*) familiarity; (*vida privada*) private life; (*Jur*) privacy

íntimo, -a ['intimo, a] *adj* intimate

intolerable [intole'raβle] *adj* intolerable, unbearable

intoxicación [intoksika'θjon] *nf* poisoning; **~ alimenticia** food poisoning

intranet [intra'net] *nf* intranet

intranquilo, -a [intran'kilo, a] *adj* worried

intransitable [intransi'taβle] *adj* impassable

intrépido, -a [in'trepiðo, a] *adj* intrepid

intriga [in'triɣa] *nf* intrigue; (*plan*) plot; **intrigar** /1h/ *vt, vi* to intrigue

intrínseco, -a [in'trinseko, a] *adj* intrinsic

introducción [introðuk'θjon] *nf* introduction

introducir [introðu'θir] /3n/ *vt* (*gen*) to introduce; (*moneda*) to insert; (*Inform*) to input, enter

intromisión [intromi'sjon] *nf* interference, meddling

introvertido, -a [introβer'tiðo, a] *adj, nm/f* introvert

intruso, -a [in'truso, a] *adj* intrusive
▷ *nm/f* intruder

intuición [intwi'θjon] *nf* intuition

inundación [inunda'θjon] *nf* flood(ing); **inundar** /1a/ *vt* to flood; (*fig*) to swamp, inundate

inusitado, -a [inusi'taðo, a] *adj* unusual

inútil [i'nutil] *adj* useless; (*esfuerzo*) vain, fruitless

inutilizar [inutili'θar] /1f/ *vt* to make unusable

invadir [imba'ðir] /3a/ *vt* to invade

inválido, -a [im'baliðo, a] *adj* invalid
▷ *nm/f* invalid

invasión [imba'sjon] *nf* invasion

invasor, a [imba'sor, a] *adj* invading
▷ *nm/f* invader

invención [imben'θjon] *nf* invention

inventar [imben'tar] /1a/ *vt* to invent

inventario [imben'tarjo] *nm* inventory

invento [im'bento] *nm* invention

inventor, a [imben'tor, a] *nm/f* inventor

invernadero [imberna'ðero] *nm* greenhouse

inverosímil [imbero'simil] *adj* implausible

inversión [imber'sjon] *nf* (*Com*) investment

inverso, a [im'berso, a] *adj* inverse, opposite; **en el orden ~** in reverse order; **a la inversa** inversely, the other way round

inversor, -a [imber'sor, a] *nm/f* (*Com*) investor

invertir [imber'tir] /3i/ *vt* (*Com*) to invest; (*volcar*) to turn upside down; (*tiempo etc*) to spend

investigación [imbestiɣa'θjon] *nf* investigation; (*Univ*) research; **~ y desarrollo** (*Com*) research and development (R & D)

investigar [imbesti'ɣar] /1h/ *vt* to investigate; (*estudiar*) to do research into

invierno [im'bjerno] *nm* winter

invisible [imbi'siβle] *adj* invisible

invitación [imbita'θjon] *nf* invitation

invitado, -a [imbi'taðo, a] *nm/f* guest

invitar [imbi'tar] /1a/ *vt* to invite; (*incitar*) to entice; **~ a algo** to pay for sth

invocar [imbo'kar] /1g/ *vt* to invoke, call on

involucrar [imbolu'krar] /1a/ *vt*: **~ a algn en algo** to involve sb in sth; **involucrarse** *vr* to get involved

involuntario, -a [imbolun'tarjo, a] *adj* involuntary; (*ofensa etc*) unintentional

inyección [injek'θjon] *nf* injection

inyectar [injek'tar] /1a/ *vt* to inject

iPod® ['ipoð] (*pl* **iPods**) *nm* iPod®

PALABRA CLAVE

ir [ir] /3s/ *vi* **1** to go; **ir caminando** to walk; **fui en tren** I travelled by train; **¡(ahora) voy!** (I'm just) coming!

2: **ir (a) por: ir (a) por el médico** to fetch the doctor

3 (*progresar: persona, cosa*) to go; **el trabajo va muy bien** work is going very well; **¿cómo te va?** how are things going?; **me va muy bien** I'm getting on very well; **le fue fatal** it went awfully badly for him

4 (*funcionar*): **el coche no va muy bien** the car isn't running very well

5: **te va estupendamente ese color** that colour suits you fantastically well

6 (*aspecto*): **iba muy bien vestido** he was very well dressed

7 (*locuciones*): **¿vino? — ¡que va!** did he come? — of course not!; **vamos, no llores** come on, don't cry; **¡vaya coche!** (*admiración*) what a car!, that's some car!

8: **no vaya a ser: tienes que correr, no vaya a ser que pierdas el tren** you'll have to run so as not to miss the train

9: **no me** etc **va ni me viene** I etc don't care

▶vb auxiliar **1**: **ir a: voy/iba a hacerlo hoy** I am/was going to do it today
2 (+ gerundio): **iba anocheciendo** it was getting dark; **todo se me iba aclarando** everything was gradually becoming clearer to me
3 (+ pp = pasivo): **van vendidos 300 ejemplares** 300 copies have been sold so far

▶**irse** vr **1**: **¿por dónde se va al zoológico?** which is the way to the zoo?
2 (marcharse) to leave; **ya se habrán ido** they must already have left o gone

ira ['ira] nf anger, rage
Irak [i'rak] nm Iraq; **irakí** adj, nmf Iraqui
Irán [i'ran] nm Iran; **iraní** adj, nmf Iranian
Iraq [i'rak] nm = **Irak**
iris ['iris] nm inv (arco iris) rainbow; (Anat) iris
Irlanda [ir'landa] nf Ireland; **~ del Norte** Northern Ireland; **irlandés, -esa** adj Irish ▷ nm/f Irishman/woman; **los irlandeses** the Irish
ironía [iro'nia] nf irony; **irónico, -a** adj ironic(al)
IRPF nm abr (ESP) = **impuesto sobre la renta de las personas físicas**
irreal [irre'al] adj unreal
irregular [irreɣu'lar] adj irregular; (situación) abnormal
irremediable [irreme'ðjaβle] adj irremediable; (vicio) incurable
irreparable [irrepa'raβle] adj (daños) irreparable; (pérdida) irrecoverable
irrespetuoso, -a [irrespe'twoso, a] adj disrespectful
irresponsable [irrespon'saβle] adj irresponsible
irreversible [irreβer'siβle] adj irreversible
irrigar [irri'ɣar] /1h/ vt to irrigate
irrisorio, -a [irri'sorjo, a] adj derisory, ridiculous

irritar [irri'tar] /1a/ vt to irritate, annoy
irrupción [irrup'θjon] nf irruption; (invasión) invasion
isla ['isla] nf island
Islam [is'lam] nm Islam; **islámico, -a** adj Islamic
islandés, -esa [islan'des, esa] adj Icelandic ▷ nm/f Icelander
Islandia [is'landja] nf Iceland
isleño, -a [is'leɲo, a] adj island cpd ▷ nm/f islander
Israel [isra'el] nm Israel; **israelí** adj, nmf Israeli
istmo ['istmo] nm isthmus
Italia [i'talja] nf Italy; **italiano, -a** adj, nm/f Italian
itinerario [itine'rarjo] nm itinerary, route
ITV nf abr (= Inspección Técnica de Vehículos) ≈ MOT (test)
IVA ['iβa] nm abr (= Impuesto sobre el Valor Añadido) VAT
izar [i'θar] /1f/ vt to hoist
izdo, izq.º abr (= izquierdo) L, l
izquierda [iθ'kjerða] nf V **izquierdo**
izquierdo, -a [iθ'kjerðo, a] adj left ▷ nf left; (Pol) left (wing); **a la izquierda** on the left; (torcer etc) (to the) left

jabalí [xaβa'li] *nm* wild boar
jabalina [xaβa'lina] *nf* javelin
jabón [xa'βon] *nm* soap
jaca ['xaka] *nf* pony
jacal [xa'kal] *nm* (*LAM*) shack
jacinto [xa'θinto] *nm* hyacinth
jactarse [xak'tarse] /1a/ *vr*: **~ (de)** to boast *o* brag (about *o* of)
jadear [xaðe'ar] /1a/ *vi* to pant, gasp for breath
jaguar [xa'ɣwar] *nm* jaguar
jaiba ['xaiβa] *nf* (*LAM*) crab
jalar [xa'lar] /1a/ *vt* (*LAM*) to pull
jalea [xa'lea] *nf* jelly
jaleo [xa'leo] *nm* racket, uproar; **armar un ~** to kick up a racket
jalón [xa'lon] *nm* (*LAM*) tug
jamás [xa'mas] *adv* never
jamón [xa'mon] *nm* ham; **~ (de) York** boiled ham; **~ dulce/serrano** boiled/ cured ham
Japón [xa'pon] *nm*: Japan; **japonés, -esa** *adj, nm/f* Japanese ▷ *nm* (*Ling*) Japanese

jaque ['xake] *nm*: **~ mate** checkmate
jaqueca [xa'keka] *nf* (very bad) headache, migraine
jarabe [xa'raβe] *nm* syrup
jardín [xar'ðin] *nm* garden; **~ de (la) infancia** (*ESP*) *o* **de niños** (*LAM*) *o* **infantil** nursery school; **jardinaje** *nm* gardening; **jardinería** *nf* gardening; **jardinero, -a** *nm/f* gardener
jarra ['xarra] *nf* jar; (*jarro*) jug
jarro ['xarro] *nm* jug
jarrón [xa'rron] *nm* vase
jaula ['xaula] *nf* cage
jauría [xau'ria] *nf* pack of hounds
jazmín [xaθ'min] *nm* jasmine
J. C. *abr* = **Jesucristo**
jeans [jins, dʒins] *nmpl* (*LAM*) jeans, denims; **unos ~** a pair of jeans
jefatura [xefa'tura] *nf*: **~ de policía** police headquarters *sg*
jefe, -a ['xefe, a] *nm/f* (*gen*) chief, head; (*patrón*) boss; **~ de cocina** chef; **~ de estación** stationmaster; **~ de estado** head of state; **~ de estudios** (*Escol*) director of studies; **~ de gobierno** head of government
jengibre [xen'xiβre] *nm* ginger
jeque ['xeke] *nm* sheik(h)
jerárquico, -a [xe'rarkiko, a] *adj* hierarchic(al)
jerez [xe'reθ] *nm* sherry
jerga ['xerɣa] *nf* jargon
jeringa [xe'ringa] *nf* syringe; (*LAM*) annoyance, bother; **jeringuilla** *nf* syringe
jeroglífico [xero'ɣlifiko] *nm* hieroglyphic
jersey [xer'sei] (*pl* **jerseys**) *nm* jersey, pullover, jumper
Jerusalén [xerusa'len] *n* Jerusalem
Jesucristo [xesu'kristo] *nm* Jesus Christ
jesuita [xe'swita] *adj, nm* Jesuit
Jesús [xe'sus] *nm* Jesus; **¡~!** good heavens!; (*al estornudar*) bless you!
jinete, -a [xi'nete, a] *nm/f* horseman/ woman
jipijapa [xipi'xapa] *nm* (*LAM*) straw hat

jirafa [xiˈrafa] nf giraffe

jirón [xiˈron] nm rag, shred

jitomate [xitoˈmate] nm (LAM) tomato

joder [xoˈðer] /2a/ (fam!) vt to fuck (!)

jogging [ˈjoɣin] nm (LAM) tracksuit (BRIT), sweat suit (US)

jornada [xorˈnaða] nf (viaje de un día) day's journey; (camino o viaje entero) journey; (día de trabajo) working day

jornal [xorˈnal] nm (day's) wage; **jornalero, -a** nm/f (day) labourer

joroba [xoˈroβa] nf hump; **jorobado, -a** adj hunchbacked ▷ nm/f hunchback

jota [ˈxota] nf letter J; (danza) Aragonese dance; **no saber ni ~** to have no idea

joven [ˈxoβen] adj young ▷ nm young man, youth ▷ nf young woman, girl

joya [ˈxoja] nf jewel, gem; (fig: persona) gem; **~s de fantasía** imitation jewellery sg; **joyería** nf (joyas) jewellery; (tienda) jeweller's (shop); **joyero** nm (persona) jeweller; (caja) jewel case

Juan [xwan] nm: **Noche de San ~** V **noche**

juanete [xwaˈnete] nm (del pie) bunion

jubilación [xuβilaˈθjon] nf (retiro) retirement

jubilado, -a [xuβiˈlado, a] adj retired ▷ nm/f pensioner (BRIT), senior citizen

jubilar [xuβiˈlar] /1a/ vt to pension off, retire; (fam) to discard; **jubilarse** vr to retire

júbilo [ˈxuβilo] nm joy, rejoicing; **jubiloso, -a** adj jubilant

judía [xuˈðia] nf V **judío**

judicial [xuðiˈθjal] adj judicial

judío, -a [xuˈðio, a] adj Jewish ▷ nm Jew ▷ nf Jewish woman; (Culin) bean; **judía blanca** haricot bean; **judía verde** French o string bean

judo [ˈjuðo] nm judo

juego [ˈxweɣo] vb V **jugar** ▷ nm (gen) play; (pasatiempo, partido) game; (en casino) gambling; (conjunto) set; **~ de** **mesa** board game; **~ de palabras** pun, play on words; **J~s Olímpicos** Olympic Games; **fuera de ~** (Deporte: persona) offside; (: pelota) out of play

juerga [ˈxwerɣa] nf binge; (fiesta) party; **ir de ~** to go out on a binge

jueves [ˈxweβes] nm inv Thursday

juez [xweθ] nmf judge; **~ de instrucción** examining magistrate; **~ de línea** linesman; **~ de salida** starter

jugada [xuˈɣaða] nf play; **buena ~** good move (o shot o stroke) etc

jugador, a [xuɣaˈðor, a] nm/f player; (en casino) gambler

jugar [xuˈɣar] /1h, 1n/ vt to play; (en casino) to gamble; (apostar) to bet; **~ al fútbol** to play football

juglar [xuˈɣlar] nm minstrel

jugo [ˈxuɣo] nm (Bot) juice; (fig) essence, substance; **~ de naranja** (esp LAM) orange juice; **jugoso, -a** adj juicy; (fig) substantial, important

juguete [xuˈɣete] nm toy; **juguetear** /1a/ vi to play; **juguetería** nf toyshop

juguetón, -ona [xuɣeˈton, ona] adj playful

juicio [ˈxwiθjo] nm judgement; (sana razón) sanity, reason; (opinión) opinion

julio [ˈxuljo] nm July

jumper [ˈdʒumper] nm (LAM) pinafore dress (BRIT), jumper (US)

junco [ˈxunko] nm rush, reed

jungla [ˈxunɡla] nf jungle

junio [ˈxunjo] nm June

junta [ˈxunta] nf V **junto**

juntar [xunˈtar] /1a/ vt to join, unite; (maquinaria) to assemble, put together; (dinero) to collect; **juntarse** vr to join, meet; (reunirse: personas) to meet, assemble; (arrimarse) to approach, draw closer; **~se con algn** to join sb

junto, -a [ˈxunto, a] adj joined; (unido) united; (anexo) near, close; (contiguo, próximo) next, adjacent ▷ nf (asamblea) meeting, assembly; (comité, consejo) board, council, committee; (articulación) joint ▷ adv: **todo ~** all at once ▷ *prep:* **~ a** near (to), next to; **~s** together; **~ con** (together) with

jurado [xu'raðo] *nm* (*Jur: individuo*) juror; (: *grupo*) jury; (*de concurso: grupo*) panel (of judges); (: *individuo*) member of a panel

juramento [xura'mento] *nm* oath; (*maldición*) oath, curse; **prestar ~** to take the oath; **tomar ~ a** to swear in, administer the oath to

jurar [xu'rar] /1a/ *vt, vi* to swear; **~ en falso** to commit perjury; **jurárselas a algn** to have it in for sb

jurídico, -a [xu'riðiko, a] *adj* legal

jurisdicción [xurisðik'θjon] *nf* (*poder, autoridad*) jurisdiction; (*territorio*) district

justamente [xusta'mente] *adv* justly, fairly; (*precisamente*) just, exactly

justicia [xus'tiθja] *nf* justice; (*equidad*) fairness, justice

justificación [xustifika'θjon] *nf* justification; **justificar** /1g/ *vt* to justify

justo, -a ['xusto, a] *adj* (*equitativo*) just, fair, right; (*preciso*) exact, correct; (*ajustado*) tight ▷ *adv* (*precisamente*) exactly, precisely; (*apenas a tiempo*) just in time

juvenil [xuβe'nil] *adj* youthful

juventud [xuβen'tuð] *nf* (*adolescencia*) youth; (*jóvenes*) young people *pl*

juzgado [xuθ'γaðo] *nm* tribunal; (*Jur*) court

juzgar [xuθ'γar] /1h/ *vt* to judge; **a ~ por ...** to judge by ..., judging by ...

kárate ['karate], **karate** [ka'rate] *nm* karate

Kg, kg *abr* (= *kilogramo(s)*) K, kg

kilo ['kilo] *nm* kilo; **kilogramo** *nm* kilogramme (*BRIT*), kilogram (*US*); **kilometraje** *nm* distance in kilometres, ≈ mileage; **kilómetro** *nm* kilometre (*BRIT*), kilometer (*US*); **kilovatio** *nm* kilowatt

kiosco ['kjosko] *nm* = **quiosco**

kleenex® [kli'neks] *nm* paper handkerchief, tissue

km *abr* (= *kilómetro(s)*) km

Kosovo [koso'βo] *nm* Kosovo

kv *abr* (= *kilovatio*) kw

l *abr* (= *litro(s)*) l

la [la] *artículo definido fsg* the ▷ *pron* her; (*en relación a usted*) you; (*en relación a una cosa*) it ▷ *nm* (*Mus*) A; **está en la cárcel** he's in jail; **la del sombrero rojo** the woman/girl/one in the red hat

laberinto [laβe'rinto] *nm* labyrinth

labio ['laβjo] *nm* lip

labor [la'βor] *nf* labour; (*Agr*) farm work; (*tarea*) job, task; (*Costura*) needlework; **~es domésticas** *o* **del hogar** household chores; **laborable** *adj* (*Agr*) workable; **día laborable** working day; **laboral** *adj* (*accidente, conflictividad*) industrial; (*jornada*) working

laboratorio [laβora'torjo] *nm* laboratory

laborista [laβo'rista] *adj*: **Partido L~** Labour Party

labrador, a [laβra'ðor, a] *adj* farming *cpd* ▷ *nm/f* farmer

labranza [la'βranθa] *nf* (*Agr*) cultivation

labrar [la'βrar] /1a/ *vt* (*gen*) to work; (*madera etc*) to carve; (*fig*) to cause, bring about

laca ['laka] *nf* lacquer

lacio, -a ['laθjo, a] *adj* (*pelo*) straight

lacón [la'kon] *nm* shoulder of pork

lactancia [lak'tanθja] *nf* lactation, breast-feeding

lácteo, -a ['lakteo, a] *adj*: **productos ~s** dairy products

ladear [laðe'ar] /1a/ *vt* to tip, tilt ▷ *vi* to tilt; **ladearse** *vr* to lean

ladera [la'ðera] *nf* slope

lado ['laðo] *nm* (*gen*) side; (*fig*) protection; (*Mil*) flank; **al ~ de** beside; **poner de ~** to put on its side; **poner a un ~** to put aside; **por todos ~s** on all sides, all round (BRIT)

ladrar [la'ðrar] /1a/ *vi* to bark; **ladrido** *nm* bark, barking

ladrillo [la'ðriʎo] *nm* (*gen*) brick; (*azulejo*) tile

ladrón, -ona [la'ðron, ona] *nm/f* thief

lagartija [laɣar'tixa] *nf* (small) lizard

lagarto [la'ɣarto] *nm* (*Zool*) lizard

lago ['laɣo] *nm* lake

lágrima ['laɣrima] *nf* tear

laguna [la'ɣuna] *nf* (*lago*) lagoon; (*en escrito, conocimientos*) gap

lamentable [lamen'taβle] *adj* lamentable, regrettable; (*miserable*) pitiful

lamentar [lamen'tar] /1a/ *vt* (*sentir*) to regret; (*deplorar*) to lament; **lamentarse** *vr* to lament; **lo lamento mucho** I'm very sorry

lamer [la'mer] /2a/ *vt* to lick

lámina ['lamina] *nf* (*plancha delgada*) sheet; (*para estampar, estampa*) plate

lámpara ['lampara] *nf* lamp; **~ de alcohol/gas** spirit/gas lamp; **~ de pie** standard lamp

lana ['lana] *nf* wool

lancha ['lantʃa] *nf* launch; **~ motora** motorboat

langosta [lanˈgosta] nf (crustáceo) lobster; (: de río) crayfish; **langostino** nm prawn

lanza [ˈlanθa] nf (arma) lance, spear

lanzamiento [lanθaˈmjento] nm (gen) throwing; (Naut, Com) launch, launching; **~ de pesos** putting the shot

lanzar [lanˈθar] /1f/ vt (gen) to throw; (Deporte: pelota) to bowl; to launch; (Jur) to evict; **lanzarse** vr to throw o.s.

lapa [ˈlapa] nf limpet

lapicero [lapiˈθero] nm pencil; (LAM) propelling (BRIT) o mechanical (US) pencil; (: bolígrafo) ballpoint pen, Biro®

lápida [ˈlapiða] nf stone; **~ mortuoria** headstone

lápiz [ˈlapiθ] nm pencil; **~ de color** coloured pencil; **~ de labios** lipstick; **~ de ojos** eyebrow pencil

largar [larˈɣar] /1h/ vt (soltar) to release; (aflojar) to loosen; (lanzar) to launch; (fam) to let fly; (velas) to unfurl; (LAM) to throw; **largarse** vr (fam) to beat it; **~se a** (LAM) to start to

largo, -a [ˈlarɣo, a] adj (longitud) long; (tiempo) lengthy; (fig) generous ▷ nm length; (Mus) largo; **dos años ~s** two long years; **a lo ~ de** along; (tiempo) all through, throughout; **a la larga** in the long run; **largometraje** nm full-length o feature film

> No confundir largo con la palabra inglesa large.

laringe [laˈrinxe] nf larynx; **laringitis** nf laryngitis

las [las] artículo definido fpl the ▷ pron them; **~ que cantan** the ones/women/girls who sing

lasaña [laˈsaɲa] nf lasagne, lasagna

láser [ˈlaser] nm laser

lástima [ˈlastima] nf (pena) pity; **dar ~** to be pitiful; **es una ~ que** it's a pity that; **¡qué ~!** what a pity!; **estar hecho una ~** to be a sorry sight

lastimar [lastiˈmar] /1a/ vt (herir) to wound; (ofender) to offend; **lastimarse** vr to hurt o.s.

lata [ˈlata] nf (metal) tin; (envase) tin, can; (fam) nuisance; **en ~** tinned; **dar (la) ~** to be a nuisance

latente [laˈtente] adj latent

lateral [lateˈral] adj side, lateral ▷ nm (Teat) wings pl

latido [laˈtiðo] nm (del corazón) beat

latifundio [latiˈfundjo] nm large estate

latigazo [latiˈɣaθo] nm (golpe) lash; (sonido) crack

látigo [ˈlatiɣo] nm whip

latín [laˈtin] nm Latin

latino, -a [laˈtino, a] adj Latin; **latinoamericano, -a** adj, nm/f Latin American

latir [laˈtir] /3a/ vi (corazón, pulso) to beat

latitud [latiˈtuð] nf (Geo) latitude

latón [laˈton] nm brass

laurel [lauˈrel] nm (Bot) laurel; (Culin) bay

lava [ˈlaβa] nf lava

lavabo [laˈβaβo] nm (jofaina) washbasin; (retrete) toilet (BRIT), washroom (US)

lavado [laˈβaðo] nm washing; (de ropa) laundry; (Arte) wash; **~ de cerebro** brainwashing; **~ en seco** dry-cleaning

lavadora [laβaˈðora] nf washing machine

lavanda [laˈβanda] nf lavender

lavandería [laβandeˈria] nf laundry; **~ automática** launderette

lavaplatos [laβaˈplatos] nm inv dishwasher

lavar [laˈβar] /1a/ vt to wash; (borrar) to wipe away; **lavarse** vr to wash o.s.; **~se las manos** to wash one's hands; **~se los dientes** to brush one's teeth; **~ y marcar** (pelo) to shampoo and set; **~ en seco** to dry-clean; **~ los platos** to wash the dishes

lavarropas [laβaˈrropas] nm inv (RPL) washing machine

lavavajillas [laβaβaˈxiʎas] nm inv dishwasher

laxante [lak'sante] *nm* laxative

lazarillo [laθa'riʎo] *nm*: **perro de ~** guide dog

lazo ['laθo] *nm* knot; (*lazada*) bow; (*para animales*) lasso; (*trampa*) snare; (*vínculo*) tie

le [le] *pron* (*directo*) him (*o* her); (: *en relación a usted*) you; (*indirecto*) to him (*o* her *o* it); (: *a usted*) to you

leal [le'al] *adj* loyal; **lealtad** *nf* loyalty

lección [lek'θjon] *nf* lesson

leche ['letʃe] *nf* milk; **tener mala ~** (*fam*) to be a nasty piece of work; **~ condensada/en polvo** condensed/powdered milk; **~ desnatada** skimmed milk

lechería [letʃe'ria] *nf* dairy

lecho ['letʃo] *nm* (*cama, de río*) bed; (*Geo*) layer

lechón [le'tʃon] *nm* sucking (BRIT) *o* suckling (US) pig

lechoso, -a [le'tʃoso, a] *adj* milky

lechuga [le'tʃuɣa] *nf* lettuce

lechuza [le'tʃuθa] *nf* (barn) owl

lector, a [lek'tor, a] *nm/f* reader ▷ *nm*: **~ de discos compactos** CD player

lectura [lek'tura] *nf* reading

leer [le'er] /2e/ *vt* to read

legado [le'ɣaðo] *nm* (*don*) bequest; (*herencia*) legacy; (*enviado*) legate

legajo [le'ɣaxo] *nm* file

legal [le'ɣal] *adj* legal; (*persona*) trustworthy; **legalizar** /1f/ *vt* to legalize; (*documento*) to authenticate

legaña [le'ɣaɲa] *nf* sleep (in eyes)

legión [le'xjon] *nf* legion; **legionario, -a** *adj* legionary ▷ *nm* legionnaire

legislación [lexisla'θjon] *nf* legislation

legislar [lexis'lar] /1a/ *vt* to legislate

legislatura [lexisla'tura] *nf* (*Pol*) period of office

legítimo, -a [le'xitimo, a] *adj* (*genuino*) authentic; (*legal*) legitimate

legua ['leɣwa] *nf* league

legumbres [le'ɣumbres] *nfpl* pulses

leído, -a [le'iðo, a] *adj* well-read

lejanía [lexa'nia] *nf* distance; **lejano, -a** *adj* far-off; (*en el tiempo*) distant; (*fig*) remote

lejía [le'xia] *nf* bleach

lejos ['lexos] *adv* far, far away; **a lo ~** in the distance; **de** *o* **desde ~** from a distance; **~ de** far from

lema ['lema] *nm* motto; (*Pol*) slogan

lencería [lenθe'ria] *nf* linen, drapery

lengua ['lengwa] *nf* tongue; (*Ling*) language; **morderse la ~** to hold one's tongue

lenguado [len'gwaðo] *nm* sole

lenguaje [len'gwaxe] *nm* language; **~ de programación** programming language

lengüeta [len'gweta] *nf* (*Anat*) epiglottis; (*de zapatos*) tongue; (*Mus*) reed

lente ['lente] *nm* *o* *f* lens; (*lupa*) magnifying glass; **lentes** *nmpl* glasses; **~s bifocales/de sol** (LAM) bifocals/sunglasses; **~s de contacto** contact lenses

lenteja [len'texa] *nf* lentil; **lentejuela** *nf* sequin

lentilla [len'tiʎa] *nf* contact lens

lentitud [lenti'tuð] *nf* slowness; **con ~** slowly

lento, -a ['lento, a] *adj* slow

leña ['leɲa] *nf* firewood; **leñador, a** *nm/f* woodcutter

leño ['leɲo] *nm* (*trozo de árbol*) log; (*madera*) timber; (*fig*) blockhead

Leo ['leo] *nm* Leo

león [le'on] *nm* lion; **~ marino** sea lion

leopardo [leo'parðo] *nm* leopard

leotardos [leo'tarðos] *nmpl* tights

lepra ['lepra] *nf* leprosy; **leproso, -a** *nm/f* leper

les [les] *pron* (*directo*) them; (: *en relación a ustedes*) you; (*indirecto*) to them; (: *a ustedes*) to you

lesbiana [les'βjana] *adj*, *nf* lesbian

lesión [le'sjon] *nf* wound, lesion; (*Deporte*) injury; **lesionado, -a** *adj* injured ▷ *nm/f* injured person

letal [le'tal] *adj* lethal

letanía [leta'nia] *nf* litany

letra ['letra] *nf* letter; (*escritura*) handwriting; (*Mus*) lyrics *pl*; **~ de cambio** bill of exchange; **~ de imprenta** print; **letrado, -a** *adj* learned ▷ *nm/f* lawyer; **letrero** *nm* (*cartel*) sign; (*etiqueta*) label

letrina [le'trina] *nf* latrine

leucemia [leu'θemja] *nf* leukaemia

levadura [leβa'ðura] *nf* yeast; **~ de cerveza** brewer's yeast

levantar [leβan'tar] /1a/ *vt* (*gen*) to raise; (*del suelo*) to pick up; (*hacia arriba*) to lift (up); (*plan*) to make, draw up; (*mesa*) to clear; (*campamento*) to strike; (*fig*) to cheer up, hearten; **levantarse** *vr* to get up; (*enderezarse*) to straighten up; (*rebelarse*) to rebel; **~ el ánimo** to cheer up

levante [le'βante] *nm* east; **el L~** region of Spain extending from Castellón to Murcia

levar [le'βar] /1a/ *vt, vi*: **~ (anclas)** to weigh anchor

leve ['leβe] *adj* light; (*fig*) trivial

levita [le'βita] *nf* frock coat

léxico ['leksiko] *nm* vocabulary

ley [lei] *nf* (*gen*) law; (*metal*) standard

leyenda [le'jenda] *nf* legend

leyó *etc vb V* **leer**

liar [li'ar] /1c/ *vt* to tie (up); (*unir*) to bind; (*envolver*) to wrap (up); (*enredar*) to confuse; (*cigarrillo*) to roll; **liarse** *vr* (*fam*) to get involved; **~se a palos** to get involved in a fight

Líbano ['liβano] *nm*: **el ~** the Lebanon

libélula [li'βelula] *nf* dragonfly

liberación [liβera'θjon] *nf* liberation; (*de la cárcel*) release

liberal [liβe'ral] *adj, nmf* liberal

liberar [liβe'rar] /1a/ *vt* to liberate

libertad [liβer'tað] *nf* liberty, freedom; **~ de asociación/de culto/ de prensa/de comercio/de palabra** freedom of association/of worship/ of the press/of trade/of speech; **~ condicional** probation; **~ bajo palabra** parole; **~ bajo fianza** bail

libertar [liβer'tar] /1a/ *vt* (*preso*) to set free; (*de una obligación*) to release; (*eximir*) to exempt

libertino, -a [liβer'tino, a] *adj* permissive ▷ *nm/f* permissive person

libra ['liβra] *nf* pound; **L~** (*Astro*) Libra; **~ esterlina** pound sterling

libramiento [liβra'mjento] (*LAM*) *nm* ring road (*BRIT*), beltway (*US*)

librar [li'βrar] /1a/ *vt* (*de peligro*) to save; (*batalla*) to wage, fight; (*de impuestos*) to exempt; (*cheque*) to make out; (*Jur*) to exempt; **librarse** *vr*: **~se de** to escape from, free o.s. from

libre ['liβre] *adj* free; (*lugar*) unoccupied; (*asiento*) vacant; (*de deudas*) free of debts; **~ de impuestos** free of tax; **tiro ~** free kick; **los 100 metros ~** the 100 metres freestyle (race); **al aire ~** in the open air

librería [liβre'ria] *nf* (*tienda*) bookshop; **librero, -a** *nm/f* bookseller

No confundir *librería* con la palabra inglesa *library*.

libreta [li'βreta] *nf* notebook

libro ['liβro] *nm* book; **~ de bolsillo** paperback; **~ electrónico** e-book; **~ de texto** textbook

Lic. *abr* = **Licenciado, a**

licencia [li'θenθja] *nf* (*gen*) licence; (*permiso*) permission; **~ por enfermedad/con goce de sueldo** sick/paid leave; **~ de armas/de caza** gun/game licence; **licenciado, -a** *adj* licensed ▷ *nm/f* graduate; **licenciar** /1b/ *vt* (*empleado*) to dismiss; (*permitir*) to permit, allow; (*soldado*) to discharge; (*estudiante*) to confer a degree upon; **licenciarse** *vr*: **licenciarse en derecho** to graduate in law

licenciatura [liθenθja'tura] *nf* (*título*) degree; (*estudios*) degree course

lícito, -a ['liθito, a] *adj* (*legal*) lawful; (*justo*) fair, just; (*permisible*) permissible

licor [li'kor] *nm* spirits *pl* (*BRIT*), liquor (*US*); (*con hierbas etc*) liqueur

licuadora [likwa'ðora] *nf* blender

líder ['liðer] *nmf* leader; **liderazgo, liderato** *nm* leadership

lidia ['liðja] *nf* bullfighting; (*una lidia*) bullfight; **toros de ~** fighting bulls; **lidiar** /1b/ *vt*, *vi* to fight

liebre ['ljeβre] *nf* hare

lienzo ['ljenθo] *nm* linen; (*Arte*) canvas; (*Arq*) wall

liga ['liɣa] *nf* (*de medias*) garter, suspender; (*confederación*) league; (*LAM: gomita*) rubber band

ligadura [liɣa'ðura] *nf* bond, tie; (*Med*, *Mus*) ligature

ligamento [liɣa'mento] *nm* ligament

ligar [li'ɣar] /1h/ *vt* (*atar*) to tie; (*unir*) to join; (*Med*) to bind up; (*Mus*) to slur ▷ *vi* to mix, blend; **ligarse** *vr* to commit o.s.; **(él) liga mucho** (*fam*) he pulls a lot of women

ligero, -a [li'xero, a] *adj* (*de peso*) light; (*tela*) thin; (*rápido*) swift, quick; (*ágil*) agile, nimble; (*de importancia*) slight; (*de carácter*) flippant, superficial ▷ *adv*: **a la ligera** superficially

liguero [li'ɣero] *nm* suspender (*BRIT*) o garter (*US*) belt

lija ['lixa] *nf* (*Zool*) dogfish; **(papel de) ~** sandpaper

lila ['lila] *nf* lilac

lima ['lima] *nf* file; (*Bot*) lime; **~ de uñas** nail file; **limar** /1a/ *vt* to file

limitación [limita'θjon] *nf* limitation, limit

limitar [limi'tar] /1a/ *vt* to limit; (*reducir*) to reduce, cut down ▷ *vi*: **~ con** to border on; **limitarse** *vr*: **~se a** to limit o confine o.s. to

límite ['limite] *nm* (*gen*) limit; (*fin*) end; (*frontera*) border; **~ de velocidad** speed limit

limítrofe [li'mitrofe] *adj* neighbouring

limón [li'mon] *nm* lemon ▷ *adj*: **amarillo ~** lemon-yellow; **limonada** *nf* lemonade

limosna *nf* alms *pl*; **pedir ~** to beg; **vivir de ~** to live on charity

limpiador, a [limpja'ðor, a] *adj* cleaning, cleansing ▷ *nm/f* cleaner ▷ *nm* (*LAM*) = **limpiaparabrisas**

limpiaparabrisas [limpjapara'βrisas] *nm inv* windscreen (*BRIT*) o windshield (*US*) wiper

limpiar [lim'pjar] /1b/ *vt* to clean; (*con trapo*) to wipe; (*quitar*) to clean away; (*zapatos*) to shine, polish; (*Inform*) to debug; (*fig*) to clean up

limpieza [lim'pjeθa] *nf* (*estado*) cleanliness; (*acto*) cleansing; (: *de las calles*) cleansing; (: *de zapatos*) polishing; (*habilidad*) skill; (*fig: Policía*) clean-up; (*pureza*) purity; (*Mil*): **operación de ~** mopping-up operation; **~ en seco** dry cleaning

limpio, -a ['limpjo, a] *adj* clean; (*moralmente*) pure; (*Com*) clear, net; (*fam*) honest ▷ *adv*: **jugar ~** to play fair; **pasar a ~** to make a fair copy

lince ['linθe] *nm* lynx

linchar [lin'tʃar] /1a/ *vt* to lynch

lindar [lin'dar] /1a/ *vi* to adjoin; **~ con** to border on

lindo, -a ['lindo, a] *adj* pretty, lovely ▷ *adv*: **canta muy ~** (*LAM*) he sings beautifully; **se divertían de lo ~** they enjoyed themselves enormously

línea ['linea] *nf* line; (*Inform*): **en ~** on line; **~ aérea** airline; **~ de meta** goal line; (*de carrera*) finishing line; **~ discontinua** (*Auto*) broken line; **~ recta** straight line

lingote [lin'gote] *nm* ingot

lingüista [lin'gwista] *nmf* linguist; **lingüística** *nf* linguistics *sg*

lino ['lino] *nm* linen; (*Bot*) flax

linterna [lin'terna] *nf*; torch (*BRIT*), flashlight (*US*)

lío ['lio] *nm* bundle; (*desorden*) muddle, mess; (*fam: follón*) fuss; **armar un ~** to make a fuss

liquen ['liken] *nm* lichen

liquidación [likiða'θjon] *nf* liquidation; **venta de ~** clearance sale

liquidar [liki'ðar] /1a/ vt (Com) to liquidate; (deudas) to pay off; (empresa) to wind up

líquido, -a ['likiðo, a] adj liquid; (ganancia) net ▷ nm liquid; **~ imponible** net taxable income

lira ['lira] nf (Mus) lyre; (moneda) lira

lírico, -a ['liriko, a] adj lyrical

lirio ['lirjo] nm (Bot) iris

lirón [li'ron] nm (Zool) dormouse; (fig) sleepyhead

Lisboa [lis'βoa] nf Lisbon

lisiar [li'sjar] /1b/ vt to maim

liso, -a ['liso, a] adj (terreno) flat; (cabello) straight; (superficie) even; (tela) plain

lista ['lista] nf list; (en escuela) school register; (de libros) catalogue; (tb: **~ de platos**) menu; (tb: **~ de precios**) price list; **pasar ~** to call the roll; **~ de espera** waiting list; **tela a ~s** striped material

listo, -a ['listo, a] adj (perspicaz) smart, clever; (preparado) ready

listón [lis'ton] nm (de madera, metal) strip

litera [li'tera] nf (en barco, tren) berth; (en dormitorio) bunk, bunk bed

literal [lite'ral] adj literal

literario, -a [lite'rarjo, a] adj literary

literato, -a [lite'rato, a] adj literary ▷ nm/f writer

literatura [litera'tura] nf literature

litigio [li'tixjo] nm (Jur) lawsuit; (fig): **en ~ con** in dispute with

litografía [litoɣra'fia] nf lithography; (una litografía) lithograph

litoral [lito'ral] adj coastal ▷ nm coast, seaboard

litro ['litro] nm litre, liter (US)

lívido, -a ['liβiðo, a] adj livid

llaga ['ʎaɣa] nf wound

llama ['ʎama] nf flame; (Zool) llama

llamada [ʎa'maða] nf call; **~ a cobro revertido** reverse-charge call; **~ al orden** call to order; **~ de atención** warning; **~ metropolitana, ~ local** local call; **~ por cobrar** (LAM) reverse-charge call

llamamiento [ʎama'mjento] nm call

llamar [ʎa'mar] /1a/ vt to call; (atención) to attract ▷ vi (por teléfono) to phone; (a la puerta) to knock (o ring); (por señas) to beckon; **llamarse** vr to be called, be named; **¿cómo se llama usted?** what's your name?

llamativo, -a [ʎama'tiβo, a] adj showy; (color) loud

llano, -a ['ʎano, a] adj (superficie) flat; (persona) straightforward; (estilo) clear ▷ nm plain, flat ground

llanta ['ʎanta] nf (wheel) rim; (LAM: neumático) tyre; (: cámara) (inner) tube; **~ de repuesto** (LAM) spare tyre

llanto ['ʎanto] nm weeping

llanura [ʎa'nura] nf plain

llave ['ʎaβe] nf key; (de gas, agua) tap (BRIT), faucet (US); (Mecánica) spanner; (de la luz) switch; (Mus) key; **~ inglesa** monkey wrench; **~ maestra** master key; **~ de contacto, ~ de encendido** (LAM Auto) ignition key; **~ de paso** stopcock; **echar ~ a** to lock up; **llavero** nm keyring

llegada [ʎe'ɣaða] nf arrival

llegar [ʎe'ɣar] /1h/ vi to arrive; (bastar) to be enough; **llegarse** vr: **~se a** to approach; **~ a** (alcanzar) to reach; to manage to, succeed in; **~ a saber** to find out; **~ a las manos de** to come into the hands of

llenar [ʎe'nar] /1a/ vt to fill; (superficie) to cover; (formulario) to fill in o out; (fig) to heap

lleno, -a ['ʎeno, a] adj full, filled; (repleto) full up ▷ nm (Teat) full house; **dar de ~ contra un muro** to hit a wall head-on

llevadero, -a [ʎeβa'ðero, a] adj bearable, tolerable

llevar [ʎe'βar] /1a/ vt to take; (ropa) to wear; (cargar) to carry; (quitar) to take away; (en coche) to drive; (transportar) to transport; (traer: dinero) to carry; (conducir) to lead; (Mat) to carry ▷ vi (suj: camino etc): **~ a** to lead to;

llevarse vr to carry off, take away; **llevamos dos días aquí** we have been here for two days; **él me lleva dos años** he's two years older than me; **~ los libros** (Com) to keep the books; **~se bien** to get on well (together)

llorar [ʎo'rar] /1a/ vt to cry ▷ vi to cry, weep; **~ de risa** to cry with laughter

llorón, -ona [ʎo'ron, ona] adj tearful ▷ nm/f cry-baby

lloroso, -a [ʎo'roso, a] adj (gen) weeping, tearful; (triste) sad, sorrowful

llover [ʎo'βer] /2h/ vi to rain

llovizna [ʎo'βiθna] nf drizzle;

lloviznar /1a/ vi to drizzle

llueve etc [ʎweβe] vb V **llover**

lluvia [ʎuβja] nf rain; **~ radioactiva** radioactive fallout; **lluvioso, -a** adj rainy

lo [lo] artículo definido neutro: **lo bueno** the good ▷ pron (en relación a una persona) him; (en relación a una cosa) it; **lo que** what, that which; **lo que sea** whatever; V tb **el**

loable [lo'aβle] adj praiseworthy

lobo [loβo] nm wolf; **~ de mar** (fig) sea dog

lóbulo [loβulo] nm lobe

local [lo'kal] adj local ▷ nm place, site; (oficinas) premises pl; **localidad** nf (barrio) locality; (lugar) location; (Teat) seat, ticket; **localizar** /1f/ vt (ubicar) to locate, find; (restringir) to localize; (situar) to place

loción [lo'θjon] nf lotion

loco, -a [loko, a] adj mad ▷ nm/f madman/woman; **estar ~ con** o **por algo/por algn** to be mad about sth/sb

locomotora [lokomo'tora] nf engine, locomotive

locuaz [lo'kwaθ] adj loquacious

locución [loku'θjon] nf expression

locura [lo'kura] nf madness; (acto) crazy act

locutor, a [loku'tor, a] nm/f (Radio) announcer; (comentarista) commentator; (TV) newsreader

locutorio [loku'torjo] nm (Telec) telephone box o booth

lodo [lodo] nm mud

lógico, -a [loxiko, a] adj logical ▷ nf logic

login [loxin] nm login

logotipo [loɣo'tipo] nm logo

logrado, -a [lo'ɣraðo, a] adj (interpretación, reproducción) polished, excellent

lograr [lo'ɣrar] /1a/ vt (obtener) to get, obtain; (conseguir) to achieve; **~ hacer** to manage to do; **~ que algn venga** to manage to get sb to come

logro [loɣro] nm achievement, success

lóker [loker] nm (LAM) locker

loma [loma] nf hillock, low ridge

lombriz [lom'briθ] nf (earth)worm

lomo [lomo] nm back; (Culin: de cerdo) pork loin; (: de vaca) rib steak; (de libro) spine

lona [lona] nf canvas

loncha [lontʃa] nf = **lonja**

lonchería [lontʃe'ria] nf (LAM) snack bar, diner (US)

Londres [londres] nm London

longaniza [longa'niθa] nf pork sausage

longitud [loŋxi'tuð] nf length; (Geo) longitude; **tener tres metros de ~** to be three metres long; **~ de onda** wavelength

lonja [lonxa] nf slice; (de tocino) rasher; **~ de pescado** fish market

loro [loro] nm parrot

los [los] artículo definido mpl the ▷ pron them; (en relación a ustedes) you; **mis libros y ~ tuyos** my books and yours

losa [losa] nf stone

lote [lote] nm portion; (Com) lot

lotería [lote'ria] nf lottery; (juego) lotto

○ **LOTERÍA**
○
○ Millions of euros are spent every
○ year on *loterías*, lotteries. There

is the weekly *Lotería Nacional*
which is very popular especially at
Christmas. Other weekly lotteries
are the *Bono Loto* and the *(Lotería)
Primitiva*. One of the most famous
lotteries is run by the wealthy and
influential society for the blind, *la
ONCE*, and the form is called *el cupón
de la ONCE* or *el cupón de los ciegos*.

loza ['loθa] *nf* crockery
lubina [lu'βina] *nf* sea bass
lubricante [luβri'kante] *nm*
lubricant
lubricar [luβri'kar] /1g/ *vt* to
lubricate
lucha ['lutʃa] *nf* fight, struggle;
~ de clases class struggle; **~ libre**
wrestling; **luchar** /1a/ *vi* to fight
lúcido, -a ['luθiðo, a] *adj (persona)*
lucid; *(mente)* logical; *(idea)* crystal-clear
luciérnaga [lu'θjernaɣa] *nf* glow-
worm
lucir [lu'θir] /3f/ *vt* to illuminate, light
(up); *(ostentar)* to show off ▷ *vi (brillar)*
to shine; **lucirse** *vr (irónico)* to make
a fool of o.s.
lucro ['lukro] *nm* profit, gain
lúdico, -a ['luðiko, a] *adj* playful;
(actividad) recreational
luego ['lweɣo] *adv (después)* next; *(más
tarde)* later, afterwards
lugar [lu'ɣar] *nm* place; *(sitio)* spot;
en ~ de instead of; **en primer ~** in the
first place, firstly; **dar ~ a** to give rise
to; **hacer ~** to make room; **fuera de
~** out of place; **sin ~ a dudas** without
doubt, undoubtedly; **tener ~** to take
place; **~ común** commonplace; **yo en
su ~** if I were him
lúgubre ['luɣuβre] *adj* mournful
lujo ['luxo] *nm* luxury; *(fig)* profusion,
abundance; **de ~** luxury *cpd*, de luxe;
lujoso, -a *adj* luxurious
lujuria [lu'xurja] *nf* lust
lumbre ['lumbre] *nf (luz)* light; *(fuego)*
fire; **¿tienes ~?** *(para cigarro)* have you
got a light?

luminoso, -a [lumi'noso, a] *adj*
luminous, shining
luna ['luna] *nf* moon; *(de un espejo)*
glass; *(de gafas)* lens; *(fig)* crescent;
**~ creciente/llena/menguante/
nueva** crescent/full/waning/new
moon; **~ de miel** honeymoon; **estar
en la ~** to have one's head in the clouds
lunar [lu'nar] *adj* lunar ▷ *nm (Anat)*
mole; **tela a ~es** spotted material
lunes ['lunes] *nm inv* Monday
lupa ['lupa] *nf* magnifying glass
lustre ['lustre] *nm* polish; *(fig)* lustre;
dar ~ a to polish
luto ['luto] *nm* mourning; **llevar el o
vestirse de ~** to be in mourning
Luxemburgo [luksem'burɣo] *nm*
Luxembourg
luz [luθ] *(pl* **luces)** *nf* light; **dar a ~ un
niño** to give birth to a child; **sacar
a la ~** to bring to light; **dar la ~** to
switch on the light; **encender** (*ESP*) *o*
prender (*LAM*)/**apagar la ~** to switch
the light on/off; **tener pocas luces**
to be dim *o* stupid; **~ roja/verde** red/
green light; **~ de freno** brake light;
luces de tráfico traffic lights; **traje
de luces** bullfighter's costume

m *abr* (= *metro(s)*) m; (= *minuto(s)*) min., m

macana [ma'kana] *nf* (*LAM: porra*) club

macarrones [maka'rrones] *nmpl* macaroni *sg*

macedonia [maθe'ðonja] *nf*: **~ de frutas** fruit salad

maceta [ma'θeta] *nf* (*de flores*) pot of flowers; (*para plantas*) flowerpot

machacar [matʃa'kar] /1g/ *vt* to crush, pound ▷ *vi* (*insistir*) to go on, keep on

machete [ma'tʃete] *nm* machete, (large) knife

machetear [matʃete'ar] /1a/ *vt* (*LAM*) to swot (*BRIT*), grind away (*US*)

machismo [ma'tʃismo] *nm* male chauvinism; **machista** *adj, nm* sexist

macho ['matʃo] *adj* male; (*fig*) virile ▷ *nm* male; (*fig*) he-man

macizo, -a [ma'θiθo, a] *adj* (*grande*) massive; (*fuerte, sólido*) solid ▷ *nm* mass, chunk

madeja [ma'ðexa] *nf* (*de lana*) skein, hank; (*de pelo*) mass, mop

madera [ma'ðera] *nf* wood; (*fig*) nature, character; **una ~** a piece of wood

madrastra [ma'ðrastra] *nf* stepmother

madre ['maðre] *adj* mother *cpd* ▷ *nf* mother; (*de vino etc*) dregs *pl*; **~ adoptiva/política/soltera** foster mother/mother-in-law/unmarried mother

Madrid [ma'ðrið] *n* Madrid

madriguera [maðri'ɣera] *nf* burrow

madrileño, -a [maðri'leɲo, a] *adj* of o from Madrid ▷ *nm/f* native o inhabitant of Madrid

madrina [ma'ðrina] *nf* godmother; (*Arq*) prop, shore; (*Tec*) brace; **~ de boda** bridesmaid

madrugada [maðru'ɣaða] *nf* early morning; (*alba*) dawn, daybreak

madrugador, a [maðruɣa'ðor, a] *adj* early-rising

madrugar [maðru'ɣar] /1h/ *vi* to get up early; (*fig*) to get ahead

madurar [maðu'rar] /1a/ *vt, vi* (*fruta*) to ripen; (*fig*) to mature; **madurez** *nf* ripeness; (*fig*) maturity; **maduro, -a** *adj* ripe; (*fig*) mature

maestra [ma'estra] *nf* V **maestro**

maestría [maes'tria] *nf* mastery; (*habilidad*) skill, expertise

maestro, -a [ma'estro, a] *adj* masterly; (*principal*) main ▷ *nm/f* master/mistress; (*profesor*) teacher ▷ *nm* (*autoridad*) authority; (*Mus*) maestro; (*experto*) master; **~ albañil** master mason

magdalena [maɣða'lena] *nf* fairy cake

magia ['maxja] *nf* magic; **mágico, -a** *adj* magic(al) ▷ *nm/f* magician

magisterio [maxis'terjo] *nm* (*enseñanza*) teaching; (*profesión*) teaching profession; (*maestros*) teachers *pl*

magistrado [maxis'traðo] *nm* magistrate

magistral [maxis'tral] *adj* magisterial; (*fig*) masterly

magnate [maɣ'nate] *nm* magnate, tycoon

magnético, -a [maɣ'netiko, a] *adj* magnetic

magnetofón [maɣneto'fon], **magnetófono** [maɣne'tofono] *nm* tape recorder

magnífico, -a [maɣ'nifiko, a] *adj* splendid, magnificent

magnitud [maɣni'tuð] *nf* magnitude

mago, -a ['maɣo, a] *nm/f* magician; **los Reyes M~s** the Three Wise Men

magro, -a ['maɣro, a] *adj* (*carne*) lean

mahonesa [mao'nesa] *nf* mayonnaise

maître ['metre] *nm* head waiter

maíz [ma'iθ] *nm* maize (BRIT), corn (US); sweet corn

majestad [maxes'tað] *nf* majesty

majo, -a ['maxo, a] *adj* nice; (*guapo*) attractive, good-looking; (*elegante*) smart

mal [mal] *adv* badly; (*equivocadamente*) wrongly ▷ *adj* = **malo** ▷ *nm* evil; (*desgracia*) misfortune; (*daño*) harm, damage; (*Med*) illness; **ir de ~ en peor** to go from bad to worse; **~ que bien** rightly or wrongly

malabarista [malaβa'rista] *nmf* juggler

malaria [ma'larja] *nf* malaria

malcriado, -a [mal'krjaðo, a] *adj* spoiled

maldad [mal'daθ] *nf* evil, wickedness

maldecir [malde'θir] /3o/ *vt* to curse

maldición [maldi'θjon] *nf* curse

maldito, -a [mal'dito, a] *adj* (*condenado*) damned; (*perverso*) wicked; **¡~ sea!** damn it!

malecón [male'kon] *nm* pier, jetty; (*LAM: paseo*) sea front, promenade

maleducado, -a [maleðu'kaðo, a] *adj* bad-mannered, rude

malentendido [malenten'diðo] *nm* misunderstanding

malestar [males'tar] *nm* (*gen*) discomfort; (*fig: inquietud*) uneasiness; (*Pol*) unrest

maleta [ma'leta] *nf* case, suitcase; (*Auto*) boot (BRIT), trunk (US); **hacer la ~** to pack; **maletero** *nm* (*Auto*) boot (BRIT), trunk (US); **maletín** *nm* small case, bag

maleza [ma'leθa] *nf* (*malas hierbas*) weeds *pl*; (*arbustos*) thicket

malgastar [malɣas'tar] /1a/ *vt* (*tiempo, dinero*) to waste; (*salud*) to ruin

malhechor, a [male'tʃor, a] *nm/f* delinquent

malhumorado, -a [malumo'raðo, a] *adj* bad-tempered

malicia [ma'liθja] *nf* (*maldad*) wickedness; (*astucia*) slyness, guile; (*mala intención*) malice, spite; (*carácter travieso*) mischievousness

maligno, -a [ma'liɣno, a] *adj* evil; (*malévolo*) malicious; (*Med*) malignant

malla ['maʎa] *nf* mesh; (*de baño*) swimsuit; (*de ballet, gimnasia*) leotard; **mallas** *nfpl* tights; **~ de alambre** wire mesh

Mallorca [ma'ʎorka] *nf* Majorca

malo, -a ['malo, a] *adj* bad; false ▷ *nm/f* villain; **estar ~** to be ill

malograr [malo'ɣrar] /1a/ *vt* to spoil; (*plan*) to upset; (*ocasión*) to waste

malparado, -a [malpa'raðo, a] *adj*: **salir ~** to come off badly

malpensado, -a [malpen'saðo, a] *adj* nasty

malteada [malte'aða] *nf* (LAM) milk shake

maltratar [maltra'tar] /1a/ *vt* to ill-treat, mistreat

malvado, -a [mal'βaðo, a] *adj* evil, villainous

Malvinas [mal'βinas] *nfpl*: **Islas ~** Falkland Islands

mama ['mama] *nf* (*de animal*) teat; (*de mujer*) breast

mamá [ma'ma] *nf* (*fam*) mum, mummy

m

mamar [ma'mar] /1a/ vt to suck
▷ vi to suck

mamarracho [mama'rratʃo] nm
sight, mess

mameluco [mamelu'ko] (LAM) nm
dungarees pl (BRIT), overalls pl (US)

mamífero [ma'mifero] nm mammal

mampara [mam'para] nf (entre
habitaciones) partition; (biombo) screen

mampostería [mamposte'ria] nf
masonry

manada [ma'naða] nf (Zool) herd; (: de
leones) pride; (: de lobos) pack

manantial [manan'tjal] nm spring

mancha ['mantʃa] nf stain, mark; (de
vegetación) patch; **manchar** /1a/ vt to
stain, mark; (ensuciar) to soil, dirty

manchego, -a [man'tʃeɣo, a] adj of o
from La Mancha

manco, -a ['manko, a] adj (de un
brazo) one-armed; (de una mano) one-
handed; (fig) defective, faulty

mandado [man'daðo] nm errand

mandamiento [manda'mjento]
nm (orden) order, command; (Rel)
commandment

mandar [man'dar] /1a/ vt (ordenar)
to order; (dirigir) to lead, command;
(enviar) to send; (pedir) to order, ask for
▷ vi to be in charge; (pey) to be bossy;
¿mande? pardon?, excuse me? (US); ~
hacer un traje to have a suit made

mandarina [manda'rina] nf (fruta)
tangerine, mandarin (orange)

mandato [man'dato] nm (orden)
order; (Pol: período) term of office;
(: territorio) mandate

mandíbula [man'diβula] nf jaw

mandil [man'dil] nm apron

mando ['mando] nm (Mil) command;
(de país) rule; (el primer lugar) lead;
(Pol) term of office; (Tec) control; ~
a la izquierda left-hand drive; ~ a
distancia remote control

mandón, -ona [man'don, ona] adj
bossy, domineering

manejar [mane'xar] /1a/ vt to
manage; (máquina) to work, operate;

(caballo etc) to handle; (casa) to
run, manage; (LAM Auto) to drive;
manejarse vr (comportarse) to act,
behave; (arreglárselas) to manage;
manejo nm (de bicicleta) handling;
(de negocio) management, running;
(Auto) driving; (facilidad de trato) ease,
confidence; **manejos** nmpl intrigues

manera [ma'nera] nf way, manner,
fashion; **maneras** nfpl (modales)
manners; **su ~ de ser** the way he
is; (aire) his manner; **de ninguna ~**
no way, by no means; **de otra ~**
otherwise; **de todas ~s** at any rate;
no hay ~ de persuadirle there's no
way of convincing him

manga ['manga] nf (de camisa) sleeve;
(de riego) hose

mango ['mango] nm handle; (Bot)
mango

manguera [man'gera] nf hose

maní [ma'ni] nm peanut

manía [ma'nia] nf (Med) mania; (fig:
moda) rage, craze; (disgusto) dislike;
(malicia) spite; **coger ~ a algn** to
take a dislike to sb; **tener ~ a algn** to
dislike sb; **maníaco, -a** adj maniac(al)
▷ nm/f maniac

maniático, -a [ma'njatiko, a] adj
maniac(al) ▷ nm/f maniac

manicomio [mani'komjo] nm
mental hospital (BRIT), insane
asylum (US)

manifestación [manifesta'θjon] nf
(declaración) statement, declaration;
(demostración) show, display; (Pol)
demonstration; (concentración) mass
meeting

manifestar [manifes'tar] /1j/ vt to
show, manifest; (declarar) to state,
declare; **manifiesto, -a** adj clear,
manifest ▷ nm manifesto

manillar [mani'ʎar] nm
handlebars pl

maniobra [ma'njoβra] nf
manœuvre; **maniobras** nfpl
manœuvres; **maniobrar** /1a/ vt to
manœuvre

manipulación [manipula'θjon] *nf* manipulation

manipular [manipu'lar] /1a/ *vt* to manipulate; (*manejar*) to handle

maniquí [mani'ki] *nmf* model ⊳ *nm* dummy

manivela [mani'βela] *nf* crank

manjar [man'xar] *nm* (tasty) dish

mano ['mano] *nf* hand; (*Zool*) foot, paw; (*de pintura*) coat; (*serie*) lot, series; **a ~** by hand; **a ~ derecha/izquierda** on (*o* to) the right(-hand side)/left(-hand side); **robo a ~ armada** armed robbery; **de primera ~** (at) first hand; **de segunda ~** (at) second hand; **estrechar la ~ a algn** to shake sb's hand; **~ de obra** labour, manpower

manojo [ma'noxo] *nm* handful, bunch; **~ de llaves** bunch of keys

manopla [ma'nopla] *nf* (*paño*) flannel; **manoplas** *nfpl* mittens

manosear [manose'ar] /1a/ *vt* (*tocar*) to handle, touch; (*desordenar*) to mess up, rumple; (*insistir en*) to overwork; (*acariciar*) to caress, fondle

manos libres *adj inv* (*teléfono, dispositivo*) hands-free ⊳ *nm inv* hands-free kit

manotazo [mano'taθo] *nm* slap, smack

mansalva [man'salβa]: **a ~** *adv* indiscriminately

mansión [man'sjon] *nf* mansion

manso, -a ['manso, a] *adj* gentle, mild; (*animal*) tame

manta ['manta] *nf* blanket

manteca [man'teka] *nf* fat; (*LAM*) butter; **~ de cerdo** lard

mantecado [mante'kaðo] *nm* (*ESP: dulce navideño*) Christmas sweet made from flour, almonds and lard; (*helado*) ice cream

mantel [man'tel] *nm* tablecloth

mantendré *etc* [manten'dre] *vb V* **mantener**

mantener [mante'ner] /2k/ *vt* to support, maintain; (*alimentar*) to sustain; (*conservar*) to keep; (*Tec*) to maintain, service; **mantenerse** *vr* (*seguir de pie*) to be still standing; (*no ceder*) to hold one's ground; (*subsistir*) to sustain o.s., keep going; **mantenimiento** *nm* maintenance; sustenance; (*sustento*) support

mantequilla [mante'kiʎa] *nf* butter

mantilla [man'tiʎa] *nf* mantilla; **mantillas** *nfpl* baby clothes

manto ['manto] *nm* (*capa*) cloak; (*de ceremonia*) robe, gown

mantuve *etc* [man'tuβe] *vb V* **mantener**

manual [ma'nwal] *adj* manual ⊳ *nm* manual, handbook

manuscrito, -a [manus'krito, a] *adj* handwritten ⊳ *nm* manuscript

manutención [manuten'θjon] *nf* maintenance; (*sustento*) support

manzana [man'θana] *nf* apple; (*Arq*) block

manzanilla [manθa'niʎa] *nf* (*planta*) camomile; (*infusión*) camomile tea

manzano [man'θano] *nm* apple tree

maña ['maɲa] *nf* (*destreza*) skill; (*pey*) guile; (*ardid*) trick

mañana [ma'ɲana] *adv* tomorrow ⊳ *nm* future ⊳ *nf* morning; **de** *o* **por la ~** in the morning; **¡hasta ~!** see you tomorrow!; **~ por la ~** tomorrow morning

mapa ['mapa] *nm* map

maple ['maple] *nm* (*LAM*) maple

maqueta [ma'keta] *nf* (*escala*) model

maquillador, a [makiʎa'ðor, a] *nm/f* (*Teat etc*) make-up artist ⊳ *nf* (*LAM Com*) bonded assembly plant

maquillaje [maki'ʎaxe] *nm* make-up; (*acto*) making up

maquillar [maki'ʎar] /1a/ *vt* to make up; **maquillarse** *vr* to put on (some) make-up

máquina ['makina] *nf* machine; (*de tren*) locomotive, engine; (*Foto*) camera; (*fig*) machinery; **escrito a ~** typewritten; **~ de afeitar** electric razor; **~ de coser** sewing machine; **~ de escribir** typewriter; **~ fotográfica** camera

maquinaria [maki'narja] nf (máquinas) machinery; (mecanismo) mechanism, works pl

maquinilla [maki'niʎa] nf: **~ de afeitar** razor

maquinista [maki'nista] nmf (Ferro) engine driver (BRIT), engineer (US); (Tec) operator; (Naut) engineer

mar [mar] nm sea; **~ adentro** o **afuera** out at sea; **en alta ~** on the high seas; **un ~ de** lots of; **el M~ Negro/Báltico** the Black/Baltic Sea

maraña [ma'raɲa] nf (maleza) thicket; (confusión) tangle

maravilla [mara'βiʎa] nf marvel, wonder; (Bot) marigold; **maravillar** /1a/ vt to astonish, amaze; **maravillarse** vr to be astonished, be amazed; **maravilloso, -a** adj wonderful, marvellous

marca ['marka] nf mark; (sello) stamp; (Com) make, brand; **de ~** excellent, outstanding; **~ de fábrica** trademark; **~ registrada** registered trademark

marcado, -a [mar'kaðo, a] adj marked, strong

marcador [marka'ðor] nm (Deporte) scoreboard; (: persona) scorer

marcapasos [marka'pasos] nm inv pacemaker

marcar [mar'kar] /1g/ vt to mark; (número de teléfono) to dial; (gol) to score; (números) to record, keep a tally of; (el pelo) to set ▷ vi (Deporte) to score; (Telec) to dial

marcha ['martʃa] nf march; (Tec) running, working; (Auto) gear; (velocidad) speed; (fig) progress; (curso) course; **dar ~ atrás** to reverse, put into reverse; **estar en ~** to be under way, be in motion; **poner en ~** to put into gear; **ponerse en ~** to start, get going; **marchar** /1a/ vi (ir) to go; (funcionar) to work, go; **marcharse** vr to go (away), leave

marchitar [martʃi'tar] /1a/ vt to wither, dry up; **marchitarse** vr (Bot) to wither; (fig) to fade away; **marchito, -a** adj withered, faded; (fig) in decline

marciano, -a [mar'θjano, a] adj Martian

marco ['marko] nm frame; (moneda) mark; (fig) framework

marea [ma'rea] nf tide; **~ negra** oil slick

marear [mare'ar] /1a/ vt (fig) to annoy, upset; (Med): **~ a algn** to make sb feel sick; **marearse** vr (tener náuseas) to feel sick; (desvanecerse) to feel faint; (aturdirse) to feel dizzy; (fam: emborracharse) to get tipsy

maremoto [mare'moto] nm tidal wave

mareo [ma'reo] nm (náusea) sick feeling; (en viaje) travel sickness; (aturdimiento) dizziness; (fam: lata) nuisance

marfil [mar'fil] nm ivory

margarina [marɣa'rina] nf margarine

margarita [marɣa'rita] nf (Bot) daisy; (en máquina impresora) daisy wheel

margen ['marxen] nm (borde) edge, border; (fig) margin, space ▷ nf (de río etc) bank; **dar ~ para** to give an opportunity for; **mantenerse al ~** to keep out (of things)

marginar [marxi'nar] /1a/ vt to exclude; (socialmente) to marginalize, ostracize

mariachi [ma'rjatʃi] nm (música) mariachi music; (grupo) mariachi band; (persona) mariachi musician

○ **MARIACHI**
○
○ Mariachi music is the musical style
○ most characteristic of Mexico.
○ From the state of Jalisco in the 19th
○ century, this music spread rapidly
○ throughout the country, until each
○ region had its own particular style

of the mariachi "sound". A mariachi band can be made up of several singers, up to eight violins, two trumpets, guitars, a *vihuela* (an old form of guitar), and a harp. The dance associated with this music is called the *zapateado*.

marica [maˈrika] *nm* (*fam!*) sissy
maricón [mariˈkon] *nm* (*fam!*) queer (!)
marido [maˈriðo] *nm* husband
marihuana [mariˈwənə] *nf* marijuana, cannabis
marina [maˈrina] *nf* navy; **~ mercante** merchant navy
marinero, -a [mariˈnero, a] *adj* sea *cpd* ▷ *nm* sailor, seaman
marino, -a [maˈrino, a] *adj* sea *cpd*, marine ▷ *nm* sailor
marioneta [marjoˈneta] *nf* puppet
mariposa [mariˈposa] *nf* butterfly
mariquita [mariˈkita] *nf* ladybird (*BRIT*), ladybug (*US*)
marisco [maˈrisko] *nm* (*tb*: **~s**) shellfish, seafood
marítimo, -a [maˈritimo, a] *adj* sea *cpd*, maritime
mármol [ˈmarmol] *nm* marble
marqués, -esa [marˈkes, esa] *nm/f* marquis/marchioness
marrón [maˈrron] *adj* brown
marroquí [marroˈki] *adj*, *nmf* Moroccan ▷ *nm* Morocco (leather)
Marruecos [maˈrrwekos] *nm* Morocco
martes [ˈmartes] *nm inv* Tuesday; **~ y trece** ≈ Friday 13th

martillo [marˈtiʎo] *nm* hammer
mártir [ˈmartir] *nmf* martyr; **martirio** *nm* martyrdom; (*fig*) torture, torment

marxismo [markˈsismo] *nm* Marxism
marzo [ˈmarθo] *nm* March
mas [mas] *conj* but

 PALABRA CLAVE

más [mas] *adj*, *adv* **1**: **más (que, de)** (*compar*) more (than), ...+ er (than); **más grande/inteligente** bigger/more intelligent; **trabaja más (que yo)** he works more (than me); *V tb* **cada**

2 (*superl*): **el más** the most, ...+ est; **el más grande/inteligente (de)** the biggest/most intelligent (in)

3 (*negativo*): **no tengo más dinero** I haven't got any more money; **no viene más por aquí** he doesn't come round here any more

4 (*adicional*): **no le veo más solución que ...** I see no other solution than to ...; **¿quién más?** anybody else?

5 (+ *adj*, *valor intensivo*): **¡qué perro más sucio!** what a filthy dog!; **¡es más tonto!** he's so stupid!

6 (*locuciones*): **más o menos** more or less; **los más** most people; **es más** furthermore; **más bien** rather; **¡qué más da!** what does it matter!; *V tb* **no**

7: **por más: por más que** lo intento no matter how much *o* hard I try; **por más que quisiera ayudar** much as I should like to help

8: **de más: veo que aquí estoy de más** I can see I'm not needed here; **tenemos uno de más** we've got one extra

▷ *prep*: **2 más 2 son 4** 2 and *o* plus 2 are 4

▷ *nm inv*: **este trabajo tiene sus más y sus menos** this job's got its good points and its bad points

masa [ˈmasa] *nf* (*mezcla*) dough; (*volumen*) volume, mass; (*Física*) mass; **en ~** en masse; **las ~s** (*Pol*) the masses
masacre [maˈsakre] *nf* massacre

masaje [ma'saxe] nm massage

máscara ['maskara] nf mask; **~ antigás** gas mask; **mascarilla** nf mask

masculino, -a [masku'lino, a] adj masculine; (Bio) male

masía [ma'sia] nf farmhouse

masivo, -a [ma'siβo, a] adj (en masa) mass

masoquista [maso'kista] nmf masochist

máster ['master] nm master's degree

masticar [masti'kar] /1g/ vt to chew

mástil ['mastil] nm (de navío) mast; (de guitarra) neck

mastín [mas'tin] nm mastiff

masturbarse [mastur'βarse] /1a/ vr to masturbate

mata ['mata] nf (arbusto) bush, shrub; (de hierbas) tuft

matadero [mata'ðero] nm slaughterhouse, abattoir

matador, a [mata'ðor, a] adj killing ▷ nm (Taur) matador, bullfighter

matamoscas [mata'moskas] nm inv (palo) fly swat

matanza [ma'tanθa] nf slaughter

matar [ma'tar] /1a/ vt, vi to kill; **matarse** vr (suicidarse) to kill o.s., commit suicide; (morir) to be o get killed; **~ el hambre** to stave off hunger

matasellos [mata'seλos] nm inv postmark

mate ['mate] adj matt ▷ nm (en ajedrez) (check)mate; (LAM: hierba) maté; (: vasija) gourd

matemáticas [mate'matikas] nfpl mathematics; **matemático, -a** adj mathematical ▷ nm/f mathematician

materia [ma'terja] nf (gen) matter; (Tec) material; (Escol) subject; **en ~ de** on the subject of; **~ prima** raw material; **material** adj material ▷ nm material; (Tec) equipment; **materialista** adj materialist(ic); **materialmente** adv materially; (fig) absolutely

maternal [mater'nal] adj motherly, maternal

maternidad [materni'ðað] nf motherhood, maternity; **materno, -a** adj maternal; (lengua) mother cpd

matinal [mati'nal] adj morning cpd

matiz [ma'tiθ] nm shade; **matizar** /1f/ vt (variar) to vary; (Arte) to blend; **matizar de** to tinge with

matón [ma'ton] nm bully

matorral [mato'rral] nm thicket

matrícula [ma'trikula] nf (registro) register; (Auto) registration number; (: placa) number plate; **~ de honor** (Univ) top marks in a subject at university with the right to free registration the following year; **matricular** /1a/ vt to register, enrol

matrimonio [matri'monjo] nm (pareja) (married) couple; (acto) marriage

matriz [ma'triθ] nf (Anat) womb; (Tec) mould

matrona [ma'trona] nf (mujer de edad) matron; (comadrona) midwife

matufia [ma'tufja] nf (LAM fam) put-up job

maullar [mau'λar] /1a/ vi to mew, miaow

maxilar [maksi'lar] nm jaw(bone)

máxima ['maksima] nf V **máximo**

máximo, -a ['maksimo, a] adj maximum; (más alto) highest; (más grande) greatest ▷ nm maximum ▷ nf maxim; **como ~** at most

mayo ['majo] nm May

mayonesa [majo'nesa] nf mayonnaise

mayor [ma'jor] adj main, chief; (adulto) adult; elderly; (Mus) major; (comparativo: de tamaño) bigger; (: de edad) older; (superlativo: de tamaño) biggest; (: de edad) oldest ▷ nm adult; **mayores** nmpl (antepasados) ancestors; **al por ~** wholesale; **~ de edad** adult

mayoral [majo'ral] nm foreman

mayordomo [major'ðomo] nm butler

mayoría [majo'ria] *nf* majority, greater part

mayorista [majo'rista] *nmf* wholesaler

mayoritario, -a [majori'tarjo, a] *adj* majority *cpd*

mayúsculo, -a [ma'juskulo, a] *adj* (*fig*) big, tremendous ▷ *nf* capital (letter)

mazapán [maθa'pan] *nm* marzipan

mazo ['maθo] *nm* (*martillo*) mallet; (*de flores*) bunch; (*Deporte*) bat

me [me] *pron* (*directo*) me; (*indirecto*) (to) me; (*reflexivo*) (to) myself; **¡dámelo!** give it to me!

mear [me'ar] /1a/ (*fam*) *vi* to pee, piss (!)

mecánica [me'kanika] *nf* V **mecánico**

mecánico, -a [me'kaniko, a] *adj* mechanical ▷ *nm/f* mechanic ▷ *nf* (*estudio*) mechanics *sg*; (*mecanismo*) mechanism

mecanismo [meka'nismo] *nm* mechanism; (*engranaje*) gear

mecanografía [mekanoɣra'fia] *nf* typewriting; **mecanógrafo, -a** *nm/f* (*copy*) typist

mecate [me'kate] *nm* (*LAM*) rope

mecedor [mese'ðor] *nm* (*LAM*), **mecedora** [meθe'ðora] *nf* rocking chair

mecer [me'θer] /2b/ *vt* (*cuna*) to rock; **mecerse** *vr* to rock; (*rama*) to sway

mecha ['metʃa] *nf* (*de vela*) wick; (*de bomba*) fuse

mechero [me'tʃero] *nm* (*cigarette*) lighter

mechón [me'tʃon] *nm* (*gen*) tuft; (*de pelo*) lock

medalla [me'ðaʎa] *nf* medal

media ['meðja] *nf* V **medio**

mediado, -a [me'ðjaðo, a] *adj* half-full; (*trabajo*) half-completed; **a ~s de** in the middle of, halfway through

mediano, -a [me'ðjano, a] *adj* (*regular*) medium, average; (*mediocre*) mediocre

medianoche [meðja'notʃe] *nf* midnight

mediante [me'ðjante] *adv* by (means of), through

mediar [me'ðjar] /1b/ *vi* (*interceder*) to mediate, intervene

medicamento [meðika'mento] *nm* medicine, drug

medicina [meði'θina] *nf* medicine

médico, -a ['meðiko, a] *adj* medical ▷ *nm/f* doctor

medida [me'ðiða] *nf* measure; (*medición*) measurement; (*moderación*) moderation, prudence; **en cierta/ gran ~** up to a point/to a great extent; **un traje a la ~** a made-to-measure suit; **~ de cuello** collar size; **a ~ de** in proportion to; (*de acuerdo con*) in keeping with; **a ~ que ...** (at the same time) as ...; **medidor** *nm* (*LAM*) meter

medio, -a ['meðjo, a] *adj* half (a); (*punto*) mid, middle; (*promedio*) average ▷ *adv* half- ▷ *nm* (*centro*) middle, centre; (*método*) means, way; (*ambiente*) environment ▷ *nf* stocking; (*LAM*) sock; (*promedio*) average; **medias** *nfpl* tights; **~ litro** half a litre; **las tres y media** half past three; **M~ Oriente** Middle East; **~ de transporte** means of transport; **a ~ terminar** half finished; **~ ambiente** environment; V *tb* **medios; medioambiental** *adj* environmental

mediocre [me'ðjokre] *adj* mediocre

mediodía [meðjo'ðia] *nm* midday, noon

medios ['meðjos] *nmpl* means, resources; **los ~ de comunicación** the media; **los ~ sociales** social media

medir [me'ðir] /3k/ *vt* to measure

meditar [meði'tar] /1a/ *vt* to ponder, think over, meditate on; (*planear*) to think out

mediterráneo, -a [meðite'rraneo, a] *adj* Mediterranean ▷ *nm*: **el (mar) M~** the Mediterranean (Sea)

médula ['meðula] *nf* (*Anat*) marrow; **~ espinal** spinal cord

m

medusa [me'ðusa] *nf* (*ESP*) jellyfish
megáfono [me'ɣafono] *nm* megaphone
megapíxel [meɣa'piksel] (*pl* **megapixels** *o* **megapíxeles**) *nm* megapixel
mejicano, -a [mexi'kano, a] *adj, nm/f* Mexican
Méjico ['mexiko] *nm* Mexico
mejilla [me'xiʎa] *nf* cheek
mejillón [mexi'ʎon] *nm* mussel
mejor [me'xor] *adj, adv* (*comparativo*) better; (*superlativo*) best; **a lo ~** probably; (*quizá*) maybe; **~ dicho** rather; **tanto ~** so much the better; **mejora** [me'xora] *nf* improvement; **mejorar** /1a/ *vt* to improve, make better ▷ *vi* to improve, get better; **mejorarse** *vr* to improve, get better
melancólico, -a [melan'koliko, a] *adj* (*triste*) sad, melancholy; (*soñador*) dreamy
melena [me'lena] *nf* (*de persona*) long hair; (*Zool*) mane
mellizo, -a [me'ʎiθo, a] *adj, nm/f* twin
melocotón [meloko'ton] *nm* (*ESP*) peach
melodía [melo'ðia] *nf* melody; tune
melodrama [melo'ðrama] *nm* melodrama; **melodramático, -a** *adj* melodramatic
melón [me'lon] *nm* melon
membrete [mem'brete] *nm* letterhead
membrillo [mem'briʎo] *nm* quince; **carne de ~** quince jelly
memoria [me'morja] *nf* (*gen*) memory; **memorias** *nfpl* (*de autor*) memoirs; **memorizar** /1f/ *vt* to memorize
menaje [me'naxe] *nm* (*tb:* **artículos de ~**) household items *pl*
mencionar [menθjo'nar] /1a/ *vt* to mention
mendigo, -a [men'diɣo, a] *nm/f* beggar
menear [mene'ar] /1a/ *vt* to move; **menearse** *vr* to shake; (*balancearse*)

to sway; (*moverse*) to move; (*fig*) to get a move on
menestra [me'nestra] *nf:* **~ de verduras** vegetable stew
menopausia [meno'pausja] *nf* menopause
menor [me'nor] *adj* (*más pequeño: comparativo*) smaller; (*: superlativo*) smallest; (*más joven: comparativo*) younger; (*: superlativo*) youngest; (*Mus*) minor ▷ *nmf* (*joven*) young person, juvenile; **no tengo la ~ idea** I haven't the faintest idea; **al por ~** retail; **~ de edad** minor
Menorca [me'norka] *nf* Minorca

 PALABRA CLAVE

menos [menos] *adj* 1 (*compar*): **menos (que, de)** (*cantidad*) less (than); (*número*) fewer (than); **con menos entusiasmo** with less enthusiasm; **menos gente** fewer people; V *tb* **cada**
2 (*superl*): **es el que menos culpa tiene** he is the least to blame
▶ *adv* 1 (*compar*): **menos (que, de)** less (than); **me gusta menos que el otro** I like it less than the other one
2 (*superl*): **es el menos listo (de su clase)** he's the least bright (in his class); **de todas ellas es la que menos me agrada** out of all of them she's the one I like least
3 (*locuciones*): **no quiero verle y menos visitarle** I don't want to see him let alone visit him; **tenemos siete (de) menos** we're seven short; **al/por lo menos** at (the very) least; **¡menos mal!** thank goodness!
▶ *prep* except; (*cifras*) minus; **todos menos él** everyone except (for) him; **5 menos 2** 5 minus 2; **las 7 menos 20** (*hora*) 20 to 7
▶ *conj*: **a menos que: a menos que venga mañana** unless he comes tomorrow

menospreciar [menospre'θjar] /1b/ vt to underrate, undervalue; (*despreciar*) to scorn, despise

mensaje [men'saxe] nm message; **enviar un ~ a algn** (*por móvil*) to text sb, send sb a text message; **~ de texto** text message; **~ electrónico** email; **mensajero, -a** nm/f messenger

menso, -a ['menso, a] adj (LAM fam) stupid

menstruación [menstrwa'θjon] nf menstruation

mensual [men'swal] adj monthly; **10 euros ~es** 10 euros a month; **mensualidad** nf (*salario*) monthly salary; (Com) monthly payment *o* instalment

menta ['menta] nf mint

mental [men'tal] adj mental; **mentalidad** nf mentality; **mentalizar** /1f/ vt (*sensibilizar*) to make aware; (*convencer*) to convince; (*preparar mentalmente*) to prepare mentally; **mentalizarse** vr (*concienciarse*) to become aware; **mentalizarse (de)** to get used to the idea (of); **mentalizarse de que ...** (*convencerse*) to get it into one's head that ...

mente ['mente] nf mind

mentir [men'tir] /3i/ vi to lie; **mentira** nf (*una mentira*) lie; (*acto*) lying; (*invención*) fiction; **parece mentira que ...** it seems incredible that ..., I can't believe that ...; **mentiroso, -a** adj lying ▷ nm/f liar

menú [me'nu] nm menu; (tb: **~ del día**) set meal; **~ turístico** tourist menu

menudo, -a [me'nuðo, a] adj (*pequeño*) small, tiny; (*sin importancia*) petty, insignificant; **¡~ negocio!** (fam) some deal!; **a ~** often, frequently

meñique [me'ɲike] nm little finger

mercadillo [merka'ðiʎo] nm (ESP) flea market

mercado [mer'kaðo] nm market; **~ de pulgas** (LAM) flea market

mercancía [merkan'θia] nf commodity; **mercancías** nfpl goods, merchandise sg

mercenario, -a [merθe'narjo, a] adj, nm mercenary

mercería [merθe'ria] nf haberdashery (BRIT), notions pl (US); (*tienda*) haberdasher's shop (BRIT), drapery (BRIT), notions store (US)

mercurio [mer'kurjo] nm mercury

merecer [mere'θer] /2d/ vt to deserve, merit ▷ vi to be deserving, be worthy; **merece la pena** it's worthwhile; **merecido, -a** adj (well) deserved; **llevarse su merecido** to get one's deserts

merendar [meren'dar] /1j/ vt to have for tea ▷ vi to have tea; (*en el campo*) to have a picnic; **merendero** nm (open-air) café

merengue [me'renge] nm meringue

meridiano [meri'ðjano] nm (Astro, Geo) meridian

merienda [me'rjenda] nf (light) tea, afternoon snack; (*de campo*) picnic

mérito ['merito] nm merit; (*valor*) worth, value

merluza [mer'luθa] nf hake

mermelada [merme'laða] nf jam

mero, -a ['mero, a] adj mere; (LAM fam) very

merodear [meroðe'ar] /1a/ vi (*de noche*) to prowl (about)

mes [mes] nm month

mesa ['mesa] nf table; (*de trabajo*) desk; (Geo) plateau; **~ electoral** *officials in charge of a polling station*; **~ redonda** (*reunión*) round table; **poner/quitar la ~** to lay/clear the table; **mesero, -a** nm/f (LAM) waiter/ waitress

meseta [me'seta] nf (Geo) tableland

mesilla [me'siʎa] nf: **~ de noche** bedside table

mesón [me'son] nm inn

mestizo, -a [mes'tiθo, a] adj mixed-race ▷ nm/f person of mixed race

meta ['meta] nf goal; (*de carrera*) finish

m

metabolismo [metaβo'lismo] *nm* metabolism

metáfora [me'tafora] *nf* metaphor

metal [me'tal] *nm* (*materia*) metal; (*Mus*) brass; **metálico, -a** *adj* metallic; (*de metal*) metal ▷ *nm* (*dinero contante*) cash

meteorología [meteorolo'xia] *nf* meteorology

meter [me'ter] /2a/ *vt* (*colocar*) to put, place; (*introducir*) to put in, insert; (*involucrar*) to involve; (*causar*) to make, cause; **meterse** *vr*: **~se en** to go into, enter; (*fig*) to interfere in, meddle in; **~se a** to start; **~se a escritor** to become a writer; **~se con algn** to provoke sb, pick a quarrel with sb

meticuloso, -a [metiku'loso, a] *adj* meticulous, thorough

metódico, -a [me'toðiko, a] *adj* methodical

método ['metoðo] *nm* method

metralleta [metra'ʎeta] *nf* sub-machine-gun

métrico, -a ['metriko, a] *adj* metric

metro ['metro] *nm* metre; (*tren*) underground (*BRIT*), subway (*US*)

metrosexual [metrosexu'al] *adj, nm* metrosexual

mexicano, -a [mexi'kano, a] *adj, nm/f* Mexican

México ['mexiko] *nm* Mexico; **Ciudad de ~** Mexico City

mezcla ['meθkla] *nf* mixture; **mezclar** /1a/ *vt* to mix (up); **mezclarse** *vr* to mix, mingle; **mezclar en** to get mixed up in, get involved in

mezquino, -a [meθ'kino, a] *adj* mean

mezquita [meθ'kita] *nf* mosque

mg *abr* (= *miligramo(s)*) mg

mi [mi] *adj posesivo* my ▷ *nm* (*Mus*) E

mí [mi] *pron* me, myself

mía ['mia] *pron* V **mío**

michelín [mitʃe'lin] *nm* (*fam*) spare tyre

microbio [mi'kroβjo] *nm* microbe

micrófono [mi'krofono] *nm* microphone

microonda [mikro'onda] *nf*, **microondas** [mikro'ondas] *nm inv* microwave; **(horno) ~s** microwave (oven)

microscopio [mikros'kopjo] *nm* microscope

miedo ['mjeðo] *nm* fear; (*nerviosismo*) apprehension, nervousness; **tener ~** to be afraid; **de ~** wonderful, marvellous; **hace un frío de ~** (*fam*) it's terribly cold; **miedoso, -a** *adj* fearful, timid

miel [mjel] *nf* honey

miembro ['mjembro] *nm* limb; (*socio*) member; **~ viril** penis

mientras ['mjentras] *conj* while; (*duración*) as long as ▷ *adv* meanwhile; **~ tanto** meanwhile

miércoles ['mjerkoles] *nm inv* Wednesday

mierda ['mjerða] *nf* (*fam!*) shit (!)

miga ['miɣa] *nf* crumb; (*fig: meollo*) essence; **hacer buenas ~s** (*fam*) to get on well

mil [mil] *num* thousand; **dos ~ libras** two thousand pounds

milagro [mi'laɣro] *nm* miracle; **milagroso, -a** *adj* miraculous

milésima [mi'lesima] *nf* (*de segundo*) thousandth

mili ['mili] *nf*: **hacer la ~** (*fam*) to do one's military service

milímetro [mi'limetro] *nm* millimetre (*BRIT*), millimeter (*US*)

militante [mili'tante] *adj* militant

militar [mili'tar] /1a/ *adj* military ▷ *nmf* soldier ▷ *vi* to serve in the army

milla ['miʎa] *nf* mile

millar [mi'ʎar] *num* thousand

millón [mi'ʎon] *num* million; **millonario, -a** *nm/f* millionaire

milusos [mi'lusos] *nm inv* (*LAM*) odd-job man

mimar [mi'mar] /1a/ *vt* to spoil, pamper

mimbre ['mimbre] *nm* wicker

mímica ['mimika] nf (para comunicarse) sign language; (imitación) mimicry

mimo ['mimo] nm (caricia) caress; (de niño) spoiling; (Teat) mime; (: actor) mime artist

mina ['mina] nf mine

mineral [mine'ral] adj mineral ▷ nm (Geo) mineral; (mena) ore

minero, -a [mi'nero, a] adj mining cpd ▷ nm/f miner

miniatura [minja'tura] adj inv, nf miniature

minidisco [mini'ðisko] nm diskette

minifalda [mini'falda] nf miniskirt

mínimo, -a ['minimo, a] adj ▷ nm minimum

minino, -a [mi'nino, a] nm/f (fam) puss, pussy

ministerio [minis'terjo] nm ministry (BRIT), department (US); **M~ de Asuntos Exteriores** Foreign Office (BRIT), State Department (US); **M~ de Hacienda** Treasury (BRIT), Treasury Department (US)

ministro, -a [mi'nistro, a] nm/f minister

minoría [mino'ria] nf minority

minúsculo, -a [mi'nuskulo, a] adj tiny, minute ▷ nf small letter

minusválido, -a [minus'βaliðo, a] adj (physically) handicapped o disabled ▷ nm/f disabled person

minuta [mi'nuta] nf (de comida) menu

minutero [minu'tero] nm minute hand

minuto [mi'nuto] nm minute

mío, -a ['mio, a] pron: **el ~** mine; **un amigo ~** a friend of mine; **lo ~** what is mine

miope [mi'ope] adj short-sighted

mira ['mira] nf (de arma) sight(s) pl; (fig) aim, intention

mirada [mi'raða] nf look, glance; (expresión) look, expression; **clavar la ~ en** to stare at; **echar una ~ a** to glance at

mirado, -a [mi'raðo, a] adj (sensato) sensible; (considerado) considerate; **bien/mal ~** well/not well thought of; **bien ~ ...** all things considered ...

mirador [mira'ðor] nm viewpoint, vantage point

mirar [mi'rar] /1a/ vt to look at; (observar) to watch; (considerar) to consider, think over; (vigilar, cuidar) to watch, look after ▷ vi to look; (Arq) to face; **mirarse** vr (dos personas) to look at each other; **~ bien/mal** to think highly of/have a poor opinion of; **~se al espejo** to look at o.s. in the mirror

mirilla [mi'riʎa] nf spyhole, peephole

mirlo ['mirlo] nm blackbird

misa ['misa] nf mass

miserable [mise'raβle] adj (avaro) mean, stingy; (nimio) miserable, paltry; (lugar) squalid; (fam) vile, despicable ▷ nmf (malvado) rogue

miseria [mi'serja] nf (pobreza) poverty; (tacañería) meanness, stinginess; (condiciones) squalor; **una ~** a pittance

misericordia [miseri'korðja] nf (compasión) compassion, pity; (perdón) mercy

misil [mi'sil] nm missile

misión [mi'sjon] nf mission; **misionero, -a** nm/f missionary

mismo, -a ['mismo, a] adj (semejante) same; (después de pronombre) -self; (para énfasis) very ▷ adv: **aquí/ayer/hoy ~** right here/only yesterday/this very day; **ahora ~** right now ▷ conj: **lo ~ que** just like, just as; **por lo ~** for the same reason; **el ~ traje** the same suit; **en ese ~ momento** at that very moment; **vino el ~ Ministro** the Minister himself came; **yo ~ lo vi** I saw it myself; **lo ~** the same (thing); **da lo ~** it's all the same; **quedamos en las mismas** we're no further forward

misterio [mis'terjo] nm mystery; **misterioso, -a** adj mysterious

mitad [mi'tað] nf (medio) half; (centro) middle; **a ~ de precio** (at) half-price;

en o **a ~ del camino** halfway along the road; **cortar por la ~** to cut through the middle

mitin ['mitin] nm meeting

mito ['mito] nm myth

mixto, -a ['miksto, a] adj mixed

ml abr (= mililitro(s)) ml

mm abr (= milímetro(s)) mm

mobiliario [moβi'ljarɣo] nm furniture

mochila [mo'tʃila] nf rucksack (BRIT), backpack

moco ['moko] nm mucus; **mocos** nmpl (fam) snot; **limpiarse los ~s** to blow one's nose

moda ['moða] nf fashion; (estilo) style; **de** o **a la ~** in fashion, fashionable; **pasado de ~** out of fashion

modal [mo'ðal] adj modal; **modales** nmpl manners

modelar [moðe'lar] /1a/ vt to model

modelo [mo'ðelo] adj inv ▷ nmf model

módem ['moðem] nm (Inform) modem

moderado, -a [moðe'raðo, a] adj moderate

moderar [moðe'rar] /1a/ vt to moderate; (violencia) to restrain, control; (velocidad) to reduce; **moderarse** vr to restrain o.s., control o.s.

modernizar [moðerni'θar] /1f/ vt to modernize

moderno, -a [mo'ðerno, a] adj modern; (actual) present-day

modestia [mo'ðestja] nf modesty; **modesto, -a** adj modest

modificar [moðifi'kar] /1g/ vt to modify

modisto, -a [mo'ðisto, a] nm/f (diseñador) couturier, designer; (que confecciona) dressmaker

modo ['moðo] nm way, manner; (Inform, Mus) mode; **modos** nmpl manners; **"~ de empleo"** "instructions for use"; **de ningún ~** in no way; **de todos ~s** at any rate

mofarse [mo'farse] /1a/ vr: **~ de** to mock, scoff at

mofle ['mofle] nm (LAM) silencer (BRIT), muffler (US)

mogollón [moɣo'ʎon] (fam) adv: **un ~** a hell of a lot

moho ['moo] nm mould, mildew; (en metal) rust

mojar [mo'xar] /1a/ vt to wet; (humedecer) to damp(en), moisten; (calar) to soak; **mojarse** vr to get wet

molcajete [molka'xete] (LAM) nm mortar

molde ['molde] nm mould; (de costura) pattern; (fig) model; **moldeado** nm soft perm; **moldear** /1a/ vt to mould

mole ['mole] nf mass, bulk; (edificio) pile

moler [mo'ler] /2h/ vt to grind, crush

molestar [moles'tar] /1a/ vt to bother; (fastidiar) to annoy; (incomodar) to inconvenience, put out ▷ vi to be a nuisance; **molestarse** vr to bother; (incomodarse) to go to a lot of trouble; (ofenderse) to take offence; **¿le molesta el ruido?** do you mind the noise?

No confundir *molestar* con la palabra inglesa *molest*.

molestia [mo'lestja] nf bother, trouble; (incomodidad) inconvenience; (Med) discomfort; **es una ~** it's a nuisance; **molesto, -a** adj (que fastidia) annoying; (incómodo) inconvenient; (inquieto) uncomfortable, ill at ease; (enfadado) annoyed

molido, -a [mo'liðo, a] adj: **estar ~** (fig) to be exhausted o dead beat

molinillo [moli'niʎo] nm hand mill; **~ de carne/café** mincer/coffee grinder

molino [mo'lino] nm (edificio) mill; (máquina) grinder

momentáneo, -a [momen'taneo, a] adj momentary

momento [mo'mento] nm moment; **de ~** at the moment, for the moment

momia ['momja] nf mummy

monarca [mo'narka] nmf monarch, ruler; **monarquía** nf monarchy

monasterio [monas'terjo] nm
monastery

mondar [mon'dar] /1a/ vt to peel;
mondarse vr: **~se de risa** (fam) to
split one's sides laughing

mondongo [mon'dongo] nm (LAM)
tripe

moneda [mo'neða] nf (tipo de dinero)
currency, money; (pieza) coin; **una
~ de 50 céntimos** a 50-cent coin;
monedero nm purse

monitor, a [moni'tor, a] nm/f
instructor, coach ▷ nm (TV) set;
(Inform) monitor

monja ['monxa] nf nun

monje ['monxe] nm monk

mono, -a ['mono, a] adj (bonito)
lovely, pretty; (gracioso) nice, charming
▷ nm/f monkey, ape ▷ nm dungarees
pl; (traje de faena) overalls pl

monopatín [monopa'tin] nm
skateboard

monopolio [mono'poljo] nm
monopoly; **monopolizar** /1f/ vt to
monopolize

monótono, -a [mo'notono, a] adj
monotonous

monstruo ['monstrwo] nm monster
▷ adj inv fantastic; **monstruoso, -a**
adj monstrous

montaje [mon'taxe] nm assembly;
(Teat) décor; (Cine) montage

montaña [mon'taɲa] nf (monte)
mountain; (sierra) mountains pl,
mountainous area; **~ rusa** roller
coaster; **montañero, -a** nm/f
mountaineer; **montañismo** nm
mountaineering

montar [mon'tar] /1a/ vt (subir a)
to mount, get on; (Tec) to assemble,
put together; (negocio) to set up;
(colocar) to lift on to; (Culin) to whip,
beat ▷ vi to mount, get on; (sobresalir)
to overlap; **~ en bicicleta** to ride a
bicycle; **~ en cólera** to get angry; **~ a
caballo** to ride, go horseriding

monte ['monte] nm (montaña)
mountain; (bosque) woodland; (área

sin cultivar) wild area, wild country; **~
de piedad** pawnshop

montón [mon'ton] nm heap, pile; **un
~ de** (fig) heaps of, lots of

monumento [monu'mento] nm
monument

moño ['moɲo] nm bun

moqueta [mo'keta] nf fitted carpet

mora ['mora] nf blackberry

morado, -a [mo'raðo, a] adj purple,
violet ▷ nm bruise

moral [mo'ral] adj moral ▷ nf (ética)
ethics pl; (moralidad) morals pl,
morality; (ánimo) morale

moraleja [mora'lexa] nf moral

morboso, -a [mor'βoso, a] adj
morbid

morcilla [mor'θiʎa] nf blood sausage,
≈ black pudding (BRIT)

mordaza [mor'ðaθa] nf (para la boca)
gag; (Tec) clamp

morder [mor'ðer] /2h/ vt to bite;
(fig: consumir) to eat away, eat into;
mordisco nm bite

moreno, -a [mo'reno, a] adj (color)
(dark) brown; (de tez) dark; (de pelo
moreno) dark-haired; (negro) black

morfina [mor'fina] nf morphine

moribundo, -a [mori'βundo, a]
adj dying

morir [mo'rir] /3j/ vi to die; (fuego) to
die down; (luz) to go out; **morirse** vr
to die; (fig) to be dying; **fue muerto a
tiros/en un accidente** he was shot
(dead)/was killed in an accident; **~se
por algo** to be dying for sth

moro, -a ['moro, a] adj Moorish
▷ nm/f Moor

moroso, -a [mo'roso, a] nm/f (Com)
bad debtor, defaulter

morro ['morro] nm (Zool) snout, nose;
(Auto, Aviat) nose

morsa ['morsa] nf walrus

mortadela [morta'ðela] nf
mortadella

mortal [mor'tal] adj mortal; (golpe)
deadly; **mortalidad** nf mortality

mortero [mor'tero] nm mortar

m

mosca ['moska] nf fly

Moscú [mos'ku] nm Moscow

mosquear [moske'ar] /1a/ (fam) vt (fastidiar) to annoy; **mosquearse** vr (enfadarse) to get annoyed; (ofenderse) to take offence

mosquitero [moski'tero] nm mosquito net

mosquito [mos'kito] nm mosquito

mostaza [mos'taθa] nf mustard

mosto ['mosto] nm unfermented grape juice

mostrador [mostra'ðor] nm (de tienda) counter; (de café) bar

mostrar [mos'trar] /1l/ vt to show; (exhibir) to display, exhibit; (explicar) to explain; **mostrarse** vr: **~se amable** to be kind; to prove to be kind; **no se muestra muy inteligente** he doesn't seem (to be) very intelligent

mota ['mota] nf speck, tiny piece; (en diseño) dot

mote ['mote] nm nickname

motín [mo'tin] nm (del pueblo) revolt, rising; (del ejército) mutiny

motivar [moti'βar] /1a/ vt (causar) to cause, motivate; (explicar) to explain, justify; **motivo** nm motive, reason

moto ['moto] nf, **motocicleta** [motoθi'kleta] nf motorbike (BRIT), motorcycle

motociclista [motoθi'klista] nmf motorcyclist, biker

motoneta [moto'neta] nf (LAM) (motor) scooter

motor, a [mo'tor, a] nm motor, engine ▷ nf motorboat; **~ a chorro** o **de reacción/de explosión** jet engine/internal combustion engine

movedizo, -a [moβe'ðiθo, a] adj (inseguro) unsteady; (fig) unsettled

mover [mo'βer] /2h/ vt to move; (cabeza) to shake; (accionar) to drive; (fig) to cause, provoke; **moverse** vr to move; (fig) to get a move on

móvil ['moβil] adj mobile; (pieza de máquina) moving; (mueble) movable

▷ nm (motivo) motive; (teléfono) mobile, cellphone (US)

movimiento [moβi'mjento] nm movement; (Tec) motion; (actividad) activity

mozo, -a ['moθo, a] adj (joven) young ▷ nm/f youth, young man/girl; (camarero) waiter; (camarera) waitress

MP3 nm MP3; **reproductor (de) ~** MP3 player

mucama [mu'kama] nf (LAM) maid

muchacho, -a [mu'tʃatʃo, a] nm/f (niño) boy/girl; (criado) servant/ servant o maid

muchedumbre [mutʃe'ðumbre] nf crowd

PALABRA CLAVE

mucho, -a ['mutʃo, a] adj 1 (cantidad) a lot of, much; (número) lots of, a lot of, many; **mucho dinero** a lot of money; **hace mucho calor** it's very hot; **muchas amigas** lots o a lot of o many friends

2 (sg: fam): **ésta es mucha casa para él** this house is much too big for him

▷ pron 1: **me queda mucho que hacer** I've got a lot to do; **muchos dicen que ...** a lot of people say that ...; V tb **tener**

▷ adv 1: **me gusta mucho** I like it a lot o very much; **lo siento mucho** I'm very sorry; **come mucho** he eats a lot; **¿te vas a quedar mucho?** are you going to be staying long?

2 (respuesta) very; **¿estás cansado?** — **¡mucho!** are you tired? — very!

3 (locuciones): **como mucho** at (the) most; **el mejor con mucho** by far the best; **no es rico ni mucho menos** he's far from being rich

4: **por mucho que: por mucho que le creas** however much o no matter how much you believe him

muda ['muða] nf change of clothing

mudanza [mu'ðanθa] nf (de casa) move

mudar [mu'ðar] /1a/ vt to change; (Zool) to shed ▷ vi to change; **mudarse** vr (la ropa) to change; **~se de casa** to move house

mudo, -a ['muðo, a] adj dumb; (callado) silent

mueble ['mweβle] nm piece of furniture; **muebles** nmpl furniture sg

mueca ['mweka] nf face, grimace; **hacer ~s a** to make faces at

muela ['mwela] nf tooth; **~ del juicio** wisdom tooth

muelle ['mweʎe] nm spring; (Naut) wharf; (malecón) pier

muerte ['mwerte] nf death; (homicidio) murder; **dar ~ a** to kill

muerto, -a ['mwerto, a] pp de **morir** ▷ adj dead ▷ nm/f dead man/ woman; (difunto) deceased; (cadáver) corpse; **estar ~ de cansancio** to be dead tired; **Día de los M~s** (LAM) All Souls' Day

○ **DÍA DE LOS MUERTOS**
○
○ All Souls' Day (or "Day of the Dead")
○ in Mexico coincides with All Saints'
○ Day, which is celebrated in the
○ Catholic countries of Latin America
○ on November 1st and 2nd. All Souls'
○ Day is actually a celebration which
○ begins in the evening of October
○ 31st and continues until November
○ 2nd. It is a combination of the
○ Catholic tradition of honouring
○ the Christian saints and martyrs,
○ and the ancient Mexican or Aztec
○ traditions, in which death was
○ not something sinister. For this
○ reason all the dead are honoured by
○ bringing offerings of food, flowers
○ and candles to the cemetery.

muestra ['mwestra] nf (señal) indication, sign; (demostración) demonstration; (prueba) proof; (estadística) sample; (modelo) model, pattern; (testimonio) token

muestro etc vb V **mostrar**

muevo etc vb V **mover**

mugir [mu'xir] /3c/ vi (vaca) to moo

mugre ['muɣre] nf dirt, filth

mujer [mu'xer] nf woman; (esposa) wife; **mujeriego** nm womaniser

mula ['mula] nf mule

muleta [mu'leta] nf (para andar) crutch; (Taur) stick with red cape attached

multa ['multa] nf fine; **echar** o **poner una ~ a** to fine; **multar** /1a/ vt to fine

multicines [multi'θine] nmpl multiscreen cinema

multinacional [multinaθjo'nal] nf multinational

múltiple ['multiple] adj multiple, many pl, numerous

multiplicar [multipli'kar] /1g/ vt (Mat) to multiply; (fig) to increase; **multiplicarse** vr (Bio) to multiply; (fig) to be everywhere at once

multitud [multi'tuð] nf (muchedumbre) crowd; **~ de** lots of

mundial [mun'djal] adj world-wide, universal; (guerra, récord) world cpd

mundo ['mundo] nm world; **todo el ~** everybody; **tener ~** to be experienced, know one's way around

munición [muni'θjon] nf ammunition

municipal [muniθi'pal] adj municipal; local

municipio [muni'θipjo] nm (ayuntamiento) town council, corporation; (territorio administrativo) town, municipality

muñeca [mu'ɲeka] nf (Anat) wrist; (juguete) doll

muñeco [mu'ɲeko] nm (figura) figure; (marioneta) puppet; (fig) puppet, pawn

mural [mu'ral] adj mural, wall cpd ▷ nm mural

muralla [mu'raʎa] nf (city) walls pl

murciélago [mur'θjelaɣo] nm bat

murmullo [mur'muʎo] nm murmur(ing); (cuchicheo) whispering

murmurar [murmu'rar] /1a/ vi to murmur, whisper; (cotillear) to gossip

muro ['muro] nm wall

muscular [musku'lar] adj muscular

músculo ['muskulo] nm muscle

museo [mu'seo] nm museum; **~ de arte** o **de pintura** art gallery

musgo ['musɣo] nm moss

músico, -a ['musiko, a] adj musical ▷ nm/f musician ▷ nf music

muslo ['muslo] nm thigh

musulmán, -ana [musul'man, ana] nm/f Moslem

mutación [muta'θjon] nf (Bio) mutation; (cambio) (sudden) change

mutilar [muti'lar] /1a/ vt to mutilate; (a una persona) to maim

mutuo, -a ['mutwo, a] adj mutual

muy [mwi] adv very; (demasiado) too; **M~ Señor mío** Dear Sir; **~ de noche** very late at night; **eso es ~ de él** that's just like him

N abr (= norte) N

nabo ['naβo] nm turnip

nacer [na'θer] /2d/ vi to be born; (huevo) to hatch; (vegetal) to sprout; (río) to rise; **nací en Barcelona** I was born in Barcelona; **nacido, -a** adj born; **recién nacido** newborn; **nacimiento** nm birth; (de Navidad) Nativity; (de río) source

nación [na'θjon] nf nation; **nacional** adj national; **nacionalidad** nf nationality; **nacionalismo** nm nationalism

nada ['naða] pron nothing ▷ adv not at all, in no way; **no decir ~ (más)** to say nothing (else), not to say anything (else); **¡~ más!** that's all; **de ~** don't mention it

nadador, a [naða'ðor, a] nm/f swimmer

nadar [na'ðar] /1a/ vi to swim

nadie ['naðje] pron nobody, no-one; **~ habló** nobody spoke; **no había ~**

there was nobody there, there wasn't anybody there

nado ['naðo]: **a ~** adv: **pasar a ~** to swim across

nafta ['nafta] nf (LAM) petrol (BRIT), gas(oline) (US)

naipe ['naipe] nm (playing) card; **naipes** nmpl cards

nalgas ['nalɣas] nfpl buttocks

nalguear [nalɣe'ar] /1a/ vt (LAM, CAM) to spank

nana ['nana] nf lullaby

naranja [na'ranxa] adj inv, nf orange; **media ~** (fam) better half; **naranjada** nf orangeade; **naranjo** nm orange tree

narciso [nar'θiso] nm narcissus

narcótico, -a [nar'kotiko, a] adj, nm narcotic; **narcotizar** /1f/ vt to drug; **narcotráfico** nm narcotics o drug trafficking

nariz [na'riθ] nf nose; **~ chata/respingona** snub/turned-up nose

narración [narra'θjon] nf narration

narrar [na'rrar] /1a/ vt to narrate, recount

narrativo, -a [narra'tiβo, a] adj, nf narrative

nata ['nata] nf cream (tb fig); (en leche cocida etc) skin; **~ batida** whipped cream

natación [nata'θjon] nf swimming

natal [na'tal] adj: **ciudad ~** home town; **natalidad** nf birth rate

natillas [na'tiʎas] nfpl (egg) custard sg

nativo, -a [na'tiβo, a] adj, nm/f native

natural [natu'ral] adj natural; (fruta etc) fresh ▷ nmf native ▷ nm disposition, temperament; **buen ~** good nature

naturaleza [natura'leθa] nf nature; (género) nature, kind; **~ muerta** still life

naturalmente [natural'mente] adv (de modo natural) in a natural way; **¡~!** of course!

naufragar [naufra'ɣar] /1h/ vi to sink; **naufragio** nm shipwreck

náusea ['nausea] nf nausea; **me da ~s** it makes me feel sick

nauseabundo, -a [nausea'βundo, a] adj nauseating, sickening

náutico, -a ['nautiko, a] adj nautical

navaja [na'βaxa] nf penknife; **~ (de afeitar)** razor

naval [na'βal] adj naval

Navarra [na'βarra] nf Navarre

nave ['naβe] nf (barco) ship, vessel; (Arq) nave; **~ espacial** spaceship; **~ industrial** factory premises pl

navegador [naβeɣa'ðor] nm (Inform) browser

navegante [naβe'ɣante] nmf navigator

navegar [naβe'ɣar] /1h/ vi (barco) to sail; (avión) to fly; **~ por Internet** to surf the Net

Navidad [naβi'ðað] nf Christmas; **Navidades** nfpl Christmas time sg; **¡Feliz ~!** Merry Christmas!; **navideño, -a** adj Christmas cpd

nazca etc vb V **nacer**

nazi ['naθi] adj, nmf Nazi

NE abr (= nor(d)este) NE

neblina [ne'βlina] nf mist

necesario, -a [neθe'sarjo, a] adj necessary

neceser [neθe'ser] nm toilet bag; (bolsa grande) holdall

necesidad [neθesi'ðað] nf need; (lo inevitable) necessity; (miseria) poverty; **en caso de ~** in case of need o emergency; **hacer sus ~es** to relieve o.s.

necesitado, -a [neθesi'taðo, a] adj needy, poor; **~ de** in need of

necesitar [neθesi'tar] /1a/ vt to need, require

necio, -a ['neθjo, a] adj foolish

nectarina [nekta'rina] nf nectarine

nefasto, -a [ne'fasto, a] adj ill-fated, unlucky

negación [neɣa'θjon] nf negation; (rechazo) refusal, denial

negar [ne'ɣar] /1h, 1j/ vt (renegar, rechazar) to refuse; (prohibir) to refuse,

n

deny; (*desmentir*) to deny; **negarse** *vr*:
~se a hacer algo to refuse to do sth
negativo, -a [neɣa'tiβo, a] *adj, nm*
negative ▷ *nf* negative; (*rechazo*)
refusal, denial
negligente [neɣli'xente] *adj*
negligent
negociación [neɣoθja'θjon] *nf*
negotiation
negociante [neɣo'θjante] *nmf*
businessman/woman
negociar [neɣo'θjar] /1b/ *vt, vi* to
negotiate; **~ en** to deal in, trade in
negocio [ne'ɣoθjo] *nm* (*Com*)
business; (*asunto*) affair, business;
(*operación comercial*) deal, transaction;
(*lugar*) place of business; **los ~s**
business *sg*; **hacer ~** to do business
negra ['neɣra] *nf* (*Mus*) crotchet;
V tb **negro**
negro, -a ['neɣro, a] *adj* black;
(*suerte*) awful ▷ *nm* black ▷ *nm/f*
black person
nene, -a ['nene, a] *nm/f* baby, small
child
neón [ne'on] *nm*: **luces/lámpara de
~** neon lights/lamp
neoyorquino, -a [neojor'kino, a]
adj New York *cpd*
nervio [ner'βjo] *nm* nerve;
nerviosismo *nm* nervousness, nerves
pl; **nervioso, -a** *adj* nervous
neto, -a ['neto, a] *adj* net
neumático, -a [neu'matiko, a] *adj*
pneumatic ▷ *nm* (*ESP*) tyre (*BRIT*), tire
(*US*); **~ de recambio** spare tyre
neurólogo, -a [neu'roloɣo, a] *nm/f*
neurologist
neurona [neu'rona] *nf* neuron
neutral [neu'tral] *adj* neutral;
neutralizar /1f/ *vt* to neutralize;
(*contrarrestar*) to counteract
neutro, -a ['neutro, a] *adj* (*Bio, Ling*)
neuter
neutrón [neu'tron] *nm* neutron
nevado, -a [ne'βaðo, a] *adj* snow-
covered ▷ *nf* snowstorm; (*caída de
nieve*) snowfall

nevar [ne'βar] /1j/ *vi* to snow
nevera [ne'βera] *nf* (*ESP*) refrigerator
(*BRIT*), icebox (*US*)
nevería [neβe'ria] *nf* (*LAM*) ice-cream
parlour
nexo ['nekso] *nm* link, connection
ni [ni] *conj* nor, neither; (*tb*: **ni
siquiera**) not even; **ni que** not even
if; **ni blanco ni negro** neither white
nor black
Nicaragua [nika'raɣwa] *nf*
Nicaragua; **nicaragüense** *adj, nmf*
Nicaraguan
nicho ['nitʃo] *nm* niche
nicotina [niko'tina] *nf* nicotine
nido ['niðo] *nm* nest
niebla ['njeβla] *nf* fog; (*neblina*) mist
niego *etc* ['njeɣo] *vb* V **negar**
nieto, -a ['njeto, a] *nm/f* grandson/
granddaughter; **nietos** *nmpl*
grandchildren
nieve ['njeβe] *vb* V **nevar** ▷ *nf* snow;
(*LAM*) ice cream
ninfa ['ninfa] *nf* nymph
ningún [nin'gun] *adj* V **ninguno**
ninguno, -a [nin'guno, a] *adj* no
▷ *pron* (*nadie*) nobody; (*ni uno*) none,
not one; (*ni uno ni otro*) neither; **de
ninguna manera** by no means,
not at all
niña ['niɲa] *nf* V **niño**
niñera [ni'ɲera] *nf* nursemaid, nanny
niñez [ni'ɲeθ] *nf* childhood; (*infancia*)
infancy
niño, -a ['niɲo, a] *adj* (*joven*) young;
(*inmaduro*) immature ▷ *nm* boy, child
▷ *nf* girl, child; (*Anat*) pupil
nipón, -ona [ni'pon, ona] *adj, nm/f*
Japanese
níquel ['nikel] *nm* nickel
níspero ['nispero] *nm* medlar
nítido, -a ['nitiðo, a] *adj* clear, sharp
nitrato [ni'trato] *nm* nitrate
nitrógeno [ni'troxeno] *nm* nitrogen
nivel [ni'βel] *nm* (*Geo*) level; (*norma*)
level, standard; (*altura*) height; **~ de
aceite** oil level; **~ de aire** spirit level;
~ de vida standard of living; **nivelar**

/1a/ vt to level out; (fig) to even up; (Com) to balance

no [no] adv no; (con verbo) not ▷ excl no!; **no tengo nada** I don't have anything, I have nothing; **no es el mío** it's not mine; **ahora no** not now; **¿no lo sabes?** don't you know?; **no mucho** not much; **no bien termine, lo entregaré** as soon as I finish I'll hand it over; **ayer no más** just yesterday; **¡pase no más!** come in!; **¡a que no lo sabes!** I bet you don't know!; **¡cómo no!** of course!; **la no intervención** non-intervention

noble ['noβle] adj, nmf noble; **nobleza** nf nobility

noche ['notʃe] nf night, night-time; (la tarde) evening; **de ~, por la ~** at night; **ayer por la ~** last night; **esta ~** tonight; **(en) toda la ~** all night; **hacer ~ en un sitio** to spend the night in a place; **se hace de ~** it's getting dark; **es de ~** it's dark; **N~ de San Juan** see note

● **NOCHE DE SAN JUAN**
●
● The *Noche de San Juan* on the 24th
● June is a *fiesta* coinciding with the
● summer solstice and which has
● taken the place of other ancient
● pagan festivals. Traditionally
● fire plays a major part in these
● festivities with celebrations and
● dancing taking place around
● bonfires in towns and villages
● across the country.

nocivo, -a [no'θiβo, a] adj harmful

noctámbulo, -a [nok'tambulo, a] nm/f sleepwalker

nocturno, -a [nok'turno, a] adj (de la noche) nocturnal, night cpd; (de la tarde) evening cpd ▷ nm nocturne

nogal [no'ɣal] nm walnut tree

nómada ['nomaða] adj nomadic ▷ nmf nomad

nombrar [nom'brar] /1a/ vt to name; (mencionar) to mention; (designar) to appoint

nombre ['nombre] nm name; (sustantivo) noun; **~ y apellidos** name in full; **poner ~ a** to call, name; **~ común/propio** common/proper noun; **~ de pila/de soltera** Christian/maiden name

nómina ['nomina] nf (Com) payroll; (hoja) payslip

nominal [nomi'nal] adj nominal

nominar [nomi'nar] /1a/ vt to nominate

nominativo, -a [nomina'tiβo, a] adj (Com): **un cheque ~ a X** a cheque made out to X

nordeste [nor'ðeste] adj north-east, north-eastern, north-easterly ▷ nm north-east

nórdico, -a ['norðiko, a] adj Nordic

noreste [no'reste] adj, nm = **nordeste**

noria ['norja] nf (Agr) waterwheel; (de carnaval) big (BRIT) o Ferris (US) wheel

norma ['norma] nf rule

normal [nor'mal] adj (corriente) normal; (habitual) usual, natural; **normalizar** /1f/ vt to normalize; (Com, Tec) to standardize; **normalizarse** vr to return to normal; **normalmente** adv normally

normativo, -a [norma'tiβo, a] adj: **es ~ en todos los coches nuevos** it is standard in all new cars ▷ nf rules pl, regulations pl

noroeste [noro'este] adj north-west, north-western, north-westerly ▷ nm north-west

norte ['norte] adj north, northern, northerly ▷ nm north; (fig) guide

norteamericano, -a [norteameri'kano, a] adj, nm/f (North) American

Noruega [no'rweɣa] nf Norway

noruego, -a [no'rweɣo, a] adj, nm/f Norwegian

nos [nos] pron (directo) us; (indirecto) (to) us; (reflexivo) (to) ourselves;

n

(*recíproco*) (to) each other; **~ levantamos a las siete** we get up at seven

nosotros, -as [no'sotros, as] *pron* (*sujeto*) we; (*después de prep*) us

nostalgia [nos'talxja] *nf* nostalgia

nota ['nota] *nf* note; (*Escol*) mark

notable [no'taβle] *adj* notable; (*Escol etc*) outstanding

notar [no'tar] /1a/ *vt* to notice, note; **notarse** *vr* to be obvious; **se nota que ...** one observes that ...

notario [no'tarjo] *nm* notary

noticia [no'tiθja] *nf* (*información*) piece of news; **las ~s** the news *sg*; **tener ~s de algn** to hear from sb

┃ No confundir *noticia* con la palabra inglesa *notice*.

noticiero [noti'θjero] *nm* (*LAM*) news bulletin

notificar [notifi'kar] /1g/ *vt* to notify, inform

notorio, -a [no'torjo, a] *adj* (*público*) well-known; (*evidente*) obvious

novato, -a [no'βato, a] *adj* inexperienced ▷ *nm/f* beginner, novice

novecientos, -as [noβe'θjentos, as] *num* nine hundred

novedad [noβe'ðað] *nf* (*calidad de nuevo*) newness; (*noticia*) piece of news; (*cambio*) change, (new) development

novel [no'βel] *adj* new; (*inexperto*) inexperienced ▷ *nmf* beginner

novela [no'βela] *nf* novel

noveno, -a [no'βeno, a] *num* ninth

noventa [no'βenta] *num* ninety

novia ['noβja] *nf* V **novio**

noviazgo [no'βjaθɣo] *nm* engagement

novicio, -a [no'βiθjo, a] *nm/f* novice

noviembre [no'βjembre] *nm* November

novillada [noβi'ʎaða] *nf* (*Taur*) bullfight with young bulls; **novillero** *nm* novice bullfighter; **novillo** *nm* young bull, bullock; **hacer novillos** (*fam*) to play truant (*BRIT*) o hooky (*US*)

novio, -a ['noβjo, a] *nm/f* boyfriend/ girlfriend; (*prometido*) fiancé/fiancée; (*recién casado*) bridegroom/bride; **los ~s** the newly-weds

nube ['nuβe] *nf* cloud

nublado, -a [nu'βlaðo, a] *adj* cloudy

nublar [nu'βlar] /1a/ *vt* (*oscurecer*) to darken; (*confundir*) to cloud; **nublarse** *vr* to cloud over

nuboso, -a [nu'βoso, a] *adj* cloudy

nuca ['nuka] *nf* nape of the neck

nuclear [nukle'ar] *adj* nuclear

núcleo ['nukleo] *nm* (*centro*) core; (*Física*) nucleus; **~ urbano** city centre

nudillo [nu'ðiʎo] *nm* knuckle

nudista [nu'ðista] *adj* nudist

nudo ['nuðo] *nm* knot; (*Ferro*) junction

nuera ['nwera] *nf* daughter-in-law

nuestro, -a ['nwestro, a] *adj posesivo* our ▷ *pron* ours; **~ padre** our father; **un amigo ~** a friend of ours; **es el ~** it's ours

Nueva York [-'jork] *nf* New York

Nueva Zelanda [-θe'landa] *nf* New Zealand

nueve ['nweβe] *num* nine

nuevo, -a ['nweβo, a] *adj* (*gen*) new; **de ~** again

nuez [nweθ] *nf* walnut; **~ de Adán** Adam's apple; **~ moscada** nutmeg

nulo, -a ['nulo, a] *adj* (*inepto, torpe*) useless; (*inválido*) (null and) void; (*Deporte*) drawn, tied

núm. *abr* (= *número*) no.

numerar [nume'rar] /1a/ *vt* to number

número ['numero] *nm* (*gen*) number; (*tamaño: de zapato*) size; (*ejemplar: de diario*) number, issue; **sin ~** numberless, unnumbered; **~ de matrícula/de teléfono** registration/ telephone number; **~ impar/par** odd/even number; **~ romano** Roman numeral; **~ atrasado** back number

numeroso, -a [nume'roso, a] *adj* numerous

nunca ['nunka] *adv* (*jamás*) never; **~ lo pensé** I never thought it; **no viene ~**

he never comes; **~ más** never again;
más que ~ more than ever
nupcias ['nupθjas] *nfpl* wedding *sg*,
nuptials
nutria ['nutrja] *nf* otter
nutrición [nutri'θjon] *nf* nutrition
nutrir [nu'trir] /3a/ *vt* (*alimentar*)
to nourish; (*dar de comer*) to feed;
(*fig*) to strengthen; **nutritivo, -a** *adj*
nourishing, nutritious
nylon [ni'lon] *nm* nylon
ñango, -a ['ɲaŋgo, a] *adj* (*LAM*) puny
ñapa ['ɲapa] *nf* (*LAM*) extra
ñata ['ɲata] *nf* (*LAM fam*) nose; V
tb **ñato**
ñato, -a ['ɲato, a] *adj* (*LAM*) snub-
nosed
ñoñería [ɲoɲe'ria] *nf* insipidness
ñoño, -a ['ɲoɲo, a] *adj* (*fam: tonto*)
silly, stupid; (*soso*) insipid; (*débil:
persona*) spineless; (*ESP: película,
novela*) sentimental

O *abr* (= *oeste*) W
o [o] *conj* or; **o ... o** either ... or
oasis [o'asis] *nm inv* oasis
obcecarse [oβθe'karse] /1g/ *vr* to
become obsessed
obedecer [oβeðe'θer] /2d/ *vt* to obey;
obediente *adj* obedient
obertura [oβer'tura] *nf* overture
obeso, -a [o'βeso, a] *adj* obese
obispo [o'βispo] *nm* bishop
obituario [oβi'twarjo] *nm* (*LAM*)
obituary
objetar [oβxe'tar] /1a/ *vt, vi* to object
objetivo, -a [oβxe'tiβo, a] *adj* ▷ *nm*
objective
objeto [oβ'xeto] *nm* (*cosa*) object;
(*fin*) aim
objetor, a [oβxe'tor, a] *nm/f* objector
obligación [oβliɣa'θjon] *nf*
obligation; (*Com*) bond
obligar [oβli'ɣar] /1h/ *vt* to force;
obligarse *vr*: **~se a** to commit o.s.
to; **obligatorio, -a** *adj* compulsory,
obligatory

oboe [o'βoe] nm oboe

obra ['oβra] nf work; (Arq) construction, building; (Teat) play; **~ maestra** masterpiece; **~s públicas** public works; **por ~ de** thanks to (the efforts of); **obrar** /1a/ vt to work; (tener efecto) to have an effect on ▷ vi to act, behave; (tener efecto) to have an effect; **la carta obra en su poder** the letter is in his/her possession

obrero, -a [o'βrero, a] adj working; (movimiento) labour cpd ▷ nm/f (gen) worker; (sin oficio) labourer

obsceno, -a [oβs'θeno, a] adj obscene

obscu... pref = **oscu...**

obsequiar [oβse'kjar] /1b/ vt (ofrecer) to present; (agasajar) to make a fuss of, lavish attention on; **obsequio** nm (regalo) gift; (cortesía) courtesy, attention

observación [oβserβa'θjon] nf observation; (reflexión) remark

observador, a [oβserβa'ðor, a] nm/f observer

observar [oβser'βar] /1a/ vt to observe; (notar) to notice; **observarse** vr to keep to, observe

obsesión [oβse'sjon] nf obsession; **obsesivo, -a** adj obsessive

obstáculo [oβs'takulo] nm obstacle; (impedimento) hindrance, drawback

obstante [oβs'tante]: **no ~** adv nevertheless

obstinado, -a [oβsti'naðo, a] adj obstinate; stubborn

obstinarse [oβsti'narse] /1a/ vr to be obstinate; **~ en** to persist in

obstruir [oβstru'ir] /3g/ vt to obstruct

obtener [oβte'ner] /2k/ vt to obtain; (ganar) to gain; (premio) to win

obturador [oβtura'ðor] nm (Foto) shutter

obvio, -a ['oββjo, a] adj obvious

oca ['oka] nf goose; (tb: **juego de la ~**) ≈ snakes and ladders

ocasión [oka'sjon] nf (oportunidad) opportunity, chance; (momento) occasion, time; (causa) cause; **de ~** secondhand; **ocasionar** /1a/ vt to cause

ocaso nm (fig) decline

occidente [okθi'ðente] nm west

O.C.D.E. nf abr (= Organización de Cooperación y Desarrollo Económicos) OECD

océano [o'θeano] nm ocean; **el ~ Índico** the Indian Ocean

ochenta [o'tʃenta] num eighty

ocho ['otʃo] num eight; **dentro de ~ días** within a week

ocio [o'θjo] nm (tiempo) leisure; (pey) idleness

octavilla [okta'βiʎa] nf leaflet, pamphlet

octavo, -a [ok'taβo, a] num eighth

octubre [ok'tuβre] nm October

oculista [oku'lista] nmf oculist

ocultar [okul'tar] /1a/ vt (esconder) to hide; (callar) to conceal; **oculto, -a** adj hidden; (fig) secret

ocupación [okupa'θjon] nf occupation

ocupado, -a [oku'paðo, a] adj (persona) busy; (plaza) occupied, taken; (teléfono) engaged

ocupar /1a/ vt (gen) to occupy; **ocuparse** vr: **~se de** o **en** to concern o.s. with; (cuidar) to look after

ocurrencia [oku'rrenθja] nf (idea) bright idea

ocurrir [oku'rrir] /3a/ vi to happen; **ocurrirse** vr: **se me ocurrió que ...** it occurred to me that ...

odiar [o'ðjar] /1b/ vt to hate; **odio** nm hate, hatred; **odioso, -a** adj (gen) hateful; (malo) nasty

odontólogo, -a [oðon'toloɣo, a] nm/f dentist, dental surgeon

oeste [o'este] nm west; **una película del ~** a western

ofender [ofen'der] /2a/ vt (agraviar) to offend; (insultar) to insult; **ofenderse** vr to take offence; **ofensa** nf offence; **ofensivo, -a** adj offensive ▷ nf offensive

oferta [o'ferta] *nf* offer; *(propuesta)* proposal; **la ~ y la demanda** supply and demand; **artículos en ~** goods on offer

oficial [ofi'θjal] *adj* official ▷ *nm* (*Mil*) officer

oficina [ofi'θina] *nf* office; **~ de correos** post office; **~ de información** information bureau; **~ de turismo** tourist office; **oficinista** *nmf* clerk

oficio [o'fiθjo] *nm* (*profesión*) profession; (*puesto*) post; (*Rel*) service; **ser del ~** to be an old hand; **tener mucho ~** to have a lot of experience; **~ de difuntos** funeral service

ofimática [ofi'matika] *nf* office automation

ofrecer [ofre'θer] /2d/ *vt* (*dar*) to offer; (*proponer*) to propose; **ofrecerse** *vr* (*persona*) to offer o.s., volunteer; (*situación*) to present itself; **¿qué se le ofrece?, ¿se le ofrece algo?** what can I do for you?, can I get you anything?

ofrecimiento [ofreθi'mjento] *nm* offer

oftalmólogo, -a [oftal'moloɣo, a] *nm/f* ophthalmologist

oída [o'iða] *nf*: **de ~s** by hearsay

oído [o'iðo] *nm* (*Anat, Mus*) ear; (*sentido*) hearing

oigo *etc vb* V **oír**

oír [o'ir] /3p/ *vt* (*gen*) to hear; (*escuchar*) to listen to; **¡oiga!** excuse me!; (*Telec*) hullo?; **~ misa** to attend mass; **como quien oye llover** without paying (the slightest) attention

ojal [o'xal] *nm* buttonhole

ojalá [oxa'la] *excl* if only (it were so)!, some hope! ▷ *conj* if only…!, would that…!; **~ que venga hoy** I hope he comes today

ojeada [oxe'aða] *nf* glance

ojera [o'xera] *nf*: **tener ~s** to have bags under one's eyes

ojo ['oxo] *nm* eye; (*de puente*) span; (*de cerradura*) keyhole ▷ *excl* careful!; **tener ~ para** to have an eye for; **~ de buey** porthole

okey ['okei] *excl* (*LAM*) O.K.

okupa [o'kupa] *nmf* (*fam*) squatter

ola ['ola] *nf* wave

olé [o'le] *excl* bravo!, olé!

oleada [ole'aða] *nf* big wave, swell; (*fig*) wave

oleaje [ole'axe] *nm* swell

óleo ['oleo] *nm* oil; **oleoducto** *nm* (oil) pipeline

oler [o'ler] /2i/ *vt* (*gen*) to smell; (*inquirir*) to pry into; (*fig: sospechar*) to sniff out ▷ *vi* to smell; **~ a** to smell of

olfatear [olfate'ar] /1a/ *vt* to smell; (*inquirir*) to pry into; **olfato** *nm* sense of smell

olimpiada [olim'piaða] *nf*: **la ~ o las ~s** the Olympics; **olímpico, -a** *adj* Olympic

oliva [o'liβa] *nf* (*aceituna*) olive; **aceite de ~** olive oil; **olivo** *nm* olive tree

olla ['oʎa] *nf* pan; (*comida*) stew; **~ a presión** pressure cooker; **~ podrida** *type of Spanish stew*

olmo ['olmo] *nm* elm (tree)

olor [o'lor] *nm* smell; **oloroso, -a** *adj* scented

olvidar [olβi'ðar] /1a/ *vt* to forget; (*omitir*) to omit; **olvidarse** *vr* (*fig*) to forget o.s.; **se me olvidó** I forgot

olvido [ol'βiðo] *nm* oblivion; (*despiste*) forgetfulness

ombligo [om'bliɣo] *nm* navel

omelette [ome'lete] *nf* (*LAM*) omelet(te)

omisión [omi'sjon] *nf* (*abstención*) omission; (*descuido*) neglect

omiso, -a [o'miso, a] *adj*: **hacer caso ~ de** to ignore, pass over

omitir [omi'tir] /3a/ *vt* to leave o miss out, omit

omnipotente [omnipo'tente] *adj* omnipotent

omoplato [omo'plato], **omóplato** [o'moplato] *nm* shoulder-blade

OMS *nf abr* (= *Organización Mundial de la Salud*) WHO

once ['onθe] *num* eleven; **onces** *nfpl* tea break *sg*

onda ['onda] nf wave; **~ corta/larga/
media** short/long/medium wave;
ondear /1a/ vi to wave; (tener ondas)
to be wavy; (agua) to ripple

ondulación [ondula'θjon] nf
undulation; **ondulado, -a** adj wavy

ONG nf abr (= organización no
gubernamental) NGO

ONU ['onu] nf abr (= Organización de las
Naciones Unidas) UN

opaco, -a [o'pako, a] adj opaque

opción [op'θjon] nf (gen) option;
(derecho) right, option

O.P.E.P. [o'pep] nf abr (= Organización
de Países Exportadores de Petróleo) OPEC

ópera ['opera] nf opera; **~ bufa** o
cómica comic opera

operación [opera'θjon] nf (gen)
operation; (Com) transaction, deal

operador, a [opera'ðor, a]
nm/f operator; (Cine: proyección)
projectionist; (: rodaje) cameraman

operar [ope'rar] /1a/ vt (producir) to
produce, bring about; (Med) to operate
on ▷ vi (Com) to operate, deal; **operarse**
vr to occur; (Med) to have an operation

opereta [ope'reta] nf operetta

opinar [opi'nar] /1a/ vt to think ▷ vi
to give one's opinion; **opinión** nf
(creencia) belief; (criterio) opinion

opio ['opjo] nm opium

oponer [opo'ner] /2q/ vt (resistencia)
to put up, offer; **oponerse** vr (objetar)
to object; (estar frente a frente) to be
opposed; (dos personas) to oppose
each other; **~ A a B** to set A against B;
me opongo a pensar que ... I refuse
to believe o think that ...

oportunidad [oportuni'ðað] nf
(ocasión) opportunity; (posibilidad)
chance

oportuno, -a [opor'tuno, a] adj (en su
tiempo) opportune, timely; (respuesta)
suitable; **en el momento ~** at the
right moment

oposición [oposi'θjon] nf opposition;
oposiciones nfpl (Escol) public
examinations

opositor, -a [oposi'tor, a] nm/f
(Admin) candidate to a public
examination; (adversario) opponent;
~ (a) candidate (for)

opresión [opre'sjon] nf oppression;
opresor, a nm/f oppressor

oprimir [opri'mir] /3a/ vt to squeeze;
(fig) to oppress

optar [op'tar] /1a/ vi (elegir) to choose;
~ a o **por** to opt for; **optativo, -a** adj
optional

óptico, -a ['optiko, a] adj optic(al)
▷ nm/f optician ▷ nf (ciencia) optics
sg; (tienda) optician's; (fig) viewpoint;
desde esta óptica from this point
of view

optimismo [opti'mismo] nm
optimism; **optimista** nmf optimist

opuesto, -a [o'pwesto, a] adj (contrario)
opposite; (antagónico) opposing

oración [ora'θjon] nf (Rel) prayer;
(Ling) sentence

orador, a [ora'ðor, a] nm/f orator;
(conferenciante) speaker

oral [o'ral] adj oral

orangután [orangu'tan] nm
orang-utan

orar [o'rar] /1a/ vi to pray

oratoria [ora'torja] nf oratory

órbita ['orβita] nf orbit

orden ['orðen] nm (colocación)
order ▷ nf (mandato) order; (Inform)
command; **en ~ de prioridad** in order
of priority; **el ~ del día** the agenda

ordenado, -a [orðe'naðo, a] adj
(metódico) methodical; (arreglado)
orderly

ordenador [orðena'ðor] nm
computer; **~ central** mainframe
computer

ordenar [orðe'nar] /1a/ vt (mandar)
to order; (poner orden) to put in order,
arrange; **ordenarse** vr (Rel) to be
ordained

ordeñar [orðe'ɲar] /1a/ vt to milk

ordinario, -a [orði'narjo, a] adj
(común) ordinary, usual; (vulgar)
vulgar, common

orégano [o'reɣano] nm oregano

oreja [o'rexa] nf ear; (Mecánica) lug, flange

orfanato [orfa'nato] nm orphanage

orfebrería [orfeβre'ria] nf gold/silver work

orgánico, -a [or'ɣaniko, a] adj organic

organismo [orɣa'nismo] nm (Bio) organism; (Pol) organization

organización [orɣaniθa'θjon] nf organization; **O~ de las Naciones Unidas (ONU)** United Nations Organization; **O~ del Tratado del Atlántico Norte (OTAN)** North Atlantic Treaty Organization (NATO); **organizar** /1f/ vt to organize

órgano ['orɣano] nm organ

orgasmo [or'ɣasmo] nm orgasm

orgía [or'xia] nf orgy

orgullo [or'ɣuʎo] nm pride; **orgulloso, -a** adj (gen) proud; (altanero) haughty

orientación [orjenta'θjon] nf (posición) position; (dirección) direction

oriental [orjen'tal] adj oriental; (región etc) eastern

orientar [orjen'tar] /1a/ vt (situar) to orientate; (señalar) to point; (dirigir) to direct; (guiar) to guide; **orientarse** vr to get one's bearings

oriente [o'rjente] nm east; **Cercano/ Medio/Lejano O~** Near/Middle/Far East

origen [o'rixen] nm origin

original [orixi'nal] adj (nuevo) original; (extraño) odd, strange; **originalidad** nf originality

originar [orixi'nar] /1a/ vt to start, cause; **originarse** vr to originate; **originario, -a** adj original; **ser originario de** to originate from

orilla [o'riʎa] nf (borde) border; (de río) bank; (de bosque, tela) edge; (de mar) shore

orina [o'rina] nf urine; **orinal** nm (chamber) pot; **orinar** /1a/ vi to urinate; **orinarse** vr to wet o.s.

oro ['oro] nm gold; V tb **oros**

oros ['oros] nmpl (Naipes) one of the suits in the Spanish card deck

orquesta [or'kesta] nf orchestra; **~ de cámara/sinfónica** chamber/symphony orchestra

orquídea [or'kiðea] nf orchid

ortiga [or'tiɣa] nf nettle

ortodoxo, -a [orto'ðokso, a] adj orthodox

ortografía [ortoɣra'fia] nf spelling

ortopedia [orto'peðja] nf orthop(a)edics sg; **ortopédico, -a** adj orthop(a)edic

oruga [o'ruɣa] nf caterpillar

orzuelo [or'θwelo] nm stye

os [os] pron you; (a vosotros) (to) you

osa ['osa] nf (she-)bear; **O~ Mayor/ Menor** Great/Little Bear

osadía [osa'ðia] nf daring

osar [o'sar] /1a/ vi to dare

oscilación [osθila'θjon] nf (movimiento) oscillation; (fluctuación) fluctuation

oscilar [osθi'lar] /1a/ vi to oscillate; to fluctuate

oscurecer [oskure'θer] /2d/ vt to darken ▷ vi to grow dark; **oscurecerse** vr to grow o get dark

oscuridad [oskuri'ðað] nf obscurity; (tinieblas) darkness

oscuro, -a [os'kuro, a] adj dark; (fig) obscure; **a oscuras** in the dark

óseo, -a ['oseo, a] adj bone cpd

oso ['oso] nm bear; **~ de peluche** teddy bear; **~ hormiguero** anteater

ostentar [osten'tar] /1a/ vt (gen) to show; (pey) to flaunt, show off; (poseer) to have, possess

ostión [os'tjon] nm (LAM) = **ostra**

ostra ['ostra] nf oyster

OTAN ['otan] nf abr (= Organización del Tratado del Atlántico Norte) NATO

otitis [o'titis] nf earache

otoñal [oto'nal] adj autumnal

otoño [o'toɲo] nm autumn, fall (US)

otorgar [otor'ɣar] /1h/ vt (conceder) to concede; (dar) to grant

o

otorrinolaringólogo, -a
[otorrinolarin'go loɣo, a] nm/f (Med: tb:
otorrino) ear, nose and throat specialist

○ **PALABRA CLAVE**

otro, -a ['otro, a] adj **1** (distinto:
sg) another; (: pl) other; **con otros
amigos** with other o different friends
2 (adicional): **tráigame otro café
(más), por favor** can I have another
coffee please; **otros 10 días más**
another 10 days
▶ pron **1**: **el otro** the other one; **de
otro** somebody o someone else's; **que
lo haga otro** let somebody o someone
else do it
2 (pl): **(los) otros** (the) others
3 (recíproco): **se odian (la) una a
(la) otra** they hate one another o
each other
4: **otro tanto: comer otro tanto** to
eat the same o as much again; **recibió
una decena de telegramas y otras
tantas llamadas** he got about ten
telegrams and as many calls

ovación [oβa'θjon] nf ovation
oval [o'βal], **ovalado, -a** [oβa'laðo,
a] adj oval; **óvalo** nm oval
ovario [o'βarjo] nm ovary
oveja [o'βexa] nf sheep
overol [oβe'rol] nm (LAm) overalls pl
ovillo [o'βiʎo] nm (de lana) ball
OVNI ['oβni] nm abr (= objeto volante (o
volador) no identificado) UFO
ovulación [oβula'θjon] nf ovulation;
óvulo nm ovum
oxidación [oksiða'θjon] nf rusting
oxidar [oksi'ðar] /1a/ vt to rust;
oxidarse vr to go rusty
óxido ['oksiðo] nm oxide
oxigenado, -a [oksixe'naðo, a] adj
(Química) oxygenated; (pelo) bleached
oxígeno [ok'sixeno] nm oxygen
oyente [o'jente] nmf listener
oyes etc vb V **oír**
ozono [o'θono] nm ozone

P

pabellón [paβe'ʎon] nm bell tent;
(Arq) pavilion; (de hospital etc) block,
section; (bandera) flag
pacer [pa'θer] /2d/ vi to graze
paciencia [pa'θjenθja] nf patience
paciente [pa'θjente] adj, nmf patient
pacificación [paθifika'θjon] nf
pacification
pacífico, -a [pa'θifiko, a] adj (persona)
peaceable; (existencia) peaceful; **el
(océano) P~** the Pacific (Ocean)
pacifista [paθi'fista] nmf pacifist
pacotilla [pako'tiʎa] nf: **de ~** shoddy
pactar [pak'tar] /1a/ vt to agree to,
agree on ▷ vi to come to an agreement
pacto ['pakto] nm (tratado) pact;
(acuerdo) agreement
padecer [paðe'θer] /2d/ vt (sufrir) to
suffer; (soportar) to endure, put up
with; **padecimiento** nm suffering
padrastro [pa'ðrastro] nm stepfather
padre ['paðre] nm father ▷ adj (fam):
un éxito ~ a tremendous success;

padres *nmpl* parents; **~ político** father-in-law

padrino [pa'ðrino] *nm* godfather; (*fig*) sponsor, patron; **padrinos** *nmpl* godparents; **~ de boda** best man

padrón [pa'ðron] *nm* (*censo*) census, roll

padrote [pa'ðrote] *nm* (*LAM fam*) pimp

paella [pa'eʎa] *nf* paella *dish of rice with meat, shellfish etc*

paga ['paɣa] *nf* (*dinero pagado*) payment; (*sueldo*) pay, wages *pl*

pagano, -a [pa'ɣano, a] *adj, nm/f* pagan, heathen

pagar [pa'ɣar] /1h/ *vt* to pay; (*las compras, crimen*) to pay for; (*fig: favor*) to repay ▷ *vi* to pay; **~ al contado/a plazos** to pay (in) cash/in instalments

pagaré [paɣa're] *nm* IOU

página ['paxina] *nf* page; **~ de inicio** (*Inform*) home page; **~ web** (*Internet*) web page

pago ['paɣo] *nm* (*dinero*) payment; (*fig*) return; **~ anticipado/a cuenta/a la entrega/en especie/inicial** advance payment/payment on account/cash on delivery/payment in kind/down payment; **en ~ de** in return for

pág(s). *abr* (= *página(s)*) p(p)

pague *etc* ['paɣe] *vb V* **pagar**

país [pa'is] *nm* (*gen*) country; (*región*) land; **los P~es Bajos** the Low Countries; **el P~ Vasco** the Basque Country

paisaje [pai'saxe] *nm* landscape; (*vista*) scenery

paisano, -a [pai'sano, a] *adj* of the same country ▷ *nm/f* (*compatriota*) fellow countryman/woman; **vestir de ~** (*soldado*) to be in civilian clothes; (*guardia*) to be in plain clothes

paja ['paxa] *nf* straw; (*fig*) trash, rubbish

pajarita [paxa'rita] *nf* bow tie

pájaro ['paxaro] *nm* bird; **~ carpintero** woodpecker

pajita [pa'xita] *nf* (drinking) straw

pala ['pala] *nf* spade; shovel; (*raqueta etc*) bat; (: *de tenis*) racquet; (*Culin*) slice; **~ mecánica** power shovel

palabra [pa'laβra] *nf* (*power of*) speech; (*facultad*) (power of) speech; (*derecho de hablar*) right to speak; **tomar la ~** to speak, take the floor

palabrota [pala'βrota] *nf* swearword

palacio [pa'laθjo] *nm* palace; (*mansión*) mansion, large house; **~ de justicia** courthouse; **~ municipal** town/city hall

paladar [pala'ðar] *nm* palate; **paladear** /1a/ *vt* to taste

palanca [pa'lanka] *nf* lever; (*fig*) pull, influence

palangana [palan'gana] *nf* washbasin

palco ['palko] *nm* box

Palestina [pales'tina] *nf* Palestine; **palestino, -a** *nm/f* Palestinian

paleto, -a [pa'leto, a] *nm/f* yokel, hick (*US*) ▷ *nf* (*pala*) small shovel; (*Arte*) palette; (*Deporte: de ping-pong*) bat; (*LAM: helado*) ice lolly (*BRIT*), Popsicle® (*US*)

palidecer [paliðe'θer] /2d/ *vi* to turn pale; **palidez** *nf* paleness; **pálido, -a** *adj* pale

palillo [pa'liʎo] *nm* (*para dientes*) toothpick; **~s (chinos)** chopsticks

paliza [pa'liθa] *nf* beating, thrashing

palma ['palma] *nf* (*Anat*) palm; (*árbol*) palm tree; **batir** *o* **dar ~s** to clap, applaud; **palmada** *nf* slap; **palmadas** *nfpl* clapping *sg*, applause *sg*

palmar [pal'mar] /1a/ *vi* (*tb*: **~la**) to die, kick the bucket

palmear [palme'ar] /1a/ *vi* to clap

palmera [pal'mera] *nf* (*Bot*) palm tree

palmo ['palmo] *nm* (*medida*) span; (*fig*) small amount; **~ a ~** inch by inch

palo ['palo] *nm* stick; (*poste*) post, pole; (*mango*) handle, shaft; (*golpe*) blow, hit; (*de golf*) club; (*de béisbol*) bat; (*Naut*) mast; (*Naipes*) suit

paloma [pa'loma] *nf* dove, pigeon

palomitas [palo'mitas] *nfpl*
popcorn *sg*

palpar [pal'par] /1a/ *vt* to touch, feel

palpitar [palpi'tar] /1a/ *vi* to
palpitate; (*latir*) to beat

palta ['palta] *nf* (*LAM*) avocado

paludismo [palu'ðismo] *nm* malaria

pamela [pa'mela] *nf* sun hat

pampa ['pampa] *nf* (*LAM*) pampa(s),
prairie

pan [pan] *nm* bread; (*una barra*)
loaf; **~ integral** wholemeal bread;
~ rallado breadcrumbs *pl*; **~ tostado**
toast

pana ['pana] *nf* corduroy

panadería [panaðe'ria] *nf* baker's
(shop); **panadero, -a** *nm/f* baker

Panamá [pana'ma] *nm* Panama;
panameño, -a *adj* Panamanian

pancarta [pan'karta] *nf* placard,
banner

panceta [pan'θeta] *nf* bacon

pancho, -a ['pantʃo, a] *adj*: **estar
tan ~** to remain perfectly calm ▷ *nm*
(*LAM*) hot dog

pancito [pan'sito] *nm* (*LAM*) (bread)
roll

panda ['panda] *nm* panda

pandemia [pan'demja] *nf* pandemic

pandereta [pande'reta] *nf*
tambourine

pandilla [pan'diʎa] *nf* set, group; (*de
criminales*) gang; (*pey*) clique

panecillo [pane'θiʎo] *nm* (bread) roll

panel [pa'nel] *nm* panel; **~ solar**
solar panel

panfleto [pan'fleto] *nm* pamphlet

pánico ['paniko] *nm* panic

panorama [pano'rama] *nm*
panorama; (*vista*) view

panqué [pan'ke], **panqueque**
[pan'keke] *nm* (*LAM*) pancake

pantalla [pan'taʎa] *nf* (*de cine*)
screen; (*cubreluz*) lampshade

pantalón, pantalones
[panta'lon(es)] *nm*(*pl*) trousers *pl*,
pants *pl* (*US*); **pantalones cortos**
shorts *pl*

pantano [pan'tano] *nm* (*ciénaga*)
marsh, swamp; (*depósito: de agua*)
reservoir; (*fig*) jam, difficulty

panteón [pante'on] *nm* (*monumento*)
pantheon

pantera [pan'tera] *nf* panther

pantimedias [panti'meðjas] *nfpl*
(*LAM*) = **pantis**

pantis ['pantis] *nm*(*pl*) tights (*BRIT*),
pantyhose (*US*)

pantomima [panto'mima] *nf*
pantomime

pantorrilla [panto'rriʎa] *nf* calf
(of the leg)

pants [pants] *nmpl* (*LAM*) tracksuit
(*BRIT*), sweat suit (*US*)

pantufla [pan'tufla] *nf* slipper

panty(s) ['panti(s)] *nm*(*pl*) tights
(*BRIT*), pantyhose (*US*)

panza ['panθa] *nf* belly, paunch

pañal [pa'ɲal] *nm* nappy, diaper (*US*);
(*fig*) early stages, infancy *sg*

paño ['paɲo] *nm* (*tela*) cloth; (*pedazo
de tela*) (piece of) cloth; (*trapo*) duster,
rag; **~s menores** underclothes

pañuelo [pa'ɲwelo] *nm* handkerchief,
hanky (*fam*); (*para la cabeza*) (head)
scarf

papa ['papa] *nf* (*LAM: patata*) potato
▷ *nm*: **el P~** the Pope; **~s fritas** (*LAM*)
French fries, chips (*BRIT*); (*de bolsa*)
crisps (*BRIT*), potato chips (*US*)

papá [pa'pa] *nm* (*fam*) dad, daddy,
pop (*US*)

papada [pa'paða] *nf* double chin

papagayo [papa'ɣajo] *nm* parrot

papalote [papa'lote] *nm* (*LAM*) kite

papanatas [papa'natas] *nm inv* (*fam*)
simpleton

papaya [pa'paja] *nf* papaya

papear [pape'ar] /1a/ *vt, vi* (*fam*)
to eat

papel [pa'pel] *nm* paper; (*hoja de papel*)
sheet of paper; (*Teat*) role; **~ de arroz/
envolver/fumar** rice/wrapping/
cigarette paper; **~ de aluminio/lija**
tinfoil/sandpaper; **~ higiénico** toilet
paper; **~ moneda** paper money;

~ pintado wallpaper; **~ secante** blotting paper

papeleo [pape'leo] nm red tape

papelera [pape'lera] nf wastepaper basket; **~ de reciclaje** (Inform) wastebasket

papelería [papele'ria] nf stationer's (shop)

papeleta [pape'leta] nf (Pol) ballot paper

paperas [pa'peras] nfpl mumps sg

papilla [pa'piʎa] nf (de bebé) baby food

paquete [pa'kete] nm (caja) packet; (bulto) parcel

par [par] adj (igual) like, equal; (Mat) even ▷ nm equal; (de guantes) pair; (de veces) couple; (título) peer; (Golf, Com) par; **abrir de ~ en ~** to open wide

para ['para] prep for; **no es ~ comer** it's not for eating; **decir ~ sí** to say to o.s.; **¿~ qué lo quieres?** what do you want it for?; **se casaron ~ separarse otra vez** they married only to separate again; **lo tendré ~ mañana** I'll have it for tomorrow; **ir ~ casa** to go home, head for home; **~ profesor es muy estúpido** he's very stupid for a teacher; **¿quién es usted ~ gritar así?** who are you to shout like that?; **tengo bastante ~ vivir** I have enough to live on

parabién [para'βjen] nm congratulations pl

parábola [para'raβola] nf parable; (Mat) parabola; **parabólica** nf (tb: **antena parabólica**) satellite dish

parabrisas [para'βrisas] nm inv windscreen, windshield (US)

paracaídas [paraka'iðas] nm inv parachute; **paracaidista** nmf parachutist; (Mil) paratrooper

parachoques [para'tʃokes] nm inv bumper; shock absorber

parada [pa'raða] nf V **parado**

paradero [para'ðero] nm stopping-place; (situación) whereabouts

parado, -a [pa'raðo, a] adj (persona) motionless, standing still; (fábrica) closed, at a standstill; (coche) stopped; (LAM: de pie) standing (up); (sin empleo) unemployed, idle ▷ nf stop; (acto) stopping; (de industria) shutdown, stoppage; (lugar) stopping-place; **parada de autobús** bus stop; **parada de taxis** taxi rank

paradoja [para'ðoxa] nf paradox

parador [para'ðor] nm (ESP) (luxury) hotel (owned by the state)

paragolpes [para'golpes] nm inv (LAM Auto) bumper, fender (US)

paraguas [para'ɣwas] nm inv umbrella

Paraguay [para'ɣwai] nm: Paraguay; **paraguayo, -a** adj, nm/f Paraguayan

paraíso [para'iso] nm paradise, heaven

paraje [pa'raxe] nm place, spot

paralelo, -a [para'lelo, a] adj parallel

parálisis [pa'ralisis] nf inv paralysis; **paralítico, -a** adj, nm/f paralytic

paralizar [parali'θar] /1f/ vt to paralyse; **paralizarse** vr to become paralysed; (fig) to come to a standstill

páramo ['paramo] nm bleak plateau

paranoico, -a [para'noiko, a] nm/f paranoid

parapente [para'pente] nm (deporte) paragliding; (aparato) paraglider

parapléjico, -a [para'plexiko, a] adj, nm/f paraplegic

parar [pa'rar] /1a/ vt to stop; (golpe) to ward off ▷ vi to stop; **pararse** vr to stop; (LAM) to stand up; **ha parado de llover** it has stopped raining; **van a ~ en la comisaría** they're going to end up in the police station; **~se en** to pay attention to

pararrayos [para'rrajos] nm inv lightning conductor

parásito, -a [pa'rasito, a] nm/f parasite

parasol [para'sol] nm parasol, sunshade

parcela [par'θela] nf plot, piece of ground

parche ['partʃe] nm patch

P

parchís [par'tʃis] *nm* ludo

parcial [par'θjal] *adj* (*pago*) part-; (*eclipse*) partial; (*juez*) prejudiced, biased; (*Pol*) partisan

parecer [pare'θer] /2d/ *nm* (*opinión*) opinion, view; (*aspecto*) looks *pl* ▷ *vi* (*tener apariencia*) to seem, look; (*asemejarse*) to look like, seem like; (*aparecer, llegar*) to appear; **parecerse** *vr* to look alike, resemble each other; **según parece** evidently, apparently; **~se a** to look like, resemble; **al ~** apparently; **me parece que** I think (that), it seems to me that

parecido, -a [pare'θiðo, a] *adj* similar ▷ *nm* similarity, likeness, resemblance; **bien ~** good-looking, nice-looking

pared [pa'reð] *nf* wall

parejo, -a [pa'rexo, a] *adj* equal ▷ *nf* pair; (*de personas*) couple; (*el otro: de un par*) other one (of a pair); (: *persona*) partner

parentesco [paren'tesko] *nm* relationship

paréntesis [pa'rentesis] *nm inv* parenthesis; (*en escrito*) bracket

parezco *etc vb* V **parecer**

pariente, -a [pa'rjente, a] *nm/f* relative, relation

▌ No confundir *pariente* con la palabra inglesa *parent*.

parir [pa'rir] /3a/ *vt* to give birth to ▷ *vi* (*mujer*) to give birth, have a baby

París [pa'ris] *nm* Paris

parka ['parka] *nf* (*LAM*) anorak

parking ['parkin] *nm* car park, parking lot (*US*)

parlamentar [parlamen'tar] /1a/ *vi* to parley

parlamentario, -a [parlamen'tarjo, a] *adj* parliamentary ▷ *nm/f* member of parliament

parlamento [parla'mento] *nm* parliament

parlanchín, -ina [parlan'tʃin, ina] *adj* indiscreet ▷ *nm/f* chatterbox

parlar [par'lar] /1a/ *vi* to chatter (away)

paro ['paro] *nm* (*huelga*) stoppage (of work), strike; (*desempleo*) unemployment; **~ cardiaco** cardiac arrest; **estar en ~** (*ESP*) to be unemployed; **subsidio de ~** unemployment benefit

parodia [pa'roðja] *nf* parody; **parodiar** /1b/ *vt* to parody

parpadear [parpaðe'ar] /1a/ *vi* (*los ojos*) to blink; (*luz*) to flicker

párpado ['parpaðo] *nm* eyelid

parque ['parke] *nm* (*lugar verde*) park; (*LAM: munición*) ammunition; **~ de atracciones/de bomberos** fairground/fire station; **~ infantil/ temático/zoológico** playground/ theme park/zoo

parqué [par'ke] *nm* parquet

parquímetro [par'kimetro] *nm* parking meter

parra ['parra] *nf* grapevine

párrafo ['parrafo] *nm* paragraph; **echar un ~** (*fam*) to have a chat

parranda [pa'rranda] *nf* (*fam*) spree, binge

parrilla [pa'rriʎa] *nf* (*Culin*) grill; **(carne a la) ~** grilled meat, barbecue; **parrillada** *nf* barbecue

párroco [pa'rroko] *nm* parish priest

parroquia [pa'rrokja] *nf* parish; (*iglesia*) parish church; (*Com*) clientele, customers *pl*; **parroquiano, -a** *nm/f* parishioner; client, customer

parte ['parte] *nm* message; (*informe*) report ▷ *nf* part; (*lado, cara*) side; (*de reparto*) share; (*Jur*) party; **en alguna ~ de Europa** somewhere in Europe; **en o por todas ~s** everywhere; **en gran ~** to a large extent; **la mayor ~ de los españoles** most Spaniards; **de algún tiempo a esta ~** for some time past; **de ~ de algn** on sb's behalf; **¿de ~ de quién?** (*Telec*) who is speaking?; **por ~ de** on the part of; **yo por mi ~** I for my part; **por una ~ ... por otra ~** on the one hand, ... on the other (hand); **dar ~ a algn** to report to sb; **tomar ~** to take part; **~ meteorológico** weather forecast o report

participación [partiθipa'θjon] *nf* (*acto*) participation, taking part; (*parte*) share; (*Com*) share, stock (*us*); (*de lotería*) shared prize; (*aviso*) notice, notification

participante [partiθi'pante] *nmf* participant

participar [partiθ'par] /1a/ *vt* to notify, inform ▷ *vi* to take part, participate

partícipe [par'tiθipe] *nmf* participant

particular [partiku'lar] *adj* (*especial*) particular, special; (*individual, personal*) private, personal ▷ *nm* (*punto, asunto*) particular, point; (*individuo*) individual; **tiene coche ~** he has a car of his own

partida [par'tiða] *nf* (*salida*) departure; (*Com*) entry, item; (*juego*) game; (*grupo, bando*) band, group; **mala ~** dirty trick; **~ de nacimiento/matrimonio/defunción** birth/marriage/death certificate

partidario, -a [parti'ðarjo, a] *adj* partisan ▷ *nm/f* supporter

partido [par'tiðo] *nm* (*Pol*) party; (*encuentro*) game, match; **sacar ~ de** to profit from, benefit from; **tomar ~** to take sides

partir [par'tir] /3a/ *vt* (*dividir*) to split, divide; (*compartir, distribuir*) to share (out), distribute; (*romper*) to break open, split open; (*rebanada*) to cut (off) ▷ *vi* (*ponerse en camino*) to set off, set out; **partirse** *vr* to crack o split o break (in two *etc*); **a ~ de** (*starting*) from

partitura [parti'tura] *nf* score

parto ['parto] *nm* birth, delivery; (*fig*) product, creation; **estar de ~** to be in labour

parvulario [parβu'larjo] *nm* nursery school, kindergarten

pasa ['pasa] *nf* V **paso**

pasacintas [pasa'θintas] *nm* (*LAM*) cassette player

pasada [pa'saða] *nf* V **pasado**

pasadizo [pasa'ðiθo] *nm* (*pasillo*) passage, corridor; (*callejuela*) alley

pasado, -a [pa'saðo, a] *adj* past; (*malo: comida, fruta*) bad; (*muy cocido*) overdone; (*anticuado*) out of date ▷ *nm* past; **~ mañana** the day after tomorrow; **el mes ~** last month; **de pasada** in passing, incidentally; **una mala pasada** a dirty trick

pasador [pasa'ðor] *nm* (*gen*) bolt; (*de pelo*) slide; (*horquilla*) grip

pasaje [pa'saxe] *nm* passage; (*pago de viaje*) fare; (*los pasajeros*) passengers *pl*; (*pasillo*) passageway

pasajero, -a [pasa'xero, a] *adj* passing; (*situación, estado*) temporary; (*amor, enfermedad*) brief ▷ *nm/f* passenger

pasamontañas [pasamon'taɲas] *nm inv* balaclava (helmet)

pasaporte [pasa'porte] *nm* passport

pasar [pa'sar] /1a/ *vt* (*gen*) to pass; (*tiempo*) to spend; (*durezas*) to suffer, endure; (*noticia*) to give, pass on; (*película*) to show; (*río*) to cross; (*barrera*) to pass through; (*falta*) to overlook, tolerate; (*contrincante*) to surpass, do better than; (*coche*) to overtake; (*enfermedad*) to give, infect with ▷ *vi* (*gen*) to pass; (*terminarse*) to be over; (*ocurrir*) to happen; **pasarse** *vr* (*flores*) to fade; (*comida*) to go bad, go off; (*fig*) to overdo it, go too far o over the top; **~ de** to go beyond, exceed; **¡pase!** come in!; **~ por** to fetch; **~lo bien/bomba** o **de maravilla** to have a good/great time; **~se al enemigo** to go over to the enemy; **se me pasó** I forgot; **no se le pasa nada** he misses nothing; **ya se te ~á** you'll get over it; **¿qué pasa?** what's going on?, what's up?; **¿qué te pasa?** what's wrong?

pasarela [pasa'rela] *nf* footbridge; (*en barco*) gangway

pasatiempo [pasa'tjempo] *nm* pastime, hobby

Pascua ['paskwa] *nf*: **~ (de Resurrección)** Easter; **Pascuas** *nfpl*

Christmas time sg; **¡felices ~s!** Merry Christmas!

pase ['pase] nm pass; (Cine) performance, showing

pasear [pase'ar] /1a/ vt to take for a walk; (exhibir) to parade, show off ▷ vi to walk, go for a walk; **pasearse** vr to walk, go for a walk; **~ en coche** to go for a drive; **paseo** nm (distancia corta) (short) walk, stroll; (avenida) avenue; **paseo marítimo** promenade; **dar un paseo** to go for a walk

pasillo [pa'siʎo] nm passage, corridor

pasión [pa'sjon] nf passion

pasivo, -a [pa'siβo, a] adj passive; (inactivo) inactive ▷ nm (Com) liabilities pl, debts pl

pasmoso, -a [pas'moso, a] adj amazing, astonishing

paso, -a ['paso, a] adj dried ▷ nm step; (modo de andar) walk; (huella) footprint; (rapidez) speed, pace, rate; (camino accesible) way through, passage; (cruce) crossing; (pasaje) passing, passage; (Geo) pass; (estrecho) strait ▷ nf raisin; **pasa de Corinto/ de Esmirna** currant/sultana; **a ese ~** (fig) at that rate; **estar de ~** to be passing through; **prohibido el ~** no entry; **ceda el ~** give way; **~ a nivel** (Ferro) level-crossing; **~ (de) cebra** (ESP) zebra crossing; **~ de peatones** pedestrian crossing; **~ elevado** flyover

pasota [pa'sota] adj, nmf (fam) ≈ dropout; **ser un (tipo) ~** to be a bit of a dropout; (ser indiferente) not to care about anything

pasta ['pasta] nf paste; (Culin: masa) dough; (: de bizcochos etc) pastry; (fam) dough; **pastas** nfpl (bizcochos) pastries, small cakes; (espaguetis etc) pasta sg; **~ de dientes** o **dentífrica** toothpaste

pastar [pas'tar] /1a/ vt, vi to graze

pastel [pas'tel] nm (dulce) cake; (Arte) pastel; **~ de carne** meat pie; **pastelería** nf cake shop

pastilla [pas'tiʎa] nf (de jabón, chocolate) bar; (píldora) tablet, pill

pasto ['pasto] nm (hierba) grass; (lugar) pasture, field; **pastor, a** nm/f shepherd(ess) ▷ nm clergyman, pastor; **pastor alemán** Alsatian

pata ['pata] nf (pierna) leg; (pie) foot; (de muebles) leg; **~s arriba** upside down; **meter la ~** to put one's foot in it; **~ de cabra** (Tec) crowbar; **metedura de ~** (fam) gaffe; **tener buena/mala ~** to be lucky/unlucky; **patada** nf stamp; (puntapié) kick

patata [pa'tata] nf potato; **~s fritas** o **a la española** chips, French fries; (de bolsa) crisps

paté [pa'te] nm pâté

patente [pa'tente] adj obvious, evident; (Com) patent ▷ nf patent

paternal [pater'nal] adj fatherly, paternal; **paterno, -a** adj paternal

patético, -a [pa'tetiko, a] adj pathetic, moving

patilla [pa'tiʎa] nf (de gafas) sidepiece; **patillas** nfpl sideburns

patín [pa'tin] nm skate; (de tobogán) runner; **patines de ruedas** rollerskates; **patinaje** nm skating; **patinar** /1a/ vi to skate; (resbalarse) to skid, slip; (fam) to slip up, blunder

patineta [pati'neta] nf (patinete) scooter; (LAM: monopatín) skateboard

patinete [pati'nete] nm scooter

patio ['patjo] nm (de casa) patio, courtyard; **~ de recreo** playground

pato ['pato] nm duck; **pagar el ~** (fam) to take the blame, carry the can

patoso, -a [pa'toso, a] adj clumsy

patotero [pato'tero] nm (LAM) hooligan, lout

patraña [pa'traɲa] nf story, fib

patria ['patrja] nf native land, mother country

patrimonio [patri'monjo] nm inheritance; (fig) heritage

patriota [pa'trjota] nmf patriot

patrocinar [patroθi'nar] /1a/ vt to sponsor

patrón, -ona [pa'tron, ona] nm/f (jefe) boss, chief, master/mistress; (propietario) landlord/lady; (Rel) patron saint ⊳ nm (Costura) pattern

patronato [patro'nato] nm sponsorship; (acto) patronage; (fundación) trust

patrulla [pa'truʎa] nf patrol

pausa ['pausa] nf pause; break

pauta ['pauta] nf line, guide line

pava ['paβa] nf (LAM) kettle

pavimento [paβi'mento] nm (de losa) pavement, paving

pavo ['paβo] nm turkey; **~ real** peacock

payaso, -a [pa'jaso, a] nm/f clown

payo, -a ['pajo, a] nm/f non-gipsy

paz [paθ] nf peace; (tranquilidad) peacefulness, tranquillity; **hacer las paces** to make peace; (fig) to make up; **¡déjame en ~!** leave me alone!

PC nm PC, personal computer

P.D. abr (= posdata) P.S.

peaje [pe'axe] nm toll

peatón [pea'ton] nm pedestrian; **peatonal** adj pedestrian

peca ['peka] nf freckle

pecado [pe'kaðo] nm sin; **pecador, a** adj sinful ⊳ nm/f sinner

pecaminoso, -a [pekami'noso, a] adj sinful

pecar [pe'kar] /1g/ vi (Rel) to sin; (fig): **~ de generoso** to be too generous

pecera [pe'θera] nf fish tank; (redonda) goldfish bowl

pecho ['petʃo] nm (Anat) chest; (de mujer) breast(s pl); **dar el ~ a** to breast-feed; **tomar algo a ~** to take sth to heart

pechuga [pe'tʃuɣa] nf breast

peculiar [peku'ljar] adj special, peculiar; (característico) typical, characteristic

pedal [pe'ðal] nm pedal; **pedalear** /1a/ vi to pedal

pédalo ['peðalo] nm pedalo, pedal boat

pedante [pe'ðante] adj pedantic ⊳ nmf pedant

pedazo [pe'ðaθo] nm piece, bit; **hacerse ~s** to smash, shatter

pediatra [pe'ðjatra] nmf paediatrician (BRIT), pediatrician (US)

pedido [pe'ðiðo] nm (Com) order; (petición) request

pedir [pe'ðir] /3k/ vt to ask for, request; (comida, Com: mandar) to order; (necesitar) to need, demand, require ⊳ vi to ask; **me pidió que cerrara la puerta** he asked me to shut the door; **¿cuánto piden por el coche?** how much are they asking for the car?

pedo ['peðo] (fam) nm fart (!)

pega ['peɣa] nf snag; **poner ~s** to raise objections

pegadizo, -a [peɣa'ðiθo, a] adj (canción etc) catchy

pegajoso, -a [peɣa'xoso, a] adj sticky, adhesive

pegamento [peɣa'mento] nm gum, glue

pegar [pe'ɣar] /1h/ vt (papel, sellos) to stick (on); (cartel) to post, stick up; (coser) to sew (on); (unir: partes) to join, fix together; (Inform) to paste; (Med) to give, infect with; (dar: golpe) to give, deal ⊳ vi (adherirse) to stick, adhere; (ir juntos: colores) to match, go together; (golpear) to hit; (quemar: el sol) to strike hot, burn; **pegarse** vr (gen) to stick; (dos personas) to hit each other, fight; **~ un grito** to let out a yell; **~ un salto** to jump (with fright); **~ fuego** to catch fire; **~ en** to touch; **~se un tiro** to shoot o.s.

pegatina [peɣa'tina] nf sticker

pegote [pe'ɣote] nm (fam) eyesore, sight

peinado [pei'naðo] nm hairstyle

peinar [pei'nar] /1a/ vt to comb sb's hair; (con un cierto estilo) to style; **peinarse** vr to comb one's hair

peine ['peine] nm comb; **peineta** nf ornamental comb

p.ej. abr (= por ejemplo) e.g.

Pekín [pe'kin] n Peking, Beijing

pelado, -a [pe'laðo, a] adj (cabeza) shorn; (fruta) peeled; (campo, fig) bare; (fam: sin dinero) broke

pelar [pe'lar] /1a/ vt (fruta, patatas) to peel; (cortar el pelo a) to cut the hair of; (quitar la piel: animal) to skin; **pelarse** vr (la piel) to peel off; **voy a ~me** I'm going to get my hair cut

peldaño [pel'daɲo] nm step

pelea [pe'lea] nf (lucha) fight; (discusión) quarrel, row; **peleado, -a** adj: **estar peleado (con algn)** to have fallen out (with sb); **pelear** /1a/ vi to fight; **pelearse** vr to fight; (reñir) to fall out, quarrel

pelela [pe'lela] nf (LAM) potty

peletería [pelete'ria] nf furrier's, fur shop

pelícano [pe'likano] nm pelican

película [pe'likula] nf film; (cobertura ligera) thin covering; (Foto: rollo) roll o reel of film; **~ de dibujos (animados)** cartoon film

peligro [pe'liɣro] nm danger; (riesgo) risk; **correr ~ de** to be in danger of, run the risk of; **peligroso, -a** adj dangerous; risky

pelirrojo, -a [peli'rroxo, a] adj red-haired, red-headed ▷ nm/f redhead

pellejo [pe'ʎexo] nm (de animal) skin, hide

pellizcar [peʎiθ'kar] /1g/ vt to pinch, nip

pelma ['pelma] nmf, **pelmazo, -a** [pel'maθo, a] nm/f (fam) pain (in the neck)

pelo ['pelo] nm (cabellos) hair; (de barba, bigote) whisker; (de animal: piel) fur, coat; (de perro etc) hair, coat; **venir al ~** to be exactly what one needs; **un hombre de ~ en pecho** a brave man; **por los ~s** by the skin of one's teeth; **no tener ~s en la lengua** to be outspoken, not mince words; **con ~s y señales** in minute detail; **tomar el ~ a algn** to pull sb's leg

pelota [pe'lota] nf ball; **en ~(s)** stark naked; **~ vasca** pelota; **hacer la ~ (a algn)** to creep (to sb)

pelotón [pelo'ton] nm (Mil) squad, detachment

peluca [pe'luka] nf wig

peluche [pe'lutʃe] nm: **muñeco de ~** soft toy

peludo, -a [pe'luðo, a] adj hairy, shaggy

peluquería [peluke'ria] nf hairdresser's; **peluquero, -a** nm/f hairdresser

pelusa [pe'lusa] nf (Bot) down; (Costura) fluff

pena ['pena] nf (congoja) grief, sadness; (remordimiento) regret; (dificultad) trouble; (dolor) pain; (Jur) sentence; **~ capital** capital punishment; **merecer o valer la ~** to be worthwhile; **a duras ~s** with great difficulty; **¡qué ~!** what a shame o pity!

penal [pe'nal] adj penal ▷ nm (cárcel) prison

penalidad [penali'ðað] nf (problema, dificultad) trouble, hardship; (Jur) penalty, punishment; **penalidades** nfpl trouble sg, hardship sg

penalti, penalty [pe'nalti] (pl **penalties** o **penaltys**) nm (Deporte) penalty (kick)

pendiente [pen'djente] adj pending, unsettled ▷ nm earring ▷ nf hill, slope

pene ['pene] nm penis

penetrante [pene'trante] adj (herida) deep; (persona, arma) sharp; (sonido) penetrating, piercing; (mirada) searching; (viento, ironía) biting

penetrar [pene'trar] /1a/ vt to penetrate, pierce; (entender) to grasp ▷ vi to penetrate, go in; (entrar) to enter; (líquido) to soak in; (emoción) to pierce

penicilina [peniθi'lina] nf penicillin

península [pe'ninsula] nf peninsula; **peninsular** adj peninsular

penique [pe'nike] nm penny

penitencia [peni'tenθja] *nf* penance

penoso, -a [pe'noso, a] *adj* laborious, difficult; (*lamentable*) distressing

pensador, a [pensa'ðor, a] *nm/f* thinker

pensamiento [pensa'mjento] *nm* thought; (*mente*) mind; (*idea*) idea

pensar [pen'sar] /1j/ *vt* to think; (*considerar*) to think over, think out; (*proponerse*) to intend, plan; (*imaginarse*) to think up, invent ▷ *vi* to think; **~ en** to aim at, aspire to; **pensativo, -a** *adj* thoughtful, pensive

pensión [pen'sjon] *nf* (*casa*) ≈ guest house; (*dinero*) pension; (*cama y comida*) board and lodging; **~ completa** full board; **media ~** half board; **pensionista** *nmf* (*jubilado*) (old-age) pensioner; (*el que vive en una pensión*) lodger

penúltimo, -a [pe'nultimo, a] *adj* penultimate, second last

penumbra [pe'numbra] *nf* half-light

peña ['peɲa] *nf* (*roca*) rock; (*acantilado*) cliff, crag; (*grupo*) group, circle; (LAM: *club*) folk club

peñasco [pe'ɲasko] *nm* large rock, boulder

peñón [pe'ɲon] *nm* crag; **el P~** the Rock (of Gibraltar)

peón [pe'on] *nm* labourer; (LAM) farm labourer, farmhand; (*Ajedrez*) pawn

peonza [pe'onθa] *nf* spinning top

peor [pe'or] *adj* (*comparativo*) worse; (*superlativo*) worst ▷ *adv* worse; worst; **de mal en ~** from bad to worse

pepinillo [pepi'niʎo] *nm* gherkin

pepino [pe'pino] *nm* cucumber; **(no) me importa un ~** I don't care one bit

pepita [pe'pita] *nf* (*Bot*) pip; (*Minería*) nugget

pepito [pe'pito] *nm* (ESP: tb: **~ de ternera**) steak sandwich

pequeño, -a [pe'keɲo, a] *adj* small, little

pera ['pera] *nf* pear; **peral** *nm* pear tree

percance [per'kanθe] *nm* setback, misfortune

percatarse [perka'tarse] /1a/ *vr*: **~ de** to notice, take note of

percebe [per'θeβe] *nm* barnacle

percepción [perθep'θjon] *nf* (*vista*) perception; (*idea*) notion, idea

percha ['pertʃa] *nf* coat hanger; (*ganchos*) coat hooks pl; (*de ave*) perch

percibir [perθi'βir] /3a/ *vt* to perceive, notice; (*Com*) to earn, get

percusión [perku'sjon] *nf* percussion

perdedor, a [perðe'ðor, a] *adj* losing ▷ *nm/f* loser

perder [per'ðer] /2g/ *vt* to lose; (*tiempo, palabras*) to waste; (*oportunidad*) to lose, miss; (*tren*) to miss ▷ *vi* to lose; **perderse** *vr* (*extraviarse*) to get lost; (*desaparecer*) to disappear, be lost to view; (*arruinarse*) to be ruined; **echar a ~** (*comida*) to spoil, ruin; (*oportunidad*) to waste

pérdida ['perðiða] *nf* loss; (*de tiempo*) waste; **pérdidas** *nfpl* (*Com*) losses

perdido, -a [per'ðiðo, a] *adj* lost

perdiz [per'ðiθ] *nf* partridge

perdón [per'ðon] *nm* (*disculpa*) pardon, forgiveness; (*clemencia*) mercy; **¡~!** sorry!, I beg your pardon!; **perdonar** /1a/ *vt* to pardon, forgive; (*la vida*) to spare; (*excusar*) to exempt, excuse; **¡perdone (usted)!** sorry!, I beg your pardon!

perecedero, -a [pereθe'ðero, a] *adj* perishable

perecer [pere'θer] /2d/ *vi* to perish, die

peregrinación [pereɣrina'θjon] *nf* (*Rel*) pilgrimage

peregrino, -a [pere'ɣrino, a] *adj* (*extraño*) strange ▷ *nm/f* pilgrim

perejil [pere'xil] *nm* parsley

perenne [pe'renne] *adj* perennial

pereza [pe'reθa] *nf* laziness; **perezoso, -a** *adj* lazy

perfección [perfek'θjon] *nf* perfection; **perfeccionar** /1a/ *vt* to perfect; (*mejorar*) to improve; (*acabar*) to complete, finish

p

perfecto, -a [per'fekto, a] *adj* perfect
▷ *nm* (*Ling*) perfect (tense)

perfil [per'fil] *nm* profile; (*silueta*)
silhouette, outline; (*Tec*) (cross)
section; **perfiles** *nmpl* features

perforación [perfora'θjon] *nf*
perforation; (*con taladro*) drilling

perforadora [perfora'ðora] *nf*
card-punch

perforar [perfo'rar] /1a/ *vt* to
perforate; (*agujero*) to drill, bore;
(*papel*) to punch a hole in ▷ *vi* to
drill, bore

perfume [per'fume] *nm* perfume,
scent

periferia [peri'ferja] *nf* periphery; (*de
ciudad*) outskirts *pl*

periférico, -a [peri'feriko, a] *adj*
peripheral ▷ *nm* (*LAM Auto*) ring road
(*BRIT*), beltway (*US*)

perilla [pe'riʎa] *nf* (*barba*) goatee;
(*LAM: de puerta*) doorknob, door handle

perímetro [pe'rimetro] *nm*
perimeter

periódico, -a [pe'rjoðiko, a] *adj*
periodic(al) ▷ *nm* (news)paper

periodismo [perjo'ðismo] *nm*
journalism; **periodista** *nmf* journalist

periodo [pe'rjoðo], **período**
[pe'rioðo] *nm* period

periquito [peri'kito] *nm* budgerigar,
budgie (*fam*)

perito, -a [pe'rito, a] *adj* (*experto*)
expert; (*diestro*) skilled, skilful ▷ *nm/f*
expert; skilled worker; (*técnico*)
technician

perjudicar [perxuði'kar] /1g/ *vt* (*gen*)
to damage, harm; **perjudicial** *adj*
damaging, harmful; (*en detrimento*)
detrimental; **perjuicio** *nm* damage,
harm

perjurar [perxu'rar] /1a/ *vi* to commit
perjury

perla ['perla] *nf* pearl; **me viene de ~s**
it suits me fine

permanecer [permane'θer] /2d/ *vi*
(*quedarse*) to stay, remain; (*seguir*) to
continue to be

permanente [perma'nente] *adj*
permanent; (*constante*) constant
▷ *nf* perm

permiso [per'miso] *nm* permission;
(*licencia*) permit, licence (*BRIT*),
license (*US*); **con ~** excuse me;
estar de ~ (*Mil*) to be on leave; **~ de
conducir** *o* **conductor** driving licence
(*BRIT*), driver's license (*US*); **~ por
enfermedad** (*LAM*) sick leave

permitir [permi'tir] /3a/ *vt* to
permit, allow

pernera [per'nera] *nf* trouser leg

pero ['pero] *conj* but; (*aún*) yet
▷ *nm* (*defecto*) flaw, defect; (*reparo*)
objection

perpendicular [perpendiku'lar] *adj*
perpendicular

perpetuo, -a [per'petwo, a] *adj*
perpetual

perplejo, -a [per'plexo, a] *adj*
perplexed, bewildered

perra ['perra] *nf* (*Zool*) bitch; (*fam:
dinero*) money; **estar sin una ~** to be
flat broke

perrera [pe'rrera] *nf* kennel

perrito [pe'rrito] *nm* (*tb: ~ **caliente**)
hot dog

perro ['perro] *nm* dog

persa ['persa] *adj, nmf* Persian

persecución [perseku'θjon] *nf*
pursuit, chase; (*Rel, Pol*) persecution

perseguir [perse'ɣir] /3d, 3k/ *vt* to
pursue, hunt; (*cortejar*) to chase after;
(*molestar*) to pester, annoy; (*Rel, Pol*)
to persecute

persiana [per'sjana] *nf* (*Venetian*)
blind

persistente [persis'tente] *adj*
persistent

persistir [persis'tir] /3a/ *vi* to persist

persona [per'sona] *nf* person;
~ mayor elderly person

personaje [perso'naxe] *nm*
important person, celebrity; (*Teat*)
character

personal [perso'nal] *adj* (*particular*)
personal; (*para una persona*) single,

for one person ▷ nm personnel, staff;
personalidad nf personality
personarse [perso'narse] /1a/ vr to
appear in person
personificar [personifi'kar] /1g/ vt
to personify
perspectiva [perspek'tiβa] nf
perspective; (vista, panorama) view,
panorama; (posibilidad futura) outlook,
prospect
persuadir [perswa'ðir] /3a/ vt (gen)
to persuade; (convencer) to convince;
persuadirse vr to become convinced;
persuasión nf persuasion
pertenecer [pertene'θer] /2d/ vi:
~ a to belong to; (fig) to concern;
perteneciente adj: **perteneciente
a** belonging to; **pertenencia** nf
ownership; **pertenencias** nfpl
possessions, property sg
pertenezca etc [perte'neθka] vb V
pertenecer
pértiga ['pertiɣa] nf: **salto de ~**
pole vault
pertinente [perti'nente] adj
relevant, pertinent; (apropiado)
appropriate; **~ a** concerning,
relevant to
perturbación [perturβa'θjon]
nf (Pol) disturbance; (Med) upset,
disturbance
Perú [pe'ru] nm Peru; **peruano, -a** adj,
nm/f Peruvian
perversión [perβer'sjon] nf
perversion; **perverso, -a** adj perverse;
(depravado) depraved
pervertido, -a [perβer'tiðo, a] adj
perverted ▷ nm/f pervert
pervertir [perβer'tir] /3i/ vt to
pervert, corrupt
pesa ['pesa] nf weight; (Deporte) shot
pesadez [pesa'ðeθ] nf (calidad de
pesado) heaviness; (lentitud) slowness;
(aburrimiento) tediousness
pesadilla [pesa'ðiʎa] nf nightmare,
bad dream
pesado, -a [pe'saðo, a] adj heavy;
(lento) slow; (difícil, duro) tough, hard;

(aburrido) tedious, boring; (bochornoso)
sultry
pésame ['pesame] nm expression of
condolence, message of sympathy;
dar el ~ to express one's condolences
pesar [pe'sar] /1a/ vt to weigh ▷ vi to
weigh; (ser pesado) to weigh a lot, be
heavy; (fig: opinión) to carry weight
▷ nm (sentimiento) regret; (pena) grief,
sorrow; **no pesa mucho** it's not very
heavy; **a ~ de (que)** in spite of, despite
pesca ['peska] nf (acto) fishing;
(cantidad de pescado) catch; **ir de ~** to
go fishing
pescadería [peskaðe'ria] nf fish
shop, fishmonger's
pescadilla [peska'ðiʎa] nf whiting
pescado [pes'kaðo] nm fish
pescador, a [peska'ðor, a] nm/f
fisherman/woman
pescar [pes'kar] /1g/ vt (coger) to
catch; (tratar de coger) to fish for;
(conseguir: trabajo) to manage to get
▷ vi to fish, go fishing
pesebre [pe'seβre] nm manger
peseta [pe'seta] nf peseta
pesimista [pesi'mista] adj
pessimistic ▷ nmf pessimist
pésimo, -a ['pesimo, a] adj awful,
dreadful
peso ['peso] nm weight; (balanza)
scales pl; (moneda) peso; **~ bruto/
neto** gross/net weight; **~ mosca/
pesado** fly-/heavyweight; **vender a ~**
to sell by weight
pesquero, -a [pes'kero, a] adj
fishing cpd
pestaña [pes'taɲa] nf (Anat) eyelash;
(borde) rim
peste ['peste] nf plague; (mal olor)
stink, stench
pesticida [pesti'θiða] nm pesticide
pestillo [pes'tiʎo] nm bolt; (picaporte)
(door) handle
petaca [pe'taka] nf (de cigarrillos)
cigarette case; (de pipa) tobacco
pouch; (LAM: maleta) suitcase
pétalo ['petalo] nm petal

p

petardo [pe'tarðo] *nm* firework, firecracker

petición [peti'θjon] *nf* (*pedido*) request, plea; (*memorial*) petition; (*Jur*) plea

peto ['peto] *nm* dungarees *pl*, overalls *pl* (*US*)

petróleo [pe'troleo] *nm* oil, petroleum; **petrolero, -a** *adj* petroleum *cpd* ▷ *nm* (*oil*) tanker

peyorativo, -a [pejora'tiβo, a] *adj* pejorative

pez [peθ] *nm* fish; **~ de colores** goldfish; **~ espada** swordfish

pezón [pe'θon] *nm* teat, nipple

pezuña [pe'θuɲa] *nf* hoof

pianista [pja'nista] *nmf* pianist

piano ['pjano] *nm* piano

piar [pjar] /1c/ *vi* to cheep

pibe, -a ['piβe, a] *nm/f* (*LAM*) boy/girl

picadero [pika'ðero] *nm* riding school

picadillo [pika'ðiʎo] *nm* mince, minced meat

picado, -a [pi'kaðo, a] *adj* pricked, punctured; (*Culin*) minced, chopped; (*mar*) choppy; (*diente*) bad; (*tabaco*) cut; (*enfadado*) cross

picador [pika'ðor] *nm* (*Taur*) picador; (*minero*) faceworker

picadura [pika'ðura] *nf* (*pinchazo*) puncture; (*de abeja*) sting; (*de mosquito*) bite; (*tabaco picado*) cut tobacco

picante [pi'kante] *adj* hot; (*comentario*) racy, spicy

picaporte [pika'porte] *nm* (*tirador*) handle; (*pestillo*) latch

picar [pi'kar] /1g/ *vt* (*agujerear, perforar*) to prick, puncture; (*abeja*) to sting; (*mosquito, serpiente*) to bite; (*Culin*) to mince, chop; (*incitar*) to incite, goad; (*dañar, irritar*) to annoy, bother; (*quemar: lengua*) to burn, sting ▷ *vi* (*pez*) to bite, take the bait; (*el sol*) to burn, scorch; (*abeja, Med*) to sting; (*mosquito*) to bite; **picarse** *vr* (*agriarse*) to turn sour, go off; (*ofenderse*) to take offence

picardía [pikar'ðia] *nf* villainy; (*astucia*) slyness, craftiness; (*una picardía*) dirty trick; (*palabra*) rude/bad word o expression

pícaro, -a ['pikaro, a] *adj* (*malicioso*) villainous; (*travieso*) mischievous ▷ *nm* (*astuto*) sly sort; (*sinvergüenza*) rascal, scoundrel

pichi ['pitʃi] *nm* (*ESP*) pinafore dress (*BRIT*), jumper (*US*)

pichón [pi'tʃon] *nm* young pigeon

pico ['piko] *nm* (*de ave*) beak; (*punta aguda*) sharp point; (*Tec*) pick, pickaxe; (*Geo*) peak, summit; **y ~** and a bit; **las seis y ~** six and a bit

picor [pi'kor] *nm* itch

picoso, -a [pi'koso, a] (*LAM*) *adj* (*comida*) hot

picudo, -a [pi'kuðo, a] *adj* pointed, with a point

pidió *etc vb* ∨ **pedir**

pido *etc vb* ∨ **pedir**

pie [pje] (*pl* **pies**) *nm* foot; (*fig: motivo*) motive, basis; (: *fundamento*) foothold; **ir a ~** to go on foot, walk; **estar de ~** to be standing (up); **ponerse de ~** to stand up; **al ~ de la letra** (*citar*) literally, verbatim; (*copiar*) exactly, word for word; **de ~s a cabeza** from head to foot; **en ~ de guerra** on a war footing; **dar ~ a** to give cause for; **hacer ~** (*en el agua*) to touch (the) bottom

piedad [pje'ðað] *nf* (*lástima*) pity, compassion; (*clemencia*) mercy; (*devoción*) piety, devotion

piedra ['pjeðra] *nf* stone; (*roca*) rock; (*de mechero*) flint; (*Meteorología*) hailstone; **~ preciosa** precious stone

piel [pjel] *nf* (*Anat*) skin; (*Zool*) skin, hide; fur; (*cuero*) leather; (*Bot*) skin, peel

pienso *etc* ['pjenso] *vb* ∨ **pensar**

pierdo *etc* ['pjerðo] *vb* ∨ **perder**

pierna ['pjerna] *nf* leg

pieza ['pjeθa] *nf* piece; (*habitación*) room; **~ de recambio** o **repuesto** spare (part)

pigmeo, -a [piɣ'meo, a] *adj, nm/f* pigmy

pijama [pi'xama] *nm* pyjamas *pl*

pila ['pila] *nf* (*Elec*) battery; (*montón*) heap, pile; (*de fuente*) sink

píldora ['pildora] *nf* pill; **la ~ (anticonceptiva)** the pill

pileta [pi'leta] *nf* (*LAM: de cocina*) sink; (: *piscina*) swimming pool

pillar [pi'ʎar] /1a/ *vt* (*saquear*) to pillage, plunder; (*fam: coger*) to catch; (: *agarrar*) to grasp, seize; (: *entender*) to grasp, catch on to; **pillarse** *vr*: **~se un dedo con la puerta** to catch one's finger in the door

pillo, -a ['piʎo, a] *adj* villainous; (*astuto*) sly, crafty ▷ *nm/f* rascal, rogue, scoundrel

piloto [pi'loto] *nm* pilot; (*de aparato*) (pilot) light; (*Auto*) rear light, tail light; (*conductor*) driver; **~ automático** automatic pilot

pimentón [pimen'ton] *nm* paprika

pimienta [pi'mjenta] *nf* pepper

pimiento [pi'mjento] *nm* pepper, pimiento

pin [pin] *nm* (*pl* **pins**) badge

pinacoteca [pinako'teka] *nf* art gallery

pinar [pi'nar] *nm* pinewood

pincel [pin'θel] *nm* paintbrush

pinchadiscos [pintʃa'diskos] *nm/f inv* disc jockey, DJ

pinchar [pin'tʃar] /1a/ *vt* (*perforar*) to prick, pierce; (*neumático*) to puncture; (*incitar*) to prod; (*Inform*) to click

pinchazo [pin'tʃaθo] *nm* (*perforación*) prick; (*de llanta*) puncture; (*fig*) prod

pincho ['pintʃo] *nm* savoury (snack); **~ moruno** shish kebab; **~ de tortilla** small slice of omelette

ping-pong ['pimpon] *nm* table tennis

pingüino [pin'gwino] *nm* penguin

pino ['pino] *nm* pine (tree)

pinta ['pinta] *nf* spot; (*gota*) spot, drop; (*aspecto*) appearance, look(s) *pl*; **pintado, -a** *adj* spotted; (*de muchos colores*) colourful; **pintadas** *nfpl* political graffiti *sg*

pintalabios [pinta'laβjos] *nm inv* (*ESP*) lipstick

pintar [pin'tar] /1a/ *vt* to paint ▷ *vi* to paint; (*fam*) to count, be important; **pintarse** *vr* to put on make-up

pintor, a [pin'tor, a] *nm/f* painter

pintoresco, -a [pinto'resko, a] *adj* picturesque

pintura [pin'tura] *nf* painting; **~ al óleo** oil painting

pinza ['pinθa] *nf* (*Zool*) claw; (*para colgar ropa*) clothes peg; (*Tec*) pincers *pl*; **pinzas** *nfpl* (*para depilar*) tweezers

piña ['piɲa] *nf* (*fruto del pino*) pine cone; (*fruta*) pineapple; (*fig*) group

piñata [pi'ɲata] *nf* piñata (*figurine hung up at parties to be beaten with sticks until sweets or presents fall out*)

piñón [pi'ɲon] *nm* (*Bot*) pine nut; (*Tec*) pinion

pío, -a ['pio, a] *adj* (*devoto*) pious, devout; (*misericordioso*) merciful

piojo ['pjoxo] *nm* louse

pipa ['pipa] *nf* pipe; (*Bot*) seed, pip; (*de girasol*) sunflower seed

pipí [pi'pi] *nm* (*fam*): **hacer ~** to have a wee(-wee)

pique ['pike] *nm* (*resentimiento*) pique, resentment; (*rivalidad*) rivalry, competition; **irse a ~** to sink; (*familia*) to be ruined

piqueta [pi'keta] *nf* pick(axe)

piquete [pi'kete] *nm* (*Mil*) squad, party; (*de obreros*) picket; (*LAM: de insecto*) bite

pirado, -a [pi'raðo, a] *adj* (*fam*) round the bend ▷ *nm/f* nutter

piragua [pi'raɣwa] *nf* canoe; **piragüismo** *nm* canoeing

pirámide [pi'ramiðe] *nf* pyramid

pirata [pi'rata] *adj, nm* pirate; (*tb*: **~ informático**) hacker

Pirineo(s) [piri'neo(s)] *nm(pl)* Pyrenees *pl*

pirómano, -a [pi'romano, a] *nm/f* (*Jur*) arsonist

piropo [pi'ropo] nm compliment, (piece of) flattery

pirueta [pi'rweta] nf pirouette

piruleta [piru'leta] nf lollipop

pis [pis] nm (fam) pee; **hacer ~** to have a pee; (para niños) to wee-wee

pisada [pi'saða] nf (paso) footstep; (huella) footprint

pisar [pi'sar] /1a/ vt (caminar sobre) to walk on, tread on; (apretar con el pie) to press; (fig) to trample on, walk all over ▷ vi to tread, step, walk

piscina [pis'θina] nf swimming pool

Piscis [pis'θis] nm Pisces

piso ['piso] nm (suelo) floor; (LAM) ground; (apartamento) flat, apartment; **primer ~** (ESP) first o second (US) floor; (LAM) ground o first (US) floor

pisotear [pisote'ar] /1a/ vt to trample (on o underfoot)

pista ['pista] nf track, trail; (indicio) clue; **~ de aterrizaje** runway; **~ de baile** dance floor; **~ de tenis** tennis court; **~ de hielo** ice rink

pistola [pis'tola] nf pistol; (Tec) spray-gun

pistón [pis'ton] nm (Tec) piston; (Mus) key

pitar [pi'tar] /1a/ vt (hacer sonar) to blow; (rechiflar) to whistle at, boo ▷ vi to whistle; (Auto) to sound o toot one's horn; (LAM) to smoke

pitillo [pi'tiʎo] nm cigarette

pito ['pito] nm whistle; (de coche) horn

pitón [pi'ton] nm (Zool) python

pitonisa [pito'nisa] nf fortune-teller

pitorreo [pito'rreo] nm joke, laugh; **estar de ~** to be in a joking mood

píxel ['piksel] nm (Inform) pixel

piyama [pi'jama] nm (LAM) pyjamas pl, pajamas pl (US)

pizarra [pi'θarra] nf (piedra) slate; (encerado) blackboard; **~ blanca** whiteboard; **~ interactiva** interactive whiteboard

pizarrón [piθa'rron] nm (LAM) blackboard

pizca ['piθka] nf pinch, spot; (fig) spot, speck; **ni ~** not a bit

placa ['plaka] nf plate; (distintivo) badge; **~ de matrícula** number plate

placard [pla'kar] nm (LAM) built-in cupboard

placer [pla'θer] /2w/ nm pleasure ▷ vt to please; **a ~** at one's pleasure

plaga ['playa] nf (Zool) pest; (Med) plague; (fig) swarm; (: abundancia) abundance

plagio ['plaxjo] nm plagiarism

plan [plan] nm (esquema, proyecto) plan; (idea, intento) idea, intention; **tener ~** (fam) to have a date; **tener un ~** (fam) to have an affair; **en ~ económico** (fam) on the cheap; **vamos en ~ de turismo** we're going as tourists; **si te pones en ese ~ ...** if that's your attitude ...

plana ['plana] nf V **plano**

plancha ['plantʃa] nf (para planchar) iron; (rótulo) plate, sheet; (Naut) gangway; **a la ~** (Culin) grilled; **planchar** /1a/ vt to iron ▷ vi to do the ironing

planear [plane'ar] /1a/ vt to plan ▷ vi to glide

planeta [pla'neta] nm planet

plano, -a ['plano, a] adj flat, level, even ▷ nm (Mat, Tec, Aviat) plane; (Foto) shot; (Arq) plan; (Geo) map; (de ciudad) map, street plan ▷ nf sheet of paper, page; (Tec) trowel; **primer ~** close-up; **en primera plana** on the front page

planta ['planta] nf (Bot, Tec) plant; (Anat) sole of the foot, foot; (piso) floor; (LAM: personal) staff; **~ baja** ground floor

plantar [plan'tar] /1a/ vt (Bot) to plant; (levantar) to erect, set up; **plantarse** vr to stand firm; **~ a algn en la calle** to chuck sb out; **dejar plantado a algn** (fam) to stand sb up

plantear [plante'ar] /1a/ vt (problema) to pose; (dificultad) to raise

plantilla [plan'tiʎa] nf (de zapato) insole; (personal) personnel; **ser de ~** to be on the staff

plantón [plan'ton] nm (Mil) guard, sentry; (fam) long wait; **dar (un) ~ a algn** to stand sb up

plasta ['plasta] nf soft mass, lump ▷ nmf (ESP fam) bore ▷ adj (ESP fam) boring

plástico, -a ['plastiko, a] adj plastic ▷ nm plastic

Plastilina® [plasti'lina] nf Plasticine®

plata ['plata] nf (metal) silver; (cosas hechas de plata) silverware; (LAM) cash

plataforma [plata'forma] nf platform; **~ de lanzamiento/ perforación** launch(ing) pad/ drilling rig

plátano ['platano] nm (fruta) banana; (árbol) plane tree; banana tree

platea [pla'tea] nf (Teat) pit

plática ['platika] nf talk, chat; **platicar** /1g/ vi to talk, chat

platillo [pla'tiʎo] nm saucer; **platillos** nmpl cymbals; **~ volador o volante** flying saucer

platino [pla'tino] nm platinum; **platinos** nmpl (Auto) (contact) points

plato ['plato] nm plate, dish; (parte de comida) course; (guiso) dish; **primer ~** first course; **~ combinado** set main course (served on one plate); **~ fuerte** main course

playa ['plaja] nf beach; (costa) seaside; **~ de estacionamiento** (LAM) car park

playero, -a [pla'jero, a] adj beach cpd ▷ nf (LAM: camiseta) T-shirt; **playeras** nfpl canvas shoes

plaza ['plaθa] nf square; (mercado) market(place); (sitio) room, space; (en vehículo) seat, place; (colocación) post, job; **~ de toros** bullring

plazo ['plaθo] nm (lapso de tiempo) time, period; (fecha de vencimiento) expiry date; (pago parcial) instalment; **a corto/largo ~** short-/long-term;

comprar a ~s to buy on hire purchase, pay for in instalments

plazoleta [plaθo'leta] nf small square

plebeyo, -a [ple'βejo, a] adj plebeian; (pey) coarse, common

plegable [ple'ɣaβle] adj pliable; (silla) folding

pleito ['pleito] nm (Jur) lawsuit, case; (fig) dispute, feud

plenitud [pleni'tuð] nf plenitude, fullness; (abundancia) abundance

pleno, -a ['pleno, a] adj full; (completo) complete ▷ nm plenum; **en ~ día** in broad daylight; **en ~ verano** at the height of summer; **en plena cara** full in the face

pliego ['pljeɣo] nm (hoja) sheet (of paper); (carta) sealed letter/ document; **~ de condiciones** details pl, specifications pl

pliegue ['pljeɣe] nm fold, crease; (de vestido) pleat

plomería [plome'ria] nf (LAM) plumbing; **plomero** nm (LAM) plumber

plomo ['plomo] nm (metal) lead; (Elec) fuse; **sin ~** unleaded

pluma ['pluma] nf feather; (para escribir) (estilográfica) ink pen; **~ fuente** (LAM) fountain pen

plumero [plu'mero] nm (quitapolvos) feather duster

plumón [plu'mon] nm (de ave) down

plural [plu'ral] adj plural

pluriempleo [pluriem'pleo] nm having more than one job

plus [plus] nm bonus

población [poβla'θjon] nf population; (pueblo, ciudad) town, city

poblado, -a [po'βlaðo, a] adj inhabited ▷ nm (aldea) village; (pueblo) (small) town; **densamente ~** densely populated

poblador, a [poβla'ðor, a] nm/f settler, colonist

pobre ['poβre] adj poor ▷ nmf poor person; **pobreza** nf poverty

pocilga [po'θilɣa] nf pigsty

P

PALABRA CLAVE

poco, -a ['poko, a] *adj* **1** (*sg*) little, not much; **poco tiempo** little *o* not much time; **de poco interés** of little interest, not very interesting; **poca cosa** not much

2 (*pl*) few, not many; **unos pocos** a few, some; **pocos niños comen lo que les conviene** few children eat what they should

▶ *adv* **1** little, not much; **cuesta poco** it doesn't cost much

2 (+ *adj: negativo, antónimo*): **poco amable/inteligente** not very nice/intelligent

3: **por poco me caigo** I almost fell

4: **a poco de haberse casado** shortly after getting married

5: **poco a poco** little by little

▶ *nm* a little, a bit; **un poco triste/de dinero** a little sad/money

podar [po'ðar] /1a/ *vt* to prune

podcast ['poðkast] *nm* podcast; **podcastear** /1a/ *vi* to podcast

PALABRA CLAVE

poder [po'ðer] /2s/ *vi* **1** (*capacidad*) can, be able to; **no puedo hacerlo** I can't do it, I'm unable to do it

2 (*permiso*) can, may, be allowed to; **¿se puede?** may I (*o* we)?; **puedes irte ahora** you may go now; **no se puede fumar en este hospital** smoking is not allowed in this hospital

3 (*posibilidad*) may, might, could; **puede llegar mañana** he may *o* might arrive tomorrow; **pudiste haberte hecho daño** you might *o* could have hurt yourself; **¡podías habérmelo dicho antes!** you might have told me before!

4: **puede (ser)** perhaps; **puede que lo sepa Tomás** Tomás may *o* might know

5: **¡no puedo más!** I've had enough!; **es tonto a más no poder** he's as stupid as they come

6: **poder con: no puedo con este crío** this kid's too much for me

▶ *nm* power; **el poder** the Government; **poder adquisitivo** purchasing power; **detentar** *u* **ocupar** *o* **estar en el poder** to be in power *o* office; **poder judicial** judiciary

poderoso, -a [poðe'roso, a] *adj* powerful

podio ['poðjo] *nm* podium

podium ['poðjum] = **podio**

podrido, -a [po'ðriðo, a] *adj* rotten, bad; (*fig*) rotten, corrupt

podrir [po'ðrir] = **pudrir**

poema [po'ema] *nm* poem

poesía [poe'sia] *nf* poetry

poeta [po'eta] *nm* poet; **poético, -a** *adj* poetic(al); **poetisa** *nf* (woman) poet

póker ['poker] *nm* poker

polaco, -a [po'lako, a] *adj* Polish ▷ *nm/f* Pole

polar [po'lar] *adj* polar

polea [po'lea] *nf* pulley

polémica [po'lemika] *nf* polemics *sg*; (*una polémica*) controversy

polen ['polen] *nm* pollen

policía [poli'θia] *nmf* policeman/woman ▷ *nf* police; **policíaco, -a** *adj* police *cpd*; **novela policíaca** detective story; **policial** *adj* police *cpd*

polideportivo [poliðepor'tiβo] *nm* sports centre

polígono [po'liɣono] *nm* (*Mat*) polygon; **~ industrial** industrial estate

polilla [po'liʎa] *nf* moth

polio ['poljo] *nf* polio

político, -a [po'litiko, a] *adj* political; (*discreto*) tactful; (*pariente*) in-law ▷ *nm/f* politician ▷ *nf* politics *sg*; (*económica, agraria*) policy; **padre ~** father-in-law; **política exterior/de**

ingresos y precios foreign/prices and incomes policy

póliza ['poliθa] *nf* certificate, voucher; (*impuesto*) tax *o* fiscal stamp; **~ de seguro(s)** insurance policy

polizón [poli'θon] *nm* stowaway

pollera [po'ʎera] *nf* (*LAM*) skirt

pollo ['poʎo] *nm* chicken

polo ['polo] *nm* (*Geo, Elec*) pole; (*helado*) ice lolly (*BRIT*), Popsicle® (*US*); (*Deporte*) polo; (*suéter*) polo-neck; **P~ Norte/Sur** North/South Pole

Polonia [po'lonja] *nf* Poland

poltrona [pol'trona] *nf* easy chair

polución [polu'θjon] *nf* pollution

polvera [pol'βera] *nf* powder compact

polvo ['polβo] *nm* dust; (*Química, Culin, Med*) powder; **polvos** *nmpl* (*maquillaje*) powder *sg*; **en ~** powdered; **~ de talco** talcum powder; **estar hecho ~** to be worn out *o* exhausted

pólvora ['polβora] *nf* gunpowder

polvoriento, -a [polβo'rjento, a] *adj* (*superficie*) dusty; (*sustancia*) powdery

pomada [po'maða] *nf* cream

pomelo [po'melo] *nm* grapefruit

pómez ['pomeθ] *nf*: **piedra ~** pumice stone

pomo ['pomo] *nm* knob, handle

pompa ['pompa] *nf* (*burbuja*) bubble; (*bomba*) pump; (*esplendor*) pomp, splendour

pómulo ['pomulo] *nm* cheekbone

pon [pon] *vb V* **poner**

ponchadura [pontʃa'dura] *nf* (*LAM*) puncture (*BRIT*), flat (*US*); **ponchar** /1a/ *vt* (*LAM: llanta*) to puncture

ponche ['pontʃe] *nm* punch

poncho ['pontʃo] *nm* poncho

pondré *etc* [pon'dre] *vb V* **poner**

PALABRA CLAVE

poner [po'ner] /2q/ *vt* **1** to put; (*colocar*) to place; (*telegrama*) to send; (*obra de teatro*) to put on; (*película*) to show; **ponlo más alto** turn it up; **¿qué ponen en el Excelsior?** what's on at the Excelsior?

2 (*tienda*) to open; (*instalar: etc*) to put in; (*radio, TV*) to switch *o* turn on

3 (*suponer*): **pongamos que ...** let's suppose that ...

4 (*contribuir*): **el gobierno ha puesto otro millón** the government has contributed another million

5 (*Telec*): **póngame con el Sr. López** can you put me through to Mr. López?

6: **poner de: le han puesto de director general** they've appointed him general manager

7 (+ *adj*) to make; **me estás poniendo nerviosa** you're making me nervous

8 (*dar nombre*): **al hijo le pusieron Diego** they called their son Diego

▶ *vi* (*gallina*) to lay

▶ **ponerse** *vr* (*colocarse*): **se puso a mi lado** he came and stood beside me; **tú ponte en esa silla** you go and sit on that chair; **ponerse en camino** to set off

2 (*vestido, cosméticos*) to put on; **¿por qué no te pones el vestido nuevo?** why don't you put on *o* wear your new dress?

3 (*sol*) to set

4 (+ *adj*) to get, become; to turn; **se puso muy serio** he got very serious; **después de lavarla la tela se puso azul** after washing it the material turned blue

5: **ponerse a: se puso a llorar** he started to cry; **tienes que ponerte a estudiar** you must get down to studying

pongo *etc* ['poŋgo] *vb V* **poner**

poniente [po'njente] *nm* west; (*viento*) west wind

pontífice [pon'tifiθe] *nm* pope, pontiff

pop [pop] *adj inv, nm* (*Mus*) pop

popa ['popa] *nf* stern; **a ~** astern, abaft; **de ~ a proa** fore and aft

popote [po'pote] *nm* (*LAM*) straw
popular [popu'lar] *adj* popular; (*del pueblo*) of the people; **popularidad** *nf* popularity

PALABRA CLAVE

por [por] *prep* **1** (*objetivo*) for; **luchar por la patria** to fight for one's country **2** (+ *infin*): **por no llegar tarde** so as not to arrive late; **por citar unos ejemplos** to give a few examples **3** (*causa*) out of, because of; **por escasez de fondos** through o for lack of funds **4** (*tiempo*): **por la mañana/noche** in the morning/at night; **se queda por una semana** she's staying (for) a week **5** (*lugar*): **pasar por Madrid** to pass through Madrid; **ir a Guayaquil por Quito** to go to Guayaquil via Quito; **caminar por la calle** to walk along the street; **¿hay un banco por aquí?** is there a bank near here? **6** (*cambio, precio*): **te doy uno nuevo por el que tienes** I'll give you a new one (in return) for the one you've got **7** (*valor distributivo*): **30 euros por hora/cabeza** 30 euros an o per hour/a o per head **8** (*modo, medio*) by; **por correo/avión** by post/air; **entrar por la entrada principal** to go in through the main entrance **9** (*agente*) by; **hecho por él** done by him **10**: **10 por 10 son 100** 10 times 10 is 100 **11** (*en lugar de*): **vino él por su jefe** he came instead of his boss **12**: **por mí que revienten** as far as I'm concerned they can drop dead **13**: **por qué** why; **¿por qué?** why?; **¿por qué no?** why not?

porcelana [porθe'lana] *nf* porcelain; (*china*) china
porcentaje [porθen'taxe] *nm* percentage

porción [por'θjon] *nf* (*parte*) portion, share; (*cantidad*) quantity, amount
porfiar [por'fjar] /1c/ *vi* to persist, insist; (*disputar*) to argue stubbornly
pormenor [porme'nor] *nm* detail, particular
pornografía [pornoɣra'fia] *nf* pornography
poro ['poro] *nm* pore
pororó [poro'ro] *nm* (*LAM*) popcorn
poroso, -a [po'roso, a] *adj* porous
poroto [po'roto] *nm* (*LAM*) stick, kidney bean
porque ['porke] *conj* (*a causa de*) because; (*ya que*) since; (*con el fin de*) so that, in order that
porqué [por'ke] *nm* reason, cause
porquería [porke'ria] *nf* (*suciedad*) filth, dirt; (*acción*) dirty trick; (*objeto*) small thing, trifle; (*fig*) rubbish
porra ['porra] *nf* (*arma*) stick, club
porrazo [po'rraθo] *nm* (*golpe*) blow; (*caída*) bump
porro ['porro] *nm* (*fam: droga*) joint
porrón [po'rron] *nm* glass wine jar with a long spout
portaaviones [port(a)a'βjones] *nm inv* aircraft carrier
portada [por'taða] *nf* (*de revista*) cover
portador, a [porta'ðor, a] *nm/f* carrier, bearer; (*Com*) bearer, payee
portaequipajes [portaeki'paxes] *nm inv* boot (*BRIT*), trunk (*US*); (*baca*) luggage rack
portafolio [porta'foljo] *nm* briefcase
portal [por'tal] *nm* (*entrada*) vestibule, hall; (*pórtico*) porch, doorway; (*puerta de entrada*) main door; (*Internet*) portal; **portales** *nmpl* arcade *sg*
portamaletas [portama'letas] *nm inv* (*Auto: maletero*) boot; (*: baca*) roof rack
portamonedas [portamo'neðas] *nm inv* (*LAM*) purse
portar [por'tar] /1a/ *vt* to carry; **portarse** *vr* to behave, conduct o.s.
portátil [por'tatil] *adj* portable; **(ordenador) ~** laptop (computer)

portavoz [porta'βoθ] *nmf* spokesman/woman

portazo [por'taθo] *nm*: **dar un ~** to slam the door

porte ['porte] *nm* (*Com*) transport; (*precio*) transport charges *pl*

portentoso, -a [porten'toso, a] *adj* marvellous, extraordinary

porteño, -a [por'teɲo, a] *adj* of o from Buenos Aires

portería [porte'ria] *nf* (*oficina*) porter's office; (*gol*) goal

portero, -a [por'tero, a] *nm/f* porter; (*conserje*) caretaker; (*ujier*) doorman; (*Deporte*) goalkeeper; **~ automático** (*ESP*) entry phone

pórtico ['portiko] *nm* (*porche*) portico, porch; (*fig*) gateway; (*arcada*) arcade

portorriqueño, -a [portorri'keɲo, a] *adj* Puerto Rican

Portugal [portu'ɣal] *nm* Portugal; **portugués, -esa** *adj, nm/f* Portuguese ▷ *nm* (*Ling*) Portuguese

porvenir [porβe'nir] *nm* future

pos [pos]: **en ~ de** *prep* after, in pursuit of

posaderas [posa'ðeras] *nfpl* backside *sg*, buttocks

posar [po'sar] /1a/ *vt* (*en el suelo*) to lay down, put down; (*la mano*) to place, put gently ▷ *vi* to sit, pose; **posarse** *vr* to settle; (*pájaro*) to perch; (*avión*) to land, come down

posavasos [posa'basos] *nm inv* coaster; (*para cerveza*) beermat

posdata [pos'ðata] *nf* postscript

pose ['pose] *nf* pose

poseedor, a [posee'ðor, a] *nm/f* owner, possessor; (*de récord, puesto*) holder

poseer [pose'er] /2e/ *vt* to have, possess, own; (*ventaja*) to enjoy; (*récord, puesto*) to hold

posesivo, -a [pose'siβo, a] *adj* possessive

posgrado [pos'ɣraðo] *nm* = postgrado

posibilidad [posiβili'ðað] *nf* possibility; (*oportunidad*) chance; **posibilitar** /1a/ *vt* to make possible; (*hacer factible*) to make feasible

posible [po'siβle] *adj* possible; (*factible*) feasible; **de ser ~** if possible; **en o dentro de lo ~** as far as possible

posición [posi'θjon] *nf* position; (*rango social*) status

positivo, -a [posi'tiβo, a] *adj* positive

poso ['poso] *nm* sediment; (*heces*) dregs *pl*

posponer [pospo'ner] /2q/ *vt* (*relegar*) to put behind o below; (*aplazar*) to postpone

post [post] (*pl* **posts**) *nm* (*en sitio web*) post

posta ['posta] *nf*: **a ~** on purpose, deliberately

postal [pos'tal] *adj* postal ▷ *nf* postcard

poste ['poste] *nm* (*de telégrafos*) post, pole; (*columna*) pillar

póster ['poster] (*pl* **posters**) *nm* poster

posterior [poste'rjor] *adj* back, rear; (*siguiente*) following, subsequent; (*más tarde*) later

postgrado [post'ɣraðo] *nm*: **curso de ~** postgraduate course

postizo, -a [pos'tiθo, a] *adj* false, artificial ▷ *nm* hairpiece

postre ['postre] *nm* sweet, dessert

póstumo, -a ['postumo, a] *adj* posthumous

postura [pos'tura] *nf* (*del cuerpo*) posture, position; (*fig*) attitude, position

potable [po'taβle] *adj* drinkable; **agua ~** drinking water

potaje [po'taxe] *nm* thick vegetable soup

potencia [po'tenθja] *nf* power; **potencial** *adj, nm* potential

potente [po'tente] *adj* powerful

potro ['potro] *nm* (*Zool*) colt; (*Deporte*) vaulting horse

pozo ['poθo] nm well; (de río) deep pool; (de mina) shaft

PP nm abr = **Partido Popular**

práctica ['praktika] nf V **práctico**

practicable [prakti'kaβle] adj practicable; (camino) passable

practicante [prakti'kante] nmf (Med: ayudante de doctor) medical assistant; (: enfermero) nurse; (el que practica algo) practitioner ▷ adj practising

practicar [prakti'kar] /1g/ vt to practise; (deporte) to go in for, play; (ejecutar) to carry out, perform

práctico, -a ['praktiko, a] adj practical; (instruido: persona) skilled, expert ▷ nf practice; (método) method; (arte, capacidad) skill; **en la práctica** in practice

practique etc [prak'tike] vb V **practicar**

pradera [pra'ðera] nf meadow; (de Canadá) prairie

prado ['praðo] nm (campo) meadow, field; (pastizal) pasture

Praga ['praγa] nf Prague

pragmático, -a [praγ'matiko, a] adj pragmatic

precario, -a [pre'karjo, a] adj precarious

precaución [prekau'θjon] nf (medida preventiva) preventive measure, precaution; (prudencia) caution, wariness

precedente [preθe'ðente] adj preceding; (anterior) former ▷ nm precedent

preceder [preθe'ðer] /2a/ vt, vi to precede, go/come before

precepto [pre'θepto] nm precept

precinto [pre'θinto] nm (tb: ~ de garantía) seal

precio ['preθjo] nm price; (costo) cost; (valor) value, worth; (de viaje) fare; ~ de coste o de cobertura cost price; ~ al contado cash price; ~ al detalle o al por menor retail price; ~ de salida upset price; ~ tope top price

preciosidad [preθjosi'ðað] nf (valor) (high) value, (great) worth; (encanto) charm; (cosa bonita) beautiful thing; **es una ~** it's lovely, it's really beautiful

precioso, -a [pre'θjoso, a] adj precious; (de mucho valor) valuable; (fam) lovely, beautiful

precipicio [preθi'piθjo] nm cliff, precipice; (fig) abyss

precipitación [preθipita'θjon] nf haste; (lluvia) rainfall

precipitado, -a [preθipi'taðo, a] adj hasty, rash; (salida) hasty, sudden

precipitar [preθipi'tar] /1a/ vt (arrojar) to hurl, throw; (apresurar) to hasten; (acelerar) to speed up, accelerate; **precipitarse** vr to throw o.s.; (apresurarse) to rush; (actuar sin pensar) to act rashly

precisamente [preθisa'mente] adv precisely; (justo) precisely, exactly

precisar [preθi'sar] /1a/ vt (necesitar) to need, require; (fijar) to determine exactly, fix; (especificar) to specify

precisión [preθi'sjon] nf (exactitud) precision

preciso, -a [pre'θiso, a] adj (exacto) precise; (necesario) necessary, essential

preconcebido, -a [prekonθe'βiðo, a] adj preconceived

precoz [pre'koθ] adj (persona) precocious; (calvicie) premature

predecir [preðe'θir] /3o/ vt to predict, forecast

predestinado, -a [preðesti'naðo, a] adj predestined

predicar [preði'kar] /1g/ vt, vi to preach

predicción [preðik'θjon] nf prediction

predilecto, -a [preði'lekto, a] adj favourite

predisposición [preðisposi'θjon] nf inclination; prejudice, bias

predominar [preðomi'nar] /1a/ vt to dominate ▷ vi to predominate;

(*prevalecer*) to prevail; **predominio** *nm*
predominance; prevalence

preescolar [preesko'lar] *adj*
preschool

prefabricado, -a [prefaβri'kaðo, a]
adj prefabricated

prefacio [pre'faθjo] *nm* preface

preferencia [prefe'renθja] *nf*
preference; **de ~** preferably, for
preference

preferible [prefe'riβle] *adj* preferable

preferido, -a [prefe'riðo, a] *adj, nm/f*
favourite, favorite (*us*)

preferir [prefe'rir] /3i/ *vt* to prefer

prefiero *etc* [pre'fjero] *vb* V **preferir**

prefijo [pre'fixo] *nm* (*Telec*) (dialling)
code

pregunta [pre'ɣunta] *nf* question;
hacer una ~ to ask a question; **~s
frecuentes** FAQs, frequently asked
questions; **preguntar** /1a/ *vt* to
ask; (*cuestionar*) to question ▷ *vi* to
ask; **preguntarse** *vr* to wonder;
preguntar por algn to ask for sb;
preguntón, -ona *adj* inquisitive

prehistórico, -a [preis'toriko, a] *adj*
prehistoric

prejuicio [pre'xwiθjo] *nm*
prejudgement; (*preconcepción*)
preconception; (*pey*) prejudice, bias

preludio [pre'luðjo] *nm* prelude

prematuro, -a [prema'turo, a] *adj*
premature

premeditar [premeði'tar] /1a/ *vt* to
premeditate

premiar [pre'mjar] /1b/ *vt* to reward;
(*en un concurso*) to give a prize to

premio ['premjo] *nm* reward; prize;
(*Com*) premium

prenatal [prena'tal] *adj* antenatal,
prenatal

prenda ['prenda] *nf* (*de ropa*)
garment, article of clothing;
(*garantía*) pledge; **prendas** *nfpl*
talents, gifts

prender [pren'der] /2a/ *vt* (*captar*)
to catch, capture; (*detener*) to arrest;
(*coser*) to pin, attach; (*sujetar*) to fasten

▷ *vi* to catch; (*arraigar*) to take root;
prenderse *vr* (*encenderse*) to catch fire

prendido, -a [pren'diðo, a] *adj*
(*LAM: luz*) on

prensa ['prensa] *nf* press; **la P~**
the press

preñado, -a [pre'ɲaðo, a] *adj*
pregnant; **~ de** pregnant with, full of

preocupación [preokupa'θjon] *nf*
worry, concern; (*ansiedad*) anxiety

preocupado, -a [preoku'paðo, a] *adj*
worried, concerned; anxious

preocupar [preoku'par] /1a/ *vt* to
worry; **preocuparse** *vr* to worry; **~se
de algo** (*hacerse cargo de algo*) to take
care of sth

preparación [prepara'θjon] *nf*
(*acto*) preparation; (*estado*) readiness;
(*entrenamiento*) training

preparado, -a [prepa'raðo, a] *adj*
(*dispuesto*) prepared; (*Culin*) ready (to
serve) ▷ *nm* preparation

preparar [prepa'rar] /1a/ *vt* (*disponer*)
to prepare, get ready; (*Tec: tratar*)
to prepare, process; (*entrenar*) to
teach, train; **prepararse** *vr*: **~se
a o para hacer algo** to prepare o
get ready to do sth; **preparativo,
-a** *adj* preparatory, preliminary;
preparativos *nmpl* preparations;
preparatoria *nf* (*LAM*) sixth form
college (*BRIT*), senior high school (*us*)

presa ['presa] *nf* (*cosa apresada*) catch;
(*víctima*) victim; (*de animal*) prey; (*de
agua*) dam

presagiar [presa'xjar] /1b/ *vt* to
presage; **presagio** *nm* omen

prescindir [presθin'dir] /3a/ *vi*: **~ de**
(*privarse de*) to do without, go without;
(*descartar*) to dispense with

prescribir [preskri'βir] /3a/ *vt* to
prescribe

presencia [pre'senθja] *nf* presence;
presenciar /1b/ *vt* to be present at;
(*asistir a*) to attend; (*ver*) to see, witness

presentación [presenta'θjon]
nf presentation; (*introducción*)
introduction

P

presentador, a [presenta'ðor, a] nm/f compère

presentar [presen'tar] /1a/ vt to present; (ofrecer) to offer; (mostrar) to show, display; (a una persona) to introduce; **presentarse** vr (llegar inesperadamente) to appear, turn up; (ofrecerse: como candidato) to run, stand; (aparecer) to show, appear; (solicitar empleo) to apply

presente [pre'sente] adj present ▷ nm present; **hacer ~** to state, declare; **tener ~** to remember, bear in mind

presentimiento [presenti'mjento] nm premonition, presentiment

presentir [presen'tir] /3i/ vt to have a premonition of

preservación [preserβa'θjon] nf protection, preservation

preservar [preser'βar] /1a/ vt to protect, preserve; **preservativo** nm sheath, condom

presidencia [presi'ðenθja] nf presidency; (de comité) chairmanship

presidente [presi'ðente] nmf president; (de comité) chairman/woman

presidir [presi'ðir] /3a/ vt (dirigir) to preside at, preside over; (: comité) to take the chair at; (dominar) to dominate, rule ▷ vi to preside; to take the chair

presión [pre'sjon] nf pressure; **~ atmosférica** atmospheric o air pressure; **presionar** /1a/ vt to press; (fig) to press, put pressure on ▷ vi: **presionar para** o **por** to press for

preso, -a ['preso, a] nm/f prisoner; **tomar** o **llevar ~ a algn** to arrest sb, take sb prisoner

prestación [presta'θjon] nf service; (subsidio) benefit; **prestaciones** nfpl (Auto) performance features

prestado, -a [pres'taðo, a] adj on loan; **pedir ~** to borrow

prestamista [presta'mista] nmf moneylender

préstamo ['prestamo] nm loan; **~ hipotecario** mortgage

prestar [pres'tar] /1a/ vt to lend, loan; (atención) to pay; (ayuda) to give; (servicio) to do, render; (juramento) to take, swear; **prestarse** vr (ofrecerse) to offer o volunteer

prestigio [pres'tixjo] nm prestige; **prestigioso, -a** adj (honorable) prestigious; (famoso, renombrado) renowned, famous

presumido, -a [presu'miðo, a] adj conceited

presumir [presu'mir] /3a/ vt to presume ▷ vi (darse aires) to be conceited; **presunto, -a** adj (supuesto) supposed, presumed; (así llamado) so-called; **presuntuoso, -a** adj conceited, presumptuous

presupuesto [presu'pwesto] nm (Finanzas) budget; (estimación: de costo) estimate

pretencioso, -a [preten'θjoso, a] adj pretentious

pretender [preten'der] /2a/ vt (intentar) to try to, seek to; (reivindicar) to claim; (buscar) to seek, try for; (cortejar) to woo, court; **~ que** to expect that; **pretendiente** nmf (amante) suitor; (al trono) pretender; **pretensión** nf (aspiración) aspiration; (reivindicación) claim; (orgullo) pretension

⬛ No confundir pretender con la palabra inglesa pretend.

pretexto [pre'teksto] nm pretext; (excusa) excuse

prevención [preβen'θjon] nf prevention; (precaución) precaution

prevenido, -a [preβe'niðo, a] adj prepared, ready; (cauteloso) cautious

prevenir [preβe'nir] /3r/ vt (impedir) to prevent; (predisponer) to prejudice, bias; (avisar) to warn; (preparar) to prepare, get ready; **prevenirse** vr to get ready, prepare; **~se contra** to take precautions against; **preventivo, -a** adj preventive, precautionary

prever [pre'βer] /2u/ vt to foresee
previo, -a ['preβjo, a] adj (anterior) previous; (preliminar) preliminary ▷ prep: **~ acuerdo de los otros** subject to the agreement of the others
previsión [preβi'sjon] nf (perspicacia) foresight; (predicción) forecast; **previsto, -a** adj anticipated, forecast
prima ['prima] nf V **primo**
primario, -a [pri'marjo, a] adj primary
primavera [prima'βera] nf (temporada) spring; (período) springtime
Primer Ministro [pri'mer-] nm Prime Minister
primero, -a [pri'mero, a] adj first; (fig) prime ▷ adv first; (más bien) sooner, rather ▷ nf (Auto) first gear; (Ferro) first class; **de primera** (fam) first-class, first-rate; **primera plana** front page
primitivo, -a [primi'tiβo, a] adj primitive; (original) original
primo, -a ['primo, a] adj (Mat) prime ▷ nm/f cousin; (fam) fool, idiot ▷ nf (Com) bonus; (de seguro) premium; **~ hermano** first cousin; **hacer el ~** to be taken for a ride
primogénito, -a [primo'xenito, a] adj first-born
primoroso, -a [primo'roso, a] adj exquisite, fine
princesa [prin'θesa] nf princess
principal [prinθi'pal] adj principal, main ▷ nm (jefe) chief, principal
príncipe ['prinθipe] nm prince
principiante [prinθi'pjante] nmf beginner
principio [prin'θipjo] nm (comienzo) beginning, start; (origen) origin; (base) rudiment, basic idea; (moral) principle; **a ~s de** at the beginning of; **desde el ~** from the first; **en un ~** at first
pringue ['pringe] nm (grasa) grease, fat, dripping
prioridad [priori'ðað] nf priority

prisa ['prisa] nf (apresuramiento) hurry, haste; (rapidez) speed; (urgencia) (sense of) urgency; **a o de ~** quickly; **correr ~** to be urgent; **darse ~** to hurry up; **estar de o tener ~** to be in a hurry
prisión [pri'sjon] nf (cárcel) prison; (período de cárcel) imprisonment; **prisionero, -a** nm/f prisoner
prismáticos [pris'matikos] nmpl binoculars
privado, -a [pri'βaðo, a] adj private
privar [pri'βar] /1a/ vt to deprive; **privativo, -a** adj exclusive
privilegiar [priβile'xjar] /1b/ vt to grant a privilege to; (favorecer) to favour
privilegio [priβi'lexjo] nm privilege; (concesión) concession
pro [pro] nm o f profit, advantage ▷ prep: **asociación ~ ciegos** association for the blind ▷ pref: **~ soviético/americano** pro-Soviet/-American; **en ~ de** on behalf of, for; **los ~s y los contras** the pros and cons
proa ['proa] nf (Naut) bow, prow; **de ~** bow cpd, fore; V tb **popa**
probabilidad [proβaβili'ðað] nf probability, likelihood; (oportunidad, posibilidad) chance, prospect; **probable** adj probable, likely
probador [proβa'ðor] nm (en una tienda) fitting room
probar [pro'βar] /1l/ vt (demostrar) to prove; (someter a prueba) to test, try out; (ropa) to try on; (comida) to taste ▷ vi to try; **probarse** vr: **~se un traje** to try on a suit
probeta [pro'βeta] nf test tube
problema [pro'βlema] nm problem
procedente [proθe'ðente] adj (razonable) reasonable; (conforme a derecho) proper, fitting; **~ de** coming from, originating in
proceder [proθe'ðer] /2a/ vi (avanzar) to proceed; (actuar) to act; (ser correcto) to be right (and proper), to be fitting ▷ nm (comportamiento) behaviour, conduct; **~ de** to come from, originate

in; **procedimiento** nm procedure; (proceso) process; (método) means, method

procesador [proθesa'ðor] nm: **~ de textos** word processor

procesar [proθe'sar] /1a/ vt to try, put on trial; (Inform) to process

procesión [proθe'sjon] nf procession

proceso [pro'θeso] nm process; (Jur) trial

proclamar [prokla'mar] /1a/ vt to proclaim

procrear [prokre'ar] /1a/ vt, vi to procreate

procurador, a [prokura'ðor, a] nm/f attorney

procurar [proku'rar] /1a/ vt (intentar) to try, endeavour; (conseguir) to get, obtain; (asegurar) to secure; (producir) to produce

prodigio [pro'ðixjo] nm prodigy; (milagro) wonder, marvel; **prodigioso, -a** adj prodigious, marvellous

pródigo, -a ['proðiyo, a] adj: **hijo ~** prodigal son

producción [proðuk'θjon] nf production; (suma de productos) output; **~ en serie** mass production

producir [proðu'θir] /3n/ vt to produce; (generar) to cause, bring about; **producirse** vr (cambio) to come about; (hacerse) to be produced, be made; (estallar) to break out; (accidente) to take place; (problema etc) to arise

productividad [proðuktiβi'ðað] nf productivity; **productivo, -a** adj productive; (provechoso) profitable

producto [pro'ðukto] nm product

productor, a [proðuk'tor, a] adj productive, producing ▷ nm/f producer

proeza [pro'eθa] nf exploit, feat

profano, -a [pro'fano, a] adj profane ▷ nm/f layman/woman

profecía [profe'θia] nf prophecy

profesión [profe'sjon] nf profession; (en formulario) occupation; **profesional** adj professional

profesor, a [profe'sor, a] nm/f teacher; **profesorado** nm teaching profession

profeta [pro'feta] nmf prophet

prófugo, -a ['profuxo, a] nm/f fugitive; (desertor) deserter

profundidad [profundi'ðað] nf depth; **profundizar** /1f/ (fig) vt to go into deeply ▷ vi: **profundizar en** to go into deeply; **profundo, -a** adj deep; (misterio, pensador) profound

progenitor [proxeni'tor] nm ancestor; **progenitores** nmpl parents

programa [pro'yrama] nm programme; (Inform) program; **~ de estudios** curriculum, syllabus; **programación** nf (Inform) programming; **programador, a** nm/f (computer) programmer; **programar** /1a/ vt (Inform) to program

progresar [proyre'sar] /1a/ vi to progress, make progress; **progresista** adj, nmf progressive; **progresivo, -a** adj progressive; (gradual) gradual; (continuo) continuous; **progreso** nm progress

prohibición [proiβi'θjon] nf prohibition, ban; **levantar la ~ de** to remove the ban on

prohibir [proi'βir] /3a/ vt to prohibit, ban, forbid; **se prohíbe fumar** no smoking; **"prohibido el paso"** "no entry"

prójimo ['proximo] nm fellow man

prólogo ['proloyo] nm prologue

prolongar [prolon'gar] /1h/ vt to extend; (en el tiempo) to prolong; (calle, tubo) to make longer, extend

promedio [pro'meðjo] nm average; (de distancia) middle, mid-point

promesa [pro'mesa] nf promise

prometer [prome'ter] /2a/ vt to promise ▷ vi to show promise; **prometerse** vr (dos personas) to get engaged; **prometido, -a** adj promised; engaged ▷ nm/f fiancé/fiancée

prominente [promi'nente] adj prominent

promoción [promo'θjon] nf
promotion

promotor [promo'tor] nm promoter;
(*instigador*) instigator

promover [promo'βer] /2h/ vt to
promote; (*causar*) to cause; (*motín*) to
instigate, stir up

promulgar [promul'ɣar] /1h/ vt to
promulgate; (*fig*) to proclaim

pronombre [pro'nombre] nm
pronoun

pronosticar [pronosti'kar] /1g/ vt to
predict, foretell, forecast; **pronóstico**
nm prediction, forecast; **pronóstico
del tiempo** weather forecast

pronto, -a ['pronto, a] adj (*rápido*)
prompt, quick; (*preparado*) ready ▷ adv
quickly, promptly; (*en seguida*) at once,
right away; (*dentro de poco*) soon;
(*temprano*) early ▷ nm: **de ~** suddenly;
tiene unos ~s muy malos he gets
ratty all of a sudden (*fam*); **por lo ~**
meanwhile, for the present

pronunciación [pronunθja'θjon] nf
pronunciation

pronunciar [pronun'θjar] /1b/ vt to
pronounce; (*discurso*) to make, deliver;
pronunciarse vr to revolt, rebel;
(*declararse*) to declare o.s.

propagación [propaɣa'θjon] nf
propagation

propaganda [propa'ɣanda] nf
(*política*) propaganda; (*comercial*)
advertising

propenso, -a [pro'penso, a] adj:
~ a prone o inclined to; **ser ~ a hacer
algo** to be inclined o have a tendency
to do sth

propicio, -a [pro'piθjo, a] adj
favourable, propitious

propiedad [propje'ðað] nf property;
(*posesión*) possession, ownership;
~ particular private property

propietario, -a [propje'tarjo, a]
nm/f owner, proprietor

propina [pro'pina] nf tip

propio, -a ['propjo, a] adj own,
of one's own; (*característico*)
characteristic, typical; (*conveniente*)
proper; (*mismo*) selfsame, very; **el
~ ministro** the minister himself;
¿tienes casa propia? have you a
house of your own?

proponer [propo'ner] /2q/ vt to
propose, put forward; (*problema*)
to pose; **proponerse** vr to propose,
intend

proporción [propor'θjon] nf
proportion; (*Mat*) ratio; **proporciones**
nfpl (*fig*) dimensions; size sg;
proporcionado, -a adj proportionate;
(*regular*) medium, middling; (*justo*) just
right; **proporcionar** /1a/ vt (*dar*) to
give, supply, provide

proposición [proposi'θjon] nf
proposition; (*propuesta*) proposal

propósito [pro'posito] nm purpose;
(*intento*) aim, intention ▷ adv: **a ~**
by the way, incidentally; (*a posta*) on
purpose, deliberately; **a ~ de** about,
with regard to

propuesto, -a [pro'pwesto, a] pp de
proponer ▷ nf proposal

propulsar [propul'sar] /1a/ vt
to drive, propel; (*fig*) to promote,
encourage; **propulsión** nf propulsion;
propulsión a chorro o **por reacción**
jet propulsion

prórroga ['prorroɣa] nf extension;
(*Jur*) stay; (*Com*) deferment; (*Deporte*)
extra time; **prorrogar** /1h/ vt (*período*)
to extend; (*decisión*) to defer, postpone

prosa ['prosa] nf prose

proseguir [prose'ɣir] /3d, **3k**/ vt to
continue, carry on ▷ vi to continue,
go on

prospecto [pros'pekto] nm
prospectus

prosperar [prospe'rar] /1a/ vi to
prosper, thrive, flourish; **prosperidad**
nf prosperity; (*éxito*) success;
próspero, -a adj prosperous, thriving;
(*que tiene éxito*) successful

prostíbulo [pros'tiβulo] nm brothel

prostitución [prostitu'θjon] nf
prostitution

P

prostituir [prosti'twir] /3g/ *vt*
to prostitute; **prostituirse** *vr* to
prostitute o.s., become a prostitute

prostituta [prosti'tuta] *nf* prostitute

protagonista [protaɣo'nista] *nmf*
protagonist

protección [protek'θjon] *nf*
protection

protector, a [protek'tor, a] *adj*
protective, protecting ▷ *nm/f*
protector

proteger [prote'xer] /2c/ *vt* to
protect; **protegido, -a** *nm/f* protégé/
protégée

proteína [prote'ina] *nf* protein

protesta [pro'testa] *nf* protest;
(*declaración*) protestation

protestante [protes'tante] *adj*
Protestant

protestar [protes'tar] /1a/ *vt* to
protest, declare ▷ *vi* to protest

protocolo [proto'kolo] *nm* protocol

prototipo [proto'tipo] *nm* prototype

provecho [pro'βetʃo] *nm* advantage,
benefit; (*Finanzas*) profit; **¡buen ~!**
bon appétit!; **en ~ de** to the benefit
of; **sacar ~ de** to benefit from,
profit by

provenir [proβe'nir] /3r/ *vi*: **~ de** to
come from

proverbio [pro'βerβjo] *nm* proverb

providencia [proβi'ðenθja] *nf*
providence

provincia [pro'βinθja] *nf* province

provisión [proβi'sjon] *nf* provision;
(*abastecimiento*) provision, supply;
(*medida*) measure, step

provisional [proβisjo'nal] *adj*
provisional

provocar [proβo'kar] /1g/ *vt* to
provoke; (*alentar*) to tempt, invite;
(*causar*) to bring about, lead to;
(*promover*) to promote; (*estimular*) to
rouse, stimulate; (*LAM*): **¿te provoca
un café?** would you like a coffee?;
provocativo, -a *adj* provocative

proxeneta [prokse'neta] *nmf* (*de
prostitutas*) pimp/procuress

próximamente [proksima'mente]
adv shortly, soon

proximidad [proksimi'ðað] *nf*
closeness, proximity; **próximo, -a** *adj*
near, close; (*vecino*) neighbouring; (*el
que viene*) next

proyectar [projek'tar] /1a/ *vt*
(*objeto*) to hurl, throw; (*luz*) to cast,
shed; (*Cine*) to screen, show; (*planear*)
to plan

proyectil [projek'til] *nm* projectile,
missile

proyecto [pro'jekto] *nm* plan;
(*estimación de costo*) detailed estimate

proyector [projek'tor] *nm* (*Cine*)
projector

prudencia [pru'ðenθja] *nf* (*sabiduría*)
wisdom; (*cautela*) care; **prudente** *adj*
sensible, wise; (*cauteloso*) careful

prueba ['prweβa] *vb V* **probar** ▷ *nf*
proof; (*ensayo*) test, trial; (*saboreo*)
testing, sampling; (*de ropa*) fitting; **a
~** on trial; **a ~ de** proof against; **a ~ de
agua/fuego** waterproof/fireproof;
someter a ~ to put to the test

psico... [siko] *pref* psycho...;
psicología *nf* psychology;
psicológico, -a *adj* psychological;
psicólogo, -a *nm/f* psychologist;
psicópata *nmf* psychopath; **psicosis**
nf inv psychosis

psiquiatra [si'kjatra] *nmf*
psychiatrist; **psiquiátrico, -a** *adj*
psychiatric

PSOE [pe'soe] *nm abr* = **Partido
Socialista Obrero Español**

púa *nf* (*Bot, Zool*) prickle, spine; (*para
guitarra*) plectrum; **alambre de ~s**
barbed wire

pubertad [puβer'tað] *nf* puberty

publicación [puβlika'θjon] *nf*
publication

publicar [puβli'kar] /1g/ *vt* (*editar*)
to publish; (*hacer público*) to publicize;
(*divulgar*) to make public, divulge

publicidad [puβliθi'ðað] *nf* publicity;
(*Com*) advertising; **publicitario, -a** *adj*
publicity *cpd*; advertising *cpd*

público, -a ['puβliko, a] adj public
▷ nm public; (Teat etc) audience

puchero [pu'tʃero] nm (Culin: olla)
cooking pot; (: guiso) stew; **hacer
~s** to pout

pucho ['putʃo] (LAM fam) nm cigarette,
fag (BRIT)

pude etc vb V **poder**

pudiente [pu'ðjente] adj (opulento)
wealthy

pudiera etc vb V **poder**

pudor [pu'ðor] nm modesty

pudrir [pu'ðrir] /3a/ vt to rot;
pudrirse vr to rot, decay

pueblo ['pweβlo] nm people; (nación)
nation; (aldea) village

puedo etc ['pweðo] vb V **poder**

puente ['pwente] nm bridge; **~
aéreo** shuttle service; **~ colgante**
suspension bridge; **~ levadizo**
drawbridge; **hacer ~** (fam) to take a
long weekend

⊙ **HACER PUENTE**
⊙
⊙ When a public holiday in Spain
⊙ falls on a Tuesday or Thursday it is
⊙ common practice for employers to
⊙ make the Monday or Friday a holiday
⊙ as well and to give everyone a four-
⊙ day holiday. This is known as hacer
⊙ puente. When a named public holiday
⊙ such as the Día de la Constitución falls
⊙ on a Tuesday or Thursday, people
⊙ refer to the whole holiday period as
⊙ e.g. the puente de la Constitución.

puerco, -a ['pwerko, a] adj (sucio)
dirty, filthy; (obsceno) disgusting
▷ nm/f pig/sow; **~ espín** porcupine

pueril [pwe'ril] adj childish

puerro ['pwerro] nm leek

puerta ['pwerta] nf door; (de jardín)
gate; (portal) doorway; (fig) gateway;
(gol) goal; **a la ~** at the door; **a ~
cerrada** behind closed doors; **~
corredera/giratoria** sliding/swing o
revolving door

puerto ['pwerto] nm port; (paso) pass;
(fig) haven, refuge

Puerto Rico [pwerto'riko] nm
Puerto Rico; **puertorriqueño, -a** adj,
nm/f Puerto Rican

pues [pwes] adv (entonces) then;
(¡entonces!) well, well then; (así que)
so ▷ conj (porque) since; **¡~ sí!** yes!,
certainly!

puesto, -a ['pwesto, a] pp de **poner**
▷ adj dressed ▷ nm (lugar, posición)
place; (trabajo) post, job; (Com) stall
▷ conj: **~ que** since, as ▷ nf (apuesta)
bet, stake; **tener algo ~** to have sth
on, to be wearing sth; **~ de mercado**
market stall; **~ de policía** police
station; **~ de socorro** first aid post;
puesta al día updating; **puesta en
marcha** starting; **puesta a punto**
fine tuning; **puesta del sol** sunset

púgil ['puxil] nm boxer

pulga ['pulɣa] nf flea

pulgada [pul'ɣaða] nf inch

pulgar [pul'ɣar] nm thumb

pulir [pu'lir] /3a/ vt to polish;
(alisar) to smooth; (fig) to polish up,
touch up

pulmón [pul'mon] nm lung;
pulmonía nf pneumonia

pulpa ['pulpa] nf pulp; (de fruta) flesh,
soft part

pulpería [pulpe'ria] nf (LAM) small
grocery store

púlpito ['pulpito] nm pulpit

pulpo ['pulpo] nm octopus

pulque ['pulke] nm pulque

⊙ **PULQUE**
⊙
⊙ Pulque is a thick, white, alcoholic
⊙ drink which is very popular in
⊙ Mexico. In ancient times it was
⊙ considered sacred by the Aztecs. It
⊙ is produced by fermenting the juice
⊙ of the maguey, a Mexican cactus
⊙ similar to the agave. It can be drunk
⊙ by itself or mixed with fruit or
⊙ vegetable juice.

pulsación [pulsa'θjon] *nf* beat; **pulsaciones** pulse rate

pulsar [pul'sar] /1a/ *vt* (*tecla*) to touch, tap; (*Mus*) to play; (*botón*) to press, push ▷ *vi* to pulsate; (*latir*) to beat, throb

pulsera [pul'sera] *nf* bracelet

pulso ['pulso] *nm* (*Med*) pulse; (*fuerza*) strength; (*firmeza*) steadiness, steady hand

pulverizador [pulβeriθa'ðor] *nm* spray, spray gun

pulverizar [pulβeri'θar] /1f/ *vt* to pulverize; (*líquido*) to spray

puna ['puna] *nf* (*LAM*) mountain sickness

punta ['punta] *nf* point, tip; (*extremidad*) end; (*fig*) touch, trace; **horas ~s** peak hours, rush hours; **sacar ~ a** to sharpen

puntada [pun'taða] *nf* (*Costura*) stitch

puntal [pun'tal] *nm* prop, support

puntapié [punta'pje] *nm* kick

puntería [punte'ria] *nf* (*de arma*) aim, aiming; (*destreza*) marksmanship

puntero, -a [pun'tero, a] *adj* leading ▷ *nm* (*señal, Inform*) pointer

puntiagudo, -a [puntja'ɣuðo, a] *adj* sharp, pointed

puntilla [pun'tiʎa] *nf* (*Costura*) lace edging; **(andar) de ~s** (to walk) on tiptoe

punto ['punto] *nm* (*gen*) point; (*señal diminuta*) spot, dot; (*lugar*) spot, place; (*momento*) point, moment; (*Costura*) stitch; **a ~** ready; **estar a ~ de** to be on the point of o about to; **en ~** on the dot; **hasta cierto ~** to some extent; **hacer ~** to knit; **~ de vista** point of view, viewpoint; **~ muerto** dead centre; (*Auto*) neutral (gear); **~ final** full stop; **dos ~s** colon; **~ y coma** semicolon; **~ acápite** (*LAM*) full stop, new paragraph; **~ de interrogación** question mark

puntocom [punto'kom] *nf inv, adj inv* dotcom

puntuación [puntwa'θjon] *nf* punctuation; (*puntos: en examen*) mark(s) *pl*; (*: Deporte*) score

puntual [pun'twal] *adj* (*a tiempo*) punctual; (*cálculo*) exact, accurate; **puntualidad** *nf* punctuality; exactness, accuracy

puntuar [pun'twar] /1e/ *vi* (*Deporte*) to score, count

punzante [pun'θante] *adj* (*dolor*) shooting, sharp; (*herramienta*) sharp

puñado [pu'ɲaðo] *nm* handful (*tb fig*)

puñal [pu'ɲal] *nm* dagger; **puñalada** *nf* stab

puñetazo [puɲe'taθo] *nm* punch

puño ['puɲo] *nm* (*Anat*) fist; (*cantidad*) fistful, handful; (*Costura*) cuff; (*de herramienta*) handle

pupila [pu'pila] *nf* pupil

pupitre [pu'pitre] *nm* desk

puré [pu're] *nm* purée; (*sopa*) (thick) soup; **~ de patatas** (*ESP*), **~ de papas** (*LAM*) mashed potatoes

purga ['purɣa] *nf* purge; **purgante** *adj, nm* purgative

purgatorio [purɣa'torjo] *nm* purgatory

purificar [purifi'kar] /1g/ *vt* to purify; (*refinar*) to refine

puritano, -a [puri'tano, a] *adj* (*actitud*) puritanical; (*iglesia, tradición*) puritan ▷ *nm/f* puritan

puro, -a ['puro, a] *adj* pure; (*verdad*) simple, plain ▷ *nm* cigar

púrpura ['purpura] *nf* purple

pus [pus] *nm* pus

puse *etc* ['puse] *vb V* **poner**

pusiera *etc vb V* **poder**

puta ['puta] *nf* whore, prostitute

putrefacción [putrefak'θjon] *nf* rotting, putrefaction

PVP *abr* (*ESP*: = *Precio Venta al Público*) ≈ RRP

PYME ['pime] *nf abr* (= *Pequeña y Mediana Empresa*) SME

q

comes or not
7 (*porque*): **no puedo, que tengo que quedarme en casa** I can't, I've got to stay in
▶ *pron* **1** (*cosa*) that, which; (: *+ prep*) which; **el sombrero que te compraste** the hat (that *o* which) you bought; **la cama en que dormí** the bed (that *o* which) I slept in **2** (*persona: suj*) that, who; (: *objeto*) that, whom; **el amigo que me acompañó al museo** the friend that *o* who went to the museum with me; **la chica que invité** the girl (that *o* whom) I invited

qué [ke] *adj* what?, which? ▷ *pron* what?; **¡~ divertido/asco!** how funny/revolting!; **¿~ edad tienes?** how old are you?; **¿de ~ me hablas?** what are you saying to me?; **¿~ tal?** how are you?, how are things?; **¿~ hay (de nuevo)?** what's new?

quebrado, -a [ke'βraðo, a] *adj* (*roto*) broken ▷ *nm/f* bankrupt ▷ *nm* (*Mat*) fraction

quebrantar [keβran'tar] /1a/ *vt* (*infringir*) to violate, transgress

quebrar [ke'βrar] /1j/ *vt* to break, smash ▷ *vi* to go bankrupt

quedar [ke'ðar] /1a/ *vi* to stay, remain; (*encontrarse*) to be; (*restar*) to remain, be left; **quedarse** *vr* to remain, stay (behind); **~ en** (*acordar*) to agree on/to; **~ por hacer** to be still to be done; **~ ciego/mudo** to be left blind/dumb; **no te queda bien ese vestido** that dress doesn't suit you; **quedamos a las seis** we agreed to meet at six; **~se (con) algo** to keep sth; **~se con algn** (*fam*) to swindle sb; **~se en nada** to come to nothing *o* nought

quedo, -a ['keðo, a] *adj* still ▷ *adv* softly, gently

quehacer [kea'θer] *nm* task, job; **~es (domésticos)** household chores

queja ['kexa] *nf* complaint; **quejarse** /1a/ *vr* (*enfermo*) to moan, groan;

○ **PALABRA CLAVE**

que [ke] *conj* **1** (*con oración subordinada: muchas veces no se traduce*) that; **dijo que vendría** he said (that) he would come; **espero que lo encuentres** I hope (that) you find it; *V tb* **el**
2 (*en oración independiente*): **¡que entre!** send him in; **¡que aproveche!** enjoy your meal!; **¡que se mejore tu padre!** I hope your father gets better
3 (*enfático*): **¿me quieres? — ¡que sí!** do you love me? — of course!
4 (*consecutivo: muchas veces no se traduce*) that; **es tan grande que no lo puedo levantar** it's so big (that) I can't lift it
5 (*comparaciones*) than; **yo que tú/él** if I were you/him; *V tb* **más; menos**
6 (*valor disyuntivo*): **que le guste o no** whether he likes it or not; **que venga o que no venga** whether he

(*protestar*) to complain; **quejarse de que ...** to complain (about the fact) that ...; **quejido** *nm* moan

quemado, -a [ke'maðo, a] *adj* burnt

quemadura [kema'ðura] *nf* burn, scald

quemar [ke'mar] /1a/ *vt* to burn; (*fig: malgastar*) to burn up, squander ▷ *vi* to be burning hot; **quemarse** *vr* (*consumirse*) to burn (up); (*del sol*) to get sunburnt

quemarropa [kema'rropa]: **a ~** *adv* point-blank

quepo *etc* ['kepo] *vb* V **caber**

querella [ke'reʎa] *nf* (*Jur*) charge; (*disputa*) dispute

PALABRA CLAVE

querer [ke'rer] /2t/ *vt* **1** (*desear*) to want; **quiero más dinero** I want more money; **quisiera** o **querría un té** I'd like a tea; **sin querer** unintentionally; **quiero ayudar/que vayas** I want to help/you to go

2 (*preguntas: para pedir u ofrecer algo*): **¿quiere abrir la ventana?** could you open the window?; **¿quieres echarme una mano?** can you give me a hand?

3 (*amar*) to love; **te quiero** I love you; **no estoy enamorado, pero la quiero mucho** I'm not in love, but I'm very fond of her

querido, -a [ke'riðo, a] *adj* dear ▷ *nm/f* darling; (*amante*) lover

queso ['keso] *nm* cheese; **~ rallado** grated cheese; **~ crema** (*LAM*), **~ de untar** (*ESP*) cream cheese; **~ manchego** sheep's milk cheese made in La Mancha; **dárselas con ~ a algn** (*fam*) to take sb in

quicio ['kiθjo] *nm* hinge; **sacar a algn de ~** to drive sb up the wall

quiebra ['kjeβra] *nf* break, split; (*Com*) bankruptcy; (*Econ*) slump

quiebro *etc* ['kjeβro] *nm* (*del cuerpo*) swerve

quien [kjen] *pron relativo* (*suj*) who; **hay ~ piensa que** there are those who think that; **no hay ~ lo haga** no-one will do it

quién [kjen] *pron interrogativo* who; (*complemento*) whom; **¿~ es?** who's there?

quienquiera [kjen'kjera] (*pl* **quienesquiera**) *pron* whoever

quiero *etc* *vb* V **querer**

quieto, -a ['kjeto, a] *adj* still; (*carácter*) placid; **quietud** *nf* stillness

No confundir *quieto* con la palabra inglesa *quiet*.

quilate [ki'late] *nm* carat

químico, -a ['kimiko, a] *adj* chemical ▷ *nm/f* chemist ▷ *nf* chemistry

quincalla [kin'kaʎa] *nf* hardware, ironmongery (*BRIT*)

quince ['kinθe] *num* fifteen; **~ días** a fortnight; **quinceañero, -a** *nm/f* teenager; **quincena** *nf* fortnight; (*pago*) fortnightly pay; **quincenal** *adj* fortnightly

quiniela [ki'njela] *nf* football pools *pl*; **quinielas** *nfpl* pools coupon *sg*

quinientos, -as [ki'njentos, as] *num* five hundred

quinto, -a ['kinto, a] *adj* fifth ▷ *nf* country house; (*Mil*) call-up, draft

quiosco ['kjosko] *nm* (*de música*) bandstand; (*de periódicos*) news stand (*also selling sweets, cigarettes etc*)

quirófano [ki'rofano] *nm* operating theatre

quirúrgico, -a [ki'rurxiko, a] *adj* surgical

quise *etc* ['kise] *vb* V **querer**

quisiera *etc* *vb* V **querer**

quisquilloso [kiski'ʎoso, a] *adj* (*susceptible*) touchy; (*meticuloso*) pernickety

quiste ['kiste] *nm* cyst

quitaesmalte [kitaes'malte] *nm* nail polish remover

quitamanchas [kita'mantʃas] *nm inv* stain remover

quitanieves [kita'njeβes] *nm inv* snowplough (*BRIT*), snowplow (*US*)

quitar [ki'tar] /1a/ *vt* to remove, take away; (*ropa*) to take off; (*dolor*) to relieve ▷ *vi*: **¡quita de ahí!** get away!; **quitarse** *vr* to withdraw; (*ropa*) to take off; **se quitó el sombrero** he took off his hat

Quito ['kito] *n* Quito

quizá(s) [ki'θa(s)] *adv* perhaps, maybe

r

rábano ['raβano] *nm* radish; **me importa un ~** I don't give a damn

rabia ['raβja] *nf (Med)* rabies *sg*; (*ira*) fury, rage; **rabiar** /1b/ *vi* to have rabies; to rage, be furious; **rabiar por algo** to long for sth

rabieta [ra'βjeta] *nf* tantrum, fit of temper

rabino [ra'βino] *nm* rabbi

rabioso, -a [ra'βjoso, a] *adj* rabid; (*fig*) furious

rabo ['raβo] *nm* tail

racha ['ratʃa] *nf* gust of wind; **buena/mala ~** spell of good/ bad luck

racial [ra'θjal] *adj* racial, race *cpd*

racimo [ra'θimo] *nm* bunch

ración [ra'θjon] *nf* portion; **raciones** *nfpl* rations

racional [raθjo'nal] *adj* (*razonable*) reasonable; (*lógico*) rational

racionar [raθjo'nar] /1a/ *vt* to ration (out)

racismo [ra'θismo] *nm* racism;
 racista *adj, nmf* racist

radar [ra'ðar] *nm* radar

radiador [raðja'ðor] *nm* radiator

radiante [ra'ðjante] *adj* radiant

radical [raði'kal] *adj, nmf* radical

radicar [raði'kar] /1g/ *vi*: ~ **en**
 (*dificultad, problema*) to lie in; (*solución*)
 to consist in

radio [ra'ðjo] *nf* radio; (*aparato*)
 radio (set) ▷ *nm* (*Mat*) radius;
 (*Química*) radium; **radioactividad**
 nf radioactivity; **radioactivo, -a** *adj*
 radioactive; **radiografía** *nf* X-ray;
 radioterapia *nf* radiotherapy;
 radioyente *nmf* listener

ráfaga ['rafaɣa] *nf* gust; (*de luz*) flash;
 (*de tiros*) burst

raíz [ra'iθ] *nf* root; ~ **cuadrada** square
 root; **a ~ de** as a result of

raja ['raxa] *nf* (*de melón etc*) slice;
 (*grieta*) crack; **rajar** /1a/ *vt* to split;
 (*fam*) to slash; **rajarse** *vr* to split, crack;
 rajarse de to back out of

rajatabla [raxa'taβla]: **a ~** *adv*
 (*estrictamente*) strictly, to the letter

rallador [raʎa'ðor] *nm* grater

rallar [ra'ʎar] /1a/ *vt* to grate

rama ['rama] *nf* branch; **ramaje** *nm*
 branches *pl*, foliage; **ramal** *nm* (*de
 cuerda*) strand; (*Ferro*) branch line;
 (*Auto*) branch (road)

rambla ['rambla] *nf* (*avenida*)
 avenue

ramo ['ramo] *nm* branch; (*sección*)
 department, section

rampa ['rampa] *nf* ramp; **~ de acceso**
 entrance ramp

rana ['rana] *nf* frog; **salto de ~**
 leapfrog

ranchero [ran'tʃero] *nm* (*LAM*)
 rancher; (*pequeño propietario*)
 smallholder

rancho ['rantʃo] *nm* (*grande*) ranch;
 (*pequeño*) small farm

rancio, -a ['ranθjo, a] *adj* (*comestibles*)
 rancid; (*vino*) aged, mellow; (*fig*)
 ancient

rango ['rango] *nm* rank; (*prestigio*)
 standing

ranura [ra'nura] *nf* groove; (*de
 teléfono etc*) slot

rapar [ra'par] /1a/ *vt* to shave; (*los
 cabellos*) to crop

rapaz [ra'paθ] *adj* (*Zool*) predatory
 ▷ *nm* young boy

rape ['rape] *nm* (*pez*) monkfish; **al ~**
 cropped

rapé [ra'pe] *nm* snuff

rapidez [rapi'ðeθ] *nf* speed, rapidity;
 rápido, -a *adj* fast, quick ▷ *adv*
 quickly ▷ *nm* (*Ferro*) express; **rápidos**
 nmpl rapids

rapiña [ra'pina] *nf* robbery; **ave de
 ~** bird of prey

raptar [rap'tar] /1a/ *vt* to kidnap;
 rapto *nm* kidnapping; (*impulso*)
 sudden impulse; (*éxtasis*) ecstasy,
 rapture

raqueta [ra'keta] *nf* racket

raquítico, -a [ra'kitiko, a] *adj*
 stunted; (*fig*) poor, inadequate

rareza [ra'reθa] *nf* rarity; (*fig*)
 eccentricity

raro, -a ['raro, a] *adj* (*poco común*) rare;
 (*extraño*) odd, strange; (*excepcional*)
 remarkable

ras [ras] *nm*: **a ~ de** level with; **a ~ de
 tierra** at ground level

rasar [ra'sar] /1a/ *vt* to level

rascacielos [raska'θjelos] *nm inv*
 skyscraper

rascar [ras'kar] /1g/ *vt* (*con las uñas
 etc*) to scratch; (*raspar*) to scrape;
 rascarse *vr* to scratch (o.s.)

rasgar [ras'ɣar] /1h/ *vt* to tear,
 rip (up)

rasgo ['rasɣo] *nm* (*con pluma*) stroke;
 rasgos *nmpl* features, characteristics;
 a grandes ~s in outline, broadly

rasguño [ras'ɣuno] *nm* scratch

raso, -a ['raso, a] *adj* (*liso*) flat, level; (*a
 baja altura*) very low ▷ *nm* satin; **cielo
 ~** clear sky

raspadura [raspa'ðura] *nf* (*acto*)
 scrape, scraping; (*marca*) scratch;

raspaduras *nfpl* (*de papel etc*) scrapings

raspar [ras'par] /1a/ *vt* to scrape; (*arañar*) to scratch; (*limar*) to file

rastra ['rastra] *nf* (*Agr*) rake; **a ~s** by dragging; (*fig*) unwillingly

rastrear [rastre'ar] /1a/ *vt* (*seguir*) to track

rastrero, -a [ras'trero, a] *adj* (*Bot, Zool*) creeping; (*fig*) despicable, mean

rastrillo [ras'triʎo] *nm* rake

rastro ['rastro] *nm* (*Agr*) rake; (*pista*) track, trail; (*vestigio*) trace; **el R~** *the Madrid flea market*

rasurado [rasu'raðo] *nm* (*LAM*) shaving; **rasurador** *nm*, (*LAM*) **rasuradora** [rasura'ðora] *nf* electric shaver *o* razor; **rasurar** /1a/ *vt* (*LAM*) to shave; **rasurarse** *vr* to shave

rata ['rata] *nf* rat

ratear [rate'ar] /1a/ *vt* (*robar*) to steal

ratero, -a [ra'tero, a] *adj* light-fingered ▷ *nm/f* (*carterista*) pickpocket; (*ladrón*) petty thief

rato ['rato] *nm* while, short time; **a ~s** from time to time; **al poco ~** shortly after, soon afterwards; **~s libres** *o* **de ocio** free *o* leisure time *sg*; **hay para ~** there's still a long way to go

ratón [ra'ton] *nm* mouse; **ratonera** *nf* mousetrap

raudal [rau'ðal] *nm* torrent; **a ~es** in abundance

raya ['raja] *nf* line; (*marca*) scratch; (*en tela*) stripe; (*puntuación*) dash; (*de pelo*) parting; (*límite*) boundary; (*pez*) ray; **a ~s** striped; **pasarse de la ~** to overstep the mark; **tener a ~** to keep in check; **rayar** /1a/ *vt* to line; to scratch; (*subrayar*) to underline ▷ *vi*: **rayar en** *o* **con** to border on

rayo ['rajo] *nm* (*del sol*) ray, beam; (*de luz*) shaft; (*en una tormenta*) (flash of) lightning; **~s X** X-rays

raza ['raθa] *nf* race; **~ humana** human race

razón [ra'θon] *nf* reason; (*justicia*) right, justice; (*razonamiento*)

reasoning; (*motivo*) reason, motive; (*Mat*) ratio; **a ~ de 10 cada día** at the rate of 10 a day; **en ~ de** with regard to; **dar ~ a algn** to agree that sb is right; **tener/no tener ~** to be right/ wrong; **~ directa/inversa** direct/ inverse proportion; **~ de ser** raison d'être; **razonable** *adj* reasonable; (*justo, moderado*) fair; **razonamiento** *nm* (*juicio*) judgement; (*argumento*) reasoning; **razonar** /1a/ *vt, vi* to reason, argue

re [re] *nm* (*Mus*) D

reacción [reak'θjon] *nf* reaction; **avión a ~** jet plane; **~ en cadena** chain reaction; **reaccionar** /1a/ *vi* to react

reacio, -a [re'aθjo, a] *adj* stubborn

reactivar [reakti'βar] /1a/ *vt* to reactivate

reactor [reak'tor] *nm* reactor

real [re'al] *adj* real; (*del rey, fig*) royal;

realidad [reali'ðað] *nf* reality; (*verdad*) truth

realista [rea'lista] *nmf* realist

realización [realiθa'θjon] *nf* fulfilment

realizador, a [realiθa'ðor, a] *nm/f* film-maker; (*TV etc*) producer

realizar [reali'θar] /1f/ *vt* (*objetivo*) to achieve; (*plan*) to carry out; (*viaje*) to make, undertake; **realizarse** *vr* to come about, come true

realmente [real'mente] *adv* really, actually

realzar [real'θar] /1f/ *vt* to enhance; (*acentuar*) to highlight

reanimar [reani'mar] /1a/ *vt* to revive; (*alentar*) to encourage; **reanimarse** *vr* to revive

reanudar [reanu'ðar] /1a/ *vt* (*renovar*) to renew; (*historia, viaje*) to resume

reaparición [reapari'θjon] *nf* reappearance

rearme [re'arme] *nm* rearmament

rebaja [re'βaxa] *nf* reduction, lowering; (*Com*) discount; **rebajas** *nfpl* (*Com*) sale; **"grandes ~s"** "big

reductions", "sale"; **rebajar** /1a/ vt
(bajar) to lower; (reducir) to reduce;
(disminuir) to lessen; (humillar) to
humble

rebanada [reβa'naða] nf slice

rebañar [reβa'ɲar] /1a/ vt (comida) to
scrape up; (plato) to scrape clean

rebaño [re'βaɲo] nm herd; (de ovejas)
flock

rebatir [reβa'tir] /3a/ vt to refute

rebeca [re'βeka] nf cardigan

rebelarse [reβe'larse] /1a/ vr to
rebel, revolt

rebelde [re'βelde] adj rebellious;
(niño) unruly ▷ nmf rebel; **rebeldía**
nf rebelliousness; (desobediencia)
disobedience

rebelión [reβe'ljon] nf rebellion

reblandecer [reβlande'θer] /2d/ vt
to soften

rebobinar [reβoβi'nar] /1a/ vt to
rewind

rebosante [reβo'sante] adj: **~ de** (fig)
brimming o overflowing with

rebosar [reβo'sar] /1a/ vi to overflow;
(abundar) to abound, be plentiful

rebotar [reβo'tar] /1a/ vt to bounce;
(rechazar) to repel ▷ vi (pelota) to
bounce; (bala) to ricochet; **rebote** nm
rebound; **de rebote** on the rebound

rebozado, -a [reβo'θaðo, a] adj fried
in batter o breadcrumbs o flour

rebozar [reβo'θar] /1f/ vt to wrap up;
(Culin) to fry in batter etc

rebuscado, -a [reβus'kaðo, a]
adj (amanerado) affected; (palabra)
recherché; (idea) far-fetched

rebuscar [reβus'kar] /1g/ vi (en
habitación) to search high and low

recado [re'kaðo] nm message;
(encargo) errand; **dejar/tomar un ~**
(Telec) to leave/take a message

recaer [reka'er] /2n/ vi to relapse;
~ en to fall to o on; (criminal etc) to
fall back into, relapse into; **recaída**
nf relapse

recalcar [rekal'kar] /1g/ vt (fig) to
stress, emphasize

recalentar [rekalen'tar] /1j/ vt
(comida) to warm up, reheat;
(demasiado) to overheat

recámara [re'kamara] nf (LAM)
bedroom

recambio [re'kambjo] nm spare; (de
pluma) refill

recapacitar [rekapaθi'tar] /1a/ vi
to reflect

recargado, -a [rekar'ɣaðo, a] adj
overloaded; (exagerado) over-elaborate

recargar [rekar'ɣar] /1h/ vt to
overload; (batería) to recharge; (tarjeta
de móvil) to top up; **recargo** nm
surcharge; (aumento) increase

recatado, -a [reka'taðo, a] adj
(modesto) modest, demure; (prudente)
cautious

recaudación [rekauða'θjon] nf
(acción) collection; (cantidad) takings
pl; (en deporte) gate; **recaudador, a**
nmf tax collector

recelar [reθe'lar] /1a/ vt: **~ que**
(sospechar) to suspect that; (temer) to
fear that ▷ vi: **~(se) de** to distrust;
recelo nm distrust, suspicion

recepción [reθep'θjon] nf reception;
recepcionista nmf receptionist

receptor, a [reθep'tor, a] nm/f
recipient ▷ nm (Telec) receiver

recesión [reθe'sjon] nf (Com)
recession

receta [re'θeta] nf (Culin) recipe; (Med)
prescription

No confundir receta con la palabra
inglesa receipt.

rechazar [retʃa'θar] /1f/ vt to repel;
(idea) to reject; (oferta) to turn down

rechazo [re'tʃaθo] nm (de propuesta, tb
Med: de un órgano) rejection

rechinar [retʃi'nar] /1a/ vi to creak;
(dientes) to grind

rechistar [retʃis'tar] /1a/ vi: **sin ~**
without complaint

rechoncho, -a [re'tʃontʃo, a] adj
(fam) thickset (BRIT), heavy-set (US)

rechupete [retʃu'pete]: **de ~** adj
(comida) delicious

recibidor [reθiβiˈðor] nm entrance hall

recibimiento [reθiβiˈmjento] nm reception, welcome

recibir [reθiˈβir] /3a/ vt to receive; (dar la bienvenida) to welcome ▷ vi to entertain; **recibo** nm receipt

reciclable [reθiˈklaβle] adj recyclable

reciclar [reθiˈklar] /1a/ vt to recycle

recién [reˈθjen] adv recently, newly; **~ casado** newly-wed; **el ~ llegado** the newcomer; **el ~ nacido** the newborn child

reciente [reˈθjente] adj recent; (fresco) fresh

recinto [reˈθinto] nm enclosure; (área) area, place

recio, -a [ˈreθjo, a] adj strong, tough; (voz) loud ▷ adv hard; loud(ly)

recipiente [reθiˈpjente] nm receptacle

recíproco, -a [reˈθiproko, a] adj reciprocal

recital [reθiˈtal] nm (Mus) recital; (Lit) reading

recitar [reθiˈtar] /1a/ vt to recite

reclamación [reklamaˈθjon] nf claim, demand; (queja) complaint; **libro de reclamaciones** complaints book

reclamar [reklaˈmar] /1a/ vt to claim, demand ▷ vi: **~ contra** to complain about; **reclamo** nm (anuncio) advertisement; (tentación) attraction

reclinar [rekliˈnar] /1a/ vt to recline, lean; **reclinarse** vr to lean back

reclusión [rekluˈsjon] nf (prisión) prison; (refugio) seclusion

recluta [reˈkluta] nmf recruit ▷ nf recruitment; **reclutamiento** nm recruitment; **reclutar** /1a/ vt (datos) to collect; (dinero) to collect up

recobrar [rekoˈβrar] /1a/ vt (recuperar) to recover; (rescatar) to get back; **recobrarse** vr to recover

recodo [reˈkoðo] nm (de río, camino) bend

recogedor, a [rekoxeˈðor, a] nm dustpan ▷ nm/f picker, harvester

recoger [rekoˈxer] /2c/ vt to collect; (Agr) to harvest; (levantar) to pick up; (juntar) to gather; (pasar a buscar) to come for, get; (dar asilo) to give shelter to; (faldas) to gather up; (pelo) to put up; **recogerse** vr (retirarse) to retire; **recogido, -a** adj (lugar) quiet, secluded; (pequeño) small ▷ nf (Correos) collection; (Agr) harvest

recolección [rekolekˈθjon] nf (Agr) harvesting; (colecta) collection

recomendación [rekomendaˈθjon] nf (sugerencia) suggestion, recommendation; (referencia) reference

recomendar [rekomenˈdar] /1j/ vt to suggest, recommend; (confiar) to entrust

recompensa [rekomˈpensa] nf reward, recompense; **recompensar** /1a/ vt to reward, recompense

reconciliación [rekonθiljaˈθjon] nf reconciliation

reconciliar [rekonθiˈljar] /1b/ vt to reconcile; **reconciliarse** vr to become reconciled

recóndito, -a [reˈkondito, a] adj (lugar) hidden, secret

reconocer [rekonoˈθer] /2d/ vt to recognize; (registrar) to search; (Med) to examine; **reconocido, -a** adj recognized; (agradecido) grateful; **reconocimiento** nm recognition; (registro) search; (inspección) examination; (gratitud) gratitude; (confesión) admission

reconquista [rekonˈkista] nf reconquest; **la R~** the Reconquest (of Spain)

reconstituyente [rekonstituˈjente] nm tonic

reconstruir [rekonstruˈir] /3g/ vt to reconstruct

reconversión [rekomberˈsjon] nf restructuring, reorganization; (tb: **~ industrial**) rationalization

recopilación [rekopilaˈθjon] nf (resumen) summary; (compilación)

r

compilation; **recopilar** /1a/ vt to compile

récord ['rekorð] nm record

recordar [rekor'ðar] /1l/ vt (acordarse de) to remember; (recordar a otro) to remind ▷ vi to remember

⏐ No confundir recordar con la palabra inglesa record.

recorrer [reko'rrer] /2a/ vt (país) to cross, travel through; (distancia) to cover; (registrar) to search; (repasar) to look over; **recorrido** nm run, journey; **tren de largo recorrido** main-line o inter-city (BRIT) train

recortar [rekor'tar] /1a/ vt to cut out; **recorte** nm (acción, de prensa) cutting; (de telas, chapas) trimming; **recorte presupuestario** budget cut

recostar [rekos'tar] /1l/ vt to lean; **recostarse** vr to lie down

recoveco [reko'βeko] nm (de camino, río etc) bend; (en casa) cubbyhole

recreación [rekrea'θjon] nf recreation

recrear [rekre'ar] /1a/ vt (entretener) to entertain; (volver a crear) to recreate; **recreativo, -a** adj recreational; **recreo** nm recreation; (Escol) break, playtime

recriminar [rekrimi'nar] /1a/ vt to reproach ▷ vi to recriminate; **recriminarse** vr to reproach each other

recrudecer [rekruðe'θer] /2d/ vt, vi to worsen; **recrudecerse** vr to worsen

recta ['rekta] nf V **recto**

rectángulo, -a [rek'tangulo, a] adj rectangular ▷ nm rectangle

rectificar [rektifi'kar] /1g/ vt to rectify; (volverse recto) to straighten ▷ vi to correct o.s.

rectitud [rekti'tuð] nf straightness

recto, -a ['rekto, a] adj straight; (persona) honest, upright ▷ nm rectum ▷ nf straight line; **siga todo ~** go straight on

rector, a [rek'tor, a] adj governing

recuadro [re'kwaðro] nm box; (Tip) inset

recubrir [reku'βir] /3a/ vt: **~ (con)** (pintura, crema) to cover (with)

recuento [re'kwento] nm inventory; **hacer el ~ de** to count o reckon up

recuerdo [re'kwerðo] nm souvenir; **recuerdos** nmpl memories; **¡~s a tu madre!** give my regards to your mother!

recular [reku'lar] /1a/ vi to back down

recuperación [rekupera'θjon] nf recovery

recuperar [rekupe'rar] /1a/ vt to recover; (tiempo) to make up; **recuperarse** vr to recuperate

recurrir [reku'rrir] /3a/ vi (Jur) to appeal; **~ a** to resort to; (persona) to turn to; **recurso** nm resort; (medio) means pl, resource; (Jur) appeal; **recursos naturales** natural resources

red [reð] nf net, mesh; (Ferro, Inform) network; (trampa) trap; **la R~** (Internet) the Net; **~es sociales** social networks; (páginas web) social networking sites

redacción [reðak'θjon] nf (acción) writing; (Escol) essay, composition; (limpieza de texto) editing; (personal) editorial staff

redactar [reðak'tar] /1a/ vt to draw up, draft; (periódico) to edit

redactor, a [reðak'tor, a] nm/f editor

redada [re'ðaða] nf: **~ policial** police raid, round-up

rededor [reðe'ðor] nm: **al** o **en ~** around, round about

redoblar [reðo'βlar] /1a/ vt to redouble ▷ vi (tambor) to roll

redonda [re'ðonda] nf V **redondo**

redondear [reðonde'ar] /1a/ vt to round, round off

redondel [reðon'del] nm (círculo) circle; (Taur) bullring, arena

redondo, -a [re'ðondo, a] adj (circular) round; (completo) complete ▷ nf: **a la redonda** around, round about

reducción [reðuk'θjon] nf reduction

reducido, -a [reðu'θiðo, a] adj reduced; (limitado) limited; (pequeño) small

reducir [reðu'θir] /3n/ vt to reduce, limit; **reducirse** vr to diminish

redundancia [reðun'danθja] nf redundancy

reembolsar [re(e)mbol'sar] /1a/ vt (persona) to reimburse; (dinero) to repay, pay back; (depósito) to refund; **reembolso** nm reimbursement; refund

reemplazar [re(e)mpla'θar] /1f/ vt to replace; **reemplazo** nm replacement; **de reemplazo** (Mil) reserve

reencuentro [re(e)n'kwentro] nm reunion

reescribible [reeskri'βiβle] adj rewritable

refacción [refak'θjon] nf (LAM) repair(s); **refacciones** nfpl (piezas de repuesto) spare parts

referencia [refe'renθja] nf reference; **con ~ a** with reference to

referéndum [refe'rendum] (pl **referéndums**) nm referendum

referente [refe'rente] adj: **~ a** concerning, relating to

réferi ['referi] nmf (LAM) referee

referir [refe'rir] /3i/ vt (contar) to tell, recount; (relacionar) to refer, relate; **referirse** vr: **~se a** to refer to

refilón [refi'lon]: **de ~** adv obliquely

refinado, -a [refi'naðo, a] adj refined

refinar [refi'nar] /1a/ vt to refine; **refinería** nf refinery

reflejar [refle'xar] /1a/ vt to reflect; **reflejo, -a** [re'flexo, a] adj reflected; (movimiento) reflex ▷ nm reflection; (Anat) reflex

reflexión [reflek'sjon] nf reflection; **reflexionar** /1a/ vt to reflect on ▷ vi to reflect; (detenerse) to pause (to think)

reflexivo, -a [reflek'siβo, a] adj thoughtful; (Ling) reflexive

reforma [re'forma] nf reform; (Arq etc) repair; **~ agraria** agrarian reform

reformar [refor'mar] /1a/ vt to reform; (modificar) to change, alter; (Arq) to repair; **reformarse** vr to mend one's ways

reformatorio [reforma'torjo] nm reformatory

reforzar [refor'θar] /1f, 1l/ vt to strengthen; (Arq) to reinforce; (fig) to encourage

refractario, -a [refrak'tarjo, a] adj (Tec) heat-resistant

refrán [re'fran] nm proverb, saying

refregar [refre'ɣar] /1h, 1j/ vt to scrub

refrescante [refres'kante] adj refreshing, cooling

refrescar [refres'kar] /1g/ vt to refresh ▷ vi to cool down; **refrescarse** vr to get cooler; (tomar aire fresco) to go out for a breath of fresh air; (beber) to have a drink

refresco [re'fresko] nm soft drink, cool drink; "**~s**" "refreshments"

refriega etc [re'frjeɣa] nf scuffle, brawl

refrigeración [refrixera'θjon] nf refrigeration; (de casa) air-conditioning

refrigerador [refrixera'ðor] nm refrigerator, icebox (US)

refrigerar [refrixe'rar] /1a/ vt to refrigerate; (sala) to air-condition

refuerzo etc [re'fwerθo] nm reinforcement; (Tec) support

refugiado, -a [refu'xjaðo, a] nm/f refugee

refugiarse [refu'xjarse] /1b/ vr to take refuge, shelter

refugio [re'fuxjo] nm refuge; (protección) shelter

refunfuñar [refunfu'ɲar] /1a/ vi to grunt, growl; (quejarse) to grumble

regadera [reɣa'ðera] nf watering can

regadío [reɣa'ðio] nm irrigated land

regalado, -a [reɣa'laðo, a] adj comfortable, luxurious; (gratis) free, for nothing

regalar [reɣa'lar] /1a/ vt (dar) to give (as a present); (entregar) to give away; (mimar) to pamper, make a fuss of

regaliz [reɣa'liθ] *nm* liquorice

regalo [re'ɣalo] *nm* (*obsequio*) gift, present; (*gusto*) pleasure

regañadientes [reɣaɲa'ðjentes]: **a ~** *adv* reluctantly

regañar [reɣa'ɲar] /1a/ *vt* to scold ▷ *vi* to grumble; **regañón, -ona** *adj* nagging

regar [re'ɣar] /1h, 1j/ *vt* to water, irrigate; (*fig*) to scatter, sprinkle

regatear [reɣate'ar] /1a/ *vt* (*Com*) to bargain over; (*escatimar*) to be mean with ▷ *vi* to bargain, haggle; (*Deporte*) to dribble; **regateo** *nm* bargaining; (*Deporte*) dribbling; (*con el cuerpo*) swerve, dodge

regazo [re'ɣaθo] *nm* lap

regenerar [rexene'rar] /1a/ *vt* to regenerate

régimen ['reximen] (*pl* **regímenes**) *nm* regime; (*Med*) diet

regimiento [rexi'mjento] *nm* regiment

regio, -a ['rexjo, a] *adj* royal, regal; (*fig: suntuoso*) splendid; (*LAm fam*) great, terrific

región [re'xjon] *nf* region

regir [re'xir] /3c, 3k/ *vt* to govern, rule; (*dirigir*) to manage, run ▷ *vi* to apply, be in force

registrar [rexis'trar] /1a/ *vt* (*buscar*) to search; (*en cajón*) to look through; (*inspeccionar*) to inspect; (*anotar*) to register, record; (*Inform*) to log; **registrarse** *vr* to register; (*ocurrir*) to happen

registro [re'xistro] *nm* (*acto*) registration; (*Mus, libro*) register; (*inspección*) inspection, search; **~ civil** registry office

regla ['reɣla] *nf* (*ley*) rule, regulation; (*de medir*) ruler, rule; (*Med: período*) period; **en ~** in order

reglamentación [reɣlamenta'θjon] *nf* (*acto*) regulation; (*lista*) rules *pl*

reglamentar [reɣlamen'tar] /1a/ *vt* to regulate; **reglamentario, -a** *adj* statutory; **reglamento** *nm* rules *pl*, regulations *pl*

regocijarse [reɣoθi'xarse] /1a/ *vr*: **~ de** *o* **por** to rejoice at; **regocijo** *nm* joy, happiness

regrabadora [reɣraβa'ðora] *nf* rewriter; **~ de DVD** DVD rewriter

regresar [reɣre'sar] /1a/ *vi* to come *o* go back, return; **regreso** *nm* return

reguero [re'ɣero] *nm* (*de sangre*) trickle; (*de humo*) trail

regulador [reɣula'ðor] *nm* regulator; (*de radio etc*) knob, control

regular [reɣu'lar] /1a/ *adj* regular; (*normal*) normal, usual; (*común*) ordinary; (*organizado*) regular, orderly; (*mediano*) average; (*fam*) not bad, so-so ▷ *adv*: **estar ~** to be so-so *o* all right ▷ *vt* (*controlar*) to control, regulate; (*Tec*) to adjust; **por lo ~** as a rule; **regularidad** *nf* regularity; **regularizar** /1f/ *vt* to regularize

rehabilitación [reaβilita'θjon] *nf* rehabilitation; (*Arq*) restoration

rehabilitar [reaβili'tar] /1a/ *vt* to rehabilitate; (*Arq*) to restore; (*reintegrar*) to reinstate

rehacer [rea'θer] /2r/ *vt* (*reparar*) to mend, repair; (*volver a hacer*) to redo, repeat; **rehacerse** *vr* (*Med*) to recover

rehén [re'en] *nmf* hostage

rehuir [reu'ir] /3g/ *vt* to avoid, shun

rehusar [reu'sar] /1a/ *vt*, *vi* to refuse

reina ['reina] *nf* queen; **reinado** *nm* reign

reinar [rei'nar] /1a/ *vi* to reign

reincidir [reinθi'ðir] /3a/ *vi* to relapse

reincorporarse [reinkorpo'rarse] /1a/ *vr*: **~ a** to rejoin

reino ['reino] *nm* kingdom; **~ animal/ vegetal** animal/plant kingdom; **el R~ Unido** the United Kingdom

reintegrar [reinte'ɣrar] /1a/ *vt* (*reconstituir*) to reconstruct; (*persona*) to reinstate; (*dinero*) to refund, pay back; **reintegrarse** *vr*: **~se a** to return to

reír [re'ir] *vi* to laugh; **reírse** *vr* to laugh; **~se de** to laugh at

reiterar [reite'rar] /1a/ vt to reiterate

reivindicación [reiβindika'θjon] nf (demanda) claim, demand; (justificación) vindication

reivindicar [reiβindi'kar] /1g/ vt to claim

reja ['rexa] nf (de ventana) grille, bars pl; (en la calle) grating

rejilla [re'xiʎa] nf grating, grille; (muebles) wickerwork; (de ventilación) vent; (de coche etc) luggage rack

rejoneador [rexonea'ðor] nm mounted bullfighter

rejuvenecer [rexuβene'θer] /2d/ vt, vi to rejuvenate

relación [rela'θjon] nf relation, relationship; (Mat) ratio; (narración) report; **relaciones laborales/públicas** labour/public relations; **con ~ a, en ~ con** in relation to; **relacionar** /1a/ vt to relate, connect; **relacionarse** vr to be connected o linked

relajación [relaxa'θjon] nf relaxation

relajar [rela'xar] /1a/ vt to relax; **relajarse** vr to relax

relamerse [rela'merse] /2a/ vr to lick one's lips

relámpago [re'lampaɣo] nm flash of lightning; **visita/huelga ~** lightning visit/strike

relatar [rela'tar] /1a/ vt to tell, relate

relativo, -a [rela'tiβo, a] adj relative; **en lo ~ a** concerning

relato [re'lato] nm (narración) story, tale

relegar [rele'ɣar] /1h/ vt to relegate

relevante [rele'βante] adj eminent, outstanding

relevar [rele'βar] /1a/ vt (sustituir) to relieve; **relevarse** vr to relay; **~ a algn de un cargo** to relieve sb of his post

relevo [re'leβo] nm relief; **carrera de ~s** relay race

relieve [re'ljeβe] nm (Arte, Tec) relief; (fig) prominence, importance; **bajo ~** bas-relief

religión [reli'xjon] nf religion; **religioso, -a** adj religious ▷ nm/f monk/nun

relinchar [relin'tʃar] /1a/ vi to neigh

reliquia [re'likja] nf relic; **~ de familia** heirloom

rellano [re'ʎano] nm (Arq) landing

rellenar [reʎe'nar] /1a/ vt (llenar) to fill up; (Culin) to stuff; (Costura) to pad; **relleno, -a** adj full up; (Culin) stuffed ▷ nm stuffing; (de tapicería) padding

reloj [re'lo(x)] nm clock; **poner el ~ (en hora)** to set one's watch o the clock; **~ (de pulsera)** (wrist)watch; **~ despertador** alarm (clock); **~ digital** digital watch; **relojero, -a** nm/f clockmaker; watchmaker

reluciente [relu'θjente] adj brilliant, shining

relucir [relu'θir] /3f/ vi to shine; (fig) to excel

remachar [rema'tʃar] /1a/ vt to rivet; (fig) to hammer home, drive home; **remache** nm rivet

remangar [reman'gar] /1h/ vt to roll up; **remangarse** vr to roll one's sleeves up

remanso [re'manso] nm pool

remar [re'mar] /1a/ vi to row

rematado, -a [rema'taðo, a] adj complete, utter

rematar [rema'tar] /1a/ vt to finish off; (Com) to sell off cheap ▷ vi to end, finish off; (Deporte) to shoot

remate [re'mate] nm end, finish; (punta) tip; (Deporte) shot; (Arq) top; **de o para ~** to crown it all (BRIT), to top it off

remedar [reme'ðar] /1a/ vt to imitate

remediar [reme'ðjar] /1b/ vt to remedy; (subsanar) to make good, repair; (evitar) to avoid

remedio [re'meðjo] nm remedy, help; (Jur) recourse, remedy; **poner ~ a** to correct, stop; **no tener más ~** to have no alternative; **¡qué ~!** there's no choice!; **sin ~** hopeless

r

remendar [remen'dar] /1j/ vt to repair; (con parche) to patch

remiendo etc [re'mjendo] nm mend; (con parche) patch; (cosido) darn

remilgado, -a [remil'ɣaðo, a] adj prim; (afectado) affected

remiso, -a [re'miso, a] adj slack, slow

remite [re'mite] nm (en sobre) name and address of sender; **remitente** nmf (Correos) sender; **remitir** /3a/ vt to remit, send ▷ vi to slacken; (en carta): **remite: X** sender: X

remo ['remo] nm (de barco) oar; (Deporte) rowing

remojar [remo'xar] /1a/ vt to steep, soak; (galleta etc) to dip, dunk

remojo [re'moxo] nm: **dejar la ropa en ~** to leave clothes to soak

remolacha [remo'latʃa] nf beet, beetroot (BRIT)

remolcador [remolka'ðor] nm (Naut) tug; (Auto) breakdown lorry

remolcar [remol'kar] /1g/ vt to tow

remolino [remo'lino] nm eddy; (de agua) whirlpool; (de viento) whirlwind; (de gente) crowd

remolque [re'molke] nm tow, towing; (cuerda) towrope; **llevar a ~** to tow

remontar [remon'tar] /1a/ vt to mend; **remontarse** vr to soar; **~se a** (Com) to amount to; **~ el vuelo** to soar

remorder [remor'ðer] /2h/ vt to distress, disturb; **~le la conciencia a algn** to have a guilty conscience; **remordimiento** nm remorse

remoto, -a [re'moto, a] adj remote

remover [remo'βer] /2h/ vt to stir; (tierra) to turn over; (objetos) to move round

remuneración [remunera'θjon] nf remuneration

remunerar [remune'rar] /1a/ vt to remunerate; (premiar) to reward

renacer [rena'θer] /2d/ vi to be reborn; (fig) to revive; **renacimiento** nm rebirth; **el Renacimiento** the Renaissance

renacuajo [rena'kwaxo] nm (Zool) tadpole

renal [re'nal] adj renal, kidney cpd

rencilla [ren'θiʎa] nf quarrel

rencor [ren'kor] nm rancour, bitterness; **rencoroso, -a** adj spiteful

rendición [rendi'θjon] nf surrender

rendido, -a [ren'diðo, a] adj (sumiso) submissive; (agotado) worn-out, exhausted

rendija [ren'dixa] nf (hendidura) crack

rendimiento [rendi'mjento] nm (producción) output; (Tec, Com) efficiency

rendir [ren'dir] /3k/ vt (vencer) to defeat; (producir) to produce; (dar beneficio) to yield; (agotar) to exhaust ▷ vi to pay; **rendirse** vr (someterse) to surrender; (cansarse) to wear o.s. out; **~ homenaje** o **culto a** to pay homage to

renegar [rene'ɣar] /1h, 1j/ vi (blasfemar) to blaspheme; **~ de** (renunciar) to renounce; (quejarse) to complain about

RENFE ['renfe] nf abr = **Red Nacional de Ferrocarriles Españoles**

renglón [ren'glon] nm (línea) line; (Com) item, article; **a ~ seguido** immediately after

renombre [re'nombre] nm renown

renovación [renoβa'θjon] nf (de contrato) renewal; (Arq) renovation

renovar [reno'βar] /1l/ vt to renew; (Arq) to renovate

renta ['renta] nf (ingresos) income; (beneficio) profit; (alquiler) rent; **~ vitalicia** annuity; **rentable** adj profitable

renuncia [re'nunθja] nf resignation; **renunciar** /1b/ vt to renounce, give up ▷ vi to resign; **renunciar a** (tabaco, alcohol etc) to give up; (oferta, oportunidad) to turn down; (puesto) to resign

reñido, -a [re'niðo, a] adj (batalla) bitter, hard-fought; **estar ~ con algn** to be on bad terms with sb

reñir [re'ɲir] /3h, 3k/ vt (regañar) to scold ▷ vi (estar peleado) to quarrel, fall out; (combatir) to fight

reo ['reo] nmf culprit, offender; (Jur) accused

reojo [re'oxo]: **de ~** adv out of the corner of one's eye

reparación [repara'θjon] nf (acto) mending, repairing; (Tec) repair; (fig) amends, reparation

reparador, -a [repara'ðor, a] adj refreshing; (comida) fortifying ▷ nm repairer

reparar [repa'rar] /1a/ vt to repair; (fig) to make amends for; (observar) to observe ▷ vi: **~ en** (darse cuenta de) to notice; (poner atención en) to pay attention to

reparo [re'paro] nm (advertencia) observation; (duda) doubt; (dificultad) difficulty; **poner ~s (a)** to raise objections (to)

repartidor, a [reparti'ðor, a] nm/f distributor

repartir [repar'tir] /3a/ vt to distribute, share out; (Com, Correos) to deliver; **reparto** nm distribution; (Com, Correos) delivery; (Teat, Cine) cast; (LAM: urbanización) housing estate (BRIT), real estate development (US)

repasar [repa'sar] /1a/ vt (Escol) to revise; (Mecánica) to check, overhaul; (Costura) to mend; **repaso** nm revision; (Mecánica) overhaul, checkup; (Costura) mending

repecho [re'petʃo] nm steep incline

repelente [repe'lente] adj repellent, repulsive

repeler [repe'ler] /2a/ vt to repel

repente [re'pente] nm: **de ~** suddenly

repentino, -a [repen'tino, a] adj sudden

repercusión [reperku'sjon] nf repercussion

repercutir [reperku'tir] /3a/ vi (objeto) to rebound; (sonido) to echo;

~ en (fig) to have repercussions o effects on

repertorio [reper'torjo] nm list; (Teat) repertoire

repetición [repeti'θjon] nf repetition

repetir [repe'tir] /3k/ vt to repeat; (plato) to have a second helping of ▷ vi to repeat; (sabor) to come back; **repetirse** vr to repeat o.s.

repetitivo, -a [repeti'tiβo, a] adj repetitive, repetitious

repique [re'pike] nm pealing, ringing; **repiqueteo** nm pealing; (de tambor) drumming

repisa [re'pisa] nf ledge, shelf; **~ de chimenea** mantelpiece; **~ de ventana** windowsill

repito etc vb V **repetir**

replantear [replante'ar] /1a/ vt (cuestión pública) to readdress; **replantearse** vr: **~se algo** to reconsider sth

repleto, -a [re'pleto, a] adj replete, full up

réplica ['replika] nf answer; (Arte) replica

replicar [repli'kar] /1g/ vi to answer; (objetar) to argue, answer back

repliegue [re'pljeɣe] nm (Mil) withdrawal

repoblación [repoβla'θjon] nf repopulation; (de río) restocking; **~ forestal** reafforestation

repoblar [repo'βlar] /1l/ vt to repopulate; (con árboles) to reafforest

repollito [repo'ʎito] nm (LAM): **~s de Bruselas** (Brussels) sprouts

repollo [re'poʎo] nm cabbage

reponer [repo'ner] /2q/ vt to replace, put back; (Teat) to revive; **reponerse** vr to recover; **~ que** to reply that

reportaje [repor'taxe] nm report, article

reportero, -a [repor'tero, a] nm/f reporter

reposacabezas [reposaka'βeθas] nm inv headrest

reposar [repo'sar] /1a/ *vi* to rest, repose

reposición [reposi'θjon] *nf* replacement; (*Cine*) second showing

reposo [re'poso] *nm* rest

repostar [repos'tar] /1a/ *vt* to replenish; (*Auto*) to fill up (with petrol o gasoline)

repostería [reposte'ria] *nf* confectioner's (shop)

represa [re'presa] *nf* dam; (*lago artificial*) lake, pool

represalia [repre'salja] *nf* reprisal

representación [representa'θjon] *nf* representation; (*Teat*) performance; **representante** *nmf* representative; (*Teat*) performer

representar [represen'tar] /1a/ *vt* to represent; (*Teat*) to perform; (*edad*) to look; **representarse** *vr* to imagine; **representativo, -a** *adj* representative

represión [repre'sjon] *nf* repression

reprimenda [repri'menda] *nf* reprimand, rebuke

reprimir [repri'mir] /3a/ *vt* to repress

reprobar [repro'βar] /1l/ *vt* to censure, reprove

reprochar [repro't∫ar] /1a/ *vt* to reproach; **reproche** *nm* reproach

reproducción [reproðuk'θjon] *nf* reproduction

reproducir [reproðu'θir] /3n/ *vt* to reproduce; **reproducirse** *vr* to breed; (*situación*) to recur

reproductor, a [reproðuk'tor, a] *adj* reproductive ▷ *nm*: **~ de CD** CD player

reptil [rep'til] *nm* reptile

república [re'puβlika] *nf* republic; **R~ Dominicana** Dominican Republic; **republicano, -a** *adj, nm/f* republican

repudiar [repu'ðjar] /1b/ *vt* to repudiate; (*fe*) to renounce

repuesto [re'pwesto] *nm* (*pieza de recambio*) spare (part); (*abastecimiento*) supply; **rueda de ~** spare wheel

repugnancia [repuɣ'nanθja] *nf* repugnance; **repugnante** *adj* repugnant, repulsive

repugnar [repuɣ'nar] /1a/ *vt* to disgust

repulsa [re'pulsa] *nf* rebuff

repulsión [repul'sjon] *nf* repulsion, aversion; **repulsivo, -a** *adj* repulsive

reputación [reputa'θjon] *nf* reputation

requerir [reke'rir] /3i/ *vt* (*pedir*) to ask, request; (*exigir*) to require; (*llamar*) to send for, summon

requesón [reke'son] *nm* cottage cheese

requete... [rekete] *pref* extremely

réquiem ['rekjem] *nm* requiem

requisito [reki'sito] *nm* requirement, requisite

res [res] *nf* beast, animal

resaca [re'saka] *nf* (*en el mar*) undertow, undercurrent; (*fam*) hangover

resaltar [resal'tar] /1a/ *vi* to project, stick out; (*fig*) to stand out

resarcir [resar'θir] /3b/ *vt* to compensate; **resarcirse** *vr* to make up for

resbaladero [resβala'ðero] *nm* (*LAM*) slide

resbaladizo, -a [resβala'ðiθo, a] *adj* slippery

resbalar [resβa'lar] /1a/ *vi* to slip, slide; (*fig*) to slip (up); **resbalarse** *vr* to slip, slide; (*fig*) to slip (up); **resbalón** *nm* (*acción*) slip

rescatar [reska'tar] /1a/ *vt* (*salvar*) to save, rescue; (*objeto*) to get back, recover; (*cautivos*) to ransom

rescate [res'kate] *nm* rescue; (*de objeto*) recovery; **pagar un ~** to pay a ransom

rescindir [resθin'dir] /3a/ *vt* rescind

rescisión [resθi'sjon] *nf* cancellation

resecar [rese'kar] /1g/ *vt* to dry off, dry thoroughly; (*Med*) to cut out, remove; **resecarse** *vr* to dry up

reseco, -a [re'seko, a] *adj* very dry; (*fig*) skinny

resentido, -a [resen'tiðo, a] *adj* resentful

resentimiento [resenti'mjento] *nm* resentment, bitterness

resentirse [resen'tirse] /3i/ *vr* (*debilitarse: persona*) to suffer; **~ de** (*sufrir las consecuencias de*) to feel the effects of; **~ de** *o* **por algo** to resent sth, be bitter about sth

reseña [re'seɲa] *nf* (*cuenta*) account; (*informe*) report; (*Lit*) review; **reseñar** /1a/ *vt* to describe; (*Lit*) to review

reserva [re'serβa] *nf* reserve; (*reservación*) reservation

reservación [reserβa'θjon] *nf* (LAm) reservation

reservado, -a [reser'βaðo, a] *adj* reserved; (*retraído*) cold, distant ▷ *nm* private room

reservar [reser'βar] /1a/ *vt* (*guardar*) to keep; (*Ferro, Teat etc*) to reserve, book; **reservarse** *vr* to save o.s.; (*callar*) to keep to o.s.

resfriado [res'frjaðo] *nm* cold; **resfriarse** /1c/ *vr* to cool off; (*Med*) to catch (a) cold

resguardar [resɣwar'ðar] /1a/ *vt* to protect, shield; **resguardarse** *vr*: **~se de** to guard against; **resguardo** *nm* defence; (*vale*) voucher; (*recibo*) receipt, slip

residencia [resi'ðenθja] *nf* residence; (*Univ*) hall of residence; **~ para ancianos** *o* **jubilados** residential home, old people's home; **residencial** *adj* residential

residente [resi'ðente] *adj, nmf* resident

residir [resi'ðir] /3a/ *vi* to reside, live; **~ en** to reside *o* lie in

residuo [re'siðwo] *nm* residue

resignación [resiɣna'θjon] *nf* resignation; **resignarse** /1a/ *vr*: **resignarse a** *o* **con** to resign o.s. to, be resigned to

resina [re'sina] *nf* resin

resistencia [resis'tenθja] *nf* (*dureza*) endurance, strength; (*oposición, Elec*) resistance; **resistente** *adj* strong, hardy; (*Tec*) resistant

resistir [resis'tir] /3a/ *vt* (*soportar*) to bear; (*oponerse a*) to resist, oppose; (*aguantar*) to put up with ▷ *vi* to resist; (*aguantar*) to last, endure; **resistirse** *vr*: **~se a** to refuse to, resist

resoluto, -a [reso'luto, a] *adj* resolute

resolver [resol'βer] /2h/ *vt* to resolve; (*solucionar*) to solve, resolve; (*decidir*) to decide, settle; **resolverse** *vr* to make up one's mind

resonar [reso'nar] /1l/ *vi* to ring, echo

resoplar [reso'plar] /1a/ *vi* to snort; **resoplido** *nm* heavy breathing

resorte [re'sorte] *nm* spring; (*fig*) lever

resortera [resor'tera] *nf* (LAm) catapult

respaldar [respal'dar] /1a/ *vt* to back (up), support; **~se con** *o* **en** (*fig*) to take one's stand on; **respaldo** *nm* (*de sillón*) back; (*fig*) support, backing

respectivo, -a [respek'tiβo, a] *adj* respective; **en lo ~** with regard to

respecto [res'pekto] *nm*: **al ~** on this matter; **con ~ a, ~ de** with regard to, in relation to

respetable [respe'taβle] *adj* respectable

respetar [respe'tar] /1a/ *vt* to respect; **respeto** *nm* respect; (*acatamiento*) deference; **respetos** *nmpl* respects; **respetuoso, -a** *adj* respectful

respingo [res'pingo] *nm* start, jump

respiración [respira'θjon] *nf* breathing; (*Med*) respiration; (*ventilación*) ventilation; **~ asistida** artificial respiration (*by machine*)

respirar [respi'rar] /1a/ *vi* to breathe; **respiratorio, -a** *adj* respiratory; **respiro** *nm* breathing; (*fig: descanso*) respite

resplandecer [resplande'θer] /2d/ *vi* to shine; **resplandeciente** *adj* resplendent, shining; **resplandor** *nm* brilliance, brightness; (*del fuego*) blaze

r

responder [respon'der] /2a/ vt
to answer ▷ vi to answer; (fig) to
respond; (pey) to answer back; **~ de** o
por to answer for; **respondón, -ona**
adj cheeky

responsabilidad [responsaβili'ðað]
nf responsibility

responsabilizarse
[responsaβili'θarse] /1f/ vr to make
o.s. responsible, take charge

responsable [respon'sable] adj
responsible

respuesta [res'pwesta] nf answer,
reply

resquebrajar [reskeβra'xar] /1a/ vt
to crack, split; **resquebrajarse** vr to
crack, split

resquicio [res'kiθjo] nm chink;
(hendidura) crack

resta ['resta] nf (Mat) remainder

restablecer [restaβle'θer] /2d/ vt to
re-establish, restore; **restablecerse**
vr to recover

restante [res'tante] adj remaining; **lo
~** the remainder

restar [res'tar] /1a/ vt (Mat) to
subtract; (fig) to take away ▷ vi to
remain, be left

restauración [restaura'θjon] nf
restoration

restaurante [restau'rante] nm
restaurant

restaurar [restau'rar] /1a/ vt to
restore

restituir [restitu'ir] /3g/ vt (devolver)
to return, give back; (rehabilitar) to
restore

resto ['resto] nm (residuo) rest,
remainder; (apuesta) stake; **restos**
nmpl remains

restorán [resto'ran] nm (LAM)
restaurant

restregar [restre'ɣar] /1h, 1j/ vt to
scrub, rub

restricción [restrik'θjon] nf
restriction

restringir [restrin'xir] /3c/ vt to
restrict, limit

resucitar [resuθi'tar] /1a/ vt, vi to
resuscitate, revive

resuelto, -a [re'swelto, a] pp de
resolver ▷ adj resolute, determined

resultado [resul'taðo] nm result;
(conclusión) outcome; **resultante** adj
resulting, resultant

resultar [resul'tar] /1a/ vi (ser) to
be; (llegar a ser) to turn out to be;
(salir bien) to turn out well; (Com) to
amount to; **~ de** to stem from; **me
resulta difícil hacerlo** it's difficult for
me to do it

resumen [re'sumen] nm summary,
résumé; **en ~** in short

resumir [resu'mir] /3a/ vt to sum up;
(cortar) to abridge, cut down

🔲 No confundir resumir con la
palabra inglesa resume.

resurgir [resur'xir] /3c/ vi (reaparecer)
to reappear

resurrección [resurrek'θjon] nf
resurrection

retablo [re'taβlo] nm altarpiece

retaguardia [reta'ɣwarðja] nf
rearguard

retahíla [reta'ila] nf series, string

retal [re'tal] nm remnant

retar [re'tar] /1a/ vt to challenge;
(desafiar) to defy, dare

retazo [re'taθo] nm snippet (BRIT),
fragment

retención [reten'θjon] nf (tráfico)
hold-up; **~ fiscal** deduction for tax
purposes

retener [rete'ner] /2k/ vt (intereses)
to withhold

reticente [reti'θente] adj (insinuador)
insinuating; (postura) reluctant; **ser
~ a hacer algo** to be reluctant o
unwilling to do sth

retina [re'tina] nf retina

retintín [retin'tin] nm jangle,
jingle; **decir algo con ~** to say sth
sarcastically

retirado, -a adj (lugar) remote; (vida)
quiet; (jubilado) retired ▷ nf (Mil)
retreat; (de dinero) withdrawal; (de

embajador) recall; **batirse en retirada** to retreat

retirar [reti'rar] /1a/ *vt* to withdraw; (*quitar*) to remove; (*jubilar*) to retire, pension off; **retirarse** *vr* to retreat, withdraw; (*jubilarse*) to retire; (*acostarse*) to retire, go to bed; **retiro** *nm* retreat; (*jubilación*) retirement; (*pago*) pension

reto ['reto] *nm* dare, challenge

retocar [reto'kar] /1g/ *vt* (*fotografía*) to touch up, retouch

retoño [re'toɲo] *nm* sprout, shoot; (*fig*) offspring, child

retoque [re'toke] *nm* retouching

retorcer [retor'θer] /2b, 2h/ *vt* to twist; (*manos, lavado*) to wring; **retorcerse** *vr* to become twisted; (*persona*) to writhe

retorcido, -a [retor'θiðo, a] *adj* (*tb fig*) twisted

retorcijón [retorθi'xon] *nm* (LAM: *tb*: ~ **de tripas**) stomach cramp

retorno [re'torno] *nm* return

retortijón [retorti'xon] *nm*: ~ **de tripas** stomach cramp

retozar [reto'θar] /1f/ *vi* (*juguetear*) to frolic, romp; (*saltar*) to gambol

retracción [retrak'θjon] *nf* retraction

retraerse [retra'erse] /2o/ *vr* to retreat, withdraw; **retraído, -a** *adj* shy, retiring; **retraimiento** *nm* retirement; (*timidez*) shyness

retransmisión [retransmi'sjon] *nf* repeat (broadcast)

retransmitir [retransmi'tir] /3a/ *vt* (*mensaje*) to relay; (*TV etc*) to repeat, retransmit; (: *en vivo*) to broadcast live

retrasado, -a [retra'saðo, a] *adj* late; (*fam*) backward; (*país etc*) underdeveloped

retrasar [retra'sar] /1a/ *vt* (*demorar*) to postpone, put off; (*retardar*) to slow down ▷ *vi* (*atrasarse*) to be late; (*reloj*) to be slow; (*producción*) to fall (off); (*quedarse atrás*) to lag behind; **retrasarse** *vr* to be late; to be slow; to fall (off); to lag behind

retraso [re'traso] *nm* (*demora*) delay; (*lentitud*) slowness; (*tardanza*) lateness; (*atraso*) backwardness; **retrasos** *nmpl* (Com) arrears; **llegar con ~** to arrive late; **~ mental** mental deficiency

retratar [retra'tar] /1a/ *vt* (*Arte*) to paint the portrait of; (*fotografiar*) to photograph; (*fig*) to depict, describe; **retrato** *nm* portrait; (*fig*) likeness; **retrato-robot** *nm* Identikit® picture

retrete [re'trete] *nm* toilet

retribuir [retriβu'ir] /3g/ *vt* (*recompensar*) to reward; (*pagar*) to pay

retro... [retro] *pref* retro...

retroceder [retroθe'ðer] /2a/ *vi* (*echarse atrás*) to move back(wards); (*fig*) to back down

retroceso [retro'θeso] *nm* backward movement; (*Med*) relapse; (*fig*) backing down

retrospectivo, -a [retrospek'tiβo, a] *adj* retrospective

retrovisor [retroβi'sor] *nm* rear-view mirror

retumbar [retum'bar] /1a/ *vi* to echo, resound

reuma ['reuma] *nm* rheumatism

reunión [reu'njon] *nf* (*asamblea*) meeting; (*fiesta*) party

reunir [reu'nir] /3a/ *vt* (*juntar*) to reunite, join (together); (*recoger*) to gather (together); (*personas*) to bring o get together; (*cualidades*) to combine; **reunirse** *vr* (*personas: en asamblea*) to meet, gather

revalidar [reβali'ðar] /1a/ *vt* (*ratificar*) to confirm, ratify

revalorizar [reβalori'θar] /1f/ *vt* to revalue, reassess

revancha [re'βantʃa] *nf* revenge

revelación [reβela'θjon] *nf* revelation

revelado [reβe'laðo] *nm* developing

revelar [reβe'lar] /1a/ *vt* to reveal; (*Foto*) to develop

reventa [re'βenta] *nf* (*de entradas*) touting

reventar [reβen'tar] /1j/ vt to burst, explode

reventón [reβen'ton] nm (Auto) blow-out (BRIT), flat (US)

reverencia [reβe'renθja] nf reverence; **reverenciar** /1b/ vt to revere

reverendo, -a [reβe'rendo, a] adj reverend

reverente [reβe'rente] adj reverent

reversa [re'βersa] nf (LAM) (reverse) gear

reversible [reβer'siβle] adj reversible

reverso [re'βerso] nm back, other side; (de moneda) reverse

revertir [reβer'tir] /3i/ vi to revert

revés [re'βes] nm back, wrong side; (fig) reverse, setback; (Deporte) backhand; **al ~** the wrong way round; (de arriba abajo) upside down; (ropa) inside out; **volver algo del ~** to turn sth round; (ropa) to turn sth inside out

revisar [reβi'sar] /1a/ vt (examinar) to check; (texto etc) to revise; **revisión** nf revision; **revisión salarial** wage review

revisor, a [reβi'sor, a] nm/f inspector; (Ferro) ticket collector

revista [re'βista] nf magazine, review; (Teat) revue; (inspección) inspection; **~ del corazón** magazine featuring celebrity gossip and real-life romance stories; **pasar ~ a** to review, inspect

revivir [reβi'βir] /3a/ vi to revive

revolcar [reβol'kar] /1g, 1l/ vt to knock down; **revolcarse** vr to roll about

revoltijo [reβol'tixo] nm mess, jumble

revoltoso, -a [reβol'toso, a] adj (travieso) naughty, unruly

revolución [reβolu'θjon] nf revolution; **revolucionario, -a** adj, nm/f revolutionary

revolver [reβol'βer] /2h/ vt (desordenar) to disturb, mess up; (mover) to move about ▷ vi: **~ en** to go through,

rummage (about) in; **revolverse** vr: **~se contra** to turn on o against

revólver [re'βolβer] nm revolver

revuelo [re'βwelo] nm fluttering; (fig) commotion

revuelto, -a [re'βwelto, a] pp de **revolver** ▷ adj (mezclado) mixed-up, in disorder ▷ nf (motín) revolt; (agitación) commotion

rey [rei] nm king; **Día de R~es** Twelfth Night; **los R~es Magos** the Three Wise Men, the Magi

- **REYES MAGOS**
-
- The night before the 6th of January
- (the Epiphany), which is a holiday in
- Spain, children go to bed expecting
- los Reyes Magos, the Three Wise
- Men who visited the baby Jesus, to
- bring them presents. Twelfth night
- processions, known as cabalgatas,
- take place that evening, when 3
- people dressed as los Reyes Magos
- arrive in the town by land or sea to
- the delight of the children.

reyerta [re'jerta] nf quarrel, brawl

rezagado, -a [reθa'ɣaðo, a] nm/f straggler

rezar [re'θar] /1f/ vi to pray; **~ con** (fam) to concern, have to do with; **rezo** nm prayer

rezumar [reθu'mar] /1a/ vt to ooze

ría ['ria] nf estuary

riada [ri'aða] nf flood

ribera [ri'βera] nf (de río) bank; (: área) riverside

ribete [ri'βete] nm (de vestido) border; (fig) addition

ricino [ri'θino] nm: **aceite de ~** castor oil

rico, -a ['riko, a] adj (adinerado) rich; (lujoso) luxurious; (comida) delicious; (niño) lovely, cute ▷ nm/f rich person

ridiculez [riðiku'leθ] nf absurdity

ridiculizar [riðikuli'θar] /1f/ vt to ridicule

ridículo, -a [ri'ðikulo, a] *adj*
ridiculous; **hacer el ~** to make a fool
of o.s.; **poner a algn en ~** to make
a fool of sb

riego ['rjeɣo] *nm* (*aspersión*) watering;
(*irrigación*) irrigation; **~ sanguíneo**
blood flow *o* circulation

riel [rjel] *nm* rail

rienda ['rjenda] *nf* rein; **dar ~ suelta
a** to give free rein to

riesgo ['rjesɣo] *nm* risk; **correr el ~ de**
to run the risk of

rifa ['rifa] *nf* (*lotería*) raffle; **rifar** /1a/
vt to raffle

rifle ['rifle] *nm* rifle

rigidez [rixi'ðeθ] *nf* rigidity, stiffness;
(*fig*) strictness; **rígido, -a** *adj* rigid,
stiff; (*moralmente*) strict, inflexible

rigor [ri'ɣor] *nm* strictness, rigour;
(*inclemencia*) harshness; **de ~** de
rigueur, essential; **riguroso, -a** *adj*
rigorous; (*Meteorología*) harsh; (*severo*)
severe

rimar [ri'mar] /1a/ *vi* to rhyme

rimbombante [rimbom'bante] *adj*
pompous

rímel, rímmel ['rimel] *nm* mascara

rímmel ['rimel] *nm* = **rímel**

rin [rin] *nm* (*LAM*) (wheel) rim

rincón [rin'kon] *nm* corner (*inside*)

rinoceronte [rinoθe'ronte] *nm*
rhinoceros

riña ['riɲa] *nf* (*disputa*) argument;
(*pelea*) brawl

riñón [ri'ɲon] *nm* kidney

río ['rio] *vb V* **reír** ▷ *nm* river; (*fig*)
torrent, stream; **~ abajo/arriba**
downstream/upstream; **R~ de la
Plata** River Plate

rioja [ri'oxa] *nm* rioja wine ▷ *nf*: **La
R~** La Rioja

rioplatense [riopla'tense] *adj* of *o*
from the River Plate region

riqueza [ri'keθa] *nf* wealth, riches *pl*;
(*cualidad*) richness

risa ['risa] *nf* laughter; (*una risa*) laugh;
¡qué ~! what a laugh!

risco ['risko] *nm* crag, cliff

ristra ['ristra] *nf* string

risueño, -a [ri'sweɲo, a] *adj*
(*sonriente*) smiling; (*contento*) cheerful

ritmo ['ritmo] *nm* rhythm; **a ~ lento**
slowly; **trabajar a ~ lento** to go slow;
~ cardíaco heart rate

rito ['rito] *nm* rite

ritual [ri'twal] *adj, nm* ritual

rival [ri'βal] *adj, nm* rival; **rivalidad** *nf*
rivalry; **rivalizar** /1f/ *vi*: **rivalizar con**
to rival, vie with

rizado, -a [ri'θaðo, a] *adj* curly ▷ *nm*
curls *pl*

rizar [ri'θar] /1f/ *vt* to curl; **rizarse** *vr* (*el
pelo*) to curl; (*agua*) to ripple; **rizo** *nm*
curl; (*en agua*) ripple

RNE *nf abr* = **Radio Nacional de
España**

robar [ro'βar] /1a/ *vt* to rob; (*objeto*) to
steal; (*casa etc*) to break into; (*Naipes*)
to draw

roble ['roβle] *nm* oak; **robledal** *nm*
oakwood

robo ['roβo] *nm* robbery, theft

robot [ro'βoθ] *adj, nm* robot ▷ *nm* (*tb*: **~ de
cocina**) food processor

robustecer [roβuste'θer] /2d/ *vt* to
strengthen

robusto, -a [ro'βusto, a] *adj* robust,
strong

roca ['roka] *nf* rock

roce ['roθe] *nm* (*caricia*) brush; (*Tec*)
friction; (*en la piel*) graze; **tener ~ con**
to have a brush with

rociar [ro'θjar] /1c/ *vt* to sprinkle,
spray

rocín [ro'θin] *nm* nag, hack

rocío [ro'θio] *nm* dew

rocola [ro'kola] *nf* (*LAM*) jukebox

rocoso, -a [ro'koso, a] *adj* rocky

rodaballo [roða'βaʎo] *nm* turbot

rodaja [ro'ðaxa] *nf* slice

rodaje [ro'ðaxe] *nm* (*Cine*) shooting,
filming; (*Auto*): **en ~** running in

rodar [ro'ðar] /1l/ *vt* (*vehículo*) to wheel
(along); (*escalera*) to roll down; (*viajar
por*) to travel (over) ▷ *vi* to roll; (*coche*)
to go, run; (*Cine*) to shoot, film

rodear [roðe'ar] /1a/ vt to surround ▷ vi to go round; **rodearse** vr: **~se de amigos** to surround o.s. with friends

rodeo [ro'ðeo] nm (desvío) detour; (evasión) evasion; (LAM) rodeo; **hablar sin ~s** to come to the point, speak plainly

rodilla [ro'ðiʎa] nf knee; **de ~s** kneeling; **ponerse de ~s** to kneel (down)

rodillo [ro'ðiʎo] nm roller; (Culin) rolling-pin

roedor, -a [roe'ðor, a] adj gnawing ▷ nm rodent

roer [ro'er] /2y/ vt (masticar) to gnaw; (corroer, fig) to corrode

rogar [ro'ɣar] /1h, 1l/ vt (pedir) to beg, ask for ▷ vi (suplicar) to beg, plead; **rogarse** vr: **se ruega no fumar** please do not smoke

rojizo, -a [ro'xiθo, a] adj reddish

rojo, -a ['roxo, a] adj red ▷ nm red; **al ~ vivo** red-hot

rol [rol] nm list, roll; (papel) role

rollito [ro'ʎito] nm (tb: **~ de primavera**) spring roll

rollizo, -a [ro'ʎiθo] adj (objeto) cylindrical; (persona) plump

rollo ['roʎo] nm roll; (de cuerda) coil; (de madera) log; (fam) bore; **¡qué ~!** what a carry-on!

Roma ['roma] nf Rome

romance [ro'manθe] nm (amoroso) romance; (Lit) ballad

romano, -a [ro'mano, a] adj Roman ▷ nm/f Roman; **a la romana** in batter

romanticismo [romanti'θismo] nm romanticism

romántico, -a [ro'mantiko, a] adj romantic

rombo ['rombo] nm (Mat) rhombus

romería [rome'ria] nf (Rel) pilgrimage; (excursión) trip, outing

● **ROMERÍA**
●
● Originally a pilgrimage to a shrine
● or church to express devotion to
● Our Lady or a local Saint, the romería
● has also become a rural fiesta which
● accompanies the pilgrimage.
● People come from all over to attend,
● bringing their own food and drink,
● and spend the day in celebration.

romero, -a [ro'mero, a] nm/f pilgrim ▷ nm rosemary

romo, -a ['romo, a] adj blunt; (fig) dull

rompecabezas [rompeka'βeθas] nm inv riddle, puzzle; (juego) jigsaw (puzzle)

rompehuelgas [rompe'welɣas] nm inv (LAM) strikebreaker, scab

rompeolas [rompe'olas] nm inv breakwater

romper [rom'per] /2a/ vt to break; (hacer pedazos) to smash; (papel, tela etc) to tear, rip ▷ vi (olas) to break; (sol, diente) to break through; **~ un contrato** to break a contract; **~ a** to start (suddenly) to; **~ a llorar** to burst into tears; **~ con algn** to fall out with sb

ron [ron] nm rum

roncar [ron'kar] /1g/ vi to snore

ronco, -a ['ronko, a] adj (afónico) hoarse; (áspero) raucous

ronda ['ronda] nf (de bebidas etc) round; (patrulla) patrol; **rondar** /1a/ vt to patrol ▷ vi to patrol; (fig) to prowl round

ronquido [ron'kiðo] nm snore, snoring

ronronear [ronrone'ar] /1a/ vi to purr

roña ['roɲa] nf (en veterinaria) mange; (mugre) dirt, grime; (óxido) rust

roñoso, -a [ro'ɲoso, a] adj (mugriento) filthy; (tacaño) mean

ropa ['ropa] nf clothes pl, clothing; **~ blanca** linen; **~ de cama** bed linen; **~ de color** coloureds pl; **~ interior** underwear; **~ sucia** dirty clothes pl, dirty washing; **ropaje** nm gown, robes pl

ropero [ro'pero] nm linen cupboard; (guardarropa) wardrobe

rosa ['rosa] adj inv pink ▷ nf rose

rosado, -a [ro'saðo, a] adj pink ▷ nm rosé

rosal [ro'sal] nm rosebush

rosario [ro'sarjo] nm (Rel) rosary; **rezar el ~** to say the rosary

rosca ['roska] nf (de tornillo) thread; (de humo) coil, spiral; (pan, postre) ring-shaped roll/pastry

rosetón [rose'ton] nm rosette; (Arq) rose window

rosquilla [ros'kiʎa] nf ring-shaped cake

rostro ['rostro] nm (cara) face

rotativo, -a [rota'tiβo, a] adj rotary

roto, -a ['roto, a] pp de **romper** ▷ adj broken

rotonda [ro'tonda] nf roundabout

rótula ['rotula] nf kneecap; (Tec) ball-and-socket joint

rotulador [rotula'ðor] nm felt-tip pen

rótulo ['rotulo] nm heading, title; (etiqueta) label; (letrero) sign

rotundamente [rotunda'mente] adv (negar) flatly; (responder, afirmar) emphatically; **rotundo, -a** adj round; (enfático) emphatic

rotura [ro'tura] nf (rompimiento) breaking; (Med) fracture

rozadura [roθa'ðura] nf abrasion, graze

rozar [ro'θar] /1f/ vt (frotar) to rub; (arañar) to scratch; (tocar ligeramente) to shave; **rozarse** vr to rub (together); **~ con** (fam) to rub shoulders with

Rte. abr = **remite; remitente**

RTVE nf abr = **Radiotelevisión Española**

rubí [ru'βi] nm ruby; (de reloj) jewel

rubio, -a ['ruβjo, a] adj fair-haired, blond(e) ▷ nm/f blond/blonde; **tabaco ~** Virginia tobacco

rubor [ru'βor] nm (sonrojo) blush; (timidez) bashfulness; **ruborizarse** /1f/ vr to blush

rúbrica ['ruβrika] nf (de la firma) flourish; **rubricar** /1g/ vt (firmar) to

sign with a flourish; (concluir) to sign and seal

rudimentario, -a [ruðimen'tarjo, a] adj rudimentary

rudo, -a ['ruðo, a] adj (sin pulir) unpolished; (grosero) coarse; (violento) violent; (sencillo) simple

rueda ['rweða] nf wheel; (círculo) ring, circle; (rodaja) slice, round; **~ de auxilio** (LAM) spare tyre; **~ delantera/trasera/de repuesto** front/back/spare wheel; **~ de prensa** press conference; **~ gigante** (LAM) big (BRIT) o Ferris (US) wheel

ruedo ['rweðo] nm (círculo) circle; (Taur) arena, bullring

ruego etc ['rweɣo] vb V **rogar** ▷ nm request

rugby ['ruɣβi] nm rugby

rugido [ru'xiðo] nm roar

rugir [ru'xir] /3c/ vi to roar

rugoso, -a [ru'ɣoso, a] adj (arrugado) wrinkled; (áspero) rough; (desigual) ridged

ruido ['rwiðo] nm noise; (sonido) sound; (alboroto) racket, row; (escándalo) commotion, rumpus; **ruidoso, -a** adj noisy, loud; (fig) sensational

ruin [rwin] adj contemptible, mean

ruina ['rwina] nf ruin; (hundimiento) collapse; (de persona) ruin, downfall

ruinoso, -a [rwi'noso, a] adj ruinous; (destartalado) dilapidated, tumbledown; (Com) disastrous

ruiseñor [rwise'ɲor] nm nightingale

rulero [ru'lero] nm (LAM) roller

ruleta [ru'leta] nf roulette

rulo ['rulo] nm (para el pelo) curler

Rumania [ru'manja] nf Rumania

rumba ['rumba] nf rumba

rumbo ['rumbo] nm (ruta) route, direction; (ángulo de dirección) course, bearing; (fig) course of events; **ir con ~ a** to be heading for

rumiante [ru'mjante] nm ruminant

rumiar [ru'mjar] /1b/ vt to chew; (fig) to chew over ▷ vi to chew the cud

r

rumor [ru'mor] nm (ruido sordo) low sound; (murmuración) murmur, buzz; **rumorearse** /1a/ vr: **se rumorea que** it is rumoured that

rupestre [ru'pestre] adj rock cpd

ruptura [rup'tura] nf rupture

rural [ru'ral] adj rural

Rusia ['rusja] nf Russia; **ruso, -a** adj, nm/f Russian

rústico, -a ['rustiko, a] adj rustic; (ordinario) coarse, uncouth ▷ nm/f yokel

ruta ['ruta] nf route

rutina [ru'tina] nf routine

S

S abr (= san, santo, a) St.; (= sur) S

s. abr (= siglo) c.; (= siguiente) foll.

S.A. abr (= Sociedad Anónima) Ltd., Inc. (us)

sábado ['saβaðo] nm Saturday

sábana ['saβana] nf sheet

sabañón [saβa'ɲon] nm chilblain

saber [sa'βer] /2m/ vt to know; (llegar a conocer) to find out, learn; (tener capacidad de) to know how to ▷ vi: **~ a** to taste of, taste like ▷ nm knowledge, learning; **a ~** namely; **¿sabes conducir/nadar?** can you drive/swim?; **¿sabes francés?** do you o can you speak French?; **~ de memoria** to know by heart; **hacer ~** to inform, let know

sabiduría [saβiðu'ria] nf (conocimientos) wisdom; (instrucción) learning

sabiendas [sa'βjendas]: **a ~** adv knowingly

sabio, -a ['saβjo, a] adj (docto) learned; (prudente) wise, sensible

sabor [sa'βor] *nm* taste, flavour; **saborear** /1a/ *vt* to taste, savour; (*fig*) to relish

sabotaje [saβo'taxe] *nm* sabotage

sabré *etc* [sa'βre] *vb* V **saber**

sabroso, -a [sa'βroso, a] *adj* tasty; (*fig: fam*) racy, salty

sacacorchos [saka'kortʃos] *nm inv* corkscrew

sacapuntas [saka'puntas] *nm inv* pencil sharpener

sacar [sa'kar] /1g/ *vt* to take out; (*fig: extraer*) to get (out); (*quitar*) to remove, get out; (*hacer salir*) to bring out; (*conclusión*) to draw; (*novela etc*) to publish, bring out; (*ropa*) to take off; (*obra*) to make; (*premio*) to receive; (*entradas*) to get; (*Tenis*) to serve; **~ adelante** (*niño*) to bring up; (*negocio*) to carry on, go on with; **~ a algn a bailar** to get sb up to dance; **~ una foto** to take a photo; **~ la lengua** to stick out one's tongue; **~ buenas/ malas notas** to get good/bad marks

sacarina [saka'rina] *nf* saccharin(e)

sacerdote [saθer'ðote] *nm* priest

saciar [sa'θjar] /1b/ *vt* to satisfy; **saciarse** *vr* (*de comida*) to get full up

saco ['sako] *nm* bag; (*grande*) sack; (*contenido*) bagful; (*LAM: chaqueta*) jacket; **~ de dormir** sleeping bag

sacramento [sakra'mento] *nm* sacrament

sacrificar [sakrifi'kar] /1g/ *vt* to sacrifice; **sacrificio** *nm* sacrifice

sacristía [sakris'tia] *nf* sacristy

sacudida [saku'ðiða] *nf* (*agitación*) shake, shaking; (*sacudimiento*) jolt, bump; **~ eléctrica** electric shock

sacudir [saku'ðir] /3a/ *vt* to shake; (*golpear*) to hit

Sagitario [saxi'tarjo] *nm* Sagittarius

sagrado, -a [sa'ɣraðo, a] *adj* sacred, holy

Sáhara ['saara] *nm*: **el ~** the Sahara (desert)

sal [sal] *vb* V **salir** ▷ *nf* salt; **~es de baño** bath salts

sala ['sala] *nf* large room; (*tb*: **~ de estar**) living room; (*Teat*) house, auditorium; (*de hospital*) ward; **~ de espera** waiting room; **~ de estar** living room

salado, -a [sa'laðo, a] *adj* salty; (*fig*) witty, amusing; **agua salada** salt water

salar [sa'lar] /1a/ *vt* to salt, add salt to

salariado, -a *adj* (*empleado*) salaried

salario [sa'larjo] *nm* wage, pay

salchicha [sal'tʃitʃa] *nf* (*pork*) sausage; **salchichón** *nm* (*salami*-type) sausage

saldo ['saldo] *nm* (*pago*) settlement; (*de una cuenta*) balance; (*lo restante*) remnant(s) (*pl*), remainder; (*de móvil*) credit; **saldos** *nmpl* (*en tienda*) sale

saldré *etc* [sal'dre] *vb* V **salir**

salero [sa'lero] *nm* salt cellar

salgo *etc vb* V **salir**

salida [sa'liða] *nf* (*puerta etc*) exit, way out; (*acto*) leaving, going out; (*de tren, Aviat*) departure; (*Com, Tec*) output, production; (*fig*) way out; (*Com*) opening; (*Geo, válvula*) outlet; (*de gas*) leak; **calle sin ~** cul-de-sac; **~ de baño** (*LAM*) bathrobe; **~ de incendios** fire escape

○ **PALABRA CLAVE**

salir [sa'lir] /3q/ *vi* **1** to leave; **Juan ha salido** Juan has gone out; **salió de la cocina** he came out of the kitchen
2 (*disco, libro*) to come out; **anoche salió en la tele** she appeared o was on TV last night; **salió en todos los periódicos** it was in all the papers
3 (*resultar*): **la muchacha nos salió muy trabajadora** the girl turned out to be a very hard worker; **la comida te ha salido exquisita** the food was delicious; **sale muy caro** it's very expensive
4: **salir adelante: no sé como haré para salir adelante** I don't know how I'll get by

▶ **salirse** *vr* (*líquido*) to spill; (*animal*) to escape

saliva [sa'liβa] *nf* saliva

salmo ['salmo] *nm* psalm

salmón [sal'mon] *nm* salmon

salmonete [salmo'nete] *nm* red mullet

salón [sa'lon] *nm* (*de casa*) living-room, lounge; (*muebles*) lounge suite; **~ de belleza** beauty parlour; **~ de baile** dance hall; **~ de actos/sesiones** assembly hall

salpicadera [salpika'ðera] *nf* (LAM) mudguard (BRIT), fender (US)

salpicadero [salpika'ðero] *nm* (*Auto*) dashboard

salpicar [salpi'kar] /1g/ *vt* (*rociar*) to sprinkle, spatter; (*esparcir*) to scatter

salpicón [salpi'kon] *nm* (*tb*: **~ de marisco**) seafood salad

salsa ['salsa] *nf* sauce; (*con carne asada*) gravy; (*fig*) spice

saltamontes [salta'montes] *nm inv* grasshopper

saltar [sal'tar] /1a/ *vt* to jump (over), leap (over); (*dejar de lado*) to skip, miss out ▷ *vi* to jump, leap; (*pelota*) to bounce; (*al aire*) to fly up; (*quebrarse*) to break; (*al agua*) to dive; (*fig*) to explode, blow up

salto ['salto] *nm* jump, leap; (*al agua*) dive; **~ de agua** waterfall; **~ de altura** high jump

salud [sa'luð] *nf* health; **¡(a su) ~!** cheers!, good health!; **saludable** *adj* (*de buena salud*) healthy; (*provechoso*) good, beneficial

saludar [salu'ðar] /1a/ *vt* to greet; (*Mil*) to salute; **saludo** *nm* greeting; **saludos** (*en carta*) best wishes, regards

salvación [salβa'θjon] *nf* salvation; (*rescate*) rescue

salvado [sal'βaðo] *nm* bran

salvaje [sal'βaxe] *adj* wild; (*tribu*) savage

salvamanteles [salβaman'teles] *nm inv* table mat

salvamento [salβa'mento] *nm* rescue

salvapantallas [salβapan'taʎas] *nm inv* screensaver

salvar [sal'βar] /1a/ *vt* (*rescatar*) to save, rescue; (*resolver*) to overcome, resolve; (*cubrir distancias*) to cover, travel; (*hacer excepción*) to except, exclude; (*un barco*) to salvage

salvavidas [salβa'βiðas] *adj inv*: **bote/chaleco/cinturón ~** lifeboat/ lifejacket/lifebelt

salvo, -a ['salβo, a] *adj* safe ▷ *prep* except (for), save; **a ~** out of danger; **~ que** unless

san [san] *n* saint; **~ Juan** St. John

sanar [sa'nar] /1a/ *vt* (*herida*) to heal; (*persona*) to cure ▷ *vi* (*persona*) to get well, recover; (*herida*) to heal

sanatorio [sana'torjo] *nm* sanatorium

sanción [san'θjon] *nf* sanction

sancochado, -a [sanko'tʃaðo, a] *adj* (LAM Culin) underdone, rare

sandalia [san'dalja] *nf* sandal

sandía [san'dia] *nf* watermelon

sándwich ['sandwitʃ] (*pl* **sándwichs** *o* **sandwiches**) *nm* sandwich

Sanfermines [sanfer'mines] *nmpl* festivities in celebration of San Fermín

---

○ **SANFERMINES**

○
○ The *Sanfermines* are a week of
○ *fiestas* in Pamplona, the capital of
○ Navarre, made famous by Ernest
○ Hemingway. From the 7th of July,
○ the feast of San Fermín, crowds
○ of mainly young people take to
○ the streets drinking, singing and
○ dancing. Early in the morning bulls
○ are released along the narrow
○ streets leading to the bullring, and
○ people risk serious injury by running
○ out in front of them, a custom
○ which is also typical of many
○ Spanish villages.

sangrar [san'grar] /1a/ *vt*, *vi* to bleed; **sangre** *nf* blood

sangría [san'gria] *nf* sangria (*sweetened drink of red wine with fruit*)

sangriento, -a [san'grjento, a] *adj* bloody

sanguíneo, -a [san'gineo, a] *adj* blood *cpd*

sanidad [sani'ðað] *nf*: **~ pública** public health (department)

San Isidro [sani'sidro] *nm patron saint of Madrid*

- **SAN ISIDRO**
- *San Isidro* is the patron saint of Madrid, and gives his name to the week-long festivities which take place around the 15th May. Originally an 18th-century trade fair, the *San Isidro* celebrations now include music, dance, a famous *romería*, theatre and bullfighting.

sanitario, -a [sani'tarjo, a] *adj* health *cpd*; **sanitarios** *nmpl* toilets (BRIT), restroom *sg* (US)

sano, -a ['sano, a] *adj* healthy; (*sin daños*) sound; (*comida*) wholesome; (*entero*) whole, intact; **~ y salvo** safe and sound

⬛ No confundir *sano* con la palabra inglesa *sane*.

Santiago [san'tjaɣo] *nm*: **~ (de Chile)** Santiago

santiamén [santja'men] *nm*: **en un ~** in no time at all

santidad [santi'ðað] *nf* holiness, sanctity

santiguarse [santi'ɣwarse] /1i/ *vr* to make the sign of the cross

santo, -a ['santo, a] *adj* holy; (*fig*) wonderful, miraculous ▷ *nm/f* saint ▷ *nm* saint's day; **~ y seña** password

santuario [san'twarjo] *nm* sanctuary, shrine

sapo ['sapo] *nm* toad

saque ['sake] *nm* (*Tenis*) service, serve; (*Fútbol*) throw-in; **~ de esquina** corner (kick)

saquear [sake'ar] /1a/ *vt* (*Mil*) to sack; (*robar*) to loot, plunder; (*fig*) to ransack

sarampión [saram'pjon] *nm* measles *sg*

sarcástico, -a [sar'kastiko, a] *adj* sarcastic

sardina [sar'ðina] *nf* sardine

sargento [sar'xento] *nm* sergeant

sarmiento [sar'mjento] *nm* vine shoot

sarna ['sarna] *nf* itch; (*Med*) scabies

sarpullido [sarpu'ʎiðo] *nm* (*Med*) rash

sarro ['sarro] *nm* (*en dientes*) tartar, plaque

sartén [sar'ten] *nf* frying pan

sastre ['sastre] *nm* tailor; **sastrería** *nf* (*arte*) tailoring; (*tienda*) tailor's (shop)

Satanás [sata'nas] *nm* Satan

satélite [sa'telite] *nm* satellite

sátira ['satira] *nf* satire

satisfacción [satisfak'θjon] *nf* satisfaction

satisfacer [satisfa'θer] /2r/ *vt* to satisfy; (*gastos*) to meet; (*pérdida*) to make good; **satisfacerse** *vr* to satisfy o.s., be satisfied; (*vengarse*) to take revenge; **satisfecho, -a** *adj* satisfied; (*contento*) content(ed), happy; (*tb*: **satisfecho de sí mismo**) self-satisfied, smug

saturar [satu'rar] /1a/ *vt* to saturate; **saturarse** *vr* (*mercado, aeropuerto*) to reach saturation point

sauce ['sauθe] *nm* willow; **~ llorón** weeping willow

sauna ['sauna] *nf* sauna

savia ['saβja] *nf* sap

saxofón [sakso'fon] *nm* saxophone

sazonar [saθo'nar] /1a/ *vt* to ripen; (*Culin*) to flavour, season

scooter [e'skuter] *nf* (ESP) scooter

Scotch® [skotʃ] *nm* (LAM) Sellotape® (BRIT), Scotch tape® (US)

SE *abr* (= *sudeste*) SE

○
PALABRA CLAVE

se [se] *pron* **1** *(reflexivo: sg: m)* himself; *(: f)* herself; *(: pl)* themselves; *(: cosa)* itself; *(: deVd)* yourself; *(: deVds)* yourselves; **se está preparando** she's getting (herself) ready
2 *(como complemento indirecto)* to him; to her; to them; to it; to you; **se lo dije ayer** *(aVd)* I told you yesterday; **se compró un sombrero** he bought himself a hat; **se rompió la pierna** he broke his leg
3 *(uso recíproco)* each other, one another; **se miraron (el uno al otro)** they looked at each other *o* one another
4 *(en oraciones pasivas)*: **se han vendido muchos libros** a lot of books have been sold
5 *(impers)*: **se dice que** people say that, it is said that; **allí se come muy bien** the food there is very good, you can eat very well there

sé [se] *vb* V **saber; ser**
sea *etc* ['sea] *vb* V **ser**
sebo ['seβo] *nm* fat, grease
secador [seka'ðor] *nm*: **~ para el pelo** hairdryer
secadora [seka'ðora] *nf* tumble dryer
secar [se'kar] /1g/ *vt* to dry; **secarse** *vr* to dry (off); *(río, planta)* to dry up
sección [sek'θjon] *nf* section
seco, -a ['seko, a] *adj* dry; *(carácter)* cold; *(respuesta)* sharp, curt; **decir algo a secas** to say sth curtly; **parar en ~** to stop dead
secretaría [sekreta'ria] *nf* secretariat
secretario, -a [sekre'tarjo, a] *nm/f* secretary
secreto, -a [se'kreto, a] *adj* secret; *(persona)* secretive ▷ *nm* secret; *(calidad)* secrecy
secta ['sekta] *nf* sect
sector [sek'tor] *nm* sector *(tb Inform)*
secuela [se'kwela] *nf* consequence

secuencia [se'kwenθja] *nf* sequence
secuestrar [sekwes'trar] /1a/ *vt* to kidnap; *(bienes)* to seize, confiscate; **secuestro** *nm* kidnapping; seizure, confiscation
secundario, -a [sekun'darjo, a] *adj* secondary
sed [seð] *nf* thirst; **tener ~** to be thirsty
seda ['seða] *nf* silk
sedal [se'ðal] *nm* fishing line
sedán [se'ðan] *nm* *(LAM)* saloon *(BRIT)*, sedan *(US)*
sedante [se'ðante] *nm* sedative
sede ['seðe] *nf* *(de gobierno)* seat; *(de compañía)* headquarters *pl*; **Santa S~** Holy See
sedentario, -a [seðen'tarjo, a] *adj* sedentary
sediento, -a [se'ðjento, a] *adj* thirsty
sedimento [seði'mento] *nm* sediment
seducción [seðuk'θjon] *nf* seduction
seducir [seðu'θir] /3n/ *vt* to seduce; *(cautivar)* to charm, fascinate; *(atraer)* to attract; **seductor, a** *adj* seductive; charming, fascinating; attractive ▷ *nm/f* seducer
segar [se'ɣar] /1h, 1j/ *vt* *(mies)* to reap, cut; *(hierba)* to mow, cut
seglar [se'ɣlar] *adj* secular, lay
seguido, -a [se'ɣiðo, a] *adj* *(continuo)* continuous, unbroken; *(recto)* straight ▷ *adv* *(directo)* straight (on); *(después)* after; *(LAM: a menudo)* often ▷ *nf*: **en seguida** at once, right away; **cinco días ~s** five days running, five days in a row
seguidor, a [seɣi'ðd]or, a] *nm/f* follower
seguir [se'ɣir] /3d, 3k/ *vt* to follow; *(venir después)* to follow on, come after; *(proseguir)* to continue; *(perseguir)* to chase, pursue ▷ *vi* *(gen)* to follow; *(continuar)* to continue, carry *o* go on; **seguirse** *vr* to follow; **sigo sin comprender** I still don't understand; **sigue lloviendo** it's still raining

según [se'ɣun] *prep* according to
▷ *adv*: **~ (y conforme)** it all depends
▷ *conj* as

segundo, -a [se'ɣundo, a] *adj*
second ▷ *nm* second ▷ *nf* second
meaning; **segunda (clase)** second
class; **segunda (marcha)** (*Auto*)
second (gear); **de segunda mano**
second hand

seguramente [seɣura'mente] *adv*
surely; (*con certeza*) for sure, with
certainty

seguridad [seɣuri'ðað] *nf* safety;
(*del estado, de casa etc*) security;
(*certidumbre*) certainty; (*confianza*)
confidence; (*estabilidad*) stability; **~**
social social security

seguro, -a [se'ɣuro, a] *adj* (*cierto*)
sure, certain; (*fiel*) trustworthy;
(*libre de peligro*) safe; (*bien defendido,*
firme) secure ▷ *adv* for sure, certainly
▷ *nm* (*Com*) insurance; **~ contra**
terceros/a todo riesgo third
party/comprehensive insurance; **~s**
sociales social security *sg*

seis [seis] *num* six

seísmo [se'ismo] *nm* tremor,
earthquake

selección [selek'θjon] *nf* selection;
seleccionar /1a/ *vt* to pick, choose,
select

selectividad [selektiβi'ðað] *nf* (*Univ*)
entrance examination

selecto, -a [se'lekto, a] *adj* select,
choice; (*escogido*) selected

sellar [se'ʎar] /1a/ *vt* (*documento*
oficial) to seal; (*pasaporte, visado*)
to stamp

sello ['seʎo] *nm* stamp; (*precinto*) seal

selva ['selβa] *nf* (*bosque*) forest, woods
pl; (*jungla*) jungle

semáforo [se'maforo] *nm* (*Auto*)
traffic lights *pl*; (*Ferro*) signal

semana [se'mana] *nf* week; **S~**
Santa Holy Week; **entre ~** during
the week; *see note* **"Semana Santa"**;
semanal *adj* weekly; **semanario** *nm*
weekly (magazine)

● **SEMANA SANTA**
●
●
● *Semana Santa* is a holiday in Spain.
● All regions take *Viernes Santo*, Good
● Friday, *Sábado Santo*, Holy Saturday,
● and *Domingo de Resurrección*, Easter
● Sunday. Other holidays at this time
● vary according to each region.
● There are spectacular *procesiones* all
● over the country, with members of
● *cofradías* (brotherhoods) dressing
● in hooded robes and parading their
● *pasos* (religious floats or sculptures)
● through the streets. Seville has the
● most renowned celebrations, on
● account of the religious fervour
● shown by the locals.

sembrar [sem'brar] /1j/ *vt* to sow;
(*objetos*) to sprinkle, scatter about;
(*noticias etc*) to spread

semejante [seme'xante] *adj*
(*parecido*) similar; **~s** alike, similar
▷ *nm* fellow man, fellow creature;
nunca hizo cosa ~ he never did such
a thing; **semejanza** *nf* similarity,
resemblance

semejar [seme'xar] /1a/ *vi* to seem
like, resemble; **semejarse** *vr* to look
alike, be similar

semen ['semen] *nm* semen

semestral [semes'tral] *adj* half-
yearly, bi-annual

semicírculo [semi'θirkulo] *nm*
semicircle

semidesnatado, -a
[semiðesna'taðo, a] *adj* semi-
skimmed

semifinal [semifi'nal] *nf* semifinal

semilla [se'miʎa] *nf* seed

seminario [semi'narjo] *nm* (*Rel*)
seminary; (*Escol*) seminar

sémola ['semola] *nf* semolina

senado [se'naðo] *nm* senate;
senador, a *nm/f* senator

sencillez [senθi'ʎeθ] *nf* simplicity; (*de*
persona) naturalness; **sencillo, -a** *adj*
simple; (*carácter*) natural, unaffected

S

senda ['senda] *nm* path, track
senderismo [sende'rismo] *nm* hiking
sendero [sen'dero] *nm* path, track
sendos, -as ['sendos, as] *adj pl*: **les dio ~ golpes** he hit both of them
senil [se'nil] *adj* senile
seno ['seno] *nm* (Anat) bosom, bust; (*fig*) bosom; **senos** *nmpl* breasts
sensación [sensa'θjon] *nf* sensation; (*sentido*) sense; (*sentimiento*) feeling; **sensacional** *adj* sensational
sensato, -a [sen'sato, a] *adj* sensible
sensible [sen'sible] *adj* sensitive; (*apreciable*) perceptible, appreciable; (*pérdida*) considerable; **sensiblero, -a** *adj* sentimental

> No confundir *sensible* con la palabra inglesa *sensible*.

sensitivo, -a [sensi'tiβo, a] *adj* sense *cpd*
sensorial [senso'rjal] *adj* sensory
sensual [sen'swal] *adj* sensual
sentado, -a [sen'taðo, a] *adj* (*establecido*) settled ▷ *nf* sitting; (*Pol*) sit-in; **dar por ~** to take for granted, assume; **estar ~** to sit, be sitting (down)
sentar [sen'tar] /1j/ *vt* to sit, seat; (*fig*) to establish ▷ *vi* (*vestido*) to suit; (*alimento*): **~ bien/mal a** to agree/disagree with; **sentarse** *vr* (*persona*) to sit, sit down; (*los depósitos*) to settle
sentencia [sen'tenθja] *nf* (*máxima*) maxim, saying; (*Jur*) sentence; **sentenciar** /1b/ *vt* to sentence
sentido, -a [sen'tiðo, a] *adj* (*pérdida*) regrettable; (*carácter*) sensitive ▷ *nm* sense; (*sentimiento*) feeling; (*significado*) sense, meaning; (*dirección*) direction; **mi más ~ pésame** my deepest sympathy; **~ del humor** sense of humour; **~ común** common sense; **tener ~** to make sense; **~ único** one-way (street)
sentimental [sentimen'tal] *adj* sentimental; **vida ~** love life

sentimiento [senti'mjento] *nm* feeling
sentir [sen'tir] /3i/ *vt* to feel; (*percibir*) to perceive, sense; (*lamentar*) to regret, be sorry for ▷ *vi* to feel; (*lamentarse*) to feel sorry ▷ *nm* opinion, judgement; **sentirse** *vr*: **lo siento** I'm sorry; **~se mejor/mal** to feel better/ill
seña ['sena] *nf* (*Mil*) password; **señas** *nfpl* address *sg*; **~s personales** personal description *sg*
señal [se'nal] *nf* sign; (*síntoma*) symptom; (*Ferro, Telec*) signal; (*marca*) mark; (*Com*) deposit; **en ~ de** as a token of, as a sign of; **señalar** /1a/ *vt* to mark; (*indicar*) to point out, indicate
señor, a [se'nor, a] *nm* (*hombre*) man; (*caballero*) gentleman; (*dueño*) owner, master; (*trato: antes de nombre propio*) Mr; (: *hablando directamente*) sir ▷ *nf* (*dama*) lady; (*trato: antes de nombre propio*) Mrs; (: *hablando directamente*) madam; (*esposa*) wife; **Muy ~ mío** Dear Sir; **Nuestra S~a** Our Lady
señorita [seno'rita] *nf* Miss; (*mujer joven*) young lady
señorito [seno'rito] *nm* young gentleman; (*pey*) toff
sepa *etc* ['sepa] *vb* V **saber**
separación [separa'θjon] *nf* separation; (*división*) division; (*distancia*) gap
separar [sepa'rar] /1a/ *vt* to separate; (*dividir*) to divide; **separarse** *vr* (*parte*) to come away; (*partes*) to come apart; (*persona*) to leave, go away; (*matrimonio*) to separate; **separatismo** *nm* separatism
sepia ['sepja] *nf* cuttlefish
septentrional [septentrjo'nal] *adj* northern
septiembre [sep'tjembre] *nm* September
séptimo, -a ['septimo, a] *adj, nm* seventh
sepulcral [sepul'kral] *adj* (*fig*) gloomy, dismal; (*silencio, atmósfera*) deadly; **sepulcro** *nm* tomb, grave

sepultar [sepul'tar] /1a/ vt to bury;
sepultura nf (acto) burial; (tumba)
grave, tomb

sequía [se'kia] nf drought

séquito ['sekito] nm (de rey etc)
retinue; (Pol) followers pl

PALABRA CLAVE

ser [ser] /2v/ vi 1 (descripción, identidad)
to be; **es médica/muy alta** she's a
doctor/very tall; **su familia es de
Cuzco** his family is from Cuzco; **soy
Ana** I'm Ana; (por teléfono) it's Ana
2 (propiedad): **es de Joaquín** it's
Joaquín's, it belongs to Joaquín
3 (horas, fechas, números): **es la una** it's
one o'clock; **son las seis y media** it's
half-past six; **es el 1 de junio** it's the
first of June; **somos/son seis** there
are six of us/them
4 (suceso): **¿qué ha sido eso?** what
was that?; **la fiesta es en mi casa** the
party's at my house
5 (en oraciones pasivas): **ha sido
descubierto ya** it's already been
discovered
6: **es de esperar que …** it is to be
hoped o I etc hope that …
7 (locuciones con subjun): **o sea** that is
to say; **sea él sea su hermana** either
him or his sister
8: **a o de no ser por él …** but for
him …
9: **a no ser que: a no ser que tenga
uno ya** unless he's got one already
▶ nm being; **ser humano** human being

sereno, -a [se'reno, a] adj (persona)
calm, unruffled; (tiempo) fine, settled;
(ambiente) calm, peaceful ▷ nm night
watchman

serial [se'rjal] nm serial

serie ['serje] nf series; (cadena)
sequence, succession; **fuera de ~**
out of order; (fig) special, out of the
ordinary; **fabricación en ~** mass
production

seriedad [serje'ðað] nf seriousness;
(formalidad) reliability

serigrafía [seriɣra'fia] nf silk screen
printing

serio, -a ['serjo, a] adj serious;
reliable, dependable; grave, serious;
en ~ seriously

sermón [ser'mon] nm (Rel) sermon

seropositivo, -a [seroposi'tiβo, a]
adj HIV-positive

serpentear [serpente'ar] /1a/ vi to
wriggle; (camino, río) to wind, snake

serpentina [serpen'tina] nf
streamer

serpiente [ser'pjente] nf snake; **~ de
cascabel** rattlesnake

serranía [serra'nia] nf mountainous
area

serrar [se'rrar] /1j/ vt to saw

serrín [se'rrin] nm sawdust

serrucho [se'rrutʃo] nm handsaw

service ['serβis] nm (LAM Auto) service

servicio [ser'βiθjo] nm service; (LAM
Auto) service; **servicios** nmpl toilet(s);
~ incluido service charge included; **~
militar** military service

servidumbre [serβi'ðumbre] nf
(sujeción) servitude; (criados) servants
pl, staff

servil [ser'βil] adj servile

servilleta [serβi'ʎeta] nf serviette,
napkin

servir [ser'βir] /3k/ vt to serve ▷ vi to
serve; (tener utilidad) to be of use, be
useful; **servirse** vr to serve o help o.s.;
~se de algo to make use of sth, use
sth; **sírvase pasar** please come in

sesenta [se'senta] num sixty

sesión [se'sjon] nf (Pol) session,
sitting; (Cine) showing

seso ['seso] nm brain; **sesudo, -a** adj
sensible, wise

seta ['seta] nf mushroom;
~ venenosa toadstool

setecientos, -as [sete'θjentos, as]
num seven hundred

setenta [se'tenta] num seventy

severo, -a [se'βero, a] adj severe

Sevilla [se'βiʎa] nf Seville; **sevillano, -a** adj of o from Seville ▷ nm/f native o inhabitant of Seville

sexo ['sekso] nm sex

sexto, -a ['seksto, a] num sixth

sexual [sek'swal] adj sexual; **vida ~** sex life

si [si] conj if; whether ▷ nm (Mus) B; **me pregunto si ...** I wonder o whether ...

sí [si] adv yes ▷ nm consent ▷ pron (uso impersonal) oneself; (sg: m) himself; (: f) herself; (: de cosa) itself; (: de usted) yourself; (pl) themselves; (: de ustedes) yourselves; (: recíproco) each other; **él no quiere pero yo sí** he doesn't want to but I do; **ella sí vendrá** she will certainly come, she is sure to come; **claro que sí** of course; **creo que sí** I think so

siamés, -esa [sja'mes, esa] adj, nm/f Siamese

SIDA ['siða] nm abr (= síndrome de inmunodeficiencia adquirida) AIDS

siderúrgico, -a [siðe'rurxico, a] adj iron and steel cpd

sidra ['siðra] nf cider

siembra ['sjembra] nf sowing

siempre ['sjempre] adv always; (todo el tiempo) all the time ▷ conj: **~ que ...** (+ indic) whenever ...; (+ subjun) provided that ...; **como ~** as usual; **para ~** forever

sien [sjen] nf temple

siento etc ['sjento] vb V **sentar; sentir**

sierra ['sjerra] nf (Tec) saw; (Geo) mountain range

siervo, -a ['sjerβo, a] nm/f slave

siesta ['sjesta] nf siesta, nap; **dormir la o echarse una o tomar una ~** to have an afternoon nap o a doze

siete ['sjete] num seven

sifón [si'fon] nm syphon

sigla ['siɣla] nf abbreviation

siglo ['siɣlo] nm century; (fig) age

significado [siɣnifi'kaðo] nm (de palabra etc) meaning

significar [siɣnifi'kar] /1g/ vt to mean, signify; (notificar) to make known, express

significativo, -a [siɣnifika'tiβo, a] adj significant

signo ['siɣno] nm sign; **~ de admiración o exclamación** exclamation mark; **~ de interrogación** question mark

sigo etc vb V **seguir**

siguiente [si'ɣjente] adj following; (próximo) next

siguió etc vb V **seguir**

sílaba ['silaβa] nf syllable

silbar [sil'βar] /1a/ vt, vi to whistle; **silbato** nm whistle; **silbido** nm whistle, whistling

silenciador [silenθja'ðor] nm silencer

silenciar [silen'θjar] /1b/ vt (persona) to silence; (escándalo) to hush up; **silencio** nm silence, quiet; **silencioso, -a** adj silent, quiet

silla ['siʎa] nf (asiento) chair; (tb: **~ de montar**) saddle; **~ de ruedas** wheelchair

sillón [si'ʎon] nm armchair, easy chair

silueta [si'lweta] nf silhouette; (de edificio) outline; (figura) figure

silvestre [sil'βestre] adj wild

simbólico, -a [sim'boliko, a] adj symbolic(al)

simbolizar [simboli'θar] /1f/ vt to symbolize

símbolo ['simbolo] nm symbol

similar [simi'lar] adj similar

simio ['simjo] nm ape

simpatía [simpa'tia] nf liking; (afecto) affection; (amabilidad) kindness; **simpático, -a** adj nice, pleasant; (bondadoso) kind

▌ No confundir *simpático* con la palabra inglesa *sympathetic*.

simpatizante [simpati'θante] nmf sympathizer

simpatizar [simpati'θar] /1f/ vi: **~ con** to get on well with

simple ['simple] adj simple; (elemental) simple, easy; (mero) mere; (puro) pure, sheer ▷ nmf simpleton; **simpleza** nf simpleness; (necedad) silly thing; **simplificar** /1g/ vt to simplify
simposio [sim'posjo] nm symposium
simular [simu'lar] /1a/ vt to simulate
simultáneo, -a [simul'taneo, a] adj simultaneous
sin [sin] prep without ▷ conj: ~ **que** (+ subjun) without; **la ropa está ~ lavar** the clothes are unwashed; ~ **embargo** however
sinagoga [sina'ɣoɣa] nf synagogue
sinceridad [sinθeri'ðað] nf sincerity; **sincero, -a** adj sincere
sincronizar [sinkroni'θar] /1f/ vt to synchronize
sindical [sindi'kal] adj union cpd, trade-union cpd; **sindicalista** adj ▷ nmf trade unionist
sindicato [sindi'kato] nm (de trabajadores) trade(s) o labor (US) union; (de negociantes) syndicate
síndrome ['sindrome] nm syndrome; ~ **de abstinencia** withdrawal symptoms; ~ **de la clase turista** economy-class syndrome
sinfín [sin'fin] nm: **un ~ de** a great many, no end of
sinfonía [sinfo'nia] nf symphony
singular [singu'lar] adj singular; (fig) outstanding, exceptional; (pey) peculiar, odd
siniestro, -a [si'njestro, a] adj sinister ▷ nm (accidente) accident
sinnúmero [sin'numero] nm = **sinfín**
sino ['sino] nm fate, destiny ▷ conj (pero) but; (salvo) except, save
sinónimo, -a [si'nonimo, a] adj synonymous ▷ nm synonym
síntesis ['sintesis] nf inv synthesis; **sintético, -a** adj synthetic
sintió vb V **sentir**
síntoma ['sintoma] nm symptom
sintonía [sinto'nia] nf (Radio) tuning; **sintonizar** /1f/ vt (Radio) to tune (in) to

sinvergüenza [simber'ɣwenθa] nmf rogue, scoundrel; **¡es un ~!** he's got a nerve!
siquiera [si'kjera] conj even if, even though ▷ adv at least; **ni ~** not even
Siria ['sirja] nf Syria
sirviente, -a [sir'βjente, a] nm/f servant
sirvo etc vb V **servir**
sistema [sis'tema] nm system; (método) method; **sistemático, -a** adj systematic

● **SISTEMA EDUCATIVO**
●
● The reform of the Spanish sistema
● educativo (education system) begun
● in the early 90s has replaced the
● courses EGB, BUP and COU with the
● following: Primaria a compulsory
● 6 years; Secundaria a compulsory 4
● years; Bachillerato an optional 2 year
● secondary school course, essential
● for those wishing to go on to higher
● education.

sitiar [si'tjar] /1b/ vt to besiege, lay siege to
sitio ['sitjo] nm (lugar) place; (espacio) room, space; (Mil) siege; ~ **de taxis** (LAM: parada) taxi stand o rank (BRIT); ~ **web** website
situación [sitwa'θjon] nf situation, position; (estatus) position, standing
situado, -a [si'twaðo, a] adj situated, placed
situar [si'twar] /1e/ vt to place, put; (edificio) to locate, situate
slip [es'lip] nm pants pl, briefs pl
smoking [(e)'smokin] (pl **smokings**) nm dinner jacket (BRIT), tuxedo (US)
◼ No confundir smoking con la palabra inglesa smoking.
SMS nm (mensaje) text (message), SMS (message)
snob [es'nob] = **esnob**
SO abr (= suroeste) SW
sobaco [so'βako] nm armpit

sobar [so'βar] /1a/ vt (ropa) to rumple; (comida) to play around with

soberanía [soβera'nia] nf sovereignty; **soberano, -a** adj sovereign; (fig) supreme ▷ nm/f sovereign

soberbio, -a [so'βerβjo, a] adj (orgulloso) proud; (altivo) arrogant; (fig) magnificent, superb ▷ nf pride; haughtiness, arrogance; magnificence

sobornar [soβor'nar] /1a/ vt to bribe; **soborno** nm bribe

sobra ['soβra] nf excess, surplus; **sobras** nfpl left-overs, scraps; **de ~** surplus, extra; **tengo de ~** I've more than enough; **sobrado, -a** adj (más que suficiente) more than enough; (superfluo) excessive; **sobrante** adj remaining, extra ▷ nm surplus, remainder; **sobrar** /1a/ vt to exceed, surpass ▷ vi (tener de más) to be more than enough; (quedar) to remain, be left (over)

sobrasada [soβra'saða] nf ≈ sausage spread

sobre ['soβre] prep (gen) on; (encima) on (top of); (por encima de, arriba de) over, above; (más que) more than; (además) in addition to, besides; (alrededor de) about ▷ nm envelope; **~ todo** above all

sobrecama [soβre'kama] nf bedspread

sobrecargar [soβrekar'ɣar] /1h/ vt (camión) to overload; (Com) to surcharge

sobredosis [soβre'ðosis] nf inv overdose

sobreentender [soβreenten'der] /2g/ vt to deduce, infer; **sobreentenderse** vr: **se sobreentiende que ...** it is implied that ...

sobrehumano, -a [soβreu'mano, a] adj superhuman

sobrellevar [soβreʎe'βar] /1a/ vt to bear, endure

sobremesa [soβre'mesa] nf: **durante la ~** after dinner

sobrenatural [soβrenatu'ral] adj supernatural

sobrenombre [soβre'nombre] nm nickname

sobrepasar [soβrepa'sar] /1a/ vt to exceed, surpass

sobreponer [soβrepo'ner] /2q/ vt (poner encima) to put on top; (añadir) to add; **sobreponerse** vr: **~se a** to overcome

sobresaliente [soβresa'ljente] adj outstanding, excellent

sobresalir [soβresa'lir] /3q/ vi to project, jut out; (fig) to stand out, excel

sobresaltar [soβresal'tar] /1a/ vt (asustar) to scare, frighten; (sobrecoger) to startle; **sobresalto** nm (movimiento) start; (susto) scare; (turbación) sudden shock

sobretodo [soβre'toðo] nm overcoat

sobrevenir [soβreβe'nir] /3r/ vi (ocurrir) to happen (unexpectedly); (resultar) to follow, ensue

sobrevivir [soβreβi'βir] /3a/ vi to survive

sobrevolar [soβreβo'lar] /1l/ vt to fly over

sobriedad [soβrje'ðað] nf sobriety, soberness; (moderación) moderation, restraint

sobrino, -a [so'βrino, a] nm/f nephew/niece

sobrio, -a ['soβrjo, a] adj sober; (moderado) moderate, restrained

socarrón, -ona [soka'rron, ona] adj (sarcástico) sarcastic, ironic(al)

socavón [soka'βon] nm (en la calle) hole

sociable [so'θjaβle] adj (persona) sociable, friendly; (animal) social

social [so'θjal] adj social; (Com) company cpd

socialdemócrata [soθjalde'mokrata] nmf social democrat

socialista [soθja'lista] *adj, nmf* socialist

socializar [soθjali'θar] /1f/ *vt* to socialize

sociedad [soθje'ðað] *nf* society; (Com) company; **~ anónima (S.A.)** limited company (Ltd) (BRIT), incorporated company (Inc) (US); **~ de consumo** consumer society

socio, -a ['soθjo, a] *nm/f* (miembro) member; (Com) partner

sociología [soθjolo'xia] *nf* sociology; **sociólogo, -a** *nm/f* sociologist

socorrer [soko'rrer] /2a/ *vt* to help; **socorrista** *nmf* first aider; (en piscina, playa) lifeguard; **socorro** *nm* (ayuda) help, aid; (Mil) relief; **¡socorro!** help!

soda ['soða] *nf* (sosa) soda; (bebida) soda (water)

sofá [so'fa] *nm* sofa, settee; **sofá-cama** *nm* studio couch, sofa bed

sofocar [sofo'kar] /1g/ *vt* to suffocate; (apagar) to smother, put out; **sofocarse** *vr* to suffocate; (fig) to blush, feel embarrassed; **sofoco** *nm* suffocation; (azoro) embarrassment

sofreír [sofre'ir] /3l/ *vt* to fry lightly

soft ['sof], **software** ['sofwer] *nm* (Inform) software

soga ['soɣa] *nf* rope

sois [sois] *vb V* **ser**

soja ['soxa] *nf* soya

sol [sol] *nm* sun; (luz) sunshine, sunlight; (Mus) G; **hace ~** it is sunny

solamente [sola'mente] *adv* only, just

solapa [so'lapa] *nf* (de chaqueta) lapel; (de libro) jacket

solapado, -a [sola'paðo, a] *adj* (intenciones) underhand; (gestos, movimiento) sly

solar [so'lar] *adj* solar, sun *cpd* ▷ *nm* (terreno) plot (of ground)

soldado [sol'daðo] *nm* soldier; **~ raso** private

soldador [solda'ðor] *nm* soldering iron; (persona) welder

soldar [sol'dar] /1l/ *vt* to solder, weld

soleado, -a [sole'aðo, a] *adj* sunny

soledad [sole'ðað] *nf* solitude; (estado infeliz) loneliness

solemne [so'lemne] *adj* solemn

soler [so'ler] *vi* to be in the habit of, be accustomed to; **suele salir a las ocho** she usually goes out at 8 o'clock

solfeo [sol'feo] *nm* sol-fa, singing of scales

solicitar [soliθi'tar] /1a/ *vt* (permiso) to ask for, seek; (puesto) to apply for; (votos) to canvass for; (atención) to attract

solícito, -a [so'liθito, a] *adj* (diligente) diligent; (cuidadoso) careful; **solicitud** *nf* (calidad) great care; (petición) request; (a un puesto) application

solidaridad [soliðari'ðað] *nf* solidarity; **solidario, -a** *adj* (participación) joint, common; (compromiso) mutually binding

sólido, -a ['soliðo, a] *adj* solid

soliloquio [soli'lokjo] *nm* soliloquy

solista [so'lista] *nmf* soloist

solitario, -a [soli'tarjo, a] *adj* (persona) lonely, solitary; (lugar) lonely, desolate ▷ *nm/f* (recluso) recluse; (en la sociedad) loner ▷ *nm* solitaire

sollozar [soʎo'θar] /1f/ *vi* to sob; **sollozo** *nm* sob

solo¹, -a ['solo, a] *adj* (único) single, sole; (sin compañía) alone; (solitario) lonely; **hay una sola dificultad** there is just one difficulty; **a solas** alone, by o.s.

solo², sólo ['solo] *adv* only, just

solomillo [solo'miʎo] *nm* sirloin

soltar [sol'tar] /1l/ *vt* (dejar ir) to let go of; (desprender) to unfasten, loosen; (librar) to release, set free; (risa etc) to let out

soltero, -a [sol'tero, a] *adj* single, unmarried ▷ *nm* bachelor ▷ *nf* single woman; **solterón** *nm* confirmed bachelor

solterona [solte'rona] *nf* spinster

soltura [sol'tura] *nf* looseness, slackness; (de los miembros) agility, ease of movement; (*en el hablar*) fluency, ease

soluble [so'luβle] *adj* (*Química*) soluble; (*problema*) solvable; **~ en agua** soluble in water

solución [solu'θjon] *nf* solution; **solucionar** /1a/ *vt* (*problema*) to solve; (*asunto*) to settle, resolve

solventar [solβen'tar] /1a/ *vt* (*pagar*) to settle, pay; (*resolver*) to resolve; **solvente** *adj* solvent

sombra ['sombra] *nf* shadow; (*como protección*) shade; **sombras** *nfpl* darkness *sg*, shadows; **tener buena/ mala ~** to be lucky/unlucky

sombrero [som'brero] *nm* hat

sombrilla [som'briʎa] *nf* parasol, sunshade

sombrío, -a [som'brio, a] *adj* (*oscuro*) dark; (*fig*) sombre, sad; (*persona*) gloomy

someter [some'ter] /2a/ *vt* (*país*) to conquer; (*persona*) to subject to one's will; (*informe*) to present, submit; **someterse** *vr* to give in, yield, submit; **~ a** to subject to

somier [so'mjer] (*pl* **somiers**) *nm* spring mattress

somnífero [som'nifero] *nm* sleeping pill *o* tablet

somos ['somos] *vb* V **ser**

son [son] *vb* V **ser** ▷ *nm* sound

sonaja [so'naxa] *nf* (*LAM*) = **sonajero**

sonajero [sona'xero] *nm* (baby's) rattle

sonambulismo [sonambu'lismo] *nm* sleepwalking; **sonámbulo, -a** *nm/f* sleepwalker

sonar [so'nar] /1l/ *vt* to ring ▷ *vi* to sound; (*hacer ruido*) to make a noise; (*Ling*) to be sounded, be pronounced; (*ser conocido*) to sound familiar; (*campana*) to ring; (*reloj*) to strike, chime; **sonarse** *vr*: **~se (la nariz)** to blow one's nose; **me suena ese nombre** that name rings a bell

sonda ['sonda] *nf* (*Naut*) sounding; (*Tec*) bore, drill; (*Med*) probe

sondear [sonde'ar] /1a/ *vt* to sound; to bore (into), drill; to probe, sound; (*fig*) to sound out; **sondeo** *nm* sounding; boring, drilling; (*encuesta*) poll, enquiry

sonido [so'niðo] *nm* sound

sonoro, -a [so'noro, a] *adj* sonorous; (*resonante*) loud, resonant

sonreír [sonre'ir] /3l/ *vi* to smile; **sonriente** *adj* smiling; **sonrisa** *nf* smile

sonrojar [sonro'xar] /1a/ *vt*: **~ a algn** to make sb blush; **sonrojarse** *vr*: **~se (de)** to blush (at)

sonrojo *nm* blush

soñador, a [soɲa'ðor, a] *nm/f* dreamer

soñar [so'ɲar] /1l/ *vt, vi* to dream; **~ con** to dream about *o* of

soñoliento, -a [soɲo'ljento, a] *adj* sleepy, drowsy

sopa ['sopa] *nf* soup

soplar [so'plar] /1a/ *vt* (*polvo*) to blow away, blow off; (*inflar*) to blow up; (*vela*) to blow out ▷ *vi* to blow; **soplo** *nm* blow, puff; (*de viento*) puff, gust

soplón, -ona [so'plon, ona] *nm/f* (*fam: chismoso*) telltale; (: *de policía*) informer, grass

soporífero, -a [sopo'rifero, a] *adj* sleep-inducing ▷ *nm* sleeping pill

soportable [sopor'taβle] *adj* bearable

soportar [sopor'tar] /1a/ *vt* to bear, carry; (*fig*) to bear, put up with; **soporte** *nm* support; (*fig*) pillar, support

▌ No confundir *soportar* con la palabra inglesa *support*.

soprano [so'prano] *nf* soprano

sorber [sor'βer] /2a/ *vt* (*chupar*) to sip; (*inhalar*) to sniff, inhale; (*absorber*) to soak up, absorb

sorbete [sor'βete] *nm* iced fruit drink

sorbo ['sorβo] *nm* (*trago*) gulp, swallow; (*chupada*) sip

sordera [sor'ðera] *nf* deafness

sórdido, -a ['sorðiðo, a] *adj* dirty, squalid

sordo, -a ['sorðo, a] *adj (persona)* deaf ▷ *nm/f* deaf person; **sordomudo, -a** *adj* speech-and-hearing impaired

sorna ['sorna] *nf* sarcastic tone

soroche [so'rotʃe] *nm (LAM)* mountain sickness

sorprendente [sorpren'dente] *adj* surprising

sorprender [sorpren'der] /2a/ *vt* to surprise; **sorpresa** *nf* surprise

sortear [sorte'ar] /1a/ *vt* to draw lots for; *(rifar)* to raffle; *(dificultad)* to dodge, avoid; **sorteo** *nm (en lotería)* draw; *(rifa)* raffle

sortija [sor'tixa] *nf* ring; *(rizo)* ringlet, curl

sosegado, -a [sose'ɣaðo, a] *adj* quiet, calm

sosiego [so'sjeɣo] *nm* quiet(ness), calm(ness)

soso, -a ['soso, a] *adj (Culin)* tasteless; *(fig)* dull, uninteresting

sospecha [sos'petʃa] *nf* suspicion; **sospechar** /1a/ *vt* to suspect; **sospechoso, -a** *adj* suspicious; *(testimonio, opinión)* suspect ▷ *nm/f* suspect

sostén [sos'ten] *nm (apoyo)* support; *(sujetador)* bra; *(alimentación)* sustenance, food

sostener [soste'ner] /2k/ *vt* to support; *(mantener)* to keep up, maintain; *(alimentar)* to sustain, keep going; **sostenerse** *vr* to support o.s.; *(seguir)* to continue, remain; **sostenido, -a** *adj* continuous, sustained; *(prolongado)* prolonged

sotana [so'tana] *nf (Rel)* cassock

sótano ['sotano] *nm* basement

soy [soi] *vb V* **ser**

soya ['soja] *nf (LAM)* soya (bean)

Sr. *abr (= Señor)* Mr

Sra. *abr (= Señora)* Mrs

Sras. *abr (= Señoras)* Mrs

Sres. *abr (= Señores)* Messrs

Srta. *abr = señorita*

Sta. *abr (= Santa)* St

Sto. *abr (= Santo)* St

su [su] *pron (de él)* his; *(de ella)* her; *(de una cosa)* its; *(de ellos, ellas)* their; *(de usted, ustedes)* your

suave ['swaβe] *adj* gentle; *(superficie)* smooth; *(trabajo)* easy; *(música, voz)* soft, sweet; **suavidad** *nf* gentleness; *(de superficie)* smoothness; *(de música)* softness, sweetness; **suavizante** *nm (de ropa)* softener; *(del pelo)* conditioner; **suavizar** /1f/ *vt* to soften; *(quitar la aspereza)* to smooth (out)

subasta [su'βasta] *nf* auction; **subastar** /1a/ *vt* to auction (off)

subcampeón, -ona [suβkampe'on, ona] *nm/f* runner-up

subconsciente [suβkons'θjente] *adj* subconscious

subdesarrollado, -a [suβðesarro'ʎaðo, a] *adj* underdeveloped

subdesarrollo [suβðesa'rroʎo] *nm* underdevelopment

subdirector, a [suβðirek'tor, a] *nm/f* assistant *o* deputy manager

súbdito, -a ['suβðito, a] *nm/f* subject

subestimar [suβesti'mar] /1a/ *vt* to underestimate, underrate

subir [su'βir] /3a/ *vt (objeto)* to raise, lift up; *(cuesta, calle)* to go up; *(colina, montaña)* to climb; *(precio)* to raise, put up ▷ *vi* to go/come up; *(a un coche)* to get in; *(a un autobús, tren)* to get on; *(precio)* to rise, go up; *(río, marea)* to rise; **subirse** *vr* to get up, climb

súbito, -a ['suβito, a] *adj (repentino)* sudden; *(imprevisto)* unexpected

subjetivo, -a [suβxe'tiβo, a] *adj* subjective

sublevar [suβle'βar] /1a/ *vt* to rouse to revolt; **sublevarse** *vr* to revolt, rise

sublime [su'βlime] *adj* sublime

submarinismo [suβmari'nismo] *nm* scuba diving

submarino, -a [suβma'rino, a] *adj* underwater ▷ *nm* submarine

subnormal [suβnorˈmal] *adj*
subnormal ▷ *nmf* subnormal person

subordinado, -a [suβorðiˈnaðo, a]
adj, nm/f subordinate

subrayar [suβraˈjar] /1a/ *vt* to
underline

subsanar [suβsaˈnar] /1a/ *vt* (*reparar*)
to rectify

subsidio [suβˈsiðjo] *nm* (*ayuda*) aid,
financial help; (*subvención*) subsidy,
grant; (*de enfermedad, paro etc*) benefit,
allowance

subsistencia [suβsisˈtenθja] *nf*
subsistence

subsistir [suβsisˈtir] /3a/ *vi* to
subsist; (*sobrevivir*) to survive, endure

subte [ˈsuβte] *nm* (RPL) underground
(BRIT), subway (US)

subterráneo, -a [suβteˈrraneo, a]
adj underground, subterranean ▷ *nm*
underpass, underground passage

subtitulado, -a [suβtituˈlaðo, a]
adj subtitled

subtítulo [suβˈtitulo] *nm* subtitle

suburbio [suˈβurβjo] *nm* (*barrio*)
slum quarter

subvención [suββenˈθjon] *nf*
subsidy, grant; **subvencionar** /1a/ *vt*
to subsidize

sucedáneo, -a [suθeˈðaneo, a] *adj*
substitute ▷ *nm* substitute (food)

suceder [suθeˈðer] /2a/ *vi* to happen;
(*seguir*) to succeed, follow; **lo que
sucede es que …** the fact is that
…; **sucesión** *nf* succession; (*serie*)
sequence, series

sucesivamente [suθesiβaˈmente]
adv: **y así ~** and so on

sucesivo, -a [suθeˈsiβo, a] *adj*
successive, following; **en lo ~** in
future, from now on

suceso [suˈθeso] *nm* (*hecho*) event,
happening; (*incidente*) incident

▌ No confundir *suceso* con la palabra
inglesa *success*.

suciedad [suθjeˈðað] *nf* (*estado*)
dirtiness; (*mugre*) dirt, filth

sucio, -a [ˈsuθjo, a] *adj* dirty

suculento, -a [sukuˈlento, a] *adj*
succulent

sucumbir [sukumˈbir] /3a/ *vi* to
succumb

sucursal [sukurˈsal] *nf* branch (office)

sudadera [suðaˈðera] *nf* sweatshirt

Sudáfrica [suˈðafrika] *nf* South Africa

Sudamérica [suðaˈmerika] *nf* South
America; **sudamericano, -a** *adj, nm/f*
South American

sudar [suˈðar] /1a/ *vt, vi* to sweat

sudeste [suˈðeste] *nm* south-east

sudoeste [suðoˈeste] *nm* south-west

sudoku [suˈdoku] *nm* sudoku

sudor [suˈðor] *nm* sweat; **sudoroso,
-a** *adj* sweaty, sweating

Suecia [ˈsweθja] *nf* Sweden; **sueco, -a**
adj Swedish ▷ *nm/f* Swede

suegro, -a [ˈsweɣro, a] *nm/f* father-/
mother-in-law

suela [ˈswela] *nf* sole

sueldo [ˈsweldo] *nm* pay, wage(s) (*pl*)

suelo [ˈswelo] *vb V* **soler** ▷ *nm* (*tierra*)
ground; (*de casa*) floor

suelto, -a [ˈswelto, a] *adj* loose;
(*libre*) free; (*separado*) detached; (*ágil*)
quick, agile ▷ *nm* (loose) change,
small change

sueñito [sweˈɲito] *nm* (LAM) nap

sueño [ˈsweɲo] *vb V* **soñar** ▷ *nm* sleep;
(*somnolencia*) sleepiness, drowsiness;
(*lo soñado, fig*) dream; **tener ~** to
be sleepy

suero [ˈswero] *nm* (*Med*) serum; (*de
leche*) whey

suerte [ˈswerte] *nf* (*fortuna*) luck;
(*azar*) chance; (*destino*) fate, destiny;
(*género*) sort, kind; **tener ~** to be lucky

suéter [ˈsweter] *nm* sweater

suficiente [sufiˈθjente] *adj* enough,
sufficient ▷ *nm* (*Escol*) pass

sufragio [suˈfraxjo] *nm* (*voto*) vote;
(*derecho de voto*) suffrage

sufrido, -a [suˈfriðo, a] *adj* (*de carácter
fuerte*) tough; (*paciente*) long-suffering,
patient

sufrimiento [sufriˈmjento] *nm*
suffering

sufrir [su'frir] /3a/ vt (padecer) to suffer; (soportar) to bear, put up with; (apoyar) to hold up, support ▷ vi to suffer

sugerencia [suxe'renθja] nf suggestion

sugerir [suxe'rir] /3i/ vt to suggest; (sutilmente) to hint

sugestión [suxes'tjon] nf suggestion; (sutil) hint; **sugestionar** /1a/ vt to influence

sugestivo, -a [suxes'tiβo, a] adj stimulating; (fascinante) fascinating

suicida [sui'θiða] adj suicidal ▷ nmf suicidal person; (muerto) suicide, person who has committed suicide; **suicidarse** /1a/ vr to commit suicide, kill o.s.; **suicidio** nm suicide

Suiza ['swiθa] nf Switzerland; **suizo, -a** adj, nm/f Swiss

sujeción [suxe'θjon] nf subjection

sujetador [suxeta'ðor] nm (prenda femenina) bra

sujetar [suxe'tar] /1a/ vt (fijar) to fasten; (detener) to hold down; **sujetarse** vr to subject o.s.; **sujeto, -a** adj fastened, secure ▷ nm subject; (individuo) individual; **sujeto a** subject to

suma ['suma] nf (cantidad) total, sum; (de dinero) sum; (acto) adding (up), addition; **en ~** in short

sumamente [suma'mente] adv extremely, exceedingly

sumar [su'mar] /1a/ vt to add (up) ▷ vi to add up

sumergir [sumer'xir] /3c/ vt to submerge; (hundir) to sink

suministrar [suminis'trar] /1a/ vt to supply, provide; **suministro** nm supply; (acto) supplying, providing

sumir [su'mir] /3a/ vt to sink, submerge; (fig) to plunge

sumiso, -a [su'miso, a] adj submissive, docile

sumo, -a ['sumo, a] adj great, extreme; (mayor) highest, supreme

suntuoso, -a [sun'twoso, a] adj sumptuous, magnificent

supe etc ['supe] vb V **saber**

súper ['super] adj (fam) super, great ▷ nf (gasolina) four-star (petrol)

super... [super] pref super..., over...

superar [supe'rar] /1a/ vt (sobreponerse a) to overcome; (rebasar) to surpass, do better than; (pasar) to go beyond; **superarse** vr to excel o.s.

superbueno, a [super'bweno, a] adj great, fantastic

superficial [superfi'θjal] adj superficial; (medida) surface cpd

superficie [super'fiθje] nf surface; (área) area

superfluo, -a [su'perflwo, a] adj superfluous

superior [supe'rjor] adj (piso, clase) upper; (temperatura, número, nivel) higher; (mejor: calidad, producto) superior, better ▷ nmf superior; **superioridad** nf superiority

supermercado [supermer'kaðo] nm supermarket

superponer [superpo'ner] /2q/ vt to superimpose

superstición [supersti'θjon] nf superstition; **supersticioso, -a** adj superstitious

supervisar [superβi'sar] /1a/ vt to supervise

supervivencia [superβi'βenθja] nf survival

superviviente [superβi'βjente] adj surviving

supiera etc vb V **saber**

suplantar [suplan'tar] /1a/ vt to supplant

suplementario, -a [suplemen'tarjo, a] adj supplementary

suplemento [suple'mento] nm supplement

suplente [su'plente] adj substitute ▷ nmf substitute

supletorio, -a [suple'torjo, a] adj supplementary ▷ nm supplement; **teléfono ~** extension

S

súplica ['suplika] nf request; (Jur) petition

suplicar [supli'kar] /1g/ vt (cosa) to beg (for), plead for; (persona) to beg, plead with

suplicio [su'pliθjo] nm torture

suplir [su'plir] /3a/ vt (compensar) to make good, make up for; (reemplazar) to replace, substitute ▷ vi: **~ a** to take the place of, substitute for

supo etc ['supo] vb V **saber**

suponer [supo'ner] /2q/ vt to suppose; **suposición** nf supposition

suprimir [supri'mir] /3a/ vt to suppress; (derecho, costumbre) to abolish; (palabra etc) to delete; (restricción) to cancel, lift

supuesto, -a [su'pwesto, a] pp de **suponer** ▷ adj (hipotético) supposed ▷ nm assumption, hypothesis ▷ conj: **~ que** since; **por ~** of course

sur [sur] nm south

suramericano, -a [surameri'kano, a] adj South American ▷ nm/f South American

surcar [sur'kar] /1g/ vt to plough; **surco** nm (en metal, disco) groove; (Agr) furrow

surfear [surfe'ar] /1a/ vt: **~ el Internet** to surf the internet

surgir [sur'xir] /3c/ vi to arise, emerge; (dificultad) to come up, crop up

suroeste [suro'este] nm south-west

surtido, -a [sur'tiðo, a] adj mixed, assorted ▷ nm (selección) selection, assortment; (abastecimiento) supply, stock; **surtidor** nm: **surtidor de gasolina** petrol (BRIT) o gas (US) pump

surtir [sur'tir] /3a/ vt to supply, provide ▷ vi to spout, spurt

susceptible [susθep'tiβle] adj susceptible; (sensible) sensitive; **~ de** capable of

suscitar [susθi'tar] /1a/ vt to cause, provoke; (interés, sospechas) to arouse

suscribir [suskri'βir] /3a/ vt (firmar) to sign; (respaldar) to subscribe to, endorse; **suscribirse** vr to subscribe; **suscripción** nf subscription

susodicho, -a [suso'ditʃo, a] adj above-mentioned

suspender [suspen'der] /2a/ vt (objeto) to hang (up), suspend; (trabajo) to stop, suspend; (Escol) to fail; (interrumpir) to adjourn; (atrasar) to postpone

suspense [sus'pense] nm suspense; **película/novela de ~** thriller

suspensión [suspen'sjon] nf suspension; (fig) stoppage, suspension

suspenso, -a [sus'penso, a] adj hanging, suspended; (Escol) failed ▷ nm (Escol) fail(ure); **quedar** o **estar en ~** to be pending; **película** o **novela de ~** (LAM) thriller

suspicaz [suspi'kaθ] adj suspicious, distrustful

suspirar [suspi'rar] /1a/ vi to sigh; **suspiro** nm sigh

sustancia [sus'tanθja] nf substance

sustento [sus'tento] nm support; (alimento) sustenance, food

sustituir [sustitu'ir] /3g/ vt to substitute, replace; **sustituto, -a** nm/f substitute, replacement

susto ['susto] nm fright, scare

sustraer [sustra'er] /2p/ vt to remove, take away; (Mat) to subtract

susurrar [susu'rrar] /1a/ vi to whisper; **susurro** nm whisper

sutil [su'til] adj (aroma) subtle; (tenue) thin; (inteligencia) sharp

suyo, -a ['sujo, a] adj (con artículo o después del verbo **ser**: de él) his; (: de ella) hers; (: de ellos, ellas) theirs; (: de usted, ustedes) yours; **un amigo ~** a friend of his (o hers o theirs o yours)

Tabacalera [taβaka'lera] *nf former Spanish state tobacco monopoly*

tabaco [ta'βako] *nm* tobacco; (*fam*) cigarettes *pl*

tabaquería [tabake'ria] *nf* tobacconist's (*BRIT*), cigar store (*US*)

taberna [ta'βerna] *nf* bar

tabique [ta'βike] *nm* partition

tabla [ta'βla] *nf* (*de madera*) plank; (*estante*) shelf; (*de vestido*) pleat; (*Arte*) panel; **tablas** *nfpl:* **estar** o **quedar en ~s** to draw; **tablado** *nm* (*plataforma*) platform; (*Teat*) stage

tablao [ta'βlao] *nm* (*tb:* **~ flamenco**) flamenco show

tablero [ta'βlero] *nm* (*de madera*) plank, board; (*de ajedrez, damas*) board; (*Auto*) dashboard; **~ de mandos** (*LAM Auto*) dashboard

tableta [ta'βleta] *nf* (*Med*) tablet; (*de chocolate*) bar

tablón [ta'βlon] *nm* (*de suelo*) plank; (*de techo*) beam; (*de anuncios*) notice board

tabú [ta'βu] *nm* taboo

taburete [taβu'rete] *nm* stool

tacaño, -a [ta'kaɲo, a] *adj* mean

tacha ['tatʃa] *nf* flaw; (*Tec*) stud; **tachar** /1a/ *vt* (*borrar*) to cross out; **tachar de** to accuse of

tacho ['tatʃo] *nm* (*LAM*) bucket; **~ de la basura** rubbish bin (*BRIT*), trash can (*US*)

taco ['tako] *nm* (*Billar*) cue; (*libro de billetes*) book; (*LAM*) heel; (*tarugo*) peg; (*palabrota*) swear word

tacón [ta'kon] *nm* heel; **de ~ alto** high-heeled

táctico, -a ['taktiko, a] *adj* tactical ▷ *nf* tactics *pl*

tacto ['takto] *nm* touch; (*fig*) tact

tajada [ta'xaða] *nf* slice

tajante [ta'xante] *adj* sharp

tajo ['taxo] *nm* (*corte*) cut; (*Geo*) cleft

tal [tal] *adj* such ▷ *pron* (*persona*) someone, such a one; (*cosa*) something, such a thing; **~ como** such as; **~ para cual** two of a kind ▷ *adv:* **~ como** (*igual*) just as; **~ cual** (*como es*) just as it is; **¿qué ~?** how are things?; **¿qué ~ te gusta?** how do you like it? ▷ *conj:* **con ~ (de) que** provided that

taladrar [tala'ðrar] /1a/ *vt* to drill; **taladro** *nm* drill

talante [ta'lante] *nm* (*humor*) mood; (*voluntad*) will, willingness

talar [ta'lar] /1a/ *vt* to fell, cut down; (*fig*) to devastate

talco ['talko] *nm* (*polvos*) talcum powder

talento [ta'lento] *nm* talent; (*capacidad*) ability

Talgo ['talgo] *nm abr* (= *tren articulado ligero Goicoechea Oriol*) high-speed train

talismán [talis'man] *nm* talisman

talla ['taʎa] *nf* (*estatura, fig, Med*) height, stature; (*de ropa*) size; (*palo*) measuring rod; (*Arte*) carving

tallar [ta'ʎar] /1a/ *vt* (*grabar*) to engrave; (*medir*) to measure

tallarín [taʎa'rin] *nm* noodle

talle ['taʎe] *nm* (*Anat*) waist; (*fig*) appearance

taller [ta'ʎer] nm (Tec) workshop; (de artista) studio

tallo ['taʎo] nm (de planta) stem; (de hierba) blade; (brote) shoot

talón [ta'lon] nm heel; (Com) counterfoil; (cheque) cheque (BRIT), check (US)

talonario [talo'narjo] nm (de cheques) chequebook (BRIT), checkbook (US); (de recibos) receipt book

tamaño, -a [ta'maɲo, a] adj (tan grande) such a big; (tan pequeño) such a small ▷ nm size; **de ~ natural** full-size

tamarindo [tama'rindo] nm tamarind

tambalearse [tambale'arse] /1a/ vr (persona) to stagger; (vehículo) to sway

también [tam'bjen] adv (igualmente) also, too, as well; (además) besides

tambor [tam'bor] nm drum; (Anat) eardrum; **~ del freno** brake drum

Támesis ['tamesis] nm Thames

tamizar [tami'θar] /1f/ vt to sieve

tampoco [tam'poko] adv nor, neither; **yo ~ lo compré** I didn't buy it either

tampón [tam'pon] nm tampon

tan [tan] adv so; **~ es así que** so much so that

tanda ['tanda] nf (gen) series; (turno) shift

tangente [tan'xente] nf tangent

tangerina [tanxe'rina] nf (LAM) tangerine

tangible [tan'xiβle] adj tangible

tanque ['tanke] nm tank; (Auto, Naut) tanker

tantear [tante'ar] /1a/ vt (calcular) to reckon (up); (medir) to take the measure of; (probar) to test, try out; (tomar la medida: persona) to take the measurements of; (considerar) to weigh up; (persona: opinión) to sound out ▷ vi (Deporte) to score; **tanteo** nm (cálculo aproximado) (rough) calculation; (prueba) test, trial; (Deporte) scoring

○ **PALABRA CLAVE**

tanto, -a ['tanto, a] adj (cantidad) so much, as much; **tantos** so many, as many; **20 y tantos** 20-odd ▷ adv (cantidad) so much, as much; (tiempo) so long, as long; **tanto tú como yo** both you and I; **tanto como eso** as much as that; **tanto más ... cuanto que** it's all the more ... because; **tanto mejor/peor** so much the better/the worse; **tanto si viene como si va** whether he comes or whether he goes; **tanto es así que** so much so that; **por tanto, por lo tanto** therefore ▷ conj: **en tanto que** while; **hasta tanto (que)** until such time as ▷ nm 1 (suma) certain amount; (proporción) so much; **un tanto perezoso** somewhat lazy 2 (punto) point; (: gol) goal 3 (locuciones): **al tanto** up to date; **al tanto de que** because of the fact that ▷ pron: **cada uno paga tanto** each one pays so much; **a tantos de agosto** on such and such a day in August; **entre tanto** meanwhile

tapa ['tapa] nf (de caja, olla) lid; (de botella) top; (de libro) cover; (de comida) snack

tapadera [tapa'ðera] nf lid, cover

tapar [ta'par] /1a/ vt (cubrir) to cover; (envolver) to wrap o cover up; (la vista) to obstruct; (persona, falta) to conceal; (LAM) to fill; **taparse** vr to wrap o.s. up

taparrabo [tapa'rraβo] nm loincloth

tapete [ta'pete] nm table cover

tapia ['tapja] nf (garden) wall

tapicería [tapiθe'ria] nf tapestry; (para muebles) upholstery; (tienda) upholsterer's (shop)

tapiz [ta'piθ] nm (alfombra) carpet; (tela tejida) tapestry; **tapizar** /1f/ vt (muebles) to upholster

tapón [ta'pon] nm (de botella) top; (Tec) plug; **~ de rosca o de tuerca** screw-top

taquigrafía [takiɣraˈfia] nf shorthand; **taquígrafo, -a** nm/f shorthand writer, stenographer (US)

taquilla [taˈkiʎa] nf (de estación etc) booking office; (suma recogida) takings pl

tarántula [taˈrantula] nf tarantula

tararear [tarareˈar] /1a/ vi to hum

tardar [tarˈðar] /1a/ vi (tomar tiempo) to take a long time; (llegar tarde) to be late; (demorar) to delay; **¿tarda mucho el tren?** does the train take long?; **a más** ~ at the (very) latest; **no tardes en venir** come soon

tarde [ˈtarðe] adv late ▷ nf (de día) afternoon; (de noche) evening; **de** ~ **en** ~ from time to time; **¡buenas** ~**s!** good afternoon!; **a** o **por la** ~ in the afternoon; in the evening

tardío, -a [tarˈðio, a] adj (retrasado) late; (lento) slow to arrive

tarea [taˈrea] nf task; **tareas** nfpl (Escol) homework sg; ~ **de ocasión** chore

tarifa [taˈrifa] nf (lista de precios) price list; (Com) tariff

tarima [taˈrima] nf (plataforma) platform

tarjeta [tarˈxeta] nf card; ~ **postal/ de crédito/de Navidad** postcard/ credit card/Christmas card; ~ **de embarque** boarding pass; ~ **de memoria** memory card; ~ **prepago** top-up card; ~ **SIM** SIM card

tarro [ˈtarro] nm jar, pot

tarta [ˈtarta] nf (pastel) cake; (torta) tart

tartamudear [tartamuðeˈar] /1a/ vi to stutter, stammer; **tartamudo, -a** adj stammering ▷ nm/f stammerer

tártaro, -a [ˈtartaro, a] adj: **salsa tártara** tartar(e) sauce

tasa [ˈtasa] nf (precio) (fixed) price, rate; (valoración) valuation; (medida, norma) measure, standard; ~ **de cambio** exchange rate; ~**s de aeropuerto** airport tax; ~**s universitarias** university fees; **tasar** /1a/ vt (arreglar el precio) to fix a price for; (valorar) to value, assess

tasca [ˈtaska] nf (fam) pub

tatarabuelo, -a [tataraˈβwelo, a] nm/f great-great-grandfather/ mother

tatuaje [taˈtwaxe] nm (dibujo) tattoo; (acto) tattooing

tatuar [taˈtwar] /1d/ vt to tattoo

taurino, -a [tauˈrino, a] adj bullfighting cpd

Tauro [ˈtauro] nm Taurus

tauromaquia [tauroˈmakja] nf (art of) bullfighting

taxi [ˈtaksi] nm taxi; **taxista** nmf taxi driver

taza [ˈtaθa] nf cup; (de retrete) bowl; ~ **para café** coffee cup; ~ **de café** cup of coffee; **tazón** nm mug, large cup; (escudilla) basin

te [te] pron (complemento de objeto) you; (complemento indirecto) (to) you; (reflexivo) (to) yourself; **¿te duele mucho el brazo?** does your arm hurt a lot?; **te equivocas** you're wrong; **¡cálmate!** calm yourself!

té [te] nm tea

teatral [teaˈtral] adj theatre cpd; (fig) theatrical

teatro [teˈatro] nm theatre; (Lit) plays pl, drama

tebeo [teˈβeo] nm children's comic

techo [ˈtetʃo] nm (externo) roof; (interno) ceiling

tecla [ˈtekla] nf (Inform, Mus, Tip) key; **teclado** nm keyboard (tb Inform); **teclear** /1a/ vi to strum; (fam) to drum ▷ vt (Inform) to key (in)

técnico, -a [ˈtekniko, a] adj technical ▷ nm/f technician; (experto) expert ▷ nf (procedimientos) technique; (tecnología) technology

tecnología [teknoloˈxia] nf technology; **tecnológico, -a** adj technological

tecolote [tekoˈlote] nm (LAm) owl

tedioso, -a [teˈðjoso, a] adj boring, tedious

teja [ˈtexa] nf tile; (Bot) lime (tree); **tejado** nm (tiled) roof

tejano, -a [te'xano, a] *adj, nm/f* Texan
▷ *nmpl:* **~s** (*vaqueros*) jeans

tejemaneje [texema'nexe] *nm* (*lío*)
fuss; (*intriga*) intrigue

tejer [te'xer] /2a/ *vt* to weave; (*LAM*)
to knit; (*fig*) to fabricate; **tejido** *nm*
fabric; (*estofa, tela*) (knitted) material;
(*telaraña*) web; (*Anat*) tissue

tel. *abr* (= *teléfono*) tel.

tela ['tela] *nf* (*material*) material; (*de
fruta, en líquido*) skin; **~ de araña**
cobweb, spider's web; **telar** *nm*
(*máquina*) loom

telaraña [tela'raɲa] *nf* cobweb

tele ['tele] *nf* (*fam*) TV

tele... *pref* **telebasura**
nf trash TV; **telecomunicación** *nf*
telecommunication; **telediario** *nm*
television news; **teledirigido, -a** *adj*
remote-controlled

teleférico [tele'feriko] *nm* (*de esquí*)
ski-lift

telefonear [telefone'ar] /1a/ *vi* to
telephone

telefónico, -a [tele'foniko, a] *adj*
telephone *cpd*

telefonillo [telefo'niʎo] *nm* (*de
puerta*) intercom

telefonista [telefo'nista] *nmf*
telephonist

teléfono [te'lefono] *nm* (tele)phone;
~ móvil mobile phone; **está
hablando por ~** he's on the phone;
llamar a algn por ~ to ring sb (up) o
phone sb (up); **~ celular** (*LAM*) mobile
phone; **~ con cámara** camera phone;
~ inalámbrico cordless phone

telégrafo [te'leɣrafo] *nm* telegraph

telegrama [tele'ɣrama] *nm* telegram

tele...: telenovela *nf* soap (opera);
teleobjetivo *nm* telephoto lens;
telepatía *nf* telepathy; **telepático,
-a** *adj* telepathic; **telerrealidad** *nf*
reality TV; **telescopio** *nm* telescope;
telesilla *nm* chairlift; **telespectador,
a** *nm/f* viewer; **telesquí** *nm* ski-lift;
teletarjeta *nf* phonecard; **teletipo**
nm teletype(writer); **teletrabajador,**

a *nm/f* teleworker; **teletrabajo**
nm teleworking; **televentas** *nfpl*
telesales

televidente [teleβi'ðente] *nmf*
viewer

televisar [teleβi'sar] /1a/ *vt* to televise

televisión [teleβi'sjon] *nf* television;
~ digital digital television

televisor [teleβi'sor] *nm* television
set

télex ['teleks] *nm* telex

telón [te'lon] *nm* curtain; **~ de
acero** (*Pol*) iron curtain; **~ de fondo**
backcloth, background

tema ['tema] *nm* (*asunto*) subject,
topic; (*Mus*) theme; **temático, -a** *adj*
thematic

temblar [tem'blar] /1j/ *vi* to shake,
tremble; (*de frío*) to shiver; **temblor**
nm trembling; (*de tierra*) earthquake;
tembloroso, -a *adj* trembling

temer [te'mer] /2a/ *vt* to fear ▷ *vi*
to be afraid; **temo que Juan llegue
tarde** I am afraid Juan may be late

temible [te'miβle] *adj* fearsome

temor [te'mor] *nm* (*miedo*) fear; (*duda*)
suspicion

témpano ['tempano] *nm*: **~ de hielo**
ice floe

temperamento [tempera'mento]
nm temperament

temperatura [tempera'tura] *nf*
temperature

tempestad [tempes'tað] *nf* storm

templado, -a [tem'plaðo, a] *adj*
(*agua*) lukewarm; (*clima*) mild;
(*Mus*) well-tuned; **templanza** *nf*
moderation

templar [tem'plar] /1a/ *vt* (*moderar*)
to moderate; (*furia*) to restrain;
(*calor*) to reduce; (*afinar*) to tune (up);
(*acero*) to temper; (*tuerca*) to tighten
up; **temple** *nm* (*ajuste*) tempering;
(*afinación*) tuning; (*pintura*) tempera

templo ['templo] *nm* (*iglesia*) church;
(*pagano etc*) temple

temporada [tempo'raða] *nf* time,
period; (*estación, social*) season

temporal [tempo'ral] *adj (no permanente)* temporary ▷ *nm* storm

temprano, -a [tem'prano, a] *adj* early ▷ *adv* early; *(demasiado pronto)* too soon, too early

ten [ten] *vb* V **tener**

tenaces [te'naθes] *adj pl* V **tenaz**

tenaz [te'naθ] *adj (material)* tough; *(persona)* tenacious; *(terco)* stubborn

tenaza(s) [te'naθ(as)] *nf, nfpl (Med)* forceps; *(Tec)* pliers; *(Zool)* pincers

tendedero [tende'ðero] *nm (para ropa)* drying-place; *(cuerda)* clothes line

tendencia [ten'denθja] *nf* tendency; **tener ~ a** to tend to have a tendency to

tender [ten'der] /2g/ *vt (extender)* to spread out; *(ropa)* to hang out; *(vía férrea, cable)* to lay; *(cuerda)* to stretch ▷ *vi* to tend; **tenderse** *vr* to lie down; **~ la cama/la mesa** (*LAM*) to make the bed/lay the table

tenderete [tende'rete] *nm (puesto)* stall; *(exposición)* display of goods

tendero, -a [ten'dero, a] *nm/f* shopkeeper

tendón [ten'don] *nm* tendon

tendré *etc* [ten'dre] *vb* V **tener**

tenebroso, -a [tene'βroso, a] *adj (oscuro)* dark; *(fig)* gloomy

tenedor [tene'ðor] *nm (Culin)* fork

tenencia [te'nenθja] *nf (de casa)* tenancy; *(de oficio)* tenure; *(de propiedad)* possession

PALABRA CLAVE

tener [te'ner] /2k/ *vt* **1** *(poseer, gen)* to have; (: *en la mano)* to hold; **¿tienes un boli?** have you got a pen?; **va a tener un niño** she's going to have a baby; **¡ten o tenga!, ¡aquí tienes o tiene!** here you are!

2 *(edad, medidas)* to be; **tiene siete años** she's seven (years old); **tiene 15 cm de largo** it's 15 cm long

3 *(sentimientos, sensaciones)*: **tener sed/hambre/frío/calor** to be thirsty/hungry/cold/hot; **tener razón** to be right

4 *(considerar)*: **lo tengo por brillante** I consider him to be brilliant; **tener en mucho a algn** to think very highly of sb

5 (+ *pp*): **tengo terminada ya la mitad del trabajo** I've done half the work already

6: **tener que hacer algo** to have to do sth; **tengo que acabar este trabajo hoy** I have to finish this job today

7: **¿qué tienes, estás enfermo?** what's the matter with you, are you ill?

▶ **tenerse** *vr* **1**: **tenerse en pie** to stand up

2: **tenerse por** to think o.s.

tengo *etc* ['tengo] *vb* V **tener**

tenia ['tenja] *nf* tapeworm

teniente [te'njente] *nm* lieutenant; *(ayudante)* deputy

tenis ['tenis] *nm* tennis; **~ de mesa** table tennis; **tenista** *nmf* tennis player

tenor [te'nor] *nm (sentido)* meaning; *(Mus)* tenor; **a ~ de** on the lines of

tensar [ten'sar] /1a/ *vt* to tauten; *(arco)* to draw

tensión [ten'sjon] *nf* tension; *(Tec)* stress; **~ arterial** blood pressure; **tener la ~ alta** to have high blood pressure

tenso, -a ['tenso, a] *adj* tense

tentación [tenta'θjon] *nf* temptation

tentáculo [ten'takulo] *nm* tentacle

tentador, a [tenta'ðor, a] *adj* tempting

tentar [ten'tar] /1j/ *vt (seducir)* to tempt; *(atraer)* to attract

tentempié [tentem'pje] *nm* snack

tenue ['tenwe] *adj (delgado)* thin, slender; *(neblina)* light; *(lazo, vínculo)* slight

teñir [te'ɲir] *vt* to dye; *(fig)* to tinge; **teñirse** *vr* to dye; **~se el pelo** to dye one's hair

teología [teolo'xia] *nf* theology

t

teoría [teo'ria] nf theory; **en ~** in theory; **teórico, -a** adj theoretic(al) ▷ nm/f theoretician, theorist; **teorizar** /1f/ vi to theorize

terapéutico, -a [tera'peutiko, a] adj therapeutic(al)

terapia [te'rapja] nf therapy

tercer [ter'θer] adj V **tercero**

tercermundista [terθermun'dista] adj Third World cpd

tercero, -a [ter'θero, a] adj third ▷ nm (Jur) third party

terceto [ter'θeto] nm trio

terciar [ter'θjar] /1b/ vi (participar) to take part; (hacer de árbitro) to mediate; **terciario, -a** adj tertiary

tercio ['terθjo] nm third

terciopelo [terθjo'pelo] nm velvet

terco, -a ['terko, a] adj obstinate

tergal® [ter'yal] nm Terylene®, Dacron® (us)

tergiversar [terxiβer'sar] /1a/ vt to distort

termal [ter'mal] adj thermal

termas ['termas] nfpl hot springs

térmico, -a ['termiko, a] adj thermal

terminal [termi'nal] adj terminal ▷ nm, nf terminal

terminante [termi'nante] adj (final) final, definitive; (tajante) categorical; **terminantemente** adv: **terminantemente prohibido** strictly forbidden

terminar [termi'nar] /1a/ vt (completar) to complete, finish; (concluir) to end ▷ vi (llegar a su fin) to end; (parar) to stop; (acabar) to finish; **terminarse** vr to come to an end; **~ por hacer algo** to end up (by) doing sth

término ['termino] nm end, conclusion; (parada) terminus; (límite) boundary; **en último ~** (a fin de cuentas) in the last analysis; (como último recurso) as a last resort; **~ medio** average; (fig) middle way

termo® ['termo] nm Thermos® (flask)

termómetro [ter'mometro] nm thermometer

termostato [termos'tato] nm thermostat

ternero, -a [ter'nero, a] nm/f (animal) calf ▷ nf (carne) veal, beef

ternura [ter'nura] nf (trato) tenderness; (palabra) endearment; (cariño) fondness

terrado [te'rraðo] nm terrace

terraplén [terra'plen] nm embankment

terrateniente [terrate'njente] nm landowner

terraza [te'rraθa] nf (balcón) balcony; (techo) flat roof; (Agr) terrace

terremoto [terre'moto] nm earthquake

terrenal [terre'nal] adj earthly

terreno [te'rreno] nm (tierra) land; (parcela) plot; (suelo) soil; (fig) field; **un ~** a piece of land

terrestre [te'rrestre] adj terrestrial; (ruta) land cpd

terrible [te'rriβle] adj terrible; awful

territorio [terri'torjo] nm territory

terrón [te'rron] nm (de azúcar) lump; (de tierra) clod, lump

terror [te'rror] nm terror; **terrorífico, -a** adj terrifying; **terrorista** adj, nmf terrorist; **terrorista suicida** suicide bomber

terso, -a ['terso, a] adj (liso) smooth; (pulido) polished

tertulia [ter'tulja] nf (reunión informal) social gathering; (grupo) group, circle

tesis ['tesis] nf inv thesis

tesón [te'son] nm (firmeza) firmness; (tenacidad) tenacity

tesorero, -a [teso'rero, a] nm/f treasurer

tesoro [te'soro] nm treasure; (Com, Pol) treasury

testamento [testa'mento] nm will

testarudo, -a [testa'ruðo, a] adj stubborn

testículo [tes'tikulo] nm testicle

testificar [testifi'kar] /1g/ vt to testify; (fig) to attest ▷ vi to give evidence

testigo [tes'tiɣo] nmf witness; **~ de cargo/descargo** witness for the prosecution/defence; **~ ocular** eye witness

testimonio [testi'monjo] nm testimony

teta ['teta] nf (de biberón) teat; (Anat: fam) breast

tétanos ['tetanos] nm tetanus

tetera [te'tera] nf teapot

tétrico, -a ['tetriko, a] adj gloomy, dismal

textear [tekste'ar] /1a/ vt (LAM) to text

textil [teks'til] adj textile

texto ['teksto] nm text; **textual** adj textual

textura [teks'tura] nf (de tejido) texture

tez [teθ] nf (cutis) complexion

ti [ti] pron you; (reflexivo) yourself

tía ['tia] nf (pariente) aunt; (fam: mujer) girl

tibio, -a ['tiβjo, a] adj lukewarm

tiburón [tiβu'ron] nm shark

tic [tik] nm (ruido) click; (de reloj) tick; **~ nervioso** nervous tic

tictac [tik'tak] nm (de reloj) tick tock

tiempo ['tjempo] nm time; (época, período) age, period; (Meteorología) weather; (Ling) tense; (de juego) half; **a ~** in time; **a un o al mismo ~** at the same time; **al poco ~** very soon (after); **se quedó poco ~** he didn't stay very long; **hace poco ~** not long ago; **mucho ~** a long time; **de ~ en ~** from time to time; **hace buen/mal ~** the weather is fine/bad; **estar a ~** to be in time; **hace ~** some time ago; **hacer ~** to while away the time; **motor de 2 ~s** two-stroke engine; **primer ~** first half

tienda ['tjenda] nf shop; store; **~ de campaña** tent; **~ de comestibles** grocer's (shop) (BRIT), grocery (store) (US)

tiene etc ['tjene] vb V **tener**

tienta ['tjenta] vb V **tentar** ▷ nf: **andar a ~s** to grope one's way along

tiento etc ['tjento] vb V **tentar** ▷ nm (tacto) touch; (precaución) wariness

tierno, -a ['tjerno, a] adj (blando, dulce) tender; (fresco) fresh

tierra ['tjerra] nf earth; (suelo) soil; (mundo) world; (país) country, land; **~ adentro** inland

tieso, -a ['tjeso, a] adj (rígido) rigid; (duro) stiff; (fam: orgulloso) conceited

tiesto ['tjesto] nm flowerpot

tifón [ti'fon] nm typhoon

tifus ['tifus] nm typhus

tigre ['tiɣre] nm tiger

tijera [ti'xera] nf (una tijera) (pair of) scissors pl; (Zool) claw; **tijeras** nfpl scissors; (para plantas) shears

tila ['tila] nf lime flower tea

tildar [til'dar] /1a/ vt: **~ de** to brand as

tilde ['tilde] nf (Tip) tilde

tilín [ti'lin] nm tinkle

timar [ti'mar] /1a/ vt (estafar) to swindle

timbal [tim'bal] nm small drum

timbre ['timbre] nm (sello) stamp; (campanilla) bell; (tono) timbre; (Com) stamp duty

timidez [timi'ðeθ] nf shyness; **tímido, -a** adj shy

timo ['timo] nm swindle

timón [ti'mon] nm helm, rudder; **timonel** nm helmsman

tímpano ['timpano] nm (Anat) eardrum; (Mus) small drum

tina ['tina] nf tub; (baño) bath(tub); **tinaja** nf large earthen jar

tinieblas [ti'njeβlas] nfpl darkness sg; (sombras) shadows

tino ['tino] nm (habilidad) skill; (juicio) insight

tinta ['tinta] nf ink; (Tec) dye; (Arte) colour

tinte ['tinte] nm dye

tintero [tin'tero] nm inkwell

tinto ['tinto] nm red wine

tintorería [tintore'ria] nf dry cleaner's

t

tío ['tio] nm (pariente) uncle; (fam: hombre) bloke, guy (us)

tiovivo [tio'βiβo] nm merry-go-round

típico, -a ['tipiko, a] adj typical

tipo ['tipo] nm (clase) type, kind; (hombre) fellow; (Anat) build; (: de mujer) figure; (Imprenta) type; ~ **bancario/de descuento** bank/discount rate; ~ **de interés** interest rate; ~ **de cambio** exchange rate

tipografía [tipoɣra'fia] nf printing

tíquet ['tiket] (pl **tíquets**) nm ticket; (en tienda) cash slip

tiquismiquis [tikis'mikis] nm fussy person ▷ nmpl (querellas) squabbling sg; (escrúpulos) silly scruples

tira ['tira] nf strip; (fig) abundance ▷ nm: ~ **y afloja** give and take

tirabuzón [tiraβu'θon] nm (rizo) curl

tirachinas [tira'tʃinas] nm inv catapult

tirado, -a [ti'raðo, a] adj (barato) dirt-cheap; (fam: fácil) very easy ▷ nf (acto) cast, throw; (serie) series; (Tip) printing, edition; **de una tirada** at one go; **está ~** (fam) it's a cinch

tirador [tira'ðor] nm (mango) handle

tirano, -a [ti'rano, a] adj tyrannical ▷ nm/f tyrant

tirante [ti'rante] adj (cuerda) tight, taut; (relaciones) strained ▷ nm (Arq) brace; (Tec) stay; **tirantes** nmpl braces, suspenders (us); **tirantez** nf tightness; (fig) tension

tirar [ti'rar] /1a/ vt to throw; (volcar) to upset; (derribar) to knock down o over; (bomba) to drop; (desechar) to throw out o away; (disipar) to squander; (imprimir) to print ▷ vi (disparar) to shoot; (dar un tirón) to pull; (fam: andar) to go; (tender a) to tend to; (Deporte) to shoot; **tirarse** vr to throw o.s.; ~ **abajo** to bring down, destroy; **tira más a su padre** he takes more after his father; **ir tirando** to manage

tirita [ti'rita] nf (sticking) plaster, Band-Aid® (us)

tiritar [tiri'tar] /1a/ vi to shiver

tiro ['tiro] nm (lanzamiento) throw; (disparo) shot; (Deporte) shot; (Tenis, Golf) drive; (alcance) range; ~ **al blanco** target practice; **caballo de** ~ cart-horse

tirón [ti'ron] nm (sacudida) pull, tug; **de un** ~ in one go

tiroteo [tiro'teo] nm exchange of shots, shooting

tisis ['tisis] nf consumption, tuberculosis

títere ['titere] nm puppet

titubear [tituβe'ar] /1a/ vi to stagger; (tartamudear) to stammer; (vacilar) to hesitate; **titubeo** nm staggering; stammering; hesitation

titulado, -a [titu'laðo, a] adj (libro) entitled; (persona) titled

titular [titu'lar] /1a/ adj titular ▷ nmf holder ▷ nm (de diario) headline ▷ vt to title; **titularse** vr to be entitled; **título** nm title; (de diario) headline; (certificado) professional qualification; (universitario) university degree; **a título de** in the capacity of

tiza ['tiθa] nf chalk

toalla [to'aʎa] nf towel

tobillo [to'βiʎo] nm ankle

tobogán [toβo'ɣan] nm (montaña rusa) roller-coaster; (resbaladilla) chute, slide

tocadiscos [toka'ðiskos] nm inv record player

tocado, -a [to'kaðo, a] adj (fam) touched ▷ nm headdress

tocador [toka'ðor] nm (mueble) dressing table; (cuarto) boudoir; (fam) ladies' room

tocar [to'kar] /1g/ vt to touch; (Mus) to play; (campana) to ring; (referirse a) to allude to ▷ vi (a la puerta) to knock (on o at the door); (ser el turno) to fall to, be the turn of; (ser hora) to be due; **tocarse** vr (cubrirse la cabeza) to cover one's head; (tener contacto) to touch (each other); **por lo que a mí me toca** as far as I am concerned; **te toca a ti** it's your turn

tocayo, -a [to'kaʝo, a] *nm/f*
namesake

tocino [to'θino] *nm* bacon

todavía [toða'βia] *adv* (*aun*) even;
(*aún*) still, yet; **~ más** yet o still more;
~ no not yet

PALABRA CLAVE

todo, -a ['toðo, a] *adj* **1** (*sg*) all; **toda
la carne** all the meat; **toda la noche**
all night, the whole night; **todo el
libro** the whole book; **toda una
botella** a whole bottle; **todo lo
contrario** quite the opposite; **está
toda sucia** she's all dirty; **por todo el
país** throughout the whole country
2 (*pl*) all; every; **todos los libros** all
the books; **todas las noches** every
night; **todos los que quieran salir** all
those who want to leave
▷ *pron* **1** everything, all; **todos**
everyone, everybody; **lo sabemos
todo** we know everything; **todos
querían más tiempo** everybody o
everyone wanted more time; **nos
marchamos todos** all of us left
2 (*con preposición*): **con todo él me
sigue gustando** even so I still like
him; **no me agrada del todo** I don't
entirely like it
▷ *adv* all; **vaya todo seguido** keep
straight on o ahead
▷ *nm*: **como un todo** as a whole

todopoderoso, -a [toðopoðe'roso,
a] *adj* all-powerful; (*Rel*) almighty

todoterreno [toðote'rreno] *nm* four-
wheel drive, SUV (*esp US*)

toga ['toɣa] *nf* toga; (*Escol*) gown

Tokio ['tokjo] *n* Tokyo

toldo ['toldo] *nm* (*para el sol*) sunshade;
(*en tienda*) marquee

tolerancia [tole'ranθja] *nf* tolerance;
tolerante *adj* tolerant; (*sociedad*)
liberal; (*fig*) open-minded

tolerar [tole'rar] /1a/ *vt* to tolerate;
(*resistir*) to endure

toma ['toma] *nf* (*gen*) taking; (*Med*)
dose; (*Elec*: *tb*: **~ de corriente**)
socket; **~ de tierra** (*Aviat*) landing;
tomacorriente *nm* (*LAM*) socket

tomar [to'mar] /1a/ *vt* to take;
(*aspecto*) to take on; (*beber*) to drink
▷ *vi* to take; (*LAM*) to drink; **tomarse**
vr to take; **~se por** to consider o.s. to
be; **¡toma!** here you are!; **~ a bien/a
mal** to take well/badly; **~ en serio**
to take seriously; **~ el pelo a algn** to pull
sb's leg; **~la con algn** to pick a quarrel
with sb; **~ el sol** to sunbathe

tomate [to'mate] *nm* tomato

tomillo [to'miʎo] *nm* thyme

tomo ['tomo] *nm* (*libro*) volume

ton [ton] *abr* = **tonelada** ▷ *nm*: **sin ~
ni son** without rhyme or reason

tonalidad [tonali'ðað] *nf* tone

tonel [to'nel] *nm* barrel

tonelada [tone'laða] *nf* ton; **tonelaje**
nm tonnage

tónico, -a ['toniko, a] *adj* tonic ▷ *nm*
(*Med*) tonic ▷ *nf* (*Mus*) tonic; (*fig*)
keynote

tono ['tono] *nm* tone; **fuera de ~**
inappropriate; **~ de llamada** ringtone

tontería [tonte'ria] *nf* (*estupidez*)
foolishness; (*una tontería*) silly thing;
tonterías *nfpl* rubbish *sg*, nonsense *sg*

tonto, -a ['tonto, a] *adj* stupid;
(*ridículo*) silly ▷ *nm/f* fool

topar [to'par] /1a/ *vi*: **~ contra** o **en** to
run into; **~ con** to run up against

tope ['tope] *adj* maximum ▷ *nm* (*fin*)
end; (*límite*) limit; (*Ferro*) buffer; (*Auto*)
bumper; **al ~** end to end

tópico, -a ['topiko, a] *adj* topical ▷ *nm*
platitude

topo ['topo] *nm* (*Zool*) mole; (*fig*)
blunderer

toque *etc* ['toke] *vb* V **tocar** ▷ *nm*
touch; (*Mus*) beat; (*de campana*) chime,
ring; **dar un ~ a** to test; **~ de queda**
curfew

toqué *etc* *vb* V **tocar**

toquetear [tokete'ar] /1a/ *vt* to
finger

toquilla [to'kiʎa] nf (pañuelo) headscarf; (chal) shawl

tórax ['toraks] nm inv thorax

torbellino [torbe'ʎino] nm whirlwind; (fig) whirl

torcedura [torθe'ðura] nf twist; (Med) sprain

torcer [tor'θer] /2b, 2h/ vt to twist; (la esquina) to turn; (Med) to sprain ▷ vi (desviar) to turn off; **torcerse** vr (doblar) to bend; (desviarse) to go astray; (fracasar) to go wrong; **torcido, -a** adj twisted; (fig) crooked ▷ nm curl

tordo, -a ['torðo, a] adj dappled ▷ nm thrush

torear [tore'ar] /1a/ vt (fig: evadir) to dodge; (jugar con) to tease ▷ vi to fight bulls; **toreo** nm bullfighting; **torero, -a** nm/f bullfighter

tormenta [tor'menta] nf storm; (fig: confusión) turmoil

tormento [tor'mento] nm torture; (fig) anguish

tornar [tor'nar] /1a/ vt (devolver) to return, give back; (transformar) to transform ▷ vi to go back

tornasolado, -a [tornaso'laðo, a] adj (brillante) iridescent; (reluciente) shimmering

torneo [tor'neo] nm tournament

tornillo [tor'niʎo] nm screw

torniquete [torni'kete] nm (Med) tourniquet

torno ['torno] nm (Tec) winch; (tambor) drum; **en ~ (a)** round, about

toro ['toro] nm bull; (fam) he-man; **los ~s** bullfighting sg

toronja [to'ronxa] nf grapefruit

torpe ['torpe] adj (poco hábil) clumsy, awkward; (necio) dim; (lento) slow

torpedo [tor'peðo] nm torpedo

torpeza [tor'peθa] nf (falta de agilidad) clumsiness; (lentitud) slowness; (error) mistake

torre ['torre] nf tower; (de petróleo) derrick

torrefacto, -a [torre'fakto, a] adj roasted

torrente [to'rrente] nm torrent

torrija [to'rrixa] nf fried bread; **~s** French toast sg

torsión [tor'sjon] nf twisting

torso ['torso] nm torso

torta ['torta] nf cake; (fam) slap

tortícolis [tor'tikolis] nm inv stiff neck

tortilla [tor'tiʎa] nf omelette; (LAM) maize pancake; **~ francesa/española** plain/potato omelette

tórtola ['tortola] nf turtledove

tortuga [tor'tuɣa] nf tortoise

tortuoso, -a [tor'twoso, a] adj winding

tortura [tor'tura] nf torture; **torturar** /1a/ vt to torture

tos [tos] nf inv cough; **~ ferina** whooping cough

toser [to'ser] /2a/ vi to cough

tostado, -a adj toasted; (por el sol) dark brown; (piel) tanned ▷ nf piece of toast; **tostadas** nfpl toast sg

tostador [tosta'ðor] nm, **tostadora** [tosta'ðora] nf toaster

tostar [tos'tar] /1l/ vt to toast; (café) to roast; (al sol) to tan; **tostarse** vr to get brown

total [to'tal] adj total ▷ adv in short; (al fin y al cabo) when all is said and done ▷ nm total; **en ~** in all; **~ que** to cut a long story short

totalidad [totali'ðað] nf whole

totalitario, -a [totali'tarjo, a] adj totalitarian

tóxico, -a ['toksiko, a] adj toxic ▷ nm poison; **toxicómano, -a** nm/f drug addict

toxina [to'ksina] nf toxin

tozudo, -a [to'θuðo, a] adj obstinate

trabajador, a [traβa'xar, a] nm/f worker ▷ adj hard-working; **~ autónomo** o **por cuenta propia** self-employed person

trabajar [traβa'xar] /1a/ vt to work; (arar) to till; (empeñarse en) to work at; (convencer) to persuade ▷ vi to work; (esforzarse) to strive; **trabajo** nm work;

(*tarea*) task; (*Pol*) labour; (*fig*) effort;
tomarse el trabajo de to take the
trouble to; **trabajo por turno/a
destajo** shift work/piecework;
trabajo en equipo teamwork;
trabajos forzados hard labour *sg*

trabalenguas [traβa'lengwas] *nm
inv* tongue twister

tracción [trak'θjon] *nf* traction;
~ delantera/trasera front-wheel/
rear-wheel drive

tractor [trak'tor] *nm* tractor

tradición [traði'θjon] *nf* tradition;
tradicional *adj* traditional

traducción [traðuk'θjon] *nf*
translation

traducir [traðu'θir] /3n/ *vt* to
translate; **traductor, a** *nm/f* translator

traer [tra'er] /2o/ *vt* to bring; (*llevar*) to
carry; (*ropa*) to wear; (*incluir*) to carry;
(*fig*) to cause; **traerse** *vr*: **~se algo** to
be up to sth

traficar [trafi'kar] /1g/ *vi* to trade

tráfico ['trafiko] *nm* (*Com*) trade;
(*Auto*) traffic

tragaluz [traɣa'luθ] *nm* skylight

tragamonedas [traɣamo'neðas] *nm
inv*, **tragaperras** [traɣa'perras] *nm
inv* slot machine

tragar [tra'ɣar] /1h/ *vt* to swallow;
(*devorar*) to devour, bolt down;
tragarse *vr* to swallow

tragedia [tra'xeðja] *nf* tragedy;
trágico, -a *adj* tragic

trago ['traɣo] *nm* (*de líquido*) drink;
(*comido de golpe*) gulp; (*fam: de bebida*)
swig; (*desgracia*) blow; **echar un ~** to
have a drink

traición [trai'θjon] *nf* treachery; (*Jur*)
treason; (*una traición*) act of treachery;
traicionar /1a/ *vt* to betray

traidor, a [trai'ðor, a] *adj* treacherous
▷ *nm/f* traitor

traigo *etc* ['traiɣo] *vb* V **traer**

traje ['traxe] *vb* V **traer** ▷ *nm* dress;
(*de hombre*) suit; (*traje típico*) costume;
~ de baño swimsuit; **~ de luces**
bullfighter's costume

trajera *etc* [tra'xera] *vb* V **traer**

trajín [tra'xin] *nm* (*fam: movimiento*)
bustle; **trajinar** /1a/ *vi* (*moverse*) to
bustle about

trama ['trama] *nf* (*intriga*) plot; (*de
tejido*) weft; **tramar** /1a/ *vt* to plot;
(*Tec*) to weave

tramitar [trami'tar] /1a/ *vt* (*asunto*)
to transact; (*negociar*) to negotiate

trámite ['tramite] *nm* (*paso*)
step; (*Jur*) transaction; **trámites**
nmpl (*burocracia*) procedures; (*Jur*)
proceedings

tramo ['tramo] *nm* (*de tierra*) plot; (*de
escalera*) flight; (*de vía*) section

trampa ['trampa] *nf* trap; (*en el suelo*)
trapdoor; (*engaño*) trick; (*fam*) fiddle;
trampear /1a/ *vt*, *vi* to cheat

trampolín *nm* trampoline; (*de piscina
etc*) diving board

tramposo, -a [tram'poso, a] *adj*
crooked, cheating ▷ *nm/f* crook,
cheat

tranca ['tranka] *nf* (*palo*) stick; (*de
puerta, ventana*) bar; **trancar** /1g/
vt to bar

trance ['tranθe] *nm* (*momento difícil*)
difficult moment; (*estado de hipnosis*)
trance

tranquilidad [trankili'ðað] *nf*
(*calma*) calmness, stillness; (*paz*)
peacefulness

tranquilizar [trankili'θar] /1f/ *vt*
(*calmar*) to calm (down); (*asegurar*) to
reassure; **tranquilizarse** *vr* to calm
down; **tranquilo, -a** *adj* (*calmado*)
calm; (*apacible*) peaceful; (*mar*) calm;
(*mente*) untroubled

transacción [transak'θjon] *nf*
transaction

transbordador [transβorða'ðor]
nm ferry

transbordo [trans'βorðo] *nm*
transfer; **hacer ~** to change (trains)

transcurrir [transku'rrir] /3a/ *vi*
(*tiempo*) to pass; (*hecho*) to turn out

transcurso [trans'kurso] *nm*: **~ del
tiempo** lapse (of time)

transeúnte [transe'unte] *nmf* passer-by

transferencia [transfe'renθja] *nf* transference; (*Com*) transfer

transferir [transfe'rir] /3i/ *vt* to transfer

transformación [transforma'θjon] *nf* transformation

transformador [transforma'ðor] *nm* transformer

transformar [transfor'mar] /1a/ *vt* to transform; (*convertir*) to convert

transfusión [transfu'sjon] *nf* (*tb:* **~ de sangre**) (blood) transfusion

transgénico, -a [trans'xeniko, a] *adj* genetically modified

transición [transi'θjon] *nf* transition

transigir [transi'xir] /3c/ *vi* to compromise; (*ceder*) to make concessions

transitar [transi'tar] /1a/ *vi* to go (from place to place); **tránsito** *nm* transit; (*Auto*) traffic; **transitorio, -a** *adj* transitory

transmisión [transmi'sjon] *nf* (*Radio, TV*) transmission; (*transferencia*) transfer; **~ en directo/exterior** live/outside broadcast

transmitir [transmi'tir] /3a/ *vt* to transmit; (*Radio, TV*) to broadcast

transparencia [transpa'renθja] *nf* transparency; (*claridad*) clearness, clarity; (*foto*) slide

transparentar [transparen'tar] /1a/ *vt* to reveal ▷ *vi* to be transparent; **transparente** *adj* transparent; (*aire*) clear

transpirar [transpi'rar] /1a/ *vi* to perspire

transportar [transpor'tar] /1a/ *vt* to transport; (*llevar*) to carry; **transporte** *nm* transport; (*Com*) haulage

transversal [transβer'sal] *adj* transverse, cross

tranvía [tram'bia] *nm* tram

trapeador [trapea'ðor] *nm* (*LAM*) mop; **trapear** /1a/ *vt* (*LAM*) to mop

trapecio [tra'peθjo] *nm* trapeze; **trapecista** *nmf* trapeze artist

trapero, -a [tra'pero, a] *nm/f* ragman

trapicheos [trapi'tʃeos] *nmpl* (*fam*) schemes, fiddles

trapo ['trapo] *nm* (*tela*) rag; (*de cocina*) cloth

tráquea ['trakea] *nf* windpipe

traqueteo [trake'teo] *nm* rattling

tras [tras] *prep* (*detrás*) behind; (*después*) after

trasatlántico [trasat'lantiko] *nm* (*barco*) (cabin) cruiser

trascendencia [trasθen'denθja] *nf* (*importancia*) importance; (*en filosofía*) transcendence

trascendental [trasθenden'tal] *adj* important; transcendental

trasero, -a [tra'sero, a] *adj* back, rear ▷ *nm* (*Anat*) bottom

trasfondo [tras'fondo] *nm* background

trasgredir [trasɣre'ðir] /3a/ *vt* to contravene

trashumante [trasu'mante] *adj* migrating

trasladar [trasla'ðar] /1a/ *vt* to move; (*persona*) to transfer; (*postergar*) to postpone; (*copiar*) to copy; **trasladarse** *vr* (*mudarse*) to move; **traslado** *nm* move; (*mudanza*) move, removal

traslucir [traslu'θir] /3f/ *vt* to show

trasluz [tras'luθ] *nm* reflected light; **al ~** against *o* up to the light

trasnochador, a *nm/f* (*fig*) night owl

trasnochar [trasno'tʃar] /1a/ *vi* (*acostarse tarde*) to stay up late

traspapelar [traspape'lar] /1a/ *vt* (*documento, carta*) to mislay, misplace

traspasar [traspa'sar] /1a/ *vt* (*bala*) to pierce, go through; (*propiedad*) to sell, transfer; (*calle*) to cross over; (*límites*) to go beyond; (*ley*) to break; **traspaso** *nm* (*venta*) transfer, sale

traspié [tras'pje] *nm* (*tropezón*) trip; (*fig*) blunder

trasplantar [trasplan'tar] /1a/ *vt* to transplant

traste ['traste] nm (Mus) fret; **dar al ~ con algo** to ruin sth

trastero [tras'tero] nm lumber room

trastienda [tras'tjenda] nf back room (of shop)

trasto ['trasto] nm (pey: cosa) piece of junk; (: persona) dead loss

trastornado, -a [trastor'naðo, a] adj (loco) mad; crazy

trastornar [trastor'nar] /1a/ vt (fig: ideas) to confuse; (: nervios) to shatter; (: persona) to drive crazy; **trastornarse** vr (volverse loco) to go mad o crazy; **trastorno** nm (acto) overturning; (confusión) confusion

tratable [tra'taβle] adj friendly

tratado [tra'taðo] nm (Pol) treaty; (Com) agreement

tratamiento [trata'mjento] nm treatment; **~ de textos** (Inform) word processing

tratar [tra'tar] /1a/ vt (ocuparse de) to treat; (manejar, Tec) to handle; (Med) to treat; (dirigirse a: persona) to address ▷ vi: **~ de** (hablar sobre) to deal with, be about; (intentar) to try to; **tratarse** vr to treat each other; **~ con** (Com) to trade in; (negociar con) to negotiate with; (tener tratos con) to have dealings with; **¿de qué se trata?** what's it about?; **trato** nm dealings pl; (relaciones) relationship; (comportamiento) manner; (Com, Jur) agreement

trauma ['trauma] nm trauma

través [tra'βes] nm (contratiempo) reverse; **al ~** across, crossways; **a ~ de** across; (sobre) over; (por) through

travesaño [traβe'saɲo] nm (Arq) crossbeam; (Deporte) crossbar

travesía [traβe'sia] nf (calle) cross-street; (Naut) crossing

travesura [traβe'sura] nf (broma) prank; (ingenio) wit

travieso, -a [tra'βjeso, a] adj (niño) naughty

trayecto [tra'jekto] nm (ruta) road, way; (viaje) journey; (tramo) stretch; **trayectoria** nf trajectory; (fig) path

traza ['traθa] nf (aspecto) looks pl; (señal) sign; **trazado, -a** adj: **bien trazado** shapely, well-formed ▷ nm (Arq) plan, design; (fig) outline

trazar [tra'θar] /1f/ vt (Arq) to plan; (Arte) to sketch; (fig) to trace; (plan) to draw up; **trazo** nm (línea) line; (bosquejo) sketch

trébol ['treβol] nm (Bot) clover

trece ['treθe] num thirteen

trecho ['tretʃo] nm (distancia) distance; (de tiempo) while

tregua ['treɣwa] nf (Mil) truce; (fig) lull, respite

treinta ['treinta] num thirty

tremendo, -a [tre'mendo, a] adj (terrible) terrible; (imponente: cosa) imposing; (fam: fabuloso) tremendous

tren [tren] nm train; **~ de aterrizaje** undercarriage; **~ de cercanías** suburban train

trenca ['trenka] nf duffel coat

trenza ['trenθa] nf (de pelo) plait

trepar [tre'par] /1a/ vt, vi to climb

tres [tres] num three

tresillo [tre'siʎo] nm three-piece suite; (Mus) triplet

treta ['treta] nf trick

triángulo [tri'angulo] nm triangle

tribu ['triβu] nf tribe

tribuna [tri'βuna] nf (plataforma) platform; (Deporte) stand

tribunal [triβu'nal] nm (en juicio) court; (comisión, fig) tribunal; **~ popular** jury

tributo [tri'βuto] nm (Com) tax

trigal [tri'ɣal] nm wheat field

trigo ['triɣo] nm wheat

trigueño, -a [tri'ɣeɲo, a] adj (pelo) corn-coloured

trillar [tri'ʎar] /1a/ vt (Agr) to thresh

trimestral [trimes'tral] adj quarterly; (Escol) termly

trimestre [tri'mestre] nm (Escol) term

trinar [tri'nar] /1a/ vi (ave) to sing; (rabiar) to fume, be angry

trinchar [trin'tʃar] /1a/ vt (Arq) to carve

t

trinchera [trinˈtʃera] nf (fosa) trench

trineo [triˈneo] nm sledge

trinidad [triniˈðað] nf trio; (Rel): **la T~** the Trinity

tripa [ˈtripa] nf (Anat) intestine; (fam) belly; **tripas** nfpl insides

triple [ˈtriple] adj triple

triplicado, -a [tripliˈkaðo, a] adj: **por ~** in triplicate

tripulación [tripulaˈθjon] nf crew

tripulante [tripuˈlante] nmf crewman/woman

tripular [tripuˈlar] /1a/ vt (barco) to man; (Auto) to drive

triquiñuela [trikiˈɲwela] nf trick

tris [tris] nm crack

triste [ˈtriste] adj sad; (lamentable) sorry, miserable; **tristeza** nf (aflicción) sadness; (melancolía) melancholy

triturar [trituˈrar] /1a/ vt (moler) to grind; (mascar) to chew

triunfar [triunˈfar] /1a/ vi (tener éxito) to triumph; (ganar) to win; **triunfo** nm triumph

trivial [triˈβjal] adj trivial

triza [ˈtriθa] nf: **hacer algo ~s** to smash sth to bits; (papel) to tear sth to shreds

trocear [troθeˈar] /1a/ vt to cut up

trocha [ˈtrotʃa] nf short cut

trofeo [troˈfeo] nm (premio) trophy

tromba [ˈtromba] nf: downpour

trombón [tromˈbon] nm trombone

trombosis [tromˈbosis] nf inv thrombosis

trompa [ˈtrompa] nf horn; (trompo) humming top; (hocico) snout; **cogerse una ~** (fam) to get tight

trompazo [tromˈpaθo] nm (choque) bump, bang; (puñetazo) punch

trompeta [tromˈpeta] nf trumpet; (clarín) bugle

trompicón [trompiˈkon]: **a trompicones** adv in fits and starts

trompo [ˈtrompo] nm spinning top

trompón [tromˈpon] nm bump

tronar [troˈnar] /1l/ vt (LAM) to shoot; (: examen) to flunk ▷ vi to thunder; (fig) to rage

tronchar [tronˈtʃar] /1a/ vt (árbol) to chop down; (fig: vida) to cut short; (esperanza) to shatter; (persona) to tire out; **troncharse** vr to fall down

tronco [ˈtronko] nm (de árbol, Anat) trunk

trono [ˈtrono] nm throne

tropa [ˈtropa] nf (Mil) troop; (soldados) soldiers pl

tropezar [tropeˈθar] /1f, 1j/ vi to trip, stumble; (fig) to slip up; **~ con** to run into; (topar con) to bump into; **tropezón** nm trip; (fig) blunder

tropical [tropiˈkal] adj tropical

trópico [ˈtropiko] nm tropic

tropiezo etc [troˈpjeθo] vb V **tropezar** ▷ nm (error) slip, blunder; (desgracia) misfortune; (obstáculo) snag

trotamundos [trotaˈmundos] nm inv globetrotter

trotar [troˈtar] /1a/ vi to trot; **trote** nm trot; (fam) travelling; **de mucho trote** hard-wearing

trozar [troˈθar] /1f/ vt (LAM) to cut up, cut into pieces

trozo [ˈtroθo] nm bit, piece

trucha [ˈtrutʃa] nf trout

truco [ˈtruko] nm (habilidad) knack; (engaño) trick

trueno [ˈtrweno] nm thunder; (estampido) bang

trueque [ˈtrweke] nm exchange; (Com) barter

trufa [ˈtrufa] nf (Bot) truffle

truhán, -ana [truˈan, ana] nm/f rogue

truncar [trunˈkar] /1g/ vt (cortar) to truncate; (la vida etc) to cut short; (el desarrollo) to stunt

tu [tu] adj your

tú [tu] pron you

tubérculo [tuˈβerkulo] nm (Bot) tuber

tuberculosis [tuβerkuˈlosis] nf inv tuberculosis

tubería [tuβeˈria] nf pipes pl; (conducto) pipeline

tubo [ˈtuβo] nm tube, pipe; **~ de ensayo** test-tube; **~ de escape** exhaust (pipe)

tuerca ['twerka] nf nut
tuerto, -a ['twerto, a] adj blind in one eye ▷ nm/f one-eyed person
tuerza etc ['twerθa] vb V **torcer**
tuétano ['twetano] nm marrow; (Bot) pith
tufo ['tufo] nm (pey) stench
tuitear [tuite'ar] vt, vi to tweet
tul [tul] nm tulle
tulipán [tuli'pan] nm tulip
tullido, -a [tu'ʎiðo, a] adj crippled
tumba ['tumba] nf (sepultura) tomb
tumbar [tum'bar] /1a/ vt to knock down; **tumbarse** vr (echarse) to lie down; (extenderse) to stretch out
tumbo ['tumbo] nm: **dar ~s** to stagger
tumbona [tum'bona] nf (butaca) easy chair; (de playa) deckchair (BRIT), beach chair (US)
tumor [tu'mor] nm tumour
tumulto [tu'multo] nm turmoil
tuna ['tuna] nf (Mus) student music group; V tb **tuno**

⊙ **TUNA**

A *tuna* is made up of university students, or quite often former students, who dress up in costumes from the *Edad de Oro*, the Spanish Golden Age. These musical troupes go through the town playing their guitars, lutes and tambourines and serenade the young ladies in the halls of residence, or make impromptu appearances at weddings or parties singing traditional Spanish songs for a few coins.

tunante [tu'nante] nm rogue
túnel ['tunel] nm tunnel
Túnez ['tuneθ] nm Tunis
tuning ['tunin] nm (Auto) car styling, modding (fam)
tuno, -a ['tuno, a] nm/f (fam) rogue ▷ nm (Mus) member of a "tuna"; V **tuna**

tupido, -a [tu'piðo, a] adj (denso) dense; (tela) close-woven
turbante [tur'βante] nm turban
turbar [tur'βar] /1a/ vt (molestar) to disturb; (incomodar) to upset
turbina [tur'βina] nf turbine
turbio, -a ['turβjo, a] adj cloudy; (tema) confused
turbulencia [turβu'lenθja] nf turbulence; (fig) restlessness; **turbulento, -a** adj turbulent; (fig: intranquilo) restless; (ruidoso) noisy
turco, -a ['turko, a] adj Turkish ▷ nm/f Turk
turismo [tu'rismo] nm tourism; (coche) saloon car; **turista** nmf tourist; **turístico, -a** adj tourist cpd
turnarse [tur'narse] /1a/ vr to take (it in) turns; **turno** nm (de trabajo) shift; (Deporte etc) turn
turquesa [tur'kesa] nf turquoise
Turquía [tur'kia] nf Turkey
turrón [tu'rron] nm (dulce) nougat
tutear [tute'ar] /1a/ vt to address as familiar "tú"; **tutearse** vr to be on familiar terms
tutela [tu'tela] nf (legal) guardianship; **tutelar** /1a/ adj tutelary ▷ vt to protect
tutor, a [tu'tor, a] nm/f (legal) guardian; (Escol) tutor
tuve etc ['tuβe] vb V **tener**
tuviera etc vb V **tener**
tuyo, -a ['tujo, a] adj yours, of yours ▷ pron yours; **un amigo ~** a friend of yours; **los ~s** (fam) your relations, your family
TV nf abr (= televisión) TV
TVE nf abr = **Televisión Española**
tweet [twit] (pl **tweets**) nm (en Twitter) tweet

u [u] *conj* or
ubicar [uβi'kar] /1g/ *vt* to place, situate; *(encontrar)* to find; **ubicarse** *vr* to be situated, be located
ubre ['uβre] *nf* udder
UCI *sigla f* (= *Unidad de Cuidados Intensivos*) ICU
Ud(s) *abr* = **usted**
UE *nf abr* (= *Unión Europea*) EU
ufanarse [ufa'narse] /1a/ *vr* to boast; **ufano, -a** *adj (arrogante)* arrogant; *(presumido)* conceited
UGT *nf abr* V **Unión General de Trabajadores (UGT)**
úlcera ['ulθera] *nf* ulcer
ulterior [ulte'rjor] *adj (más allá)* farther, further; *(subsecuente, siguiente)* subsequent
últimamente ['ultimamente] *adv (recientemente)* lately, recently
ultimar [ulti'mar] /1a/ *vt* to finish; *(finalizar)* to finalize; *(Lam: matar)* to kill
ultimátum [ulti'matum] *nm* ultimatum

último, -a ['ultimo, a] *adj* last; *(más reciente)* latest, most recent; *(más bajo)* bottom; *(más alto)* top; **en las últimas** on one's last legs; **por ~** finally
ultra ['ultra] *adj* ultra ▷ *nmf* extreme right-winger
ultraje [ul'traxe] *nm* outrage; insult
ultramar [ultra'mar] *nm*: **de** *o* **en ~** abroad, overseas
ultranza [ul'tranθa]: **a ~** *adv (a toda costa)* at all costs; *(completo)* outright
umbral [um'bral] *nm (gen)* threshold

un, -una [un, 'una] *artículo indefinido*
1 a; *(antes de vocal)* an; **una mujer/ naranja** a woman/an orange
2: **unos/unas: hay unos regalos para ti** there are some presents for you; **hay unas cervezas en la nevera** there are some beers in the fridge; V tb **uno**

unánime [u'nanime] *adj* unanimous; **unanimidad** *nf* unanimity
undécimo, -a [un'deθimo, a] *adj* eleventh
ungir [un'xir] /3c/ *vt* to anoint
ungüento [un'gwento] *nm* ointment
único, -a ['uniko, a] *adj* only; sole; *(sin par)* unique
unidad [uni'ðað] *nf* unity; *(Tec)* unit
unido, -a [u'niðo, a] *adj* joined, linked; *(fig)* united
unificar [unifi'kar] /1g/ *vt* to unite, unify
uniformar [unifor'mar] /1a/ *vt* to make uniform; *(persona)* to put into uniform
uniforme [uni'forme] *adj* uniform, equal; *(superficie)* even ▷ *nm* uniform
unilateral [unilate'ral] *adj* unilateral
unión [u'njon] *nf* union; *(acto)* uniting, joining; *(calidad)* unity; *(Tec)* joint; **U~ General de Trabajadores (UGT)** *(ESP)* Socialist Union Confederation; **U~ Europea** European Union
unir [u'nir] /3a/ *vt (juntar)* to join, unite; *(atar)* to tie, fasten; *(combinar)*

to combine; **unirse** vr to join together, unite; (*empresas*) to merge

unísono [u'nisono] nm: **al ~** in unison

universal [uniβer'sal] adj universal; (*mundial*) world cpd

universidad [uniβersi'ðað] nf university

universitario, -a [uniβersi'tarjo, a] adj university cpd ▷ nm/f (*profesor*) lecturer; (*estudiante*) (university) student; (*graduado*) graduate

universo [uni'βerso] nm universe

○ **PALABRA CLAVE**

uno, -a ['uno, a] adj one; **unos pocos** a few; **unos cien** about a hundred
▶ pron 1 one; **quiero uno solo** I only want one; **uno de ellos** one of them
2 (*alguien*) somebody, someone; **conozco a uno que se te parece** I know somebody o someone who looks like you; **unos querían quedarse** some (people) wanted to stay
3 (*impersonal*) one; **uno mismo** oneself
4: **unos ... otros ...** some ... others
▶ nf one; **es la una** it's one o'clock
▶ num (number) one; V tb **un**

untar [un'tar] /1a/ vt (*mantequilla*) to spread; (*engrasar*) to grease, oil

uña ['uŋa] nf (*Anat*) nail; (*garra*) claw; (*casco*) hoof; (*arrancaclavos*) claw

uranio [u'ranjo] nm uranium

urbanización [urβaniθa'θjon] nf (*colonia, barrio*) estate, housing scheme

urbanizar [urβani'θar] /1f/ vt (*zona*) to develop, urbanize

urbano, -a [ur'βano, a] adj (*de ciudad*) urban; (*cortés*) courteous, polite

urbe ['urβe] nf large city

urdir [ur'ðir] /3a/ vt to warp; (*fig*) to plot, contrive

urgencia [ur'xenθja] nf urgency; (*prisa*) haste, rush; (*emergencia*) emergency; **servicios de ~** emergency services; **"U~s"** "Casualty"; **urgente** adj urgent

urgir [ur'xir] /3c/ vi to be urgent; **me urge** I'm in a hurry for it

urinario, -a [uri'narjo, a] adj urinary ▷ nm urinal

urna ['urna] nf urn; (*Pol*) ballot box

urraca [u'rraka] nf magpie

URSS nf abr (*Historia*: = *Unión de Repúblicas Socialistas Soviéticas*) USSR

Uruguay [uru'ɣwai] nm: **El ~** Uruguay; **uruguayo, -a** adj, nm/f Uruguayan

usado, -a [u'saðo, a] adj used; (*de segunda mano*) secondhand

usar [u'sar] /1a/ vt to use; (*ropa*) to wear; (*tener costumbre*) to be in the habit of; **usarse** vr to be used; **uso** nm use; (*Mecánica etc*) usage, custom; (*moda*) fashion; **al uso** in keeping with custom; **al uso de** in the style of; **de uso externo** (*Med*) for external use

usted [us'teð] pron you sg; **~es** you pl

usual [u'swal] adj usual

usuario, -a [usw'arjo, a] nm/f user

usura [u'sura] nf usury; **usurero, -a** nm/f usurer

usurpar [usur'par] /1a/ vt to usurp

utensilio [uten'siljo] nm tool; (*Culin*) utensil

útero ['utero] nm uterus, womb

útil ['util] adj useful ▷ nm tool; **utilidad** nf usefulness; (*Com*) profit; **utilizar** /1f/ vt to use, utilize

utopía [uto'pia] nf Utopia; **utópico, -a** adj Utopian

uva ['uβa] nf grape

○ **UVA**

● In Spain *las uvas* play a big part on New Years' Eve (*Nochevieja*), when on the stroke of midnight people from every part of Spain, at home, in restaurants or in the plaza mayor eat a grape for each stroke of the clock – especially the one at Puerta del Sol in Madrid. It is said to bring luck for the following year.

u

V

va [ba] *vb V* **ir**

vaca ['baka] *nf* (*animal*) cow; (*carne*) beef

vacaciones [baka'θjones] *nfpl* holiday(s)

vacante [ba'kante] *adj* vacant, empty ▷ *nf* vacancy

vaciar [ba'θjar] /1c/ *vt* to empty (out); (*ahuecar*) to hollow out; (*moldear*) to cast; **vaciarse** *vr* to empty

vacilar [baθi'lar] /1a/ *vi* to be unsteady; to falter; to hesitate, waver; (*memoria*) to fail

vacío, -a [ba'θio, a] *adj* empty; (*puesto*) vacant; (*desocupado*) idle; (*vano*) vain ▷ *nm* emptiness; (*Física*) vacuum; (*un vacío*) (empty) space

vacuna [ba'kuna] *nf* vaccine; **vacunar** /1a/ *vt* to vaccinate

vacuno, -a [ba'kuno, a] *adj* bovine; **ganado ~** cattle

vadear [baðe'ar] /1a/ *vt* (*río*) to ford; **vado** *nm* ford; **"vado permanente"** "keep clear"

vagabundo, -a [baɣa'βundo, a] *adj* wandering ▷ *nm/f* tramp

vagancia [ba'ɣanθja] *nf* (*pereza*) idleness, laziness; (*vagabundeo*) vagrancy

vagar [ba'ɣar] /1h/ *vi* to wander; (*no hacer nada*) to idle

vagina [ba'xina] *nf* vagina

vago, -a ['baɣo, a] *adj* vague; (*perezoso*) lazy ▷ *nm/f* (*vagabundo*) tramp; (*perezoso*) lazybones *sg*, idler

vagón [ba'ɣon] *nm* (*de pasajeros*) carriage; (*de mercancías*) wagon

vaho ['bao] *nm* (*vapor*) vapour, steam; (*respiración*) breath

vaina ['baina] *nf* sheath

vainilla [bai'niʎa] *nf* vanilla

vais [bais] *vb V* **ir**

vaivén [bai'βen] *nm* to-and-fro movement; (*de tránsito*) coming and going; **vaivenes** *nmpl* (*fig*) ups and downs

vajilla [ba'xiʎa] *nf* crockery, dishes *pl*; (*una vajilla*) service

valdré *etc vb V* **valer**

vale ['bale] *nm* voucher; (*recibo*) receipt; (*pagaré*) IOU

valedero, -a [bale'ðero, a] *adj* valid

valenciano, -a [balen'θjano, a] *adj* Valencian

valentía [balen'tia] *nf* courage, bravery

valer [ba'ler] /2p/ *vt* to be worth; (*Mat*) to equal; (*costar*) to cost ▷ *vi* (*ser útil*) to be useful; (*ser válido*) to be valid; **valerse** *vr* to take care of o.s.; **~ la pena** to be worthwhile; **¿vale?** O.K.?; **más vale que nos vayamos** we'd better go; **~se de** to make use of, take advantage of; **¡eso a mí no me vale!** (*LAM fam: no importar*) I couldn't care less about that

valeroso, -a [bale'roso, a] *adj* brave, valiant

valgo *etc* ['balɣo] *vb V* **valer**

valía [ba'lia] *nf* worth

validar [bali'ðar] /1a/ *vt* to validate; **validez** *nf* validity; **válido, -a** *adj* valid

valiente [ba'ljente] adj brave, valiant
▷ nmf brave man/woman

valija [ba'lixa] nf (LAM) case, suitcase; **~ diplomática** diplomatic bag

valioso, -a [ba'ljoso, a] adj valuable

valla ['baʎa] nf fence; (Deporte) hurdle; **~ publicitaria** hoarding (esp BRIT), billboard (esp US); **vallar** /1a/ vt to fence in

valle ['baʎe] nm valley

valor [ba'lor] nm value, worth; (precio) price; (valentía) valour, courage; (importancia) importance; V tb **valores**; **valorar** /1a/ vt to value; **valores** nmpl (Com) securities

vals [bals] nm waltz

válvula ['balβula] nf valve

vamos ['bamos] vb V **ir**

vampiro, -iresa [bam'piro, i'resa] nm/f vampire

van [ban] vb V **ir**

vanguardia [ban'gwardja] nf vanguard; (Arte) avant-garde

vanidad [bani'ðað] nf vanity; **vanidoso, -a** adj vain, conceited

vano, -a ['bano, a] adj vain

vapor [ba'por] nm vapour; (vaho) steam; **al ~** (Culin) steamed; **~ de agua** water vapour; **vaporizador** nm spray; **vaporizar** /1f/ vt to vaporize; **vaporoso, -a** adj vaporous

vaquero, -a [ba'kero, a] adj cattle cpd ▷ nm cowboy; **vaqueros** nmpl jeans

vaquilla [ba'kiʎa] nf heifer

vara ['bara] nf stick; (Tec) rod

variable [ba'rjaβle] adj, nf variable (tb Inform)

variación [barja'θjon] nf variation

variar [ba'rjar] /1c/ vt to vary; (modificar) to modify; (cambiar de posición) to switch around ▷ vi to vary

varicela [bari'θela] nf chicken pox

varices [ba'riθes] nfpl varicose veins

variedad [barje'ðað] nf variety

varilla [ba'riʎa] nf stick; (Bot) twig; (Tec) rod; (de rueda) spoke

vario, -a ['barjo, a] adj varied; **~s** various, several

varita [ba'rita] nf: **~ mágica** magic wand

varón [ba'ron] nm male, man; **varonil** adj manly

Varsovia [bar'soβja] nf Warsaw

vas [bas] vb V **ir**

vasco, -a ['basko, a], **vascongado, -a** [baskon'gaðo, a] adj, nm/f Basque

vaselina [base'lina] nf Vaseline®

vasija [ba'sixa] nf (earthenware) vessel

vaso ['baso] nm glass, tumbler; (Anat) vessel

> No confundir *vaso* con la palabra inglesa *vase*.

vástago ['bastaɣo] nm (Bot) shoot; (Tec) rod; (fig) offspring

vasto, -a ['basto, a] adj vast, huge

Vaticano [bati'kano] nm: **el ~** the Vatican

vatio ['batjo] nm (Elec) watt

vaya etc ['baja] vb V **ir**

Vd abr = **usted**

Vds abr = **ustedes**; V **usted**

ve [be] vb V **ir**; **ver**

vecindad [beθin'dað] nf, **vecindario** [beθin'darjo] nm neighbourhood; (habitantes) residents pl

vecino, -a [be'θino, a] adj neighbouring ▷ nm/f neighbour; (residente) resident

veda ['beða] nf prohibition; **vedar** /1a/ vt (prohibir) to ban, prohibit; (impedir) to stop, prevent

vegetación [bexeta'θjon] nf vegetation

vegetal [bexe'tal] adj, nm vegetable

vegetariano, -a [bexeta'rjano, a] adj, nm/f vegetarian

vehículo [be'ikulo] nm vehicle; (Med) carrier

veía etc vb V **ver**

veinte ['beinte] num twenty

vejar [be'xar] /1a/ vt (irritar) to annoy, vex; (humillar) to humiliate

vejez [be'xeθ] nf old age

vejiga [be'xiɣa] nf (Anat) bladder

v

vela ['bela] nf (de cera) candle; (Naut) sail; (insomnio) sleeplessness; (vigilia) vigil; (Mil) sentry duty; **estar a dos ~s** (fam) to be skint

velado, -a [be'laðo, a] adj veiled; (sonido) muffled; (Foto) blurred ▷ nf soirée

velar [be'lar] /1a/ vt (vigilar) to keep watch over ▷ vi to stay awake; **~ por** to watch over, look after

velatorio [bela'torjo] nm (funeral) wake

velero [be'lero] nm (Naut) sailing ship; (Aviat) glider

veleta [be'leta] nf weather vane

veliz [be'lis] nm (LAm) suitcase

vello ['beʎo] nm down, fuzz

velo ['belo] nm veil

velocidad [beloθi'ðað] nf speed; (Tec) rate; (Mecánica, Auto) gear

velocímetro [belo'θimetro] nm speedometer

velorio [be'lorjo] nm (LAm) (funeral) wake

veloz [be'loθ] adj fast

ven [ben] vb V **venir**

vena ['bena] nf vein

venado [be'naðo] nm deer

vencedor, a [benθe'ðor, a] adj victorious ▷ nm/f victor, winner

vencer [ben'θer] /2b/ vt (dominar) to defeat, beat; (derrotar) to vanquish; (superar, controlar) to overcome, master ▷ vi (triunfar) to win (through), triumph; (plazo) to expire; **vencido, -a** adj (derrotado) defeated, beaten; (Com) due ▷ adv: **pagar vencido** to pay in arrears

venda ['benda] nf bandage; **vendaje** nm bandage, dressing; **vendar** /1a/ vt to bandage; **vendar los ojos** to blindfold

vendaval [benda'βal] nm (viento) gale

vendedor, a [bende'ðor, a] nm/f seller

vender [ben'der] /2a/ vt to sell; **venderse** vr (estar a la venta) to be on sale; **~ al contado/al por mayor/al por menor/a plazos** to sell for cash/wholesale/retail/on credit; **"se vende"** "for sale"

vendimia [ben'dimja] nf grape harvest

vendré etc [ben'dre] vb V **venir**

veneno [be'neno] nm poison; (de serpiente) venom; **venenoso, -a** adj poisonous; venomous

venerable [bene'raβle] adj venerable; **venerar** /1a/ vt (respetar) to revere; (reconocer) to venerate; (adorar) to worship

venéreo, -a [be'nereo, a] adj: **enfermedad venérea** venereal disease

venezolano, -a [beneθo'lano, a] adj Venezuelan

Venezuela [bene'θwela] nf Venezuela

venganza [ben'ganθa] nf vengeance, revenge; **vengar** /1h/ vt to avenge; **vengarse** vr to take revenge; **vengativo, -a** adj (persona) vindictive

vengo etc vb V **venir**

venia ['benja] nf (perdón) pardon; (permiso) consent

venial [be'njal] adj venial

venida [be'niða] nf (llegada) arrival; (regreso) return

venidero, -a [beni'ðero, a] adj coming, future

venir [be'nir] /3r/ vi to come; (llegar) to arrive; (ocurrir) to happen; **venirse** vr: **~se abajo** to collapse; **~ bien** to be suitable; **~ mal** to be unsuitable o inconvenient; **el año que viene** next year

venta ['benta] nf (Com) sale; **~ a plazos** hire purchase; **"en ~"** "for sale"; **~ al contado/al por mayor/al por menor o al detalle** cash sale/wholesale/retail; **~ a domicilio** door-to-door selling; **estar de o en ~** to be (up) for sale o on the market

ventaja [ben'taxa] nf advantage; **ventajoso, -a** adj advantageous

ventana [ben'tana] nf window; **ventanilla** nf (de taquilla) window

ventilación [bentila'θjon] *nf*
ventilation; (*corriente*) draught
ventilador [bentila'ðor] *nm* fan
ventilar [benti'lar] /1a/ *vt* to
ventilate; (*poner a secar*) to put out to
dry; (*fig*) to air, discuss
ventisca [ben'tiska] *nf* blizzard
ventrílocuo, -a [ben'trilokwo, a]
nm/f ventriloquist
ventura [ben'tura] *nf* (*felicidad*)
happiness; (*buena suerte*) luck; (*destino*)
fortune; **a la (buena) ~** at random;
venturoso, -a *adj* happy; (*afortunado*)
lucky, fortunate
veo *etc vb V* **ver**
ver [ber] /2u/ *vt, vi* to see; (*mirar*) to
look at, watch; (*investigar*) to look
into; (*entender*) to see, understand;
verse *vr* (*encontrarse*) to meet; (*dejarse
ver*) to be seen; (*hallarse: en un apuro*)
to find o.s., be; **a ~** let's see; **no tener
nada que ~ con** to have nothing to do
with; **a mi modo de ~** as I see it; **ya
veremos** we'll see
vera ['bera] *nf* edge, verge; (*de río*) bank
veraneante [berane'ante] *nmf*
holidaymaker, (summer) vacationer
(*US*)
veranear [berane'ar] /1a/ *vi* to
spend the summer; **veraneo** *nm*
summer holiday; **veraniego, -a** *adj*
summer *cpd*
verano [be'rano] *nm* summer
veras ['beras] *nfpl*: **de ~** really, truly
verbal [ber'βal] *adj* verbal
verbena [ber'βena] *nf* street party;
(*baile*) open-air dance
verbo ['berβo] *nm* verb
verdad [ber'ðað] *nf* truth; (*fiabilidad*)
reliability; **de ~** real, proper; **a decir
~, no quiero** to tell (you) the truth,
I don't want to; **verdadero, -a** *adj*
(*veraz*) true, truthful; (*fiable*) reliable;
(*fig*) real
verde ['berðe] *adj* green; (*chiste etc*)
blue, dirty ▷ *nm* green; **viejo ~** dirty
old man; **verdear** /1a/ *vi* to turn
green; **verdor** *nm* greenness

verdugo [ber'ðuɣo] *nm* executioner
verdulero, -a [berðu'lero, a] *nm/f*
greengrocer
verdura [ber'ðura] *nf* greenness;
verduras *nfpl* (*Culin*) greens
vereda [be'reða] *nf* path; (*LAM*)
pavement, sidewalk (*US*)
veredicto [bere'ðikto] *nm* verdict
vergonzoso, -a [berɣon'θoso, a] *adj*
shameful; (*tímido*) timid, bashful
vergüenza [ber'ɣwenθa] *nf* shame,
sense of shame; (*timidez*) bashfulness;
(*pudor*) modesty; **me da ~ decírselo**
I feel too shy *o* it embarrasses me to
tell him
verídico, -a [be'riðiko, a] *adj* true,
truthful
verificar [berifi'kar] /1a/ *vt* to
check; (*corroborar*) to verify (*tb
Inform*); (*llevar a cabo*) to carry out;
verificarse *vr* (*profecía etc*) to come
o prove true
verja ['berxa] *nf* (*cancela*) iron gate;
(*cerca*) railing(s); (*rejado*) grating
vermut [ber'mu] (*pl* **vermuts**) *nm*
vermouth
verosímil [bero'simil] *adj* likely,
probable; (*relato*) credible
verruga [be'rruɣa] *nf* wart
versátil [ber'satil] *adj* versatile
versión [ber'sjon] *nf* version
verso ['berso] *nm* verse; **un ~** a line
of poetry
vértebra ['berteβra] *nf* vertebra
verter [ber'ter] /2g/ *vt* (*vaciar*) to
empty, pour (out); (*sin querer*) to spill;
(*basura*) to dump ▷ *vi* to flow
vertical [berti'kal] *adj* vertical
vértice ['bertiθe] *nm* vertex, apex
vertidos [ber'tiðos] *nmpl* waste *sg*
vertiente [ber'tjente] *nf* slope;
(*fig*) aspect
vértigo ['bertiɣo] *nm* vertigo; (*mareo*)
dizziness
vesícula [be'sikula] *nf* blister
vespino® [bes'pino] *nm o f* ≈ moped
vestíbulo [bes'tiβulo] *nm* hall; (*de
teatro*) foyer

V

vestido [bes'tiðo] *nm* (*ropa*) clothes *pl*, clothing; (*de mujer*) dress, frock

vestidor [besti'ðor] *nm* (LAM Deporte) changing (BRIT) *o* locker (US) room

vestimenta [besti'menta] *nf* clothing

vestir [bes'tir] /3k/ *vt* (*poner: ropa*) to put on; (*llevar: ropa*) to wear; (*pagar: la ropa*) to clothe; (*sastre*) to make clothes for ▷ *vi* to dress; (*verse bien*) to look good; **vestirse** *vr* to get dressed, dress o.s.; **estar vestido de** to be dressed *o* clad in; (*como disfraz*) to be dressed as

vestuario [bes'twarjo] *nm* clothes *pl*, wardrobe; (Teat) *o para actores*) dressing room; (*Deporte*) changing room

vetar [be'tar] /1a/ *vt* to veto

veterano, -a [bete'rano, a] *adj*, *nm/f* veteran

veterinario, -a [beteri'narjo, a] *nm/f* vet(erinary surgeon) ▷ *nf* veterinary science

veto ['beto] *nm* veto

vez [beθ] *nf* time; (*turno*) turn; **a la ~ que** at the same time as; **a su ~** in its turn; **una ~** once; **dos veces** twice; **de una ~** in one go; **de una ~ para siempre** once and for all; **en ~ de** instead of; **a veces** sometimes; **otra ~** again; **una y otra ~** repeatedly; **de en cuando** from time to time; **7 veces 9** 7 times 9; **hacer las veces de** to stand in for; **tal ~** perhaps

vía ['bia] *nf* track, route; (Ferro) line; (*fig*) way; (Anat) passage, tube ▷ *prep* via, by way of; **por ~ judicial** by legal means; **en ~s de** in the process of; **~ aérea** airway; **V~ Láctea** Milky Way; **~ pública** public highway *o* thoroughfare

viable ['bjaβle] *adj* (*plan etc*) feasible

viaducto [bja'ðukto] *nm* viaduct

viajante [bja'xante] *nm* commercial traveller

viajar [bja'xar] /1a/ *vi* to travel; **viaje** *nm* journey; (*gira*) tour; (Naut) voyage; **estar de viaje** to be on a journey;

viaje de ida y vuelta round trip; **viaje de novios** honeymoon; **viajero, -a** *adj* travelling (BRIT), traveling (US); (Zool) migratory ▷ *nm/f* (*quien viaja*) traveller; (*pasajero*) passenger

víbora ['biβora] *nf* viper; (LAM: *venenoso*) poisonous snake

vibración [biβra'θjon] *nf* vibration

vibrar [bi'βrar] /1a/ *vt* to vibrate ▷ *vi* to vibrate

vicepresidente [biθepresi'ðente] *nmf* vice president

viceversa [biθe'βersa] *adv* vice versa

vicio ['biθjo] *nm* vice; (*mala costumbre*) bad habit; **vicioso, -a** *adj* (*muy malo*) vicious; (*corrompido*) depraved ▷ *nm/f* depraved person

víctima ['biktima] *nf* victim

victoria [bik'torja] *nf* victory; **victorioso, -a** *adj* victorious

vid [bið] *nf* vine

vida ['biða] *nf* life; (*duración*) lifetime; **de por ~** for life; **en la/mi ~** never; **estar con ~** to be still alive; **ganarse la ~** to earn one's living

vídeo ['biðeo] *nm* video; **película de ~** videofilm; **videocámara** *nf* camcorder; **videoclub** *nm* video club; **videojuego** *nm* video game; **videollamada** *nf* video call; **videoteléfono** *nf* videophone

vidrio ['biðrjo] *nm* glass

vieira ['bjeira] *nf* scallop

viejo, -a ['bjexo, a] *adj* old ▷ *nm/f* old man/woman; **hacerse** *o* **ponerse ~** to grow *o* get old

Viena ['bjena] *nf* Vienna

viene *etc* ['bjene] *vb* V **venir**

vienés, -esa [bje'nes, esa] *adj* Viennese

viento ['bjento] *nm* wind; **hacer ~** to be windy

vientre ['bjentre] *nm* belly; (*matriz*) womb

viernes ['bjernes] *nm inv* Friday; **V~ Santo** Good Friday

Vietnam [bjet'nam] *nm*: Vietnam; **vietnamita** *adj* Vietnamese

viga ['biɣa] nf beam, rafter; (de metal) girder

vigencia [bi'xenθja] nf validity; **estar/entrar en ~** to be in/come into effect o force; **vigente** adj valid, in force; (imperante) prevailing

vigésimo, -a [bi'xesimo, a] num twentieth

vigía [bi'xia] nm look-out

vigilancia [bixi'lanθja] nf: **tener a algn bajo ~** to keep watch on sb

vigilar [bixi'lar] /1a/ vt to watch over ▷ vi to be vigilant; (hacer guardia) to keep watch; **~ por** to take care of

vigilia [vi'xilja] nf wakefulness; (Rel) vigil; (: ayuno) fast

vigor [bi'ɣor] nm vigour, vitality; **en ~** in force; **entrar/poner en ~** to come/put into effect; **vigoroso, -a** adj vigorous

VIH nm abr (= virus de inmunodeficiencia humana) HIV; **~ negativo/positivo** HIV-negative/-positive

vil [bil] adj vile, low

villa ['biʎa] nf (casa) villa; (pueblo) small town; (municipalidad) municipality

villancico [biʎan'θiko] nm (Christmas) carol

vilo ['bilo]: **en ~** adv in the air, suspended; (fig) on tenterhooks, in suspense

vinagre [bi'naɣre] nm vinegar

vinagreta [bina'ɣreta] nf vinaigrette, French dressing

vinculación [binkula'θjon] nf (lazo) link, bond; (acción) linking

vincular [binku'lar] /1a/ vt to link, bind; **vínculo** nm link, bond

vine etc vb V **venir**

vinicultor, -a [binikul'tor, a] nm/f wine grower

vinicultura [binikul'tura] nf wine growing

viniera etc vb V **venir**

vino ['bino] vb V **venir** ▷ nm wine; **~ de solera/seco/tinto** vintage/dry/red wine

viña ['biɲa] nf, **viñedo** [bi'ɲeðo] nm vineyard

viola ['bjola] nf viola

violación [bjola'θjon] nf violation; **~ (sexual)** rape

violar [bjo'lar] /1a/ vt to violate; (cometer estupro) to rape

violencia [bjo'lenθja] nf (fuerza) violence, force; (embarazo) embarrassment; (acto injusto) unjust act; **violentar** /1a/ vt to force; (casa) to break into; (agredir) to assault; (violar) to violate; **violento, -a** adj violent; (furioso) furious; (situación) embarrassing; (acto) forced, unnatural

violeta [bjo'leta] nf violet

violín [bjo'lin] nm violin

violón [bjo'lon] nm double bass

viral [bi'ral] adj viral

virar [bi'rar] /1a/ vi to change direction

virgen ['birxen] adj virgin ▷ nmf virgin

Virgo ['birɣo] nm Virgo

viril [bi'ril] adj virile; **virilidad** nf virility

virtud [bir'tuð] nf virtue; **en ~ de** by virtue of; **virtuoso, -a** adj virtuous ▷ nm/f virtuoso

viruela [bi'rwela] nf smallpox

virulento, -a [biru'lento, a] adj virulent

virus ['birus] nm inv virus

visa ['bisa] nf (LAM), **visado** [bi'saðo] nm (ESP) visa

víscera ['bisθera] nf internal organ; **vísceras** nfpl entrails

visceral [bisθe'ral] adj (odio) deep-rooted; **reacción ~** gut reaction

visera [bi'sera] nf visor

visibilidad [bisiβili'ðað] nf visibility; **visible** adj visible; (fig) obvious

visillo [bi'siʎo] nm lace curtain

visión [bi'sjon] nf (Anat) vision, (eye) sight; (fantasía) vision, fantasy

visita [bi'sita] nf call, visit; (persona) visitor; **visitante** adj visiting ▷ nmf visitor; **visitar** /1a/ vt to visit, call on

visón [bi'son] nm mink

visor [bi'sor] nm (Foto) viewfinder

víspera ['bispera] nf day before; **la ~ o en ~s de** on the eve of

vista ['bista] nf sight, vision; (*capacidad de ver*) (eye)sight; (*mirada*) look(s); **a primera ~** at first glance; **hacer la ~ gorda** to turn a blind eye; **volver la ~** to look back; **está a la ~ que** it's obvious that; **en ~ de** in view of; **en ~ de que** in view of the fact that; **¡hasta la ~!** so long!, see you!; **con ~s a** with a view to; **vistazo** nm glance; **dar o echar un vistazo a** to glance at

visto, -a ['bisto, a] vb V **vestir** ▷ pp de **ver** ▷ adj seen; (*considerado*) considered ▷ nm: **~ bueno** approval; **por lo ~** apparently; **está ~ que** it's clear that; **está bien/mal ~** it's acceptable/unacceptable; **~ que** since, considering that

vistoso, -a [bis'toso, a] adj colourful

visual [bi'swal] adj visual

vital [bi'tal] adj life cpd, living cpd; (*fig*) vital; (*persona*) lively, vivacious; **vitalicio, -a** adj for life; **vitalidad** nf vitality; (*de persona, negocio*) energy; (*de ciudad*) liveliness

vitamina [bita'mina] nf vitamin

vitorear [bitore'ar] /1a/ vt to cheer, acclaim

vitrina [bi'trina] nf glass case; (*en casa*) display cabinet; (LAM) shop window

viudo, -a ['bjuðo, a] adj widowed ▷ nm widower ▷ nf widow

viva ['biβa] excl hurrah!; **¡~ el rey!** long live the King!

vivaracho, -a [biβa'ratʃo, a] adj jaunty, lively; (*ojos*) bright, twinkling

vivaz [bi'βaθ] adj lively

víveres ['biβeres] nmpl provisions

vivero [bi'βero] nm (*Horticultura*) nursery; (*para peces*) fish farm; (*fig*) hotbed

viveza [bi'βeθa] nf liveliness; (*agudeza: mental*) sharpness

vivienda [bi'βjenda] nf housing; (*casa*) house; (*piso*) flat (BRIT), apartment (US)

viviente [bi'βjente] adj living

vivir [bi'βir] /3a/ vt to live o go through ▷ vi: **~ (de)** to live (by, off, on) ▷ nm life, living

vivo, -a ['biβo, a] adj living, alive; (*fig*) vivid; (*persona: astuto*) smart, clever; **en ~** (TV etc) live

vocablo [bo'kaβlo] nm (*palabra*) word; (*término*) term

vocabulario [bokaβu'larjo] nm vocabulary

vocación [boka'θjon] nf vocation; **vocacional** nf (LAM) ≈ technical college

vocal [bo'kal] adj vocal ▷ nf vowel; **vocalizar** /1f/ vt to vocalize

vocero, -a [bo'θero, a] nm/f (LAM) spokesman/woman

voces ['boθes] nfpl de **voz**

vodka ['boðka] nm vodka

vol abr = **volumen**

volado, -a [bo'laðo, a] adv (LAM) in a rush, hastily

volador, a [bola'ðor, a] adj flying

volandas [bo'landas]: **en ~** adv in o through the air

volante [bo'lante] adj flying ▷ nm (*de máquina, coche*) steering wheel; (*de reloj*) balance

volar [bo'lar] /1l/ vt to blow up ▷ vi to fly

volátil [bo'latil] adj volatile

volcán [bol'kan] nm volcano; **volcánico, -a** adj volcanic

volcar [bol'kar] /1g, 1l/ vt to upset, overturn; (*tumbar, derribar*) to knock over; (*vaciar*) to empty out ▷ vi to overturn; **volcarse** vr to tip over

voleibol [bolei'βol] nm volleyball

volqué [bol'ke] vb V **volcar**

voltaje [bol'taxe] nm voltage

voltear [bolte'ar] /1a/ vt to turn over; (*volcar*) to knock over

voltereta [bolte'reta] nf somersault

voltio ['boltjo] nm volt

voluble [bo'luβle] adj fickle

volumen [bo'lumen] nm volume; **voluminoso, -a** adj voluminous; (*enorme*) massive

voluntad [bolun'taθ] *nf* will, willpower; (*deseo*) desire, wish

voluntario, -a [bolun'tarjo, a] *adj* voluntary ▷ *nm/f* volunteer

volver [bol'βer] /2h/ *vt* to turn; (*boca abajo*) to turn (over); (*voltear*) to turn round, turn upside down; (*poner del revés*) to turn inside out; (*devolver*) to return ▷ *vi* to return, go/come back; **volverse** *vr* to turn round; **~ la espalda** to turn one's back; **~ a hacer** to do again; **~ en sí** to come to o round; **~ triste** *etc* **a algn** to make sb sad *etc*; **~se loco** to go mad

vomitar [bomi'tar] /1a/ *vt, vi* to vomit; **vómito** *nm* vomit

voraz [bo'raθ] *adj* voracious

vos [bos] *pron* (*LAM*) you

vosotros, -as [bo'sotros, as] *pron* you *pl*; (*reflexivo*): **entre ~** among yourselves

votación [bota'θjon] *nf* (*acto*) voting; (*voto*) vote

votar [bo'tar] /1a/ *vi* to vote; **voto** *nm* vote; (*promesa*) vow; **votos** *nmpl* (good) wishes

voy [boi] *vb V* **ir**

voz [boθ] *nf* voice; (*grito*) shout; (*chisme*) rumour; (*Ling*) word; **dar voces** to shout, yell; **en ~ baja** in a low voice; **de viva ~** verbally; **en ~ alta** aloud; **~ de mando** command

vuelco *etc* ['bwelko] *vb V* **volcar** ▷ *nm* spill, overturning

vuelo ['bwelo] *vb V* **volar** ▷ *nm* flight; (*encaje*) lace, frill; **coger al ~** to catch in flight; **~ libre** hang-gliding; **~ regular** scheduled flight

vuelque *etc* ['bwelke] *vb V* **volcar**

vuelta ['bwelta] *nf* turn; (*curva*) bend, curve; (*regreso*) return; (*revolución*) revolution; (*circuito*) lap; (*de papel, tela*) reverse; (*cambio*) change; **~ ciclista** (*Deporte*) (cycle) tour; **a la ~** (*ESP*) on one's return; **a ~ de la esquina** round the corner; **a ~ de correo** by return of post; **dar ~s** to turn, revolve; (*cabeza*) to spin; **dar(se) la ~** (*volverse*)

to turn round; **dar ~s a una idea** to turn over an idea (in one's mind); **dar una ~** to go for a walk; (*en coche*) to go for a drive

vuelto ['bwelto] *pp de* **volver**

vuelvo *etc* ['bwelβo] *vb V* **volver**

vuestro, -a ['bwestro, a] *adj* your ▷ *pron*: **el ~/la vuestra/los ~s/las vuestras** yours; **un amigo ~** a friend of yours

vulgar [bul'ɣar] *adj* (*ordinario*) vulgar; (*común*) common; **vulgaridad** *nf* commonness; (*acto*) vulgarity; (*expresión*) coarse expression

vulnerable [bulne'raβle] *adj* vulnerable

vulnerar [bulne'rar] /1a/ *vt* (*Jur, Com*) to violate; (*derechos*) to violate, to interfere with; (*reputación*) to harm, damage

W X

walkie-talkie [walki'talki] *nm* walkie-talkie

walkman® ['wal(k)man] *nm* Walkman®

wáter ['bater] *nm (taza)* toilet; *(LAM: lugar)* toilet *(BRIT)*, rest room *(US)*

web [web] *nm o f (página)* website; *(red)* (World Wide) Web; **webcam** *nf* webcam; **webmaster** *nmf* webmaster; **website** *nm* website

western ['western] *(pl* **westerns***)* *nm* western

whisky ['wiski] *nm* whisky

wifi ['waifai] *nm* Wi-Fi

windsurf ['winsurf] *nm* windsurfing; **hacer ~** to go windsurfing

xenofobia [seno'foβja] *nf* xenophobia

xilófono [si'lofono] *nm* xylophone

xocoyote, -a [ksoko'jote, a] *nm/f* *(LAM)* baby of the family, youngest child

yoga ['joɣa] *nm* yoga
yogur(t) [jo'ɣur(t)] *nm* yogurt
yuca ['juka] *nf* (*Bot*) yucca; (*alimento*)
cassava, manioc root
Yugoslavia [juɣos'laβja] *nf* (*Historia*)
Yugoslavia
yugular [juɣu'lar] *adj* jugular
yunque ['junke] *nm* anvil
yuyo ['jujo] *nm* (*LAm: mala hierba*) weed

y [i] *conj* and; (*hora*): **la una y cinco**
five past one
ya [ja] *adv* (*gen*) already; (*ahora*) now;
(*en seguida*) at once; (*pronto*) soon
▷ *excl* all right! ▷ *conj* (*ahora que*) now
that; **ya lo sé** I know; **¡ya está bien!**
that's (quite) enough!; **¡ya voy!**
coming!; **ya que** since
yacer [ja'θer] /2x/ *vi* to lie
yacimiento [jaθi'mjento] *nm*
deposit; (*arqueológico*) site
yanqui ['janki] *adj* ▷ *nmf* Yankee
yate ['jate] *nm* yacht
yazco *etc* ['jaθko] *vb* V **yacer**
yedra ['jeðra] *nf* ivy
yegua ['jeɣwa] *nf* mare
yema ['jema] *nf* (*del huevo*) yolk; (*Bot*)
leaf bud; (*fig*) best part; **~ del dedo**
fingertip
yerno ['jerno] *nm* son-in-law
yeso ['jeso] *nm* plaster
yo [jo] *pron personal* I; **soy yo** it's me
yodo ['joðo] *nm* iodine

Z

zafar [θa'far] /1a/ vt (soltar) to untie; (superficie) to clear; **zafarse** vr (escaparse) to escape; (Tec) to slip off

zafiro [θa'firo] nm sapphire

zaga ['θaɣa] nf: **a la ~** behind, in the rear

zaguán [θa'ɣwan] nm hallway

zalamero, -a [θala'mero, a] adj flattering; (relamido) suave

zamarra [θa'marra] nf (chaqueta) sheepskin jacket

zambullirse [θambu'ʎirse] /3h/ vr to dive

zampar [θam'par] /1a/ vt to gobble

zanahoria [θana'orja] nf carrot

zancadilla [θanka'ðiʎa] nf trip

zanco ['θanko] nm stilt

zángano ['θangano] nm drone

zanja ['θanxa] nf ditch; **zanjar** /1a/ vt (conflicto) to resolve

zapata [θa'pata] nf (Mecánica) shoe

zapatería [θapate'ria] nf (oficio) shoemaking; (tienda) shoe-shop; (fábrica) shoe factory; **zapatero, -a** nm/f shoemaker

zapatilla [θapa'tiʎa] nf slipper; (de deporte) training shoe

zapato [θa'pato] nm shoe

zapping ['θapin] nm channel-hopping; **hacer ~** to channel-hop, flick through the channels

zar [θar] nm tsar, czar

zarandear [θarande'ar] /1a/ vt (fam) to shake vigorously

zarpa ['θarpa] nf (garra) claw

zarpar [θar'par] /1a/ vi to weigh anchor

zarza ['θarθa] nf (Bot) bramble

zarzamora [θarθa'mora] nf blackberry

zarzuela [θar'θwela] nf Spanish light opera

zigzag [θiɣ'θaɣ] adj zigzag

zinc [θink] nm zinc

zíper ['siper] nm (LAM) zip, zipper (US)

zócalo ['θokalo] nm (Arq) plinth, base; (de pared) skirting board

zoclo ['θoklo] nm (LAM) skirting board (BRIT), baseboard (US)

zodíaco [θo'ðiako] nm zodiac

zona ['θona] nf area, zone; **~ fronteriza** border area; **~ roja** (LAM) red-light district

zonzo, -a ['θonθo, a] (LAM) adj silly ▷ nm/f fool

zoo ['θoo] nm zoo

zoología [θoolo'xia] nf zoology; **zoológico, -a** adj zoological ▷ nm (tb: **parque zoológico**) zoo; **zoólogo, -a** nm/f zoologist

zoom [θum] nm zoom lens

zopilote [θopi'lote] nm (LAM) buzzard

zoquete [θo'kete] nm (fam) blockhead

zorro, -a ['θorro, a] adj crafty ▷ nm/f fox/vixen

zozobrar [θoθo'βrar] /1a/ vi (hundirse) to capsize; (fig) to fail

zueco ['θweko] nm clog

zumbar [θum'bar] /1a/ vt (golpear) to hit ▷ vi to buzz; **zumbido** nm buzzing

zumo ['θumo] nm juice

zurcir [θur'θir] /3b/ vt (coser) to darn

zurdo, -a ['θurðo, a] adj (persona) left-handed

zurrar [θu'rrar] /1a/ vt (fam) to wallop

Spanish in focus

Introduction

Spanish in focus gives you a fascinating introduction to the Spanish-speaking world. The following pages look at where Spanish is spoken throughout the world, helping you to get to know the language and the people that speak it. Practical language tips and notes on common translation difficulties will allow you to become more confident in Spanish and a useful correspondence section gives you all the information you need to be able to communicate effectively.

We've also included a number of links to useful websites, which will give you the opportunity to read and learn more about Spanish-speaking countries and the Spanish language.

We hope that you will enjoy using your *Spanish in focus* supplement. We are sure that it will help you to find out more about Spanish-speaking countries and become more confident in writing and speaking Spanish.

¡Vamos!

Spain and its regions

Spellings
The English spellings of Seville, Majorca and Andalusia are not used in Spanish; *Sevilla*, *Mallorca* and *Andalucía* are the Spanish forms. Remember the accent on *Málaga*, *Córdoba* and *Cádiz* in Spanish.

3

Spain and its regions

The six biggest Spanish cities

City	Name of inhabitants	Population
Madrid	los madrileños	3,273,049
Barcelona	los barceloneses	1,619,337
Valencia	los valencianos	809,267
Sevilla	los sevillanos	704,198
Zaragoza	los zaragozanos	675,211
Málaga	los malagueños	568,507

Spain shares the Iberian Peninsula with Portugal, its neighbour to the west. The Spanish state consists of the mainland; the Balearic Islands in the Mediterranean; and the Canary Islands in the Atlantic, off north-west Africa. The towns of Ceuta and Melilla, on the coast of Morocco, are also Spanish.

The head of state is the King, Juan Carlos I. The Prime Minister, leader of the party that has the majority in parliament, heads the government and is elected every four years.

Spain is organized into seventeen administrative regions called *comunidades autónomas*. Each region, made up of several smaller *provincias*, has its own parliament and can legislate in areas such as housing, infrastructure, health and education. Central government retains jurisdiction for matters such as defence, foreign affairs and the legal system, which affect the country as a whole.

Regional identity is strong in many parts of Spain, and though the majority of people speak Castilian Spanish (*castellano*) as their first language, other languages and dialects are also important, and for significant numbers of people are their mother tongue. Three of these languages are called *lenguas cooficiales*: Basque (*euskera*), Catalan (*catalán*) and Galician (*gallego*). They have official status under the Constitution and are therefore used in official documents, education and so on.

A snapshot of Spain

- Spain is the second biggest country by area in Western Europe, covering 504 800 km² (well over twice the size of the UK).

- Spain's highest mountain is in the Canary Islands: Teide (3718 m), in Tenerife.

- The river Ebro is around 910km long, rising in the Cantabrian Mountains and flowing into the Mediterranean.

- 40.8 million people live in Spain. The population is one of the slowest-growing in the world.

- The main religion in Spain is Roman Catholicism.

- Spain is the world's tenth largest economy (the US is first and the UK fourth).

- Only France is more popular with foreign tourists; almost 52 million visit Spain every year. The British and Germans head the list, and Andalusia is the most popular destination.

Useful links:
www.ine.es
   The Spanish statistical office.

www.cervantes.es
   Information about Spanish language and culture.

The Spanish-speaking world

Spellings

Don't forget the accent on *Perú*, *Panamá* and *México* in Spanish. *República Dominicana* is the Spanish-speaking Dominican Republic (not to be confused with English-speaking Dominica). Cuba's capital, Havana, is *la Habana* in Spanish.

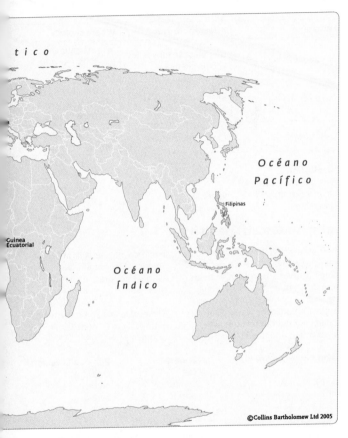

t i c o

*Océano
Pacífico*

Filipinas

Guinea
Ecuatorial

*Océano
Índico*

©Collins Bartholomew Ltd 2005

Countries or regions where Spanish is the main language or an official language

Countries or regions where many of the population speak Spanish

Other languages of Spain

Language	Brief description	Where spoken
Basque (*euskera*)	Not related to any other known language	In the Basque Country (on the border with France)
Catalan (*catalán*)	Closely related to both French and Spanish	In Catalonia (north-eastern Spain), Valencia and the Balearics
Galician (*gallego*)	Close to Portuguese	In Galicia (north-west Spain)

A useful link:
www.lamoncloa.gob.es
Information on the Prime Minister and government.

Latin American Spanish

There are 417 million speakers of Spanish worldwide; only Chinese has more. Latin American Spanish differs from the Spanish spoken in Europe (peninsular Spanish). There is also a huge variation in the type of Spanish spoken throughout the Americas. For example, a 'light bulb' is *un foco* in Mexico, but *una bujía* in Central America. Accents and pronunciation can also vary dramatically throughout the region.

Some words are common to most Latin American countries. For example:

Latin American Spanish	English	Peninsular Spanish
carro	car	*coche*
computadora	computer	*ordenador*
papa	potato	*patata*

> **Two Amerindian languages**
> *Náhuatl* was the language of the Aztecs and is still spoken by a million Mexicans. It gave us words such as 'tomato', 'avocado', 'chocolate' and 'chilli'.
> *Quechua* is still used by 13 million descendants of the Incas in the Andean region. 'Llama', 'condor' and 'puma' all come from Quechua.

A snapshot of Spanish-speaking America

- Argentina is the biggest Spanish-speaking country by area in South and Central America, covering 2 780 000 km². Next come Mexico (1 958 000 km²) and Peru (1 285 000 km²).

- Mexico has by far the biggest population (101 million), but is outstripped by tiny El Salvador in terms of population density (310 people per km², compared with 246 in the UK and just 31 in the US).

- The highest mountain in the world outside the Himalayas, Cerro Aconcagua (6959 m) lies in Argentina, on the border with Chile. The lowest point in South America, Península Valdés (40 m below sea level), is also in Argentina

- At an altitude of 3630 m, the Bolivian city of La Paz is the highest capital in the Americas.

- The Atacama Desert (lying mainly in northern Chile) is the driest place on earth.

- The second longest river in the world, the Amazon, rises in the Peruvian Andes and flows east through Brazil to the Atlantic. Angel Falls in Venezuela is the world's highest waterfall.

- Latin America has only two landlocked countries: Bolivia and Paraguay.

- Chile is over 4000 km long but only 177 km wide on average.

- Mexico is the world's ninth largest economy (the US is first and the UK fourth).

- The USA has the fifth largest Spanish-speaking population in the world (28 million, or 10% of the population).

A useful link:

http://lanic.utexas.edu/index.html
Aspects of life in Spanish-speaking America.

Improving your pronunciation

There are a number of different methods you can use to improve your accent and increase your confidence in speaking Spanish:

- read out loud to yourself to improve your confidence

- listen to Spanish-language radio

- watch Spanish-language films

- chat with Spanish-speakers

A useful link:
www.mediatico.com

Some special Spanish sounds

- **Z and c.** Most Spaniards say *z* and the *c* in *ce* and *ci* like 'th' in English '**th**in' (e.g. *cena* = 'thena'; *diez* = 'dieth'). Latin Americans tend to use an 's' sound, as in English '**s**ame'.

- **Ll.** The pronunciation of this (e.g. *llamar, ella*) is rather variable – all over the Spanish-speaking world you'll hear speakers who pronounce it like English '**y**et', while others pronounce it like 'mi**ll**ion'.

- **J and g.** *J* in any position and *g* before *e* or *i* sound similar to English 'lo**ch**' (e.g. *jefe, ajo, gente*) in Spain, but in Latin America they are softer, more like English *h*.

- **B and v.** These sound exactly the same: at the start of a word and after *m* and *n* (e.g. *vaso,*

ambulancia) they are similar to English **b**oy. Otherwise to say them try saying a 'b', but don't let your lips touch (e.g. *obra, uva*).

- **D.** Between vowels and after consonants other than *l* or *n* (e.g. *modo, ardiente*), *d* is very like 'th' in English '**th**ough'.

- **H.** In Spanish, *h* is always silent (e.g. *hablar* is pronounced 'ablar').

- **R and rr.** *Rr* is strongly trilled, like Scots *r* (e.g. *perro*). *R* is said with a single trill (e.g. *pero*), but sounds like *rr* at the start of a word and after *l, n* or *s* (e.g. *rápido*).

- **Ñ.** A *tilde* changes the sound of *n* to one similar to English 'o**ni**on' (e.g. *baño*).

Improving your fluency

Conversational words and phrases

In English we insert lots of words and phrases, such as *so, then, by the way* into our conversation, to give our thoughts a structure and often to show our attitude. The Spanish words shown below do the same thing. If you use them they will make you sound more fluent and natural.

- *además*
  Además, *no tienes nada que perder.*
  (= besides)

- *está bien*
  *¡***Está bien***! Lo haré.* (= all right!)

- *bueno*
  *¡***Bueno***! Haremos lo que tú quieras.*
  (= all right!)

- *por cierto*
  Por cierto, *¿has sacado las entradas?*
  (= by the way)

- *claro*
  *¿Te gusta el fútbol? – ¡***Claro que sí/no***!*
  (= of course!/of course not!)

- *desde luego*
  *¡***Desde luego*** que me gusta!* (= of course)

- *entonces*
  *Si no es tu padre, ¿***entonces*** quién es?*
  (= then)
  *¿***Entonces***, vienes o te quedas?* (= so)

- *pues*
  Pues, *como te iba contando …* (= well)

- *por supuesto*
  Por supuesto *que iré.* (= of course)

- *de todas formas/maneras*
  De todas formas/maneras *iremos.*
  (= anyway, in any case)

- *vale*
  *¿Vamos a tomar algo? – ¡***Vale***!* (= OK)

- *venga*
  *¡***Venga***, vámonos!* (= come on; *used in Spain*)

Improving your fluency

Varying the words you use to get your message across will make you sound more fluent in Spanish. For example, you already know *Me gusta el mar*, but for a change you could say *Me encanta el mar* to mean the same thing. Here are some other suggestions:

Saying what you like or dislike

Me ha gustado mucho tu regalo.	I was delighted with ...
Estaba encantado/encantada con el regalo.	I (really) liked ...
No me gusta comer fuera de casa.	I don't like ...
Mi vecina *me cae muy mal*.	I don't like ... (at all).
Detesto cualquier tipo de violencia.	I hate ...

Expressing your opinion

Creo que es demasiado caro.	I think ...
Pienso que es normal.	I think ...
Me parece que le va a encantar tu visita.	I think ...
Estoy seguro/segura de que no es culpa tuya.	I'm sure ...
En mi opinión, fue un error.	In my opinion ...

Agreeing or disagreeing

Tienes razón.	You're right.
Estoy (No estoy) de acuerdo contigo.	I (don't) agree with you.
¡Claro que sí!	Of course!
¡Naturalmente!	Of course!
En eso te equivocas.	You're wrong there.

Correspondence

The following section on correspondence has been designed to help you communicate confidently in written as well as spoken Spanish. Sample letters, emails and sections on text messaging and making telephone calls will ensure that you have all the vocabulary you need to correspond successfully in Spanish.

Text messaging

Abbreviation	Spanish	English
+trd	*más tarde*	later
2	*tú*	you
a2	*adiós*	goodbye
bboo	*besos*	love (from)
find	*fin de semana*	weekend
gnl	*genial*	wonderful
h lgo HL	*hasta luego*	see you later
LAP	*lo antes posible*	asap (as soon as possible)
msj	*mensaje*	message
NLS	*no lo sé*	I don't know
q acc? q hcs?	*¿qué haces?*	what are you doing?
QT1BD	*¡que tengas un buen día!*	have a good day!
q tl?	*¿qué tal?*	how are you?
salu2	*saludos*	best wishes
tq	*te quiero*	I love you
x	*por*	for, by etc
xdon	*perdón*	sorry
xq	*porque*	because
xq?	*¿por qué?*	why?

13

Writing an email

A:	belen.huertas@glnet.es
Cc:	
Copia oculta:	
Asunto:	Concierto

Nuevo mensaje
Responder al autor
Responder a todos
Reenviar
Archivo adjunto

Hola, ¿qué tal el fin de semana?

Me sobran dos entradas para el concierto de mañana, de unos amigos que no pueden venir. Si te interesa, o conoces a alguien que quiera ir, avísame en cuanto puedas.

Un beso,

E.

Saying your email address
In Spanish, when you tell someone your email address, you say:
belen punto huertas arroba glnet punto es

archivo	file	*responder a todos*	reply to all
edición (f)	edit	*reenviar*	forward
ver	view	*archivo adjunto*	attachment
herramientas (fpl)	tools	*A*	to
correo	mail	*CC*	cc (carbon copy)
ayuda	help	*copia oculta*	bcc (blind carbon copy)
enviar	send	*asunto*	subject
nuevo mensaje (m)	new	*de*	from
responder	reply	*fecha*	date

Here is some additional useful Internet vocabulary:

adelante	forward	e-mail or email (m)	email; email address
atrás	back	enlaces (mpl)	links
banda ancha	broadband	historial (m)	history
bajarse algo de Internet	to download something from the Internet	icono	icon
borrar	to delete	Internet (m or f)	the Internet
buscador (m)	search engine	mandar un e-mail or un email a alguien	to email someone
buscar	to search		
clicar en or hacer clic en	to click on	navegar por Internet	to surf the Net
copia de seguridad	backup	página de inicio	home page
copiar	to copy	página web	web page
correo basura	spam	preguntas frecuentes	FAQs
cortar y pegar	to cut and paste	sitio web	website
descargarse algo de Internet	to download something from the Internet	el or la web	the (World-Wide) Web

Writing a personal letter

Town/city you are writing from, and the date; your full address is not given ➡

Barcelona,
5 de junio de 2012

Queridos amigos: ⬅ Use a colon here

Muchas gracias por la preciosa pulsera que me mandasteis por mi cumpleaños, que me ha gustado muchísimo. Voy a disfrutar de verdad poniéndomela para mi fiesta del sábado, y estoy segura de que a Cristina le va a dar una envidia tremenda.

En realidad no hay demasiadas cosas nuevas que contaros, ya que últimamente parece que no hago otra cosa que estudiar para los exámenes, que ya están a la vuelta de la esquina. No sabéis las ganas que tengo de terminarlos todos y poder empezar a pensar en las vacaciones.

Paloma me encarga que os dé recuerdos de su parte.

Muchos besos de

Ana

Writing a personal letter

Other ways of starting a personal letter	Other ways of ending a personal letter
Querido Juan Mi querida Marta Queridísimo Antonio	Con mucho cariño Un fuerte abrazo de ... Un beso muy fuerte Afectuosamente

Some useful phrases

Muchas gracias por la carta.	Thank you for your letter.
Me alegró mucho recibir noticias tuyas.	It was great to hear from you.
Perdona que no te haya escrito antes.	Sorry for not writing sooner.
Dale un beso a Eduardo de mi parte.	Give my love to Eduardo.
Mamá te manda recuerdos.	Mum sends her best wishes.
Escríbeme pronto.	Write soon.

Writing a formal letter

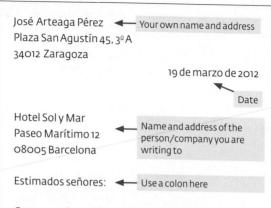

José Arteaga Pérez ← Your own name and address
Plaza San Agustín 45, 3º A
34012 Zaragoza

19 de marzo de 2012
← Date

Hotel Sol y Mar ← Name and address of the
Paseo Marítimo 12   person/company you are
08005 Barcelona   writing to

Estimados señores: ← Use a colon here

Como continuación a nuestra conversación telefónica de esta mañana, les escribo para confirmarles la reserva de una habitación doble con baño para las noches del miércoles 4 y el jueves 5 de julio de 2012.

Como hemos acordado, le adjunto un cheque de 30 € como garantía para la reserva.

Sin otro particular, les envío un atento saludo.

José Arteaga Pérez

In much of the Spanish-speaking world, and especially in Spain, most people use two *apellidos*, or surnames. The first is their father's first surname, and the second their mother's first surname. For example, the children of Juan Arteaga López, married to Carmen Pérez Rodríguez, would be called Arteaga Pérez. A married woman normally retains her own surname instead of taking her husband's.

Writing a formal letter

Other ways of starting a formal letter	Other ways of ending a formal letter
Estimado señor (García) *Estimados señores* *Muy señor mío/Muy señores míos* (used especially in Spain) *De nuestra consideración* (used especially in Latin America)	*Reciba un atento saludo de …* *Un cordial saludo* *Le/les saluda atentamente*

Some useful phrases

Agradecemos su carta de …	Thank you for your letter of …
En relación con …	With reference to …
Les ruego que me envíen …	Please send me …
Sin otro particular, quedo a la espera de su respuesta.	I look forward to hearing from you.
Muchas gracias de antemano por …	Thank you in advance for …

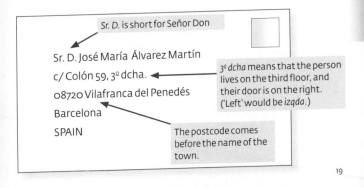

Sr. D. is short for Señor Don

Sr. D. José María Álvarez Martín
c/ Colón 59, 3º dcha.
08720 Vilafranca del Penedés
Barcelona
SPAIN

3º dcha means that the person lives on the third floor, and their door is on the right. ('Left' would be *izqda*.)

The postcode comes before the name of the town.

19

Making a call

Asking for information

¿Cuál es el prefijo de Léon?
¿Qué hay que hacer para obtener línea externa?
¿Podría decirme cuál es la extensión del Sr. Ruiz?

What's the code for Léon?

How do I get an outside line?
Please could you tell me what Sr. Ruiz's extension number is?

When your number answers

Hola, ¿está Susana?
Por favor, ¿podría hablar con Carlos García?
¿Es usted la Sra. Reyes?
¿Puede decirle que me llame?

Le vuelvo a llamar dentro de media hora.
¿Podría dejar un recado?

Hello! Is Susana there?
Could I speak to Carlos García, please?
Is that Sra. Reyes?
Could you ask him/her to call me back?

I'll call back in half an hour.
Could I leave a message, please?

When you answer the telephone

¿Diga?/ ¿Dígame?/¿Sí?
¿Aló?
¿Hola?
¿Bueno?

Hello?

(used in Spain)
(used in Latin America)
(used in the Southern Cone)
(used in Mexico)

¿Con quién hablo?
Soy Marcos.
Sí, soy yo.
¿Quiere dejar un mensaje?

Who's speaking?
It's Marcos speaking.
Speaking.
Would you like to leave a message?

Making a call

What you may hear

¿De parte de quién?	Who's calling?
Le paso.	I'm putting you through now.
No cuelgue.	Please hold.
No contesta.	There's no reply.
Comunica.	The line is engaged (Brit)/busy (US).
¿Quiere dejar un mensaje?	Would you like to leave a message?

If you have a problem

Perdone, me he equivocado de número.	Sorry, I dialled the wrong number.
No se oye bien.	This is a bad line.
Se corta.	You're breaking up.
Me estoy quedando sin batería.	My battery's low.
Se oye muy mal.	I can't hear you.

Saying your phone number

To tell someone your phone number in Spanish, you divide the number up into pairs instead of saying each digit separately. For example:

88 73 14

ochenta y ocho / setenta y tres / catorce

If there's an extra number, you make a group of three and say those numbers separately. For example:

959 48 32 94

nueve-cinco-nueve / cuarenta y ocho / treinta y dos / noventa y cuatro

Spanish phrases and sayings

In Spanish, as in many languages, people use vivid expressions based on images from their experience of real life. We've grouped the common expressions below according to the type of image they use. For fun, we have given you the word-for-word translation as well as the true English equivalent.

Food and drink

en todas partes cuecen habas
word for word:
→ it's the same the whole world over
broad beans are cooked everywhere

llamar al pan pan y al vino vino
word for word:
→ to call a spade a spade
to call bread bread and wine wine

eso es pedir peras al olmo
word for word:
→ that's asking the impossible
that's asking the elm tree for pears

llegar para los postres
word for word:
→ to come very late
to arrive in time for pudding

ahogarse en un vaso de agua
word for word:
→ to make a mountain out of a molehill
to drown in a glass of water

Animals and insects

aburrirse como una ostra
word for word:
→ to be bored stiff
to get as bored as an oyster

si los burros volaran
word for word:
→ pigs might fly
if donkeys could fly

estar más loco que una cabra
word for word:
→ to be as mad as a hatter
to be madder than a goat

a paso de tortuga
word for word:
→ at a snail's pace
at a tortoise's pace

Spanish phrases and sayings

Objects

consultar algo con la almohada → to sleep on something

   word for word: *to discuss something with one's pillow*

empezar la casa por el tejado → to put the cart before the horse

   word for word: *to start the house with the roof*

estar en la luna → to have one's head in the clouds

   word for word: *to be on the moon*

Weather

ha llovido mucho desde entonces → a lot of water has flowed under the bridge since then

   word for word: *it's rained a lot since then*

nunca llueve a gusto de todos → you can't please everyone

   word for word: *it never rains to everyone's liking*

una tormenta en un vaso de agua → a storm in a teacup

   word for word: *a storm in a glass of water*

Parts of the body

romperse la cabeza → to rack one's brains

   word for word: *to break one's head*

tener la cabeza sobre los hombros → to have one's head screwed on (the right way)

   word for word: *to have one's head on one's shoulders*

costar un ojo de la cara → to cost an arm and a leg

   word for word: *to cost an eye from one's face*

me costó un riñón → it cost me a fortune

   word for word: *it cost me a kidney*

Spanish phrases and sayings

Clothes

cambiar de chaqueta → to change sides
    word for word: *to change one's jacket*

estar hasta el gorro → to be fed up
    word for word: *to be up to one's hat*

querer nadar y guardar la ropa → to want to have it both ways
    word for word: *to want to swim and keep one's clothes on*

estar todavía en pañales → to be still wet behind the ears
    word for word: *to be still in nappies*

Colours

no distinguir lo blanco de lo negro → to be unable to tell right from wrong
    word for word: *not to be able to tell what's white from what's black*

ponerse de mil colores → to go bright red
    word for word: *to turn a thousand colours*

verlo todo de color de rosa → to see everything through rose-tinted spectacles
    word for word: *to see everything in pink*

estar más rojo que un cangrejo → to be lobster-pink or lobster-red
    word for word: *to be redder than a crab*

Some common translation difficulties

On the following pages we have shown some of the translation difficulties that you are most likely to come across. We hope that the tips we have given will help you to avoid these common pitfalls when writing and speaking Spanish.

'I, you, he, she, they...?'

Yo, tú, él and so on are not normally used before a verb if the ending or context make it clear who is performing the action:

I speak Spanish.	→	*Hablo español.*
We have two cars.	→	*Tenemos dos coches.*

But use *yo, tú, él* and the other subject pronouns for emphasis, contrast or where it helps make it clear who is being talked about:

You don't need to come.	→	**Tú** *no tienes que venir.*
He drives but she doesn't.	→	**Él** *conduce pero ella no.*

Usted and **ustedes**, the polite words for 'you', are used more than the other pronouns.

Personal *a*

When the direct object of a verb is a specific person or pet, put *a* in front of it (except after *tener*):

I look after **my little sister**.	→	*Cuido **a mi hermana pequeña**.*
They love **their dog**.	→	*Quieren mucho **a su perro**.*

Some common translation difficulties

In Spanish the word for 'you' and the form of the verb depend on who you are talking to:

- With one person you know well, use the **tú** form of the verb:

  Will you lend me this CD? → *¿Me **prestas** este CD?*

- With one person you do not know so well, use **usted** and the **usted** form of the verb:

  Have you met my wife? → *¿**Usted conoce** a mi mujer?*

- With more than one person you know well, in Spain use the **vosotros/as** form of the verb:

  Do you understand, children? → *¿**Entendéis**, niños?*

Elsewhere, use **ustedes** and the **ustedes** form:

  Are you coming too? → *¿Vienen también **ustedes**?*

- With more than one person you do not know so well, use **ustedes** and the **ustedes** form:

  Please come this way. → *Pasen **ustedes** por aquí.*

Vos and tú

In Argentina and parts of Central America, *vos* is preferred to *tú*.

Some common translation difficulties

Showing possession

In English, you can use 's and s' to show who or what something belongs to; in Spanish, you have to use a different construction:

my brother**'s** car	→	*el coche **de** mi hermano*
the girl**s'** bedroom	→	*el cuarto **de** las niñas*

Translating 'to'

To is generally translated by **a** but remember:

- When you are talking about the time, use **menos**:

five **to** ten	→	*las diez **menos** cinco*
at a quarter **to** seven	→	*a las siete **menos** cuarto*

- In front of verbs, it is often just shown by the Spanish verb ending:

to sing	→	*cantar*
to eat	→	*comer*
I want **to go out**.	→	*Quiero **salir**.*

- When you mean 'in order to', use **para**:

I did it **(in order) to** help you.	→	*Lo hice **para** ayudaros.*

Some common translation difficulties

'There is' and 'there are'

In Spanish these are both translated by **hay**:

There is a gentleman at the door.	→	**Hay** un señor en la puerta.
There are five books on the table.	→	**Hay** cinco libros en la mesa.

Translating 'and'

The normal word for 'and' is *y*, but to avoid two 'i' sounds coming together, you use *e* instead before words beginning with *i* or *hi* (but not *hie*):

Spain **and** Italy	→	España **e** Italia
grapes **and** figs	→	uvas **e** higos

Translating 'or'

The normal word for 'or' is *o*, but to avoid two 'o' sounds coming together, you use *u* instead before words beginning with *o* or *ho*:

for one reason **or** another	→	por un motivo **u** otro

Translating '-ing'

In Spanish you use the infinitive (the Spanish verb ending in *-ar*, *-er* or *-ir*) after verbs like *gustar*, *encantar*, *preferir*, *ver* and *oír* as well as after prepositions, even though in English we use the *-ing* form of the verb:

I like **going** to the cinema.	→	Me gusta **ir** al cine.
We love **dancing**.	→	Nos encanta **bailar**.
We prefer **travelling** by train.	→	Preferimos **viajar** en tren.
I've heard her **singing**.	→	La he oído **cantar**.
Before **leaving**…	→	Antes de **salir**…

Some common translation difficulties

To be: ser or estar?

There are two main verbs which mean 'be' in Spanish, ser and estar.

Ser is used:

- to link nouns and pronouns (words like 'he' and 'him'):

Pablo **is** a teacher.	→	*Pablo **es** profesor.*
It's me.	→	***Soy** yo.*
It's five o'clock.	→	***Son** las cinco.*
Three and two **are** five.	→	*Tres y dos **son** cinco.*

- with adjectives that give the idea of inherent and fundamental characteristics:

He's tall.	→	***Es** alto.*
Marta**'s** very attractive.	→	*Marta **es** muy guapa.*
They're fair.	→	***Son** rubios.*
He's a bachelor.	→	***Es** soltero.*
They're Italian.	→	***Son** italianos.*

Estar is used:

- when describing more temporary qualities:

The coffee**'s** cold.	→	*El café **está** frío.*
She's in a bad mood.	→	***Está** de mal humor.*
You're looking very pretty today.	→	***Estás** muy guapa hoy.*

- to talk about location and with past participles (the –ado/-ido form of regular verbs) used as adjectives:

I'm in Madrid.	→	***Estoy** en Madrid.*
Madrid **is** in Spain.	→	*Madrid **está** en España.*
She's married.	→	***Está** casada.*
The window**'s** broken.	→	*La ventana **está** rota.*

Some common translation difficulties

Other verbs can be used in certain contexts instead of *ser* and *estar* to translate 'to be':

• Use **tener** in phrases describing how you feel:

I'm hot/cold.	→	**Tengo** *calor/frío.*
We're hungry/thirsty.	→	**Tenemos** *hambre/sed.*
Don't be afraid.	→	**No tengas** *miedo.*
You're right.	→	**Tienes** *razón.*

• Use **tener** when talking about your age:

How old **are you**?	→	¿Cuántos años **tienes**?
I'm fifteen.	→	**Tengo** *quince (años).*

• Use **hacer** when talking about the weather:

What's the weather like?	→	¿Qué tiempo **hace**?
It's lovely.	→	**Hace** *bueno.*
It's hot.	→	**Hace** *calor.*
It's windy.	→	**Hace** *viento.*

Many English verbs can be followed by a preposition or adverb such as 'on' or 'back' – 'to go on', 'to give back'. These additions often give the verb a new meaning. There is no similar way of doing this in Spanish – you just use a different word, for example:

to go	→	*ir*
to go on	→	*seguir, continuar*
to give	→	*dar*
to give back	→	*devolver*

Some common translation difficulties

More on prepositions

Sentences that contain a verb and preposition in English might not contain a preposition in Spanish, and vice versa. The dictionary can help you with these.

For example:

• Verb + preposition:

   to look **for** something   →   *buscar algo*

Verb without preposition:

• Verb without preposition:

   to attend something   →   *asistir **a** algo*

Verb + preposition:

'Can', 'be able'

There are different ways of saying what someone can do in Spanish:

• Use **poder** to talk about someone's physical ability to do something:

   I can't go out with you.   →   **No puedo** salir contigo.

• Use **saber** to talk about things you *know how to* do:

   Can you swim?   →   ¿**Sabes** nadar?

• Don't translate *can* when it's used with verbs of sensing, seeing and hearing:

   I **can't see** anything.   →   **No veo** nada.
   Can't you **hear** me?   →   ¿Es que **no** me **oyes**?

A useful link:
<u>www.spanish.about.com/od/learnspanishgrammar</u>

A [eɪ] n (Mus) la m; **A road** n (BRIT Aut) ≈ carretera nacional

AAA n abbr (= American Automobile Association) ≈ RACE m (SP)

aback [ə'bæk] adv: **to be taken ~** quedar(se) desconcertado

abandon [ə'bændən] vt abandonar; (renounce) renunciar a

abattoir ['æbətwɑːʳ] n (BRIT) matadero

abbey ['æbɪ] n abadía

abbreviation [əbriːvɪ'eɪʃən] n (short form) abreviatura

abdomen ['æbdəmən] n abdomen m

abduct [æb'dʌkt] vt raptar, secuestrar

abide [ə'baɪd] vt: **I can't ~ it/him** no lo/le puedo ver or aguantar; **abide by** vt fus atenerse a

ability [ə'bɪlɪtɪ] n habilidad f, capacidad f; (talent) talento

able ['eɪbl] adj capaz; (skilled) hábil; **to be ~ to do sth** poder hacer algo

abnormal [æb'nɔːməl] adj anormal

aboard [ə'bɔːd] adv a bordo ▷ prep a bordo de

abolish [ə'bɒlɪʃ] vt suprimir, abolir

abolition [æbəu'lɪʃən] n supresión f, abolición f

abort [ə'bɔːt] vt abortar; (Comput) interrumpir ▷ vi (Comput) interrumpir el programa; **abortion** n aborto; **to have an abortion** abortar

KEYWORD

a [ə] indef art (before vowel and silent h **an**) **1** un(a); **a book** un libro; **an apple** una manzana; **she's a nurse** (ella) es enfermera
2 (instead of the number "one") un(a); **a year ago** hace un año; **a hundred/thousand pounds** cien/mil libras
3 (in expressing ratios, prices etc): **three a day/week** tres al día/a la semana; **10 km an hour** 10 km por hora; **£5 a person** £5 por persona; **30p a kilo** 30p el kilo

A2 n (BRIT Scol) segunda parte de los "A levels" (módulos 4–6)

AA n abbr (BRIT: = Automobile Association) ≈ RACE m (SP); (= Alcoholics Anonymous) A.A.

 KEYWORD

about [ə'baut] adv **1** (approximately) más o menos, aproximadamente; **about a hundred/thousand** etc unos/as or como cien/mil etc; **it takes about 10 hours** se tarda unas or más o menos 10 horas; **at about two o'clock** sobre las dos; **I've just about finished** casi he terminado
2 (referring to place) por todas partes; **to leave things lying about** dejar las cosas (tiradas) por ahí; **to run about** correr por todas partes; **to walk about** pasearse, ir y venir
3: **to be about to do sth** estar a punto de hacer algo

▶ prep **1** (*relating to*) de, sobre, acerca de; **a book about London** un libro sobre or acerca de Londres; **what is it about?** ¿de qué se trata?; **we talked about it** hablamos de eso or ello; **what** or **how about doing this?** ¿qué tal si hacemos esto?

2 (*referring to place*) por; **to walk about the town** caminar por la ciudad

above [ə'bʌv] adv encima, por encima, arriba ▷ prep encima de; (*greater than: in number*) más de; (: *in rank*) superior a; **mentioned ~** susodicho; **~ all** sobre todo

abroad [ə'brɔ:d] adv (*be*) en el extranjero; (*go*) al extranjero

abrupt [ə'brʌpt] adj (*sudden*) brusco

abscess ['æbsɪs] n absceso

absence ['æbsəns] n ausencia

absent ['æbsənt] adj ausente; **absent-minded** adj distraído

absolute ['æbsəlu:t] adj absoluto; **absolutely** adv totalmente; **oh yes, absolutely!** ¡claro or por supuesto que sí!

absorb [əb'zɔ:b] vt absorber; **to be ~ed in a book** estar absorto en un libro; **absorbent** adj absorbente; **absorbent cotton** n (*us*) algodón m hidrófilo; **absorbing** adj absorbente

abstain [əb'steɪn] vi: **to ~ (from)** abstenerse (de)

abstract ['æbstrækt] adj abstracto

absurd [əb'sə:d] adj absurdo

abundance [ə'bʌndəns] n abundancia

abundant [ə'bʌndənt] adj abundante

abuse [ə'bju:s] n (*insults*) insultos mpl; (*misuse*) abuso ▷ vt [ə'bju:z] (*ill-treat*) maltratar; (*take advantage of*) abusar de; **abusive** adj ofensivo

abysmal [ə'bɪzməl] adj pésimo; (*failure*) garrafal; (*ignorance*) supino

academic [ækə'dɛmɪk] adj académico, universitario; (*pej: issue*) puramente teórico ▷ n estudioso/a; (*lecturer*) profesor(a) m/f universitario/a; **academic year** n (*Univ*) año académico

academy [ə'kædəmɪ] n (*learned body*) academia; (*school*) instituto, colegio

accelerate [æk'sɛləreɪt] vi acelerar; **acceleration** n aceleración f; **accelerator** n (*BRIT*) acelerador m

accent ['æksɛnt] n acento; (*fig*) énfasis m

accept [ək'sɛpt] vt aceptar; (*concede*) admitir; **acceptable** adj aceptable; **acceptance** n aceptación f

access ['æksɛs] n acceso ▷ vt: **to have ~ to** tener acceso a; **accessible** adj (*place, person*) accesible; (*knowledge etc*) asequible

accessory [æk'sɛsərɪ] n accesorio; (*Law*): **~ to** cómplice de

accident ['æksɪdənt] n accidente m; (*chance*) casualidad f; **by ~** (*unintentionally*) sin querer; (*by coincidence*) por casualidad; **accidental** adj accidental, fortuito; **accidentally** adv sin querer; por casualidad; **Accident and Emergency Department** n (*BRIT*) Urgencias fpl; **accident insurance** n seguro contra accidentes

acclaim [ə'kleɪm] vt aclamar, aplaudir ▷ n aclamación f, aplausos mpl

accommodate [ə'kɔmədeɪt] vt alojar, hospedar; (*car, hotel etc*) tener cabida para; (*oblige, help*) complacer; **this car ~s four people comfortably** en este coche caben cuatro personas cómodamente

accommodation n, (*us*) **accommodations** npl [əkɔmə'deɪʃən(z)] alojamiento

accompaniment [ə'kʌmpənɪmənt] n acompañamiento

accompany [ə'kʌmpənɪ] vt acompañar

accomplice [ə'kʌmplɪs] n cómplice mf

accomplish [ə'kʌmplɪʃ] vt (finish) concluir; **accomplishment** n (bringing about) realización f; (skill) talento

accord [ə'kɔːd] n acuerdo ▷ vt conceder; **of his own ~** espontáneamente; **accordance** n: **in accordance with** de acuerdo con; **according to** prep según; (in accordance with) conforme a; **accordingly** adv (thus) por consiguiente; (appropriately) de acuerdo con esto

account [ə'kaunt] n (Comm) cuenta; (report) informe m; **accounts** npl (Comm) cuentas fpl; **of little ~** de poca importancia; **on ~** a crédito; **to buy sth on ~** comprar algo a crédito; **on no ~** bajo ningún concepto; **on ~ of** a causa de, por motivo de; **to take into ~, take ~ of** tener en cuenta; **account for** vt fus (explain) explicar; **accountable** adj: **accountable (for)** responsable (de); **accountant** n contable mf, contador(a) m/f (LAM); **account number** n (at bank etc) número de cuenta

accumulate [ə'kjuːmjuleɪt] vt acumular ▷ vi acumularse

accuracy ['ækjurəsɪ] n (of total) exactitud f; (of description etc) precisión f

accurate ['ækjurɪt] adj (number) exacto; (answer) acertado; (shot) certero; **accurately** adv con precisión

accusation [ækju'zeɪʃən] n acusación f

accuse [ə'kjuːz] vt acusar; (blame) echar la culpa a; **to ~ sb (of sth)** acusar a algn (de algo); **accused** n acusado/a

accustomed [ə'kʌstəmd] adj: **~ to** acostumbrado a

ace [eɪs] n as m

ache [eɪk] n dolor m ▷ vi doler; **my head ~s** me duele la cabeza

achieve [ə'tʃiːv] vt (reach) alcanzar; (victory, success) lograr, conseguir;

achievement n (completion) realización f; (success) éxito

acid ['æsɪd] adj ácido; (bitter) agrio ▷ n (Chem, inf: LSD) ácido

acknowledge [ək'nɔlɪdʒ] vt (letter: also: **~ receipt of**) acusar recibo de; (fact) reconocer; **acknowledgement** n acuse m de recibo

acne ['æknɪ] n acné m

acorn ['eɪkɔːn] n bellota

acoustic [ə'kuːstɪk] adj acústico

acquaintance [ə'kweɪntəns] n conocimiento; (person) conocido/a; **to make sb's ~** conocer a algn

acquire [ə'kwaɪər] vt adquirir

acquisition [ækwɪ'zɪʃən] n adquisición f

acquit [ə'kwɪt] vt absolver, exculpar; **to ~ o.s. well** salir con éxito

acre ['eɪkər] n acre m

acronym ['ækrənɪm] n siglas fpl

across [ə'krɔs] prep (on the other side of) al otro lado de; (crosswise) a través de ▷ adv de un lado a otro, de una parte a otra a través, al través; **to run/swim ~** atravesar corriendo/nadando; **~ from** enfrente de; **the lake is 12 km ~** el lago tiene 12 km de ancho

acrylic [ə'krɪlɪk] adj acrílico

act [ækt] n acto, acción f; (Theat) acto; (in music-hall etc) número; (Law) decreto, ley f ▷ vi (behave) comportarse; (Theat) actuar; (pretend) fingir; (take action) tomar medidas ▷ vt (part) hacer; **to catch sb in the ~** coger a algn in fraganti or con las manos en la masa; **to ~ Hamlet** hacer el papel de Hamlet; **to ~ as** actuar or hacer de; **act up** vi (inf: person) portarse mal; **acting** adj suplente ▷ n: **to do some acting** hacer algo de teatro

action ['ækʃən] n acción f, acto; (Mil) acción f; (Law) proceso, demanda; **out of ~** (person) fuera de combate; (thing) averiado, estropeado; **to take ~** tomar medidas; **action replay** n (TV) repetición f

activate ['æktɪveɪt] vt activar

active ['æktɪv] adj activo, enérgico; (volcano) en actividad; **actively** adv (participate) activamente; (discourage, dislike) enérgicamente

activist ['æktɪvɪst] n activista mf

activity [æk'tɪvɪtɪ] n actividad f; **activity holiday** n vacaciones con actividades organizadas

actor ['æktər] n actor m

actress ['æktrɪs] n actriz f

actual ['æktjuəl] adj verdadero, real

> Be careful not to translate actual by the Spanish word actual.

actually ['æktjuəlɪ] adv realmente, en realidad

> Be careful not to translate actually by the Spanish word actualmente.

acupuncture ['ækjupʌŋktʃər] n acupuntura

acute [ə'kju:t] adj agudo

ad [æd] n abbr = **advertisement**

adamant ['ædəmənt] adj firme, inflexible

adapt [ə'dæpt] vt adaptar ▷ vi: **to ~ (to)** adaptarse (a), ajustarse (a); **adapter, adaptor** n (Elec) adaptador m; (for several plugs) ladrón m

add [æd] vt añadir, agregar (esp LAm); **add up** vt (figures) sumar ▷ vi (fig): **it doesn't ~ up** no tiene sentido; **it doesn't ~ up to much** es poca cosa, no tiene gran or mucha importancia

addict ['ædɪkt] n adicto/a; (enthusiast) entusiasta mf; **addicted** [ə'dɪktɪd] adj: **to be addicted to** ser adicto a; ser aficionado a; **addiction** [ə'dɪkʃən] n (to drugs etc) adicción f; **addictive** [ə'dɪktɪv] adj que causa adicción

addition [ə'dɪʃən] n (adding up) adición f; (thing added) añadidura, añadido; **in ~** además, por añadidura; **in ~ to** además de; **additional** adj adicional

additive ['ædɪtɪv] n aditivo

address [ə'dres] n dirección f, señas fpl; (speech) discurso ▷ vt (letter) dirigir; (speak to) dirigirse a, dirigir la palabra

a; **to ~ o.s. to sth** (issue, problem) abordar; **address book** n agenda (de direcciones)

adequate ['ædɪkwɪt] adj (satisfactory) adecuado; (enough) suficiente

adhere [əd'hɪər] vi: **to ~ to** adherirse a; (fig: abide by) observar

adhesive [əd'hi:zɪv] n adhesivo; **adhesive tape** n (BRIT) cinta adhesiva; (US Med) esparadrapo

adjacent [ə'dʒeɪsənt] adj: **~ to** contiguo a, inmediato a

adjective ['ædʒektɪv] n adjetivo

adjoining [ə'dʒɔɪnɪŋ] adj contiguo, vecino

adjourn [ə'dʒə:n] vt aplazar ▷ vi suspenderse

adjust [ə'dʒʌst] vt (change) modificar; (arrange) arreglar; (machine) ajustar ▷ vi: **to ~ (to)** adaptarse (a); **adjustable** adj ajustable; **adjustment** n adaptación f; (of prices, wages) ajuste m

administer [əd'mɪnɪstər] vt administrar

administration [ædmɪnɪ'streɪʃən] n administración f; (government) gobierno

administrative [əd'mɪnɪstrətɪv] adj administrativo

administrator [əd'mɪnɪstreɪtər] n administrador(a) m/f

admiral ['ædmərəl] n almirante m

admiration [ædmə'reɪʃən] n admiración f

admire [əd'maɪər] vt admirar; **admirer** n admirador(a) m/f

admission [əd'mɪʃən] n (to exhibition, nightclub) entrada; (enrolment) ingreso; (confession) confesión f

admit [əd'mɪt] vt dejar entrar, dar entrada a; (permit) admitir; (acknowledge) reconocer; **to be ~ted to hospital** ingresar en el hospital; **admit to** vt fus confesarse culpable de; **admittance** n entrada; **admittedly** adv es cierto que

adolescent [ædəʊ'lɛsnt] *adj, n* adolescente *mf*

adopt [ə'dɔpt] *vt* adoptar; **adopted** *adj* adoptivo; **adoption** *n* adopción *f*

adore [ə'dɔːʳ] *vt* adorar

adorn [ə'dɔːn] *vt* adornar

Adriatic [eɪdrɪ'ætɪk] *n*: **the ~ (Sea)** el (Mar) Adriático

adrift [ə'drɪft] *adv* a la deriva

ADSL *n abbr* (= *asymmetrical digital subscriber line*) ADSL *m*

adult ['ædʌlt] *n* adulto/a ▷ *adj*: **~ education** educación *f* para adultos

adultery [ə'dʌltərɪ] *n* adulterio

advance [əd'vɑːns] *n* adelanto, progreso; (*money*) anticipo; (*Mil*) avance *m* ▷ *vt* avanzar, adelantar; (*money*) anticipar ▷ *vi* avanzar, adelantarse; **in ~** por adelantado; **to make ~s to sb** hacer una proposición a algn; (*amorously*) insinuarse a algn; **advanced** *adj* avanzado; (*Scol: studies*) adelantado

advantage [əd'vɑːntɪdʒ] *n* (*also Tennis*) ventaja; **to take ~ of** aprovecharse de

advent ['ædvənt] *n* advenimiento; **A~** Adviento

adventure [əd'vɛntʃəʳ] *n* aventura; **adventurous** *adj* aventurero

adverb ['ædvəːb] *n* adverbio

adversary ['ædvəsərɪ] *n* adversario, contrario

adverse ['ædvəːs] *adj* adverso, contrario

advert ['ædvəːt] *n abbr* (BRIT) = **advertisement**

advertise ['ædvətaɪz] *vi* (*in newspaper etc*) poner un anuncio, anunciarse; **to ~ for** buscar por medio de anuncios ▷ *vt* anunciar; **advertisement** [əd'vəːtɪsmənt] *n* anuncio; **advertiser** *n* anunciante *mf*; **advertising** *n* publicidad *f*; anuncios *mpl*; (*industry*) industria publicitaria

advice [əd'vaɪs] *n* consejo, consejos *mpl*; (*notification*) aviso; **a piece of ~** un consejo; **to take legal ~** consultar a un abogado

advisable [əd'vaɪzəbl] *adj* aconsejable, conveniente

advise [əd'vaɪz] *vt* aconsejar; **to ~ sb of sth** informar a algn de algo; **to ~ sb against sth/doing sth** desaconsejar algo a algn/ aconsejar a algn que no haga algo; **adviser** *n* consejero/a; (*business adviser*) asesor/a *m/f*; **advisory** *adj* consultivo

advocate ['ædvəkeɪt] *vt* abogar por ▷ *n* ['ædvəkɪt] abogado/a; (*supporter*): **~ of** defensor/a *m/f* de

Aegean [iː'dʒiːən] *n*: **the ~ (Sea)** el (Mar) Egeo

aerial ['ɛərɪəl] *n* antena ▷ *adj* aéreo

aerobics [ɛə'rəʊbɪks] *nsg* aerobic *m*

aeroplane ['ɛərəpleɪn] *n* (BRIT) avión *m*

aerosol ['ɛərəsɔl] *n* aerosol *m*

affair [ə'fɛəʳ] *n* asunto; (*also:* **love ~**) aventura *f* amorosa

affect [ə'fɛkt] *vt* afectar, influir en; (*move*) conmover; **affected** *adj* afectado

affection *n* afecto, cariño; **affectionate** *adj* afectuoso, cariñoso

afflict [ə'flɪkt] *vt* afligir

affluent ['æfluənt] *adj* acomodado; **the ~ society** la sociedad opulenta

afford [ə'fɔːd] *vt* (*provide*) proporcionar; **can we ~ a car?** ¿podemos permitirnos el gasto de comprar un coche?; **affordable** *adj* asequible

Afghanistan [æf'gænɪstæn] *n* Afganistán *m*

afraid [ə'freɪd] *adj*: **to be ~ of** (*person*) tener miedo a; (*thing*) tener miedo de; **to be ~ to** tener miedo de, temer; **I am ~ that** me temo que; **I'm ~ so** me temo que sí; **I'm ~ not** lo siento, pero no

Africa ['æfrɪkə] *n* África; **African** *adj, n* africano/a; **African-American** *adj, n* afroamericano/a

after ['ɑːftər] prep (time) después de; (place, order) detrás de, tras ▷ adv después ▷ conj después (de) que; **what/who are you ~?** ¿qué/a quién buscas?; **~ having done/he left** después de haber hecho/después de que se marchó; **to ask ~ sb** preguntar por algn; **~ all** después de todo, al fin y al cabo; **~ you!** ¡pase usted!; **after-effects** npl secuelas fpl, efectos mpl; **aftermath** n consecuencias fpl, resultados mpl; **afternoon** n tarde f; **after-shave (lotion)** n aftershave m; **aftersun (lotion)** n aftersun m inv; **afterwards** adv después, más tarde

again [ə'gɛn] adv otra vez, de nuevo; **to do sth ~** volver a hacer algo; **~ and ~** una y otra vez

against [ə'gɛnst] prep (opposed) en contra de, (close to) contra, junto a

age [eɪdʒ] n edad f; (period) época ▷ vi envejecer(se) ▷ vt envejecer; **he is 20 years of ~** tiene 20 años; **under ~** menor de edad; **to come of ~** llegar a la mayoría de edad; **it's been ~s since I saw you** hace siglos que no te veo; **age group** n: **to be in the same age group** tener la misma edad; **age limit** n límite m de edad, edad f tope

agency ['eɪdʒənsɪ] n agencia

agenda [ə'dʒɛndə] n orden m del día
Be careful not to translate agenda by the Spanish word agenda.

agent ['eɪdʒənt] n agente mf; (representative) representante mf delegado/a

aggravate ['ægrəveɪt] vt agravar; (annoy) irritar

aggression [ə'grɛʃən] n agresión f

aggressive [ə'grɛsɪv] adj agresivo; (vigorous) enérgico

agile ['ædʒaɪl] adj ágil

agitated ['ædʒɪteɪtɪd] adj agitado

AGM n abbr (= annual general meeting) junta f general

ago [ə'gəu] adv: **two days ~** hace dos días; **not long ~** hace poco; **how long ~?** ¿hace cuánto tiempo?

agony ['ægənɪ] n (pain) dolor m atroz; (distress) angustia; **to be in ~** retorcerse de dolor

agree [ə'griː] vt (price) acordar, quedar en ▷ vi (statements etc) coincidir, concordar; **to ~ (with)** (person) estar de acuerdo (con), ponerse de acuerdo (con); **to ~ to do** aceptar hacer; **to ~ to sth** consentir en algo; **to ~ that** (admit) estar de acuerdo en que; **garlic doesn't ~ with me** el ajo no me sienta bien; **agreeable** adj agradable; (person) simpático; (willing) de acuerdo, conforme; **agreed** adj (time, place) convenido; **agreement** n acuerdo; (Comm) contrato; **in agreement** de acuerdo, conforme

agricultural [ægrɪ'kʌltʃərəl] adj agrícola

agriculture ['ægrɪkʌltʃər] n agricultura

ahead [ə'hɛd] adv delante; **~ of** delante de; (fig: schedule etc) antes de; **~ of time** antes de la hora; **go right** or **straight ~** siga adelante

aid [eɪd] n ayuda, auxilio ▷ vt ayudar, auxiliar; **in ~ of** a beneficio de

aide [eɪd] n ayudante mf

AIDS [eɪdz] n abbr (= acquired immune (or immuno-)deficiency syndrome) SIDA m

ailing ['eɪlɪŋ] adj (person, economy) enfermizo

ailment ['eɪlmənt] n enfermedad f, achaque m

aim [eɪm] vt (gun) apuntar; (missile, remark) dirigir; (blow) asestar ▷ vi (also: **take ~**) apuntar ▷ n puntería; (objective) propósito, meta; **to ~ at** (objective) aspirar a, pretender; **to ~ to do** tener la intención de hacer, aspirar a hacer

ain't [eɪnt] (inf) = **are not; aren't; isn't**

air [ɛər] n aire m; (appearance) aspecto ▷ vt (room) ventilar; (clothes, bed, grievances, ideas) airear ▷ cpd aéreo; **throw sth into the ~** (ball etc) lanzar algo al aire; **by ~** (travel) en avión; **to**

be on the ~ (Radio, TV: programme) estarse emitiendo; (: station) estar en antena; **airbag** n airbag m inv; **air bed** n (BRIT) colchoneta inflable or neumática; **airborne** adj (in the air) en el aire; **as soon as the plane was airborne** tan pronto como el avión estuvo en el aire; **air-conditioned** adj climatizado; **air conditioning** n aire m acondicionado; **aircraft** n (pl inv) avión m; **airfield** n campo de aviación; **Air Force** n fuerzas aéreas fpl, aviación f; **air hostess** (BRIT) n azafata; **airing cupboard** n (BRIT) armario m para oreo; **airlift** n puente m aéreo; **airline** n línea aérea; **airliner** n avión m de pasajeros; **airmail** n: **by airmail** por avión; **airplane** n (US) avión m; **airport** n aeropuerto; **air raid** n ataque m aéreo; **airsick** adj: **to be airsick** marearse (en avión); **airspace** n espacio aéreo; **airstrip** n pista de aterrizaje; **air terminal** n terminal f; **airtight** adj hermético; **air traffic controller** n controlador(a) m/f aéreo/a; **airy** adj (room) bien ventilado; (manners) desenfadado

aisle [aɪl] n (of church) nave f lateral; (of theatre, plane) pasillo; **aisle seat** n (on plane) asiento de pasillo

ajar [ə'dʒɑːr] adj entreabierto

à la carte [ælæ'kɑːt] adv a la carta

alarm [ə'lɑːm] n alarma; (anxiety) inquietud f ▷ vt asustar, alarmar; **alarm call** n (in hotel etc) alarma; **alarm clock** n despertador m; **alarmed** adj (person) alarmado, asustado; (house, car etc) con alarma; **alarming** adj alarmante

Albania [æl'beɪnɪə] n Albania

albeit [ɔːl'biːɪt] conj aunque

album ['ælbəm] n álbum m; (L.P.) elepé m

alcohol ['ælkəhɒl] n alcohol m; **alcohol-free** adj sin alcohol; **alcoholic** adj, n alcohólico/a

alcove ['ælkəʊv] n nicho, hueco

ale [eɪl] n cerveza

alert [ə'lɜːt] adj alerta inv; (sharp) despierto, atento ▷ n alerta m, alarma ▷ vt poner sobre aviso; **to be on the ~** estar alerta or sobre aviso

algebra ['ældʒɪbrə] n álgebra

Algeria [æl'dʒɪərɪə] n Argelia

alias ['eɪlɪəs] adv alias, conocido por ▷ n alias m; (of criminal) apodo; (of writer) seudónimo

alibi ['ælɪbaɪ] n coartada

alien ['eɪlɪən] n (foreigner) extranjero/a; (extraterrestrial) extraterrestre mf ▷ adj: **~ to** ajeno a; **alienate** vt enajenar, alejar

alight [ə'laɪt] adj ardiendo ▷ vi apearse, bajar

align [ə'laɪn] vt alinear

alike [ə'laɪk] adj semejantes, iguales ▷ adv igualmente, del mismo modo; **to look ~** parecerse

alive [ə'laɪv] adj vivo; (lively) alegre

○ **KEYWORD**

all [ɔːl] adj todo/a sg, todos/as pl; **all day** todo el día; **all night** toda la noche; **all men** todos los hombres; **all five came** vinieron los cinco; **all the books** todos los libros; **all the time/ his life** todo el tiempo/toda su vida ▷ pron 1 todo; **I ate it all, I ate all of it** me lo comí todo; **all of us went** fuimos todos; **all the boys went** fueron todos los chicos; **is that all?** ¿eso es todo?, ¿algo más?; (in shop) ¿algo más?, ¿alguna cosa más?
2 (in phrases): **above all** sobre todo; por encima de todo; **after all** después de todo; **at all: anything at all** lo que sea; **not at all** (in answer to question) en absoluto; (in answer to thanks) ¡de nada!, ¡no hay de qué!; **I'm not at all tired** no estoy nada cansado/a; **anything at all will do** cualquier cosa viene bien; **all in all** a fin de cuentas
▷ adv: **all alone** completamente solo/a; **it's not as hard as all that**

no es tan difícil como lo pintas; **all the more/the better** tanto más/mejor; **all but** casi; **the score is two all** están empatados a dos

Allah ['ælə] n Alá m

allegation [ælɪ'geɪʃən] n alegato

alleged [ə'lɛdʒd] adj supuesto, presunto; **allegedly** [ə'lɛdʒɪdlɪ] adv supuestamente, según se afirma

allegiance [ə'li:dʒəns] n lealtad f

allergic [ə'lə:dʒɪk] adj: **~ to** alérgico a

allergy ['ælədʒɪ] n alergia

alleviate [ə'li:vɪeɪt] vt aliviar

alley ['ælɪ] n callejuela

alliance [ə'laɪəns] n alianza

allied ['ælaɪd] adj aliado

alligator ['ælɪgeɪtər] n caimán m

all-in ['ɔ:lɪn] adj, adv (BRIT: charge) todo incluido

allocate ['æləkeɪt] vt (share out) repartir; (devote) asignar

allot [ə'lɔt] vt asignar

all-out ['ɔ:laut] adj (effort etc) supremo

allow [ə'lau] vt permitir, dejar; (a claim) admitir; (sum to spend, time estimated) dar, conceder; (concede): **to ~ that** reconocer que; **to ~ sb to do** permitir a algn hacer; **he is ~ed to ...** se le permite ...; **allow for** vt fus tener en cuenta; **allowance** n subvención f, pensión f; (tax allowance) desgravación f; **to make allowances for** (person) disculpar a; (thing) tener en cuenta

all right adv bien; (as answer) ¡de acuerdo!, ¡está bien!

ally n ['ælaɪ] aliado/a ▷ vt [ə'laɪ]: **to ~ o.s. with** aliarse con

almighty [ɔ:l'maɪtɪ] adj todopoderoso; (row etc) imponente

almond ['ɑ:mənd] n almendra

almost ['ɔ:lməust] adv casi; **he ~ fell** casi or por poco se cae

alone [ə'ləun] adj solo ▷ adv solo; **to leave sb ~** dejar a algn en paz; **to leave sth ~** no tocar algo; **let ~ ...** y mucho menos ...

along [ə'lɔŋ] prep a lo largo de, por ▷ adv: **is he coming ~ with us?** ¿viene con nosotros?; **he was limping ~** iba cojeando; **~ with** junto con; **all ~** (all the time) desde el principio; **alongside** prep al lado de ▷ adv (Naut) de costado

aloof [ə'lu:f] adj distante ▷ adv: **to stand ~** mantenerse a distancia

aloud [ə'laud] adv en voz alta

alphabet ['ælfəbɛt] n alfabeto

Alps [ælps] npl: **the ~** los Alpes

already [ɔ:l'rɛdɪ] adv ya

alright ['ɔ:l'raɪt] adv (BRIT) = **all right**

also ['ɔ:lsəu] adv también, además

altar ['ɔ:ltər] n altar m

alter ['ɔ:ltər] vt cambiar, modificar ▷ vi cambiar, modificarse; **alteration** n cambio, modificación f; **alterations** npl (Sewing) arreglos mpl

alternate [ɔl'tə:nɪt] adj alterno ▷ vi ['ɔltəneɪt]: **to ~ (with)** alternar (con); **on ~ days** en días alternos

alternative [ɔl'tə:nətɪv] adj alternativo ▷ n alternativa; **~ medicine** medicina alternativa; **alternatively** adv: **alternatively one could ...** por otra parte se podría ...

although [ɔ:l'ðəu] conj aunque

altitude ['æltɪtju:d] n altura

altogether [ɔ:ltə'gɛðər] adv completamente, del todo; (on the whole, in all) en total, en conjunto

aluminium [ælju'mɪnɪəm], (US) **aluminum** [ə'lu:mɪnəm] n aluminio

always ['ɔ:lweɪz] adv siempre

Alzheimer's ['ælts haɪməz] n (also: **~ disease**) (enfermedad f de) m Alzheimer

am [æm] vb see **be**

a.m. adv abbr (= ante meridiem) de la mañana

amalgamate [ə'mælgəmeɪt] vi amalgamarse ▷ vt amalgamar

amass [ə'mæs] vt amontonar, acumular

amateur ['æmətə^r] n aficionado/a, amateur mf

amaze [ə'meɪz] vt asombrar, pasmar; **to be ~d (at)** asombrarse (de); **amazed** adj asombrado; **amazement** n asombro, sorpresa; **amazing** adj extraordinario; (bargain, offer) increíble

Amazon ['æməzən] n (Geo) Amazonas m

ambassador [æm'bæsədə^r] n embajador(a) m/f

amber ['æmbə^r] n ámbar m; **at ~** (BRIT Aut) en amarillo

ambiguous [æm'bɪɡjʊəs] adj ambiguo

ambition [æm'bɪʃən] n ambición f; **ambitious** adj ambicioso

ambulance ['æmbjʊləns] n ambulancia

ambush ['æmbʊʃ] n emboscada ▷ vt tender una emboscada a

amen [ɑː'mɛn] excl amén

amend [ə'mɛnd] vt enmendar; **to make ~s** dar cumplida satisfacción; **amendment** n enmienda

amenities [ə'miːnɪtɪz] npl comodidades fpl

America [ə'mɛrɪkə] n América (del Norte); (USA) Estados mpl Unidos; **American** adj, n (norte) americano/a, estadounidense mf; **American football** n (BRIT) fútbol m americano

amicable ['æmɪkəbl] adj amistoso, amigable

amid(st) [ə'mɪd(st)] prep entre, en medio de

ammunition [æmjʊ'nɪʃən] n municiones fpl

amnesty ['æmnɪstɪ] n amnistía

among(st) [ə'mʌŋ(st)] prep entre, en medio de

amount [ə'maʊnt] n cantidad f; (of bill etc) suma, importe m ▷ vi: **to ~ to** sumar; (be same as) equivaler a, significar

amp(ère) ['æmp(ɛə^r)] n amperio

ample ['æmpl] adj (spacious) amplio; (abundant) abundante; **to have ~ time** tener tiempo de sobra

amplifier ['æmplɪfaɪə^r] n amplificador m

amputate ['æmpjuteɪt] vt amputar

Amtrak ['æmtræk] n (US) empresa nacional de ferrocarriles de los EE.UU.

amuse [ə'mjuːz] vt divertir; (distract) distraer, entretener; **amusement** n diversión f; (pastime) pasatiempo; (laughter) risa; **amusement arcade** n salón m de juegos; **amusement park** n parque m de atracciones

amusing [ə'mjuːzɪŋ] adj divertido

an [æn, ən, n] indef art see **a**

anaemia [ə'niːmɪə] n anemia

anaemic [ə'niːmɪk] adj anémico; (fig) flojo

anaesthetic [ænɪs'θɛtɪk] n anestesia

analog(ue) ['ænəlɔɡ] adj analógico

analogy [ə'nælədʒɪ] n analogía

analyse ['ænəlaɪz] vt (BRIT) analizar; **analysis** (pl **analyses**) n análisis m inv; **analyst** ['ænəlɪst] n (political analyst, psychoanalyst) analista mf

analyze ['ænəlaɪz] vt (US) = **analyse**

anarchy ['ænəkɪ] n anarquía, desorden m

anatomy [ə'nætəmɪ] n anatomía

ancestor ['ænsɪstə^r] n antepasado

anchor ['æŋkə^r] n ancla, áncora ▷ vi (also: **to drop ~**) anclar; **to weigh ~** levar anclas

anchovy ['æntʃəvɪ] n anchoa

ancient ['eɪnʃənt] adj antiguo

and [ænd] conj y; (before i, hi) e; **~ so on** etcétera; **try ~ come** procura venir; **better ~ better** cada vez mejor

Andes ['ændiːz] npl: **the ~** los Andes

Andorra [æn'dɔːrə] n Andorra

anemia [ə'niːmɪə] n (US) = **anaemia**

anemic [ə'niːmɪk] adj (US) = **anaemic**

anesthetic [ænɪs'θɛtɪk] n (US) = **anaesthetic**

angel ['eɪndʒəl] n ángel m

anger ['æŋɡə^r] n cólera

angina [æn'dʒaɪnə] n angina (del pecho)

angle ['æŋgl] n ángulo; **from their ~** desde su punto de vista

angler ['æŋglər] n pescador(a) m/f (de caña)

Anglican ['æŋglɪkən] adj, n anglicano/a

angling ['æŋglɪŋ] n pesca con caña

angrily ['æŋgrɪlɪ] adv enojado, enfadado

angry ['æŋgrɪ] adj enfadado, enojado (esp LAM); **to be ~ with sb/ at sth** estar enfadado con algn/por algo; **to get ~** enfadarse, enojarse (esp LAM)

anguish ['æŋgwɪʃ] n (physical) tormentos mpl; (mental) angustia

animal ['ænɪməl] n animal m; (pej: person) bestia

animated ['ænɪmeɪtɪd] adj animado

animation [ænɪ'meɪʃən] n animación f

aniseed ['ænɪsiːd] n anís m

ankle ['æŋkl] n tobillo m

annex n ['æneks] (BRIT: also: **annexe**: building) edificio anexo ▷ vt [æ'neks] (territory) anexionar

anniversary [ænɪ'vəːsərɪ] n aniversario

announce [ə'nauns] vt anunciar; **announcement** n anuncio; (declaration) declaración f; **announcer** n (Radio) locutor(a) m/f; (TV) presentador(a) m/f

annoy [ə'nɔɪ] vt molestar, fastidiar; **don't get ~ed!** ¡no se enfade!; **annoying** adj molesto, fastidioso; (person) pesado

annual ['ænjuəl] adj anual ▷ n (Bot) anual m; (book) anuario; **annually** adv anualmente, cada año

annum ['ænəm] n see **per annum**

anonymous [ə'nɒnɪməs] adj anónimo

anorak ['ænəræk] n anorak m

anorexia [ænə'rɛksɪə] n (Med) anorexia

anorexic [ænə'rɛksɪk] adj, n anoréxico/a

another [ə'nʌðər] adj: **~ book** otro libro ▷ pron otro; see also **one**

answer ['ɑːnsər] n respuesta, contestación f; (to problem) solución f ▷ vi contestar, responder ▷ vt (reply to) contestar a, responder a; (problem) resolver; **in ~ to your letter** contestando or en contestación a su carta; **to ~ the phone** contestar el teléfono; **to ~ the bell** or **the door** abrir la puerta; **answer back** vi replicar, ser respondón/ona; **answer for** vt fus responder de or por; **answer to** vt fus (description) corresponder a; **answerphone** n (esp BRIT) contestador m (automático)

ant [ænt] n hormiga

Antarctic [ænt'ɑːktɪk] n: **the ~** el Antártico

antelope ['æntɪləup] n antílope m

antenatal [æntɪ'neɪtl] adj prenatal

antenna (pl **antennae**) [æn'tɛnə, -niː] n antena

anthem ['ænθəm] n: **national ~** himno nacional

anthology [æn'θɔlədʒɪ] n antología

anthrax ['ænθræks] n ántrax m

anthropology [ænθrə'pɔlədʒɪ] n antropología

anti... [æntɪ] pref anti...; **antibiotic** [æntɪbaɪ'ɔtɪk] adj, n antibiótico; **antibody** ['æntɪbɔdɪ] n anticuerpo

anticipate [æn'tɪsɪpeɪt] vt prever; (expect) esperar, contar con; (forestall) anticiparse a, adelantarse a; **anticipation** [æntɪsɪ'peɪʃən] n previsión f; esperanza; anticipación f

anticlimax [æntɪ'klaɪmæks] n decepción f

anticlockwise [æntɪ'klɔkwaɪz] adv en dirección contraria a la de las agujas del reloj

antics ['æntɪks] npl gracias fpl

anti: antidote ['æntɪdəut] n antídoto; **antifreeze** ['æntɪfriːz] n anticongelante m; **antihistamine**

[æntɪˈhɪstəmiːn] n antihistamínico;
antiperspirant [ˈæntɪpəˈspɪrənt] n
antitranspirante m

antique [ænˈtiːk] n antigüedad f ▷ adj
antiguo; **antique shop** n tienda de
antigüedades

antiseptic [æntɪˈsɛptɪk] adj, n
antiséptico

antisocial [æntɪˈsəʊʃəl] adj antisocial

antivirus [æntɪˈvaɪərəs] adj
antivirus; **~ software** antivirus m

antlers [ˈæntləz] npl cornamenta

anxiety [æŋˈzaɪətɪ] n (worry)
inquietud f; (eagerness) ansia, anhelo

anxious [ˈæŋkʃəs] adj (worried)
inquieto; (keen) deseoso; **to be ~ to do**
tener muchas ganas de hacer

○ **KEYWORD**

any [ˈɛnɪ] adj 1 (in questions etc) algún/
alguna; **have you any butter/
children?** ¿tienes mantequilla/
hijos?; **if there are any tickets left** si
quedan billetes, si queda algún billete
2 (with negative): **I haven't any
money/books** no tengo dinero/libros
3 (no matter which) cualquier; **any
excuse will do** valdrá or servirá
cualquier excusa; **choose any book
you like** escoge el libro que quieras
4 (in phrases): **in any case** de todas
formas, en cualquier caso; **any day
now** cualquier día (de estos); **at any
moment** en cualquier momento, de
un momento a otro; **at any rate** en
todo caso; **any time: come (at) any
time** ven cuando quieras; **he might
come (at) any time** podría llegar de
un momento a otro
▷ pron 1 (in questions etc): **have you
got any?** ¿tienes alguno/a?; **can any
of you sing?** ¿sabe cantar alguno de
vosotros/ustedes?
2 (with negative): **I haven't any (of
them)** no tengo ninguno
3 (no matter which one(s)): **take any of
those books (you like)** toma el libro

que quieras de ésos
▷ adv 1 (in questions etc): **do you
want any more soup/sandwiches?**
¿quieres más sopa/bocadillos?; **are
you feeling any better?** ¿te sientes
algo mejor?
2 (with negative): **I can't hear him any
more** ya no le oigo; **don't wait any
longer** no esperes más

anybody [ˈɛnɪbɔdɪ] pron cualquiera;
(in interrogative sentences) alguien; (in
negative sentences): **I don't see ~** no
veo a nadie

anyhow [ˈɛnɪhaʊ] adv de todos
modos, de todas maneras; (carelessly)
de cualquier manera; (haphazardly)
de cualquier modo; **I shall go ~** iré de
todas maneras

anyone [ˈɛnɪwʌn] pron = **anybody**

anything [ˈɛnɪθɪŋ] pron cualquier
cosa; (in interrogative sentences)
algo; (in negative sentences) nada;
(everything) todo; **~ else?** ¿algo más?;
can you see ~? ¿ves algo?; **he'll eat ~**
come de todo or lo que sea

anytime [ˈɛnɪtaɪm] adv (at any
moment) en cualquier momento, de
un momento a otro; (whenever) no
importa cuándo, cuando quiera

anyway [ˈɛnɪweɪ] adv (at any rate)
de todos modos, de todas formas;
(besides) además; **~, I couldn't come
even if I wanted to** además, no
podría venir aunque quisiera; **I shall
go ~** iré de todos modos; **why are
you phoning, ~?** ¿entonces, por qué
llamas?, ¿por qué llamas, pues?

anywhere [ˈɛnɪwɛəʳ] adv
dondequiera; (interrogative) en algún
sitio; (negative sense) en ningún sitio;
(everywhere) en or por todas partes; **I
don't see him ~** no le veo en ningún
sitio; **are you going ~?** ¿vas a algún
sitio?; **~ in the world** en cualquier
parte del mundo

apart [əˈpɑːt] adv aparte,
separadamente; **10 miles ~** separados

por 10 millas; **to take ~** desmontar; **~ from** prep aparte de

apartment [əˈpɑːtmənt] n (US) piso, departamento (LAM), apartamento; (room) cuarto; **apartment block,** (US) **apartment building** n bloque m de apartamentos

apathy [ˈæpəθɪ] n apatía, indiferencia

ape [eɪp] n mono ▷ vt imitar, remedar

aperitif [əˈperitiːf] n aperitivo

aperture [ˈæpətʃuəʳ] n rendija, resquicio; (Phot) abertura

APEX [ˈeɪpeks] n abbr (Aviat: = advance purchase excursion) tarifa f APEX

apologize [əˈpɒlədʒaɪz] vi: **to ~ (for sth to sb)** disculparse (con algn por algo)

apology [əˈpɒlədʒɪ] n disculpa, excusa

Be careful not to translate apology by the Spanish word apología.

apostrophe [əˈpɒstrəfɪ] n apóstrofo m

app n abbr (inf: Comput: = application) aplicación f

appal [əˈpɔːl] vt horrorizar, espantar; **appalling** adj espantoso; (awful) pésimo

apparatus [æpəˈreɪtəs] n (equipment) equipo; (organization) aparato; (in gymnasium) aparatos mpl

apparent [əˈpærənt] adj aparente; (obvious) evidente; **apparently** adv por lo visto, al parecer

appeal [əˈpiːl] vi (Law) apelar ▷ n (Law) apelación f; (request) llamamiento; (plea) petición f; (charm) atractivo; **to ~ for** solicitar; **to ~ to** (thing) atraer; **it doesn't ~ to me** no me atrae, no me llama la atención; **appealing** adj (nice) atractivo

appear [əˈpɪəʳ] vi aparecer, presentarse; (Law) comparecer; (publication) salir (a luz), publicarse; (seem) parecer; **to ~ on TV/in "Hamlet"** salir por la tele/hacer un papel en "Hamlet"; **it would ~ that** parecería que; **appearance** n aparición f; (look, aspect) apariencia, aspecto; **to keep up appearances** salvar las apariencias; **to all appearances** al parecer

appendices [əˈpendɪsiːz] npl of **appendix**

appendicitis [əpendɪˈsaɪtɪs] n apendicitis f

appendix (pl **appendices**) [əˈpendɪks, -dɪsiːz] n apéndice m

appetite [ˈæpɪtaɪt] n apetito; (fig) deseo, anhelo

appetizer [ˈæpɪtaɪzəʳ] n (drink) aperitivo; (food) tapas fpl (SP)

applaud [əˈplɔːd] vt, vi aplaudir

applause [əˈplɔːz] n aplausos mpl

apple [ˈæpl] n manzana; **apple pie** n pastel m de manzana, pay m de manzana (LAM)

appliance [əˈplaɪəns] n aparato

applicable [əˈplɪkəbl] adj aplicable; **to be ~ to** referirse a

applicant [ˈæplɪkənt] n candidato/a; solicitante mf

application [æplɪˈkeɪʃən] n (also Comput) aplicación f; (for a job, a grant etc) solicitud f; **application form** n solicitud f

apply [əˈplaɪ] vt: **to ~ (to)** aplicar (a); (fig) emplear (para) ▷ vi: **to ~ to** (ask) dirigirse a; (be suitable for) ser aplicable a; **to ~ for** (permit, grant, job) solicitar; **to ~ o.s. to** aplicarse a, dedicarse a

appoint [əˈpɔɪnt] vt (to post) nombrar

Be careful not to translate appoint by the Spanish word apuntar.

appointment n (engagement) cita; (act) nombramiento; (post) puesto; **to make an ~ (with)** (doctor) pedir hora (con); (friend) citarse (con)

appraisal [əˈpreɪzl] n evaluación f

appreciate [əˈpriːʃɪeɪt] vt apreciar, tener en mucho; (be grateful for) agradecer; (be aware of) comprender ▷ vi (Comm) aumentar en valor; **appreciation** n apreciación f; (gratitude) reconocimiento, agradecimiento; (*Comm*) aumento en valor

apprehension [æprɪ'hɛnʃən] *n* (*fear*) aprensión *f*

apprehensive [æprɪ'hɛnsɪv] *adj* aprensivo

apprentice [ə'prɛntɪs] *n* aprendiz(a) *m/f*

approach [ə'prəutʃ] *vi* acercarse ▷ *vt* acercarse a; (*ask, apply to*) dirigirse a; (*problem*) abordar ▷ *n* acercamiento; (*access*) acceso; (*to problem etc*) enfoque *m*

appropriate [ə'prəuprɪɪt] *adj* apropiado, conveniente ▷ *vt* [-rɪeɪt] (*take*) apropiarse de

approval [ə'pruːvəl] *n* aprobación *f*, visto bueno; **on ~** (*Comm*) a prueba

approve [ə'pruːv] *vt* aprobar; **approve of** *vt fus* aprobar; **they don't ~ of her** (ella) no les parece bien

approximate [ə'prɒksɪmɪt] *adj* aproximado; **approximately** *adv* aproximadamente, más o menos

Apr. *abbr* (= *April*) abr

apricot ['eɪprɪkɔt] *n* albaricoque *m* (*SP*), damasco (*LAM*)

April ['eɪprəl] *n* abril *m*; **April Fools' Day** *n* ≈ día *m* de los (Santos) Inocentes

apron ['eɪprən] *n* delantal *m*

apt [æpt] *adj* acertado, oportuno; **~ to do** (*likely*) propenso a hacer

aquarium [ə'kwɛərɪəm] *n* acuario

Aquarius [ə'kwɛərɪəs] *n* Acuario

Arab ['ærəb] *adj*, *n* árabe *mf*

Arabia [ə'reɪbɪə] *n* Arabia; **Arabian** *adj* árabe; **Arabic** ['ærəbɪk] *adj* árabe, arábigo ▷ *n* árabe *m*; **Arabic numerals** numeración *f* arábiga

arbitrary ['ɑːbɪtrərɪ] *adj* arbitrario

arbitration [ɑːbɪ'treɪʃən] *n* arbitraje *m*

arc [ɑːk] *n* arco

arcade [ɑː'keɪd] *n* (*round a square*) soportales *mpl*; (*shopping arcade*) galería comercial

arch [ɑːtʃ] *n* arco; (*of foot*) puente *m* ▷ *vt* arquear

archaeology [ɑːkɪ'ɔlədʒɪ] *n* arqueología

archbishop [ɑːtʃ'bɪʃəp] *n* arzobispo

archeology *etc* [ɑːkɪ'ɔlədʒɪ] (*US*) *see* **archaeology** *etc*

architect ['ɑːkɪtɛkt] *n* arquitecto/a; **architectural** *adj* arquitectónico; **architecture** *n* arquitectura

archive ['ɑːkaɪv] *n* (*often pl*: *also Comput*) archivo

Arctic ['ɑːktɪk] *adj* ártico ▷ *n*: **the ~** el Ártico

are [ɑːʳ] *vb see* **be**

area ['ɛərɪə] *n* área; (*Math etc*) superficie *f*; (*zone*) región *f*, zona; (*of knowledge, experience*) campo; **area code** *n* (*US Tel*) prefijo

arena [ə'riːnə] *n* arena; (*of circus*) pista

aren't [ɑːnt] = **are not**

Argentina [ɑːdʒən'tiːnə] *n* Argentina; **Argentinian** [ɑːdʒən'tɪnɪən] *adj*, *n* argentino/a

arguably ['ɑːgjuəblɪ] *adv*: **it is ~ ...** es discutiblemente ...

argue ['ɑːgjuː] *vi* (*quarrel*) discutir; (*reason*) razonar, argumentar; **to ~ that** sostener que

argument ['ɑːgjumənt] *n* (*reasons*) argumento; (*quarrel*) discusión *f*

Aries ['ɛərɪz] *n* Aries *m*

arise [ə'raɪz] (*pt* **arose**, *pp* **arisen** [ə'rɪzn]) *vi* surgir, presentarse

arithmetic [ə'rɪθmətɪk] *n* aritmética

arm [ɑːm] *n* brazo ▷ *vt* armar; **~ in ~** cogidos del brazo; **armchair** *n* sillón *m*, butaca

armed [ɑːmd] *adj* armado; **armed robbery** *n* robo a mano armada

armour, (*US*) **armor** ['ɑːməʳ] *n* armadura

armpit ['ɑːmpɪt] *n* sobaco, axila

armrest ['ɑːmrɛst] *n* reposabrazos *m inv*

army ['ɑːmɪ] *n* ejército; (*fig*) multitud *f*

A road *n* (*BRIT*) ≈ carretera *f* nacional

aroma [əˈrəʊmə] n aroma m, fragancia; **aromatherapy** n aromaterapia

arose [əˈrəʊz] pt of **arise**

around [əˈraʊnd] adv alrededor; (in the area) a la redonda ▷ prep alrededor de

arouse [əˈraʊz] vt despertar; (anger) provocar

arrange [əˈreɪndʒ] vt arreglar, ordenar; (programme) organizar; **to ~ to do sth** quedar en hacer algo; **arrangement** n arreglo; (agreement) acuerdo; **arrangements** npl (preparations) preparativos mpl

array [əˈreɪ] n: **~ of** (things) serie f or colección f de; (people) conjunto de

arrears [əˈrɪəz] npl atrasos mpl; **to be in ~ with one's rent** estar retrasado en el pago del alquiler

arrest [əˈrɛst] vt detener; (sb's attention) llamar ▷ n detención f; **under ~** detenido

arrival [əˈraɪvəl] n llegada; **new ~** recién llegado/a

arrive [əˈraɪv] vi llegar; **arrive at** vt fus (decision, solution) llegar a

arrogance [ˈærəgəns] n arrogancia, prepotencia (LAM)

arrogant [ˈærəgənt] adj arrogante

arrow [ˈærəʊ] n flecha

arse [ɑːs] n (BRIT infl) culo, trasero

arson [ˈɑːsn] n incendio provocado

art [ɑːt] n arte m; (skill) destreza; **art college** n escuela f de Bellas Artes

artery [ˈɑːtərɪ] n arteria

art gallery n pinacoteca; (Comm) galería de arte

arthritis [ɑːˈθraɪtɪs] n artritis f

artichoke [ˈɑːtɪtʃəʊk] n alcachofa; **Jerusalem ~** aguaturma

article [ˈɑːtɪkl] n artículo

articulate adj [ɑːˈtɪkjulɪt] (speech) claro ▷ vt [ɑːˈtɪkjuleɪt] expresar

artificial [ɑːtɪˈfɪʃəl] adj artificial

artist [ˈɑːtɪst] n artista mf; (Mus) intérprete mf; **artistic** adj artístico

art school n escuela de bellas artes

as [æz] conj **1** (referring to time: while) mientras; **as the years go by** con el paso de los años; **he came in as I was leaving** entró cuando me marchaba; **as from tomorrow** a partir de or desde mañana

2 (in comparisons): **as big as** tan grande como; **twice as big as** el doble de grande que; **as much money/many books as** tanto dinero/tantos libros como; **as soon as** en cuanto

3 (since, because) como, ya que; **as I don't speak German I can't understand him** no le entiendo ya que no hablo alemán

4 (referring to manner, way): **do as you wish** haz lo que quieras; **as she said** como dijo

5 (concerning): **as for or to that** por or en lo que respecta a eso

6: **as if or though** como si; **he looked as if he was ill** parecía como si estuviera enfermo, tenía aspecto de enfermo; see also **long**; **such**; **well**

▶ prep (in the capacity of): **he works as a barman** trabaja de barman; **as chairman of the company, he ...** como presidente de la compañía, ...; **he gave it to me as a present** me lo dio de regalo

a.s.a.p. abbr (= as soon as possible) cuanto antes

asbestos [æzˈbɛstəs] n asbesto, amianto

ascent [əˈsɛnt] n subida; (slope) cuesta, pendiente f

ash [æʃ] n ceniza; (tree) fresno

ashamed [əˈʃeɪmd] adj avergonzado; **to be ~ of** avergonzarse de

ashore [əˈʃɔːʳ] adv en tierra; (swim etc) a tierra

ashtray [ˈæʃtreɪ] n cenicero

Ash Wednesday n miércoles m de Ceniza

Asia ['eɪʃə] n Asia; **Asian** adj, n asiático/a

aside [ə'saɪd] adv a un lado ▷ n aparte m

ask [ɑːsk] vt (question) preguntar; (invite) invitar; **to ~ sb sth/to do sth** preguntar algo a algn/pedir a algn que haga algo; **to ~ sb about sth** preguntar algo a algn; **to ~ (sb) a question** hacer una pregunta (a algn); **to ~ sb out to dinner** invitar a cenar a algn; **ask for** vt fus pedir; **it's just ~ing for trouble** or **for it** es buscarse problemas

asleep [ə'sliːp] adj dormido; **to fall ~** dormirse, quedarse dormido

asparagus [əs'pærəgəs] n espárragos mpl

aspect ['æspɛkt] n aspecto, apariencia; (direction in which a building etc faces) orientación f

aspirations [æspə'reɪʃənz] npl aspiraciones fpl; (ambition) ambición f

aspire [əs'paɪəʳ] vi: **to ~ to** aspirar a, ambicionar

aspirin ['æsprɪn] n aspirina

ass [æs] n asno, burro; (inf) imbécil mf; (us inf!) culo, trasero

assassin [ə'sæsɪn] n asesino/a; **assassinate** vt asesinar

assault [ə'sɔːlt] n asalto; (Law) agresión f ▷ vt asaltar; (sexually) violar

assemble [ə'sɛmbl] vt reunir, juntar; (Tech) montar ▷ vi reunirse, juntarse

assembly [ə'sɛmblɪ] n reunión f, asamblea; (parliament) parlamento; (construction) montaje m

assert [ə'sɜːt] vt afirmar; (insist on) hacer valer; **assertion** n afirmación f

assess [ə'sɛs] vt valorar, calcular; (tax, damages) fijar; (for tax) gravar; **assessment** n valoración f; gravamen m

asset ['æsɛt] n ventaja; **assets** npl (funds) activo sg, fondos mpl

assign [ə'saɪn] vt (date) fijar; (task) asignar; (resources) destinar; **assignment** n tarea

assist [ə'sɪst] vt ayudar; **assistance** n ayuda, auxilio; **assistant** n ayudante mf; (BRIT: also: **shop assistant**) dependiente/a m/f

associate [adj, n ə'səuʃɪɪt, vt, vi ə'səuʃɪeɪt] adj asociado ▷ n colega mf ▷ vt asociar; (ideas) relacionar ▷ vi: **to ~ with sb** tratar con algn

association [əsəusɪ'eɪʃən] n asociación f

assorted [ə'sɔːtɪd] adj surtido, variado

assortment [ə'sɔːtmənt] n (of shapes, colours) surtido; (of books) colección f; (of people) mezcla

assume [ə'sjuːm] vt suponer; (responsibilities etc) asumir; (attitude, name) adoptar, tomar

assumption [ə'sʌmpʃən] n suposición f, presunción f; (act) asunción f

assurance [ə'ʃuərəns] n garantía, promesa; (confidence) confianza, aplomo; (insurance) seguro

assure [ə'ʃuəʳ] vt asegurar

asterisk ['æstərɪsk] n asterisco

asthma ['æsmə] n asma

astonish [ə'stɒnɪʃ] vt asombrar, pasmar; **astonished** adj estupefacto, pasmado; **to be astonished (at)** asombrarse (de); **astonishing** adj asombroso, pasmoso; **I find it astonishing that ...** me asombra or pasma que ...; **astonishment** n asombro, sorpresa

astound [ə'staund] vt asombrar, pasmar

astray [ə'streɪ] adv: **to go ~** extraviarse; **to lead ~** llevar por mal camino

astrology [əs'trɒlədʒɪ] n astrología

astronaut ['æstrənɔːt] n astronauta mf

astronomer [əs'trɒnəməʳ] n astrónomo/a

astronomical [æstrə'nɒmɪkəl] adj astronómico

astronomy [əs'trɒnəmɪ] n astronomía

astute [əs'tjuːt] adj astuto
asylum [ə'saɪləm] n (refuge) asilo;
(hospital) manicomio

KEYWORD

at [æt] prep 1 (referring to position) en;
(direction) a; **at the top** en lo alto; **at
home/school** en casa/la escuela; **to
look at sth/sb** mirar algo/a algn
2 (referring to time): **at four o'clock**
a las cuatro; **at night** por la noche;
at Christmas en Navidad; **at times**
a veces
3 (referring to rates, speed etc): **at £1 a
kilo** a una libra el kilo; **two at a time**
de dos en dos; **at 50 km/h** a 50 km/h
4 (referring to manner): **at a stroke** de
un golpe; **at peace** en paz
5 (referring to activity): **to be at work**
estar trabajando; (in office) estar en el
trabajo; **to play at cowboys** jugar a
los vaqueros; **to be good at sth** ser
bueno en algo
6 (referring to cause): **shocked/
surprised/annoyed at sth**
asombrado/sorprendido/fastidiado
por algo; **I went at his suggestion**
fui a instancias suyas
▶ n (symbol @) arroba

ate [ɛt, eɪt] pt of **eat**
atheist ['eɪθɪɪst] n ateo/a
Athens ['æθɪnz] n Atenas f
athlete ['æθliːt] n atleta mf
athletic [æθ'lɛtɪk] adj atlético;
athletics n atletismo
Atlantic [ət'læntɪk] adj atlántico ▷ n:
the ~ (Ocean) el (Océano) Atlántico
atlas ['ætləs] n atlas m inv
A.T.M. n abbr (= Automated Telling
Machine) cajero automático
atmosphere ['ætməsfɪəʳ] n
atmósfera; (fig) ambiente m
atom ['ætəm] n átomo; **atomic**
[ə'tɔmɪk] adj atómico; **atom(ic)
bomb** n bomba atómica
A to Z® n (map) callejero

atrocity [ə'trɔsɪtɪ] n atrocidad f
attach [ə'tætʃ] vt sujetar; (document,
email, letter) adjuntar; **to be ~ed to
sb/sth** (like) tener cariño a algn/
algo; **attachment** n (tool) accesorio;
(Comput) archivo o documento
adjunto; (love): **attachment (to)**
apego (a)
attack [ə'tæk] vt (Mil) atacar;
(criminal) agredir, asaltar; (criticize)
criticar; (task etc) emprender ▷ n
ataque m, asalto; (on sb's life)
atentado; (fig: criticism) crítica; **heart
~** infarto (de miocardio); **attacker** n
agresor(a) m/f, asaltante mf
attain [ə'teɪn] vt (also: **~ to**) alcanzar;
(achieve) lograr, conseguir
attempt [ə'tɛmpt] n tentativa,
intento; (attack) atentado ▷ vt
intentar
attend vt asistir a; (patient) atender;
attend to vt fus (needs, affairs etc)
ocuparse de; (speech etc) prestar
atención a; (customer) atender a;
attendance n asistencia, presencia;
(people present) concurrencia;
attendant n sirviente/a m/f,
ayudante mf ▷ adj concomitante
attention [ə'tɛnʃən] n atención f
▷ excl (Mil) ¡firme(s)!; **for the ~ of ...**
(Admin) a la atención de ...
attic ['ætɪk] n desván m
attitude ['ætɪtjuːd] n actitud f;
(disposition) disposición f
attorney [ə'təːnɪ] n (lawyer)
abogado/a; **Attorney General** n
(BRIT) ≈ fiscal mf general del Estado;
(US) ≈ ministro/a de Justicia
attract [ə'trækt] vt atraer;
(attention) llamar; **attraction** n
encanto; (Physics) atracción f;
(towards sth) atracción f; **attractive**
adj atractivo
attribute ['ætrɪbjuːt] n atributo
▷ vt [ə'trɪbjuːt]: **to ~ sth to** atribuir
algo a
aubergine ['əubəʒiːn] n (BRIT)
berenjena; (colour) morado

auburn ['ɔːbən] adj color castaño rojizo

auction ['ɔːkʃən] n (also: **sale by ~**) subasta ▷ vt subastar

audible ['ɔːdɪbl] adj audible, que se puede oír

audience ['ɔːdɪəns] n público; (Radio) radioescuchas mpl; (TV) telespectadores mpl; (interview) audiencia

audit ['ɔːdɪt] vt revisar, intervenir

audition [ɔːˈdɪʃən] n audición f

auditor ['ɔːdɪtə'] n interventor(a) m/f, censor(a) m/f de cuentas

auditorium [ɔːdɪˈtɔːrɪəm] n auditorio

Aug. abbr (= August) ag

August ['ɔːgəst] n agosto

aunt [ɑːnt] n tía; **auntie, aunty** ['ɑːntɪ] n diminutive of **aunt**

au pair ['əuˈpɛə'] n (also: **~ girl**) chica f au pair

aura ['ɔːrə] n aura f, (atmosphere) ambiente m

austerity [ɔsˈtɛrɪtɪ] n austeridad f

Australia [ɔsˈtreɪlɪə] n Australia; **Australian** adj, n australiano/a

Austria ['ɔstrɪə] n Austria; **Austrian** adj, n austríaco/a

authentic [ɔːˈθɛntɪk] adj auténtico

author ['ɔːθə'] n autor(a) m/f

authority [ɔːˈθɔrɪtɪ] n autoridad f; **the authorities** npl las autoridades

authorize ['ɔːθəraɪz] vt autorizar

auto ['ɔːtəu] n (US) coche m, carro (LAM), automóvil m; **autobiography** [ɔːtəbaɪˈɔgrəfɪ] n autobiografía; **autograph** ['ɔːtəgrɑːf] n autógrafo ▷ vt (photo etc) dedicar; **automatic** [ɔːtəˈmætɪk] adj automático ▷ n (gun) pistola automática; **automatically** adv automáticamente; **automobile** ['ɔːtəməbiːl] n (US) coche m, carro (LAM), automóvil m; **autonomous** [ɔːˈtɔnəməs] adj autónomo; **autonomy** [ɔːˈtɔnəmɪ] n autonomía

autumn ['ɔːtəm] n otoño

auxiliary [ɔːgˈzɪlɪərɪ] adj auxiliar

avail [əˈveɪl] vt: **to ~ o.s. of** aprovechar(se) de ▷ n: **to no ~** en vano, sin resultado

availability [əveɪləˈbɪlɪtɪ] n disponibilidad f

available [əˈveɪləbl] adj disponible

avalanche ['ævəlɑːnʃ] n alud m, avalancha

Ave. abbr (= avenue) Av., Avda

avenue ['ævənjuː] n avenida; (fig) camino

average ['ævərɪdʒ] n promedio, media ▷ adj (mean) medio; (ordinary) regular, corriente ▷ vt alcanzar un promedio de; **on ~** por término medio

avert [əˈvəːt] vt prevenir; (blow) desviar; (one's eyes) apartar

avid ['ævɪd] adj ávido

avocado [ævəˈkɑːdəu] n (BRIT: also: **~ pear**) aguacate m, palta (LAM)

avoid [əˈvɔɪd] vt evitar, eludir

await [əˈweɪt] vt esperar, aguardar

awake [əˈweɪk] (pt **awoke**, pp **awoken** or **awaked**) adj despierto ▷ vt despertar ▷ vi despertarse; **to be ~** estar despierto

award [əˈwɔːd] n premio; (Law) fallo, sentencia ▷ vt otorgar, conceder; (Law: damages) adjudicar

aware [əˈwɛə'] adj consciente; **to become ~ of** darse cuenta de, enterarse de; **awareness** n conciencia, conocimiento

away [əˈweɪ] adv fuera; (far away) lejos; **two kilometres ~** a dos kilómetros (de distancia); **two hours ~ by car** a dos horas en coche; **the holiday was two weeks ~** faltaban dos semanas para las vacaciones; **he's ~ for a week** estará ausente una semana; **to work/pedal ~** seguir trabajando/pedaleando; **to fade ~** desvanecerse; (sound) apagarse

awe [ɔː] n respeto, admiración f respetuosa; **awesome** ['ɔːsəm] adj (esp US: excellent) formidable

awful ['ɔ:fəl] adj terrible; **an ~ lot of** (people, cars, dogs) la mar de, muchísimos; **awfully** adv (very) terriblemente

awkward ['ɔ:kwəd] adj desmañado, torpe; (shape, situation) incómodo; (question) difícil

awoke [ə'wəuk] pt of **awake**

awoken [ə'wəukən] pp of **awake**

axe, (US) **ax** [æks] n hacha ▷ vt (project etc) cortar; (jobs) reducir

axle ['æksl] n eje m, árbol m

ay(e) [aɪ] excl (yes) sí

azalea [ə'zeɪlɪə] n azalea

B [bi:] n (Mus) si m

baby ['beɪbɪ] n bebé mf; (US inf: darling) mi amor; **baby carriage** n (US) cochecito; **baby-sit** vi hacer de canguro; **baby-sitter** n canguro mf; **baby wipe** n toallita húmeda (para bebés)

bachelor ['bætʃələʳ] n soltero; **B~ of Arts/Science (BA/BSc)** licenciado/a en Filosofía y Letras/Ciencias

back [bæk] n (of person) espalda; (of animal) lomo; (of hand, page) dorso; (as opposed to front) parte f de atrás; (of chair) respaldo; (of page) reverso; (Football) defensa m ▷ vt (candidate: also: ~ **up**) respaldar, apoyar; (horse: at races) apostar a; (car) dar marcha atrás a or con ▷ vi (car etc) dar marcha atrás ▷ adj (garden, room) de atrás ▷ adv (not forward) (hacia) atrás; **he's ~** (returned) ha vuelto; **~ seats/ wheels** (Aut) asientos mpl traseros, ruedas fpl traseras; **~ payments**

pagos *mpl* con efecto retroactivo; **~ rent** renta atrasada; **he ran ~** volvió corriendo; **throw the ball ~** (*restitution*) devuelve la pelota; **can I have it ~?** ¿me lo devuelve?; **he called ~** (*again*) volvió a llamar; **back down** *vi* echarse atrás; **back out** *vi* (*of promise*) volverse atrás; **back up** *vt* (*person*) apoyar, respaldar; (*theory*) defender; (*Comput*) hacer una copia de reserva de; **backache** *n* dolor *m* de espalda; **backbencher** *n* (BRIT) diputado sin cargo oficial en el gobierno o la oposición; **backbone** *n* columna vertebral; **back door** *n* puerta *f* trasera; **backfire** *vi* (*Aut*) petardear; (*plans*) fallar, salir mal; **backgammon** *n* backgammon *m*; **background** *n* fondo; (*of events*) antecedentes *mpl*; (*basic knowledge*) bases *fpl*; (*experience*) conocimientos *mpl*, educación *f*; **family background** origen *m*, antecedentes *mpl* familiares; **backing** *n* (*fig*) apoyo, respaldo; (*Comm*) respaldo financiero; (*Mus*) acompañamiento; **backlog** *n*: **backlog of work** trabajo atrasado; **backpack** *n* mochila; **backpacker** *n* mochilero/a; **backslash** *n* pleca, barra inversa; **backstage** *adv* entre bastidores; **backstroke** *n* espalda; **backup** *adj* suplementario; (*Comput: disk, file*) de reserva ▷ *n* (*support*) apoyo; (*also*: **backup file**) copia de reserva; **backward** *adj* (*person, country*) atrasado; **backwards** *adv* hacia atrás; (*read a list*) al revés; (*fall*) de espaldas; **backyard** *n* patio trasero

bacon ['beɪkən] *n* tocino, beicon *m*

bacteria [bæk'tɪərɪə] *npl* bacterias *fpl*

bad [bæd] *adj* malo; (*serious*) grave; (*meat, food*) podrido, pasado; **to go ~** pasarse

badge [bædʒ] *n* insignia; (*metal badge*) chapa; (*of policeman*) placa

badger ['bædʒə'] *n* tejón *m*

badly ['bædlɪ] *adv* mal; **to reflect ~ on sb** influir negativamente en la reputación de

algn; **~ wounded** gravemente herido; **he needs it ~** le hace mucha falta; **to be ~ off (for money)** andar mal de dinero

bad-mannered ['bæd'mænəd] *adj* mal educado

badminton ['bædmɪntən] *n* bádminton *m*

bad-tempered ['bæd'tɛmpəd] *adj* de mal genio *or* carácter; (*temporarily*) de mal humor

bag [bæg] *n* bolsa; (*handbag*) bolso; (*satchel*) mochila; (*case*) maleta; **~s of** (*inf*) un montón de

baggage ['bægɪdʒ] *n* equipaje *m*; **baggage allowance** *n* límite *m* de equipaje; **baggage (re)claim** *n* recogida de equipajes

baggy ['bægɪ] *adj* (*trousers*) ancho, holgado

bagpipes ['bægpaɪps] *npl* gaita *sg*

bail [beɪl] *n* fianza ▷ *vt* (*prisoner: also*: **grant ~ to**) poner en libertad bajo fianza; (*boat: also*: **~ out**) achicar; **on ~** (*prisoner*) bajo fianza; **to ~ sb out** pagar la fianza de algn

bait [beɪt] *n* cebo ▷ *vt* poner el cebo en

bake [beɪk] *vt* cocer (al horno) ▷ *vi* cocerse; **baked beans** *npl* judías *fpl* en salsa de tomate; **baked potato** *n* patata al horno; **baker** *n* panadero/a; **bakery** *n* panadería; (*for cakes*) pastelería; **baking** *n* (*act*) cocción *f*; (*batch*) hornada; **baking powder** *n* levadura (en polvo)

balance ['bæləns] *n* equilibrio; (*Comm: sum*) balance *m*; (*remainder*) resto; (*scales*) balanza ▷ *vt* equilibrar; (*budget*) nivelar; (*account*) saldar; (*compensate*) compensar; **~ of trade/payments** balanza de comercio/pagos; **balanced** *adj* (*personality, diet*) equilibrado; (*report*) objetivo; **balance sheet** *n* balance *m*

balcony ['bælkənɪ] *n* (*open*) balcón *m*; (*closed*) galería; (*in theatre*) anfiteatro

bald [bɔːld] *adj* calvo; (*tyre*) liso

ball [bɔːl] n (football) balón m; (for tennis, golf etc) pelota; (of wool, string) ovillo; (dance) baile m; **to play ~ (with sb)** jugar a la pelota (con algn); (fig) cooperar

ballerina [bælə'riːnə] n bailarina

ballet ['bæleɪ] n ballet m; **ballet dancer** n bailarín/ina m/f (de ballet)

balloon [bə'luːn] n globo

ballot ['bælət] n votación f

ballroom ['bɔːlrʊm] n salón m de baile

Baltic ['bɔːltɪk] n: **the ~ (Sea)** el (Mar) Báltico

bamboo [bæm'buː] n bambú m

ban [bæn] n prohibición f ▷ vt prohibir; (exclude) excluir

banana [bə'nɑːnə] n plátano, banana (LAM)

band [bænd] n (group) banda; (strip) faja, tira; (at a dance) orquesta; (Mil) banda; (rock band) grupo

bandage ['bændɪdʒ] n venda, vendaje m ▷ vt vendar

Band-Aid® ['bændeɪd] n (US) tirita

bandit ['bændɪt] n bandido

bang [bæŋ] n (of gun, exhaust) estallido; (of door) portazo; (blow) golpe m ▷ vt (door) cerrar de golpe; (one's head) golpear ▷ vi estallar; see also **bangs**

Bangladesh [bæŋglə'deʃ] n Bangladesh f

bangle ['bæŋgl] n brazalete m, ajorca

bangs [bæŋz] npl (US) flequillo sg

banish ['bænɪʃ] vt desterrar

banister(s) ['bænɪstə(z)] n(pl) barandilla f, pasamanos m inv

banjo ['bændʒəʊ] (pl **banjoes** or **banjos**) n banjo

bank [bæŋk] n (Comm) banco; (of river, lake) ribera, orilla; (of earth) terraplén m ▷ vi (Aviat) ladearse; **bank on** vt fus contar con; **bank account** n cuenta bancaria; **bank balance** n saldo; **bank card** n tarjeta bancaria; **bank charges** npl comisión fsg; **banker** n banquero; **bank holiday** n (BRIT)

día m festivo or de fiesta; ver nota "**bank holiday**"; **banking** n banca; **bank manager** n director(a) m/f (de sucursal) de banco; **banknote** n billete m de banco

○ **BANK HOLIDAY**
○
○ El término bank holiday se aplica en
○ el Reino Unido a todo día festivo
○ oficial en el que cierran bancos y
○ comercios. Los más destacados
○ coinciden con Navidad, Semana
○ Santa, finales de mayo y finales
○ de agosto. Al contrario que en los
○ países de tradición católica, no se
○ celebran las festividades dedicadas
○ a los santos.

bankrupt ['bæŋkrʌpt] adj quebrado, insolvente; **to go ~** hacer bancarrota; **to be ~** estar en quiebra; **bankruptcy** n quiebra

bank statement n extracto de cuenta

banner ['bænər] n pancarta

bannister(s) ['bænɪstə(z)] n(pl) = **banister(s)**

banquet ['bæŋkwɪt] n banquete m

baptism ['bæptɪzəm] n bautismo; (act) bautizo

baptize [bæp'taɪz] vt bautizar

bar [bɑːr] n barra; (on door) tranca; (of window, cage) reja; (of soap) pastilla; (of chocolate) tableta; (fig: hindrance) obstáculo; (prohibition) prohibición f; (pub) bar m; (counter) barra, mostrador m; (Mus) barra ▷ vt (road) obstruir; (person) excluir; (activity) prohibir; **behind ~s** entre rejas; **the B~** (Law) la abogacía; **~ none** sin excepción

barbaric [bɑː'bærɪk] adj bárbaro

barbecue ['bɑːbɪkjuː] n barbacoa

barbed wire ['bɑːbd-] n alambre m de espino

barber ['bɑːbər] n peluquero, barbero; **barber's (shop)**, (US) **barber (shop)** n peluquería

bar code n código de barras
bare [bɛəʳ] adj desnudo; (trees) sin hojas ▷ vt desnudar; **to ~ one's teeth** enseñar los dientes; **barefoot** adj, adv descalzo; **barely** adv apenas
bargain ['bɑːgɪn] n pacto; (transaction) negocio; (good buy) ganga ▷ vi negociar; (haggle) regatear; **into the ~** además, por añadidura; **bargain for** vt fus (inf): **he got more than he ~ed for** le resultó peor de lo que esperaba
barge [bɑːdʒ] n barcaza; **barge in** vi irrumpir; (in conversation) entrometerse
bark [bɑːk] n (of tree) corteza; (of dog) ladrido ▷ vi ladrar
barley ['bɑːlɪ] n cebada
barmaid ['bɑːmeɪd] n camarera
barman ['bɑːmən] n camarero, barman m
barn [bɑːn] n granero
barometer [bə'rɒmɪtəʳ] n barómetro
baron ['bærən] n barón m; (fig) magnate m; **baroness** n baronesa
barracks ['bærəks] npl cuartel msg
barrage ['bærɑːʒ] n (Mil) cortina de fuego; (dam) presa; (of criticism etc) lluvia, aluvión m
barrel ['bærəl] n barril m; (of gun) cañón m
barren ['bærən] adj estéril
barrette [bə'rɛt] n (US) pasador m (LAM, SP), broche m (MEX)
barricade [bærɪ'keɪd] n barricada
barrier ['bærɪəʳ] n barrera
barring ['bɑːrɪŋ] prep excepto, salvo
barrister ['bærɪstəʳ] n (BRIT) abogado/a
barrow ['bærəu] n (cart) carretilla
bartender ['bɑːtɛndəʳ] n (US) camarero, barman m
base [beɪs] n base f ▷ vt: **to ~ sth on** basar or fundar algo en ▷ adj bajo, infame
baseball ['beɪsbɔːl] n béisbol m; **baseball cap** n gorra f de béisbol
basement ['beɪsmənt] n sótano

bases ['beɪsiːz] npl of **basis**
bash [bæʃ] vt (inf) golpear
basic ['beɪsɪk] adj básico; **basically** adv fundamentalmente, en el fondo; **basics** npl: **the basics** los fundamentos
basil ['bæzl] n albahaca
basin ['beɪsn] n cuenco, tazón m; (Geo) cuenca; (also: **wash~**) lavabo
basis ['beɪsɪs] (pl **bases**) n base f; **on a part-time/trial ~** a tiempo parcial/a prueba
basket ['bɑːskɪt] n cesta, cesto; **basketball** n baloncesto
bass [beɪs] n (Mus) bajo
bastard ['bɑːstəd] n bastardo/a; (inf!) hijo de puta (!)
bat [bæt] n (Zool) murciélago; (for ball games) palo; (BRIT: for table tennis) pala ▷ vt: **he didn't ~ an eyelid** ni pestañeó
batch [bætʃ] n lote m; (of bread) hornada
bath [bɑːθ] n (act) baño; (bathtub) bañera, tina (esp LAM) ▷ vt bañar; **to have a ~** bañarse, darse un baño; see also **baths**
bathe [beɪð] vi bañarse ▷ vt (wound etc) lavar
bathing ['beɪðɪŋ] n baño; **bathing costume**, (US) **bathing suit** n traje m de baño
bath: bathrobe n albornoz m; **bathroom** n (cuarto de) baño; **baths** [bɑːðz] npl piscina sg; **bath towel** n toalla de baño; **bathtub** n bañera
baton ['bætən] n (Mus) batuta; (weapon) porra
batter ['bætəʳ] vt maltratar; (wind, rain) azotar ▷ n batido; **battered** adj (hat, pan) estropeado
battery ['bætərɪ] n batería; (of torch) pila; **battery farming** n cría intensiva
battle ['bætl] n batalla; (fig) lucha ▷ vi luchar; **battlefield** n campo m de batalla
bay [beɪ] n (Geo) bahía; **to hold sb at ~** mantener a alguien a raya

bazaar [bəˈzɑːʳ] n bazar m
BBC n abbr (= British Broadcasting Corporation) BBC f

 KEYWORD

be [biː] (pt **was, were**, pp **been**) aux vb **1** (with present participle, forming continuous tenses): **what are you doing?** ¿qué estás haciendo?, ¿qué haces?; **they're coming tomorrow** vienen mañana; **I've been waiting for you for hours** llevo horas esperándote
2 (with pp: forming passives) ser (but often replaced by active or reflexive constructions); **to be murdered** ser asesinado; **the box had been opened** habían abierto la caja; **the thief was nowhere to be seen** no se veía al ladrón por ninguna parte
3 (in tag questions): **it was fun, wasn't it?** fue divertido, ¿no? or ¿verdad?; **he's good-looking, isn't he?** es guapo, ¿no te parece?; **she's back again, is she?** entonces, ¿ha vuelto?
4 (+ to + infin): **the house is to be sold** (necessity) hay que vender la casa; (future) van a vender la casa; **he's not to open it** no tiene que abrirlo
▶ vb +complement **1** (with n or num complement) ser; **he's a doctor** es médico; **2 and 2 are 4** 2 y 2 son 4
2 (with adj complement, expressing permanent or inherent quality) ser; (: expressing state seen as temporary or reversible) estar; **I'm English** soy inglés/esa; **she's tall/pretty** es alta/bonita; **he's young** es joven; **be careful/good/quiet** ten cuidado/pórtate bien/cállate; **I'm tired** estoy cansado/a; **it's dirty** está sucio/a
3 (of health) estar; **how are you?** ¿cómo estás?; **he's very ill** está muy enfermo; **I'm better now** ya estoy mejor
4 (of age) tener; **how old are you?** ¿cuántos años tienes?; **I'm sixteen**

(years old) tengo dieciséis años
5 (cost) costar; ser; **how much was the meal?** ¿cuánto fue or costó la comida?; **that'll be £5.75, please** son £5.75, por favor; **this shirt is £17** esta camisa cuesta £17
▶ vi **1** (exist, occur etc) existir, haber; **the best singer that ever was** el mejor cantante que existió jamás; **is there a God?** ¿hay un Dios?, ¿existe Dios?; **be that as it may** sea como sea; **so be it** así sea
2 (referring to place) estar; **I won't be here tomorrow** no estaré aquí mañana
3 (referring to movement): **where have you been?** ¿dónde has estado?
▶ impers vb **1** (referring to time): **it's 5 o'clock** son las 5; **it's the 28th of April** estamos a 28 de abril
2 (referring to distance): **it's 10 km to the village** el pueblo está a 10 km
3 (referring to the weather): **it's too hot/cold** hace demasiado calor/frío; **it's windy today** hace viento hoy
4 (emphatic): **it's me** soy yo; **it was Maria who paid the bill** fue María la que pagó la cuenta

beach [biːtʃ] n playa ▷ vt varar
beacon [ˈbiːkən] n (lighthouse) faro; (marker) guía
bead [biːd] n cuenta; (of dew, sweat) gota; **beads** npl (necklace) collar m
beak [biːk] n pico
beam [biːm] n (Arch) viga; (of light) rayo, haz m de luz ▷ vi brillar; (smile) sonreír
bean [biːn] n judía; **runner/broad ~** habichuela/haba; **coffee ~** grano de café; **bean sprouts** npl brotes mpl de soja
bear [bɛəʳ] (pt **bore**, pp **borne**) n oso ▷ vt (weight etc) llevar; (cost) pagar; (responsibility) tener; (endure) soportar, aguantar; (children) tener; (fruit) dar ▷ vi: **to ~ right/left** torcer a la derecha/izquierda

beard [bɪəd] n barba

bearer ['bɛərəʳ] n portador(a) m/f

bearing ['bɛərɪŋ] n porte m; (connection) relación f

beast [biːst] n bestia; (inf) bruto, salvaje m

beat [biːt] (pt **beat**, pp **beaten** ['biːtn]) n (of heart) latido; (Mus) ritmo, compás m; (of policeman) ronda ▷ vt (hit) golpear, pegar; (eggs) batir; (defeat) vencer, derrotar; (better) sobrepasar; (drum) redoblar ▷ vi (heart) latir; **off the ~en track** aislado; **to ~ it** largarse; **beat up** vt (inf: person) dar una paliza a; **beating** n paliza

beautiful ['bjuːtɪful] adj hermoso, bello; **beautifully** adv de maravilla

beauty ['bjuːtɪ] n belleza; **beauty parlour**, (US) **beauty parlor** n salón m de belleza; **beauty salon** n salón m de belleza; **beauty spot** n (Tourism) lugar m pintoresco

beaver ['biːvəʳ] n castor m

became [bɪ'keɪm] pt of **become**

because [bɪ'kɔz] conj porque; **~ of** prep debido a, a causa de

beckon ['bɛkən] vt (also: **~ to**) llamar con señas

become [bɪ'kʌm] (irreg: like **come**) vi (+ noun) hacerse, llegar a ser; (+ adj) ponerse, volverse ▷ vt (suit) favorecer, sentar bien a; **to ~ fat** engordar

bed [bɛd] n cama; (of flowers) macizo; (of sea, lake) fondo; (of river) lecho; (of coal, clay) capa; **to go to ~** acostarse; **bed and breakfast** n ≈ pensión f; ver nota **"bed and breakfast"**; **bedclothes** npl ropa de cama; **bedding** n ropa de cama; **bed linen** n (BRIT) ropa f de cama; **bedroom** n dormitorio; **bedside** n: **at sb's bedside** a la cabecera de alguien; **bedside lamp** n lámpara de noche; **bedside table** n mesilla de noche; **bedsit(ter)** n (BRIT) estudio; **bedspread** n cubrecama m, colcha; **bedtime** n hora de acostarse

○ **BED AND BREAKFAST**
○
○ Se llama Bed and Breakfast a la casa
○ de hospedaje particular, o granja
○ si es en el campo, que ofrece cama
○ y desayuno a tarifas inferiores a
○ las de un hotel. El servicio se suele
○ anunciar con carteles colocados en
○ las ventanas del establecimiento,
○ en el jardín o en la carretera y en
○ ellos aparece a menudo únicamente
○ el símbolo "B & B".

bee [biː] n abeja

beech [biːtʃ] n haya

beef [biːf] n carne f de vaca; **roast ~** rosbif m; **beefburger** n hamburguesa

been [biːn] pp of **be**

beer [bɪəʳ] n cerveza; **beer garden** n (BRIT) terraza f de verano, jardín m (de un bar)

beet [biːt] n (US) remolacha

beetle ['biːtl] n escarabajo

beetroot ['biːtruːt] n (BRIT) remolacha

before [bɪ'fɔːʳ] prep (of time) antes de; (of space) delante de ▷ conj antes (de) que ▷ adv (time) antes; (space) delante, adelante; **~ going** antes de marcharse; **~ she goes** antes de que se vaya; **the week ~** la semana anterior; **I've never seen it ~** no lo he visto nunca; **beforehand** adv de antemano, con anticipación

beg [bɛg] vi pedir limosna ▷ vt pedir, rogar; (entreat) suplicar; **to ~ sb to do sth** rogar a algn que haga algo; see also **pardon**

began [bɪ'gæn] pt of **begin**

beggar ['bɛgəʳ] n mendigo/a

begin [bɪ'gɪn] (pt **began**, pp **begun**) vt, vi empezar, comenzar; **to ~ doing** or **to do sth** empezar a hacer algo; **beginner** n principiante mf; **beginning** n principio, comienzo

begun [bɪ'gʌn] pp of **begin**

behalf [bɪ'hɑːf] n: **on ~ of** en nombre de, por; (for benefit of) en beneficio de; **on my/his ~** por mí/él

behave [bɪ'heɪv] vi (person) portarse, comportarse; (well: also: **~ o.s.**) portarse bien; **behaviour,** (US) **behavior** n comportamiento, conducta

behind [bɪ'haɪnd] prep detrás de ▷ adv detrás, por detrás, atrás ▷ n trasero; **to be ~ (schedule)** ir retrasado; **~ the scenes** (fig) entre bastidores

beige [beɪʒ] adj (color) beige

Beijing ['beɪ'dʒɪŋ] n Pekín m

being ['biːɪŋ] n ser m; **to come into ~** nacer, aparecer

belated [bɪ'leɪtɪd] adj atrasado, tardío

belch [bɛltʃ] vi eructar ▷ vt (also: **~ out**: smoke etc) arrojar

Belgian ['bɛldʒən] adj, n belga mf

Belgium ['bɛldʒəm] n Bélgica

belief [bɪ'liːf] n opinión f; (trust, faith) fe f

believe [bɪ'liːv] vt, vi creer; **to ~ in** creer en; **believer** n partidario/a; (Rel) creyente mf, fiel mf

bell [bɛl] n campana; (small) campanilla; (on door) timbre m

bellboy ['bɛlbɔɪ], (US) **bellhop** ['bɛlhɔp] n botones m inv

bellow ['bɛləʊ] vi bramar; (person) rugir

bell pepper n (esp US) pimiento, pimentón m (LAM)

belly ['bɛlɪ] n barriga, panza; **belly button** (inf) n ombligo

belong [bɪ'lɔŋ] vi: **to ~ to** pertenecer a; (club etc) ser socio de; **this book ~s here** este libro va aquí; **belongings** npl pertenencias fpl

beloved [bɪ'lʌvɪd] adj, n querido/a

below [bɪ'ləʊ] prep bajo, debajo de; (less than) inferior a ▷ adv abajo, (por) debajo; **see ~** véase más abajo

belt [bɛlt] n cinturón m; (Tech) correa, cinta ▷ vt (thrash) pegar con correa; **beltway** n (US Aut) carretera de circunvalación

bemused [bɪ'mjuːzd] adj perplejo

bench [bɛntʃ] n banco; (BRIT Pol): **the Government/Opposition ~es**

(los asientos de) los miembros del Gobierno/de la Oposición; **the B~** (Law) la magistratura

bend [bɛnd] (pt, pp **bent**) vt doblar ▷ vi inclinarse ▷ n (in road, river) recodo; (in pipe) codo; **bend down** vi inclinarse, doblarse; **bend over** vi inclinarse

beneath [bɪ'niːθ] prep bajo, debajo de; (unworthy of) indigno de ▷ adv abajo, (por) debajo

beneficial [bɛnɪ'fɪʃəl] adj: **~ to** beneficioso para

benefit ['bɛnɪfɪt] n beneficio; (allowance of money) subsidio ▷ vt beneficiar ▷ vi: **he'll ~ from it** le sacará provecho

benign [bɪ'naɪn] adj benigno; (smile) afable

bent [bɛnt] pt, pp of **bend** ▷ n inclinación f ▷ adj: **to be ~ on** estar empeñado en

bereaved [bɪ'riːvd] n: **the ~** los allegados mpl del difunto

beret ['bɛreɪ] n boina

Berlin [bə:'lɪn] n Berlín m

Bermuda [bə:'mjuːdə] n las (Islas) Bermudas

berry ['bɛrɪ] n baya

berth [bə:θ] n (bed) litera; (cabin) camarote m; (for ship) amarradero ▷ vi atracar, amarrar

beside [bɪ'saɪd] prep junto a, al lado de; **to be ~ o.s. with anger** estar fuera de sí; **that's ~ the point** eso no tiene nada que ver; **besides** adv además ▷ prep además de

best [bɛst] adj (el/la) mejor ▷ adv (lo) mejor; **the ~ part of** (most) la mayor parte a; **at ~** en el mejor de los casos; **to make the ~ of sth** sacar el mejor partido de algo; **to do one's ~** hacer todo lo posible; **to the ~ of my knowledge** que yo sepa; **to the ~ of my ability** como mejor puedo; **best-before date** n fecha de consumo preferente; **best man** n padrino de boda; **bestseller** n éxito de ventas, bestseller m

bet [bɛt] n apuesta ▷ vt, vi (pt, pp **bet** or **betted**): **to ~ (on)** apostar (a)

betray [bɪˈtreɪ] vt traicionar; (trust) faltar a

better [ˈbɛtəʳ] adj mejor ▷ adv mejor ▷ vt superar ▷ n: **to get the ~ of sb** quedar por encima de algn; **you had ~ do it** más vale que lo hagas; **he thought ~ of it** cambió de parecer; **to get ~** mejorar(se)

betting [ˈbɛtɪŋ] n juego, apuestas fpl; **betting shop** n (BRIT) casa de apuestas

between [bɪˈtwiːn] prep entre ▷ adv (time) mientras tanto; (place) en medio

beverage [ˈbɛvərɪdʒ] n bebida

beware [bɪˈwɛəʳ] vi: **to ~ (of)** tener cuidado (con); **"~ of the dog"** "perro peligroso"

bewildered [bɪˈwɪldəd] adj aturdido, perplejo

beyond [bɪˈjɔnd] prep más allá de; (past: understanding) fuera de; (after: date) después de, más allá de; (above) superior a ▷ adv (in space) más allá; (in time) posteriormente; **~ doubt** fuera de toda duda; **~ repair** irreparable

bias [ˈbaɪəs] n (prejudice) prejuicio; (preference) predisposición f

bias(s)ed [ˈbaɪəst] adj parcial

bib [bɪb] n babero

Bible [ˈbaɪbl] n Biblia

bicarbonate of soda [baɪˈkɑːbənɪt-] n bicarbonato sódico

biceps [ˈbaɪsɛps] n bíceps m

bicycle [ˈbaɪsɪkl] n bicicleta; **bicycle pump** n bomba de bicicleta

bid [bɪd] n oferta, postura; (attempt) tentativa, conato ▷ vi hacer una oferta ▷ vt (offer) ofrecer; **to ~ sb good day** dar a algn los buenos días; **bidder** n: **the highest bidder** el mejor postor

bidet [ˈbiːdeɪ] n bidet m

big [bɪg] adj grande; (brother, sister) mayor; **bigheaded** adj engreído; **big toe** n dedo gordo (del pie)

bike [baɪk] n bici f; **bike lane** n carril m bici

bikini [bɪˈkiːnɪ] n bikini m

bilateral [baɪˈlætərl] adj (agreement) bilateral

bilingual [baɪˈlɪŋgwəl] adj bilingüe

bill [bɪl] n cuenta; (invoice) factura; (Pol) proyecto de ley; (US: banknote) billete m; (of bird) pico; (Theat) programa m; **"post no ~s"** "prohibido fijar carteles"; **to fit** or **fill the ~** (fig) cumplir con los requisitos; **billboard** n valla publicitaria; **billfold** n (US) cartera

billiards [ˈbɪljədz] n billar m

billion [ˈbɪljən] n (BRIT) billón m; (US) mil millones mpl

bin [bɪn] n cubo or bote m (LAM) de la basura; (litterbin) papelera

bind (pt, pp **bound**) [baɪnd, baund] vt atar; (book) encuadernar; (oblige) obligar ▷ n (inf: nuisance) lata

binge [bɪndʒ] n: **to go on a ~** ir de juerga

bingo [ˈbɪŋgəu] n bingo m

binoculars [bɪˈnɔkjuləz] npl prismáticos mpl

bio...: biochemistry [baɪəˈkɛmɪstrɪ] n bioquímica; **biodegradable** [ˈbaɪəudɪˈgreɪdəbl] adj biodegradable; **biofuel** [ˈbaɪəufjuəl] n biocombustible m, biocarburante m; **biography** [baɪˈɔgrəfɪ] n biografía; **biological** [baɪəˈlɔdʒɪkəl] adj biológico; **biology** [baɪˈɔlədʒɪ] n biología; **biometric** [baɪəˈmɛtrɪk] adj biométrico

birch [bəːtʃ] n abedul m

bird [bəːd] n ave f, pájaro; (BRIT inf: girl) chica; **bird flu** n gripe aviar; **bird of prey** n ave f de presa; **bird-watching** n: **he likes to go bird-watching on Sundays** los domingos le gusta ir a ver pájaros

Biro® [ˈbaɪrəu] n bolígrafo

birth [bəːθ] n nacimiento; (Med) parto; **to give ~ to** parir, dar a luz a; (fig) dar origen a; **birth certificate** n partida de nacimiento; **birth control** n control m de natalidad; (*methods*) métodos mpl anticonceptivos; **birthday** n cumpleaños m inv; **birthmark** n antojo, marca de nacimiento; **birthplace** n lugar m de nacimiento

biscuit ['bɪskɪt] n (*BRIT*) galleta

bishop ['bɪʃəp] n obispo; (*Chess*) alfil m

bistro ['bi:strəʊ] n café-bar m

bit [bɪt] pt of **bite** ▷ n trozo, pedazo, pedacito; (*Comput*) bit m; (*for horse*) freno, bocado; **a ~ of** un poco de; **a ~ mad** un poco loco; **~ by ~** poco a poco

bitch [bɪtʃ] n (*dog*) perra; (*inf!: woman*) zorra (!)

bite [baɪt] vt, vi (*pt* **bit**, *pp* **bitten**) morder; (*insect etc*) picar ▷ n (*of insect*) picadura; (*mouthful*) bocado; **to ~ one's nails** morderse las uñas; **let's have a ~ (to eat)** vamos a comer algo

bitten ['bɪtn] pp of **bite**

bitter ['bɪtə'] adj amargo; (*wind, criticism*) cortante, penetrante; (*battle*) encarnizado ▷ n (*BRIT: beer*) cerveza típica británica a base de lúpulos

bizarre [bɪ'zɑ:'] adj raro, extraño

black [blæk] adj negro ▷ n color m negro; (*person*): **B~** negro/a ▷ vt (*BRIT Industry*) boicotear; **to give sb a ~ eye** ponerle a algn el ojo morado; **~ coffee** café m solo; **~ and blue** adj amoratado; **black out** vi (*faint*) desmayarse; **blackberry** n zarzamora; **blackbird** n mirlo; **blackboard** n pizarra; **blackcurrant** n grosella negra; **black ice** n hielo invisible en la carretera; **blackmail** n chantaje m ▷ vt chantajear; **black market** n mercado negro; **blackout** n (*Elec*) apagón m; (*TV*) bloqueo informativo; (*fainting*) desmayo, pérdida de conocimiento; **black pepper** n pimienta f negra; **black pudding** n morcilla; **Black Sea** n: **the Black Sea** el Mar Negro

bladder ['blædə'] n vejiga

blade [bleɪd] n hoja; **a ~ of grass** una brizna de hierba

blame [bleɪm] n culpa ▷ vt: **to ~ sb for sth** echar a algn la culpa de algo; **to be to ~ (for)** tener la culpa (de)

bland [blænd] adj (*taste*) soso

blank [blæŋk] adj (*look*) sin expresión ▷ n blanco, espacio en blanco; (*cartridge*) cartucho sin bala or de fogueo; **my mind is a ~** no puedo recordar nada

blanket ['blæŋkɪt] n manta, cobija (*LAM*); (*of snow*) capa; (*of fog*) manto

blast [blɑ:st] n (*of wind*) ráfaga, soplo; (*of explosive*) explosión f ▷ vt (*blow up*) volar

blatant ['bleɪtənt] adj descarado

blaze [bleɪz] n (*fire*) fuego; (*fig*) arranque m ▷ vi (*fire*) arder en llamas; (*fig*) brillar ▷ vt: **to ~ a trail** (*fig*) abrir (un) camino; **in a ~ of publicity** bajo los focos de la publicidad

blazer ['bleɪzə'] n chaqueta de uniforme de colegial o de socio de club

bleach [bli:tʃ] n (*also:* **household ~**) lejía ▷ vt blanquear; **bleachers** npl (*US Sport*) gradas fpl

bleak [bli:k] adj (*countryside*) desierto; (*weather*) desapacible; (*smile*) triste; (*prospect, future*) poco prometedor(a)

bled [bled] pt, pp of **bleed**

bleed [bli:d] (*pt, pp* **bled**) vt sangrar ▷ vi sangrar; **my nose is ~ing** me está sangrando la nariz

blemish ['blemɪʃ] n marca, mancha; (*on reputation*) tacha

blend [blend] n mezcla ▷ vt mezclar ▷ vi (*colours etc*) combinarse, mezclarse; **blender** n (*Culin*) batidora

bless (*pt, pp* **blessed** *or* **blest**) [bles, blest] vt bendecir; **~ you!** (*after sneeze*) ¡Jesús!; **blessing** n bendición f; (*advantage*) beneficio, ventaja; **it was a blessing in disguise** no hay mal que por bien no venga

blew [blu:] pt of **blow**

blight [blaɪt] vt (*hopes etc*) frustrar, arruinar

blind [blaɪnd] adj ciego ▷ n (*for window*) persiana ▷ vt cegar; (*dazzle*) deslumbrar; **to ~ sb to ...** (deceive) cegar a algn a ...; **the blind** npl los ciegos; **blind alley** n callejón m sin salida; **blindfold** n venda ▷ adv con los ojos vendados ▷ vt vendar los ojos a

blink [blɪŋk] vi parpadear, pestañear; (light) oscilar

bliss [blɪs] n felicidad f

blister ['blɪstə^r] n ampolla ▷ vi ampollarse

blizzard ['blɪzəd] n ventisca

bloated ['bləʊtɪd] adj hinchado

blob [blɒb] n (drop) gota; (stain, spot) mancha

block [blɒk] n (also Comput) bloque m; (in pipes) obstáculo; (of buildings) manzana, cuadra (LAM) ▷ vt obstruir, cerrar; (progress) estorbar; **~ of flats** (BRIT) bloque m de pisos; **mental ~** bloqueo mental; **block up** vt tapar, obstruir; (pipe) atascar; **blockade** [blɒ'keɪd] n bloqueo ▷ vt bloquear; **blockage** n estorbo, obstrucción f; **blockbuster** n (book) best-seller m; (film) éxito de público; **block capitals** npl mayúsculas fpl; **block letters** npl mayúsculas fpl

blog [blɒg] n blog m ▷ vi bloguear; **he ~s about politics** tiene un blog sobre política

blogger ['blɒgə^r] n (inf: person) blogero/a

bloke [bləʊk] n (BRIT inf) tipo, tío

blond, blonde [blɒnd] adj, n rubio/a

blood [blʌd] n sangre f; **blood donor** n donante mf de sangre; **blood group** n grupo sanguíneo; **blood poisoning** n septicemia, envenenamiento de la sangre; **blood pressure** n tensión f, presión f sanguínea; **bloodshed** n baño de sangre; **bloodshot** adj inyectado en sangre; **bloodstream** n corriente f sanguínea; **blood test** n análisis m de sangre; **blood transfusion** n transfusión f de sangre; **blood type** n grupo sanguíneo; **blood vessel** n vaso sanguíneo; **bloody** adj sangriento; (BRIT inf!): **this bloody**

... este condenado or puñetero or fregado (LAM ... !) ▷ adv (BRIT inf!): **bloody strong/good** terriblemente fuerte/bueno

bloom [blu:m] n floración f ▷ vi florecer

blossom ['blɒsəm] n flor f ▷ vi florecer

blot [blɒt] n borrón m ▷ vt (stain) manchar

blouse [blauz] n blusa

blow [bləʊ] (pt **blew**, pp **blown**) n golpe m ▷ vi soplar; (fuse) fundirse ▷ vt (fuse) quemar; (instrument) tocar; **to ~ one's nose** sonarse; **blow away** vt llevarse, arrancar; **blow out** vt apagar ▷ vi apagarse; **blow up** vi estallar ▷ vt volar; (tyre) inflar; (Phot) ampliar; **blow-dry** n secado con secador de mano

blown [bləʊn] pp of **blow**

blue [blu:] adj azul; **~ film** película porno; **~ joke** chiste verde; **to come out of the ~** (fig) ser completamente inesperado; **bluebell** n campanilla, campánula azul; **blueberry** n arándano; **blue cheese** n queso azul; **blues** npl: **the blues** (Mus) el blues; **to have the blues** estar triste; **bluetit** n herrerillo m (común)

bluff [blʌf] vi tirarse un farol, farolear ▷ n farol m; **to call sb's ~** coger a algn en un renuncio

blunder ['blʌndə^r] n patinazo, metedura de pata ▷ vi cometer un error, meter la pata

blunt [blʌnt] adj (knife) desafilado; (person) franco, directo

blur [blə:^r] n aspecto borroso; **to become a ~** hacerse borroso ▷ vt (vision) enturbiar; **blurred** adj borroso

blush [blʌʃ] vi ruborizarse, ponerse colorado ▷ n rubor m; **blusher** n colorete m

board [bɔ:d] n tabla, tablero; (on wall) tablón m; (for chess etc) tablero; (committee) junta, consejo; (in firm) mesa or junta directiva; (Naut, Aviat): **on ~** a bordo ▷ vt (ship) embarcarse en; (*train*) subir a; **full ~** (*BRIT*) pensión f completa; **half ~** (*BRIT*) media pensión; **to go by the ~** (*fig*) irse por la borda; **board game** n juego de tablero; **boarding card** n (*BRIT Aviat, Naut*) tarjeta de embarque; **boarding pass** n (*US*) = **boarding card**; **boarding school** n internado; **board room** n sala de juntas

boast [bəust] vi: **to ~ (about** or **of)** alardear (de)

boat [bəut] n barco, buque m; (*small*) barca, bote m

bob [bɔb] vi (*also*: **~ up and down**) menearse, balancearse

body ['bɔdɪ] n cuerpo; (*corpse*) cadáver m; (*of car*) caja, carrocería; (*fig: public body*) organismo; **body-building** n culturismo; **bodyguard** n guardaespaldas m inv; **bodywork** n carrocería

bog [bɔg] n pantano, ciénaga ▷ vt: **to get ~ged down** (*fig*) empantanarse, atascarse

bogus ['bəugəs] adj falso, fraudulento

boil [bɔɪl] vt hervir; (*eggs*) pasar por agua ▷ vi hervir; (*fig: with anger*) estar furioso ▷ n (*Med*) furúnculo, divieso; **to come to the** (*BRIT*) or **a** (*US*) **~** comenzar a hervir; **~ed egg** huevo pasado por agua; **~ed potatoes** patatas fpl or papas fpl (*LAM*) cocidas; **boil over** vi (*liquid*) salirse; (*anger, resentment*) llegar al colmo; **boiler** n caldera; **boiling** adj: **I'm boiling (hot)** (*inf*) estoy asado; **boiling point** n punto de ebullición f

bold [bəuld] adj valiente, audaz; (*pej*) descarado; (*colour*) llamativo

Bolivia [bə'lɪvɪə] n Bolivia; **Bolivian** adj, n boliviano/a

bollard ['bɔləd] n (*BRIT Aut*) poste m

bolt [bəult] n (*lock*) cerrojo; (*with nut*) perno, tornillo ▷ adv: **~ upright** rígido, erguido ▷ vt (*door*) echar el cerrojo a; (*food*) engullir ▷ vi fugarse; (*horse*) desbocarse

bomb [bɔm] n bomba ▷ vt bombardear

bombard [bɔm'bɑːd] vt bombardear; (*fig*) asediar

bomb: bomber n (*Aviat*) bombardero; **bomb scare** n amenaza de bomba

bond [bɔnd] n (*binding promise*) fianza; (*Finance*) bono; (*link*) vínculo, lazo; **in ~** (*Comm*) en depósito bajo fianza

bone [bəun] n hueso; (*of fish*) espina ▷ vt deshuesar; quitar las espinas a

bonfire ['bɔnfaɪə] n hoguera, fogata

bonnet ['bɔnɪt] n gorra; (*BRIT: of car*) capó m

bonus ['bəunəs] n (*payment*) paga extraordinaria, plus m; (*fig*) bendición f

boo [buː] excl ¡uh! ▷ vt abuchear

book [buk] n libro; (*of stamps etc*) librillo; **~s** (*Comm*) cuentas fpl, contabilidad f ▷ vt (*ticket, seat, room*) reservar; **book in** vi (*at hotel*) registrarse; **book up** vt: **the hotel is ~ed up** el hotel está completo; **bookcase** n librería, estante m para libros; **booking** n reserva; **booking office** n (*BRIT: Rail*) despacho de billetes or boletos (*LAM*); (: *Theat*) taquilla, boletería (*LAM*); **book-keeping** n contabilidad f; **booklet** n folleto; **bookmaker** n corredor m de apuestas; **bookmark** n (*Comput*) favorito, marcador m; **bookseller** n librero/a; **bookshelf** n estante m; **bookshop** n librería

book store n = **bookshop**

boom [buːm] n (*noise*) trueno, estampido; (*in prices etc*) alza rápida; (*Econ*) boom m ▷ vi (*cannon*) hacer gran estruendo, retumbar; (*Econ*) estar en alza

boost [buːst] n estímulo, empuje m ▷ vt estimular, empujar

boot [buːt] n bota; (*BRIT: of car*) maleta, maletero ▷ vt (*Comput*) arrancar; **to ~** (*in addition*) además, por añadidura

booth [buːð] n (*telephone booth, voting booth*) cabina

booze [buːz] (inf) n bebida
border ['bɔːdər] n borde m, margen m; (of a country) frontera; (for flowers) arriate m ▷ adj fronterizo; **the B~s** región fronteriza entre Escocia e Inglaterra; **border on** vt fus lindar con; **borderline** n (fig) frontera; **on the borderline** en el límite
bore [bɔːr] pt of **bear** ▷ vt (hole) hacer; (person) aburrir ▷ n (person) pelmazo, pesado; (of gun) calibre m; **bored** adj aburrido; **he's bored to tears** or **to death** or **stiff** está aburrido como una ostra, está muerto de aburrimiento; **boredom** n aburrimiento
boring ['bɔːrɪŋ] adj aburrido
born [bɔːn] adj: **to be ~** nacer; **I was ~ in 1960** nací en 1960
borne [bɔːn] pp of **bear**
borough ['bʌrə] n municipio
borrow ['bɔrəu] vt: **to ~ sth (from sb)** tomar algo prestado (a alguien)
Bosnia ['bɔznɪə] n Bosnia; **Bosnia-Herzegovina, Bosnia-Hercegovina** ['bɔznɪəhɜːtsəˈɡəuviːnə] n Bosnia-Herzegovina; **Bosnian** adj, n bosnio/a
bosom ['buzəm] n pecho
boss [bɔs] n jefe/a m/f ▷ vt (also: ~ **about** or **around**) mangonear; **bossy** adj mandón/ona
both [bəuθ] adj, pron ambos/as, los/las dos; **~ of us went, we ~ went** fuimos los dos, ambos fuimos ▷ adv: **~ A and B** tanto A como B
bother ['bɔðər] vt (worry) preocupar; (disturb) molestar, fastidiar ▷ vi: **to ~ o.s.** molestarse ▷ n (trouble) dificultad f; (nuisance) molestia, lata; **to ~ doing** tomarse la molestia de hacer
bottle ['bɔtl] n botella; (small) frasco; (baby's) biberón m ▷ vt embotellar; **bottle bank** n contenedor m de vidrio; **bottle-opener** n abrebotellas m inv
bottom ['bɔtəm] n (of box, sea) fondo; (buttocks) trasero, culo; (of page, mountain, tree) pie m; (of list) final m ▷ adj (lowest) más bajo; (last) último
bought [bɔːt] pt, pp of **buy**

boulder ['bəuldər] n canto rodado
bounce [bauns] vi (ball) (re)botar; (cheque) ser rechazado ▷ vt hacer (re)botar ▷ n (rebound) (re)bote m; **bouncer** n (inf) gorila m
bound [baund] pt, pp of **bind** ▷ n (leap) salto; (gen pl: limit) límite m ▷ vi (leap) saltar ▷ adj: **~ by** rodeado de; **to be ~ to do sth** (obliged) tener el deber de hacer algo; **he's ~ to come** es seguro que vendrá; **"out of ~s to the public"** "prohibido el paso"; **~ for** con destino a
boundary ['baundrɪ] n límite m, frontera
bouquet ['bukeɪ] n (of flowers) ramo
bourbon ['buəbən] n (US: also: ~ **whiskey**) whisky m americano, bourbon m
bout [baut] n (of malaria etc) ataque m; (Boxing etc) combate m, encuentro
boutique [buːˈtiːk] n boutique f, tienda de ropa
bow¹ [bəu] n (knot) lazo; (weapon, Mus) arco
bow² [bau] n (of the head) reverencia; (Naut: also: ~**s**) proa ▷ vi inclinarse, hacer una reverencia
bowels ['bauəlz] npl intestinos mpl, vientre m; (fig) entrañas fpl
bowl [bəul] n tazón m, cuenco; (ball) bola ▷ vi (Cricket) arrojar la pelota; see also **bowls**; **bowler** n (Cricket) lanzador m (de la pelota); (BRIT: also: **bowler hat**) hongo, bombín m; **bowling** n (game) bolos mpl; **bowling alley** n bolera; **bowling green** n pista para bochas; **bowls** n juego de los bolos, bochas fpl
bow tie ['bəu-] n corbata de lazo, pajarita
box [bɔks] n (also: **cardboard ~**) caja, cajón m; (Theat) palco ▷ vt encajonar ▷ vi (Sport) boxear; **boxer** n (person) boxeador m; (dog) bóxer m; **boxer shorts** npl bóxers; **a pair of boxer shorts** unos bóxers; **boxing** n (Sport) boxeo; **Boxing Day** n (BRIT) día m de San Esteban; **boxing gloves** npl guantes mpl de boxeo; **boxing ring**

n ring *m*, cuadrilátero; **box office** *n* taquilla, boletería (*LAM*)

boy [bɔɪ] *n* (*young*) niño; (*older*) muchacho, chico; (*son*) hijo; **boy band** *n* boy band *m* (*grupo musical de chicos*)

boycott ['bɔɪkɔt] *n* boicot *m* ▷ *vt* boicotear

boyfriend ['bɔɪfrɛnd] *n* novio

bra [brɑː] *n* sostén *m*, sujetador *m*

brace [breɪs] *n* (*BRIT: on teeth*) corrector *m*, aparato; (*tool*) berbiquí *m* ▷ *vt* asegurar, reforzar; **to ~ o.s. (for)** (*fig*) prepararse (para); *see also* **braces**

bracelet ['breɪslɪt] *n* pulsera, brazalete *m*

braces ['breɪsɪz] *npl* (*on teeth*) corrector *m*; (*BRIT: for trousers*) tirantes *mpl*

bracket ['brækɪt] *n* (*Tech*) soporte *m*, puntal *m*; (*group*) clase *f*, categoría; (*also:* **brace ~**) soporte *m*, abrazadera; (*also:* **round ~**) paréntesis *m inv*; **in ~s** entre paréntesis

brag [bræg] *vi* jactarse

braid [breɪd] *n* (*trimming*) galón *m*; (*of hair*) trenza

brain [breɪn] *n* cerebro; **brains** *npl* sesos *mpl*; **she's got ~s** es muy lista

braise [breɪz] *vt* cocer a fuego lento

brake [breɪk] *n* (*on vehicle*) freno ▷ *vi* frenar; **brake light** *n* luz *f* de frenado

bran [bræn] *n* salvado

branch [brɑːntʃ] *n* rama; (*Comm*) sucursal *f* ▷ *vi* ramificarse; (*fig*) extenderse; **branch off** *vi*: **a small road ~es off to the right** hay una carretera pequeña que sale hacia la derecha; **branch out** *vi* (*fig*) extenderse

brand [brænd] *n* marca; (*fig: type*) tipo ▷ *vt* (*cattle*) marcar con hierro candente; **brand name** *n* marca; **brand-new** *adj* flamante, completamente nuevo

brandy ['brændɪ] *n* coñac *m*

brash [bræʃ] *adj* (*cheeky*) descarado

brass [brɑːs] *n* latón *m*; **the ~** (*Mus*) los cobres; **brass band** *n* banda de metal

brat [bræt] *n* (*pej*) mocoso/a

brave [breɪv] *adj* valiente, valeroso ▷ *vt* (*challenge*) desafiar; (*resist*) aguantar; **bravery** *n* valor *m*, valentía

Brazil [brə'zɪl] *n* (el) Brasil; **Brazilian** *adj*, *n* brasileño/a

breach [briːtʃ] *vt* abrir brecha en ▷ *n* (*gap*) brecha; (*breaking*): **~ of contract** infracción *f* de contrato; **~ of the peace** perturbación *f* del orden público

bread [brɛd] *n* pan *m*; **breadbin** *n* panera; **breadbox** *n* (*US*) panera; **breadcrumbs** *npl* migajas *fpl*; (*Culin*) pan *msg* rallado

breadth [brɛtθ] *n* anchura; (*fig*) amplitud *f*

break [breɪk] (*pt* **broke**, *pp* **broken**) *vt* romper; (*promise*) faltar a; (*law*) violar, infringir; (*record*) batir ▷ *vi* romperse, quebrarse; (*storm*) estallar; (*weather*) cambiar; (*news etc*) darse a conocer ▷ *n* (*gap*) abertura; (*fracture*) fractura; (*time*) intervalo; (*: at school*) (período de) recreo; (*chance*) oportunidad *f*; **break down** *vt* (*figures, data*) analizar, descomponer ▷ *vi* estropearse; (*Aut*) averiarse; (*person*) romper a llorar; (*talks*) fracasar; **break in** *vt* (*horse etc*) domar ▷ *vi* (*burglar*) forzar una entrada; **break into** *vt fus* (*house*) forzar; **break off** *vi* (*speaker*) pararse, detenerse; (*branch*) partir; **break out** *vi* estallar; (*prisoner*) escaparse; **to ~ out in spots** salir a algn granos; **break up** *vi* (*marriage*) deshacerse; (*ship*) hacerse pedazos; (*crowd, meeting*) disolverse; (*Scol*) terminar (el curso); (*line*) cortarse ▷ *vt* (*rocks etc*) partir; (*journey*) partir; (*fight etc*) acabar con; **the line's** or **you're ~ing up** se corta; **breakdown** *n* (*Aut*) avería; (*in communications*) interrupción *f*; (*Med: also:* **nervous breakdown**) colapso, crisis *f* nerviosa; (*of marriage, talks*) fracaso; (*of figures*) desglose *m*;

breakdown truck, breakdown van n (camión m) grúa

breakfast ['brɛkfəst] n desayuno

break: break-in n robo con allanamiento de morada; **breakthrough** n (fig) avance m

breast [brɛst] n (of woman) pecho, seno; (chest) pecho; (of bird) pechuga; **breast-feed** vt, vi (irreg: like **feed**) amamantar, dar el pecho

breaststroke ['brɛststrəuk] n braza de pecho

breath [brɛθ] n aliento, respiración f; **to take a deep ~** respirar hondo; **out of ~** sin aliento, sofocado

Breathalyser® ['brɛθəlaɪzəʳ] n (BRIT) alcoholímetro m

breathe [bri:ð] vt, vi respirar; **breathe in** vt, vi aspirar; **breathe out** vt, vi espirar; **breathing** n respiración f

breath: breathless adj sin aliento, jadeante; **breathtaking** adj imponente, pasmoso; **breath test** n prueba de la alcoholemia

bred [brɛd] pt, pp of **breed**

breed [bri:d] (pt, pp **bred**) vt criar ▷ vi reproducirse, procrear ▷ n raza, casta

breeze [bri:z] n brisa

breezy ['bri:zɪ] adj de mucho viento, ventoso; (person) despreocupado

brew [bru:] vt (tea) hacer; (beer) elaborar ▷ vi (fig: trouble) prepararse; (storm) amenazar; **brewery** n fábrica de cerveza

bribe [braɪb] n soborno ▷ vt sobornar, cohechar; **bribery** n soborno, cohecho

bric-a-brac ['brɪkəbræk] n inv baratijas fpl

brick [brɪk] n ladrillo; **bricklayer** n albañil m

bride n novia; **bridegroom** n novio; **bridesmaid** n dama de honor

bridge [brɪdʒ] n puente m; (Naut) puente m de mando; (of nose) caballete m; (Cards) bridge m ▷ vt (fig): **to ~ a gap** llenar un vacío

bridle ['braɪdl] n brida, freno

brief [bri:f] adj breve, corto ▷ n (Law) escrito ▷ vt informar; **briefcase** n cartera, portafolio(s) m inv (LAM); **briefing** n (Press) informe m; **briefly** adv (smile, glance) brevemente; (explain, say) en pocas palabras

briefs npl (for men) calzoncillos mpl; (for women) bragas fpl

brigadier [brɪgə'dɪəʳ] n general m de brigada

bright [braɪt] adj brillante; (room) luminoso; (day) de sol; (person: clever) listo, inteligente; (: lively) alegre; (colour) vivo; (future) prometedor(a)

brilliant ['brɪljənt] adj brillante; (clever) genial

brim [brɪm] n borde m; (of hat) ala

brine [braɪn] n (Culin) salmuera

bring [brɪŋ] (pt, pp **brought**) vt (thing) traer; (person) conducir; **bring about** vt ocasionar, producir; **bring back** vt volver a traer; (return) devolver; **bring down** vt (government, plane) derribar; (price) rebajar; **bring in** vt (harvest) recoger; (person) hacer entrar or pasar; (object) traer; (Pol: bill, law) presentar; (produce: income) producir, rendir; **bring on** vt (illness, attack) producir, causar; (player, substitute) sacar (de la reserva), hacer salir; **bring out** vt (object) sacar; (book) publicar; **bring round** vt (unconscious person) hacer volver en sí; (convince) convencer; **bring up** vt (person) educar, criar; (question) sacar a colación; (food: vomit) devolver, vomitar

brink [brɪŋk] n borde m

brisk [brɪsk] adj (walk) enérgico, vigoroso; (speedy) rápido; (wind) fresco; (trade) activo; (abrupt) brusco

bristle ['brɪsl] n cerda ▷ vi (fur) erizarse; **to ~ in anger** temblar de rabia

Brit [brɪt] n abbr (inf: = British person) británico/a

Britain ['brɪtən] n (also: **Great ~**) Gran Bretaña

British [ˈbrɪtɪʃ] adj británico; **the British** npl los británicos; **the British Isles** npl las Islas Británicas

Briton [ˈbrɪtən] n británico/a

brittle [ˈbrɪtl] adj quebradizo, frágil

broad [brɔːd] adj ancho; (range) amplio; (accent) cerrado; **in ~ daylight** en pleno día; **broadband** n banda ancha; **broad bean** n haba; **broadcast** (pt, pp **broadcast**) n emisión f ▷ vt (Radio) emitir; (TV) transmitir ▷ vi emitir; transmitir; **broaden** vt ampliar ▷ vi ensancharse; **to broaden one's mind** hacer más tolerante a algn; **broadly** adv en general; **broad-minded** adj tolerante, liberal

broccoli [ˈbrɔkəlɪ] n brécol m

brochure [ˈbrəʊʃjuəʳ] n folleto

broil [brɔɪl] vt (US) asar a la parrilla

broiler [ˈbrɔɪləʳ] n (grill) parilla

broke [brəʊk] pt of **break** ▷ adj (inf) pelado, sin blanca

broken [ˈbrəʊkən] pp of **break** ▷ adj roto; **~ leg** pierna rota; **in ~ English** en un inglés chapurreado

broken-down [ˈbrəʊkn'daʊn] adj (car) averiado; (machine) estropeado

broker [ˈbrəʊkəʳ] n corredor(a) m/f de bolsa

bronchitis [brɔŋ'kaɪtɪs] n bronquitis f

bronze [brɔnz] n bronce m

brooch [brəʊtʃ] n broche m

brood [bruːd] n camada, cría ▷ vi (hen) empollar; **to ~ over** dar vueltas a

broom [brum] n escoba; (Bot) retama

Bros. abbr (Comm: = Brothers) Hnos

broth [brɔθ] n caldo

brothel [ˈbrɔθl] n burdel m

brother [ˈbrʌðəʳ] n hermano; **brother-in-law** n cuñado

brought [brɔːt] pt, pp of **bring**

brow [brau] n (forehead) frente f; (eyebrow) ceja; (of hill) cumbre f

brown [braun] adj marrón; (hair) castaño; (tanned) moreno ▷ n (colour) marrón m ▷ vt (Culin) dorar; **brown bread** n pan m integral

Brownie [ˈbrauni] n niña exploradora

brown rice n arroz m integral

brown sugar n azúcar m moreno

browse [brauz] vi (animal) pacer; (among books) hojear libros; **to ~ through a book** hojear un libro; **browser** n (Comput) navegador m

bruise [bruːz] n (on person) cardenal m ▷ vt magullar

brunette [bruː'nɛt] n morena

brush [brʌʃ] n cepillo; (for painting, shaving etc) brocha; (artist's) pincel m ▷ vt (sweep) barrer; (groom) cepillar; **to ~ past, ~ against** rozar al pasar

Brussels [ˈbrʌslz] n Bruselas

Brussels sprout n col f de Bruselas

brutal [ˈbruːtl] adj brutal

BSc abbr (= Bachelor of Science) licenciado en Ciencias

BSE n abbr (= bovine spongiform encephalopathy) encefalopatía espongiforme bovina

bubble [ˈbʌbl] n burbuja ▷ vi burbujear, borbotar; **bubble bath** n espuma para el baño; **bubble gum** n chicle m (de globo); **bubblejet printer** [ˈbʌbldʒet-] n impresora de inyección por burbujas

buck [bʌk] n (rabbit) macho; (deer) gamo; (US inf) dólar m ▷ vi corcovear; **to pass the ~ (to sb)** echar (a algn) el muerto

bucket [ˈbʌkɪt] n cubo, balde m (esp LAM)

buckle [ˈbʌkl] n hebilla ▷ vt abrochar con hebilla ▷ vi combarse

bud [bʌd] n (of plant) brote m, yema; (of flower) capullo ▷ vi brotar, echar brote

Buddhism [ˈbudɪzm] n Budismo

Buddhist [ˈbudɪst] adj, n budista mf

buddy [ˈbʌdɪ] n (US) compañero, compinche m

budge [bʌdʒ] vt mover; (fig) hacer ceder ▷ vi moverse

budgerigar [ˈbʌdʒərɪgaːʳ] n periquito

budget [ˈbʌdʒɪt] n presupuesto ▷ vi; **to ~ for sth** presupuestar algo

budgie [ˈbʌdʒɪ] n = **budgerigar**

buff [bʌf] adj (colour) color de ante ▷ n (enthusiast) entusiasta mf

buffalo ['bʌfələu] (pl **buffalo** or **buffaloes**) n (BRIT) búfalo; (US: bison) bisonte m

buffer ['bʌfəʳ] n (Rail) tope m; (Comput) memoria intermedia, buffer m

buffet ['bufeɪ] n (BRIT: bar) bar m, cafetería; (food) buffet m; **buffet car** n (BRIT Rail) coche-restaurante m

bug [bʌg] n (insect) bicho, sabandija; (germ) microbio, bacilo; (spy device) micrófono oculto; (Comput) error m ▷ vt (annoy) fastidiar; (room) poner un micrófono oculto en

build [bɪld] n (of person) tipo ▷ vt (pt, pp **built**) construir, edificar; **build up** vt (morale, forces, production) acrecentar; (stocks) acumular; **builder** n (contractor) contratista mf

building ['bɪldɪŋ] n construcción f; (habitation, offices) edificio; **building site** n obra, solar m (SP); **building society** n (BRIT) sociedad f de préstamo inmobiliario

built [bɪlt] pt, pp of **build**; **built-in** adj (cupboard) empotrado; (device) interior, incorporado; **built-up** adj (area) urbanizado

bulb [bʌlb] n (Bot) bulbo; (Elec) bombilla, bombillo (LAM), foco (LAM)

Bulgaria [bʌlˈgɛərɪə] n Bulgaria; **Bulgarian** adj búlgaro ▷ n búlgaro/a

bulge [bʌldʒ] n bulto ▷ vi bombearse, pandearse; **to ~ (with)** rebosar (de)

bulimia [bəˈlɪmɪə] n bulimia

bulimic adj, n bulímico/a

bulk [bʌlk] n (mass) bulto, volumen m; **in ~** (Comm) a granel; **the ~ of** la mayor parte de; **bulky** adj voluminoso, abultado

bull [bul] n toro

bulldozer ['buldəuzəʳ] n buldozer m

bullet ['bulɪt] n bala; **~ wound** balazo

bulletin ['bulɪtɪn] n comunicado, parte m; (journal) boletín m; **bulletin board** n (US) tablón m de anuncios; (Comput) tablero de noticias

bullfight ['bulfaɪt] n corrida de toros; **bullfighter** n torero; **bullfighting** n los toros mpl, el toreo

bully ['bulɪ] n valentón m, matón m ▷ vt intimidar, tiranizar; **bullying** n (at school) acoso escolar

bum [bʌm] n (inf: BRIT: backside) culo; (esp US: tramp) vagabundo

bumblebee ['bʌmblbiː] n abejorro

bump [bʌmp] n (blow) tope m, choque m; (jolt) sacudida; (on road etc) bache m; (on head) chichón m ▷ vt (strike) chocar contra; **bump into** vt fus chocar contra, tropezar con; (person) topar con; **bumper** n (BRIT) parachoques m inv ▷ adj: **bumper crop/harvest** cosecha abundante; **bumpy** adj (road) lleno de baches

bun [bʌn] n (BRIT: cake) pastel m; (US: bread) bollo; (of hair) moño

bunch [bʌntʃ] n (of flowers) ramo; (of keys) manojo; (of bananas) piña; (of people) grupo; (pej) pandilla; **bunches** npl (in hair) coletas fpl

bundle ['bʌndl] n bulto, fardo; (of sticks) haz m; (of papers) legajo ▷ vt (also: **~ up**) atar, envolver; **to ~ sth/sb into** meter algo/a algn precipitadamente en

bungalow ['bʌŋgələu] n bungalow m, chalé m

bungee jumping ['bʌndʒiːˈdʒʌmpɪŋ] n puenting m, banyi m

bunion ['bʌnjən] n juanete m

bunk [bʌŋk] n litera; **~ beds** npl literas fpl

bunker ['bʌŋkəʳ] n (coal store) carbonera; (Mil) refugio; (Golf) bunker m

bunny ['bʌnɪ] n (also: **~ rabbit**) conejito

buoy [bɔɪ] n boya; **buoyant** adj (ship) capaz de flotar; (carefree) boyante, optimista; (Comm: market, prices etc) sostenido; (: economy) boyante

burden ['bəːdn] n carga ▷ vt cargar

bureau (pl **bureaux**) ['bjuərəu, -z] n (BRIT: writing desk) escritorio, buró m;

(US: *chest of drawers*) cómoda; (*office*) oficina, agencia

bureaucracy [bjʊəˈrɔkrəsɪ] n burocracia

bureaucrat [ˈbjʊərəkræt] n burócrata *mf*

bureau de change [-dəˈʃɑ̃ʒ] (pl **bureaux de change**) n caja *f* de cambio

bureaux [ˈbjʊərəuz] npl of **bureau**

burger [ˈbəːgəʳ] n hamburguesa

burglar [ˈbəːgləʳ] n ladrón/ona *m/f*; **burglar alarm** n alarma *f* contra robo; **burglary** n robo con allanamiento or fractura, robo de una casa

burial [ˈbɛrɪəl] n entierro

burn [bəːn] (pt, pp **burned** or **burnt**) vt quemar; (*house*) incendiar ▷ vi quemarse, arder; incendiarse; (*sting*) escocer ▷ n (Med) quemadura; **burn down** vt incendiar; **burn out** vt (*writer etc*): **to ~ o.s. out** agotarse; **burning** adj (*building, forest*) en llamas; (*hot: sand etc*) abrasador(a); (*ambition*) ardiente

Burns' Night [bəːnz-] n ver nota "Burns' Night"

BURNS' NIGHT

Cada veinticinco de enero los escoceses celebran la llamada *Burns' Night* (noche de Burns), en honor al poeta escocés Robert Burns (1759-1796). Es tradición hacer una cena en la que, al son de la música de la gaita escocesa, se sirve *haggis*, plato tradicional de asadura de cordero cocida en el estómago del animal, acompañado de nabos y puré de patatas. Durante la misma se recitan poemas del autor y varios discursos conmemorativos de carácter festivo.

burnt [bəːnt] pt, pp of **burn**

burp [bəːp] (inf) n eructo ▷ vi eructar

burrow [ˈbʌrəu] n madriguera ▷ vt hacer una madriguera

burst [bəːst] (pt, pp **burst**) vt (*balloon, pipe*) reventar; (*banks etc*) romper ▷ vi reventarse; romperse; (*tyre*) pincharse ▷ n (*explosion*) estallido; (*also:* **~ pipe**) reventón m; **to ~ out laughing** soltar la carcajada; **to ~ into tears** deshacerse en lágrimas; **to be ~ing with** reventar de; **a ~ of energy** una explosión de energía; **a ~ of speed** un acelerón; **to ~ open** abrirse de golpe; **burst into** vt fus (*room etc*) irrumpir en

bury [ˈbɛrɪ] vt enterrar; (*body*) enterrar, sepultar

bus [bʌs] n autobús m; **bus conductor** n cobrador(a) *m/f*

bush [buʃ] n arbusto; (*scrub land*) monte m bajo; **to beat about the ~** andar(se) con rodeos

business [ˈbɪznɪs] n (*matter, affair*) asunto; (*trading*) comercio, negocios mpl; (*firm*) empresa, casa; (*occupation*) oficio; **to be away on ~** estar en viaje de negocios; **it's my ~ to ...** me toca or corresponde ...; **it's none of my ~** no es asunto mío; **he means ~** habla en serio; **business class** n (Aviat) clase *f* preferente; **businesslike** adj eficiente; **businessman** n hombre m de negocios; **business trip** n viaje m de negocios; **businesswoman** n mujer *f* de negocios

busker [ˈbʌskəʳ] n (BRIT) músico/a ambulante

bus: bus pass n bonobús; **bus shelter** n parada cubierta; **bus station** n estación *f* or terminal *f* de autobuses; **bus-stop** n parada de autobús

bust [bʌst] n (Anat) pecho; (*sculpture*) busto ▷ adj (inf: *broken*) roto, estropeado; **to go ~** quebrar

bustling [ˈbʌslɪŋ] adj (*town*) animado, bullicioso

busy [ˈbɪzɪ] adj ocupado, atareado; (*shop, street*) concurrido, animado ▷ vt: **to ~ o.s. with** ocuparse en; **the line's ~** está comunicando; **busy signal** n (US Tel) señal *f* de comunicando

KEYWORD

but [bʌt] *conj* **1** pero; **he's not very bright, but he's hard-working** no es muy inteligente, pero es trabajador **2** (*in direct contradiction*) sino; **he's not English but French** no es inglés sino francés; **he didn't sing but he shouted** no cantó sino que gritó **3** (*showing disagreement, surprise etc*): **but that's far too expensive!** ¡pero eso es carísimo!; **but it does work!** ¡(pero) sí que funciona!
▶ *prep* (*apart from, except*) menos, salvo; **we've had nothing but trouble** no hemos tenido más que problemas; **no-one but him can do it** nadie más que él puede hacerlo; **who but a lunatic would do such a thing?** ¡sólo un loco haría una cosa así!; **but for you/your help** si no fuera por ti/tu ayuda; **anything but that** cualquier cosa menos eso
▶ *adv* (*just, only*): **she's but a child** no es más que una niña; **had I but known** si lo hubiera sabido; **I can but try** al menos lo puedo intentar; **it's all but finished** está casi acabado

butcher [ˈbʊtʃəʳ] *n* carnicero/a ▶ *vt* hacer una carnicería con; (*cattle etc for meat*) matar; **~'s (shop)** carnicería
butler [ˈbʌtləʳ] *n* mayordomo
butt [bʌt] *n* (*cask*) tonel *m*; (*of gun*) culata; (*of cigarette*) colilla; (BRIT *fig: target*) blanco ▶ *vt* dar cabezadas contra
butter [ˈbʌtəʳ] *n* mantequilla ▶ *vt* untar con mantequilla; **buttercup** *n* ranúnculo
butterfly [ˈbʌtəflaɪ] *n* mariposa; (Swimming: *also*: **~ stroke**) (braza de) mariposa
buttocks [ˈbʌtəks] *npl* nalgas *fpl*
button [ˈbʌtn] *n* botón *m* ▶ *vt* (*also*: **~ up**) abotonar, abrochar ▶ *vi* abrocharse
buy [baɪ] (*pt, pp* **bought**) *vt* comprar ▶ *n* compra; **to ~ sb sth/sth from sb**

comprarle algo a algn; **to ~ sb a drink** invitar a algn a tomar algo; **buy out** *vt* (*partner*) comprar la parte de; **buy up** *vt* (*property*) acaparar; (*stock*) comprar todas las existencias de; **buyer** *n* comprador(a) *m/f*; **buyer's market** mercado favorable al comprador
buzz [bʌz] *n* zumbido; (*inf: phone call*) llamada (telefónica) ▶ *vi* zumbar; **buzzer** *n* timbre *m*

KEYWORD

by [baɪ] *prep* **1** (*referring to cause, agent*) por; de; **abandoned by his mother** abandonado por su madre; **a painting by Picasso** un cuadro de Picasso
2 (*referring to method, manner, means*): **by bus/car/train** en autobús/coche/ tren; **to pay by cheque** pagar con cheque; **by moonlight/candlelight** a la luz de la luna/una vela; **by saving hard, he ...** ahorrando, ...
3 (*via, through*) por; **we came by Dover** vinimos por Dover
4 (*close to, past*): **the house by the river** la casa junto al río; **she rushed by me** pasó a mi lado como una exhalación; **I go by the post office every day** paso por delante de Correos todos los días
5 (*time: not later than*) para; (: *during*): **by daylight** de día; **by 4 o'clock** para las cuatro; **by this time tomorrow** mañana a estas horas; **by the time I got here it was too late** cuando llegué ya era demasiado tarde
6 (*amount*): **by the metre/kilo** por metro/kilo; **paid by the hour** pagado por hora
7 (*in measurements, sums*): **to divide/ multiply by 3** dividir/multiplicar por 3; **a room 3 metres by 4** una habitación de 3 metros por 4; **it's broader by a metre** es un metro más ancho
8 (*according to*) según, de acuerdo con; **it's 3 o'clock by my watch** según mi

reloj, son las tres; **it's all right by me** por mí, está bien

9: (all) by oneself *etc* todo solo; **he did it (all) by himself** lo hizo él solo; **he was standing (all) by himself in a corner** estaba de pie solo en un rincón

10: by the way a propósito, por cierto; **this wasn't my idea, by the way** pues, no fue idea mía

▶ *adv* 1 *see* **go, pass**

2: by and by finalmente; **they'll come back by and by** acabarán volviendo; **by and large** en líneas generales, en general

by-election *n* (*BRIT*) elección *f* parcial
bypass ['baɪpɑːs] *n* carretera de circunvalación; (*Med*) (operación *f* de) bypass *m* ▷ *vt* evitar
byte [baɪt] *n* (*Comput*) byte *m*, octeto

C, c [si:] *n* (*Mus*) do *m*
cab [kæb] *n* taxi *m*; (*of truck*) cabina
cabaret ['kæbəreɪ] *n* cabaret *m*
cabbage ['kæbɪdʒ] *n* col *f*, berza
cabin ['kæbɪn] *n* cabaña; (*on ship*) camarote *m*; **cabin crew** *n* tripulación *f* de cabina
cabinet ['kæbɪnɪt] *n* (*Pol*) consejo de ministros; (*furniture*) armario; (*also:* **display ~**) vitrina; **cabinet minister** *n* ministro/a (del gabinete)
cable ['keɪbl] *n* cable *m* ▷ *vt* cablegrafiar; **cable car** *n* teleférico; **cable television** *n* televisión *f* por cable
cactus (*pl* **cacti**) ['kæktəs, -taɪ] *n* cacto
café ['kæfeɪ] *n* café *m*
cafeteria [kæfɪ'tɪərɪə] *n* cafetería (*con autoservicio para comer*)
caffeine ['kæfiːn] *n* cafeína
cage [keɪdʒ] *n* jaula
cagoule [kə'guːl] *n* chubasquero

cake [keɪk] n (large) tarta; (small) pastel m; (of soap) pastilla

calcium ['kælsɪəm] n calcio

calculate ['kælkjuleɪt] vt calcular; **calculation** n cálculo, cómputo; **calculator** n calculadora

calendar ['kæləndəʳ] n calendario

calf [kɑːf] (pl **calves**) n (of cow) ternero, becerro; (of other animals) cría; (also: **~skin**) piel f de becerro; (Anat) pantorrilla

calibre, (US) **caliber** ['kælɪbəʳ] n calibre m

call [kɔːl] vt llamar; (meeting, strike) convocar ▷ vi (shout) llamar; (telephone) llamar (por teléfono); (visit: also: **~ in, ~ round**) hacer una visita ▷ n llamada; (of bird) canto; **to be ~ed** llamarse; **on ~** (nurse, doctor etc) de guardia; **call back** vi (return) volver; (Tel) volver a llamar; **call for** vt fus (demand) pedir, exigir; (fetch) pasar a recoger; **call in** vt (doctor, expert, police) llamar; **call off** vt (cancel: meeting, race) cancelar; (: deal) anular; (: strike) desconvocar; **call on** vt fus (visit) ir a ver; (turn to) acudir a; **call out** vi gritar; **call up** vt (Mil) llamar a filas; **callbox** n (BRIT) cabina telefónica; **call centre** n (BRIT) centro de atención al cliente; **caller** n visita f; (Tel) usuario/a

callous ['kæləs] adj insensible, cruel

calm [kɑːm] adj tranquilo, (sea) tranquilo, en calma ▷ n calma, tranquilidad f ▷ vt calmar, tranquilizar; **calm down** vi calmarse, tranquilizarse ▷ vt calmar, tranquilizar; **calmly** adv tranquilamente, con calma

Calor gas® ['kæləʳ-] n butano

calorie ['kælərɪ] n caloría

calves [kɑːvz] npl of **calf**

camcorder ['kæmkɔːdəʳ] n videocámara

came [keɪm] pt of **come**

camel ['kæməl] n camello

camera ['kæmərə] n cámara or máquina fotográfica; (Cine, TV)

cámara; **in ~** (Law) a puerta cerrada; **cameraman** n cámara m; **camera phone** n teléfono m con cámara

camouflage ['kæməflɑːʒ] n camuflaje m ▷ vt camuflar

camp [kæmp] n campamento, camping m; (Mil) campamento; (for prisoners) campo; (fig: faction) bando ▷ vi acampar ▷ adj afectado, afeminado; **to go ~ing** ir de or hacer camping

campaign [kæm'peɪn] n (Mil, Pol etc) campaña ▷ vi: **to ~ (for/against)** hacer campaña (a favor de/en contra de); **campaigner** n: **campaigner for** defensor(a) m/f de

camp: campbed n (BRIT) cama plegable; **camper** n campista mf; (vehicle) caravana; **campground** n (US) camping m, campamento; **camping** n camping m; **campsite** n camping m

campus ['kæmpəs] n campus m

can¹ [kæn] n (of oil, water) bidón m; (tin) lata, bote m ▷ vt enlatar

○ **KEYWORD**

can² [kæn] (negative **cannot, can't**, conditional, pt **could**) aux vb **1** (be able to) poder; **you can do it if you try** puedes hacerlo si lo intentas; **I can't see you** no te veo

2 (know how to) saber; **I can swim/ play tennis/drive** sé nadar/jugar al tenis/conducir; **can you speak French?** ¿hablas or sabes hablar francés?

3 (may) poder; **can I use your phone?** ¿me dejas or puedo usar tu teléfono?

4 (expressing disbelief, puzzlement etc): **it can't be true!** ¡no puede ser (verdad)!; **what CAN he want?** ¿qué querrá?

5 (expressing possibility, suggestion etc): **he could be in the library** podría estar en la biblioteca; **she could have been delayed** puede que se haya retrasado

Canada ['kænədə] n Canadá m;
  Canadian [kə'neɪdɪən] adj, n
  canadiense mf
canal [kə'næl] n canal m
canary [kə'nɛərɪ] n canario
Canary Islands npl las (Islas) Canarias
cancel ['kænsəl] vt cancelar;
  (train) suprimir; (cross out) tachar;
  cancellation [kænsə'leɪʃən] n
  cancelación f; supresión f
cancer ['kænsəʳ] n cáncer m; **C~**
  (Astro) Cáncer m
candidate ['kændɪdeɪt] n
  candidato/a
candle ['kændl] n vela; (in church)
  cirio; **candlestick** n (single) candelero;
  (: low) palmatoria; (bigger, ornate)
  candelabro
candy ['kændɪ] n azúcar m cande; (US)
  caramelo; **candy bar** (US) n barrita
  (dulce); **candyfloss** n (BRIT) algodón
  m (azucarado)
cane [keɪn] n (Bot) caña; (stick) vara,
  palmeta ▷ vt (BRIT Scol) castigar (con
  palmeta)
canister ['kænɪstəʳ] n bote m, lata
cannabis ['kænəbɪs] n canabis m
canned [kænd] adj en lata, de lata
cannon ['kænən] (pl **cannon** or
  cannons) n cañón m
cannot ['kænɔt] = **can not**
canoe [kə'nu:] n canoa; (Sport)
  piragua; **canoeing** n piragüismo
canon ['kænən] n (clergyman)
  canónigo; (standard) canon m
can opener n abrelatas m inv
can't [kænt] = **can not**
canteen [kæn'ti:n] n (eating place)
  comedor m; (BRIT: of cutlery) juego
canter ['kæntəʳ] vi ir a medio galope
canvas ['kænvəs] n (material) lona;
  (painting) lienzo; (Naut) velamen m
canvass ['kænvəs] vi (Pol): **to ~
  for** solicitar votos por ▷ vt (Comm)
  sondear
canyon ['kænjən] n cañón m
cap [kæp] n (hat) gorra; (of pen)
  capuchón m; (of bottle) tapón m, tapa;

(BRIT: contraceptive) diafragma m ▷ vt
  (outdo) superar; (limit) recortar
capability [keɪpə'bɪlɪtɪ] n
  capacidad f
capable ['keɪpəbl] adj capaz
capacity [kə'pæsɪtɪ] n capacidad f;
  (position) calidad f
cape [keɪp] n capa; (Culin: also: ~s)
  alcaparra; (prank) travesura
caper ['keɪpəʳ] n (Culin: also: ~s)
  alcaparra; (prank) travesura
capital ['kæpɪtl] n (also: ~ **city**) capital
  f; (money) capital m; (also: ~ **letter**)
  mayúscula; **capitalism** n capitalismo;
  capitalist adj, n capitalista mf;
  capital punishment n pena de
  muerte
Capitol ['kæpɪtl] n: **the ~** el
  Capitolio

  ○ **CAPITOL**
  ○
  ● El Capitolio (Capitol) es el edificio en
  ● el que se reúne el Congreso de los
  ● Estados Unidos (Congress), situado
  ● en la ciudad de Washington. Por
  ● extensión, también se suele llamar
  ● así al edificio en el que tienen lugar
  ● las sesiones parlamentarias de
  ● la cámara de representantes de
  ● muchos de los estados.

Capricorn ['kæprɪkɔ:n] n
  Capricornio
capsize [kæp'saɪz] vt volcar, hacer
  zozobrar ▷ vi volcarse, zozobrar
capsule ['kæpsju:l] n cápsula
captain ['kæptɪn] n capitán m
caption ['kæpʃən] n (heading) título;
  (to picture) leyenda
captivity [kæp'tɪvɪtɪ] n cautiverio
capture ['kæptʃəʳ] vt capturar; (place)
  tomar; (attention) captar, llamar ▷ n
  captura; toma; (Comput: also: **data ~**)
  formulación f de datos
car [kɑ:ʳ] n coche m, carro (LAM),
  automóvil m; (US Rail) vagón m
carafe [kə'ræf] n jarra
caramel ['kærəməl] n caramelo

carat ['kærət] n quilate m
caravan ['kærəvæn] n (BRIT) caravana, rulot m; (of camels) caravana; **caravan site** n (BRIT) camping m para caravanas
carbohydrates [kɑ:bəu'haɪdreɪts] npl (foods) hidratos mpl de carbono
carbon ['kɑ:bən] n carbono; **carbon dioxide** n dióxido de carbono, anhídrido carbónico; **carbon footprint** n huella de carbono; **carbon monoxide** n monóxido de carbono
car boot sale n mercadillo (de objetos usados expuestos en el maletero del coche)
carburettor, (US) **carburetor** [kɑ:bju'retə'] n carburador m
card [kɑ:d] n (thin cardboard) cartulina; (playing card) carta, naipe m; (visiting card, greetings card etc) tarjeta; (index card) ficha; **cardboard** n cartón m, cartulina; **card game** n juego de naipes or cartas
cardigan ['kɑ:dɪgən] n rebeca
cardinal ['kɑ:dɪnl] adj cardinal; (importance, principal) esencial ▷ n cardenal m
cardphone ['kɑ:dfəun] n cabina que funciona con tarjetas telefónicas
care [kɛə'] n cuidado; (worry) preocupación f; (charge) cargo, custodia ▷ vi: **to ~ about** preocuparse por; **~ of** (c/o) en casa de, al cuidado de; **in sb's ~** a cargo de algn; **to take ~ to** cuidarse de, tener cuidado de; **to take ~ of** vt cuidar; **I don't ~** no me importa; **I couldn't ~ less** me trae sin cuidado; **care for** vt fus cuidar; (like) querer
career [kə'rɪə'] n profesión f ▷ vi (also: **~ along**) correr a toda velocidad
care: **carefree** adj despreocupado; **careful** adj cuidadoso; (cautious) cauteloso; **(be) careful!** ¡(ten) cuidado!; **carefully** adv con cuidado, cuidadosamente; **caregiver** (US) n (professional) enfermero/a; (unpaid) persona que cuida a un pariente o vecino; **careless** adj descuidado; (heedless) poco atento; **carelessness** n descuido, falta de atención; **carer** n (professional) enfermero/a; (unpaid) persona que cuida a un pariente o vecino; **caretaker** n portero/a, conserje mf
car-ferry ['kɑ:fɛrɪ] n transbordador m para coches
cargo ['kɑ:gəu] (pl **cargoes**) n cargamento, carga
car hire n alquiler m de coches
Caribbean [kærɪ'bi:ən] adj caribe, caribeño; **the ~ (Sea)** el (Mar) Caribe
caring ['kɛərɪŋ] adj humanitario
carnation [kɑ:'neɪʃən] n clavel m
carnival ['kɑ:nɪvəl] n carnaval m; (US) parque m de atracciones
carol ['kærəl] n: **(Christmas) ~** villancico
carousel [kærə'sɛl] n (US) tiovivo, caballitos mpl
car park n (BRIT) aparcamiento, parking m
carpenter ['kɑ:pɪntə'] n carpintero/a
carpet ['kɑ:pɪt] n alfombra ▷ vt alfombrar; **fitted ~** moqueta
car rental n (US) alquiler m de coches
carriage ['kærɪdʒ] n (BRIT Rail) vagón m; (horse-drawn) coche m; (for goods) transporte m; **~ paid** porte pagado; **carriageway** n (BRIT: part of road) calzada
carrier ['kærɪə'] n transportista mf; (company) empresa de transportes; (Med) portador(a) m/f; **carrier bag** n (BRIT) bolsa de papel or plástico
carrot ['kærət] n zanahoria
carry ['kærɪ] vt (person) llevar; (transport) transportar; (involve: responsibilities etc) entrañar ▷ vi (sound) oírse; **to get carried away** (fig) entusiasmarse; **carry on** vi (continue) seguir (adelante), continuar ▷ vt seguir, continuar; **carry out** vt (orders) cumplir; (investigation) llevar a cabo, realizar

cart [kɑ:t] n carro, carreta ▷ vt (inf: transport) cargar con

carton ['kɑ:tən] n caja (de cartón); (of milk etc) bote m

cartoon [kɑ:'tu:n] n (Press) chiste m; (comic strip) tira cómica; (film) dibujos mpl animados

cartridge ['kɑ:trɪdʒ] n cartucho

carve [kɑ:v] vt (meat) trinchar; (wood) tallar; (stone) cincelar, esculpir; (on tree) grabar; **carving** n (in wood etc) escultura; (design) talla

car wash n túnel m de lavado

case [keɪs] n (container) caja; (Med) caso; (for jewels etc) estuche m; (Law) causa, proceso; (BRIT: also: **suit~**) maleta; **in ~ of** en caso de; **in any ~** en todo caso; **just in ~** por si acaso

cash [kæʃ] n (dinero en) efectivo; (inf: money) dinero ▷ vt cobrar, hacer efectivo; **to pay (in) ~** pagar al contado; **~ on delivery (COD)** entrega contra reembolso; **cashback** n (discount) devolución f; (at supermarket etc) retirada de dinero en efectivo de un establecimiento donde se ha pagado con tarjeta; también dinero retirado; **cash card** n tarjeta f de(l) cajero (automático); **cash desk** n (BRIT) caja; **cash dispenser** n cajero automático

cashew [kæ'ʃu:] n (also: **~ nut**) anacardo

cashier [kæ'ʃɪər] n cajero/a

cashmere ['kæʃmɪər] n cachemira

cash point n cajero automático

cash register n caja

casino [kə'si:nəu] n casino

casket ['kɑ:skɪt] n cofre m, estuche m; (US: coffin) ataúd m

casserole ['kæsərəul] n (food, pot) cazuela

cassette [kæ'sɛt] n cas(s)et(t)e m or f; **cassette player, cassette recorder** n cas(s)et(t)e m

cast [kɑ:st] (pt, pp **cast**) vt (throw) echar, arrojar, lanzar; (Theat): **to ~ sb as Othello** dar a algn el papel de Otelo

▷ n (Theat) reparto; (also: **plaster ~**) vaciado; **to ~ one's vote** votar; **cast off** vi (Naut) soltar amarras; (Knitting) cerrar los puntos

castanets [kæstə'nɛts] npl castañuelas fpl

caster sugar ['kɑ:stər-] n (BRIT) azúcar m extrafino

Castile [kæs'ti:l] n Castilla; **Castilian** adj, n castellano/a

cast-iron ['kɑ:staɪən] adj (lit) (hecho) de hierro fundido or colado; (fig: alibi) irrebatible; (will) férreo

castle ['kɑ:sl] n castillo; (Chess) torre f

casual ['kæʒjul] adj fortuito; (irregular: work etc) eventual, temporero; (unconcerned) despreocupado; (clothes) de sport

> Be careful not to translate casual by the Spanish word casual.

casualty ['kæʒjultɪ] n víctima, herido; (dead) muerto; **casualty ward** n urgencias fpl

cat [kæt] n gato

Catalan ['kætəlæn] adj, n catalán/ ana m/f

catalogue, (US) **catalog** ['kætələɡ] n catálogo ▷ vt catalogar

Catalonia [kætə'ləunɪə] n Cataluña

catalytic converter [kætə'lɪtɪkkən'və:tər] n catalizador m

cataract ['kætərækt] n (Med) cataratas fpl

catarrh [kə'tɑ:r] n catarro

catastrophe [kə'tæstrəfɪ] n catástrofe f

catch [kætʃ] (pt, pp **caught**) vt coger (SP), agarrar (LAM); (arrest) atrapar; (grasp) asir; (breath) recobrar; (person: by surprise) pillar; (attract: attention) captar; (Med) pillar, coger; (also: **~ up**) alcanzar ▷ vi (fire) encenderse; (in branches etc) engancharse ▷ n (fish etc) captura; (act of catching) cogida; (of lock) pestillo, cerradura; **to ~ fire** prenderse; (house) incendiarse; **to**

~ sight of divisar; **catch up** vi (fig) ponerse al día; **catching** adj (Med) contagioso

category ['kætɪgərɪ] n categoría

cater ['keɪtə^r] vi: **to ~ for** (BRIT) abastecer a; (needs) atender a; (consumers) proveer a

caterpillar ['kætəpɪlə^r] n oruga

cathedral [kə'θi:drəl] n catedral f

cattle ['kætl] npl ganado sg

catwalk ['kætwɔ:k] n pasarela

caught [kɔ:t] pt, pp of **catch**

cauliflower ['kɔlɪflauə^r] n coliflor f

cause [kɔ:z] n causa; (reason) motivo, razón f ▷ vt causar

caution ['kɔ:ʃən] n cautela, prudencia; (warning) advertencia, amonestación f ▷ vt amonestar; **cautious** adj cauteloso, prudente, precavido

cave [keɪv] n cueva, caverna; **cave in** vi (roof etc) derrumbarse, hundirse

caviar(e) ['kævɪɑ:^r] n caviar m

cavity ['kævɪtɪ] n hueco, cavidad f

cc abbr (= cubic centimetres) cc, cm³; (on letter etc) = **carbon copy**

CCTV n abbr = **closed-circuit television**

CD n abbr (= compact disc) CD m; **CD player** n reproductor m de CD; **CD-ROM** n abbr (= compact disc read-only memory) CD-ROM m; **CD writer** n grabadora f de CDs

cease [si:s] vt cesar; **ceasefire** n alto m el fuego

cedar ['si:də^r] n cedro

ceilidh ['keɪlɪ] n baile con música y danzas tradicionales escocesas o irlandesas

ceiling ['si:lɪŋ] n techo; (fig) límite m

celebrate ['sɛlɪbreɪt] vt celebrar ▷ vi: **let's ~!** ¡vamos a celebrarlo!; **celebration** n celebración f

celebrity [sɪ'lɛbrɪtɪ] n (person) famoso/a

celery ['sɛlərɪ] n apio

cell [sɛl] n celda; (Biol) célula; (Elec) elemento

cellar ['sɛlə^r] n sótano; (for wine) bodega

cello ['tʃɛləu] n violoncelo

Cellophane® ['sɛləfeɪn] n celofán m

cellphone ['sɛlfəun] n móvil

Celsius ['sɛlsɪəs] adj centígrado

Celtic ['kɛltɪk, 'sɛltɪk] adj celta

cement [sə'mɛnt] n cemento

cemetery ['sɛmɪtrɪ] n cementerio

censor ['sɛnsə^r] n censor(a) m/f ▷ vt (cut) censurar; **censorship** n censura

census ['sɛnsəs] n censo

cent [sɛnt] n (US: unit of dollar) centavo; (unit of euro) céntimo; see also **per**

centenary [sɛn'ti:nərɪ], (US) **centennial** [sɛn'tɛnɪəl] n centenario

center ['sɛntə^r] n (US) = **centre**

centi...: centigrade ['sɛntɪgreɪd] adj centígrado; **centimetre,** (US) **centimeter** ['sɛntɪmi:tə^r] n centímetro; **centipede** ['sɛntɪpi:d] n ciempiés m inv

central ['sɛntrəl] adj central; (house etc) céntrico; **Central America** n Centroamérica; **central heating** n calefacción f central; **central reservation** n (BRIT Aut) mediana

centre, (US) **center** ['sɛntə^r] n centro ▷ vt centrar; **centre-forward** n (Sport) delantero centro; **centre-half** n (Sport) medio centro

century ['sɛntjurɪ] n siglo; **20th ~** siglo veinte

CEO n abbr = **chief executive officer**

ceramic [sɪ'ræmɪk] adj de cerámica

cereal ['si:rɪəl] n cereal m

ceremony ['sɛrɪmənɪ] n ceremonia; **to stand on ~** hacer ceremonias, andarse con cumplidos

certain ['sə:tən] adj seguro; (particular) cierto; **for ~** a ciencia cierta; **a ~ Mr Smith** un tal Sr. Smith; **certainly** adv desde luego, por supuesto; **certainty** n certeza, certidumbre f, seguridad f

certificate [sə'tɪfɪkɪt] n certificado

certify ['sə:tɪfaɪ] vt certificar; (declare insane) declarar loco

cf. abbr (= compare) cfr

CFC n abbr (= chlorofluorocarbon) CFC m

chain [tʃeɪn] n cadena; (of mountains) cordillera; (of events) sucesión f ▷ vt (also: **~ up**) encadenar; **chain-smoke** vi fumar un cigarrillo tras otro

chair [tʃeəʳ] n silla; (armchair) sillón m; (of university) cátedra ▷ vt (meeting) presidir; **chairlift** n telesilla m; **chairman** n presidente m; **chairperson** n presidente/a m/f; **chairwoman** n presidenta

chalet ['ʃæleɪ] n chalet m (de madera)

chalk [tʃɔːk] n (Geo) creta; (for writing) tiza, gis m (LAM); **chalkboard** (US) n pizarrón (LAM), pizarra (SP)

challenge ['tʃælɪndʒ] n desafío, reto ▷ vt desafiar, retar; (statement, right) poner en duda; **to ~ sb to do sth** retar a algn a que haga algo; **challenging** adj que supone un reto; (tone) de desafío

chamber ['tʃeɪmbəʳ] n cámara, sala; **chambermaid** n camarera

champagne [ʃæm'peɪn] n champaña m, champán m

champion ['tʃæmpɪən] n campeón/ona m/f; (of cause) defensor(a) m/f; **championship** n campeonato

chance [tʃɑːns] n (opportunity) ocasión f, oportunidad f; (likelihood) posibilidad f; (risk) riesgo ▷ vt arriesgar, probar ▷ adj fortuito, casual; **to ~ it** arriesgarse, intentarlo; **to take a ~** arriesgarse; **by ~** por casualidad

chancellor ['tʃɑːnsələʳ] n canciller m; **C~ of the Exchequer** (BRIT) Ministro de Economía y Hacienda; see also **Downing Street**

chandelier [ʃændə'lɪəʳ] n araña (de luces)

change [tʃeɪndʒ] vt cambiar; (clothes, house) cambiarse de, mudarse de; (transform) transformar ▷ vi cambiar(se); (change trains) hacer transbordo; (be transformed): **to ~ into** transformarse en ▷ n cambio; (alteration) modificación f, transformación f; (coins) suelto; (money returned) vuelta, vuelto (LAM); **to ~ one's mind** cambiar de opinión or idea; **to ~ gear** (Aut) cambiar de marcha; **for a ~** para variar; **change over** vi (from sth to sth) cambiar; (players etc) cambiar(se) ▷ vt cambiar; **changeable** adj (weather) cambiable; **change machine** n máquina de cambio; **changing room** n (BRIT) vestuario

channel ['tʃænl] n (TV) canal m; (of river) cauce m; (fig: medium) medio ▷ vt (river etc) encauzar; **the (English) C~** el Canal (de la Mancha); **the C~ Islands** las Islas Anglonormandas; **the C ~ Tunnel** el túnel del Canal de la Mancha, el Eurotúnel

chant [tʃɑːnt] n (also Rel) canto; (of crowd) gritos mpl ▷ vt (slogan, word) repetir a gritos

chaos ['keɪɔs] n caos m

chaotic [keɪ'ɔtɪk] adj caótico

chap [tʃæp] n (BRIT inf: man) tío, tipo

chapel ['tʃæpəl] n capilla

chapped [tʃæpt] adj agrietado

chapter ['tʃæptəʳ] n capítulo

character ['kærɪktəʳ] n carácter m, naturaleza, índole f; (in novel, film) personaje m; (individuality) carácter m; **characteristic** [kærɪktə'rɪstɪk] adj característico ▷ n característica; **characterize** vt caracterizar

charcoal ['tʃɑːkəʊl] n carbón m vegetal; (Art) carboncillo

charge [tʃɑːdʒ] n (Law) cargo, acusación f; (cost) precio, coste m; (responsibility) cargo ▷ vt (Law): **to ~ (with)** acusar (de); (gun, battery) cargar; (Mil: enemy) cargar; (price) pedir; (customer) cobrar ▷ vi precipitarse; **charge card** n tarjeta de cuenta; **charger** n (also: **battery charger**) cargador m (de baterías)

charismatic [kærɪz'mætɪk] *adj* carismático

charity ['tʃærɪtɪ] *n* caridad *f*; (*organization*) organización *f* benéfica; (*money, gifts*) limosnas *fpl*; **charity shop** *n* (BRIT) tienda de artículos de segunda mano que dedica su recaudación a causas benéficas

charm [tʃɑːm] *n* encanto, atractivo; (*spell*) hechizo; (*object*) amuleto; (*on bracelet*) dije *m* ▷ *vt* encantar; **charming** *adj* encantador(a)

chart [tʃɑːt] *n* (*table*) cuadro; (*graph*) gráfica, (*map*) carta de navegación ▷ *vt* (*course*) trazar; (*progress*) seguir; (*sales*) hacer una gráfica de; **to be in the ~s** (*record, pop group*) estar en la lista de éxitos

charter ['tʃɑːtəʳ] *vt* (*bus*) alquilar; (*plane, ship*) fletar ▷ *n* (*document*) carta; **chartered accountant** *n* (BRIT) contable *mf* diplomado/a; **charter flight** *n* vuelo chárter

chase [tʃeɪs] *vt* (*pursue*) perseguir; (*hunt*) cazar ▷ *n* persecución *f*

chat [tʃæt] *vi* (*also*: **have a ~**) charlar; (*Internet*) chatear ▷ *n* charla; **chat up** *vt* (*inf: girl*) ligar con, enrollarse con; **chat room** *n* (*Internet*) chat *m*, canal *m* de charla; **chat show** *n* (BRIT) programa *m* de entrevistas

chatter ['tʃætəʳ] *vi* (*person*) charlar; (*teeth*) castañetear ▷ *n* (*of birds*) parloteo; (*of people*) charla, cháchara

chauffeur ['ʃəufəʳ] *n* chófer *m*

chauvinist ['ʃəuvɪnɪst] *n* (*also*: **male ~**) machista *m*; (*nationalist*) chovinista *mf*

cheap [tʃiːp] *adj* barato; (*joke*) de mal gusto; (*poor quality*) de mala calidad ▷ *adv* barato; **cheap day return** *n* billete de ida y vuelta el mismo día; **cheaply** *adv* barato, a bajo precio

cheat [tʃiːt] *vi* hacer trampa ▷ *vt* estafar ▷ *n* (*person*) tramposo/a; **to ~ sb (out of sth)** estafar (algo) a algn; **cheat on** *vt fus* engañar

check [tʃɛk] *vt* (*examine*) controlar; (*facts*) comprobar; (*count*) contar; (*halt*) frenar; (*restrain*) refrenar, restringir ▷ *n* (*inspection*) control *m*, inspección *f*; (*curb*) freno; (*bill*) nota, cuenta; (*US*) = **cheque**; (*pattern: gen pl*) cuadro; **check in** *vi* (*in hotel*) registrarse; (*at airport*) facturar ▷ *vt* (*luggage*) facturar; **check off** *vt* (*esp US: check*) comprobar; (*cross off*) tachar; **check out** *vi* (*of hotel*) desocupar la habitación; **check up** *vi*: **to ~ up on sth** comprobar algo; **to ~ up on sb** investigar a algn; **checkbook** *n* (*US*) = **chequebook**; **checked** *adj* a cuadros *inv*; **checkers** *n* (*US*) damas *fpl*; **check-in** *n* (*also*: **check-in desk**: *at airport*) mostrador *m* de facturación; **checking account** *n* (*US*) cuenta corriente; **checklist** *n* lista; **checkmate** *n* jaque *m* mate; **checkout** *n* caja; **checkpoint** *n* (punto de) control *m*; **checkroom** *n* (*US*) consigna; **checkup** *n* (*Med*) reconocimiento general

cheddar ['tʃedəʳ] *n* (*also*: **~ cheese**) queso *m* cheddar

cheek [tʃiːk] *n* mejilla; (*impudence*) descaro; **what a ~!** ¡qué cara!; **cheekbone** *n* pómulo; **cheeky** *adj* fresco, descarado

cheer [tʃɪəʳ] *vt* vitorear, ovacionar; (*gladden*) alegrar, animar ▷ *vi* dar vivas ▷ *n* viva *m*; **cheer up** *vi* animarse ▷ *vt* alegrar, animar; **cheerful** *adj* alegre

cheerio [tʃɪərɪ'əu] *excl* (BRIT) ¡hasta luego!

cheerleader ['tʃɪəliːdəʳ] *n* animador(a) *m/f*

cheese [tʃiːz] *n* queso; **cheeseburger** *n* hamburguesa con queso; **cheesecake** *n* pastel *m* de queso

chef [ʃɛf] *n* jefe/a *m/f* de cocina

chemical ['kɛmɪkəl] *adj* químico ▷ *n* producto químico

chemist ['kɛmɪst] *n* (BRIT: *pharmacist*) farmacéutico/a; (*scientist*) químico/a;

~'s (shop) n (BRIT) farmacia; **chemistry** n química

cheque, (US) **check** [tʃɛk] n cheque m; **chequebook** n talonario (de cheques), chequera (LAM); **cheque card** n (BRIT) tarjeta de identificación bancaria

cherry ['tʃɛrɪ] n cereza; (also: **~ tree**) cerezo

chess [tʃɛs] n ajedrez m

chest [tʃɛst] n (Anat) pecho; (box) cofre m; **~ of drawers** n cómoda

chestnut ['tʃɛsnʌt] n castaña; (also: **~ tree**) castaño

chew [tʃuː] vt mascar, masticar; **chewing gum** n chicle m

chic [ʃiːk] adj elegante

chick [tʃɪk] n pollito, polluelo; (US inf) chica

chicken ['tʃɪkɪn] n gallina, pollo; (food) pollo; (inf: coward) gallina mf; **chicken out** vi (inf) rajarse; **chickenpox** n varicela

chickpea ['tʃɪkpiː] n garbanzo

chief [tʃiːf] n jefe a m/f ▷ adj principal; **chief executive (officer)** n director m general; **chiefly** adv principalmente

child (pl **children**) [tʃaɪld, 'tʃɪldrən] n niño/a; (offspring) hijo/a; **child abuse** n (with violence) malos tratos mpl a niños; (sexual) abuso m sexual de niños; **child benefit** n (BRIT) subsidio por cada hijo pequeño; **childbirth** n parto; **childcare** n cuidado de los niños; **childhood** n niñez f, infancia; **childish** adj pueril, infantil; **child minder** n (BRIT) madre f de día; **children** ['tʃɪldrən] npl of **child**

Chile ['tʃɪlɪ] n Chile m; **Chilean** adj, n chileno/a

chill [tʃɪl] n frío; (Med) resfriado ▷ vt enfriar; (Culin) refrigerar; **chill out** vi (esp US inf) tranquilizarse

chilly ['tʃɪlɪ] adj frío

chimney ['tʃɪmnɪ] n chimenea

chimpanzee [tʃɪmpæn'ziː] n chimpancé m

chin [tʃɪn] n mentón m, barbilla

China ['tʃaɪnə] n China

china ['tʃaɪnə] n porcelana; (crockery) loza

Chinese [tʃaɪˈniːz] adj chino ▷ n (pl inv) chino/a; (Ling) chino

chip [tʃɪp] n (gen pl: Culin: BRIT) patata or (LAM) papa frita; (: US: also: **potato ~**) patata or (LAM) papa frita; (of wood) astilla; (stone) lasca; (in gambling) ficha; (Comput) chip m ▷ vt (cup, plate) desconchar; **chip shop** n ver nota **"chip shop"**

CHIP SHOP

Se denomina chip shop o fish-and-chip shop a un tipo de tienda popular de comida rápida en la que se despachan platos tradicionales británicos, principalmente filetes de pescado rebozado frito y patatas fritas.

chiropodist [kɪˈrɔpədɪst] n (BRIT) podólogo/a

chisel ['tʃɪzl] n (for wood) escoplo; (for stone) cincel m

chives ['tʃaɪvz] npl cebollinos mpl

chlorine ['klɔːriːn] n cloro

choc-ice ['tʃɔkaɪs] n (BRIT) helado m cubierto de chocolate

chocolate ['tʃɔklɪt] n chocolate m; (sweet) bombón m

choice [tʃɔɪs] n elección f; (preference) preferencia ▷ adj escogido

choir ['kwaɪəʳ] n coro

choke [tʃəʊk] vi ahogarse; (on food) atragantarse ▷ vt ahogar; (block) atascar ▷ n (Aut) estárter m

cholesterol [kɔˈlɛstərəl] n colesterol m

chook [tʃuk] (AUST, NZ inf) n gallina; (as food) pollo

choose (pt **chose**, pp **chosen**) [tʃuːz, tʃəʊz, tʃəʊzn] vt escoger, elegir; (team) seleccionar; **to ~ to do sth** optar por hacer algo

chop [tʃɔp] vt (wood) cortar, talar; (Culin: also: ~ **up**) picar ▷ n (Culin) chuleta; **chop down** vt (tree) talar; **chop off** vt cortar (de un tajo); **chopsticks** npl palillos mpl

chord [kɔːd] n (Mus) acorde m

chore [tʃɔːʳ] n faena, tarea; (routine task) trabajo rutinario

chorus ['kɔːrəs] n coro; (repeated part of song) estribillo

chose [tʃəuz] pt of **choose**

chosen ['tʃəuzn] pp of **choose**

Christ [kraist] n Cristo

christen ['krɪsn] vt bautizar; **christening** n bautizo

Christian ['krɪstɪən] adj, n cristiano/a; **Christianity** [krɪstɪ'ænɪtɪ] n cristianismo; **Christian name** n nombre m de pila

Christmas ['krɪsməs] n Navidad f; **Merry ~!** ¡Felices Navidades!; **Christmas card** n crismas m inv, tarjeta de Navidad; **Christmas carol** n villancico m; **Christmas Day** n día m de Navidad; **Christmas Eve** n Nochebuena; **Christmas pudding** n (esp BRIT) pudín m de Navidad; **Christmas tree** n árbol m de Navidad

chrome [krəum] n = **chromium**

chromium ['krəumɪəm] n cromo; (also: ~ **plating**) cromado

chronic ['krɔnɪk] adj crónico

chrysanthemum [krɪ'sænθəməm] n crisantemo

chubby ['tʃʌbɪ] adj rechoncho

chuck [tʃʌk] (inf) vt lanzar, arrojar; (BRIT: also: ~ **in**, ~ **up**) abandonar; **chuck out** vt (person) echar (fuera); (rubbish etc) tirar

chuckle ['tʃʌkl] vi reírse entre dientes

chum [tʃʌm] n amiguete/a m/f

chunk [tʃʌŋk] n pedazo, trozo

church [tʃəːtʃ] n iglesia; **churchyard** n cementerio

churn [tʃəːn] n (for butter) mantequera; (for milk) lechera

chute [ʃuːt] n (also: **rubbish ~**) vertedero

chutney ['tʃʌtnɪ] n salsa picante de frutas y especias

CIA n abbr (US: = Central Intelligence Agency) CIA f

CID n abbr (BRIT: = Criminal Investigation Department) ≈ B.I.C. f (SP)

cider ['saɪdəʳ] n sidra

cigar [sɪ'gɑːʳ] n puro

cigarette [sɪgə'rɛt] n cigarrillo; **cigarette lighter** n mechero

cinema ['sɪnəmə] n cine m

cinnamon ['sɪnəmən] n canela

circle ['səːkl] n círculo; (in theatre) anfiteatro ▷ vi dar vueltas ▷ vt (surround) rodear, cercar; (move round) dar la vuelta a

circuit ['səːkɪt] n circuito; (track) pista; (lap) vuelta

circular ['səːkjuləʳ] adj circular ▷ n circular f

circulate ['səːkjuleɪt] vi circular; (person: socially) alternar, circular ▷ vt poner en circulación; **circulation** [səːkju'leɪʃən] n circulación f; (of newspaper etc) tirada

circumstances ['səːkəmstənsɪz] npl circunstancias fpl; (financial condition) situación f económica

circus ['səːkəs] n circo

cite [saɪt] vt citar

citizen ['sɪtɪzn] n (Pol) ciudadano/a; (of city) habitante mf, vecino/a; **citizenship** n ciudadanía; (BRIT Scol) civismo

citrus fruits ['sɪtrəs-] npl cítricos mpl

city ['sɪtɪ] n ciudad f; **the C~** centro financiero de Londres; **city centre** n centro de la ciudad

City Technology College n (BRIT) ≈ Centro de formación profesional

civic ['sɪvɪk] adj cívico; (authorities) municipal

civil ['sɪvɪl] adj civil; (polite) atento, cortés; **civilian** [sɪ'vɪlɪən] adj civil ▷ n civil mf

civilization [sɪvɪlaɪ'zeɪʃən] n civilización f

civilized ['sɪvɪlaɪzd] *adj* civilizado

civil: civil law *n* derecho civil; **civil rights** *npl* derechos *mpl* civiles; **civil servant** *n* funcionario/a (del Estado); **Civil Service** *n* administración *f* pública; **civil war** *n* guerra civil

CJD *n abbr* (= *Creutzfeldt-Jakob disease*) enfermedad de Creutzfeldt-Jakob

claim [kleɪm] *vt* exigir, reclamar; (*rights etc*) reivindicar; (*assert*) pretender ▷ *vi* (*for insurance*) reclamar ▷ *n* (*for expenses*) reclamación *f*; (*Law*) demanda; (*pretension*) pretensión *f*; **claim form** *n* solicitud *f*

clam [klæm] *n* almeja

clamp [klæmp] *n* abrazadera; (*laboratory clamp*) grapa ▷ *vt* afianzar (con abrazadera)

clan [klæn] *n* clan *m*

clap [klæp] *vi* aplaudir

claret ['klærət] *n* burdeos *m inv*

clarify ['klærɪfaɪ] *vt* aclarar

clarinet [klærɪ'net] *n* clarinete *m*

clarity ['klærɪtɪ] *n* claridad *f*

clash [klæʃ] *n* estruendo; (*fig*) choque *m* ▷ *vi* enfrentarse; (*beliefs*) chocar; (*disagree*) estar en desacuerdo; (*colours*) desentonar; (*two events*) coincidir

clasp [klɑːsp] *n* (*hold*) apretón *m*; (*of necklace, bag*) cierre *m* ▷ *vt* (*hand*) apretar; (*embrace*) abrazar

class [klɑːs] *n* clase *f* ▷ *vt* clasificar

classic ['klæsɪk] *n* clásico; **classical** *adj* clásico

classification [klæsɪfɪ'keɪʃən] *n* clasificación *f*

classify ['klæsɪfaɪ] *vt* clasificar

classmate ['klɑːsmeɪt] *n* compañero/a de clase

classroom ['klɑːsrum] *n* aula; **classroom assistant** *n* profesor(a) *m/f* de apoyo

classy ['klɑːsɪ] *adj* (*inf*) elegante, con estilo

clatter ['klætə'] *n* ruido, estruendo ▷ *vi* hacer ruido *or* estruendo

clause [klɔːz] *n* cláusula; (*Ling*) oración *f*

claustrophobic [klɔːstrə'fəubɪk] *adj* claustrofóbico; **I feel ~** me entra claustrofobia

claw [klɔː] *n* (*of cat*) uña; (*of bird of prey*) garra; (*of lobster*) pinza

clay [kleɪ] *n* arcilla

clean [kliːn] *adj* limpio; (*record, reputation*) bueno, intachable; (*joke*) decente ▷ *vt* limpiar; (*hands etc*) lavar; **clean up** *vt* limpiar, asear; **cleaner** *n* encargado/a de la limpieza; (*also*: **dry cleaner**) tintorero/a; (*substance*) producto para la limpieza; **cleaning** *n* limpieza

cleanser ['klenzə'] *n* (*cosmetic*) loción *f* or crema limpiadora

clear [klɪə'] *adj* claro; (*road, way*) libre ▷ *vt* (*space*) despejar, limpiar; (*Law: suspect*) absolver; (*obstacle*) salvar, saltar por encima de; (*cheque*) aceptar ▷ *vi* (*fog etc*) despejarse ▷ *adv*: **~ of** a distancia de; **to ~ the table** recoger *or* quitar la mesa; **clear away** *vt* (*things, clothes etc*) quitar (de en medio); (*dishes*) retirar; **clear up** *vt* limpiar; (*mystery*) aclarar, resolver; **clearance** *n* (*removal*) despeje *m*; (*permission*) acreditación *f*; **clear-cut** *adj* bien definido, claro; **clearing** *n* (*in wood*) claro; **clearly** *adv* claramente; (*evidently*) sin duda; **clearway** *n* (BRIT) carretera en la que no se puede estacionar

clench [klentʃ] *vt* apretar, cerrar

clergy ['klɜːdʒɪ] *n* clero

clerk [klɑːk, US klə:k] *n* oficinista *mf*; (US) dependiente/a *m/f*

clever ['klevə'] *adj* (*mentally*) inteligente, listo; (*skilful*) hábil; (*device, arrangement*) ingenioso

cliché ['kliːʃeɪ] *n* cliché *m*, frase *f* hecha

click [klɪk] *vt* (*tongue*) chasquear ▷ *vi* (*Comput*) hacer clic; **to ~ one's heels** taconear; **to ~ on an icon** hacer clic en un icono

client ['klaɪənt] *n* cliente *mf*

cliff [klɪf] *n* acantilado

climate ['klaɪmɪt] n clima m; **climate change** n cambio climático

climax ['klaɪmæks] n (of battle, career) apogeo; (of film, book) punto culminante, clímax; (sexual) orgasmo

climb [klaɪm] vi subir, trepar ▷ vt (stairs) subir; (tree) trepar a; (mountain) escalar ▷ n subida, ascenso; **to ~ over a wall** saltar una tapia; **climb down** vi (fig) volverse atrás; **climber** n escalador(a) m/f; **climbing** n escalada

clinch [klɪntʃ] vt (deal) cerrar; (argument) remachar

cling (pt, pp **clung**) [klɪŋ, klʌŋ] vi: **to ~ (to)** agarrarse (a); (clothes) pegarse (a)

clinic ['klɪnɪk] n clínica

clip [klɪp] n (for hair) horquilla; (also: **paper ~**) sujetapapeles m inv, clip m ▷ vt (cut) cortar; (also: **~ together**) unir; **clipping** n (from newspaper) recorte m

cloak [kləʊk] n capa, manto ▷ vt (fig) encubrir, disimular; **cloakroom** n guardarropa m; (BRIT: WC) lavabo, aseos mpl, baño (esp LAM)

clock [klɒk] n reloj m; **clock in, clock on** vi fichar, picar; **clock off, clock out** vi fichar or picar la salida; **clockwise** adv en el sentido de las agujas del reloj; **clockwork** n aparato de relojería ▷ adj (toy, train) de cuerda

clog [klɒg] n zueco, chanclo ▷ vt atascar ▷ vi (also: **~ up**) atascarse

clone [kləʊn] n clon m ▷ vt clonar

close [kləʊs, kləʊz] adj (near) (**~ to**) cerca (de); (friend) íntimo; (connection) estrecho; (examination) detallado, minucioso; (weather) bochornoso ▷ adv cerca; **~ to** prep cerca de ▷ vt cerrar; (end) concluir, terminar ▷ vi (shop etc) cerrar; (end) concluir(se), terminar(se) ▷ n (end) fin m, final m, conclusión f; **to have a ~ shave** (fig) escaparse por un pelo; **~ by, ~ at hand** muy cerca; **close down** vi cerrar definitivamente; **closed** [kləʊzd] adj (shop etc) cerrado

closed-circuit ['kləʊzd'sə:kɪt] adj: **~ television** televisión f por circuito cerrado

closely ['kləʊslɪ] adv (study) con detalle; (watch) de cerca

closet ['klɒzɪt] n armario

close-up ['kləʊsʌp] n primer plano

closing time ['kləʊzɪŋ-] n hora de cierre

closure ['kləʊʒəʳ] n cierre m

clot [klɒt] n (also: **blood ~**) coágulo; (inf: idiot) imbécil mf ▷ vi (blood) coagularse

cloth [klɒθ] n (material) tela, paño; (rag) trapo

clothes [kləʊðz] npl ropa sg; **clothes line** n cuerda (para tender la ropa); **clothes peg**, (US) **clothes pin** n pinza

clothing ['kləʊðɪŋ] n = **clothes**

cloud [klaʊd] n nube f; **cloud over** vi (also fig) nublarse; **cloudy** adj nublado; (liquid) turbio

clove [kləʊv] n clavo; **~ of garlic** diente m de ajo

clown [klaʊn] n payaso ▷ vi (also: **~ about, ~ around**) hacer el payaso

club [klʌb] n (society) club m; (weapon) porra, cachiporra; (also: **golf ~**) palo ▷ vt aporrear ▷ vi: **to ~ together** (join forces) unir fuerzas; **clubs** npl (Cards) tréboles mpl; **club class** n (Aviat) clase f preferente

clue [klu:] n pista; (in crosswords) indicación f; **I haven't a ~** no tengo ni idea

clump [klʌmp] n (of trees) grupo

clumsy ['klʌmzɪ] adj (person) torpe; (tool) difícil de manejar

clung [klʌŋ] pt, pp of **cling**

cluster ['klʌstəʳ] n grupo ▷ vi agruparse, apiñarse

clutch [klʌtʃ] n (Aut) embrague m; **to fall into sb's ~es** caer en las garras de algn ▷ vt agarrar

cm abbr (= centimetre) cm

Co. abbr = **county; company**

c/o abbr (= care of) c/a, a/c

coach [kəʊtʃ] n autocar m (SP), autobús m; (horse-drawn) coche m;

(of train) vagón m, coche m; (Sport) entrenador(a) m/f, instructor(a) m/f ▷ vt (Sport) entrenar; (student) preparar, enseñar; **coach station** n (BRIT) estación f de autobuses etc; **coach trip** n excursión f en autocar

coal [kəul] n carbón m

coalition [kəuə'lɪʃən] n coalición f

coarse [kɔːs] adj basto, burdo; (vulgar) grosero, ordinario

coast [kəust] n costa, litoral m ▷ vi (Aut) ir en punto muerto; **coastal** adj costero; **coastguard** n guardacostas m inv; **coastline** n litoral m

coat [kəut] n abrigo; (of animal) pelo, pelaje, lana; (of paint) mano f, capa ▷ vt cubrir, revestir; **coat hanger** n percha, gancho (LAM); **coating** n capa, baño

coax [kəuks] vt engatusar

cob [kɔb] n see **corn**

cobbled ['kɔbld] adj: ~ **street** calle f empedrada, calle f adoquinada

cobweb ['kɔbwɛb] n telaraña

cocaine [kə'keɪn] n cocaína

cock [kɔk] n (rooster) gallo; (male bird) macho ▷ vt (gun) amartillar; **cockerel** n gallito

cockney ['kɔknɪ] n habitante de ciertos barrios de Londres

cockpit ['kɔkpɪt] n cabina

cockroach ['kɔkrəutʃ] n cucaracha

cocktail ['kɔkteɪl] n cóctel m

cocoa ['kəukəu] n cacao; (drink) chocolate m

coconut ['kəukənʌt] n coco

COD abbr = **cash on delivery**; (US: = **collect on delivery**) C.A.E.

cod [kɔd] n bacalao

code [kəud] n código; (cipher) clave f; (Tel) prefijo

coeducational [kəuɛdju'keɪʃənl] adj mixto

coffee ['kɔfɪ] n café m; **coffee bar** n (BRIT) cafetería; **coffee bean** n grano de café; **coffee break** n descanso (para tomar café); **coffee maker** n máquina de hacer café, cafetera;

coffeepot n cafetera; **coffee shop** n café m; **coffee table** n mesita baja

coffin ['kɔfɪn] n ataúd m

cog [kɔg] n diente m

cognac ['kɔnjæk] n coñac m

coherent [kəu'hɪərənt] adj coherente

coil [kɔɪl] n rollo; (Aut, Elec) bobina, carrete m; (contraceptive) DIU m ▷ vt enrollar

coin [kɔɪn] n moneda ▷ vt (word) inventar, acuñar

coincide [kəuɪn'saɪd] vi coincidir; **coincidence** [kəu'ɪnsɪdəns] n casualidad f

Coke® [kəuk] n Coca Cola® f

coke [kəuk] n (coal) coque m

colander ['kɔləndər] n escurridor m

cold [kəuld] adj frío ▷ n frío; (Med) resfriado; **it's ~** hace frío; **to be ~** tener frío; **to catch a ~** resfriarse, acatarrarse; **in ~ blood** a sangre fría; **cold sore** n herpes m labial

coleslaw ['kəulslɔː] n ensalada de col con zanahoria

colic ['kɔlɪk] n cólico

collaborate [kə'læbəreɪt] vi colaborar

collapse [kə'læps] vi hundirse, derrumbarse; (Med) sufrir un colapso ▷ n hundimiento, derrumbamiento; (Med) colapso

collar ['kɔlər] n (of coat, shirt) cuello; (for dog) collar m; **collarbone** n clavícula

colleague ['kɔliːg] n colega mf; (at work) compañero/a m/f

collect [kə'lɛkt] vt reunir; (as a hobby) coleccionar; (BRIT: call and pick up) recoger; (debts) recaudar; (donations, subscriptions) colectar ▷ vi (crowd) reunirse ▷ adv (US Tel): **to call ~** llamar a cobro revertido; **collection** n colección f; (of post) recogida; **collective** adj colectivo; **collector** n coleccionista mf

college ['kɔlɪdʒ] n colegio; (of technology, agriculture etc) escuela

collide [kə'laɪd] vi chocar
collision [kə'lɪʒən] n choque m
cologne [kə'ləʊn] n (also: **eau de ~**) (agua de) colonia
Colombia [kə'lɒmbɪə] n Colombia; **Colombian** adj, n colombiano/a
colon ['kəʊlən] n (sign) dos puntos; (Med) colon m
colonel ['kɜːnl] n coronel m
colonial [kə'ləʊnɪəl] adj colonial
colony ['kɒlənɪ] n colonia
colour, (us) **color** ['kʌlər] n color m ▷ vt colorear; (dye) teñir; (fig: account) adornar; (: judgement) distorsionar ▷ vi (blush) sonrojarse; **colour in** vt colorear; **colour-blind** adj daltónico; **coloured** adj de color; (photo) en color; (inf: of race) de color; **colour film** n película en color; **colourful** adj lleno de color; (person) pintoresco; **colouring** n colorido, color; (substance) colorante m; **colour television** n televisión f en color
column ['kɒləm] n columna
coma ['kəʊmə] n coma m
comb [kəʊm] n peine m; (ornamental) peineta ▷ vt (hair) peinar; (area) registrar a fondo
combat ['kɒmbæt] n combate m ▷ vt combatir
combination [kɒmbɪ'neɪʃən] n combinación f
combine [kəm'baɪn] vt combinar; (qualities) reunir ▷ vi combinarse ▷ n ['kɒmbaɪn] (Econ) cartel m

KEYWORD

come [kʌm] (pt **came**, pp **come**) vi 1 (movement towards) venir; **to come running** venir corriendo
2 (arrive) llegar; **he's come here to work** ha venido aquí para trabajar; **to come home** volver a casa
3 (reach): **to come to** llegar a; **the bill came to £40** la cuenta ascendía a cuarenta libras
4 (occur): **an idea came to me** se me

ocurrió una idea
5 (be, become): **to come loose/ undone** etc aflojarse/desabrocharse, desatarse etc; **I've come to like him** por fin ha llegado a gustarme
come across vt fus (person) encontrarse con; (thing) encontrar
come along vi (BRIT: progress) ir
come back vi (return) volver
come down vi (price) bajar; (building: be demolished) ser derribado
come from vt fus (place, source) ser de
come in vi (visitor) entrar; (train, report) llegar; (fashion) ponerse de moda; (on deal etc) entrar
come off vi (button) soltarse, desprenderse; (attempt) salir bien
come on vi (pupil, work, project) marchar; (lights) encenderse; (electricity) volver; **come on!** ¡vamos!
come out vi (fact) salir a la luz; (book, sun) salir; (stain) quitarse
come round vi (after faint, operation) volver en sí
come to vi (wake) volver en sí
come up vi (sun) salir; (problem) surgir; (event) aproximarse; (in conversation) mencionarse
come up with vt fus (idea) sugerir; (money) conseguir

comeback ['kʌmbæk] n: **to make a ~** (Theat) volver a las tablas
comedian [kə'miːdɪən] n humorista mf
comedy ['kɒmɪdɪ] n comedia
comet ['kɒmɪt] n cometa m
comfort ['kʌmfət] n bienestar m; (relief) alivio ▷ vt consolar; **comfortable** adj cómodo; (income) adecuado; **comfort station** n (us) servicios mpl
comic ['kɒmɪk] adj (also: **~al**) cómico ▷ n (comedian) cómico; (magazine) tebeo; (for adults) cómic m; **comic book** n (us) libro m de cómics; **comic strip** n tira cómica
comma ['kɒmə] n coma f

command [kə'mɑːnd] n orden f,
mandato; (Mil: authority) mando;
(mastery) dominio ▷ vt (troops)
mandar; (give orders to) mandar,
ordenar; **commander** n (Mil)
comandante mf, jefe/a m/f

commemorate [kə'mɛmərɛɪt] vt
conmemorar

commence [kə'mɛns] vt, vi
comenzar; **commencement** n (US)
(Univ) (ceremonia de) graduación f

commend [kə'mɛnd] vt elogiar,
alabar; (recommend) recomendar

comment ['kɔmɛnt] n comentario
▷ vi: **to ~ (on)** hacer comentarios
(sobre); **"no ~"** (written) "sin
comentarios"; (spoken) "no tengo
nada que decir"; **commentary** n
comentario; **commentator** n
comentarista m f

commerce ['kɔmə:s] n comercio

commercial [kə'mə:ʃəl] adj
comercial ▷ n (TV) anuncio;
commercial break n intermedio para
publicidad

commission [kə'mɪʃən] n
(committee, fee, order for work of art
etc) comisión f ▷ vt (work of art)
encargar; **out of ~** fuera de servicio;
commissioner n (Police) comisario
m de policía

commit [kə'mɪt] vt (act) cometer;
(resources) dedicar; (to sb's care)
entregar; **to ~ o.s. (to do)**
comprometerse (a hacer); **to ~
suicide** suicidarse; **commitment** n
compromiso

committee [kə'mɪtɪ] n comité m

commodity [kə'mɔdɪtɪ] n mercancía

common ['kɔmən] adj común;
(pej) ordinario ▷ n campo común;
commonly adv comúnmente;
commonplace adj corriente;
Commons npl (BRIT Pol): **the
Commons** (la Cámara de) los
Comunes; **common sense** n sentido
común; **Commonwealth** n: **the
Commonwealth** la Commonwealth

communal ['kɔmjuːnl] adj comunal;
(kitchen) común

commune ['kɔmjuːn] n (group)
comuna ▷ vi [kə'mjuːn]: **to ~ with**
comunicarse con

communicate [kə'mjuːnɪkeɪt]
vt comunicar ▷ vi: **to ~ (with)**
comunicarse (con); (in writing) estar en
contacto (con)

communication [kəmjuːnɪ'keɪʃən]
n comunicación f

communion [kə'mjuːnɪən] n (also:
Holy C~) comunión f

communism ['kɔmjunɪzəm] n
comunismo; **communist** adj, n
comunista mf

community [kə'mjuːnɪtɪ] n
comunidad f; (large group) colectividad
f; **community centre** n centro social;
community service n trabajo m
comunitario (prestado en lugar de
cumplir una pena de prisión)

commute [kə'mjuːt] vi viajar a diario
de casa al trabajo ▷ vt conmutar;
commuter n persona que viaja a diario
de casa al trabajo

compact [kəm'pækt] adj compacto
▷ n ['kɔmpækt] (also: **powder ~**)
polvera; **compact disc** n compact
disc m; **compact disc player** n
lector m or reproductor m de discos
compactos

companion [kəm'pænɪən] n
compañero/a

company ['kʌmpənɪ] n compañía;
(Comm) empresa, compañía; **to keep
sb ~** acompañar a algn; **company
car** n coche m de la empresa;
company director n director(a) m/f
de empresa

comparable ['kɔmpərəbl] adj
comparable

comparative [kəm'pærətɪv] adj
relativo; (study, linguistics) comparado;
comparatively adv (relatively)
relativamente

compare [kəm'pɛəʳ] vt comparar
▷ vi: **to ~ (with)** poder compararse

(con); **~d with** or **to** comparado con
or a; **comparison** [kəm'pærɪsn] *n*
comparación *f*

compartment [kəm'pɑːtmənt] *n*
compartim(i)ento

compass ['kʌmpəs] *n* brújula;
compasses *npl* compás *m*

compassion [kəm'pæʃən] *n*
compasión *f*

compatible [kəm'pætɪbl] *adj*
compatible

compel [kəm'pɛl] *vt* obligar;
compelling *adj* (*fig: argument*)
convincente

compensate ['kɔmpənseɪt] *vt*
compensar ▷ *vi*: **to ~ for** compensar;
compensation *n* (*for loss*)
indemnización *f*

compete [kəm'piːt] *vi* (*take part*)
competir; (*vie with*) competir, hacer la
competencia

competent ['kɔmpɪtənt] *adj*
competente, capaz

competition [kɔmpɪ'tɪʃən]
n (*contest*) concurso; (*rivalry*)
competencia

competitive [kəm'pɛtɪtɪv] *adj* (*Econ,
Sport*) competitivo

competitor [kəm'pɛtɪtə] *n* (*rival*)
competidor(a) *m/f*; (*participant*)
concursante *mf*

complacent [kəm'pleɪsənt] *adj*
autocomplaciente

complain [kəm'pleɪn] *vi* quejarse;
(*Comm*) reclamar; **complaint** *n*
queja; (*Comm*) reclamación *f*; (*Med*)
enfermedad *f*

complement ['kɔmplɪmənt] *n*
complemento; (*esp ship's crew*)
dotación *f* ▷ *vt* ['kɔmplɪmɛnt]
(*enhance*) complementar;
complementary [kɔmplɪ'mɛntərɪ]
adj complementario

complete [kəm'pliːt] *adj* (*full*)
completo; (*finished*) acabado ▷ *vt*
(*fulfil*) completar; (*finish*) acabar;
(*a form*) rellenar; **completely** *adv*
completamente; **completion** *n*

terminación *f*; **on completion of
contract** cuando se realice el contrato

complex ['kɔmplɛks] *n* complejo

complexion [kəm'plɛkʃən] *n* (*of face*)
tez *f*, cutis *m*

compliance [kəm'plaɪəns] *n*
(*submission*) sumisión *f*; (*agreement*)
conformidad *f*; **in ~ with** de acuerdo
con

complicate ['kɔmplɪkeɪt] *vt*
complicar; **complicated** *adj*
complicado; **complication**
[kɔmplɪ'keɪʃən] *n* complicación *f*

compliment ['kɔmplɪmənt] *n*
(*formal*) cumplido ▷ *vt* felicitar;
complimentary [kɔmplɪ'mɛntərɪ]
adj elogioso; (*copy*) de regalo

comply [kəm'plaɪ] *vi*: **to ~ with**
acatar

component [kəm'pəunənt] *adj*
componente ▷ *n* (*Tech*) pieza

compose [kəm'pəuz] *vt* componer;
to be ~d of componerse de; **to ~ o.s.**
tranquilizarse; **composer** *n* (*Mus*)
compositor(a) *m/f*; **composition**
[kɔmpə'zɪʃən] *n* composición *f*

composure [kəm'pəuʒə] *n*
serenidad *f*, calma

compound ['kɔmpaund] *n*
(*Chem*) compuesto; (*Ling*) término
compuesto; (*enclosure*) recinto ▷ *adj*
compuesto; (*fracture*) complicado

comprehension [kɔmprɪ'hɛnʃən] *n*
comprensión *f*

comprehensive [kɔmprɪ'hɛnsɪv]
adj (*broad*) exhaustivo; **~ (school)** *n*
centro estatal de enseñanza secundaria ≈
Instituto Nacional de Bachillerato (*SP*)

compress [kəm'prɛs] *vt* comprimir;
(*Comput*) comprimir ▷ *n* ['kɔmprɛs]
(*Med*) compresa

comprise [kəm'praɪz] *vt* (*also*: **be ~d
of**) comprender, constar de

compromise ['kɔmprəmaɪz] *n*
(*agreement*) arreglo ▷ *vt* comprometer
▷ *vi* transigir

compulsive [kəm'pʌlsɪv] *adj*
compulsivo; (*viewing, reading*) obligado

compulsory [kəmˈpʌlsərɪ] *adj* obligatorio

computer [kəmˈpju:tər] *n* ordenador *m*, computador *m*, computadora; **computer game** *n* juego de ordenador; **computerize** *vt* (*data*) computerizar; (*system*) informatizar; **computer programmer** *n* programador(a) *m/f*; **computer programming** *n* programación *f*; **computer science** *n* informática; **computer studies** *npl* informática *fsg*, computación *fsg* (*LAM*); **computing** [kəmˈpju:tɪŋ] *n* (*activity*) informática

con [kɔn] *vt* estafar ▷ *n* estafa; **to ~ sb into doing sth** (*inf*) engañar a algn para que haga algo

conceal [kənˈsi:l] *vt* ocultar

concede [kənˈsi:d] *vt* (*point, argument*) reconocer; (*territory*) ceder; **to ~ (defeat)** darse por vencido; **to ~ that** admitir que

conceited [kənˈsi:tɪd] *adj* orgulloso

conceive [kənˈsi:v] *vt*, *vi* concebir

concentrate [ˈkɔnsəntreɪt] *vi* concentrarse ▷ *vt* concentrar

concentration [kɔnsənˈtreɪʃən] *n* concentración *f*

concept [ˈkɔnsɛpt] *n* concepto

concern [kənˈsə:n] *n* (*matter*) asunto; (*Comm*) empresa; (*anxiety*) preocupación *f* ▷ *vt* (*worry*) preocupar; (*involve*) afectar; (*relate to*) tener que ver con; **to be ~ed (about)** interesarse (por), preocuparse (por); **concerning** *prep* sobre, acerca de

concert [ˈkɔnsət] *n* concierto; **concert hall** *n* sala de conciertos

concerto [kənˈtʃə:təu] *n* concierto

concession [kənˈsɛʃən] *n* concesión *f*; **tax ~** privilegio fiscal

concise [kənˈsaɪs] *adj* conciso

conclude [kənˈklu:d] *vt* concluir; (*treaty etc*) firmar; (*agreement*) llegar a; (*decide*): **to ~ that ...** llegar a la conclusión de que ...; **conclusion** [kənˈklu:ʒən] *n* conclusión *f*

concrete [ˈkɔnkri:t] *n* hormigón *m* ▷ *adj* de hormigón; (*fig*) concreto

concussion [kənˈkʌʃən] *n* conmoción *f* cerebral

condemn [kənˈdɛm] *vt* condenar; (*building*) declarar en ruina

condensation [kɔndɛnˈseɪʃən] *n* condensación *f*

condense [kənˈdɛns] *vi* condensarse ▷ *vt* condensar; (*text*) abreviar

condition [kənˈdɪʃən] *n* condición *f*; (*of health*) estado; (*disease*) enfermedad *f* ▷ *vt* condicionar; **on ~ that** a condición (de) que; **conditional** *adj* condicional; **conditioner** *n* suavizante *m*

condo [ˈkɔndəu] *n abbr* (*US inf*); = **condominium**

condom [ˈkɔndəm] *n* condón *m*

condominium [kɔndəˈmɪnɪəm] *n* (*US: building*) bloque *m* de pisos *or* apartamentos (*propiedad de quienes lo habitan*), condominio (*LAM*); (: *apartment*) piso *or* apartamento (en propiedad), condominio (*LAM*)

condone [kənˈdəun] *vt* condonar

conduct [ˈkɔndʌkt] *n* conducta, comportamiento ▷ *vt* [kənˈdʌkt] (*lead*) conducir; (*manage*) llevar, dirigir; (*Mus*) dirigir; **to ~ o.s.** comportarse; **conducted tour** *n* (*BRIT*) visita con guía; **conductor** *n* (*of orchestra*) director(a) *m/f*; (*US: on train*) revisor(a) *m/f*; (*on bus*) cobrador *m*; (*Elec*) conductor *m*

cone [kəun] *n* cono; (*pine cone*) piña; (*for ice cream*) cucurucho

confectionery [kənˈfɛkʃənrɪ] *n* dulces *mpl*

confer [kənˈfə:r] *vt*: **to ~ (on)** otorgar (a) ▷ *vi* conferenciar

conference [ˈkɔnfərns] *n* (*meeting*) reunión *f*; (*convention*) congreso

confess [kənˈfɛs] *vt* confesar ▷ *vi* confesar; **confession** *n* confesión *f*

confide [kənˈfaɪd] *vi*: **to ~ in** confiar en

confidence ['kɒnfɪdns] n (*also*: **self-~**) confianza; (*secret*) confidencia; **in ~** (*speak, write*) en confianza; **confident** *adj* seguro de sí mismo; **confidential** [kɒnfɪ'dɛnʃəl] *adj* confidencial

confine [kən'faɪn] vt (*limit*) limitar; (*shut up*) encerrar; **confined** *adj* (*space*) reducido

confirm [kən'fə:m] vt confirmar; **confirmation** [kɒnfə'meɪʃən] n confirmación f

confiscate ['kɒnfɪskeɪt] vt confiscar

conflict ['kɒnflɪkt] n conflicto ▷ vi [kən'flɪkt] (*opinions*) estar reñido

conform [kən'fɔ:m] vi: **to ~ to** ajustarse a

confront [kən'frʌnt] vt (*problems*) hacer frente a; (*enemy, danger*) enfrentarse con; **confrontation** [kɒnfrən'teɪʃən] n enfrentamiento

confuse [kən'fju:z] vt (*perplex*) desconcertar; (*mix up*) confundir; (*complicate*) complicar; **confused** *adj* confuso; (*person*) desconcertado; **confusing** *adj* confuso; **confusion** n confusión f

congestion [kən'dʒɛstʃən] n congestión f

congratulate [kən'grætjuleɪt] vt felicitar; **congratulations** [kəngrætju'leɪʃənz] npl: **congratulations (on)** felicitaciones fpl (por); **congratulations!** ¡enhorabuena!

congregation [kɒŋgrɪ'geɪʃən] n (*in church*) fieles mpl

congress ['kɒŋgrɛs] n congreso; (*us Pol*): **C~** el Congreso (de los Estados Unidos); **congressman** n (*us*) miembro del Congreso; **congresswoman** n (*us*) diputada, miembro f del Congreso

conifer ['kɒnɪfəʳ] n conífera

conjugate ['kɒndʒugeɪt] vt conjugar

conjugation [kɒndʒə'geɪʃən] n conjugación f

conjunction [kən'dʒʌŋkʃən] n conjunción f; **in ~ with** junto con

conjure ['kʌndʒəʳ] vi hacer juegos de manos

connect [kə'nɛkt] vt juntar, unir; (*Elec*) conectar; (*fig*) relacionar, asociar ▷ vi: **to ~ with** (*train*) enlazar con; **to be ~ed with** (*associated*) estar relacionado con; **I am trying to ~ you** (*Tel*) estoy intentando ponerle al habla; **connecting flight** n vuelo m de enlace; **connection** n juntura, unión f; (*Elec*) conexión f; (*Rail*) enlace m; (*Tel*) comunicación f; (*fig*) relación f

conquer ['kɒŋkəʳ] vt (*territory*) conquistar; (*enemy, feelings*) vencer

conquest ['kɒŋkwɛst] n conquista

cons [kɒnz] npl see **mod cons; pro**

conscience ['kɒnʃəns] n conciencia

conscientious [kɒnʃɪ'ɛnʃəs] *adj* concienzudo; (*objection*) de conciencia

conscious ['kɒnʃəs] *adj* consciente; (*deliberate: insult, error*) premeditado, intencionado; **consciousness** n conciencia; (*Med*) conocimiento

consecutive [kən'sɛkjutɪv] *adj* consecutivo; **on 3 ~ occasions** en 3 ocasiones consecutivas

consensus [kən'sɛnsəs] n consenso

consent [kən'sɛnt] n consentimiento ▷ vi: **to ~ to** consentir en

consequence ['kɒnsɪkwəns] n consecuencia

consequently ['kɒnsɪkwəntlɪ] *adv* por consiguiente

conservation [kɒnsə'veɪʃən] n conservación f

conservative [kən'sə:vətɪv] *adj, n* conservador(a); (*cautious*) moderado; **C~** *adj* (*BRIT Pol*) conservador(a) m/f

conservatory [kən'sə:vətrɪ] n (*greenhouse*) invernadero

consider [kən'sɪdəʳ] vt considerar; (*take into account*) tener en cuenta; (*study*) estudiar, examinar; **to ~ doing sth** pensar en (la posibilidad de) hacer algo; **considerable** *adj* considerable; **considerably** *adv* bastante,

considerablemente; **considerate**
adj considerado; **consideration**
[kənsɪdə'reɪʃən] *n* consideración *f*;
to be under consideration estar
estudiándose; **considering** *prep*:
considering (that) teniendo en
cuenta (que)

consignment [kən'saɪnmənt] *n*
envío

consist [kən'sɪst] *vi*: **to ~ of**
consistir en

consistency [kən'sɪstənsɪ] *n* (*of
person etc*) consecuencia, coherencia;
(*thickness*) consistencia

consistent [kən'sɪstənt] *adj*
(*person, argument*) consecuente,
coherente

consolation [kɔnsə'leɪʃən] *n*
consuelo

console [kən'səʊl] *vt* consolar ▷ *n*
['kɔnsəʊl] consola

consonant ['kɔnsənənt] *n*
consonante *f*

conspicuous [kən'spɪkjuəs] *adj*
(*visible*) visible

conspiracy [kən'spɪrəsɪ] *n* conjura,
complot *m*

constable ['kʌnstəbl] *n* (*BRIT*)
agente *mf* (de policía); **chief ~** ≈ jefe
mf de policía

constant ['kɔnstənt] *adj* constante;
constantly *adv* constantemente

constipated ['kɔnstɪpeɪtəd] *adj*
estreñido

> Be careful not to translate
> *constipated* by the Spanish word
> *constipado*.

constipation [kɔnstɪ'peɪʃən] *n*
estreñimiento

constituency [kən'stɪtjuənsɪ]
n (*Pol*) distrito electoral; (*people*)
electorado

constitute ['kɔnstɪtjuːt] *vt*
constituir

constitution [kɔnstɪ'tjuːʃən] *n*
constitución *f*

constraint [kən'streɪnt] *n* (*force*)
fuerza; (*limit*) restricción *f*

construct [kən'strʌkt] *vt* construir;
construction *n* construcción *f*;
constructive *adj* constructivo

consul ['kɔnsl] *n* cónsul *mf*;
consulate ['kɔnsjuːlɪt] *n* consulado

consult [kən'sʌlt] *vt* consultar;
consultant *n* (*BRIT Med*) especialista
mf; (*other specialist*) asesor(a) *m/f*;
consultation *n* consulta; **consulting
room** *n* (*BRIT*) consultorio

consume [kən'sjuːm] *vt* (*eat*)
comerse; (*drink*) beberse; (*fire
etc*) consumir; (*Comm*) consumir;
consumer *n* consumidor(a) *m/f*

consumption [kən'sʌmpʃən] *n*
consumo

cont. *abbr* (= *continued*) sigue

contact ['kɔntækt] *n* contacto;
(*person: pej*) enchufe *m* ▷ *vt* ponerse en
contacto con; **~ lenses** *n pl* lentes *fpl*
de contacto

contagious [kən'teɪdʒəs] *adj*
contagioso

contain [kən'teɪn] *vt* contener;
to ~ o.s. contenerse; **container**
n recipiente *m*; (*for shipping etc*)
contenedor *m*

contaminate [kən'tæmɪneɪt] *vt*
contaminar

cont'd *abbr* (= *continued*) sigue

contemplate ['kɔntəmpleɪt] *vt*
contemplar; (*reflect upon*) considerar

contemporary [kən'tɛmpərərɪ] *adj*,
n contemporáneo/a

contempt [kən'tɛmpt] *n* desprecio;
~ of court (*Law*) desacato (a los
tribunales *or* a la justicia)

contend [kən'tɛnd] *vt* (*argue*) afirmar
▷ *vi*: **to ~ with/for** luchar contra/por

content [kən'tɛnt] *adj* (*happy*)
contento; (*satisfied*) satisfecho ▷ *vt*
contentar; satisfacer ▷ *n* ['kɔntɛnt]
contenido; **contents** *npl* contenido
msg; **(table of) ~s** índice *m* de
materias; **contented** *adj* contento;
satisfecho

contest ['kɔntɛst] *n* contienda;
(*competition*) concurso ▷ *vt* [kən'tɛst]

(*dispute*) impugnar; (*Pol: election, seat*) presentarse como candidato/a a

> Be careful not to translate *contest* by the Spanish word *contestar*.

contestant [kənˈtɛstənt] *n* concursante *mf*; (*in fight*) contendiente *mf*

context [ˈkɔntɛkst] *n* contexto

continent [ˈkɔntɪnənt] *n* continente *m*; **the C~** (BRIT) el continente europeo; **continental** *adj* continental; **continental breakfast** *n* desayuno estilo europeo; **continental quilt** *n* (BRIT) edredón *m*

continual [kənˈtɪnjuəl] *adj* continuo; **continually** *adv* continuamente

continue [kənˈtɪnjuː] *vi, vt* seguir, continuar

continuity [kɔntɪˈnjuːtɪ] *n* (*also Cine*) continuidad *f*

continuous [kənˈtɪnjuəs] *adj* continuo; **continuous assessment** *n* (BRIT) evaluación *f* continua; **continuously** *adv* continuamente

contour [ˈkɔntuəʳ] *n* contorno; (*also:* **~ line**) curva de nivel

contraception [kɔntrəˈsɛpʃən] *n* contracepción *f*

contraceptive [kɔntrəˈsɛptɪv] *adj, n* anticonceptivo

contract [*n* ˈkɔntrækt, *vi, vt* kɔnˈtrækt] *n* contrato ▷ *vi* (*Comm*): **to ~ to do sth** comprometerse por contrato a hacer algo; (*become smaller*) contraerse, encogerse ▷ *vt* contraer; **contractor** *n* contratista *mf*

contradict [kɔntrəˈdɪkt] *vt* contradecir; **contradiction** *n* contradicción *f*

contrary¹ [ˈkɔntrərɪ] *adj* contrario ▷ *n* lo contrario; **on the ~** al contrario; **unless you hear to the ~** a no ser que le digan lo contrario

contrary² [kənˈtrɛərɪ] *adj* (*perverse*) terco

contrast [ˈkɔntrɑːst] *n* contraste *m* ▷ *vt* [kənˈtrɑːst] contrastar; **in ~ to** or **with** a diferencia de

contribute [kənˈtrɪbjuːt] *vi* contribuir ▷ *vt*: **to ~ to** contribuir a; (*newspaper*) colaborar en; (*discussion*) intervenir en; **contribution** *n* (*money*) contribución *f*; (*to debate*) intervención *f*; (*to journal*) colaboración *f*; **contributor** *n* (*to newspaper*) colaborador(a) *m/f*

control [kənˈtrəul] *vt* controlar; (*traffic etc*) dirigir; (*machinery*) manejar; (*temper*) dominar; (*disease, fire*) dominar, controlar ▷ *n* control *m*; (*of car*) conducción *f*; (*check*) freno; **controls** *npl* (*of vehicle*) instrumentos *mpl* de mando; (*of radio*) controles *mpl*; (*governmental*) medidas *fpl* de control; **everything is under ~** todo está bajo control; **to be in ~ of** estar al mando de; **the car went out of ~** perdió el control del coche; **control tower** *n* (*Aviat*) torre *f* de control

controversial [kɔntrəˈvəːʃl] *adj* polémico

controversy [ˈkɔntrəvəːsɪ] *n* polémica

convenience [kənˈviːnɪəns] *n* (*comfort*) comodidad *f*; (*advantage*) ventaja; **at your earliest ~** (*Comm*) tan pronto como le sea posible; **all modern ~s** (BRIT) todo confort

convenient [kənˈviːnɪənt] *adj* (*useful*) útil; (*place*) conveniente; (*time*) oportuno

convent [ˈkɔnvənt] *n* convento

convention [kənˈvɛnʃən] *n* convención *f*; (*meeting*) asamblea; **conventional** *adj* convencional

conversation [kɔnvəˈseɪʃən] *n* conversación *f*

conversely [kɔnˈvəːslɪ] *adv* a la inversa

conversion [kənˈvəːʃən] *n* conversión *f*

convert [kənˈvəːt] *vt* (*Rel, Comm*) convertir; (*alter*) transformar ▷ *n* [ˈkɔnvəːt] converso/a; **convertible** *adj* convertible ▷ *n* descapotable *m*

convey [kən'veɪ] vt transportar; (thanks) comunicar; (idea) expresar; **conveyor belt** n cinta transportadora

convict [kən'vɪkt] vt (find guilty) declarar culpable a ▷ n ['kɒnvɪkt] presidiario/a; **conviction** [kən'vɪkʃən] n condena; (belief) convicción f

convince [kən'vɪns] vt convencer; **to ~ sb (of sth/that)** convencer a algn (de algo/de que); **convinced** adj: **convinced of/that** convencido de/de que; **convincing** adj convincente

convoy ['kɒnvɔɪ] n convoy m

cook [kuk] vt (stew etc) guisar; (meal) preparar ▷ vi hacerse; (person) cocinar ▷ n cocinero/a; **cookbook** n libro de cocina; **cooker** n cocina; **cookery** n cocina; **cookery book** n (BRIT) = **cookbook**

cookie ['kukɪ] n (US) galleta; (Comput) cookie f

cooking ['kukɪŋ] n cocina

cool [ku:l] adj fresco; (not afraid) tranquilo; (unfriendly) frío ▷ vt enfriar ▷ vi enfriarse; **cool down** vi enfriarse; (fig: person, situation) calmarse; **cool off** vi (become calmer) calmarse, apaciguarse; (lose enthusiasm) perder (el) interés, enfriarse

cop [kɒp] n (inf) poli m

cope [kəup] vi: **to ~ with** (problem) hacer frente a

copper ['kɒpəʳ] n (metal) cobre m; (inf) poli m

copy ['kɒpɪ] n copia; (of book) ejemplar m ▷ vt (also Comput) copiar; **copyright** n derechos mpl de autor

coral ['kɒrəl] n coral m

cord [kɔ:d] n cuerda; (Elec) cable m; (fabric) pana; **cords** npl (trousers) pantalones mpl de pana; **cordless** adj sin hilos

corduroy ['kɔ:dərɔɪ] n pana

core [kɔ:ʳ] n centro, núcleo; (of fruit) corazón m; (of problem etc) meollo ▷ vt quitar el corazón de

coriander [kɒrɪ'ændəʳ] n culantro

cork [kɔ:k] n corcho; (tree) alcornoque m; **corkscrew** n sacacorchos m inv

corn [kɔ:n] n (BRIT: wheat) trigo; (US: maize) maíz m; (on foot) callo; **~ on the cob** (Culin) maíz en la mazorca

corned beef ['kɔ:nd-] n carne f de vaca acecinada

corner ['kɔ:nəʳ] n (outside) esquina; (inside) rincón m; (in road) curva; (Football) córner m ▷ vt (trap) arrinconar; (Comm) acaparar ▷ vi (in car) tomar las curvas; **corner shop** n (BRIT) tienda de la esquina

cornflakes ['kɔ:nfleɪks] npl copos mpl de maíz, cornflakes mpl

cornflour ['kɔ:nflauəʳ] n (BRIT) harina de maíz

cornstarch ['kɔ:nstɑ:tʃ] n (US) = **cornflour**

Cornwall ['kɔ:nwəl] n Cornualles m

coronary ['kɒrənərɪ] n: **~ (thrombosis)** infarto

coronation [kɒrə'neɪʃən] n coronación f

coroner ['kɒrənəʳ] n juez mf de instrucción

corporal ['kɔ:pərl] n cabo ▷ adj: **~ punishment** castigo corporal

corporate ['kɔ:pərɪt] adj (action, ownership) colectivo; (finance, image) corporativo

corporation [kɔ:pə'reɪʃən] n (of town) ayuntamiento; (Comm) corporación f

corps (pl **corps**) [kɔ:ʳ, kɔ:z] n cuerpo; **press ~** gabinete m de prensa

corpse [kɔ:ps] n cadáver m

correct [kə'rekt] adj correcto; (accurate) exacto ▷ vt corregir; **correction** n (act) corrección f; (instance) rectificación f

correspond [kɒrɪs'pɒnd] vi: **to ~ (with)** (write) escribirse (con); (be in accordance) corresponder (con); **to ~ (to)** (be equivalent to) corresponder (a); **correspondence** n correspondencia; **correspondent** n corresponsal mf; **corresponding** adj correspondiente

corridor ['kɒrɪdɔːʳ] n pasillo

corrode [kə'rəud] vt corroer ▷ vi corroerse

corrupt [kə'rʌpt] adj corrompido; (person) corrupto ▷ vt corromper; (Comput) degradar; **corruption** n corrupción f; (of data) alteración f

Corsica ['kɔːsɪkə] n Córcega

cosmetic [kɒz'mɛtɪk] n ▷ adj cosmético; **cosmetic surgery** n cirugía f estética

cosmopolitan [kɒzmə'pɒlɪtn] adj cosmopolita

cost [kɒst] (pt, pp **cost**) n (price) precio ▷ vi costar, valer ▷ vt preparar el presupuesto de; (Law) costas fpl; **how much does it ~?** ¿cuánto cuesta?; **to ~ sb time/effort** costarle a algn tiempo/esfuerzo; **it ~ him his life** le costó la vida; **at all ~s** cueste lo que cueste

co-star ['kəustaːʳ] n coprotagonista mf

Costa Rica ['kɒstə'riːkə] n Costa Rica; **Costa Rican** adj, n costarriqueño/a

costly ['kɒstlɪ] adj costoso

costume ['kɒstjuːm] n traje m; (BRIT: also: **swimming ~**) traje de baño

cosy, (US) **cozy** ['kəuzɪ] adj cómodo; (room, atmosphere) acogedor(a)

cot [kɒt] n (BRIT: child's) cuna; (US: folding bed) cama plegable

cottage ['kɒtɪdʒ] n casita de campo; **cottage cheese** n requesón m

cotton ['kɒtn] n algodón m; (thread) hilo; **cotton on** vi (inf): **to ~ on (to sth)** caer en la cuenta (de algo); **cotton bud** n (BRIT) bastoncillo m de algodón; **cotton candy** n (US) algodón m (azucarado); **cotton wool** n (BRIT) algodón m (hidrófilo)

couch [kautʃ] n sofá m; (in doctor's surgery) camilla; (psychiatrist's) diván m

cough [kɒf] vi toser ▷ n tos f; **cough mixture** n jarabe m para la tos

could [kud] pt of **can²**; **couldn't** = **could not**

council ['kaunsl] n consejo; **city** or **town ~** ayuntamiento, consejo municipal; **council estate** n (BRIT) barriada de viviendas sociales de alquiler; **council house** n (BRIT) vivienda social de alquiler; **councillor** n concejal mf; **council tax** n (BRIT) contribución f municipal (dependiente del valor de la vivienda)

counsel ['kaunsl] n (advice) consejo; (lawyer) abogado/a ▷ vt aconsejar; **counselling**, (US) **counseling** n (Psych) asistencia f psicológica; **counsellor**, (US) **counselor** n consejero/a; abogado/a

count [kaunt] vt contar; (include) incluir ▷ vi contar ▷ n cuenta; (of votes) escrutinio; (nobleman) conde m; **count in** (inf) vt: **to ~ sb in on sth** contar con algn para algo; **count on** vt fus contar con; **countdown** n cuenta atrás

counter ['kauntəʳ] n (in shop) mostrador m; (in games) ficha ▷ vt contrarrestar ▷ adv: **~ to** contrario a

counter-clockwise ['kauntə'klɒkwaɪz] adv en sentido contrario al de las agujas del reloj

counterfeit ['kauntəfɪt] n falsificación f ▷ vt falsificar ▷ adj falso, falsificado

counterpart ['kauntəpaːt] n homólogo/a

countess ['kauntɪs] n condesa

countless ['kauntlɪs] adj innumerable

country ['kʌntrɪ] n país m; (native land) patria; (as opposed to town) campo; (region) región f, tierra; **country and western (music)** n música country; **country house** n casa de campo; **countryside** n campo

county ['kauntɪ] n condado

coup [kuː] (pl **coups**) n golpe m; (triumph) éxito; (also: **~ d'état**) golpe de estado

couple ['kʌpl] n (of things) par m; (of people) pareja; (married couple) matrimonio; **a ~ of** un par de

coupon ['ku:pɔn] n cupón m; (voucher) valé m

courage ['kʌrɪdʒ] n valor m, valentía; **courageous** [kə'reɪdʒəs] adj valiente

courgette [kuə'ʒet] n (BRIT) calabacín m

courier ['kurɪər] n mensajero/a; (for tourists) guía mf (de turismo)

course [kɔːs] n (direction) dirección f; (of river) curso; (Scol) curso; (of ship) rumbo; (Golf) campo; (part of meal) plato; **of ~** adv desde luego, naturalmente; **of ~!** ¡claro!; **~ of treatment** (Med) tratamiento

court [kɔːt] n (royal) corte f; (Law) tribunal m, juzgado; (Tennis) pista, cancha (LAM) ▷ vt (woman) cortejar; **to take to ~** demandar

courtesy ['kɔːtəsɪ] n cortesía; **by ~ of** (por) cortesía de; **courtesy bus, courtesy coach** n autobús m gratuito

court: courthouse n (US) palacio de justicia; **courtroom** n sala de justicia; **courtyard** n patio

cousin ['kʌzn] n primo/a; **first ~** primo/a carnal

cover ['kʌvər] vt cubrir; (with lid) tapar; (distance) cubrir, recorrer; (include) abarcar; (protect) abrigar; (journalist) investigar; (issues) tratar ▷ n cubierta; (lid) tapa; (for chair etc) funda; (envelope) sobre m; (of magazine) portada; (shelter) abrigo; (insurance) cobertura; **to take ~** (shelter) protegerse, resguardarse; **under ~** (indoors) bajo techo; **under ~ of darkness** al amparo de la oscuridad; **under separate ~** (Comm) por separado; **cover up** vi: **to ~ up for sb** encubrir a algn; **coverage** n (in media) cobertura informativa; **cover charge** n precio del cubierto; **cover-up** n encubrimiento

cow [kau] n vaca ▷ vt intimidar

coward ['kauəd] n cobarde mf; **cowardly** adj cobarde

cowboy ['kaubɔɪ] n vaquero

cozy ['kəuzɪ] adj (US) = **cosy**

crab [kræb] n cangrejo

crack [kræk] n grieta; (noise) crujido; (drug) crack m ▷ vt agrietar, romper; (nut) cascar; (whip etc) chasquear; (knuckles) crujir; (joke) contar ▷ adj (athlete) de primera clase; **crack down on** vt fus adoptar medidas severas contra; **cracked** adj (cup, window) rajado; (wall) resquebrajado; **cracker** n (biscuit) crácker m; (Christmas cracker) petardo sorpresa

crackle ['krækl] vi crepitar

cradle ['kreɪdl] n cuna

craft [krɑːft] n (skill) arte m; (trade) oficio; (cunning) astucia; (boat) embarcación f; **craftsman** n artesano; **craftsmanship** n destreza

cram [kræm] vt (fill): **to ~ sth with** llenar algo (a reventar) de; (put): **to ~ sth into** meter algo a la fuerza en ▷ vi (for exams) empollar

cramp [kræmp] n (Med) calambre m; **cramped** adj apretado

cranberry ['krænbərɪ] n arándano agrio

crane [kreɪn] n (Tech) grúa; (bird) grulla

crap [kræp] n (inf!) mierda (!)

crash [kræʃ] n (noise) estrépito; (of cars, plane) accidente m; (of business) quiebra ▷ vt (plane) estrellar ▷ vi (plane) estrellarse; (two cars) chocar; **crash course** n curso acelerado; **crash helmet** n casco (protector)

crate [kreɪt] n cajón m de embalaje; (for bottles) caja

crave [kreɪv] vt, vi: **to ~ (for)** ansiar, anhelar

crawl [krɔːl] vi (drag o.s.) arrastrarse; (child) andar a gatas, gatear; (vehicle) avanzar (lentamente) ▷ n (Swimming) crol m

crayfish ['kreɪfɪʃ] n (pl inv: freshwater) cangrejo (de río); (: saltwater) cigala

crayon ['kreɪən] n lápiz m de color

craze [kreɪz] n (fashion) moda

crazy ['kreɪzɪ] adj (person) loco; (idea) disparatado; **to be ~ about sb/sth** (inf) estar loco por algn/algo

creak [kri:k] vi crujir; (hinge etc) chirriar, rechinar

cream [kri:m] n (of milk) nata, crema; (lotion) crema; (fig) flor f y nata ▷ adj (colour) color m crema; **cream cheese** n queso blanco cremoso; **creamy** adj cremoso

crease [kri:s] n (fold) pliegue m; (in trousers) raya; (wrinkle) arruga ▷ vt (wrinkle) arrugar ▷ vi (wrinkle up) arrugarse

create [kri:'eɪt] vt crear; **creation** n creación f; **creative** adj creativo; **creator** n creador(a) m/f

creature ['kri:tʃəʳ] n (animal) animal m; (insect) bicho; (person) criatura

crèche, creche [krɛʃ] n (BRIT) guardería (infantil)

credentials [krɪ'dɛnʃlz] npl referencias fpl

credibility [krɛdɪ'bɪlɪtɪ] n credibilidad f

credible ['krɛdɪbl] adj creíble

credit ['krɛdɪt] n crédito; (merit) honor m, mérito ▷ vt (Comm) abonar; (believe) creer, dar crédito a ▷ adj crediticio; **to be in ~** (person, bank account) tener saldo a favor; **to ~ sb with** (fig) reconocer a algn el mérito de; see also **credits**; **credit card** n tarjeta de crédito; **credit crunch** n crisis f crediticia

credits ['krɛdɪts] npl (Cine) títulos mpl or rótulos mpl de crédito, ficha técnica

creek [kri:k] n cala, ensenada; (US) riachuelo

creep (pt, pp **crept**) [kri:p, krɛpt] vi (animal) deslizarse

cremate [krɪ'meɪt] vt incinerar

crematorium [krɛmə'tɔ:rɪəm] (pl **crematoria**) n crematorio

crept [krɛpt] pt, pp of **creep**

crescent ['krɛsnt] n media luna; (street) calle f (en forma de semicírculo)

cress [krɛs] n berro

crest [krɛst] n (of bird) cresta; (of hill) cima, cumbre f; (of coat of arms) blasón m

crew [kru:] n (of ship etc) tripulación f; (Cine etc) equipo; **crew-neck** n cuello a la caja

crib [krɪb] n cuna ▷ vt (inf) plagiar

cricket ['krɪkɪt] n (insect) grillo; (game) críquet m; **cricketer** n jugador(a) m/f de críquet

crime [kraɪm] n crimen m; (less serious) delito; **criminal** ['krɪmɪnl] n criminal mf, delincuente mf ▷ adj criminal; (law) penal

crimson ['krɪmzn] adj carmesí

cringe [krɪndʒ] vi encogerse

cripple ['krɪpl] n (inf!) lisiado/a, cojo/a ▷ vt lisiar, mutilar

crisis ['kraɪsɪs] (pl **crises**) n crisis f

crisp [krɪsp] adj fresco; (toast, snow) crujiente; (manner) seco; **crispy** adj crujiente

criterion [kraɪ'tɪərɪən] (pl **criteria**) n criterio

critic ['krɪtɪk] n crítico/a; **critical** adj crítico; (illness) grave; **criticism** ['krɪtɪsɪzm] n crítica; **criticize** ['krɪtɪsaɪz] vt criticar

Croat ['krəuæt] adj, n = **Croatian**

Croatia [krəu'eɪʃə] n Croacia; **Croatian** adj, n croata mf ▷ n (Ling) croata m

crockery ['krɔkərɪ] n loza, vajilla

crocodile ['krɔkədaɪl] n cocodrilo

crocus ['krəukəs] n crocus m, croco

croissant ['krwasā] n croissant m, medialuna (esp LAM)

crook [kruk] n ladrón/ona m/f; (of shepherd) cayado; **crooked** ['krukɪd] adj torcido; (inf) corrupto

crop [krɔp] n (produce) cultivo; (amount produced) cosecha; (riding crop) látigo de montar ▷ vt cortar, recortar; **crop up** vi surgir, presentarse

cross [krɔs] n cruz f ▷ vt (street etc) cruzar, atravesar ▷ adj de mal humor, enojado; **cross off** vt tachar; **cross out** vt tachar; **cross over** vi cruzar; **cross-Channel ferry** n transbordador m que cruza el Canal de la Mancha; **cross-country (race)**

n carrera a campo traviesa, cross *m*; **crossing** *n* (*sea passage*) travesía; (*also*: **pedestrian crossing**) paso de peatones; **crossing guard** *n* (*US*) *persona encargada de ayudar a los niños a cruzar la calle*; **crossroads** *nsg* cruce *m*; (*fig*) encrucijada; **crosswalk** *n* (*US*) paso de peatones; **crossword** *n* crucigrama *m*

crotch [krɔtʃ] *n* (*of garment*) entrepierna

crouch [krautʃ] *vi* agacharse, acurrucarse

crouton ['kru:tɒn] *n* cubito de pan frito

crow [krəu] *n* (*bird*) cuervo; (*of cock*) canto, cacareo ▷ *vi* (*cock*) cantar

crowd [kraud] *n* muchedumbre *f* ▷ *vt* (*gather*) amontonar; (*fill*) llenar ▷ *vi* (*gather*) reunirse; (*pile up*) amontonarse; **crowded** *adj* (*full*) atestado; (*densely populated*) superpoblado

crown [kraun] *n* corona; (*of head*) coronilla; (*of hill*) cumbre *f*; (*for tooth*) funda ▷ *vt* coronar; **and to ~ it all …** (*fig*) y para colmo *or* remate …; **crown jewels** *npl* joyas *fpl* reales

crucial ['kru:ʃl] *adj* decisivo

crucifix ['kru:sɪfɪks] *n* crucifijo

crude [kru:d] *adj* (*materials*) bruto; (*basic*) tosco; (*vulgar*) ordinario ▷ *n* (*also*: **~ oil**) (petróleo) crudo

cruel ['kruəl] *adj* cruel; **cruelty** *n* crueldad *f*

cruise [kru:z] *n* crucero ▷ *vi* (*ship*) navegar; (*car*) ir a velocidad constante

crumb [krʌm] *n* miga, migaja

crumble ['krʌmbl] *vt* desmenuzar ▷ *vi* (*building*) desmoronarse

crumpet ['krʌmpɪt] *n* ≈ bollo para tostar

crumple ['krʌmpl] *vt* (*paper*) estrujar; (*material*) arrugar

crunch [krʌntʃ] *vt* (*with teeth*) mascar; (*underfoot*) hacer crujir ▷ *n* (*fig*) hora de la verdad; **crunchy** *adj* crujiente

crush [krʌʃ] *n* (*crowd*) aglomeración *f* ▷ *vt* aplastar; (*paper*) estrujar; (*cloth*)

arrugar; (*fruit*) exprimir; (*opposition*) aplastar; (*hopes*) destruir; **to have a ~ on sb** estar enamorado de algn

crust [krʌst] *n* corteza; **crusty** *adj* (*bread*) crujiente; (*person*) de mal carácter

crutch [krʌtʃ] *n* muleta

cry [kraɪ] *vi* llorar; (*shout: also*: **~ out**) gritar ▷ *n* grito; (*of animal*) aullido; **cry out** *vi* (*call out, shout*) lanzar un grito, echar un grito ▷ *vt* gritar

crystal ['krɪstl] *n* cristal *m*

cub [kʌb] *n* cachorro; (*also*: **~ scout**) niño explorador

Cuba ['kju:bə] *n* Cuba; **Cuban** *adj, n* cubano/a

cube [kju:b] *n* cubo ▷ *vt* (*Math*) elevar al cubo

cubicle ['kju:bɪkl] *n* (*at pool*) caseta; (*for bed*) cubículo

cuckoo ['kuku:] *n* cuco

cucumber ['kju:kʌmbər] *n* pepino

cuddle ['kʌdl] *vt* abrazar ▷ *vi* abrazarse

cue [kju:] *n* (*snooker cue*) taco; (*Theat etc*) entrada

cuff [kʌf] *n* (*BRIT: of shirt, coat etc*) puño; (*US: of trousers*) vuelta; (*blow*) bofetada; **off the ~** *adv* improvisado; **cufflinks** *npl* gemelos *mpl*

cuisine [kwɪ'zi:n] *n* cocina

cul-de-sac ['kʌldəsæk] *n* callejón *m* sin salida

cull [kʌl] *vt* (*kill selectively: animals*) matar selectivamente ▷ *n* matanza selectiva

culminate ['kʌlmɪneɪt] *vi*: **to ~ in** culminar en

culprit ['kʌlprɪt] *n* culpable *mf*

cult [kʌlt] *n* culto

cultivate ['kʌltɪveɪt] *vt* (*also fig*) cultivar

cultural ['kʌltʃərəl] *adj* cultural

culture ['kʌltʃər] *n* (*also fig*) cultura; (*Biol*) cultivo

cumin ['kʌmɪn] *n* (*spice*) comino

cunning ['kʌnɪn] *n* astucia ▷ *adj* astuto

cup [kʌp] n taza; (prize, event) copa
cupboard ['kʌbəd] n armario; (in kitchen) alacena
cup final n (Football) final f de copa
curator [kjuə'reɪtəʳ] n director(a) m/f
curb [kə:b] vt refrenar ▷ n freno; (US) bordillo
curdle ['kə:dl] vi cuajarse
cure [kjuəʳ] vt curar ▷ n cura, curación f; (fig: solution) remedio
curfew ['kə:fju:] n toque m de queda
curiosity [kjuərɪ'ɔsɪtɪ] n curiosidad f
curious ['kjuərɪəs] adj curioso; **I'm ~ about him** me intriga
curl [kə:l] n rizo ▷ vt (hair) rizar ▷ vi rizarse; **curl up** vi (person) hacerse un ovillo; **curler** n bigudí m, rulo; **curly** adj rizado
currant ['kʌrnt] n pasa; (black, red) grosella
currency ['kʌrnsɪ] n moneda; **to gain ~** (fig) difundirse
current ['kʌrnt] n corriente f ▷ adj actual; **in ~ use** de uso corriente; **current account** n (BRIT) cuenta corriente; **current affairs** npl (noticias fpl de) actualidad f; **currently** adv actualmente
curriculum [kə'rɪkjuləm] (pl **curriculums** or **curricula**) n plan m de estudios; **curriculum vitae** [-'vi:taɪ] n currículum m (vitae)
curry ['kʌrɪ] n curry m ▷ vt: **to ~ favour with** buscar el favor de; **curry powder** n curry m en polvo
curse [kə:s] vi echar pestes, soltar palabrotas ▷ vt maldecir ▷ n maldición f; (swearword) palabrota, taco
cursor ['kə:səʳ] n (Comput) cursor m
curt [kə:t] adj seco
curtain ['kə:tn] n cortina; (Theat) telón m; **to draw the ~s** (together) cerrar las cortinas; (apart) abrir las cortinas
curve [kə:v] n curva ▷ vi (road) hacer una curva; (line etc) curvarse; **curved** adj curvo

cushion ['kuʃən] n cojín m; (Snooker) banda ▷ vt (shock) amortiguar
custard ['kʌstəd] n natillas fpl
custody ['kʌstədɪ] n custodia; **to take sb into ~** detener a algn
custom ['kʌstəm] n costumbre f; (Comm) clientela
customer ['kʌstəməʳ] n cliente mf
customized ['kʌstəmaɪzd] adj (car etc) hecho a encargo
customs ['kʌstəmz] npl aduana sg; **customs officer** n aduanero/a
cut [kʌt] (pt, pp **cut**) vt cortar; (price) rebajar; (reduce) reducir ▷ vi cortar ▷ n corte m; (in skin) cortadura; (in salary etc) rebaja; (in spending) reducción f, recorte m; (slice of meat) tajada; **to ~ and paste** (Comput) cortar y pegar; **cut back** vt (plants) podar; (production, expenditure) reducir; **cut down** vt (tree) derribar; (consumption, expenses) reducir; **cut off** vt cortar; (fig) aislar; **we've been ~ off** (Tel) nos han cortado la comunicación; **cut out** vt (shape) recortar; (delete) suprimir; **cut up** vt cortar (en pedazos); **cutback** n reducción f
cute [kju:t] adj mono
cutlery ['kʌtlərɪ] n cubiertos mpl
cutlet ['kʌtlɪt] n chuleta
cut-price ['kʌt'praɪs] adj a precio reducido
cutting ['kʌtɪŋ] adj (remark) mordaz ▷ n (BRIT: from newspaper) recorte m; (from plant) esqueje m
CV n abbr = **curriculum vitae**
cyber attack ['saɪbərətæk] n ciberataque m
cyberbullying ['saɪbəbulɪɪŋ] n ciberacoso
cybercafé ['saɪbə,kæfeɪ] n cibercafé m
cyberspace ['saɪbəspeɪs] n ciberespacio
cycle ['saɪkl] n ciclo; (bicycle) bicicleta ▷ vi ir en bicicleta; **cycle hire** n alquiler m de bicicletas; **cycle lane** n carril m bici; **cycle path** n

carril-bici *m*; **cycling** *n* ciclismo;
 cyclist *n* ciclista *mf*
cyclone ['saɪkləun] *n* ciclón *m*
cylinder ['sɪlɪndəʳ] *n* cilindro
cymbals ['sɪmblz] *npl* platillos *mpl*
cynical ['sɪnɪkl] *adj* cínico
Cypriot ['sɪprɪət] *adj*, *n* chipriota *mf*
Cyprus ['saɪprəs] *n* Chipre *f*
cyst [sɪst] *n* quiste *m*; **cystitis**
 [sɪs'taɪtɪs] *n* cistitis *f*
czar [zɑːʳ] *n* zar *m*
Czech [tʃɛk] *adj* checo ▷ *n* checo/a;
 the ~ Republic la República Checa

D, d [diː] *n* (*Mus*) re *m*
dab [dæb] *vt*: **to ~ ointment onto
 a wound** aplicar pomada sobre una
 herida; **to ~ with paint** dar unos
 toques de pintura
dad [dæd], **daddy** ['dædɪ] *n* papá *m*
daffodil ['dæfədɪl] *n* narciso
daft [dɑːft] *adj* tonto
dagger ['dægəʳ] *n* puñal *m*, daga; **to
 look ~s at sb** fulminar a algn con
 la mirada
daily ['deɪlɪ] *adj* diario, cotidiano ▷ *adv*
 todos los días, cada día
dairy ['dɛərɪ] *n* (*shop*) lechería; (*on
 farm*) vaquería; **dairy produce** *n*
 productos *mpl* lácteos
daisy ['deɪzɪ] *n* margarita
dam [dæm] *n* presa ▷ *vt* embalsar
damage ['dæmɪdʒ] *n* daño; (*fig*)
 perjuicio; (*to machine*) avería ▷ *vt*
 dañar; perjudicar; averiar; **~ to
 property** daños materiales;
 damages *npl* (*Law*) daños y perjuicios

damn [dæm] vt condenar; (curse)
maldecir ⊳ n (inf): **I don't give a ~** me
importa un pito ⊳ adj (inf: also: **~ed**)
maldito; **~ (it)!** ¡maldito sea!

damp [dæmp] adj húmedo, mojado
⊳ n humedad f ⊳ vt (also: **~en**: cloth,
rag) mojar; (: enthusiasm) enfriar

dance [dɑːns] n baile m ⊳ vi bailar;
dance floor n pista f de baile; **dancer**
n bailador(a) m/f; (professional)
bailarín/ina m/f; **dancing** n baile m

dandelion ['dændɪlaɪən] n diente
m de león

dandruff ['dændrəf] n caspa

D & T (BRIT Scol) n abbr (= design and
technology) diseño y pretecnología

Dane [deɪn] n danés/esa m/f

danger ['deɪndʒə'] n peligro; (risk)
riesgo; **~!** (on sign) ¡peligro!; **to be in
~ of** correr riesgo de; **dangerous** adj
peligroso

dangle ['dæŋgl] vt colgar ⊳ vi pender,
estar colgado

Danish ['deɪnɪʃ] adj danés/esa ⊳ n
(Ling) danés m

dare [dɛə'] vt: **to ~ sb to do** desafiar
a algn a hacer ⊳ vi: **to ~ (to) do sth**
atreverse a hacer algo; **I ~ say** (I
suppose) puede ser; **daring** adj (person)
osado; (plan, escape) atrevido ⊳ n
atrevimiento, osadía

dark [dɑːk] adj oscuro; (hair,
complexion) moreno ⊳ n: **in the
~** a oscuras; **in the ~ about** (fig)
ignorante de; **after ~** después
del anochecer; **darken** vt (colour)
hacer más oscuro ⊳ vi oscurecerse;
darkness n oscuridad f; **darkroom** n
cuarto oscuro

darling ['dɑːlɪŋ] adj, n querido/a

dart [dɑːt] n dardo; (in sewing) pinza
⊳ vi precipitarse; **dartboard** n diana;
darts n dardos mpl

dash [dæʃ] n (small quantity: of liquid)
gota, chorrito; (sign) raya ⊳ vt (hopes)
defraudar ⊳ vi precipitarse, ir de prisa

dashboard ['dæʃbɔːd] n (Aut)
salpicadero

data ['deɪtə] npl datos mpl; **database**
n base f de datos; **data processing** n
proceso or procesamiento de datos

date [deɪt] n (day) fecha; (with friend)
cita; (fruit) dátil m ⊳ vt fechar; (inf:
girl etc) salir con; **~ of birth** fecha de
nacimiento; **to ~** adv hasta la fecha;
dated adj anticuado

daughter ['dɔːtə'] n hija; **daughter-
in-law** n nuera, hija política

daunting ['dɔːntɪŋ] adj desalentador/a

dawn [dɔːn] n alba, amanecer m; (fig)
nacimiento ⊳ vi amanecer; (fig): **it
~ed on him that ...** cayó en la cuenta
de que ...

day [deɪ] n día m; (working day) jornada;
the ~ before el día anterior; **the ~
after tomorrow** pasado mañana;
the ~ before yesterday anteayer;
the following ~ el día siguiente; **by
~** de día; **day-care centre** n centro
de día; (for children) guardería infantil;
daydream vi soñar despierto;
daylight n luz f (del día); **day return**
n (BRIT) billete m de ida y vuelta (en un
día); **daytime** n día m; **day-to-day**
adj cotidiano; **day trip** n excursión f
(de un día)

dazed [deɪzd] adj aturdido

dazzle ['dæzl] vt deslumbrar;
dazzling adj (light, smile)
deslumbrante; (colour) fuerte

DC abbr (Elec) = **direct current**

dead [dɛd] adj muerto; (limb) dormido;
(battery) agotado ⊳ adv (completely)
totalmente; (exactly) justo; **to shoot
sb ~** matar a algn a tiros; **~ tired**
muerto (de cansancio); **to stop ~**
parar en seco; **dead end** n callejón
m sin salida; **deadline** n fecha tope;
deadly adj mortal, fatal; **deadly dull**
aburridísimo; **Dead Sea** n: **the Dead
Sea** el Mar Muerto

deaf [dɛf] adj sordo; **deafen** vt
ensordecer; **deafening** adj
ensordecedor/a

deal [diːl] n (agreement) pacto,
convenio ⊳ vt (pt, pp **dealt**) dar; (card)

repartir; **a great ~ (of)** bastante, mucho; **deal with** vt fus (people) tratar con; (problem) ocuparse de; (subject) tratar de; **dealer** n comerciante mf; (Cards) mano f; **dealings** npl (Comm) transacciones fpl; (relations) relaciones fpl

dealt [dɛlt] pt, pp of **deal**

dean [di:n] n (Rel) deán m; (Scol) decano/a

dear [dɪər] adj querido; (expensive) caro ⊳ n: **my ~ ** querido/a; **~ me!** ¡Dios mío!; **D~ Sir/Madam** (in letter) Muy señor mío, Estimado señor/Estimada señora, De mi/nuestra (mayor) consideración (esp LAM); **D~ Mr/Mrs X** Estimado/a señor(a) X; **dearly** adv (love) mucho; (pay) caro

death [dɛθ] n muerte f; **death penalty** n pena de muerte; **death sentence** n condena a muerte

debate [dɪˈbeɪt] n debate m ⊳ vt discutir

debit [ˈdɛbɪt] n debe m ⊳ vt: **to ~ a sum to sb** or **to sb's account** cargar una suma en cuenta a algn; **debit card** n tarjeta f de débito

debris [ˈdɛbri:] n escombros mpl

debt [dɛt] n deuda f; **to be in ~** tener deudas

debug [ˈdi:ˈbʌg] vt (Comput) depurar, limpiar

début [ˈdeɪbju:] n presentación f

Dec. abbr (= December) dic

decade [ˈdɛkeɪd] n década, decenio m

decaffeinated [dɪˈkæfɪneɪtɪd] adj descafeinado

decay [dɪˈkeɪ] n (of building) desmoronamiento m; (of tooth) caries f inv ⊳ vi (rot) pudrirse

deceased [dɪˈsi:st] n: **the ~** el/la difunto/a

deceit [dɪˈsi:t] n engaño

deceive [dɪˈsi:v] vt engañar

December [dɪˈsɛmbər] n diciembre m

decency [ˈdi:sənsɪ] n decencia

decent [ˈdi:sənt] adj (proper) decente; (person) amable, bueno

deception [dɪˈsɛpʃən] n engaño

Be careful not to translate deception by the Spanish word decepción.

deceptive [dɪˈsɛptɪv] adj engañoso

decide [dɪˈsaɪd] vt (person) decidir; (question, argument) resolver ⊳ vi decidir; **to ~ to do/that** decidir hacer que; **to ~ on sth** tomar una decisión sobre algo

decimal [ˈdɛsɪməl] adj decimal ⊳ n decimal f

decision [dɪˈsɪʒən] n decisión f

decisive [dɪˈsaɪsɪv] adj decisivo; (manner, person) decidido

deck [dɛk] n (Naut) cubierta; (of bus) piso; (of cards) baraja; **record ~** platina; **deckchair** n tumbona

declaration [dɛkləˈreɪʃən] n declaración f

declare [dɪˈklɛər] vt declarar

decline [dɪˈklaɪn] n disminución f ⊳ vt rehusar ⊳ vi (person, business) decaer; (strength) disminuir

decorate [ˈdɛkəreɪt] vt (paint) pintar; (paper) empapelar; (adorn): **to ~ (with)** adornar (de), decorar (de); **decoration** n adorno; (act) decoración f; (medal) condecoración f; **decorator** n (workman) pintor m decorador

decrease [ˈdi:kri:s] n disminución f ⊳ vt [di:ˈkri:s] disminuir, reducir ⊳ vi reducirse

decree [dɪˈkri:] n decreto

dedicate [ˈdɛdɪkeɪt] vt dedicar; **dedicated** adj dedicado; (Comput) especializado; **dedicated word processor** procesador m de textos especializado or dedicado; **dedication** n (devotion) dedicación f; (in book) dedicatoria f

deduce [dɪˈdju:s] vt deducir

deduct [dɪˈdʌkt] vt restar; (from wage etc) descontar; **deduction** n (amount deducted) descuento; (conclusion) deducción f, conclusión f

deed [di:d] n hecho, acto; (feat) hazaña; (Law) escritura

deem [diːm] vt (formal) juzgar, considerar

deep [diːp] adj profundo; (voice) bajo; (breath) profundo ▷ adv: **the spectators stood 20 ~** los espectadores se formaron de 20 en fondo; **to be four metres ~** tener cuatro metros de profundidad; **deep-fry** vt freír en aceite abundante; **deeply** adv (breathe) a pleno pulmón; (interested, moved, grateful) profundamente, hondamente

deer (pl **deer**) [dɪəʳ] n ciervo

default [dɪˈfɔːlt] n (Comput) defecto; **by ~** por incomparecencia

defeat [dɪˈfiːt] n derrota ▷ vt derrotar, vencer

defect [ˈdiːfɛkt] n defecto ▷ vi [dɪˈfɛkt]: **to ~ to the enemy** pasarse al enemigo; **defective** [dɪˈfɛktɪv] adj defectuoso

defence, (US) **defense** [dɪˈfɛns] n defensa

defend [dɪˈfɛnd] vt defender; **defendant** n acusado/a; (in civil case) demandado/a; **defender** n defensor(a) m/f; (Sport) defensa mf

defense [dɪˈfɛns] n (US) = **defence**

defensive [dɪˈfɛnsɪv] adj defensivo ▷ n: **on the ~** a la defensiva

defer [dɪˈfəːʳ] vt aplazar

defiance [dɪˈfaɪəns] n desafío; **in ~ of** en contra de; **defiant** [dɪˈfaɪənt] adj (challenging) retador(a), desafiante

deficiency [dɪˈfɪʃənsɪ] n (lack) falta; (defect) defecto; **deficient** [dɪˈfɪʃənt] adj (lacking) insuficiente; **deficient in** deficiente en

deficit [ˈdɛfɪsɪt] n déficit m

define [dɪˈfaɪn] vt definir; (limits etc) determinar

definite [ˈdɛfɪnɪt] adj (fixed) determinado; (clear, obvious) claro; **he was ~ about it** no dejó lugar a dudas (sobre ello); **definitely** adv: **he's definitely mad** no cabe duda de que está loco

definition [dɛfɪˈnɪʃən] n definición f

deflate [diːˈfleɪt] vt desinflar

deflect [dɪˈflɛkt] vt desviar

defraud [dɪˈfrɔːd] vt: **to ~ sb of sth** estafar algo a algn

defriend [diːˈfrɛnd] vt (Internet) quitar de amigo a; **he has ~ed her on Facebook** la ha quitado de amiga en Facebook

defrost [diːˈfrɔst] vt (frozen food, fridge) descongelar

defuse [diːˈfjuːz] vt desarmar; (situation) calmar

defy [dɪˈfaɪ] vt (resist) oponerse a; (challenge) desafiar; **it defies description** resulta imposible describirlo

degree [dɪˈɡriː] n grado; (Scol) título; **to have a ~ in maths** ser licenciado/a en matemáticas; **by ~s** (gradually) poco a poco, por etapas; **to some ~** hasta cierto punto

dehydrated [diːhaɪˈdreɪtɪd] adj deshidratado; (milk) en polvo

de-icer [diːˈaɪsəʳ] n descongelador m

delay [dɪˈleɪ] vt demorar, aplazar; (person) entretener; (train) retrasar ▷ vi tardar ▷ n demora, retraso; **without ~** en seguida, sin tardar

delegate [ˈdɛlɪɡɪt] n delegado/a ▷ vt [ˈdɛlɪɡeɪt] (person) delegar en; (task) delegar

delete [dɪˈliːt] vt suprimir, tachar

deli [ˈdɛlɪ] n = **delicatessen**

deliberate [dɪˈlɪbərɪt] adj (intentional) intencionado; (slow) pausado, lento ▷ vi [dɪˈlɪbəreɪt] deliberar; **deliberately** adv (on purpose) a propósito

delicacy [ˈdɛlɪkəsɪ] n delicadeza; (choice food) manjar m

delicate [ˈdɛlɪkɪt] adj delicado; (fragile) frágil

delicatessen [dɛlɪkəˈtɛsn] n tienda especializada en alimentos de calidad

delicious [dɪˈlɪʃəs] adj delicioso

delight [dɪˈlaɪt] n (feeling) placer m, deleite m; (object) encanto, delicia ▷ vt encantar, deleitar; **to**

take ~ in deleitarse en; **delighted**
adj: **delighted (at** or **with/to do)**
encantado (con/de hacer); **delightful**
adj encantador(a), delicioso

delinquent [dɪ'lɪŋkwənt] adj, n
delincuente mf

deliver [dɪ'lɪvəʳ] vt (distribute) repartir;
(hand over) entregar; (message)
comunicar; (speech) pronunciar;
(Med) asistir al parto de; **delivery**
n reparto; entrega; (of speaker)
modo de expresarse; (Med) parto,
alumbramiento; **to take delivery
of** recibir

delusion [dɪ'luːʒən] n ilusión f,
engaño

de luxe [də'lʌks] adj de lujo

delve [dɛlv] vi: **to ~ into** hurgar en

demand [dɪ'mɑːnd] vt exigir; (rights)
reclamar ▷ n exigencia; (claim)
reclamación f; (Econ) demanda; **to
be in ~** ser muy solicitado; **on ~** a
solicitud; **demanding** adj (boss)
exigente; (work) absorbente

demise [dɪ'maɪz] n (death)
fallecimiento

demo ['dɛməu] n abbr (inf:
= demonstration) manifestación f

democracy [dɪ'mɔkrəsɪ] n
democracia

democrat ['dɛməkræt] n demócrata
mf; **democratic** [dɛmə'krætɪk]
adj democrático; **the Democratic
Party** el partido demócrata
(estadounidense)

demolish [dɪ'mɔlɪʃ] vt derribar,
demoler; (fig: argument) destruir

demolition [dɛmə'lɪʃən] n derribo,
demolición f

demon ['diːmən] n (evil spirit)
demonio

demonstrate ['dɛmənstreɪt]
vt demostrar ▷ vi manifestarse;
demonstration [dɛmən'streɪʃən] n
(Pol) manifestación f; (proof) prueba,
demostración f; **demonstrator** n (Pol)
manifestante mf

demote [dɪ'məut] vt degradar

den [dɛn] n (of animal) guarida

denial [dɪ'naɪəl] n (refusal) denegación
f; (of report etc) desmentido

denim ['dɛnɪm] n tela vaquera;
denims npl vaqueros mpl

Denmark ['dɛnmɑːk] n Dinamarca

denomination [dɪnɔmɪ'neɪʃən] n
valor m; (Rel) confesión f

denounce [dɪ'nauns] vt denunciar

dense [dɛns] adj (thick) espeso; (foliage
etc) tupido; (stupid) torpe

density ['dɛnsɪtɪ] n densidad f;
single/double-~ disk (Comput)
disco de densidad sencilla/de doble
densidad

dent [dɛnt] n abolladura ▷ vt (also:
make a ~ in) abollar

dental ['dɛntl] adj dental; **dental
floss** n seda dental; **dental surgery** n
clínica dental, consultorio dental

dentist ['dɛntɪst] n dentista mf

dentures ['dɛntʃəz] npl dentadura
sg (postiza)

deny [dɪ'naɪ] vt negar; (charge)
rechazar

deodorant [diː'əudərənt] n
desodorante m

depart [dɪ'pɑːt] vi irse, marcharse;
(train) salir; **to ~ from** (fig: differ from)
apartarse de

department [dɪ'pɑːtmənt] n (Comm)
sección f; (Scol) departamento; (Pol)
ministerio; **department store** n
grandes almacenes mpl

departure [dɪ'pɑːtʃəʳ] n partida, ida;
(of train) salida; **a new ~** un nuevo
rumbo; **departure lounge** n (at
airport) sala de embarque

depend [dɪ'pɛnd] vi: **to ~ (up)on**
depender de; (rely on) contar con; **it ~s**
depende, según; **~ing on the result**
según el resultado; **dependant** n
dependiente mf; **dependent** adj: **to
be dependent (on)** depender (de) ▷ n
= **dependant**

depict [dɪ'pɪkt] vt (in picture) pintar;
(describe) representar

deport [dɪ'pɔːt] vt deportar

deposit [dɪˈpɔzɪt] n depósito; (Chem) sedimento; (of ore, oil) yacimiento ▷ vt depositar; **deposit account** n (BRIT) cuenta de ahorros

depot [ˈdɛpəu] n (storehouse) depósito; (for vehicles) parque m

depreciate [dɪˈpriːʃɪeɪt] vi depreciarse, perder valor

depress [dɪˈprɛs] vt deprimir; (press down) apretar; **depressed** adj deprimido; **depressing** adj deprimente; **depression** n depresión f

deprive [dɪˈpraɪv] vt: **to ~ sb of** privar a algn de; **deprived** adj necesitado

dept. abbr (= department) dto

depth [dɛpθ] n profundidad f; **at a ~ of three metres** a tres metros de profundidad; **to be out of one's ~** (swimmer) perder pie; (fig) sentirse perdido

deputy [ˈdɛpjuti] adj: **~ head** subdirector(a) m/f ▷ n sustituto/a, suplente mf; (Pol) diputado/a

derail [dɪˈreɪl] vt: **to be ~ed** descarrilarse

derelict [ˈdɛrɪlɪkt] adj abandonado

derive [dɪˈraɪv] vt derivar; (benefit etc) obtener ▷ vi: **to ~ from** derivarse de

descend [dɪˈsɛnd] vt, vi descender, bajar; **to ~ from** descender de; **descendant** n descendiente mf

descent [dɪˈsɛnt] n descenso; (origin) descendencia

describe [dɪsˈkraɪb] vt describir; **description** [dɪsˈkrɪpʃən] n descripción f; (sort) clase f, género

desert [n ˈdɛzət, vt, vi dɪˈzəːt] n desierto ▷ vt abandonar ▷ vi (Mil) desertar; **deserted** adj desierto

deserve [dɪˈzəːv] vt merecer, ser digno de

design [dɪˈzaɪn] n (sketch) bosquejo; (of dress, car) diseño; (pattern) dibujo ▷ vt diseñar; **design and technology** n (BRIT Scol) diseño y tecnología

designate [ˈdɛzɪgneɪt] vt (appoint) nombrar; (destine) designar ▷ adj [ˈdɛzɪgnɪt] designado

designer [dɪˈzaɪnər] n diseñador/a (m/f)

desirable [dɪˈzaɪərəbl] adj (proper) deseable; (attractive) atractivo

desire [dɪˈzaɪər] n deseo ▷ vt desear

desk [dɛsk] n (in office) escritorio; (for pupil) pupitre m; (in hotel, at airport) recepción f; (BRIT: in shop, restaurant) caja

desktop [ˈdɛsktɔp] n (Comput) escritorio; **desktop publishing** n autoedición f

despair [dɪsˈpɛər] n desesperación f ▷ vi: **to ~ of** desesperar de

despatch [dɪsˈpætʃ] n, vt = **dispatch**

desperate [ˈdɛspərɪt] adj desesperado; (fugitive) peligroso; **to be ~ for sth/to do** necesitar urgentemente algo/hacer; **desperately** adv desesperadamente; (very) terriblemente, gravemente

desperation [dɛspəˈreɪʃən] n desesperación f; **in ~** desesperado

despise [dɪsˈpaɪz] vt despreciar

despite [dɪsˈpaɪt] prep a pesar de, pese a

dessert [dɪˈzəːt] n postre m; **dessertspoon** n cuchara (de postre)

destination [dɛstɪˈneɪʃən] n destino

destined [ˈdɛstɪnd] adj: **~ for London** con destino a Londres

destiny [ˈdɛstɪnɪ] n destino

destroy [dɪsˈtrɔɪ] vt destruir; **destruction** [dɪsˈtrʌkʃən] n destrucción f

destructive [dɪsˈtrʌktɪv] adj destructivo, destructor(a)

detach [dɪˈtætʃ] vt separar; (unstick) despegar; **detached** adj (attitude) objetivo, imparcial; **detached house** n chalé m, chalet m

detail [ˈdiːteɪl] n detalle m ▷ vt detallar; (Mil) destacar; **in ~** detalladamente; **to go into ~(s)** entrar en detalles; **detailed** adj detallado

detain [dɪˈteɪn] vt retener; (in captivity) detener

detect [dɪ'tɛkt] vt descubrir; (Med, Police) identificar; (Mil, Radar, Tech) detectar; **detection** n descubrimiento; identificación f; **detective** n detective m; **detective story** n novela policíaca

detention [dɪ'tɛnʃən] n detención f, arresto; (Scol) castigo

deter [dɪ'tə:ʳ] vt (dissuade) disuadir

detergent [dɪ'tə:dʒənt] n detergente m

deteriorate [dɪ'tɪərɪəreɪt] vi deteriorarse

determination [dɪtə:mɪ'neɪʃən] n resolución f

determine [dɪ'tə:mɪn] vt determinar; **determined** adj: **to be determined to do sth** estar decidido or resuelto a hacer algo

deterrent [dɪ'tɛrənt] n fuerza de disuasión

detest [dɪ'tɛst] vt aborrecer

detour [ˈdi:tuəʳ] n (us Aut: diversion) desvío

detract [dɪ'trækt] vt: **to ~ from** quitar mérito a, restar valor a

detrimental [dɛtrɪ'mɛntl] adj: **~ (to)** perjudicial a

devastating [ˈdɛvəsteɪtɪŋ] adj devastador/a; (fig) arrollador/a

develop [dɪ'vɛləp] vt desarrollar; (Phot) revelar; (disease) contraer; (habit) adquirir ▷ vi desarrollarse; (advance) progresar; **developing country** n país m en (vías de) desarrollo; **development** n desarrollo; (advance) progreso; (of affair, case) desenvolvimiento; (of land) urbanización f

device [dɪ'vaɪs] n (apparatus) aparato, mecanismo

devil [ˈdɛvl] n diablo, demonio

devious [ˈdi:vɪəs] adj taimado

devise [dɪ'vaɪz] vt idear, inventar

devote [dɪ'vəut] vt: **to ~ sth to** dedicar algo a; **devoted** adj (loyal) leal, fiel; **to be devoted to sb** querer con devoción a algn; **the book is devoted to politics** el libro trata de política; **devotion** n dedicación f; (Rel) devoción f

devour [dɪ'vauəʳ] vt devorar

devout [dɪ'vaut] adj devoto

dew [dju:] n rocío

diabetes [daɪə'bi:ti:z] n diabetes f

diabetic [daɪə'bɛtɪk] n diabético/a

diagnose [ˈdaɪəgnəuz] vt diagnosticar

diagnosis (pl **diagnoses**) [daɪəg'nəusɪs, -si:z] n diagnóstico

diagonal [daɪ'ægənl] adj diagonal ▷ n diagonal f

diagram [ˈdaɪəgræm] n diagrama m, esquema m

dial [ˈdaɪəl] n esfera; (of radio) dial; (of phone) disco ▷ vt (number) marcar

dialect [ˈdaɪəlɛkt] n dialecto

dialling code [ˈdaɪəlɪŋ-] n prefijo

dialling tone n señal f or tono de marcar

dialogue, (us) **dialog** [ˈdaɪəlɔg] n diálogo

diameter [daɪ'æmɪtəʳ] n diámetro

diamond [ˈdaɪəmənd] n diamante m; **diamonds** npl (Cards) diamantes mpl

diaper [ˈdaɪəpəʳ] n (us) pañal m

diarrhoea, (us) **diarrhea** [daɪə'ri:ə] n diarrea

diary [ˈdaɪərɪ] n (daily account) diario; (book) agenda

dice [daɪs] n (pl inv) dados mpl ▷ vt (Culin) cortar en cuadritos

dictate [dɪk'teɪt] vt dictar; **dictation** n dictado

dictator [dɪk'teɪtəʳ] n dictador m

dictionary [ˈdɪkʃənrɪ] n diccionario

did [dɪd] pt of **do**

didn't [ˈdɪdənt] = **did not**

die [daɪ] vi morir; **to be dying for sth/to do sth** morirse por algo/de ganas de hacer algo; **die down** vi apagarse; (wind) amainar; **die out** vi desaparecer

diesel [ˈdi:zl] n diesel m

diet [ˈdaɪət] n dieta; (restricted food) régimen m ▷ vi (also: **be on a ~**) estar a dieta, hacer régimen

differ ['dɪfə'] vi (be different) ser distinto, diferenciarse; (disagree) discrepar; **difference** ['dɪfrəns] n diferencia; (quarrel) desacuerdo; **different** adj diferente, distinto; **differentiate** [dɪfə'renʃɪeɪt] vi: **to differentiate between** distinguir entre; **differently** adv de otro modo, en forma distinta

difficult ['dɪfɪkəlt] adj difícil; **difficulty** n dificultad f

dig [dɪg] vt (pt, pp **dug**) (hole) cavar; (ground) remover ▷ n (prod) empujón m; (archaeological) excavación f; (remark) indirecta; **to ~ one's nails into** clavar las uñas en; see also **digs**; **dig up** vt desenterrar; (plant) desarraigar

digest [daɪ'dʒɛst] vt (food) digerir; (facts) asimilar ▷ n ['daɪdʒɛst] resumen m; **digestion** n digestión f

digit ['dɪdʒɪt] n (number) dígito; (finger) dedo; **digital** adj digital; **digital camera** n cámara digital; **digital TV** n televisión f digital

dignified ['dɪgnɪfaɪd] adj grave, solemne

dignity ['dɪgnɪtɪ] n dignidad f

digs [dɪgz] npl (BRIT inf) pensión f, alojamiento

dilemma [daɪ'lɛmə] n dilema m

dill [dɪl] n eneldo

dilute [daɪ'lu:t] vt diluir

dim [dɪm] adj (light) débil; (outline) borroso; (stupid) lerdo; (room) oscuro ▷ vt (light) bajar

dime [daɪm] n (US) moneda de diez centavos

dimension [dɪ'mɛnʃən] n dimensión f

diminish [dɪ'mɪnɪʃ] vt, vi disminuir

din [dɪn] n estruendo, estrépito

dine [daɪn] vi cenar; **diner** n (person) comensal mf

dinghy ['dɪŋgɪ] n bote m; (also: **rubber ~**) lancha (neumática)

dingy ['dɪndʒɪ] adj (room) sombrío; (dirty) sucio

dining car ['daɪnɪŋ-] n (BRIT) coche-restaurante m

dining room n comedor m

dining table n mesa f de comedor

dinkum ['dɪŋkəm] adj (AUST, NZ inf: also: **fair ~**) de verdad, auténtico; **fair ~?** ¿de verdad?

dinner ['dɪnə'] n (evening meal) cena; (lunch) comida; (public) cena, banquete m; **dinner jacket** n smoking m; **dinner party** n cena; **dinner time** n (evening) hora de cenar; (midday) hora de comer

dinosaur ['daɪnəsɔ:'] n dinosaurio

dip [dɪp] n (slope) pendiente f; (in sea) chapuzón m ▷ vt (in water) mojar; (ladle etc) meter; (BRIT Aut): **to ~ one's lights** poner la luz de cruce ▷ vi descender, bajar

diploma [dɪ'pləumə] n diploma m

diplomacy [dɪ'pləuməsɪ] n diplomacia

diplomat ['dɪpləmæt] n diplomático/a; **diplomatic** [dɪplə'mætɪk] adj diplomático

dipstick ['dɪpstɪk] n (Aut) varilla de nivel (del aceite)

dire [daɪə'] adj calamitoso

direct [daɪ'rɛkt] adj directo; (manner, person) franco ▷ vt dirigir; **can you ~ me to …?** ¿puede indicarme dónde está …?; **to ~ sb to do sth** mandar a algn hacer algo; **direct debit** n domiciliación f bancaria de recibos

direction [dɪ'rɛkʃən] n dirección f; **sense of ~** sentido de la orientación; **directions** npl instrucciones fpl; **~s for use** modo de empleo

directly [dɪ'rɛktlɪ] adv (in straight line) directamente; (at once) en seguida

director [dɪ'rɛktə'] n director(a) m/f

directory [dɪ'rɛktərɪ] n (Tel) guía (telefónica); (Comput) directorio; **directory enquiries, (US) directory assistance** n (service) (servicio m de) información

dirt [də:t] n suciedad f; **dirty** adj sucio; (joke) verde, colorado (LAM) ▷ vt ensuciar; (stain) manchar

disability [dɪsə'bɪlɪtɪ] n incapacidad f

disabled [dɪsˈeɪbld] *adj* (*physically*)
minusválido/a; (*mentally*) deficiente
mental
disadvantage [dɪsədˈvɑːntɪdʒ] *n*
desventaja, inconveniente *m*
disagree [dɪsəˈɡriː] *vi* (*differ*) discrepar;
to ~ (with) no estar de acuerdo (con);
disagreeable *adj* desagradable;
disagreement *n* desacuerdo
disappear [dɪsəˈpɪə^r] *vi* desaparecer;
disappearance *n* desaparición *f*
disappoint [dɪsəˈpɔɪnt] *vt*
decepcionar; defraudar;
disappointed *adj* decepcionado;
disappointing *adj* decepcionante;
disappointment *n* decepción *f*
disapproval [dɪsəˈpruːvəl] *n*
desaprobación *f*
disapprove [dɪsəˈpruːv] *vi*: **to ~ of**
desaprobar
disarm [dɪsˈɑːm] *vt* desarmar;
disarmament *n* desarme *m*
disaster [dɪˈzɑːstə^r] *n* desastre *m*
disastrous [dɪˈzɑːstrəs] *adj*
desastroso
disbelief [dɪsbəˈliːf] *n* incredulidad *f*
disc [dɪsk] *n* disco; (*Comput*); = **disk**
discard [dɪsˈkɑːd] *vt* tirar; (*fig*)
descartar
discharge [dɪsˈtʃɑːdʒ] *vt* (*task,
duty*) cumplir; (*patient*) dar de alta;
(*employee*) despedir; (*soldier*) licenciar;
(*defendant*) poner en libertad ▷ *n*
[ˈdɪstʃɑːdʒ] (*Elec*) descarga; (*dismissal*)
despedida; (*of duty*) desempeño; (*of
debt*) pago, descargo
discipline [ˈdɪsɪplɪn] *n* disciplina ▷ *vt*
disciplinar
disc jockey *n* pinchadiscos *m inv f inv*
disclose [dɪsˈkləuz] *vt* revelar
disco [ˈdɪskəu] *n abbr* = **discothèque**
discoloured, (*us*) **discolored**
[dɪsˈkʌləd] *adj* descolorido
discomfort [dɪsˈkʌmfət] *n*
incomodidad *f*; (*unease*) inquietud *f*;
(*physical*) malestar *m*
disconnect [dɪskəˈnɛkt] *vt* separar;
(*Elec etc*) desconectar

discontent [dɪskənˈtɛnt] *n*
descontento
discontinue [dɪskənˈtɪnjuː] *vt*
interrumpir; (*payments*) suspender
discothèque [ˈdɪskəutɛk] *n*
discoteca
discount [ˈdɪskaunt] *n* descuento
▷ *vt* [dɪsˈkaunt] descontar
discourage [dɪsˈkʌrɪdʒ] *vt*
desalentar; **to ~ sb from doing**
disuadir a algn de hacer
discover [dɪsˈkʌvə^r] *vt* descubrir;
discovery *n* descubrimiento
discredit [dɪsˈkrɛdɪt] *vt* desacreditar
discreet [dɪˈskriːt] *adj* (*tactful*)
discreto; (*careful*) circunspecto,
prudente
discrepancy [dɪˈskrɛpənsɪ] *n*
(*difference*) diferencia
discretion [dɪˈskrɛʃən] *n* (*tact*)
discreción *f*; **at the ~ of** a criterio de
discriminate [dɪˈskrɪmɪneɪt] *vi*:
to ~ between distinguir entre;
to ~ against discriminar contra;
discrimination [dɪskrɪmɪˈneɪʃən]
n (*discernment*) perspicacia; (*bias*)
discriminación *f*
discuss [dɪsˈkʌs] *vt* discutir; (*a theme*)
tratar; **discussion** *n* discusión *f*
disease [dɪˈziːz] *n* enfermedad *f*
disembark [dɪsɪmˈbɑːk] *vt, vi*
desembarcar
disgrace [dɪsˈgreɪs] *n* ignominia;
(*shame*) vergüenza, escándalo
▷ *vt* deshonrar; **disgraceful** *adj*
vergonzoso
disgruntled [dɪsˈgrʌntld] *adj*
disgustado, descontento
disguise [dɪsˈgaɪz] *n* disfraz *m* ▷ *vt*
disfrazar; **in ~** disfrazado
disgust [dɪsˈgʌst] *n* repugnancia ▷ *vt*
repugnar, dar asco a
⬛ Be careful not to translate *disgust*
by the Spanish word *disgustar*.
disgusted [dɪsˈgʌstɪd] *adj* indignado
⬛ Be careful not to translate
disgusted by the Spanish word
disgustado.

disgusting [dɪs'gʌstɪŋ] *adj*
repugnante, asqueroso

dish [dɪʃ] *n* plato; **to do** *or* **wash the**
~es fregar los platos; **dishcloth** *n*
(*for washing*) bayeta; (*for drying*) paño
de cocina

dishonest [dɪs'ɔnɪst] *adj* (*person*)
poco honrado, tramposo; (*means*)
fraudulento

dishtowel ['dɪʃtauəl] *n* (US) bayeta

dishwasher ['dɪʃwɔʃəʳ] *n* lavaplatos
m inv

disillusion [dɪsɪ'lu:ʒən] *vt*
desilusionar

disinfectant [dɪsɪn'fɛktənt] *n*
desinfectante *m*

disintegrate [dɪs'ɪntɪgreɪt] *vi*
disgregarse, desintegrarse

disk [dɪsk] *n* (*Comput*) disco, disquete
m; **single-/double-sided ~** disco
de una cara/dos caras; **disk drive**
n unidad *f* (de disco); **diskette** *n*
disquete *m*

dislike [dɪs'laɪk] *n* antipatía, aversión
f ▷ *vt* tener antipatía a

dislocate ['dɪsləkeɪt] *vt* dislocar

disloyal [dɪs'lɔɪəl] *adj* desleal

dismal ['dɪzml] *adj* (*dark*) sombrío,
(*depressing*) triste; (*very bad*) fatal

dismantle [dɪs'mæntl] *vt*
desmontar, desarmar

dismay [dɪs'meɪ] *n* consternación *f*
▷ *vt* consternar

dismiss [dɪs'mɪs] *vt* (*worker*) despedir;
(*idea*) rechazar; (*Law*) rechazar;
(*possibility*) descartar; **dismissal** *n*
despido

disobedient [dɪsə'bi:dɪənt] *adj*
desobediente

disobey [dɪsə'beɪ] *vt* desobedecer

disorder [dɪs'ɔ:dəʳ] *n* desorden *m*;
(*rioting*) disturbio; (*Med*) trastorno

disorganized [dɪs'ɔ:gənaɪzd] *adj*
desorganizado

disown [dɪs'əun] *vt* renegar de

dispatch [dɪs'pætʃ] *vt* enviar ▷ *n*
(*sending*) envío; (*Press*) informe *m*;
(*Mil*) parte *m*

dispel [dɪs'pɛl] *vt* disipar

dispense [dɪs'pɛns] *vt* (*medicine*)
preparar; **dispense with** *vt fus*
prescindir de; **dispenser** *n* (*container*)
distribuidor *m* automático

disperse [dɪs'pə:s] *vt* dispersar ▷ *vi*
dispersarse

display [dɪs'pleɪ] *n* (*in shop window*)
escaparate *m*; (*exhibition*) exposición
f; (*Comput*) visualización *f*; (*of feeling*)
manifestación *f* ▷ *vt* exponer;
manifestar; (*ostentatiously*) lucir

displease [dɪs'pli:z] *vt* (*offend*)
ofender; (*annoy*) fastidiar

disposable [dɪs'pəuzəbl] *adj*
desechable; **~ personal income**
ingresos *mpl* personales disponibles

disposal [dɪs'pəuzl] *n* (*of rubbish*)
destrucción *f*; **at one's ~** a la
disposición de algn

dispose [dɪs'pəuz] *vi*: **~ of** (*unwanted*
goods) deshacerse de; (*Comm: sell*)
traspasar, vender

disposition [dɪspə'zɪʃən] *n*
disposición *f*; (*temperament*)
carácter *m*

disproportionate [dɪsprə'pɔ:ʃənət]
adj desproporcionado

dispute [dɪs'pju:t] *n* disputa; (*also:*
industrial ~) conflicto (laboral) ▷ *vt*
(*argue*) disputar; (*question*) cuestionar

disqualify [dɪs'kwɔlɪfaɪ] *vt* (*Sport*)
desclasificar; **to ~ sb for sth/from**
doing sth incapacitar a algn para
algo/para hacer algo

disregard [dɪsrɪ'gɑ:d] *vt* (*ignore*) no
hacer caso de

disrupt [dɪs'rʌpt] *vt* (*plans*)
desbaratar, trastornar; (*meeting, public*
transport, conversation) interrumpir;
disruption *n* desbaratamiento;
trastorno; interrupción *f*

dissatisfaction [dɪssætɪs'fækʃən] *n*
disgusto, descontento

dissatisfied [dɪs'sætɪsfaɪd] *adj*
insatisfecho

dissect [dɪ'sɛkt] *vt* disecar

dissent [dɪ'sɛnt] *n* disensión *f*

dissertation [dɪsə'teɪʃən] n tesina
dissolve [dɪ'zɔlv] vt disolver ▷ vi
disolverse
distance ['dɪstns] n distancia; **in the**
~ a lo lejos
distant ['dɪstnt] adj lejano; (manner)
reservado, frío
distil, (US) **distill** [dɪs'tɪl] vt destilar;
distillery n destilería
distinct [dɪs'tɪŋkt] adj (different)
distinto; (clear) claro; (unmistakeable)
inequívoco; **as ~ from** a diferencia
de; **distinction** n distinción f; (in
exam) sobresaliente m; **distinctive**
adj distintivo
distinguish [dɪs'tɪŋgwɪʃ] vt
distinguir; **distinguished** adj
(eminent) distinguido
distort [dɪs'tɔːt] vt deformar; (sound)
distorsionar
distract [dɪs'trækt] vt distraer;
distracted adj distraído; **distraction**
n distracción f; (confusion)
aturdimiento
distraught [dɪs'trɔːt] adj turbado,
enloquecido
distress [dɪs'trɛs] n (anguish)
angustia ▷ vt afligir; **distressing** adj
angustioso; doloroso
distribute [dɪs'trɪbjuːt] vt distribuir;
(share out) repartir; **distribution**
[dɪstrɪ'bjuːʃən] n distribución f;
distributor n (Aut) distribuidor m;
(Comm) distribuidora
district ['dɪstrɪkt] n (of country) zona,
región f; (of town) barrio; (Admin)
distrito; **district attorney** n (US)
fiscal mf
distrust [dɪs'trʌst] n desconfianza
▷ vt desconfiar de
disturb [dɪs'təːb] vt (person: bother,
interrupt) molestar; (disorganize)
desordenar; **disturbance** n (political
etc) disturbio; (of mind) trastorno;
disturbed adj (worried, upset)
preocupado, angustiado; **to be**
emotionally/mentally disturbed
tener problemas emocionales/ser un

trastornado mental; **disturbing** adj
inquietante, perturbador(a)
ditch [dɪtʃ] n zanja; (irrigation ditch)
acequia ▷ vt (inf: partner) deshacerse
de; (: plan, car etc) abandonar
ditto ['dɪtəu] adv ídem, lo mismo
dive [daɪv] n (from board) salto;
(underwater) buceo; (of submarine)
inmersión f ▷ vi (swimmer: into water)
saltar; (: underwater) zambullirse,
bucear; (fish, submarine) sumergirse;
(bird) lanzarse en picado; **to ~ into** (bag
etc) meter la mano en; (place) meterse
de prisa en; **diver** n (underwater) buzo
diverse [daɪ'vəːs] adj diversos/as,
varios/as
diversion [daɪ'vəːʃən] n (BRIT Aut)
desviación f; (distraction) diversión f;
(Mil) diversión f
diversity [daɪ'vəːsɪtɪ] n diversidad f
divert [daɪ'vəːt] vt (train, plane, traffic)
desviar
divide [dɪ'vaɪd] vt dividir; (separate)
separar ▷ vi dividirse; (road) bifurcarse;
divided highway n (US) carretera de
doble calzada
divine [dɪ'vaɪn] adj divino
diving ['daɪvɪŋ] n (Sport) salto;
(underwater) buceo; **diving board** n
trampolín m
division [dɪ'vɪʒən] n división f;
(sharing out) reparto; (disagreement)
diferencias fpl; (Comm) sección f
divorce [dɪ'vɔːs] n divorcio ▷ vt
divorciarse de; **divorced** adj
divorciado; **divorcee** [dɪvɔː'siː] n
divorciado/a
DIY adj, n abbr = **do-it-yourself**
dizzy ['dɪzɪ] adj (person) mareado; **to**
feel ~ marearse
DJ n abbr (= disc jokey) DJ mf
DNA n abbr (= deoxyribonucleic acid)
ADN m

○ **KEYWORD**

do [duː] (pt **did**, pp **done**) n (inf: party
etc): **we're having a little do on**

Saturday damos una fiestecita el sábado; **it was rather a grand do** fue un acontecimiento a lo grande

▶ *aux vb* **1** (*in negative constructions, not translated*): **I don't understand** no entiendo

2 (*to form questions, not translated*): **didn't you know?** ¿no lo sabías?; **what do you think?** ¿qué opinas?

3 (*for emphasis, in polite expressions*): **people do make mistakes sometimes** a veces sí se cometen errores; **she does seem rather late** a mí también me parece que se ha retrasado; **do sit down/help yourself** siéntate/sírvete por favor; **do take care!** ¡ten cuidado! ¿eh?

4 (*used to avoid repeating vb*): **she sings better than I do** canta mejor que yo; **do you agree? — yes, I do/no, I don't** ¿estás de acuerdo? — sí (lo estoy)/no (lo estoy); **she lives in Glasgow — so do I** vive en Glasgow — yo también; **he didn't like it and neither did we** no le gustó y a nosotros tampoco; **who made this mess? — I did** ¿quién hizo esta chapuza? — yo; **he asked me to help him and I did** me pidió que le ayudara y lo hice

5 (*in question tags*): **you like him, don't you?** te gusta, ¿verdad? *or* ¿no?; **I don't know him, do I?** creo que no le conozco

▶ *vt* **1**: **what are you doing tonight?** ¿qué haces esta noche?; **what can I do for you?** (*in shop*) ¿en qué puedo servirle?; **to do the washing-up/cooking** fregar los platos/cocinar; **to do one's teeth/hair/nails** lavarse los dientes/arreglarse el pelo/arreglarse las uñas

2 (*Aut etc*): **the car was doing 100** el coche iba a 100; **we've done 200 km already** ya hemos hecho 200 km; **he can do 100 in that car** puede ir a 100 en ese coche

▶ *vi* **1** (*act, behave*) hacer; **do as I do** haz como yo

2 (*get on, fare*): **he's doing well/badly at school** va bien/mal en la escuela; **the firm is doing well** la empresa anda *or* va bien; **how do you do?** mucho gusto; (*less formal*) ¿qué tal?

3 (*suit*): **will it do?** ¿sirve?, ¿está *or* va bien?

4 (*be sufficient*) bastar; **will £10 do?** ¿será bastante con £10?; **that'll do** así está bien; **that'll do!** (*in annoyance*) ¡ya está bien!, ¡basta ya!; **to make do (with)** arreglárselas (con)

do up *vt* (*laces*) atar; (*zip, dress, shirt*) abrochar; (*renovate: room, house*) renovar

do with *vt fus* (*need*): **I could do with a drink/some help** no me vendría mal un trago/un poco de ayuda; (*be connected with*) tener que ver con; **what has it got to do with you?** ¿qué tiene que ver contigo?

do without *vi*: **if you're late for dinner then you'll do without** si llegas tarde tendrás que quedarte sin cenar ▶ *vt fus* pasar sin; **I can do without a car** puedo pasar sin coche

dock [dɔk] *n* (*Naut*) muelle *m*; (*Law*) banquillo (de los acusados) ▶ *vi* (*enter dock*) atracar (en el muelle); **docks** *npl* muelles *mpl*, puerto *sg*

doctor ['dɔktə'] *n* médico; (*Ph.D. etc*) doctor(a) *m/f* ▶ *vt* (*drink etc*) adulterar; **Doctor of Philosophy** *n* Doctor *m* (en Filosofía y Letras)

document ['dɔkjumənt] *n* documento; **documentary** [dɔkju'mentərɪ] *adj* documental ▶ *n* documental *m*; **documentation** [dɔkjumɛn'teɪʃən] *n* documentación *f*

dodge [dɔdʒ] *n* (*fig*) truco ▶ *vt* evadir; (*blow*) esquivar

dodgy ['dɔdʒɪ] *adj* (BRIT *inf*: *uncertain*) dudoso; (*shady*) sospechoso; (*risky*) arriesgado

does [dʌz] *vb see* **do**

doesn't ['dʌznt] = **does not**

dog [dɒg] n perro ▷ vt seguir (de cerca); (memory etc) perseguir; **doggy bag** n bolsa para llevarse las sobras de la comida

do-it-yourself [duːɪtjɔːˈsɛlf] n bricolaje m

dole [dəul] n (BRIT: payment) subsidio de paro; **on the ~** parado; **dole out** vt repartir

doll [dɒl] n muñeca

dollar [ˈdɒləʳ] n dólar m

dolphin [ˈdɒlfɪn] n delfín m

dome [dəum] n (Arch) cúpula

domestic [dəˈmɛstɪk] adj (animal, duty) doméstico; (flight, news, policy) nacional; **domestic appliance** n aparato m doméstico, aparato m de uso doméstico

dominant [ˈdɒmɪnənt] adj dominante

dominate [ˈdɒmɪneɪt] vt dominar

domino [ˈdɒmɪnəu] (pl **dominoes**) n ficha de dominó; **dominoes** n (game) dominó

donate [dəˈneɪt] vt donar; **donation** n donativo

done [dʌn] pp of **do**

donkey [ˈdɒŋkɪ] n burro

donor [ˈdəunəʳ] n donante mf; **donor card** n carnet m de donante de órganos

don't [dəunt] = **do not**

doodle [ˈduːdl] vi pintar dibujitos or garabatos

doom [duːm] n (fate) suerte f ▷ vt: **to be ~ed to failure** estar condenado al fracaso

door [dɔːʳ] n puerta; **doorbell** n timbre m; **door handle** n tirador m; (of car) manija; **doorknob** n pomo m de la puerta, manilla f (LAM); **doorstep** n peldaño; **doorway** n entrada, puerta

dope [dəup] n (inf: illegal drug) droga; (: person) imbécil mf ▷ vt (horse etc) drogar

dormitory [ˈdɔːmɪtrɪ] n (BRIT) dormitorio; (US) colegio mayor

DOS [dɒs] n abbr = **disk operating system**

dosage [ˈdəusɪdʒ] n dosis f inv

dose [dəus] n dosis f inv

dot [dɒt] n punto ▷ vi: **~ted with** salpicado de; **on the ~** en punto; **dotcom** n puntocom f; **dotted line** n: **to sign on the dotted line** firmar

double [ˈdʌbl] adj doble ▷ adv (twice): **to cost ~** costar el doble ▷ n doble m ▷ vt doblar ▷ vi doblarse; **on the ~, (BRIT) at the ~** corriendo; **double back** vi (person) volver sobre sus pasos; **double bass** n contrabajo; **double bed** n cama de matrimonio; **double-check** vt volver a revisar ▷ vi: **I'll double-check** voy a revisarlo otra vez; **double-click** (Comput) vi hacer doble clic; **double-cross** vt (trick) engañar; (betray) traicionar; **doubledecker** n autobús m de dos pisos; **double glazing** n (BRIT) doble acristalamiento; **double room** n habitación f doble; **doubles** n (Tennis) juego de dobles; **double yellow lines** npl (BRIT Aut) línea doble amarilla de prohibido aparcar ≈ línea f sg amarilla continua

doubt [daut] n duda ▷ vt dudar; (suspect) dudar de; **to ~ that** dudar que; **doubtful** adj dudoso; (unconvinced): **to be doubtful about sth** tener dudas sobre algo; **doubtless** adv sin duda

dough [dəu] n masa, pasta; **doughnut** n dónut m

dove [dʌv] n paloma

down [daun] n (feathers) plumón m, flojel m; (hill) loma ▷ adv (also: **~wards**) abajo, hacia abajo; (on the ground) por/en tierra ▷ prep abajo ▷ vt (inf: drink) beberse; **~ with X!** ¡abajo X!; **down-and-out** n (tramp) vagabundo/a; **downfall** n caída, ruina; **downhill** adv: **to go downhill** ir cuesta abajo

Downing Street [ˈdaunɪŋ-] n (BRIT) Downing Street f

DOWNING STREET

Downing Street es la calle de Londres en la que tienen su residencia oficial tanto el Primer Ministro (*Prime Minister*) como el Ministro de Economía (*Chancellor of the Exchequer*). El primero vive en el n° 10 y el segundo en el n° 11. Es una calle cerrada al público que se encuentra en el barrio de Westminster, en el centro de Londres. *Downing Street* se usa también en lenguaje periodístico para referirse al jefe del gobierno británico.

down: download vt (*Comput*) descargar; **downloadable** adj (*Comput*) descargable; **downright** adj (*nonsense, lie*) manifiesto; (*refusal*) terminante

Down's syndrome [daunz-] n síndrome m de Down

down: downstairs adv (*below*) (en el piso de) abajo; (*motion*) escaleras abajo; **down-to-earth** adj práctico; **downtown** adv en el centro de la ciudad; **down under** adv en Australia (*or* Nueva Zelanda); **downward** ['daunwəd] adv hacia abajo; **downwards** ['daunwədz] adv hacia abajo

doz. abbr = **dozen**

doze [dəuz] vi dormitar

dozen ['dʌzn] n docena; **a ~ books** una docena de libros; **~s of** cantidad de

Dr, Dr. abbr (= *doctor*) Dr; (*in street names*) = **drive**

drab [dræb] adj gris, monótono

draft [drɑːft] n (*first copy*) borrador m; (*us: call-up*) quinta ▷ vt (*write roughly*) hacer un borrador de; *see also* **draught**

drag [dræg] vt arrastrar; (*river*) dragar, rastrear ▷ vi arrastrarse por el suelo ▷ n (*inf*) lata; (*women's clothing*): **in ~** vestido de mujer; **to ~ and drop** (*Comput*) arrastrar y soltar

dragon ['drægən] n dragón m

dragonfly ['drægənflaɪ] n libélula

drain [dreɪn] n desaguadero; (*in street*) sumidero ▷ vt (*land, marshes*) desecar; (*reservoir*) desecar; (*fig*) agotar ▷ vi escurrirse; **to be a ~ on** consumir, agotar; **drainage** n (*act*) desagüe m; (*Med, Agr*) drenaje m; (*sewage*) alcantarillado; **drainpipe** n tubo de desagüe

drama ['drɑːmə] n (*art*) teatro; (*play*) drama m; **dramatic** [drə'mætɪk] adj dramático; (*sudden, marked*) espectacular

drank [dræŋk] pt of **drink**

drape [dreɪp] vt (*cloth*) colocar; (*flag*) colgar

drastic ['dræstɪk] adj (*measure, reduction*) severo; (*change*) radical

draught, (*us*) **draft** [drɑːft] n (*of air*) corriente f de aire; (*Naut*) calado; **on ~** (*beer*) de barril; **draught beer** n cerveza de barril; **draughts** n (*BRIT*) juego de damas

draw [drɔː] (*pt* **drew**, *pp* **drawn**) vt (*take out*) sacar; (*attract*) atraer; (*picture*) dibujar; (*money*) retirar ▷ vi (*Sport*) empatar ▷ n (*Sport*) empate m; (*lottery*) sorteo; **draw out** vi (*lengthen*) alargarse; **draw up** vi (*stop*) pararse ▷ vt (*document*) redactar; **drawback** n inconveniente m, desventaja

drawer n cajón m

drawing ['drɔːɪŋ] n dibujo; **drawing pin** n (*BRIT*) chincheta; **drawing room** n salón m

drawn [drɔːn] pp of **draw**

dread [dred] n pavor m, terror m ▷ vt temer, tener miedo *or* pavor a; **dreadful** adj espantoso

dream [driːm] n sueño ▷ vt, vi soñar; **dreamer** n soñador(a) m/f

dreamt [dremt] pt, pp of **dream**

dreary ['drɪərɪ] adj monótono

drench [drentʃ] vt empapar

dress [dres] n vestido; (*clothing*) ropa ▷ vt vestir; (*wound*) vendar ▷ vi vestirse; **to ~ o.s., get ~ed** vestirse;

dress up vi vestirse de etiqueta; (in fancy dress) disfrazarse; **dress circle** n (BRIT) principal m; **dresser** n (furniture) aparador m; (: US) tocador m; **dressing** n (Med) vendaje m; (Culin) aliño; **dressing gown** n (BRIT) bata; **dressing room** n (Theat) camarín m; (Sport) vestuario; **dressing table** n tocador m; **dressmaker** n modista, costurera

drew [druː] pt of **draw**

dribble ['drɪbl] vi (baby) babear ▷ vt (ball) regatear

dried [draɪd] adj seco; (milk) en polvo

drier ['draɪəʳ] n = **dryer**

drift [drɪft] n (of current etc) flujo; (of snow) ventisquero; (meaning) significado ▷ vi (boat) ir a la deriva; (sand, snow) amontonarse

drill [drɪl] n taladro; (bit) broca; (of dentist) fresa; (for mining etc) perforadora, barrena; (Mil) instrucción f ▷ vt perforar, taladrar; (soldiers) ejercitar ▷ vi (for oil) perforar

drink [drɪŋk] n bebida ▷ vt, vi beber; **to have a ~** tomar algo; tomar una copa or un trago; **a ~ of water** un trago de agua; **drink-driving** n: **to be charged with drink-driving** ser acusado de conducir borracho or en estado de embriaguez; **drinker** n bebedor(a) m/f; **drinking water** n agua potable

drip [drɪp] n (act) goteo; (one drip) gota; (Med) gota a gota m ▷ vi gotear

drive [draɪv] n (journey) viaje m (en coche); (also: **~way**) entrada; (energy) energía, vigor m; (Comput: also: **disk ~**) unidad f (de disco) ▷ vt (car) conducir; (nail) clavar; (push) empujar; (Tech: motor) impulsar ▷ vi (Aut: at controls) conducir, manejar (LAM); (: travel) pasearse en coche; **left-/right-hand ~** conducción f a la izquierda/derecha; **to ~ sb mad** volverle loco a algn; **drive out** vt (force out) expulsar, echar; **drive-in** adj (esp US): **drive-in cinema** autocine m

driven ['drɪvn] pp of **drive**

driver ['draɪvəʳ] n conductor(a) m/f, chofer m (LAM); **driver's license** n (US) carnet m or permiso de conducir

driveway ['draɪvweɪ] n camino de entrada

driving ['draɪvɪŋ] n conducir m, manejar m (LAM); **driving instructor** n instructor(a) m/f de autoescuela; **driving lesson** n clase f de conducir; **driving licence** n (BRIT) carnet m or permiso de conducir; **driving test** n examen m de conducir

drizzle ['drɪzl] n llovizna

droop [druːp] vi (flower) marchitarse; (shoulders) encorvarse; (head) inclinarse

drop [drɔp] n (of water) gota; (fall: in price) bajada ▷ vt dejar caer; (voice, eyes, price) bajar; (set down from car) dejar ▷ vi (object) caer; (price, temperature) bajar; (wind) amainar; **drop in** vi (inf: visit): **to ~ in (on)** pasar por casa (de); **drop off** vi (sleep) dormirse ▷ vt (passenger) dejar; **drop out** vi (withdraw) retirarse

drought [draut] n sequía

drove [drəuv] pt of **drive**

drown [draun] vt ahogar ▷ vi ahogarse

drowsy ['drauzɪ] adj soñoliento; **to be ~** tener sueño

drug [drʌg] n medicamento; (narcotic) droga ▷ vt drogar; **to be on ~s** drogarse; **drug addict** n drogadicto/a; **drug dealer** n traficante mf de drogas; **druggist** n (US) farmacéutico/a; **drugstore** n (US) tienda (de comestibles, periódicos y medicamentos)

drum [drʌm] n tambor m; (for oil, petrol) bidón m; **drums** npl batería sg; **drummer** n tambor mf

drunk [drʌŋk] pp of **drink** ▷ adj borracho ▷ n (also: **drunkard**) borracho/a; **drunken** adj borracho

dry [draɪ] adj seco; (day) sin lluvia; (climate) árido, seco ▷ vt secar; (tears) enjugarse ▷ *vi* secarse; **dry up** *vi* (*river*) secarse; **dry-cleaner's** *n* tintorería; **dry-cleaning** *n* lavado en seco; **dryer** *n* (*for hair*) secador *m*; (*for clothes*) secadora

DSS *n abbr* (BRIT) = **Department of Social Security**; *see* **social security**

DTP *n abbr* = **desktop publishing**

dual ['djuəl] *adj* doble; **dual carriageway** *n* (BRIT) ≈ autovía

dubious ['dju:bɪəs] *adj* (*questionable: reputation*) dudoso; (: *character*) sospechoso; (*unsure*) indeciso

duck [dʌk] *n* pato ▷ *vi* agacharse

due [dju:] *adj* (*proper*) debido ▷ *adv*: **~ north** derecho al norte; **in ~ course** a su debido tiempo; **~ to** debido a; **the train is ~ to arrive at 8.00** el tren tiene (prevista) la llegada a las ocho; **the rent's ~ on the 30th** hay que pagar el alquiler el día 30

duel ['djuəl] *n* duelo

duet [dju:'ɛt] *n* dúo

dug [dʌg] *pt, pp of* **dig**

duke [dju:k] *n* duque *m*

dull [dʌl] *adj* (*light*) apagado; (*stupid*) torpe; (*boring*) pesado; (*sound, pain*) sordo; (*weather, day*) gris ▷ *vt* (*pain, grief*) aliviar; (*mind, senses*) entorpecer

dumb [dʌm] *adj* mudo; (*stupid*) estúpido

dummy ['dʌmɪ] *n* (*tailor's model*) maniquí *m*; (BRIT: *for baby*) chupete *m* ▷ *adj* falso, postizo

dump [dʌmp] *n* (*place*) basurero, vertedero *m* ▷ *vt* (*put down*) dejar; (*get rid of*) deshacerse de; (*Comput*) tirar (a la papelera); (*Comm: goods*) inundar el mercado de

dumpling ['dʌmplɪŋ] *n bola de masa hervida*

dune [dju:n] *n* duna

dungarees [dʌŋgə'ri:z] *npl* mono *sg*, overol *msg* (LAM)

dungeon ['dʌndʒən] *n* calabozo

duplex ['dju:plɛks] *n* dúplex *m*

duplicate ['dju:plɪkət] *n* duplicado ▷ *vt* ['dju:plɪkeɪt] duplicar; (*photocopy*) fotocopiar; (*repeat*) repetir; **in ~** por duplicado

durable ['djuərəbl] *adj* duradero

duration [djuə'reɪʃən] *n* duración *f*

during ['djuərɪŋ] *prep* durante

dusk [dʌsk] *n* crepúsculo, anochecer *m*

dust [dʌst] *n* polvo ▷ *vt* (*furniture*) desempolvar; (*cake etc*) espolvorear de; **dustbin** *n* (BRIT) cubo de la basura, balde *m* (LAM); **duster** *n* paño, trapo; **dustman** *n* basurero; **dustpan** *n* cogedor *m*; **dusty** *adj* polvoriento

Dutch [dʌtʃ] *adj* holandés/esa ▷ *n* (*Ling*) holandés *m* ▷ *adv*: **to go ~** pagar a escote; **the Dutch** *npl* los holandeses; **Dutchman, Dutchwoman** *n* holandés/esa *m/f*

duty ['dju:tɪ] *n* deber *m*; (*tax*) derechos *mpl* de aduana; **on ~** de servicio; (*at night etc*) de guardia; **off ~** libre (de servicio); **duty-free** *adj* libre de impuestos

duvet ['du:veɪ] *n* (BRIT) edredón *m* (*nórdico*)

DVD *n abbr* (= *digital versatile or video disc*) DVD *m*; **DVD player** *n* lector *m* de DVD; **DVD writer** *n* grabadora de DVD

dwarf (*pl* **dwarves**) [dwɔ:f, dwɔ:vz] *n* (*infl*) enano/a ▷ *vt* empequeñecer

dwell (*pt, pp* **dwelt**) [dwɛl, dwɛlt] *vi* morar; **dwell on** *vt fus* explayarse en

dwindle ['dwɪndl] *vi* disminuir

dye [daɪ] *n* tinte *m* ▷ *vt* teñir

dying ['daɪɪŋ] *adj* moribundo

dynamic [daɪ'næmɪk] *adj* dinámico

dynamite ['daɪnəmaɪt] *n* dinamita

dyslexia [dɪs'lɛksɪə] *n* dislexia

dyslexic [dɪs'lɛksɪk] *adj, n* disléxico/a

de primavera/del siglo diecinueve; **early retirement** n jubilación f anticipada

earmark ['ɪəmɑːk] vt: **to ~ for** reservar para, destinar a

earn [əːn] vt (salary) percibir; (interest) devengar; (praise) ganarse

earnest ['əːnɪst] adj (wish) fervoroso; (person) serio, formal ▷ n: **in ~** adv en serio

earnings ['əːnɪŋz] npl (personal) ingresos mpl; (of company etc) ganancias fpl

ear: earphones npl auriculares mpl; **earplugs** npl tapones mpl para los oídos; **earring** n pendiente m, arete m (LAM)

earth [əːθ] n tierra; (BRIT Elec) toma de tierra ▷ vt (BRIT Elec) conectar a tierra; **earthquake** n terremoto

ease [iːz] n facilidad f; (comfort) comodidad f ▷ vt (problem) mitigar; (pain) aliviar; **to ~ sth in/out** meter/sacar algo con cuidado; **at ~!** (Mil) ¡descansen!

easily ['iːzɪlɪ] adv fácilmente

east [iːst] n este m ▷ adj del este, oriental ▷ adv al este, hacia el este; **the E~** el Oriente; (Pol) el Este; **eastbound** adj en dirección este

Easter ['iːstəʳ] n Pascua (de Resurrección); **Easter egg** n huevo de Pascua

eastern ['iːstən] adj del este, oriental

Easter Sunday n Domingo de Resurrección

easy ['iːzɪ] adj fácil; (life) holgado, cómodo; (relaxed) natural ▷ adv: **to take it** or **things ~** (not worry) no preocuparse; (rest) descansar; **easy-going** adj acomodadizo

eat (pt **ate**, pp **eaten**) [iːt, eit, 'iːtn] vt comer; **eat out** vi comer fuera

eavesdrop ['iːvzdrɔp] vi: **to ~ (on sb)** escuchar a escondidas or con disimulo (a algn)

e-book ['iːbuk] n libro electrónico

E [iː] n (Mus) mi m

each [iːtʃ] adj cada inv ▷ pron cada uno; **~ other** el uno al otro; **they hate ~ other** se odian (entre ellos or mutuamente)

eager ['iːgəʳ] adj (keen) entusiasmado; **to be ~ to do sth** estar deseoso de hacer algo; **to be ~ for** tener muchas ganas de

eagle ['iːgl] n águila

ear [ɪəʳ] n oreja; (sense of hearing) oído; (of corn) espiga; **earache** n dolor m de oídos; **eardrum** n tímpano

earl [əːl] n conde m

earlier ['əːlɪəʳ] adj anterior ▷ adv antes

early ['əːlɪ] adv temprano; (ahead of time) con tiempo, con anticipación ▷ adj temprano; (reply) pronto; (man) primitivo; (first: Christians, settlers) primero; **to have an ~ night** acostarse temprano; **in the ~** or **~ in the spring/19th century** a principios

e-business ['iːbɪznɪs] n (commerce) comercio electrónico; (company) negocio electrónico

EC n abbr (= European Community) CE f

eccentric [ɪk'sɛntrɪk] adj, n excéntrico/a

echo ['ɛkəʊ] (pl **echoes**) n eco m ▷ vt (sound) repetir ▷ vi resonar, hacer eco

eclipse [ɪ'klɪps] n eclipse m

eco-friendly ['iːkəʊfrɛndlɪ] adj ecológico

ecological [iːkə'lɒdʒɪkl] adj ecológico

ecology [ɪ'kɒlədʒɪ] n ecología

e-commerce ['iːkɒmɜːs] n comercio electrónico

economic [iːkə'nɒmɪk] adj económico; (business etc) rentable; **economical** adj económico; **economics** n (Scol) economía

economist [ɪ'kɒnəmɪst] n economista mf

economize [ɪ'kɒnəmaɪz] vi economizar, ahorrar

economy [ɪ'kɒnəmɪ] n economía; **economy class** n (Aviat etc) clase f turista; **economy class syndrome** n síndrome m de la clase turista

ecstasy ['ɛkstəsɪ] n éxtasis m inv; (drug) éxtasis m inv; **ecstatic** [ɛks'tætɪk] adj extático

eczema ['ɛksɪmə] n eczema m

edge [ɛdʒ] n (of knife etc) filo m; (of object) borde m; (of lake etc) orilla ▷ vt (Sewing) ribetear; **on ~** (fig) = **edgy**; **to ~ away from** alejarse poco a poco de

edgy ['ɛdʒɪ] adj nervioso, inquieto

edible ['ɛdɪbl] adj comestible

Edinburgh ['ɛdɪnbərə] n Edimburgo

edit ['ɛdɪt] vt (be editor of) dirigir; (re-write) redactar; (Comput) editar; **edition** [ɪ'dɪʃən] n edición f; **editor** n (of newspaper) director(a) m/f; (of book) redactor(a) m/f; **editorial** [ɛdɪ'tɔːrɪəl] adj editorial ▷ n editorial m

educate ['ɛdjʊkeɪt] vt educar; (instruct) instruir; **educated** ['ɛdjʊkeɪtɪd] adj culto

education [ɛdjʊ'keɪʃən] n educación f; (schooling) enseñanza; (Scol) pedagogía; **educational** adj (policy etc) de educación, educativo; (teaching) docente; (instructive) educativo

eel [iːl] n anguila

eerie ['ɪərɪ] adj espeluznante

effect [ɪ'fɛkt] n efecto ▷ vt efectuar, llevar a cabo; **effects** npl (property) efectos mpl; **to take ~** (law) entrar en vigor or vigencia; (drug) surtir efecto; **in ~** en realidad; **effective** adj eficaz; (real) efectivo; **effectively** adv eficazmente; (in reality) de hecho

efficiency [ɪ'fɪʃənsɪ] n eficiencia; (of machine) rendimiento

efficient [ɪ'fɪʃənt] adj eficiente; (machine, car) de buen rendimiento; **efficiently** adv eficientemente, de manera eficiente

effort ['ɛfət] n esfuerzo; **effortless** adj sin ningún esfuerzo

e.g. adv abbr (= exempli gratia) p.ej.

egg [ɛg] n huevo; **hard-boiled/ soft-boiled/poached ~** huevo duro or (LAM) a la copa or (LAM) tibio/ pasado por agua/escalfado; **eggcup** n huevera; **eggplant** n (esp US) berenjena; **eggshell** n cáscara de huevo; **egg white** n clara de huevo; **egg yolk** n yema de huevo

ego ['iːgəʊ] n ego

Egypt ['iːdʒɪpt] n Egipto; **Egyptian** [ɪ'dʒɪpʃən] adj, n egipcio/a

eight [eɪt] num ocho; **eighteen** num dieciocho; **eighteenth** adj decimoctavo; **the eighteenth floor** la planta dieciocho; **the eighteenth of August** el dieciocho de agosto; **eighth** [eɪtθ] adj octavo; **eightieth** ['eɪtɪɪθ] adj octogésimo; **eighty** ['eɪtɪ] num ochenta

Eire ['ɛərə] n Eire m

either ['aɪðəʳ] adj cualquiera de los dos ...; (both, each) cada ▷ pron: **~ (of them)** cualquiera (de los dos) ▷ adv tampoco ▷ conj: **~ yes or no** o sí o no;

on ~ side en ambos lados; **I don't like ~** no me gusta ninguno de los dos; **no, I don't ~** no, yo tampoco

eject [ɪ'dʒɛkt] *vt* echar; (*tenant*) desahuciar

elaborate *adj* [ɪ'læbərɪt] (*design, pattern*) complejo ▷ *vt* [ɪ'læbəreɪt] elaborar; (*expand*) ampliar; (*refine*) refinar ▷ *vi* explicarse con muchos detalles

elastic [ɪ'læstɪk] *adj, n* elástico; **elastic band** (*BRIT*) gomita

elbow ['ɛlbəʊ] *n* codo

elder ['ɛldə'] *adj* mayor ▷ *n* (*tree*) saúco; (*person*) mayor; **elderly** *adj* de edad, mayor ▷ *npl*: **the elderly** los mayores, los ancianos

eldest ['ɛldɪst] *adj, n* el/la mayor

elect [ɪ'lɛkt] *vt* elegir; **to ~ to do** optar por hacer ▷ *adj*: **the president ~** el presidente electo; **election** *n* elección *f*; **electoral** *adj* electoral; **electorate** *n* electorado

electric [ɪ'lɛktrɪk] *adj* eléctrico; **electrical** *adj* eléctrico; **electric blanket** *n* manta eléctrica; **electric fire** *n* estufa eléctrica; **electrician** [ɪlɛk'trɪʃən] *n* electricista *mf*; **electricity** [ɪlɛk'trɪsɪtɪ] *n* electricidad *f*; **electric shock** *n* electrochoque *m*; **electrify** [ɪ'lɛktrɪfaɪ] *vt* (*Rail*) electrificar; (*fig: audience*) electrizar

electronic [ɪlɛk'trɔnɪk] *adj* electrónico; **electronic mail** *n* correo electrónico; **electronics** *n* electrónica

elegance ['ɛlɪgəns] *n* elegancia

elegant ['ɛlɪgənt] *adj* elegante

element ['ɛlɪmənt] *n* elemento; (*of heater, kettle etc*) resistencia

elementary [ɛlɪ'mɛntərɪ] *adj* elemental; (*primitive*) rudimentario; **elementary school** *n* (*US*) escuela de enseñanza primaria

elephant ['ɛlɪfənt] *n* elefante *m*

elevate ['ɛlɪveɪt] *vt* elevar; (*in rank*) ascender

elevator ['ɛlɪveɪtə'] *n* (*US*) ascensor *m*

eleven [ɪ'lɛvn] *num* once; **eleventh** [ɪ'lɛvnθ] *adj* undécimo

eligible ['ɛlɪdʒəbl] *adj*: **an ~ young man/woman** un buen partido; **to be ~ for sth** llenar los requisitos para algo

eliminate [ɪ'lɪmɪneɪt] *vt* (*a suspect, possibility*) descartar

elm [ɛlm] *n* olmo

eloquent ['ɛləkwənt] *adj* elocuente

else [ɛls] *adv*: **something ~** otra cosa *or* algo más; **somewhere ~** en otra parte; **everywhere ~** en todas partes menos aquí; **where ~?** ¿dónde más?, ¿en qué otra parte?; **there was little ~ to do** apenas quedaba otra cosa que hacer; **nobody ~** nadie más; **elsewhere** *adv* (*be*) en otra parte; (*go*) a otra parte

elusive [ɪ'luːsɪv] *adj* esquivo; (*answer*) difícil de encontrar

email ['iːmeɪl] *n abbr* (= *electronic mail*) email *m*, correo electrónico; **email address** *n* dirección *f* electrónica, email *m*

embankment [ɪm'bæŋkmənt] *n* terraplén *m*

embargo [ɪm'bɑːgəʊ] (*pl* **embargoes**) *n* prohibición *f*; (*Comm, Naut*) embargo; **to put an ~ on sth** poner un embargo en algo

embark [ɪm'bɑːk] *vi* embarcarse ▷ *vt* embarcar; **to ~ on** (*journey*) emprender, iniciar

embarrass [ɪm'bærəs] *vt* avergonzar, dar vergüenza a; **embarrassed** *adj* azorado, violento; **to be embarrassed** sentirse azorado *or* violento; **embarrassing** *adj* (*situation*) violento; (*question*) embarazoso; **embarrassment** *n* vergüenza

Be careful not to translate *embarrassed* by the Spanish word *embarazada*.

embassy ['ɛmbəsɪ] *n* embajada

embrace [ɪm'breɪs] *vt* abrazar, dar un abrazo a; (*include*) abarcar ▷ *vi* abrazarse ▷ *n* abrazo

embroider [ɪmˈbrɔɪdəʳ] vt bordar;
embroidery n bordado
embryo [ˈɛmbrɪəʊ] n embrión m
emerald [ˈɛmərəld] n esmeralda
emerge [ɪˈmɜːdʒ] vi salir; (arise) surgir
emergency [ɪˈmɜːdʒənsɪ] n crisis
f inv; **in an ~** en caso de urgencia;
(to declare a) state of ~ (declarar)
estado de emergencia or de excepción;
emergency brake n (US) freno de
mano; **emergency exit** n salida de
emergencia; **emergency landing**
n aterrizaje m forzoso; **emergency
room** (US Med) n sala f de urgencias;
emergency service n servicio de
urgencia
emigrate [ˈɛmɪɡreɪt] vi emigrar;
emigration n emigración f
eminent [ˈɛmɪnənt] adj eminente
emission [ɪˈmɪʃən] n emisión f
emit [ɪˈmɪt] vt emitir; (smell, smoke)
despedir
emoticon [ɪˈməʊtɪkɒn] n emoticón m
emotion [ɪˈməʊʃən] n emoción f;
emotional adj (person) sentimental;
(scene) conmovedor(a), emocionante
emperor [ˈɛmpərəʳ] n emperador m
emphasis (pl **emphases**) [ˈɛmfəsɪs,
-siːz] n énfasis m inv
emphasize [ˈɛmfəsaɪz] vt (word,
point) subrayar, recalcar; (feature)
hacer resaltar
empire [ˈɛmpaɪəʳ] n imperio
employ [ɪmˈplɔɪ] vt emplear;
employee [ɪmplɔɪˈiː] n empleado/a;
employer n patrón/ona m/f;
(businessman) empresario/a;
employment n empleo; **to find
employment** encontrar trabajo;
employment agency n agencia de
colocaciones or empleo
empower [ɪmˈpaʊəʳ] vt: **to ~ sb
to do sth** autorizar a algn para
hacer algo
empress [ˈɛmprɪs] n emperatriz f
emptiness [ˈɛmptɪnɪs] n vacío
empty [ˈɛmptɪ] adj vacío; (street, area)
desierto; (threat) vano ▷ vt vaciar;

(place) dejar vacío ▷ vi vaciarse; (house)
quedar(se) vacío or desocupado;
empty-handed adj con las manos
vacías
EMU n abbr (= European Monetary
Union) UME f
emulsion [ɪˈmʌlʃən] n emulsión f
enable [ɪˈneɪbl] vt: **to ~ sb to do sth**
permitir a algn hacer algo
enamel [ɪˈnæməl] n esmalte m
enchanting [ɪnˈtʃɑːntɪŋ] adj
encantador(a)
encl. abbr (= enclosed) adj
enclose [ɪnˈkləʊz] vt (land) cercar;
(with letter etc) adjuntar; **please find
~d** le mandamos adjunto
enclosure [ɪnˈkləʊʒəʳ] n cercado,
recinto
encore [ɒŋˈkɔːʳ] excl ¡otra!, ¡bis! ▷ n
bis m
encounter [ɪnˈkaʊntəʳ] n encuentro
▷ vt encontrar, encontrarse con;
(difficulty) tropezar con
encourage [ɪnˈkʌrɪdʒ] vt alentar,
animar; (growth) estimular;
encouragement n estímulo; (of
industry) fomento
encouraging [ɪnˈkʌrɪdʒɪŋ] adj
alentador(a)
encyclop(a)edia [ɛnsaɪkləʊˈpiːdɪə]
n enciclopedia
end [ɛnd] n fin m; (of table) extremo;
(of street) final m; (Sport) lado ▷ vt
terminar, acabar; (also: **bring to an ~,
put an ~ to**) acabar con ▷ vi terminar,
acabar; **in the ~** al final; on ~
(object) de punta, de cabeza; **to stand on ~**
(hair) erizarse; **for hours on ~** hora
tras hora; **end up** vi: **to ~ up in**
terminar en; (place) ir a parar a
endanger [ɪnˈdeɪndʒəʳ] vt poner en
peligro; **an ~ed species** una especie
en peligro de extinción
endearing [ɪnˈdɪərɪŋ] adj entrañable
endeavour, (US) **endeavor**
[ɪnˈdɛvəʳ] n esfuerzo; (attempt)
tentativa ▷ vi: **to ~ to do** esforzarse
por hacer; (try) procurar hacer

ending ['ɛndɪŋ] n (of book) desenlace m; (Ling) terminación f
endless ['ɛndlɪs] adj interminable, inacabable
endorse [ɪn'dɔːs] vt (cheque) endosar; (approve) aprobar; **endorsement** n (on driving licence) nota de sanción
endurance [ɪn'djuərəns] n resistencia
endure [ɪn'djuəʳ] vt (bear) aguantar, soportar ▷ vi (last) perdurar
enemy ['ɛnəmɪ] adj, n enemigo/a
energetic [ɛnə'dʒɛtɪk] adj enérgico
energy ['ɛnədʒɪ] n energía
enforce [ɪn'fɔːs] vt (law) hacer cumplir
engaged [ɪn'geɪdʒd] adj (BRIT: busy, in use) ocupado; (betrothed) prometido; **to get ~** prometerse; **engaged tone** n (BRIT Tel) señal f de comunicando
engagement [ɪn'geɪdʒmənt] n (appointment) compromiso, cita; (to marry) compromiso; (period) noviazgo; **engagement ring** n anillo de pedida
engaging [ɪn'geɪdʒɪŋ] adj atractivo
engine ['ɛndʒɪn] n (Aut) motor m; (Rail) locomotora
engineer [ɛndʒɪ'nɪəʳ] n ingeniero/a; (BRIT: for repairs) técnico/a; (US Rail) maquinista mf; **engineering** n ingeniería
England ['ɪŋglənd] n Inglaterra
English ['ɪŋglɪʃ] adj inglés/esa ▷ n (Ling) el inglés; **the English** npl los ingleses; **English Channel** n: **the English Channel** el Canal de la Mancha; **Englishman, Englishwoman** n inglés/esa m/f
engrave [ɪn'greɪv] vt grabar
engraving [ɪn'greɪvɪŋ] n grabado
enhance [ɪn'hɑːns] vt aumentar; (beauty) realzar
enjoy [ɪn'dʒɔɪ] vt (health, fortune) disfrutar de, gozar de; **I ~ doing ...** me gusta hacer ...; **to ~ o.s.** divertirse; **enjoyable** adj agradable; (amusing) divertido; **enjoyment** n (joy) placer m
enlarge [ɪn'lɑːdʒ] vt aumentar; (broaden) extender; (Phot) ampliar ▷ vi: **to ~ on** (subject) tratar con más detalles; **enlargement** n (Phot) ampliación f
enlist [ɪn'lɪst] vt alistar; (support) conseguir ▷ vi alistarse
enormous [ɪ'nɔːməs] adj enorme
enough [ɪ'nʌf] adj: **~ time/books** bastante tiempo/bastantes libros ▷ n: **have you got ~?** ¿tiene usted bastante? ▷ adv: **big ~** bastante grande; **he has not worked ~** no ha trabajado bastante; **(that's) ~!** ¡basta ya!, ¡ya está bien!; **that's ~, thanks** con eso basta, gracias; **I've had ~** estoy harto; **... which, funnily ~ ...** ... lo que, por extraño que parezca ...
enquire [ɪn'kwaɪəʳ] vt, vi = **inquire**
enrage [ɪn'reɪdʒ] vt enfurecer
enrich [ɪn'rɪtʃ] vt enriquecer
enrol, (US) **enroll** [ɪn'rəul] vt (member) inscribir; (Scol) matricular ▷ vi inscribirse; (Scol) matricularse; **enrolment**, (US) **enrollment** n inscripción f; matriculación f
en route [ɔn'ruːt] adv durante el viaje
en suite [ɔn'swiːt] adj: **with ~ bathroom** con baño
ensure [ɪn'ʃuəʳ] vt asegurar
entail [ɪn'teɪl] vt suponer
enter ['ɛntəʳ] vt (room, profession) entrar en; (club) hacerse socio de; (army) alistarse en; (sb for a competition) inscribir; (write down) anotar, apuntar; (Comput) introducir ▷ vi entrar
enterprise ['ɛntəpraɪz] n empresa; (spirit) iniciativa; **free ~** la libre empresa; **private ~** la iniciativa privada; **enterprising** adj emprendedor(a)
entertain [ɛntə'teɪn] vt (amuse) divertir; (receive: guest) recibir (en casa); (idea) abrigar; **entertainer** n artista mf; **entertaining** adj divertido, entretenido; **entertainment** n (amusement) diversión f; (show) espectáculo
enthusiasm [ɪn'θuːzɪæzəm] n entusiasmo

enthusiast [ɪn'θuːzɪæst] n
entusiasta mf; **enthusiastic**
[ɪnθuːzɪ'æstɪk] adj entusiasta; **to
be enthusiastic about sb/sth** estar
entusiasmado con algn/algo
entire [ɪn'taɪəʳ] adj entero; **entirely**
adv totalmente
entitle [ɪn'taɪtl] vt: **to ~ sb to sth** dar a
algn derecho a algo; **entitled** adj (book)
titulado; **to be entitled to sth/to do
sth** tener derecho a algo/a hacer algo
entrance ['entrəns] n entrada ▷ vt
[ɪn'trɑːns] encantar, hechizar; **to
gain ~ to** (university etc) ingresar en;
entrance examination n examen m
de ingreso; **entrance fee** n (to a show)
entrada; (to a club) cuota; **entrance
ramp** n (us Aut) rampa de acceso
entrant ['entrənt] n (in race,
competition) participante mf; (in exam)
candidato/a
entrepreneur [ɔntrəprə'nəːʳ] n
empresario/a
entrust [ɪn'trʌst] vt: **to ~ sth to sb**
confiar algo a algn
entry ['entrɪ] n entrada; (in register,
diary, ship's log) apunte m; (in account
book, ledger, list) partida; **no ~**
prohibido el paso; (Aut) dirección
prohibida; **entry phone** n portero
automático
envelope ['envələup] n sobre m
envious ['envɪəs] adj envidioso; (look)
de envidia
environment [ɪn'vaɪərnmənt]
n (surroundings) entorno;
Department of the E~
ministerio del medio ambiente;
environmental [ɪnvaɪərn'mentl] adj
(medio)ambiental; **environmentally**
[ɪnvaɪərn'mentlɪ] adv:
environmentally sound/friendly
ecológico
envisage [ɪn'vɪzɪdʒ] vt prever
envoy ['envɔɪ] n enviado/a
envy ['envɪ] n envidia ▷ vt tener
envidia a; **to ~ sb sth** envidiar algo
a algn

epic ['epɪk] n épica ▷ adj épico
epidemic [epɪ'demɪk] n epidemia
epilepsy ['epɪlepsɪ] n epilepsia
epileptic [epɪ'leptɪk] adj, n
epiléptico/a; **epileptic fit** n
ataque m de epilepsia, acceso m
epiléptico
episode ['epɪsəud] n episodio
equal ['iːkwl] adj igual; (treatment)
equitativo ▷ n igual mf ▷ vt ser igual
a; (fig) igualar; **to be ~ to** (task) estar
a la altura de; **equality** [iː'kwɔlɪtɪ]
n igualdad f; **equalize** vi (Sport)
empatar; **equally** adv igualmente;
(share etc) a partes iguales
equation [ɪ'kweɪʒən] n (Math)
ecuación f
equator [ɪ'kweɪtəʳ] n ecuador m
equip [ɪ'kwɪp] vt equipar; (person)
proveer; **to be well ~ped** estar bien
equipado; **equipment** n equipo
equivalent [ɪ'kwɪvələnt] adj, n
equivalente m; **to be ~ to** equivaler a
ER abbr (BRIT: = Elizabeth Regina) la reina
Isabel; (US Med) = **emergency room**
era ['ɪərə] n era, época
erase [ɪ'reɪz] vt borrar; **eraser** n goma
de borrar
erect [ɪ'rekt] adj erguido ▷ vt erigir,
levantar; (assemble) montar; **erection**
n (of building) construcción f; (of
machinery) montaje m; (Med) erección f
ERM n abbr (= Exchange Rate
Mechanism) (mecanismo de cambios
del) SME m
erode [ɪ'rəud] vt (Geo) erosionar;
(metal) corroer, desgastar
erosion [ɪ'rəuʒən] n erosión f;
desgaste m
erotic [ɪ'rɔtɪk] adj erótico
errand ['ernd] n recado, mandado
(LAm)
erratic [ɪ'rætɪk] adj desigual, poco
uniforme
error ['erəʳ] n error m, equivocación f
erupt [ɪ'rʌpt] vi entrar en erupción;
(fig) estallar; **eruption** n erupción f; (of
anger, violence) estallido

escalate ['ɛskəleɪt] vi extenderse, intensificarse

escalator ['ɛskəleɪtər] n escalera mecánica

escape [ɪ'skeɪp] n fuga ▷ vi escaparse; (flee) huir, evadirse ▷ vt evitar, eludir; (consequences) escapar a; **his name ~s me** no me sale su nombre; **to ~ from** (place) escaparse de; (person) huir de

escort n ['ɛskɔ:t] acompañante mf; (Mil) escolta ▷ vt [ɪ'skɔ:t] acompañar

especially [ɪ'spɛʃlɪ] adv especialmente; (above all) sobre todo; (particularly) en especial

espionage ['ɛspɪənɑ:ʒ] n espionaje m

essay ['ɛseɪ] n (Scol) redacción f; (: longer) trabajo

essence ['ɛsns] n esencia

essential [ɪ'sɛnʃl] adj (necessary) imprescindible; (basic) esencial ▷ n (often pl) lo esencial; **essentially** adv esencialmente

establish [ɪ'stæblɪʃ] vt establecer; (prove) demostrar; (relations) entablar; **establishment** n establecimiento; **the Establishment** la clase dirigente

estate [ɪ'steɪt] n (land) finca, hacienda; (inheritance) herencia; **housing ~** (BRIT) urbanización f; **estate agent** n (BRIT) agente mf inmobiliario/a; **estate car** n (BRIT) ranchera, coche m familiar

estimate ['ɛstɪmət] n estimación f; (assessment) tasa, cálculo; (Comm) presupuesto ▷ vt ['ɛstɪmeɪt] estimar; tasar, calcular

etc abbr (= et cetera) etc

eternal [ɪ'tə:nl] adj eterno

eternity [ɪ'tə:nɪtɪ] n eternidad f

ethical ['ɛθɪkl] adj ético; **ethics** ['ɛθɪks] n ética ▷ npl moralidad f

Ethiopia [i:θɪ'əupɪə] n Etiopía

ethnic ['ɛθnɪk] adj étnico; **ethnic minority** n minoría étnica

e-ticket ['i:tɪkɪt] n billete electrónico, boleto electrónico (LAM)

etiquette ['ɛtɪkɛt] n etiqueta

EU n abbr (= European Union) UE f

euro ['juərəu] n euro

Europe ['juərəp] n Europa; **European** [juərə'pi:ən] adj, n europeo/a; **European Community** n Comunidad f Europea; **European Union** n Unión f Europea

Eurostar® ['juərəustɑ:r] n Eurostar® m

evacuate [ɪ'vækjueɪt] vt evacuar; (place) desocupar

evade [ɪ'veɪd] vt evadir, eludir

evaluate [ɪ'væljueɪt] vt evaluar; (value) tasar; (evidence) interpretar

evaporate [ɪ'væpəreɪt] vi evaporarse; (fig) desvanecerse

eve [i:v] n: **on the ~ of** en vísperas de

even ['i:vn] adj (level) llano; (smooth) liso; (speed, temperature) uniforme; (number) par ▷ adv hasta, incluso; **~ if, ~ though** aunque + subjun, así + subjun (LAM); **~ more** aun más; **~ so** aun así; **not ~** ni siquiera; **~ he was there** hasta él estaba allí; **~ on Sundays** incluso los domingos; **to get ~ with sb** ajustar cuentas con algn

evening ['i:vnɪŋ] n tarde f; (night) noche f; **in the ~** por la tarde; **this ~** esta tarde or noche; **tomorrow/ yesterday ~** mañana/ayer por la tarde or noche; **evening class** n clase f nocturna; **evening dress** n (man's) traje m de etiqueta; (woman's) traje m de noche

event [ɪ'vɛnt] n suceso, acontecimiento; (Sport) prueba; **in the ~ of** en caso de; **eventful** adj (life) azaroso; (day) ajetreado; (game) lleno de emoción; (journey) lleno de incidentes

eventual [ɪ'vɛntʃuəl] adj final; **eventually** adv (finally) por fin; (in time) con el tiempo

⚠ Be careful not to translate eventual by the Spanish word eventual.

ever ['ɛvər] adv nunca, jamás; (at all times) siempre ▷ conj después de que; **for ~** (para) siempre; **the best ~** lo nunca visto; **have you ~ seen it?** ¿lo has visto alguna vez?; **better than ~** mejor que nunca; **~ since** adv desde entonces; **evergreen** n árbol m de hoja perenne

○ **KEYWORD**

every ['ɛvrɪ] adj 1 (each) cada; **every one of them** (persons) todos ellos/as; (objects) cada uno de ellos/as; **every shop in the town was closed** todas las tiendas de la ciudad estaban cerradas
2 (all possible) todo/a; **I gave you every assistance** te di toda la ayuda posible; **I have every confidence in him** tiene toda mi confianza; **we wish you every success** te deseamos toda suerte de éxitos
3 (showing recurrence) todo/a; **every day/week** todos los días/todas las semanas; **every other car had been broken into** habían forzado uno de cada dos coches; **she visits me every other/third day** me visita cada dos/ tres días; **every now and then** de vez en cuando

everybody ['ɛvrɪbɔdɪ] pron todos pron pl, todo el mundo
everyday ['ɛvrɪdeɪ] adj (daily: use, occurrence, experience) cotidiano; (usual: expression) corriente
everyone ['ɛvrɪwʌn] pron
= **everybody**
everything ['ɛvrɪθɪŋ] pron todo
everywhere ['ɛvrɪwɛəʳ] adv (be) en todas partes; (go) a o por todas partes; **~ you go you meet …** en todas partes encuentras …
evict [ɪ'vɪkt] vt desahuciar
evidence ['ɛvɪdəns] n (proof) prueba; (of witness) testimonio; **to give ~** prestar declaración, dar testimonio
evident ['ɛvɪdənt] adj evidente, manifiesto; **evidently** adv por lo visto
evil ['iːvl] adj malo; (influence) funesto ▷ n mal m

evoke [ɪ'vəuk] vt evocar
evolution [iːvə'luːʃən] n evolución f
evolve [ɪ'vɔlv] vt desarrollar ▷ vi evolucionar, desarrollarse
ewe [juː] n oveja
ex [eks] (inf) n: **my ex** mi ex
ex- [eks] pref (husband, president etc) ex-
exact [ɪg'zækt] adj exacto ▷ vt: **to ~ sth (from)** exigir algo (de); **exactly** adv exactamente; **exactly!** ¡exacto!
exaggerate [ɪg'zædʒəreɪt] vt, vi exagerar; **exaggeration** [ɪgzædʒə'reɪʃən] n exageración f
exam [ɪg'zæm] n abbr (Scol)
= **examination**
examination [ɪgzæmɪ'neɪʃən] n examen m; (Med) reconocimiento
examine [ɪg'zæmɪn] vt examinar; (inspect) inspeccionar; (Med) reconocer; **examiner** n examinador(a) m/f
example [ɪg'zɑːmpl] n ejemplo; **for ~** por ejemplo
exasperate [ɪg'zɑːspəreɪt] vt exasperar; **~d by** or **at** or **with** exasperado por or con
excavate ['ɛkskəveɪt] vt excavar
exceed [ɪk'siːd] vt exceder; (number) pasar de; (speed limit) sobrepasar; (powers) excederse en; (hopes) superar; **exceedingly** adv sumamente, sobremanera
excel [ɪk'sɛl] vi sobresalir; **to ~ o.s.** lucirse
excellence ['ɛksələns] n excelencia
excellent ['ɛksələnt] adj excelente
except [ɪk'sɛpt] prep (also: **~ for, ~ing**) excepto, salvo ▷ vt exceptuar, excluir; **~ if/when** excepto si/cuando; **~ that** salvo que; **exception** n excepción f; **to take exception to** ofenderse por; **exceptional** adj excepcional; **exceptionally** adv excepcionalmente, extraordinariamente
excerpt ['ɛksəːpt] n extracto
excess [ɪk'sɛs] n exceso; **excess baggage** n exceso de equipaje; **excessive** adj excesivo

exchange [ɪks'tʃeɪndʒ] n intercambio; (also: **telephone ~**) central f (telefónica) ▷ vt: **to ~ (for)** cambiar (por); **exchange rate** n tipo de cambio

excite [ɪk'saɪt] vt (stimulate) estimular; **to get ~d** emocionarse; **excitement** n emoción f; **exciting** adj emocionante

exclaim [ɪk'skleɪm] vi exclamar

exclamation [ɛksklə'meɪʃən] n exclamación f; **exclamation mark, (US) exclamation point** n signo de admiración

exclude [ɪk'sklu:d] vt excluir; (except) exceptuar

excluding [ɪks'klu:dɪŋ] prep: **~ VAT** IVA no incluido

exclusion [ɪk'sklu:ʒən] n exclusión f; **to the ~ of** con exclusión de

exclusive [ɪk'sklu:sɪv] adj exclusivo; (club, district) selecto; **~ of tax** excluyendo impuestos; **exclusively** adv únicamente

excruciating [ɪk'skru:ʃɪeɪtɪŋ] adj (pain) agudísimo, atroz

excursion [ɪk'skə:ʃən] n excursión f

excuse n [ɪk'skju:s] disculpa, excusa; (evasion) pretexto ▷ vt [ɪk'skju:z] disculpar, perdonar; (justify) justificar; **to ~ sb from doing sth** dispensar a algn de hacer algo; **~ me!** ¡perdone!; (attracting attention) ¡oiga (, por favor)!; **if you will ~ me** con su permiso

ex-directory ['ɛksdɪ'rɛktərɪ] adj (BRIT): **~ (phone) number** número que no figura en la guía (telefónica)

execute ['ɛksɪkju:t] vt (plan) realizar; (order) cumplir; (person) ajusticiar, ejecutar; **execution** n realización f; cumplimiento; ejecución f

executive [ɪg'zɛkjutɪv] n (Comm) ejecutivo/a; (Pol) poder m ejecutivo ▷ adj ejecutivo

exempt [ɪg'zɛmpt] adj: **~ from** exento de ▷ vt: **to ~ sb from** eximir a algn de

exercise ['ɛksəsaɪz] n ejercicio ▷ vt ejercer; (patience etc) proceder con; (dog) sacar de paseo ▷ vi hacer ejercicio; **exercise book** n cuaderno de ejercicios

exert [ɪg'zə:t] vt ejercer; **to ~ o.s.** esforzarse; **exertion** [ɪg'zə:ʃən] n esfuerzo

exhale [ɛks'heɪl] vt despedir ▷ vi espirar

exhaust [ɪg'zɔ:st] n (pipe) (tubo de) escape m; (fumes) gases mpl de escape ▷ vt agotar; **exhausted** adj agotado; **exhaustion** [ɪg'zɔ:stʃən] n agotamiento; **nervous exhaustion** agotamiento nervioso

exhibit [ɪg'zɪbɪt] n (Art) obra expuesta; (Law) objeto expuesto ▷ vt (show: emotions) manifestar; (: courage, skill) demostrar; (paintings) exponer; **exhibition** [ɛksɪ'bɪʃən] n exposición f

exhilarating [ɪg'zɪləreɪtɪŋ] adj estimulante, tónico

exile ['ɛksaɪl] n exilio; (person) exiliado/a ▷ vt desterrar, exiliar

exist [ɪg'zɪst] vi existir; **existence** n existencia; **existing** adj existente, actual

exit ['ɛksɪt] n salida ▷ vi (Theat) hacer mutis; (Comput) salir (del sistema); **exit ramp** n (US Aut) vía de acceso

▌ Be careful not to translate *exit* by the Spanish word *éxito*.

exotic [ɪg'zɔtɪk] adj exótico

expand [ɪk'spænd] vt ampliar, extender; (number) aumentar ▷ vi (trade etc) ampliarse, expandirse; (gas, metal) dilatarse; **to ~ on** (notes, story etc) ampliar

expansion [ɪk'spænʃən] n ampliación f; aumento; (of trade) expansión f

expect [ɪk'spɛkt] vt esperar; (count on) contar con; (suppose) suponer ▷ vi: **to be ~ing** estar encinta; **expectation** [ɛkspɛk'teɪʃən] n (hope) esperanza; (belief) expectativa

expedition [ɛkspə'dɪʃən] *n* expedición *f*

expel [ɪk'spɛl] *vt* expulsar

expenditure [ɪk'spɛndɪtʃəʳ] *n* gastos *mpl*, desembolso; (*of time, effort*) gasto

expense [ɪk'spɛns] *n* gasto, gastos *mpl*; (*high cost*) coste *m*; **expenses** *npl* (Comm) gastos *mpl*; **at the ~ of** a costa de; **expense account** *n* cuenta de gastos (de representación)

expensive [ɪk'spɛnsɪv] *adj* caro, costoso

experience [ɪk'spɪərɪəns] *n* experiencia ▷ *vt* experimentar; (*suffer*) sufrir; **experienced** *adj* experimentado

experiment [ɪk'spɛrɪmənt] *n* experimento ▷ *vi* hacer experimentos; **experimental** [ɪkspɛrɪ'mɛntl] *adj* experimental; **the process is still at the experimental stage** el proceso está todavía en prueba

expert ['ɛkspə:t] *adj* experto, perito ▷ *n* experto/a, perito/a; (*specialist*) especialista *mf*; **expertise** [ɛkspə:'ti:z] *n* pericia

expire [ɪk'spaɪəʳ] *vi* caducar, vencerse; **expiry** [ɪk'spaɪərɪ] *n* vencimiento; **expiry date** *n* (*of medicine, food item*) fecha de caducidad

explain [ɪk'spleɪn] *vt* explicar; **explanation** [ɛksplə'neɪʃən] *n* explicación *f*

explicit [ɪk'splɪsɪt] *adj* explícito

explode [ɪk'spləud] *vi* estallar, explotar; (*with anger*) reventar

exploit ['ɛksplɔɪt] *n* hazaña ▷ *vt* [ɪk'splɔɪt] explotar; **exploitation** [ɛksplɔɪ'teɪʃən] *n* explotación *f*

explore [ɪk'splɔ:ʳ] *vt* explorar; (*fig*) examinar, sondear; **explorer** *n* explorador(a) *m/f*

explosion [ɪk'spləuʒən] *n* explosión *f*; **explosive** [ɪk'spləusɪv] *adj, n* explosivo

export *vt* [ɛk'spɔ:t] exportar ▷ *n* ['ɛkspɔ:t] exportación *f* ▷ *cpd* de

exportación; **exporter** [ɛk'spɔ:təʳ] *n* exportador(a) *m/f*

expose [ɪk'spəuz] *vt* exponer; (*unmask*) desenmascarar; **exposed** *adj* expuesto

exposure [ɪk'spəuʒəʳ] *n* exposición *f*; (Phot: *speed*) (tiempo *m* de) exposición *f*; (: *shot*) fotografía; **to die from ~** (Med) morir de frío

express [ɪk'sprɛs] *adj* (*definite*) expreso, explícito; (BRIT: *letter etc*) urgente ▷ *vt* (*train*) rápido ▷ *vt* expresar; **expression** [ɪk'sprɛʃən] *n* expresión *f*; **expressway** *n* (US: *urban motorway*) autopista

exquisite [ɛk'skwɪzɪt] *adj* exquisito

extend [ɪk'stɛnd] *vt* (*visit, street*) prolongar; (*building*) ampliar; (*invitation*) ofrecer ▷ *vi* (*land*) extenderse; **the contract ~s to/ for …** el contrato se prolonga hasta/ por …

extension [ɪk'stɛnʃən] *n* extensión *f*; (*building*) ampliación *f*; (Tel: *line*) extensión *f*; (: *telephone*) supletorio *m*; (*of deadline*) prórroga

extensive [ɪk'stɛnsɪv] *adj* extenso; (*damage*) importante; (*knowledge*) amplio

extent [ɪk'stɛnt] *n* (*breadth*) extensión *f*; (*scope*) alcance *m*; **to some ~** hasta cierto punto; **to the ~ of …** hasta el punto de …; **to such an ~ that …** hasta tal punto que …; **to what ~?** ¿hasta qué punto?

exterior [ɛk'stɪərɪəʳ] *adj* exterior, externo ▷ *n* exterior *m*

external [ɛk'stə:nl] *adj* externo

extinct [ɪk'stɪŋkt] *adj* (*volcano*) extinguido; (*race*) extinguido; **extinction** *n* extinción *f*

extinguish [ɪk'stɪŋgwɪʃ] *vt* extinguir, apagar

extra ['ɛkstrə] *adj* adicional ▷ *adv* (*in addition*) más ▷ *n* (*addition*) extra *m*; (Theat) extra *mf*, comparsa *mf*

extract *vt* [ɪk'strækt] sacar; (*tooth*) extraer ▷ *n* ['ɛkstrækt] extracto

extradite ['ɛkstrədaɪt] vt extraditar

extraordinary [ɪk'strɔːdnrɪ] adj extraordinario; (odd) raro

extravagance [ɪk'strævəgəns] n derroche m; (thing bought) extravagancia

extravagant [ɪk'strævəgənt] adj (wasteful) derrochador(a); (taste, gift) excesivamente caro; (price) exorbitante

extreme [ɪk'striːm] adj extremo; extremado ▷ n extremo; **extremely** adv sumamente, extremadamente

extremist [ɪk'striːmɪst] adj, n extremista mf

extrovert ['ɛkstrəvəːt] n extrovertido/a

eye [aɪ] n ojo ▷ vt mirar; **to keep an ~ on** vigilar; **eyeball** n globo ocular; **eyebrow** n ceja; **eyedrops** npl gotas fpl para los ojos; **eyelash** n pestaña; **eyelid** n párpado; **eyeliner** n lápiz m de ojos; **eyeshadow** n sombra de ojos; **eyesight** n vista; **eye witness** n testigo mf ocular

F [ɛf] n (Mus) fa m

fabric ['fæbrɪk] n tejido, tela

 Be careful not to translate fabric by the Spanish word fábrica.

fabulous ['fæbjuləs] adj fabuloso

face [feɪs] n (Anat) cara, rostro; (of clock) esfera ▷ vt (direction) estar de cara a; (situation) hacer frente a; (facts) aceptar; **~ down** (person, card) boca abajo; **to lose ~** desprestigiarse; **to make** or **pull a ~** hacer muecas; **in the ~ of** (difficulties etc) ante; **on the ~ of it** a primera vista; **~ to ~** cara a cara; **face up to** vt fus hacer frente a, enfrentarse a; **face cloth** n (BRIT) toallita; **face pack** n (BRIT) mascarilla

facial ['feɪʃəl] adj de la cara ▷ n (also: **beauty ~**) tratamiento facial, limpieza

facilitate [fə'sɪlɪteɪt] vt facilitar

facility [fə'sɪlɪtɪ] n facilidad f; **facilities** npl instalaciones fpl; **credit ~** facilidades de crédito

fact [fækt] n hecho; **in ~** en realidad

faction ['fækʃən] n facción f

factor ['fæktə'] n factor m

factory ['fæktərɪ] n fábrica

factual ['fæktjuəl] adj basado en los hechos

faculty ['fækəltɪ] n facultad f; (US: teaching staff) personal m docente

fad [fæd] n novedad f, moda

fade [feɪd] vi desteñirse; (sound, hope) desvanecerse; (light) apagarse; (flower) marchitarse; **fade away** vi (sound) apagarse

fag [fæg] n (BRIT inf: cigarette) pitillo (SP), cigarro

Fahrenheit ['fɑ:rənhaɪt] n Fahrenheit m

fail [feɪl] vt suspender; (memory etc) fallar a ▷ vi suspender; (be unsuccessful) fracasar; (strength, brakes, engine) fallar; **to ~ to do sth** (neglect) dejar de hacer algo; (be unable) no poder hacer algo; **without ~** sin falta; **failing** n falta, defecto ▷ prep a falta de; **failure** ['feɪljə'] n fracaso m; (person) fracasado/a; (mechanical etc) fallo

faint [feɪnt] adj débil; (recollection) vago; (mark) apenas visible ▷ n desmayo ▷ vi desmayarse; **to feel ~** estar mareado, marearse; **faintest** adj: **I haven't the faintest idea** no tengo la más remota idea; **faintly** adv débilmente; (vaguely) vagamente

fair [feə'] adj justo; (hair, person) rubio; (weather) bueno; (good enough) suficiente; (sizeable) considerable ▷ adv: **to play ~** jugar limpio ▷ n feria, (BRIT: funfair) parque m de atracciones; **fairground** n recinto ferial; **fair-haired** adj (person) rubio; **fairly** adv (justly) con justicia; (quite) bastante; **fair trade** n comercio justo; **fairway** n (Golf) calle f

fairy ['feərɪ] n hada; **fairy tale** n cuento de hadas

faith [feɪθ] n fe f; (trust) confianza; (sect) religión f; **faithful** adj, adj (loyal: troops etc) leal; (spouse) fiel; (account) exacto; **faithfully** adv fielmente;

yours faithfully (BRIT: in letters) le saluda atentamente

fake [feɪk] n (painting etc) falsificación f; (person) impostor(a) m/f ▷ adj falso ▷ vt fingir; (painting etc) falsificar

falcon ['fɔ:lkən] n halcón m

fall [fɔ:l] n caída; (US) otoño ▷ vi (pt **fell**, pp **fallen**) caer; (accidentally) caerse; (price) bajar; **falls** npl (waterfall) cataratas fpl, salto sg de agua; **to ~ flat** vi (on one's face) caerse de bruces; (joke, story) no hacer gracia; **fall apart** vi deshacerse; **fall down** vi (person) caerse; (building) derrumbarse; **fall for** vt fus (trick) tragar; (person) enamorarse de; **fall off** vi caerse; (diminish) disminuir; **fall out** vi (friends etc) reñir; (hair, teeth) caerse; **fall over** vi caer(se); **fall through** vi (plan, project) fracasar

fallen ['fɔ:lən] pp of **fall**

fallout ['fɔ:laut] n lluvia radioactiva

false [fɔ:ls] adj falso; **under ~ pretences** con engaños; **false alarm** n falsa alarma; **false teeth** npl (BRIT) dentadura sg postiza

fame [feɪm] n fama

familiar [fə'mɪlɪə'] adj familiar; (well-known) conocido; (tone) de confianza; **to be ~ with** (subject) conocer (bien); **familiarize** [fə'mɪlɪəraɪz] vt: **to familiarize o.s. with** familiarizarse con

family ['fæmɪlɪ] n familia; **family doctor** n médico/a de cabecera; **family planning** n planificación f familiar

famine ['fæmɪn] n hambre f, hambruna

famous ['feɪməs] adj famoso, célebre

fan [fæn] n abanico; (Elec) ventilador m; (Sport) hincha mf; (of pop star) fan mf ▷ vt abanicar; (fire, quarrel) atizar

fanatic [fə'nætɪk] n fanático/a

fan belt n correa del ventilador

fan club n club m de fans

fancy ['fænsɪ] n (whim) capricho, antojo; (imagination) imaginación f

▷ *adj* (*luxury*) de lujo ▷ *vt* (*feel like, want*) tener ganas de; (*imagine*) imaginarse; **to take a ~ to sb** tomar cariño a algn; **he fancies her** le gusta (ella) mucho; **fancy dress** n disfraz m

fan heater n calefactor m de aire

fantasize ['fæntəsaɪz] vi fantasear, hacerse ilusiones

fantastic [fæn'tæstɪk] adj fantástico

fantasy ['fæntəzɪ] n fantasía

fanzine ['fænzi:n] n fanzine m

FAQs npl abbr (= frequently asked questions) preguntas fpl frecuentes

far [fɑːʳ] adj (distant) lejano ▷ adv lejos; **~ away, ~ off** (a lo) lejos; **~ better** mucho mejor; **~ from** lejos de; **by ~** con mucho; **go as ~ as the farm** vaya hasta la granja; **as ~ as I know** que yo sepa; **how ~?** ¿hasta dónde?; (fig) ¿hasta qué punto?

farce [fɑːs] n farsa

fare [fɛəʳ] n (on trains, buses) precio (del billete); (in taxi: cost) tarifa; (food) comida; **half/full ~** medio billete m/ billete m completo

Far East n: **the ~** el Extremo or Lejano Oriente

farewell [fɛə'wɛl] excl, n adiós m

farm [fɑːm] n granja, finca, estancia (LAm), chacra (LAm) ▷ vt cultivar; **farmer** n granjero/a, estanciero/a (LAm); **farmhouse** n granja, casa de hacienda (LAm); **farming** n agricultura; (tilling) cultivo; **sheep farming** cría de ovejas; **farmyard** n corral m

far-reaching [fɑː'riːtʃɪŋ] adj (reform, effect) de gran alcance

fart [fɑːt] (inf!) vi tirarse un pedo (!)

farther ['fɑːðəʳ] adv más lejos, más allá ▷ adj más lejano

farthest ['fɑːðɪst] superlative of **far**

fascinate ['fæsɪneɪt] vt fascinar; **fascinated** adj fascinado; **fascinating** adj fascinante; **fascination** [fæsɪ'neɪʃən] n fascinación f; **fascinator** n (hat) tocado (de plumas, flores o cintas)

fascist ['fæʃɪst] adj, n fascista mf

fashion ['fæʃən] n moda; (fashion industry) industria de la moda; (manner) manera ▷ vt formar; **in ~** a la moda; **out of ~** pasado de moda; **fashionable** adj de moda; **fashion show** n desfile m de modelos

fast [fɑːst] adj (also Phot: film) rápido; (dye, colour) sólido; (clock): **to be ~** estar adelantado ▷ adv rápidamente, de prisa; (stuck, held) firmemente ▷ n ayuno ▷ vi ayunar; **~ asleep** profundamente dormido

fasten ['fɑːsn] vt asegurar, sujetar; (coat, belt) abrochar ▷ vi cerrarse

fast food n comida rápida, platos mpl preparados

fat [fæt] adj gordo; (book) grueso; (profit) grande, pingüe ▷ n grasa; (on person) carnes fpl; (lard) manteca

fatal ['feɪtl] adj (mistake) fatal; (injury) mortal; **fatality** [fə'tælɪtɪ] n (road death etc) víctima f mortal; **fatally** adv **fatally injured** herido de muerte

fate [feɪt] n destino

father ['fɑːðəʳ] n padre m; **Father Christmas** n Papá m Noel; **father-in-law** n suegro

fatigue [fə'tiːg] n fatiga, cansancio

fatten ['fætn] vt, vi engordar; **chocolate is ~ing** el chocolate engorda

fatty ['fætɪ] adj (food) graso ▷ n (inf) gordito/a, gordinflón/ona m/f

faucet ['fɔːsɪt] n (US) grifo, llave f, canilla (LAm)

fault [fɔːlt] n (blame) culpa; (defect: in character) defecto; (Geo) falla ▷ vt criticar; **it's my ~** es culpa mía; **to find ~ with** criticar, poner peros a; **at ~** culpable; **faulty** adj defectuoso

fauna ['fɔːnə] n fauna

favour, (US) **favor** ['feɪvəʳ] n favor m; (approval) aprobación f ▷ vt (proposition) estar a favor de, aprobar; (assist) favorecer; **to do sb a ~** hacer un favor a algn; **to find ~ with sb** (person) caer en gracia a algn; **in ~ of**

a favor de; **favourable** adj favorable; **favourite** ['feɪvərɪt] adj, n favorito/a, preferido/a

fawn [fɔːn] n cervato ▷ adj (also: **~-coloured**) de color cervato, leonado ▷ vi: **to ~ (up)on** adular

fax [fæks] n fax m ▷ vt mandar or enviar por fax

FBI n abbr (US: = Federal Bureau of Investigation) FBI m

fear [fɪə^r] n miedo, temor m ▷ vt temer; **for ~ of** por temor a; **fearful** adj temeroso; (awful) espantoso; **fearless** adj audaz

feasible ['fiːzəbl] adj factible

feast [fiːst] n banquete m; (Rel: also: **~ day**) fiesta ▷ vi festejar

feat [fiːt] n hazaña

feather ['fɛðə^r] n pluma

feature ['fiːtʃə^r] n característica; (article) reportaje m ▷ vt (film) presentar ▷ vi figurar; **features** npl (of face) facciones fpl; **feature film** n largometraje m

Feb. abbr (= February) feb

February ['fɛbruərɪ] n febrero

fed [fɛd] pt, pp of **feed**

federal ['fɛdərəl] adj federal

federation [fɛdə'reɪʃən] n federación f

fee [fiː] n (professional) honorarios mpl; (of school) matrícula; (also: **membership ~**) cuota

feeble ['fiːbl] adj débil

feed [fiːd] n comida; (of animal) pienso; (on printer) dispositivo de alimentación ▷ vt (pt, pp **fed**) alimentar; (BRIT: breastfeed) dar el pecho a; (animal, baby) dar de comer a; **feed into** vt (data, information) suministrar a; **feedback** n reacción f; feedback m

feel [fiːl] n (sensation) sensación f; (sense of touch) tacto ▷ vt (pt, pp **felt**) tocar; (cold, heat etc) sentir; (think, believe) creer; **to ~ hungry/cold** tener hambre/frío; **to ~ lonely/better** sentirse solo/mejor; **I don't ~ well** no me siento bien; **it ~s soft** es suave

al tacto; **to ~ like** (want) tener ganas de; **feeling** n (physical) sensación f; (foreboding) presentimiento; (emotion) sentimiento

feet [fiːt] npl of **foot**

fell [fɛl] pt of **fall** ▷ vt (tree) talar

fellow ['fɛləu] n tipo, tío (SP); (of learned society) socio/a; **fellow citizen** n conciudadano/a; **fellow countryman** n compatriota m; **fellow men** npl semejantes mpl; **fellowship** n compañerismo; (grant) beca

felony ['fɛlənɪ] n crimen m

felt [fɛlt] pt, pp of **feel** ▷ n fieltro

felt-tip pen ['fɛlttɪp-] n rotulador m

female ['fiːmeɪl] n (woman) mujer f; (Zool) hembra ▷ adj femenino

feminine ['fɛmɪnɪn] adj femenino

feminist ['fɛmɪnɪst] n feminista mf

fence [fɛns] n valla, cerca ▷ vt (also: **~ in**) cercar ▷ vi hacer esgrima; **fencing** n esgrima

fend [fɛnd] vi: **to ~ for o.s.** valerse por sí mismo; **fend off** vt (attack, attacker) rechazar; (awkward question) esquivar

fender ['fɛndə^r] n (US Aut) parachoques m inv

fennel ['fɛnl] n hinojo

ferment vi [fə'mɛnt] fermentar ▷ n ['fɜːmɛnt] (fig) agitación f

fern [fɜːn] n helecho

ferocious [fə'rəuʃəs] adj feroz

ferret ['fɛrɪt] n hurón m

ferry ['fɛrɪ] n (small) barca de pasaje, balsa; (large: also: **~boat**) transbordador m, ferry m ▷ vt transportar

fertile ['fɜːtaɪl] adj fértil; (Biol) fecundo; **fertilize** ['fɜːtɪlaɪz] vt (Biol) fecundar; (Agr) abonar; **fertilizer** n abono

festival ['fɛstɪvəl] n (Rel) fiesta; (Art, Mus) festival m

festive ['fɛstɪv] adj festivo; **the ~ season** (BRIT: Christmas) las Navidades

fetch [fɛtʃ] vt ir a buscar; (sell for) venderse por

fête [feɪt] n fiesta

fetus ['fiːtəs] n (US) = **foetus**

feud [fjuːd] n (hostility) enemistad f; (quarrel) disputa

fever ['fiːvəʳ] n fiebre f; **feverish** adj febril

few [fjuː] adj (not many) pocos ▷ pron algunos; **a ~** adj unos pocos; **fewer** adj menos; **fewest** adj los/las menos

fiancé [fɪ'ãːŋseɪ] n novio, prometido; **fiancée** n novia, prometida

fiasco [fɪ'æskəʊ] n fiasco

fib [fɪb] n mentirijilla

fibre, (US) **fiber** ['faɪbəʳ] n fibra; **fibreglass**, (US) **fiberglass** n fibra de vidrio

fickle ['fɪkl] adj inconstante

fiction ['fɪkʃən] n ficción f; **fictional** adj novelesco

fiddle ['fɪdl] n (Mus) violín m; (cheating) trampa ▷ vt (BRIT: accounts) falsificar; **fiddle with** vt fus juguetear con

fidelity [fɪ'dɛlɪtɪ] n fidelidad f

field [fiːld] n campo; (fig) campo, esfera; (Sport) campo, cancha (LAM); **field marshal** n mariscal m

fierce [fɪəs] adj feroz; (wind, attack) violento; (heat) intenso; (fighting, enemy) encarnizado

fifteen [fɪf'tiːn] num quince; **fifteenth** adj decimoquinto; **the fifteenth floor** la planta quince; **the fifteenth of August** el quince de agosto

fifth [fɪfθ] adj quinto

fiftieth ['fɪftɪɪθ] adj quincuagésimo

fifty ['fɪftɪ] num cincuenta; **fifty-fifty** adj (deal, split) a medias ▷ adv: **to go fifty-fifty with sb** ir a medias con algn

fig [fɪg] n higo

fight [faɪt] (pt, pp **fought**) n pelea; (Mil) combate m; (struggle) lucha ▷ vt luchar contra; (cancer, alcoholism) combatir ▷ vi pelear, luchar; **fight back** vi defenderse; (after illness) recuperarse ▷ vt (tears) contener; **fight off** vt (attack, attacker) rechazar; (disease, sleep, urge) luchar contra; **fighting** n combate m, pelea

figure ['fɪgəʳ] n (Drawing, Geom) figura dibujo; (number, cipher) cifra; (person, outline) figura ▷ vt (esp US: think, calculate) calcular, imaginarse ▷ vi (appear) figurar; **figure out** vt (work out) resolver

file [faɪl] n (tool) lima; (dossier) expediente m; (folder) carpeta; (Comput) fichero; (row) fila ▷ vt limar; (Law: claim) presentar; (store) archivar; **filing cabinet** n archivo

Filipino [fɪlɪ'piːnəʊ] adj filipino ▷ n (person) filipino/a

fill [fɪl] vt llenar; (vacancy) cubrir ▷ n: **to eat one's ~** comer hasta hartarse; **fill in** vt rellenar; **fill out** vt (form, receipt) rellenar; **fill up** vt llenar (hasta el borde) ▷ vi (Aut) echar gasolina

fillet ['fɪlɪt] n filete m; **fillet steak** n filete m de ternera

filling ['fɪlɪŋ] n (Culin) relleno; (for tooth) empaste m; **filling station** n estación f de servicio

film [fɪlm] n película ▷ vt (scene) filmar ▷ vi rodar; **film star** n estrella de cine

filter ['fɪltəʳ] n filtro ▷ vt filtrar; **filter lane** n (BRIT) carril m de selección

filth [fɪlθ] n suciedad f; **filthy** adj sucio; (language) obsceno

fin [fɪn] n aleta

final ['faɪnl] adj (last) final, último; (definitive) definitivo ▷ n (Sport) final f; **finals** npl (Scol) exámenes mpl finales

finale [fɪ'nɑːlɪ] n final m

final: **finalist** n (Sport) finalista mf; **finalize** vt ultimar; **finally** adv (lastly) por último, finalmente; (eventually) por fin

finance [faɪ'næns] n (money, funds) fondos mpl ▷ vt financiar; **finances** npl finanzas fpl; **financial** [faɪ'nænʃəl] adj financiero; **financial year** n ejercicio (financiero)

find [faɪnd] (pt, pp **found**) vt encontrar, hallar; (come upon) descubrir ▷ n hallazgo;

descubrimiento; **to ~ sb guilty** (*Law*) declarar culpable a algn; **find out** *vt* averiguar; (*truth, secret*) descubrir ▷ *vi*: **to ~ out about** enterarse de; **findings** *npl* (*Law*) veredicto *sg*, fallo *sg*; (*of report*) recomendaciones *fpl*

fine [faɪn] *adj* (*delicate*) fino ▷ *adv* (*well*) bien ▷ *n* (*Law*) multa ▷ *vt* (*Law*) multar; **he's ~** está muy bien; **fine arts** *npl* bellas artes *fpl*

finger ['fɪŋgəʳ] *n* dedo ▷ *vt* (*touch*) manosear; **little/index ~** (*dedo*) meñique *m*/índice *m*; **fingernail** *n* uña; **fingerprint** *n* huella dactilar; **fingertip** *n* yema del dedo

finish ['fɪnɪʃ] *n* (*end*) fin *m*; (*Sport*) meta; (*polish etc*) acabado ▷ *vt, vi* terminar; **to ~ doing sth** acabar de hacer algo; **to ~ first/second/third** llegar el primero/segundo/tercero; **finish off** *vt* acabar, terminar; (*kill*) rematar; **finish up** *vt* acabar, terminar ▷ *vi* ir a parar, terminar

Finland ['fɪnlənd] *n* Finlandia

Finn [fɪn] *n* finlandés/esa *m/f*; **Finnish** *adj* finlandés/esa ▷ *n* (*Ling*) finlandés *m*

fir [fəːʳ] *n* abeto

fire [faɪəʳ] *n* fuego; (*accidental, damaging*) incendio; (*heater*) estufa ▷ *vt* (*gun*) disparar; (*interest*) despertar; (*dismiss*) despedir ▷ *vi* encenderse; **on ~** ardiendo, en llamas; **fire alarm** *n* alarma de incendios; **firearm** *n* arma de fuego; **fire brigade,** (*us*) **fire department** *n* (cuerpo de) bomberos *mpl*; **fire engine** *n* coche *m* de bomberos; **fire escape** *n* escalera de incendios; **fire exit** *n* salida de incendios; **fire extinguisher** *n* extintor *m*; **fireman** *n* bombero; **fireplace** *n* chimenea; **fire station** *n* parque *m* de bomberos; **firetruck** *n* (*us*) = **fire engine**; **firewall** *n* (*Internet*) firewall *m*; **firewood** *n* leña; **fireworks** *npl* fuegos *mpl* artificiales

firm [fəːm] *adj* firme ▷ *n* empresa; **firmly** *adv* firmemente

first [fəːst] *adj* primero ▷ *adv* (*before others*) primero; (*when listing reasons etc*) en primer lugar, primeramente ▷ *n* (*person: in race*) primero/a; (*Aut*) primera; **at ~** al principio; **~ of all** ante todo; **first aid** *n* primeros auxilios *mpl*; **first aid kit** *n* botiquín *m*; **first-class** *adj* de primera clase; **first-hand** *adj* de primera mano; **first lady** *n* (*esp us*) primera dama; **firstly** *adv* en primer lugar; **first name** *n* nombre *m* de pila; **first-rate** *adj* de primera (clase)

fiscal ['fɪskəl] *adj* fiscal; **~ year** año fiscal, ejercicio

fish [fɪʃ] *n* (*pl inv*) pez *m*; (*food*) pescado ▷ *vt* pescar en ▷ *vi* pescar; **to go ~ing** ir de pesca; **~ and chips** pescado frito con patatas fritas; **fisherman** *n* pescador *m*; **fish fingers** *npl* (*brit*) palitos *mpl* de pescado (empanado); **fishing boat** *n* barca de pesca; **fishing line** *n* sedal *m*; **fishmonger** *n* (*brit*) pescadero/a; **fishmonger's (shop)** *n* (*brit*) pescadería; **fish sticks** *npl* (*us*) = **fish fingers**; **fishy** *adj* (*fig*) sospechoso

fist [fɪst] *n* puño

fit [fɪt] *adj* (*Med, Sport*) en (buena) forma; (*proper*) adecuado, apropiado ▷ *vt* (*clothes*) quedar bien a; (*instal*) poner; (*equip*) proveer; (*match: facts*) cuadrar *or* corresponder *or* coincidir con ▷ *vi* (*clothes*) quedar bien; (*in space, gap*) caber; (*facts*) coincidir ▷ *n* (*Med*) ataque *m*; **~ to** apto para; **~ for** apropiado para; **a ~ of anger/ enthusiasm** un arranque de cólera/ entusiasmo; **this dress is a good ~** este vestido me queda bien; **by ~s and starts** a rachas; **fit in** *vi* encajar; **fitness** *n* (*Med*) forma física; **fitted** *adj* (*jacket, shirt*) entallado; (*sheet*) de cuatro picos; **fitted carpet** *n* moqueta; **fitted kitchen** *n* cocina amueblada; **fitting** *adj* apropiado ▷ *n* (*of dress*) prueba; **fitting room** *n* (*in shop*) probador *m*; **fittings** *npl* instalaciones *fpl*

five [faɪv] *num* cinco; **fiver** *n* (*inf: BRIT*) billete *m* de cinco libras; (: *US*) billete *m* de cinco dólares

fix [fɪks] *vt* (*secure*) fijar, asegurar; (*mend*) arreglar; (*meal, drink*) preparar ▷ *n*: **to be in a ~** estar en un aprieto; **fix up** *vt* (*date, meeting*) arreglar; **to ~ sb up with sth** conseguirle algo a algn; **fixed** *adj* (*prices etc*) fijo; **fixture** *n* (*Sport*) encuentro

fizzy ['fɪzɪ] *adj* (*drink*) gaseoso

flag [flæg] *n* bandera; (*stone*) losa ▷ *vi* decaer; **flag down** *vt*: **to ~ sb down** hacer señas a algn para que se pare; **flagpole** *n* asta de bandera

flair [flɛəʳ] *n* aptitud *f* especial

flak [flæk] *n* (*Mil*) fuego antiaéreo; (*inf: criticism*) lluvia de críticas

flake [fleɪk] *n* (*of rust, paint*) desconchón *m*; (*of snow*) copo; (*of soap powder*) escama ▷ *vi* (*also*: **~ off**) desconcharse

flamboyant [flæm'bɔɪənt] *adj* (*dress*) vistoso; (*person*) extravagante

flame [fleɪm] *n* llama

flamingo [flə'mɪŋɡəu] *n* flamenco

flammable ['flæməbl] *adj* inflamable

flan [flæn] *n* (*BRIT*) tarta

> Be careful not to translate *flan* by the Spanish word *flan*.

flank [flæŋk] *n* flanco ▷ *vt* flanquear

flannel ['flænl] *n* (*BRIT: also*: **face ~**) toallita; (*fabric*) franela; **flannels** *npl* pantalones *mpl* de franela

flap [flæp] *n* (*of pocket, envelope*) solapa ▷ *vt* (*wings*) batir ▷ *vi* (*sail, flag*) ondear

flare [flɛəʳ] *n* llamarada; (*Mil*) bengala; (*in skirt etc*) vuelo; **flares** *npl* (*trousers*) pantalones *mpl* de campana; **flare up** *vi* encenderse; (*fig: person*) encolerizarse; (: *revolt*) estallar

flash [flæʃ] *n* relámpago; (*also*: **news ~**) noticias *fpl* de última hora; (*Phot*) flash *m* ▷ *vt* (*light, headlights*) lanzar destellos con ▷ *vi* brillar; (*hazard light etc*) lanzar destellos; **in a ~** en un instante; **he ~ed by** *or* **past** pasó como un rayo; **flashback** *n* flashback

m; **flashbulb** *n* bombilla de flash; **flashlight** *n* linterna

flask [flɑːsk] *n* petaca; (*also*: **vacuum ~**) termo

flat [flæt] *adj* llano; (*smooth*) liso; (*tyre*) desinflado; (*battery*) descargado; (*beer*) sin gas; (*Mus: instrument*) desafinado ▷ *n* (*BRIT: apartment*) piso (*SP*), departamento (*LAM*), apartamento; (*Aut*) pinchazo; (*Mus*) bemol *m*; **(to work) ~ out** (trabajar) a tope; **flatten** *vt* (*also*: **flatten out**) allanar; (*smooth out*) alisar; (*house, city*) arrasar

flatter ['flætəʳ] *vt* adular, halagar; **flattering** *adj* halagüeño(a); (*clothes etc*) que favorece

flaunt [flɔːnt] *vt* ostentar, lucir

flavour, (*US*) **flavor** ['fleɪvəʳ] *n* sabor *m*, gusto ▷ *vt* sazonar, condimentar; **strawberry ~ed** con sabor a fresa; **flavouring**, (*US*) **flavoring** *n* (*in product*) aromatizante *m*

flaw [flɔː] *n* defecto; **flawless** *adj* impecable

flea [fliː] *n* pulga; **flea market** *n* rastro, mercadillo

flee (*pt, pp* **fled**) [fliː, flɛd] *vt* huir de ▷ *vi* huir

fleece [fliːs] *n* vellón *m*; (*wool*) lana; (*top*) forro polar ▷ *vt* (*inf*) desplumar

fleet [fliːt] *n* flota; (*of cars, lorries etc*) parque *m*

fleeting ['fliːtɪŋ] *adj* fugaz

Flemish ['flɛmɪʃ] *adj* flamenco

flesh [flɛʃ] *n* carne *f*; (*skin*) piel *f*; (*of fruit*) pulpa

flew [fluː] *pt of* **fly**

flex [flɛks] *n* cable *m* ▷ *vt* (*muscles*) tensar; **flexibility** *n* flexibilidad *f*; **flexible** *adj* flexible; **flexitime** *n* horario flexible

flick [flɪk] *n* capirotazo ▷ *vt* dar un golpecito a; **flick through** *vt fus* hojear

flicker ['flɪkəʳ] *vi* (*light*) parpadear; (*flame*) vacilar

flies [flaɪz] *npl of* **fly**

light [flaɪt] n vuelo; (*escape*) huida, fuga; (*also*: **~ of steps**) tramo (de escaleras); **flight attendant** n auxiliar mf de vuelo

flimsy ['flɪmzɪ] adj (*thin*) muy ligero; (*excuse*) flojo

flinch [flɪntʃ] vi encogerse; **to ~ from** retroceder ante

fling [flɪŋ] (pt, pp **flung**) vt arrojar

flint [flɪnt] n pedernal m; (*in lighter*) piedra

flip [flɪp] vt: **to ~ a coin** echar a cara o cruz

flip-flops ['flɪpflɒps] npl (*esp BRIT*) chancletas fpl

flipper ['flɪpə^r] n aleta

flirt [fləːt] vi coquetear, flirtear ▷ n coqueta f

float [fləʊt] n flotador m; (*in procession*) carroza; (*sum of money*) reserva ▷ vi (*currency*) flotar; (*swimmer*) hacer la plancha

flock [flɒk] n (*of sheep*) rebaño; (*of birds*) bandada ▷ vi: **to ~ to** acudir en tropel a

flood [flʌd] n inundación f; (*of letters, imports etc*) avalancha ▷ vt inundar ▷ vi (*place*) inundarse; (*people*): **to ~ into** inundar; **flooding** n inundaciones fpl; **floodlight** n foco

floor [flɔː^r] n suelo; (*storey*) piso; (*of sea, valley*) fondo ▷ vt (*with blow*) derribar; (*fig: baffle*) dejar anonadado; **ground ~**, (*US*) **first ~** planta baja; **first ~**, (*US*) **second ~** primer piso; **floorboard** n tabla; **flooring** n suelo; (*material*) solería; **floor show** n cabaret m

flop [flɒp] n fracaso ▷ vi (*fail*) fracasar; **floppy** adj flojo ▷ n (*Comput: also*: **floppy disk**) floppy m

flora ['flɔːrə] n flora

floral ['flɔːrl] adj (*pattern*) floreado

florist ['flɒrɪst] n florista mf; **~'s (shop)** n floristería

flotation [fləʊ'teɪʃən] n (*of shares*) emisión f; (*of company*) lanzamiento

flour ['flaʊə^r] n harina

flourish ['flʌrɪʃ] vi florecer ▷ n ademán m, movimiento (ostentoso)

flow [fləʊ] n (*movement*) flujo; (*of traffic*) circulación f; (*Elec*) corriente f ▷ vi (*river, blood*) fluir; (*traffic*) circular

flower ['flaʊə^r] n flor f ▷ vi florecer; **flower bed** n macizo; **flowerpot** n tiesto

flown [fləʊn] pp of **fly**

fl. oz. abbr = **fluid ounce**

flu [fluː] n: **to have ~** tener la gripe

fluctuate ['flʌktjueɪt] vi fluctuar

fluent ['fluːənt] adj (*speech*) elocuente; **he speaks ~ French, he's ~ in French** domina el francés

fluff [flʌf] n pelusa; **fluffy** adj de pelo suave

fluid ['fluːɪd] adj (*movement*) fluido, líquido; (*situation*) inestable ▷ n fluido, líquido; **fluid ounce** n onza f líquida

fluke [fluːk] n (*inf*) chiripa

flung [flʌŋ] pt, pp of **fling**

fluorescent [fluə'rɛsnt] adj fluorescente

fluoride ['fluəraɪd] n fluoruro

flurry ['flʌrɪ] n (*of snow*) ventisca; **~ of activity** frenesí m de actividad

flush [flʌʃ] n rubor m; (*fig: of youth, beauty*) resplandor m ▷ vt limpiar con agua ▷ vi ruborizarse ▷ adj: **~ with** a ras de; **to ~ the toilet** tirar de la cadena (del wáter)

flute [fluːt] n flauta travesera

flutter ['flʌtə^r] n (*of wings*) revoloteo, aleteo ▷ vi revolotear

fly [flaɪ] (pt **flew**, pp **flown**) n mosca; (*on trousers: also*: **flies**) bragueta ▷ vt (*plane*) pilotar; (*cargo*) transportar (en avión); (*distance*) recorrer (en avión) ▷ vi volar; (*passenger*) ir en avión; (*escape*) evadirse; (*flag*) ondear; **fly away** vi (*bird, insect*) irse volando; **fly off** vi irse volando; **fly-drive** n: **fly-drive holiday** vacaciones que incluyen vuelo y alquiler de coche; **flying** n (*activity*) (el) volar ▷ adj: **flying visit** visita relámpago; **with flying colours** con lucimiento;

flying saucer *n* platillo volante;
flyover *n* (BRIT) paso elevado *or* (LAM)
a desnivel
FM *abbr* (*Radio*: = *frequency modulation*)
FM
foal [fəul] *n* potro
foam [fəum] *n* espuma ▷ *vi* hacer
espuma
focus ['fəukəs] (*pl* **focuses**) *n* foco;
(*centre*) centro ▷ *vt* (*field glasses etc*)
enfocar ▷ *vi*: **to ~ (on)** enfocar (a);
(*issue etc*) centrarse en; **in/out of ~**
enfocado/desenfocado
foetus, (US) **fetus** ['fi:təs] *n* feto
fog [fɔg] *n* niebla; **foggy** *adj*: **it's**
foggy hay niebla; **fog lamp**, (US) **fog**
light *n* (*Aut*) faro antiniebla
foil [fɔil] *vt* frustrar ▷ *n* hoja; (*also*:
kitchen ~) papel *m* (de) aluminio;
(*Fencing*) florete *m*
fold [fəuld] *n* (*bend, crease*) pliegue *m*;
(*Agr*) redil *m* ▷ *vt* doblar; **to ~ one's**
arms cruzarse de brazos; **fold up** *vi*
plegarse, doblarse; (*business*) quebrar
▷ *vt* (*map etc*) plegar; **folder** *n* (*for*
papers) carpeta; (*Comput*) directorio;
folding *adj* (*chair, bed*) plegable
foliage ['fəulɪɪdʒ] *n* follaje *m*
folk [fəuk] *npl* gente *f* ▷ *adj* popular,
folklórico; **folks** *npl* familia, parientes
mpl; **folklore** ['fəuklɔːʳ] *n* folclore *m*;
folk music *n* música folk; **folk song** *n*
canción *f* popular *or* folk
follow ['fɔləu] *vt* seguir ▷ *vi* seguir;
(*result*) resultar; **he ~ed suit** hizo
lo mismo; **follow up** *vt* (*letter, offer*)
responder a; (*case*) investigar;
follower *n* seguidor(a) *m/f*; (*Pol*)
partidario/a; **following** *adj* siguiente
▷ *n* seguidores *mpl*, afición *f*; **follow-**
up *n* continuación *f*
fond [fɔnd] *adj* (*loving*) cariñoso; **to be**
~ of sb tener cariño a algn; **she's ~ of**
swimming tiene afición a la natación,
le gusta nadar
food [fu:d] *n* comida; **food mixer**
n batidora; **food poisoning** *n*
intoxicación *f* alimentaria; **food**

processor *n* robot *m* de cocina; **food**
stamp *n* (US) vale *m* para comida
fool [fu:l] *n* tonto/a; (*Culin*) puré *m*
de frutas con nata ▷ *vt* engañar;
fool about, fool around *vi* hacer el
tonto; **foolish** *adj* tonto; (*careless*)
imprudente; **foolproof** *adj* (*plan etc*)
infalible
foot [fut] (*pl* **feet**) *n* (*Anat*) pie *m*;
(*measure*) pie *m* (= 304 mm); (*of animal,*
table) pata ▷ *vt* (*bill*) pagar; **on ~**
a pie; **footage** *n* (*Cine*) imágenes
fpl; **foot-and-mouth (disease)** *n*
fiebre *f* aftosa; **football** *n* balón *m*;
(*game*: BRIT) fútbol *m*; (: US) fútbol
m americano; **footballer** *n* (BRIT)
= **football player**; **football match**
n partido de fútbol; **football player**
n futbolista *mf*, jugador(a) *m/f* de
fútbol; **footbridge** *n* puente *m* para
peatones; **foothills** *npl* estribaciones
fpl; **foothold** *n* pie *m* firme; **footing**
n (*fig*) nivel *m*; **to lose one's footing**
perder pie; **footnote** *n* nota (de pie
de página); **footpath** *n* sendero;
footprint *n* huella, pisada; **footstep**
n paso; **footwear** *n* calzado

KEYWORD

for [fɔː] *prep* **1** (*indicating destination,*
intention) para; **the train for London**
el tren con destino a Londres; **he**
left for Rome marchó para Roma; **he**
went for the paper fue por el
periódico; **is this for me?** ¿es esto
para mí?; **it's time for lunch** es la
hora de comer
2 (*indicating purpose*) para; **what('s**
it) for? ¿para qué (es)?; **to pray for**
peace rezar por la paz
3 (*on behalf of, representing*): **the MP**
for Hove el diputado por Hove; **he**
works for the government/a local
firm trabaja para el gobierno/en una
empresa local; **I'll ask him for you**
se lo pediré por ti; **G for George** G
de Gerona

4 (*because of*) por esta razón; **for fear of being criticized** por temor a ser criticado

5 (*with regard to*) para; **it's cold for July** hace frío para julio; **he has a gift for languages** tiene don de lenguas

6 (*in exchange for*) por; **I sold it for £5** lo vendí por £5; **to pay 50 pence for a ticket** pagar 50 peniques por un billete

7 (*in favour of*): **are you for or against us?** ¿estás con nosotros o contra nosotros?; **I'm all for it** estoy totalmente a favor; **vote for X** vote (a) X

8 (*referring to distance*): **there are roadworks for 5 km** hay obras en 5 km; **we walked for miles** caminamos kilómetros y kilómetros

9 (*referring to time*): **he was away for two years** estuvo fuera (durante) dos años; **it hasn't rained for three weeks** no ha llovido durante or en tres semanas; **I have known her for years** la conozco desde hace años; **can you do it for tomorrow?** ¿lo podrás hacer para mañana?

10 (*with infinitive clauses*): **it is not for me to decide** la decisión no es cosa mía; **it would be best for you to leave** sería mejor que te fueras; **there is still time for you to do it** todavía te queda tiempo para hacerlo; **for this to be possible ...** para que esto sea posible ...

11 (*in spite of*) a pesar de; **for all his complaints** a pesar de sus quejas ▶ *conj* (*since, as: formal*) puesto que

forbid (*pt* **forbad(e)**, *pp* **forbidden**) [fə'bɪd, -'bæd, -'bɪdn] *vt* prohibir; **to ~ sb to do sth** prohibir a algn hacer algo; **forbidden** *pt of* **forbid** ▶ *adj* (*food, area*) prohibido; (*word, subject*) tabú

force [fɔːs] *n* fuerza ▷ *vt* forzar; **to ~ o.s. to do** hacer un esfuerzo por

hacer; **forced** *adj* forzado; **forceful** *adj* enérgico

ford [fɔːd] *n* vado

fore [fɔːʳ] *n*: **to come to the ~** empezar a destacar; **forearm** *n* antebrazo; **forecast** *n* pronóstico ▷ *vt* (*irreg: like* **cast**) pronosticar; **forecourt** *n* patio; (*of garage*) área de entrada; **forefinger** *n* (dedo) índice *m*; **forefront** *n*: **in the forefront of** en la vanguardia de; **foreground** *n* (*also* Comput) primer plano *m*; **forehead** ['fɔrɪd] *n* frente *f*

foreign ['fɔrɪn] *adj* extranjero; (*trade*) exterior; **foreign currency** *n* divisas *fpl*; **foreigner** *n* extranjero/a; **foreign exchange** *n* divisas *fpl*; **Foreign Office** *n* (BRIT) Ministerio de Asuntos Exteriores; **Foreign Secretary** *n* (BRIT) Ministro/a de Asuntos Exteriores

fore: foreman *n* capataz *m*; **foremost** *adj* principal ▷ *adv*: **first and foremost** ante todo; **forename** *n* nombre *m* (de pila)

forensic [fə'rɛnsɪk] *adj* forense

foresee (*pt* **foresaw**, *pp* **foreseen**) [fɔː'siː, -'sɔː, -'siːn] *vt* prever; **foreseeable** *adj* previsible

forest ['fɔrɪst] *n* bosque *m*; **forestry** *n* silvicultura

forever [fə'rɛvəʳ] *adv* para siempre; (*endlessly*) constantemente

foreword ['fɔːwəːd] *n* prefacio

forfeit ['fɔːfɪt] *vt* perder (derecho a)

forgave [fə'geɪv] *pt of* **forgive**

forge [fɔːdʒ] *n* herrería ▷ *vt* (*signature, money*) falsificar; (*metal*) forjar; **forger** *n* falsificador(a) *m/f*; **forgery** *n* falsificación *f*

forget (*pt* **forgot**, *pp* **forgotten**) [fə'gɛt, -'gɔt, -'gɔtn] *vt* olvidar ▷ *vi* olvidarse; **forgetful** *adj* olvidadizo, despistado

forgive (*pt* **forgave**, *pp* **forgiven**) [fə'gɪv, -'geɪv, -'gɪvn] *vt* perdonar; **to ~ sb for sth/for doing sth** perdonar algo a algn/a algn por haber hecho algo

forgot [fə'gɒt] pt of **forget**

forgotten [fə'gɒtn] pp of **forget**

fork [fɔːk] n (for eating) tenedor m; (for gardening) horca; (of roads) bifurcación f ▷ vi (road) bifurcarse

forlorn [fə'lɔːn] adj (person) triste, melancólico; (cottage) abandonado; (attempt) desesperado

form [fɔːm] n forma; (BRIT Scol) curso; (document) formulario, planilla (LAM) ▷ vt formar; **in top ~** en plena forma; **to ~ a circle/a queue** hacer una curva/una cola

formal ['fɔːməl] adj (offer, receipt) por escrito; (person etc) correcto; (occasion, dinner) ceremonioso; **~ dress** traje m de vestir; **formality** [fɔː'mælɪtɪ] n ceremonia

format ['fɔːmæt] n formato ▷ vt (Comput) formatear

formation [fɔː'meɪʃən] n formación f

former ['fɔːmə'] adj anterior; (earlier) antiguo; (ex) ex; **the ~ ... the latter ...** aquél ... éste ...; **formerly** adv antes

formidable ['fɔːmɪdəbl] adj formidable

formula ['fɔːmjulə] n fórmula

fort [fɔːt] n fuerte m

forthcoming [fɔːθ'kʌmɪŋ] adj próximo, venidero; (character) comunicativo

fortieth ['fɔːtɪɪθ] adj cuadragésimo

fortify ['fɔːtɪfaɪ] vt fortalecer

fortnight ['fɔːtnaɪt] n (BRIT) quincena; **it's a ~ since ...** hace quince días que ...; **fortnightly** adj quincenal ▷ adv quincenalmente

fortress ['fɔːtrɪs] n fortaleza

fortunate ['fɔːtʃənɪt] adj: **it is ~ that ...** (es una) suerte que ...; **fortunately** adv afortunadamente

fortune ['fɔːtʃən] n suerte f; (wealth) fortuna; **fortune-teller** n adivino/a

forty ['fɔːtɪ] num cuarenta

forum ['fɔːrəm] n foro

forward ['fɔːwəd] adj (position) avanzado; (movement) hacia delante; (front) delantero; (not shy) atrevido ▷ n (Sport) delantero ▷ vt (letter) remitir; (career) promocionar; **to move ~** avanzar; **forwarding address** n destinatario; **forward slash** n barra diagonal

fossick ['fɒsɪk] vi (AUST, NZ inf) buscar; **to ~ for sth** buscar algo

fossil ['fɒsl] n fósil m

foster ['fɒstə'] vt (child) acoger en familia; (idea) fomentar; **foster child** n hijo/a adoptivo/a; **foster mother** n madre f adoptiva

fought [fɔːt] pt, pp of **fight**

foul [faul] adj sucio, puerco; (weather, smell etc) asqueroso; (language) grosero; (temper) malísimo ▷ n (Football) falta ▷ vt (dirty) ensuciar; **foul play** n (Law) muerte f violenta

found [faund] pt, pp of **find** ▷ vt fundar; **foundation** [faun'deɪʃən] n (act) fundación f; (basis) base f; (also: **foundation cream**) crema de base; **foundations** npl (of building) cimientos mpl

founder ['faundə'] n fundador(a) m/f ▷ vi irse a pique

fountain ['fauntɪn] n fuente f; **fountain pen** n (pluma) estilográfica, plumafuente f (LAM)

four [fɔː'] num cuatro; **on all ~s** a gatas; **four-letter word** n taco; **four-poster** n (also: **four-poster bed**) cama de columnas; **fourteen** num catorce; **fourteenth** adj decimocuarto; **fourth** adj cuarto; **four-wheel drive** n tracción f a las cuatro ruedas

fowl [faul] n ave f (de corral)

fox [fɒks] n zorro ▷ vt confundir

foyer ['fɔɪeɪ] n vestíbulo

fraction ['frækʃən] n fracción f

fracture ['fræktʃə'] n fractura

fragile ['frædʒaɪl] adj frágil

fragment ['frægmənt] n fragmento

fragrance ['freɪɡrəns] n fragancia

frail [freɪl] adj frágil, quebradizo

frame [freɪm] n (Tech) armazón f; (of picture, door etc) marco; (of spectacles:

also: **~s**) montura ▷ *vt* enmarcar;
framework *n* marco
France [frɑːns] *n* Francia
franchise ['fræntʃaɪz] *n* (*Pol*) derecho
al voto, sufragio; (*Comm*) licencia,
concesión *f*
frank [fræŋk] *adj* franco ▷ *vt* (*letter*)
franquear; **frankly** *adv* francamente
frantic ['fræntɪk] *adj* (*need, desire*)
desesperado; (*search*) frenético
fraud [frɔːd] *n* fraude *m*; (*person*)
impostor(a) *m/f*
fraught [frɔːt] *adj*: **~ with** cargado de
fray [freɪ] *vi* deshilacharse
freak [friːk] *n* (*person*) fenómeno;
(*event*) suceso anormal
freckle ['frɛkl] *n* peca
free [friː] *adj* libre; (*gratis*) gratuito
▷ *vt* (*prisoner etc*) poner en libertad;
(*jammed object*) soltar; **~ (of charge),
for ~** gratis; **freedom** *n* libertad *f*;
Freefone® *n* número gratuito; **free
gift** *n* regalo; **free kick** *n* tiro libre;
freelance *adj* independiente ▷ *adv* por
cuenta propia; **freely** *adv* libremente;
(*liberally*) generosamente; **Freepost®**
n porte *m* pagado; **free-range** *adj*
(*hen, egg*) de granja; **freeway** *n* (*US*)
autopista; **free will** *n* libre albedrío;
of one's own free will por su propia
voluntad
freeze [friːz] (*pt* **froze**, *pp* **frozen**) *vi*
helarse, congelarse ▷ *vt* helar; (*prices,
food, salaries*) congelar ▷ *n* helada; (*on
arms, wages*) congelación *f*; **freezer** *n*
congelador *m*
freezing ['friːzɪŋ] *adj* helado;
freezing point *n* punto de
congelación
freight [freɪt] *n* (*goods*) carga; (*money
charged*) flete *m*; **freight train** *n* (*US*)
tren *m* de mercancías
French [frɛntʃ] *adj* francés/esa ▷ *n*
(*Ling*) francés *m*; **the French** *npl*
los franceses; **French bean** *n* judía
verde; **French bread** *n* pan *m* francés;
French dressing *n* (*Culin*) vinagreta;
French fried potatoes, (*US*) **French**

fries *npl* patatas *fpl or* (*LAM*) papas
fpl fritas; **Frenchman** *n* francés
m; **French stick** *n* barra de pan;
French window *n* puerta ventana;
Frenchwoman *n* francesa
frenzy ['frɛnzɪ] *n* frenesí *m*
frequency ['friːkwənsɪ] *n* frecuencia
frequent *adj* ['friːkwənt] frecuente
▷ *vt* [frɪ'kwɛnt] frecuentar;
frequently *adv* frecuentemente, a
menudo
fresh [frɛʃ] *adj* fresco; (*bread*) tierno;
(*new*) nuevo; **freshen** *vi* (*wind*)
arreciar; (*air*) refrescar; **freshen up**
vi (*person*) arreglarse; **fresher** *n* (*BRIT
Scol: inf*) estudiante *mf* de primer
año; **freshly** *adv*: **freshly painted/
arrived** recién pintado/llegado;
freshman *n* (*US Scol*); = **fresher**;
freshwater *adj* (*fish*) de agua dulce
fret [frɛt] *vi* inquietarse
Fri. *abbr* (= *Friday*) vier
friction ['frɪkʃən] *n* fricción *f*
Friday ['fraɪdɪ] *n* viernes *m inv*
fridge [frɪdʒ] *n* (*BRIT*) nevera, frigo,
refrigeradora (*LAM*), heladera (*LAM*)
fried [fraɪd] *adj*: **~ egg** huevo frito
friend [frɛnd] *n* amigo/a ▷ *vt* (*Internet*)
añadir como amigo a; **friendly** *adj*
simpático; (*government*) amigo; (*place*)
acogedor(a); (*match*) amistoso;
friendship *n* amistad *f*
fries [fraɪz] *npl* (*esp US*) = **French fried
potatoes**
frigate ['frɪgɪt] *n* fragata
fright [fraɪt] *n* susto; **to take ~**
asustarse; **frighten** *vt* asustar;
frightened *adj* asustado; **frightening**
adj: **it's frightening** da miedo;
frightful *adj* espantoso, horrible
frill [frɪl] *n* volante *m*
fringe [frɪndʒ] *n* (*BRIT: of hair*)
flequillo; (*of forest etc*) borde *m*,
margen *m*
Frisbee® ['frɪzbɪ] *n* frisbee® *m*
fritter ['frɪtə'] *n* buñuelo
frivolous ['frɪvələs] *adj* frívolo
fro [frəu] *see* **to**

frock [frɔk] n vestido
frog [frɔg] n rana; **frogman** n hombre-rana m

KEYWORD

from [frɔm] prep **1** (indicating starting place) de, desde; **where do you come from?** ¿de dónde eres?; **from London to Glasgow** de Londres a Glasgow; **to escape from sth/sb** escaparse de algo/algn
2 (indicating origin etc) de; **a letter/telephone call from my sister** una carta/llamada de mi hermana; **tell him from me that ...** dígale de mi parte que ...
3 (indicating time): **from one o'clock to or until or till nine** de la una a las nueve, desde la una hasta las nueve; **from January (on)** a partir de enero
4 (indicating distance) de; **the hotel is 1 km from the beach** el hotel está a 1 km de la playa
5 (indicating price, number etc) de; **prices range from £10 to £50** los precios van desde £10 a or hasta £50; **the interest rate was increased from 9% to 10%** el tipo de interés fue incrementado de un 9% a un 10%
6 (indicating difference) de; **he can't tell red from green** no sabe distinguir el rojo del verde; **to be different from sb/sth** ser diferente de algn/algo
7 (because of, on the basis of): **from what he says** por lo que dice; **weak from hunger** debilitado por el hambre

front [frʌnt] n (foremost part) parte f delantera; (of house) fachada; (promenade: also: **sea ~**) paseo marítimo; (Mil, Pol, Meteorology) frente m; (fig: appearances) apariencia ▷ adj (wheel, leg) delantero; (row, line) primero; **in ~ (of)** delante (de); **front door** n puerta principal; **frontier** ['frʌntɪə'] n frontera; **front page** n

primera plana; **front-wheel drive** n tracción f delantera
frost [frɔst] n helada; (also: **hoar~**) escarcha; **frostbite** n congelación f; **frosting** n (esp US: icing) glaseado; **frosty** adj (weather) de helada; (welcome etc) glacial
froth [frɔθ] n espuma
frown [fraun] vi fruncir el ceño
froze [frəuz] pt of **freeze**
frozen ['frəuzn] pp of **freeze**
fruit [fruːt] n (pl inv) fruta; **fruit juice** n jugo or (SP) zumo de fruta; **fruit machine** n (BRIT) máquina tragaperras; **fruit salad** n macedonia or (LAM) ensalada de frutas
frustrate [frʌs'treɪt] vt frustrar; **frustrated** adj frustrado
fry [fraɪ] (pt, pp **fried**) vt freír ▷ n: **small ~** gente f menuda; **frying pan** n sartén f
ft. abbr = **foot**; **feet**
fudge [fʌdʒ] n (Culin) caramelo blando
fuel [fjuəl] n (for heating) combustible m; (coal) carbón m; (wood) leña; (for engine) carburante m; **fuel tank** n depósito de combustible
fulfil [ful'fɪl] vt (function) desempeñar; (condition) cumplir; (wish, desire) realizar
full [ful] adj lleno; (fig) pleno; (complete) completo; (maximum) máximo; (information) detallado; (price) íntegro ▷ adv: **~ well** perfectamente; **I'm ~ (up)** estoy lleno; **~ employment** pleno empleo; **a ~ two hours** dos horas enteras; **at ~ speed** a toda velocidad; **in ~** (reproduce, quote) íntegramente; **full-length** adj (portrait) de cuerpo entero; **full moon** n luna llena; **full-scale** adj (attack, war, search, retreat) en gran escala; (plan, model) de tamaño natural; **full stop** n punto; **full-time** adj (work) de tiempo completo ▷ adv: **to work full-time** trabajar a tiempo completo; **fully** adv completamente; (at least) al menos

fumble ['fʌmbl] vi: **to ~ with** manejar torpemente

fume [fjuːm] vi estar furioso, echar humo; **fumes** npl humo sg, gases mpl

fun [fʌn] n (amusement) diversión f; **to have ~** divertirse; **for ~** por gusto; **to make ~ of** reírse de

function ['fʌŋkʃən] n función f ⊳ vi funcionar

fund [fʌnd] n fondo; (reserve) reserva; **funds** npl (money) fondos mpl

fundamental [fʌndə'mɛntl] adj fundamental

funeral ['fjuːnərəl] n (burial) entierro; (ceremony) funerales mpl; **funeral director** n director(a) m/f de pompas fúnebres; **funeral parlour** n (BRIT) funeraria

funfair ['fʌnfɛəʳ] n (BRIT) parque m de atracciones

fungus (pl **fungi**) ['fʌŋgəs, -gaɪ] n hongo; (mould) moho

funnel ['fʌnl] n embudo; (of ship) chimenea

funny ['fʌnɪ] adj gracioso, divertido; (strange) curioso, raro

fur [fəːʳ] n piel f; (BRIT: on tongue etc) sarro; **fur coat** n abrigo de pieles

furious ['fjuərɪəs] adj furioso; (effort, argument) violento

furnish ['fəːnɪʃ] vt amueblar; (supply) proporcionar; (information) facilitar; **furnishings** npl mobiliario sg

furniture ['fəːnɪtʃəʳ] n muebles mpl; **piece of ~** mueble m

furry ['fəːrɪ] adj peludo

further ['fəːðəʳ] adj (new) nuevo ⊳ adv más lejos; (more) más; (moreover) además ⊳ vt hacer avanzar; **how much ~ is it?** ¿a qué distancia queda?; **~ to your letter of ...** (Comm) con referencia a su carta de ...; **to ~ one's interests** fomentar sus intereses; **further education** n educación f postescolar; **furthermore** adv además

furthest ['fəːðɪst] superlative of **far**

fury ['fjuərɪ] n furia

fuse, (US) **fuze** [fjuːz] n fusible m; (for bomb etc) mecha ⊳ vt (metal) fundir; (fig) fusionar ⊳ vi fundirse; fusionarse; (BRIT Elec): **to ~ the lights** fundir los plomos; **fuse box** n caja de fusibles

fusion ['fjuːʒən] n fusión f

fuss [fʌs] n (excitement) conmoción f; (complaint) alboroto; **to make a ~** armar jaleo; **fussy** adj (person) quisquilloso

future ['fjuːtʃəʳ] adj futuro; (coming) venidero ⊳ n futuro, porvenir; **in ~** de ahora en adelante; **futures** npl (Comm) operaciones fpl a término, futuros mpl

fuze [fjuːz] n, vb (US) = **fuse**

fuzzy ['fʌzɪ] adj (Phot) borroso; (hair) muy rizado

g

G [dʒiː] n (Mus) sol m

g. abbr (= gram(s), gravity) g

gadget ['gædʒɪt] n aparato

Gaelic ['geɪlɪk] adj, n (Ling) gaélico

gag [gæg] n (on mouth) mordaza; (joke) chiste m ▷ vt amordazar

gain [geɪn] n ganancia ▷ vt ganar ▷ vi (watch) adelantarse; **to ~ by sth** ganar con algo; **to ~ ground** ganar terreno; **to ~ 3 lbs (in weight)** engordar 3 libras; **gain (up)on** vt fus alcanzar

gal., gall. abbr = **gallon**

gala ['gɑːlə] n gala

galaxy ['gæləksɪ] n galaxia

gale [geɪl] n (wind) vendaval m; **~ force 10** vendaval de fuerza 10

gall bladder n vesícula biliar

gallery ['gælərɪ] n (also: **art ~**: state-owned) pinacoteca or museo de arte; (: private) galería de arte

gallon ['gæln] n galón m (= 8 pintas; Brit = 4,546 litros; US = 3,785 litros)

gallop ['gæləp] n galope m ▷ vi galopar

gallstone ['gɔːlstəun] n cálculo biliar

gamble ['gæmbl] n (risk) jugada arriesgada; (bet) apuesta ▷ vt: **to ~ on** apostar a; (fig) contar con ▷ vi jugar; (take a risk) jugárselas; (Comm) especular; **to ~ on the Stock Exchange** jugar a la bolsa; **gambler** n jugador(a) m/f; **gambling** n juego

game [geɪm] n juego; (match) partido; (of cards) partida; (Hunting) caza ▷ adj valiente; (ready): **to be ~ for anything** estar dispuesto a todo; **~s** (Scol) deportes mpl; **games console** n consola de juegos; **game show** n programa m concurso inv, concurso

gaming ['geɪmɪŋ] n (with video games) juegos mpl de ordenador or computadora

gammon ['gæmən] n (bacon) tocino ahumado; (ham) jamón m ahumado

gang [gæŋ] n (of criminals etc) banda; (of kids) pandilla; (of workmen) brigada

gangster ['gæŋstəʳ] n gángster m

gap [gæp] n hueco; (in trees, traffic) claro; (in time) intervalo

gape [geɪp] vi mirar boquiabierto

gap year n año sabático (antes de empezar a estudiar en la universidad)

garage ['gærɑːʒ] n garaje m; (for repairs) taller m; **garage sale** n venta de objetos usados (en el jardín de una casa particular)

garbage ['gɑːbɪdʒ] n (US) basura; (nonsense) bobadas fpl; **garbage can** n (US) cubo or balde m (LAM) or bote m (LAM) de la basura; **garbage collector** n (US) basurero/a

garden ['gɑːdn] n jardín m; **gardens** npl (public) parque m; **garden centre** n (BRIT) centro de jardinería; **gardener** n jardinero/a; **gardening** n jardinería

garlic ['gɑːlɪk] n ajo

garment ['gɑːmənt] n prenda (de vestir)

garnish ['gɑːnɪʃ] vt (Culin) aderezar

garrison ['gærɪsn] n guarnición f

gas [gæs] n gas m; (US: gasoline) gasolina ▷ vt asfixiar con gas; **gas cooker** n (BRIT) cocina de gas; **gas cylinder** n bombona de gas; **gas fire** n estufa de gas

gasket ['gæskɪt] n (Aut) junta

gasoline ['gæsəliːn] n (US) gasolina

gasp [gɑːsp] n grito sofocado ▷ vi (pant) jadear

gas: gas pedal n (esp US) acelerador m; **gas station** n (US) gasolinera; **gas tank** n (US Aut) depósito (de gasolina)

gate [geɪt] n (also at airport) puerta; (metal) verja

gatecrash ['geɪtkræʃ] vt colarse en

gateway ['geɪtweɪ] n puerta

gather ['gæðəʳ] vt (flowers, fruit) coger (SP), recoger (LAM); (assemble) reunir; (pick up) recoger; (Sewing) fruncir; (understand) sacar en consecuencia ▷ vi (assemble) reunirse; **to ~ speed** ganar velocidad; **gathering** n reunión f, asamblea

gauge, (US) **gage** [geɪdʒ] n (instrument) indicador m ▷ vt medir; (fig) juzgar

gave [geɪv] pt of **give**

gay [geɪ] adj (homosexual) gay; (colour, person) alegre

gaze [geɪz] n mirada fija ▷ vi: **to ~ at sth** mirar algo fijamente

GB abbr (= Great Britain) GB

GCSE n abbr (BRIT: = General Certificate of Secondary Education) certificado del último ciclo de la enseñanza secundaria obligatoria

gear [gɪəʳ] n equipo; (Tech) engranaje m; (Aut) velocidad f, marcha ▷ vt (fig: adapt): **to ~ sth to** adaptar or ajustar algo a; **top** or (US) **high/low ~** cuarta/primera; **in ~** con la marcha metida; **gear up** vi prepararse; **gear box** n caja de cambios; **gear lever**, (US) **gear shift** n palanca de cambio; **gear stick** n (BRIT) = **gear lever**

geese [giːs] npl of **goose**

gel [dʒɛl] n gel m

gem [dʒɛm] n piedra preciosa

Gemini ['dʒɛmɪnaɪ] n Géminis m

gender ['dʒɛndəʳ] n género

gene [dʒiːn] n gen(e) m

general ['dʒɛnərl] n general m ▷ adj general; **in ~** en general; **general anaesthetic**, (US) **general anesthetic** n anestesia general; **general election** n elecciones fpl generales; **generalize** vi generalizar; **generally** adv generalmente, en general; **general practitioner** n médico/a de medicina general; **general store** n tienda (que vende de todo) (LAM, SP), almacén m (SC, SP)

generate ['dʒɛnəreɪt] vt generar

generation [dʒɛnə'reɪʃən] n generación f

generator ['dʒɛnəreɪtəʳ] n generador m

generosity [dʒɛnə'rɔsɪtɪ] n generosidad f

generous ['dʒɛnərəs] adj generoso

genetic [dʒɪ'nɛtɪk] adj genético; **~ engineering** ingeniería genética; **~ fingerprinting** identificación f genética; **genetically modified organism** n organismo transgénico; **genetics** n genética

genitals ['dʒɛnɪtlz] npl (órganos mpl) genitales mpl

genius ['dʒiːnɪəs] n genio

genome ['giːnəʊm] n genoma m

gent [dʒɛnt] n abbr (BRIT inf); = **gentleman**

gentle ['dʒɛntl] adj (sweet) dulce; (touch etc) ligero, suave

▌ Be careful not to translate gentle by the Spanish word gentil.

gentleman ['dʒɛntlmən] n señor m; (well-bred man) caballero

gently ['dʒɛntlɪ] adv suavemente

gents [dʒɛnts] n servicios mpl (de caballeros)

genuine ['dʒɛnjuɪn] adj auténtico; (person) sincero; **genuinely** adv sinceramente

geographic(al) [dʒɪə'græfɪk(l)] adj geográfico

geography [dʒɪˈɔgrəfɪ] n geografía
geology [dʒɪˈɔlədʒɪ] n geología
geometry [dʒɪˈɔmətrɪ] n geometría
geranium [dʒɪˈreɪnjəm] n geranio
gerbil [ˈdʒɜːbl] n gerbo
geriatric [dʒɛrɪˈætrɪk] adj, n
geriátrico/a
germ [dʒəːm] n (microbe) microbio,
bacteria; (seed) germen m
German [ˈdʒəːmən] adj alemán/ana
▷ n alemán/ana m/f; (Ling) alemán m;
German measles n rubeola, rubéola
Germany [ˈdʒəːmənɪ] n Alemania
gesture [ˈdʒɛstjəʳ] n gesto

KEYWORD

get [gɛt] (pt, pp **got**, pp **gotten** (US))
vi **1** (become, be) ponerse, volverse; **to
get old/tired** envejecer/cansarse; **to
get drunk** emborracharse; **to
get dirty** ensuciarse; **when do I
get paid?** ¿cuándo me pagan or se
me paga?; **it's getting late** se está
haciendo tarde
2 (go): **to get to/from** llegar a/de; **to
get home** llegar a casa
3 (begin) empezar a; **to get to
know sb** (llegar a) conocer a algn;
I'm getting to like him me está
empezando a gustar; **let's get going**
or **started** ¡vamos (a empezar)!
4 (modal aux vb): **you've got to do it**
tienes que hacerlo
▷ vt **1**: **to get sth done** (finish) hacer
algo; (have done) mandar hacer algo;
to get one's hair cut cortarse el
pelo; **to get the car going** or **to go**
arrancar el coche; **to get sb to do
sth** conseguir or hacer que algn haga
algo; **to get sth/sb ready** preparar
algo/a algn
2 (obtain: money, permission, results)
conseguir; (find: job, flat) encontrar;
(fetch: person, doctor) buscar; (: object)
ir a buscar, traer; **to get sth for sb**
conseguir algo para algn; **get me Mr
Jones, please** (Tel) póngame or (LAM)

comuníqueme con el Sr. Jones, por
favor; **can I get you a drink?** ¿quieres
algo de beber?
3 (receive: present, letter) recibir;
(acquire: reputation) alcanzar; (: prize)
ganar; **what did you get for your
birthday?** ¿qué te regalaron por
tu cumpleaños?; **how much did
you get for the painting?** ¿cuánto
sacaste por el cuadro?
4 (catch) coger (SP), agarrar (LAM);
(hit: target etc) dar en; **to get sb by
the arm/throat** coger or agarrar a
algn por el brazo/cuello; **get him!**
¡cógelo! (SP), ¡atrápalo! (LAM); **the
bullet got him in the leg** la bala le dio
en la pierna
5 (take, move) llevar; **to get sth to sb**
hacer llegar algo a algn; **do you think
we'll get it through the door?** ¿crees
que lo podremos meter por la puerta?
6 (catch, take: plane, bus etc) coger
(SP), tomar (LAM); **where do I get
the train for Birmingham?** ¿dónde
se coge or se toma el tren para
Birmingham?
7 (understand) entender; (hear) oír;
I've got it! ¡ya lo tengo!, ¡eureka!;
I don't get your meaning no te
entiendo; **I'm sorry, I didn't get your
name** lo siento, no me he enterado
de tu nombre
8 (have, possess): **to have got** tener
get away vi marcharse; (escape)
escaparse
get away with vt fus hacer
impunemente
get back vi (return) volver ▷ vt
recobrar
get in vi entrar; (train) llegar; (arrive
home) volver a casa, regresar
get into vt fus entrar en; (vehicle) subir
a; **to get into a rage** enfadarse
get off vi (from train etc) bajar(se);
(depart: person, car) marcharse ▷ vt
(remove) quitar ▷ vt fus (train, bus)
bajar(se) de
get on vi (at exam etc): **how are you**

getting on? ¿cómo te va?; **to get on (with)** (*agree*) llevarse bien (con) ▷ vt fus subir(se) a

get out vi salir; (*of vehicle*) bajar(se) ▷ vt sacar

get out of vt fus salir de; (*duty etc*) escaparse de

get over vt fus (*illness*) recobrarse de

get through vi (*Tel*) (lograr) comunicar

get up vi (*rise*) levantarse ▷ vt fus subir

getaway ['gɛtəweɪ] n fuga

Ghana ['gɑːnə] n Ghana

ghastly ['gɑːstlɪ] adj horrible

ghetto ['gɛtəu] n gueto

ghost [gəust] n fantasma m

giant ['dʒaɪənt] n gigante mf ▷ adj gigantesco, gigante

gift [gɪft] n regalo; (*ability*) don m; **gifted** adj dotado; **gift shop,** (US) **gift store** n tienda de regalos; **gift token**, **gift voucher** n vale-regalo m

gig [gɪg] n (*inf: concert*) actuación

gigabyte ['gɪgəbaɪt] n gigabyte m

gigantic [dʒaɪˈgæntɪk] adj gigantesco

giggle ['gɪgl] vi reírse tontamente

gills [gɪlz] npl (*of fish*) branquias fpl, agallas fpl

gilt [gɪlt] adj, n dorado

gimmick ['gɪmɪk] n reclamo

gin [dʒɪn] n ginebra

ginger ['dʒɪndʒər] n jengibre m

gipsy ['dʒɪpsɪ] n gitano/a

giraffe [dʒɪˈrɑːf] n jirafa

girl [gəːl] n (*small*) niña; (*young woman*) chica, joven f, muchacha; **an English ~** una (chica) inglesa; **girl band** n girl band m (*grupo musical de chicas*); **girlfriend** n (*of girl*) amiga; (*of boy*) novia

gist [dʒɪst] n lo esencial

give (pt **gave**, pp **given**) [gɪv, geɪv, 'gɪvn] vt dar; (*deliver*) entregar; (*as gift*) regalar ▷ vi (*break*) romperse; (*stretch: fabric*) dar de sí; **to ~ sb sth, ~ sth to sb** dar algo a algn; **give**

away vt (*give free*) regalar; (*betray*) traicionar; (*disclose*) revelar; **give back** vt devolver; **give in** vi ceder ▷ vt entregar; **give out** vt distribuir; **give up** vi rendirse, darse por vencido ▷ vt renunciar a; **to ~ up smoking** dejar de fumar; **to ~ o.s. up** entregarse

given ['gɪvn] pp of **give** ▷ adj (*fixed: time, amount*) determinado ▷ conj **~ (that) ...** dado (que) ...; **~ the circumstances ...** dadas las circunstancias ...

glacier ['glæsɪər] n glaciar m

glad [glæd] adj contento; **gladly** adv con mucho gusto

glamorous ['glæmərəs] adj con glamour, glam(o)uroso

glamour, (US) **glamor** ['glæmər] n encanto, atractivo

glance [glɑːns] n ojeada, mirada ▷ vi: **to ~ at** echar una ojeada a

gland [glænd] n glándula

glare [glɛər] n deslumbramiento, brillo ▷ vi deslumbrar; **to ~ at** mirar con odio; **glaring** adj (*mistake*) manifiesto

glass [glɑːs] n vidrio, cristal m; (*for drinking*) vaso; (*with stem*) copa; **glasses** ['glɑːsəz] npl gafas fpl

glaze [gleɪz] vt (*window*) acristalar; (*pottery*) vidriar ▷ n barniz m

gleam [gliːm] vi relucir

glen [glɛn] n cañada

glide [glaɪd] vi deslizarse; (*Aviat: bird*) planear; **glider** n (*Aviat*) planeador m

glimmer ['glɪmər] n luz f tenue; (*of hope*) rayo

glimpse [glɪmps] n vislumbre m ▷ vt vislumbrar, entrever

glint [glɪnt] vi centellear

glisten ['glɪsn] vi relucir, brillar

glitter ['glɪtər] vi relucir, brillar

global ['gləubl] adj mundial; **globalization** [gləubəlaɪzeɪʃən] n globalización f; **global warming** n (re) calentamiento global or de la tierra

globe [gləub] n globo; (*model*) globo terráqueo

gloom [gluːm] n penumbra; (sadness) desaliento, melancolía; **gloomy** adj (dark) oscuro; (sad) triste; (pessimistic) pesimista

glorious ['glɔːrɪəs] adj glorioso; (weather, sunshine) espléndido

glory ['glɔːrɪ] n gloria

gloss [glɒs] n (shine) brillo; (also: ~ paint) (pintura) esmalte m

glossary ['glɒsərɪ] n glosario

glossy ['glɒsɪ] adj lustroso; (magazine) de papel satinado or cuché

glove [glʌv] n guante m; **glove compartment** n (Aut) guantera

glow [gləu] vi brillar

glucose ['gluːkəus] n glucosa

glue [gluː] n pegamento ▷ vt pegar

GM adj abbr (= genetically-modified) transgénico

gm abbr (= gram) g

GMT abbr (= Greenwich Mean Time) GMT

gnaw [nɔː] vt roer

go [gəu] (pt **went**, pp **gone**) vi ir; (travel) viajar; (depart) irse, marcharse; (work) funcionar, marchar; (be sold) venderse; (time) pasar; (become) ponerse; (break etc) estropearse, romperse ▷ n: **to have a go (at)** probar suerte (con); **to be on the go** no parar; **whose go is it?** ¿a quién le toca?; **he's going to do it** va a hacerlo; **to go for a walk** ir a dar un paseo; **to go dancing** ir a bailar; **how did it go?** ¿qué tal salió or resultó?, ¿cómo ha ido?; **go ahead** vi seguir adelante; **go around** vi = **go round**; **go away** vi irse, marcharse; **go back** vi volver; **go by** vi (years, time) pasar ▷ vt fus guiarse por; **go down** vi bajar; (ship) hundirse; (sun) ponerse ▷ vt fus bajar por; **go for** vt fus (fetch) ir por; (like) gustar; (attack) atacar; **go in** vi entrar; **go into** vt fus entrar en; (investigate) investigar; (embark on) dedicarse a; **go off** vi irse, marcharse; (food) pasarse; (explode) estallar; (event) realizarse ▷ vt fus perder el interés por; **I'm going off him/the idea** ya no me gusta tanto él/la idea; **go on** vi (continue) seguir, continuar; (happen) pasar, ocurrir; **to go on doing sth** seguir haciendo algo; **go out** vi salir; (fire, light) apagarse; **go over** vi (ship) zozobrar ▷ vt fus (check) revisar; **go past** vi, vt fus pasar; **go round** vi (circulate: news, rumour) correr; (suffice) alcanzar, bastar; (revolve) girar, dar vueltas; (make a detour): **to go round (by)** dar la vuelta (por); (visit): **to go round (to sb's)** pasar a ver (a algn) ▷ vt fus: **to go round the back** pasar por detrás; **go through** vt fus (town etc) atravesar; **go up** vi subir; **go with** vt fus (accompany) ir con; (fit, suit) hacer juego con, acompañar a; **go without** vt fus pasarse sin

go-ahead ['gəuəhɛd] adj emprendedor(a) ▷ n luz f verde

goal [gəul] n meta; (score) gol m; **goalkeeper** n portero; **goal post** n poste m (de la portería)

goat [gəut] n cabra f

gobble ['gɒbl] vt (also: ~ **down**, ~ **up**) engullir

god [gɒd] n dios m; **G~** Dios m; **godchild** n ahijado/a; **goddaughter** n ahijada; **goddess** n diosa; **godfather** n padrino; **godmother** n madrina; **godson** n ahijado

goggles ['gɒglz] npl gafas fpl

going ['gəuɪŋ] n (conditions) cosas fpl ▷ adj: **the ~ rate** la tarifa corriente or en vigor

gold [gəuld] n oro ▷ adj de oro; **golden** adj (made of gold) de oro; (colour) dorado; **goldfish** n pez m de colores; **goldmine** n mina de oro; **gold-plated** adj chapado en oro

golf [gɒlf] n golf m; **golf ball** n (for game) pelota de golf; (on typewriter) esfera impresora; **golf club** n club m de golf; (stick) palo (de golf); **golf course** n campo de golf; **golfer** n golfista mf

gone [gɒn] pp of **go**

gong [gɒŋ] n gong m

good [gud] adj bueno; (before m sg n) buen; (well-behaved) educado ▷ n bien m; **~!** ¡qué bien!; **he's ~ at it** se le da bien; **to be ~ for** servir para; **it's ~ for you** te hace bien; **would you be ~ enough to …?** ¿podría hacerme el favor de …?, ¿sería tan amable de …?; **a ~ deal (of)** mucho; **a ~ many** muchos; **to make ~** reparar; **it's no ~ complaining** no sirve de nada quejarse; **for ~** (for ever) para siempre, definitivamente; **~ morning/afternoon** ¡buenos días/buenas tardes!; **~ evening!** ¡buenas noches!; **~ night!** ¡buenas noches!

goodbye [gud'baɪ] excl ¡adiós!; **to say ~ (to)** (person) despedirse (de)

good: Good Friday n Viernes m Santo; **good-looking** adj guapo; **good-natured** adj (person) de buen carácter; **goodness** n (of person) bondad f; **for goodness sake!** ¡por Dios!; **goodness gracious!** ¡madre mía!; **goods** npl (Comm etc) mercancías fpl; **goods train** n (BRIT) tren m de mercancías; **goodwill** n buena voluntad f

google ['guːgəl] vt, vi buscar en Google®

goose (pl **geese**) [guːs, giːs] n ganso, oca

gooseberry ['guzbərɪ] n grosella espinosa or silvestre; **to play ~** hacer de carabina

gorge [gɔːdʒ] n garganta ▷ vr: **to ~ o.s. (on)** atracarse (de)

gorgeous ['gɔːdʒəs] adj precioso; (weather) estupendo; (person) guapísimo

gorilla [gə'rɪlə] n gorila m

gosh [gɒʃ] (inf) excl ¡cielos!

gospel ['gɒspl] n evangelio

gossip ['gɒsɪp] n cotilleo; (person) cotilla mf ▷ vi cotillear; **gossip column** n ecos mpl de sociedad

got [gɒt] pt, pp of **get**

gotten ['gɒtn] (US) pp of **get**

gourmet ['guəmeɪ] n gastrónomo/a

govern ['gʌvən] vt gobernar; **government** n gobierno; **governor** n gobernador(a) m/f; (of school etc) miembro del consejo; (of jail) director(a) m/f

gown [gaun] n vestido; (of teacher, judge) toga

GP n abbr (Med) = **general practitioner**

GPS n abbr (= global positioning system) GPS m

grab [græb] vt agarrar, coger (SP); **to ~ at** intentar agarrar

grace [greɪs] n gracia ▷ vt honrar; (adorn) adornar; **5 days' ~** un plazo de 5 días; **graceful** adj grácil, ágil; (style, shape) elegante, gracioso; **gracious** ['greɪʃəs] adj amable

grade [greɪd] n (quality) clase f, calidad f; (in hierarchy) grado; (Scol: mark) nota; (US: Scol) curso ▷ vt clasificar; **grade crossing** n (US) paso a nivel; **grade school** n (US) escuela primaria

gradient ['greɪdɪənt] n pendiente f

gradual ['grædjuəl] adj gradual; **gradually** adv gradualmente

graduate n ['grædjuɪt] licenciado/a, graduado/a ▷ vi ['grædjueɪt] licenciarse, graduarse; **graduation** [grædju'eɪʃən] n graduación f; (US Scol) entrega de los títulos de bachillerato

graffiti [grə'fiːtɪ] npl pintadas fpl

graft [grɑːft] n (Agr, Med) injerto; (bribery) corrupción f ▷ vt injertar; **hard ~** (inf) trabajo duro

grain [greɪn] n (single particle) grano; (no pl: cereals) cereales mpl; (in wood) veta

gram [græm] n gramo

grammar ['græmə^r] n gramática; **grammar school** n (BRIT) ≈ instituto (de segunda enseñanza)

gramme [græm] n = **gram**

gran [græn] n (BRIT inf) abuelita

grand [grænd] adj magnífico, imponente; (wonderful) estupendo; (gesture etc) grandioso; **grandad** (inf) n = **granddad**; **grandchild** (pl

grandchildren) n nieto/a; **granddad** n yayo, abuelito; **granddaughter** n nieta; **grandfather** n abuelo; **grandma** n yaya, abuelita; **grandmother** n abuela; **grandpa** n = **granddad**; **grandparents** npl abuelos mpl; **grand piano** n piano de cola; **Grand Prix** [ˈɡrɑ̃ːˈpriː] n (Aut) gran premio, Grand Prix m; **grandson** n nieto

granite [ˈɡrænɪt] n granito

granny [ˈɡrænɪ] n abuelita, yaya

grant [ɡrɑːnt] vt (concede) conceder; (admit): **to ~ (that)** reconocer (que) ▷ n (Scol) beca; **to take sth for ~ed** dar algo por sentado

grape [ɡreɪp] n uva

grapefruit [ˈɡreɪpfruːt] n pomelo (sc, sp), toronja (LAM)

graph [ɡrɑːf] n gráfica; **graphic** [ˈɡræfɪk] adj gráfico; **graphics** n artes fpl gráficas ▷ npl (drawings, Comput) gráficos mpl

grasp [ɡrɑːsp] vt agarrar, asir; (understand) comprender ▷ n (grip) asimiento; (understanding) comprensión f

grass [ɡrɑːs] n hierba; (lawn) césped m; **grasshopper** n saltamontes m inv

grate [ɡreɪt] n parrilla ▷ vi chirriar ▷ vt (Culin) rallar

grateful [ˈɡreɪtful] adj agradecido

grater [ˈɡreɪtəʳ] n rallador m

gratitude [ˈɡrætɪtjuːd] n agradecimiento

grave [ɡreɪv] n tumba ▷ adj serio, grave

gravel [ˈɡrævl] n grava

gravestone [ˈɡreɪvstəʊn] n lápida

graveyard [ˈɡreɪvjɑːd] n cementerio

gravity [ˈɡrævɪtɪ] n gravedad f

gravy [ˈɡreɪvɪ] n salsa de carne

gray [ɡreɪ] adj (US) = **grey**

graze [ɡreɪz] vi pacer ▷ vt (touch lightly, scrape) rozar ▷ n (Med) rozadura

grease [ɡriːs] n (fat) grasa; (lubricant) lubricante m ▷ vt engrasar; **greasy** adj grasiento

great [ɡreɪt] adj grande; (inf) estupendo; **Great Britain** n Gran Bretaña; **great-grandfather** n bisabuelo; **great-grandmother** n bisabuela; **greatly** adv muy; (with verb) mucho

Greece [ɡriːs] n Grecia

greed [ɡriːd] n (also: **~iness**) codicia; (for food) gula; (for power etc) avidez f; **greedy** adj codicioso; (for food) glotón/ona

Greek [ɡriːk] adj griego ▷ n griego/a; (Ling) griego

green [ɡriːn] adj verde; (inexperienced) novato ▷ n verde m; (stretch of grass) césped m; (of golf course) green m; **the G~ party** (Pol) el partido verde; **greens** npl verduras fpl; **green card** n (Aut) carta verde; (US: work permit) permiso de trabajo para los extranjeros en EE. UU.; **greengage** n (ciruela) claudia; **greengrocer** n (BRIT) verdulero/a; **greenhouse** n invernadero; **greenhouse effect** n efecto invernadero

Greenland [ˈɡriːnlənd] n Groenlandia

green salad n ensalada f (de lechuga, pepino, pimiento verde, etc)

greet [ɡriːt] vt saludar; (news) recibir; **greeting** n (welcome) bienvenida; **greeting(s) card** n tarjeta de felicitación

grew [ɡruː] pt of **grow**

grey [ɡreɪ] adj gris; **grey-haired** adj canoso; **greyhound** n galgo

grid [ɡrɪd] n rejilla; (Elec) red f; **gridlock** n retención f

grief [ɡriːf] n dolor m, pena

grievance [ˈɡriːvəns] n motivo de queja, agravio

grieve [ɡriːv] vi afligirse, acongojarse ▷ vt afligir, apenar; **to ~ for** llorar por

grill [ɡrɪl] n (on cooker) parrilla ▷ vt (BRIT) asar a la parrilla; (question) interrogar

grille [ɡrɪl] n rejilla

grim [grɪm] adj (place) lúgubre;
(person) adusto

grime [graɪm] n mugre f

grin [grɪn] n sonrisa abierta ▷ vi: **to ~
(at)** sonreír abiertamente (a)

grind [graɪnd] (pt, pp **ground**) vt
(coffee, pepper etc) moler; (US: meat)
picar; (make sharp) afilar ▷ n: **the daily
~** (inf) la rutina diaria

grip [grɪp] n (hold) asimiento; (handle)
asidero ▷ vt agarrar; **to get to ~s
with** enfrentarse con; **to lose one's
~** (fig) perder el control; **gripping** adj
absorbente

grit [grɪt] n gravilla; (courage) valor m
▷ vt (road) poner gravilla en; **to ~ one's
teeth** apretar los dientes

grits [grɪts] npl (US) maíz msg a medio
moler

groan [grəʊn] n gemido, quejido ▷ vi
gemir, quejarse

grocer ['grəʊsəʳ] n tendero (de
ultramarinos); **~'s (shop)** n
tienda de ultramarinos or (LAM) de
abarrotes; **groceries** npl comestibles
mpl; **grocery** n (shop) tienda de
ultramarinos

groin [grɔɪn] n ingle f

groom [gruːm] n mozo/a de cuadra;
(also: **bride~**) novio ▷ vt (horse)
almohazar; (fig): **to ~ sb for** preparar a
algn para; **well-~ed** acicalado

groove [gruːv] n ranura; surco

grope [grəʊp] vi: **to ~ for** buscar
a tientas

gross [grəʊs] adj (neglect, injustice)
grave; (vulgar: behaviour) grosero;
(: appearance) de mal gusto;
(Comm) bruto; **grossly** adv (greatly)
enormemente

grotesque [grə'tɛsk] adj grotesco

ground [graʊnd] pt, pp of **grind** ▷ n
suelo, tierra; (Sport) campo, terreno;
(reason: gen pl) motivo, razón f;
(US: also: **~ wire**) tierra ▷ vt (plane)
mantener en tierra; (US Elec) conectar
con tierra; **grounds** npl (of coffee etc)
poso sg; (gardens etc) jardines mpl,

parque m; **on the ~** en el suelo; **to
gain/lose ~** ganar/perder terreno; **to
the ~** al suelo; **ground floor** n (BRIT)
planta baja; **groundsheet** (BRIT) n
tela impermeable; **groundwork** n
trabajo preliminar

group [gruːp] n grupo; (Mus: pop
group) conjunto, grupo ▷ vi (also: **~
together**) agrupar ▷ vi agruparse

grouse [graʊs] n (pl inv: bird) urogallo
▷ vi (complain) quejarse

grovel ['grɔvl] vi (fig) arrastrarse

grow (pt **grew**, pp **grown**) [grəʊ,
gruː, grəʊn] vi crecer; (increase)
aumentar; (expand) desarrollarse;
(become) volverse ▷ vt cultivar; (hair,
beard) dejar crecer; **to ~ rich/weak**
enriquecerse/debilitarse; **grow on**
vt fus: **that painting is ~ing on me**
ese cuadro me gusta cada vez más;
grow up vi crecer, hacerse hombre/
mujer

growl [graʊl] vi gruñir

grown [grəʊn] pp of **grow**; **grown-up**
n adulto/a, mayor mf

growth [grəʊθ] n crecimiento,
desarrollo; (what has grown) brote m;
(Med) tumor m

grub [grʌb] n gusano; (inf: food)
comida

grubby ['grʌbɪ] adj sucio, mugriento

grudge [grʌdʒ] n rencor ▷ vt: **to ~ sb
sth** dar algo a algn de mala gana; **to
bear sb a ~** guardar rencor a algn

gruelling, (US) **grueling** adj
agotador

gruesome ['gruːsəm] adj horrible

grumble ['grʌmbl] vi refunfuñar,
quejarse

grumpy ['grʌmpɪ] adj gruñón/ona

grunt [grʌnt] vi gruñir

guarantee [gærən'tiː] n garantía
▷ vt garantizar

guard [gɑːd] n guardia; (person)
guarda mf; (BRIT Rail) jefe m de tren;
(on machine) cubierta de protección;
(fireguard) pantalla ▷ vt guardar; **to
be on one's ~** (fig) estar en guardia;

g

guardian n guardián/ana m/f; (of minor) tutor(a) m/f

guerrilla [gəˈrɪlə] n guerrillero/a

guess [gɛs] vi, vt adivinar; (suppose) suponer ▷ n suposición f, conjetura; **to take** or **have a ~** tratar de adivinar

guest [gɛst] n invitado/a; (in hotel) huésped(a) m/f; **guest room** n cuarto de huéspedes

guidance [ˈgaɪdəns] n (advice) consejos mpl

guide [gaɪd] n (person) guía mf; (book, fig) guía f; (also: **girl ~**) exploradora ▷ vt guiar; **guidebook** n guía; **guide dog** n perro guía; **guided tour** n visita f con guía; **guidelines** npl (fig) directrices fpl

guild [gɪld] n gremio

guilt [gɪlt] n culpabilidad f; **guilty** adj culpable

guinea pig n cobaya; (fig) conejillo de Indias

guitar [gɪˈtɑːʳ] n guitarra; **guitarist** n guitarrista mf

gulf [gʌlf] n golfo; (abyss) abismo

gull [gʌl] n gaviota

gulp [gʌlp] vi tragar saliva ▷ vt (also: **~ down**) tragarse

gum [gʌm] n (Anat) encía; (glue) goma, cemento (Lam); (sweet) gominola; (also: **chewing~**) chicle m ▷ vt pegar con goma

gun [gʌn] n (small) pistola; (shotgun) escopeta; (rifle) fusil m; (cannon) cañón m; **gunfire** n disparos mpl; **gunman** n pistolero; **gunpoint** n: **at gunpoint** a mano armada; **gunpowder** n pólvora; **gunshot** n disparo

gush [gʌʃ] vi chorrear, salir a raudales; (fig) deshacerse en efusiones

gust [gʌst] n (of wind) ráfaga

gut [gʌt] n intestino; (Mus etc) cuerda de tripa; **guts** npl (courage) agallas fpl, valor m; (inf: innards: of people, animals) tripas fpl

gutter [ˈgʌtəʳ] n (of roof) canalón m; (in street) cuneta

guy [gaɪ] n (also: **~rope**) viento, cuerda; (inf: man) tío (sp), tipo

Guy Fawkes' Night [gaɪˈfɔːks-] n ver nota **"Guy Fawkes' Night"**

● **GUY FAWKES' NIGHT**
●
● La noche del cinco de noviembre,
● Guy Fawkes' Night, se celebra el
● fracaso de la conspiración de la
● pólvora (Gunpowder Plot), el intento
● fallido de volar el parlamento de
● Jaime 1 en 1605. Esa noche se lanzan
● fuegos artificiales y se queman
● en muchas hogueras muñecos de
● trapo que representan a Guy Fawkes,
● uno de los cabecillas. Días antes los
● niños tienen por costumbre pedir a
● los viandantes "a penny for the guy",
● dinero para comprar los cohetes.

gym [dʒɪm] n (also: **gymnasium**) gimnasio; (also: **gymnastics**) gimnasia; **gymnasium** n gimnasio; **gymnast** n gimnasta mf; **gymnastics** n gimnasia; **gym shoes** npl zapatillas fpl de gimnasia

gynaecologist, (us) **gynecologist** [gaɪnɪˈkɔlədʒɪst] n ginecólogo/a

gypsy [ˈdʒɪpsɪ] n = **gipsy**

h

haberdashery [ˈhæbəˈdæʃərɪ] n
(BRIT) mercería
habit [ˈhæbɪt] n hábito, costumbre f;
(drug habit) adicción f
habitat [ˈhæbɪtæt] n hábitat m
hack [hæk] vt (cut) cortar; (slice)
tajar ▷ n (pej: writer) escritor(a) m/f a
sueldo; **hacker** n (Comput) pirata m
informático
had [hæd] pt, pp of **have**
haddock [ˈhædək] (pl **haddock** or
haddocks) n especie de merluza
hadn't [ˈhædnt] = **had not**
haemorrhage, (US) **hemorrhage**
[ˈhɛmərɪdʒ] n hemorragia
haemorrhoids, (US)
hemorrhoids [ˈhɛmərɔɪdz] npl
hemorroides fpl
haggle [ˈhægl] vi regatear
Hague [heɪg] n: **The ~** La Haya
hail [heɪl] n (weather) granizo ▷ vt
saludar; (call) llamar a ▷ vi granizar;
hailstone n (piedra de) granizo

hair [hɛəʳ] n pelo, cabellos mpl; (one
hair) pelo, cabello; (on legs etc) vello;
to do one's ~ arreglarse el pelo;
grey ~ canas fpl; **hairband** n cinta;
hairbrush n cepillo (para el pelo);
haircut n corte m de pelo; **hairdo** n
peinado; **hairdresser** n peluquero/a;
hairdresser's peluquería; **hairdryer**
n secador m (de pelo); **hair gel** n
fijador; **hair spray** n laca; **hairstyle**
n peinado; **hairy** adj peludo, velludo;
(inf: frightening) espeluznante
haka [ˈhɑːkə] n (NZ) haka m or f
hake [heɪk] n merluza
half [hɑːf] (pl **halves**) n mitad f; (of
beer) ≈ caña (SP), media pinta; (Rail)
billete m de niño ▷ adj medio ▷ adv
medio, a medias; **two and a ~** dos y
media; **~ a dozen** media docena; **~ a
pound** media libra, ≈ 250 gr.; **to cut
sth in ~** cortar algo por la mitad; **half
board** n (BRIT: in hotel) media pensión;
half-brother n hermanastro;
half day n medio día m, media
jornada; **half fare** n medio pasaje m;
half-hearted adj indiferente, poco
entusiasta; **half-hour** n media hora;
half-price adj a mitad de precio;
half term n (BRIT Scol) vacaciones
de mediados del trimestre; **half-time**
n descanso; **halfway** adv a medio
camino
hall [hɔːl] n (for concerts) sala; (entrance
way) vestíbulo
hallmark [ˈhɔːlmɑːk] n sello
hallo [həˈləu] excl = **hello**
hall of residence n (BRIT) residencia
universitaria
Hallowe'en [hæləuˈiːn] n víspera de
Todos los Santos

● **HALLOWE'EN**
●
● La tradición anglosajona dice
● que en la noche del 31 de octubre,
● *Hallowe'en*, víspera de Todos los
● Santos, es fácil ver a brujas y
● fantasmas. Es una ocasión festiva

en la que los niños se disfrazan y van de puerta en puerta llevando un farol hecho con una calabaza en forma de cabeza humana. Cuando se les abre la puerta gritan "*trick or treat*" para indicar que gastarán una broma a quien no les dé un pequeño regalo (como golosinas o dinero).

hallucination [həluːsɪˈneɪʃən] *n* alucinación *f*

hallway [ˈhɔːlweɪ] *n* vestíbulo

halo [ˈheɪləʊ] *n* (*of saint*) aureola, halo

halt [hɔːlt] *n* (*stop*) alto, parada ▷ *vt* parar ▷ *vi* pararse

halve [hɑːv] *vt* partir por la mitad

halves [hɑːvz] *pl of* **half**

ham [hæm] *n* jamón *m* (cocido)

hamburger [ˈhæmbəːgəʳ] *n* hamburguesa

hamlet [ˈhæmlɪt] *n* aldea

hammer [ˈhæməʳ] *n* martillo ▷ *vt* (*nail*) clavar; **to ~ a point home to sb** remacharle un punto a algn

hammock [ˈhæmək] *n* hamaca

hamper [ˈhæmpəʳ] *vt* estorbar ▷ *n* cesto

hamster [ˈhæmstəʳ] *n* hámster *m*

hamstring [ˈhæmstrɪŋ] *n* (*Anat*) tendón *m* de la corva

hand [hænd] *n* mano *f*; (*of clock*) aguja; (*writing*) letra; (*worker*) obrero ▷ *vt* dar, pasar; **to give sb a ~** echar una mano a algn, ayudar a algn; **at ~** a mano; **in ~** entre manos; **on ~** (*person, services*) a mano, al alcance; **to ~** (*information etc*) a mano; **on the one ~ ..., on the other ~ ...** por una parte ... por otra (parte) ...; **hand down** *vt* pasar, bajar; (*tradition*) transmitir; (*heirloom*) dejar en herencia; (*us: sentence, verdict*) imponer; **hand in** *vt* entregar; **hand out** *vt* distribuir; **hand over** *vt* (*deliver*) entregar; **handbag** *n* bolso, cartera (*LAM*); **hand baggage** *n* = **hand luggage**; **handbook** *n* manual *m*; **handbrake** *n* freno de mano;

handcuffs *npl* esposas *fpl*; **handful** *n* puñado

handicap [ˈhændɪkæp] *n* desventaja; (*Sport*) hándicap *m* ▷ *vt* estorbar; **handicapped** *adj*: **to be mentally handicapped** ser discapacitado/a mental; **to be physically handicapped** ser minusválido/a

handkerchief [ˈhæŋkətʃɪf] *n* pañuelo

handle [ˈhændl] *n* (*of door etc*) pomo, tirador *m*; (*of cup etc*) asa; (*of knife etc*) mango; (*for winding*) manivela ▷ *vt* (*touch*) tocar; (*deal with*) encargarse de; (*treat: people*) manejar; **"~ with care"** (manéjese) con cuidado"; **to fly off the ~** perder los estribos; **handlebar(s)** *n(pl)* manillar *msg*

hand: hand luggage *n* equipaje *m* de mano; **handmade** *adj* hecho a mano; **handout** *n* (*charity*) limosna; (*leaflet*) folleto

hands-free [ˈhændzfriː] *adj* (*Tel: telephone*) manos libres; **~ kit** manos libres *m inv*

handsome [ˈhænsəm] *adj* guapo

handwriting [ˈhændraɪtɪŋ] *n* letra

handy [ˈhændɪ] *adj* (*close at hand*) a mano; (*machine, tool etc*) práctico; (*skilful*) hábil, diestro

hang [hæŋ] (*pt, pp* **hung**) *vt* colgar; (*criminal*) ahorcar; **to get the ~ of sth** (*inf*) coger el tranquillo a algo; **hang about, hang around** *vi* haraganear; **hang down** *vi* colgar, pender; **hang on** *vi* (*wait*) esperar; **hang out** *vt* (*washing*) tender, colgar ▷ *vi* (*inf: live*) vivir; **to ~ out of sth** colgar fuera de algo; **hang round** *vi* = **hang about**; **hang up** *vt* colgar ▷ (*Tel*) colgar

hanger [ˈhæŋəʳ] *n* percha

hang-gliding [ˈhæŋglaɪdɪŋ] *n* vuelo con ala delta

hangover [ˈhæŋəʊvəʳ] *n* (*after drinking*) resaca

hankie, hanky [ˈhæŋkɪ] *n abbr* = **handkerchief**

happen ['hæpən] *vi* suceder, ocurrir; (*chance*): **he ~ed to hear/see** dio la casualidad de que oyó/vio, **as it ~s** da la casualidad de que

happily ['hæpɪlɪ] *adv* (*luckily*) afortunadamente; (*cheerfully*) alegremente

happiness ['hæpɪnɪs] *n* felicidad *f*; (*joy*) alegría

happy ['hæpɪ] *adj* feliz; (*cheerful*) alegre; **to be ~ (with)** estar contento (con); **yes, I'd be ~ to** sí, con mucho gusto; **~ birthday!** ¡feliz cumpleaños!

harass ['hærəs] *vt* acosar, hostigar; **harassment** *n* persecución *f*

harbour, (*US*) **harbor** ['hɑːbə'] *n* puerto ▷ *vt* (*fugitive*) dar abrigo a; (*hope etc*) abrigar

hard [hɑːd] *adj* duro; (*difficult*) difícil; (*work*) arduo; (*person*) severo ▷ *adv* (*work*) mucho, duro; (*think*) profundamente; **to look ~ at sb/ sth** clavar los ojos en algn/algo; **to try ~** esforzarse; **no ~ feelings!** ¡sin rencor(es)!; **to be ~ of hearing** ser duro de oído; **to be ~ done by** ser tratado injustamente; **hardback** *n* libro de tapa dura; **hardboard** *n* aglomerado *m* (*de madera*); **hard disk** *n* (*Comput*) disco duro; **harden** *vt* endurecer; (*fig*) curtir ▷ *vi* endurecerse; (*fig*) curtirse

hardly ['hɑːdlɪ] *adv* apenas; **~ ever** casi nunca

hard: hardship *n* (*troubles*) penas *fpl*; (*financial*) apuro; **hard shoulder** *n* (*Aut*) arcén *m*; **hard-up** *adj* (*inf*) sin un duro (*SP*), sin plata (*LAM*); **hardware** *n* ferretería; (*Comput*) hardware *m*; **hardware shop**, (*US*) **hardware store** *n* ferretería; **hard-working** *adj* trabajador(a)

hardy ['hɑːdɪ] *adj* fuerte; (*plant*) resistente

hare [hɛə'] *n* liebre *f*

harm [hɑːm] *n* daño, mal *m* ▷ *vt* (*person*) hacer daño a; (*health, interests*) perjudicar; (*thing*) dañar; **out of ~'s**

way a salvo; **harmful** *adj* dañino; **harmless** *adj* (*person*) inofensivo; (*joke etc*) inocente

harmony ['hɑːmənɪ] *n* armonía

harness ['hɑːnɪs] *n* arreos *mpl* ▷ *vt* (*horse*) enjaezar; (*resources*) aprovechar

harp [hɑːp] *n* arpa ▷ *vi*: **to ~ on (about)** machacar (con)

harsh [hɑːʃ] *adj* (*cruel*) duro, cruel; (*severe*) severo

harvest ['hɑːvɪst] *n* (*harvest time*) siega; (*of cereals etc*) cosecha; (*of grapes*) vendimia ▷ *vt* cosechar

has [hæz] *vb see* **have**

hasn't ['hæznt] = **has not**

hassle ['hæsl] *n* (*inf*) lío, rollo ▷ *vt* incordiar

haste [heɪst] *n* prisa; **hasten** ['heɪsn] *vt* acelerar ▷ *vi* darse prisa; **hastily** *adv* de prisa; **hasty** *adj* apresurado

hat [hæt] *n* sombrero

hatch *n* (*Naut: also:* **~way**) escotilla ▷ *vi* salir del cascarón ▷ *vt* incubar; (*scheme, plot*) tramar; **5 eggs have ~ed** han salido 5 pollos

hatchback ['hætʃbæk] *n* (*Aut*) tres *or* cinco puertas *m*

hate [heɪt] *vt* odiar, aborrecer ▷ *n* odio; **hatred** ['heɪtrɪd] *n* odio

haul [hɔːl] *vt* tirar ▷ *n* (*of fish*) redada; (*of stolen goods etc*) botín *m*

haunt [hɔːnt] *vt* (*ghost*) aparecer en; (*obsess*) obsesionar ▷ *n* guarida; **haunted** *adj* (*castle etc*) embrujado; (*look*) de angustia

 KEYWORD

have [hæv] (*pt, pp* **had**) *aux vb* **1** haber; **to have arrived/eaten** haber llegado/comido; **having finished** *or* **when he had finished, he left** cuando hubo acabado, se fue

2 (*in tag questions*): **you've done it, haven't you?** lo has hecho, ¿verdad? *or* ¿no?

3 (*in short answers and questions*): **I haven't** no; **so I have** pues, es verdad; **we haven't paid — yes we have!** no hemos pagado — ¡sí que hemos pagado!; **I've been there before, have you?** he estado allí antes, ¿y tú?

▶ *modal aux vb* (*be obliged*): **to have (got) to do sth** tener que hacer algo; **you haven't to tell her** no hay que *or* no debes decírselo

▶ *vt* **1** (*possess*); **he has (got) blue eyes/dark hair** tiene los ojos azules/ el pelo negro

2 (*referring to meals etc*): **to have breakfast/lunch/dinner** desayunar/ comer/cenar; **to have a drink/a cigarette** tomar algo/fumar un cigarrillo

3 (*receive*) recibir; **may I have your address?** ¿puedes darme tu dirección?; **you can have it for £5** te lo puedes quedar por £5; **I must have it by tomorrow** lo necesito para mañana; **to have a baby** tener un niño *or* bebé

4 (*maintain, allow*): **I won't have it!** ¡no lo permitiré!; **I won't have this nonsense!** ¡no permitiré estas tonterías!; **we can't have that** no podemos permitir eso

5: **to have sth done** hacer *or* mandar hacer algo; **to have one's hair cut** cortarse el pelo; **to have sb do sth** hacer que algn haga algo

6 (*experience, suffer*): **to have a cold/ flu** tener un resfriado/la gripe; **she had her bag stolen/her arm broken** le robaron el bolso/se rompió un brazo; **to have an operation** operarse

7 (*+ noun*): **to have a swim/walk/ bath/rest** nadar/dar un paseo/darse un baño/descansar; **let's have a look** vamos a ver; **to have a meeting/ party** celebrar una reunión/una fiesta; **let me have a try** déjame intentarlo

haven ['heɪvn] *n* puerto; (*fig*) refugio

haven't ['hævnt] = **have not**
havoc ['hævək] *n* estragos *mpl*
Hawaii [hə'waɪiː] *n* (Islas *fpl*) Hawai *m*
hawk [hɔːk] *n* halcón *m*
hawthorn ['hɔːθɔːn] *n* espino
hay [heɪ] *n* heno; **hay fever** *n* fiebre *f* del heno; **haystack** *n* almiar *m*
hazard ['hæzəd] *n* peligro ▷ *vt* aventurar; **hazardous** *adj* peligroso; **hazard warning lights** *npl* (*Aut*) señales *fpl* de emergencia
haze [heɪz] *n* neblina
hazel ['heɪzl] *n* (*tree*) avellano ▷ *adj* (*eyes*) color *m* de avellano; **hazelnut** *n* avellana
hazy ['heɪzɪ] *adj* brumoso; (*idea*) vago
he [hiː] *pron* él; **he who ...** aquél que ..., quien ...

head [hɛd] *n* cabeza; (*leader*) jefe/a *m/f* ▷ *vt* (*list*) encabezar; (*group*) capitanear; **~s (or tails)** cara (o cruz); **~ first** de cabeza; **~ over heels in love** perdidamente enamorado; **to ~ the ball** cabecear (el balón); **head for** *vt fus* dirigirse a; (*disaster*) ir camino de; **head off** *vt* (*threat, danger*) evitar; **headache** *n* dolor *m* de cabeza; **heading** *n* título; **headlamp** *n* (*BRIT*) = **headlight**; **headlight** *n* faro; **headline** *n* titular *m*; **head office** *n* oficina central, central *f*; **headphones** *npl* auriculares *mpl*; **headquarters** *np* sede *f* central; (*Mil*) cuartel *m* general; **headroom** *n* (*in car*) altura interior; (*under bridge*) (límite *m* de) altura; **headscarf** *n* pañuelo; **headset** *n* cascos *mpl*; **head teacher** *n* director(a); **head waiter** *n* maître *m*
heal [hiːl] *vt* curar ▷ *vi* cicatrizar
health [hɛlθ] *n* salud *f*; **health care** *n* asistencia sanitaria; **health centre** *n* ambulatorio, centro médico; **health food** *n* alimentos *mpl* orgánicos; **Health Service** *n* (*BRIT*) servicio de salud pública, ≈ Insalud *m* (*SP*); **healthy** *adj* sano; saludable
heap [hiːp] *n* montón *m* ▷ *vt* amontonar; **~s of** (*inf: lots*) montones

de; **to ~ favours/praise/gifts** etc **on sb** colmar a algn de favores/elogios/regalos etc

hear [hɪəʳ] (pt, pp **heard**) vt oír; (news) saber ▷ vi oír; **to ~ about** oír hablar de; **to ~ from sb** tener noticias de algn

heard [hə:d] pt, pp of **hear**

hearing [ˈhɪərɪŋ] n (sense) oído; (Law) vista; **hearing aid** n audífono

hearse [hə:s] n coche m fúnebre

heart [hɑ:t] n corazón m; (fig) valor m; (of lettuce) cogollo; **hearts** npl (Cards) corazones mpl; **at ~** en el fondo; **by ~** (learn, know) de memoria; **to take ~** cobrar ánimos; **heart attack** n infarto (de miocardio); **heartbeat** n latido (del corazón); **heartbroken** adj: **she was heartbroken about it** eso le partió el corazón; **heartburn** n acedía; **heart disease** n enfermedad f cardíaca

hearth [hɑ:θ] n (fireplace) chimenea

heartless [ˈhɑ:tlɪs] adj despiadado

hearty [ˈhɑ:tɪ] adj (person) campechano; (laugh) sano; (dislike, support) absoluto

heat [hi:t] n calor m; (Sport: also: **qualifying ~**) prueba eliminatoria ▷ vt calentar; **heat up** vi calentarse ▷ vt calentar; **heated** adj caliente; (fig) acalorado; **heater** n calentador m, estufa

heather [ˈhɛðəʳ] n brezo

heating [ˈhi:tɪŋ] n calefacción f

heatwave [ˈhi:tweɪv] n ola de calor

heaven [ˈhɛvn] n cielo; (Rel) paraíso; **heavenly** adj celestial

heavily [ˈhɛvɪlɪ] adv pesadamente; (drink, smoke) en exceso; (sleep, sigh) profundamente

heavy [ˈhɛvɪ] adj pesado; (work) duro; (sea, rain, meal) fuerte; (drinker, smoker) empedernido; (responsibility) grave; (schedule) ocupado; (weather) bochornoso; **~ goods vehicle** n vehículo pesado

Hebrew [ˈhi:bru:] adj, n (Ling) hebreo

hectare [ˈhɛktɑ:ʳ] n (BRIT) hectárea

hectic [ˈhɛktɪk] adj agitado

he'd [hi:d] = **he would**; **he had**

hedge [hɛdʒ] n seto ▷ vi contestar con evasivas; **to ~ one's bets** (fig) cubrirse

hedgehog [ˈhɛdʒhɔg] n erizo

heed [hi:d] vt (also: **take ~ of**) hacer caso de

heel [hi:l] n talón m; (of shoe) tacón m ▷ vt (shoe) poner tacón a

hefty [ˈhɛftɪ] adj (person) fornido; (price) alto

height [haɪt] n (of person) talla, estatura; (of building) altura; (high ground) cerro; (altitude) altitud f; **at the ~ of summer** en los días más calurosos del verano; **heighten** vt elevar; (fig) aumentar

heir [ɛəʳ] n heredero; **heiress** n heredera

held [hɛld] pt, pp of **hold**

helicopter [ˈhɛlɪkɔptəʳ] n helicóptero

hell [hɛl] n infierno; **oh ~!** (inf) ¡demonios!

he'll [hi:l] = **he will**; **he shall**

hello [həˈləu] excl ¡hola!; (to attract attention) ¡oiga!; (surprise) ¡caramba!

helmet [ˈhɛlmɪt] n casco

help [hɛlp] n ayuda; (cleaner etc) criada, asistenta ▷ vt ayudar; **~!** ¡socorro!; **~ yourself** sírvete; **he can't ~ it** no lo puede evitar; **help out** vi ayudar, echar una mano ▷ vt: **to ~ sb out** ayudar a algn, echar una mano a algn; **helper** n ayudante mf; **helpful** adj útil; (person) servicial; **helping** n ración f; **helpless** adj (incapable) incapaz; (defenceless) indefenso; **helpline** n teléfono de asistencia al público

hem [hɛm] n dobladillo ▷ vt poner or coser el dobladillo a

hemisphere [ˈhɛmɪsfɪəʳ] n hemisferio

hemorrhage [ˈhɛmərɪdʒ] n (US) = **haemorrhage**

hemorrhoids [ˈhɛmərɔɪdz] npl (US) = **haemorrhoids**

h

hen [hɛn] n gallina; (*female bird*) hembra

hence [hɛns] adv (*therefore*) por lo tanto; **two years ~** de aquí a dos años

hen night n (*inf*) despedida de soltera

hepatitis [hɛpə'taɪtɪs] n hepatitis f inv

her [hə:ʳ] pron (*direct*) la; (*indirect*) le; (*stressed, after prep*) ella ⊳ adj su; see also **me; my**

herb [hə:b] n hierba; **herbal** ['hə:bl] adj de hierbas; **herbal tea** n infusión f de hierbas

herd [hə:d] n rebaño

here [hɪəʳ] adv aquí; **~!** (*present*) ¡presente!; **~ is/are** aquí está/están; **~ she is** aquí está

hereditary [hɪ'rɛdɪtrɪ] adj hereditario

heritage ['hɛrɪtɪdʒ] n patrimonio

hernia ['hə:nɪə] n hernia

hero ['hɪərəu] (*pl* **heroes**) n héroe m; (*in book, film*) protagonista m; **heroic** [hɪ'rəuɪk] adj heroico

heroin ['hɛrəuɪn] n heroína

heroine ['hɛrəuɪn] n heroína; (*in book, film*) protagonista

heron ['hɛrən] n garza

herring ['hɛrɪŋ] (*pl inv*) n arenque m

hers [hə:z] pron (el) suyo/(la) suya etc; see also **mine**

herself [hə:'sɛlf] pron (*reflexive*) se; (*emphatic*) ella misma; (*after prep*) sí (misma); see also **oneself**

he's [hi:z] = **he is; he has**

hesitant ['hɛzɪtənt] adj indeciso

hesitate ['hɛzɪteɪt] vi vacilar; (*in speech*) titubear; (*be unwilling*) resistirse a; **hesitation** [hɛzɪ'teɪʃən] n indecisión f

heterosexual [hɛtərəu'sɛksjuəl] adj, n heterosexual mf

hexagon ['hɛksəgən] n hexágono

hey [heɪ] excl ¡oye!, ¡oiga!

heyday ['heɪdeɪ] n: **the ~ of** el apogeo de

HGV n abbr = **heavy goods vehicle**

hi [haɪ] excl ¡hola!

hibernate ['haɪbəneɪt] vi invernar

hiccough, hiccup ['hɪkʌp] vi hipar

hid [hɪd] pt of **hide**

hidden ['hɪdn] pp of **hide** ⊳ adj: **~ agenda** plan m encubierto

hide [haɪd] (*pt* **hid**, *pp* **hidden**) n (*skin*) piel f ⊳ vt esconder; ocultar ⊳ vi: **to ~ (from sb)** esconderse or ocultarse (de algn)

hideous ['hɪdɪəs] adj horrible

hiding ['haɪdɪŋ] n (*beating*) paliza; **to be in ~** (*concealed*) estar escondido

hi-fi ['haɪfaɪ] n estéreo, hifi m ⊳ adj de alta fidelidad

high [haɪ] adj alto; (*speed, number*) grande; (*price*) elevado; (*wind*) fuerte; (*voice*) agudo ⊳ adv alto, a gran altura; **it is 20 m ~** tiene 20 m de altura; **~ in the air** en las alturas; **highchair** n silla alta (para niños); **high-class** adj (*hotel*) de lujo; (*person*) distinguido, de categoría; (*food*) de alta categoría; **higher education** n educación f or enseñanza superior; **high heels** npl (*heels*) tacones mpl altos; (*shoes*) zapatos mpl de tacón; **high jump** n (*Sport*) salto de altura; **highlands** npl tierras fpl altas; **the Highlands** (*in Scotland*) las Tierras Altas de Escocia; **highlight** n (*fig: of event*) punto culminante ⊳ vt subrayar; **highlights** npl (*in hair*) reflejos mpl; **highlighter** n rotulador; **highly** adv sumamente; **highly paid** muy bien pagado; **to speak highly of** hablar muy bien de; **highness** n altura; **Her** or **His Highness** Su Alteza; **high-rise** n (*also:* **high-rise block, high-rise building**) torre f de pisos; **high school** n ≈ Instituto Nacional de Bachillerato (*SP*); **high season** n (*BRIT*) temporada alta; **high street** n (*BRIT*) calle f mayor; **high-tech** (*inf*) adj al-tec (*inf*), de alta tecnología; **highway** n carretera; (*US*) autopista; **Highway Code** n (*BRIT*) código de la circulación

hijack ['haɪdʒæk] vt secuestrar; **hijacker** n secuestrador(a) m/f

hike [haɪk] vi (go walking) ir de
excursión (a pie) ▷ n caminata;
hiker n excursionista mf; **hiking** n
senderismo

hilarious [hɪˈlɛərɪəs] adj
divertidísimo

hill [hɪl] n colina; (high) montaña;
(slope) cuesta; **hillside** n ladera; **hill
walking** n senderismo (de montaña);
hilly adj montañoso

him [hɪm] pron (direct) le, lo; (indirect)
le; (stressed, after prep) él; see also **me**;
himself pron (reflexive) se; (emphatic)
él mismo; (after prep) sí (mismo); see
also **oneself**

hind [haɪnd] adj posterior

hinder [ˈhɪndər] vt estorbar, impedir

hindsight [ˈhaɪndsaɪt] n: **with ~** en
retrospectiva

Hindu [ˈhɪnduː] n hindú mf; **Hinduism**
[ˈhɪnduːɪzm] n (Rel) hinduismo

hinge [hɪndʒ] n bisagra, gozne m ▷ vi
(fig): **to ~ on** depender de

hint [hɪnt] n indirecta; (advice) consejo
▷ vt: **to ~ that** insinuar que ▷ vi: **to
~ at** aludir a

hip [hɪp] n cadera

hippie [ˈhɪpɪ] n hippie mf, jipi mf

hippo [ˈhɪpəu] (pl **hippos**) n
hipopótamo; **hippopotamus** (pl
hippopotamuses or **hippopotami**)
[hɪpəˈpɔtəməs, -ˈpɔtəmaɪ] n
hipopótamo

hippy [ˈhɪpɪ] n = **hippie**

hire [ˈhaɪər] vt (BRIT: car, equipment)
alquilar; (worker) contratar ▷ n alquiler
m; **for ~** se alquila; (taxi) libre; **hire(d)
car** n (BRIT) coche m de alquiler;
hire purchase n (BRIT) compra a
plazos; **to buy sth on hire purchase**
comprar algo a plazos

his [hɪz] pron (el) suyo/(la) suya etc
▷ adj su; see also **my**; **mine**

Hispanic [hɪsˈpænɪk] adj hispánico

hiss [hɪs] vi silbar

historian [hɪsˈtɔːrɪən] n
historiador(a) m/f

historic(al) [hɪsˈtɔːrɪk(l)] adj histórico

history [ˈhɪstərɪ] n historia

hit [hɪt] vt (strike) golpear, pegar;
(reach: target) alcanzar; (collide with:
car) chocar contra; (fig: affect) afectar
▷ n golpe m; (success) éxito; (on website)
visita; (in web search) correspondencia;
to ~ it off with sb llevarse bien con
algn; **hit back** vi defenderse; (fig)
devolver golpe por golpe

hitch [hɪtʃ] vt (fasten) atar, amarrar;
(also: **~ up**) arremangarse ▷ n
(difficulty) problema, pega; **to ~ a lift**
hacer autostop

hitch-hike [ˈhɪtʃhaɪk] vi hacer
autostop; **hitch-hiker** n autostopista
mf; **hitch-hiking** n autostop m

hi-tech [haɪˈtɛk] adj de alta
tecnología

hitman [ˈhɪtmæn] n asesino a sueldo

HIV n abbr (= human immunodeficiency
virus) VIH m; **~-negative** VIH
negativo; **~-positive** VIH positivo,
seropositivo

hive [haɪv] n colmena

hoard [hɔːd] n (treasure) tesoro;
(stockpile) provisión f ▷ vt acumular

hoarse [hɔːs] adj ronco

hoax [həuks] n engaño

hob [hɔb] n quemador m

hobble [ˈhɔbl] vi cojear

hobby [ˈhɔbɪ] n pasatiempo, afición f

hobo [ˈhəubəu] n (US) vagabundo

hockey [ˈhɔkɪ] n hockey m; **hockey
stick** n palo m de hockey

hog [hɔg] n cerdo, puerco ▷ vt (fig)
acaparar; **to go the whole ~** echar el
todo por el todo

Hogmanay [hɔgməˈneɪ] n
Nochevieja

○ **HOGMANAY**
○
○ La Nochevieja o New Year's Eve se
○ conoce como Hogmanay en Escocia,
○ donde se festeje de forma especial.
○ La familia y los amigos se suelen
○ juntar para oír las campanadas del
○ reloj y luego se hace el first-footing,

costumbre que consiste en visitar a los amigos y vecinos llevando algo de beber (generalmente whisky) y un trozo de carbón que se supone que traerá buena suerte para el año entrante.

hoist [hɔɪst] n (crane) grúa ▷ vt levantar, alzar

hold [həuld] (pt, pp **held**) vt sostener; (contain) contener; (have: power, qualification) tener; (keep back) retener; (believe) sostener; (meeting) celebrar ▷ vi (withstand: pressure) resistir; (be valid) ser válido; (stick) pegarse ▷ n (grasp) asimiento; (fig) dominio; **~ the line!** (Tel) ¡no cuelgue!; **to ~ one's own** (fig) defenderse; **to catch** or **get (a) ~ of** agarrarse or asirse de; **hold back** vt retener; (secret) ocultar; **hold on** vi agarrarse bien; (wait) esperar; **~ on!** (Tel) ¡(espere) un momento!; **hold out** vt ofrecer ▷ vi (resist) resistir; **hold up** vt (raise) levantar; (support) apoyar; (delay) retrasar; (rob) asaltar; **holdall** n (BRIT) bolsa; **holder** n (of ticket, record) poseedor/a m/f; (of passport, post, office, title etc) titular mf

hole [həul] n agujero

holiday ['hɔlɪdɪ] n vacaciones fpl; (day off) día m de) fiesta, día m festivo or feriado (LAM); **on ~** de vacaciones; **holiday camp** n (BRIT) colonia or centro vacacional; **holiday job** n (BRIT) trabajo para las vacaciones; **holidaymaker** n (BRIT) turista mf; **holiday resort** n centro turístico

Holland ['hɔlənd] n Holanda

hollow ['hɔləu] adj hueco; (fig) vacío; (eyes) hundido; (sound) sordo ▷ n hueco; (in ground) hoyo ▷ vt: **to ~ out** ahuecar

holly ['hɔlɪ] n acebo

Hollywood ['hɔlɪwud] n Hollywood m

holocaust ['hɔləkɔːst] n holocausto

holy ['həulɪ] adj santo, sagrado; (water) bendito

home [həum] n casa; (country) patria; (institution) asilo ▷ adj (domestic) casero, de casa; (Econ, Pol) nacional ▷ adv (direction) a casa; **at ~** en casa; **to go/come ~** ir/volver a casa; **make yourself at ~** ¡estás en tu casa!; **home address** n domicilio; **homeland** n tierra natal; **homeless** adj sin hogar, sin casa; **homely** adj (simple) sencillo; **home-made** adj casero; **home match** n partido en casa; **Home Office** n (BRIT) Ministerio del Interior; **home owner** n propietario/a de una casa; **home page** n (Comput) página de inicio; **Home Secretary** n (BRIT) Ministro del Interior; **homesick** adj: **to be homesick** tener morriña or nostalgia; **home town** n ciudad f natal; **homework** n deberes mpl

homicide ['hɔmɪsaɪd] n (US) homicidio

homoeopathic, (US) **homeopathic** [həumɪəu'pæθɪk] adj homeopático

homoeopathy, (US) **homeopathy** [həumɪ'ɔpəθɪ] n homeopatía

homosexual [hɔməu'sɛksjuəl] adj, n homosexual mf

honest ['ɔnɪst] adj honrado; (sincere) franco, sincero; **honestly** adv honradamente; francamente; **honesty** n honradez f

honey ['hʌnɪ] n miel f; **honeymoon** n luna de miel; **honeysuckle** n madreselva

Hong Kong ['hɔŋ'kɔŋ] n Hong-Kong m

honorary ['ɔnərərɪ] adj no remunerado; (duty, title) honorífico; **~ degree** n doctorado honoris causa

honour, (US) **honor** ['ɔnə'] vt honrar; (commitment, promise) cumplir con ▷ n honor m, honra; **honourable,** (US) **honorable** ['ɔnərəbl] adj honorable; **honours degree** n (Univ) licenciatura superior

hood [hud] n capucha; (BRIT Aut) capota; (US Aut) capó m; (of cooker) campana de humos; **hoodie** ['hudɪ] n (pullover) sudadera f con capucha; (young person) capuchero/a

hoof (pl **hoofs** or **hooves**) [hu:f, hu:vz] n pezuña

hook [huk] n gancho; (on dress) corchete m, broche m; (for fishing) anzuelo ▷ vt enganchar

hooligan ['hu:lɪgən] n gamberro

hoop [hu:p] n aro

hooray [hu:'reɪ] excl = **hurrah**

hoot [hu:t] vi (BRIT Aut) tocar la bocina; (siren) sonar; (owl) ulular

hooves [hu:vz] pl of **hoof**

hop [hɔp] vi saltar, brincar; (on one foot) saltar con un pie

hope [həup] vt, vi esperar ▷ n esperanza; **I ~ so/not** espero que sí/no; **hopeful** adj (person) optimista; (situation) prometedor(a); **hopefully** adv con esperanza; **hopefully he will recover** esperamos que se recupere; **hopeless** adj desesperado

hops [hɔps] npl lúpulo sg

horizon [hə'raɪzn] n horizonte m; **horizontal** [hɔrɪ'zɔntl] adj horizontal

hormone ['hɔ:məun] n hormona

horn [hɔ:n] n cuerno; (Mus: also: **French ~**) trompa; (Aut) bocina, claxon m

horoscope ['hɔrəskəup] n horóscopo

horrendous [hɔ'rɛndəs] adj horrendo

horrible ['hɔrɪbl] adj horrible

horrid ['hɔrɪd] adj horrible, horroroso

horrific [hɔ'rɪfɪk] adj (accident) horroroso; (film) horripilante

horrifying ['hɔrɪfaɪɪŋ] adj horroroso

horror ['hɔrəʳ] n horror m; **horror film** n película de terror or miedo

hors d'œuvre [ɔ:'də:vrə] n entremeses mpl

horse [hɔ:s] n caballo; **horseback** n: **on horseback** a caballo; **horse chestnut** n (tree) castaño de Indias; (nut) castaña de Indias; **horsepower** n caballo (de fuerza), potencia en caballos; **horse-racing** n carreras fpl

de caballos; **horseradish** n rábano picante; **horse riding** n (BRIT) equitación f

hose [həuz] n (also: **~pipe**) manguera

hospital ['hɔspɪtl] n hospital m

hospitality [hɔspɪ'tælɪtɪ] n hospitalidad f

host [həust] n anfitrión m; (TV, Radio) presentador(a) m/f; (Rel) hostia; (large number): **a ~ of** multitud de

hostage ['hɔstɪdʒ] n rehén m

hostel ['hɔstl] n hostal m; **(youth) ~** albergue m juvenil

hostess ['həustɪs] n anfitriona; (BRIT: air hostess) azafata; (TV, Radio) presentadora

hostile ['hɔstaɪl] adj hostil

hostility [hɔ'stɪlɪtɪ] n hostilidad f

hot [hɔt] adj caliente; (weather) caluroso, de calor; (as opposed to only warm) muy caliente; (spicy) picante; **to be ~** (person) tener calor; (object) estar caliente; (weather) hacer calor; **hot dog** n perrito caliente

hotel [həu'tɛl] n hotel m

hotspot ['hɔt'spɔt] n (Comput: also: **wireless ~**) punto de acceso inalámbrico

hot-water bottle [hɔt'wɔ:tə-] n bolsa de agua caliente

hound [haund] vt acosar ▷ n perro de caza

hour ['auəʳ] n hora; **hourly** adj (de) cada hora

house [haus] n casa; (Pol) cámara; (Theat) sala ▷ vt [hauz] (person) alojar; **it's on the ~** (fig) la casa invita; **household** n familia; **householder** n propietario/a; (head of house) cabeza de familia; **housekeeper** n ama de llaves; **housekeeping** n (work) trabajos mpl domésticos; **housewife** n ama de casa; **house wine** n vino m de la casa; **housework** n faenas fpl (de la casa)

housing ['hauzɪŋ] n (act) alojamiento; (houses) viviendas *fpl*; **housing development,** (*BRIT*) **housing estate** *n* urbanización *f*

hover ['hɔvər] *vi* flotar (en el aire); **hovercraft** *n* aerodeslizador *m*

how [hau] *adv* cómo; **~ are you?** ¿cómo estás?; **~ long have you been here?** ¿cuánto (tiempo) hace que estás aquí?, ¿cuánto (tiempo) llevas aquí?; **~ lovely!** ¡qué bonito!; **~ many/much?** ¿cuántos/cuánto?; **~ much does it cost?** ¿cuánto cuesta?; **~ old are you?** ¿cuántos años tienes?; **~ is school?** ¿qué tal la escuela?; **~ was the film?** ¿qué tal la película?

however [hau'ɛvər] *adv* de cualquier manera; (+ *adjective*) por muy ... que; (*in questions*) cómo ▷ *conj* sin embargo, no obstante; **~ I do it** lo haga como lo haga; **~ cold it is** por mucho frío que haga; **~ did you do it?** ¿cómo lo hiciste?

howl [haul] *n* aullido ▷ *vi* aullar; (*person*) dar alaridos; (*wind*) ulular

HP *n abbr* (*BRIT*) = **hire purchase**

hp *abbr* = **horsepower**

HQ *n abbr* = **headquarters**

hr(s) *abbr* (= *hour(s)*) h

HTML *n abbr* (= *hypertext markup language*) HTML *m*

hubcap ['hʌbkæp] *n* tapacubos *m inv*

huddle ['hʌdl] *vi*: **to ~ together** amontonarse

huff [hʌf] *n*: **in a ~** enojado

hug [hʌg] *vt* abrazar ▷ *n* abrazo

huge [hju:dʒ] *adj* enorme

hull [hʌl] *n* (*of ship*) casco

hum [hʌm] *vt* tararear, canturrear ▷ *vi* tararear, canturrear; (*insect*) zumbar

human ['hju:mən] *adj* humano

humane [hju:'meɪn] *adj* humano, humanitario

humanitarian [hju:mænɪ'tɛərɪən] *adj* humanitario

humanity [hju:'mænɪtɪ] *n* humanidad *f*

human rights *npl* derechos *mpl* humanos

humble ['hʌmbl] *adj* humilde

humid ['hju:mɪd] *adj* húmedo; **humidity** [hju:'mɪdɪtɪ] *n* humedad *f*

humiliate [hju:'mɪlɪeɪt] *vt* humillar

humiliating [hju:'mɪlɪeɪtɪŋ] *adj* humillante, vergonzoso

humiliation [hju:mɪlɪ'eɪʃən] *n* humillación *f*

hummus ['huməs] *n* humus *m*

humorous ['hju:mərəs] *adj* gracioso, divertido

humour, (*US*) **humor** ['hju:mər] *n* humorismo, sentido del humor; (*mood*) humor *m* ▷ *vt* (*person*) complacer

hump [hʌmp] *n* (*in ground*) montículo; (*camel's*) giba

hunch [hʌntʃ] *n* (*premonition*) presentimiento

hundred ['hʌndrəd] *num* ciento; (*before n*) cien; **~s of** centenares de; **hundredth** *adj* centésimo

hung [hʌŋ] *pt, pp of* **hang**

Hungarian [hʌŋ'gɛərɪən] *adj* húngaro ▷ *n* húngaro/a

Hungary ['hʌŋgərɪ] *n* Hungría

hunger ['hʌŋgər] *n* hambre *f* ▷ *vi*: **to ~ for** (*fig*) tener hambre de, anhelar

hungry ['hʌŋgrɪ] *adj* hambriento; **to be ~** tener hambre

hunt [hʌnt] *vt* (*seek*) buscar; (*Sport*) cazar ▷ *vi* (*search*): **to ~ (for)** buscar; (*Sport*) cazar ▷ *n* caza, cacería; **hunter** *n* cazador(a) *m/f*; **hunting** *n* caza

hurdle ['hə:dl] *n* (*Sport*) valla; (*fig*) obstáculo

hurl [hə:l] *vt* lanzar, arrojar

hurrah [hu'rɑ:], **hurray** [hu'reɪ] *n* ¡viva!

hurricane ['hʌrɪkən] *n* huracán *m*

hurry ['hʌrɪ] *n* prisa ▷ *vt* (*person*) dar prisa a; (*work*) apresurar, hacer de prisa; **to be in a ~** tener prisa; **hurry up** *vi* darse prisa, apurarse (*LAM*)

hurt [hə:t] (*pt, pp* **hurt**) *vt* hacer daño a ▷ *vi* doler ▷ *adj* lastimado

husband ['hʌzbənd] *n* marido

hush [hʌʃ] *n* silencio ▷ *vt* hacer callar; **~!** ¡chitón!, ¡cállate!

husky ['hʌskɪ] *adj* ronco ▷ *n* perro
esquimal
hut [hʌt] *n* cabaña; (*shed*) cobertizo
hyacinth ['haɪəsɪnθ] *n* jacinto
hydrangea [haɪ'dreɪnʒə] *n* hortensia
hydrofoil ['haɪdrəfoɪl] *n*
aerodeslizador *m*
hydrogen ['haɪdrədʒən] *n* hidrógeno
hygiene ['haɪdʒiːn] *n* higiene *f*;
hygienic [haɪ'dʒiːnɪk] *adj* higiénico
hymn [hɪm] *n* himno
hype [haɪp] *n* (*inf*) bombo
hyperlink ['haɪpəlɪŋk] *n*
hiperenlace *m*
hyphen ['haɪfn] *n* guión *m*
hypnotize ['hɪpnətaɪz] *vt* hipnotizar
hypocrite ['hɪpəkrɪt] *n* hipócrita *mf*
hypocritical [hɪpə'krɪtɪkl] *adj*
hipócrita
hypothesis (*pl* **hypotheses**)
[haɪ'pɔθɪsɪs, -siːz] *n* hipótesis *f inv*
hysterical [hɪ'sterɪkl] *adj* histérico
hysterics [hɪ'sterɪks] *npl* histeria *sg*,
histerismo *sg*; **to be in ~** (*fig*) morirse
de risa

I [aɪ] *pron* yo
ice [aɪs] *n* hielo ▷ *vt* (*cake*) alcorzar ▷ *vi*
(*also*: **~ over, ~ up**) helarse; **iceberg**
n iceberg *m*; **ice cream** *n* helado; **ice
cube** *n* cubito de hielo; **ice hockey** *n*
hockey *m* sobre hielo
Iceland ['aɪslənd] *n* Islandia;
Icelander *n* islandés/esa *m/f*;
Icelandic *adj* islandés/esa ▷ *n* (*Ling*)
islandés *m*
ice: ice lolly *n* (*BRIT*) polo; **ice rink** *n*
pista de hielo; **ice-skating** *n* patinaje
m sobre hielo
icing ['aɪsɪŋ] *n* (*Culin*) alcorza; **icing
sugar** *n* (*BRIT*) azúcar *m* glas(eado)
icon ['aɪkɔn] *n* icono
ICT *n abbr* (= *Information and
Communication(s) Technology*) TIC *f*;
(*BRIT Scol*) informática
icy ['aɪsɪ] *adj* helado
I'd [aɪd] = **I would; I had**
ID card *n* (*identity card*) DNI *m*
idea [aɪ'dɪə] *n* idea

ideal [aɪ'dɪəl] n ideal m ▷ adj ideal;
  ideally [aɪ'dɪəlɪ] adv
identical [aɪ'dɛntɪkl] adj idéntico
identification [aɪdɛntɪfɪ'keɪʃən]
  n identificación f; **means of ~**
  documentos mpl personales
identify [aɪ'dɛntɪfaɪ] vt identificar
identity [aɪ'dɛntɪtɪ] n identidad f;
  identity card n carnet m de identidad;
  identity theft n robo de identidad
ideology [aɪdɪ'ɔlədʒɪ] n ideología
idiom ['ɪdɪəm] n modismo; (style of
  speaking) lenguaje m

> Be careful not to translate idiom by
> the Spanish word idioma.

idiot ['ɪdɪət] n idiota mf
idle ['aɪdl] adj (inactive) ocioso; (lazy)
  holgazán/ana; (unemployed) parado,
  desocupado; (talk) frívolo ▷ vi (machine)
  funcionar or marchar en vacío
idol ['aɪdl] n ídolo
idyllic [ɪ'dɪlɪk] adj idílico
i.e. abbr (= id est) es decir
if [ɪf] conj si; **if necessary** si resultase
  necesario; **if I were you** yo en tu
  lugar; **if only** si solamente; **as if**
  como si
ignite [ɪg'naɪt] vt (set fire to) encender
  ▷ vi encenderse
ignition [ɪg'nɪʃən] n (Aut: process)
  ignición f; (: mechanism) encendido; **to**
  switch on/off the ~ arrancar/apagar
  el motor
ignorance ['ɪgnərəns] n ignorancia
ignorant ['ɪgnərənt] adj ignorante;
  to be ~ of ignorar
ignore [ɪg'nɔːʳ] vt (person) no hacer
  caso de; (fact) pasar por alto
ill [ɪl] adj enfermo, malo ▷ n mal m
  ▷ adv mal; **to take** or **be taken ~** caer
  or ponerse enfermo
I'll [aɪl] = **I will; I shall**
illegal [ɪ'liːgl] adj ilegal
illegible [ɪ'lɛdʒɪbl] adj ilegible
illegitimate [ɪlɪ'dʒɪtɪmət] adj
  ilegítimo
ill health n mala salud f; **to be in ~**
  estar mal de salud

illiterate [ɪ'lɪtərət] adj analfabeto
illness ['ɪlnɪs] n enfermedad f
illuminate [ɪ'luːmɪneɪt] vt (room,
  street) iluminar, alumbrar
illusion [ɪ'luːʒən] n ilusión f
illustrate ['ɪləstreɪt] vt ilustrar
illustration [ɪlə'streɪʃən] n (example)
  ejemplo, ilustración f; (in book) lámina
I'm [aɪm] = **I am**
image ['ɪmɪdʒ] n imagen f
imaginary [ɪ'mædʒɪnərɪ] adj
  imaginario
imagination [ɪmædʒɪ'neɪʃən] n
  imaginación f; (inventiveness) inventiva
imaginative [ɪ'mædʒɪnətɪv] adj
  imaginativo
imagine [ɪ'mædʒɪn] vt imaginarse
imbalance [ɪm'bæləns] n
  desequilibrio
imitate ['ɪmɪteɪt] vt imitar; **imitation**
  [ɪmɪ'teɪʃən] n imitación f; (copy) copia
immaculate [ɪ'mækjulət] adj
  inmaculado
immature [ɪmə'tjuəʳ] adj (person)
  inmaduro
immediate [ɪ'miːdɪət] adj
  inmediato; (pressing) urgente,
  apremiante; (nearest: family)
  próximo; (: neighbourhood) inmediato;
  immediately adv (at once) en
  seguida; (directly) inmediatamente;
  immediately next to justo al lado de
immense [ɪ'mɛns] adj inmenso,
  enorme; **immensely** adv
  enormemente
immerse [ɪ'məːs] vt (submerge)
  sumergir; **to be ~d in** (fig) estar
  absorto en
immigrant ['ɪmɪgrənt] n inmigrante
  mf; **immigration** [ɪmɪ'greɪʃən] n
  inmigración f
imminent ['ɪmɪnənt] adj inminente
immoral [ɪ'mɔrl] adj inmoral
immortal [ɪ'mɔːtl] adj inmortal
immune [ɪ'mjuːn] adj: **~ (to)** inmune
  (a); **immune system** n sistema m
  inmunitario
immunize ['ɪmjunaɪz] vt inmunizar

mpact [ˈɪmpækt] *n* impacto
mpair [ɪmˈpɛəʳ] *vt* perjudicar
mpartial [ɪmˈpɑːʃl] *adj* imparcial
mpatience [ɪmˈpeɪʃəns] *n*
impaciencia
mpatient [ɪmˈpeɪʃənt] *adj*
impaciente; **to get** *or* **grow ~**
impacientarse
mpeccable [ɪmˈpɛkəbl] *adj*
impecable
mpending [ɪmˈpɛndɪŋ] *adj*
inminente
mperative [ɪmˈpɛrətɪv] *adj* (*tone*)
imperioso; (*necessary*) imprescindible
mperfect [ɪmˈpəːfɪkt] *adj* (*goods etc*)
defectuoso ▷ *n* (*Ling: also:* **~ tense**)
imperfecto
mperial [ɪmˈpɪərɪəl] *adj* imperial
mpersonal [ɪmˈpəːsənl] *adj*
impersonal
mpersonate [ɪmˈpəːsəneɪt] *vt*
hacerse pasar por
mpetus [ˈɪmpətəs] *n* ímpetu *m*; (*fig*)
impulso
mplant [ɪmˈplɑːnt] *vt* (*Med*) injertar,
implantar; (*fig: idea, principle*) inculcar
mplement *n* [ˈɪmplɪmənt]
herramienta ▷ *vt* [ˈɪmplɪmɛnt] hacer
efectivo; (*carry out*) realizar
mplicate [ˈɪmplɪkeɪt] *vt* (*compromise*)
comprometer; **to ~ sb in sth**
comprometer a algn en algo
mplication [ɪmplɪˈkeɪʃən] *n*
consecuencia; **by ~** indirectamente
mplicit [ɪmˈplɪsɪt] *adj* implícito;
absoluto
mply [ɪmˈplaɪ] *vt* (*involve*) suponer;
(*hint*) insinuar
mpolite [ɪmpəˈlaɪt] *adj* mal educado
mport *vt* [ɪmˈpɔːt] importar ▷ *n*
[ˈɪmpɔːt] (*Comm*) importación *f*;
(*: article*) producto importado;
(*meaning*) significado, sentido
mportance [ɪmˈpɔːtəns] *n*
importancia
mportant [ɪmˈpɔːtənt] *adj*
importante; **it's not ~** no importa, no
tiene importancia

importer [ɪmˈpɔːtəʳ] *n* importador(a)
m/f
impose [ɪmˈpəuz] *vt* imponer ▷ *vi*: **to
~ on sb** abusar de algn; **imposing** *adj*
imponente, impresionante
impossible [ɪmˈpɔsɪbl] *adj* imposible;
(*person*) insoportable
impotent [ˈɪmpətənt] *adj* impotente
impoverished [ɪmˈpɔvərɪʃt] *adj*
necesitado
impractical [ɪmˈpræktɪkl] *adj*
(*person*) poco práctico
impress [ɪmˈprɛs] *vt* impresionar;
(*mark*) estampar; **to ~ sth on sb**
convencer a algn de la importancia
de algo
impression [ɪmˈprɛʃən] *n* impresión
f; **to be under the ~ that** tener la
impresión de que
impressive [ɪmˈprɛsɪv] *adj*
impresionante
imprison [ɪmˈprɪzn] *vt* encarcelar;
imprisonment *n* encarcelamiento;
(*term of imprisonment*) cárcel *f*
improbable [ɪmˈprɔbəbl] *adj*
improbable, inverosímil
improper [ɪmˈprɔpəʳ] *adj* (*incorrect*)
impropio; (*unseemly*) indecoroso;
(*indecent*) indecente; (*dishonest:
activities*) deshonesto
improve [ɪmˈpruːv] *vt* mejorar;
(*foreign language*) perfeccionar ▷ *vi*
mejorar; **improvement** *n* mejora;
perfeccionamiento
improvise [ˈɪmprəvaɪz] *vt, vi*
improvisar
impulse [ˈɪmpʌls] *n* impulso; **to act
on ~** actuar sin reflexionar; **impulsive**
[ɪmˈpʌlsɪv] *adj* irreflexivo

 KEYWORD

in [ɪn] *prep* **1** (*indicating place, position,
with place names*) en; **in the house/
garden** en (la) casa/el jardín; **in
here/there** aquí/ahí or allí dentro;
in London/England en Londres/
Inglaterra

2 (*indicating time*) en; **in spring** en (la) primavera; **in 1988/May** en 1988/mayo; **in the afternoon** por la tarde; **at four o'clock in the afternoon** a las cuatro de la tarde; **I did it in three hours/days** lo hice en tres horas/días; **I'll see you in two weeks** *or* **in two weeks' time** te veré dentro de dos semanas

3 (*indicating manner etc*) en; **in a loud/soft voice** en voz alta/baja; **in pencil/ink** a lápiz/bolígrafo; **the boy in the blue shirt** el chico de la camisa azul

4 (*indicating circumstances*): **in the sun/shade** al sol/a la sombra; **in the rain** bajo la lluvia; **a change in policy** un cambio de política

5 (*indicating mood, state*): **in tears** llorando; **in anger/despair** enfadado/desesperado; **to live in luxury** vivir lujosamente

6 (*with ratios, numbers*): **1 in 10 households, 1 household in 10** una de cada 10 familias; **20 pence in the pound** 20 peniques por libra; **they lined up in twos** se alinearon de dos en dos

7 (*referring to people, works*) en; entre; **the disease is common in children** la enfermedad es común entre los niños; **in (the works of) Dickens** en (las obras de) Dickens

8 (*indicating profession etc*): **to be in teaching** dedicarse a la enseñanza

9 (*after superlative*) de; **the best pupil in the class** el/la mejor alumno/a de la clase

10 (*with present participle*): **in saying this** al decir esto

▶ *adv*: **to be in** (*person: at home*) estar en casa; (: *at work*) estar; (*train, ship, plane*) haber llegado; (*in fashion*) estar de moda; **she'll be in later today** llegará más tarde hoy; **to ask sb in** hacer pasar a algn; **to run/limp** *etc* **in** entrar corriendo/cojeando *etc*

▶ *n*: **the ins and outs** (*of proposal, situation etc*) los detalles

inability [ɪnəˈbɪlɪtɪ] *n*: **~ (to do)** incapacidad *f* (de hacer)

inaccurate [ɪnˈækjurət] *adj* inexacto, incorrecto

inadequate [ɪnˈædɪkwət] *adj* (*insufficient*) insuficiente; (*person*) incapaz

inadvertently [ɪnədˈvəːtntlɪ] *adv* por descuido

inappropriate [ɪnəˈprəuprɪət] *adj* inadecuado

inaugurate [ɪˈnɔːgjureɪt] *vt* inaugurar; (*president, official*) investir

Inc. *abbr* = **incorporated**

incapable [ɪnˈkeɪpəbl] *adj*: **~ (of doing sth)** incapaz (de hacer algo)

incense *n* [ˈɪnsɛns] incienso ▷ *vt* [ɪnˈsɛns] (*anger*) indignar, encolerizar

incentive [ɪnˈsɛntɪv] *n* incentivo, estímulo

inch [ɪntʃ] *n* pulgada; **to be within an ~ of** estar a dos dedos de; **he didn't give an ~** no hizo la más mínima concesión

incidence [ˈɪnsɪdns] *n* (*of crime, disease*) incidencia

incident [ˈɪnsɪdnt] *n* incidente *m*

incidentally [ɪnsɪˈdɛntəlɪ] *adv* (*by the way*) por cierto

inclination [ɪnklɪˈneɪʃən] *n* (*tendency*) tendencia, inclinación *f*

incline [*n* ˈɪnklaɪn, *vt, vi* ɪnˈklaɪn] *n* pendiente *f*, cuesta ▷ *vt* (*head*) poner de lado ▷ *vi* inclinarse; **to be ~d to** (*tend*) ser propenso a

include [ɪnˈkluːd] *vt* incluir; (*in letter*) adjuntar; **including** *prep* incluso, inclusive; **including tip** propina incluida

inclusion [ɪnˈkluːʒən] *n* inclusión *f*

inclusive [ɪnˈkluːsɪv] *adj* inclusivo; **~ of tax** incluidos los impuestos

income [ˈɪnkʌm] *n* (*personal*) ingresos *mpl*; (*from property etc*) renta; (*profit*) rédito; **income support** *n* (BRIT)

≈ ayuda familiar; **income tax** n
impuesto sobre la renta

ncoming ['ɪnkʌmɪŋ] adj (passengers,
flight) de llegada; (government)
entrante; (tenant) nuevo

ncompatible [ɪnkəm'pætɪbl] adj
incompatible

ncompetence [ɪn'kɔmpɪtəns] n
incompetencia

ncompetent [ɪn'kɔmpɪtənt] adj
incompetente

ncomplete [ɪnkəm'pliːt] adj
incompleto; (unfinished) sin terminar

nconsistent [ɪnkən'sɪstənt] adj
inconsecuente; (contradictory)
incongruente; **~ with** que no
concuerda con

nconvenience [ɪnkən'viːnjəns] n
inconvenientes mpl; (trouble) molestia
▷ vt incomodar

nconvenient [ɪnkən'viːnjənt] adj
incómodo, poco práctico; (time, place)
inoportuno

ncorporate [ɪn'kɔːpəreɪt] vt
incorporar; (contain) comprender;
(add) agregar

ncorporated [ɪn'kɔːpəreɪtɪd] adj:
~ company (US) ≈ Sociedad f Anónima
(S.A.)

ncorrect [ɪnkə'rɛkt] adj incorrecto

ncrease [n 'ɪnkriːs, vi, vt ɪn'kriːs] n
aumento ▷ vi aumentar; (grow) crecer;
(price) subir ▷ vt aumentar; (price)
subir; **increasingly** adv cada vez más

ncredible adj increíble; **incredibly**
adv increíblemente

ncur [ɪn'kəːʳ] vt (expenses) incurrir
en; (loss) sufrir; (anger, disapproval)
provocar

ndecent [ɪn'diːsnt] adj indecente

ndeed [ɪn'diːd] adv efectivamente, en
realidad; (in fact) en efecto; (furthermore)
es más; **yes ~!** ¡claro que sí!

ndefinitely [ɪn'dɛfɪnɪtlɪ] adv (wait)
indefinidamente

ndependence [ɪndɪ'pɛndns] n
independencia; **Independence Day** n
Día m de la Independencia

independent [ɪndɪ'pɛndənt] adj
independiente; **independent school**
n (BRIT) escuela f privada, colegio m
privado

index ['ɪndɛks] n (pl indexes: in book)
indices m; (in library etc) catálogo; (pl
indexes: ratio, sign) exponente m

India ['ɪndɪə] n la India; **Indian** adj, n
indio/a; (inf!): **Red Indian** piel roja mf

indicate ['ɪndɪkeɪt] vt indicar;
indication [ɪndɪ'keɪʃən] n indicio,
señal f; **indicative** [ɪn'dɪkətɪv]
adj: **to be indicative of sth** indicar
algo; **indicator** n indicador m; (Aut)
intermitente m

indices ['ɪndɪsiːz] npl of **index**

indict [ɪn'daɪt] vt acusar; **indictment**
n acusación f

indifference [ɪn'dɪfrəns] n
indiferencia

indifferent [ɪn'dɪfrənt] adj
indiferente; (poor) regular

indigenous [ɪn'dɪdʒɪnəs] adj
indígena

indigestion [ɪndɪ'dʒɛstʃən] n
indigestión f

indignant [ɪn'dɪɡnənt] adj: **to be ~
about sth** indignarse por algo

indirect [ɪndɪ'rɛkt] adj indirecto

indispensable [ɪndɪ'spɛnsəbl] adj
indispensable, imprescindible

individual [ɪndɪ'vɪdjuəl] n individuo
▷ adj individual; (personal) personal;
(particular) particular; **individually**
adv individualmente

Indonesia [ɪndəˈniːziə] n Indonesia
indoor [ˈɪndɔːʳ] adj (swimming pool)
cubierto; (plant) de interior; (sport)
bajo cubierta; **indoors** [ɪnˈdɔːz] adv
dentro
induce [ɪnˈdjuːs] vt inducir, persuadir;
(bring about) producir
indulge [ɪnˈdʌldʒ] vt (whim)
satisfacer; (person) complacer; (child)
mimar ▷ vi: **to ~ in** darse el gusto de;
indulgent adj indulgente
industrial [ɪnˈdʌstrɪəl] adj industrial;
industrial estate n (BRIT) polígono or
(LAM) zona industrial; **industrialist** n
industrial mf; **industrial park** n (US)
= **industrial estate**
industry [ˈɪndəstrɪ] n industria;
(diligence) aplicación f
inefficient [ɪnɪˈfɪʃənt] adj ineficaz,
ineficiente
inequality [ɪnɪˈkwɔlɪtɪ] n
desigualdad f
inevitable [ɪnˈɛvɪtəbl] adj inevitable;
(necessary) forzoso; **inevitably** adv
inevitablemente
inexpensive [ɪnɪkˈspɛnsɪv] adj
económico
inexperienced [ɪnɪkˈspɪərɪənst] adj
inexperto
inexplicable [ɪnɪkˈsplɪkəbl] adj
inexplicable
infamous [ˈɪnfəməs] adj infame
infant [ˈɪnfənt] n niño/a; (baby)
niño/a pequeño/a, bebé mf
infantry [ˈɪnfəntrɪ] n infantería
infant school n (BRIT) escuela
infantil
infect [ɪnˈfɛkt] vt (wound) infectar;
(food) contaminar; (person, animal)
contagiar; **infection** [ɪnˈfɛkʃən] n
infección f; (fig) contagio; **infectious**
[ɪnˈfɛkʃəs] adj contagioso
infer [ɪnˈfəːʳ] vt deducir, inferir
inferior [ɪnˈfɪərɪəʳ] adj, n inferior mf
infertile [ɪnˈfəːtaɪl] adj estéril;
(person) infecundo
infertility [ɪnfəːˈtɪlɪtɪ] n esterilidad f;
infecundidad f

infested [ɪnˈfɛstɪd] adj: **~ (with)**
plagado (de)
infinite [ˈɪnfɪnɪt] adj infinito;
infinitely adv infinitamente
infirmary [ɪnˈfəːmərɪ] n hospital m
inflamed [ɪnˈfleɪmd] adj: **to become**
~ inflamarse
inflammation [ɪnfləˈmeɪʃən] n
inflamación f
inflatable [ɪnˈfleɪtəbl] adj inflable
inflate [ɪnˈfleɪt] vt (tyre) inflar; (fig)
hinchar; **inflation** [ɪnˈfleɪʃən] n (Econ)
inflación f
inflexible [ɪnˈflɛksɪbl] adj inflexible
inflict [ɪnˈflɪkt] vt: **to ~ on** infligir en
influence [ˈɪnflʊəns] n influencia ▷ vt
influir en, influenciar; **under the ~**
of alcohol en estado de embriaguez;
influential [ɪnflʊˈɛnʃl] adj influyente
influx [ˈɪnflʌks] n afluencia
info [ˈɪnfəu] n (inf) = **information**
inform [ɪnˈfɔːm] vt: **to ~ sb of sth**
informar a algn sobre or de algo ▷ vi:
to ~ on sb delatar a algn
informal [ɪnˈfɔːml] adj (manner,
tone) desenfadado; (dress, occasion)
informal; (visit, meeting) extraoficial
information [ɪnfəˈmeɪʃən]
n información f; (knowledge)
conocimientos mpl; **a piece of**
~ un dato; **information office**
n información f; **information**
technology n informática
informative [ɪnˈfɔːmətɪv] adj
informativo
infra-red [ɪnfrəˈrɛd] adj infrarrojo
infrastructure [ˈɪnfrəstrʌktʃəʳ] n
infraestructura
infrequent [ɪnˈfriːkwənt] adj
infrecuente
infuriate [ɪnˈfjuərɪeɪt] vt: **to**
become ~d ponerse furioso
infuriating [ɪnˈfjuərɪeɪtɪŋ] adj (habit,
noise) enloquecedor(a)
ingenious [ɪnˈdʒiːnjəs] adj
ingenioso
ingredient [ɪnˈɡriːdɪənt] n
ingrediente m

nhabit [ɪn'hæbɪt] vt vivir en;
inhabitant n habitante mf

nhale [ɪn'heɪl] vt inhalar ▷ vi (breathe
in) aspirar; (in smoking) tragar; **inhaler**
n inhalador m

nherent [ɪn'hɪərənt] adj: **~ in** or **to**
inherente a

nherit [ɪn'hɛrɪt] vt heredar;
inheritance n herencia; (fig)
patrimonio

nhibit [ɪn'hɪbɪt] vt inhibir, impedir;
inhibition [ɪnhɪ'bɪʃən] n cohibición f

nitial [ɪ'nɪʃl] adj primero ▷ n inicial
f ▷ vt firmar con las iniciales; **initials**
npl iniciales fpl; (abbreviation) siglas fpl;
initially adv en un principio

nitiate [ɪ'nɪʃɪeɪt] vt iniciar; **to ~
proceedings against sb** (Law) poner
una demanda contra algn

nitiative [ɪ'nɪʃətɪv] n iniciativa; **to
take the ~** tomar la iniciativa

nject [ɪn'dʒɛkt] vt inyectar; **injection**
[ɪn'dʒɛkʃən] n inyección f

njure [ɪ'ndʒər] vt herir; (hurt) lastimar;
(fig: reputation etc) perjudicar; **injured**
adj herido; **injury** n herida, lesión f;
(wrong) perjuicio, daño

Be careful not to translate injury
by the Spanish word injuria.

njustice [ɪn'dʒʌstɪs] n injusticia

nk [ɪŋk] n tinta; **ink-jet printer**
['ɪŋkdʒɛt-] n impresora de chorro
de tinta

nland adj ['ɪnlənd] interior ▷ adv
[ɪn'lænd] tierra adentro; **Inland
Revenue** n (BRIT) ≈ Hacienda,
≈ Agencia Tributaria

n-laws ['ɪnlɔːz] npl suegros mpl

nmate ['ɪnmeɪt] n (in prison) preso/a,
presidiario/a; (in asylum) internado/a

nn [ɪn] n posada, mesón m

nner ['ɪnər] adj interior; (feelings)
íntimo; **inner-city** adj (schools,
problems) de las zonas céntricas
pobres, de los barrios céntricos pobres

nning ['ɪnɪŋ] n (US Baseball) inning m,
entrada; **~s** (Cricket) entrada, turno

nnocence ['ɪnəsns] n inocencia

innocent ['ɪnəsnt] adj inocente

innovation [ɪnəu'veɪʃən] n novedad f

innovative ['ɪnəuvətɪv] adj
innovador

in-patient ['ɪnpeɪʃənt] n (paciente
mf) interno/a

input ['ɪnput] n entrada; (of resources)
inversión f; (Comput) entrada de datos

inquest ['ɪnkwɛst] n (coroner's)
investigación f post-mortem

inquire [ɪn'kwaɪər] vi preguntar
▷ vt: **to ~ when/where/whether**
preguntar cuándo/dónde/si; **to ~
about** (person) preguntar por; (fact)
informarse de; **inquiry** n pregunta;
(Law) investigación f, pesquisa;
"Inquiries" "Información"

insane [ɪn'seɪn] adj loco; (Med)
demente

insanity [ɪn'sænɪtɪ] n demencia,
locura

insect ['ɪnsɛkt] n insecto; **insect
repellent** n loción f contra los
insectos

insecure [ɪnsɪ'kjuər] adj inseguro

insecurity [ɪnsɪ'kjuərɪtɪ] n
inseguridad f

insensitive [ɪn'sɛnsɪtɪv] adj
insensible

insert vt [ɪn'səːt] (into sth) introducir;
(Comput) insertar ▷ n ['ɪnsəːt]
encarte m

inside ['ɪn'saɪd] n interior m ▷ adj
interior, interno ▷ adv (within) (por)
dentro; (with movement) hacia dentro
▷ prep dentro de; (of time): **~ 10
minutes** en menos de 10 minutos;
~ out adv (turn) al revés; (know) a
fondo; **inside lane** n (Aut: BRIT) carril
m izquierdo; (: in US, Europe etc) carril
m derecho

insight ['ɪnsaɪt] n perspicacia

insignificant [ɪnsɪg'nɪfɪknt] adj
insignificante

insincere [ɪnsɪn'sɪər] adj poco sincero

insist [ɪn'sɪst] vi insistir; **to ~ on
doing** empeñarse en hacer; **to ~
that** insistir en que; (claim) exigir que;

insistent adj insistente; (noise, action) persistente

insomnia [ɪnˈsɔmnɪə] n insomnio

inspect [ɪnˈspɛkt] vt inspeccionar, examinar; (troops) pasar revista a; **inspection** [ɪnˈspɛkʃən] n inspección f, examen m; (of troops) revista; **inspector** n inspector(a) m/f; (BRIT: on buses, trains) revisor(a) m/f

inspiration [ɪnspəˈreɪʃən] n inspiración f; **inspire** [ɪnˈspaɪəʳ] vt inspirar; **inspiring** adj inspirador(a)

instability [ɪnstəˈbɪlɪtɪ] n inestabilidad f

install, (US) **instal** [ɪnˈstɔːl] vt instalar; **installation** [ɪnstəˈleɪʃən] n instalación f

instalment, (US) **installment** [ɪnˈstɔːlmənt] n plazo; (of story) entrega; (of TV serial etc) capítulo; **in ~s** (pay, receive) a plazos

instance [ˈɪnstəns] n ejemplo, caso; **for ~** por ejemplo; **in the first ~** en primer lugar

instant [ˈɪnstənt] n instante m, momento ▷ adj inmediato; (coffee) instantáneo; **instantly** adv en seguida, al instante; **instant messaging** n mensajería instantánea

instead [ɪnˈstɛd] adv en cambio; **~ of** en lugar de, en vez de

instinct [ˈɪnstɪŋkt] n instinto; **instinctive** adj instintivo

institute [ˈɪnstɪtjuːt] n instituto; (professional body) colegio ▷ vt (begin) iniciar, empezar; (proceedings) entablar

institution [ɪnstɪˈtjuːʃən] n institución f; (Med: home) asilo; (: asylum) manicomio

instruct [ɪnˈstrʌkt] vt: **to ~ sb in sth** instruir a algn en or sobre algo; **to ~ sb to do sth** dar instrucciones a algn or mandar a algn hacer algo; **instruction** [ɪnˈstrʌkʃən] n (teaching) instrucción f; **instructions** npl órdenes fpl; **instructions (for use)** modo sg de empleo; **instructor** n instructor(a) m/f

instrument [ˈɪnstrəmənt] n instrumento; **instrumental** [ɪnstrəˈmɛntl] adj (Mus) instrumental; **to be instrumental ir** ser el artífice de

insufficient [ɪnsəˈfɪʃənt] adj insuficiente

insulate [ˈɪnsjuleɪt] vt aislar; **insulation** [ɪnsjuˈleɪʃən] n aislamiento

insulin [ˈɪnsjulɪn] n insulina

insult n [ˈɪnsʌlt] insulto ▷ vt [ɪnˈsʌlt] insultar; **insulting** adj insultante

insurance [ɪnˈʃuərəns] n seguro; **fire/life ~** seguro contra incendios/ de vida; **insurance company** n compañía f de seguros; **insurance policy** n póliza (de seguros)

insure [ɪnˈʃuəʳ] vt asegurar

intact [ɪnˈtækt] adj íntegro; (untouched) intacto

intake [ˈɪnteɪk] n (of food) ingestión f; (BRIT Scol): **an ~ of 200 a year** 200 matriculados al año

integral [ˈɪntɪgrəl] adj (whole) íntegro; (part) integrante

integrate [ˈɪntɪgreɪt] vt integrar ▷ vi integrarse

integrity [ɪnˈtɛgrɪtɪ] n honradez f, rectitud f

intellect [ˈɪntəlɛkt] n intelecto; **intellectual** [ɪntəˈlɛktjuəl] adj, n intelectual mf

intelligence [ɪnˈtɛlɪdʒəns] n inteligencia

intelligent [ɪnˈtɛlɪdʒənt] adj inteligente

intend [ɪnˈtɛnd] vt (gift etc): **to ~ sth for** destinar algo a; **to ~ to do sth** tener intención de or pensar hacer algo

intense [ɪnˈtɛns] adj intenso

intensify [ɪnˈtɛnsɪfaɪ] vt intensificar; (increase) aumentar

intensity [ɪnˈtɛnsɪtɪ] n intensidad f

intensive [ɪnˈtɛnsɪv] adj intensivo; **intensive care** n: **to be in intensive care** estar bajo cuidados intensivos;

intensive care unit unidad f de vigilancia intensiva

ntent [ɪnˈtɛnt] n propósito; (Law) premeditación f ▷ adj (absorbed) absorto; (attentive) atento; **to all ~s and purposes** a efectos prácticos; **to be ~ on doing sth** estar resuelto or decidido a hacer algo

ntention [ɪnˈtɛnʃən] n intención f, propósito; **intentional** adj deliberado

nteract [ɪntərˈækt] vi influirse mutuamente; **interaction** [ɪntərˈækʃən] n interacción f, acción f recíproca; **interactive** adj (Comput) interactivo

ntercept [ɪntəˈsɛpt] vt interceptar; (stop) detener

nterchange n [ˈɪntətʃeɪndʒ] intercambio; (on motorway) intersección f

ntercourse [ˈɪntəkɔːs] n (also: **sexual ~**) relaciones fpl sexuales

nterest [ˈɪntrɪst] n (Comm) interés m ▷ vt interesar; **interested** adj interesado; **to be interested in** interesarse por; **interesting** adj interesante; **interest rate** n tipo de interés

nterface [ˈɪntəfeɪs] n (Comput) junción f

nterfere [ɪntəˈfɪəʳ] vi: **to ~ in** entrometerse en; **to ~ with** (hinder) estorbar; (damage) estropear

nterference [ɪntəˈfɪərəns] n intromisión f; (Radio, TV) interferencia f

nterim [ˈɪntərɪm] adj provisional ▷ n: **in the ~** en el ínterin

nterior [ɪnˈtɪərɪəʳ] n interior m ▷ adj interior; **interior design** n interiorismo, decoración f de interiores

ntermediate [ɪntəˈmiːdɪət] adj intermedio

ntermission [ɪntəˈmɪʃən] n (Theat) descanso

ntern vt [ɪnˈtəːn] internar ▷ n [ˈɪntəːn] (esp US: doctor) médico/a

interno/a; (: on work placement) becario/a

internal [ɪnˈtəːnl] adj interior; (injury, structure, memo) internal; **~ injuries** heridas fpl or lesiones fpl internas; **Internal Revenue Service** n (US) ≈ Hacienda, ≈ Agencia Tributaria

international [ɪntəˈnæʃənl] adj internacional; **~ (game)** partido internacional

internet, Internet [ˈɪntənɛt] n: **the ~** (el or la) Internet; **internet café** n cibercafé m; **Internet Service Provider** n proveedor m de (acceso a) Internet; **internet user** n internauta mf

interpret [ɪnˈtəːprɪt] vt interpretar; (translate) traducir; (understand) entender ▷ vi hacer de intérprete; **interpretation** [ɪntəːprɪˈteɪʃən] n interpretación f; traducción f; **interpreter** n intérprete mf

interrogate [ɪnˈtɛrəgeɪt] vt interrogar; **interrogation** [ɪntɛrəʊˈgeɪʃən] n interrogatorio; **interrogative** [ɪntəˈrɔgətɪv] adj interrogativo

interrupt [ɪntəˈrʌpt] vt, vi interrumpir; **interruption** [ɪntəˈrʌpʃən] n interrupción f

intersection [ɪntəˈsɛkʃən] n (of roads) cruce m

interstate [ˈɪntəsteɪt] n (US) carretera interestatal

interval [ˈɪntəvl] n intervalo; (BRIT Theat, Sport) descanso; (Scol) recreo; **at ~s** a ratos, de vez en cuando

intervene [ɪntəˈviːn] vi intervenir; (take part) participar; (occur) sobrevenir

interview [ˈɪntəvjuː] n entrevista ▷ vt entrevistar a; **interviewer** n entrevistador(a) m/f

intimate adj [ˈɪntɪmət] íntimo; (friendship) estrecho; (knowledge) profundo ▷ vt [ˈɪntɪmeɪt] dar a entender

intimidate [ɪnˈtɪmɪdeɪt] vt intimidar,
amedrentar; **intimidating** adj
amedrentador, intimidante

into [ˈɪntuː] prep en; (towards) a;
(inside) hacia el interior de; **~ three
pieces/French** en tres pedazos/
al francés

intolerant [ɪnˈtɔlərənt] adj: **~ (of)**
intolerante (con)

intranet [ˈɪntrənet] n intranet f

intransitive [ɪnˈtrænsɪtɪv] adj
intransitivo

intricate [ˈɪntrɪkət] adj (design,
pattern) intrincado

intrigue [ɪnˈtriːg] n intriga ▷ vt
fascinar; **intriguing** adj fascinante

introduce [ɪntrəˈdjuːs] vt
introducir, meter; (speaker, TV show
etc) presentar; **to ~ sb (to sb)**
presentar algn (a algn); **to ~ sb to**
(pastime, technique) introducir a algn
a; **introduction** [ɪntrəˈdʌkʃən]
n introducción f; (of person)
presentación f; **introductory**
[ɪntrəˈdʌktərɪ] adj introductorio;
an introductory offer una oferta
introductoria

intrude [ɪnˈtruːd] vi (person)
entrometerse; **to ~ on** estorbar;
intruder n intruso/a

intuition [ɪntjuːˈɪʃən] n intuición f

inundate [ˈɪnʌndeɪt] vt: **to ~ with**
inundar de

invade [ɪnˈveɪd] vt invadir

invalid n [ˈɪnvəlɪd] minusválido/a
▷ adj [ɪnˈvælɪd] (not valid) inválido,
nulo

invaluable [ɪnˈvæljuəbl] adj
inestimable

invariably [ɪnˈvɛərɪəblɪ] adv sin
excepción, siempre; **she is ~ late**
siempre llega tarde

invasion [ɪnˈveɪʒən] n invasión f

invent [ɪnˈvent] vt inventar;
invention [ɪnˈvɛnʃən] n invento; (lie)
invención f; **inventor** [ɪnˈvɛntər] n
inventor(a) m/f

inventory [ˈɪnvəntrɪ] n inventario

inverted commas [ɪnˈvəːtɪd-] npl
(BRIT) comillas fpl

invest [ɪnˈvest] vt invertir ▷ vi: **to ~ in**
(company etc) invertir dinero en; (fig:
sth useful) comprar; **to ~ sb with sth**
conferir algo a algn

investigate [ɪnˈvestɪgeɪt] vt
investigar; **investigation**
[ɪnvestɪˈgeɪʃən] n investigación f,
pesquisa

investigator [ɪnˈvestɪgeɪtər] n
investigador(a) m/f; **private ~**
investigador(a) m/f privado/a

investment [ɪnˈvestmənt] n
inversión f

investor [ɪnˈvestər] n inversor(a) m/f

invisible [ɪnˈvɪzɪbl] adj invisible

invitation [ɪnvɪˈteɪʃən] n invitación f

invite [ɪnˈvaɪt] vt invitar; (opinions etc)
solicitar, pedir; **inviting** adj atractivo;
(food) apetitoso

invoice [ˈɪnvɔɪs] n factura ▷ vt facturar

involve [ɪnˈvɔlv] vt suponer,
implicar, tener que ver con; (concern,
affect) corresponder a; **to ~ sb (in
sth)** involucrar a algn (en algo),
comprometer a algn (con algo);
involved adj complicado; **to be
involved in sth** (take part) estar
involucrado en algo; (engrossed in)
estar muy metido; **involvement**
[ɪnˈvɔlvmənt] n participación f,
dedicación f; (obligation) compromiso;
(difficulty) apuro

inward [ˈɪnwəd] adj (movement)
interior, interno; (thought, feeling)
íntimo; **inwards** adv hacia dentro

iPod® [ˈaɪpɔd] n iPod® m

IQ n abbr (= intelligence quotient) C.I. m

IRA n abbr (= Irish Republican Army)
IRA m

Iran [ɪˈrɑːn] n Irán m; **Iranian**
[ɪˈreɪnɪən] adj iraní ▷ n iraní mf

Iraq [ɪˈrɑːk] n Irak m; **Iraqi** [ɪˈrɑːkɪ]
adj, n irakí mf

Ireland [ˈaɪələnd] n Irlanda

iris (pl **irises**) [ˈaɪrɪs, -ɪz] n (Anat) iris
m; (Bot) lirio

Irish ['aɪrɪʃ] adj irlandés/esa ▷ npl: **the ~** los irlandeses; **Irishman** n irlandés m; **Irishwoman** n irlandesa

iron ['aɪən] n hierro; (for clothes) plancha ▷ adj de hierro ▷ vt (clothes) planchar

ironic(al) [aɪ'rɔnɪk(l)] adj irónico

ironic: ironically adv irónicamente

ironing ['aɪənɪŋ] n (act) planchado; (ironed clothes) ropa planchada; (clothes to be ironed) ropa por planchar; **ironing board** n tabla de planchar

irony ['aɪrənɪ] n ironía

irrational [ɪ'ræʃənl] adj irracional

irregular [ɪ'regjulər] adj irregular; (surface) desigual; (action, event) anómalo; (behaviour) poco ortodoxo

irrelevant [ɪ'reləvənt] adj: **to be ~** estar fuera de lugar

irresistible [ɪrɪ'zɪstɪbl] adj irresistible

irresponsible [ɪrɪ'spɔnsɪbl] adj (act) irresponsable; (person) poco serio

irrigation [ɪrɪ'geɪʃən] n riego

irritable ['ɪrɪtəbl] adj (person) de mal humor

irritate ['ɪrɪteɪt] vt fastidiar; (Med) picar; **irritating** adj fastidioso; **irritation** [ɪrɪ'teɪʃən] n fastidio; picazón f

IRS n abbr (US) = **Internal Revenue Service**

is [ɪz] vb see **be**

ISDN n abbr (= Integrated Services Digital Network) RDSI f

Islam ['ɪzlɑːm] n Islam m; **Islamic** [ɪz'læmɪk] adj islámico

island ['aɪlənd] n isla; **islander** n isleño/a

isle [aɪl] n isla

isn't ['ɪznt] = **is not**

isolated ['aɪsəleɪtɪd] adj aislado

isolation [aɪsə'leɪʃən] n aislamiento

ISP n abbr = **Internet Service Provider**

Israel ['ɪzreɪl] n Israel m; **Israeli** [ɪz'reɪlɪ] adj, n israelí mf

issue ['ɪʃjuː] n cuestión f; (outcome) resultado; (of banknotes etc) emisión f; (of newspaper etc) número ▷ vt

(rations, equipment) distribuir, repartir; (orders) dar; (certificate, passport) expedir; (decree) promulgar; (magazine) publicar; (cheque) extender; (banknotes, stamp) emitir; **at ~** en cuestión; **to take ~ with sb (over)** disentir con algn (en); **to make an ~ of sth** dar a algo más importancia de lo necesario

IT n abbr = **information technology**

KEYWORD

it [ɪt] pron 1 (specific subject: not generally translated) él/ella; (direct object) lo/la; (indirect object) le; (after prep) él/ella; (abstract concept) ello; **it's on the table** está en la mesa; **I can't find it** no lo (or la) encuentro; **give it to me** dámelo (or dámela); **I spoke to him about it** le hablé del asunto; **what did you learn from it?** ¿qué aprendiste de él (or ella)?; **did you go to it?** (party, concert etc) ¿fuiste?
2 (impersonal): **it's raining** llueve, está lloviendo; **it's 6 o'clock/the 10th of August** son las 6/es el 10 de agosto; **how far is it?** — **it's 10 miles/2 hours on the train** ¿a qué distancia está? — a 10 millas/2 horas en tren; **who is it?** — **it's me** ¿quién es? — soy yo

Italian [ɪ'tæljən] adj italiano ▷ n italiano/a; (Ling) italiano

italic [ɪ'tælɪk] adj cursivo; **italics** npl cursiva sg

Italy ['ɪtəlɪ] n Italia

itch [ɪtʃ] n picazón f ▷ vi (part of body) picar; **to be ~ing to do sth** rabiar por or morirse de ganas de hacer algo; **itchy** adj: **to be itchy** picar; **my hand is itchy** me pica la mano

it'd ['ɪtd] = **it would; it had**

item ['aɪtəm] n artículo; (on agenda) asunto (a tratar); (also: **news ~**) noticia

itinerary [aɪ'tɪnərərɪ] n itinerario

it'll ['ɪtl] = **it will; it shall**

its [ɪts] *adj* su
it's [ɪts] = **it is; it has**
itself [ɪt'sɛlf] *pron* (*reflexive*) sí
mismo/a; (*emphatic*) él mismo/a
ITV *n abbr* (BRIT: = Independent Television)
cadena de televisión comercial
I've [aɪv] = **I have**
ivory ['aɪvərɪ] *n* marfil *m*
ivy ['aɪvɪ] *n* hiedra

jab [dʒæb] *n* (*Med: inf*) pinchazo ▷ *vt*:
to ~ sth into sth clavar algo en algo
jack [dʒæk] *n* (*Aut*) gato; (*Cards*) sota
jacket ['dʒækɪt] *n* chaqueta,
americana, saco (LAM); (*of book*)
sobrecubierta; **jacket potato** *n*
patata asada (con piel)
jackpot ['dʒækpɔt] *n* premio gordo
Jacuzzi® [dʒə'kuːzɪ] *n* jacuzzi® *m*
jagged ['dʒægɪd] *adj* dentado
jail [dʒeɪl] *n* cárcel *f* ▷ *vt* encarcelar; **jail**
sentence *n* pena *f* de cárcel
jam [dʒæm] *n* mermelada; (*also:* **traffic**
~) embotellamiento; (*difficulty*) apuro
▷ *vt* (*passage etc*) obstruir; (*mechanism,*
drawer etc) atascar; (*Radio*) interferir
▷ *vi* atascarse, trabarse; **to ~ sth into**
sth meter algo a la fuerza en algo
Jamaica [dʒə'meɪkə] *n* Jamaica
jammed [dʒæmd] *adj* atascado
Jan. *abbr* (= January) ene
janitor ['dʒænɪtəʳ] *n* (*caretaker*)
portero, conserje *m*

January ['dʒænjuərɪ] n enero

Japan [dʒə'pæn] n (el) Japón; **Japanese** [dʒæpə'niːz] adj japonés/ esa ▷ n (pl inv) japonés/esa m/f; (Ling) japonés m

jar n (glass: large) jarra; (: small) tarro ▷ vi (sound) chirriar; (colours) desentonar

jargon ['dʒɑːgən] n jerga

javelin ['dʒævlɪn] n jabalina

jaw [dʒɔː] n mandíbula

jazz [dʒæz] n jazz m

jealous ['dʒɛləs] adj celoso; (envious) envidioso; **jealousy** n celos mpl; envidia

jeans [dʒiːnz] npl (pantalones mpl) vaqueros mpl or tejanos mpl, bluejean m inv (LAM)

Jello® ['dʒɛləu] n (US) gelatina

jelly ['dʒɛlɪ] n (jam) jalea; (dessert etc) gelatina; **jellyfish** n medusa

jeopardize ['dʒɛpədaɪz] vt arriesgar, poner en peligro

jerk [dʒəːk] n (jolt) sacudida; (wrench) tirón m; (US inf) imbécil mf ▷ vt tirar bruscamente de ▷ vi (vehicle) dar una sacudida

Jersey ['dʒəːzɪ] n Jersey m

jersey ['dʒəːzɪ] n jersey m; (fabric) tejido de punto

Jesus ['dʒiːzəs] n Jesús m

jet [dʒɛt] n (of gas, liquid) chorro; (Aviat) avión m a reacción; **jet lag** n desorientación f por desfase horario; **jet-ski** vi practicar el motociclismo acuático

jetty ['dʒɛtɪ] n muelle m, embarcadero

Jew [dʒuː] n judío/a

jewel ['dʒuːəl] n joya; (in watch) rubí m; **jeweller**, (US) **jeweler** n joyero/a; **jeweller's (shop)** joyería; **jewellery**, (US) **jewelry** n joyas fpl, alhajas fpl

Jewish ['dʒuːɪʃ] adj judío

jigsaw ['dʒɪgsɔː] n (also: ~ puzzle) rompecabezas m inv, puzle m

job [dʒɔb] n (task) tarea; (post) empleo; **it's a good ~ that ...** menos mal que ...; **just the ~!** ¡justo lo que necesito!;

that's not my ~ eso no me incumbe or toca a mí; **job centre** n (BRIT) oficina de empleo; **jobless** adj sin trabajo

jockey ['dʒɔkɪ] n jockey mf ▷ vi: **to ~ for position** maniobrar para sacar delantera

jog [dʒɔg] vt empujar (ligeramente) ▷ vi (run) hacer footing; **to ~ sb's memory** refrescar la memoria a algn; **jogging** n footing m

join [dʒɔɪn] vt (things) unir, juntar; (club) hacerse socio de; (Pol: party) afiliarse a; (meet: people) reunirse con; (fig) unirse a ▷ vi (roads) empalmar; (rivers) confluir ▷ n juntura; **join in** vi tomar parte, participar ▷ vt fus tomar parte or participar en; **join up** vi unirse; (Mil) alistarse

joiner ['dʒɔɪnə'] n carpintero/a

joint [dʒɔɪnt] n (Tech) juntura, unión f; (Anat) articulación f; (BRIT Culin) pieza de carne (para asar); (inf: place) garito; (of cannabis) porro ▷ adj (common) común; (combined) conjunto; **joint account** n (with bank etc) cuenta común; **jointly** adv en común; (together) conjuntamente

joke [dʒəuk] n chiste m; (also: **practical ~**) broma ▷ vi bromear; **to play a ~ on** gastar una broma a; **joker** n (Cards) comodín m

jolly ['dʒɔlɪ] adj (merry) alegre; (enjoyable) divertido ▷ adv (inf) muy

jolt [dʒəult] n (shake) sacudida; (shock) susto ▷ vt (physically) sacudir; (emotionally) asustar

Jordan ['dʒɔːdən] n (country) Jordania; (river) Jordán m

journal ['dʒəːnl] n (magazine) revista; (diary) diario; **journalism** n periodismo; **journalist** n periodista mf

journey ['dʒəːnɪ] n viaje m; (distance covered) trayecto

joy [dʒɔɪ] n alegría; **joyrider** n persona que se da una vuelta en un coche robado

joystick ['dʒɔɪstɪk] n (Aviat) palanca de mando; (Comput) palanca de control

Jr *abbr* = **junior**

judge [dʒʌdʒ] *n* juez *mf* ▷ *vt* juzgar; (*estimate*) considerar; **judg(e)ment** *n* juicio

judo ['dʒuːdəu] *n* judo

jug [dʒʌg] *n* jarra

juggle ['dʒʌgl] *vi* hacer juegos malabares; **juggler** *n* malabarista *mf*

juice [dʒuːs] *n* jugo, zumo (*SP*); **juicy** *adj* jugoso

Jul. *abbr* (= *July*) jul

July [dʒuː'laɪ] *n* julio

jumble ['dʒʌmbl] *n* revoltijo ▷ *vt* (*also*: ~ **up**) revolver; **jumble sale** *n* (*BRIT*) mercadillo

○ **JUMBLE SALE**
○
○ En cada *jumble sale* pueden
○ comprarse todo tipo de objetos
○ baratos de segunda mano,
○ especialmente ropa, juguetes,
○ libros, vajillas y muebles. Suelen
○ organizarse en los locales de un
○ colegio, iglesia, ayuntamiento o
○ similar, con fines benéficos, bien
○ en ayuda de una organización
○ benéfica conocida o para solucionar
○ problemas más concretos de la
○ comunidad.

jumbo ['dʒʌmbəu], **jumbo jet** *n* jumbo

jump [dʒʌmp] *vi* saltar, dar saltos; (*increase*) aumentar ▷ *vt* saltar ▷ *n* salto; (*increase*) aumento; **to ~ the queue** (*BRIT*) colarse

jumper ['dʒʌmpəʳ] *n* (*BRIT*: *pullover*) jersey *m*, suéter *m*; (*US*: *dress*) pichi *m*

jump leads, (*US*) **jumper cables** *npl* cables *mpl* puente de batería

Jun. *abbr* = **junior**

junction ['dʒʌŋkʃən] *n* (*BRIT*: *of roads*) cruce *m*; (*Rail*) empalme *m*

June [dʒuːn] *n* junio

jungle ['dʒʌŋgl] *n* selva, jungla

junior ['dʒuːnɪəʳ] *adj* (*in age*) menor, más joven; (*position*) subalterno ▷ *n*

menor *mf*, joven *mf*; **junior high school** *n* (*US*) centro de educación secundaria; **junior school** *n* (*BRIT*) escuela primaria

junk [dʒʌŋk] *n* (*cheap goods*) baratijas *fpl*; (*rubbish*) basura; **junk food** *n* comida basura *or* de plástico

junkie ['dʒʌŋkɪ] *n* (*inf*) yonqui *mf*

junk mail *n* propaganda (buzoneada)

Jupiter ['dʒuːpɪtəʳ] *n* (*Mythology, Astro*) Júpiter *m*

jurisdiction [dʒuərɪs'dɪkʃən] *n* jurisdicción *f*; **it falls** *or* **comes within/outside our ~** es/no es de nuestra competencia

jury ['dʒuərɪ] *n* jurado

just [dʒʌst] *adj* justo ▷ *adv* (*exactly*) exactamente; (*only*) sólo, solamente; **he's ~ done it/left** acaba de hacerlo/irse; **~ right** perfecto; **~ two o'clock** las dos en punto; **she's ~ as clever as you** es tan lista como tú; **~ as well that ...** menos mal que ...; **~ as he was leaving** en el momento en que se marchaba; **~ before/enough** justo antes/lo suficiente; **~ here** aquí mismo; **he ~ missed** falló por poco; **~ listen to this** escucha esto un momento

justice ['dʒʌstɪs] *n* justicia; (*US*: *judge*) juez *mf*; **to do ~ to** (*fig*) hacer justicia a

justification [dʒʌstɪfɪ'keɪʃən] *n* justificación *f*

justify ['dʒʌstɪfaɪ] *vt* justificar; (*text*) alinear

jut [dʒʌt] *vi* (*also*: ~ **out**) sobresalir

juvenile ['dʒuːvənaɪl] *adj* (*humour, mentality*) infantil ▷ *n* menor *mf* de edad

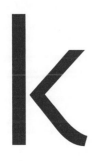

K

K _abbr_ (= _one thousand_) mil; (= _kilobyte_) K
kangaroo [kæŋgəˈruː] _n_ canguro
karaoke [kɑːrəˈəʊkɪ] _n_ karaoke
karate [kəˈrɑːtɪ] _n_ karate _m_
kebab [kəˈbæb] _n_ pincho moruno
keel [kiːl] _n_ quilla; **on an even ~** (_fig_) en equilibrio
keen [kiːn] _adj_ (_interest, desire_) grande, vivo; (_eye, intelligence_) agudo; (_competition_) reñido; (_edge_) afilado; (BRIT: _eager_) entusiasta; **to be ~ to do** _or_ **on doing sth** tener muchas ganas de hacer algo; **to be ~ on sth/sb** interesarse por algo/algn
keep [kiːp] (_pt, pp_ **kept**) _vt_ (_retain, preserve_) guardar; (_hold back_) quedarse con; (_shop_) ser propietario de; (_feed: family etc_) mantener; (_promise_) cumplir; (_chickens, bees etc_) criar ▷ _vi_ (_food_) conservarse; (_remain_) seguir, continuar ▷ _n_ (_of castle_) torreón _m_; (_food etc_) comida, sustento; **to ~ doing sth** seguir haciendo algo; **to**

~ sb from doing sth impedir a algn hacer algo; **to ~ sb happy** tener a algn contento; **to ~ a place tidy** mantener un lugar limpio; **to ~ sth to o.s.** no decirle algo a nadie; **to ~ time** (_clock_) mantener la hora exacta; **keep away** _vt_: **to ~ sth/sb away from sb** mantener algo/a algn apartado de algn ▷ _vi_: **to ~ away (from)** mantenerse apartado (de); **keep back** _vt_ (_crowd, tears_) contener; (_money_) quedarse con; (_conceal: information_): **to ~ sth back from sb** ocultar algo a algn ▷ _vi_ hacerse a un lado; **keep off** _vt_ (_dog, person_) mantener a distancia ▷ _vi_ evitar; **~ your hands off!** ¡no toques!; **"~ off the grass"** "prohibido pisar el césped"; **keep on** _vi_: **to ~ on doing** seguir _or_ continuar haciendo; **to ~ on (about sth)** no parar de hablar (de algo); **keep out** _vi_ (_stay out_) permanecer fuera; **"~ out"** "prohibida la entrada"; **keep up** _vt_ mantener, conservar ▷ _vi_ no rezagarse; **to ~ up with** (_pace_) ir al paso de; (_level_) mantenerse a la altura de; **keeper** _n_ guarda _mf_; **keeping** _n_ (_care_) cuidado; **in keeping with** de acuerdo con
kennel [ˈkɛnl] _n_ perrera; **kennels** _npl_ residencia canina
Kenya [ˈkɛnjə] _n_ Kenia
kept [kɛpt] _pt, pp_ de **keep**
kerb [kəːb] _n_ (BRIT) bordillo
kerosene [ˈkɛrəsiːn] _n_ keroseno
ketchup [ˈkɛtʃəp] _n_ salsa de tomate, ketchup _m_
kettle [ˈkɛtl] _n_ hervidor _m_
key [kiː] _n_ llave _f_; (_Mus_) tono; (_of piano, typewriter_) tecla; (_on map_) clave _f_ ▷ _cpd_ (_vital: position, issue, industry etc_) clave ▷ _vt_ (_also_: **~ in**) teclear; **keyboard** _n_ teclado; **keyhole** _n_ ojo (de la cerradura); **keyring** _n_ llavero
kg _abbr_ (= _kilogram_) kg
khaki [ˈkɑːkɪ] _n_ caqui
kick [kɪk] _vt_ (_person_) dar una patada a; (_inf: habit_) quitarse de ▷ _vi_ (_horse_) dar coces ▷ _n_ patada; puntapié _m_; (_thrill_):

he does it for ~s lo hace por pura diversión; **kick off** vi (Sport) hacer el saque inicial; **kick-off** n saque inicial; **the kick-off is at 10 o'clock** el partido empieza a las diez

kid [kɪd] n (inf: child) chiquillo/a; (animal) cabrito; (leather) cabritilla ▷ vi (inf) bromear

kidnap ['kɪdnæp] vt secuestrar; **kidnapping** n secuestro

kidney ['kɪdnɪ] n riñón m; **kidney bean** n judía, alubia

kill [kɪl] vt matar; (murder) asesinar ▷ n matanza; **to ~ time** matar el tiempo; **killer** n asesino/a; **killing** n (one) asesinato; (several) matanza; **to make a killing** hacer su agosto

kiln [kɪln] n horno

kilo ['kiːləʊ] n abbr (= kilogram(me)) kilo; **kilobyte** ['kɪləʊbaɪt] n (Comput) kilobyte m; **kilogram(me)** ['kɪləʊgræm] n kilogramo; **kilometre**, (US) **kilometer** ['kɪləmiːtəˀ] n kilómetro; **kilowatt** ['kɪləʊwɔt] n kilovatio

kilt [kɪlt] n falda escocesa

kin [kɪn] n parientes mpl

kind [kaɪnd] adj amable, atento ▷ n clase f, especie f; (species) género; **in ~** (Comm) en especie; **a ~ of** una especie de; **to be two of a ~** ser tal para cual

kindergarten ['kɪndəgɑːtn] n jardín m de infancia

kindly ['kaɪndlɪ] adj bondadoso; (gentle) cariñoso ▷ adv bondadosamente, amablemente; **will you ~ ...** sería usted tan amable de ...

kindness ['kaɪndnɪs] n bondad f, amabilidad f; (act) favor m

king [kɪŋ] n rey m; **kingdom** n reino; **kingfisher** n martín m pescador; **king-size(d)** adj de tamaño gigante; **king-size bed** cama de matrimonio extragrande

kiosk ['kiːɔsk] n quiosco; (BRIT Tel) cabina

kipper ['kɪpəˀ] n arenque m ahumado

kiss [kɪs] n beso ▷ vt besar; **~ of life** (artificial respiration) respiración f boca a boca; **to ~ (each other)** besarse

kit [kɪt] n equipo; (set of tools etc) (caja de) herramientas fpl; (assembly kit) juego de armar

kitchen ['kɪtʃɪn] n cocina

kite [kaɪt] n (toy) cometa

kitten ['kɪtn] n gatito/a

kiwi ['kiːwiː] n (also: **~ fruit**) kiwi m

km abbr (= kilometre) km

km/h abbr (= kilometres per hour) km/h

knack [næk] n: **to have the ~ of doing sth** tener facilidad para hacer algo

knee [niː] n rodilla; **kneecap** n rótula

kneel (pt, pp knelt) [niːl, nɛlt] vi (also: **~ down**) arrodillarse

knelt [nɛlt] pt, pp of **kneel**

knew [njuː] pt of **know**

knickers ['nɪkəz] npl (BRIT) bragas fpl

knife [naɪf] (pl **knives**) n cuchillo ▷ vt acuchillar

knight [naɪt] n caballero; (Chess) caballo

knit [nɪt] vt tejer, tricotar ▷ vi hacer punto, tricotar; (bones) soldarse; **knitting** n labor f de punto; **knitting needle**, (US) **knit pin** n aguja de hacer punto or tejer; **knitwear** n prendas fpl de punto

knives [naɪvz] pl of **knife**

knob [nɔb] n (of door) pomo; (of stick) puño; (on radio, TV) botón m

knock [nɔk] vt (strike) golpear; (bump into) chocar contra; (inf) criticar ▷ vi (at door etc): **to ~ at/ on** llamar a ▷ n golpe m; (on door) llamada; **knock down** vt atropellar; **knock off** vi (inf: finish) salir del trabajo ▷ vt (inf: steal) birlar; **knock out** vt dejar sin sentido; (Boxing) poner fuera de combate, dejar K.O.; (in competition) eliminar; **knock over** vt (object) tirar; (pedestrian) atropellar; **knockout** n (Boxing) K.O. m, knockout m

knot [nɔt] n nudo ▷ vt anudar

know (*pt* **knew**, *pp* **known**) [nəu, nju:, nəun] *vt* saber; (*person, author, place*) conocer; (*recognize*) reconocer ▷ *vi*: **to ~ how to swim** saber nadar; **to ~ about** *or* **of sb/ sth** saber de algn/algo; **know-all** *n* sabelotodo *m inv f inv*; **know-how** *n* conocimientos *mpl*; **knowing** *adj* (*look etc*) de complicidad; **knowingly** *adv* (*purposely*) a sabiendas; (*smile, look*) con complicidad; **know-it-all** *n* (*US*) = **know-all**

knowledge ['nɔlɪdʒ] *n* conocimiento; (*learning*) saber *m*, conocimientos *mpl*; **knowledgeable** *adj* entendido

known [nəun] *pp of* **know** ▷ *adj* (*thief, facts*) conocido; (*expert*) reconocido

knuckle ['nʌkl] *n* nudillo

koala [kəu'ɑ:lə] *n* (*also:* **~ bear**) koala *m*

Koran [kɔ'rɑ:n] *n* Corán *m*

Korea [kə'rɪə] *n* Corea; **Korean** *adj, n* coreano/a

kosher ['kəuʃəʳ] *adj* autorizado por la ley judía

Kosovar ['kɔsəvɑ:ʳ], **Kosovan** ['kɔsəvən] *adj* kosovar; **Kosovo** ['kɒsəvəu] *n* Kosovo *m*

Kremlin ['kremlɪn] *n*: **the ~** el Kremlin

Kuwait [ku'weɪt] *n* Kuwait *m*

L *abbr* (*BRIT Aut* = *learner*) L

lab [læb] *n abbr* = **laboratory**

label ['leɪbl] *n* etiqueta ▷ *vt* poner una etiqueta a

labor ['leɪbəʳ] *n, vb* (*US*) = **labour**

laboratory [lə'bɔrətərɪ] *n* laboratorio

Labor Day *n* (*US*) día *m* de los trabajadores (*primer lunes de septiembre*)

labor union *n* (*US*) sindicato

labour, (*US*) **labor** ['leɪbəʳ] *n* (*task*) trabajo; (*also:* **~ force**) mano *f* de obra; (*Med*) (dolores *mpl* de) parto ▷ *vi*: **to ~ (at)** trabajar (en) ▷ *vt*: **to ~ a point** insistir en un punto; **to be in ~** (*Med*) estar de parto; **the L~ party** (*BRIT*) el partido laborista, los laboristas *mpl*; **labourer** *n* peón *m*; (*on farm*) peón *m*; (*day labourer*) jornalero

lace [leɪs] *n* encaje *m*; (*of shoe etc*) cordón *m* ▷ *vt* (shoes: *also:* **~ up**) atarse

lack [læk] *n* (*absence*) falta ▷ *vt* faltarle a algn, carecer de; **through** *or* **for**

~ of por falta de; **to be ~ing** faltar, no haber; **to be ~ing in sth** faltarle a algn algo

lacquer ['lækə^r] n laca

lacy ['leɪsɪ] adj (like lace) como de encaje

lad [læd] n muchacho, chico

ladder ['lædə^r] n escalera (de mano); (BRIT: in tights) carrera

ladle ['leɪdl] n cucharón m

lady ['leɪdɪ] n señora; (distinguished, noble) dama; **young ~** señorita; **the ladies' (room)** los servicios de señoras; **"ladies and gentlemen ..."** "señoras y caballeros ..."; **ladybird, (US) ladybug** n mariquita

lag [læg] vi (also: **~ behind**) retrasarse, quedarse atrás ▷ vt (pipes) revestir

lager ['lɑːgə^r] n cerveza (rubia)

lagoon [lə'guːn] n laguna

laid [leɪd] pt, pp of **lay**

laid-back [leɪd'bæk] adj (inf) relajado

lain [leɪn] pp of **lie**

lake [leɪk] n lago

lamb [læm] n cordero; (meat) carne f de cordero

lame [leɪm] adj cojo; (excuse) poco convincente

lament [lə'mɛnt] n lamento ▷ vt lamentarse de

lamp [læmp] n lámpara; **lamppost** n (BRIT) farola; **lampshade** n pantalla

land [lænd] n tierra; (country) país m; (piece of land) terreno; (estate) tierras fpl, finca ▷ vi (from ship) desembarcar; (Aviat) aterrizar; (fig: fall) caer ▷ vt (passengers, goods) desembarcar; **to ~ sb with sth** (inf) hacer cargar a algn con algo; **landing** n aterrizaje m; (of staircase) rellano; **landing card** n tarjeta de desembarque; **landlady** n (owner) dueña; (of boarding house) patrona; **landline** n (teléfono) fijo; **landlord** n propietario; (of pub etc) patrón m; **landmark** n lugar m conocido; **to be a landmark** (fig) hacer época; **landowner** n terrateniente mf; **landscape** n paisaje

m; **landslide** n (Geo) corrimiento de tierras; (fig: Pol) victoria arrolladora

lane [leɪn] n (in country) camino; (Aut) carril m; (in race) calle f

language ['læŋgwɪdʒ] n lenguaje m; (national tongue) idioma m, lengua; **bad ~** palabrotas fpl; **language laboratory** n laboratorio de idiomas; **language school** n academia de idiomas

lantern ['læntn] n linterna, farol m

lap [læp] n (of track) vuelta; (of body) regazo ▷ vi (waves) chapotear; **to sit on sb's ~** sentarse en las rodillas de algn; **lap up** vt beber a lengüetadas or con la lengua

lapel [lə'pɛl] n solapa

lapse [læps] n fallo; (moral) desliz m ▷ vi (expire) caducar; (time) pasar, transcurrir; **to ~ into bad habits** volver a las andadas; **~ of time** lapso, intervalo

lard [lɑːd] n manteca (de cerdo)

larder ['lɑːdə^r] n despensa

large [lɑːdʒ] adj grande; **at ~** (free) en libertad; (generally) en general; **largely** adv (mostly) en su mayor parte; (introducing reason) en gran parte; **large-scale** adj (map, drawing) a gran escala; (reforms, business activities) importante

▌ Be careful not to translate large by the Spanish word largo.

lark [lɑːk] n (bird) alondra; (joke) broma

larrikin ['lærɪkɪn] n (AUST, NZ inf) gamberro/a

laryngitis [lærɪn'dʒaɪtɪs] n laringitis f

lasagne [lə'zænjə] n lasaña

laser ['leɪzə^r] n láser m; **laser printer** n impresora láser

lash [læʃ] n latigazo; (also: **eye~**) pestaña ▷ vt azotar; (tie) atar; **lash out** vi: **to ~ out (at sb)** (hit) arremeter (contra algn); **to ~ out against sb** lanzar invectivas contra algn

lass [læs] n chica

last [lɑːst] adj último; (final) final ▷ adv (finally) por último ▷ vi durar;

(*continue*) continuar, seguir; **~ night** anoche; **~ week** la semana pasada; **at ~** por fin; **~ but one** penúltimo; **lastly** *adv* por último, finalmente; **last-minute** *adj* de última hora

latch [lætʃ] *n* pestillo; **latch on to** *vt fus* (*person*) pegarse a; (*idea*) aferrarse a

late [leɪt] *adj* (*not on time*) tarde, atrasado; (*deceased*) fallecido ▷ *adv* tarde; (*behind time, schedule*) con retraso; **of ~** últimamente; **~ at night** a última hora de la noche; **in ~ May** hacia fines de mayo; **the ~ Mr X** el difunto Sr. X; **latecomer** *n* recién llegado/a; **lately** *adv* últimamente; **later** *adj* (*date etc*) posterior; (*version etc*) más reciente ▷ *adv* más tarde, después; **latest** ['leɪtɪst] *adj* último; **at the latest** a más tardar

lather ['lɑːðə'] *n* espuma (de jabón) ▷ *vt* enjabonar

Latin ['lætɪn] *n* latín *m* ▷ *adj* latino; **Latin America** *n* América Latina; **Latin American** *adj, n* latinoamericano/a

latitude ['lætɪtjuːd] *n* latitud *f*; (*fig*) libertad *f*

latter ['lætə'] *adj* último; (*of two*) segundo ▷ *n*: **the ~** el último, éste

laugh [lɑːf] *n* risa ▷ *vi* reírse, reír; **(to do sth) for a ~** (hacer algo) en broma; **laugh at** *vt fus* reírse de; **laughter** *n* risa

launch [lɔːntʃ] *n* (*boat*) lancha ▷ *vt* (*ship*) botar; (*rocket, plan*) lanzar; (*fig*) comenzar; **launch into** *vt fus* lanzarse a

launder ['lɔːndə'] *vt* lavar

Launderette® [lɔːn'drɛt], (*US*) **Laundromat®** ['lɔːndrəmæt] *n* lavandería (automática)

laundry ['lɔːndrɪ] *n* lavandería; (*clothes: dirty*) ropa sucia; (*: clean*) colada

lava ['lɑːvə] *n* lava

lavatory ['lævətərɪ] *n* wáter *m*

lavender ['lævəndə'] *n* lavanda

lavish ['lævɪʃ] *adj* abundante; **~ with** pródigo en ▷ *vt*: **to ~ sth on sb** colmar a algn de algo

law [lɔː] *n* ley *f*; (*study*) derecho; (*of game*) regla; **lawful** *adj* legítimo, lícito; **lawless** *adj* (*act*) ilegal

lawn [lɔːn] *n* césped *m*; **lawnmower** *n* cortacésped *m*

lawsuit ['lɔːsuːt] *n* pleito

lawyer ['lɔːjə'] *n* abogado/a; (*for sales, wills etc*) notario/a

lax [læks] *adj* (*discipline*) relajado; (*person*) negligente

laxative ['læksətɪv] *n* laxante *m*

lay [leɪ] *pt of* **lie** ▷ *adj* laico; (*not expert*) lego ▷ *vt* (*pt, pp* **laid**) (*place*) colocar; (*eggs, table*) poner; (*trap*) tender; (*carpet*) extender; **lay down** *vt* (*pen etc*) dejar; (*rules etc*) establecer; **to ~ down the law** imponer las normas; **lay off** *vt* (*workers*) despedir; **lay on** *vt* (*meal, facilities*) proveer; **lay out** *vt* (*display*) exponer; **lay-by** *n* (*BRIT Aut*) área de descanso

layer ['leɪə'] *n* capa

layman ['leɪmən] *n* lego

layout ['leɪaut] *n* (*design*) plan *m*, trazado; (*Press*) composición *f*

lazy ['leɪzɪ] *adj* perezoso, vago

lb. *abbr* (*weight*) = **pound**

lead¹ (*pt, pp* **led**) [liːd, lɛd] *n* (*front position*) delantera; (*clue*) pista; (*Elec*) cable *m*; (*for dog*) correa; (*Theat*) papel *m* principal ▷ *vt* conducir; (*be leader of*) dirigir; (*Sport*) ir en cabeza de ▷ *vi* ir primero; **to be in the ~** (*Sport*) llevar la delantera; (*fig*) ir a la cabeza; **lead up to** *vt fus* (*events*) conducir a; (*in conversation*) preparar el terreno para

lead² [lɛd] *n* (*metal*) plomo; (*in pencil*) mina

leader ['liːdə'] *n* jefe/a *m/f*, líder *m*; **leadership** *n* dirección *f*; **qualities of leadership** iniciativa *sg*

lead-free ['lɛdfriː] *adj* sin plomo

leading ['liːdɪŋ] *adj* (*main*) principal; (*first*) primero; (*front*) delantero

lead singer [liːd-] *n* cantante *mf*

leaf [li:f] (pl **leaves**) n hoja; **to turn over a new ~** hacer borrón y cuenta nueva; **leaf through** vt fus (book) hojear

leaflet ['li:flɪt] n folleto

league [li:g] n sociedad f; (Football) liga; **to be in ~ with** estar confabulado con

leak [li:k] n (of liquid, gas) escape m, fuga; (in pipe) agujero; (in roof) gotera; (fig: of information, in security) filtración f ▷ vi (ship) hacer agua; (pipe) tener un escape; (roof) tener goteras; (also: **~ out**: liquid, gas) escaparse ▷ vt (fig) filtrar

lean [li:n] (pt, pp **leaned** or **leant**) adj (thin) flaco; (meat) magro ▷ vt: **to ~ sth on sth** apoyar algo en algo ▷ vi (slope) inclinarse; **to ~ against** apoyarse contra; **to ~ on** apoyarse en; **lean forward** vi inclinarse hacia adelante; **lean over** vi inclinarse; **leaning** n: **leaning (towards)** inclinación f (hacia)

leant [lɛnt] pt, pp of **lean**

leap [li:p] n salto ▷ vi (pt, pp **leaped** or **leapt**) saltar

leapt [lɛpt] pt, pp of **leap**

leap year n año bisiesto

learn (pt, pp **learned** or **learnt**) [lə:n, -t] vt aprender; (come to know of) enterarse de ▷ vi aprender; **to ~ how to do sth** aprender a hacer algo; **learner** n (BRIT: also: **learner driver**) conductor(a) m/f en prácticas; see also **L-plates**; **learning** n saber m, conocimientos mpl

learnt [lə:nt] pp of **learn**

lease [li:s] n arriendo ▷ vt arrendar

leash [li:ʃ] n correa

least [li:st] adj (slightest) menor, más pequeño; (smallest amount of) mínimo ▷ adv menos; **the ~ expensive car** el coche menos caro; **at ~** por lo menos, al menos; **not in the ~** en absoluto

leather ['lɛðəʳ] n cuero

leave [li:v] (pt, pp **left**) vt dejar; (go away from) abandonar ▷ vi irse; (train)

salir ▷ n permiso; **to be left** quedar, sobrar; **there's some milk left over** sobra or queda algo de leche; **on ~** de permiso; **leave behind** vt (on purpose) dejar (atrás); (accidentally) olvidar; **leave out** vt omitir

leaves [li:vz] pl of **leaf**

Lebanon ['lɛbənən] n: **the ~** el Líbano

lecture ['lɛktʃəʳ] n conferencia; (Scol) clase f ▷ vi dar clase(s) ▷ vt (reprove) echar una reprimenda a; **to give a ~ on** dar una conferencia sobre; **lecture hall** n sala de conferencias; (Univ) aula; **lecturer** n conferenciante mf; (BRIT: at university) profesor(a) m/f; **lecture theatre** n = **lecture hall**

led [lɛd] pt, pp of **lead**¹

ledge [lɛdʒ] n (on wall) repisa; (of window) alféizar m; (of mountain) saliente m

leek [li:k] n puerro

left [lɛft] pt, pp of **leave** ▷ adj izquierdo; (remaining): **there are two ~** quedan dos ▷ n izquierda ▷ adv a la izquierda; **on** or **to the ~** a la izquierda; **the L~** (Pol) la izquierda; **left-hand** adj: **the left-hand side** la izquierda; **left-hand drive** n conducción f por la izquierda; **left-handed** adj zurdo; **left-luggage locker** n (BRIT) consigna f automática; **left-luggage (office)** n (BRIT) consigna; **left-overs** npl sobras fpl; **left-wing** adj (Pol) de izquierda(s), izquierdista

leg [lɛg] n pierna; (of animal, chair) pata; (Culin: of meat) pierna; (: of chicken) pata; (of journey) etapa

legacy ['lɛgəsɪ] n herencia

legal ['li:gl] adj (permitted by law) lícito; (of law) legal; **legal holiday** n (US) fiesta oficial; **legalize** vt legalizar; **legally** adv legalmente

legend ['lɛdʒənd] n leyenda; **legendary** adj legendario

leggings ['lɛgɪŋz] npl mallas fpl, leggins mpl

legible ['lɛdʒəbl] adj legible

legislation [lɛdʒɪsˈleɪʃən] n
legislación f
legislative [ˈlɛdʒɪslətɪv] adj
legislativo
legitimate [lɪˈdʒɪtɪmət] adj legítimo
leisure [ˈlɛʒəʳ] n ocio, tiempo libre;
at ~ con tranquilidad; **leisure centre**
n polideportivo; **leisurely** adj sin
prisa; lento
lemon [ˈlɛmən] n limón m; **lemonade**
n (fizzy) gaseosa; **lemon tea** n té m
con limón
lend [lɛnd] (pt, pp **lent**) vt: **to ~ sth to
sb** prestar algo a algn
length [lɛŋθ] n (size) largo, longitud
f; (of rope etc) largo; (of wood, string)
trozo; (amount of time) duración f; **at ~**
(at last) por fin, finalmente; (lengthily)
largamente; **lengthen** vt alargar ▷ vi
alargarse; **lengthways** adv a lo largo;
lengthy adj largo, extenso
lens [lɛnz] n (of spectacles) lente f; (of
camera) objetivo
Lent [lɛnt] n Cuaresma
lent [lɛnt] pt, pp of **lend**
lentil [ˈlɛntl] n lenteja
Leo [ˈliːəu] n Leo
leopard [ˈlɛpəd] n leopardo
leotard [ˈliːətɑːd] n malla
leprosy [ˈlɛprəsɪ] n lepra
lesbian [ˈlɛzbɪən] n lesbiana
less [lɛs] adj (in size, degree etc) menor;
(in quantity) menos ▷ pron, adv menos;
~ than half menos de la mitad; **~
than ever** menos que nunca; **~ 5%**
menos el cinco por ciento; **~ and ~**
cada vez menos; **the ~ he works ...**
cuanto menos trabaja ...; **lessen** vi
disminuir, reducirse ▷ vt disminuir,
reducir; **lesser** [ˈlɛsəʳ] adj menor; **to
a lesser extent** or **degree** en menor
grado
lesson [ˈlɛsn] n clase f; **it taught him
a ~** (fig) le sirvió de lección
let (pt, pp **let**) [lɛt] vt (allow) dejar,
permitir; (BRIT: lease) alquilar; **to ~
sb do sth** dejar que algn haga algo;
to ~ sb know sth comunicar algo a

algn; **~'s go** ¡vamos!; **~ him come** que
venga; **"to ~"** "se alquila"; **let down** vt
(tyre) desinflar; (disappoint) defraudar;
let in vt dejar entrar; (visitor etc)
hacer pasar; **let off** vt dejar escapar;
(firework etc) disparar; (bomb) accionar;
let out vt dejar salir
lethal [ˈliːθl] adj (weapon) mortífero;
(poison, wound) mortal
letter [ˈlɛtəʳ] n (of alphabet) letra;
(correspondence) carta; **letterbox** n
(BRIT) buzón m
lettuce [ˈlɛtɪs] n lechuga
leukaemia, (US) **leukemia**
[luːˈkiːmɪə] n leucemia
level [ˈlɛvl] adj (flat) llano ▷ adv a nivel
▷ n nivel m; (height) altura ▷ vt nivelar,
allanar; (destroy: building) derribar;
to be ~ with estar a nivel de; **A ~s**
(BRIT) ≈ exámenes mpl de bachillerato
superior; **on the ~** (fig: honest) en
serio; **level crossing** (BRIT) paso
a nivel
lever [ˈliːvəʳ] n palanca ▷ vt: **to ~ up**
levantar con palanca; **leverage** n (fig:
influence) influencia
levy [ˈlɛvɪ] n impuesto ▷ vt exigir,
recaudar
liability [laɪəˈbɪlətɪ] n (pej: person,
thing) estorbo, lastre m; (Law:
responsibility) responsabilidad f;
(handicap) desventaja
liable [ˈlaɪəbl] adj (subject): **~ to** sujeto
a; (responsible): **~ for** responsable de;
(likely): **~ to do** propenso a hacer
liaise [liːˈeɪz] vi: **to ~ (with)** colaborar
(con)
liar [ˈlaɪəʳ] n mentiroso/a
liberal [ˈlɪbərl] adj liberal; (generous):
~ with generoso con; **Liberal
Democrat** n (BRIT) demócrata mf
liberal
liberate [ˈlɪbəreɪt] vt (people: from
poverty etc) librar; (prisoner) libertar;
(country) liberar
liberation [lɪbəˈreɪʃən] n liberación f
liberty [ˈlɪbətɪ] n libertad f; **to be at ~**
(criminal) estar en libertad; **to be at ~**

to do estar libre para hacer; **to take the ~ of doing sth** tomarse la libertad de hacer algo

Libra ['li:brə] n Libra

librarian [laɪ'brɛərɪən] n bibliotecario/a

library ['laɪbrərɪ] n biblioteca

⬛ Be careful not to translate *library* by the Spanish word *librería*.

Libya ['lɪbɪə] n Libia

lice [laɪs] pl of **louse**

licence, (US) **license** ['laɪsns] n licencia; (*permit*) permiso; (*also:* **driving ~**, (US) **driver's license**) carnet de conducir, permiso de manejar (LAM)

license ['laɪsns] n (US) = **licence** ▷ vt autorizar, dar permiso a; **licensed** adj (*for alcohol*) autorizado para vender bebidas alcohólicas; **license plate** n (US) placa (de matrícula); **licensing hours** npl (BRIT) horas durante las cuales se permite la venta y consumo de alcohol (en un bar etc)

lick [lɪk] vt lamer; (*inf: defeat*) dar una paliza a; **to ~ one's lips** relamerse

lid [lɪd] n (*of box, case, pan*) tapa, tapadera

lie [laɪ] n mentira ▷ vi (*pt* **lay**, *pp* **lain**) mentir; (*rest*) estar echado, estar acostado; (*of object: be situated*) estar, encontrarse; **to tell ~s** mentir; **to ~ low** (*fig*) mantenerse a escondidas; **lie about, lie around** vi (*things*) estar tirado; (BRIT: *people*) estar acostado or tumbado; **lie down** vi echarse, tumbarse

Liechtenstein ['lɪktənstaɪn] n Liechtenstein m

lie-in ['laɪɪn] n (BRIT): **to have a ~** quedarse en la cama

lieutenant [lɛf'tɛnənt] [(US) luː'tɛnənt] n (Mil) teniente m

life (*pl* **lives**) [laɪf, laɪvz] n vida; **life assurance** n (BRIT) seguro de vida; **lifebelt** n (BRIT) cinturón m salvavidas; **lifeboat** n lancha de socorro; **lifeguard** n vigilante mf, socorrista

mf; **life insurance** n = **life assurance**; **life jacket** n chaleco salvavidas; **lifelike** adj natural; **life preserver** n (US) = **lifebelt**; **life sentence** n cadena perpetua; **lifestyle** n estilo de vida; **lifetime** n: **in his lifetime** durante su vida

lift [lɪft] vt levantar; (*copy*) plagiar ▷ vi (*fog*) disiparse ▷ n (BRIT: *elevator*) ascensor m; **to give sb a ~** (BRIT) lleva a algn en coche; **lift up** vt levantar; **lift-off** n despegue m

light [laɪt] n luz f; (*lamp*) luz f, lámpara; (*headlight*) faro; (*for cigarette etc*): **have you got a ~?** ¿tienes fuego? ▷ vt (*pt*, *pp* **lit**) (*candle, cigarette, fire*) encender; (*room*) alumbrar ▷ adj (*colour*) claro; (*room*) con mucha luz; **lights** npl (*traffic lights*) semáforos mpl; **in the ~ of** a la luz de; **to come to ~** salir a la luz; **light up** vi (*smoke*) encender un cigarrillo; (*face*) iluminarse ▷ vt (*illuminate*) iluminar, alumbrar; (*set fire to*) encender; **light bulb** n bombilla, bombillo (LAM), foco (LAM); **lighten** vt (*make less heavy*) aligerar; **lighter** n (*also:* **cigarette lighter**) encendedor m, mechero; **light-hearted** adj (*person*) alegre; (*remark etc*) divertido; **lighthouse** n faro; **lighting** n (*system*) alumbrado; **lightly** adv ligeramente; (*not seriously*) con poca seriedad; **to get off lightly** ser castigado con poca severidad

lightning ['laɪtnɪŋ] n relámpago, rayo

lightweight adj (*suit*) ligero ▷ n (*Boxing*) peso ligero

like [laɪk] vt (*person*) querer a ▷ prep como ▷ adj parecido, semejante ▷ n: **his ~s and dislikes** sus gustos y aversiones; **the ~s of him** personas como él; **I would ~, I'd ~** me gustaría; (*for purchase*) quisiera; **would you ~ a coffee?** ¿te apetece un café?; **I ~ swimming** me gusta nadar; **to be ~ look ~ sb/sth** parecerse a algn/algo; **that's just ~ him** es muy de él, es típico de él; **do it ~ this** hazlo así; **it is nothing ~ ...** no tiene parecido alguno con ...; **what's he ~?** ¿cómo es (él)?; **likeable** adj simpático, agradable

ikelihood ['laɪklɪhud] n probabilidad f

ikely ['laɪklɪ] adj probable; **he's ~ to leave** es probable or (LAm) capaz que se vaya; **not ~!** ¡ni hablar!

ikewise ['laɪkwaɪz] adv igualmente; **to do ~** hacer lo mismo

iking ['laɪkɪŋ] n: ~ (for) (person) cariño (a); (thing) afición (a); **to be to sb's ~** ser del gusto de algn

ilac ['laɪlək] n (tree) lilo; (flower) lila

ilo® ['laɪləu] n colchoneta inflable

ily ['lɪlɪ] n lirio, azucena; **~ of the valley** n lirio de los valles

imb [lɪm] n miembro

imbo ['lɪmbəu] n: **to be in ~** (fig) quedar a la expectativa

ime [laɪm] n (tree) limero; (fruit) lima; (Geo) cal f

imelight ['laɪmlaɪt] n: **to be in the ~** (fig) ser el centro de atención

imestone ['laɪmstəun] n piedra caliza

imit ['lɪmɪt] n límite m ▷ vt limitar; **limited** adj limitado; **to be limited to** limitarse a

imousine ['lɪməziːn] n limusina

imp [lɪmp] n: **to have a ~** tener cojera ▷ vi cojear ▷ adj flojo

ine [laɪn] n línea; (rope) cuerda; (for fishing) sedal m; (wire) hilo; (row, series) fila, hilera; (of writing) renglón m; (on face) arruga; (Rail) vía ▷ vt (Sewing): **to ~ (with)** forrar (de); **to ~ the streets** ocupar las aceras; **in ~ with** de acuerdo con; **line up** vi hacer cola ▷ vt alinear; **to have sth ~d up** tener algo arreglado

inear ['lɪnɪər] adj lineal

inen ['lɪnɪn] n ropa blanca; (cloth) lino

iner ['laɪnər] n vapor m de línea transatlántico; **dustbin ~** bolsa de la basura

line-up ['laɪnʌp] n (US: queue) cola; (Sport) alineación f

linger ['lɪŋgər] vi retrasarse, tardar en marcharse; (smell, tradition) persistir

lingerie ['lænʒəriː] n ropa interior (de mujer), lencería

linguist ['lɪŋgwɪst] n lingüista mf; **linguistic** adj lingüístico

lining ['laɪnɪŋ] n forro

link [lɪŋk] n (of chain) eslabón m; (relationship) relación f; (bond) vínculo, lazo; (Internet) enlace m ▷ vt vincular, unir; (associate): **to ~ with** or **to** relacionar con; **links** npl (Golf); **link up** vt acoplar ▷ vi unirse

lion ['laɪən] n león m; **lioness** n leona

lip [lɪp] n labio; **lip-read** vi leer los labios; **lip salve** n crema protectora para labios; **lipstick** n lápiz m or barra de labios, carmín m

liqueur [lɪ'kjuər] n licor m

liquid ['lɪkwɪd] adj, n líquido; **liquidizer** ['lɪkwɪdaɪzər] n (Culin) licuadora

liquor ['lɪkər] n licor m, bebidas fpl alcohólicas; **liquor store** n (US) bodega, tienda de vinos y bebidas alcohólicas

Lisbon ['lɪzbən] n Lisboa

lisp [lɪsp] n ceceo ▷ vi cecear

list [lɪst] n lista ▷ vt (write down) hacer una lista de; (mention) enumerar

listen ['lɪsn] vi escuchar, oír; **listener** n oyente mf

lit [lɪt] pt, pp of **light**

liter ['liːtər] n (US) = **litre**

literacy ['lɪtərəsɪ] n capacidad f de leer y escribir

literal ['lɪtərl] adj literal; **literally** adv literalmente

literary ['lɪtərərɪ] adj literario

literate ['lɪtərət] adj que sabe leer y escribir; (educated) culto

literature ['lɪtərɪtʃər] n literatura; (brochures etc) folletos mpl

litre, (US)**liter** ['liːtər] n litro

litter ['lɪtər] n (rubbish) basura; (young animals) camada, cría; **litter bin** n

(BRIT) papelera; **littered** adj: **littered with** lleno de

little ['lɪtl] adj (small) pequeño; (not much) poco; (diminutive): **~ house** casita ▷ adv poco; **a ~** un poco (de); **a ~ bit** un poquito; **~ by ~** poco a poco; **little finger** n dedo meñique

live¹ [laɪv] adj (animal) vivo; (wire) conectado; (broadcast) en directo; (unexploded) sin explotar

live² [lɪv] vi vivir; **to ~ together** vivir juntos; **live up to** vt fus (fulfil) cumplir con

livelihood ['laɪvlɪhud] n sustento

lively ['laɪvlɪ] adj vivo; (place, book etc) animado

liven up ['laɪvn-] vt animar ▷ vi animarse

liver ['lɪvəʳ] n hígado

lives [laɪvz] npl of **life**

livestock ['laɪvstɔk] n ganado

living ['lɪvɪŋ] adj (alive) vivo ▷ n: **to earn** or **make a ~** ganarse la vida; **living room** n sala (de estar)

lizard ['lɪzəd] n lagartija

load [ləud] n carga; (weight) peso ▷ vt (also Comput) cargar; **a ~ of, ~s of** (fig) (gran) cantidad de, montones de; **to ~ (up) with** cargar con or de; **loaded** adj cargado

loaf (pl **loaves**) [ləuf] n (barra de) pan m

loan [ləun] n préstamo ▷ vt prestar; **on ~** prestado

loathe [ləuð] vt aborrecer; (person) odiar

loaves [ləuvz] pl of **loaf**

lobby ['lɔbɪ] n vestíbulo, sala de espera; (Pol: pressure group) grupo de presión ▷ vt presionar

lobster ['lɔbstəʳ] n langosta

local ['ləukl] adj local ▷ n (pub) bar m; **the locals** npl los vecinos, los del lugar; **local anaesthetic,** (US) **local anesthetic** n (Med) anestesia local; **local authority** n municipio, ayuntamiento (SP); **local government** n gobierno municipal; **locally** ['ləukəlɪ] adv en la vecindad

locate [ləu'keɪt] vt (find) localizar; (situate): **to be ~d in** estar situado en

location [ləu'keɪʃən] n situación f; **on ~** (Cine) en exteriores

loch [lɔx] n lago

lock [lɔk] n (of door, box) cerradura; (of canal) esclusa; (of hair) mechón m ▷ vt (with key) cerrar con llave ▷ vi (door etc) cerrarse con llave; (wheels) trabarse; **lock in** vt encerrar; **lock out** vt (person) cerrar la puerta a; **lock up** vt (criminal) meter en la cárcel; (mental patient) encerrar; (house) cerrar (con llave) ▷ vi echar la llave

locker ['lɔkəʳ] n casillero; **locker-room** n (US Sport) vestuario

locksmith ['lɔksmɪθ] n cerrajero/a

locomotive [ləukə'məutɪv] n locomotora

lodge [lɔdʒ] n casa del guarda ▷ vi (person): **to ~ (with)** alojarse (en casa de) ▷ vt presentar; **lodger** ['lɔdʒəʳ] n huésped mf

lodging ['lɔdʒɪŋ] n alojamiento, hospedaje m

loft [lɔft] n desván m

log [lɔg] n (of wood) leño, tronco; (written account) diario ▷ vt anotar; **log in, log on** vi (Comput) iniciar la sesión; **log off, log out** vi (Comput) finalizar la sesión

logic ['lɔdʒɪk] n lógica; **logical** adj lógico

login ['lɔgɪn] n (Comput) login m

lollipop ['lɔlɪpɔp] n pirulí m; **lollipop man, lollipop lady** n (BRIT) persona encargada de ayudar a los niños a cruzar la calle

lolly ['lɔlɪ] n (inf: ice cream) polo; (: lollipop) piruleta; (: money) guita

London ['lʌndən] n Londres m; **Londoner** n londinense mf

lone [ləun] adj solitario

loneliness ['ləunlɪnɪs] n soledad f, aislamiento

lonely ['ləunlɪ] adj (situation) solitario; (person) solo; (place) aislado

long [lɔŋ] adj largo ▷ adv mucho tiempo, largamente ▷ vi: **to ~ for sth**

anhelar algo; **so** or **as ~ as** mientras, con tal de que; **don't be ~!** ¡no tardes!, ¡vuelve pronto!; **how ~ is the street?** ¿cuánto tiene la calle de largo?; **how ~ is the lesson?** ¿cuánto dura la clase?; **six metres ~** que mide seis metros, de seis metros de largo; **six months ~** que dura seis meses, de seis meses de duración; **all night ~** toda la noche; **he no ~er comes** ya no viene; **~ before** mucho antes; **before ~** (+ future) dentro de poco; (+ past) poco tiempo después; **at ~ last** al fin, por fin; **long-distance** adj (race) de larga distancia; (call) interurbano; **long-haul** adj (flight) de larga distancia; **longing** n anhelo, ansia; (nostalgia) nostalgia ▷ adj anhelante

longitude ['lɔŋgɪtjuːd] n longitud f

long: long jump n salto de longitud; **long-life** adj (batteries) de larga duración; (milk) uperizado; **long-sighted** adj (BRIT) présbita; **long-standing** adj de mucho tiempo; **long-term** adj a largo plazo

loo [luː] n (BRIT inf) wáter m

look [luk] vi mirar; (seem) parecer; (building etc): **to ~ south/on to the sea** dar al sur/al mar ▷ n mirada; (glance) vistazo; (appearance) aire m, aspecto; **looks** npl belleza sg; **~ (here)!** (expressing annoyance etc) ¡oye!; **~!** (expressing surprise) ¡mira!; **look after** vt fus (care for) cuidar a; (deal with) encargarse de; **look around** vi echar una mirada alrededor; **look at** vt fus mirar; **look back** vi mirar hacia atrás; **look down on** vt fus (fig) despreciar, mirar con desprecio; **look for** vt fus buscar; **look forward to** vt fus esperar con ilusión; (in letters): **we ~ forward to hearing from you** quedamos a la espera de su respuesta or contestación; **look into** vt fus investigar; **look out** vi (beware): **to ~ out (for)** tener cuidado (de); **look out for** vt fus (seek) buscar; (await) esperar; **look round** vi volver la cabeza; **look**

through vt fus (papers, book) hojear; **look to** vt fus ocuparse de; (rely on) contar con; **look up** vi mirar hacia arriba; (improve) mejorar ▷ vt (word) buscar; **look up to** vt fus admirar

look-out n (tower etc) puesto de observación; (person) vigía mf; **to be on the ~ for sth** estar al acecho de algo

loom [luːm] vi: **~ (up)** (threaten) surgir, amenazar; (event: approach) aproximarse

loony ['luːnɪ] adj, n (inf!) loco/a

loop [luːp] n lazo; **loophole** n laguna

loose [luːs] adj suelto; (clothes) ancho; (morals, discipline) relajado; **to be at a ~ end** or (US) **at ~ ends** no saber qué hacer; **loosely** adv libremente, aproximadamente; **loosen** vt aflojar

loot [luːt] n botín m ▷ vt saquear

lop-sided ['lɔpˈsaɪdɪd] adj torcido; (fig) desequilibrado

lord [lɔːd] n señor m; **L~ Smith** Lord Smith; **the L~** el Señor; **the (House of) L~s** (BRIT) la Cámara de los Lores

lorry ['lɔrɪ] n (BRIT) camión m; **lorry driver** n camionero/a

lose (pt, pp **lost**) [luːz, lɔst] vt perder ▷ vi perder, ser vencido; **to ~ (time)** (clock) atrasarse; **lose out** vi salir perdiendo; **loser** n perdedor(a) m/f

loss [lɔs] n pérdida; **heavy ~es** (Mil) grandes pérdidas fpl; **to be at a ~** no saber qué hacer; **to make a ~** sufrir pérdidas

lost [lɔst] pt, pp of **lose** ▷ adj perdido; **lost property**, (US) **lost and found** n objetos mpl perdidos

lot [lɔt] n (at auction) lote m; **the ~** el todo, todos mpl, todas fpl; **a ~** mucho, bastante; **a ~ of**, **~s of** muchos/as; (with singular noun) mucho/a; **I read a ~** leo bastante; **to draw ~s (for sth)** echar suertes (para decidir algo)

lotion ['ləʊʃən] n loción f

lottery ['lɔtərɪ] n lotería

loud [laud] adj (voice, sound) fuerte; (laugh, shout) estrepitoso; (gaudy) chillón/ona ▷ adv (speak etc) fuerte;

out ~ en voz alta; **loudly** adv
(noisily) fuerte; (aloud) en alta voz;
loudspeaker n altavoz m

lounge [laundʒ] n salón m, sala de
estar; (of hotel) salón m; (of airport) sala
de embarque ▷ vi (also: **~ about, ~
around**) holgazanear

louse (pl **lice**) [laus, laɪs] n piojo

lousy ['lauzɪ] adj (fig) vil, asqueroso;
(ill) fatal

love [lʌv] n (romantic, sexual) amor m;
(kind, caring) cariño ▷ vt amar, querer;
~ from Anne (in letter) con cariño de
Anne; **I ~ to read** me encanta leer;
to be in ~ with estar enamorado
de; **to make ~** hacer el amor; **I ~ you**
te quiero; **for the ~ of** por amor a;
"15 ~ " (Tennis) "15 a cero"; **I ~ paella**
me encanta la paella; **love affair** n
aventura sentimental or amorosa;
love life n vida sentimental

lovely ['lʌvlɪ] adj (delightful)
encantador(a); (beautiful) precioso

lover ['lʌvəʳ] n amante mf; (amateur):
a ~ of un(a) aficionado/a or un(a)
amante de

loving ['lʌvɪŋ] adj amoroso, cariñoso

low [ləu] adj, adv bajo ▷ n (Meteorology)
área de baja presión; **to feel ~** sentirse
deprimido; **to turn (down) ~** bajar;
low-alcohol adj bajo en alcohol; **low-
calorie** adj bajo en calorías

lower ['ləuəʳ] adj más bajo; (less
important) menos importante ▷ vt
bajar; (reduce) reducir; **to ~ o.s. to** (fig)
rebajarse a

low-fat adj (milk, yoghurt) desnatado;
(diet) bajo en calorías

loyal ['lɔɪəl] adj leal; **loyalty** n lealtad
f; **loyalty card** n tarjeta cliente

LP n abbr (= long-playing record) elepé m

L-plates ['ɛlpleɪts] npl (BRIT) (placas
fpl de) la L

L-PLATES

En el Reino Unido las personas
que están aprendiendo a conducir
han de llevar indicativos blancos
con una L en rojo llamados
normalmente L-plates (de learner)
en la parte delantera y trasera de
los automóviles que conducen. No
tienen que ir a clases teóricas, sino
que desde el principio se les entrega
un carnet de conducir provisional
(provisional driving licence) para
que realicen sus prácticas, que
han de estar supervisadas por un
conductor con carnet definitivo
(full driving licence). Tampoco
se les permite hacer prácticas
en autopistas aunque vayan
acompañados.

Lt. abbr (= lieutenant) Tte.

Ltd abbr (Comm: = limited company)
S.A.

luck [lʌk] n suerte f; **good/bad ~**
buena/mala suerte; **good ~!** ¡(que
tengas) suerte!; **bad** or **hard** or
tough ~! ¡qué pena!; **luckily** adv
afortunadamente; **lucky** adj
afortunado; (at cards etc) con suerte;
(object) que trae suerte

lucrative ['lu:krətɪv] adj lucrativo

ludicrous ['lu:dɪkrəs] adj absurdo

luggage ['lʌgɪdʒ] n equipaje m;
luggage rack n (on car) baca,
portaequipajes m inv

lukewarm ['lu:kwɔ:m] adj tibio

lull [lʌl] n tregua ▷ vt (child) acunar;
(person, fear) calmar; **to ~ sb to sleep**
arrullar a algn; **to ~ sb into a false
sense of security** dar a algn una falsa
sensación de seguridad

lullaby ['lʌləbaɪ] n nana

lumber ['lʌmbəʳ] n (junk) trastos mpl
viejos; (wood) maderos mpl

luminous ['lu:mɪnəs] adj luminoso

lump [lʌmp] n terrón m; (fragment)
trozo; (swelling) bulto ▷ vt (also:
~ together) juntar; **lump sum** n
suma global; **lumpy** adj (sauce) lleno
de grumos

lunatic ['lu:nətɪk] adj, n (inf!) loco/a

lunch [lʌntʃ] *n* almuerzo, comida ▷ *vi* almorzar; **lunch break, lunch hour** *n* hora del almuerzo

lunchtime ['lʌntʃtaɪm] *n* hora del almuerzo *or* de comer

lung [lʌŋ] *n* pulmón *m*

lure [luəʳ] *n* (*bait*) cebo; (*decoy*) señuelo; (*attraction*) atracción *f* ▷ *vt* convencer con engaños

lurk [lə:k] *vi* (*wait*) estar al acecho; (*fig*) acechar

lush [lʌʃ] *adj* exuberante

lust [lʌst] *n* lujuria; (*greed*) codicia

Luxembourg ['lʌksəmbə:g] *n* Luxemburgo

luxurious [lʌg'zjuərɪəs] *adj* lujoso

luxury ['lʌkʃərɪ] *n* lujo ▷ *cpd* de lujo

Lycra® ['laɪkrə] *n* licra®

lying ['laɪɪŋ] *n* mentiras *fpl* ▷ *adj* mentiroso

lyric ['lɪrɪk] *adj* lírico; **lyrics** *npl* (*of song*) letra *sg*

m *abbr* (= *metre*) m.; = **mile; million**

MA *n abbr* (*Scol*) = **Master of Arts**

ma [mɑ:] *n* (*inf*) mamá

mac [mæk] *n* (*BRIT*) impermeable *m*

macaroni [mækə'rəunɪ] *n* macarrones *mpl*

Macedonia [mæsɪ'dəunɪə] *n* Macedonia; **Macedonian** [mæsɪ'dəunɪən] *adj* macedonio ▷ *n* macedonio/a; (*Ling*) macedonio

machine [mə'ʃi:n] *n* máquina ▷ *vt* (*dress etc*) coser a máquina; (*Tech*) trabajar a máquina; **machine gun** *n* ametralladora; **machinery** *n* maquinaria; (*fig*) mecanismo; **machine washable** *adj* lavable a máquina

macho ['mætʃəu] *adj* macho

mackerel ['mækrl] *n* (*pl inv*) caballa

mackintosh ['mækɪntɔʃ] *n* (*BRIT*) impermeable *m*

mad [mæd] *adj* loco; (*idea*) disparatado; (*angry*) furioso; **to be ~ (keen) about** *or* **on sth** estar loco por algo

madam ['mædəm] n señora

mad cow disease n encefalopatía espongiforme bovina

made [meɪd] pt, pp of **make**; **made-to-measure** adj (BRIT) hecho a la medida; **made-up** adj (story) ficticio

madly ['mædlɪ] adv locamente

madman ['mædmən] n loco

madness ['mædnɪs] n locura

Madrid [mə'drɪd] n Madrid m

Mafia ['mæfɪə] n Mafia

mag [mæg] n abbr (BRIT inf); = **magazine**

magazine [mægə'ziːn] n revista

maggot ['mægət] n gusano

magic ['mædʒɪk] n magia ▷ adj mágico; **magical** adj mágico; **magician** [mə'dʒɪʃən] n mago/a

magistrate ['mædʒɪstreɪt] n juez mf (municipal)

magnet ['mægnɪt] n imán m; **magnetic** [mæg'nɛtɪk] adj magnético

magnificent [mæg'nɪfɪsnt] adj magnífico

magnify ['mægnɪfaɪ] vt (object) ampliar; (sound) aumentar; **magnifying glass** n lupa

magpie ['mægpaɪ] n urraca

mahogany [mə'hɔgənɪ] n caoba

maid [meɪd] n criada; **old ~** (pej) solterona

maiden name n apellido de soltera

mail [meɪl] n correo; (letters) cartas fpl ▷ vt echar al correo; **mailbox** (US) buzón m; **mailing list** n lista de direcciones; **mailman** n (US) cartero; **mail-order** n pedido postal

main [meɪn] adj principal, mayor ▷ n (pipe) cañería principal or maestra; (US) red f eléctrica; **the ~s** (BRIT Elec) la red eléctrica; **in the ~** en general; **main course** n (Culin) plato principal; **mainland** n continente m; **mainly** adv principalmente; **main road** n carretera principal; **mainstream** n corriente f principal; **main street** n calle f mayor

maintain [meɪn'teɪn] vt mantener

maintenance ['meɪntənəns] n mantenimiento; (alimony) pensión f alimenticia

maisonette [meɪzə'nɛt] n dúplex m

maize [meɪz] n (BRIT) maíz m, choclo (LAM)

majesty ['mædʒɪstɪ] n majestad f; **Your M~** Su Majestad

major ['meɪdʒəʳ] n (Mil) comandante m ▷ adj principal; (Mus) mayor

Majorca [mə'jɔːkə] n Mallorca

majority [mə'dʒɔrɪtɪ] n mayoría

make [meɪk] (pt, pp **made**) vt (manufacture) hacer, fabricar; (mistake) cometer; (speech) pronunciar; (cause to be): **to ~ sb sad** poner triste o entristecer a algn; (force): **to ~ sb do sth** obligar a algn a hacer algo; (equal): **2 and 2 ~ 4** 2 y 2 son 4 ▷ n marca; **to ~ a fool of sb** poner a algn en ridículo; **to ~ a profit/loss** obtener ganancias/ sufrir pérdidas; **to ~ it** (arrive) llegar; (achieve sth) tener éxito; **what time do you ~ it?** ¿qué hora tienes?; **to ~ do with** contentarse con; **make off** vi largarse; **make out** vt (decipher) descifrar; (understand) entender; (see) distinguir; (cheque) extender; **make up** vt (invent) inventar; (parcel) hacer ▷ vi reconciliarse; (with cosmetics) maquillarse; **make up for** vt fus compensar; **makeover** n cambio de imagen; **to give sb a makeover** hacerle a algn un cambio de imagen; **maker** n fabricante mf; (of film, programme) autor(a) m/f; **makeshift** adj improvisado; **make-up** n maquillaje m

making ['meɪkɪŋ] n (fig): **in the ~** en vías de formación; **to have the ~s of** (person) tener madera de

malaria [mə'lɛərɪə] n malaria

Malaysia [mə'leɪzɪə] n Malaisia, Malaysia

male [meɪl] n (Biol, Elec) macho ▷ adj (sex, attitude) masculino; (child etc) varón

malicious [mə'lɪʃəs] *adj* malicioso; rencoroso

malignant [mə'lɪgnənt] *adj* (*Med*) maligno

mall [mɔːl] *n* (*us: also:* **shopping ~**) centro comercial

mallet ['mælɪt] *n* mazo

malnutrition [mælnjuː'trɪʃən] *n* desnutrición *f*

malpractice [mæl'præktɪs] *n* negligencia profesional

malt [mɔːlt] *n* malta; (*whisky*) whisky *m* de malta

Malta ['mɔːltə] *n* Malta; **Maltese** [mɔːl'tiːz] *adj* maltés/esa ▷ *n* (*pl inv*) maltés/esa *m/f*

mammal ['mæml] *n* mamífero

mammoth ['mæməθ] *n* mamut *m* ▷ *adj* gigantesco

man [*pl* **men**] [mæn, mɛn] *n* hombre *m*; (*mankind*) el hombre ▷ *vt* (*Naut*) tripular; (*Mil*) defender; (*operate: machine*) manejar; **an old ~** un viejo; **~ and wife** marido y mujer

manage ['mænɪdʒ] *vi* arreglárselas ▷ *vt* (*be in charge of*) dirigir; (*person etc*) manejar; **manageable** *adj* manejable; **management** *n* dirección *f*; **manager** *n* director(a) *m/f*; (*of pop star*) mánager *mf*; (*Sport*) entrenador(a) *m/f*; **manageress** *n* directora; (*Sport*) entrenadora; **managerial** [mænə'dʒɪərɪəl] *adj* directivo; **managing director** *n* director(a) *m/f* general

mandarin ['mændərɪn] *n* (*also:* **~ orange**) mandarina; (*person*) mandarín *m*

mandate ['mændeɪt] *n* mandato

mandatory ['mændətərɪ] *adj* obligatorio

mane [meɪn] *n* (*of horse*) crin *f*; (*of lion*) melena

maneuver [mə'nuːvər] *vb, n* (*us*) = **manoeuvre**

mangetout [mɔnʒ'tuː] *n* tirabeque *m*

mango ['mæŋgəʊ] (*pl* **mangoes**) *n* mango

man: **manhole** *n* boca de alcantarilla; **manhood** *n* edad *f* viril; (*manliness*) virilidad *f*

mania ['meɪnɪə] *n* manía; **maniac** ['meɪnɪæk] *n* maníaco/a; (*fig*) maniático

manic ['mænɪk] *adj* frenético

manicure ['mænɪkjʊər] *n* manicura

manifest ['mænɪfɛst] *vt* manifestar, mostrar ▷ *adj* manifiesto

manifesto [mænɪ'fɛstəʊ] *n* manifiesto

manipulate [mə'nɪpjuleɪt] *vt* manipular

man: **mankind** [mæn'kaɪnd] *n* humanidad *f*, género humano; **manly** *adj* varonil; **man-made** *adj* artificial

manner ['mænər] *n* manera, modo; (*behaviour*) conducta, manera de ser; (*type*) clase *f*; **manners** *npl* modales *mpl*; **bad ~s** falta *sg* de educación

manoeuvre, (*us*) **maneuver** [mə'nuːvər] *vt, vi* maniobrar ▷ *n* maniobra

manpower ['mænpaʊər] *n* mano *f* de obra

mansion ['mænʃən] *n* mansión *f*

manslaughter ['mænslɔːtər] *n* homicidio involuntario

mantelpiece ['mæntlpiːs] *n* repisa de la chimenea

manual ['mænjuəl] *adj* manual ▷ *n* manual *m*

manufacture [mænju'fæktʃər] *vt* fabricar ▷ *n* fabricación *f*; **manufacturer** *n* fabricante *mf*

manure [mə'njuər] *n* estiércol *m*

manuscript ['mænjuskrɪpt] *n* manuscrito

many ['mɛnɪ] *adj* muchos/as ▷ *pron* muchos/as; **a great ~** muchísimos, un buen número de; **~ a time** muchas veces

map [mæp] *n* mapa *m*; **map out** *vt* proyectar

maple ['meɪpl] *n* arce *m*, maple *m* (*LAM*)

mar [mɑːr] *vt* estropear

m

Mar. *abbr* (= March) mar

marathon ['mærəθən] *n* maratón *m*

marble ['mɑ:bl] *n* mármol *m*; (*toy*) canica

March [mɑ:tʃ] *n* marzo

march [mɑ:tʃ] *vi* (*Mil*) marchar; (*demonstrators*) manifestarse ▷ *n* marcha; (*demonstration*) manifestación *f*

mare [mɛəʳ] *n* yegua

margarine [mɑ:dʒə'ri:n] *n* margarina

margin ['mɑ:dʒɪn] *n* margen *m*; (*Comm: profit margin*) margen *m* de beneficios; **marginal** *adj* marginal; **marginally** *adv* ligeramente

marigold ['mærɪgəuld] *n* caléndula

marijuana [mærɪ'wɑ:nə] *n* marihuana

marina [mə'ri:nə] *n* puerto deportivo

marinade [mærɪ'neɪd] *n* adobo

marinate ['mærɪneɪt] *vt* adobar

marine [mə'ri:n] *adj* marino ▷ *n* soldado de infantería de marina

marital ['mærɪtl] *adj* matrimonial; **~ status** estado civil

maritime ['mærɪtaɪm] *adj* marítimo

marjoram ['mɑ:dʒərəm] *n* mejorana

mark [mɑ:k] *n* marca, señal *f*; (*in snow, mud etc*) huella; (*stain*) mancha; (*BRIT Scol*) nota ▷ *vt* (*Sport: player*) marcar; (*stain*) manchar; (*BRIT Scol*) calificar, corregir; **to ~ time** marcar el paso; (*fig*) marcar(se) un ritmo; **marked** *adj* marcado, acusado; **marker** *n* (*sign*) marcador *m*; (*bookmark*) registro

market ['mɑ:kɪt] *n* mercado ▷ *vt* (*Comm*) comercializar; **marketing** *n* marketing *m*; **marketplace** *n* mercado; **market research** *n* (*Comm*) estudios *mpl* de mercado

marmalade ['mɑ:məleɪd] *n* mermelada de naranja

maroon [mə'ru:n] *vt*: **to be ~ed** (*shipwrecked*) quedar aislado; (*fig*) quedar abandonado ▷ *n* (*colour*) granate *m*

marquee [mɑ:'ki:] *n* entoldado

marriage ['mærɪdʒ] *n* (*state*) matrimonio; (*wedding*) boda; (*act*) casamiento; **marriage certificate** *n* partida de casamiento

married ['mærɪd] *adj* casado; (*life, love*) conyugal

marrow ['mærəu] *n* médula; (*vegetable*) calabacín *m*

marry ['mærɪ] *vt* casarse con; (*father, priest etc*) casar ▷ *vi* (*also*: **get married**) casarse

Mars [mɑ:z] *n* Marte *m*

marsh [mɑ:ʃ] *n* pantano; (*salt marsh*) marisma

marshal ['mɑ:ʃl] *n* (*Mil*) mariscal *m*; (*at sports meeting, demonstration etc*) oficial *m*; (*US: of police, fire department*) jefe/a *m/f* ▷ *vt* (*facts*) ordenar; (*soldiers*) formar

martyr ['mɑ:təʳ] *n* mártir *mf*

marvel ['mɑ:vl] *n* maravilla, prodigio ▷ *vi*: **to ~ (at)** maravillarse (de); **marvellous,** (*US*) **marvelous** ['mɑ:vləs] *adj* maravilloso

Marxism ['mɑ:ksɪzəm] *n* marxismo

Marxist ['mɑ:ksɪst] *adj, n* marxista *mf*

marzipan ['mɑ:zɪpæn] *n* mazapán *m*

mascara [mæs'kɑ:rə] *n* rimel *m*

mascot ['mæskət] *n* mascota

masculine ['mæskjulɪn] *adj* masculino

mash [mæʃ] *vt* machacar; **mashed potatoes** *npl* puré *m* de patatas *or* (*LAM*) papas

mask [mɑ:sk] *n* máscara ▷ *vt* (*hide: feelings*) esconder; **to ~ one's face** (*cover*) ocultarse la cara

mason ['meɪsn] *n* (*also*: **stone~**) albañil *m*; (*also*: **free~**) masón *m*; **masonry** *n* (*in building*) mampostería

mass [mæs] *n* (*people*) muchedumbre *f*; (*Physics*) masa; (*Rel*) misa; (*great quantity*) montón *m* ▷ *vi* reunirse; (*Mil*) concentrarse; **the ~es** las masas

massacre ['mæsəkəʳ] *n* masacre *f*

massage ['mæsɑ:ʒ] *n* masaje *m* ▷ *vt* dar masajes *or* un masaje a

massive ['mæsɪv] *adj* enorme; (*support, intervention*) masivo

mass media npl medios mpl de comunicación de masas

mass-produce ['mæsprə'dju:s] vt fabricar en serie

mast [mɑ:st] n (Naut) mástil m; (Radio etc) torre f

master ['mɑ:stəʳ] n (of servant, animal) amo; (of situation) dueño; (Art, Mus) maestro; (in secondary school) profesor m; (title for boys): **M~ X** Señorito X ▷ vt dominar; **mastermind** n inteligencia superior ▷ vt dirigir, planear; **Master of Arts** n licenciatura superior en Letras; see also **master's degree**; **Master of Science** n licenciatura superior en Ciencias; see also **master's degree**; **masterpiece** n obra maestra; **master's degree** n máster m

○ **MASTER'S DEGREE**
○
○ Los estudios de postgrado
○ británicos que llevan a la obtención
○ de un master's degree consisten
○ generalmente en una combinación
○ de curso(s) académico(s) y tesina
○ (dissertation) sobre un tema original,
○ o bien únicamente la redacción
○ de una tesina. El primer caso es el
○ más frecuente para los títulos de
○ MA (Master of Arts) y MSc (Master
○ of Science), mientras que los de
○ MLitt (Master of Letters) o MPhil
○ (Master of Philosophy) se obtienen
○ normalmente mediante tesina.
○ En algunas universidades, como
○ las escocesas, el título de master's
○ degree no es de postgrado, sino que
○ corresponde a la licenciatura.

masturbate ['mæstəbeɪt] vi masturbarse

mat [mæt] n alfombrilla; (also: **door~**) felpudo ▷ adj = **matt**

match [mætʃ] n cerilla, fósforo; (game) partido; (fig) igual mf ▷ vt emparejar; (go well with) hacer juego con; (equal)

igualar; (correspond to) corresponderse con; (pair: also: **~ up**) casar con ▷ vi hacer juego; **to be a good ~** hacer buena pareja; **matchbox** n caja de cerillas; **matching** adj que hace juego

mate [meɪt] n (workmate) colega mf; (inf: friend) amigo/a; (animal) macho/hembra; (in merchant navy) primer oficial m, segundo de a bordo ▷ vi acoplarse, aparearse ▷ vt acoplar, aparear

material [mə'tɪərɪəl] n (substance) materia; (equipment) material m; (cloth) tela, tejido ▷ adj material; (important) esencial; **materials** npl materiales mpl

materialize [mə'tɪərɪəlaɪz] vi materializarse

maternal [mə'tə:nl] adj maternal

maternity [mə'tə:nɪtɪ] n maternidad f; **maternity hospital** n hospital m de maternidad; **maternity leave** n baja por maternidad

math [mæθ] n abbr (US: = mathematics) matemáticas fpl

mathematical [mæθə'mætɪkl] adj matemático

mathematician [mæθəmə'tɪʃən] n matemático/a

mathematics [mæθə'mætɪks] n matemáticas fpl

maths [mæθs] n abbr (BRIT: = mathematics) matemáticas fpl

matinée ['mætɪneɪ] n sesión f de tarde

matron ['meɪtrən] n (in hospital) enfermera jefe; (in school) ama de llaves

matt [mæt] adj mate

matter ['mætəʳ] n cuestión f, asunto; (Physics) sustancia, materia; (Med: pus) pus m ▷ vi importar; **it doesn't ~** no importa; **what's the ~?** ¿qué pasa?; **no ~ what** pase lo que pase; **as a ~ of course** por rutina; **as a ~ of fact** en realidad; **printed ~** impresos mpl; **reading ~** material m de lectura

mattress ['mætrɪs] n colchón m

mature [məˈtjuəʳ] *adj* maduro
▷ *vi* madurar; **mature student** *n* estudiante de más de 21 años; **maturity** *n* madurez f

maul [mɔːl] *vt* magullar

mauve [məuv] *adj* de color malva

max *abbr* = **maximum**

maximize [ˈmæksɪmaɪz] *vt* (*profits etc*) llevar al máximo; (*chances*) maximizar

maximum [ˈmæksɪməm] *adj* máximo ▷ *n* máximo

May [meɪ] *n* mayo

may [meɪ] *vi* (*indicating possibility*): **he ~ come** puede que venga; (*be allowed to*): **~ I smoke?** ¿puedo fumar?; (*wishes*): **~ God bless you!** ¡que Dios le bendiga!

maybe [ˈmeɪbiː] *adv* quizá(s)

May Day *n* el primero de Mayo

mayhem [ˈmeɪhɛm] *n* caos *m* total

mayonnaise [meɪəˈneɪz] *n* mayonesa

mayor [mɛəʳ] *n* alcalde *m*; **mayoress** *n* alcaldesa

maze [meɪz] *n* laberinto

MD *n abbr* (*Comm*) = **managing director**

me [miː] *pron* (*direct*) me; (*stressed, after pronoun*) mí; **can you hear me?** ¿me oyes?; **he heard ME!** me oyó a mí; **it's me** soy yo; **give them to me** dámelos; **with/without me** conmigo/sin mí

meadow [ˈmɛdəu] *n* prado, pradera

meagre, (*us*) **meager** [ˈmiːɡəʳ] *adj* escaso, pobre

meal [miːl] *n* comida; (*flour*) harina; **mealtime** *n* hora de comer

mean [miːn] *adj* (*with money*) tacaño; (*unkind*) mezquino, malo; (*average*) medio ▷ *vt* (*signify*) querer decir, significar; (*intend*): **to ~ to do sth** tener la intención de *or* pensar hacer algo ▷ *n* medio, término medio; **do you ~ it?** ¿lo dices en serio?; **what do you ~?** ¿qué quiere decir?; **to be meant for sb/sth** ser para algn/algo; *see also* **means**

meaning [ˈmiːnɪŋ] *n* significado, sentido; **meaningful** *adj* significativo; **meaningless** *adj* sin sentido

means *npl* medio *sg*, manera *sg*; (*resource*) recursos *mpl*, medios *mpl*; **by ~ of** mediante, por medio de; **by all ~!** ¡naturalmente!, ¡claro que sí!

meant [mɛnt] *pt*, *pp of* **mean**

meantime [ˈmiːntaɪm], **meanwhile** [ˈmiːnwaɪl] *adv* (*also:* **in the ~**) mientras tanto

measles [ˈmiːzlz] *n* sarampión *m*

measure [ˈmɛʒəʳ] *vt* medir ▷ *vi* medir ▷ *n* medida; (*ruler*) cinta métrica, metro; **measurement** *n* (*measure*) medida; (*act*) medición *f*; **to take sb's measurements** tomar las medidas a algn

meat [miːt] *n* carne *f*; **cold ~s** fiambres *mpl*; **meatball** *n* albóndiga

Mecca [ˈmɛkə] *n* la Meca

mechanic [mɪˈkænɪk] *n* mecánico/a; **mechanical** *adj* mecánico

mechanism [ˈmɛkənɪzəm] *n* mecanismo

medal [ˈmɛdl] *n* medalla; **medallist**, (*us*) **medalist** [ˈmɛdlɪst] *n* (*Sport*) medallista *mf*

meddle [ˈmɛdl] *vi*: **to ~ in** entrometerse en; **to ~ with sth** manosear algo

media [ˈmiːdɪə] *npl* medios *mpl* de comunicación

mediaeval [mɛdɪˈiːvl] *adj* = **medieval**

mediate [ˈmiːdɪeɪt] *vi* mediar

medical [ˈmɛdɪkl] *adj* médico ▷ *n* reconocimiento médico; **medical certificate** *n* certificado *m* médico

medicated [ˈmɛdɪkeɪtɪd] *adj* medicinal

medication [mɛdɪˈkeɪʃən] *n* medicación *f*

medicine [ˈmɛdsɪn] *n* medicina; (*drug*) medicamento

medieval [mɛdɪˈiːvl] *adj* medieval

mediocre [miːdɪˈəukəʳ] *adj* mediocre

meditate [ˈmɛdɪteɪt] *vi* meditar

meditation [mɛdɪ'teɪʃən] n
meditación f

Mediterranean [mɛdɪtə'reɪnɪən]
adj mediterráneo; **the ~ (Sea)** el (mar
m) Mediterráneo

medium ['miːdɪəm] adj mediano
▷ n (means) medio; (person) médium
mf; **medium-sized** adj de tamaño
mediano; (clothes) de (la) talla
mediana; **medium wave** n onda
media

meek [miːk] adj manso, sumiso

meet [miːt] (pt, pp **met**) vt encontrar;
(accidentally) encontrarse con; (by
arrangement) reunirse con; (for the
first time) conocer; (go and fetch) ir a
buscar; (opponent) enfrentarse con;
(obligations) cumplir ▷ vi encontrarse;
(in session) reunirse; (join: objects)
unirse; (get to know) conocerse; **meet
up** vi: **to ~ up with sb** reunirse con
algn; **meet with** vt fus (difficulty)
tropezar con; **meeting** n encuentro;
(arranged) cita, compromiso (LAM);
(formal session, business meeting)
reunión f; (Pol) mitin m; **meeting
place** n lugar m de reunión or
encuentro

megabyte ['mɛgə'baɪt] n (Comput)
megabyte m, megaocteto

megaphone ['mɛgəfəun] n
megáfono

megapixel ['mɛgəpɪksl] n megapíxel
m

melancholy ['mɛlənkəlɪ] n
melancolía ▷ adj melancólico

melody ['mɛlədɪ] n melodía

melon ['mɛlən] n melón m

melt [mɛlt] vi (metal) fundirse; (snow)
derretirse ▷ vt fundir

member ['mɛmbəˀ] n miembro; (of
club) socio/a; **M~ of Parliament**
(BRIT) diputado/a; **M~ of the
European Parliament** (BRIT)
eurodiputado/a; **M~ of the Scottish
Parliament** (BRIT) diputado/a del
Parlamento escocés; **membership** n
(members) miembros mpl; (numbers)

número de miembros or socios;
membership card n carnet m de
socio

memento [mə'mɛntəu] n recuerdo

memo ['mɛməu] n apunte m, nota

memorable ['mɛmərəbl] adj
memorable

memorandum (pl **memoranda**)
[mɛmə'rændəm, -də] n nota (de
servicio); (Pol) memorándum m

memorial [mɪ'mɔːrɪəl] n
monumento conmemorativo ▷ adj
conmemorativo

memorize ['mɛməraɪz] vt aprender
de memoria

memory ['mɛmərɪ] n recuerdo;
(Comput) memoria; **memory card** n
tarjeta de memoria; **memory stick** n
(Comput) llave f de memoria

men [mɛn] pl of **man**

menace ['mɛnəs] n amenaza ▷ vt
amenazar

mend [mɛnd] vt reparar, arreglar;
(darn) zurcir ▷ vi reponerse ▷ n
remiendo; (darn) zurcido; **to be on
the ~** ir mejorando; **to ~ one's ways**
enmendarse

meningitis [mɛnɪn'dʒaɪtɪs] n
meningitis f

menopause ['mɛnəupɔːz] n
menopausia

men's room n (US): **the ~** el servicio
de caballeros

menstruation [mɛnstru'eɪʃən] n
menstruación f

menswear ['mɛnzweəˀ] n confección
f de caballero

mental ['mɛntl] adj mental; **mental
hospital** n (hospital m) psiquiátrico;
mentality [mɛn'tælɪtɪ] n mentalidad
f; **mentally** adv: **to be mentally ill**
tener una enfermedad mental

menthol ['mɛnθɔl] n mentol m

mention ['mɛnʃən] n mención f ▷ vt
mencionar; (speak of) hablar de; **don't
~ it!** ¡de nada!

menu ['mɛnjuː] n (set menu) menú m;
(printed) carta; (Comput) menú m

m

MEP n abbr = **Member of the European Parliament**

mercenary ['mə:sɪnərɪ] adj, n mercenario/a

merchandise ['mə:tʃəndaɪz] n mercancías fpl

merchant ['mə:tʃənt] n comerciante mf; **merchant navy**, (us) **merchant marine** n marina mercante

merciless ['mə:sɪlɪs] adj despiadado

mercury ['mə:kjʊrɪ] n mercurio

mercy ['mə:sɪ] n compasión f; (Rel) misericordia f; **at the ~ of** a la merced de

mere [mɪər] adj simple, mero; **merely** adv simplemente, sólo

merge [mə:dʒ] vt (join) unir ▷ vi unirse; (Comm) fusionarse; **merger** n (Comm) fusión f

meringue [mə'ræŋ] n merengue m

merit ['mɛrɪt] n mérito ▷ vt merecer

mermaid ['mə:meɪd] n sirena

merry ['mɛrɪ] adj alegre; **M~ Christmas!** ¡Felices Pascuas!; **merry-go-round** n tiovivo

mesh [mɛʃ] n malla

mess [mɛs] n confusión f; (of objects) revoltijo m; (dirt) porquería; (Mil) comedor m; **mess about, mess around** vi (inf) perder el tiempo; (pass the time) pasar el rato; **mess up** vt (inf: spoil) estropear; (dirty) ensuciar; **mess with** vt fus (inf: challenge, confront) meterse con (inf); (interfere with) interferir con

message ['mɛsɪdʒ] n mensaje m, recado ▷ vt (inf: person) mandar un mensaje a; (: comment) mandar

messenger ['mɛsɪndʒər] n mensajero/a

Messrs abbr (on letters: = Messieurs) Sres.

messy ['mɛsɪ] adj (dirty) sucio; (untidy) desordenado

met [mɛt] pt, pp of **meet**

metabolism [mɛ'tæbəlɪzəm] n metabolismo

metal ['mɛtl] n metal m; **metallic** [mɛ'tælɪk] adj metálico

metaphor ['mɛtəfər] n metáfora

meteor ['mi:tɪər] n meteoro; **meteorite** ['mi:tɪəraɪt] n meteorito

meteorology [mi:tɪə'rɒlədʒɪ] n meteorología

meter ['mi:tər] n (instrument) contador m; (us: unit); = **metre** ▷ vt (us Post) franquear

method ['mɛθəd] n método; **methodical** adj metódico

meths [mɛθs] n (BRIT) = **methylated spirit**

methylated spirit ['mɛθɪleɪtɪd-] n (BRIT) alcohol m metilado or desnaturalizado

meticulous [mɛ'tɪkjʊləs] adj meticuloso

metre, (us) **meter** ['mi:tər] n metro

metric ['mɛtrɪk] adj métrico

metropolitan [mɛtrə'pɒlɪtən] adj metropolitano

Metropolitan Police n (BRIT): **the ~** la policía londinense

Mexican ['mɛksɪkən] adj, n mexicano/a, mejicano/a

Mexico ['mɛksɪkəʊ] n México, Méjico

mg abbr (= milligram) mg

mice [maɪs] pl of **mouse**

micro... [maɪkrəʊ] pref micro...; **microchip** n microplaqueta; **microphone** n micrófono; **microscope** n microscopio; **microwave** n (also: **microwave oven**) horno microondas

mid [mɪd] adj: **in ~ May** a mediados de mayo; **in ~ afternoon** a media tarde; **in ~ air** en el aire; **midday** n mediodía m

middle ['mɪdl] n centro; (half-way point) medio; (waist) cintura ▷ adj en medio; **in the ~ of the night** en plena noche; **middle-aged** adj de mediana edad; **Middle Ages** npl: **the Middle Ages** la Edad Media; **middle class** n: **the middle class(es)** la clase media ▷ adj: **middle-class** de clase media; **Middle East** n Oriente m Medio; **middle name** n segundo

nombre m; **middle school** n (US)
colegio para niños de doce a catorce años;
(BRIT) colegio para niños de ocho o nueve a
doce o trece años

midge [mɪdʒ] n mosquito

midget ['mɪdʒɪt] n (inf!) enano/a

midnight ['mɪdnaɪt] n medianoche f

midst [mɪdst] n: **in the ~ of** en medio
de; (situation, action) en mitad de

midsummer [mɪd'sʌmə'] n: **a ~ day**
un día de pleno verano

midway [mɪd'weɪ] adj, adv: **~
(between)** a medio camino (entre);
~ through a la mitad (de)

midweek [mɪd'wi:k] adv entre
semana

midwife (pl **midwives**) ['mɪdwaɪf,
-waɪvz] n matrona, comadrona

midwinter [mɪd'wɪntə'] n: **in ~** en
pleno invierno

might [maɪt] vb see **may** ▷ n fuerza,
poder m; **mighty** adj fuerte, poderoso

migraine ['mi:greɪn] n jaqueca

migrant ['maɪgrənt] adj migratorio;
(worker) emigrante

migrate [maɪ'greɪt] vi emigrar

migration [maɪ'greɪʃən] n
emigración f

mike [maɪk] n abbr (= microphone)
micro

mild [maɪld] adj (person) apacible;
(climate) templado; (slight) ligero;
(taste) suave; (illness) leve; **mildly** adv
ligeramente; suavemente; **to put it
mildly** por no decir algo peor

mile [maɪl] n milla; **mileage** n
número de millas; (Aut) kilometraje
m; **mileometer** [maɪ'lɔmɪtə'] n
(BRIT) = **milometer**; **milestone** n
mojón m

military ['mɪlɪtərɪ] adj militar

militia [mɪ'lɪʃə] n milicia

milk [mɪlk] n leche f ▷ vt (cow)
ordeñar; (fig) explotar; **milk chocolate**
n chocolate m con leche; **milkman** n
lechero; **milky** adj lechoso

mill [mɪl] n (windmill etc) molino;
(coffee mill) molinillo; (factory)

fábrica ▷ vt moler ▷ vi (also: **~ about**)
arremolinarse

millennium (pl **millenniums** or
millennia) [mɪ'lɛnɪəm, -'lɛnɪə] n
milenio, milenario

milli... ['mɪlɪ] pref mili...;
milligram(me) ['mɪlɪgræm] n
miligramo; **millilitre,** (US) **milliliter**
['mɪlɪli:tə'] n mililitro; **millimetre,**
(US) **millimeter** ['mɪlɪmi:tə'] n
milímetro

million ['mɪljən] n millón m; **a ~
times** un millón de veces; **millionaire**
[mɪljə'nɛə'] n millonario/a; **millionth**
adj millonésimo

milometer [maɪ'lɔmɪtə'] n (BRIT)
cuentakilómetros m inv

mime [maɪm] n mímica; (actor)
mimo/a ▷ vt remedar ▷ vi actuar
de mimo

mimic ['mɪmɪk] n imitador(a) m/f
▷ adj mímico ▷ vt remedar, imitar

min. abbr (= minute(s)) m.; = **minimum**

mince [mɪns] vt picar ▷ n (BRIT Culin)
carne f picada; **mincemeat** n conserva
de fruta picada; (US: meat) carne f
picada; **mince pie** n pastelillo relleno
de fruta picada

mind [maɪnd] n mente f; (contrasted
with matter) espíritu m ▷ vt (attend
to, look after) ocuparse de, cuidar; (be
careful of) tener cuidado con; (object
to): **I don't ~ the noise** no me molesta
el ruido; **it is on my ~** me preocupa;
to bear sth in ~ tomar or tener algo
en cuenta; **to make up one's ~**
decidirse; **I don't ~** me es igual; **~
you, ...** te advierto que ...; **never ~!**
¡es igual!, ¡no importa!; (don't worry)
¡no te preocupes!; **"~ the step"**
"cuidado con el escalón"; **mindless**
adj (violence, crime) sin sentido; (work)
de autómata

mine [maɪn] pron (el) mío/(la) mía
etc ▷ adj: **this book is ~** este libro es
mío ▷ n mina ▷ vt (coal) extraer; (ship,
beach) minar; **minefield** n campo de
minas; **miner** n minero/a

mineral ['mɪnərəl] *adj* mineral ▷ *n* mineral *m*; **mineral water** *n* agua mineral

mingle ['mɪŋgl] *vi*: **to ~ with** mezclarse con

miniature ['mɪnətʃəʳ] *adj* (en) miniatura ▷ *n* miniatura

minibar ['mɪnɪbɑːʳ] *n* minibar *m*

minibus ['mɪnɪbʌs] *n* microbús *m*

minicab ['mɪnɪkæb] *n* taxi *m* (*que sólo puede pedirse por teléfono*)

minimal ['mɪnɪml] *adj* mínimo

minimize ['mɪnɪmaɪz] *vt* minimizar; (*play down*) empequeñecer

minimum ['mɪnɪməm] *n* mínimo ▷ *adj* mínimo

mining ['maɪnɪŋ] *n* minería

miniskirt ['mɪnɪskəːt] *n* minifalda

minister ['mɪnɪstəʳ] *n* (BRIT Pol) ministro/a; (: *junior*) secretario/a de Estado; (Rel) pastor *m* ▷ *vi*: **to ~ to** atender a

ministry ['mɪnɪstrɪ] *n* (BRIT Pol) ministerio; (Rel) sacerdocio

minor ['maɪnəʳ] *adj* (*repairs, injuries*) leve; (*poet, planet*) menor; (*Mus*) menor ▷ *n* (Law) menor *mf* de edad

Minorca [mɪ'nɔːkə] *n* Menorca

minority [maɪ'nɔrɪtɪ] *n* minoría

mint [mɪnt] *n* (*plant*) menta, hierbabuena; (*sweet*) caramelo de menta ▷ *vt* (*coins*) acuñar; **the (Royal) M~**, (US): **the (US) M~** la Casa de la Moneda; **in ~ condition** en perfecto estado

minus ['maɪnəs] *n* (*also*: **~ sign**) signo menos ▷ *prep* menos; **12 ~ 6 equals 6** 12 menos 6 son 6; **~ 24°C** menos 24 grados

minute[1] ['mɪnɪt] *n* minuto; (*fig*) momento; **minutes** *npl* (*of meeting*) actas *fpl*; **at the last ~** a última hora

minute[2] [maɪ'njuːt] *adj* diminuto; (*search*) minucioso

miracle ['mɪrəkl] *n* milagro

miraculous [mɪ'rækjuləs] *adj* milagroso

mirage ['mɪrɑːʒ] *n* espejismo

mirror ['mɪrəʳ] *n* espejo; (*in car*) retrovisor *m*

misbehave [mɪsbɪ'heɪv] *vi* portarse mal

misc. *abbr* = **miscellaneous**

miscarriage ['mɪskærɪdʒ] *n* (*Med*) aborto (no provocado); **~ of justice** error *m* judicial

miscellaneous [mɪsɪ'leɪnɪəs] *adj* varios/as, diversos/as

mischief ['mɪstʃɪf] *n* travesura; (*maliciousness*) malicia; **mischievous** ['mɪstʃɪvəs] *adj* travieso

misconception ['mɪskən'sɛpʃən] *n* idea equivocada; equivocación *f*

misconduct [mɪs'kɔndʌkt] *n* mala conducta; **professional ~** falta profesional

miser ['maɪzəʳ] *n* avaro/a

miserable ['mɪzərəbl] *adj* (*unhappy*) triste, desgraciado; (*wretched*) miserable

misery ['mɪzərɪ] *n* tristeza; (*wretchedness*) miseria, desdicha

misfortune [mɪs'fɔːtʃən] *n* desgraci

misgiving [mɪs'gɪvɪŋ] *n* (*apprehension*) presentimiento; **to have ~s about sth** tener dudas sobre algo

misguided [mɪs'gaɪdɪd] *adj* equivocado

mishap ['mɪshæp] *n* desgracia, contratiempo

misinterpret [mɪsɪn'təːprɪt] *vt* interpretar mal

misjudge [mɪs'dʒʌdʒ] *vt* juzgar mal

mislay [mɪs'leɪ] *vt* extraviar, perder

mislead [mɪs'liːd] *vt* llevar a conclusiones erróneas; **misleading** *adj* engañoso

misplace [mɪs'pleɪs] *vt* extraviar

misprint ['mɪsprɪnt] *n* errata, error *n* de imprenta

misrepresent [mɪsrɛprɪ'zɛnt] *vt* falsificar

Miss [mɪs] *n* Señorita

miss [mɪs] *vt* (*train etc*) perder; (*target*) errar; (*regret the absence of*): **I ~ him** le

echo de menos ▷ vi fallar ▷ n (shot) tiro
fallido; **miss out** vt (BRIT) omitir; **miss
out on** vt fus (fun, party, opportunity)
perderse

missile ['mɪsaɪl] n (Aviat) misil m;
(object thrown) proyectil m

missing ['mɪsɪŋ] adj (pupil) ausente;
(thing) perdido; **~ in action**
desaparecido en combate

mission ['mɪʃən] n misión f;
missionary n misionero/a

misspell [mɪs'spɛl] vt (irreg: like spell)
escribir mal

mist [mɪst] n (light) neblina; (heavy)
niebla; (at sea) bruma ▷ vi (also: **~ over,
~ up**: BRIT: windows) empañarse

mistake [mɪs'teɪk] n error m ▷ vt
(irreg: like take) entender mal; **by
~** por equivocación; **to make a ~**
equivocarse; **to ~ A for B** confundir
A con B; **mistaken** pp of **mistake**
▷ adj equivocado; **to be mistaken**
equivocarse, engañarse

mister ['mɪstər] n (inf) señor m; see
also **Mr**

mistletoe ['mɪsltəu] n muérdago

mistook [mɪs'tuk] pt of **mistake**

mistress ['mɪstrɪs] n (lover) amante f;
(of house) señora (de la casa); (BRIT: in
primary school) maestra; (: in secondary
school) profesora

mistrust [mɪs'trʌst] vt desconfiar de

misty ['mɪstɪ] adj (day) de niebla;
(glasses) empañado

misunderstand [mɪsʌndə'stænd]
vt, vi (irreg: like understand)
entender mal; **misunderstanding** n
malentendido

misunderstood [mɪsʌndə'stud] pt,
pp of **misunderstand** ▷ adj (person)
incomprendido

misuse n [mɪs'juːs] mal uso; (of power)
abuso; (of funds) malversación f ▷ vt
[mɪs'juːz] abusar de; (funds) malversar

mix [mɪks] vt mezclar; (combine)
unir ▷ vi mezclarse; (people) llevarse
bien ▷ n mezcla; **mix up** vt mezclar;
(confuse) confundir; **mixed** adj mixto;

(feelings etc) encontrado; **mixed
grill** n (BRIT) parrillada mixta; **mixed
salad** n ensalada mixta; **mixed-up**
adj (confused) confuso, revuelto;
mixer n (for food) batidora; (person):
he's a good mixer tiene don de
gentes; **mixture** n mezcla; **mix-up** n
confusión f

ml abbr (= millilitre(s)) ml

mm abbr (= millimetre) mm

moan [məun] n gemido ▷ vi gemir;
(inf: complain): **to ~ (about)** quejarse
(de)

moat [məut] n foso

mob [mɔb] n multitud f ▷ vt acosar

mobile ['məubaɪl] adj móvil ▷ n móvil
m; **mobile home** n caravana; **mobile
phone** n teléfono móvil

mobility [məu'bɪlɪtɪ] n movilidad f

mobilize ['məubɪlaɪz] vt movilizar

mock [mɔk] vt (make ridiculous)
ridiculizar; (laugh at) burlarse de
▷ adj fingido; **~ exams** (BRIT: Scol)
exámenes mpl de prueba; **mockery**
n burla

mod cons ['mɔd'kɔnz] npl abbr
= **modern conveniences**; see
convenience

mode [məud] n modo

model ['mɔdl] n modelo; (for fashion,
art) modelo mf ▷ adj modelo inv ▷ vt
modelar; **to ~ o.s. on** tomar como
modelo a ▷ vi ser modelo; **to ~
clothes** pasar modelos, ser modelo

modem ['məudəm] n módem m

moderate adj, n ['mɔdərət]
moderado/a ▷ vi ['mɔdəreɪt]
moderarse, calmarse ▷ vt ['mɔdəreɪt]
moderar

moderation [mɔdə'reɪʃən] n
moderación f; **in ~** con moderación

modern ['mɔdən] adj moderno;
modernize vt modernizar

modest ['mɔdɪst] adj modesto;
(small) módico; **modesty** ['mɔdɪstɪ]
n modestia

modification [mɔdɪfɪ'keɪʃən] n
modificación f

modify ['mɒdɪfaɪ] vt modificar
module ['mɒdjuːl] n módulo
mohair ['məuhɛəʳ] n mohair m
Mohammed [mə'hæmɛd] n
Mahoma m
moist [mɔɪst] adj húmedo; **moisture**
['mɔɪstʃəʳ] n humedad f; **moisturizer**
['mɔɪstʃəraɪzəʳ] n crema hidratante
mold [məuld] n, vt (US) = **mould**
mole [məul] n (animal) topo; (spot)
lunar m
molecule ['mɒlɪkjuːl] n molécula
molest [məu'lɛst] vt importunar;
(sexually) abusar sexualmente de
  ▌ Be careful not to translate molest
  by the Spanish word molestar.
molten ['məultən] adj fundido;
(lava) líquido
mom [mɒm] n (US) = **mum**
moment ['məumənt] n momento;
at or **for the ~** de momento, por
ahora; **momentarily** ['məuməntrɪlɪ]
adv momentáneamente; (US:
very soon) de un momento a otro;
momentary adj momentáneo;
momentous [məu'mɛntəs] adj
trascendental, importante
momentum [məu'mɛntəm] n
momento; (fig) ímpetu m; **to gather ~**
cobrar velocidad; (fig) cobrar fuerza
mommy ['mɒmɪ] n (US) = **mummy**
Mon. abbr (= Monday) lun.
Monaco ['mɒnəkəu] n Mónaco
monarch ['mɒnək] n monarca mf;
monarchy n monarquía
monastery ['mɒnəstərɪ] n
monasterio
Monday ['mʌndɪ] n lunes m inv
monetary ['mʌnɪtərɪ] adj monetario
money ['mʌnɪ] n dinero; **to make ~**
ganar dinero; **money belt** n riñonera;
money order n giro
mongrel ['mʌŋgrəl] n (dog) perro
cruzado
monitor ['mɒnɪtəʳ] n (Scol) monitor
m; (also: **television ~**) receptor m de
control; (of computer) monitor m ▷ vt
controlar

monk [mʌŋk] n monje m
monkey ['mʌŋkɪ] n mono
monologue ['mɒnəlɒg] n monólogo
monopoly [mə'nɒpəlɪ] n monopolio
monotonous [mə'nɒtənəs] adj
monótono
monsoon [mɒn'suːn] n monzón m
monster ['mɒnstəʳ] n monstruo
month [mʌnθ] n mes m; **300 dollars
a ~** 300 dólares al mes; **every ~** cada
mes; **monthly** adj mensual ▷ adv
mensualmente
monument ['mɒnjumənt] n
monumento
mood [muːd] n humor m; **to be in
a good/bad ~** estar de buen/mal
humor; **moody** adj (changeable) de
humor variable; (sullen) malhumorado
moon [muːn] n luna; **moonlight** n
luz f de la luna
moor [muəʳ] n páramo ▷ vt (ship)
amarrar ▷ vi echar las amarras
moose [muːs] n (pl inv) alce m
mop [mɒp] n fregona; (of hair) melena
▷ vt fregar; **mop up** vt limpiar
mope [məup] vi estar deprimido
moped ['məupɛd] n ciclomotor m
moral ['mɒrl] adj moral ▷ n moraleja;
morals npl moralidad f, moral f
morale [mɒ'rɑːl] n moral f
morality [mə'rælɪtɪ] n moralidad f
morbid ['mɔːbɪd] adj (interest)
morboso; (Med) mórbido

KEYWORD

more [mɔːʳ] adj 1 (greater in number
etc) más; **more people/work than
before** más gente/trabajo que antes
2 (additional) más; **do you want
(some) more tea?** ¿quieres más té?;
is there any more wine? ¿queda
vino?; **it'll take a few more weeks**
tardará unas semanas más; **it's 2 kms
more to the house** faltan 2 kms para
la casa; **more time/letters than we
expected** más tiempo del que/más
cartas de las que esperábamos

▶ pron (greater amount, additional amount) más; **more than 10** más de 10; **it cost more than the other one/than we expected** costó más que el otro/más de lo que esperábamos; **is there any more?** ¿hay más?; **many/much more** muchos/as más, mucho/a más
▶ adv más; **more dangerous/easily (than)** más peligroso/fácilmente (que); **more and more expensive** cada vez más caro; **more or less** más o menos; **more than ever** más que nunca

moreover [mɔːˈrəuvəʳ] adv además, por otra parte

morgue [mɔːg] n depósito de cadáveres

morning [ˈmɔːnɪŋ] n mañana; (early morning) madrugada; **in the ~** por la mañana; **7 o'clock in the ~** las 7 de la mañana; **morning sickness** n náuseas fpl del embarazo

Moroccan [məˈrɔkən] adj, n marroquí mf

Morocco [məˈrɔkəu] n Marruecos m

moron [ˈmɔːrɔn] n (inf!) imbécil mf

morphine [ˈmɔːfiːn] n morfina

Morse [mɔːs] n (also: ~ **code**) (código) morse m

mortal [ˈmɔːtl] adj, n mortal m

mortar [ˈmɔːtəʳ] n argamasa

mortgage [ˈmɔːgɪdʒ] n hipoteca ▷ vt hipotecar

mortician [mɔːˈtɪʃən] n (US) director(a) m/f de pompas fúnebres

mortified [ˈmɔːtɪfaɪd] adj: **I was ~** me dio muchísima vergüenza

mortuary [ˈmɔːtjuərɪ] n depósito de cadáveres

mosaic [məuˈzeɪɪk] n mosaico

Moslem [ˈmɔzləm] adj, n = **Muslim**

mosque [mɔsk] n mezquita

mosquito [mɔsˈkiːtəu] (pl **mosquitoes**) n mosquito, zancudo (LAM)

moss [mɔs] n musgo

most [məust] adj la mayor parte de, la mayoría de ▷ pron la mayor parte, la mayoría ▷ adv el más; (very) muy; **the ~** (also: + adjective) el más; **~ of them** la mayor parte de ellos; **I saw the ~** yo fui el que más vi; **at the (very) ~** a lo sumo, todo lo más; **to make the ~ of** aprovechar (al máximo); **a ~ interesting book** un libro interesantísimo; **mostly** adv en su mayor parte, principalmente

MOT n abbr (BRIT) = **Ministry of Transport**; **the ~ (test)** ≈ la ITV

motel [məuˈtɛl] n motel m

moth [mɔθ] n mariposa nocturna; (clothes moth) polilla

mother [ˈmʌðəʳ] n madre f ▷ adj materno ▷ vt (care for) cuidar (como una madre); **motherhood** n maternidad f; **mother-in-law** n suegra; **mother-of-pearl** n nácar m; **Mother's Day** n Día m de la Madre; **mother-to-be** n futura madre; **mother tongue** n lengua materna

motif [məuˈtiːf] n motivo

motion [ˈməuʃən] n movimiento; (gesture) ademán m, señal f; (at meeting) moción f ▷ vt, vi: **to ~ (to) sb to do sth** hacer señas a algn para que haga algo; **motionless** adj inmóvil; **motion picture** n película

motivate [ˈməutɪveɪt] vt motivar

motivation [məutɪˈveɪʃən] n motivación f

motive [ˈməutɪv] n motivo

motor [ˈməutəʳ] n motor m; (BRIT inf: vehicle) coche m, carro (LAM), automóvil m, auto m (LAM) ▷ adj motor (f: motora or motriz); **motorbike** n moto f; **motorboat** n lancha motora; **motorcar** n (BRIT) coche m, carro (LAM), automóvil m, auto m (LAM); **motorcycle** n motocicleta; **motorcyclist** n motociclista mf; **motoring** n (BRIT) automovilismo; **motorist** n conductor(a) m/f, automovilista mf; **motor racing** n (BRIT) carreras fpl de coches,

m

automovilismo; **motorway** n (BRIT) autopista

motto ['mɔtəu] (pl **mottoes**) n lema m; (watchword) consigna

mould, (US) **mold** [məuld] n molde m; (mildew) moho ▷ vt moldear; (fig) formar; **mouldy** adj enmohecido

mound [maund] n montón m, montículo

mount [maunt] n monte m ▷ vt montar en, subir a; (picture) enmarcar ▷ vi (also: ~ **up**: increase) aumentar; (on horse) montar

mountain ['mauntin] n montaña ▷ cpd de montaña; **mountain bike** n bicicleta de montaña; **mountaineer** n alpinista mf, andinista mf (LAM); **mountaineering** n montañismo, alpinismo, andinismo (LAM); **mountainous** adj montañoso; **mountain range** n sierra

mourn [mɔːn] vt llorar, lamentar ▷ vi: **to ~ for** llorar la muerte de; **mourner** n doliente mf; **mourning** n luto; **in mourning** de luto

mouse (pl **mice**) [maus, mais] n (also Comput) ratón m; **mouse mat** n (Comput) alfombrilla, almohadilla

mousse [muːs] n (Culin) mousse f; (for hair) espuma (moldeadora)

moustache [məs'taːʃ], (US) **mustache** ['mʌstæʃ] n bigote m

mouth (pl **mouths**) [mauθ, -ðz] n boca; (of river) desembocadura; **mouthful** n bocado; **mouth organ** n armónica; **mouthpiece** n (of musical instrument) boquilla; (spokesman) portavoz mf; **mouthwash** n enjuague m bucal

move [muːv] n (movement) movimiento; (in game) jugada; (: turn to play) turno; (change of house) mudanza ▷ vt mover; (emotionally) conmover; (Pol: resolution etc) proponer ▷ vi moverse; (traffic) circular; (also: ~ **house**) trasladarse, mudarse; **to get a ~ on** darse prisa; **to ~ sb to do sth** mover a algn a hacer

algo; **move back** vi volver; **move in** vi (to a house) instalarse; **move off** vi ponerse en camino; **move on** vi seguir viaje; **move out** vi (of house) mudarse; **move over** vi hacerse a un lado, correrse; **move up** vi (employee) ascender; **movement** n movimiento

movie ['muːvi] n película; **to go to the ~s** ir al cine; **movie theater** n (US) cine m

moving ['muːviŋ] adj (emotional) conmovedor(a); (that moves) móvil

mow (pt **mowed**, pp **mowed** or **mown** [məu, -n] vt (grass) cortar; (corn) segar; **mower** n (also: **lawnmower**) cortacésped m

Mozambique [məuzæm'biːk] n Mozambique m

MP n abbr (BRIT) = **Member of Parliament**

mpg n abbr (= miles per gallon) 30 mpg = 9.4 l. per 100 km

mph abbr (= miles per hour) 60 mph = 96 km/h

MP3 ['ɛmpiː'θriː] n MP3 m; **MP3 player** n reproductor m MP3

Mr, Mr. ['mistər] n: **Mr Smith** (el) Sr. Smith

Mrs, Mrs. ['misiz] n: **~ Smith** (la) Sra. de Smith

Ms, Ms. [miz] n (Miss or Mrs) abreviatura con la que se evita hacer expreso el estado civil de una mujer; **Ms Smith** (la) Sra. Smith

MSP n abbr (BRIT) = **Member of the Scottish Parliament**

Mt abbr (Geo: = mount) m.

much [mʌtʃ] adj mucho ▷ adv, n, pron mucho; (before pp) muy; **how ~ is it?** ¿cuánto es?, ¿cuánto cuesta?; **too ~** demasiado; **it's not ~** no es mucho; **as ~ as** tanto como; **however ~ he tries** por mucho que se esfuerce

muck [mʌk] n suciedad f; **muck up** vt (inf) estropear; **mucky** adj (dirty) sucio

mucus ['mjuːkəs] n mucosidad f, moco

mud [mʌd] n barro, lodo

muddle ['mʌdl] n desorden m, confusión f; (mix-up) embrollo, lío ▷ vt (also: ~ **up**) embrollar, confundir

muddy ['mʌdɪ] adj fangoso, cubierto de lodo

mudguard ['mʌdgɑːd] n guardabarros m inv

muesli ['mjuːzlɪ] n muesli m

muffin ['mʌfɪn] n bollo, ≈ magdalena

muffled ['mʌfld] adj apagado; (noise etc) amortiguado

muffler ['mʌflər] n (scarf) bufanda; (us: Aut) silenciador m

mug [mʌg] n (cup) taza alta; (for beer) jarra; (inf: face) jeta ▷ vt (assault) atracar; **mugger** ['mʌgər] n atracador(a) m/f; **mugging** n atraco callejero

muggy ['mʌgɪ] adj bochornoso

mule [mjuːl] n mula

multicoloured, (us) **multicolored** ['mʌltɪkʌləd] adj multicolor

multimedia ['mʌltɪ'miːdɪə] adj multimedia inv

multinational [mʌltɪ'næʃənl] n multinacional f ▷ adj multinacional

multiple ['mʌltɪpl] adj múltiple ▷ n múltiplo; **multiple choice** n (also: **multiple choice test**) examen m de tipo test; **multiple sclerosis** n esclerosis f múltiple

multiplex ['mʌltɪpleks] n (also: ~ **cinema**) multicines m inv

multiplication [mʌltɪplɪ'keɪʃən] n multiplicación f

multiply ['mʌltɪplaɪ] vt multiplicar ▷ vi multiplicarse

multistorey [mʌltɪ'stɔːrɪ] adj (brit) de muchos pisos

mum [mʌm] n (brit) mamá f ▷ adj: **to keep ~ (about sth)** no decir ni mu (de algo)

mumble ['mʌmbl] vt decir entre dientes ▷ vi hablar entre dientes, musitar

mummy ['mʌmɪ] n (brit: mother) mamá f; (embalmed) momia

mumps [mʌmps] n paperas fpl

munch [mʌntʃ] vt, vi mascar

municipal [mjuː'nɪsɪpl] adj municipal

mural ['mjuərl] n (pintura) mural m

murder ['məːdər] n asesinato; (in law) homicidio ▷ vt asesinar, matar; **murderer** n asesino

murky ['məːkɪ] adj (water, past) turbio; (room) sombrío

murmur ['məːmər] n murmullo ▷ vt, vi murmurar

muscle ['mʌsl] n músculo; (fig: strength) garra, fuerza; **muscular** ['mʌskjulər] adj muscular; (person) musculoso

museum [mjuː'zɪəm] n museo

mushroom ['mʌʃrum] n seta, hongo; (small) champiñón m ▷ vi crecer de la noche a la mañana

music ['mjuːzɪk] n música; **musical** adj musical; (sound) melodioso; (person) con talento musical ▷ n (show) (comedia) musical m; **musical instrument** n instrumento musical; **musician** [mjuː'zɪʃən] n músico/a

Muslim ['mʌzlɪm] adj, n musulmán/ ana m/f

muslin ['mʌzlɪn] n muselina

mussel ['mʌsl] n mejillón m

must [mʌst] aux vb (obligation): **I ~ do it** debo hacerlo, tengo que hacerlo; (probability): **he ~ be there by now** ya debe (de) estar allí ▷ n: **it's a ~** es imprescindible

mustache ['mʌstæʃ] n (us) = **moustache**

mustard ['mʌstəd] n mostaza

mustn't ['mʌsnt] = **must not**

mute [mjuːt] adj, n mudo/a

mutilate ['mjuːtɪleɪt] vt mutilar

mutiny ['mjuːtɪnɪ] n motín m ▷ vi amotinarse

mutter ['mʌtər] vt, vi murmurar

mutton ['mʌtn] n (carne f de) cordero

mutual ['mjuːtʃuəl] adj mutuo; (friend) común

muzzle ['mʌzl] n hocico; (*protective device*) bozal m; (*of gun*) boca ▷ vt (*dog*) poner un bozal a

my [maɪ] *adj* mi(s); **my house/ brother/sisters** mi casa/hermano/ mis hermanas; **I've washed my hair/ cut my finger** me he lavado el pelo/ cortado un dedo; **is this my pen or yours?** ¿este bolígrafo es mío o tuyo?

myself [maɪ'sɛlf] *pron* (*reflexive*) me; (*emphatic*) yo mismo; (*after prep*) mí (mismo); *see also* **oneself**

mysterious [mɪs'tɪərɪəs] *adj* misterioso

mystery ['mɪstərɪ] n misterio

mystical ['mɪstɪkl] *adj* místico

mystify ['mɪstɪfaɪ] vt (*perplex*) dejar perplejo

myth [mɪθ] n mito; **mythology** [mɪ'θɒlədʒɪ] n mitología

n/a *abbr* (= *not applicable*) no interesa

nag [næg] vt (*scold*) regañar

nail [neɪl] n (*human*) uña; (*metal*) clavo ▷ vt clavar; **to ~ sb down to a date/price** hacer que algn se comprometa a una fecha/un precio; **nailbrush** n cepillo para las uñas; **nailfile** n lima para las uñas; **nail polish** n esmalte m or laca para las uñas; **nail polish remover** n quitaesmalte m; **nail scissors** npl tijeras fpl para las uñas; **nail varnish** n (BRIT) = **nail polish**

naïve [naɪ'iːv] *adj* ingenuo

naked ['neɪkɪd] *adj* (*nude*) desnudo; (*flame*) expuesto al aire

name [neɪm] n nombre m; (*surname*) apellido; (*reputation*) fama, renombre m ▷ vt (*child*) poner nombre a; (*criminal*) identificar; (*price, date etc*) fijar; **by ~** de nombre; **in the ~ of** en nombre de; **what's your ~?** ¿cómo se llama usted?; **to give one's ~ and**

address dar sus señas; **namely** adv a saber

nanny ['nænɪ] n niñera

nap [næp] n (sleep) sueñecito, siesta

napkin ['næpkɪn] n (also: **table ~**) servilleta

nappy ['næpɪ] n (BRIT) pañal m

narcotic [nɑ:'kɔtɪk] adj, n narcótico; **narcotics** npl estupefacientes mpl, narcóticos mpl

narrative ['nærətɪv] n narrativa ⊳ adj narrativo

narrator [nə'reɪtəʳ] n narrador(a) m/f

narrow ['nærəu] adj estrecho ⊳ vi estrecharse; (diminish) reducirse; **to have a ~ escape** escaparse por los pelos; **narrow down** vt (search, investigation, possibilities) restringir, limitar; (list) reducir; **narrowly** adv (miss) por poco; **narrow-minded** adj de miras estrechas

nasal ['neɪzl] adj nasal

nasty ['nɑːstɪ] adj (remark) feo; (person) antipático; (revolting: taste, smell) asqueroso; (wound, disease etc) peligroso, grave

nation ['neɪʃən] n nación f

national ['næʃənl] adj nacional ⊳ n súbdito/a; **national anthem** n himno nacional; **national dress** n traje m típico del país; **National Health Service** n (BRIT) servicio nacional de salud, ≈ INSALUD m (SP); **National Insurance** n (BRIT) seguro social nacional; **nationalist** adj, n nacionalista mf; **nationality** n nacionalidad f; **nationalize** vt nacionalizar; **National Trust** n (BRIT) organización encargada de preservar el patrimonio histórico británico

nationwide ['neɪʃənwaɪd] adj a escala nacional

native ['neɪtɪv] n (local inhabitant) natural mf ⊳ adj (indigenous) indígena; (country) natal; (innate) natural, innato; **a ~ of Russia** un(a) natural de Rusia; **Native American** adj, n americano/a indígena, amerindio/a;

native speaker n hablante mf nativo/a

NATO ['neɪtəu] n abbr (= North Atlantic Treaty Organization) OTAN f

natural ['nætʃrəl] adj natural; **natural gas** n gas m natural; **natural history** n historia natural; **naturally** adv (speak etc) naturalmente; (of course) desde luego, por supuesto; **natural resources** npl recursos mpl naturales

nature ['neɪtʃəʳ] n naturaleza; (group, sort) género, clase f; (character) modo de ser, carácter m; **by ~** por naturaleza; **nature reserve** n reserva natural

naughty ['nɔːtɪ] adj (child) travieso

nausea ['nɔːsɪə] n náusea

naval ['neɪvl] adj naval, de marina

navel ['neɪvl] n ombligo

navigate ['nævɪgeɪt] vt gobernar ⊳ vi navegar; (Aut) ir de copiloto; **navigation** [nævɪ'geɪʃən] n (action) navegación f; (science) náutica

navy ['neɪvɪ] n marina de guerra; (ships) armada, flota

Nazi ['nɑːtsɪ] n nazi mf

NB abbr (= nota bene) nótese

near [nɪəʳ] adj (place, relation) cercano; (time) próximo ⊳ adv cerca ⊳ prep (also: **~ to**: space) cerca de, junto a; (time) cerca de ⊳ vt acercarse a, aproximarse a; **nearby** [nɪə'baɪ] adj cercano, próximo ⊳ adv cerca; **nearly** adv casi, por poco; **I nearly fell** por poco me caigo; **near-sighted** adj miope, corto de vista

neat [niːt] adj (place) ordenado, bien cuidado; (person) pulcro; (plan) ingenioso; (spirits) solo; **neatly** adv (tidily) con esmero; (skilfully) ingeniosamente

necessarily ['nɛsɪsrɪlɪ] adv necesariamente

necessary ['nɛsɪsrɪ] adj necesario, preciso

necessity [nɪ'sɛsɪtɪ] n necesidad f

neck [nɛk] n (Anat) cuello; (of animal) pescuezo ⊳ vi besuquearse; **~ and ~**

parejos; **necklace** ['nɛklɪs] n collar m; **necktie** n (US) corbata

nectarine ['nɛktərɪn] n nectarina

need [niːd] n (lack) escasez f, falta; (necessity) necesidad f ▷ vt (require) necesitar; **I ~ to do it** tengo que hacerlo; **you don't ~ to go** no hace falta que vayas

needle ['niːdl] n aguja ▷ vt (fig: inf) picar, fastidiar

needless ['niːdlɪs] adj innecesario; **~ to say** huelga decir que

needlework ['niːdlwəːk] n (activity) costura, labor f de aguja

needn't ['niːdnt] = need not

needy ['niːdɪ] adj necesitado

negative ['nɛgətɪv] n (Phot) negativo; (Ling) negación f ▷ adj negativo

neglect [nɪ'glɛkt] vt (one's duty) faltar a, no cumplir con; (child) descuidar, desatender ▷ n (state) abandono; (personal) dejadez f; (of child) desatención f; (of duty) incumplimiento

negotiate [nɪ'gəʊʃɪeɪt] vt (treaty, loan) negociar; (obstacle) franquear; (bend in road) tomar ▷ vi: **to ~ (with)** negociar (con)

negotiation [nɪgəʊʃɪ'eɪʃən] n negociación f; **negotiations** npl negociaciones

negotiator [nɪ'gəʊʃɪeɪtər] n negociador(a) m/f

neighbour, (US) **neighbor** ['neɪbər] n vecino/a; **neighbourhood,** (US) **neighborhood** n (place) vecindad f, barrio; (people) vecindario; **neighbouring,** (US) **neighboring** ['neɪbərɪŋ] adj vecino

neither ['naɪðər] adj n ▷ conj: **I didn't move and ~ did John** no me he movido, ni Juan tampoco ▷ pron ninguno ▷ adv: **~ good nor bad** ni bueno ni malo

neon ['niːɔn] n neón m

Nepal [nɪ'pɔːl] n Nepal m

nephew ['nɛvjuː] n sobrino

nerve [nəːv] n (Anat) nervio; (courage) valor m; (impudence) descaro, frescura; **nerves** (nervousness) nerviosismo msg, nervios mpl; **a fit of ~s** un ataque de nervios

nervous ['nəːvəs] adj (anxious) nervioso; (Anat) nervioso; (timid) tímido, miedoso; **nervous breakdown** n crisis f nerviosa

nest [nɛst] n (of bird) nido ▷ vi anidar

net [nɛt] n red f; (fabric) tul m ▷ adj (Comm) neto, líquido ▷ vt coger (SP) or agarrar (LAM) con red; (Sport) marcar; **netball** n balonred m

Netherlands ['nɛðələndz] npl: **the ~** los Países Bajos

nett [nɛt] adj = net

nettle ['nɛtl] n ortiga

network ['nɛtwəːk] n red f

neurotic [njuə'rɔtɪk] adj, n neurótico/a

neuter ['njuːtər] adj (Ling) neutro ▷ vt castrar, capar

neutral ['njuːtrəl] adj (person) neutral; (colour etc) neutro; (Elec) neutro ▷ n (Aut) punto muerto

never ['nɛvər] adv nunca, jamás; **I ~ went** no fui nunca; **~ in my life** jamás en la vida; see also **mind**; **never-ending** adj interminable, sin fin; **nevertheless** [nɛvəðə'lɛs] adv sin embargo, no obstante

new [njuː] adj nuevo; (recent) reciente; **New Age** n Nueva era; **newborn** adj recién nacido; **newcomer** ['njuːkʌmər] n recién venido or llegado; **newly** adv recién

news [njuːz] n noticias fpl; **a piece of ~** una noticia; **the ~** (Radio, TV) las noticias fpl; **news agency** n agencia de noticias; **newsagent** n (BRIT) vendedor(a) m/f de periódicos; **newscaster** n presentador(a) m/f, locutor(a) m/f; **news dealer** n (US) = newsagent; **newsletter** n hoja informativa, boletín m; **newspaper** n periódico, diario; **newsreader** n = newscaster

newt [njuːt] *n* tritón *m*

New Year *n* Año Nuevo; **New Year's Day** *n* Día *m* de Año Nuevo; **New Year's Eve** *n* Nochevieja

New Zealand [-'ziːlənd] *n* Nueva Zelanda (*SP*), Nueva Zelandia (*LAM*); **New Zealander** *n* neozelandés/esa *m/f*

next [nɛkst] *adj* (*house, room*) vecino, de al lado; (*meeting*) próximo; (*page*) siguiente ▷ *adv* después; **the ~ day** el día siguiente; **~ time** la próxima vez; **~ year** el año próximo *or* que viene; **~ to** junto a, al lado de; **~ to nothing** casi nada; **next door** *adv* en la casa de al lado ▷ *adj* vecino, de al lado; **next-of-kin** *n* pariente(s) *m(pl)* más cercano(s)

NHS *n abbr* (*BRIT*) = **National Health Service**

nibble ['nɪbl] *vt* mordisquear

nice [naɪs] *adj* (*likeable*) simpático; (*kind*) amable; (*pleasant*) agradable; (*attractive*) bonito; **nicely** *adv* amablemente; (*of health etc*) bien

niche [niːʃ] *n* (*Arch*) nicho, hornacina

nick [nɪk] *n* (*wound*) rasguño; (*cut, indentation*) mella, muesca ▷ *vt* (*inf*) birlar; **in the ~ of time** justo a tiempo

nickel ['nɪkl] *n* níquel *m*; (*US*) moneda de 5 centavos

nickname ['nɪkneɪm] *n* apodo, mote *m* ▷ *vt* apodar

nicotine ['nɪkətiːn] *n* nicotina

niece [niːs] *n* sobrina

Nigeria [naɪ'dʒɪərɪə] *n* Nigeria

night [naɪt] *n* noche *f*; (*evening*) tarde *f*; **the ~ before last** anteanoche; **at ~, by ~** de noche, por la noche; **night club** *n* club nocturno, discoteca; **nightdress** *n* (*BRIT*) camisón *m*

nightgown ['naɪtgaun], **nightie** ['naɪtɪ] (*BRIT*) *n* = **nightdress**

night: **night life** *n* vida nocturna; **nightly** *adj* de todas las noches ▷ *adv* todas las noches, cada noche; **nightmare** *n* pesadilla; **night school** *n* clase(s) *f(pl)* nocturna(s); **night shift**

n turno nocturno *or* de noche; **night-time** *n* noche *f*

nil [nɪl] *n* (*BRIT Sport*) cero, nada

nine [naɪn] *num* nueve; **nineteen** ['naɪn'tiːn] *num* diecinueve; **nineteenth** [naɪn'tiːnθ] *adj* decimonoveno, decimonono; **ninetieth** ['naɪntɪɪθ] *adj* nonagésimo; **ninety** *num* noventa

ninth [naɪnθ] *adj* noveno

nip [nɪp] *vt* (*pinch*) pellizcar; (*bite*) morder

nipple ['nɪpl] *n* (*Anat*) pezón *m*

nitrogen ['naɪtrədʒən] *n* nitrógeno

 KEYWORD

no [nəu] *adv* (*opposite of "yes"*) no; **are you coming? — no (I'm not)** ¿vienes? — no; **would you like some more? — no thank you** ¿quieres más? — no gracias

▶ *adj* **1** (*not any*): **I have no money/time/books** no tengo dinero/tiempo/libros; **no other man would have done it** ningún otro lo hubiera hecho

2: **"no entry"** "prohibido el paso"; **"no smoking"** "prohibido fumar"

▶ *n* (*pl* **noes**) no *m*

nobility [nəu'bɪlɪtɪ] *n* nobleza

noble ['nəubl] *adj* noble

nobody ['nəubədɪ] *pron* nadie

nod [nɔd] *vi* saludar con la cabeza; (*in agreement*) asentir con la cabeza ▷ *vt*: **to ~ one's head** inclinar la cabeza ▷ *n* inclinación *f* de cabeza; **nod off** *vi* cabecear

noise [nɔɪz] *n* ruido; (*din*) escándalo, estrépito; **noisy** *adj* ruidoso; (*child*) escandaloso

nominal ['nɔmɪnl] *adj* nominal

nominate ['nɔmɪneɪt] *vt* (*propose*) proponer; (*appoint*) nombrar; **nomination** [nɔmɪ'neɪʃən] *n* propuesta; nombramiento; **nominee** [nɔmɪ'niː] *n* candidato/a

none [nʌn] *pron* ninguno/a ▷ *adv* de ninguna manera; **~ of you** ninguno de vosotros; **I've ~ left** no me queda ninguno/a; **he's ~ the worse for it** no le ha perjudicado; **I have ~** no tengo ninguno; **~ at all** (*not one*) ni uno

nonetheless [nʌnðə'les] *adv* sin embargo, no obstante

non-fiction *n* no ficción *f*

nonsense ['nɒnsəns] *n* tonterías *fpl*, disparates *fpl*; **~!** ¡qué tonterías!

non-: **non-smoker** ['nɒn'sməukəʳ] *n* no fumador(a) *m/f*; **non-smoking** *adj* (de) no fumador; **non-stick** ['nɒn'stɪk] *adj* (*pan, surface*) antiadherente

noodles ['nu:dlz] *npl* tallarines *mpl*

noon [nu:n] *n* mediodía *m*

no-one ['nəuwʌn] *pron* = **nobody**

nor [nɔ:ʳ] *conj* = **neither** ▷ *adv* see **neither**

norm [nɔ:m] *n* norma

normal ['nɔ:ml] *adj* normal; **normally** *adv* normalmente

north [nɔ:θ] *n* norte *m* ▷ *adj* (del) norte ▷ *adv* al *or* hacia el norte; **North America** *n* América del Norte; **North American** *adj*, *n* norteamericano/a; **northbound** ['nɔ:θbaund] *adj* (*traffic*) que se dirige al norte; (*carriageway*) de dirección norte; **north-east** *n* nor(d) este *m*; **northeastern** *adj* nor(d)este, del nor(d)este; **northern** ['nɔ:ðən] *adj* norteño, del norte; **Northern Ireland** *n* Irlanda del Norte; **North Korea** *n* Corea del Norte; **North Pole** *n*: **the North Pole** el Polo Norte; **North Sea** *n*: **the North Sea** el mar del Norte; **north-west** *n* noroeste *m*; **northwestern** ['nɔ:θ'westən] *adj* noroeste, del noroeste

Norway ['nɔ:wei] *n* Noruega

Norwegian [nɔ:'wi:dʒən] *adj* noruego/a ▷ *n* noruego/a; (*Ling*) noruego

nose [nəuz] *n* (*Anat*) nariz *f*; (*Zool*) hocico; (*sense of smell*) olfato; **nose about, nose around** *vi* curiosear;

nosebleed *n* hemorragia nasal; **nosey** *adj* curioso, fisgón/ona

nostalgia [nɒs'tældʒiə] *n* nostalgia

nostalgic [nɒs'tældʒik] *adj* nostálgico

nostril ['nɒstril] *n* ventana *or* orificio de la nariz

nosy ['nəuzi] *adj* = **nosey**

not [nɒt] *adv* no; **~ that ...** no es que ...; **it's too late, isn't it?** es demasiado tarde, ¿verdad?; **why ~?** ¿por qué no?

notable ['nəutəbl] *adj* notable; **notably** *adv* especialmente

notch [nɒtʃ] *n* muesca, corte *m*

note [nəut] *n* (*Mus, record, letter*) nota; (*banknote*) billete *m*; (*tone*) tono ▷ *vt* (*observe*) notar, observar; (*write down*) apuntar, anotar; **notebook** *n* libreta, cuaderno; **noted** *adj* célebre, conocido; **notepad** *n* bloc *m*; **notepaper** *n* papel *m* para cartas

nothing ['nʌθiŋ] *n* nada; (*zero*) cero; **he does ~** no hace nada; **~ new** nada nuevo; **~ much** no mucho; **for ~** (*free*) gratis; (*in vain*) en balde

notice ['nəutis] *n* (*announcement*) anuncio; (*warning*) aviso; (*dismissal*) despido; (*resignation*) dimisión *f* ▷ *vt* (*observe*) notar, observar; **to bring sth to sb's ~** (*attention*) llamar la atención de algn sobre algo; **to take ~ of** hacer caso de, prestar atención a; **at short ~** con poca antelación; **until further ~** hasta nuevo aviso; **to hand in one's ~** dimitir, renunciar; **noticeable** *adj* evidente, obvio

▌ Be careful not to translate *notice* by the Spanish word *noticia*.

notify ['nəutifai] *vt*: **to ~ sb (of sth)** comunicar (algo) a algn

notion ['nəuʃən] *n* noción *f*, idea; (*opinion*) opinión *f*

notions ['nəuʃənz] *npl* (*us*) mercería

notorious [nəu'tɔ:riəs] *adj* notorio

notwithstanding [nɒtwiθ'stændiŋ] *adv* no obstante, sin embargo; **~ this** a pesar de esto

nought [nɔːt] n cero

noun [naun] n nombre m, sustantivo

nourish ['nʌrɪʃ] vt nutrir; (fig) alimentar; **nourishment** n alimento, sustento

Nov. abbr (= November) nov.

novel ['nɔvl] n novela ▷ adj (new) nuevo, original; (unexpected) insólito; **novelist** n novelista mf; **novelty** n novedad f

November [nəu'vɛmbəʳ] n noviembre m

novice ['nɔvɪs] n (Rel) novicio/a

now [nau] adv (at the present time) ahora; (these days) actualmente, hoy día ▷ conj: **~ (that)** ya que, ahora que; **right ~** ahora mismo; **by ~** ya; **I'll do it just ~** ahora mismo lo hago; **~ and then**, **~ and again** de vez en cuando; **from ~ on** de ahora en adelante; **nowadays** ['nauədeɪz] adv hoy (en) día, actualmente

nowhere ['nəuwɛəʳ] adv (direction) a ninguna parte; (location) en ninguna parte

nozzle ['nɔzl] n boquilla

nr abbr (BRIT) = **near**

nuclear ['njuːklɪəʳ] adj nuclear

nucleus (pl nuclei) ['njuːklɪəs, 'njuːklɪaɪ] n núcleo

nude [njuːd] adj, n desnudo m; **in the ~** desnudo

nudge [nʌdʒ] vt dar un codazo a

nudist ['njuːdɪst] n nudista mf

nudity ['njuːdɪtɪ] n desnudez f

nuisance ['njuːsns] n molestia, fastidio; (person) pesado, latoso; **what a ~!** ¡qué lata!

numb [nʌm] adj: **to be ~ with cold** estar entumecido de frío; **~ with fear/grief** paralizado de miedo/dolor

number ['nʌmbəʳ] n número; (quantity) cantidad f ▷ vt (pages etc) numerar, poner número a; (amount to) sumar, ascender a; **to be ~ed among** figurar entre; **a ~ of** varios, algunos; **they were ten in ~** eran diez; **number plate** n (BRIT) matrícula, placa;

Number Ten n (BRIT: 10 Downing Street) residencia del primer ministro

numerical [njuː'mɛrɪkl] adj numérico

numerous ['njuːmərəs] adj numeroso

nun [nʌn] n monja, religiosa

nurse [nəːs] n enfermero/a; (nanny) niñera ▷ vt (patient) cuidar, atender

nursery ['nəːsərɪ] n (institution) guardería infantil; (room) cuarto de los niños; (for plants) criadero, semillero; **nursery rhyme** n canción f infantil; **nursery school** n escuela infantil; **nursery slope** n (BRIT Ski) cuesta para principiantes

nursing ['nəːsɪŋ] n (profession) profesión f de enfermera; (care) asistencia, cuidado; **nursing home** n clínica de reposo

nurture ['nəːtʃəʳ] vt (child, plant) alimentar, nutrir

nut [nʌt] n (Tech) tuerca; (Bot) nuez f

nutmeg ['nʌtmɛg] n nuez f moscada

nutrient ['njuːtrɪənt] adj nutritivo ▷ n elemento nutritivo

nutrition [njuː'trɪʃən] n nutrición f, alimentación f

nutritious [njuː'trɪʃəs] adj nutritivo

nuts [nʌts] adj (inf) chiflado

NVQ n abbr (BRIT: = national vocational qualification) título de formación profesional

nylon ['naɪlɔn] n nilón m ▷ adj de nilón

n

O

oak [əuk] *n* roble *m* ▷ *adj* de roble
OAP *n abbr* (BRIT) = **old-age pensioner**
oar [ɔːʳ] *n* remo
oasis (*pl* **oases**) [əu'eisis, əu'eisi:z] *n* oasis *m inv*
oath [əuθ] *n* juramento; (*swear word*) palabrota; **on** (BRIT) *or* **under ~** bajo juramento
oatmeal ['əutmi:l] *n* harina de avena
oats [əuts] *npl* avena
obedience [ə'bi:diəns] *n* obediencia
obedient [ə'bi:diənt] *adj* obediente
obese [əu'bi:s] *adj* obeso
obesity [əu'bi:siti] *n* obesidad *f*
obey [ə'bei] *vt* obedecer; (*instructions*) cumplir
obituary [ə'bitjuəri] *n* necrología
object *n* ['ɔbdʒikt] objeto; (*purpose*) objeto, propósito; (*Ling*) complemento ▷ *vi* [əb'dʒɛkt]: **to ~ to** (*attitude*) estar en contra de; (*proposal*) oponerse a; **to ~ that** objetar que; **expense is no ~** no

importa lo que cueste; **I ~!** ¡protesto!;
objection [əb'dʒɛkʃən] *n* objeción *f*;
I have no objection to ... no tengo inconveniente en que ...; **objective** *adj, n* objetivo
obligation [ɔbli'geiʃən] *n* obligación *f*; (*debt*) deber *m*; **"without ~"** "sin compromiso"
obligatory [ə'bligətəri] *adj* obligatorio
oblige [ə'blaidʒ] *vt* (*do a favour for*) complacer, hacer un favor a; **to ~ sb to do sth** obligar a algn a hacer algo; **to be ~d to sb for sth** estarle agradecido a algn por algo
oblique [ə'bli:k] *adj* oblicuo; (*allusion*) indirecto
obliterate [ə'blitəreit] *vt* borrar
oblivious [ə'bliviəs] *adj*: **~ of** inconsciente de
oblong ['ɔblɔŋ] *adj* rectangular ▷ *n* rectángulo
obnoxious [əb'nɔkʃəs] *adj* odioso, detestable; (*smell*) nauseabundo
oboe ['əubəu] *n* oboe *m*
obscene [əb'si:n] *adj* obsceno
obscure [əb'skjuəʳ] *adj* oscuro ▷ *vt* oscurecer; (*hide: sun*) ocultar
observant [əb'zə:vnt] *adj* observador(a)
observation [ɔbzə'veiʃən] *n* (*Med*) observación *f*
observatory [əb'zə:vətri] *n* observatorio
observe [əb'zə:v] *vt* observar; (*rule*) cumplir; **observer** *n* observador(a) *m/f*
obsess [əb'sɛs] *vt* obsesionar; **obsession** [əb'sɛʃən] *n* obsesión *f*; **obsessive** *adj* obsesivo
obsolete ['ɔbsəli:t] *adj* obsoleto
obstacle ['ɔbstəkl] *n* obstáculo; (*nuisance*) estorbo
obstinate ['ɔbstinit] *adj* terco, obstinado
obstruct [əb'strʌkt] *vt* obstruir; (*hinder*) estorbar, obstaculizar; **obstruction** [əb'strʌkʃən] *n*

obstrucción f; (object) estorbo, obstáculo

obtain [əb'teɪn] vt obtener; (achieve) conseguir

obvious ['ɔbvɪəs] adj obvio, evidente; **obviously** adv evidentemente; **obviously not!** ¡por supuesto que no!

occasion [ə'keɪʒən] n oportunidad f, ocasión f; (event) acontecimiento; **occasional** adj poco frecuente, ocasional; **occasionally** adv de vez en cuando

occult [ɔ'kʌlt] adj oculto

occupant ['ɔkjupənt] n (of house) inquilino/a; (of boat, car) ocupante mf

occupation [ɔkju'peɪʃən] n (job) trabajo; (pastime) ocupaciones fpl

occupy ['ɔkjupaɪ] vt (seat, post, time) ocupar; (house) habitar; **to ~ o.s. with** or **by doing** (as job) dedicarse a hacer; (to pass time) entretenerse haciendo

occur [ə'kəːʳ] vi ocurrir, suceder; **to ~ to sb** ocurrírsele a algn; **occurrence** [ə'kʌrəns] n suceso

ocean ['əuʃən] n océano

o'clock [ə'klɔk] adv: **it is five ~** son las cinco

Oct. abbr (= October) oct.

October [ɔk'təubəʳ] n octubre m

octopus ['ɔktəpəs] n pulpo

odd [ɔd] adj (strange) extraño, raro; (number) impar; (sock, shoe etc) suelto; **60-~** 60 y pico; **at ~ times** de vez en cuando; **to be the ~ one out** estar de más; **oddly** adv extrañamente; **odds** npl (in betting) puntos mpl de ventaja; **it makes no odds** da lo mismo; **at odds** reñidos/as; **odds and ends** cachivaches mpl

odometer [ɔ'dɔmɪtəʳ] n (US) cuentakilómetros m inv

odour, (US) **odor** ['əudəʳ] n olor m; (unpleasant) hedor m

KEYWORD

of [ɔv, əv] prep **1** de; **a friend of ours** un amigo nuestro; **a boy of 10** un chico de 10 años; **that was kind of you** eso fue muy amable de tu parte **2** (expressing quantity, amount, dates etc) de; **a kilo of flour** un kilo de harina; **there were three of them** había tres; **three of us went** tres de nosotros fuimos; **the 5th of July** el 5 de julio **3** (from, out of) de; **made of wood** (hecho) de madera

off [ɔf] adj, adv (engine, light) apagado; (tap) cerrado; (BRIT: food: bad) pasado, malo; (: milk) cortado; (cancelled) suspendido ▷ prep de; **to be ~** (leave) irse, marcharse; **to be ~ sick** estar enfermo or de baja; **a day ~** un día libre; **to have an ~ day** tener un mal día; **he had his coat ~** se había quitado el abrigo; **10% ~** (Comm) (con el) 10% de descuento; **5 km ~ (the road)** a 5 km (de la carretera); **~ the coast** frente a la costa; **I'm ~ meat** (no longer eat/like it) paso de la carne; **on the ~ chance** por si acaso; **on and ~** de vez en cuando

offence, (US) **offense** [ə'fɛns] n (crime) delito; **to take ~ at** ofenderse por

offend [ə'fɛnd] vt (person) ofender; **offender** n delincuente mf

offense [ə'fɛns] n (US) = **offence**

offensive [ə'fɛnsɪv] adj ofensivo; (smell etc) repugnante ▷ n (Mil) ofensiva

offer ['ɔfəʳ] n oferta, ofrecimiento; (proposal) propuesta ▷ vt ofrecer; **"on ~"** (Comm) "en oferta"

offhand [ɔf'hænd] adj informal ▷ adv de improviso

office ['ɔfɪs] n (place) oficina; (room) despacho; (position) cargo, oficio; **doctor's ~** (US) consultorio; **to take ~** entrar en funciones; **office block,** (US) **office building** n bloque m de oficinas; **office hours** npl horas fpl de oficina; (US Med) horas fpl de consulta

officer ['ɔfɪsəʳ] n (Mil etc) oficial mf; (of organization) director(a) m/f; (also: **police ~**) agente mf de policía

o

office worker n oficinista mf
official [əˈfɪʃl] adj oficial, autorizado
▷ n funcionario/a
off-licence n (BRIT: shop) tienda de bebidas alcohólicas

○ **OFF-LICENCE**
○
○ En el Reino Unido una off-licence
○ es una tienda especializada en la
○ venta de bebidas alcohólicas para el
○ consumo fuera del establecimiento.
○ De ahí su nombre, pues se necesita
○ un permiso especial para tal venta,
○ que está estrictamente regulada.
○ Suelen vender además bebidas sin
○ alcohol, tabaco, chocolate, patatas
○ fritas etc y a menudo son parte de
○ grandes cadenas nacionales.

off: off-peak adj (electricity) de banda económica; (ticket) billete de precio reducido por viajar fuera de las horas punta; **off-putting** adj (BRIT: person) poco amable, difícil; (remark) desalentador(a); **off-season** [ˈɔfsiːzn] adj, adv fuera de temporada; **offset** [ˈɔfsɛt] vt (irreg: like **set**) contrarrestar, compensar; **offshore** [ɔfˈʃɔːʳ] adj (breeze, island) costero; (fishing) de bajura; **offside** [ˈɔfsaɪd] adj (Sport) fuera de juego; (Aut: in UK) del lado derecho; (: in US, Europe etc) del lado izquierdo
offspring [ˈɔfsprɪŋ] n descendencia
often [ˈɔfn] adv a menudo, con frecuencia; **how ~ do you go?** ¿cada cuánto vas?
oh [əu] excl ¡ah!
oil [ɔɪl] n aceite m; (petroleum) petróleo ▷ vt engrasar; **oil filter** n (Aut) filtro de aceite; **oil painting** n pintura al óleo; **oil refinery** n refinería de petróleo; **oil rig** n torre f de perforación; **oil slick** n marea negra; **oil tanker** n petrolero; (truck) camión m cisterna; **oil well** n pozo (de petróleo); **oily** adj aceitoso; (food) grasiento

ointment [ˈɔɪntmənt] n ungüento
O.K., okay [ˈəuˈkeɪ] excl O.K., ¡está bien!, ¡vale! ▷ adj bien ▷ vt dar el visto bueno a
old [əuld] adj viejo; (former) antiguo; **how ~ are you?** ¿cuántos años tienes?, ¿qué edad tienes?; **he's 10 years ~** tiene 10 años; **~er brother** hermano mayor; **old age** n vejez f; **old-age pension** n (BRIT) jubilación f, pensión f; **old-age pensioner** n (BRIT) jubilado/a; **old-fashioned** adj anticuado, pasado de moda; **old people's home** n (esp BRIT) residencia f de ancianos
olive [ˈɔlɪv] n (fruit) aceituna; (tree) olivo ▷ adj (also: **~-green**) verde oliva inv; **olive oil** n aceite m de oliva
Olympic [əuˈlɪmpɪk] adj olímpico; **the ~ Games, the ~s** n pl las Olimpiadas
omelet(te) [ˈɔmlɪt] n tortilla, tortilla de huevo (LAM)
omen [ˈəumən] n presagio
ominous [ˈɔmɪnəs] adj de mal agüero, amenazador(a)
omit [əuˈmɪt] vt omitir

○ **KEYWORD**

on [ɔn] prep 1 (indicating position) en; sobre; **on the wall** en la pared; **it's on the table** está sobre or en la mesa; **on the left** a la izquierda
2 (indicating means, method, condition etc): **on foot** a pie; **on the train/plane** (go) en tren/avión; (be) en el tren/el avión; **on the radio/television** por or en la radio/televisión; **on the telephone** al teléfono; **to be on drugs** drogarse; (Med) estar a tratamiento; **to be on holiday/business** estar de vacaciones/en viaje de negocios
3 (referring to time): **on Friday** el viernes; **on Fridays** los viernes; **on June 20th** el 20 de junio; **a week on Friday** del viernes en una semana;

on arrival al llegar; **on seeing this** al ver esto

4 (*about, concerning*) sobre, acerca de; **a book on physics** un libro de *or* sobre física

▶ *adv* **1** (*referring to dress*): **to have one's coat on** tener *or* llevar el abrigo puesto; **she put her gloves on** se puso los guantes

2 (*referring to covering*): **"screw the lid on tightly"** "cerrar bien la tapa"

3 (*further, continuously*): **to walk/run on** seguir caminando/corriendo *etc*

▶ *adj* **1** (*functioning, in operation: machine, radio, TV, light*) encendido (*SP*), prendido (*LAM*); (: *tap*) abierto; (: *brakes*) echado, puesto; **is the meeting still on?** (*in progress*) ¿todavía continúa la reunión?; (*not cancelled*) ¿va a haber reunión al fin?; **there's a good film on at the cinema** ponen una buena película en el cine

2: **that's not on!** (*inf: not possible*) ¡eso ni hablar!; (: *not acceptable*) ¡eso no se hace!

once [wʌns] *adv* una vez; (*formerly*) antiguamente ▷ *conj* una vez que; **~ he had left/it was done** una vez que se había marchado/se hizo; **at ~** en seguida, inmediatamente; (*simultaneously*) a la vez; **~ a week** una vez a la semana; **~ more** otra vez; **~ and for all** de una vez por todas; **~ upon a time** érase una vez

oncoming ['ɔnkʌmɪŋ] *adj* (*traffic*) que viene de frente

KEYWORD

one [wʌn] *num* un/una; **one hundred and fifty** ciento cincuenta; **one by one** uno a uno

▶ *adj* **1** (*sole*) único; **the one book which** el único libro que; **the one man who** el único que

2 (*same*) mismo/a; **they came in the one car** vinieron en un solo coche

▶ *pron* **1**: **this one** este, éste; **that one** ese, ése; (*more remote*) aquel, aquél; **I've already got (a red) one** ya tengo uno/a (rojo/a); **one by one** uno/a por uno/a

2: **one another** (*us*) nos; (*you*) os (*SP*); (*you: formal, them*) se; **do you two ever see one another?** ¿os veis alguna vez? (*SP*), ¿se ven alguna vez?; **the two boys didn't dare look at one another** los dos chicos no se atrevieron a mirarse (el uno al otro); **they all kissed one another** se besaron unos a otros

3 (*impers*): **one never knows** nunca se sabe; **to cut one's finger** cortarse el dedo; **one needs to eat** hay que comer

one: one-off *n* (*BRIT inf: event*) caso especial; **oneself** *pron* (*reflexive*) se; (*after prep*) sí; (*emphatic*) uno/a mismo/a; **to hurt oneself** hacerse daño; **to keep sth for oneself** guardarse algo; **to talk to oneself** hablar solo; **one-shot** [wʌn'ʃɔt] *n* (*US*) = **one-off**; **one-sided** *adj* (*argument*) parcial; (*decision, view*) unilateral; (*game, contest*) desigual; **one-to-one** *adj* (*relationship*) individualizado; **one-way** *adj* (*street, traffic*) de dirección única

ongoing ['ɔngəʊɪŋ] *adj* continuo

onion ['ʌnjən] *n* cebolla

online [ɔn'laɪn] *adj, adv* (*Comput*) en línea

onlooker ['ɔnlʊkəʳ] *n* espectador(a) *m/f*

only ['əʊnlɪ] *adv* solamente, solo, sólo (*to avoid confusion with adj*) ▷ *adj* único, solo ▷ *conj* solamente que, pero; **an ~ child** un hijo único; **not ~ ... but also ...** no sólo ... sino también ...

on-screen [ɔn'skriːn] *adj* (*Comput etc*) en pantalla; (*romance, kiss*) cinematográfico

onset ['ɔnsɛt] *n* comienzo

onto ['ɔntʊ] *prep* = **on to**

onward(s) ['ɒnwəd(z)] adv (move) (hacia) adelante; **from that time onward** desde entonces en adelante

oops [ups] excl (also: **~-a-daisy!**) ¡huy!

ooze [uːz] vi rezumar

opaque [əu'peɪk] adj opaco

open ['əupn] adj abierto; (car) descubierto; (road, view) despejado; (meeting) público; (admiration) manifiesto ▷ vt abrir ▷ vi abrirse; (book etc: commence) comenzar; **in the ~ (air)** al aire libre; **open up** vt abrir; (blocked road) despejar ▷ vi abrirse; **opening** n abertura; (beginning) comienzo; (opportunity) oportunidad f; **opening hours** npl horario de apertura; **open learning** n enseñanza flexible a tiempo parcial; **openly** adv abiertamente; **open-minded** adj de amplias miras, sin prejuicios; **open-necked** adj sin corbata; **open-plan** adj diáfano, sin tabiques; **Open University** n (BRIT) ≈ Universidad f Nacional de Enseñanza a Distancia, UNED f

○ **OPEN UNIVERSITY**
○
○ La Open University, fundada en 1969,
○ está especializada en impartir
○ cursos a distancia y a tiempo
○ parcial con sus propios materiales
○ de apoyo diseñados para tal fin,
○ entre ellos programas de radio y
○ televisión emitidos por la BBC. Los
○ trabajos se envían por correo y se
○ complementan con la asistencia
○ obligatoria a cursos de verano. Para
○ obtener la licenciatura es necesario
○ estudiar un mínimo de módulos y
○ alcanzar un determinado número
○ de créditos.

opera ['ɒpərə] n ópera; **opera house** n teatro de la ópera; **opera singer** n cantante mf de ópera

operate ['ɒpəreɪt] vt (machine) hacer funcionar; (company) dirigir ▷ vi funcionar; **to ~ on sb** (Med) operar a algn; **operating theatre,** (US) **operating room** n quirófano, sala de operaciones

operation [ɒpə'reɪʃən] n operación f; (of machine) funcionamiento; **to be in ~** estar funcionando or en funcionamiento; **to have an ~** (Med) ser operado; **operational** adj operacional, en buen estado

operative ['ɒpərətɪv] adj en vigor

operator ['ɒpəreɪtər] n (of machine) operario/a, maquinista mf; (Tel) operador(a) m/f, telefonista mf

opinion [ə'pɪnjən] n opinión f; **in my ~** en mi opinión, a mi juicio; **opinion poll** n encuesta, sondeo

opponent [ə'pəunənt] n adversario/a, contrincante mf

opportunity [ɒpə'tjuːnɪtɪ] n oportunidad f; **to take the ~ to do** or **of doing** aprovechar la ocasión para hacer

oppose [ə'pəuz] vt oponerse a; **to be ~d to sth** oponerse a algo; **as ~d to** a diferencia de

opposite ['ɒpəzɪt] adj opuesto, contrario; (house etc) de enfrente ▷ adv en frente ▷ prep en frente de, frente a ▷ n lo contrario

opposition [ɒpə'zɪʃən] n oposición f

oppress [ə'prɛs] vt oprimir

opt [ɒpt] vi: **to ~ for** optar por; **to ~ to do** optar por hacer; **opt out** vi: **to ~ out of** optar por no hacer

optician [ɒp'tɪʃən] n óptico/a

optimism ['ɒptɪmɪzəm] n optimismo

optimist ['ɒptɪmɪst] n optimista mf; **optimistic** [ɒptɪ'mɪstɪk] adj optimista

optimum ['ɒptɪməm] adj óptimo

option ['ɒpʃən] n opción f; **optional** adj opcional

or [ɔːr] conj o; (before o, ho) u; (with negative): **he hasn't seen or heard anything** no ha visto ni oído nada; **or else** si no

oral ['ɔːrəl] *adj* oral ▷ *n* examen *m* oral

orange ['ɔrɪndʒ] *n* (*fruit*) naranja ▷ *adj* (de color) naranja *inv*; **orange juice** *n* jugo *m* de naranja, zumo *m* de naranja (*SP*); **orange squash** *n* bebida de naranja

orbit ['ɔːbɪt] *n* órbita ▷ *vt, vi* orbitar

orchard ['ɔːtʃəd] *n* huerto

orchestra ['ɔːkɪstrə] *n* orquesta; (*US: seating*) platea

orchid ['ɔːkɪd] *n* orquídea

ordeal [ɔːˈdiːl] *n* experiencia terrible

order ['ɔːdəʳ] *n* orden *m*; (*command*) orden *f*; (*state*) estado; (*Comm*) pedido ▷ *vt* (*also:* **put in ~**) ordenar, poner en orden; (*Comm*) pedir; (*command*) mandar, ordenar; **in ~** en orden; (*of document*) en regla; **in (working) ~** en funcionamiento; **to be out of ~** estar desordenado; (*not working*) no funcionar; **in ~ to do** para hacer; **on ~** (*Comm*) pedido; **to ~ sb to do sth** mandar a algn hacer algo; **order form** *n* hoja de pedido; **orderly** *n* (*Mil*) ordenanza *m*; (*Med*) auxiliar *mf* (de hospital) ▷ *adj* ordenado

ordinary ['ɔːdnrɪ] *adj* corriente, normal; (*pej*) común y corriente; **out of the ~** fuera de lo común

ore [ɔːʳ] *n* mineral *m*

oregano [ɔrɪˈgɑːnəu] *n* orégano

organ ['ɔːgən] *n* órgano

organic [ɔːˈgænɪk] *adj* orgánico

organism *n* organismo

organization [ɔːgənaɪˈzeɪʃən] *n* organización *f*

organize ['ɔːgənaɪz] *vt* organizar; **organized** ['ɔːgənaɪzd] *adj* organizado; **to get organized** organizarse; **organizer** *n* organizador(a) *m/f*

orgasm ['ɔːgæzəm] *n* orgasmo

orgy ['ɔːdʒɪ] *n* orgía

oriental [ɔːrɪˈɛntl] *adj* oriental

orientation [ɔːrɪenˈteɪʃən] *n* orientación *f*

origin ['ɔrɪdʒɪn] *n* origen *m*

original [əˈrɪdʒɪnl] *adj* original; (*first*) primero; (*earlier*) primitivo ▷ *n* original *m*; **originally** *adv* al principio

originate [əˈrɪdʒɪneɪt] *vi*: **to ~ from, to ~ in** surgir de, tener su origen en

Orkneys ['ɔːknɪz] *npl*: **the ~** (*also:* **the Orkney Islands**) las Orcadas

ornament ['ɔːnəmənt] *n* adorno; (*trinket*) chuchería; **ornamental** [ɔːnəˈmɛntl] *adj* decorativo, de adorno

ornate [ɔːˈneɪt] *adj* recargado

orphan ['ɔːfn] *n* huérfano/a

orthodox ['ɔːθədɔks] *adj* ortodoxo

orthopaedic, (*US*) **orthopedic** [ɔːθəˈpiːdɪk] *adj* ortopédico

osteopath ['ɔstɪəpæθ] *n* osteópata *mf*

ostrich ['ɔstrɪtʃ] *n* avestruz *m*

other ['ʌðəʳ] *adj* otro ▷ *pron*: **the ~ one** el/la otro/a; **~ than** aparte de; **otherwise** *adv, conj* de otra manera; (*if not*) si no

otter ['ɔtəʳ] *n* nutria

ouch [autʃ] *excl* ¡ay!

ought [ɔːt] *aux vb*: **I ~ to do it** debería hacerlo; **this ~ to have been corrected** esto debiera de haberse corregido; **he ~ to win** (*probability*) debiera ganar

ounce [auns] *n* onza (=28.35g: 16oz = 1lb)

our ['auəʳ] *adj* nuestro; *see also* **my**; **ours** *pron* (el) nuestro/(la) nuestra *etc*; *see also* **mine**; **ourselves** *pron pl* (*reflexive, after prep*) nosotros/as; (*emphatic*) nosotros /as mismos/as; *see also* **oneself**

oust [aust] *vt* desalojar

out [aut] *adv* fuera, afuera; (*not at home*) fuera (de casa); (*light, fire*) apagado; **~ there** allí (fuera); **he's ~** (*absent*) no está, ha salido; **to be ~ in one's calculations** equivocarse (en sus cálculos); **to run ~** salir corriendo; **~ loud** en alta voz; **~ of** (*outside*) fuera de; (*because of: anger etc*) por; **~ of petrol** sin gasolina;

"~ of order" "no funciona"; **outback** n interior m; **outbound** adj (flight) de salida; (flight: not return) de ida; **outbound from/for** con salida de/ hacia; **outbreak** n (of war) comienzo; (of disease) epidemia; (of violence etc) ola; **outburst** n explosión f, arranque m; **outcast** n paria mf; **outcome** n resultado; **outcry** n protestas fpl; **outdated** adj anticuado; **outdoor** adj al aire libre; (clothes) de calle; **outdoors** adv al aire libre

outer ['autə'] adj exterior, externo; **outer space** n espacio exterior

outfit n (clothes) traje m

out: outgoing adj (president, tenant) saliente; (character) extrovertido; **outgoings** npl (BRIT) gastos mpl; **outhouse** n dependencia; **outing** n excursión f, paseo; **outlaw** n proscrito/a ▷ vt (practice) declarar ilegal; **outlay** n inversión f; **outlet** n salida; (of pipe) desagüe m; (US Elec) toma de corriente; (also: **retail outlet**) punto de venta; **outline** n (shape) contorno, perfil m; (sketch, plan) esbozo ▷ vt (plan etc) esbozar; **in outline** (fig) a grandes rasgos; **outlook** n (fig: prospects) perspectivas fpl; (: for weather) pronóstico; (: opinion) punto de vista; **outnumber** vt exceder or superar en número; **out-of-date** adj (passport) caducado; (clothes, customs) pasado de moda; **out-of-doors** adv al aire libre; **out-of-the-way** adj apartado; **out-of-town** adj (shopping centre etc) en las afueras; **outpatient** n paciente mf externo/a; **outpost** n puesto avanzado; **output** n (volumen m de) producción f, rendimiento; (: Comput) salida

outrage ['autreɪdʒ] n escándalo; (atrocity) atrocidad f ▷ vt ultrajar; **outrageous** [aut'reɪdʒəs] adj (clothes) extravagante; (behaviour) escandaloso

outright adv [aut'raɪt] (ask, deny) francamente; (refuse) rotundamente;

(win) de manera absoluta; (be killed) en el acto ▷ adj ['autraɪt] completo; (refusal) rotundo

outset ['autset] n principio

outside [aut'saɪd] n exterior m ▷ adj exterior, externo ▷ adv fuera ▷ prep fuera de; (beyond) más allá de; **at the ~** (fig) a lo sumo; **outside lane** n (Aut: in Britain) carril m de la derecha; (: in US, Europe etc) carril m de la izquierda; **outside line** n (Tel) línea (exterior); **outsider** n (stranger) forastero/a

out: outsize adj (clothes) de talla grande; **outskirts** npl alrededores mpl, afueras fpl; **outspoken** adj muy franco; **outstanding** adj excepcional, destacado; (unfinished) pendiente

outward ['autwəd] adj externo; (journey) de ida

outweigh [aut'weɪ] vt pesar más que

oval ['əuvl] adj ovalado ▷ n óvalo

ovary ['əuvərɪ] n ovario

oven ['ʌvn] n horno; **oven glove** n guante m para el horno, manopla para el horno; **ovenproof** adj resistente al horno; **oven-ready** adj listo para el horno

over ['əuvə'] adv encima, por encima ▷ adj (finished) terminado; (surplus) de sobra ▷ prep (por) encima de; (above) sobre; (on the other side of) al otro lado de; (more than) más de; (during) durante; **~ here** (por) aquí; **~ there** (por) allí or allá; **all ~** (everywhere) por todas partes; **~ and ~ (again)** una y otra vez; **~ and above** además de; **to ask sb ~** invitar a algn a casa; **to bend ~** inclinarse

overall ['əuvərɔːl] adj (length) total; (study) de conjunto ▷ adv ['əuvər'ɔːl] en conjunto ▷ n (BRIT) guardapolvo; **overalls** npl mono sg, overol msg (LAM)

over: overboard adv (Naut) por la borda; **overcame** pt of **overcome**; **overcast** adj encapotado; **overcharge** vt: **to overcharge sb** cobrar un precio excesivo a algn; **overcoat** n abrigo; **overcome** vt (*irreg: like* **come**) vencer; (*difficulty*) superar; **overcrowded** *adj* atestado de gente; (*city, country*) superpoblado; **overdo** *vt* (*irreg: like* **do**) exagerar; (*overcook*) cocer demasiado; **to overdo it** (*work etc*) pasarse; **overdone** *adj* (*vegetables*) recocido; (*steak*) demasiado hecho; **overdose** *n* sobredosis *f inv*; **overdraft** *n* saldo deudor; **overdrawn** *adj* (*account*) en descubierto; **overdue** *adj* retrasado; **overestimate** *vt* sobreestimar

overflow [əuvə'fləu] *vi* desbordarse ▷ *n* ['əuvəfləu] (*also:* **~ pipe**) (cañería de) desagüe *m*

over: overgrown [əuvə'grəun] *adj* (*garden*) cubierto de hierba; **overhaul** *vt* [əuvə'hɔːl] revisar, repasar ▷ *n* ['əuvəhɔːl] revisión *f*

overhead *adv* [əuvə'hɛd] por arriba *or* encima ▷ *adj* ['əuvəhɛd] (*cable*) aéreo ▷ *n* ['əuvəhɛd] (*us*) = **overheads**; **overhead projector** *n* retroproyector; **overheads** *npl* gastos *mpl* generales

over: overhear *vt* (*irreg: like* **hear**) oír por casualidad; **overheat** *vi* (*engine*) recalentarse; **overland** *adj*, *adv* por tierra; **overlap** *vi* [əuvə'læp] superponerse; **overleaf** *adv* al dorso; **overload** *vt* sobrecargar; **overlook** *vt* (*have view of*) dar a, tener vistas a; (*miss*) pasar por alto; (*excuse*) perdonar

overnight [əuvə'naɪt] *adv* durante la noche; (*fig*) de la noche a la mañana ▷ *adj* de noche; **to stay ~** pasar la noche; **overnight bag** *n* fin *m* de semana, neceser *m* de viaje

overpass *n* (*us*) paso elevado *or* a desnivel

overpower [əuvə'pauə'] *vt* dominar; (*fig*) embargar; **overpowering** *adj* (*heat*) agobiante; (*smell*) penetrante

over: overreact [əuvərɪ'ækt] *vi* reaccionar de manera exagerada; **overrule** *vt* (*decision*) anular; (*claim*) denegar; **overrun** *vt* (*irreg: like* **run**: *country*) invadir; (: *time limit*) rebasar,

exceder; **overseas** [əuvə'siːz] *adv* (*abroad*) en el extranjero ▷ *adj* (*trade*) exterior; (*visitor*) extranjero; **oversee** (*irreg: like* **see**) *vt* supervisar; **overshadow** *vt* (*fig*) eclipsar; **to be overshadowed by** estar a la sombra de; **oversight** *n* descuido; **oversleep** *vi* (*irreg: like* **sleep**) dormir más de la cuenta, no despertarse a tiempo; **overspend** *vi* (*irreg: like* **spend**) gastar más de la cuenta; **we have overspent by five dollars** hemos excedido el presupuesto en cinco dólares

overt [əu'vəːt] *adj* abierto

over: overtake *vt* (*irreg: like* **take**) sobrepasar; (BRIT Aut) adelantar; **overthrow** *vt* (*irreg: like* **throw**: *government*) derrocar; **overtime** *n* horas *fpl* extraordinarias; **overtook** [əuvə'tuk] *pt of* **overtake**; **overturn** *vt* volcar; (*fig: plan*) desbaratar; (: *government*) derrocar ▷ *vi* volcar; **overweight** *adj* demasiado gordo *or* pesado; **overwhelm** *vt* aplastar; **overwhelming** *adj* (*victory, defeat*) arrollador(a); (*desire*) irresistible

owe [əu] *vt* deber; **to ~ sb sth, to ~ sth to sb** deber algo a algn; **owing to** *prep* debido a, por causa de

owl [aul] *n* búho; (*also:* **barn ~**) lechuza

own [əun] *vt* tener, poseer ▷ *adj* propio; **a room of my ~** mi propia habitación; **to get one's ~ back** tomarse la revancha; **on one's ~** solo, a solas; **own up** *vi* confesar; **owner** *n* dueño/a; **ownership** *n* posesión *f*

ox (*pl* **oxen**) [ɔks, 'ɔksn] *n* buey *m*

Oxbridge ['ɔksbrɪdʒ] *n universidades de Oxford y Cambridge*

oxen ['ɔksən] *npl of* **ox**

oxygen ['ɔksɪdʒən] *n* oxígeno

oyster ['ɔɪstə'] *n* ostra

oz. *abbr* = **ounce**

ozone ['əuzəun] *n* ozono; **ozone-friendly** *adj* que no daña la capa de ozono; **ozone layer** *n* capa de ozono

o

P

p *abbr* (*BRIT*) = **penny; pence**
PA *n abbr* = **personal assistant; public address system**
p.a. *abbr* = **per annum**
pace [peɪs] *n* paso ▷ *vi*: **to ~ up and down** pasearse de un lado a otro; **to keep ~ with** llevar el mismo paso que; **pacemaker** *n* (*Med*) marcapasos *m inv*; (*Sport: also*: **pacesetter**) liebre *f*
pacific [pə'sɪfɪk] *adj* pacífico ▷ *n*: **the P~ (Ocean)** el (océano) Pacífico
pacifier ['pæsɪfaɪə'] *n* (*US: dummy*) chupete *m*
pack [pæk] *n* (*packet*) paquete *m*; (*of hounds*) jauría; (*of people*) manada; (*of thieves etc*) banda; (*of cards*) baraja; (*bundle*) fardo; (*US: of cigarettes*) paquete *m* ▷ *vt* (*fill*) llenar; (*in suitcase etc*) meter, poner; (*cram*) llenar, atestar; **to ~ (one's bags)** hacer las maletas; **to ~ sb off** (*inf*) despachar a algn; **pack in** *vi* (*inf: break down*) estropearse ▷ *vt* (*inf*) dejar; **~ it in!**

¡para!, ¡basta ya!; **pack up** *vi* (*inf: machine*) estropearse; (*person*) irse ▷ *vt* (*belongings, clothes*) recoger; (*goods, presents*) empaquetar, envolver
package ['pækɪdʒ] *n* paquete *m*; (*bulky*) bulto; (*also*: **~ deal**) acuerdo global ▷ *vt* (*Comm: goods*) envasar, embalar; **package holiday** *n* viaje *m* organizado (con todo incluido); **package tour** *n* viaje *m* organizado
packaging ['pækɪdʒɪŋ] *n* envase *m*
packed [pækt] *adj* abarrotado; **packed lunch** *n* almuerzo frío
packet ['pækɪt] *n* paquete *m*
packing ['pækɪŋ] *n* embalaje *m*
pact [pækt] *n* pacto
pad [pæd] *n* (*of paper*) bloc *m*; (*cushion*) cojinete *m*; (*inf: flat*) casa ▷ *vt* rellenar; **padded** *adj* (*jacket*) acolchado; (*bra*) reforzado
paddle ['pædl] *n* (*oar*) canalete *m*, pala; (*US: for table tennis*) pala ▷ *vt* remar ▷ *vi* (*with feet*) chapotear; **paddling pool** *n* (*BRIT*) piscina para niños
paddock ['pædək] *n* (*field*) potrero
padlock ['pædlɔk] *n* candado
paedophile, (*US*) **pedophile** ['piːdəʊfaɪl] *adj* de pedófilos ▷ *n* pedófilo/a
page [peɪdʒ] *n* página; (*of newspaper*) plana; (*also*: **~ boy**) paje *m* ▷ *vt* (*in hotel etc*) llamar por altavoz a
pager ['peɪdʒə'] *n* busca *m*
paid [peɪd] *pt, pp of* **pay** ▷ *adj* (*work*) remunerado; (*holiday*) pagado; (*official*) a sueldo; **to put ~ to** (*BRIT*) acabar con
pain [peɪn] *n* dolor *m*; **to be in ~** sufrir *see also* **pains**; **painful** *adj* doloroso; (*difficult*) penoso; (*disagreeable*) desagradable; **painkiller** *n* analgésico; **pains** *npl*: **to take pains to do sth** tomarse el trabajo de hacer algo; **painstaking** ['peɪnzteɪkɪŋ] *adj* (*person*) concienzudo, esmerado
paint [peɪnt] *n* pintura ▷ *vt* pintar; **to ~ the door blue** pintar la puerta

de azul; **paintbrush** n (artist's) pincel m; (decorator's) brocha; **painter** n pintor(a) m/f; **painting** n pintura

pair [pɛəʳ] n (of shoes, gloves etc) par m; (of people) pareja; **a ~ of scissors** unas tijeras; **a ~ of trousers** unos pantalones, un pantalón

pajamas [pɪˈdʒɑːməz] npl (US) pijama msg

Pakistan [pɑːkɪˈstɑːn] n Paquistán m; **Pakistani** adj, n paquistaní mf

pal [pæl] n (inf) amiguete/a m/f, colega mf

palace [ˈpæləs] n palacio

pale [peɪl] adj pálido; (colour) claro ▷ n: **to be beyond the ~** pasarse de la raya

Palestine [ˈpælɪstaɪn] n Palestina; **Palestinian** [pælɪsˈtɪnɪən] adj, n palestino/a

palm [pɑːm] n (Anat) palma; (also: **~ tree**) palmera, palma ▷ vt: **to ~ sth off on sb** (BRIT inf) endosarle algo a algn

pamper [ˈpæmpəʳ] vt mimar

pamphlet [ˈpæmflət] n folleto

pan [pæn] n (also: **sauce~**) cacerola, cazuela, olla; (also: **frying ~**) sartén f

pancake [ˈpænkeɪk] n crepe f

panda [ˈpændə] n panda m

pandemic [pænˈdɛmɪk] n pandemia; **flu ~** pandemia de gripe

pane [peɪn] n cristal m

panel [ˈpænl] n (of wood) panel m; (Radio, TV) panel m de invitados

panhandler [ˈpænhændləʳ] n (US inf) mendigo/a

panic [ˈpænɪk] n pánico ▷ vi dejarse llevar por el pánico

panorama [pænəˈrɑːmə] n panorama m

pansy [ˈpænzɪ] n (Bot) pensamiento; (inf!) maricón m

pant [pænt] vi jadear

panther [ˈpænθəʳ] n pantera

panties [ˈpæntɪz] npl bragas fpl

pantomime [ˈpæntəmaɪm] n (BRIT) representación f musical navideña

○ **PANTOMIME**
○
○ En época navideña los teatros
○ británicos ponen en escena
○ representaciones llamadas
○ pantomimes, versiones libres
○ de cuentos tradicionales como
○ Aladino o El gato con botas. En ella
○ nunca faltan personajes como la
○ dama (dame), papel que siempre
○ interpreta un actor; el protagonista
○ joven (principal boy), normalmente
○ interpretado por una actriz, y el
○ malvado (villain). Es un espectáculo
○ familiar dirigido a los niños pero
○ con grandes dosis de humor para
○ adultos en el que se alienta la
○ participación del público.

pants [pænts] npl (BRIT: underwear: woman's) bragas fpl; (: man's) calzoncillos mpl; (US: trousers) pantalones mpl

paper [ˈpeɪpəʳ] n papel m; (also: **news~**) periódico, diario; (study, article) artículo; (exam) examen m ▷ adj de papel ▷ vt empapelar; **(identity) ~s** npl papeles mpl, documentos mpl; **paperback** n libro de bolsillo; **paper bag** n bolsa de papel; **paper clip** n clip m; **paper shop** n (BRIT) tienda de periódicos; **paperwork** n trabajo administrativo

paprika [ˈpæprɪkə] n pimentón m

par [pɑːʳ] n par f; (Golf) par m; **to be on a ~ with** estar a la par con

paracetamol [pærəˈsiːtəmɔl] n (BRIT) paracetamol m

parachute [ˈpærəʃuːt] n paracaídas m inv

parade [pəˈreɪd] n desfile m ▷ vt (show off) hacer alarde de ▷ vi desfilar; (Mil) pasar revista

paradise [ˈpærədaɪs] n paraíso

paradox [ˈpærədɔks] n paradoja

paraffin [ˈpærəfɪn] n (BRIT): **~ (oil)** parafina

paragraph [ˈpærəgrɑːf] n párrafo

p

parallel ['pærəlɛl] adj: ~ **(with/to)**
en paralelo (con/a); (fig) semejante
(a) ▷ n (line) paralela; (fig) paralelo;
(Geo) paralelo

paralysis [pə'rælɪsɪs] n parálisis f
inv; **paralyze** vt paralizar; **paralyzed**
paralizado

paramedic [pærə'mɛdɪk] n auxiliar
mf sanitario/a

paranoid ['pærənɔɪd] adj (person,
feeling) paranoico

parasite ['pærəsaɪt] n parásito/a

parcel ['pɑːsl] n paquete m ▷ vt (also: ~
up) empaquetar, embalar

pardon ['pɑːdn] n (Law) indulto
▷ vt perdonar; ~ **me!, I beg your ~!**
¡perdone usted!; **(I beg your) ~?**, (us):
~ **me?** ¿cómo (dice)?

parent ['pɛərənt] n (mother) madre f;
(father) padre m; **parents** npl padres
mpl; **parental** [pə'rɛntl] adj paternal/
maternal

> Be careful not to translate parent
> by the Spanish word pariente.

Paris ['pærɪs] n París m

parish ['pærɪʃ] n parroquia

Parisian [pə'rɪzɪən] adj, n parisiense
mf

park [pɑːk] n parque m ▷ vt, vi aparcar,
estacionar

parking ['pɑːkɪŋ] n aparcamiento,
estacionamiento; **"no ~"** prohibido
aparcar or estacionarse"; **parking lot**
n (us) parking m; **parking meter** n
parquímetro; **parking ticket** n multa
de aparcamiento

parkway ['pɑːkweɪ] n (us) alameda

parliament ['pɑːləmənt] n
parlamento, (Spanish) las Cortes
fpl; ver nota **"parliament"**;
parliamentary adj parlamentario

- **PARLIAMENT**
-
- El Parlamento británico (Parliament)
- tiene como sede el palacio de
- Westminster, también llamado
- Houses of Parliament. Consta de
- dos cámaras; la Cámara de los
- Comunes (House of Commons)
- está formada por 650 diputados
- (Members of Parliament) que
- acceden a ella tras ser elegidos por
- sufragio universal en su respectiva
- área o circunscripción electoral
- (constituency). Se reúne 175 días al
- año y sus sesiones son presididas
- y moderadas por el Presidente de
- la Cámara (Speaker). La cámara
- alta es la Cámara de los Lores
- (House of Lords) y sus miembros son
- nombrados por el monarca o bien
- han heredado su escaño. Su poder
- es limitado, aunque actúa como
- tribunal supremo de apelación,
- excepto en Escocia.

Parmesan [pɑːmɪ'zæn] n (also: ~
cheese) queso parmesano

parole [pə'rəul] n: **on ~** en libertad
condicional

parrot ['pærət] n loro, papagayo

parsley ['pɑːslɪ] n perejil m

parsnip ['pɑːsnɪp] n chirivía

parson ['pɑːsn] n cura m

part [pɑːt] n parte f; (Mus) parte f;
(bit) trozo; (of machine) pieza; (Theat
etc) papel m; (of serial) entrega;
(us: in hair) raya ▷ adv = **partly** ▷ vt
separar ▷ vi (people) separarse; (crowd)
apartarse; **to take ~ in** participar or
tomar parte en; **to take sb's ~** tomar
partido por algn; **for my ~** por mi
parte; **for the most ~** en su mayor
parte; **~ of speech** (Ling) categoría
gramatical; **part with** vt fus ceder,
entregar; (money) pagar; (get rid of)
deshacerse de

partial ['pɑːʃl] adj parcial; **to be ~ to**
(like) ser aficionado a

participant [pɑː'tɪsɪpənt] n (in
competition) concursante mf

participate [pɑː'tɪsɪpeɪt] vi: **to ~ in**
participar en

particle ['pɑːtɪkl] n partícula; (of
dust) mota

articular [pəˈtɪkjuləʳ] *adj* (*special*) particular; (*concrete*) concreto; (*given*) determinado; (*fussy*) quisquilloso; (*demanding*) exigente; **particulars** *npl* (*information*) datos *mpl*; (*details*) pormenores *mpl*; **in ~** en particular; **particularly** *adv* (*in particular*) sobre todo; (*difficult, good etc*) especialmente

arting [ˈpɑːtɪŋ] *n* (*act of*) separación *f*; (*farewell*) despedida; (BRIT: *in hair*) raya ▷ *adj* de despedida

artition [pɑːˈtɪʃən] *n* (*Pol*) división *f*; (*wall*) tabique *m*

artly [ˈpɑːtlɪ] *adv* en parte

artner [ˈpɑːtnəʳ] *n* (*Comm*) socio/a; (*Sport*) pareja; (*at dance*) pareja; (*spouse*) cónyuge *mf*; (*friend etc*) compañero/a; **partnership** *n* asociación *f*; (*Comm*) sociedad *f*

artridge [ˈpɑːtrɪdʒ] *n* perdiz *f*

art-time [ˈpɑːtˈtaɪm] *adj, adv* a tiempo parcial

arty [ˈpɑːtɪ] *n* (*Pol*) partido; (*celebration*) fiesta; (*group*) grupo; (*Law*) parte *f* ▷ *adj* (*Pol*) de partido

ass [pɑːs] *vt* (*time, object*) pasar; (*place*) pasar por; (*exam, law*) aprobar; (*overtake, surpass*) rebasar; (*approve*) aprobar ▷ *vi* pasar; (*Scol*) aprobar ▷ *n* (*permit*) permiso; (*membership card*) carnet *m*; (*in mountains*) puerto; (*Sport*) pase *m*; (*Scol: also*: **~ mark**) aprobado; **to ~ sth through sth** pasar algo por algo; **to make a ~ at sb** (*inf*) insinuársele a algn; **pass away** *vi* fallecer; **pass by** *vi* pasar ▷ *vt* (*ignore*) pasar por alto; **pass on** *vt*: **to ~ on (to)** transmitir (a); **pass out** *vi* desmayarse; **pass over** *vt* omitir, pasar por alto; **pass up** *vt* (*opportunity*) dejar pasar, no aprovechar; **passable** *adj* (*road*) transitable; (*tolerable*) pasable

assage [ˈpæsɪdʒ] *n* pasillo; (*act of passing*) tránsito; (*fare, in book*) pasaje *m*; (*by boat*) travesía

assenger [ˈpæsɪndʒəʳ] *n* pasajero/a, viajero/a

passer-by [pɑːsəˈbaɪ] *n* transeúnte *mf*

passing place *n* (*Aut*) apartadero

passion [ˈpæʃən] *n* pasión *f*; **passionate** *adj* apasionado; **passion fruit** *n* fruta de la pasión, granadilla

passive [ˈpæsɪv] *adj* (*also Ling*) pasivo

passport [ˈpɑːspɔːt] *n* pasaporte *m*; **passport control** *n* control *m* de pasaporte; **passport office** *n* oficina de pasaportes

password [ˈpɑːswɜːd] *n* contraseña

past [pɑːst] *prep* (*further than*) más allá de; (*later than*) después de ▷ *adj* pasado; (*president etc*) antiguo ▷ *n* (*time*) pasado; (*of person*) antecedentes *mpl*; **quarter/half ~ four** las cuatro y cuarto/media; **he's ~ forty** tiene más de cuarenta años; **for the ~ few/ three days** durante los últimos días/ últimos tres días; **to run ~** pasar corriendo

pasta [ˈpæstə] *n* pasta

paste [peɪst] *n* pasta; (*glue*) engrudo ▷ *vt* pegar

pastel [ˈpæstl] *adj* pastel; (*painting*) al pastel

pasteurized [ˈpæstəraɪzd] *adj* pasteurizado

pastime [ˈpɑːstaɪm] *n* pasatiempo

pastor [ˈpɑːstəʳ] *n* pastor *m*

past participle *n* (*Ling*) participio *m* (de) pasado *or* (de) pretérito *or* pasivo

pastry [ˈpeɪstrɪ] *n* (*dough*) pasta; (*cake*) pastel *m*

pasture [ˈpɑːstʃəʳ] *n* pasto

pasty *n* [ˈpæstɪ] empanada ▷ *adj* [ˈpeɪstɪ] (*complexion*) pálido

pat [pæt] *vt* dar una palmadita a; (*dog etc*) acariciar

patch [pætʃ] *n* (*of material*) parche *m*; (*mended part*) remiendo; (*of land*) terreno ▷ *vt* remendar; **(to go through) a bad ~** (pasar por) una mala racha; **patchy** *adj* desigual

pâté [ˈpæteɪ] *n* paté *m*

patent [ˈpeɪtnt] *n* patente *f* ▷ *vt* patentar ▷ *adj* patente, evidente

P

paternal [pəˈtə:nl] *adj* paternal; (*relation*) paterno

paternity [pəˈtə:nɪtɪ] *n* paternidad *f*; **paternity leave** *n* permiso *m* por paternidad, licencia por paternidad

path [pɑ:θ] *n* camino, sendero; (*trail, track*) pista; (*of missile*) trayectoria

pathetic [pəˈθɛtɪk] *adj* patético; (*very bad*) malísimo

pathway [ˈpɑ:θweɪ] *n* sendero, vereda

patience [ˈpeɪʃns] *n* paciencia; (BRIT *Cards*) solitario

patient [ˈpeɪʃnt] *n* paciente *mf* ▷ *adj* paciente, sufrido

patio [ˈpætɪəu] *n* patio

patriotic [pætrɪˈɔtɪk] *adj* patriótico

patrol [pəˈtrəul] *n* patrulla ▷ *vt* patrullar por; **patrol car** *n* coche *m* patrulla

patron [ˈpeɪtrən] *n* (*in shop*) cliente *mf*; (*of charity*) patrocinador(a) *m/f*; **~ of the arts** mecenas *m*

patronizing [ˈpætrənaɪzɪŋ] *adj* condescendiente

pattern [ˈpætən] *n* (*Sewing*) patrón *m*; (*design*) dibujo; **patterned** (*material*) estampado

pause [pɔ:z] *n* pausa ▷ *vi* hacer una pausa

pave [peɪv] *vt* pavimentar; **to ~ the way for** preparar el terreno para

pavement [ˈpeɪvmənt] *n* (BRIT) acera, vereda (LAM), andén *m* (LAM), banqueta (LAM)

pavilion [pəˈvɪlɪən] *n* (*Sport*) vestuarios *mpl*

paving [ˈpeɪvɪŋ] *n* pavimento, enlosado

paw [pɔ:] *n* pata

pawn [pɔ:n] *n* (*Chess*) peón *m*; (*fig*) instrumento ▷ *vt* empeñar; **pawnbroker** [ˈpɔ:nbrəukəʳ] *n* prestamista *mf*

pay [peɪ] (*pt, pp* **paid**) *n* (*wage etc*) sueldo, salario ▷ *vt* pagar ▷ *vi* (*be profitable*) rendir; **to ~ attention (to)** prestar atención (a); **pay back**

vt (*money*) reembolsar; (*person*) pagar; **pay for** *vt fus* pagar; **pay in** *vt* ingresar; **pay off** *vt* saldar ▷ *vi* (*scheme, decision*) dar resultado; **pay out** *vt* (*money*) gastar, desembolsar; **pay up** *vt* pagar; **payable** *adj* pagadero; **to make a cheque payable to sb** extender un cheque a favor de algn; **pay day** *n* día *m* de paga; **pay envelope** *n* (US) = **pay packet**; **payment** *n* pago; **monthly payment** mensualidad *f*; **payout** *n* pago; (*in competition*) premio en metálico; **pay packet** *n* (BRIT) sobre *m* (de la paga); **pay-phone** *n* teléfono público; **payroll** *n* plantilla, nómina; **pay slip** *n* nómina, hoja del sueldo; **pay television** *n* televisión *f* de pago

PC *n abbr* (= *personal computer*) PC *m*, OP *m*; (BRIT) = **police constable** ▷ *adj abb* = **politically correct**

pc *abbr* = **per cent**

PDA *n abbr* (= *personal digital assistant*) agenda electrónica

PE *n abbr* (= *physical education*) ed. física

pea [pi:] *n* guisante *m*, chícharo (LAM), arveja (LAM)

peace [pi:s] *n* paz *f*; (*calm*) paz *f*, tranquilidad *f*; **peaceful** *adj* (*gentle*) pacífico; (*calm*) tranquilo, sosegado

peach [pi:tʃ] *n* melocotón *m*, durazno (LAM)

peacock [ˈpi:kɔk] *n* pavo real

peak [pi:k] *n* (*of mountain*) cumbre *f*, cima; (*of cap*) visera; (*fig*) cumbre *f*; **peak hours** *npl* horas *fpl* punta

peanut [ˈpi:nʌt] *n* cacahuete *m*, maní *m* (LAM); **peanut butter** *n* mantequilla de cacahuete

pear [pɛəʳ] *n* pera

pearl [pə:l] *n* perla

peasant [ˈpɛznt] *n* campesino/a

peat [pi:t] *n* turba

pebble [ˈpɛbl] *n* guijarro

peck [pɛk] *vt* (*also:* **~ at**) picotear ▷ *n* picotazo; (*kiss*) besito; **peckish** *adj* (BRIT *inf*): **I feel peckish** tengo ganas de picar algo

peculiar [pɪˈkjuːlɪəʳ] *adj* (*odd*) extraño, raro; (*typical*) propio, característico; **~ to** propio de

pedal [ˈpɛdl] *n* pedal *m* ▷ *vi* pedalear

pedalo [ˈpɛdələu] *n* patín *m* a pedal

pedestal [ˈpɛdəstl] *n* pedestal *m*

pedestrian [pɪˈdɛstrɪən] *n* peatón *m* ▷ *adj* pedestre; **pedestrian crossing** *n* (BRIT) paso de peatones; **pedestrianized** *adj*: **a pedestrianized street** una calle peatonal; **pedestrian precinct**, (US) **pedestrian zone** *n* zona reservada para peatones

pedigree [ˈpɛdɪgriː] *n* genealogía; (*of animal*) pedigrí *m* ▷ *cpd* (*animal*) de raza, de casta

pedophile [ˈpiːdəufaɪl] *n* (US) = **paedophile**

pee [piː] *vi* (*inf*) mear

peek [piːk] *vi* mirar a hurtadillas

peel [piːl] *n* piel *f*; (*of orange, lemon*) cáscara; (*: removed*) peladuras *fpl* ▷ *vt* pelar ▷ *vi* (*paint etc*) desconcharse; (*wallpaper*) despegarse, desprenderse; (*skin*) pelar

peep [piːp] *n* (*look*) mirada furtiva; (*sound*) pío ▷ *vi* (*look*) mirar furtivamente

peer [pɪəʳ] *vi*: **to ~ at** escudriñar ▷ *n* (*noble*) par *m*; (*equal*) igual *m*; (*contemporary*) contemporáneo/a

peg [pɛg] *n* (*for coat etc*) gancho, colgador *m*; (BRIT: *also*: **clothes ~**) pinza

pelican [ˈpɛlɪkən] *n* pelícano; **pelican crossing** *n* (BRIT Aut) paso de peatones señalizado

pelt [pɛlt] *vt*: **to ~ sb with sth** arrojarle algo a algn ▷ *vi* (*rain: also*: **~ down**) llover a cántaros; (*inf: run*) correr ▷ *n* pellejo

pelvis [ˈpɛlvɪs] *n* pelvis *f*

pen [pɛn] *n* (*also*: **ballpoint ~**) bolígrafo; (*also*: **fountain ~**) pluma; (*for sheep*) redil *m*

penalty [ˈpɛnltɪ] *n* pena; (*fine*) multa

pence [pɛns] *pl of* **penny**

pencil [ˈpɛnsl] *n* lápiz *m* ▷ *vt* (*also*: **~ in**) escribir con lápiz; (*fig*) apuntar con carácter provisional; **pencil case** *n* estuche *m*; **pencil sharpener** *n* sacapuntas *m inv*

pendant [ˈpɛndnt] *n* pendiente *m*

pending [ˈpɛndɪŋ] *prep* antes de ▷ *adj* pendiente

penetrate [ˈpɛnɪtreɪt] *vt* penetrar

penfriend [ˈpɛnfrɛnd] *n* (BRIT) amigo/a por correspondencia

penguin [ˈpɛŋgwɪn] *n* pingüino

penicillin [pɛnɪˈsɪlɪn] *n* penicilina

peninsula [pəˈnɪnsjulə] *n* península

penis [ˈpiːnɪs] *n* pene *m*

penitentiary [pɛnɪˈtɛnʃərɪ] *n* (US) cárcel *f*, presidio

penknife [ˈpɛnnaɪf] *n* navaja

penniless [ˈpɛnɪlɪs] *adj* sin dinero

penny (*pl* **pennies** *or* (Brit) **pence**) [ˈpɛnɪ, ˈpɛnɪz, pɛns] *n* (BRIT) penique *m*; (US) centavo

penpal [ˈpɛnpæl] *n* amigo/a por correspondencia

pension [ˈpɛnʃən] *n* (*allowance, state payment*) pensión *f*; (*old-age*) jubilación *f*; **pensioner** *n* (BRIT) jubilado/a

pentagon [ˈpɛntəgən] *n* pentágono; **the P~** (US Pol) el Pentágono

> **PENTAGON**
>
> Se conoce como el Pentágono
> (*the Pentagon*) al edificio de
> planta pentagonal que acoge
> las dependencias del Ministerio
> de Defensa estadounidense
> (*Department of Defense*) en Arlington,
> Virginia. En lenguaje periodístico se
> aplica también a la dirección militar
> del país.

penthouse [ˈpɛnthaus] *n* ático (de lujo)

penultimate [pɛˈnʌltɪmət] *adj* penúltimo

people [ˈpiːpl] *npl* gente *f*; (*citizens*) pueblo *sg*, ciudadanos *mpl*; (*Pol*): **the**

~ el pueblo ▷ *n* (*nation, race*) pueblo, nación *f*; **several ~ came** vinieron varias personas; **~ say that ...** dice la gente que ...

pepper ['pɛpəʳ] *n* (*spice*) pimienta; (*vegetable*) pimiento ▷ *vt*: **to ~ with** (*fig*) salpicar de; **peppermint** *n* (*sweet*) pastilla de menta

per [pəːʳ] *prep* por; **~ day/person** por día/persona; **~ annum** al año

perceive [pə'siːv] *vt* percibir; (*realize*) darse cuenta de

per cent, (*us*) **percent** *n* por ciento

percentage [pə'sɛntɪdʒ] *n* porcentaje *m*

perception [pə'sɛpʃən] *n* percepción *f*; (*insight*) perspicacia

perch [pəːtʃ] *n* (*fish*) perca; (*for bird*) percha ▷ *vi*: **to ~ (on)** (*bird*) posarse (en); (*person*) encaramarse (en)

percussion [pə'kʌʃən] *n* percusión *f*

perfect *adj* ['pəːfɪkt] perfecto ▷ *n* (*also*: **~ tense**) perfecto ▷ *vt* [pə'fɛkt] perfeccionar; **perfection** *n* perfección *f*; **perfectly** *adv* perfectamente

perform [pə'fɔːm] *vt* (*carry out*) realizar, llevar a cabo; (*Theat*) representar; (*piece of music*) interpretar ▷ *vi* (*Tech*) funcionar; **performance** *n* (*of a play*) representación *f*; (*of player etc*) actuación *f*; (*of engine*) rendimiento; **performer** *n* (*actor*) actor *m*, actriz *f*

perfume ['pəːfjuːm] *n* perfume *m*

perhaps [pə'hæps] *adv* quizá(s), tal vez

perimeter [pə'rɪmɪtəʳ] *n* perímetro

period ['pɪərɪəd] *n* período; (*Scol*) clase *f*; (*full stop*) punto; (*Med*) regla ▷ *adj* (*costume, furniture*) de época; **periodical** [pɪərɪ'ɔdɪkl] *adj* periódico; **periodically** *adv* de vez en cuando, cada cierto tiempo

perish ['pɛrɪʃ] *vi* perecer; (*decay*) echarse a perder

perjury ['pəːdʒərɪ] *n* (*Law*) perjurio

perk [pəːk] *n* extra *m*

perm [pəːm] *n* permanente *f*

permanent ['pəːmənənt] *adj* permanente; **permanently** *adv* (*lastingly*) para siempre, de modo definitivo; (*all the time*) permanentemente

permission [pə'mɪʃən] *n* permiso

permit *n* ['pəːmɪt] permiso, licencia ▷ *vt* [pə'mɪt] permitir

perplex [pə'plɛks] *vt* dejar perplejo

persecute ['pəːsɪkjuːt] *vt* perseguir

persecution [pəːsɪ'kjuːʃən] *n* persecución *f*

persevere [pəːsɪ'vɪəʳ] *vi* perseverar

Persian ['pəːʃən] *adj, n* persa *mf*; **the ~ Gulf** el Golfo Pérsico

persist [pə'sɪst] *vi* persistir; **to ~ in doing sth** empeñarse en hacer algo; **persistent** *adj* persistente; (*determined*) porfiado

person ['pəːsn] *n* persona; **in ~** en persona; **personal** *adj* personal, individual; (*visit*) en persona; **personal assistant** *n* ayudante *mf* personal; **personal computer** *n* ordenador *m* personal; **personality** [pəːsə'nælɪtɪ] *n* personalidad *f*; **personally** *adv* personalmente; (*in person*) en persona; **to take sth personally** tomarse algo a mal; **personal organizer** *n* agenda; **personal stereo** *n* walkman® *m*

personnel [pəːsə'nɛl] *n* personal *m*

perspective [pə'spɛktɪv] *n* perspectiva

perspiration [pəːspɪ'reɪʃən] *n* transpiración *f*

persuade [pə'sweɪd] *vt*: **to ~ sb to do sth** persuadir a algn para que haga algo

persuasion [pə'sweɪʒən] *n* persuasión *f*; (*persuasiveness*) persuasiva

persuasive [pə'sweɪsɪv] *adj* persuasivo

perverse [pə'vəːs] *adj* perverso; (*wayward*) travieso

pervert *n* ['pəːvəːt] pervertido/a ▷ *vt* [pə'vəːt] pervertir

essimism [ˈpɛsɪmɪzəm] n
pesimismo

essimist [ˈpɛsɪmɪst] n pesimista
mf; **pessimistic** [pɛsɪˈmɪstɪk] adj
pesimista

ester [ˈpɛstəʳ] vt molestar, acosar

esticide [ˈpɛstɪsaɪd] n pesticida m

et [pɛt] n animal m doméstico;
(favourite) favorito/a ▷ vt acariciar
▷ cpd: **teacher's ~** favorito/a (del
profesor); **~ hate** manía

etal [ˈpɛtl] n pétalo

etite [pəˈtiːt] adj chiquita

etition [pəˈtɪʃən] n petición f

etrified [ˈpɛtrɪfaɪd] adj horrorizado

etrol [ˈpɛtrəl] (BRIT) n gasolina

etroleum [pəˈtrəʊlɪəm] n petróleo

etrol: petrol pump n (BRIT: in garage)
surtidor m de gasolina; **petrol station**
n (BRIT) gasolinera; **petrol tank** n
(BRIT) depósito (de gasolina)

etticoat [ˈpɛtɪkəʊt] n combinación
f, enagua(s) f(pl) (LAM)

etty [ˈpɛtɪ] adj (mean) mezquino;
(unimportant) insignificante

ew [pjuː] n banco

ewter [ˈpjuːtəʳ] n peltre m

hantom [ˈfæntəm] n fantasma m

harmacist [ˈfɑːməsɪst] n
farmacéutico/a

harmacy [ˈfɑːməsɪ] n (us) farmacia

hase [feɪz] n fase f; **phase in** vt
introducir progresivamente; **phase
out** vt (machinery, product) retirar
progresivamente; (job, subsidy)
eliminar por etapas

heasant [ˈfɛznt] n faisán m

henomena [fəˈnɒmɪnə] npl of
phenomenon

henomenal [fɪˈnɒmɪnl] adj
fenomenal, extraordinario

henomenon (pl **phenomena**)
[fəˈnɒmɪnən, -nə] n fenómeno

hilippines [ˈfɪlɪpiːnz] npl: **the ~** (las
Islas) Filipinas

hilosopher [fɪˈlɒsəfəʳ] n filósofo/a

philosophical [fɪləˈsɒfɪkl] adj
filosófico

philosophy [fɪˈlɒsəfɪ] n filosofía

phlegm [flɛm] n flema

phobia [ˈfəʊbjə] n fobia

phone [fəʊn] n teléfono ▷ vt
telefonear, llamar por teléfono; **to be
on the ~** tener teléfono; (be calling)
estar hablando por teléfono; **phone
back** vt, vi volver a llamar; **phone up**
vt, vi llamar por teléfono; **phone book**
n guía telefónica; **phone box, phone
booth** n cabina telefónica; **phone call**
n llamada (telefónica); **phonecard** n
tarjeta telefónica; **phone number** n
número de teléfono

phonetics [fəˈnɛtɪks] n fonética

phoney [ˈfəʊnɪ] adj = **phony**

phony [ˈfəʊnɪ] adj falso

photo [ˈfəʊtəʊ] n foto f; **photo album**
n álbum m de fotos; **photocopier**
n fotocopiadora; **photocopy** n
fotocopia ▷ vt fotocopiar

photograph [ˈfəʊtəgræf] n
fotografía ▷ vt fotografiar;
photographer [fəˈtɒgrəfəʳ] n fotógrafo/a;
photography [fəˈtɒgrəfɪ] n
fotografía

phrase [freɪz] n frase f ▷ vt expresar;
phrase book n libro de frases

physical [ˈfɪzɪkl] adj físico; **physical
education** n educación f física;
physically adv físicamente

physician [fɪˈzɪʃən] n médico/a

physicist [ˈfɪzɪsɪst] n físico/a

physics [ˈfɪzɪks] n física

physiotherapist [fɪzɪəʊˈθɛrəpɪst] n
fisioterapeuta mf; **physiotherapy** n
fisioterapia

physique [fɪˈziːk] n físico

pianist [ˈpɪənɪst] n pianista mf

piano [pɪˈænəʊ] n piano

pick [pɪk] n (tool: also: **~axe**) pico,
piqueta ▷ vt (select) elegir, escoger;
(gather) coger (SP), recoger (LAM);
(lock) abrir con ganzúa; **take your ~**
escoja lo que quiera; **the ~ of** lo mejor
de; **to ~ one's nose/teeth** hurgarse

p

la nariz/escarbarse los dientes;
pick on vt fus (person) meterse con;
pick out vt escoger; (distinguish)
identificar; **pick up** vi (improve: sales) ir
mejor; (: patient) reponerse; (: Finance)
recobrarse ▷ vt recoger; (learn)
aprender; (Police: arrest) detener;
(Radio, TV, Tel) captar; **to ~ up speed**
acelerarse; **to ~ o.s. up** levantarse

pickle ['pɪkl] n (also: **~s**: as condiment)
escabeche m; (fig: mess) apuro ▷ vt
conservar en escabeche; (in vinegar)
conservar en vinagre

pickpocket ['pɪkpɔkɪt] n carterista
mf

pickup ['pɪkʌp] n (also: **~ truck, ~ van**)
furgoneta, camioneta

picnic ['pɪknɪk] n merienda ▷ vi hacer
un picnic; **picnic area** n zona de
picnic; (Aut) área de descanso

picture ['pɪktʃə'] n cuadro; (painting)
pintura; (photograph) fotografía; (film)
película; (TV) imagen f; (fig: description)
descripción f; (: situation) situación f
▷ vt (imagine) imaginar; **the ~s** (BRIT)
el cine; **picture frame** n marco;
picture messaging n (envío de)
mensajes mpl con imágenes

picturesque [pɪktʃə'rɛsk] adj
pintoresco

pie [paɪ] n (of meat etc: large) pastel m;
(: small) empanada; (sweet) tarta

piece [piːs] n pedazo, trozo; (of cake)
trozo; (item): **a ~ of furniture/advice**
un mueble/un consejo ▷ vt: **to ~
together** juntar; (Tech) armar; **to
take to ~s** desmontar

pie chart n gráfico de sectores or
de tarta

pier [pɪə'] n muelle m, embarcadero

pierce [pɪəs] vt perforar; **to have
one's ears ~d** hacerse los agujeros
de las orejas

pig [pɪg] n cerdo, chancho (LAM);
(person: greedy) tragón/ona m/f,
comilón/ona m/f; (: nasty) cerdo/a

pigeon ['pɪdʒən] n paloma; (as food)
pichón m

piggy bank ['pɪgɪbæŋk] n hucha (en
forma de cerdito)

pigsty ['pɪgstaɪ] n pocilga

pigtail ['pɪgteɪl] n (girl's) trenza

pike [paɪk] n (fish) lucio

pilchard ['pɪltʃəd] n sardina

pile [paɪl] n montón m; (of carpet)
pelo; **pile up** vi (accumulate: work)
amontonarse, acumularse ▷ vt
(put in a heap: books, clothes) apilar,
amontonar; (accumulate) acumular;
piles npl (Med) almorranas fpl,
hemorroides mpl; **pile-up** n (Aut)
accidente m múltiple

pilgrimage ['pɪlgrɪmɪdʒ] n
peregrinación f, romería

pill [pɪl] n píldora; **the ~** la píldora

pillar ['pɪlə'] n pilar m

pillow ['pɪləu] n almohada;
pillowcase ['pɪləukeɪs] n funda (de
almohada)

pilot ['paɪlət] n piloto mf ▷ adj (scheme
etc) piloto inv ▷ vt pilotar; **pilot light**
n piloto

pimple ['pɪmpl] n grano

PIN n abbr (= personal identification
number) PIN m

pin [pɪn] n alfiler m ▷ vt prender con
(alfiler); **~s and needles** hormigueo
sg; **to ~ sth on sb** (fig) cargar a algn
con la culpa de algo; **pin down** vt (fig):
to ~ sb down hacer que algn concrete

pinafore ['pɪnəfɔː'] n delantal m

pinch [pɪntʃ] n (of salt etc) pizca ▷ vt
pellizcar; (inf: steal) birlar; **at a ~** en
caso de apuro

pine [paɪn] n (also: **~ tree**) pino ▷ vi: **to
~ for** suspirar por

pineapple ['paɪnæpl] n piña,
ananá(s) m (LAM)

ping [pɪŋ] n (noise) sonido agudo;
Ping-Pong® n pingpong m

pink [pɪŋk] adj (de color) rosa inv ▷ n
(colour) rosa m; (Bot) clavel m

pinpoint ['pɪnpɔɪnt] vt precisar

pint [paɪnt] n pinta (Brit = 0,57 l, US
= 0,47 l); (BRIT inf: of beer) pinta de
cerveza, ≈ jarra (SP)

pioneer [paɪə'nɪəʳ] n pionero/a
pious ['paɪəs] adj piadoso, devoto
pip [pɪp] n (seed) pepita; **the ~s** (BRIT) la señal
pipe [paɪp] n tubería, cañería; (for smoking) pipa ▷ vt conducir en cañerías; **pipeline** n (for oil) oleoducto; (for natural gas) gaseoducto; **piper** n gaitero/a
pirate ['paɪərət] n pirata mf ▷ vt (record, video, book) hacer una copia pirata de, piratear
Pisces ['paɪsiːz] n Piscis m
piss [pɪs] vi (inf) mear; **pissed** adj (inf: drunk) mamado, pedo
pistol ['pɪstl] n pistola
piston ['pɪstən] n pistón m, émbolo
pit [pɪt] n hoyo; (also: **coal ~**) mina; (in garage) foso de inspección; (also: **orchestra ~**) foso de la orquesta ▷ vt: **to ~ one's wits against sb** medir fuerzas con algn
pitch [pɪtʃ] n (Mus) tono; (BRIT Sport) campo, terreno; (tar) brea ▷ vt (throw) arrojar, lanzar ▷ vi (fall) caer(se); **to ~ a tent** montar una tienda (de campaña); **pitch-black** adj negro como boca de lobo
pitfall ['pɪtfɔːl] n riesgo
pith [pɪθ] n (of orange) piel f blanca
pitiful ['pɪtɪful] adj (touching) lastimoso, conmovedor(a)
pity ['pɪtɪ] n compasión f, piedad f ▷ vt compadecer(se de); **what a ~!** ¡qué pena!
pizza ['piːtsə] n pizza
placard ['plækɑːd] n (in march etc) pancarta
place [pleɪs] n lugar m, sitio; (seat) plaza, asiento; (post) puesto; (home): **at/to his ~** en/a su casa ▷ vt (object) poner, colocar; (identify) reconocer; **to take ~** tener lugar; **to be ~d** (in race, exam) colocarse; **out of ~** (not suitable) fuera de lugar; **in the first ~** en primer lugar; **to change ~s with sb** cambiarse de sitio con algn; **~ of birth** lugar m de nacimiento; **place**

mat n (wooden etc) salvamanteles m inv; (in linen etc) mantel m individual; **placement** n colocación f; (at work) emplazamiento
placid ['plæsɪd] adj apacible
plague [pleɪg] n plaga; (Med) peste f ▷ vt (fig) acosar, atormentar
plaice [pleɪs] n (pl inv) platija
plain [pleɪn] adj (clear) claro, evidente; (simple) sencillo; (not handsome) poco atractivo ▷ adv claramente ▷ n llano, llanura; **plain chocolate** n chocolate m oscuro or amargo; **plainly** adv claramente
plaintiff ['pleɪntɪf] n demandante mf
plait [plæt] n trenza
plan [plæn] n (drawing) plano; (scheme) plan m, proyecto ▷ vt proyectar ▷ vi hacer proyectos; **to ~ to do** pensar hacer
plane [pleɪn] n (Aviat) avión m; (tree) plátano; (tool) cepillo; (Math) plano
planet ['plænɪt] n planeta m
plank [plæŋk] n tabla
planning ['plænɪŋ] n planificación f; **family ~** planificación familiar
plant [plɑːnt] n planta; (machinery) maquinaria; (factory) fábrica ▷ vt plantar; (field) sembrar; (bomb) colocar
plantation [plæn'teɪʃən] n plantación f; (estate) hacienda
plaque [plæk] n placa
plaster ['plɑːstəʳ] n (for walls) yeso; (also: **~ of Paris**) yeso mate; (BRIT: also: **sticking ~**) tirita ▷ vt enyesar; (cover): **to ~ with** llenar or cubrir de; **plaster cast** n (Med) escayola; (model, statue) vaciado de yeso
plastic ['plæstɪk] n plástico ▷ adj de plástico; **plastic bag** n bolsa de plástico; **plastic surgery** n cirugía plástica
plate [pleɪt] n (dish) plato; (metal, in book) lámina; (dental plate) placa de dentadura postiza
plateau (pl **plateaus** or **plateaux**) ['plætəu, -z] n meseta, altiplanicie f

P

platform ['plætfɔːm] n (Rail) andén m; (stage) plataforma; (at meeting) tribuna; (Pol) programa m (electoral)

platinum ['plætɪnəm] n platino

platoon [plə'tuːn] n pelotón m

platter ['plætər] n fuente f

plausible ['plɔːzɪbl] adj verosímil; (person) convincente

play [pleɪ] n juego; (Theat) obra ▷ vt (game) jugar; (football, tennis, cards) jugar a; (compete against) jugar contra; (instrument) tocar; (Theat: part) hacer el papel de ▷ vi jugar; (band) tocar; (tape, record) sonar; **to ~ safe** ir a lo seguro; **play back** vt (tape) poner; **play up** vi (cause trouble) dar guerra; **player** n jugador(a) m/f; (Theat) actor m, actriz f; (Mus) músico/a; **playful** adj juguetón/ona; **playground** n (in school) patio de recreo; (in park) parque m infantil; **playgroup** n jardín m de infancia; **playing card** n naipe m, carta; **playing field** n campo de deportes; **playschool** n = **playgroup**; **playtime** n (Scol) (hora de) recreo; **playwright** n dramaturgo/a

plc abbr (BRIT: = public limited company) S.A.

plea [pliː] n súplica, petición f; (Law) alegato, defensa

plead [pliːd] vt (give as excuse) poner como pretexto; (Law): **to ~ sb's case** defender a algn ▷ vi (Law) declararse; (beg): **to ~ with sb** suplicar or rogar a algn

pleasant ['plɛznt] adj agradable

please [pliːz] excl ¡por favor! ▷ vt (give pleasure to) dar gusto a, agradar ▷ vi (think fit): **do as you ~** haz lo que quieras or lo que te dé la gana; **~ yourself!** ¡haz lo que quieras!, ¡como quieras!; **pleased** adj (happy) alegre, contento; **pleased (with)** satisfecho (de); **pleased to meet you** ¡encantado!, ¡tanto or mucho gusto!

pleasure ['plɛʒər] n placer m, gusto; **"it's a ~"** "el gusto es mío"

pleat [pliːt] n pliegue m

pledge [plɛdʒ] n (promise) promesa, voto ▷ vt prometer

plentiful ['plɛntɪful] adj copioso, abundante

plenty ['plɛntɪ] n: **~ of** mucho(s)/a(s)

pliers ['plaɪəz] npl alicates mpl, tenazas fpl

plight [plaɪt] n condición f or situación f difícil

plod [plɔd] vi caminar con paso pesado; (fig) trabajar laboriosamente

plonk [plɔŋk] (inf) n (BRIT: wine) vino peleón ▷ vt: **to ~ sth down** dejar caer algo

plot [plɔt] n (scheme) complot m, conjura; (of story, play) argumento; (of land) terreno ▷ vt (mark out) trazar; (conspire) tramar, urdir ▷ vi conspirar

plough, (US) **plow** [plau] n arado ▷ vt (earth) arar

plow [plau] n, vb (US) = **plough**

ploy [plɔɪ] n truco, estratagema

pluck [plʌk] vt (fruit) coger (SP), recoger (LAM); (musical instrument) puntear; (bird) desplumar; **to ~ up courage** hacer de tripas corazón; **to ~ one's eyebrows** depilarse las cejas

plug [plʌg] n tapón m; (Elec) enchufe m, clavija; (Aut: also: **spark(ing) ~**) bujía ▷ vt (hole) tapar; (inf: advertise) dar publicidad a; **plug in** vt (Elec) enchufar; **plughole** n desagüe m

plum [plʌm] n (fruit) ciruela

plumber ['plʌmər] n fontanero/a, plomero/a (LAM)

plumbing ['plʌmɪŋ] n (trade) fontanería, plomería (LAM); (piping) cañerías

plummet ['plʌmɪt] vi: **to ~ (down)** caer a plomo

plump [plʌmp] adj rechoncho, rollizo; **plump for** vt fus (inf: choose) optar por

plunge [plʌndʒ] n zambullida ▷ vt sumergir, hundir ▷ vi (fall) caer; (dive) saltar; (person) arrojarse; **to take the ~** lanzarse

plural ['pluərl] adj plural ▷ n plural m

plus [plʌs] n (also: **~ sign**) signo más ▷ prep más, y, además de; **ten/twenty ~** más de diez/veinte

ply [plaɪ] vt (a trade) ejercer ▷ vi (ship) ir y venir; **to ~ sb with drink** no dejar de ofrecer copas a algn; **plywood** n madera contrachapada

PM n abbr (BRIT) = **Prime Minister**

p.m. adv abbr (= post meridiem) de la tarde or noche

PMS n abbr (= premenstrual syndrome) SPM m

PMT n abbr (= premenstrual tension) SPM m

pneumatic drill n taladradora neumática

pneumonia [njuːˈməʊnɪə] n pulmonía

poach [pəʊtʃ] vt (cook) escalfar; (steal) cazar/pescar en vedado ▷ vi cazar/pescar en vedado; **poached** adj (egg) escalfado

PO Box n abbr (= Post Office Box) apdo., aptdo.

pocket ['pɒkɪt] n bolsillo; (fig) bolsa ▷ vt meter en el bolsillo; (steal) embolsarse; **to be out of ~** salir perdiendo; **pocketbook** n (US) cartera; **pocket money** n asignación f

pod [pɒd] n vaina

podcast ['pɒdkɑːst] n podcast m ▷ vi podcastear

podiatrist [pɒˈdiːətrɪst] n (US) podólogo/a

podium ['pəʊdɪəm] n podio

poem ['pəʊɪm] n poema m

poet ['pəʊɪt] n poeta mf; **poetic** [pəʊˈɛtɪk] adj poético; **poetry** n poesía

poignant ['pɔɪnjənt] adj conmovedor(a)

point [pɔɪnt] n punto; (tip) punta; (purpose) fin m, propósito; (use) utilidad f; (significant part) lo esencial; (also: **decimal ~**); **2 ~ 3 (2.3)** dos coma tres (2,3) ▷ vt (gun etc): **to ~ sth at sb** apuntar con algo a algn ▷ vi: **to ~ at** señalar; **points** npl (Aut) contactos

mpl; (Rail) agujas fpl; **to be on the ~ of doing sth** estar a punto de hacer algo; **to make a ~ of doing sth** poner empeño en hacer algo; **to get the ~** comprender; **to come to the ~** ir al meollo; **there's no ~ (in doing)** no tiene sentido (hacer); **point out** vt señalar; **point-blank** adv (say, refuse) sin más hablar; (also: **at point-blank range**) a quemarropa; **pointed** adj (shape) puntiagudo, afilado; (remark) intencionado; **pointer** n (needle) aguja, indicador m; **pointless** adj sin sentido; **point of view** n punto de vista

poison ['pɔɪzn] n veneno ▷ vt envenenar; **poisonous** adj venenoso; (fumes etc) tóxico

poke [pəʊk] vt (jab with finger, stick etc) empujar; (put): **to ~ sth in(to)** introducir algo en; **poke about** vi fisgonear; **poke out** vi (stick out) salir

poker ['pəʊkər] n atizador m; (Cards) póker m

Poland ['pəʊlənd] n Polonia

polar ['pəʊlər] adj polar; **polar bear** n oso polar

Pole [pəʊl] n polaco/a

pole [pəʊl] n palo; (Geo) polo; (Tel) poste m; **pole bean** n (US) judía trepadora; **pole vault** n salto con pértiga

police [pəˈliːs] n policía ▷ vt vigilar; **police car** n coche-patrulla m; **police constable** n (BRIT) guardia m, policía m; **police force** n cuerpo de policía; **policeman** n guardia m, policía m; **police officer** n guardia mf, policía mf; **police station** n comisaría; **policewoman** n (mujer f) policía

policy ['pɒlɪsɪ] n política; (also: **insurance ~**) póliza

polio ['pəʊlɪəʊ] n polio f

Polish ['pəʊlɪʃ] adj polaco ▷ n (Ling) polaco

polish ['pɒlɪʃ] n (for shoes) betún m; (for floor) cera (de lustrar); (shine) brillo, lustre *m*; (*fig*: *refinement*) refinamiento ▷ *vt* (*shoes*) limpiar; (*make shiny*) pulir, sacar brillo a; **polish off** *vt* (*food*) despachar; **polished** *adj* (*fig*: *person*) refinado

polite [pə'laɪt] *adj* cortés, atento; **politeness** *n* cortesía

political [pə'lɪtɪkl] *adj* político; **politically** *adv* políticamente; **politically correct** *adj* políticamente correcto

politician [pɔlɪ'tɪʃən] *n* político/a

politics ['pɔlɪtɪks] *n* política

poll [pəul] *n* (*votes*) votación *f*; (*also*: **opinion ~**) sondeo, encuesta ▷ *vt* (*votes*) obtener

pollen ['pɔlən] *n* polen *m*

polling station *n* centro electoral

pollute [pə'lu:t] *vt* contaminar

pollution [pə'lu:ʃən] *n* contaminación *f*

polo ['pəuləu] *n* (*sport*) polo; **polo-neck** *adj* de cuello vuelto ▷ *n* (*sweater*) suéter *m* de cuello vuelto; **polo shirt** *n* polo, niqui *m*

polyester [pɔlɪ'ɛstəʳ] *n* poliéster *m*

polystyrene [pɔlɪ'staɪri:n] *n* poliestireno

polythene ['pɔlɪθi:n] *n* (*BRIT*) polietileno; **polythene bag** *n* bolsa de plástico

pomegranate ['pɔmɪɡrænɪt] *n* granada

pompous ['pɔmpəs] *adj* pomposo

pond [pɔnd] *n* (*natural*) charca; (*artificial*) estanque *m*

ponder ['pɔndəʳ] *vt* meditar

pony ['pəunɪ] *n* poney *m*; **ponytail** *n* coleta; **pony trekking** *n* (*BRIT*) excursión *f* a caballo

poodle ['pu:dl] *n* caniche *m*

pool [pu:l] *n* (*natural*) charca; (*also*: **swimming ~**) piscina, alberca (*LAm*) ▷ *vt* juntar; **(football) ~s** *npl* quinielas *fpl*

poor [puəʳ] *adj* pobre; (*bad*) malo ▷ *npl*: **the ~** los pobres; **poorly** *adj* mal, enfermo ▷ *adv* mal

pop [pɔp] *n* (*sound*) ruido seco; (*Mus*) (música) pop *m*; (*inf*: *father*) papá *m*; (*drink*) gaseosa ▷ *vt* (*burst*) hacer reventar ▷ *vi* reventar; (*cork*) saltar; **pop in** *vi* entrar un momento; **pop out** *vi* salir un momento; **popcorn** *n* palomitas *fpl* (de maíz)

poplar ['pɔpləʳ] *n* álamo

popper ['pɔpəʳ] *n* corchete *m*, botón *m* automático

poppy ['pɔpɪ] *n* amapola; *see also* **Remembrance Day**

Popsicle® ['pɔpsɪkl] *n* (*US*) polo

pop star *n* estrella del pop

popular ['pɔpjuləʳ] *adj* popular; **popularity** [pɔpju'lærɪtɪ] *n* popularidad *f*

population [pɔpju'leɪʃən] *n* población *f*

porcelain ['pɔ:slɪn] *n* porcelana

porch [pɔ:tʃ] *n* pórtico, entrada; (*US*) veranda

pore [pɔ:ʳ] *n* poro ▷ *vi*: **to ~ over** enfrascarse en

pork [pɔ:k] *n* (carne *f* de) cerdo *or* chancho (*LAm*); **pork chop** *n* chuleta de cerdo; **pork pie** *n* (*BRIT Culin*) empanada de carne de cerdo

porn [pɔ:n] *adj* (*inf*) porno *inv* ▷ *n* porno; **pornographic** [pɔ:nə'ɡræfɪk] *adj* pornográfico; **pornography** [pɔ:'nɔɡrəfɪ] *n* pornografía

porridge ['pɔrɪdʒ] *n* gachas *fpl* de avena

port [pɔ:t] *n* puerto; (*Naut*: *left side*) babor *m*; (*wine*) oporto; **~ of call** puerto de escala

portable ['pɔ:təbl] *adj* portátil

porter ['pɔ:təʳ] *n* (*for luggage*) maletero; (*doorkeeper*) portero/a, conserje *mf*

portfolio [pɔ:t'fəuliəu] *n* (*case, of artist*) cartera, carpeta; (*Pol, Finance*) cartera

portion ['pɔ:ʃən] *n* porción *f*; (*helping*) ración *f*

portrait ['pɔ:treɪt] *n* retrato

portray [pɔːˈtreɪ] vt retratar; (in writing) representar

Portugal [ˈpɔːtjuɡl] n Portugal m

Portuguese [pɔːtjuˈɡiːz] adj portugués/esa ▷ n (pl inv) portugués/esa m/f; (Ling) portugués m

pose [pəuz] n postura, actitud f ▷ vi (pretend): **to ~ as** hacerse pasar por ▷ vt (question) plantear; **to ~ for** posar para

posh [pɔʃ] adj (inf) elegante, de lujo

position [pəˈzɪʃən] n posición f; (job) puesto ▷ vt colocar

positive [ˈpɔzɪtɪv] adj positivo; (certain) seguro; (definite) definitivo; **positively** adv (affirmatively, enthusiastically) de forma positiva; (inf: really) absolutamente

possess [pəˈzɛs] vt poseer; **possession** [pəˈzɛʃən] n posesión f; **possessions** npl (belongings) pertenencias fpl; **possessive** adj posesivo

possibility [pɔsɪˈbɪlɪtɪ] n posibilidad f

possible [ˈpɔsɪbl] adj posible; **as big as ~** lo más grande posible; **possibly** adv posiblemente; **I cannot possibly come** me es imposible venir

post [pəust] n (BRIT: system) correos mpl; (: letters, delivery) correo; (job, situation) puesto; (pole) poste m; (on blog, social network) post m ▷ vt (BRIT) mandar por correo; (on blog, social network) colgar; (BRIT: appoint): **to ~ to** destinar a; **postage** n porte m, franqueo; **postal** adj postal, de correos; **postal order** n giro postal; **postbox** n (BRIT) buzón m; **postcard** n (tarjeta) postal f; **postcode** n (BRIT) código postal

poster [ˈpəustəʳ] n cartel m

postgraduate [ˈpəustˈɡrædjuɪt] n posgraduado/a

postman [ˈpəustmən] (irreg: like **man**) n (BRIT) cartero

postmark [ˈpəustmɑːk] n matasellos m inv

post-mortem [pəustˈmɔːtəm] n autopsia

post office n (building) (oficina de) correos m; (organization): **the Post Office** Dirección f General de Correos

postpone [pəsˈpəun] vt aplazar

posture [ˈpɔstʃəʳ] n postura, actitud f

postwoman [ˈpəustwumən] (irreg: like **woman**) n (BRIT) cartera

pot [pɔt] n (for cooking) olla; (teapot) tetera; (coffeepot) cafetera; (for flowers) maceta; (for jam) tarro, pote m (LAM); (inf: marijuana) costo, chocolate m ▷ vt (plant) poner en tiesto; **to go to ~** (inf) irse al traste

potato [pəˈteɪtəu] (pl potatoes) n patata, papa (LAM); **potato peeler** n pelapatatas m inv

potent [ˈpəutnt] adj potente, poderoso; (drink) fuerte

potential [pəˈtɛnʃl] adj potencial, posible ▷ n potencial m

pothole [ˈpɔthəul] n (in road) bache m; (BRIT: underground) gruta

pot plant n planta de interior

potter [ˈpɔtəʳ] n alfarero/a ▷ vi: **to ~ around, ~ about** entretenerse haciendo cosillas; **pottery** [ˈpɔtərɪ] n cerámica; (factory) alfarería

potty [ˈpɔtɪ] n orinal m de niño

pouch [pautʃ] n (Zool) bolsa; (for tobacco) petaca

poultry [ˈpəultrɪ] n aves fpl de corral; (meat) pollo

pounce [pauns] vi: **to ~ on** precipitarse sobre

pound [paund] n libra ▷ vt (beat) golpear; (crush) machacar ▷ vi (beat) dar golpes; **pound sterling** n libra esterlina

pour [pɔːʳ] vt echar; (tea) servir ▷ vi correr, fluir; **to ~ sb a drink** servirle a algn una copa; **pour in** vi (people) entrar en tropel; **pour out** vi salir en tropel ▷ vt (drink) echar, servir; (fig): **to ~ out one's feelings** desahogarse; **pouring** adj: **pouring rain** lluvia torrencial

p

pout [paut] *vi* hacer pucheros

poverty ['pɒvətɪ] *n* pobreza, miseria

powder ['paudə^r] *n* polvo; (*also*: **face ~**) polvos *mpl* ▷ *vt* empolvar; **to ~ one's face** empolvarse la cara; **powdered milk** *n* leche *f* en polvo

power ['pauə^r] *n* poder *m*; (*strength*) fuerza; (*nation*) potencia; (*drive*) empuje *m*; (*Tech*) potencia; (*Elec*) energía ▷ *vt* impulsar; **to be in ~** (*Pol*) estar en el poder; **power cut** *n* (*BRIT*) apagón *m*; **power failure** *n* = **power cut**; **powerful** *adj* poderoso; (*engine*) potente; (*play, speech*) convincente; **powerless** *adj* impotente; **power point** *n* (*BRIT*) enchufe *m*; **power station** *n* central *f* eléctrica

pp *n abbr* (= *per procurationem*; *by proxy*) p.p.; = **pages**

PR *n abbr* (= *public relations*) relaciones *fpl* públicas

practical ['præktɪkl] *adj* práctico; **practical joke** *n* broma pesada; **practically** *adv* (*almost*) casi, prácticamente

practice ['præktɪs] *n* (*habit*) costumbre *f*; (*exercise*) práctica; (*training*) adiestramiento; (*Med*: *of profession*) práctica, ejercicio; (*Med, Law*: *business*) consulta ▷ *vt, vi* (*US*) = **practise**; **in ~** (*in reality*) en la práctica; **out of ~** desentrenado

practise, (*US*) **practice** ['præktɪs] *vt* (*carry out*) practicar; (*profession*) ejercer; (*train at*) practicar ▷ *vi* ejercer; (*train*) practicar; **practising**, (*US*) **practicing** *adj* (*Christian etc*) practicante; (*lawyer*) en ejercicio

practitioner [præk'tɪʃənə^r] *n* (*Med*) médico/a

pragmatic [præg'mætɪk] *adj* pragmático

prairie ['prɛərɪ] *n* pampa

praise [preɪz] *n* alabanza(s) *f(pl)*, elogio(s) *m(pl)* ▷ *vt* alabar, elogiar

pram [præm] *n* (*BRIT*) cochecito de niño

prank [præŋk] *n* travesura

prawn [prɔːn] *n* gamba; **prawn cocktail** *n* cóctel *m* de gambas

pray [preɪ] *vi* rezar; **prayer** [prɛə^r] *n* oración *f*, rezo; (*entreaty*) ruego, súplica

preach [priːtʃ] *vi* predicar; **preacher** *n* predicador(a) *m/f*

precarious [prɪ'kɛərɪəs] *adj* precario

precaution [prɪ'kɔːʃən] *n* precaución *f*

precede [prɪ'siːd] *vt, vi* preceder; **precedent** ['prɛsɪdənt] *n* precedente *m*; **preceding** [prɪ'siːdɪŋ] *adj* precedente

precinct ['priːsɪŋkt] *n* recinto

precious ['prɛʃəs] *adj* precioso

precise [prɪ'saɪs] *adj* preciso, exacto; **precisely** *adv* exactamente, precisamente

precision [prɪ'sɪʒən] *n* precisión *f*

predator ['prɛdətə^r] *n* depredador *m*

predecessor ['priːdɪsɛsə^r] *n* antecesor(a) *m/f*

predicament [prɪ'dɪkəmənt] *n* apuro

predict [prɪ'dɪkt] *vt* pronosticar; **predictable** *adj* previsible; **prediction** [prɪ'dɪkʃən] *n* predicción *f*

predominantly [prɪ'dɔmɪnəntlɪ] *adv* en su mayoría

preface ['prɛfəs] *n* prefacio

prefect ['priːfɛkt] *n* (*BRIT*: *in school*) monitor(a) *m/f*

prefer [prɪ'fəː^r] *vt* preferir; **to ~ coffee to tea** preferir el café al té; **preferable** ['prɛfrəbl] *adj* preferible; **preferably** ['prɛfrəblɪ] *adv* preferentemente, más bien; **preference** ['prɛfrəns] *n* preferencia; (*priority*) prioridad *f*

prefix ['priːfɪks] *n* prefijo

pregnancy ['prɛgnənsɪ] *n* (*of woman*) embarazo; (*of animal*) preñez *f*

pregnant ['prɛgnənt] *adj* (*woman*) embarazada; (*animal*) preñada

prehistoric ['priːhɪs'tɔrɪk] *adj* prehistórico

prejudice ['prɛdʒudɪs] *n* prejuicio; **prejudiced** *adj* (*person*) predispuesto

preliminary [prɪˈlɪmɪnərɪ] adj preliminar

prelude [ˈprɛljuːd] n preludio

premature [ˈprɛmətjuəʳ] adj prematuro

premier [ˈprɛmɪəʳ] adj primero, principal ▷ n (Pol) primer(a) ministro/a

première [ˈprɛmɪɛəʳ] n estreno

Premier League n primera división

premises [ˈprɛmɪsɪs] npl local msg; **on the ~** en el lugar mismo

premium [ˈpriːmɪəm] n premio; (insurance) prima; **to be at a ~** estar muy solicitado

premonition [prɛməˈnɪʃən] n presentimiento

preoccupied [priːˈɔkjupaɪd] adj ensimismado

prepaid [priːˈpeɪd] adj porte pagado

preparation [prɛpəˈreɪʃən] n preparación f; **preparations** npl preparativos mpl

preparatory school n (BRIT) colegio privado de enseñanza primaria; (US) colegio privado de enseñanza secundaria

prepare [prɪˈpɛəʳ] vt preparar, disponer; (Culin) preparar ▷ vi: **to ~ for** (action) prepararse or disponerse para; (event) hacer preparativos para; **prepared** adj (willing): **to be prepared to help sb** estar dispuesto a ayudar a algn; **prepared for** listo para

preposition [prɛpəˈzɪʃən] n preposición f

prep school [prɛp-] n = **preparatory school**

prerequisite [priːˈrɛkwɪzɪt] n requisito previo

preschool [ˈpriːˈskuːl] adj preescolar

prescribe [prɪˈskraɪb] vt (Med) recetar

prescription [prɪˈskrɪpʃən] n (Med) receta

presence [ˈprɛzns] n presencia; **in sb's ~** en presencia de algn; **~ of mind** aplomo

present adj [ˈprɛznt] (in attendance) presente; (current) actual ▷ n [ˈprɛznt] (gift) regalo; (actuality): **the ~** la actualidad, el presente ▷ vt [prɪˈzɛnt] (introduce) presentar; (expound) exponer; (give) presentar, dar, ofrecer; (Theat) representar; **to give sb a ~** regalar algo a algn; **at ~** actualmente; **presentable** [prɪˈzɛntəbl] adj: **to make o.s. presentable** arreglarse; **presentation** [prɛznˈteɪʃən] n presentación f; (of case) exposición f; **present-day** adj actual; **presenter** [prɪˈzɛntəʳ] n (Radio, TV) locutor(a) m/f; **presently** adv (soon) dentro de poco; (now) ahora; **present participle** n participio (de) presente

preservation [prɛzəˈveɪʃən] n conservación f

preservative [prɪˈzəːvətɪv] n conservante m

preserve [prɪˈzəːv] vt (keep safe) preservar, proteger; (maintain) mantener; (food) conservar ▷ n (for game) coto, vedado; (often pl: jam) confitura

preside [prɪˈzaɪd] vi presidir

president [ˈprɛzɪdənt] n presidente mf; (US: of company) director(a) m/f; **presidential** [prɛzɪˈdɛnʃl] adj presidencial

press [prɛs] n (tool, machine, newspapers) prensa; (printer's) imprenta; (of hand) apretón m ▷ vt (push) empujar; (squeeze: button) apretar; (iron: clothes) planchar; (pressure) presionar; (insist): **to ~ sth on sb** insistir en que algn acepte algo ▷ vi (squeeze) apretar; **we are ~ed for time** tenemos poco tiempo; **to ~ sb to do** or **into doing sth** (urge, entreat) presionar a algn para que haga algo; **press conference** n rueda de prensa; **pressing** adj apremiante; **press stud** n (BRIT) botón m de presión; **press-up** n (BRIT) flexión f

pressure [ˈprɛʃəʳ] n presión f; **to put ~ on sb** presionar a algn; **pressure cooker** n olla a presión; **pressure group** n grupo de presión

prestige [prɛs'ti:ʒ] n prestigio
prestigious [prɛs'tɪdʒəs] adj
prestigioso
presumably [prɪ'zju:məblɪ] adv es
de suponer que, cabe presumir que
presume [prɪ'zju:m] vt: **to ~ (that)**
presumir (que), suponer (que)
pretence, (US) **pretense** [prɪ'tɛns]
n fingimiento; **under false ~s** con
engaños
pretend [prɪ'tɛnd] vt, vi fingir
> Be careful not to translate pretend
by the Spanish word pretender.
pretense [prɪ'tɛns] n (US)
= **pretence**
pretentious [prɪ'tɛnʃəs] adj
pretencioso; (ostentatious) ostentoso,
aparatoso
pretext ['pri:tɛkst] n pretexto
pretty ['prɪtɪ] adj bonito, lindo (LAM)
> adv bastante
prevail [prɪ'veɪl] vi (gain mastery)
prevalecer; (be current) predominar;
prevailing adj (dominant)
predominante
prevalent ['prɛvələnt] adj
(widespread) extendido
prevent [prɪ'vɛnt] vt: **to ~ (sb) from
doing sth** impedir (a algn) hacer algo;
to ~ sth from happening evitar que
ocurra algo; **prevention** [prɪ'vɛnʃən]
n prevención f; **preventive** adj
preventivo
preview ['pri:vju:] n (of film)
preestreno
previous ['pri:vɪəs] adj previo,
anterior; **previously** adv antes
prey [preɪ] n presa > vi: **to ~ on** (feed
on) alimentarse de; **it was ~ing on his
mind** le obsesionaba
price [praɪs] n precio > vt (goods) fijar
el precio de; **priceless** adj que no tiene
precio; **price list** n tarifa
prick [prɪk] n (sting) picadura > vt
pinchar; (hurt) picar; **to ~ up one's
ears** aguzar el oído
prickly ['prɪklɪ] adj espinoso; (fig:
person) enojadizo

pride [praɪd] n orgullo; (pej) soberbia
> vt: **to ~ o.s. on** enorgullecerse de
priest [pri:st] n sacerdote m
primarily ['praɪmərɪlɪ] adv ante todo
primary ['praɪmərɪ] adj (first in
importance) principal > n (US: also:
~ election) (elección f) primaria;
primary school n (BRIT) escuela
primaria
prime [praɪm] adj primero, principal;
(excellent) selecto, de primera clase
> n: **in the ~ of life** en la flor de la
vida > vt (wood, also fig) preparar;
~ example ejemplo típico; **Prime
Minister** n primer(a) ministro/a; ver
nota **"Downing Street"**
primitive ['prɪmɪtɪv] adj primitivo;
(crude) rudimentario
primrose ['prɪmrəuz] n primavera,
prímula
prince [prɪns] n príncipe m
princess [prɪn'sɛs] n princesa
principal ['prɪnsɪpl] adj principal
> n director(a) m/f; **principally** adv
principalmente
principle ['prɪnsɪpl] n principio; **in ~**
en principio; **on ~** por principio
print [prɪnt] n (impression) marca,
impresión f; (footprint) huella;
(fingerprint) huella dactilar; (letters)
letra de molde; (fabric) estampado;
(Art) grabado; (Phot) impresión f > vt
imprimir; (write in capitals) escribir en
letras de molde; **out of ~** agotado;
print out vt (Comput) imprimir;
printer n (person) impresor(a) m/f;
(machine) impresora; **printout** n
(Comput) copia impresa
prior ['praɪər] adj anterior, previo;
(more important) más importante; **~ to
doing** antes de or hasta hacer
priority [praɪ'ɔrɪtɪ] n prioridad f;
to have or **take ~ over sth** tener
prioridad sobre algo
prison ['prɪzn] n cárcel f, prisión f
> cpd carcelario; **prisoner** n (in prison)
preso/a; (captured person) prisionero/a
pristine ['prɪsti:n] adj pristino

privacy ['prɪvəsɪ] n intimidad f
private ['praɪvɪt] adj (personal)
particular; (property, industry, discussion
etc) privado; (person) reservado; (place)
tranquilo ▷ n soldado raso; **"~"** (on
envelope) "confidencial"; (on door)
"privado"; **in ~** en privado; **privately**
adv en privado; (in o.s.) en secreto;
private property n propiedad f
privada; **private school** n colegio
privado
privatize ['praɪvɪtaɪz] vt privatizar
privilege ['prɪvɪlɪdʒ] n privilegio;
(prerogative) prerrogativa
prize [praɪz] n premio ▷ adj de primera
clase ▷ vt apreciar, estimar; **prize-
giving** n distribución f de premios;
prizewinner n premiado/a
pro [prəu] n (Sport) profesional mf; **the
~s and cons** los pros y los contras
probability [prɔbə'bɪlɪtɪ] n
probabilidad f; **in all ~** lo más probable
probable ['prɔbəbl] adj probable
probably ['prɔbəblɪ] adv
probablemente
probation [prə'beɪʃən] n: **on ~**
(employee) a prueba; (Law) en libertad
condicional
probe [prəub] n (Med, Space) sonda;
(enquiry) investigación f ▷ vt sondar;
(investigate) investigar
problem ['prɔbləm] n problema m
procedure [prə'si:dʒə'] n
procedimiento; (bureaucratic)
trámites mpl
proceed [prə'si:d] vi proceder;
(continue): **to ~ (with)** continuar (con);
proceedings npl acto(s) m(pl); (Law)
proceso sg; **proceeds** ['prəusi:dz] npl
ganancias fpl, ingresos mpl
process ['prəuses] n proceso ▷ vt
tratar, elaborar
procession [prə'seʃən] n desfile m;
funeral ~ cortejo fúnebre
proclaim [prə'kleɪm] vt (announce)
anunciar
prod [prɔd] vt empujar ▷ n
empujoncito; codazo

produce n ['prɔdju:s] (Agr) productos
mpl agrícolas ▷ vt [prə'dju:s] producir;
(Theat) presentar; **producer** n
(Theat) director(a) m/f; (Agr, Cine)
productor(a) m/f
product ['prɔdʌkt] n producto;
production [prə'dʌkʃən] n (act)
producción f; (Theat) representación
f; **productive** [prə'dʌktɪv] adj
productivo; **productivity**
[prɔdʌk'tɪvɪtɪ] n productividad f
Prof. [prɔf] abbr (= professor) Prof
profession [prə'feʃən] n profesión f;
professional n profesional mf; (skilled
person) perito
professor [prə'fesə'] n (BRIT)
catedrático/a; (US: teacher) profesor(a)
m/f
profile ['prəufaɪl] n perfil m
profit ['prɔfɪt] n (Comm) ganancia ▷ vi:
to ~ by or **from** aprovechar or sacar
provecho de; **profitable** adj (Econ)
rentable
profound [prə'faund] adj profundo
programme, (US or Comput)
program ['prəugræm] n programa
m ▷ vt programar; **programmer,**
(US) **programer** ['prəugræmə'] n
programador(a) m/f; **programming,**
(US) **programing** ['prəugræmɪŋ] n
programación f
progress n ['prəugres] progreso;
(development) desarrollo ▷ vi [prə'gres]
progresar, avanzar; **in ~** en curso;
progressive [prə'gresɪv] adj
progresivo; (person) progresista
prohibit [prə'hɪbɪt] vt prohibir; **to
~ sb from doing sth** prohibir a algn
hacer algo
project n ['prɔdʒekt] proyecto ▷ vt
[prə'dʒekt] proyectar ▷ vi (stick
out) salir, sobresalir; **projection**
[prə'dʒekʃən] n proyección f;
(overhang) saliente m; **projector**
[prə'dʒektə'] n proyector m
prolific [prə'lɪfɪk] adj prolífico
prolong [prə'lɔŋ] vt prolongar,
extender

P

prom [prɔm] n abbr (BRIT)
= **promenade**; = **promenade
concert**; (US: ball) baile m de gala; ver
nota **"prom"**

○ **PROM**
○
○ Los conciertos de música clásica
○ más conocidos en Inglaterra son
○ los llamados *Proms* (o *promenade
○ concerts*), que tienen lugar en el
○ *Royal Albert Hall* de Londres, aunque
○ también se llama así a cualquier
○ concierto de esas características.
○ Su nombre se debe al hecho de que
○ en un principio el público paseaba
○ durante las actuaciones; en la
○ actualidad parte de la gente que
○ acude a ellos permanece de pie.
○ En Estados Unidos se llama *prom*
○ a un baile de gala en un colegio o
○ universidad.

promenade [prɔmə'nɑ:d] n (by sea)
paseo marítimo
prominent ['prɔmɪnənt] adj
(standing out) saliente; (important)
eminente, importante
promiscuous [prə'mɪskjuəs] adj
(sexually) promiscuo
promise ['prɔmɪs] n promesa
▷ vt, vi prometer; **promising** adj
prometedor(a)
promote [prə'məut] vt (Mil)
ascender; (employee) ascender; (ideas)
fomentar; **promotion** [prə'məuʃən]
n promoción f; (Mil) ascenso
prompt [prɔmpt] adj pronto ▷ adv:
at six o'clock ~ a las seis en punto ▷ n
(Comput) aviso, guía ▷ vt (urge) mover,
incitar; (when talking) instar; (Theat)
apuntar; **to ~ sb to do sth** instar
a algn a hacer algo; **promptly** adv
(punctually) puntualmente; (rapidly)
rápidamente
prone [prəun] adj (lying) postrado;
~ to propenso a
prong [prɔŋ] n diente m, punta

pronoun ['prəunaun] n
pronombre m
pronounce [prə'nauns] vt
pronunciar
pronunciation [prənʌnsɪ'eɪʃən] n
pronunciación f
proof [pru:f] n prueba ▷ adj:
~ against a prueba de
prop [prɔp] n apoyo m; (fig) sostén m;
props npl accesorios mpl, at(t)rezzo
msg; **prop up** vt (roof, structure)
apuntalar; (economy) respaldar
propaganda [prɔpə'gændə] n
propaganda
propeller [prə'pɛlər] n hélice f
proper ['prɔpər] adj (suited, right)
propio; (exact) justo; (seemly)
correcto, decente; (authentic)
verdadero; **properly** adv (adequately)
correctamente; (decently)
decentemente; **proper noun** n
nombre m propio
property ['prɔpətɪ] n propiedad f;
personal ~ bienes mpl muebles
prophecy ['prɔfɪsɪ] n profecía
prophet ['prɔfɪt] n profeta mf
proportion [prə'pɔ:ʃən] n
proporción f; (share) parte f;
proportions npl (size) dimensiones
fpl; **proportional** adj: **proportional
(to)** en proporción (con)
proposal [prə'pəuzl] n (offer of
marriage) oferta de matrimonio; (plan)
proyecto
propose [prə'pəuz] vt proponer ▷ vi
declararse; **to ~ to do** tener intención
de hacer
proposition [prɔpə'zɪʃən] n
propuesta
proprietor [prə'praɪətər] n
propietario/a, dueño/a
prose [prəuz] n prosa
prosecute ['prɔsɪkju:t] vt
(Law) procesar; **prosecution**
[prɔsɪ'kju:ʃən] n proceso, causa;
(accusing side) acusación f; **prosecutor**
n acusador(a) m/f; (also: **public
prosecutor**) fiscal mf

prospect n ['prɔspɛkt] (chance) posibilidad f; (outlook) perspectiva ▷ vi [prə'spɛkt] buscar; **prospects** npl (for work etc) perspectivas fpl; **prospective** [prə'spɛktɪv] adj futuro

prospectus [prə'spɛktəs] n prospecto

prosper ['prɔspə'] vi prosperar; **prosperity** [prɔ'spɛrɪtɪ] n prosperidad f; **prosperous** adj próspero

prostitute ['prɔstɪtju:t] n prostituta; **male ~** prostituto

protect [prə'tɛkt] vt proteger; **protection** [prə'tɛkʃən] n protección f; **protective** adj protector(a)

protein ['prəuti:n] n proteína

protest n ['prəutɛst] protesta ▷ vi [prə'tɛst]: **to ~ about** or **at/against** protestar de/contra ▷ vt (insist): **to ~ (that)** insistir en (que)

Protestant ['prɔtɪstənt] adj, n protestante mf

protester, protestor n manifestante mf

protractor [prə'træktə'] n (Geom) transportador m

proud [praud] adj orgulloso; (pej) soberbio, altanero

prove [pru:v] vt probar; (show) demostrar ▷ vi: **to ~ correct** resultar correcto; **to ~ o.s.** ponerse a prueba

proverb ['prɔvə:b] n refrán m

provide [prə'vaɪd] vt proporcionar, dar; **to ~ sb with sth** proveer a algn de algo; **provide for** vt fus (person) mantener a; (problem etc) tener en cuenta; **provided** conj: **provided (that)** con tal de que, a condición de que; **providing** [prə'vaɪdɪŋ] conj: **providing (that)** a condición de que, con tal de que

province ['prɔvɪns] n provincia; (fig) esfera; **provincial** [prə'vɪnʃəl] adj provincial; (pej) provinciano

provision [prə'vɪʒən] n (supply) suministro, abastecimiento;

provisions npl provisiones fpl, víveres mpl; **provisional** adj provisional

provocative [prə'vɔkətɪv] adj provocativo

provoke [prə'vəuk] vt (arouse) provocar, incitar; (anger) enojar

prowl [praul] vi (also: **~ about, ~ around**) merodear ▷ n: **on the ~** de merodeo

proximity [prɔk'sɪmɪtɪ] n proximidad f

proxy ['prɔksɪ] n: **by ~** por poderes

prudent ['pru:dnt] adj prudente

prune [pru:n] n ciruela pasa ▷ vt podar

pry [praɪ] vi: **to ~ into** entrometerse en

PS abbr (= postscript) P.D.

pseudonym ['sju:dənɪm] n seudónimo

PSHE n abbr (BRIT Scol: = personal, social, and health education) formación social y sanitaria para la vida adulta

psychiatric [saɪkɪ'ætrɪk] adj psiquiátrico

psychiatrist [saɪ'kaɪətrɪst] n psiquiatra mf

psychic ['saɪkɪk] adj (also: **~al**) psíquico

psychoanalysis (pl **psychoanalyses**) [saɪkəuə'nælɪsɪs, -si:z] n psicoanálisis m inv

psychological [saɪkə'lɔdʒɪkl] adj psicológico

psychologist [saɪ'kɔlədʒɪst] n psicólogo/a

psychology [saɪ'kɔlədʒɪ] n psicología

psychotherapy [saɪkəu'θɛrəpɪ] n psicoterapia

pt abbr = **pint; point**

PTO abbr (= please turn over) sigue

pub [pʌb] n abbr (= public house) pub m, bar m

puberty ['pju:bətɪ] n pubertad f

public ['pʌblɪk] adj público ▷ n: **the ~** el público; **in ~** en público; **to make sth ~** revelar or hacer público algo

P

publication [pʌblɪˈkeɪʃən] *n*
publicación *f*

public: public company *n* sociedad
f anónima; **public convenience** *n*
(BRIT) aseos *mpl* públicos, sanitarios
mpl (LAM); **public holiday** *n* día *m*
de fiesta, (día) feriado (LAM); **public
house** *n* (BRIT) pub *m*, bar *m*

publicity [pʌbˈlɪsɪtɪ] *n* publicidad *f*

publicize [ˈpʌblɪsaɪz] *vt* publicitar

public: public limited company *n*
sociedad *f* anónima (S.A.); **publicly**
adv públicamente, en público;
public opinion *n* opinión *f* pública;
public relations *n* relaciones *fpl*
públicas; **public school** *n* (BRIT)
colegio privado; (US) instituto; **public
transport** *n* transporte *m* público

publish [ˈpʌblɪʃ] *vt* publicar;
publisher *n* (person) editor(a) *m/f*;
(firm) editorial *f*; **publishing** *n*
(industry) industria del libro

pub lunch *n* almuerzo que se sirve en un
pub; **to go for a ~** almorzar o comer
en un pub

pudding [ˈpudɪŋ] *n* pudín *m*; (BRIT:
sweet) postre *m*; **black ~** morcilla

puddle [ˈpʌdl] *n* charco

Puerto Rico [-ˈriːkəu] *n* Puerto Rico

puff [pʌf] *n* soplo; (of smoke) bocanada;
(of breathing, engine) resoplido ▷ *vt*:
to ~ one's pipe dar chupadas a la
pipa ▷ *vi* (pant) jadear; **puff pastry** *n*
hojaldre *m*

pull [pul] *n* ▷ *vt* tirar de; (haul) tirar,
arrastrar ▷ *vi* tirar, jalar (LAM); **to
give sth a ~** (tug) dar un tirón a algo;
to ~ to pieces hacer pedazos; **to ~
one's punches** andarse con bromas;
to ~ one's weight hacer su parte;
to ~ o.s. together tranquilizarse,
sobreponerse; **to ~ sb's leg** tomar
el pelo a algn; **pull apart** *vt* (break)
romper; **pull away** *vi* (vehicle: move off)
salir, arrancar; (draw back) apartarse
bruscamente; **pull back** *vt* (lever etc)
tirar hacia sí; (curtains) descorrer ▷ *vi*
(refrain) contenerse; (Mil: withdraw)

retirarse; **pull down** *vt* (house)
derribar; **pull in** *vi* (Aut: at the kerb)
parar (junto a la acera); (Rail) llegar;
pull off *vt* (deal etc) cerrar; **pull out** *vi*
(car, train etc) salir ▷ *vt* sacar, arrancar;
pull over *vi* (Aut) hacerse a un lado;
pull up *vi* (stop) parar ▷ *vt* (uproot)
arrancar, desarraigar

pulley [ˈpulɪ] *n* polea

pullover [ˈpuləuvəʳ] *n* jersey *m*,
suéter *m*

pulp [pʌlp] *n* (of fruit) pulpa

pulpit [ˈpulpɪt] *n* púlpito

pulse [pʌls] *n* (Anat) pulso; (of music,
engine) pulsación *f*; (Bot) legumbre *f*;
pulses *npl* legumbres

puma [ˈpjuːmə] *n* puma *m*

pump [pʌmp] *n* bomba; (shoe)
zapatilla de tenis ▷ *vt* sacar con una
bomba; **pump up** *vt* inflar

pumpkin [ˈpʌmpkɪn] *n* calabaza

pun [pʌn] *n* juego de palabras

punch [pʌntʃ] *n* (blow) golpe *m*,
puñetazo; (tool) punzón *m*; (drink)
ponche *m* ▷ *vt*: **to ~ sb/sth** (hit) dar
un puñetazo o golpear a algn/algo;
punch-up *n* (BRIT inf) riña

punctual [ˈpʌŋktjuəl] *adj* puntual

punctuation [pʌŋktjuˈeɪʃən] *n*
puntuación *f*

puncture [ˈpʌŋktʃəʳ] (BRIT) *n*
pinchazo ▷ *vt* pinchar

punish [ˈpʌnɪʃ] *vt* castigar;
punishment *n* castigo

punk [pʌŋk] *n* (also: ~ **rocker**) punki
mf; (also: ~ **rock**) música punk; (US inf:
hoodlum) matón *m*

pup [pʌp] *n* cachorro

pupil [ˈpjuːpl] *n* alumno/a; (of eye)
pupila

puppet [ˈpʌpɪt] *n* títere *m*

puppy [ˈpʌpɪ] *n* cachorro, perrito

purchase [ˈpəːtʃɪs] *n* compra ▷ *vt*
comprar

pure [pjuəʳ] *adj* puro; **purely** *adv*
puramente

purify [ˈpjuərɪfaɪ] *vt* purificar, depurar

purity [ˈpjuərɪtɪ] *n* pureza

purple ['pəːpl] *adj* morado
purpose ['pəːpəs] *n* propósito; **on ~** a propósito, adrede
purr [pəːʳ] *vi* ronronear
purse [pəːs] *n* monedero; (*US: handbag*) bolso, cartera (*LAM*) ▷ *vt* fruncir
pursue [pəˈsjuː] *vt* seguir
pursuit [pəˈsjuːt] *n* (*chase*) caza; (*occupation*) actividad *f*
pus [pʌs] *n* pus *m*
push [puʃ] *n* empujón *m*; (*drive*) empuje *m* ▷ *vt* empujar; (*button*) apretar; (*promote*) promover ▷ *vi* empujar; **to ~ for** (*better pay, conditions*) reivindicar; **push in** *vi* colarse; **push off** *vi* (*inf*) largarse; **push on** *vi* seguir adelante; **push over** *vt* (*cause to fall*) hacer caer, derribar; (*knock over*) volcar; **push through** *vi* (*crowd*) abrirse paso a empujones ▷ *vt* (*measure*) despachar; **pushchair** *n* (*BRIT*) silla de niño; **pusher** *n* (*also*: **drug pusher**) traficante *mf* de drogas; **push-up** *n* (*US*) flexión *f*
puss [pus], **pussy(-cat)** ['pusɪ-] *n* minino
put (*pt, pp* **put**) [put] *vt* (*place*) poner, colocar; (*put into*) meter; (*express, say*) expresar; (*a question*) hacer; (*estimate*) calcular; **put aside** *vt* (*lay down: book etc*) dejar *or* poner a un lado; (*save*) ahorrar; (*in shop*) guardar; **put away** *vt* (*store*) guardar; **put back** *vt* (*replace*) devolver a su lugar; (*postpone*) aplazar; **put by** *vt* (*money*) guardar; **put down** *vt* (*on ground*) poner en el suelo; (*animal*) sacrificar; (*in writing*) apuntar; (*revolt etc*) sofocar; (*attribute*) atribuir; **put forward** *vt* (*ideas*) presentar, proponer; **put in** *vt* (*application, complaint*) presentar; (*time*) dedicar; **put off** *vt* (*postpone*) aplazar; (*discourage*) desanimar; **put on** *vt* ponerse; (*light etc*) encender; (*play etc*) presentar; (*brake*) echar; (*record, kettle etc*) poner; (*assume*) adoptar; **put out** *vt* (*fire, light*) apagar; (*rubbish* *etc*) sacar; (*cat etc*) echar; (*one's hand*) alargar; **put through** *vt* (*call*) poner; (*plan etc*) hacer aprobar; **put together** *vt* unir, reunir; (*assemble: furniture*) armar, montar; (*meal*) preparar; **put up** *vt* (*raise*) levantar, alzar; (*hang*) colgar; (*build*) construir; (*increase*) aumentar; (*accommodate*) alojar; **put up with** *vt fus* aguantar
putt [pʌt] *n* putt *m*; **putting green** *n* green *m*, minigolf *m*
puzzle ['pʌzl] *n* rompecabezas *m inv*; (*also*: **crossword ~**) crucigrama *m*; (*mystery*) misterio ▷ *vt* dejar perplejo, confundir ▷ *vi*: **to ~ over** devanarse los sesos sobre; **puzzling** *adj* misterioso, extraño
pyjamas, (*US*) **pajamas** [pɪˈdʒɑːməz] *npl* pijama *msg*
pylon ['paɪlən] *n* torre *f* de conducción eléctrica
pyramid ['pɪrəmɪd] *n* pirámide *f*

p

q

quack [kwæk] n graznido; (*pej: doctor*) curandero/a

quadruple [kwɔ'dru:pl] vt, vi cuadruplicar

quail [kweɪl] n codorniz f ▷ vi amedrentarse

quaint [kweɪnt] adj extraño; (*picturesque*) pintoresco

quake [kweɪk] vi temblar ▷ n abbr = **earthquake**

qualification [kwɔlɪfɪ'keɪʃən] n (*ability*) capacidad f; (*often pl: diploma etc*) título; (*reservation*) salvedad f

qualified ['kwɔlɪfaɪd] adj capacitado; (*limited*) limitado; (*professionally*) titulado

qualify ['kwɔlɪfaɪ] vt (*capacitate*) capacitar; (*modify*) matizar ▷ vi: **to ~ (for)** (*in competition*) calificarse (para); (*be eligible*) reunir los requisitos (para); **to ~ (as)** (*pass examination*) calificarse (de), graduarse (en)

quality ['kwɔlɪtɪ] n calidad f; (*moral*) cualidad f

qualm [kwɑ:m] n escrúpulo

quantify ['kwɔntɪfaɪ] vt cuantificar

quantity ['kwɔntɪtɪ] n cantidad f; **in ~** en grandes cantidades

quarantine ['kwɔrnti:n] n cuarentena

quarrel ['kwɔrl] n riña, pelea ▷ vi reñir, pelearse

quarry ['kwɔrɪ] n cantera

quart [kwɔ:t] n cuarto de galón = 1.136 l

quarter ['kwɔ:tə^r] n cuarto, cuarta parte f; (*us: coin*) moneda de 25 centavos; (*of year*) trimestre m; (*district*) barrio ▷ vt dividir en cuartos; (*Mil: lodge*) alojar; **quarters** npl (*barracks*) cuartel msg; (*living quarters*) alojamiento sg; **a ~ of an hour** un cuarto de hora; **quarter final** n cuarto de final; **quarterly** adj trimestral ▷ adv cada 3 meses, trimestralmente

quartet(te) [kwɔ:'tɛt] n cuarteto

quartz [kwɔ:ts] n cuarzo

quay [ki:] n (*also*: **~side**) muelle m

queasy ['kwi:zɪ] adj: **to feel ~** tener náuseas

queen [kwi:n] n reina; (*Cards etc*) dama

queer [kwɪə^r] adj raro, extraño ▷ n (*pej, infl*) marica (!) m

quench [kwɛntʃ] vt: **to ~ one's thirst** apagar la sed

query ['kwɪərɪ] n (*question*) pregunta ▷ vt dudar de

quest [kwɛst] n busca, búsqueda

question ['kwɛstʃən] n pregunta; (*matter*) asunto, cuestión f ▷ vt (*doubt*) dudar de; (*interrogate*) interrogar, hacer preguntas a; **beyond ~** fuera de toda duda; **out of the ~** imposible, ni hablar; **questionable** adj dudoso; **question mark** n punto de interrogación; **questionnaire** [kwɛstʃə'nɛə^r] n cuestionario

queue [kju:] (*BRIT*) n cola ▷ vi hacer cola

quiche [ki:ʃ] n quiche m

quick [kwɪk] *adj* rápido; (*agile*) ágil; (*mind*) listo ▷ *n*: **cut to the ~** (*fig*) herido en lo más vivo; **be ~!** ¡date prisa!; **quickly** *adv* rápidamente, de prisa

quid [kwɪd] *n* (*pl inv*: BRIT *inf*) libra

quiet ['kwaɪət] *adj* (*voice, music etc*) bajo; (*person, place*) tranquilo ▷ *n* silencio; (*calm*) tranquilidad *f*; **quietly** *adv* tranquilamente; (*silently*) silenciosamente

> Be careful not to translate *quiet* by the Spanish word *quieto*.

quilt [kwɪlt] *n* edredón *m*

quirky ['kwɜːkɪ] *adj* raro, estrafalario

quit [kwɪt] (*pt, pp* **quit** *or* **quitted**) *vt* dejar, abandonar; (*premises*) desocupar ▷ *vi* (*give up*) renunciar; (*resign*) dimitir

quite [kwaɪt] *adv* (*rather*) bastante; (*entirely*) completamente; **~ a few of them** un buen número de ellos; **~ (so)!** ¡así es!, ¡exactamente!; **that's not ~ right** eso no está del todo bien

quits [kwɪts] *adj*: **~ (with)** en paz (con); **let's call it ~** quedamos en paz

quiver ['kwɪvə^r] *vi* estremecerse

quiz [kwɪz] *n* concurso

quota ['kwəʊtə] *n* cuota

quotation [kwəʊ'teɪʃən] *n* cita; (*estimate*) presupuesto; **quotation marks** *npl* comillas *fpl*

quote [kwəʊt] *n* cita ▷ *vt* (*sentence*) citar; (*Comm: sum, figure*) cotizar ▷ *vi*: **to ~ from** citar de; **quotes** *npl* (*inverted commas*) comillas *fpl*

rabbi ['ræbaɪ] *n* rabino

rabbit ['ræbɪt] *n* conejo

rabies ['reɪbiːz] *n* rabia

RAC *n abbr* (BRIT: = *Royal Automobile Club*) ≈ RACE *m* (SP)

raccoon [rə'kuːn] *n* mapache *m*

race [reɪs] *n* carrera; (*species*) raza ▷ *vt* (*horse*) hacer correr; (*engine*) acelerar ▷ *vi* (*compete*) competir; (*run*) correr; (*pulse*) latir a ritmo acelerado; **race car** *n* (US) = **racing car**; **racecourse** *n* hipódromo; **racehorse** *n* caballo de carreras; **racetrack** *n* hipódromo; (*for cars*) circuito de carreras

racial ['reɪʃl] *adj* racial

racing ['reɪsɪŋ] *n* carreras *fpl*; **racing car** *n* (BRIT) coche *m* de carreras; **racing driver** *n* (BRIT) piloto *mf* de carreras

racism ['reɪsɪzəm] *n* racismo

racist ['reɪsɪst] *adj, n* racista *mf*

rack [ræk] *n* (*also*: **luggage ~**) rejilla (portaequipajes); (*shelf*) estante *m*;

(also: **roof ~**) baca; (also: **clothes ~**) perchero ▷ vt atormentar; **to ~ one's brains** devanarse los sesos

racket ['rækɪt] n (for tennis) raqueta; (inf: noise) ruido, estrépito; (: swindle) estafa, timo

racquet ['rækɪt] n raqueta

radar ['reɪdɑː] n radar m

radiation [reɪdɪ'eɪʃən] n radiación f

radiator ['reɪdɪeɪtə*] n radiador m

radical ['rædɪkl] adj radical

radio ['reɪdɪəʊ] n radio f; **on the ~** en or por la radio; **radioactive** adj radi(o)activo; **radio station** n emisora

radish ['rædɪʃ] n rábano

RAF n abbr (BRIT) = **Royal Air Force**

raffle ['ræfl] n rifa, sorteo

raft [rɑːft] n balsa; (also: **life ~**) balsa salvavidas

rag [ræg] n (piece of cloth) trapo; (torn cloth) harapo; (pej: newspaper) periodicucho; (for charity) actividades estudiantiles benéficas; **rags** npl harapos mpl

rage [reɪdʒ] n rabia, furor m ▷ vi (person) rabiar, estar furioso; (storm) bramar; **it's all the ~** es lo último; (very fashionable) está muy de moda

ragged ['rægɪd] adj (edge) desigual, mellado; (cuff) roto; (appearance) andrajoso, harapiento

raid [reɪd] n (Mil) incursión f; (criminal) asalto; (by police) redada ▷ vt invadir, atacar; asaltar

rail [reɪl] n (on stair) barandilla, pasamanos m inv; (on bridge) pretil m; (of balcony, ship) barandilla; **railcard** n (BRIT) tarjeta para obtener descuentos en el tren; **railing(s)** n(pl) verja sg; **railway,** (US) **railroad** n ferrocarril m, vía férrea; **railway line** n (BRIT) línea (de ferrocarril); **railway station** n (BRIT) estación f de ferrocarril

rain [reɪn] n lluvia ▷ vi llover; **in the ~** bajo la lluvia; **it's ~ing** llueve, está lloviendo; **rainbow** n arco iris; **raincoat** n impermeable m; **raindrop** n gota de lluvia; **rainfall** n lluvia;

rainforest n selva tropical; **rainy** adj lluvioso

raise [reɪz] n aumento ▷ vt levantar; (increase) aumentar; (improve: morale) subir; (: standards) mejorar; (doubts) suscitar; (a question) plantear; (cattle, family) criar; (crop) cultivar; (army) reclutar; (loan) obtener; **to ~ one's voice** alzar la voz

raisin ['reɪzn] n pasa de Corinto

rake [reɪk] n (tool) rastrillo; (person) libertino ▷ vt (garden) rastrillar

rally ['rælɪ] n reunión f; (Pol) mitin m; (Aut) rallye m; (Tennis) peloteo ▷ vt reunir ▷ vi recuperarse

RAM [ræm] n abbr (= random access memory) RAM f

ram [ræm] n carnero; (Tech) pisón m; (also: **battering ~**) ariete m ▷ vt (crash into) dar contra, chocar con; (push: fist etc) empujar con fuerza

Ramadan ['ræmədæn] n Ramadán m

ramble ['ræmbl] n caminata, excursión f en el campo ▷ vi (pej: also: **~ on**) divagar; **rambler** n excursionista mf; (Bot) trepadora; **rambling** adj (speech) inconexo; (Bot) trepador(a); (house) laberíntico

ramp [ræmp] n rampa; **on/off ~** n (US Aut) vía de acceso/salida

rampage [ræm'peɪdʒ] n: **to be on the ~** desmandarse ▷ vi: **they went rampaging through the town** recorrieron la ciudad armando alboroto

ran [ræn] pt of **run**

ranch [rɑːntʃ] n hacienda, estancia

random ['rændəm] adj fortuito, sin orden; (Comput, Math) aleatorio ▷ n: **at ~** al azar

rang [ræŋ] pt of **ring**

range [reɪndʒ] n (of mountains) cadena de montañas, cordillera; (of missile) alcance m; (of voice) registro; (series) serie f; (of products) surtido; (Mil: also: **shooting ~**) campo de tiro; (also: **kitchen ~**) fogón m ▷ vt (place) colocar; (arrange) arreglar ▷ vi: **to ~**

over (extend) extenderse por; **to ~ from ... to ...** oscilar entre ... y ...

ranger ['reɪndʒəʳ] n guardabosques m inv

rank [ræŋk] n (row) fila; (Mil) rango; (status) categoría; (BRIT: also: **taxi ~**) parada ▷ vi: **to ~ among** figurar entre ▷ adj fétido, rancio; **the ~ and file** (fig) las bases

ransom ['rænsəm] n rescate m; **to hold sb to ~** (fig) poner a algn entre la espada y la pared

rant [rænt] vi despotricar

rap [ræp] vt golpear, dar un golpecito en ▷ n (music) rap m

rape [reɪp] n violación f; (Bot) colza ▷ vt violar

rapid ['ræpɪd] adj rápido; **rapidly** adv rápidamente; **rapids** npl (Geo) rápidos mpl

rapist ['reɪpɪst] n violador m

rapport [ræ'pɔːʳ] n entendimiento

rare [rɛəʳ] adj raro, poco común; (Culin: steak) poco hecho; **rarely** adv pocas veces

rash [ræʃ] adj imprudente, precipitado ▷ n (Med) sarpullido, erupción f (cutánea)

rasher ['ræʃəʳ] n loncha

raspberry ['rɑːzbərɪ] n frambuesa

rat [ræt] n rata

rate [reɪt] n (ratio) razón f; (price) precio; (: of hotel) tarifa; (of interest) tipo; (speed) velocidad f ▷ vt (value) tasar; (estimate) estimar; **rates** npl (BRIT) impuesto sg municipal; (fees) tarifa sg; **to ~ sb/sth highly** tener a algn/algo en alta estima

rather ['rɑːðəʳ] adv: **it's ~ expensive** es algo caro; (too much) es demasiado caro; **there's ~ a lot** hay bastante; **I would** or **I'd ~ go** preferiría ir; **or ~** o mejor dicho

rating ['reɪtɪŋ] n tasación f; **ratings** npl (Radio, TV) niveles mpl de audiencia

ratio ['reɪʃɪəu] n razón f; **in the ~ of 100 to 1** a razón de or en la proporción de 100 a 1

ration ['ræʃən] n ración f ▷ vt racionar; **rations** npl víveres mpl

rational ['ræʃənl] adj (solution, reasoning) lógico, razonable; (person) cuerdo, sensato

rattle ['rætl] n golpeteo; (of train etc) traqueteo; (object: of baby) sonaja, sonajero ▷ vi (small objects) castañetear; (car, bus): **to ~ along** traquetear ▷ vt hacer sonar agitando

rave [reɪv] vi (in anger) encolerizarse; (with enthusiasm) entusiasmarse; (Med) delirar, desvariar ▷ n (inf: party) rave m

raven ['reɪvən] n cuervo

ravine [rə'viːn] n barranco

raw [rɔː] adj crudo; (not processed) bruto; (sore) vivo; (inexperienced) novato, inexperto; **~ materials** materias primas

ray [reɪ] n rayo; **~ of hope** (rayo de) esperanza

razor ['reɪzəʳ] n (open) navaja; (safety razor) máquina de afeitar; (electric razor) máquina (eléctrica) de afeitar; **razor blade** n hoja de afeitar

Rd abbr = **road**

RE n abbr (BRIT: Scol) = **religious education**; (: Mil) = **Royal Engineers**

re [riː] prep con referencia a

reach [riːtʃ] n alcance m; (of river etc) extensión f entre dos recodos ▷ vt alcanzar, llegar a; (achieve) lograr ▷ vi extenderse; **within ~** al alcance (de la mano); **out of ~** fuera del alcance; **reach out** vt (hand) tender ▷ vi: **to ~ out for sth** alargar or tender la mano para tomar algo

react [riː'ækt] vi reaccionar; **reaction** [riː'ækʃən] n reacción f; **reactor** [riː'æktəʳ] n (also: **nuclear reactor**) reactor m (nuclear)

read (pt, pp **read**) [riːd, rɛd] vi leer ▷ vt leer; (understand) entender; (study) estudiar; **read out** vt leer en alta voz; **reader** n lector(a) m/f; (BRIT: at university) profesor(a) m/f

r

readily ['rɛdɪlɪ] adv (willingly) de buena gana; (easily) fácilmente; (quickly) en seguida

reading ['riːdɪŋ] n lectura; (on instrument) indicación f

ready ['rɛdɪ] adj listo, preparado; (willing) dispuesto; (available) disponible ▷ adv: **~-cooked** listo para comer ▷ n: **at the ~** (Mil) listo para tirar ▷ vt preparar; **to get ~** vi prepararse; **ready-made** adj confeccionado

real [rɪəl] adj verdadero, auténtico; **in ~ terms** en términos reales; **real ale** n cerveza elaborada tradicionalmente; **real estate** n bienes mpl raíces; **realistic** [rɪə'lɪstɪk] adj realista

reality [riː'ælɪtɪ] n realidad f; **reality TV** n telerrealidad f

realization [rɪəlaɪ'zeɪʃən] n comprensión f; (of a project) realización f; (Comm) realización f

realize ['rɪəlaɪz] vt (understand) darse cuenta de

really ['rɪəlɪ] adv realmente; (for emphasis) verdaderamente; **what ~ happened** (actually) lo que pasó en realidad; **~?** ¿de veras?; **~!** (annoyance) ¡vamos!, ¡por favor!

realm [rɛlm] n reino; (fig) esfera

reappear [riːə'pɪər] vi reaparecer

rear [rɪər] adj trasero ▷ n parte f trasera ▷ vt (cattle, family) criar ▷ vi (also: **~ up**: animal) encabritarse

rearrange [riːə'reɪndʒ] vt ordenar or arreglar de nuevo

rear: **rear-view mirror** n (Aut) espejo retrovisor; **rear-wheel drive** n tracción f trasera

reason ['riːzn] n razón f ▷ vi: **to ~ with sb** tratar de que algn entre en razón; **it stands to ~ that ...** es lógico que ...; **reasonable** adj razonable; (sensible) sensato; **reasonably** adv razonablemente; **reasoning** n razonamiento, argumentos mpl

reassurance [riːə'ʃuərəns] n consuelo

reassure [riːə'ʃuər] vt tranquilizar; **to ~ sb that** tranquilizar a algn asegurándole que

rebate ['riːbeɪt] n (on tax etc) desgravación f

rebel n ['rɛbl] rebelde mf ▷ vi [rɪ'bɛl] rebelarse, sublevarse; **rebellion** n rebelión f, sublevación f; **rebellious** adj rebelde; (child) revoltoso

rebuild [riː'bɪld] vt reconstruir

recall [rɪ'kɔːl] vt (remember) recordar; (ambassador etc) retirar ▷ n recuerdo

recd., rec'd abbr (= received) recibido

receipt [rɪ'siːt] n (document) recibo; (act of receiving) recepción f; **receipts** npl (Comm) ingresos mpl

> Be careful not to translate *receipt* by the Spanish word *receta*.

receive [rɪ'siːv] vt recibir; (guest) acoger; (wound) sufrir; **receiver** n (Tel) auricular m; (Radio) receptor m; (of stolen goods) perista mf; (Law) administrador m jurídico

recent ['riːsnt] adj reciente; **recently** adv recientemente; **recently arrived** recién llegado

reception [rɪ'sɛpʃən] n recepción f; (welcome) acogida; **reception desk** n recepción f; **receptionist** n recepcionista mf

recession [rɪ'sɛʃən] n recesión f

recharge [riː'tʃɑːdʒ] vt (battery) recargar

recipe ['rɛsɪpɪ] n receta; (for disaster, success) fórmula

recipient [rɪ'sɪpɪənt] n recibidor(a) m/f; (of letter) destinatario/a

recital [rɪ'saɪtl] n recital m

recite [rɪ'saɪt] vt (poem) recitar

reckless ['rɛkləs] adj temerario, imprudente; (speed) peligroso

reckon ['rɛkən] vt calcular; (consider) considerar ▷ vi: **I ~ that ...** me parece que ...

reclaim [rɪ'kleɪm] vt (land) recuperar; (: from sea) rescatar; (demand back) reclamar

recline [rɪ'klaɪn] vi reclinarse

recognition [rekəg'nɪʃən] n
reconocimiento; **transformed
beyond ~** irreconocible

recognize ['rekəgnaɪz] vt: **to ~ (by/
as)** reconocer (por/como)

recollection [rekə'lekʃən] n recuerdo

recommend [rekə'mend] vt
recomendar; **recommendation**
[rekəmen'deɪʃən] n recomendación f

reconcile ['rekənsaɪl] vt (two people)
reconciliar; (two facts) conciliar; **to ~
o.s. to sth** resignarse or conformarse
a algo

reconsider [ri:kən'sɪdər] vt repensar

reconstruct [ri:kən'strʌkt] vt
reconstruir

record n ['rekɔːd] (Mus) disco; (of
meeting etc) acta; (register) registro,
partida; (file) archivo; (also: **police
or criminal ~**) antecedentes mpl
penales; (written) expediente m;
(Sport) récord m; (Comput) registro
▷ vt [rɪ'kɔːd] registrar; (Mus: song
etc) grabar; **in ~ time** en un tiempo
récord; **off the ~** adj no oficial;
adv confidencialmente; **recorded
delivery** n (BRIT Post) entrega
con acuse de recibo; **recorder** n
(Mus) flauta de pico; **recording** n
(Mus) grabación f; **record player** n
tocadiscos m inv

recount vt [rɪ'kaʊnt] contar

recover [rɪ'kʌvər] vt recuperar
▷ vi recuperarse; **recovery** n
recuperación f

recreate [ri:krɪ'eɪt] vt recrear

recreation [rekrɪ'eɪʃən] n recreo;
recreational adj de, recreo;
recreational drug n droga recreativa;
recreational vehicle n (US) caravana
or roulotte f pequeña

recruit [rɪ'kruːt] n recluta mf
▷ vt reclutar; (staff) contratar;
recruitment n reclutamiento

rectangle ['rektæŋgl] n rectángulo;
rectangular [rek'tæŋgjulər] adj
rectangular

rectify ['rektɪfaɪ] vt rectificar

rector ['rektər] n (Rel) párroco

recur [rɪ'kɜːr] vi repetirse; (pain, illness)
producirse de nuevo; **recurring** adj
(problem) repetido, constante

recyclable [riː'saɪkləbl] adj reciclable

recycle [riː'saɪkl] vt reciclar

recycling [riː'saɪklɪŋ] n reciclaje m

red [red] n rojo ▷ adj rojo; (hair)
pelirrojo; (wine) tinto; **to be in the
~** (account) estar en números rojos;
(business) tener un saldo negativo;
to give sb the ~ carpet treatment
recibir a algn con todos los honores;
Red Cross n Cruz f Roja; **redcurrant**
n grosella roja

redeem [rɪ'diːm] vt redimir; (promises)
cumplir; (sth in pawn) desempeñar;
(Rel: fig) rescatar

red: redhead n pelirrojo/a; **red-hot** adj
candente; **red light** n: **to go through**
or **jump a red light** (Aut) saltarse un
semáforo; **red-light district** n barrio
chino; **red meat** n carne f roja

reduce [rɪ'djuːs] vt reducir; **to ~ sb to
silence/despair/tears** hacer callar/
desesperarse/llorar a algn; **reduced**
adj (decreased) reducido, rebajado;
at a reduced price con rebaja or
descuento; **"greatly reduced
prices"** "grandes rebajas"; **reduction**
[rɪ'dʌkʃən] n reducción f; (of price)
rebaja; (discount) descuento

redundancy [rɪ'dʌndənsɪ] n
despido; (unemployment) desempleo

redundant [rɪ'dʌndənt] adj (BRIT:
worker) parado, sin trabajo; (detail,
object) superfluo; **to be made ~** (BRIT)
quedar(se) sin trabajo

reed [riːd] n (Bot) junco, caña; (Mus)
lengüeta

reef [riːf] n (at sea) arrecife m

reel [riːl] n carrete m, bobina; (of film)
rollo ▷ vt (Tech) devanar; (also: **~ in**)
sacar ▷ vi (sway) tambalear(se)

ref [ref] n abbr (inf): = **referee**

refectory [rɪ'fektərɪ] n comedor m

refer [rɪ'fɜːr] vt (send: patient) referir;
(: matter) remitir ▷ vi: **to ~ to** (allude

to) referirse a, aludir a; (*apply to*) relacionarse con; (*consult*) remitirse a

referee [rɛfə'riː] *n* árbitro; (BRIT: *for job application*): **to be a ~ for sb** proporcionar referencias a algn ▷ *vt* (*match*) arbitrar en

reference ['rɛfrəns] *n* referencia; (*for job application: letter*) carta de recomendación; **with ~ to** (Comm: *in letter*) me remito a; **reference number** *n* número de referencia

refill *vt* [riː'fɪl] rellenar ▷ *n* ['riːfɪl] repuesto, recambio

refine [rɪ'faɪn] *vt* refinar; **refined** *adj* (*person, taste*) refinado, fino; **refinery** *n* refinería

reflect [rɪ'flɛkt] *vt* reflejar ▷ *vi* (*think*) reflexionar, pensar; **it ~s badly/well on him** le perjudica/le hace honor; **reflection** [rɪ'flɛkʃən] *n* (*act*) reflexión *f*; (*image*) reflejo; (*discredit*) crítica; **on reflection** pensándolo bien

reflex ['riːflɛks] *adj, n* reflejo

reform [rɪ'fɔːm] *n* reforma ▷ *vt* reformar

refrain [rɪ'freɪn] *vi*: **to ~ from doing** abstenerse de hacer ▷ *n* estribillo

refresh [rɪ'frɛʃ] *vt* refrescar; **refreshing** *adj* refrescante; **refreshments** *npl* refrescos *mpl*

refrigerator [rɪ'frɪdʒəreɪtər] *n* frigorífico, refrigeradora (LAM), heladera (LAM)

refuel [riː'fjuəl] *vi* repostar (combustible)

refuge ['rɛfjuːdʒ] *n* refugio, asilo; **to take ~ in** refugiarse en; **refugee** [rɛfju'dʒiː] *n* refugiado/a

refund *n* ['riːfʌnd] reembolso ▷ *vt* [rɪ'fʌnd] devolver, reembolsar

refurbish [riː'fəːbɪʃ] *vt* restaurar, renovar

refusal [rɪ'fjuːzəl] *n* negativa; **to have first ~ on sth** tener la primera opción a algo

refuse¹ ['rɛfjuːs] *n* basura

refuse² [rɪ'fjuːz] *vt* (*reject*) rechazar; (*invitation*) declinar; (*permission*)

denegar; (*say no to*) negarse a ▷ *vi* negarse; (*horse*) rehusar; **to ~ to do sth** negarse a or rehusar hacer algo

regain [rɪ'geɪn] *vt* recobrar, recuperar

regard [rɪ'gɑːd] *n* mirada; (*esteem*) respeto; (*attention*) consideración *f* ▷ *vt* (*consider*) considerar; **to give one's ~s to** saludar de su parte a; **"with kindest ~s"** "con muchos recuerdos"; **as ~s, with ~ to** con respecto a, en cuanto a; **regarding** *prep* con respecto a, en cuanto a; **regardless** *adv* a pesar de todo; **regardless of** sin reparar en

regenerate [rɪ'dʒɛnəreɪt] *vt* regenerar

reggae ['rɛgeɪ] *n* reggae *m*

regiment ['rɛdʒɪmənt] *n* regimiento

region ['riːdʒən] *n* región *f*; **in the ~ of** (*fig*) alrededor de; **regional** *adj* regional

register ['rɛdʒɪstər] *n* registro ▷ *vt* registrar; (*birth*) declarar; (*car*) matricular; (*letter*) certificar; (*instrument*) marcar, indicar ▷ *vi* (*at hotel*) registrarse; (*as student*) matricularse; (*make impression*) producir impresión; **registered** *adj* (*letter*) certificado

registrar ['rɛdʒɪstrɑːʳ] *n* secretario/a (del registro civil)

registration [rɛdʒɪs'treɪʃən] *n* (*act*) declaración *f*; (*Aut: also*: **~ number**) matrícula

registry office *n* (BRIT) registro civil; **to get married in a ~** casarse por lo civil

regret [rɪ'grɛt] *n* sentimiento, pesar *m* ▷ *vt* sentir, lamentar; **regrettable** *adj* lamentable

regular ['rɛgjulər] *adj* regular; (*soldier*) profesional; (*usual*) habitual ▷ *n* (*client etc*) cliente *a m/f* habitual; **regularly** *adv* con regularidad

regulate ['rɛgjuleɪt] *vt* controlar; **regulation** [rɛgju'leɪʃən] *n* (*rule*) regla, reglamento

rehabilitation ['ri:əbɪlɪ'teɪʃən] n
rehabilitación f

rehearsal [rɪ'həːsəl] n ensayo

rehearse [rɪ'həːs] vt ensayar

reign [reɪn] n reinado; (fig) predominio
▷ vi reinar; (fig) imperar

reimburse [ri:ɪm'bəːs] vt
reembolsar

rein [reɪn] n (for horse) rienda

reincarnation [ri:ɪnkɑː'neɪʃən] n
reencarnación f

reindeer ['reɪndɪə'] n (pl inv) reno

reinforce [ri:ɪn'fɔːs] vt reforzar

reinforcement [ri:ɪn'fɔːsmənt] n
refuerzo; **reinforcements** npl (Mil)
refuerzos mpl

reinstate [ri:ɪn'steɪt] vt (worker)
reintegrar (a su puesto); (tax, law)
reinstaurar

reject n ['ri:dʒɛkt] (thing) desecho ▷ vt
[rɪ'dʒɛkt] rechazar; (proposition, offer
etc) descartar; **rejection** [rɪ'dʒɛkʃən]
n rechazo

rejoice [rɪ'dʒɔɪs] vi: **to ~ at** or **over**
regocijarse or alegrarse de

relate [rɪ'leɪt] vt (tell) contar,
relatar; (connect) relacionar ▷ vi
relacionarse; **related** adj afín; (person)
emparentado; **to be related to**
(connected) guardar relación con;
(by family) ser pariente de; **relating**:
relating to prep referente a

relation [rɪ'leɪʃən] n (person) pariente
mf; (link) relación f; **relations** npl
(relatives) familiares mpl; **relationship**
n relación f; (personal) relaciones
fpl; (also: **family relationship**)
parentesco

relative ['rɛlətɪv] n pariente mf,
familiar mf ▷ adj relativo; **relatively**
adv (fairly, rather) relativamente

relax [rɪ'læks] vi descansar; (quieten
down) relajarse ▷ vt relajar; (grip)
aflojar; **relaxation** [ri:læk'seɪʃən] n
descanso; (easing) relajamiento m;
(entertainment) diversión f; **relaxed** adj
relajado; (tranquil) tranquilo; **relaxing**
adj relajante

relay n ['ri:leɪ] (race) carrera de relevos
▷ vt [rɪ'leɪ] (Radio, TV) retransmitir

release [rɪ'li:s] n (liberation) liberación
f; (discharge) puesta en libertad; (of
gas etc) escape m; (of film etc) estreno;
(of record) lanzamiento ▷ vt (prisoner)
poner en libertad; (film) estrenar;
(book) publicar; (piece of news) difundir;
(gas etc) despedir, arrojar; (free: from
wreckage etc) liberar; (Tech: catch, spring
etc) desenganchar

relegate ['rɛləɡeɪt] vt relegar; (Sport):
to be ~d bajar a

relent [rɪ'lɛnt] vi ablandarse;
relentless adj implacable

relevant ['rɛləvənt] adj (fact)
pertinente; **~ to** relacionado con

reliable [rɪ'laɪəbl] adj (person, firm) de
confianza, de fiar; (method, machine)
seguro; (source) fidedigno

relic ['rɛlɪk] n (Rel) reliquia; (of the
past) vestigio

relief [rɪ'li:f] n (from pain, anxiety)
alivio; (help, supplies) socorro, ayuda;
(Art, Geo) relieve m

relieve [rɪ'li:v] vt (pain, patient)
aliviar; (bring help to) ayudar, socorrer;
(take over from) sustituir a; (: guard)
relevar; **to ~ sb of sth** quitar algo a
algn; **to ~ o.s.** hacer sus necesidades;
relieved adj: **to be relieved** sentir
un gran alivio

religion [rɪ'lɪdʒən] n religión f

religious [rɪ'lɪdʒəs] adj religioso;
religious education n educación
f religiosa

relish ['rɛlɪʃ] n (Culin) salsa; (enjoyment)
entusiasmo ▷ vt (food, challenge etc)
saborear; **to ~ doing** gozar haciendo

relocate [ri:ləu'keɪt] vt trasladar ▷ vi
trasladarse

reluctance [rɪ'lʌktəns] n renuencia

reluctant [rɪ'lʌktənt] adj reacio; **to
be ~ to do sth** resistirse a hacer algo;
reluctantly adv de mala gana

rely [rɪ'laɪ]: **to ~ on** vt fus depender de;
you can ~ on my discretion puedes
contar con mi discreción

r

remain [rɪ'meɪn] vi (*survive*) quedar;
(*be left*) sobrar; (*continue*) quedar(se),
permanecer; **remainder** n resto;
remaining adj restante, que
queda(n); **remains** npl restos mpl
remand [rɪ'mɑːnd] n: **on ~** detenido
(bajo custodia) ▷ vt: **to ~ in custody**
mantener bajo custodia
remark [rɪ'mɑːk] n comentario
▷ vt comentar; **remarkable** adj
(*outstanding*) extraordinario
remarry [riː'mærɪ] vi volver a
casarse
remedy ['rɛmədɪ] n remedio ▷ vt
remediar, curar
remember [rɪ'mɛmbər] vt recordar,
acordarse de; (*bear in mind*) tener
presente; **~ me to your wife and
children!** ¡déle recuerdos a su familia!
**Remembrance Day,
Remembrance Sunday** n (BRIT)
ver nota **"Remembrance Day"**

- **REMEMBRANCE DAY**
-
- En el Reino Unido el domingo
- más cercano al 11 de noviembre es
- *Remembrance Day* o *Remembrance
- Sunday*, aniversario de la firma
- del armisticio de 1918 que puso
- fin a la Primera Guerra Mundial.
- Tal día se recuerda a todos
- aquellos que murieron en las
- dos guerras mundiales con dos
- minutos de silencio a las once de
- la mañana (hora en que se firmó el
- armisticio), durante los actos de
- conmemoración celebrados en los
- monumentos a los caídos. Allí se
- colocan coronas de amapolas, flor
- que también se suele llevar prendida
- en el pecho tras pagar un donativo
- para los inválidos de guerra.

remind [rɪ'maɪnd] vt: **to ~ sb to do
sth** recordar a algn que haga algo; **to
~ sb of sth** recordar algo a algn; **she
~s me of her mother** me recuerda a

su madre; **reminder** n notificación f;
(*memento*) recuerdo
reminiscent [rɛmɪ'nɪsnt] adj: **to be
~ of sth** recordar algo
remnant ['rɛmnənt] n resto; (*of
cloth*) retal m
remorse [rɪ'mɔːs] n remordimientos
mpl
remote [rɪ'məut] adj (*distant*)
lejano; (*person*) distante; **remote
control** n mando a distancia;
remotely adv remotamente; (*slightly*)
levemente
removal [rɪ'muːvəl] n (*taking away*)
(el) quitar; (BRIT: *from house*) mudanza,
(*from office: dismissal*) destitución f;
(*Med*) extirpación f; **removal man** n
(BRIT) mozo de mudanzas; **removal
van** n (BRIT) camión m de mudanzas
remove [rɪ'muːv] vt quitar; (*employee*)
destituir; (*name: from list*) tachar,
borrar; (*doubt*) disipar; (*Med*) extirpar
Renaissance [rɪ'neɪsɔ̃s] n: **the ~** el
Renacimiento
rename [riː'neɪm] vt poner nuevo
nombre a
render ['rɛndər] vt (*thanks*) dar;
(*aid*) proporcionar; prestar; **to ~ sth
useless** hacer algo inútil
renew [rɪ'njuː] vt renovar; (*resume*)
reanudar; (*extend date*) prorrogar;
renewable adj renovable; **renewable
energy, renewables** energías
renovables
renovate ['rɛnəveɪt] vt renovar
renowned [rɪ'naund] adj
renombrado
rent [rɛnt] n (*for house*) arriendo, renta
▷ vt alquilar; **rental** n (*for television,
car*) alquiler m
reorganize [riː'ɔːɡənaɪz] vt
reorganizar
rep [rɛp] n abbr (Comm);
= **representative**
repair [rɪ'pɛər] n reparación f ▷ vt
reparar; **in good/bad ~** en buen/
mal estado; **repair kit** n caja de
herramientas

repay [rɪ'peɪ] vt (money) devolver, reembolsar; (person) pagar; (debt) liquidar; (sb's efforts) devolver, corresponder a; **repayment** n reembolso, devolución f; (sum of money) recompensa

repeat [rɪ'piːt] n (Radio, TV) reposición f ▷ vt repetir ▷ vi repetirse; **repeatedly** adv repetidas veces; **repeat prescription** n (BRIT) receta renovada

repellent [rɪ'pɛlənt] adj repugnante ▷ n: **insect ~** crema/loción f antiinsectos

repercussion [riːpə'kʌʃən] n repercusión f; **to have ~s** repercutir

repetition [rɛpɪ'tɪʃən] n repetición f

repetitive [rɪ'pɛtɪtɪv] adj repetitivo

replace [rɪ'pleɪs] vt (put back) devolver a su sitio; (take the place of) reemplazar, sustituir; **replacement** n (act) reposición f; (thing) recambio; (person) suplente mf

replay ['riːpleɪ] n (Sport) partido de desempate; (TV) repetición f

replica ['rɛplɪkə] n réplica, reproducción f

reply [rɪ'plaɪ] n respuesta, contestación f ▷ vi contestar, responder

report [rɪ'pɔːt] n informe m; (Press etc) reportaje m; (BRIT: also: **school ~**) informe m escolar; (of gun) detonación f ▷ vt informar sobre; (Press etc) hacer un reportaje sobre; (notify: accident, culprit) denunciar ▷ vi (make a report) presentar un informe; (present o.s.): **to ~ (to sb)** presentarse (ante algn); **report card** n (US, SCOTTISH) cartilla escolar; **reportedly** adv según se dice; **reporter** n periodista mf

represent [rɛprɪ'zɛnt] vt representar; (Comm) ser agente de; **representation** [rɛprɪzɛn'teɪʃən] n representación f; **representative** n (US Pol) representante mf, diputado/a; (Comm) representante mf ▷ adj:

representative (of) representativo (de)

repress [rɪ'prɛs] vt reprimir; **repression** [rɪ'prɛʃən] n represión f

reprimand ['rɛprɪmɑːnd] n reprimenda ▷ vt reprender

reproduce [riːprə'djuːs] vt reproducir ▷ vi reproducirse; **reproduction** [riːprə'dʌkʃən] n reproducción f

reptile ['rɛptaɪl] n reptil m

republic [rɪ'pʌblɪk] n república; **republican** adj, n republicano/a

reputable ['rɛpjutəbl] adj (make etc) de renombre

reputation [rɛpju'teɪʃən] n reputación f

request [rɪ'kwɛst] n solicitud f, petición f ▷ vt: **to ~ sth of or from sb** solicitar algo a algn; **request stop** n (BRIT) parada discrecional

require [rɪ'kwaɪəʳ] vt (need: person) necesitar, tener necesidad de; (: thing, situation) exigir; (want) pedir; **to ~ sb to do sth/sth of sb** exigir que algn haga algo; **requirement** n requisito; (need) necesidad f

resat [riː'sæt] pt, pp of **resit**

rescue ['rɛskjuː] n rescate m ▷ vt rescatar

research [rɪ'səːtʃ] n investigaciones fpl ▷ vt investigar

resemblance [rɪ'zɛmbləns] n parecido

resemble [rɪ'zɛmbl] vt parecerse a

resent [rɪ'zɛnt] vt resentirse por, ofenderse por; **resentful** adj resentido; **resentment** n resentimiento

reservation [rɛzə'veɪʃən] n reserva; **reservation desk** n (US: in hotel) recepción f

reserve [rɪ'zəːv] n reserva; (Sport) suplente mf ▷ vt (seats etc) reservar; **reserved** adj reservado

reservoir ['rɛzəvwɑːʳ] n (artificial lake) embalse m, represa; (tank) depósito

residence ['rɛzɪdəns] n (formal: home) domicilio; (length of stay)

r

permanencia; **residence permit** n (BRIT) permiso de residencia
resident ['rɛzɪdənt] n vecino/a; (in hotel) huésped(a) m/f ▷ adj residente; (population) permanente; **residential** [rɛzɪ'dɛnʃəl] adj residencial
residue ['rɛzɪdjuː] n resto
resign [rɪ'zaɪn] vt renunciar a ▷ vi: **to ~ (from)** dimitir (de); **to ~ o.s. to** resignarse a; **resignation** [rɛzɪg'neɪʃən] n dimisión f; (state of mind) resignación f
resin ['rɛzɪn] n resina
resist [rɪ'zɪst] vt (temptation, damage) resistir; **resistance** n resistencia
resit ['riːsɪt] (pt, pp **resat**) vt (BRIT: exam) volver a presentarse a; (: subject) recuperar, volver a examinarse de (SP)
resolution [rɛzə'luːʃən] n resolución f
resolve [rɪ'zɔlv] n resolución f ▷ vt resolver ▷ vi: **to ~ to do** resolver hacer
resort [rɪ'zɔːt] n (town) centro turístico; (recourse) recurso ▷ vi: **to ~ to** recurrir a; **in the last ~** como último recurso
resource [rɪ'sɔːs] n recurso; **resourceful** adj ingenioso
respect [rɪs'pɛkt] n respeto ▷ vt respetar; **respectable** adj respetable; (amount etc) apreciable; (passable) tolerable; **respectful** adj respetuoso; **respective** adj respectivo; **respectively** adv respectivamente
respite ['rɛspaɪt] n respiro
respond [rɪs'pɔnd] vi responder; (react) reaccionar; **response** [rɪs'pɔns] n respuesta; (reaction) reacción f
responsibility [rɪspɔnsɪ'bɪlɪtɪ] n responsabilidad f
responsible [rɪs'pɔnsɪbl] adj (liable): **~ (for)** responsable (de); (character) serio, formal; (job) de responsabilidad; **responsibly** adv con seriedad
responsive [rɪs'pɔnsɪv] adj sensible
rest [rɛst] n descanso, reposo; (Mus) pausa, silencio; (support) apoyo; (remainder) resto ▷ vi descansar; (be

supported): **to ~ on** apoyarse en ▷ vt: **to ~ sth on/against** apoyar algo en o▮ sobre/contra; **the ~ of them** (people, objects) los demás; **it ~s with him** depende de él
restaurant ['rɛstərɔŋ] n restaurante m; **restaurant car** n (BRIT) coche-comedor m
restless ['rɛstlɪs] adj inquieto
restoration [rɛstə'reɪʃən] n restauración f; (giving back) devolución f
restore [rɪ'stɔːʳ] vt (building) restaurar; (sth stolen) devolver; (health▮ restablecer
restrain [rɪs'treɪn] vt (feeling) contener, refrenar; (person): **to ~ (from doing)** disuadir (de hacer); **restraint** n (moderation) moderación ▮ (of style) reserva
restrict [rɪs'trɪkt] vt restringir, limitar **restriction** [rɪs'trɪkʃən] n restricción f, limitación f
rest room n (US) aseos mpl
restructure [riː'strʌktʃəʳ] vt reestructurar
result [rɪ'zʌlt] n resultado ▷ vi: **to ~ in** terminar en, tener por resultado; **as a ~ of** a or como consecuencia de
resume [rɪ'zjuːm] vt reanudar ▷ vi (meeting) continuar

> ▮ Be careful not to translate resume by the Spanish word resumir.

résumé ['reɪzjuːmeɪ] n resumen m
resuscitate [rɪ'sʌsɪteɪt] vt resucitar
retail ['riːteɪl] cpd al por menor; **retailer** n detallista mf
retain [rɪ'teɪn] vt (keep) retener, conservar
retaliation [rɪtælɪ'eɪʃən] n represalias fpl
retarded [rɪ'tɑːdɪd] adj (inf!) retrasado (mental) (!)
retire [rɪ'taɪəʳ] vi (give up work) jubilarse; (withdraw) retirarse; (go to bed) acostarse; **retired** adj (person) jubilado; **retirement** n jubilación f
retort [rɪ'tɔːt] vi replicar

retreat [rɪ'triːt] n (place) retiro; (Mil) retirada ▷ vi retirarse

retrieve [rɪ'triːv] vt recobrar; (situation, honour) salvar; (Comput) recuperar; (error) reparar

retrospect ['rɛtrəspɛkt] n: **in ~** retrospectivamente; **retrospective** [rɛtrə'spɛktɪv] adj retrospectivo; (law) retroactivo

return [rɪ'təːn] n (going or coming back) vuelta, regreso; (of sth stolen etc) devolución f; (Finance: from land, shares) ganancia, ingresos mpl ▷ cpd (journey) de regreso; (BRIT: ticket) de ida y vuelta; (match) de vuelta ▷ vi (person etc: come or go back) volver, regresar; (symptoms etc) reaparecer ▷ vt devolver; (favour, love etc) corresponder a; (verdict) pronunciar; (Pol: candidate) elegir; **returns** npl (Comm) ingresos mpl; **in ~ (for)** a cambio (de); **by ~ of post** a vuelta de correo; **many happy ~s (of the day)!** ¡feliz cumpleaños!; **return ticket** n (esp BRIT) billete m (SP) or boleto m (LAM) de ida y vuelta, billete m redondo (MEX)

reunion [riː'juːniən] n (of family) reunión f; (of two people, school) reencuentro

reunite [riːjuː'naɪt] vt reunir; (reconcile) reconciliar

revamp [riː'væmp] vt renovar

reveal [rɪ'viːl] vt revelar; **revealing** adj revelador(a)

revel ['rɛvl] vi: **to ~ in sth/in doing sth** gozar de algo/haciendo algo

revelation [rɛvə'leɪʃən] n revelación f

revenge [rɪ'vɛndʒ] n venganza; **to take ~ on** vengarse de

revenue ['rɛvənjuː] n ingresos mpl, rentas fpl

Reverend ['rɛvərənd] adj (in titles): **the ~ John Smith** (Anglican) el Reverendo John Smith; (Catholic) el Padre John Smith; (Protestant) el Pastor John Smith

reversal [rɪ'vəːsl] n (of order) inversión f; (of policy) cambio de rumbo; (of decision) revocación f

reverse [rɪ'vəːs] n (opposite) contrario; (back: of cloth) revés m; (: of coin) reverso; (: of paper) dorso; (Aut: also: **~ gear**) marcha atrás ▷ adj (order) inverso; (direction) contrario ▷ vt (decision) dar marcha atrás a; (Aut) dar marcha atrás a; (position, function) invertir ▷ vi (BRIT Aut) poner en marcha atrás; **reverse-charge call** n (BRIT) llamada a cobro revertido; **reversing lights** npl (BRIT Aut) luces fpl de marcha atrás

revert [rɪ'vəːt] vi: **to ~ to** volver or revertir a

review [rɪ'vjuː] n (magazine, also Mil) revista; (of book, film) reseña; (US: examination) repaso, examen m ▷ vt repasar, examinar; (Mil) pasar revista a; (book, film) reseñar

revise [rɪ'vaɪz] vt (manuscript) corregir; (opinion) modificar; (price, procedure) revisar; (BRIT: study: subject) repasar; **revision** [rɪ'vɪʒən] n corrección f; modificación f; (of subject) repaso

revival [rɪ'vaɪvəl] n (recovery) reanimación f; (of interest) renacimiento; (Theat) reestreno; (of faith) despertar m

revive [rɪ'vaɪv] vt resucitar; (custom) restablecer; (hope, courage) reanimar; (play) reestrenar ▷ vi (person) volver en sí; (business) reactivarse

revolt [rɪ'vəult] n rebelión f ▷ vi rebelarse, sublevarse ▷ vt dar asco a, repugnar; **revolting** adj asqueroso, repugnante

revolution [rɛvə'luːʃən] n revolución f; **revolutionary** adj, n revolucionario/a

revolve [rɪ'vɔlv] vi dar vueltas, girar; **to ~ (a)round** girar en torno a

revolver [rɪ'vɔlvəʳ] n revólver m

reward [rɪ'wɔːd] n premio, recompensa ▷ vt: **to ~ (for)**

r

recompensar or premiar (por);
rewarding adj (fig) gratificante
rewind [riːˈwaɪnd] vt rebobinar
rewritable [riːˈraɪtəbl] adj
reescribible
rewrite [riːˈraɪt] vt (irreg: like **write**)
reescribir
rheumatism [ˈruːmətɪzəm] n
reumatismo, reúma
rhinoceros [raɪˈnɔsərəs] n
rinoceronte m
rhubarb [ˈruːbɑːb] n ruibarbo
rhyme [raɪm] n rima; (verse) poesía
rhythm [ˈrɪðm] n ritmo
rib [rɪb] n (Anat) costilla ▷ vt (mock)
tomar el pelo a
ribbon [ˈrɪbən] n cinta; **in ~s** (torn)
hecho trizas
rice [raɪs] n arroz m; **rice pudding** n
arroz m con leche
rich [rɪtʃ] adj rico; (soil) fértil; (food)
pesado; (: sweet) empalagoso; **to be ~
in sth** abundar en algo
rid (pt, pp **rid**) [rɪd] vt: **to ~ sb of sth**
librar a algn de algo; **to get ~ of**
deshacerse or desembarazarse de
riddle [ˈrɪdl] n (conundrum) acertijo;
(mystery) enigma m, misterio ▷ vt: **to
be ~d with** ser lleno or plagado de
ride [raɪd] (pt **rode**, pp **ridden**) n paseo;
(distance covered) viaje m, recorrido
▷ vi (on horse, as sport) montar; (go
somewhere: on horse, bicycle) dar un
paseo, pasearse; (journey: on bicycle,
motor cycle, bus) viajar ▷ vt (a horse)
montar a; (distance) recorrer; **to ~ a
bicycle** andar en bicicleta; **to take sb
for a ~** (fig) tomar el pelo a algn; **rider**
n (on horse) jinete m; (on bicycle) ciclista
mf; (on motorcycle) motociclista mf
ridge [rɪdʒ] n (of hill) cresta; (of roof)
caballete m; (wrinkle) arruga
ridicule [ˈrɪdɪkjuːl] n irrisión f, burla
▷ vt poner en ridículo a, burlarse de;
ridiculous [rɪˈdɪkjuləs] adj ridículo
riding [ˈraɪdɪŋ] n equitación f; **I like
~** me gusta montar a caballo; **riding
school** n escuela de equitación

rife [raɪf] adj: **to be ~** ser muy común;
to be ~ with abundar en
rifle [ˈraɪfl] n rifle m, fusil m ▷ vt
saquear
rift [rɪft] n (fig: between friends)
desavenencia
rig [rɪg] n (also: **oil ~**: at sea) plataforma
petrolera ▷ vt (election etc) amañar los
resultados de
right [raɪt] adj (true, correct) correcto,
exacto; (suitable) indicado, debido;
(proper) apropiado; (just) justo; (morally
good) bueno; (not left) derecho ▷ n
(title, claim) derecho; (not left) derecha
▷ adv bien, correctamente; (not on
the left) a la derecha ▷ vt (put straight)
enderezar; (correct) corregir ▷ excl
¡bueno!, ¡está bien!; **to be ~** (person)
tener razón; (answer) ser correcto; **by
~s** en justicia; **on the ~** a la derecha;
to be in the ~ tener razón; **~ now**
ahora mismo; **~ in the middle**
exactamente en el centro; **~ away** en
seguida; **right angle** n ángulo recto;
rightful adj legítimo; **right-hand**
adj: **right-hand drive** conducción
f por la derecha; **the right-hand
side** derecha; **right-handed** adj
(person) que usa la mano derecha,
diestro; **rightly** adv correctamente,
debidamente; (with reason) con razón;
right of way n (on path etc) derecho de
paso; (Aut) prioridad f de paso; **right-
wing** adj (Pol) derechista
rigid [ˈrɪdʒɪd] adj rígido; (person, ideas)
inflexible
rigorous [ˈrɪgərəs] adj riguroso
rim [rɪm] n borde m; (of spectacles) aro;
(of wheel) llanta
rind [raɪnd] n (of bacon, cheese)
corteza; (of lemon etc) cáscara
ring [rɪŋ] (pt **rang**, pp **rung**) n (of metal)
aro; (on finger) anillo; (of people) corro;
(of objects) círculo; (gang) banda; (for
boxing) cuadrilátero; (of circus) pista;
(bull ring) ruedo, plaza; (sound of bell)
toque m ▷ vi (on telephone) llamar por
teléfono; (large bell) repicar; (doorbell,

phone) sonar; (*also*: **~ out**) sonar; (*ears*) zumbar ▷ *vt* (BRIT *Tel*) llamar; (*bell etc*) hacer sonar; (*doorbell*) tocar; **to give sb a ~** (BRIT *Tel*) llamar a algn; en un telefonazo a algn; **ring back** *vt*, *vi* (*Tel*) devolver la llamada; **ring off** *vi* (BRIT *Tel*) colgar, cortar la comunicación; **ring up** *vt* (BRIT *Tel*) llamar, telefonear; **ringing tone** *n* (*Tel*) tono de llamada; **ringleader** *n* cabecilla *mf*; **ring road** *n* (BRIT) carretera periférica *or* de circunvalación; **ringtone** *n* tono de llamada

rink [rɪŋk] *n* (*also*: **ice ~**) pista de hielo

rinse [rɪns] *n* (*of dishes*) enjuague *m*; (*of clothes*) aclarado; (*hair colouring*) reflejo ▷ *vt* enjuagar, aclarar; (*hair*) dar reflejos a

riot ['raɪət] *n* motín *m*, disturbio ▷ *vi* amotinarse; **to run ~** desmandarse

rip [rɪp] *n* rasgón *m* ▷ *vt* rasgar, desgarrar ▷ *vi* rasgarse; **rip off** *vt* (*inf: cheat*) estafar; **rip up** *vt* hacer pedazos

ripe [raɪp] *adj* maduro

rip-off ['rɪpɔf] *n* (*inf*): **it's a ~!** ¡es una estafa!, ¡es un timo!

ripple ['rɪpl] *n* onda, rizo; (*sound*) murmullo ▷ *vi* rizarse

rise (*pt* **rose**, *pp* **risen**) [raɪz, rəuz, 'rɪzn] *n* (*slope*) cuesta, pendiente *f*; (*hill*) altura; (*in wages*) aumento; (*in prices, temperature*) subida; (*fig: to power etc*) ascenso ▷ *vi* subir; (*waters*) crecer; (*sun*) salir; (*person: from bed etc*) levantarse; (*also*: **~ up**: *rebel*) sublevarse; (*in rank*) ascender; **to give ~ to** dar lugar *or* origen a; **to ~ to the occasion** ponerse a la altura de las circunstancias; **risen** ['rɪzn] *pp of* **rise**; **rising** *adj* (*increasing: number*) creciente; (: *prices*) en aumento *or* alza; (*tide*) creciente; (*sun, moon*) naciente

risk [rɪsk] *n* riesgo, peligro ▷ *vt* arriesgar; **to take** *or* **run the ~ of doing** correr el riesgo de hacer; **at ~** en peligro; **at one's own ~** bajo su propia responsabilidad; **risky** *adj* arriesgado, peligroso

rite [raɪt] *n* rito; **last ~s** últimos sacramentos *mpl*

ritual ['rɪtjuəl] *adj* ritual ▷ *n* ritual *m*, rito

rival ['raɪvl] *n* rival *mf*; (*in business*) competidor(a) *m/f* ▷ *adj* rival, opuesto ▷ *vt* competir con; **rivalry** *n* competencia

river ['rɪvər] *n* río ▷ *cpd* (*port, traffic*) de río; **up/down ~** río arriba/abajo; **riverbank** *n* orilla (del río)

rivet ['rɪvɪt] *n* roblón *m*, remache *m* ▷ *vt* (*fig*) fascinar

road [rəud] *n* camino; (*motorway etc*) carretera; (*in town*) calle *f*; **major/minor ~** carretera general/ secundaria; **roadblock** *n* barricada; **road map** *n* mapa *m* de carreteras; **road rage** *n* conducta agresiva de los conductores; **road safety** *n* seguridad *f* vial; **roadside** *n* borde *m* (del camino); **roadsign** *n* señal *f* de tráfico; **road tax** *n* (BRIT) impuesto de rodaje; **roadworks** *npl* obras *fpl*

roam [rəum] *vi* vagar

roar [rɔːr] *n* rugido; (*of vehicle, storm*) estruendo; (*of laughter*) carcajada ▷ *vi* rugir; hacer estruendo; **to ~ with laughter** reírse a carcajadas; **roaring** *adj*: **to do a roaring trade** hacer buen negocio

roast [rəust] *n* carne *f* asada, asado ▷ *vt* asar; (*coffee*) tostar; **roast beef** *n* rosbif *m*

rob [rɔb] *vt* robar; **to ~ sb of sth** robar algo a algn; (*fig: deprive*) quitar algo a algn; **robber** *n* ladrón/ona *m/f*; **robbery** *n* robo

robe [rəub] *n* (*for ceremony etc*) toga; (*also*: **bath ~**) bata, albornoz *m*

robin ['rɔbɪn] *n* petirrojo

robot ['rəubɔt] *n* robot *m*

robust [rəu'bʌst] *adj* robusto, fuerte

rock [rɔk] *n* roca; (*boulder*) peña, peñasco; (BRIT: *sweet*) ≈ pirulí *m* ▷ *vt* (*swing gently*) mecer; (*shake*) sacudir ▷ *vi* mecerse, balancearse; sacudirse; **on the ~s** (*drink*) con hielo; **their**

r

marriage is on the ~s su matrimonio se está yendo a pique; **rock and roll** n rocanrol m; **rock climbing** n (Sport) escalada

rocket ['rɔkɪt] n cohete m

rocking chair ['rɔkɪŋ-] n mecedora

rocky ['rɔkɪ] adj rocoso

rod [rɔd] n vara, varilla; (also: **fishing ~**) caña

rode [rəʊd] pt of **ride**

rodent ['rəʊdnt] n roedor m

rogue [rəʊg] n pícaro, pillo

role [rəʊl] n papel m; **role-model** n modelo a imitar

roll [rəʊl] n rollo; (of bank notes) fajo; (also: **bread ~**) panecillo; (register) lista, nómina; (sound: of drums etc) redoble m ▷ vt hacer rodar; (also: **~ up**: string) enrollar; (: cigarettes) liar; (also: **~ out**: pastry) aplanar ▷ vi rodar; (drum) redoblar; (ship) balancearse; **roll over** vi dar una vuelta; **roll up** vi (inf: arrive) aparecer ▷ vt (carpet, cloth, map) arrollar; (sleeves) arremangar

roller n rodillo; (wheel) rueda; (for road) apisonadora; (for hair) rulo; **Rollerblades®** npl patines mpl en línea; **roller coaster** n montaña rusa; **roller skates** npl patines mpl de rueda; **roller-skating** n patinaje sobre ruedas; **to go roller-skating** ir a patinar (sobre ruedas)

rolling pin n rodillo (de cocina)

ROM [rɔm] n abbr (Comput: = read-only memory) (memoria) ROM f

Roman ['rəʊmən] adj, n romano/a; **Roman Catholic** adj, n católico/a (romano/a)

romance [rə'mæns] n (love affair) amor m; (charm) lo romántico; (novel) novela de amor

Romania [ru:'meɪnɪə] n = **Rumania**

Roman numeral n número romano

romantic [rə'mæntɪk] adj romántico

Rome [rəʊm] n Roma

roof [ru:f] n techo; (of house) tejado ▷ vt techar, poner techo a; **~ of the**

mouth paladar m; **roof rack** n (Aut) baca, portaequipajes msg

rook [ruk] n (bird) graja; (Chess) torre f

room [ru:m] n cuarto, habitación f, pieza (esp LAM); (also: **bed~**) dormitorio; (in school etc) sala; (space) sitio; **roommate** n compañero/a de cuarto; **room service** n servicio de habitaciones; **roomy** adj espacioso

rooster ['ru:stə'] n gallo

root [ru:t] n raíz f ▷ vi arraigar(se)

rope [rəʊp] n cuerda; (Naut) cable m ▷ vt (box) atar or amarrar con (una) cuerda; (climbers: also: **~ together**) encordarse; (an area: also: **~ off**) acordonar; **to know the ~s** (fig) conocer los trucos (del oficio)

rort [rɔ:t] (AUST, NZ inf) n estafa ▷ vt estafar

rose [rəʊz] pt of **rise** ▷ n rosa; (also: **~bush**) rosal m; (on watering can) roseta

rosé ['rəʊzeɪ] n vino rosado

rosemary ['rəʊzmərɪ] n romero

rosy ['rəʊzɪ] adj rosado, sonrosado; **the future looks ~** el futuro parece prometedor

rot [rɔt] n podredumbre f; (fig: pej) tonterías fpl ▷ vt pudrir ▷ vi pudrirse

rota ['rəʊtə] n lista (de tareas)

rotate [rəʊ'teɪt] vt (revolve) hacer girar, dar vueltas a; (jobs) alternar ▷ vi girar, dar vueltas

rotten ['rɔtn] adj podrido; (fig) corrompido; (inf: bad) pésimo; **to feel ~** (ill) sentirse fatal

rough [rʌf] adj (skin, surface) áspero; (terrain) accidentado; (road) desigual; (voice) bronco; (person, manner) tosco, grosero; (weather) borrascoso; (treatment) brutal; (sea) embravecido; (town, area) peligroso; (cloth) basto; (plan) preliminar; (guess) aproximado ▷ n (Golf): **in the ~** en las hierbas altas; **to ~ it** vivir sin comodidades; **to sleep ~** (BRIT) pasar la noche al raso; **roughly** adv (handle) torpemente; (make) toscamente; (approximately) aproximadamente; **roughly speaking** más o menos

roulette [ruːˈlɛt] n ruleta

round [raund] adj redondo ▷ n círculo; (of policeman) ronda; (of milkman) recorrido; (of doctor) visitas fpl; (game: in competition, cards) partida; (of ammunition) cartucho; (Boxing) asalto; (of talks) ronda ▷ vt (corner) doblar ▷ prep alrededor de; (surrounding): **~ his neck/the table** en su cuello/alrededor de la mesa; (in a circular movement): **to move ~ the room/sail ~ the world** dar una vuelta a la habitación/circunnavegar el mundo; (in various directions): **to move ~ a room/house** moverse por toda la habitación/casa ▷ adv: **all ~** por todos lados; **all the year ~** durante todo el año; **the long way ~** por el camino menos directo; **it's just ~ the corner** (fig) está a la vuelta de la esquina; **~ the clock** adv las 24 horas; **to go ~ to sb's (house)** ir a casa de algn; **to go ~ the back** pasar por atrás; **enough to go ~** bastante (para todos); **a ~ of applause** una salva de aplausos; **a ~ of drinks/sandwiches** una ronda de bebidas/bocadillos; **a ~ of toast** (BRIT) una tostada; **round off** vt (speech etc) acabar, poner término a; **round up** vt (cattle) acorralar; (people) reunir; (prices) redondear; **roundabout** n (BRIT: Aut) glorieta, rotonda; (: at fair) tiovivo ▷ adj (route, means) indirecto; **round trip** n viaje m de ida y vuelta; **roundup** n rodeo; (of criminals) redada; **a roundup of the latest news** un resumen de las últimas noticias

rouse [rauz] vt (wake up) despertar; (stir up) suscitar

route [ruːt] n ruta, camino; (of bus) recorrido; (of shipping) derrota

routine [ruːˈtiːn] adj rutinario ▷ n rutina; (Theat) número

row¹ [rəu] n (line) fila, hilera; (Knitting) vuelta ▷ vi (in boat) remar ▷ vt (boat) conducir remando; **four days in a ~** cuarto días seguidos

row² [rau] n (noise) escándalo; (dispute) bronca, pelea; (scolding) reprimenda ▷ vi reñir(se)

rowboat [ˈrəubəut] n (US) bote m de remos

rowing [ˈrəuɪŋ] n remo; **rowing boat** n (BRIT) bote m or barco de remos

royal [ˈrɔɪəl] adj real; **Royal Air Force** n Fuerzas Aéreas Británicas fpl; **royalty** n (royal persons) (miembros mpl de la) familia real; (payment to author) derechos mpl de autor

rpm abbr (= revolutions per minute) r.p.m.

RSVP abbr (= répondez s'il vous plaît) SRC

Rt. Hon. abbr (BRIT: = Right Honourable) tratamiento honorífico de diputado

rub [rʌb] vt frotar; (hard) restregar ▷ n: **to give sth a ~** frotar algo; **to ~ sb up** or (US)**~ sb the wrong way** sacar de quicio a algn; **rub in** vt (ointment) frotar; **rub off** vt borrarse; **rub out** vt borrar

rubber [ˈrʌbəʳ] n caucho, goma; (BRIT: eraser) goma de borrar; **rubber band** n goma, gomita; **rubber gloves** npl guantes mpl de goma

rubbish [ˈrʌbɪʃ] (BRIT) n (from household) basura; (waste) desperdicios mpl; (fig: pej) tonterías fpl; (trash) basura, porquería; **rubbish bin** n cubo or bote m (LAM) de la basura; **rubbish dump** n vertedero, basurero

rubble [ˈrʌbl] n escombros mpl

ruby [ˈruːbɪ] n rubí m

rucksack [ˈrʌksæk] n mochila

rudder [ˈrʌdəʳ] n timón m

rude [ruːd] adj (impolite: person) maleducado; (: word, manners) grosero; (indecent) indecente

ruffle [ˈrʌfl] vt (hair) despeinar; (clothes) arrugar; (fig: person) agitar

rug [rʌg] n alfombra; (BRIT: for knees) manta

rugby [ˈrʌgbɪ] n rugby m

rugged ['rʌgɪd] adj (landscape)
accidentado; (features) robusto

ruin ['ruːɪn] n ruina ▷ vt arruinar;
(spoil) estropear; **ruins** npl ruinas fpl,
restos mpl

rule [ruːl] n (norm) norma, costumbre
f; (regulation, ruler) regla; (government)
dominio ▷ vt (country, person) gobernar
▷ vi gobernar; (Law) fallar; **as a ~** por
regla general; **rule out** vt excluir;
ruler n (sovereign) soberano; (for
measuring) regla; **ruling** adj (party)
gobernante; (class) dirigente ▷ n (Law)
fallo, decisión f

rum [rʌm] n ron m

Rumania [ruːˈmeɪnɪə] n Rumanía;
Rumanian adj, n rumano/a

rumble ['rʌmbl] n ruido sordo ▷ vi
retumbar, hacer un ruido sordo;
(stomach, pipe) sonar

rumour, (US) **rumor** ['ruːməʳ] n
rumor m ▷ vt: **it is ~ed that ...** se
rumorea que ...; **~ has it that ...** corre
la voz de que ...

rump steak n filete m de lomo

run [rʌn] (pt ran, pp run) n (Sport)
carrera; (outing) paseo, excursión f;
(distance travelled) trayecto; (series)
serie f; (Theat) temporada; (Ski) pista;
(in tights, stockings) carrera ▷ vt
(operate: business) dirigir; (: competition,
course) organizar; (: hotel, house)
administrar, llevar; (Comput) ejecutar;
(to pass: hand) pasar; (Press: feature)
publicar ▷ vi correr; (work: machine)
funcionar, marchar; (bus, train: operate)
circular, ir; (: travel) ir; (: continue: play)
seguir en cartel; (: contract) ser válido;
(flow: river, bath) fluir; (colours, washing)
desteñirse; (in election) ser candidato;
there was a ~ on (meat, tickets) hubo
mucha demanda de; **in the long ~** a
la larga; **on the ~** en fuga; **I'll ~ you
to the station** te llevaré a la estación
en coche; **to ~ a risk** correr un riesgo;
to ~ a bath llenar la bañera; **run
after** vt fus (to catch up) correr tras;
(chase) perseguir; **run away** vi huir;

run down vt (reduce: production)
ir reduciendo; (factory) restringir
la producción de; (Aut) atropellar;
(criticize) criticar; **to be ~ down**
(person: tired) encontrarse agotado;

run into vt fus (meet: person, trouble)
tropezar con; (collide with) chocar con;
run off vt (water) dejar correr ▷ vi huir
corriendo; **run out** vi (person) salir
corriendo; (liquid) irse; (lease) caducar,
vencer; (money) acabarse; **run out
of** vt fus quedar sin; **run over** vt (Aut)
atropellar ▷ vt fus (revise) repasar; **run
through** vt fus (instructions) repasar; **run
up** vt (debt) incurrir en; **to ~ up
against** (difficulties) tropezar con;
runaway adj (horse) desbocado;
(truck) sin frenos; (person) fugitivo

rung [rʌŋ] pp of **ring** ▷ n (of ladder)
escalón m, peldaño

runner ['rʌnəʳ] n (in race: person)
corredor(a) m/f; (: horse) caballo;
(on sledge) patín m; **runner bean**
n (BRIT) judía verde; **runner-up** n
subcampeón/ona m/f

running ['rʌnɪŋ] n (sport) atletismo;
(race) carrera ▷ adj (costs, water)
corriente; (commentary) en directo; **to
be in/out of the ~ for sth** tener/no
tener posibilidades de ganar algo; **6
days ~** 6 días seguidos

runny ['rʌnɪ] adj líquido; (eyes) lloroso;
to have a ~ nose tener mocos

run-up ['rʌnʌp] n: **~ to** (election etc)
período previo a

runway ['rʌnweɪ] n (Aviat) pista (de
aterrizaje)

rupture ['rʌptʃəʳ] n (Med) hernia ▷ vt:
to ~ o.s. causarse una hernia

rural ['ruərl] adj rural

rush [rʌʃ] n ímpetu m; (hurry) prisa;
(Comm) demanda repentina; (Bot)
junco; (current) corriente f fuerte; (of
feeling) torrente m ▷ vt apresurar; (work)
hacer de prisa ▷ vi correr, precipitarse;
rush hour n horas fpl punta

Russia ['rʌʃə] n Rusia; **Russian** adj
ruso ▷ n ruso/a; (Ling) ruso

rust [rʌst] *n* herrumbre *f*, moho ▷ *vi* oxidarse
rusty ['rʌstɪ] *adj* oxidado
ruthless ['ruːθlɪs] *adj* despiadado
RV *n abbr* (US) = **recreational vehicle**
rye [raɪ] *n* centeno

S

Sabbath ['sæbəθ] *n* domingo; (*Jewish*) sábado
sabotage ['sæbətɑːʒ] *n* sabotaje *m* ▷ *vt* sabotear
saccharin(e) ['sækərɪn] *n* sacarina
sachet ['sæʃeɪ] *n* sobrecito
sack [sæk] *n* (*bag*) saco, costal *m* ▷ *vt* (*dismiss*) despedir; (*plunder*) saquear; **to get the ~** ser despedido
sacred ['seɪkrɪd] *adj* sagrado, santo
sacrifice ['sækrɪfaɪs] *n* sacrificio ▷ *vt* sacrificar
sad [sæd] *adj* (*unhappy*) triste; (*deplorable*) lamentable
saddle ['sædl] *n* silla (de montar); (*of cycle*) sillín *m* ▷ *vt* (*horse*) ensillar; **to be ~d with sth** (*inf*) quedar cargado con algo
sadistic [sə'dɪstɪk] *adj* sádico
sadly ['sædlɪ] *adv* tristemente; **~ lacking (in)** muy deficiente (en)
sadness ['sædnɪs] *n* tristeza
safari [sə'fɑːrɪ] *n* safari *m*

safe [seɪf] *adj (out of danger)* fuera de peligro; *(not dangerous, sure)* seguro; *(unharmed)* ileso ▷ *n* caja de caudales, caja fuerte; **~ and sound** sano y salvo; **(just) to be on the ~ side** para mayor seguridad; **safely** *adv* seguramente, con seguridad; **to arrive safely** llegar bien; **safe sex** *n* sexo seguro *or* sin riesgo

safety ['seɪftɪ] *n* seguridad *f*; **safety belt** *n* cinturón *m* (de seguridad); **safety pin** *n* imperdible *m*, seguro (*LAM*)

saffron ['sæfrən] *n* azafrán *m*

sag [sæg] *vi* aflojarse

sage [seɪdʒ] *n (herb)* salvia; *(man)* sabio

Sagittarius [sædʒɪ'teərɪəs] *n* Sagitario

Sahara [sə'hɑːrə] *n*: **the ~ (Desert)** el Sáhara

said [sɛd] *pt, pp* of **say**

sail [seɪl] *n (on boat)* vela ▷ *vt (boat)* gobernar ▷ *vi (travel: ship)* navegar; *(Sport)* hacer vela; **they ~ed into Copenhagen** arribaron a Copenhague; **sailboat** *n (US)* velero, barco de vela; **sailing** *n (Sport)* vela; **to go sailing** hacer vela; **sailing boat** *n* velero, barco de vela; **sailor** *n* marinero, marino

saint [seɪnt] *n* santo

sake [seɪk] *n*: **for the ~ of** por

salad ['sæləd] *n* ensalada; **salad cream** *n (BRIT)* mayonesa; **salad dressing** *n* aliño

salami [sə'lɑːmɪ] *n* salami *m*, salchichón *m*

salary ['sælərɪ] *n* sueldo

sale [seɪl] *n* venta; *(at reduced prices)* liquidación *f*, saldo; *(auction)* subasta; **sales** *npl (total amount sold)* ventas *fpl*, facturación *f*; **"for ~"** "se vende"; **on ~** en venta; **on ~ or return** *(goods)* venta por reposición; **sales assistant** *n (BRIT)* dependiente/a *m/f*; **sales clerk** *n (US)* dependiente/a *m/f*; **salesman** *n* vendedor *m*; *(in shop)* dependiente *m*; **salesperson** *(irreg)* *n* vendedor(a)

m/f, dependiente/a *m/f*; **sales rep** *n* representante *mf*, agente *mf* comercial

saline ['seɪlaɪn] *adj* salino

saliva [sə'laɪvə] *n* saliva

salmon ['sæmən] *n (pl inv)* salmón *m*

salon ['sælɔn] *n (hairdressing salon, beauty salon)* salón *m*

saloon [sə'luːn] *n (US)* bar *m*, taberna; *(BRIT Aut)* (coche *m* de) turismo; *(ship's lounge)* cámara, salón *m*

salt [sɔːlt] *n* sal *f* ▷ *vt* salar; *(put salt on)* poner sal en; **saltwater** *adj* de agua salada; **salty** *adj* salado

salute [sə'luːt] *n* saludo; *(of guns)* salva ▷ *vt* saludar

salvage ['sælvɪdʒ] *n (saving)* salvamento, recuperación *f*; *(things saved)* objetos *mpl* salvados ▷ *vt* salvar

Salvation Army *n* Ejército de Salvación

same [seɪm] *adj* mismo ▷ *pron*: **the ~** el mismo/la misma; **the ~ book as** el mismo libro que; **at the ~ time** *(at the same moment)* al mismo tiempo; *(yet)* sin embargo; **all** *or* **just the ~** sin embargo, aun así; **to do the ~ (as sb)** hacer lo mismo (que otro); **and the ~ to you!** ¡igualmente!

sample ['sɑːmpl] *n* muestra ▷ *vt (food, wine)* probar

sanction ['sæŋkʃən] *n* sanción *f* ▷ *vt* sancionar; **sanctions** *npl (Pol)* sanciones *fpl*

sanctuary ['sæŋktjuərɪ] *n* santuario; *(refuge)* asilo, refugio; *(for wildlife)* reserva

sand [sænd] *n* arena; *(beach)* playa; **sands** *npl* playa *sg* de arena ▷ *vt (also: ~ down: wood etc)* lijar

sandal ['sændl] *n* sandalia

sand: sandbox *n (US)* = **sandpit**; **sandcastle** *n* castillo de arena; **sand dune** *n* duna; **sandpaper** *n* papel *m* de lija; **sandpit** *n (for children)* cajón *m* de arena; **sandstone** *n* piedra arenisca

sandwich ['sændwɪtʃ] *n* bocadillo *(SP)*, sandwich *m (LAM)* ▷ *vt (also: ~ in)*

intercalar; **to be ~ed between** estar
apretujado entre; **cheese/ham ~**
sandwich de queso/jamón
sandy ['sændı] adj arenoso; (colour)
rojizo
sane [seɪn] adj cuerdo, sensato
Be careful not to translate sane by
the Spanish word sano.
sang [sæŋ] pt of **sing**
sanitary towel, (US) **sanitary
napkin** n paño higiénico,
compresa
sanity ['sænıtı] n cordura; (of
judgment) sensatez f
sank [sæŋk] pt of **sink**
Santa Claus [sæntə'klɔːz] n San
Nicolás m, Papá Noel m
sap [sæp] n (of plants) savia ▷ vt
(strength) minar, agotar
sapphire ['sæfaɪər] n zafiro
sarcasm ['sɑːkæzm] n sarcasmo
sarcastic [sɑː'kæstɪk] adj sarcástico
sardine [sɑː'diːn] n sardina
SASE n abbr (US: = self-addressed
stamped envelope) sobre con las propias
señas de uno y con sello
sat [sæt] pt, pp of **sit**
Sat. abbr (= Saturday) sáb.
satchel ['sætʃl] n (child's) cartera,
mochila (LAM)
satellite ['sætəlaɪt] n satélite m;
satellite dish n (antena) parabólica;
satellite television n televisión f
por satélite
satin ['sætɪn] n raso ▷ adj de raso
satire ['sætaɪər] n sátira
satisfaction [sætɪs'fækʃən] n
satisfacción f
satisfactory [sætɪs'fæktərɪ] adj
satisfactorio
satisfied ['sætɪsfaɪd] adj satisfecho;
to be ~ (with sth) estar satisfecho
(de algo)
satisfy ['sætɪsfaɪ] vt satisfacer;
(convince) convencer
satnav ['sætnæv] n abbr (= satellite
navigation) navegador m (GPS)
Saturday ['sætədɪ] n sábado

sauce [sɔːs] n salsa; (sweet) crema;
saucepan n cacerola, olla
saucer ['sɔːsər] n platillo
Saudi Arabia n Arabia Saudí or
Saudita
sauna ['sɔːnə] n sauna
sausage ['sɔsɪdʒ] n salchicha;
sausage roll n empanadilla de
salchicha
sautéed ['səuteɪd] adj salteado
savage ['sævɪdʒ] adj (cruel, fierce)
feroz, furioso; (primitive) salvaje ▷ n
salvaje mf ▷ vt (attack) embestir
save [seɪv] vt (rescue) salvar, rescatar;
(money, time) ahorrar; (put by) guardar;
(Comput) salvar (y guardar); (avoid:
trouble) evitar; (Sport) parar ▷ vi (also:
~ up) ahorrar ▷ n (Sport) parada ▷ prep
salvo, excepto
saving ['seɪvɪŋ] n (on price etc)
economía; **savings** npl ahorros
mpl; **savings account** n cuenta
de ahorros; **savings and loan
association** n (US) sociedad f de
ahorro y préstamo
savoury, (US) **savory** ['seɪvərɪ] adj
sabroso; (dish: not sweet) salado
saw [sɔː] pt of **see** ▷ n (tool) sierra ▷ vt
serrar; **sawdust** n (a)serrín m
sawn [sɔːn] pp of **saw**
saxophone ['sæksəfəun] n saxófono
say (pt, pp **said**) [seɪ, sɛd] n: **to have
one's ~** expresar su opinión ▷ vt, vi
decir; **to have a** or **some ~ in sth**
tener voz y voto en algo; **to ~ yes/no**
decir que sí/no; **that is to ~** es decir;
that goes without ~ing ni que decir
tiene; **saying** n dicho, refrán m
scab [skæb] n costra; (pej) esquirol(a)
m/f
scaffolding ['skæfəldɪŋ] n andamio,
andamiaje m
scald [skɔːld] n escaldadura ▷ vt
escaldar
scale [skeɪl] n escala; (Mus) escala;
(of fish) escama; (of salaries, fees etc)
escalafón m ▷ vt (mountain) escalar;
(tree) trepar; **scales** npl (small) balanza

S

sg; (large) báscula sg; **on a large ~** a gran escala; **~ of charges** tarifa, lista de precios

scallion ['skæljən] n (US) cebolleta

scallop ['skɔləp] n (Zool) venera; (Sewing) festón m

scalp [skælp] n cabellera ▷ vt escalpar

scalpel ['skælpl] n bisturí m

scam [skæm] n (inf) estafa, timo

scampi ['skæmpɪ] npl gambas fpl

scan [skæn] vt (examine) escudriñar; (glance at quickly) dar un vistazo a; (TV, Radar) explorar, registrar ▷ n (Med) examen m ultrasónico; **to have a ~** pasar por el escáner

scandal ['skændl] n escándalo; (gossip) chismes mpl

Scandinavia [skændɪ'neɪvɪə] n Escandinavia; **Scandinavian** adj, n escandinavo/a

scanner ['skænəʳ] n (Radar, Med, Comput) escáner m

scapegoat ['skeɪpgəʊt] n cabeza de turco, chivo expiatorio

scar [skɑ:] n cicatriz f ▷ vt marcar con una cicatriz

scarce [skeəs] adj escaso; **to make o.s. ~** (inf) esfumarse; **scarcely** adv apenas

scare [skeəʳ] n susto, sobresalto; (panic) pánico ▷ vt asustar, espantar; **to ~ sb stiff** dar a algn un susto de muerte; **bomb ~** amenaza de bomba; **scarecrow** n espantapájaros m inv; **scared** adj: **to be scared** estar asustado

scarf (pl **scarves**) [skɑ:f, skɑ:vz] n (long) bufanda; (square) pañuelo

scarlet ['skɑ:lɪt] adj escarlata

scarves [skɑ:vz] npl of **scarf**

scary ['skeərɪ] adj (inf) de miedo

scatter ['skætəʳ] vt (spread) esparcir, desparramar; (put to flight) dispersar ▷ vi desparramarse; dispersarse

scenario [sɪ'nɑ:rɪəu] n (Theat) argumento; (Cine) guión m; (fig) escenario

scene [si:n] n (Theat) escena; (of crime, accident) escenario; (sight, view) vista, panorama; (fuss) escándalo; **scenery** n (Theat) decorado; (landscape) paisaje m; **scenic** adj pintoresco

▮ Be careful not to translate *scenery* by the Spanish word *escenario*.

scent [sent] n perfume m, olor m; (fig: track) rastro, pista

sceptical, (US) **skeptical** ['skeptɪkl] adj escéptico

schedule ['ʃedju:l, US 'skedju:l] n (of trains) horario; (of events) programa m; (list) lista ▷ vt (visit) fijar la hora de; **on ~** a la hora, sin retraso; **to be ahead of/behind ~** ir adelantado/retrasado

scheduled ['ʃedju:ld, US 'skedju:ld] adj (date, time) fijado; **~ flight** vuelo regular

scheme [ski:m] n (plan) plan m, proyecto; (plot) intriga; (arrangement) disposición f; (pension scheme etc) sistema m ▷ vi (intrigue) intrigar

schizophrenic [skɪtsə'frenɪk] adj esquizofrénico

scholar ['skɔləʳ] n (pupil) alumno/a; (learned person) sabio/a, erudito/a; **scholarship** n erudición f; (grant) beca

school [sku:l] n escuela, colegio; (in university) facultad f; **schoolbook** n libro de texto; **schoolboy** n alumno; **schoolchild** schoolchildren n alumno/a; **schoolgirl** n alumna; **schooling** n enseñanza; **schoolteacher** n (primary) maestro/a; (secondary) profesor(a) m/f

science ['saɪəns] n ciencia; **science fiction** n ciencia-ficción f; **scientific** [saɪən'tɪfɪk] adj científico; **scientist** n científico/a

sci-fi ['saɪfaɪ] n abbr (inf) = **science fiction**

scissors ['sɪzəz] npl tijeras fpl; **a pair of ~** unas tijeras

scold [skəʊld] vt regañar

scone [skɔn] n pastel de pan

scoop [sku:p] n (for flour etc) pala; (Press) exclusiva

scooter ['sku:tə^r] n (motor cycle) Vespa®; (toy) patinete m

scope [skəup] n (of plan, undertaking) ámbito; (of person) competencia; (opportunity) libertad f (de acción)

scorching ['skɔ:tʃɪŋ] adj abrasador(a)

score [skɔ:^r] n (points etc) puntuación f; (Mus) partitura; (twenty) veintena ▷ vt (goal, point) ganar; (mark, cut) rayar ▷ vi marcar un tanto; (Football) marcar un gol; (keep score) llevar el tanteo; **on that ~** en lo que se refiere a eso; **to ~ 6 out of 10** obtener una puntuación de 6 sobre 10; **score out** vt tachar; **scoreboard** n marcador m; **scorer** n marcador(a) m/f; (keeping score) encargado/a del marcador

scorn [skɔ:n] n desprecio

Scorpio ['skɔ:piəu] n Escorpión m

scorpion ['skɔ:piən] n alacrán m

Scot [skɒt] n escocés/esa m/f

Scotch tape® n (US) cinta adhesiva, celo, scotch®m

Scotland ['skɒtlənd] n Escocia

Scots [skɒts] adj escocés/esa; **Scotsman** n escocés m; **Scotswoman** n escocesa

Scottish ['skɒtɪʃ] adj escocés/esa; **the ~ Parliament** el Parlamento escocés

scout [skaut] n explorador m; **girl ~** (US) niña exploradora

scowl [skaul] vi fruncir el ceño; **to ~ at sb** mirar con ceño a algn

scramble ['skræmbl] n (climb) subida (difícil); (struggle) pelea ▷ vi: **to ~ out/through** salir/abrirse paso con dificultad; **to ~ for** pelear por; **scrambled eggs** npl huevos mpl revueltos

scrap [skræp] n (bit) pedacito; (fig) pizca; (fight) riña, bronca; (also: **~ iron**) chatarra, hierro viejo ▷ vt (discard) desechar, descartar ▷ vi reñir, armar (una) bronca; **scraps** npl (waste) sobras fpl, desperdicios mpl; **scrapbook** n álbum m de recortes

scrape [skreɪp] n (fig) lío, apuro ▷ vt raspar; (skin etc) rasguñar; (also: **~ against**) rozar; **to get into a ~** meterse en un lío; **scrape through** vi (in exam) aprobar por los pelos

scrap paper n pedazos mpl de papel

scratch [skrætʃ] n rasguño; (from claw) arañazo ▷ vt (paint, car) rayar; (with claw, nail) rasguñar, arañar ▷ vi rascarse; **to start from ~** partir de cero; **to be up to ~** cumplir con los requisitos; **scratch card** n (BRIT) tarjeta f de "rasque y gane"

scream [skri:m] n chillido ▷ vi chillar

screen [skri:n] n (Cine, TV) pantalla; (movable) biombo ▷ vt (conceal) tapar; (from the wind etc) proteger; (film) proyectar; (fig: person: for security) investigar; **screening** n (Med) exploración f; **screenplay** n guión m; **screen saver** n (Comput) salvapantallas m inv

screw [skru:] n tornillo; (propeller) hélice f ▷ vt atornillar; **screw up** vt (paper, material etc) arrugar; **to ~ up one's eyes** arrugar el entrecejo; **screwdriver** n destornillador m

scribble ['skrɪbl] n garabatos mpl ▷ vi garabatear ▷ vt: **to ~ sth down** garabatear algo

script [skrɪpt] n (Cine etc) guión m; (writing) escritura, letra

scroll [skrəul] n rollo

scrub [skrʌb] n (land) maleza ▷ vt fregar, restregar; (reject) cancelar, anular

scruffy ['skrʌfɪ] adj desaliñado

scrum(mage) ['skrʌm(ɪdʒ)] n (Rugby) melée f

scrutiny ['skru:tɪnɪ] n escrutinio, examen m

scuba diving ['sku:bə'daɪvɪŋ] n submarinismo

sculptor ['skʌlptə^r] n escultor(a) m/f

sculpture ['skʌlptʃə^r] n escultura

scum [skʌm] n (on liquid) espuma; (pej: people) escoria

scurry ['skʌrɪ] vi: **to ~ off** escabullirse

sea [si:] n mar m (or also f); **by ~** (travel) en barco; **on the ~** (boat) en el mar; (town) junto al mar; **to be all at ~** (fig) estar despistado; **out to ~** or **at ~** en alta mar; **seafood** n mariscos mpl; **sea front** n paseo marítimo; **seagull** n gaviota

seal [si:l] n (animal) foca; (stamp) sello ▷ vt (close) cerrar; **seal off** vt obturar

sea level n nivel m del mar

seam [si:m] n costura; (of metal) juntura; (of coal) veta, filón m

search [sə:tʃ] n (for person, thing) busca, búsqueda; (of drawer, pockets) registro ▷ vt (look in) buscar en; (examine) examinar; (person, place) registrar ▷ vi: **to ~ for** buscar; **in ~ of** en busca de; **search engine** n (Internet) buscador m; **search party** n equipo de salvamento

sea: seashore n playa, orilla del mar; **seasick** adj mareado; **seaside** n playa, orilla del mar; **seaside resort** n centro turístico costero

season ['si:zn] n (of year) estación f; (sporting etc) temporada ▷ vt (food) sazonar; **to be in/out of ~** estar en sazón/fuera de temporada; **seasonal** adj estacional; **seasoning** n condimento; **season ticket** n abono

seat [si:t] n (in bus, train) asiento; (chair) silla; (Parliament) escaño; (buttocks) trasero ▷ vt sentar; (have room for) tener cabida para; **to be ~ed** sentarse; **seat belt** n cinturón m de seguridad; **seating** n asientos mpl

sea: sea water n agua m del mar; **seaweed** n alga marina

sec. abbr = **second**

secluded [sɪ'klu:dɪd] adj retirado

second ['sɛkənd] adj segundo ▷ adv en segundo lugar ▷ n segundo; (Aut: also: **~ gear**) segunda; (Comm) artículo con algún desperfecto; (BRIT Scol: degree) título universitario de segunda clase ▷ vt (motion) apoyar; **to have ~ thoughts** cambiar de opinión; **on ~ thoughts** or (US) **thought** pensándolo bien; **secondary** adj secundario; **secondary school** n escuela secundaria; **second-class** adj de segunda clase ▷ adv: **to travel second-class** viajar en segunda; **secondhand** adj de segunda mano, usado; **secondly** adv en segundo lugar; **second-rate** adj de segunda categoría

secrecy ['si:krəsɪ] n secreto

secret ['si:krɪt] adj, n secreto; **in ~** en secreto

secretary ['sɛkrətərɪ] n secretario/a; **S~ of State** (BRIT Pol) Ministro (con cartera)

secretive ['si:krətɪv] adj reservado, sigiloso

secret service n servicio secreto

sect [sɛkt] n secta

section ['sɛkʃən] n sección f; (part) parte f; (of document) artículo; (of opinion) sector m

sector ['sɛktər] n sector m

secular ['sɛkjulər] adj secular, seglar

secure [sɪ'kjuər] adj seguro; (firmly fixed) firme, fijo ▷ vt (fix) asegurar, afianzar; (get) conseguir

security [sɪ'kjuərɪtɪ] n seguridad f; (for loan) fianza; (: object) prenda; **securities** npl (Comm) valores mpl, títulos mpl; **security guard** n guardia mf de seguridad

sedan [sɪ'dæn] n (US Aut) sedán m

sedate [sɪ'deɪt] adj tranquilo ▷ vt administrar sedantes a, sedar

sedative ['sɛdɪtɪv] n sedante m

seduce [sɪ'dju:s] vt seducir; **seductive** [sɪ'dʌktɪv] adj seductor/a

see [si:] (pt **saw**, pp **seen**) vt ver; (understand) ver, comprender ▷ vi ver ▷ n sede f; **to ~ sb to the door** acompañar a algn a la puerta; **to ~ that** (ensure) asegurarse de que; **~ you soon/later/tomorrow!** ¡hasta pronto/luego/mañana!; **see off** vt despedir; **see out** vt (take to the door) acompañar hasta la puerta; **see**

through vt fus calar ▷ vt llevar a cabo; **see to** vt fus atender a, encargarse de
seed [siːd] n semilla; (in fruit) pepita; (fig) germen m; (Tennis) preseleccionado/a; **to go to ~** (plant) granar; (fig) descuidarse
seeing [ˈsiːɪŋ] conj: **~ (that)** visto que, en vista de que
seek (pt, pp **sought**) [siːk, sɔːt] vt buscar; (post) solicitar
seem [siːm] vi parecer; **there ~s to be ...** parece que hay ...; **seemingly** adv aparentemente, según parece
seen [siːn] pp of **see**
seesaw [ˈsiːsɔː] n subibaja m
segment [ˈsɛɡmənt] n segmento; (of citrus fruit) gajo
segregate [ˈsɛɡrɪɡeɪt] vt segregar
seize [siːz] vt (grasp) agarrar, asir; (take possession of) secuestrar; (: territory) apoderarse de; (opportunity) aprovecharse de
seizure [ˈsiːʒəʳ] n (Med) ataque m; (Law) incautación f
seldom [ˈsɛldəm] adv rara vez
select [sɪˈlɛkt] adj selecto, escogido ▷ vt escoger, elegir; (Sport) seleccionar; **selection** n selección f, elección f; (Comm) surtido; **selective** adj selectivo
self [sɛlf] n uno mismo ▷ pref auto...; **the ~** el yo; **self-assured** adj seguro de sí mismo; **self-catering** adj (BRIT): **self-catering apartment** apartamento con cocina propia; **self-centred**, (US) **self-centered** adj egocéntrico; **self-confidence** n confianza en sí mismo; **self-confident** adj seguro de sí (mismo), lleno de confianza en sí mismo; **self-conscious** adj cohibido; **self-contained** adj (BRIT: flat) con entrada particular; **self-control** n autodominio; **self-defence**, (US) **self-defense** n defensa propia; **self-employed** adj que trabaja por cuenta propia; **self-esteem** n amor m propio; **self-indulgent** adj indulgente consigo mismo; **self-interest** n egoísmo; **selfish** adj egoísta; **self-pity** n lástima de sí mismo; **self-raising**, (US) **self-rising** adj: **self-raising flour** harina con levadura; **self-respect** n amor m propio; **self-service** adj de autoservicio

sell (pt, pp **sold**) [sɛl, səuld] vt vender ▷ vi venderse; **to ~ at** or **for £10** venderse a 10 libras; **sell off** vt liquidar; **sell out** vi: **the tickets are all sold out** las entradas están agotadas; **sell-by date** n fecha de caducidad; **seller** n vendedor(a) m/f
Sellotape® [ˈsɛləuteɪp] n (BRIT) celo, scotch® m
selves [sɛlvz] npl of **self**
semester [sɪˈmɛstəʳ] n (US) semestre m
semi... [sɛmɪ] pref semi..., medio...; **semicircle** n semicírculo; **semidetached (house)** n casa adosada; **semi-final** n semifinal f
seminar [ˈsɛmɪnɑːʳ] n seminario
semi-skimmed [ˈsɛmɪˈskɪmd] adj semidesnatado; **semi-skimmed (milk)** n leche semidesnatada
senate [ˈsɛnɪt] n senado; see also **Congress**; **senator** n senador(a) m/f
send (pt, pp **sent**) [sɛnd, sɛnt] vt mandar, enviar; **send back** vt devolver; **send for** vt fus mandar traer; **send in** vt (report, application, resignation) mandar; **send off** vt (goods) despachar; (BRIT Sport: player) expulsar; **send on** vt (letter, luggage) remitir; **send out** vt (invitation) mandar; (signal) emitir; **send up** vt (person, price) hacer subir; (BRIT: parody) parodiar; **sender** n remitente mf; **send-off** n: **a good send-off** una buena despedida
senile [ˈsiːnaɪl] adj senil
senior [ˈsiːnɪəʳ] adj (older) mayor, más viejo; (: on staff) de más antigüedad; (of higher rank) superior; **senior citizen** n persona de la tercera edad; **senior high school** n (US) ≈ instituto de enseñanza media

sensation [sɛn'seɪʃən] n sensación f;
sensational adj sensacional
sense [sɛns] n (faculty, meaning)
sentido; (feeling) sensación f; (good
sense) sentido común, juicio ▷ vt
sentir, percibir; **it makes ~** tiene
sentido; **senseless** adj estúpido,
insensato; (unconscious) sin
conocimiento; **sense of humour** n
(BRIT) sentido del humor
sensible ['sɛnsɪbl] adj sensato;
(reasonable) razonable, lógico

Be careful not to translate sensible
by the Spanish word sensible.

sensitive ['sɛnsɪtɪv] adj sensible;
(touchy) susceptible
sensual ['sɛnsjuəl] adj sensual
sensuous ['sɛnsjuəs] adj sensual
sent [sɛnt] pt, pp of **send**
sentence ['sɛntəns] n (Ling) oración
f; (Law) sentencia, fallo ▷ vt: **to ~ sb to
death/to five years** condenar a algn
a muerte/a cinco años de cárcel
sentiment ['sɛntɪmənt] n
sentimiento; (opinion) opinión f;
sentimental [sɛntɪ'mɛntl] adj
sentimental
Sep. abbr (= September) sep., set.
separate adj ['sɛprɪt] separado;
(distinct) distinto; **~s** npl (clothes)
coordinados mpl ▷ vt ['sɛpəreɪt]
separar; (part) dividir ▷ vi ['sɛpəreɪt]
separarse; **separately** adv por
separado; **separation** [sɛpə'reɪʃən] n
separación f
September [sɛp'tɛmbər] n se(p)
tiembre m
septic ['sɛptɪk] adj séptico; **septic
tank** n fosa séptica
sequel ['si:kwl] n consecuencia,
resultado; (of story) continuación f
sequence ['si:kwəns] n sucesión f,
serie f; (Cine) secuencia
sequin ['si:kwɪn] n lentejuela
Serb [sə:b] adj, n = **Serbian**
Serbian ['sə:bɪən] adj serbio ▷ n
serbio/a; (Ling) serbio
sergeant ['sɑ:dʒənt] n sargento

serial ['sɪərɪəl] n (TV) serie f; **serial
killer** n asesino/a múltiple; **serial
number** n número de serie
series ['sɪəri:z] n (pl inv) serie f
serious ['sɪərɪəs] adj serio; (grave)
grave; **seriously** adv en serio; (ill,
wounded etc) gravemente
sermon ['sə:mən] n sermón m
servant n servidor(a) m/f; (also:
house ~) criado/a
serve [sə:v] vt servir; (customer)
atender; (train) tener parada en;
(apprenticeship) hacer; (prison term)
cumplir ▷ vi (servant, soldier etc) servir;
(Tennis) sacar ▷ n (Tennis) saque m; **it
~s him right** se lo tiene merecido;
server n (Comput) servidor m
service ['sə:vɪs] n servicio; (Rel) misa;
(Aut) mantenimiento; (of dishes) juego
▷ vt (car, washing machine) revisar;
(: repair) reparar; **services** npl (Econ:
tertiary sector) sector m terciario or
(de) servicios; (BRIT: on motorway)
área de servicio; **the S~s** las fuerzas
armadas; **to be of ~ to sb** ser útil
a algn; **~ included/not included**
servicio incluido/no incluido; **service
area** n (on motorway) área de servicios;
service charge n (BRIT) servicio;
serviceman n militar m; **service
station** n estación f de servicio
serviette [sə:vɪ'ɛt] n (BRIT) servilleta
session ['sɛʃən] n sesión f; **to be in ~**
estar en sesión
set [sɛt] (pt, pp **set**) n juego; (Radio)
aparato; (TV) televisor m; (of utensils)
batería; (of cutlery) cubierto; (of books)
colección f; (Tennis) set m; (group of
people) grupo; (Cine) plató m; (Theat)
decorado; (Hairdressing) marcado
▷ adj (fixed) fijo; (ready) listo ▷ vt (place)
poner, colocar; (fix) fijar; (adjust)
ajustar, arreglar; (decide: rules etc)
establecer, decidir ▷ vi (sun) ponerse;
(jam, jelly) cuajarse; (concrete) fraguar;
to be ~ on doing sth estar empeñado
en hacer algo; **to ~ to music** poner
música a; **to ~ on fire** incendiar,

prender fuego a; **to ~ free** poner en libertad; **to ~ sth going** poner algo en marcha; **to ~ sail** zarpar, hacerse a la mar; **set aside** vt poner aparte, dejar de lado; **set down** vt (bus, train) dejar; **set in** vi (infection) declararse; (complications) comenzar; **the rain has ~ in for the day** parece que va a llover todo el día; **set off** vi partir ▷ vt (bomb) hacer estallar; (cause to start) poner en marcha; (show up well) hacer resaltar; **set out** vi partir ▷ vt (arrange) disponer; (state) exponer; **to ~ out to do sth** proponer hacer algo; **set up** vt establecer; **setback** n revés m, contratiempo; **set menu** n menú m

settee [sɛ'tiː] n sofá m

setting ['sɛtɪŋ] n (scenery) marco; (of jewel) engaste m, montadura

settle ['sɛtl] vt (argument, matter) resolver; (pay: bill, accounts) pagar, liquidar; (Med: calm) calmar, sosegar ▷ vi (dust etc) depositarse; (weather) estabilizarse; **to ~ for sth** convenir en aceptar algo; **to ~ on sth** decidirse por algo; **settle down** vi (get comfortable) ponerse cómodo, acomodarse; (calm down) calmarse, tranquilizarse; (live quietly) echar raíces; **settle in** vi instalarse; **settle up** vi: **to ~ up with sb** ajustar cuentas con algn; **settlement** n (payment) liquidación f; (agreement) acuerdo, convenio; (village etc) poblado

setup ['sɛtʌp] n sistema m

seven ['sɛvn] num siete; **seventeen** num diecisiete; **seventeenth** adj decimoséptimo; **seventh** adj séptimo; **seventieth** adj septuagésimo; **seventy** num setenta

sever ['sɛvər] vt cortar; (relations) romper

several ['sɛvərl] adj, pron varios/as m/f pl, algunos/as m/f pl; **~ of us** varios de nosotros

severe [sɪ'vɪər] adj severo; (serious) grave; (hard) duro; (pain) intenso

sew (pt **sewed**, pp **sewn**) [səu, səud, səun] vt, vi coser

sewage ['suːɪdʒ] n aguas fpl residuales

sewer ['suːər] n alcantarilla, cloaca

sewing ['səuɪŋ] n costura; **sewing machine** n máquina de coser

sewn [səun] pp of **sew**

sex [sɛks] n sexo; **to have ~** hacer el amor; **sexism** n sexismo; **sexist** adj, n sexista mf; **sexual** ['sɛksjuəl] adj sexual; **sexual intercourse** relaciones fpl sexuales; **sexuality** [sɛksju'ælɪtɪ] n sexualidad f; **sexy** adj sexy

shabby ['ʃæbɪ] adj (person) desharrapado; (clothes) raído, gastado

shack [ʃæk] n choza, chabola

shade [ʃeɪd] n sombra; (for lamp) pantalla; (for eyes) visera; (of colour) tono m, tonalidad f ▷ vt dar sombra a; **shades** npl (US: sunglasses) gafas fpl de sol; **in the ~** a la sombra; **a ~ more** (small quantity) un poquito más

shadow ['ʃædəu] n sombra ▷ vt (follow) seguir y vigilar; **shadow cabinet** n (BRIT Pol) gobierno en la oposición

shady ['ʃeɪdɪ] adj sombreado; (fig: dishonest) sospechoso; (deal) turbio

shaft [ʃɑːft] n (of arrow, spear) astil m; (Aut, Tech) eje m, árbol m; (of mine) pozo; (of lift) hueco, caja; (of light) rayo

shake [ʃeɪk] (pt **shook**, pp **shaken**) vt sacudir; (building) hacer temblar ▷ vi (tremble) temblar; **to ~ one's head** (in refusal) negar con la cabeza; (in dismay) mover or menear la cabeza, incrédulo; **to ~ hands with sb** estrechar la mano a algn; **shake off** vt sacudirse; (fig) deshacerse de; **shake up** vt agitar; **shaky** adj (unstable) inestable, poco firme; (trembling) tembloroso

shall [ʃæl] aux vb: **I ~ go** iré; **~ I help you?** ¿quieres que te ayude?; **I'll buy three, ~ I?** compro tres, ¿no te parece?

shallow ['ʃæləu] adj poco profundo; (fig) superficial

S

sham [ʃæm] n fraude m, engaño
shambles ['ʃæmblz] n confusión f
shame [ʃeɪm] n vergüenza ▷ vt
avergonzar; **it is a ~ that/to do** es
una lástima or pena que/hacer; **what
a ~!** ¡qué lástima or pena!; **shameful**
adj vergonzoso; **shameless** adj
descarado
shampoo [ʃæm'pu:] n champú m ▷ vt
lavar con champú
shandy ['ʃændɪ] n clara, cerveza con
gaseosa
shan't [ʃɑ:nt] = **shall not**
shape [ʃeɪp] n forma ▷ vt formar, dar
forma a; (sb's ideas) formar; (sb's life)
determinar; **to take ~** tomar forma
share [ʃɛəʳ] n (part) parte f, porción
f; (contribution) cuota; (Comm)
acción f ▷ vt dividir; (have in common)
compartir; **to ~ out (among
or between)** repartir (entre);
shareholder n (BRIT) accionista mf
shark [ʃɑ:k] n tiburón m
sharp [ʃɑ:p] adj (razor, knife) afilado;
(point) puntiagudo; (outline) definido;
(pain) intenso; (Mus) desafinado;
(contrast) marcado; (voice) agudo;
(person: quick-witted) avispado;
(: dishonest) poco escrupuloso ▷ n
(Mus) sostenido ▷ adv: **at two o'clock
~** a las dos en punto; **sharpen** vt afilar;
(pencil) sacar punta a; (fig) agudizar;
sharpener n (also: **pencil sharpener**)
sacapuntas m inv; **sharply** adv
(abruptly) bruscamente; (clearly)
claramente; (harshly) severamente
shatter ['ʃætəʳ] vt hacer añicos or
pedazos; (fig: ruin) destruir, acabar
con ▷ vi hacerse añicos; **shattered**
adj (grief-stricken) destrozado,
deshecho; (exhausted) agotado,
hecho polvo
shave [ʃeɪv] vt afeitar, rasurar ▷ vi
afeitarse ▷ n: **to have a ~** afeitarse;
shaver n (also: **electric shaver**)
máquina de afeitar (eléctrica)
shaving ['ʃeɪvɪŋ] n (action) afeitado;
shavings npl (of wood etc) virutas fpl;

shaving cream n crema (de afeitar);
shaving foam n espuma de afeitar
shawl [ʃɔ:l] n chal m
she [ʃi:] pron ella
sheath [ʃi:θ] n vaina; (contraceptive)
preservativo
shed (pt, pp **shed**) [ʃɛd] n cobertizo
▷ vt (skin) mudar; (tears) derramar;
(workers) despedir
she'd [ʃi:d] = **she had; she would**
sheep [ʃi:p] n (pl inv) oveja; **sheepdog**
n perro pastor; **sheepskin** n piel f
de carnero
sheer [ʃɪəʳ] adj (utter) puro, completo;
(steep) escarpado; (material) diáfano
▷ adv verticalmente
sheet [ʃi:t] n (on bed) sábana; (of paper)
hoja; (of glass, metal) lámina
sheik(h) [ʃeɪk] n jeque m
shelf (pl **shelves**) [ʃɛlf, ʃɛlvz] n
estante m
shell [ʃɛl] n (on beach) concha; (of egg,
nut etc) cáscara; (explosive) proyectil m,
obús m; (of building) armazón m ▷ vt
(peas) desenvainar; (Mil) bombardear
she'll [ʃi:l] = **she will; she shall**
shellfish ['ʃɛlfɪʃ] n (pl inv) crustáceo;
(pl: as food) mariscos mpl
shelter ['ʃɛltəʳ] n abrigo, refugio ▷ vt
(aid) amparar, proteger; (give lodging
to) abrigar ▷ vi abrigarse, refugiarse;
sheltered adj (life) protegido; (spot)
abrigado
shelves [ʃɛlvz] npl of **shelf**
shelving ['ʃɛlvɪŋ] n estantería
shepherd ['ʃɛpəd] n pastor m ▷ vt
(guide) guiar, conducir; **shepherd's
pie** n pastel de carne y puré de patatas
sheriff ['ʃɛrɪf] n (US) sheriff m
sherry ['ʃɛrɪ] n jerez m
she's [ʃi:z] = **she is; she has**
Shetland ['ʃɛtlənd] n (also: **the ~s,
the ~ Isles**) las Islas fpl Shetland
shield [ʃi:ld] n escudo; (Tech) blindaje
m ▷ vt: **to ~ (from)** proteger (de)
shift [ʃɪft] n (change) cambio; (at work)
turno ▷ vt trasladar; (remove) quitar
▷ vi moverse

shin [ʃɪn] n espinilla
shine [ʃaɪn] (pt, pp **shone**) n brillo, lustre m ▷ vi brillar, relucir ▷ vt (shoes) lustrar, sacar brillo a; **to ~ a torch on sth** dirigir una linterna hacia algo
shingles ['ʃɪŋglz] n (Med) herpes msg
shiny ['ʃaɪnɪ] adj brillante, lustroso
ship [ʃɪp] n buque m, barco m ▷ vt (goods) embarcar; (send) transportar or enviar por vía marítima; **shipment** n (goods) envío; **shipping** n (act) embarque m; (traffic) buques mpl; **shipwreck** n naufragio ▷ vt: **to be shipwrecked** naufragar; **shipyard** n astillero
shirt [ʃə:t] n camisa; **in ~ sleeves** en mangas de camisa
shit [ʃɪt] (inf!) excl ¡mierda! (!)
shiver ['ʃɪvə'] n escalofrío ▷ vi temblar, estremecerse; (with cold) tiritar
shock [ʃɔk] n (impact) choque m; (Elec) descarga (eléctrica); (emotional) conmoción f; (start) sobresalto, susto; (Med) postración f nerviosa ▷ vt dar un susto a; (offend) escandalizar; **shocking** adj (awful) espantoso; (improper) escandaloso
shoe (pt, pp **shod**) [ʃu:, ʃɔd] n zapato; (for horse) herradura ▷ vt (horse) herrar; **shoelace** n cordón m; **shoe polish** n betún m; **shoeshop** n zapatería
shone [ʃɔn] pt, pp of **shine**
shonky ['ʃɔŋkɪ] adj (AUST, NZ inf) chapucero
shook [ʃuk] pt of **shake**
shoot [ʃu:t] (pt, pp **shot**) n (on branch, seedling) retoño, vástago ▷ vt disparar; (kill) matar a tiros; (execute) fusilar; (Cine: film, scene) rodar, filmar ▷ vi (Football) chutar; **shoot down** vt (plane) derribar; **shoot up** vi (prices) dispararse; **shooting** n (shots) tiros mpl; (Hunting) caza con escopeta
shop [ʃɔp] n tienda; (workshop) taller m ▷ vi (also: **go ~ping**) ir de compras; **shop assistant** n (BRIT) dependiente/a m/f; **shopkeeper** n tendero/a; **shoplifting** n ratería, robo (en las tiendas); **shopping** n (goods)

compras fpl; **shopping bag** n bolsa (de compras); **shopping centre,** (US) **shopping center** n centro comercial; **shopping mall** n centro comercial; **shopping trolley** n (BRIT) carrito de la compra; **shop window** n escaparate m, vidriera (LAM)
shore [ʃɔ:'] n orilla ▷ vt: **to ~ (up)** reforzar; **on ~** en tierra
short [ʃɔ:t] adj corto; (in time) breve, de corta duración; (person) bajo; (curt) brusco, seco; **(a pair of) ~s** (unos) pantalones mpl cortos; **to be ~ of sth** estar falto de algo; **in ~** en pocas palabras; **~ of doing ...** a menos que hagamos etc ...; **everything ~ of ...** todo menos ...; **it is ~ for** es la forma abreviada de; **to cut ~** (speech, visit) interrumpir, terminar inesperadamente; **to fall ~ of** no alcanzar; **to run ~ of sth** acabársele algo; **to stop ~** parar en seco; **to stop ~ of** detenerse antes de; **shortage** ['ʃɔ:tɪdʒ] n falta; **shortbread** n galleta de mantequilla especie de mantecada; **shortcoming** n defecto, deficiencia; **short(crust) pastry** n (BRIT) pasta quebradiza; **shortcut** n atajo; **shorten** vt acortar; (visit) interrumpir; **shortfall** n déficit m; **shorthand** n (BRIT) taquigrafía; **short-lived** adj efímero; **shortly** adv en breve, dentro de poco; **short-sighted** adj (BRIT) miope; (fig) imprudente; **short-sleeved** adj de manga corta; **short story** n cuento; **short-tempered** adj enojadizo; **short-term** adj (effect) a corto plazo
shot [ʃɔt] pt, pp of **shoot** ▷ n (sound) tiro, disparo; (try) tentativa; (injection) inyección f; (Phot) toma, fotografía; **like a ~** (without any delay) como un rayo; **shotgun** n escopeta
should [ʃud] aux vb: **I ~ go now** debo irme ahora; **he ~ be there now** debe de haber llegado (ya); **I ~ go if I were you** yo en tu lugar me iría; **I ~ like to** me gustaría

S

shoulder [ˈʃəʊldəʳ] n hombro ▷ vt (fig) cargar con; **shoulder blade** n omóplato

shouldn't [ˈʃʊdnt] = **should not**

shout [ʃaut] n grito ▷ vt gritar ▷ vi gritar, dar voces

shove [ʃʌv] n empujón m ▷ vt empujar; (inf: put): **to ~ sth in** meter algo a empellones

shovel [ˈʃʌvl] n pala; (mechanical) excavadora ▷ vt mover con pala

show [ʃəʊ] (pt **showed**, pp **shown**) n (of emotion) demostración f; (semblance) apariencia; (exhibition) exposición f; (Theat) función f, espectáculo ▷ vt mostrar, enseñar; (courage etc) mostrar, manifestar; (exhibit) exponer; (film) proyectar ▷ vi mostrarse; (appear) aparecer; **on ~** (exhibits etc) expuesto; **it's just for ~** es sólo para impresionar; **show in** vt (person) hacer pasar; **show off** vi (pej) presumir ▷ vt (display) lucir; **show out** vt: **to ~ sb out** acompañar a algn a la puerta; **show up** vi (stand out) destacar; (inf: turn up) presentarse ▷ vt (unmask) desenmascarar; **show business** n el mundo del espectáculo

shower [ˈʃaʊəʳ] n (rain) chaparrón m, chubasco; (of stones etc) lluvia; (also: ~ **bath**) ducha ▷ vi llover ▷ vt: **to ~ sb with sth** colmar a algn de algo; **to have** or **take a ~** ducharse; **shower cap** n gorro de baño; **shower gel** n gel de ducha

showing [ˈʃəʊɪŋ] n (of film) proyección f

show jumping n hípica

shown [ʃəʊn] pp of **show**

show-off [ˈʃəʊɒf] n (inf: person) fanfarrón/ona m/f; **showroom** n sala de muestras

shrank [ʃræŋk] pt of **shrink**

shred [ʃred] n (gen pl) triza, jirón m ▷ vt hacer trizas; (Culin) desmenuzar

shrewd [ʃruːd] adj astuto

shriek [ʃriːk] n chillido ▷ vi chillar

shrimp [ʃrɪmp] n camarón m

shrine [ʃraɪn] n santuario, sepulcro

shrink (pt **shrank**, pp **shrunk**) [ʃrɪŋk, ʃræŋk, ʃrʌŋk] vi encogerse; (be reduced) reducirse ▷ vt encoger ▷ n (inf, pej) loquero/a; **to ~ from (doing) sth** no atreverse a hacer algo

shrivel [ˈʃrɪvl], **shrivel up** vt (dry) secar ▷ vi secarse

shroud [ʃraud] n sudario ▷ vt: **~ed in mystery** envuelto en el misterio

Shrove Tuesday [ˈʃrəʊv-] n martes m de carnaval

shrub [ʃrʌb] n arbusto

shrug [ʃrʌg] n encogimiento de hombros ▷ vt, vi: **to ~ (one's shoulders)** encogerse de hombros; **shrug off** vt negar importancia a

shrunk [ʃrʌŋk] pp of **shrink**

shudder [ˈʃʌdəʳ] n estremecimiento, escalofrío ▷ vi estremecerse

shuffle [ˈʃʌfl] vt (cards) barajar; **to ~ (one's feet)** arrastrar los pies

shun [ʃʌn] vt rehuir, esquivar

shut (pt, pp **shut**) [ʃʌt] vt cerrar ▷ vi cerrarse; **shut down** vt, vi cerrar; **shut up** vi (inf: keep quiet) callarse ▷ vt (close) cerrar; (silence) callar; **shutter** n contraventana; (Phot) obturador m

shuttle [ˈʃʌtl] n lanzadera; (also: ~ **service**: Aviat) puente m aéreo; **shuttlecock** n volante m

shy [ʃaɪ] adj tímido

sibling [ˈsɪblɪŋ] n (formal) hermano/a

sick [sɪk] adj (ill) enfermo/a; (nauseated) mareado; (humour) morboso; **to be ~** (BRIT) vomitar; **to feel ~** tener náuseas; **to be ~ of** (fig) estar harto de; **sickening** adj (fig) asqueroso; **sick leave** n baja por enfermedad; **sickly** adj enfermizo; (taste) empalagoso; **sickness** n enfermedad f, mal m; (vomiting) náuseas fpl

side [saɪd] n lado; (of body) costado; (of lake) orilla; (team) equipo; (of hill) ladera ▷ adj (door, entrance) lateral ▷ vi: **to ~ with sb** tomar partido por algn; **by the ~ of** al lado de; **~ by ~** juntos/ as; **from all ~s** de todos lados; **to**

take ~s (with) tomar partido (por);
sideboard n aparador m; **sideboards,**
(BRIT) **sideburns** npl patillas fpl;
sidelight n (Aut) luz f lateral; **sideline**
n (Sport) línea de banda; (fig) empleo
suplementario; **side road** n (BRIT)
calle f lateral; **side street** n calle f
lateral; **sidetrack** vt (fig) desviar (de
su propósito); **sidewalk** ['saɪdwɔːk] n
(US) acera; **sideways** adv de lado
siege [siːdʒ] n cerco, sitio
sieve [sɪv] n colador m ▷ vt cribar
sift [sɪft] vt cribar ▷ vi: **to ~**
through (information) examinar
cuidadosamente
sigh [saɪ] n suspiro ▷ vi suspirar
sight [saɪt] n (faculty) vista; (spectacle)
espectáculo; (on gun) mira, alza ▷ vt
divisar; **in ~** a la vista; **out of ~** fuera
de (la) vista; **sightseeing** n turismo;
to go sightseeing hacer turismo
sign [saɪn] n (with hand) señal f, seña;
(trace) huella, rastro; (notice) letrero;
(written) signo ▷ vt firmar; (Sport)
fichar; **sign in** vi firmar el registro (al
entrar); **sign on** vi (Mil) alistarse; (as
unemployed) apuntarse al paro ▷ vt
(Mil) alistar; (employee) contratar; **to**
~ on for a course matricularse en un
curso; **sign over** vt: **to ~ sth over to**
sb traspasar algo a algn; **sign up** vi
(Mil) alistarse; (for course) inscribirse
▷ vt (player) fichar
signal ['sɪɡnl] n señal f ▷ vi señalizar
▷ vt (person) hacer señas a; (message)
transmitir
signature ['sɪɡnətʃər] n firma
significance [sɪɡ'nɪfɪkəns] n
(importance) trascendencia
significant [sɪɡ'nɪfɪkənt] adj
significativo; (important) trascendente
signify ['sɪɡnɪfaɪ] vt significar
sign language n mímica, lenguaje m
por or de señas
signpost ['saɪnpəust] n indicador m
Sikh [siːk] adj, n sij mf
silence ['saɪlns] n silencio ▷ vt hacer
callar, acallar; (guns) reducir al silencio

silent ['saɪlnt] adj silencioso; (not
speaking) callado; (film) mudo; **to**
keep or **remain ~** guardar silencio
silhouette [sɪluː'ɛt] n silueta
silicon chip n chip m, plaqueta de
silicio
silk [sɪlk] n seda ▷ cpd de seda
silly ['sɪlɪ] adj (person) tonto; (idea)
absurdo
silver ['sɪlvər] n plata; (money) moneda
suelta ▷ adj de plata; **silver-plated**
adj plateado
SIM card [sɪm-] n (Tel) SIM card m or
f, tarjeta SIM
similar ['sɪmɪlər] adj: **~ to** parecido or
semejante a; **similarity** [sɪmɪ'lærɪtɪ]
n semejanza; **similarly** adv del mismo
modo
simmer ['sɪmər] vi hervir a fuego lento
simple ['sɪmpl] adj (easy) sencillo;
(foolish) simple; (Comm) simple;
simplicity [sɪm'plɪsɪtɪ] n sencillez f;
simplify ['sɪmplɪfaɪ] vt simplificar;
simply adv (live, talk) sencillamente;
(just, merely) sólo
simulate ['sɪmjuleɪt] vt simular
simultaneous [sɪməl'teɪnɪəs] adj
simultáneo; **simultaneously** adv
simultáneamente
sin [sɪn] n pecado ▷ vi pecar
since [sɪns] adv desde entonces
▷ prep desde ▷ conj (time) desde que;
(because) ya que, puesto que; **~ then,**
ever ~ desde entonces
sincere [sɪn'sɪər] adj sincero;
sincerely adv: **yours sincerely** (in
letters) le saluda atentamente
sing (pt **sang**, pp **sung**) [sɪŋ, sæŋ, sʌŋ]
vt cantar ▷ vi cantar
Singapore [sɪŋə'pɔːr] n Singapur m
singer ['sɪŋər] n cantante mf
singing ['sɪŋɪŋ] n canto
single ['sɪŋgl] adj único, solo;
(unmarried) soltero; (not double)
individual, sencillo ▷ n (BRIT: also:
~ ticket) billete m sencillo; (record)
sencillo, single m; **singles** npl
(Tennis) individual msg; **single out** vt

(*choose*) escoger; **single bed** *n* cama individual; **single file** *n*: **in single file** en fila de uno; **single-handed** *adv* sin ayuda; **single-minded** *adj* resuelto, firme; **single parent** *n* (*mother*) madre *f* soltera; (*father*) padre *m* soltero; **single-parent family** familia monoparental; **single room** *n* habitación *f* individual

singular ['sɪŋɡjʊləʳ] *adj* raro, extraño; (*outstanding*) excepcional ▷ *n* (*Ling*) singular *m*

sinister ['sɪnɪstəʳ] *adj* siniestro

sink [sɪŋk] (*pt* **sank**, *pp* **sunk**) *n* fregadero ▷ *vt* (*ship*) hundir, echar a pique; (*foundations*) excavar; (*piles etc*): **to ~ sth into** hundir algo en ▷ *vi* hundirse; **sink in** *vi* (*fig*) penetrar, calar

sinus ['saɪnəs] *n* (*Anat*) seno

sip [sɪp] *n* sorbo ▷ *vt* sorber, beber a sorbitos

sir [səːʳ] *n* señor *m*; **S~ John Smith** Sir John Smith; **yes ~** sí, señor

siren ['saɪərn] *n* sirena

sirloin ['səːlɔɪn] *n* solomillo

sirloin steak *n* filete *m* de solomillo

sister ['sɪstəʳ] *n* hermana; (*BRIT: nurse*) enfermera jefe; **sister-in-law** *n* cuñada

sit (*pt*, *pp* **sat**) [sɪt, sæt] *vi* sentarse; (*be sitting*) estar sentado; (*assembly*) reunirse; (*for painter*) posar ▷ *vt* (*exam*) presentarse a; **sit back** *vi* (*in seat*) recostarse; **sit down** *vi* sentarse; **sit on** *vt fus* (*jury, committee*) ser miembro de, formar parte de; **sit up** *vi* incorporarse; (*not go to bed*) no acostarse

sitcom ['sɪtkɔm] *n abbr* (TV: = *situation comedy*) telecomedia

site [saɪt] *n* sitio; (*also*: **building ~**) solar *m* ▷ *vt* situar

sitting ['sɪtɪŋ] *n* (*of assembly etc*) sesión *f*; (*in canteen*) turno; **sitting room** *n* sala de estar

situated ['sɪtjueɪtɪd] *adj* situado

situation [sɪtju'eɪʃən] *n* situación *f*; **"~s vacant"** (*BRIT*) "ofertas de trabajo"

six [sɪks] *num* seis; **sixteen** *num* dieciséis; **sixteenth** *adj* decimosexto; **sixth** [sɪksθ] *adj* sexto; **sixth form** *n* (*BRIT*) clase *f* de alumnos del sexto año (*de 16 a 18 años de edad*); **sixth-form college** *n* instituto *m* para alumnos de 16 a 18 años; **sixtieth** *adj* sexagésimo; **sixty** *num* sesenta

size [saɪz] *n* tamaño; (*extent*) extensión *f*; (*of clothing*) talla; (*of shoes*) número; **sizeable** *adj* importante, considerable

sizzle ['sɪzl] *vi* crepitar

skate [skeɪt] *n* patín *m*; (*fish: pl inv*) raya ▷ *vi* patinar; **skateboard** *n* monopatín *m*; **skateboarding** *n* monopatín *m*; **skater** *n* patinador(a) *m/f*; **skating** *n* patinaje *m*; **skating rink** *n* pista de patinaje

skeleton ['skɛlɪtn] *n* esqueleto; (*Tech*) armazón *m*; (*outline*) esquema *m*

sketch [skɛtʃ] *n* (*drawing*) dibujo; (*outline*) esbozo, bosquejo; (*Theat*) pieza corta, sketch *m* ▷ *vt* dibujar; (*plan etc: also*: **~ out**) esbozar

skewer ['skjuːəʳ] *n* broqueta

ski [skiː] *n* esquí *m* ▷ *vi* esquiar; **ski boot** *n* bota de esquí

skid [skɪd] *n* patinazo ▷ *vi* patinar

ski: skier *n* esquiador(a) *m/f*; **skiing** *n* esquí *m*

skilful, (*US*) **skillful** ['skɪlful] *adj* diestro, experto

ski lift *n* telesilla *m*, telesquí *m*

skill [skɪl] *n* destreza, pericia; (*technique*) técnica; **skilled** *adj* hábil, diestro; (*worker*) cualificado

skim [skɪm] *vt* (*milk*) desnatar; (*glide over*) rozar, rasar ▷ *vi*: **to ~ through** (*book*) hojear; **skimmed milk** *n* leche *f* desnatada or descremada

skin [skɪn] *n* piel *f*; (*complexion*) cutis *m* ▷ *vt* (*fruit etc*) pelar; (*animal*) despellejar; **skinhead** *n* cabeza *mf* rapada, skin(head) *mf*; **skinny** *adj* flaco

skip [skɪp] *n* brinco, salto; (*container*) contenedor *m* ▷ *vi* brincar; (*with* rope) saltar a la comba ▷ vt (*pass over*) omitir, saltarse

ski: ski pass n forfait m (de esquí); **ski pole** n bastón m de esquiar

skipper ['skɪpəʳ] n (*Naut, Sport*) capitán m

skipping rope ['skɪpɪŋ-] n (*BRIT*) comba

skirt [skə:t] n falda, pollera (*LAM*) ▷ vt (*go round*) ladear

skirting board ['skə:tɪŋ-] n (*BRIT*) rodapié m

ski slope n pista de esquí

ski suit n traje m de esquiar

skull [skʌl] n calavera; (*Anat*) cráneo

skunk [skʌŋk] n mofeta

sky [skaɪ] n cielo; **skyscraper** n rascacielos m inv

slab [slæb] n (*stone*) bloque m; (*flat*) losa; (*of cake*) trozo

slack [slæk] adj (*loose*) flojo; (*slow*) de poca actividad; (*careless*) descuidado; **slacks** npl pantalones mpl

slain [sleɪn] pp of **slay**

slam [slæm] vt (*throw*) arrojar (violentamente); (*criticize*) vapulear, vituperar ▷ vi cerrarse de golpe; **to ~ the door** dar un portazo

slander ['slɑ:ndəʳ] n calumnia, difamación f

slang [slæŋ] n argot m; (*jargon*) jerga

slant [slɑ:nt] n sesgo, inclinación f; (*fig*) punto de vista, interpretación f

slap [slæp] n palmada; (*in face*) bofetada ▷ vt dar una palmada/bofetada a; (*paint etc*): **to ~ sth on sth** embadurnar algo con algo ▷ adv (*directly*) de lleno

slash [slæʃ] vt acuchillar; (*fig: prices*) fulminar

slate [sleɪt] n pizarra ▷ vt (*BRIT fig: criticize*) vapulear

slaughter ['slɔ:təʳ] n (*of animals*) matanza; (*of people*) carnicería ▷ vt matar; **slaughterhouse** n matadero

Slav [slɑ:v] adj eslavo

slave [sleɪv] n esclavo/a ▷ vi (*also: ~ away*) trabajar como un negro; **slavery** n esclavitud f

slay (pt **slew**, pp **slain**) [sleɪ, slu:, sleɪn] vt matar

sleazy ['sli:zɪ] adj (*fig: place*) sórdido

sledge [slɛdʒ], (*US*) **sled** [slɛd] n trineo

sleek [sli:k] adj (*shiny*) lustroso

sleep [sli:p] (pt, pp **slept**) n sueño ▷ vi dormir; **to go to ~** dormirse; **sleep in** vi (*oversleep*) quedarse dormido; **sleeper** n (*person*) durmiente mf; (*BRIT: Rail: on track*) traviesa; (*: train*) coche-cama m; **sleeping bag** n saco de dormir; **sleeping car** n coche-cama m; **sleeping pill** n somnífero; **sleepover** n: **we're having a sleepover at Fiona's** nos quedamos a dormir en casa de Fiona; **sleepwalk** vi caminar dormido; (*habitually*) ser sonámbulo; **sleepy** adj soñoliento; (*place*) soporífero

sleet [sli:t] n aguanieve f

sleeve [sli:v] n manga; (*Tech*) manguito; (*of record*) funda; **sleeveless** adj sin mangas

sleigh [sleɪ] n trineo

slender ['slɛndəʳ] adj delgado; (*means*) escaso

slept [slɛpt] pt, pp of **sleep**

slew [slu:] vi (*veer*) torcerse ▷ pt of **slay**

slice [slaɪs] n (*of meat*) tajada; (*of bread*) rebanada; (*of lemon*) rodaja; (*utensil*) paleta ▷ vt cortar; rebanar

slick [slɪk] adj (*skilful*) hábil, diestro; (*clever*) astuto ▷ n (*also: oil ~*) marea negra

slide [slaɪd] (pt, pp **slid**) n (*in playground*) tobogán m; (*Phot*) diapositiva; (*BRIT: also: hair ~*) pasador m ▷ vt correr, deslizar ▷ vi (*slip*) resbalarse; (*glide*) deslizarse; **sliding** adj (*door*) corredizo

slight [slaɪt] adj (*slim*) delgado; (*frail*) delicado; (*pain etc*) leve; (*trifling*) insignificante; (*small*) pequeño ▷ n desaire m ▷ vt (*offend*) ofender, desairar; **not in the ~est** en absoluto; **slightly** adv ligeramente, un poco

slim [slɪm] *adj* delgado, esbelto ▷ *vi* adelgazar; **slimming** *n* adelgazamiento

slimy ['slaɪmɪ] *adj* cenagoso

sling (*pt, pp* **slung**) [slɪŋ, slʌŋ] *n* (*Med*) cabestrillo; (*weapon*) honda ▷ *vt* tirar, arrojar

slip [slɪp] *n* (*slide*) resbalón *m*; (*mistake*) descuido; (*underskirt*) combinación *f*; (*of paper*) papelito ▷ *vt* (*slide*) deslizar ▷ *vi* deslizarse; (*stumble*) resbalar(se); (*decline*) decaer; (*move smoothly*): **to ~ into/out of** (*room etc*) colarse en/salirse de; **to give sb the ~** dar esquinazo a algn; **a ~ of the tongue** un lapsus; **slip up** *vi* (*make mistake*) equivocarse; meter la pata

slipper ['slɪpər] *n* zapatilla, pantufla

slippery ['slɪpərɪ] *adj* resbaladizo

slip road *n* (*BRIT*) carretera de acceso

slit [slɪt] (*pt, pp* **slit**) *n* raja; (*cut*) corte *m* ▷ *vt* rajar, cortar

slog [slɔg] (*BRIT*) *vi* sudar tinta ▷ *n*: **it was a ~** costó trabajo (hacerlo)

slogan ['sləʊgən] *n* eslogan *m*, lema *m*

slope [sləʊp] *n* (*up*) cuesta, pendiente *f*; (*down*) declive *m*; (*side of mountain*) falda, vertiente *f* ▷ *vi*: **to ~ down** estar en declive; **to ~ up** subir (en pendiente); **sloping** *adj* en pendiente; en declive

sloppy ['slɔpɪ] *adj* (*work*) descuidado; (*appearance*) desaliñado

slot [slɔt] *n* ranura ▷ *vt*: **to ~ into** encajar en; **slot machine** *n* (*BRIT: vending machine*) máquina expendedora; (*for gambling*) máquina tragaperras

Slovakia [sləʊ'vækɪə] *n* Eslovaquia

Slovene [sləʊ'viːn] *adj* esloveno ▷ *n* esloveno/a; (*Ling*) esloveno

Slovenia [sləʊ'viːnɪə] *n* Eslovenia; **Slovenian** *adj, n* = **Slovene**

slow [sləʊ] *adj* lento; (*watch*): **to be ~** ir atrasado ▷ *adv* lentamente, despacio ▷ *vt* (*also*: **~ down, ~ up**: *engine, machine*) reducir la marcha de ▷ *vi* (*also*: **~ down, ~ up**) ir más despacio;

"~" (*road sign*) "disminuir la velocidad"; **slowly** *adv* lentamente, despacio; **slow motion** *n*: **in slow motion** a cámara lenta

slug [slʌg] *n* babosa; (*bullet*) posta; **sluggish** *adj* lento; (*lazy*) perezoso

slum [slʌm] *n* casucha

slump [slʌmp] *n* (*economic*) depresión *f* ▷ *vi* hundirse; (*prices*) caer en picado

slung [slʌŋ] *pt, pp of* **sling**

slur [sləːr] *n* calumnia ▷ *vt* (*word*) pronunciar mal; **to cast a ~ on sb** manchar la reputación de algn, difamar a algn

sly [slaɪ] *adj* astuto; (*nasty*) malicioso

smack [smæk] *n* (*slap*) bofetada ▷ *vt* dar una manotada a ▷ *vi*: **to ~ of** saber a, oler a

small [smɔːl] *adj* pequeño; **small ads** *npl* (*BRIT*) anuncios *mpl* por palabras; **small change** *n* suelto, cambio

smart [smɑːt] *adj* elegante; (*clever*) listo, inteligente; (*quick*) rápido, vivo ▷ *vi* escocer, picar; **smartcard** *n* tarjeta inteligente; **smart phone** *n* smartphone *m*

smash [smæʃ] *n* (*also*: **~-up**) choque *m*; (*sound*) estrépito ▷ *vt* (*break*) hacer pedazos; (*car etc*) estrellar; (*Sport: record*) batir ▷ *vi* hacerse pedazos; (*against wall etc*) estrellarse; **smashing** *adj* (*inf*) estupendo

smear [smɪər] *n* mancha; (*Med*) frotis *m inv* (cervical) ▷ *vt* untar; **smear test** *n* (*Med*) citología, frotis *m inv* (cervical)

smell [smɛl] (*pt, pp* **smelt** *or* **smelled**) *n* olor *m*; (*sense*) olfato ▷ *vt, vi* oler; **smelly** *adj* maloliente

smelt [smɛlt] *pt, pp of* **smell**

smile [smaɪl] *n* sonrisa ▷ *vi* sonreír

smirk [sməːk] *n* sonrisa falsa *or* afectada

smog [smɔg] *n* smog *m*

smoke [sməʊk] *n* humo ▷ *vi* fumar; (*chimney*) echar humo ▷ *vt* (*cigarettes*) fumar; **smoke alarm** *n* detector *m* de humo, alarma contra incendios; **smoked** *adj* (*bacon, glass*) ahumado;

smoker n fumador(a) m/f; **smoking** n: **"no smoking"** "prohibido fumar"; **smoky** adj (room) lleno de humo

> Be careful not to translate smoking by the Spanish word smoking.

smooth [smuːð] adj liso; (sea) tranquilo; (flavour, movement) suave; (person: pej) meloso ▷ vt alisar; (also: ~ **out**: creases) alisar; (difficulties) allanar

smother ['smʌðəʳ] vt sofocar; (repress) contener

SMS n abbr (= short message service) SMS m; **SMS message** n (mensaje m) SMS m

smudge [smʌdʒ] n mancha ▷ vt manchar

smug [smʌg] adj engreído

smuggle ['smʌgl] vt pasar de contrabando; **smuggling** n contrabando

snack [snæk] n bocado; **snack bar** n cafetería

snag [snæg] n problema m

snail [sneɪl] n caracol m

snake [sneɪk] n serpiente f

snap [snæp] n (sound) chasquido; (photograph) foto f ▷ adj (decision) instantáneo ▷ vt (break) quebrar ▷ vi quebrarse; (fig: person) contestar bruscamente; **to ~ shut** cerrarse de golpe; **snap at** vt fus: **to ~ (at sb)** (dog) intentar morder (a algn); **snap up** vt agarrar; **snapshot** n foto f (instantánea)

snarl [snɑːl] vi gruñir

snatch [snætʃ] n (small piece) fragmento ▷ vt (snatch away) arrebatar; (grasp) agarrar; **to ~ some sleep** buscar tiempo para dormir

sneak [sniːk] vi: **to ~ in/out** entrar/ salir a hurtadillas ▷ n (inf) soplón/ona m/f; **to ~ up on sb** aparecérsele de improviso a algn; **sneakers** npl (us) zapatos mpl de lona

sneer [snɪəʳ] vi sonreír con desprecio; **to ~ at sth/sb** burlarse or mofarse de algo/algn

sneeze [sniːz] vi estornudar

sniff [snɪf] vi sorber (por la nariz) ▷ vt husmear, oler; (glue, drug) esnifar

snigger ['snɪgəʳ] vi reírse con disimulo

snip [snɪp] n (piece) recorte m; (bargain) ganga ▷ vt tijeretear

sniper ['snaɪpəʳ] n francotirador(a) m/f

snob [snɔb] n (e)snob mf

snooker ['snuːkəʳ] n snooker m, billar inglés

snoop [snuːp] vi: **to ~ about** fisgonear

snooze [snuːz] n siesta ▷ vi echar una siesta

snore [snɔːʳ] vi roncar ▷ n ronquido

snorkel ['snɔːkl] n tubo de respiración

snort [snɔːt] n bufido ▷ vi bufar

snow [snəʊ] n nieve f ▷ vi nevar; **snowball** n bola de nieve ▷ vi ir aumentando; **snowstorm** n tormenta de nieve, nevasca

snub [snʌb] vt: **to ~ sb** desairar a algn ▷ n desaire m, repulsa

snug [snʌg] adj (cosy) cómodo; (fitted) ajustado

○ **KEYWORD**

so [səʊ] adv **1** (thus, likewise) así, de este modo; **if so** de ser así; **I like swimming — so do I** a mí me gusta nadar — a mí también; **I've got work to do — so has Paul** tengo trabajo que hacer — Paul también; **it's five o'clock — so it is!** son las cinco — ¡pues es verdad!; **I hope/think so** espero/creo que sí; **so far** hasta ahora; (in past) hasta este momento **2** (in comparisons etc: to such a degree) tan; **so quickly (that)** tan rápido (que); **she's not so clever as her brother** no es tan lista como su hermano; **we were so worried** estábamos preocupadísimos **3**: **so much** adj tanto/a; adv tanto; **so many** tantos/as **4** (phrases): **10 or so** unos 10, 10 o así; **so long!** (inf: goodbye) ¡hasta luego!

▶ conj **1** (*expressing purpose*): **so as to do** para hacer; **so (that)** para que + subjun

2 (*expressing result*) así que; **so you see, I could have gone** así que ya ves, (yo) podría haber ido

soak [səuk] vt (*drench*) empapar; (*put in water*) remojar ▷ vi remojarse, estar a remojo; **soak up** vt absorber; **soaking** adj (*also:* **soaking wet**) calado or empapado (hasta los huesos or el tuétano)

so-and-so ['səuənsəu] n (*somebody*) fulano/a de tal

soap [səup] n jabón m; **soap opera** n telenovela; **soap powder** n jabón m en polvo

soar [sɔːʳ] vi (*on wings*) remontarse; (*building etc*) elevarse; (*price*) dispararse

sob [sɔb] n sollozo ▷ vi sollozar

sober ['səubəʳ] adj (*serious*) serio; (*not drunk*) sobrio; (*colour, style*) discreto; **sober up** vi pasársele a algn la borrachera

so-called ['səu'kɔːld] adj llamado

soccer ['sɔkəʳ] n fútbol m

sociable ['səuʃəbl] adj sociable

social ['səuʃl] adj social ▷ n velada, fiesta; **socialism** n socialismo; **socialist** adj, n socialista mf; **socialize** vi hacer vida social; **social life** n vida social; **socially** adv socialmente; **social media** npl medios sociales; **social networking** n interacción f social a través de la red; **social networking site** n red f social; **social security** n seguridad f social; **social services** npl servicios mpl sociales; **social work** n asistencia social; **social worker** n asistente/a m/f social

society [sə'saɪətɪ] n sociedad f; (*club*) asociación f; (*also:* **high ~**) alta sociedad

sociology [səusɪ'ɔlədʒɪ] n sociología

sock [sɔk] n calcetín m

socket ['sɔkɪt] n (*Elec*) enchufe m

soda ['səudə] n (*Chem*) sosa; (*also:* **~ water**) soda; (*us: also:* **~ pop**) gaseosa

sodium ['səudɪəm] n sodio

sofa ['səufə] n sofá m; **sofa bed** n sofá-cama m

soft [sɔft] adj (*teacher, parent*) blando; (*gentle, not loud*) suave; **soft drink** n bebida no alcohólica; **soft drugs** npl drogas fpl blandas; **soften** ['sɔfn] vt ablandar; suavizar ▷ vi ablandarse; suavizarse; **softly** adv suavemente; (*gently*) delicadamente, con delicadeza; **software** n (*Comput*) software m

soggy ['sɔgɪ] adj empapado

soil [sɔɪl] n (*earth*) tierra, suelo ▷ vt ensuciar

solar ['səuləʳ] adj solar; **solar power** n energía solar; **solar system** n sistema m solar

sold [səuld] pt, pp of **sell**

soldier ['səuldʒəʳ] n soldado; (*army man*) militar m

sold out adj (*Comm*) agotado

sole [səul] n (*of foot*) planta; (*of shoe*) suela; (*fish: pl inv*) lenguado ▷ adj único; **solely** adv únicamente, sólo, solamente; **I will hold you solely responsible** le consideraré el único responsable

solemn ['sɔləm] adj solemne

solicitor [sə'lɪsɪtəʳ] n (BRIT: *for wills etc*) ≈ notario/a; (*in court*) ≈ abogado/a

solid ['sɔlɪd] adj sólido; (*gold etc*) macizo ▷ n sólido

solitary ['sɔlɪtərɪ] adj solitario, solo

solitude ['sɔlɪtjuːd] n soledad f

solo ['səuləu] n solo ▷ adv (*fly*) en solitario; **soloist** n solista mf

soluble ['sɔljubl] adj soluble

solution [sə'luːʃən] n solución f

solve [sɔlv] vt resolver, solucionar

solvent ['sɔlvənt] adj (*Comm*) solvente ▷ n (*Chem*) solvente m

sombre, (us) **somber** ['sɔmbəʳ] adj sombrío

◯ **KEYWORD**

some [sʌm] *adj* **1** (*a certain amount or number of*): **some tea/water/biscuits** té/agua/(unas) galletas; **there's some milk in the fridge** hay leche en el frigo; **there were some people outside** había algunas personas fuera; **I've got some money, but not much** tengo algo de dinero, pero no mucho **2** (*certain: in contrasts*) algunos/as; **some people say that ...** hay quien dice que ...; **some films were excellent, but most were mediocre** hubo películas excelentes, pero la mayoría fueron mediocres **3** (*unspecified*): **some woman was asking for you** una mujer estuvo preguntando por ti; **some day** algún día; **some day next week** un día de la semana que viene; **he was asking for some book (or other)** pedía no sé qué libro

▶ *pron* **1** (*a certain number*): **I've got some** (*books etc*) tengo algunos/as **2** (*a certain amount*) algo; **I've got some** (*money, milk*) tengo algo; **could I have some of that cheese?** ¿me puede dar un poco de ese queso?; **I've read some of the book** he leído parte del libro

▶ *adv*: **some 10 people** unas 10 personas, una decena de personas; **somebody** *pron* alguien; **somehow** *adv* de alguna manera; (*for some reason*) por una u otra razón; **someone** *pron* = **somebody**; **someplace** *adv* (*US*) = **somewhere**; **something** *pron* algo; **would you like something to eat/drink?** ¿te gustaría cenar/tomar algo?; **sometime** *adv* (*in future*) algún día, en algún momento; **sometime last month** durante el mes pasado; **sometimes** *adv* a veces; **somewhat** *adv* algo; **somewhere** *adv* (*be*) en alguna parte; (*go*) a alguna parte; **somewhere else** (*be*) en otra parte; (*go*) a otra parte

son [sʌn] *n* hijo
song [sɒŋ] *n* canción f
son-in-law ['sʌnɪnlɔ:] *n* yerno
soon [su:n] *adv* pronto, dentro de poco; **~ afterwards** poco después; *see also* **as**; **sooner** *adv* (*time*) antes, más temprano; **I would sooner do that** preferiría hacer eso; **sooner or later** tarde o temprano
soothe [su:ð] *vt* tranquilizar; (*pain*) aliviar
sophisticated [sə'fɪstɪkeɪtɪd] *adj* sofisticado
sophomore ['sɒfəmɔ:ʳ] *n* (*US*) estudiante *mf* de segundo año
soprano [sə'prɑ:nəu] *n* soprano f
sorbet ['sɔ:beɪ] *n* sorbete m
sordid ['sɔ:dɪd] *adj* (*place etc*) sórdido; (*motive etc*) mezquino
sore [sɔ:ʳ] *adj* (*painful*) doloroso, que duele ▷ *n* llaga
sorrow ['sɒrəu] *n* pena, dolor m
sorry ['sɒrɪ] *adj* (*regretful*) arrepentido; (*condition, excuse*) lastimoso; **~!** ¡perdón!, ¡perdone!; **~?** ¿cómo?; **I feel ~ for him** me da lástima *or* pena
sort [sɔ:t] *n* clase f, género, tipo ▷ *vt* (*also*: **~ out**: *papers*) clasificar; (*organize*) ordenar, organizar; (*resolve: problem, situation etc*) arreglar, solucionar
SOS *n* SOS m
so-so ['səusəu] *adv* regular, así así
sought [sɔ:t] *pt, pp of* **seek**
soul [səul] *n* alma f
sound [saund] *adj* (*healthy*) sano; (*safe, not damaged*) en buen estado; (*dependable: person*) de fiar; (*sensible*) sensato, razonable ▷ *adv*: **~ asleep** profundamente dormido ▷ *n* (*noise*) sonido, ruido; (*volume: on TV etc*) volumen m; (*Geo*) estrecho ▷ *vt* (*alarm*) sonar ▷ *vi* sonar, resonar; (*fig: seem*) parecer; **to ~ like** sonar a; **soundtrack** *n* (*of film*) banda sonora
soup [su:p] *n* (*thick*) sopa; (*thin*) caldo
sour ['sauəʳ] *adj* agrio; (*milk*) cortado; **it's just ~ grapes!** (*fig*) ¡están verdes!

s

source [sɔːs] n fuente f
south [sauθ] n sur m ▷ adj del sur
▷ adv al sur, hacia el sur; **South Africa**
n Sudáfrica f; **South African** adj, n
sudafricano/a; **South America** n
América del Sur, Sudamérica; **South
American** adj, n sudamericano/a;
southbound adj (con) rumbo al sur;
south-east n sudeste m, sureste
m ▷ adj (counties etc) (del) sudeste,
(del) sureste; **southeastern** adj (del)
sudeste, (del) sureste; **southern** adj
del sur, meridional; **South Korea** n
Corea del Sur; **South Pole** n Polo
Sur; **southward(s)** adv hacia el
sur; **south-west** n suroeste m;
southwestern adj suroeste
souvenir [suːvəˈnɪəʳ] n recuerdo
sovereign [ˈsɔvrɪn] adj, n soberano/a
sow¹ [sau] n cerda, puerca
sow² (pt **sowed**, pp **sown**) [səu, səun]
vt sembrar
soya [ˈsɔɪə], (US) **soy** [sɔɪ] n soja
spa [spaː] n balneario
space [speɪs] n espacio; (room) sitio
▷ vt (also: ~ **out**) espaciar; **spacecraft**
n nave f espacial; **spaceship** n
= **spacecraft**
spacious [ˈspeɪʃəs] adj amplio
spade [speɪd] n (tool) pala; **spades**
npl (Cards: British) picas fpl; (: Spanish)
espadas fpl
spaghetti [spəˈgɛtɪ] n espaguetis mpl
Spain [speɪn] n España
spam n (junk email) correo basura
span [spæn] n (of bird, plane)
envergadura; (of arch) luz f; (in time)
lapso ▷ vt extenderse sobre, cruzar;
(fig) abarcar
Spaniard [ˈspænjəd] n español(a) m/f
Spanish [ˈspænɪʃ] adj español(a)
▷ n (Ling) español m, castellano; **the
Spanish** npl los españoles
spank [spæŋk] vt zurrar
spanner [ˈspænəʳ] n (BRIT) llave f
inglesa
spare [spɛəʳ] adj de reserva; (surplus)
sobrante, de más ▷ n (part) pieza de

repuesto ▷ vt (do without) pasarse sin;
(refrain from hurting) perdonar; **to ~**
(surplus) sobrante, de sobra; **spare
part** n pieza de repuesto; **spare room**
n cuarto de los invitados; **spare time**
n tiempo libre; **spare tyre,** (US) **spare
tire** n (Aut) neumático or llanta (LAM)
de recambio; **spare wheel** n (Aut)
rueda de recambio
spark [spaːk] n chispa; (fig) chispazo
sparking plug [ˈspaːk(ɪŋ)-] n
= **spark plug**
sparkle [ˈspaːkl] n centelleo, destello
▷ vi (shine) relucir, brillar
spark plug n bujía
sparrow [ˈspærəu] n gorrión m
sparse [spaːs] adj esparcido, escaso
spasm [ˈspæzəm] n (Med) espasmo
spat [spæt] pt, pp of **spit**
spate [speɪt] n (fig): ~ **of** torrente m de
spatula [ˈspætjulə] n espátula
speak (pt **spoke**, pp **spoken**) [spiːk,
spəuk, ˈspəukn] vt (language) hablar;
(truth) decir ▷ vi hablar; (make a speech)
intervenir; **to ~ to sb/of** or **about
sth** hablar con algn/de o sobre algo;
~ **up!** ¡habla más alto!; **speaker**
n (in public) orador(a) m/f; (also:
loudspeaker) altavoz m; (for stereo
etc) bafle m; **the Speaker** (Pol: BRIT) el
Presidente de la Cámara de los Comunes;
(: US) el Presidente del Congreso
spear [spɪəʳ] n lanza ▷ vt alancear
special [ˈspɛʃl] adj especial; (edition
etc) extraordinario; (delivery)
urgente; **special delivery** n (Post):
by special delivery por entrega
urgente; **special effects** npl (Cine)
efectos mpl especiales; **specialist**
n especialista mf; **speciality** n
especialidad f; **specialize** vi: **to
specialize (in)** especializarse (en);
specially adv especialmente; **special
offer** n (Comm) oferta especial;
special school n (BRIT) colegio m de
educación especial; **specialty** n (US)
= **speciality**
species [ˈspiːʃiːz] n especie f

specific [spə'sɪfɪk] adj específico;
specifically adv específicamente
specify ['spɛsɪfaɪ] vt, vi especificar,
precisar
specimen ['spɛsɪmən] n ejemplar
m; (Med: of urine) espécimen m; (: of
blood) muestra
speck [spɛk] n grano, mota
spectacle ['spɛktəkl] n espectáculo;
spectacles npl (BRIT: glasses) gafas
fpl (SP), anteojos mpl; **spectacular**
[spɛk'tækjuləʳ] adj espectacular;
(success) impresionante
spectator [spɛk'teɪtəʳ] n
espectador(a) m/f
spectrum (pl **spectra**) ['spɛktrəm,
-trə] n espectro
speculate ['spɛkjuleɪt] vi especular;
to ~ about especular sobre
sped [spɛd] pt, pp of **speed**
speech [spiːtʃ] n (faculty) habla;
(formal talk) discurso; (language)
lenguaje m; **speechless** adj mudo,
estupefacto
speed [spiːd] n velocidad f; (haste)
prisa; (promptness) rapidez f; **at full** or
top ~ a la máxima velocidad; **speed up**
vi acelerarse ▷ vt acelerar; **speedboat**
n lancha motora; **speeding** n (Aut)
exceso de velocidad; **speed limit** n
límite m de velocidad, velocidad f
máxima; **speedometer** [spɪ'dɔmɪtəʳ]
n velocímetro; **speedy** adj (fast) veloz,
rápido; (prompt) pronto
spell [spɛl] n (also: **magic ~**) encanto,
hechizo; (period of time) rato, período
▷ vt deletrear; (fig) anunciar, presagiar;
to cast a ~ on sb hechizar a algn; **he
can't ~** comete faltas de ortografía;
spell out vt (explain): **to ~ sth out
for sb** explicar algo a algn en detalle;
spellchecker n (Comput) corrector m
(ortográfico); **spelling** n ortografía
spelt [spɛlt] pt, pp of **spell**
spend (pt, pp **spent**) [spɛnd, spɛnt]
vt (money) gastar; (time) pasar; (life)
dedicar; **spending** n: **government
spending** gastos mpl del gobierno

spent [spɛnt] pt, pp of **spend** ▷ adj
(cartridge, bullets, match) usado
sperm [spəːm] n esperma
sphere [sfɪəʳ] n esfera
spice [spaɪs] n especia ▷ vt especiar
spicy ['spaɪsɪ] adj picante
spider ['spaɪdəʳ] n araña
spike [spaɪk] n (point) punta; (Bot)
espiga
spill (pt, pp **spilt** or **spilled**) [spɪl,
spɪlt, spɪld] vt derramar, verter
▷ vi derramarse; **spill over** vi
desbordarse
spin [spɪn] (pt, pp **spun**) n (Aviat)
barrena; (trip in car) paseo (en coche)
▷ vt (wool etc) hilar; (wheel) girar ▷ vi
girar, dar vueltas
spinach ['spɪnɪtʃ] n espinacas fpl
spinal ['spaɪnl] adj espinal
spin doctor n (inf) informador(a)
parcial al servicio de un partido político
spin-dryer n (BRIT) secadora
centrífuga
spine [spaɪn] n espinazo, columna
vertebral; (thorn) espina
spiral ['spaɪərl] n espiral f ▷ vi (prices)
dispararse
spire ['spaɪəʳ] n aguja, chapitel m
spirit ['spɪrɪt] n (soul) alma f; (ghost)
fantasma m; (attitude) espíritu m;
(courage) valor m, ánimo; **spirits**
npl (drink) alcohol msg, bebidas fpl
alcohólicas; **in good ~s** alegre, de
buen ánimo
spiritual ['spɪrɪtjuəl] adj espiritual
▷ n espiritual m
spit (pt, pp **spat**) [spɪt, spæt] n (for
roasting) asador m, espetón m;
(saliva) saliva ▷ vi escupir; (sound)
chisporrotear
spite [spaɪt] n rencor m, ojeriza ▷ vt
fastidiar; **in ~ of** a pesar de, pese a;
spiteful adj rencoroso, malévolo
splash [splæʃ] n (sound) chapoteo; (of
colour) mancha ▷ vt salpicar ▷ vi (also:
~ about) chapotear; **splash out** vi
(BRIT inf) derrochar dinero
splendid ['splɛndɪd] adj espléndido

s

splinter ['splɪntə'] n astilla; (in finger) espigón m ▷ vi astillarse, hacer astillas

split [splɪt] (pt, pp **split**) n hendedura, raja; (fig) división f; (Pol) escisión f ▷ vt partir, rajar; (party) dividir; (work, profits) repartir ▷ vi dividirse, escindirse; **split up** vi (couple) separarse; (meeting) acabarse

spoil (pt, pp **spoilt** or **spoiled**) [spɔɪl, spɔɪlt, spɔɪld] vt (damage) dañar; (ruin) estropear, echar a perder; (child) mimar, consentir

spoilt [spɔɪlt] pt, pp of **spoil** ▷ adj (child) mimado, consentido; (ballot paper) invalidado

spoke [spəuk] pt of **speak** ▷ n rayo, radio

spoken ['spəukn] pp of **speak**

spokesman ['spəuksmən] n portavoz m

spokesperson ['spəukspə:sn] n portavoz mf, vocero/a (LAM)

spokeswoman ['spəukswumən] n portavoz f

sponge [spʌndʒ] n esponja; (also: ~ **cake**) bizcocho ▷ vt (wash) lavar con esponja ▷ vi: **to ~ on** or (US) **off sb** vivir a costa de algn; **sponge bag** n (BRIT) neceser m

sponsor ['spɒnsə'] n patrocinador(a) m/f ▷ vt patrocinar; apadrinar; **sponsorship** n patrocinio

spontaneous [spɒn'teɪnɪəs] adj espontáneo

spooky ['spu:kɪ] adj (inf) espeluznante, horripilante

spoon [spu:n] n cuchara; **spoonful** n cucharada

sport [spɔ:t] n deporte m; **to be a good ~** (person) ser muy majo; **sport jacket** n (US) = **sports jacket**; **sports car** n coche m sport; **sports centre** n (BRIT) polideportivo; **sports jacket,** (US) **sport jacket** n chaqueta deportiva; **sportsman** n deportista m; **sports utility vehicle** n todoterreno m inv; **sportswear** n ropa de deporte; **sportswoman** n deportista; **sporty** adj deportivo

spot [spɒt] n sitio, lugar m; (dot: on pattern) punto, mancha; (pimple) grano ▷ vt (notice) notar, observar; **on the ~** en el acto; **spotless** adj (clean) inmaculado; (reputation) intachable; **spotlight** n foco, reflector m; (Aut) faro auxiliar

spouse [spauz] n cónyuge mf

sprain [spreɪn] n torcedura ▷ vt: **to ~ one's ankle** torcerse el tobillo

sprang [spræŋ] pt of **spring**

sprawl [sprɔ:l] vi tumbarse

spray [spreɪ] n rociada; (of sea) espuma; (container) atomizador m; (of paint) pistola rociadora; (of flowers) ramita ▷ vt rociar; (crops) regar

spread [sprɛd] (pt, pp **spread**) n extensión f; (inf: food) comilona ▷ vt extender; (butter) untar; (wings, sails) desplegar; (scatter) esparcir ▷ vi (also: ~ **out**: stain) extenderse; (news) diseminarse; **middle-age ~** gordura de la mediana edad; **repayments will be ~ over 18 months** los pagos se harán a lo largo de 18 meses; **spread out** vi (move apart) separarse; **spreadsheet** n (Comput) hoja de cálculo

spree [spri:] n: **to go on a ~** ir de juerga or farra (LAM)

spring [sprɪŋ] (pt **sprang**, pp **sprung**) n (season) primavera; (leap) salto, brinco; (coiled metal) resorte m; (of water) fuente f, manantial m ▷ vi saltar, brincar; **spring up** vi (thing: appear) aparecer; (problem) surgir; **spring onion** n cebolleta

sprinkle ['sprɪŋkl] vt (pour: liquid) rociar; (: salt, sugar) espolvorear; **to ~ water** etc **on, ~ with water** etc rociar or salpicar de agua etc

sprint [sprɪnt] n (e)sprint m ▷ vi esprintar

sprung [sprʌŋ] pp of **spring**

spun [spʌn] pt, pp of **spin**

spur [spə:'] n espuela; (fig) estímulo, aguijón m ▷ vt (also: ~ **on**) estimular, incitar; **on the ~ of the moment** de improviso

spurt [spə:t] *n* chorro; (*of energy*) arrebato ▷ *vi* chorrear

spy [spaɪ] *n* espía *mf* ▷ *vi*: **to ~ on** espiar a ▷ *vt* (*see*) divisar, lograr ver

sq. *abbr* (*Math etc*); = **square**

squabble ['skwɔbl] *vi* reñir, pelear

squad [skwɔd] *n* (*Mil*) pelotón *m*; (*Police*) brigada; (*Sport*) equipo

squadron ['skwɔdrn] *n* (*Mil*) escuadrón *m*; (*Aviat, Naut*) escuadra

squander ['skwɔndəʳ] *vt* (*money*) derrochar, despilfarrar; (*chances*) desperdiciar

square [skwɛəʳ] *n* cuadro; (*in town*) plaza; (*inf: person*) carca *mf* ▷ *adj* cuadrado; (*inf: ideas, tastes*) trasnochado ▷ *vt* (*arrange*) arreglar; (*Math*) cuadrar; (*reconcile*) compaginar; **all ~** igual(es); **a ~ meal** una comida decente; **two metres ~** dos metros por dos; **one ~ metre** un metro cuadrado; **square root** *n* raíz *f* cuadrada

squash [skwɔʃ] *n* (*vegetable*) calabaza; (*Sport*) squash *m*; (*BRIT: drink*): **lemon/ orange ~** zumo (*SP*) or jugo (*LAM*) de limón/naranja ▷ *vt* aplastar

squat [skwɔt] *adj* achaparrado ▷ *vi* agacharse, sentarse en cuclillas; **squatter** *n* okupa *mf*

squeak [skwi:k] *vi* (*hinge, wheel*) chirriar, rechinar; (*mouse*) chillar

squeal [skwi:l] *vi* chillar, dar gritos agudos

squeeze [skwi:z] *n* presión *f*; (*of hand*) apretón *m*; (*Comm*) restricción *f* ▷ *vt* (*hand, arm*) apretar

squid [skwɪd] *n* (*inv*) calamar *m*

squint [skwɪnt] *vi* bizquear, ser bizco ▷ *n* (*Med*) estrabismo

squirm [skwə:m] *vi* retorcerse, revolverse

squirrel ['skwɪrəl] *n* ardilla

squirt [skwə:t] *vi* salir a chorros ▷ *vt* chiscar

Sr *abbr* = **senior**

Sri Lanka [srɪ'læŋkə] *n* Sri Lanka *m*

St *abbr* (= *saint*) Sto./a.; (= *street*) c/

stab [stæb] *n* (*with knife etc*) puñalada; (*of pain*) pinchazo; **to have a ~ at (doing) sth** (*inf*) probar (a hacer) algo ▷ *vt* apuñalar

stability [stə'bɪlɪtɪ] *n* estabilidad *f*

stable ['steɪbl] *adj* estable ▷ *n* cuadra, caballeriza

stack [stæk] *n* montón *m*, pila ▷ *vt* amontonar, apilar

stadium ['steɪdɪəm] *n* estadio

staff [stɑ:f] *n* (*work force*) personal *m*, plantilla; (*BRIT Scol*) cuerpo docente ▷ *vt* proveer de personal

stag [stæg] *n* ciervo, venado

stage [steɪdʒ] *n* escena; (*point*) etapa; (*platform*) plataforma; **the ~** el teatro ▷ *vt* (*play*) poner en escena, representar; (*organize*) montar, organizar; **in ~s** por etapas

stagger ['stægəʳ] *vi* tambalear ▷ *vt* (*amaze*) asombrar; (*hours, holidays*) escalonar; **staggering** *adj* asombroso

stagnant ['stægnənt] *adj* estancado

stag night, stag party *n* despedida de soltero

stain [steɪn] *n* mancha; (*colouring*) tintura ▷ *vt* manchar; (*wood*) teñir; **stained glass** *n* vidrio *m* de color; **stainless steel** *n* acero inoxidable

stair [stɛəʳ] *n* (*step*) peldaño; **stairs** *npl* escaleras *fpl*

staircase ['stɛəkeɪs], **stairway** ['stɛəweɪ] *n* escalera

stake [steɪk] *n* estaca, poste *m*; (*Comm*) interés *m*; (*Betting*) apuesta ▷ *vt* (*bet*) apostar; **to be at ~** estar en juego; **to ~ a claim (to sth)** presentar reclamación por or reclamar (algo)

stale [steɪl] *adj* (*bread*) duro; (*food*) pasado; (*smell*) rancio; (*beer*) agrio

stalk [stɔ:k] *n* tallo, caña ▷ *vt* acechar, cazar al acecho

stall *n* (*in market*) puesto; (*in stable*) casilla (de establo) ▷ *vt* (*Aut*) calar; (*fig*) dar largas a ▷ *vi* (*Aut*) pararse, calarse; (*fig*) buscar evasivas

s

stamina ['stæmɪnə] n resistencia
stammer ['stæmə'] n tartamudeo
▷ vi tartamudear
stamp [stæmp] n sello, estampilla
(LAM); (mark) marca, huella; (on
document) timbre m ▷ vi (also: ~ **one's
foot**) patear ▷ vt (letter) poner sellos
en, franquear; (with rubber stamp)
marcar con sello; **~ed addressed
envelope (sae)** sobre m franqueado
con la dirección propia; **stamp out**
vt (fire) apagar con el pie; (crime,
opposition) acabar con
stampede [stæm'piːd] n estampida
stance [stæns] n postura
stand [stænd] (pt, pp **stood**) n
(attitude) posición f, postura; (for
taxis) parada; (also: **music ~**) atril m;
(Sport) tribuna; (at exhibition) stand
m ▷ vi (be) estar, encontrarse; (be on
foot) estar de pie; (rise) levantarse;
(remain) quedar en pie ▷ vt (place)
poner, colocar; (tolerate, withstand)
aguantar, soportar; **to make a ~** (fig)
mantener una postura firme; **to ~ for
parliament** (BRIT) presentarse (como
candidato) a las elecciones; **stand
back** vi retirarse; **stand by** vi (be ready)
estar listo ▷ vt fus (opinion) mantener;
stand down vi (withdraw) ceder el
puesto; (Mil, Law) retirarse; **stand
for** vt fus (signify) significar; (tolerate)
aguantar, permitir; **stand in for** vt
fus suplir a; **stand out** vi destacarse;
stand up vi levantarse, ponerse de
pie; **stand up for** vt fus defender;
stand up to vt fus hacer frente a
standard ['stændəd] n patrón m,
norma; (flag) estandarte m ▷ adj (size
etc) normal, corriente, estándar;
standards npl (morals) valores mpl
morales; **standard of living** n nivel
m de vida
standing ['stændɪŋ] adj (on foot) de
pie, en pie; (permanent) permanente
▷ n reputación f; **of many years' ~**
que lleva muchos años; **standing
order** n (BRIT: at bank) giro bancario

stand: standpoint n punto de vista;
standstill n: **at a standstill** (industry,
traffic) paralizado; **to come to a
standstill** pararse, quedar paralizado
stank [stæŋk] pt of **stink**
staple ['steɪpl] n (for papers) grapa
▷ adj (crop, industry, food etc) básico
▷ vt grapar
star [stɑː'] n estrella; (celebrity)
estrella, astro ▷ vi: **to ~ in** ser la
estrella de; **the stars** npl (Astrology)
el horóscopo
starboard ['stɑːbəd] n estribor m
starch [stɑːtʃ] n almidón m
stardom ['stɑːdəm] n estrellato
stare [stɛə'] n mirada fija ▷ vi: **to ~
at** mirar fijo
stark [stɑːk] adj (bleak) severo,
escueto ▷ adv: **~ naked** en cueros
start [stɑːt] n principio, comienzo;
(departure) salida; (sudden movement)
sobresalto; (advantage) ventaja ▷ vt
empezar, comenzar; (cause) causar;
(found) fundar; (engine) poner en
marcha ▷ vi comenzar, empezar;
(with fright) asustarse, sobresaltarse;
(train etc) salir; **to ~ doing** or **to do
sth** empezar a hacer algo; **start off**
vi empezar, comenzar; (leave) salir,
ponerse en camino; **start out** vi
(begin) empezar; (set out) partir, salir;
start up vi empezar; (car) ponerse
en marcha ▷ vt comenzar; (car) poner
en marcha; **starter** n (Aut) botón m
de arranque; (Sport: official) juez mf de
salida; (: runner) corredor(a) m/f; (BRIT
Culin) entrada, entrante m; **starting
point** n punto de partida
startle ['stɑːtl] vt sobresaltar;
startling adj alarmante
starvation [stɑː'veɪʃən] n hambre f
starve [stɑːv] vi pasar hambre; (to
death) morir de hambre ▷ vt hacer
pasar hambre
state [steɪt] n estado ▷ vt (say,
declare) afirmar; **to be in a ~** estar
agitado; **the S~s** los Estados Unidos;
statement n afirmación f; **state**

school n escuela or colegio estatal;
statesman n estadista m

static ['stætɪk] n (Radio) parásitos mpl
▷ adj estático

station ['steɪʃən] n estación f; (Radio)
emisora; (rank) posición f social ▷ vt
colocar, situar; (Mil) apostar

stationary ['steɪʃnərɪ] adj
estacionario, fijo

stationer's (shop) n (BRIT) papelería

stationery ['steɪʃənərɪ] n papel m de
escribir; (writing materials) artículos
mpl de escritorio

station wagon n (US) coche m
familiar con ranchera

statistic [stə'tɪstɪk] n estadística;
statistics n (science) estadística

statue ['stætjuː] n estatua

stature ['stætʃə'] n estatura; (fig) talla

status ['steɪtəs] n estado; (reputation)
estatus m; **status quo** n (e)statu
quo m

statutory ['stætjutrɪ] adj estatutario

staunch [stɔːntʃ] adj leal,
incondicional

stay [steɪ] n estancia ▷ vi quedar(se);
(as guest) hospedarse; **to ~ put** seguir
en el mismo sitio; **to ~ the night/5
days** pasar la noche/estar or quedarse
5 días; **stay away** vi (from person,
building) no acercarse; (from event) no
acudir; **stay behind** vi quedar atrás;
stay in vi quedarse en casa; **stay on**
vi quedarse; **stay out** vi (of house) no
volver a casa; (strikers) no volver al
trabajo; **stay up** vi (at night) velar, no
acostarse

steadily ['stɛdɪlɪ] adv (firmly)
firmemente; (unceasingly) sin parar;
(fixedly) fijamente

steady ['stɛdɪ] adj (fixed) firme;
(regular) regular; (boyfriend etc) formal,
fijo; (person, character) sensato,
juicioso ▷ vt (stabilize) estabilizar;
(nerves) calmar

steak [steɪk] n filete m; (beef) bistec m

steal (pt **stole**, pp **stolen**) [stiːl, stəul,
'stəuln] vt, vi robar

steam [stiːm] n vapor m; (mist) vaho,
humo ▷ vt (Culin) cocer al vapor ▷ vi
echar vapor; **steam up** vi (window)
empañarse; **to get ~ed up about sth**
(fig) ponerse negro por algo; **steamy**
adj (room) lleno de vapor; (window)
empañado; (heat, atmosphere)
bochornoso

steel [stiːl] n acero ▷ adj de acero

steep [stiːp] adj escarpado, abrupto;
(stair) empinado; (price) exorbitante,
excesivo ▷ vt empapar, remojar

steeple ['stiːpl] n aguja

steer [stɪə'] vt (car) conducir (SP),
manejar (LAM); (person) dirigir ▷ vi
conducir (SP), manejar (LAM);
steering n (Aut) dirección f; **steering
wheel** n volante m

stem [stɛm] n (of plant) tallo; (of glass)
pie m ▷ vt detener; (blood) restañar

step [stɛp] n paso; (stair) peldaño,
escalón m ▷ vi: **to ~ forward** dar
un paso adelante; **steps** npl (BRIT)
= **stepladder**; **to be in/out of ~ with**
estar acorde con/estar en disonancia
con; **step down** vi (fig) retirarse;
step in vi entrar; (fig) intervenir;
step up vt (increase) aumentar;
stepbrother n hermanastro;
stepchild (pl **stepchildren**) n
hijastro/a; **stepdaughter** n
hijastra; **stepfather** n padrastro;
stepladder n escalera doble or de
tijera; **stepmother** n madrastra;
stepsister n hermanastra; **stepson**
n hijastro

stereo ['stɛrɪəu] n estéreo ▷ adj (also:
~phonic) estéreo, estereofónico

stereotype ['stɪərɪətaɪp] n
estereotipo ▷ vt estereotipar

sterile ['stɛraɪl] adj estéril; **sterilize**
['stɛrɪlaɪz] vt esterilizar

sterling ['stəːlɪŋ] adj (silver) de ley ▷ n
(Econ) libras fpl esterlinas; **a pound ~**
una libra esterlina

stern [stəːn] adj severo, austero ▷ n
(Naut) popa

steroid ['stɪərɔɪd] n esteroide m

s

stew [stju:] n estofado ⊳ vt, vi estofar, guisar; (fruit) cocer

steward ['stju:əd] n camarero; **stewardess** n azafata

stick [stɪk] (pt, pp **stuck**) n palo; (as weapon) porra; (also: **walking ~**) bastón m ⊳ vt (glue) pegar; (inf: put) meter; (: tolerate) aguantar, soportar ⊳ vi pegarse; (come to a stop) quedarse parado; **it stuck in my mind** se me quedó grabado; **stick out** vi sobresalir; **stick up** vi sobresalir; **stick up for** vt fus defender; **sticker** n (label) etiqueta adhesiva; (with slogan) pegatina; **sticking plaster** n (BRIT) esparadrapo; **stick insect** n insecto palo; **stick shift** n (US Aut) palanca de cambios

sticky ['stɪkɪ] adj pegajoso; (label) adhesivo; (fig) difícil

stiff [stɪf] adj rígido, tieso; (hard) duro; (difficult) difícil; (person) inflexible; (price) exorbitante ⊳ adv: **scared/bored ~** muerto de miedo/aburrimiento

stifling ['staɪflɪŋ] adj (heat) sofocante, bochornoso

stigma ['stɪgmə] n estigma m

stiletto [stɪ'lɛtəu] n (BRIT: also: **~ heel**) tacón m de aguja

still [stɪl] adj inmóvil, quieto ⊳ adv todavía; (even) aún; (nonetheless) sin embargo, aun así

stimulate ['stɪmjuleɪt] vt estimular

stimulus (pl **stimuli**) ['stɪmjuləs, -laɪ] n estímulo, incentivo

sting [stɪŋ] (pt, pp **stung**) n (wound) picadura; (pain) escozor m, picazón m; (organ) aguijón m ⊳ vt picar ⊳ vi picar

stink (pt **stank**, pp **stunk**) [stɪŋk, stæŋk, stʌŋk] n hedor m, tufo ⊳ vi heder, apestar

stir [stə:ʳ] n (fig: agitation) conmoción f ⊳ vt (tea etc) remover; (fig: emotions) provocar ⊳ vi moverse; **stir up** vt (trouble) fomentar; **stir-fry** vt sofreír removiendo ⊳ n plato preparado sofriendo y removiendo los ingredientes

stitch [stɪtʃ] n (Sewing) puntada; (Knitting) punto; (Med) punto (de sutura); (pain) punzada ⊳ vt coser; (Med) suturar

stock [stɔk] n (Comm: reserves) existencias fpl, stock m; (: selection) surtido; (Agr) ganado, ganadería; (Culin) caldo; (fig: lineage) estirpe f; (Finance) capital m ⊳ adj (reply etc) clásico ⊳ vt (have in stock) tener existencias de; **stocks** npl: **~s and shares** acciones y valores; **in ~** en existencia or almacén; **out of ~** agotado; **to take ~ of** (fig) considerar, examinar; **stockbroker** ['stɔkbrəukəʳ] n agente mf or corredor(a) m/f de bolsa; **stock cube** n pastilla or cubito de caldo; **stock exchange** n bolsa; **stockholder** ['stɔkhəuldəʳ] n (US) accionista mf

stocking ['stɔkɪŋ] n media

stock market n bolsa (de valores)

stole [stəul] pt of **steal** ⊳ n estola

stolen ['stəuln] pp of **steal**

stomach ['stʌmək] n (Anat) estómago; (belly) vientre m ⊳ vt tragar, aguantar; **stomachache** n dolor m de estómago

stone [stəun] n piedra; (in fruit) hueso; (BRIT: weight) = 6.348 kg; 14lb ⊳ adj de piedra ⊳ vt apedrear; (fruit) deshuesar

stood [stud] pt, pp of **stand**

stool [stu:l] n taburete m

stoop [stu:p] vi (also: **~ down**) doblarse, agacharse; (also: **have a ~**) ser cargado de espaldas; (bend) inclinarse

stop [stɔp] n parada; (in punctuation) punto ⊳ vt parar, detener; (break off) suspender; (block: pay) suspender; (: cheque) invalidar; (also: **put a ~ to**) poner término a ⊳ vi pararse, detenerse; (end) acabarse; **to ~ doing sth** dejar de hacer algo; **stop by** vi pasar por; **stop off** vi interrumpir el viaje; **stopover** n parada intermedia; (Aviat) escala; **stoppage** n (strike) paro; (blockage) obstrucción f

storage ['stɔːrɪdʒ] n almacenaje m

store [stɔːʳ] n (stock) provisión f; (depot) almacén m; (BRIT: large shop) almacén m; (US) tienda; (reserve) reserva, repuesto ▷ vt almacenar; **stores** npl víveres mpl; **who knows what is in ~ for us** quién sabe lo que nos espera; **storekeeper** n (US) tendero/a

storey, (US) **story** ['stɔːrɪ] n piso

storm [stɔːm] n tormenta; (fig: of applause) salva; (: of criticism) nube f ▷ vi (fig) rabiar ▷ vt tomar por asalto; **stormy** adj tempestuoso

story ['stɔːrɪ] n historia; (lie) cuento; (US) = **storey**

stout [staut] adj (strong) sólido; (fat) gordo, corpulento ▷ n cerveza negra

stove [stəuv] n (for cooking) cocina; (for heating) estufa

straight [streɪt] adj recto, derecho; (frank) franco, directo ▷ adv derecho, directamente; (drink) solo; **to put** or **get sth ~** dejar algo en claro; **~ away, ~ off** en seguida; **straighten** vt (also: **straighten out**) enderezar, poner derecho ▷ vi (also: **straighten up**) enderezarse, ponerse derecho; **straightforward** [streɪtˈfɔːwəd] adj (simple) sencillo; (honest) sincero

strain [streɪn] n tensión f; (Tech) presión f; (Med) torcedura; (of virus) variedad f ▷ vt (back etc) torcerse; (resources) agotar; (stretch) estirar; (filter) filtrar; **strained** adj (muscle) torcido; (laugh) forzado; (relations) tenso; **strainer** n colador m

strait [streɪt] n (Geo) estrecho; **to be in dire ~s** (fig) estar en un gran aprieto

strand [strænd] n (of thread) hebra; (of rope) ramal m; **a ~ of hair** un pelo; **stranded** adj (person: without money) desamparado; (: without transport) colgado

strange [streɪndʒ] adj (not known) desconocido; (odd) extraño, raro; **strangely** adv de un modo raro; see also **enough**; **stranger** n

desconocido/a; (from another area) forastero/a

  Be careful not to translate stranger by the Spanish word extranjero.

strangle ['stræŋgl] vt estrangular

strap [stræp] n correa; (of slip, dress) tirante m

strategic [strəˈtiːdʒɪk] adj estratégico

strategy ['strætɪdʒɪ] n estrategia

straw [strɔː] n paja; (also: **drinking ~**) caña, pajita; **that's the last ~!** ¡eso es el colmo!

strawberry ['strɔːbərɪ] n fresa, frutilla (LAM)

stray [streɪ] adj (animal) extraviado; (bullet) perdido; (scattered) disperso ▷ vi extraviarse, perderse

streak [striːk] n raya ▷ vt rayar ▷ vi: **to ~ past** pasar como un rayo

stream [striːm] n riachuelo, arroyo; (jet) chorro; (flow) corriente f; (of people) oleada ▷ vt (Scol) dividir en grupos por habilidad ▷ vi correr, fluir; **to ~ in/out** (people) entrar/salir en tropel

street [striːt] n calle f; **streetcar** n (US) tranvía m; **street light** n farol m (LAM), farola (SP); **street map** n plano (de la ciudad); **street plan** n plano callejero

strength [strɛŋθ] n fuerza; (of girder, knot etc) resistencia; (fig: power) poder m; **strengthen** vt fortalecer, reforzar

strenuous ['strɛnjuəs] adj (energetic) enérgico

stress [strɛs] n presión f; (mental strain) estrés m; (Ling, Poetry) acento ▷ vt subrayar, recalcar; **stressed** adj (tense) estresado, agobiado; (syllable) acentuado; **stressful** adj (job) estresante

stretch [strɛtʃ] n (of sand etc) trecho ▷ vi estirarse; (extend) **to ~ to** or **as far as** extenderse hasta ▷ vt extender, estirar; (make demands of) exigir el máximo esfuerzo a; **stretch out** vi tenderse ▷ vt (arm etc) extender; (spread) estirar

S

stretcher ['strɛtʃəʳ] n camilla
strict [strɪkt] adj estricto; (discipline, ban) severo; **strictly** adv estrictamente; (totally) terminantemente
stride (pt **strode**, pp **stridden**) [straɪd, strəud, 'strɪdn] n zancada, tranco ▷ vi dar zancadas, andar a trancos
strike [straɪk] (pt, pp **struck**) n huelga; (of oil etc) descubrimiento; (attack) ataque m ▷ vt golpear, pegar; (oil etc) descubrir; (agreement, deal) alcanzar ▷ vi declarar la huelga; (attack) atacar; (clock) dar la hora; **on ~** (workers) en huelga; **to ~ a match** encender una cerilla; **striker** n huelguista mf; (Sport) delantero; **striking** ['straɪkɪŋ] adj (colour) llamativo; (obvious) notorio
string (pt, pp **strung**) [strɪŋ, strʌŋ] n cuerda; (row) hilera ▷ vt: **to ~ together** ensartar; **to ~ out** extenderse; **the strings** npl (Mus) los instrumentos de cuerda; **to pull ~s** (fig) mover palancas
strip [strɪp] n tira; (of land) franja; (of metal) cinta, lámina ▷ vt desnudar; (also: **~ down**: machine) desmontar ▷ vi desnudarse; **strip off** vt (paint etc) quitar ▷ vi (person) desnudarse
stripe [straɪp] n raya; (Mil) galón m; **striped** adj a rayas, rayado
stripper ['strɪpəʳ] n artista mf de striptease
strip-search ['strɪpsəːtʃ] vt: **to ~ sb** desnudar y registrar a algn
strive (pt **strove**, pp **striven**) [straɪv, strəuv, 'strɪvn] vi: **to ~ to do sth** esforzarse or luchar por hacer algo
strode [strəud] pt of **stride**
stroke [strəuk] n (blow) golpe m; (Swimming) brazada; (Med) apoplejía ▷ vt acariciar; **at a ~** de golpe
stroll [strəul] n paseo, vuelta ▷ vi dar un paseo or una vuelta; **stroller** n (us: pushchair) cochecito
strong [strɔŋ] adj fuerte; **they are 50 ~** son 50; **stronghold** n fortaleza; (fig) baluarte m; **strongly** adv

fuertemente, con fuerza; (believe) firmemente
strove [strəuv] pt of **strive**
struck [strʌk] pt, pp of **strike**
structure ['strʌktʃəʳ] n estructura; (building) construcción f
struggle ['strʌgl] n lucha ▷ vi luchar
strung [strʌŋ] pt, pp of **string**
stub [stʌb] n (of ticket etc) matriz f; (of cigarette) colilla ▷ vt: **to ~ one's toe on sth** dar con el dedo del pie contra algo; **stub out** vt apagar
stubble ['stʌbl] n rastrojo; (on chin) barba (incipiente)
stubborn ['stʌbən] adj terco, testarudo
stuck [stʌk] pt, pp of **stick** ▷ adj (jammed) atascado
stud [stʌd] n (shirt stud) corchete m; (of boot) taco; (earring) pendiente m (de bolita); (also: **~ farm**) caballeriza; (also: **~ horse**) caballo semental ▷ vt (fig): **~ded with** salpicado de
student ['stjuːdənt] n estudiante mf ▷ adj estudiantil; **student driver** n (us Aut) aprendiz(a) m/f de conductor; **students' union** n (BRIT: association) sindicato de estudiantes; (: building) centro de estudiantes
studio ['stjuːdɪəu] n estudio; (artist's) taller m; **studio flat** n estudio
study ['stʌdɪ] n estudio ▷ vt estudiar; (examine) examinar, investigar ▷ vi estudiar
stuff [stʌf] n materia; (substance) material m, sustancia; (things, belongings) cosas fpl ▷ vt llenar; (Culin) rellenar; (animal) disecar; **stuffing** n relleno; **stuffy** adj (room) mal ventilado; (person) de miras estrechas
stumble ['stʌmbl] vi tropezar, dar un traspié; **stumble across** vt fus (fig) tropezar con
stump [stʌmp] n (of tree) tocón m; (of limb) muñón m ▷ vt: **to be ~ed for an answer** quedarse sin saber qué contestar
stun [stʌn] vt aturdir

stung [stʌŋ] *pt, pp of* **sting**

stunk [stʌŋk] *pp of* **stink**

stunned [stʌnd] *adj (dazed)* aturdido, atontado; *(amazed)* pasmado; *(shocked)* anonadado

stunning ['stʌnɪŋ] *adj (fig: news)* pasmoso; *(: outfit etc)* sensacional

stunt [stʌnt] *n (in film)* escena peligrosa; *(also:* **publicity ~)** truco publicitario

stupid ['stjuːpɪd] *adj* estúpido, tonto; **stupidity** [stjuːˈpɪdɪtɪ] *n* estupidez *f*

sturdy ['stəːdɪ] *adj* robusto, fuerte

stutter ['stʌtəʳ] *n* tartamudeo ▷ *vi* tartamudear

style [staɪl] *n* estilo; **stylish** *adj* elegante, a la moda; **stylist** *n (hair stylist)* peluquero/a

sub... [sʌb] *pref* sub...; **subconscious** *adj* subconsciente

subdued [səbˈdjuːd] *adj (light)* tenue; *(person)* sumiso, manso

subject *n* ['sʌbdʒɪkt] súbdito; *(Scol)* tema *m*, materia; *(Grammar)* sujeto ▷ *vt* [səbˈdʒɛkt]: **to ~ sb to sth** someter a algn a algo ▷ *adj* ['sʌbdʒɪkt]: **to be ~ to** *(law)* estar sujeto a; *(person)* ser propenso a; **subjective** [səbˈdʒɛktɪv] *adj* subjetivo; **subject matter** *n (content)* contenido

subjunctive [səbˈdʒʌŋktɪv] *adj, n* subjuntivo

submarine [sʌbməˈriːn] *n* submarino

submission [səbˈmɪʃən] *n* sumisión *f*

submit [səbˈmɪt] *vt* someter ▷ *vi* someterse

subordinate [səˈbɔːdɪnət] *adj, n* subordinado/a

subscribe [səbˈskraɪb] *vi* suscribir; **to ~ to** *(fund, opinion)* suscribir, aprobar; *(newspaper)* suscribirse a

subscription [səbˈskrɪpʃən] *n* abono; *(to magazine)* suscripción *f*

subsequent ['sʌbsɪkwənt] *adj* subsiguiente, posterior;

subsequently *adv* posteriormente, más tarde

subside [səbˈsaɪd] *vi* hundirse; *(flood)* bajar; *(wind)* amainar

subsidiary [səbˈsɪdɪərɪ] *n* sucursal *f*, filial *f*

subsidize ['sʌbsɪdaɪz] *vt* subvencionar

subsidy ['sʌbsɪdɪ] *n* subvención *f*

substance ['sʌbstəns] *n* sustancia

substantial [səbˈstænʃl] *adj* sustancial, sustancioso; *(fig)* importante

substitute ['sʌbstɪtjuːt] *n (person)* suplente *mf*; *(thing)* sustituto ▷ *vt*: **to ~ A for B** sustituir B por A, reemplazar A por B; **substitution** *n* sustitución *f*

subtle ['sʌtl] *adj* sutil

subtract [səbˈtrækt] *vt* restar; sustraer

suburb ['sʌbəːb] *n* barrio residencial; **the ~s** las afueras (de la ciudad); **suburban** [səˈbəːbən] *adj* suburbano; *(train etc)* de cercanías

subway ['sʌbweɪ] *n (BRIT)* paso subterráneo or inferior; *(US)* metro

succeed [səkˈsiːd] *vi (person)* tener éxito; *(plan)* salir bien ▷ *vt* suceder a; **to ~ in doing** lograr hacer

success [səkˈsɛs] *n* éxito; **successful** *adj (venture)* de éxito, exitoso *(esp LAM)*; **successfully** *adv* con éxito

> Be careful not to translate *success* by the Spanish word *suceso*.

succession [səkˈsɛʃən] *n* sucesión *f*, serie *f*

successive [səkˈsɛsɪv] *adj* sucesivo

successor [səkˈsɛsəʳ] *n* sucesor(a) *m/f*

succumb [səˈkʌm] *vi* sucumbir

such [sʌtʃ] *adj* tal, semejante; *(of that kind)*: **~ a book** tal libro; *(so much)*: **~ courage** tanto valor ▷ *adv* tan; **~ a long trip** un viaje tan largo; **~ a lot of** tanto; **~ as** *(like)* tal como; **as ~** como tal; **such-and-such** *adj* tal o cual

suck [sʌk] *vt* chupar; *(bottle)* sorber; *(breast)* mamar

Sudan [suˈdæn] *n* Sudán *m*

sudden ['sʌdn] *adj* (*rapid*) repentino, súbito; (*unexpected*) imprevisto; **all of a ~** de repente; **suddenly** *adv* de repente

sudoku [su'dəuku:] *n* sudoku *m*

sue [su:] *vt* demandar

suede [sweɪd] *n* ante *m*, gamuza (*LAM*)

suffer ['sʌfəʳ] *vt* sufrir, padecer; (*tolerate*) aguantar, soportar ▷ *vi* sufrir, padecer; **to ~ from** padecer, sufrir; **suffering** *n* sufrimiento

suffice [sə'faɪs] *vi* bastar, ser suficiente

sufficient [sə'fɪʃənt] *adj* suficiente, bastante

suffocate ['sʌfəkeɪt] *vi* ahogarse, asfixiarse

sugar ['ʃugəʳ] *n* azúcar *m* ▷ *vt* echar azúcar a, azucarar

suggest [sə'dʒɛst] *vt* sugerir; **suggestion** [sə'dʒɛstʃən] *n* sugerencia

suicide ['suɪsaɪd] *n* suicidio; (*person*) suicida *mf*; **to commit ~** suicidarse; **suicide attack** *n* atentado suicida; **suicide bomber** *n* terrorista *mf* suicida; **suicide bombing** *n* atentado *m* suicida

suit [su:t] *n* traje *m*; (*Law*) pleito; (*Cards*) palo ▷ *vt* convenir; (*clothes*) sentar bien a, ir bien a; (*adapt*): **to ~ sth to** adaptar or ajustar algo a; **well ~ed** (*couple*) hechos el uno para el otro; **suitable** *adj* conveniente; (*apt*) indicado; **suitcase** *n* maleta, valija (*LAM*)

suite [swi:t] *n* (*of rooms*) suite *f*; (*Mus*) suite *f*; (*furniture*): **bedroom/dining room ~** (juego de) dormitorio/comedor *m*; **a three-piece ~** un tresillo

sulfur ['sʌlfəʳ] *n* (*US*) = **sulphur**

sulk [sʌlk] *vi* estar de mal humor

sulphur, (*US*) **sulfur** ['sʌlfəʳ] *n* azufre *m*

sultana [sʌl'tɑːnə] *n* (*fruit*) pasa de Esmirna

sum [sʌm] *n* suma; (*total*) total *m*; **sum up** *vt* resumir ▷ *vi* hacer un resumen

summarize ['sʌməraɪz] *vt* resumir

summary ['sʌmərɪ] *n* resumen *m* ▷ *adj* (*justice*) sumario

summer ['sʌməʳ] *n* verano ▷ *adj* de verano; **in (the) ~** en (el) verano; **summer holidays** *npl* vacaciones *fpl* de verano; **summertime** *n* (*season*) verano

summit ['sʌmɪt] *n* cima, cumbre *f*; (*also*: **~ conference**) (conferencia) cumbre *f*

summon ['sʌmən] *vt* (*person*) llamar; (*meeting*) convocar

sun [sʌn] *n* sol *m*

Sun. *abbr* (= *Sunday*) dom.

sun: sunbathe *vi* tomar el sol; **sunbed** *n* cama solar; **sunblock** *n* filtro solar; **sunburn** *n* (*painful*) quemadura del sol; (*tan*) bronceado; **sunburnt, sunburned** *adj* (*tanned*) bronceado; (*painfully*) quemado por el sol

Sunday ['sʌndɪ] *n* domingo

sunflower ['sʌnflauəʳ] *n* girasol *m*

sung [sʌŋ] *pp of* **sing**

sunglasses ['sʌnglɑːsɪz] *npl* gafas *fpl* de sol

sunk [sʌŋk] *pp of* **sink**

sun: sunlight *n* luz *f* del sol; **sun lounger** *n* tumbona, perezosa (*LAM*); **sunny** ['sʌnɪ] *adj* soleado; (*day*) de sol; (*fig*) alegre; **sunrise** *n* salida del sol; **sun roof** *n* (*Aut*) techo corredizo or solar; **sunscreen** *n* filtro solar; **sunset** *n* puesta del sol; **sunshade** *n* (*over table*) sombrilla; **sunshine** ['sʌnʃaɪn] *n* sol *m*; **sunstroke** *n* insolación *f*; **suntan** *n* bronceado; **suntan lotion** *n* bronceador *m*; **suntan oil** *n* aceite *m* bronceador

super ['su:pəʳ] *adj* (*inf*) genial

superb [su:'pə:b] *adj* magnífico, espléndido

superficial [su:pə'fɪʃəl] *adj* superficial

superintendent [su:pərɪn'tɛndənt]
n director(a) *m/f*; (*also:* **police ~**)
subjefe/a *m/f*

superior [su'pɪərɪə^r] *adj* superior;
(*smug*) desdeñoso ▷ *n* superior *m*

superlative [su'pə:lətɪv] *n*
superlativo

supermarket ['su:pəmɑ:kɪt] *n*
supermercado

supernatural [su:pə'nætʃərəl]
adj sobrenatural ▷ *n*: **the ~** lo
sobrenatural

superpower ['su:pəpauə^r] *n* (*Pol*)
superpotencia

superstition [su:pə'stɪʃən] *n*
superstición *f*

superstitious [su:pə'stɪʃəs] *adj*
supersticioso

superstore ['su:pəstɔ:^r] *n* (*BRIT*)
hipermercado

supervise ['su:pəvaɪz] *vt* supervisar;
supervision [su:pə'vɪʒən] *n*
supervisión *f*; **supervisor** *n*
supervisor(a) *m/f*

supper ['sʌpə^r] *n* cena

supple ['sʌpl] *adj* flexible

supplement *n* ['sʌplɪmənt]
suplemento *m* ▷ *vt* [sʌplɪ'mɛnt] suplir

supplier [sə'plaɪə^r] *n* (*Comm*)
distribuidor(a) *m/f*

supply [sə'plaɪ] *vt* (*provide*)
suministrar; (*equip*): **to ~ (with)**
proveer (de) ▷ *n* provisión *f*; (*of gas,*
water etc) suministro; **supplies** *npl*
(*food*) víveres *mpl*; (*Mil*) pertrechos *mpl*

support [sə'pɔ:t] *n* apoyo; (*Tech*)
soporte *m* ▷ *vt* apoyar; (*financially*)
mantener; (*uphold*) sostener;
supporter *n* (*Pol etc*) partidario/a;
(*Sport*) aficionado/a

> Be careful not to translate *support*
> by the Spanish word *soportar*.

suppose [sə'pəuz] *vt* suponer; (*imagine*) imaginarse; **to be ~d to do**
sth deber hacer algo; **supposedly**
[sə'pəuzɪdlɪ] *adv* según cabe
suponer; **supposing** *conj* en caso
de que

suppress [sə'prɛs] *vt* suprimir; (*yawn*)
ahogar

supreme [su'pri:m] *adj* supremo

surcharge ['sə:tʃɑ:dʒ] *n* sobretasa,
recargo

sure [ʃuə^r] *adj* seguro; (*definite,*
convinced) cierto; **to make ~ of sth/**
that asegurarse de algo/asegurar
que; **~!** (*of course*) ¡claro!, ¡por
supuesto!; **~ enough** efectivamente;
surely *adv* (*certainly*) seguramente

surf [sə:f] *n* olas *fpl* ▷ *vt*: **to ~ the Net**
navegar por Internet

surface ['sə:fɪs] *n* superficie *f* ▷ *vt*
(*road*) revestir ▷ *vi* salir a la superficie;
surface mail *n* vía terrestre

surfboard ['sə:fbɔ:d] *n* tabla (de surf)

surfer ['sə:fə^r] *n* surfista *mf*; **web** or
net ~ internauta *mf*

surfing ['sə:fɪŋ] *n* surf *m*

surge [sə:dʒ] *n* oleada, oleaje *m* ▷ *vi*
(*wave*) romper; (*people*) avanzar a
tropel

surgeon ['sə:dʒən] *n* cirujano/a

surgery ['sə:dʒərɪ] *n* cirugía; (*BRIT:*
room) consultorio

surname ['sə:neɪm] *n* apellido

surpass [sə:'pɑ:s] *vt* superar, exceder

surplus ['sə:pləs] *n* excedente *m*;
(*Comm*) superávit *m* ▷ *adj* excedente,
sobrante

surprise [sə'praɪz] *n* sorpresa ▷ *vt*
sorprender; **surprised** *adj* (*look,*
smile) de sorpresa; **to be surprised**
sorprenderse; **surprising** *adj*
sorprendente; **surprisingly** *adv* (*easy,*
helpful) de modo sorprendente

surrender [sə'rɛndə^r] *n* rendición *f*,
entrega ▷ *vi* rendirse, entregarse

surround [sə'raund] *vt* rodear,
circundar; (*Mil etc*) cercar;
surrounding *adj* circundante;
surroundings *npl* alrededores *mpl*,
cercanías *fpl*

surveillance [sə:'veɪləns] *n*
vigilancia

survey *n* ['sə:veɪ] inspección *f*
reconocimiento; (*inquiry*) encuesta

s

▷ vt [sə:'veɪ] examinar, inspeccionar; (look at) mirar, contemplar; **surveyor** n agrimensor(a) m/f

survival [sə'vaɪvl] n supervivencia

survive [sə'vaɪv] vi sobrevivir; (custom etc) perdurar ▷ vt sobrevivir a; **survivor** n superviviente mf

suspect adj, n ['sʌspɛkt] sospechoso/a ▷ vt [səs'pɛkt] sospechar

suspend [səs'pɛnd] vt suspender; **suspended sentence** n (Law) libertad f condicional; **suspenders** npl (BRIT) ligas fpl; (US) tirantes mpl

suspense [səs'pɛns] n incertidumbre f, duda; (in film etc) suspense m; **to keep sb in ~** mantener a algn en suspense

suspension [səs'pɛnʃən] n suspensión f; (of driving licence) privación f; **suspension bridge** n puente m colgante

suspicion [səs'pɪʃən] n sospecha; (distrust) recelo; **suspicious** adj receloso; (causing suspicion) sospechoso

sustain [səs'teɪn] vt sostener, apoyar; (suffer) sufrir, padecer

SUV ['ɛs'juː'viː] n abbr (= sports utility vehicle) todoterreno m inv, cuatro por cuatro m inv

swallow ['swɔləu] n (bird) golondrina ▷ vt tragar

swam [swæm] pt of **swim**

swamp [swɔmp] n pantano, ciénaga ▷ vt abrumar, agobiar

swan [swɔn] n cisne m

swap [swɔp] n canje m ▷ vt: **to ~ (for)** canjear (por), cambiar (por)

swarm [swɔ:m] n (of bees) enjambre m; (fig) multitud f ▷ vi (bees) formar un enjambre; (fig) pulular

sway [sweɪ] vi mecerse, balancearse ▷ vt (influence) mover, influir en

swear (pt swore, pp sworn) [swɛə^r, swɔ:^r, swɔ:n] vi jurar ▷ vt: jurar; **swear in** vt: **to be sworn in** prestar juramento; **swearword** n taco, palabrota

sweat [swɛt] n sudor m ▷ vi sudar

sweater ['swɛtə^r] n suéter m

sweatshirt ['swɛtʃə:t] n sudadera

sweaty ['swɛtɪ] adj sudoroso

Swede [swi:d] n sueco/a

swede [swi:d] n (BRIT) nabo

Sweden ['swi:dn] n Suecia

Swedish ['swi:dɪʃ] adj, n (Ling) sueco

sweep [swi:p] (pt, pp **swept**) n (act) barrida; (also: **chimney ~**) deshollinador(a) m/f ▷ vt barrer; (with arm) empujar; (current) arrastrar ▷ vi barrer

sweet [swi:t] n (BRIT: candy) dulce m, caramelo; (: pudding) postre m ▷ adj dulce; (charming: smile, character) dulce, amable; **sweetcorn** n maíz m (dulce); **sweetener** ['swi:tnə^r] n (Culin) edulcorante m; **sweetheart** n novio/a; **sweetshop** n (BRIT) confitería, bombonería

swell [swɛl] (pt swelled, pp swollen or swelled) n (of sea) marejada, oleaje m ▷ adj (us inf: excellent) estupendo, fenomenal ▷ vt hinchar, inflar ▷ vi (also: **~ up**) hincharse; (numbers) aumentar; (sound, feeling) ir aumentando; **swelling** n (Med) hinchazón f

swept [swɛpt] pt, pp of **sweep**

swerve [swə:v] vi desviarse bruscamente

swift [swɪft] n (bird) vencejo ▷ adj rápido, veloz

swim [swɪm] (pt swam, pp swum) n: **to go for a ~** ir a nadar or a bañarse ▷ vi nadar; (head, room) dar vueltas ▷ vt pasar a nado; **to go ~ming** ir a nadar; **swimmer** n nadador(a) m/f; **swimming** n natación f; **swimming costume** n bañador m, traje m de baño; **swimming pool** n piscina, alberca (LAM); **swimming trunks** npl bañador msg; **swimsuit** n = **swimming costume**

swing [swɪŋ] (pt, pp swung) n (in playground) columpio; (movement) balanceo, vaivén m; (change of direction) viraje m; (rhythm) ritmo ▷ vt balancear; (also: **~ round**) voltear, girar ▷ vi balancearse, columpiarse; (also: **~ round**) dar media vuelta; **to be in full ~** estar en plena marcha

swipe card [swaɪp-] n tarjeta magnética deslizante, tarjeta swipe

swirl [swɜːl] vi arremolinarse

Swiss [swɪs] adj, n (pl inv) suizo/a

switch [swɪtʃ] n (for light, radio etc) interruptor m; (change) cambio ▷ vt (change) cambiar de; **switch off** vt apagar; (engine) parar; **switch on** vt encender, prender (LAM); (engine, machine) arrancar; **switchboard** n (Tel) centralita (de teléfonos), conmutador m (LAM)

Switzerland ['swɪtsələnd] n Suiza

swivel ['swɪvl] vi (also: **~ round**) girar

swollen ['swəʊlən] pp of **swell**

swoop [swuːp] n (by police etc) redada ▷ vi (also: **~ down**) caer en picado

swop [swɔp] n, vb = **swap**

sword [sɔːd] n espada; **swordfish** n pez m espada

swore [swɔːʳ] pt of **swear**

sworn [swɔːn] pp of **swear** ▷ adj (statement) bajo juramento; (enemy) implacable

swum [swʌm] pp of **swim**

swung [swʌŋ] pt, pp of **swing**

syllable ['sɪləbl] n sílaba

syllabus ['sɪləbəs] n programa m de estudios

symbol ['sɪmbl] n símbolo

symbolic(al) [sɪm'bɒlɪk(l)] adj simbólico; **to be symbolic of sth** simbolizar algo

symmetrical [sɪ'mɛtrɪkl] adj simétrico

symmetry ['sɪmɪtrɪ] n simetría

sympathetic [sɪmpə'θɛtɪk] adj (understanding) comprensivo; **to be ~ towards** (person) ser comprensivo con

> Be careful not to translate *sympathetic* by the Spanish word *simpático*.

sympathize ['sɪmpəθaɪz] vi: **to ~ with** (person) compadecerse de; (feelings) comprender; (cause) apoyar

sympathy ['sɪmpəθɪ] n (pity) compasión f

symphony ['sɪmfənɪ] n sinfonía

symptom ['sɪmptəm] n síntoma m, indicio

synagogue ['sɪnəgɒg] n sinagoga

syndicate ['sɪndɪkɪt] n sindicato; (Press) agencia (de noticias)

syndrome ['sɪndrəʊm] n síndrome m

synonym ['sɪnənɪm] n sinónimo

synthetic [sɪn'θɛtɪk] adj sintético

Syria ['sɪrɪə] n Siria

syringe [sɪ'rɪndʒ] n jeringa

syrup ['sɪrəp] n jarabe m, almíbar m

system ['sɪstəm] n sistema m; (Anat) organismo; **systematic** [sɪstə'mætɪk] adj sistemático; metódico; **systems analyst** n analista mf de sistemas

s

t

ta [tɑ:] *excl* (BRIT *inf*) ¡gracias!
tab [tæb] *n* lengüeta; (*label*) etiqueta; **to keep ~s on** (*fig*) vigilar
table ['teɪbl] *n* mesa; (*of statistics etc*) cuadro, tabla ▷ *vt* (BRIT: *motion etc*) presentar; **to lay** *or* **set the ~** poner la mesa; **tablecloth** *n* mantel *m*; **table d'hôte** [tɑ:bl'dəut] *n* menú *m*; **table lamp** *n* lámpara de mesa; **tablemat** *n* (*for plate*) posaplatos *m inv*; (*for hot dish*) salvamanteles *m inv*; **tablespoon** *n* cuchara grande; (*also*: **tablespoonful**: *as measurement*) cucharada grande
tablet ['tæblɪt] *n* (*Med*) pastilla, comprimido; (*of stone*) lápida
table tennis *n* ping-pong *m*, tenis *m* de mesa
tabloid ['tæblɔɪd] *n* periódico popular sensacionalista
taboo [tə'bu:] *adj*, *n* tabú *m*
tack [tæk] *n* (*nail*) tachuela ▷ *vt* (*nail*) clavar con tachuelas; (*stitch*) hilvanar ▷ *vi* virar

tackle ['tækl] *n* (*gear*) equipo; (*fishing tackle, for lifting*) aparejo ▷ *vt* (*difficulty*) enfrentarse a; (*challenge: person*) hacer frente a; (*grapple with*) agarrar; (*Football*) entrar a; (*Rugby*) placar
tacky ['tækɪ] *adj* pegajoso; (*inf*) hortera *inv*, de mal gusto
tact [tækt] *n* tacto, discreción *f*; **tactful** *adj* discreto, diplomático
tactics ['tæktɪks] *npl* táctica *sg*
tactless ['tæktlɪs] *adj* indiscreto
tadpole ['tædpəul] *n* renacuajo
taffy ['tæfɪ] *n* (US) melcocha
tag [tæg] *n* (*label*) etiqueta
tail [teɪl] *n* cola; (*of shirt, coat*) faldón *m* ▷ *vt* (*follow*) vigilar a; **tails** *npl* (*formal suit*) levita
tailor ['teɪləʳ] *n* sastre *m*
Taiwan [taɪ'wɑ:n] *n* Taiwán *m*; **Taiwanese** *adj*, *n* taiwanés/esa
take [teɪk] (*pt* **took**, *pp* **taken**) *vt* tomar; (*grab*) coger (SP), agarrar (LAM); (*gain: prize*) ganar; (*require: effort, courage*) exigir; (*support weight of*) aguantar; (*hold: passengers etc*) tener cabida para; (*accompany, bring, carry*) llevar; (*exam*) presentarse a; **to ~ sth from** (*drawer etc*) sacar algo de; (*person*) quitar algo a, coger algo a (SP); **I ~ it that ...** supongo que ...; **take after** *vt fus* parecerse a; **take apart** *vt* desmontar; **take away** *vt* (*remove*) quitar; (*carry off*) llevar; **take back** *vt* (*return*) devolver; (*one's words*) retractar; **take down** *vt* (*building*) derribar; (*message etc*) apuntar; **take in** *vt* (*deceive*) engañar; (*understand*) entender; (*include*) abarcar; (*lodger*) acoger, recibir; **take off** *vi* (*Aviat*) despegar ▷ *vt* (*remove*) quitar; **take on** *vt* (*work*) emprender; (*employee*) contratar; (*opponent*) desafiar; **take out** *vt* sacar; **take over** *vt* (*business*) tomar posesión de ▷ *vi*: **to ~ over from sb** reemplazar a algn; **take up** *vt* (*a dress*) acortar; (*occupy: time, space*) ocupar; (*engage in: hobby etc*) dedicarse a; (*accept*) aceptar; **to ~ sb up on**

aceptar algo de algn; **takeaway** adj (BRIT: food) para llevar ▷ n tienda or restaurante m de comida para llevar; **taken** pp of **take**; **takeoff** n (Aviat) despegue m; **takeover** n (Comm) absorción f; **takings** npl (Comm) ingresos mpl

talc [tælk] n (also: **~um powder**) talco

tale [teɪl] n (story) cuento; (account) relación f; **to tell ~s** (fig) contar chismes

talent ['tælnt] n talento; **talented** adj de talento

talk [tɔːk] n charla; (gossip) habladurías fpl, chismes mpl; (conversation) conversación f ▷ vi hablar; **talks** npl (Pol etc) conversaciones fpl; **to ~ about** hablar de; **to ~ sb into doing sth** convencer a algn para que haga algo; **to ~ sb out of doing sth** disuadir a algn de que haga algo; **to ~ shop** hablar del trabajo; **talk over** vt discutir; **talk show** n programa m magazine

tall [tɔːl] adj alto; (tree) grande; **to be 6 feet ~** ≈ medir 1 metro 80, tener 1 metro 80 de alto

tambourine [tæmbə'riːn] n pandereta

tame [teɪm] adj domesticado; (fig: story, style, person) soso, anodino

tamper ['tæmpəʳ] vi: **to ~ with** (lock etc) intentar forzar

tampon ['tæmpən] n tampón m

tan [tæn] n (also: **sun~**) bronceado ▷ vi ponerse moreno ▷ adj (colour) marrón

tandem ['tændəm] n tándem m

tangerine [tændʒə'riːn] n mandarina

tangle ['tæŋgl] n enredo; **to get in(to) a ~** enredarse

tank [tæŋk] n (also: **water ~**) depósito, tanque m; (for fish) acuario; (Mil) tanque m

tanker ['tæŋkəʳ] n (ship) petrolero; (truck) camión m cisterna

tanned [tænd] adj (skin) moreno

tantrum ['tæntrəm] n rabieta

Tanzania [tænzə'nɪə] n Tanzania

tap [tæp] n (BRIT: on sink etc) grifo, canilla (LAM); (gentle blow) golpecito; (gas tap) llave f ▷ vt (shoulder etc) dar palmaditas en; (resources) utilizar, explotar; (telephone conversation) intervenir; **on ~** (fig: resources) a mano; **beer on ~** cerveza de barril; **tap dancing** n claqué m

tape [teɪp] n cinta; (also: **magnetic ~**) cinta magnética; (sticky tape) cinta adhesiva ▷ vt (record) grabar (en cinta); **on ~** (song etc) grabado (en cinta); **tape measure** n cinta métrica, metro; **tape recorder** n grabadora

tapestry ['tæpɪstrɪ] n (object) tapiz m; (art) tapicería

tar [tɑːʳ] n alquitrán m, brea

target ['tɑːgɪt] n blanco

tariff ['tærɪf] n (on goods) arancel m; (BRIT: in hotels etc) tarifa

tarmac ['tɑːmæk] n (BRIT: on road) asfalto; (Aviat) pista (de aterrizaje)

tarpaulin [tɑː'pɔːlɪn] n lona (impermeabilizada)

tarragon ['tærəgən] n estragón m

tart [tɑːt] n (Culin) tarta; (BRIT inf, pej: woman) fulana ▷ adj agrio, ácido

tartan ['tɑːtn] n tartán m, tela escocesa

task [tɑːsk] n tarea; **to take to ~** reprender

taste [teɪst] n sabor m, gusto; (fig) muestra, idea ▷ vt probar ▷ vi: **to ~ of or like** (fish etc) saber a; **you can ~ the garlic (in it)** se nota el sabor a ajo; **in good/bad ~** de buen/mal gusto; **tasteful** adj de buen gusto; **tasteless** adj (food) soso; (remark) de mal gusto; **tasty** adj sabroso, rico

tatters ['tætəz] npl: **in ~** hecho jirones

tattoo [tə'tuː] n tatuaje m; (spectacle) espectáculo militar ▷ vt tatuar

taught [tɔːt] pt, pp of **teach**

taunt [tɔːnt] n pulla ▷ vt lanzar pullas a

Taurus ['tɔːrəs] n Tauro

taut [tɔːt] adj tirante, tenso

t

tax [tæks] *n* impuesto ▷ *vt* gravar (con un impuesto); (*fig: test*) poner a prueba; (*: patience*) agotar; **tax-free** *adj* libre de impuestos

taxi ['tæksɪ] *n* taxi *m* ▷ *vi* (*Aviat*) rodar por la pista; **taxi driver** *n* taxista *mf*; **taxi rank**, (*BRIT*) **taxi stand** *n* parada de taxis

tax payer *n* contribuyente *mf*

TB *n abbr* = **tuberculosis**

tea [tiː] *n* té *m*; (*BRIT: snack*) ≈ merienda; **high ~** (*BRIT*) ≈ merienda-cena; **tea bag** *n* bolsita de té; **tea break** *n* (*BRIT*) descanso para el té

teach (*pt, pp* **taught**) [tiːtʃ, tɔːt] *vt*: **to ~ sb sth, ~ sth to sb** enseñar algo a algn ▷ *vi* enseñar; (*be a teacher*) ser profesor(a); **teacher** *n* (*in secondary school*) profesor(a) *m/f*; (*in primary school*) maestro/a; **teaching** *n* enseñanza

tea: tea cloth *n* (*BRIT*) paño de cocina, trapo de cocina (*LAm*); **teacup** *n* taza de té; **tea leaves** *npl* hojas *fpl* de té

team [tiːm] *n* equipo; (*of animals*) pareja; **team up** *vi* asociarse

teapot ['tiːpɔt] *n* tetera

tear¹ [tɪəʳ] *n* lágrima; **in ~s** llorando

tear² [tɛəʳ] (*pt* **tore**, *pp* **torn**) *n* rasgón *m*, desgarrón *m* ▷ *vt* romper, rasgar ▷ *vi* rasgarse; **tear apart** *vt* (*also fig*) hacer pedazos; **tear down** *vt* (*building, statue*) derribar; (*poster, flag*) arrancar; **tear off** *vt* (*sheet of paper etc*) arrancar; (*one's clothes*) quitarse a tirones; **tear up** *vt* (*sheet of paper etc*) romper

tearful ['tɪəful] *adj* lloroso

tear gas *n* gas *m* lacrimógeno

tearoom ['tiːruːm] *n* salón *m* de té

tease [tiːz] *vt* tomar el pelo a

tea: teaspoon *n* cucharita; (*also:* **teaspoonful**: *as measurement*) cucharadita; **teatime** *n* hora del té; **tea towel** *n* (*BRIT*) paño de cocina

technical ['tɛknɪkl] *adj* técnico

technician [tɛk'nɪʃn] *n* técnico/a

technique [tɛk'niːk] *n* técnica

technology [tɛk'nɔlədʒɪ] *n* tecnología

teddy (bear) ['tɛdɪ-] *n* osito de peluche

tedious ['tiːdɪəs] *adj* pesado, aburrido

tee [tiː] *n* (*Golf*) tee *m*

teen [tiːn] *adj* = **teenage** ▷ *n* (*US*) = **teenager**

teenage ['tiːneɪdʒ] *adj* (*fashions etc*) juvenil; **teenager** ['tiːneɪdʒəʳ] *n* adolescente *mf*

teens [tiːnz] *npl*: **to be in one's ~** ser adolescente

teeth [tiːθ] *npl of* **tooth**

teetotal ['tiː'təutl] *adj* abstemio

telecommunications ['tɛlɪkəmjuːnɪ'keɪʃənz] *n* telecomunicaciones *fpl*

telegram ['tɛlɪgræm] *n* telegrama *m*

telegraph pole *n* poste *m* telegráfico

telephone ['tɛlɪfəun] *n* teléfono ▷ *vt* llamar por teléfono, telefonear; **to be on the ~** (*subscriber*) tener teléfono; (*be speaking*) estar hablando por teléfono; **telephone book** *n* guía *f* telefónica; **telephone booth**, (*BRIT*) **telephone box** *n* cabina telefónica; **telephone call** *n* llamada telefónica; **telephone directory** *n* guía telefónica; **telephone number** *n* número de teléfono

telesales ['tɛlɪseɪlz] *npl* televentas *fpl*

telescope ['tɛlɪskəup] *n* telescopio

televise ['tɛlɪvaɪz] *vt* televisar

television ['tɛlɪvɪʒən] *n* televisión *f*; **to watch ~** mirar *or* ver la televisión; **television programme** *n* programa *m* de televisión

tell (*pt, pp* **told**) [tɛl, təuld] *vt* decir; (*relate: story*) contar; (*distinguish*): **to ~ sth from** distinguir algo de ▷ *vi* (*talk*): **to ~ (of)** contar; (*have effect*) tener efecto; **to ~ sb to do sth** decir a algn que haga algo; **tell off** *vt*: **to ~ sb off** regañar a algn; **teller** *n* (*in bank*) cajero/a

telly ['tɛlɪ] *n* (*BRIT inf*) tele *f*

temp [tɛmp] n abbr (BRIT: = temporary office worker) empleado/a eventual

temper ['tɛmpə^r] n (mood) humor m; (bad humour) (mal) genio; (fit of anger) ira ▷ vt (moderate) moderar; **to be in a ~** estar furioso; **to lose one's ~** enfadarse, enojarse (LAM)

temperament ['tɛmprəmənt] n (nature) temperamento; **temperamental** [tɛmprə'mɛntl] adj temperamental

temperature ['tɛmprətʃə^r] n temperatura; **to have** or **run a ~** tener fiebre

temple ['tɛmpl] n (building) templo; (Anat) sien f

temporary ['tɛmpərərɪ] adj provisional; (passing) transitorio; (worker) eventual; (job) temporal

tempt [tɛmpt] vt tentar; **to ~ sb into doing sth** tentar or inducir a algn a hacer algo; **temptation** n tentación f; **tempting** adj tentador(a); (food) apetitoso

ten [tɛn] num diez

tenant ['tɛnənt] n inquilino/a

tend [tɛnd] vt cuidar ▷ vi: **to ~ to do sth** tener tendencia a hacer algo; **tendency** ['tɛndənsɪ] n tendencia

tender ['tɛndə^r] adj tierno, blando; (delicate) delicado; (meat) tierno; (sore) sensible ▷ n (Comm: offer) oferta; (money): **legal ~** moneda de curso legal ▷ vt ofrecer

tendon ['tɛndən] n tendón m

tenner ['tɛnə^r] n (billete m de) diez libras fpl

tennis ['tɛnɪs] n tenis m; **tennis ball** n pelota de tenis; **tennis court** n cancha de tenis; **tennis match** n partido de tenis; **tennis player** n tenista mf; **tennis racket** n raqueta de tenis

tenor ['tɛnə^r] n (Mus) tenor m

tenpin bowling ['tɛnpɪn-] n bolos mpl

tense [tɛns] adj tenso; (person) nervioso ▷ n (Ling) tiempo

tension ['tɛnʃən] n tensión f

tent [tɛnt] n tienda (de campaña), carpa (LAM)

tentative ['tɛntətɪv] adj (person) indeciso; (provisional) provisional

tenth [tɛnθ] adj décimo

tent: tent peg n clavija, estaca; **tent pole** n mástil m

tepid ['tɛpɪd] adj tibio

term [tə:m] n (word) término; (period) período; (Scol) trimestre m ▷ vt llamar; **terms** npl (conditions) condiciones fpl; **in the short/long ~** a corto/largo plazo; **to be on good ~s with sb** llevarse bien con algn; **to come to ~s with** (problem) aceptar

terminal ['tə:mɪnl] adj (disease) mortal; (patient) terminal ▷ n (Elec) borne m; (Comput) terminal m; (also: **air ~**) terminal f; (BRIT: also: **coach ~**) (estación f) terminal f

terminate ['tə:mɪneɪt] vt poner término a

termini ['tə:mɪnaɪ] npl of **terminus**

terminology [tə:mɪ'nɔlədʒɪ] n terminología

terminus (pl **termini**) ['tə:mɪnəs, 'tə:mɪnaɪ] n término, (estación f) terminal f

terrace ['tɛrəs] n terraza; (BRIT: row of houses) hilera de casas adosadas; **the ~s** (BRIT Sport) las gradas fpl; **terraced** adj (garden) escalonado; (house) adosado

terrain [tɛ'reɪn] n terreno

terrestrial [tɪ'rɛstrɪəl] adj (life) terrestre; (BRIT: channel) de transmisión (por) vía terrestre

terrible ['tɛrɪbl] adj terrible, horrible; (inf) malísimo; **terribly** adv terriblemente; (very badly) malísimamente

terrier ['tɛrɪə^r] n terrier m

terrific [tə'rɪfɪk] adj fantástico, fenomenal

terrify ['tɛrɪfaɪ] vt aterrorizar; **to be terrified** estar aterrado

or aterrorizado; **terrifying** *adj*
aterrador(a)

territorial [tɛrɪˈtɔːrɪəl] *adj* territorial
territory [ˈtɛrɪtərɪ] *n* territorio
terror [ˈtɛrəʳ] *n* terror *m*; **terrorism**
n terrorismo; **terrorist** *n* terrorista
mf; **terrorist attack** *n* atentado
(terrorista)
test [tɛst] *n* (*trial, check*) prueba; (*Chem,
Med*) prueba; (*exam*) examen *m*, test
m; (*also:* **driving ~**) examen *m* de
conducir ▷ *vt* probar, poner a prueba;
(*Med*) examinar
testicle [ˈtɛstɪkl] *n* testículo
testify [ˈtɛstɪfaɪ] *vi* (*Law*) prestar
declaración; **to ~ to sth** atestiguar
algo
testimony [ˈtɛstɪmənɪ] *n* (*Law*)
testimonio
test: test match *n* partido
internacional; **test tube** *n* probeta
tetanus [ˈtɛtənəs] *n* tétano
text [tɛkst] *n* texto; (*on mobile*)
mensaje *m* de texto ▷ *vt*: **to ~ sb**
enviar un mensaje (de texto) a algn;
textbook *n* libro de texto
textiles [ˈtɛkstaɪlz] *npl* tejidos *mpl*
text message *n* mensaje *m* de texto
text messaging [-ˈmɛsɪdʒɪŋ] *n*
(envío de) mensajes *mpl* de texto
texture [ˈtɛkstʃəʳ] *n* textura
Thai [taɪ] *adj, n* tailandés/esa *m/f*
Thailand [ˈtaɪlænd] *n* Tailandia
than [ðæn, ðən] *conj* que; (*with
numerals*): **more ~ 10/once** más de
10/una vez; **I have more/less ~ you**
tengo más/menos que tú; **it is better
to phone ~ to write** es mejor llamar
por teléfono que escribir
thank [θæŋk] *vt* dar las gracias a,
agradecer; **~ you (very much)**
(muchas) gracias; **~ God!** ¡gracias a
Dios!; *see also* **thanks**; **thankfully** *adv*:
thankfully there were few victims
afortunadamente hubo pocas víctimas
thanks [θæŋks] *npl* gracias *fpl* ▷ *excl*
¡gracias!; **many ~, ~ a lot** ¡muchas
gracias!; **~ to** *prep* gracias a

Thanksgiving (Day)
[ˈθæŋksɡɪvɪŋ-] *n* día *m* de Acción
de Gracias

○ **THANKSGIVING DAY**

En Estados Unidos el cuarto jueves
de noviembre es *Thanksgiving
Day*, fiesta oficial en la que se
conmemora la celebración que
tuvieron los primeros colonos
norteamericanos (*Pilgrims* o *Pilgrim
Fathers*) tras la estupenda cosecha
de 1621, por la que se dan gracias
a Dios. En Canadá se celebra
una fiesta semejante el segundo
lunes de octubre, aunque no
está relacionada con dicha fecha
histórica.

KEYWORD

that [ðæt] (*pl* **those**) *adj*
(*demonstrative*) ese/a; (: *more remote*)
aquel/aquella; **leave that book
on the table** deja ese libro sobre la
mesa; **that one** ese/esa, ése/ésa (*to
avoid confusion with adj*); (*more remote*)
aquel/aquella, aquél/aquélla (*to avoid
confusion with adj*); **that one over
there** ese/esa de ahí, ése/ésa de ahí;
aquel/aquella de allí, aquél/aquélla de
allí; *see also* **those**
▷ *pron* **1** (*demonstrative*) ese/a, ése/a
(*to avoid confusion with adj*), eso
(*neuter*); (: *more remote*) aquel/aquella,
aquél/aquélla (*to avoid confusion with
adj*), aquello (*neuter*); **what's that?**
¿qué es eso (*or* aquello)?; **who's that?**
¿quién es?; (*pointing etc*) ¿quién es
ese/a?; **is that you?** ¿eres tú?; **will
you eat all that?** ¿vas a comer todo
eso?; **that's my house** esa es mi
casa; **that's what he said** eso es lo
que dijo; **that is (to say)** es decir; *see
also* **those**
2 (*relative, subject, object*) que; (: *with*

preposition) (ella) que, ella cual; **the book (that) I read** el libro que leí; **the books that are in the library** los libros que están en la biblioteca; **all (that) I have** todo lo que tengo; **the box (that) I put it in** la caja en la que *or* donde lo puse; **the people (that) I spoke to** la gente con la que hablé
3 (*relative, of time*) que; **the day (that) he came** el día (en) que vino
▶ *conj* que; **he thought that I was ill** creyó que yo estaba enfermo
▶ *adv* (*demonstrative*): **I can't work that much** no puedo trabajar tanto; **I didn't realize it was that bad** no creí que fuera tan malo; **that high** así de alto

thatched [θætʃt] *adj* (*roof*) de paja; **~ cottage** casita con tejado de paja

thaw [θɔ:] *n* deshielo ▷ *vi* (*ice*) derretirse; (*food*) descongelarse ▷ *vt* descongelar

KEYWORD

the [ði:, ðə] *def art* **1** el *m*, la *f*, los *mpl*, las *fpl* (NB = el used immediately before feminine noun beginning with stressed (h) *a*; *a + el = al*; *de + el = del*): **the boy/girl** el chico/la chica; **the books/flowers** los libros/las flores; **to the postman/ from the drawer** al cartero/del cajón; **I haven't the time/money** no tengo tiempo/dinero
2 (+ *adj to form noun*) los; lo; **the rich and the poor** los ricos y los pobres; **to attempt the impossible** intentar lo imposible
3 (*in titles, surnames*): **Elizabeth the First** Isabel Primera; **Peter the Great** Pedro el Grande
4 (*in comparisons*): **the more he works the more he earns** cuanto más trabaja más gana

theatre, (*us*) **theater** [ˈθɪətəʳ] *n* teatro; (*also*: **lecture ~**) aula; (*Med*: *also*: **operating ~**) quirófano

theft [θeft] *n* robo
their [ðɛəʳ] *adj* su; **theirs** *pron* (el) suyo/(la) suya *etc*; *see also* **my**; **mine**
them [ðɛm, ðəm] *pron* (*direct*) los/las; (*indirect*) les; (*stressed, after prep*) ellos/ ellas; *see also* **me**
theme [θi:m] *n* tema *m*; **theme park** *n* parque *m* temático
themselves [ðəmˈsɛlvz] *pron pl* (*subject*) ellos mismos/ellas mismas; (*complement*) se; (*after prep*) sí (mismos/as); *see also* **oneself**
then [ðɛn] *adv* (*at that time*) entonces; (*next*) pues; (*later*) luego, después; (*and also*) además ▷ *conj* (*therefore*) en ese caso, entonces ▷ *adj*: **the ~ president** el entonces presidente; **from ~ on** desde entonces
theology [θɪˈɔlədʒɪ] *n* teología
theory [ˈθɪərɪ] *n* teoría
therapist [ˈθɛrəpɪst] *n* terapeuta *mf*
therapy [ˈθɛrəpɪ] *n* terapia

KEYWORD

there [ˈðɛəʳ] *adv* **1**: **there is, there are** hay; **there is no-one here** no hay nadie aquí; **there is no bread left** no queda pan; **there has been an accident** ha habido un accidente
2 (*referring to place*) ahí; (: *distant*) allí; **it's there** está ahí; **put it in/on/ up/down there** ponlo ahí dentro/ encima/arriba/abajo; **I want that book there** quiero ese libro de ahí; **there he is!** ¡ahí está!
3: **there, there** (*esp to child*) venga, venga, bueno; **thereabouts** *adv* por ahí; **thereafter** *adv* después; **thereby** *adv* así, de ese modo

therefore [ˈðɛəfɔ:ʳ] *adv* por lo tanto
there's = **there is**; **there has**
thermal [ˈθə:ml] *adj* termal; (*paper*) térmico
thermometer [θəˈmɔmɪtəʳ] *n* termómetro

t

thermostat [ˈθəːməustæt] *n*
termostato

these [ðiːz] *adj pl* estos/as ▷ *pron pl*
estos/as, éstos/as (*to avoid confusion
with adj*); **~ children/flowers** estos
chicos/estas flores; *see also* **this**

thesis (*pl* **theses**) [ˈθiːsɪs, -siːz] *n*
tesis *f inv*

they [ðeɪ] *pron pl* ellos/ellas; **~ say
that ...** (*it is said that*) se dice que ...;
they'd [ðeɪd] = **they had; they
would; they'll** = **they shall; they
will; they're** = **they are; they've**
= **they have**

thick [θɪk] *adj* (*dense*) espeso;
(: *vegetation, beard*) tupido; (*stupid*)
torpe ▷ *n*: **in the ~ of the battle** en
lo más reñido de la batalla; **it's 20
cm ~** tiene 20 cm de espesor; **thicken**
vi espesarse ▷ *vt* (*sauce etc*) espesar;
thickness *n* espesor *m*, grueso

thief (*pl* **thieves**) [θiːf, θiːvz] *n* ladrón/
ona *m/f*

thigh [θaɪ] *n* muslo

thin [θɪn] *adj* delgado; (*hair*) escaso;
(*crowd*) disperso ▷ *vt*: **to ~ (down)**
diluir

thing [θɪŋ] *n* cosa; (*object*) objeto,
artículo; (*contraption*) chisme *m*;
(*mania*) manía; **things** *npl* (*belongings*)
cosas *fpl*; **the best ~ would be to ...**
lo mejor sería ...; **how are ~s?** ¿qué tal
van las cosas?

think (*pl* **thought**) [θɪŋk, θɔːt] *vi*
pensar ▷ *vt* pensar, creer; **what did
you ~ of them?** ¿qué te parecieron?;
to ~ about sth/sb pensar en algo/
algn; **I'll ~ about it** lo pensaré; **to ~
of doing sth** pensar en hacer algo; **I
~ so/not** creo que sí/no; **to ~ well of
sb** tener buen concepto de algn; **think
over** *vt* reflexionar sobre, meditar;
think up *vt* imaginar

third [θəːd] *adj* (*before n*) tercer(a);
(*following n*) tercero/a ▷ *n* tercero/a;
(*fraction*) tercio; (BRIT: *degree*) título
universitario de tercera clase; **thirdly**
adv en tercer lugar; **third party**

insurance *n* (BRIT) seguro a terceros;
Third World *n*: **the Third World** el
Tercer Mundo

thirst [θəːst] *n* sed *f*; **thirsty** *adj*
(*person*) sediento; **to be thirsty**
tener sed

thirteen [θəːˈtiːn] *num* trece;
thirteenth [θəːˈtiːnθ] *adj*
decimotercero

thirtieth [ˈθəːtɪəθ] *adj* trigésimo

thirty [ˈθəːtɪ] *num* treinta

 KEYWORD

this [ðɪs] (*pl* **these**) *adj* (*demonstrative*)
este/a; **this man/woman** este
hombre/esta mujer; **this one (here)**
este/a, éste/a (*to avoid confusion with
adj*), esto (de aquí); *see also* **these**
▷ *pron* (*demonstrative*) este/a, éste/a
(*to avoid confusion with adj*), esto *neuter*;
who is this? ¿quién es esteesta?;
what is this? ¿qué es esto?; **this is
where I live** aquí vivo; **this is what
he said** esto es lo que dijo; **this is Mr
Brown** (*in introductions*) le presento al
Sr. Brown; (*photo*) este es el Sr. Brown;
(*on telephone*) habla el Sr. Brown; *see
also* **these**
▷ *adv* (*demonstrative*): **this high/long**
así de alto/largo; **this far** hasta aquí

thistle [ˈθɪsl] *n* cardo

thorn [θɔːn] *n* espina

thorough [ˈθʌrə] *adj* (*search*)
minucioso; (*knowledge*) profundo;
(*research*) a fondo; **thoroughly** *adv*
(*search*) minuciosamente; (*study*)
profundamente; (*wash*) a fondo;
(*utterly: bad, wet etc*) completamente,
totalmente

those [ðəuz] *adj pl* esos/esas;
aquellos/as ▷ *pron pl* esos/esas, ésos/
ésas (*to avoid confusion with adj*); (*more
remote*) aquellos/as, aquéllos/as (*to
avoid confusion with adj*); **leave ~
books on the table** deja esos libros
sobre la mesa

though [ðəʊ] *conj* aunque ▷ *adv* sin embargo, aún así; **even ~** aunque; **it's not so easy, ~** sin embargo no es tan fácil

thought [θɔːt] *pt, pp of* **think** ▷ *n* pensamiento; (*opinion*) opinión *f*; **thoughtful** *adj* pensativo; (*considerate*) atento; **thoughtless** *adj* desconsiderado

thousand ['θaʊzənd] *num* mil; **two ~** dos mil; **~s of** miles de; **thousandth** *num* milésimo

thrash [θræʃ] *vt* dar una paliza a

thread [θrɛd] *n* hilo; (*of screw*) rosca ▷ *vt* (*needle*) enhebrar

threat [θrɛt] *n* amenaza; **threaten** *vi* amenazar ▷ *vt*: **to threaten sb with sth/to do** amenazar a algn con algo/ con hacer; **threatening** ['θrɛtnɪŋ] *adj* amenazador(a)

three [θriː] *num* tres; **three-dimensional** *adj* tridimensional; **three-piece** ['θriː'piːs] *cpd*: **three-piece suite** tresillo; **three-quarters** *npl* tres cuartas partes; **three-quarters full** tres cuartas partes lleno

threshold ['θrɛʃhəʊld] *n* umbral *m*

threw [θruː] *pt of* **throw**

thrill [θrɪl] *n* (*excitement*) emoción *f* ▷ *vt* emocionar; **to be ~ed** (*with gift etc*) estar encantado; **thriller** *n* película/novela de suspense; **thrilling** *adj* emocionante

thriving ['θraɪvɪŋ] *adj* próspero

throat [θrəʊt] *n* garganta; **I have a sore ~** me duele la garganta

throb [θrɒb] *vi* latir; (*with pain*) dar punzadas

throne [θrəʊn] *n* trono

through [θruː] *prep* por, a través de; (*time*) durante; (*by means of*) por medio de, mediante; (*owing to*) gracias a ▷ *adj* (*ticket, train*) directo ▷ *adv* completamente, de parte a parte; de principio a fin; **to put sb ~ to sb** (*Tel*) poner *or* pasar a algn con algn; **to be ~** (*Tel*) tener comunicación;

(*have finished*) haber terminado; **"no ~ road"** (*BRIT*) "calle sin salida"; **throughout** *prep* (*place*) por todas partes de, por todo; (*time*) durante todo ▷ *adv* por *or* en todas partes

throw (*pt* **threw**, *pp* **thrown**) [θrəʊ, θruː, θrəʊn] *n* tiro; (*Sport*) lanzamiento ▷ *vt* tirar, echar; (*Sport*) lanzar; (*rider*) derribar; (*fig*) desconcertar; **to ~ a party** dar una fiesta; **throw away** *vt* tirar; **throw in** *vt* (*Sport: ball*) sacar; (*include*) incluir; **throw off** *vt* deshacerse de; **throw out** *vt* tirar; **throw up** *vi* vomitar

thru [θruː] *prep, adj, adv* (*US*) = **through**

thrush [θrʌʃ] *n* zorzal *m*, tordo

thrust [θrʌst] (*pt, pp* **thrust**) *vt* empujar

thud [θʌd] *n* golpe *m* sordo

thug [θʌg] *n* gamberro/a

thumb [θʌm] *n* (*Anat*) pulgar *m* ▷ *vt*: **to ~ a lift** hacer dedo; **thumbtack** *n* (*US*) chincheta

thump [θʌmp] *n* golpe *m*; (*sound*) ruido seco *or* sordo ▷ *vt, vi* golpear

thunder ['θʌndəʳ] *n* trueno ▷ *vi* tronar; (*train etc*): **to ~ past** pasar como un trueno; **thunderstorm** ['θʌndəstɔːm] *n* tormenta

Thur(s). *abbr* (= *Thursday*) juev.

Thursday ['θəːzdɪ] *n* jueves *m inv*

thus [ðʌs] *adv* así, de este modo

thwart [θwɔːt] *vt* frustrar

thyme [taɪm] *n* tomillo

Tibet [tɪ'bɛt] *n* el Tíbet

tick [tɪk] *n* (*sound: of clock*) tictac *m*; (*mark*) señal *f* (de visto bueno), palomita (*LAM*); (*Zool*) garrapata; (*BRIT inf*): **in a ~** en un instante ▷ *vi* hacer tictac ▷ *vt* marcar; **tick off** *vt* marcar; (*person*) reñir

ticket ['tɪkɪt] *n* billete *m*, boleto (*LAM*); (*for cinema etc*) entrada, boleto (*LAM*); (*in shop, on goods*) etiqueta; (*for library*) tarjeta; **to get a parking ~** (*Aut*) ser multado por estacionamiento ilegal; **ticket barrier** *n* (*BRIT Rail*) barrera

más allá de la cual se necesita billete/
boleto; **ticket collector** n revisor(a)
m/f; **ticket inspector** n revisor(a)
m/f, inspector(a) m/f de boletos (LAM);
ticket machine n máquina de billetes
(SP) or boletos (LAM); **ticket office** n
(Theat) taquilla, boletería (LAM); (Rail)
despacho de billetes or boletos (LAM)

tickle ['tɪkl] vt hacer cosquillas a ▷ vi
hacer cosquillas; **ticklish** adj (which
tickles: blanket) que pica; (: cough)
irritante; (fig: problem) delicado; **to be
ticklish** tener cosquillas

tide [taɪd] n marea; (fig: of events)
curso, marcha

tidy ['taɪdɪ] adj (room) ordenado;
(drawing, work) limpio; (person) (bien)
arreglado ▷ vt (also: ~ **up**) poner
en orden

tie [taɪ] n (string etc) atadura; (BRIT:
necktie) corbata; (fig: link) vínculo,
lazo; (Sport: draw) empate m ▷ vt
atar ▷ vi (Sport) empatar; **to ~ in
a bow** hacer un lazo; **to ~ a knot
in sth** hacer un nudo en algo; **tie
down** vt atar; (fig): **to ~ sb down to**
obligar a algn a; **tie up** vt (dog) atar;
(arrangements) concluir; **to be ~d up**
(busy) estar ocupado

tier [tɪəʳ] n grada; (of cake) piso

tiger ['taɪgəʳ] n tigre m

tight [taɪt] adj (rope) tirante; (money)
escaso; (clothes, budget) ajustado;
(programme) apretado; (budget)
ajustado; (security) estricto; (inf:
drunk) borracho ▷ adv (squeeze) muy
fuerte; (shut) herméticamente;
tighten vt (rope) estirar; (screw)
apretar ▷ vi estirarse; apretarse;
tightly adv (grasp) muy fuerte;
tights npl (BRIT) medias fpl,
panties mpl

tile [taɪl] n (on roof) teja; (on floor)
baldosa; (on wall) azulejo

till [tɪl] n caja (registradora) ▷ vt (land)
cultivar ▷ prep, conj = **until**

tilt [tɪlt] vt inclinar ▷ vi inclinarse

timber ['tɪmbəʳ] n (material) madera

time [taɪm] n tiempo; (epoch: often
pl) época; (by clock) hora; (moment)
momento; (occasion) vez f; (Mus)
compás m ▷ vt calcular or medir
el tiempo de; (race) cronometrar;
(remark etc) elegir el momento para;
a long ~ mucho tiempo; **four at a
~** cuarto a la vez; **for the ~ being**
de momento, por ahora; **at ~s** a
veces; **from ~ to ~** de vez en cuando;
in ~ (soon enough) a tiempo; (after
some time) con el tiempo; (Mus) al
compás; **in a week's ~** dentro de
una semana; **in no ~** en un abrir y
cerrar de ojos; **any ~** cuando sea;
on ~ a la hora; **5 ~s 5** 5 por 5; **what
~ is it?** ¿qué hora es?; **to have a
good ~** pasarlo bien, divertirse; **time
limit** n plazo; **timely** adj oportuno;
timer n (in kitchen) temporizador m;
timetable n horario; **time zone** n
huso horario

timid ['tɪmɪd] adj tímido

timing ['taɪmɪŋ] n (Sport)
cronometraje m; **the ~ of his
resignation** el momento que eligió
para dimitir

tin [tɪn] n estaño; (also: ~ **plate**)
hojalata; (BRIT: can) lata; **tinfoil** n
papel m de estaño

tingle ['tɪŋgl] vi (cheeks, skin: from
cold) sentir comezón; (: from bad
circulation) sentir hormigueo; **to ~
with** estremecerse de

tinker ['tɪŋkəʳ]: ~ **with** vt fus jugar
con, tocar

tinned [tɪnd] adj (BRIT: food) en lata,
en conserva

tin opener [-əʊpnəʳ] n (BRIT)
abrelatas m inv

tint [tɪnt] n matiz m; (for hair) tinte
m; **tinted** adj (hair) teñido; (glass,
spectacles) ahumado

tiny ['taɪnɪ] adj minúsculo, pequeñito

tip [tɪp] n (end) punta; (gratuity)
propina; (BRIT: for rubbish) vertedero;
(advice) consejo ▷ vt (waiter) dar una
propina a; (tilt) inclinar; (empty: also:

~ out) vaciar; echar; **tip off** vt avisar, poner sobre aviso a

tiptoe ['tɪptəʊ] n: **on ~** de puntillas

tire ['taɪər] n (US) = **tyre** ▷ vt cansar ▷ vi cansarse; (become bored) aburrirse; **tired** adj cansado; **to be tired of sth** estar harto de algo; **tire pressure** n (US) = **tyre pressure**; **tiring** adj cansado

tissue ['tɪʃuː] n tejido; (paper handkerchief) pañuelo de papel, kleenex®m; **tissue paper** n papel m de seda

tit [tɪt] n (bird) herrerillo común; **to give ~ for tat** dar ojo por ojo

title ['taɪtl] n título

T-junction ['tiː'dʒʌŋkʃən] n cruce m en T

TM abbr (= trademark) marca de fábrica; = **transcendental meditation**

KEYWORD

to [tuː, tə] prep 1 (direction) a; **to go to France/London/school/the station** ir a Francia/Londres/al colegio/a la estación; **to go to Claude's/the doctor's** ir a casa de Claude/al médico; **the road to Edinburgh** la carretera de Edimburgo 2 (as far as) hasta, a; **from here to London** de aquí a or hasta Londres; **to count to 10** contar hasta 10; **from 40 to 50 people** entre 40 y 50 personas 3 (with expressions of time): **a quarter/twenty to five** las cinco menos cuarto/veinte 4 (for, of): **the key to the front door** la llave de la puerta principal; **she is secretary to the director** es la secretaria del director; **a letter to his wife** una carta a or para su mujer 5 (expressing indirect object) a; **to give sth to sb** darle algo a algn; **to talk to sb** hablar con algn; **to be a danger to sb** ser un peligro para algn; **to carry out repairs to sth** hacer reparaciones en algo

6 (in relation to): **3 goals to 2** 3 goles a 2; **30 miles to the gallon** ≈ 9,4 litros a los cien (kilómetros)

7 (purpose, result): **to come to sb's aid** venir en auxilio or ayuda de algn; **to sentence sb to death** condenar a algn a muerte; **to my great surprise** con gran sorpresa mía

▷ infin particle 1 (simple infin): **to go/eat** ir/comer 2 (following another vb; see also relevant vb): **to want/try/start to do** querer/intentar/empezar a hacer 3 (with vb omitted): **I don't want to** no quiero 4 (purpose, result) para; **I did it to help you** lo hice para ayudarte; **he came to see you** vino a verte 5 (equivalent to relative clause): **I have things to do** tengo cosas que hacer; **the main thing is to try** lo principal es intentarlo 6 (after adj etc): **ready to go** listo para irse; **too old to ...** demasiado viejo (como) para ...

▷ adv: **pull/push the door to** tirar de/empujar la puerta

toad [təʊd] n sapo; **toadstool** n seta venenosa

toast [təʊst] n (Culin) tostada; (drink, speech) brindis m inv ▷ vt (Culin) tostar; (drink to) brindar por; **toaster** n tostador m

tobacco [tə'bækəʊ] n tabaco

toboggan [tə'bɒgən] n tobogán m

today [tə'deɪ] adv, n (also fig) hoy m

toddler ['tɒdlə'] n niño/a (que empieza a andar)

toe [təʊ] n dedo (del pie); (of shoe) punta ▷ vt: **to ~ the line** (fig) acatar las normas; **toenail** n uña del pie

toffee ['tɒfɪ] n caramelo

together [tə'geðə'] adv juntos; (at same time) al mismo tiempo, a la vez; **~ with** junto con

toilet ['tɔɪlət] n (BRIT: lavatory) servicios mpl, baño ▷ cpd (bag, soap *etc*) de aseo; **toilet bag** *n* neceser *m*, bolsa de aseo; **toilet paper** *n* papel *m* higiénico; **toiletries** *npl* artículos *mpl* de tocador; **toilet roll** *n* rollo de papel higiénico

token ['təukən] *n* (*sign*) señal *f*, muestra; (*souvenir*) recuerdo; (*disc*) ficha ▷ *cpd* (*fee, strike*) simbólico; **book/record ~** (*BRIT*) vale *m* para comprar libros/discos

Tokyo ['təukjəu] *n* Tokio, Tokío

told [təuld] *pt, pp of* **tell**

tolerant ['tɔlərnt] *adj*: **~ of** tolerante con

tolerate ['tɔləreɪt] *vt* tolerar

toll [təul] *n* (*of casualties*) número de víctimas; (*tax, charge*) peaje *m* ▷ *vi* (*bell*) doblar; **toll call** *n* (*us Tel*) conferencia, llamada interurbana; **toll-free** *adj, adv* (*us*) gratis

tomato [tə'mɑːtəu] (*pl* **tomatoes**) *n* tomate *m*; **tomato sauce** *n* salsa de tomate

tomb [tuːm] *n* tumba; **tombstone** *n* lápida

tomorrow [tə'mɔrəu] *adv, n* (*also fig*) mañana; **the day after ~** pasado mañana; **~ morning** mañana por la mañana

ton [tʌn] *n* tonelada; **~s of** (*inf*) montones de

tone [təun] *n* tono ▷ *vi* armonizar; **tone down** *vt* (*criticism*) suavizar; (*colour*) atenuar

tongs [tɔŋz] *npl* (*for coal*) tenazas *fpl*; (*for hair*) tenacillas *fpl*

tongue [tʌŋ] *n* lengua; **~ in cheek** en broma

tonic ['tɔnɪk] *n* (*Med*) tónico; (*also:* **~ water**) (agua) tónica

tonight [tə'naɪt] *adv, n* esta noche

tonsil ['tɔnsl] *n* amígdala; **tonsillitis** [tɔnsɪ'laɪtɪs] *n* amigdalitis *f*

too [tuː] *adv* (*excessively*) demasiado; (*also*) también; **~ much** demasiado; **~ many** demasiados/as

took [tuk] *pt of* **take**

tool [tuːl] *n* herramienta; **tool box** *n* caja de herramientas; **tool kit** *n* juego de herramientas

tooth (*pl* **teeth**) [tuːθ, tiːθ] *n* (*Anat, Tech*) diente *m*; (*molar*) muela; **toothache** *n* dolor *m* de muelas; **toothbrush** *n* cepillo de dientes; **toothpaste** *n* pasta de dientes; **toothpick** *n* palillo

top [tɔp] *n* (*of mountain*) cumbre *f*, cima; (*of head*) coronilla; (*of ladder*) (lo) alto; (*of cupboard, table*) superficie *f*; (*lid: of box, jar*) tapa; (: *of bottle*) tapón *m*; (*of list, table, queue, page*) cabeza; (*toy*) peonza; (*Dress: blouse*) blusa; (: *T-shirt*) camiseta ▷ *adj* de arriba; (*in rank*) principal, primero; (*best*) mejor ▷ *vt* (*exceed*) exceder; (*be first in*) encabezar; **on ~** sobre, encima de; **from ~ to bottom** de pies a cabeza; **top up** *vt* volver a llenar; (*mobile phone*) recargar el saldo de; **top floor** *n* último piso; **top hat** *n* sombrero de copa

topic ['tɔpɪk] *n* tema *m*; **topical** *adj* actual

topless ['tɔplɪs] *adj* (*bather etc*) topless *inv*

topping ['tɔpɪŋ] *n* (*Culin*): **with a ~ of cream** con nata por encima

topple ['tɔpl] *vt* derribar ▷ *vi* caerse

top-up card *n* (*for mobile phone*) tarjeta prepago

torch [tɔːtʃ] *n* antorcha; (*BRIT: electric*) linterna

tore [tɔːʳ] *pt of* **tear**[1]

torment *n* ['tɔːmɛnt] tormento ▷ *vt* [tɔː'mɛnt] atormentar; (*fig: annoy*) fastidiar

torn [tɔːn] *pp of* **tear**[1]

tornado [tɔː'neɪdəu] (*pl* **tornadoes**) *n* tornado

torpedo [tɔː'piːdəu] (*pl* **torpedoes**) *n* torpedo

torrent ['tɔrnt] *n* torrente *m*; **torrential** [tɔ'rɛnʃl] *adj* torrencial

tortoise ['tɔːtəs] *n* tortuga

torture ['tɔːtʃəʳ] *n* tortura ▷ *vt* torturar; (*fig*) atormentar

Tory ['tɔːrɪ] *adj, n* (*BRIT Pol*) conservador(a) *m/f*

toss [tɔs] *vt* tirar, echar; (*head*) sacudir; **to ~ a coin** echar a cara o cruz; **to ~ up for sth** jugar algo a cara o cruz; **to ~ and turn** (*in bed*) dar vueltas (en la cama)

total ['təutl] *adj* total, entero; (*emphatic: failure etc*) completo, total ▷ *n* total *m*, suma ▷ *vt* (*add up*) sumar; (*amount to*) ascender a

totalitarian [təutælɪ'tɛərɪən] *adj* totalitario

totally ['təutəlɪ] *adv* totalmente

touch [tʌtʃ] *n* tacto; (*contact*) contacto ▷ *vt* tocar; (*emotionally*) conmover; **a ~ of** (*fig*) una pizca *or* un poquito de; **to get in ~ with sb** ponerse en contacto con algn; **to lose ~** (*friends*) perder contacto; **touch down** *vi* (*on land*) aterrizar; **touchdown** *n* aterrizaje *m*; (*US Football*) ensayo; **touched** *adj* conmovido; **touching** *adj* conmovedor(a); **touchline** *n* (*Sport*) línea de banda; **touch-sensitive** *adj* sensible al tacto

tough [tʌf] *adj* (*meat*) duro; (*task, problem, situation*) difícil; (*person*) fuerte

tour ['tuər] *n* viaje *m*; (*also*: **package ~**) viaje *m* con todo incluido; (*of town, museum*) visita ▷ *vt* viajar por; **to go on a ~ of** (*region, country*) ir de viaje por; (*museum, castle*) visitar; **to go on ~** partir *or* ir de gira; **tour guide** *n* guía *mf* turístico/a

tourism ['tuərɪzm] *n* turismo

tourist ['tuərɪst] *n* turista *mf* ▷ *cpd* turístico; **tourist office** *n* oficina de turismo

tournament ['tuənəmənt] *n* torneo

tour operator *n* touroperador(a) *m/f*, operador(a) *m/f* turístico/a

tow [təu] *n* ▷ *vt* remolcar; **"on** *or* (*US*) **in ~"** (*Aut*) "a remolque"; **tow away** *vt* llevarse a remolque

toward(s) [tə'wɔːd(z)] *prep* hacia; (*of attitude*) respecto a, con; (*of purpose*) para

towel ['tauəl] *n* toalla; **towelling** *n* (*fabric*) felpa

tower ['tauər] *n* torre *f*; **tower block** *n* (*BRIT*) bloque *m* de pisos

town [taun] *n* ciudad *f*; **to go to ~** ir a la ciudad; (*fig*) tirar la casa por la ventana; **town centre** *n* centro de la ciudad; **town hall** *n* ayuntamiento

tow truck *n* (*US*) camión *m* grúa

toxic ['tɔksɪk] *adj* tóxico

toy [tɔɪ] *n* juguete *m*; **toy with** *vt fus* jugar con; (*idea*) acariciar; **toyshop** *n* juguetería

trace [treɪs] *n* rastro ▷ *vt* (*draw*) trazar, delinear; (*locate*) encontrar

track [træk] *n* (*mark*) huella, pista; (*path*) camino, senda; (*: of bullet etc*) trayectoria; (*: of suspect, animal*) pista, rastro; (*Rail*) vía; (*Comput, Sport*) pista; (*on album*) canción *f* ▷ *vt* seguir la pista de; **to keep ~ of** mantenerse al tanto de, seguir; **track down** *vt* (*person*) localizar; (*sth lost*) encontrar; **tracksuit** *n* chándal *m*

tractor ['træktər] *n* tractor *m*

trade [treɪd] *n* comercio; (*skill, job*) oficio ▷ *vi* negociar, comerciar ▷ *vt* (*exchange*): **to ~ sth (for sth)** cambiar algo (por algo); **trade in** *vt* (*old car etc*) ofrecer como parte del pago; **trademark** *n* marca de fábrica; **trader** *n* comerciante *mf*; **tradesman** *n* (*shopkeeper*) comerciante *mf*; **trade union** *n* sindicato

trading ['treɪdɪŋ] *n* comercio

tradition [trə'dɪʃən] *n* tradición *f*; **traditional** *adj* tradicional

traffic ['træfɪk] *n* tráfico, circulación *f* ▷ *vi*: **to ~ in** (*pej: liquor, drugs*) traficar en; **air ~** tráfico aéreo; **traffic circle** *n* (*US*) rotonda, glorieta; **traffic island** *n* refugio, isleta; **traffic jam** *n* embotellamiento; **traffic lights** *npl* semáforo *sg*; **traffic warden** *n* guardia *mf* de tráfico

tragedy ['trædʒədɪ] *n* tragedia

tragic ['trædʒɪk] *adj* trágico

trail [treɪl] n (tracks) rastro, pista; (path) camino, sendero; (dust, smoke) estela ▷ vt (drag) arrastrar; (follow) seguir la pista de ▷ vi arrastrarse; (in contest etc) ir perdiendo; **trailer** n (Aut) remolque m; (caravan) caravana; (Cine) trailer m, avance m

train [treɪn] n tren m; (of dress) cola ▷ vt (educate) formar; (sportsman) entrenar; (dog) amaestrar; (point: gun etc): **to ~ on** apuntar a ▷ vi (Sport) entrenarse; (be educated, learn a skill) formarse; **to ~ as a teacher** etc estudiar para profesor etc; **one's ~ of thought** el razonamiento de algn; **trainee** [treɪ'ni:] n trabajador(a) m/f en prácticas; **trainer** n (Sport) entrenador(a) m/f; (of animals) domador(a) m/f; **trainers** npl (shoes) zapatillas fpl (de deporte); **training** n formación f; entrenamiento; **to be in training** (Sport) estar entrenando; **training course** n curso de formación; **training shoes** npl zapatillas fpl (de deporte)

trait [treɪt] n rasgo

traitor ['treɪtəʳ] n traidor(a) m/f

tram [træm] n (BRIT: also: **~car**) tranvía m

tramp [træmp] n (person) vagabundo/a; (inf, pej: woman) puta

trample ['træmpl] vt: **to ~ (underfoot)** pisotear

trampoline ['træmpəli:n] n trampolín m

tranquil ['træŋkwɪl] adj tranquilo; **tranquillizer, (US) tranquilizer** n (Med) tranquilizante m

transaction [træn'zækʃən] n transacción f, operación f

transatlantic ['trænzət'læntɪk] adj transatlántico

transcript ['trænskrɪpt] n copia

transfer n ['trænsfəʳ] transferencia; (Sport) traspaso; (picture, design) calcomanía ▷ vt [træns'fɜːʳ] trasladar; **to ~ the charges** (BRIT Tel) llamar a cobro revertido

transform [træns'fɔːm] vt transformar; **transformation** n transformación f

transfusion [træns'fju:ʒən] n transfusión f

transit ['trænzɪt] n: **in ~** en tránsito

transition [træn'zɪʃən] n transición f

transitive ['trænzɪtɪv] adj (Ling) transitivo

translate [trænz'leɪt] vt: **to ~ (from/ into)** traducir (de/a); **translation** [trænz'leɪʃən] n traducción f; **translator** n traductor(a) m/f

transmission [trænz'mɪʃən] n transmisión f

transmit [trænz'mɪt] vt transmitir; **transmitter** n transmisor m

transparent [træns'pærnt] adj transparente

transplant n ['trænspla:nt] (Med) transplante m

transport n ['trænspɔːt] transporte m ▷ vt [træns'pɔːt] transportar; **transportation** [trænspɔː'teɪʃən] n transporte m

transvestite [trænz'vestaɪt] n travesti mf

trap [træp] n (snare, trick) trampa ▷ vt (person) coger (SP) or agarrar (LAM) en una trampa; (trick) engañar; (confine) atrapar

trash [træʃ] n basura; (inf: nonsense) tonterías fpl; **the book/film is ~** el libro/la película no vale nada; **trash can** n (US) cubo, balde m (LAM) or bote m (LAM) de la basura

trauma ['trɔ:mə] n trauma m; **traumatic** [trɔː'mætɪk] adj traumático

travel ['trævl] n viaje m ▷ vi viajar ▷ vt (distance) recorrer; **travel agency** n agencia de viajes; **travel agent** n agente mf de viajes; **travel insurance** n seguro de viaje; **traveller, (US) traveler** ['trævləʳ] n viajero/a; **traveller's cheque, (US) traveler's check** n cheque m de viaje; **travelling, (US) traveling** ['trævlɪŋ] *n* los viajes, el viajar; **travel-sick** *adj*: **to get travel-sick** marearse al viajar; **travel sickness** *n* mareo

tray [treɪ] *n* bandeja; (*on desk*) cajón *m*

treacherous ['trɛtʃərəs] *adj* traidor(a); **road conditions are ~** el estado de las carreteras es peligroso

treacle ['triːkl] *n* (*BRIT*) melaza

tread (*pt* **trod**, *pp* **trodden**) [trɛd, trɔd, 'trɔdn] *n* paso, pisada; (*of tyre*) banda de rodadura ▷ *vi* pisar; **tread on** *vt fus* pisar

treasure ['trɛʒəʳ] *n* tesoro ▷ *vt* (*value*) apreciar, valorar; **treasurer** *n* tesorero/a

treasury ['trɛʒərɪ] *n*: **the T~** ≈ el Ministerio de Economía y de Hacienda

treat [triːt] *n* (*present*) regalo ▷ *vt* tratar; **to ~ sb to sth** invitar a algn a algo; **treatment** *n* tratamiento

treaty ['triːtɪ] *n* tratado

treble ['trɛbl] *adj* triple ▷ *vt* triplicar ▷ *vi* triplicarse

tree [triː] *n* árbol *m*; **tree trunk** *n* tronco de árbol

trek [trɛk] *n* (*long journey*) expedición *f*; (*tiring walk*) caminata

tremble ['trɛmbl] *vi* temblar

tremendous [trɪ'mɛndəs] *adj* tremendo; enorme; (*excellent*) estupendo

trench [trɛntʃ] *n* zanja

trend [trɛnd] *n* (*tendency*) tendencia; (*of events*) curso; (*fashion*) moda; **trendy** *adj* de moda

trespass ['trɛspəs] *vi*: **to ~ on** entrar sin permiso en; **"no ~ing"** "prohibido el paso"

trial ['traɪəl] *n* (*Law*) juicio, proceso; (*test: of machine etc*) prueba; **trial period** *n* periodo de prueba

triangle ['traɪæŋgl] *n* (*Math, Mus*) triángulo

triangular [traɪ'æŋgjuləʳ] *adj* triangular

tribe [traɪb] *n* tribu *f*

tribunal [traɪ'bjuːnl] *n* tribunal *m*

tribute ['trɪbjuːt] *n* homenaje *m*, tributo; **to pay ~ to** rendir homenaje a

trick [trɪk] *n* trampa; (*conjuring trick, deceit*) truco; (*joke*) broma; (*Cards*) baza ▷ *vt* engañar; **to play a ~ on sb** gastar una broma a algn; **that should do the ~** eso servirá

trickle ['trɪkl] *n* (*of water etc*) hilo ▷ *vi* gotear

tricky ['trɪkɪ] *adj* difícil; (*problem*) delicado

tricycle ['traɪsɪkl] *n* triciclo

trifle ['traɪfl] *n* bagatela; (*Culin*) dulce de bizcocho, gelatina, fruta y natillas ▷ *adv*: **a ~ long** un pelín largo

trigger ['trɪgəʳ] *n* (*of gun*) gatillo

trim [trɪm] *adj* (*house, garden*) en buen estado; (*figure*): **to be ~** tener buen talle ▷ *n* (*haircut etc*) recorte *m* ▷ *vt* (*neaten*) arreglar; (*cut*) recortar; (*decorate*) adornar; (*Naut: a sail*) orientar

trio ['triːəu] *n* trío

trip [trɪp] *n* viaje *m*; (*excursion*) excursión *f*; (*stumble*) traspié *m* ▷ *vi* (*stumble*) tropezar; (*go lightly*) andar a paso ligero; **on a ~** de viaje; **trip up** *vi* tropezar, caerse ▷ *vt* hacer tropezar *or* caer

triple ['trɪpl] *adj* triple

triplets ['trɪplɪts] *npl* trillizos/as *m/f pl*

tripod ['traɪpɔd] *n* trípode *m*

triumph ['traɪʌmf] *n* triunfo ▷ *vi*: **to ~ (over)** vencer; **triumphant** [traɪ'ʌmfənt] *adj* triunfante

trivial ['trɪvɪəl] *adj* insignificante

trod [trɔd] *pt of* **tread**

trodden ['trɔdn] *pp of* **tread**

trolley ['trɔlɪ] *n* carrito

trolley bus *n* trolebús *m*

trombone [trɔm'bəun] *n* trombón *m*

troop [truːp] *n* grupo, banda; **troops** *npl* (*Mil*) tropas *fpl*

trophy ['trəufɪ] *n* trofeo

tropical ['trɔpɪkl] *adj* tropical

trot [trɔt] *n* trote *m* ▷ *vi* trotar; **on the ~** (*BRIT fig*) seguidos/as

trouble ['trʌbl] n problema m,
dificultad f; (worry) preocupación f;
(bother, effort) molestia, esfuerzo;
(unrest) inquietud f; (Med): **stomach ~**
problemas mpl gástricos ▷ vt molestar;
(worry) preocupar, inquietar ▷ vi: **to ~
to do sth** molestarse en hacer algo;
troubles npl (Pol etc) conflictos mpl; **to
be in ~** estar en un apuro; **it's no ~!** ¡no
es molestia (ninguna)!; **what's the
~?** ¿qué pasa?; **troubled** adj (person)
preocupado; (epoch, life) agitado;
troublemaker n agitador(a) m/f;
troublesome adj molesto

trough [trɔf] n (also: **drinking ~**)
abrevadero; (also: **feeding ~**)
comedero

trousers ['trauzəz] npl pantalones
mpl; **short ~** pantalones mpl cortos

trout [traut] n (pl inv) trucha

trowel ['trauəl] n paleta

truant ['truənt] n: **to play ~** (BRIT)
hacer novillos

truce [tru:s] n tregua

truck [trʌk] n (US) camión m; (Rail)
vagón m; **truck driver** n camionero/a

true [tru:] adj verdadero; (accurate)
exacto; (genuine) auténtico; (faithful)
fiel; **to come ~** realizarse

truly ['tru:lɪ] adv realmente; **yours ~**
(in letter-writing) atentamente

trumpet ['trʌmpɪt] n trompeta

trunk [trʌŋk] n (of tree, person) tronco;
(of elephant) trompa; (case) baúl m; (US
Aut) maletero

trunks [trʌŋks] npl (also:
swimming ~) bañador m

trust [trʌst] n confianza f; (Law)
fideicomiso ▷ vt (rely on) tener
confianza en; **to ~ sth to sb** (entrust)
confiar algo a algn; **to ~ (that)** (hope)
esperar (que); **you'll have to take
it on ~** tienes que aceptarlo a ojos
cerrados; **trusted** adj de confianza;
trustworthy adj digno de confianza

truth (pl **truths**) [tru:θ, tru:ðz] n
verdad f; **truthful** adj (person) sincero;
(account) fidedigno

try [traɪ] n tentativa, intento; (Rugby)
ensayo ▷ vt (Law) juzgar, procesar;
(test: sth new) probar, someter a
prueba; (attempt) intentar; (strain:
patience) hacer perder ▷ vi probar; **to
give sth a ~** intentar hacer algo; **to
~ to do sth** intentar hacer algo; **~
again!** ¡vuelve a probar!; **~ harder!**
¡esfuérzate más!; **well, I tried** al
menos lo intenté; **try on** vt (clothes)
probarse; **trying** adj cansado; (person)
pesado

T-shirt ['ti:ʃə:t] n camiseta

tub [tʌb] n cubo (SP), balde m (LAM);
(bath) bañera, tina (LAM)

tube [tju:b] n tubo; (BRIT: underground)
metro

tuberculosis [tjubə:kju'ləusɪs] n
tuberculosis f inv

tube station n (BRIT) estación f
de metro

tuck [tʌk] vt (put) poner; **tuck away**
vt esconder; **tuck in** vt meter; (child)
arropar ▷ vi (eat) comer con apetito

tucker ['tʌkər] n (AUST, NZ inf) papeo

tuck shop n (Scol) tienda de
golosinas

Tue(s). abbr (= Tuesday) mart.

Tuesday ['tju:zdɪ] n martes m inv

tug [tʌg] n (ship) remolcador m ▷ vt
remolcar

tuition [tju:'ɪʃən] n (BRIT) enseñanza;
(: private tuition) clases fpl particulares;
(US: school fees) matrícula

tulip ['tju:lɪp] n tulipán m

tumble ['tʌmbl] n (fall) caída ▷ vi
caerse; **to ~ to sth** (inf) caer en la
cuenta de algo; **tumble dryer** n (BRIT)
secadora

tumbler ['tʌmblər] n vaso

tummy ['tʌmɪ] n (inf) barriga

tumour, (US) **tumor** ['tju:mər] n
tumor m

tuna ['tju:nə] n (pl inv: also: **~ fish**)
atún m

tune [tju:n] n melodía ▷ vt (Mus)
afinar; (Radio, TV, Aut) sintonizar;
to be in/out of ~ (instrument) estar

afinado/desafinado; (*singer*) afinar/desafinar; **to be in/out of ~ with** (*fig*) armonizar/desentonar con; **tune in** *vi* (*Radio, TV*): **to ~ in (to)** sintonizar (con); **tune up** *vi* (*musician*) afinar (su instrumento)

tunic ['tjuːnɪk] *n* túnica

Tunisia [tjuːˈnɪzɪə] *n* Túnez *m*

tunnel ['tʌnl] *n* túnel *m*; (*in mine*) galería ▷ *vi* construir un túnel/una galería

turbulence ['təːbjuləns] *n* (*Aviat*) turbulencia

turf [təːf] *n* césped *m*; (*clod*) tepe *m* ▷ *vt* cubrir con césped

Turk [təːk] *n* turco/a

Turkey ['təːkɪ] *n* Turquía

turkey ['təːkɪ] *n* pavo

Turkish ['təːkɪʃ] *adj* turco ▷ *n* (*Ling*) turco

turmoil ['təːmɔɪl] *n*: **in ~** revuelto

turn [təːn] *n* turno; (*in road*) curva; (*Theat*) número; (*Med*) ataque *m* ▷ *vt* girar, volver; (*collar, steak*) dar la vuelta a; (*change*): **to ~ sth into** convertir algo en ▷ *vi* volver; (*person: look back*) volverse; (*reverse direction*) dar la vuelta); (*milk*) cortarse; **a good ~** un favor; **it gave me quite a ~** me dio un susto; **"no left ~"** (*Aut*) "prohibido girar a la izquierda"; **it's your ~** te toca a ti; **in ~** por turnos; **to take ~s** turnarse; **turn around** *vi* (*person*) volverse, darse la vuelta ▷ *vt* (*object*) dar la vuelta a, voltear (*LAM*); **turn away** *vi* apartar la vista ▷ *vt* rechazar; **turn back** *vi* volverse atrás ▷ *vt* hacer retroceder; (*clock*) retrasar; **turn down** *vt* (*refuse*) rechazar; (*reduce*) bajar; (*fold*) doblar; **turn in** *vi* (*inf: go to bed*) acostarse ▷ *vt* (*fold*) doblar hacia dentro; **turn off** *vi* (*from road*) desviarse ▷ *vt* (*light, radio etc*) apagar; (*engine*) parar; **turn on** *vt* (*light, radio etc*) encender, prender (*LAM*); (*engine*) poner en marcha; **turn out** *vt* (*light, gas*) apagar; (*produce*) producir ▷ *vi*: **to ~ out to be ...** resultar ser ...; **turn**

over *vi* (*person*) volverse ▷ *vt* (*mattress, card*) dar la vuelta a; (*page*) volver; **turn round** *vi* volverse; (*rotate*) girar; **turn to** *vt fus*: **to ~ to sb** acudir a algn; **turn up** *vi* (*person*) llegar, presentarse; (*lost object*) aparecer ▷ *vt* (*radio*) subir;

turning *n* (*bend*) curva; **turning point** *n* (*fig*) momento decisivo

turnip ['təːnɪp] *n* nabo

turn: turnout ['təːnaut] *n* (*attendance*) asistencia; (*number of people attending*) número de asistentes; (*spectators*) público; **turnover** *n* (*Comm: amount of money*) facturación *f*; (*of goods*) movimiento; **turnstile** *n* torniquete *m*; **turn-up** *n* (*BRIT: on trousers*) vuelta

turquoise ['təːkwɔɪz] *n* (*stone*) turquesa ▷ *adj* color turquesa *inv*

turtle ['təːtl] *n* tortuga (marina)

turtleneck (sweater) ['təːtlnɛk-] *n* (*jersey m de*) cuello cisne

tusk [tʌsk] *n* colmillo

tutor ['tjuːtəʳ] *n* profesor(a) *m/f*; **tutorial** [tjuːˈtɔːrɪəl] *n* (*Scol*) seminario

tuxedo [tʌkˈsiːdəu] *n* (*US*) smóking *m*, esmoquin *m*

TV [tiːˈviː] *n abbr* (= *television*) televisión *f*

tweed [twiːd] *n* tweed *m*

tweet [twiːt] *n* (*on Twitter*) tweet *m* ▷ *vt, vi* (*on Twitter*) tuitear

tweezers ['twiːzəz] *npl* pinzas *fpl* (*de depilar*)

twelfth [twɛlfθ] *num* duodécimo

twelve [twɛlv] *num* doce; **at ~ o'clock** (*midday*) a mediodía; (*midnight*) a medianoche

twentieth ['twɛntɪɪθ] *num* vigésimo

twenty ['twɛntɪ] *num* veinte; **in ~ fourteen** en dos mil catorce

twice [twaɪs] *adv* dos veces; **~ as much** dos veces más

twig [twɪg] *n* ramita

twilight ['twaɪlaɪt] *n* crepúsculo

twin [twɪn] *adj, n* gemelo/a ▷ *vt* hermanar; **twin-bedded room** *n* = **twin room**; **twin beds** *npl* camas *fpl* gemelas

twinkle ['twɪŋkl] vi centellear; (eyes) parpadear

twin room n habitación f con dos camas

twist [twɪst] n (action) torsión f; (in road, coil) vuelta; (in wire, flex) doblez f; (in story) giro ▷ vt torcer; (roll around) enrollar; (fig) deformar ▷ vi serpentear

twit [twɪt] n (inf) tonto

twitch [twɪtʃ] n sacudida; (nervous) tic m nervioso ▷ vi moverse nerviosamente

two [tuː] num dos; **to put ~ and ~ together** (fig) atar cabos

type [taɪp] n (category) tipo, género; (model) modelo; (Typ) tipo, letra ▷ vt (letter etc) escribir a máquina; **typewriter** n máquina de escribir

typhoid ['taɪfɔɪd] n (fiebre f) tifoidea

typhoon [taɪ'fuːn] n tifón m

typical ['tɪpɪkl] adj típico; **typically** adv típicamente

typing ['taɪpɪŋ] n mecanografía

typist ['taɪpɪst] n mecanógrafo/a

tyre, (US) **tire** ['taɪəʳ] n neumático, llanta (LAm); **tyre pressure** n presión f de los neumáticos

U

UFO ['juːfəʊ] n abbr (= unidentified flying object) OVNI m

Uganda [juː'gændə] n Uganda

ugly ['ʌglɪ] adj feo; (dangerous) peligroso

UHT adj abbr = **ultra heat treated**; **~ milk** leche f uperizada

UK n abbr (= United Kingdom) R.U.

ulcer ['ʌlsəʳ] n úlcera; **mouth ~** llaga bucal

ultimate ['ʌltɪmət] adj último, final; (greatest) mayor; **ultimately** adv (in the end) por último, al final; (fundamentally) a fin de cuentas

ultimatum (pl **ultimatums** or **ultimata**) [ʌltɪ'meɪtəm, -tə] n ultimátum m

ultrasound ['ʌltrəsaʊnd] n (Med) ultrasonido

ultraviolet ['ʌltrə'vaɪəlɪt] adj ultravioleta

umbrella [ʌm'brɛlə] n paraguas m inv

umpire ['ʌmpaɪəʳ] n árbitro

UN *n abbr* (= United Nations) ONU *f*
unable [ʌn'eɪbl] *adj*: **to be ~ to do sth** no poder hacer algo
unacceptable [ʌnək'sɛptəbl] *adj* (*proposal, behaviour, price*) inaceptable; **it's ~ that** no se puede aceptar que
unanimous [juː'nænɪməs] *adj* unánime
unarmed [ʌn'ɑːmd] *adj* (*person*) desarmado
unattended [ʌnə'tɛndɪd] *adj* desatendido
unattractive [ʌnə'træktɪv] *adj* poco atractivo
unavailable [ʌnə'veɪləbl] *adj* (*article, room, book*) no disponible; (*person*) ocupado
unavoidable [ʌnə'vɔɪdəbl] *adj* inevitable
unaware [ʌnə'wɛəʳ] *adj*: **to be ~ of** ignorar; **unawares** *adv*: **to catch sb unawares** pillar a algn desprevenido
unbearable [ʌn'bɛərəbl] *adj* insoportable
unbeatable [ʌn'biːtəbl] *adj* invencible; (*price*) inmejorable
unbelievable [ʌnbɪ'liːvəbl] *adj* increíble
unborn [ʌn'bɔːn] *adj* que va a nacer
unbutton [ʌn'bʌtn] *vt* desabrochar
uncalled-for [ʌn'kɔːldfɔːʳ] *adj* gratuito, inmerecido
uncanny [ʌn'kænɪ] *adj* extraño
uncertain [ʌn'sɜːtn] *adj* incierto; (*indecisive*) indeciso; **uncertainty** *n* incertidumbre *f*
unchanged [ʌn'tʃeɪndʒd] *adj* sin cambiar *or* alterar
uncle ['ʌŋkl] *n* tío
unclear [ʌn'klɪəʳ] *adj* poco claro; **I'm still ~ about what I'm supposed to do** todavía no tengo muy claro lo que tengo que hacer
uncomfortable [ʌn'kʌmfətəbl] *adj* incómodo; (*uneasy*) inquieto
uncommon [ʌn'kɔmən] *adj* poco común, raro

unconditional [ʌnkən'dɪʃənl] *adj* incondicional
unconscious [ʌn'kɔnʃəs] *adj* sin sentido; (*unaware*) inconsciente ▷ *n*: **the ~** el inconsciente
uncontrollable [ʌnkən'trəuləbl] *adj* (*temper*) indomable; (*laughter*) incontenible
unconventional [ʌnkən'vɛnʃənl] *adj* poco convencional
uncover [ʌn'kʌvəʳ] *vt* descubrir; (*take lid off*) destapar
undecided [ʌndɪ'saɪdɪd] *adj* (*person*) indeciso; (*question*) no resuelto
undeniable [ʌndɪ'naɪəbl] *adj* innegable
under ['ʌndəʳ] *prep* debajo de; (*less than*) menos de; (*according to*) según, de acuerdo con ▷ *adv* debajo, abajo; **~ there** ahí debajo; **~ construction** en construcción; **undercover** *adj* clandestino; **underdone** *adj* (*Culin*) poco hecho; **underestimate** *vt* subestimar; **undergo** *vt* (*irreg: like* **go**) sufrir; (*treatment*) recibir; **undergraduate** *n* estudiante *mf*; **underground** *n* (BRIT: *railway*) metro; (*Pol*) movimiento clandestino ▷ *adj* subterráneo ▷ *adv* (*work*) en la clandestinidad; **undergrowth** *n* maleza; **underline** *vt* subrayar; **undermine** *vt* socavar, minar; **underneath** [ʌndə'niːθ] *adv* debajo ▷ *prep* debajo de, bajo; **underpants** *npl* calzoncillos *mpl*; **underpass** *n* (BRIT) paso subterráneo; **underprivileged** *adj* desposeído; **underscore** *vt* subrayar, sostener; **undershirt** *n* (US) camiseta; **underskirt** *n* (BRIT) enaguas *fpl*
understand [ʌndə'stænd] *vt, vi* entender, comprender; (*assume*) tener entendido; **understandable** *adj* comprensible; **understanding** *adj* comprensivo ▷ *n* comprensión *f*, entendimiento; (*agreement*) acuerdo
understatement [ʌndə'steɪtmənt] *n* modestia (excesiva); **to say it was**

good is quite an ~ decir que estuvo bien es quedarse corto

understood [ʌndə'stud] *pt*, *pp* *of* **understand** ▷ *adj* entendido; *(implied)*: **it is ~ that** se sobreentiende que

undertake [ʌndə'teɪk] *vt (irreg: like* **take***)* emprender; **to ~ to do sth** comprometerse a hacer algo

undertaker ['ʌndəteɪkəʳ] *n* director(a) *m/f* de pompas fúnebres

undertaking ['ʌndəteɪkɪŋ] *n* empresa; *(promise)* promesa

under: underwater *adv* bajo el agua ▷ *adj* submarino; **underway** *adj*: **to be underway** *(meeting)* estar en marcha; *(investigation)* estar llevándose a cabo; **underwear** *n* ropa interior *or* íntima *(LAM)*; **underwent** *vb see* **undergo**; **underworld** *n (of crime)* hampa, inframundo

undesirable [ʌndɪ'zaɪərəbl] *adj* indeseable

undisputed [ʌndɪ'spju:tɪd] *adj* incontestable

undo [ʌn'du:] *vt (irreg: like* **do***: laces)* desatar; *(button etc)* desabrochar; *(spoil)* deshacer

undone [ʌn'dʌn] *pp of* **undo** ▷ *adj*: **to come ~** *(clothes)* desabrocharse; *(parcel)* desatarse

undoubtedly [ʌn'dautɪdlɪ] *adv* indudablemente, sin duda

undress [ʌn'drɛs] *vi* desnudarse

unearth [ʌn'ə:θ] *vt* desenterrar

uneasy [ʌn'i:zɪ] *adj* intranquilo; *(worried)* preocupado; **to feel ~ about doing sth** sentirse incómodo con la idea de hacer algo

unemployed [ʌnɪm'plɔɪd] *adj* parado, sin trabajo ▷ *n*: **the ~** los parados

unemployment [ʌnɪm'plɔɪmənt] *n* paro, desempleo; **unemployment benefit** *n (BRIT)* subsidio de desempleo *or* paro

unequal [ʌn'i:kwəl] *adj (length, objects etc)* desigual; *(amounts)* distinto

uneven [ʌn'i:vn] *adj* desigual; *(road etc)* con baches

unexpected [ʌnɪk'spɛktɪd] *adj* inesperado; **unexpectedly** *adv* inesperadamente

unfair [ʌn'fɛəʳ] *adj*: **~ (to sb)** injusto (con algn)

unfaithful [ʌn'feɪθful] *adj* infiel

unfamiliar [ʌnfə'mɪlɪəʳ] *adj* extraño, desconocido; **to be ~ with sth** desconocer *or* ignorar algo

unfashionable [ʌn'fæʃnəbl] *adj* pasado *or* fuera de moda

unfasten [ʌn'fɑ:sn] *vt* desatar

unfavourable, *(US)* **unfavorable** [ʌn'feɪvərəbl] *adj* desfavorable

unfinished [ʌn'fɪnɪʃt] *adj* inacabado, sin terminar

unfit [ʌn'fɪt] *adj* en baja forma; *(incompetent)* incapaz; **~ for work** no apto para trabajar

unfold [ʌn'fəuld] *vt* desdoblar ▷ *vi* abrirse

unforgettable [ʌnfə'gɛtəbl] *adj* inolvidable

unfortunate [ʌn'fɔ:tʃnət] *adj* desgraciado; *(event, remark)* inoportuno; **unfortunately** *adv* desgraciadamente

unfriend [ʌn'frɛnd] *vt (Internet)* quitar de amigo a; **he has ~ed her on Facebook** la ha quitado de amiga en Facebook

unfriendly [ʌn'frɛndlɪ] *adj* antipático; *(behaviour, remark)* hostil, poco amigable

unfurnished [ʌn'fə:nɪʃt] *adj* sin amueblar

unhappiness [ʌn'hæpɪnɪs] *n* tristeza

unhappy [ʌn'hæpɪ] *adj (sad)* triste; *(unfortunate)* desgraciado; *(childhood)* infeliz; **~ with** *(arrangements etc)* poco contento con, descontento con

unhealthy [ʌn'hɛlθɪ] *adj* malsano; *(person)* enfermizo; *(interest)* morboso

unheard-of [ʌn'hə:dɔv] *adj* inaudito, sin precedente

unhelpful [ʌn'hɛlpful] *adj* (person) poco servicial; (advice) inútil

unhurt [ʌn'hɜːt] *adj* ileso

unidentified [ʌnaɪ'dɛntɪfaɪd] *adj* no identificado; **~ flying object (UFO)** objeto volante no identificado

uniform ['juːnɪfɔːm] *n* uniforme *m* ▷ *adj* uniforme

unify ['juːnɪfaɪ] *vt* unificar, unir

unimportant [ʌnɪm'pɔːtənt] *adj* sin importancia

uninhabited [ʌnɪn'hæbɪtɪd] *adj* desierto

unintentional [ʌnɪn'tɛnʃənəl] *adj* involuntario

union ['juːnjən] *n* unión *f*; (also: **trade ~**) sindicato ▷ *cpd* sindical; **Union Jack** *n* bandera del Reino Unido

unique [juː'niːk] *adj* único

unisex ['juːnɪsɛks] *adj* unisex

unit ['juːnɪt] *n* unidad *f*; (team, squad) grupo; **kitchen ~** módulo de cocina

unite [juː'naɪt] *vt* unir ▷ *vi* unirse; **united** *adj* unido; **United Kingdom** *n* Reino Unido

United Nations (Organization) *n* Naciones Unidas *fpl*

United States (of America) *n* Estados Unidos *mpl* (de América)

unity ['juːnɪtɪ] *n* unidad *f*

universal [juːnɪ'vɜːsl] *adj* universal

universe ['juːnɪvɜːs] *n* universo

university [juːnɪ'vɜːsɪtɪ] *n* universidad *f*

unjust [ʌn'dʒʌst] *adj* injusto

unkind [ʌn'kaɪnd] *adj* poco amable; (comment etc) cruel

unknown [ʌn'nəun] *adj* desconocido

unlawful [ʌn'lɔːful] *adj* ilegal, ilícito

unleaded [ʌn'lɛdɪd] *n* (also: **~ petrol**) gasolina sin plomo

unleash [ʌn'liːʃ] *vt* desatar

unless [ʌn'lɛs] *conj* a menos que; **~ he comes** a menos que venga; **~ otherwise stated** salvo indicación contraria

unlike [ʌn'laɪk] *adj* distinto ▷ *prep* a diferencia de

unlikely [ʌn'laɪklɪ] *adj* improbable

unlimited [ʌn'lɪmɪtɪd] *adj* ilimitado

unlisted [ʌn'lɪstɪd] *adj* (us Tel) que no figura en la guía

unload [ʌn'ləud] *vt* descargar

unlock [ʌn'lɔk] *vt* abrir (con llave)

unlucky [ʌn'lʌkɪ] *adj* desgraciado; (object, number) que da mala suerte; **to be ~** tener mala suerte

unmarried [ʌn'mærɪd] *adj* soltero

unmistakable [ʌnmɪs'teɪkəbl] *adj* inconfundible

unnatural [ʌn'nætʃrəl] *adj* antinatural; (manner) afectado; (habit) perverso

unnecessary [ʌn'nɛsəsərɪ] *adj* innecesario, inútil

UNO ['juːnəu] *n abbr* (= *United Nations Organization*) ONU *f*

unofficial [ʌnə'fɪʃl] *adj* no oficial

unpack [ʌn'pæk] *vi* deshacer las maletas ▷ *vt* deshacer

unpaid [ʌn'peɪd] *adj* (bill, debt) sin pagar, impagado; (Comm) pendiente; (holiday) sin sueldo; (work) sin pago, voluntario

unpleasant [ʌn'plɛznt] *adj* (disagreeable) desagradable; (person, manner) antipático

unplug [ʌn'plʌg] *vt* desenchufar, desconectar

unpopular [ʌn'pɔpjulər] *adj* poco popular

unprecedented [ʌn'prɛsɪdəntɪd] *adj* sin precedentes

unpredictable [ʌnprɪ'dɪktəbl] *adj* imprevisible

unprotected ['ʌnprə'tɛktɪd] *adj* (sex) sin protección

unqualified [ʌn'kwɔlɪfaɪd] *adj* sin título, no cualificado; (success) total

unravel [ʌn'rævl] *vt* desenmarañar

unreal [ʌn'rɪəl] *adj* irreal

unrealistic [ʌnrɪə'lɪstɪk] *adj* poco realista

unreasonable [ʌn'riːznəbl] *adj* irrazonable; **to make ~ demands on sb** hacer demandas excesivas a algn

u

unrelated [ʌnrɪˈleɪtɪd] *adj* sin relación; (*family*) no emparentado

unreliable [ʌnrɪˈlaɪəbl] *adj* (*person*) informal; (*machine*) poco fiable

unrest [ʌnˈrɛst] *n* inquietud *f*, malestar *m*; (*Pol*) disturbios *mpl*

unroll [ʌnˈrəʊl] *vt* desenrollar

unruly [ʌnˈruːlɪ] *adj* indisciplinado

unsafe [ʌnˈseɪf] *adj* peligroso

unsatisfactory [ˈʌnsætɪsˈfæktərɪ] *adj* poco satisfactorio

unscrew [ʌnˈskruː] *vt* destornillar

unsettled [ʌnˈsɛtld] *adj* inquieto; (*weather*) variable

unsettling [ʌnˈsɛtlɪŋ] *adj* perturbador(a), inquietante

unsightly [ʌnˈsaɪtlɪ] *adj* desagradable

unskilled [ʌnˈskɪld] *adj*: **~ workers** mano *f* de obra no cualificada

unspoiled [ˈʌnˈspɔɪld], **unspoilt** [ˈʌnˈspɔɪlt] *adj* (*place*) que no ha perdido su belleza natural

unstable [ʌnˈsteɪbl] *adj* inestable

unsteady [ʌnˈstɛdɪ] *adj* inestable

unsuccessful [ʌnsəkˈsɛsfʊl] *adj* (*attempt*) infructuoso; (*writer, proposal*) sin éxito; **to be ~** (*in attempting sth*) no tener éxito, fracasar

unsuitable [ʌnˈsuːtəbl] *adj* inapropiado; (*time*) inoportuno

unsure [ʌnˈʃʊəʳ] *adj* inseguro, poco seguro

untidy [ʌnˈtaɪdɪ] *adj* (*room*) desordenado; (*appearance*) desaliñado

untie [ʌnˈtaɪ] *vt* desatar

until [ənˈtɪl] *prep* hasta ▷ *conj* hasta que; **~ he comes** hasta que venga; **~ now** hasta ahora; **~ then** hasta entonces

untrue [ʌnˈtruː] *adj* (*statement*) falso

unused [ʌnˈjuːzd] *adj* sin usar

unusual [ʌnˈjuːʒuəl] *adj* insólito, poco común; **unusually** *adv*: **he arrived unusually early** llegó más temprano que de costumbre

unveil [ʌnˈveɪl] *vt* (*statue*) descubrir

unwanted [ʌnˈwɒntɪd] *adj* (*person, effect*) no deseado

unwell [ʌnˈwɛl] *adj*: **to feel ~** estar indispuesto, sentirse mal

unwilling [ʌnˈwɪlɪŋ] *adj*: **to be ~ to do sth** estar poco dispuesto a hacer algo

unwind [ʌnˈwaɪnd] (*irreg: like* **wind²**) *vt* desenvolver ▷ *vi* (*relax*) relajarse

unwise [ʌnˈwaɪz] *adj* imprudente

unwittingly [ʌnˈwɪtɪŋlɪ] *adv* inconscientemente, sin darse cuenta

unwrap [ʌnˈræp] *vt* desenvolver

unzip [ʌnˈzɪp] *vt* abrir la cremallera de; (*Comput*) descomprimir

 KEYWORD

up [ʌp] *prep*: **to go/be up sth** subir/ estar subido en algo; **he went up the stairs/the hill** subió las escaleras/ la colina; **we walked/climbed up the hill** subimos la colina; **they live further up the street** viven más arriba en la calle; **go up that road and turn left** sigue por esa calle y gira a la izquierda

▶ *adv* **1** (*upwards, higher*) más arriba; **up in the mountains** en lo alto (de la montaña); **put it a bit higher up** ponlo un poco más arriba *or* alto; **up there** ahí *or* allí arriba; **up above** en lo alto, por encima, arriba

2: **to be up** (*out of bed*) estar levantado; (*prices, level*) haber subido

3: **up to** (*as far as*) hasta; **up to now** hasta ahora *or* la fecha

4: **to be up to** (*depending on*): **it's up to you** depende de ti; **he's not up to it** (*job, task etc*) no es capaz de hacerlo; **his work is not up to the required standard** su trabajo no da la talla; **what is he up to?** (*inf: doing*) ¿qué estará tramando?

▶ *n*: **ups and downs** altibajos *mpl*

up-and-coming [ʌpəndˈkʌmɪŋ] *adj* prometedor(a)

upbringing ['ʌpbrɪŋɪŋ] n educación f
update [ʌp'deɪt] vt poner al día
upfront [ʌp'frʌnt] adj claro, directo ▷ adv a las claras; (pay) por adelantado; **to be ~ about sth** admitir algo claramente
upgrade [ʌp'greɪd] vt ascender; (Comput) modernizar
upheaval [ʌp'hiːvl] n trastornos mpl; (Pol) agitación f
uphill [ʌp'hɪl] adj cuesta arriba; (fig: task) penoso, difícil ▷ adv: **to go ~** ir cuesta arriba
upholstery [ʌp'həʊlstərɪ] n tapicería
upload ['ʌpləʊd] vt (Comput) subir
upmarket [ʌp'mɑːkɪt] adj (product) de categoría
upon [ə'pɔn] prep sobre
upper ['ʌpəʳ] adj superior, de arriba ▷ n (of shoe: also: ~s) pala; **upper-class** adj de clase alta
upright ['ʌpraɪt] adj vertical; (fig) honrado
uprising ['ʌpraɪzɪŋ] n sublevación f
uproar ['ʌprɔːʳ] n escándalo
upset n ['ʌpsɛt] (to plan etc) revés m, contratiempo; (Med) trastorno ▷ vt [ʌp'sɛt] (irreg: like **set**: glass etc) volcar; (plan) alterar; (person) molestar ▷ adj [ʌp'sɛt] preocupado, perturbado; (stomach) revuelto
upside-down ['ʌpsaɪd'daʊn] adv al revés; **to turn a place ~** (fig) revolverlo todo
upstairs [ʌp'stɛəz] adv arriba ▷ adj (room) de arriba ▷ n el piso superior
up-to-date ['ʌptə'deɪt] adj actual, moderno
uptown ['ʌptaʊn] adv (US) hacia las afueras ▷ adj exterior, de las afueras
upward(s) ['ʌpwəd(z)] adv hacia arriba; (more than): **~ of** más de
uranium [juə'reɪnɪəm] n uranio
Uranus [juə'reɪnəs] n Urano
urban ['əːbən] adj urbano
urge [əːdʒ] n (desire) deseo ▷ vt: **to ~ sb to do sth** animar a algn a hacer algo

urgency ['əːdʒənsɪ] n urgencia
urgent ['əːdʒənt] adj urgente
urinal ['juərɪnl] n (building) urinario; (vessel) orinal m
urinate ['juərɪneɪt] vi orinar
urine ['juərɪn] n orina
US n abbr (= United States) EE.UU.
us [ʌs] pron sg; (after prep) nosotros/as; see also **me**
USA n abbr = **United States of America**; (Mil) = **United States Army**
USB abbr (= universal serial bus) USB m; **USB stick** n memoria USB, llave f de memoria
use n [juːs] uso, empleo; (usefulness) utilidad f ▷ vt [juːz] usar, emplear; **in ~** en uso; **out of ~** en desuso; **to be of ~** servir; **it's no ~** (pointless) es inútil; (not useful) no sirve; **to be ~d to** estar acostumbrado a (SP), acostumbrar; **she ~d to do it** (ella) solía or acostumbraba hacerlo; **use up** vt (food) consumir; (money) gastar; **used** [juːzd] adj (car) usado; **useful** adj útil; **useless** adj (unusable) inservible; **user** n usuario/a; **user-friendly** adj (Comput) fácil de utilizar
usual ['juːʒuəl] adj normal, corriente; **as ~** como de costumbre; **usually** adv normalmente
ute [juːt] n abbr (AUST, NZ inf: = utility truck) camioneta
utensil [juː'tɛnsl] n utensilio; **kitchen ~s** batería de cocina
utility [juː'tɪlɪtɪ] n utilidad f; (public utility) (empresa de) servicio público
utilize ['juːtɪlaɪz] vt utilizar
utmost ['ʌtməʊst] adj mayor ▷ n: **to do one's ~** hacer todo lo posible
utter ['ʌtəʳ] adj total, completo ▷ vt pronunciar, proferir; **utterly** adv completamente, totalmente
U-turn ['juː'təːn] n cambio de sentido

u

v. *abbr* (= *verse*) vers.°; (= *see*) V, vid., vide; (= *versus*) vs.; = **volt**

vacancy ['veɪkənsɪ] *n* (*job*) vacante *f*; (*room*) cuarto libro; **"no vacancies"** "completo"

vacant ['veɪkənt] *adj* desocupado, libre; (*expression*) distraído

vacate [və'keɪt] *vt* (*house*) desocupar; (*job*) dejar (vacante)

vacation [və'keɪʃən] *n* vacaciones *fpl*; **vacationer** [və'keɪʃənəʳ], **vacationist** [və'keɪʃənɪst] *n* (*US*) turista *mf*

vaccination [væksɪ'neɪʃən] *n* vacunación *f*

vaccine ['væksiːn] *n* vacuna *f*

vacuum ['vækjum] *n* vacío; **vacuum cleaner** *n* aspiradora *f*

vagina [və'dʒaɪnə] *n* vagina *f*

vague [veɪg] *adj* vago; (*memory*) borroso; (*ambiguous*) impreciso; (*person: absent-minded*) distraído; (: *evasive*): **to be ~** no decir las cosas claramente

vain [veɪn] *adj* (*conceited*) presumido; (*useless*) vano, inútil; **in ~** en vano

Valentine's Day *n* día de los enamorados (*el 14 de febrero, día de San Valentín*)

valid ['vælɪd] *adj* válido; (*ticket*) valedero; (*law*) vigente

valley ['vælɪ] *n* valle *m*

valuable ['væljuəbl] *adj* (*jewel*) de valor; (*time*) valioso; **valuables** *npl* objetos *mpl* de valor

value ['væljuː] *n* valor *m*; (*importance*) importancia ▷ *vt* (*fix price of*) tasar, valorar; (*esteem*) apreciar; **values** *npl* (*moral*) valores *mpl* morales

valve [vælv] *n* válvula

vampire ['væmpaɪəʳ] *n* vampiro

van [væn] *n* (*Aut*) furgoneta, camioneta (*LAM*)

vandal ['vændl] *n* vándalo/a; **vandalism** *n* vandalismo; **vandalize** *vt* dañar, destruir

vanilla [və'nɪlə] *n* vainilla

vanish ['vænɪʃ] *vi* desaparecer

vanity ['vænɪtɪ] *n* vanidad *f*

vapour, (*US*) **vapor** ['veɪpəʳ] *n* vapor *m*; (*on breath, window*) vaho

variable ['vɛərɪəbl] *adj* variable

variant ['vɛərɪənt] *n* variante *f*

variation [vɛərɪ'eɪʃən] *n* variación *f*

varied ['vɛərɪd] *adj* variado

variety [və'raɪətɪ] *n* variedad *f*, diversidad *f*

various ['vɛərɪəs] *adj* varios/as, diversos/as

varnish ['vɑːnɪʃ] *n* barniz *m*; (*also*: **nail ~**) esmalte *m* ▷ *vt* barnizar; (*nails*) pintar (con esmalte)

vary ['vɛərɪ] *vt* variar; (*change*) cambiar ▷ *vi* variar

vase [vɑːz] *n* florero, jarrón *m*

⬛ Be careful not to translate *vase* by the Spanish word *vaso*.

Vaseline® ['væsɪliːn] *n* vaselina®

vast [vɑːst] *adj* enorme

VAT [væt] *n abbr* (*BRIT*: = *value added tax*) IVA *m*

vault [vɔːlt] n (of roof) bóveda; (tomb) panteón m; (in bank) cámara acorazada ▷ vt (also: **~ over**) saltar (por encima de)

VCR n abbr = **video cassette recorder**

VDU n abbr (= visual display unit) UPV f

veal [viːl] n ternera

veer [vɪər] vi (vehicle) virar; (wind) girar

vegan ['viːgən] n vegetariano/a estricto/a

vegetable ['vɛdʒtəbl] n (Bot) vegetal m; (edible plant) legumbre f, hortaliza ▷ adj vegetal

vegetarian [vɛdʒɪ'tɛərɪən] adj, n vegetariano/a

vegetation [vɛdʒɪ'teɪʃən] n vegetación f

vehicle ['viːɪkl] n vehículo; (fig) medio

veil [veɪl] n velo ▷ vt velar

vein [veɪn] n vena; (of ore etc) veta

Velcro® ['vɛlkrəu] n velcro®m

velvet ['vɛlvɪt] n terciopelo

vending machine ['vɛndɪŋ-] n máquina expendedora, expendedor m

vendor ['vɛndər] n vendedor(a) m/f; **street ~** vendedor(a) m/f callejero/a

vengeance ['vɛndʒəns] n venganza; **with a ~** (fig) con creces

venison ['vɛnɪsn] n carne f de venado

venom ['vɛnəm] n veneno

vent [vɛnt] n (opening) abertura; (air-hole) respiradero; (in wall) rejilla (de ventilación) ▷ vt (fig: feelings) desahogar

ventilation [vɛntɪ'leɪʃən] n ventilación f

venture ['vɛntʃər] n empresa ▷ vt (opinion) ofrecer ▷ vi arriesgarse, lanzarse; **a business ~** una empresa comercial

venue ['vɛnjuː] n (meeting place) lugar m de reunión

Venus ['viːnəs] n Venus m

verb [vəːb] n verbo; **verbal** adj verbal

verdict ['vəːdɪkt] n veredicto, fallo; (fig) opinión f, juicio

verge [vəːdʒ] n (BRIT) borde m; **to be on the ~ of doing sth** estar a punto de hacer algo

verify ['vɛrɪfaɪ] vt comprobar, verificar

versatile ['vəːsətaɪl] adj (person) polifacético; (machine, tool etc) versátil

verse [vəːs] n poesía; (stanza) estrofa; (in bible) versículo

version ['vəːʃən] n versión f

versus ['vəːsəs] prep contra

vertical ['vəːtɪkl] adj vertical

very ['vɛrɪ] adv muy ▷ adj: **the ~ book which** el mismo libro que; **the ~ last** el último (de todos); **at the ~ least** al menos; **~ much** muchísimo

vessel ['vɛsl] n (ship) barco; (container) vasija

vest [vɛst] n (BRIT) camiseta; (US: waistcoat) chaleco

vet [vɛt] n abbr = **veterinary surgeon** ▷ vt revisar; **to ~ sb for a job** someter a investigación a algn para un trabajo

veteran ['vɛtərn] n veterano/a

veterinary surgeon n (BRIT) veterinario/a

veto ['viːtəu] n veto ▷ vt prohibir

via ['vaɪə] prep por, por vía de

viable ['vaɪəbl] adj viable

vibrate [vaɪ'breɪt] vi vibrar

vibration [vaɪ'breɪʃən] n vibración f

vicar ['vɪkər] n párroco

vice [vaɪs] n (evil) vicio; (Tech) torno de banco; **vice-chairman** n vicepresidente m

vice versa ['vaɪsɪ'vəːsə] adv viceversa

vicinity [vɪ'sɪnɪtɪ] n: **in the ~ (of)** cercano/a

vicious ['vɪʃəs] adj (remark) malicioso; (blow) brutal; (dog, horse) resabido; **a ~ circle** un círculo vicioso

victim ['vɪktɪm] n víctima

victor ['vɪktər] n vencedor(a) m/f

Victorian [vɪk'tɔːrɪən] adj victoriano/a

victorious [vɪk'tɔːrɪəs] adj vencedor(a)

victory ['vɪktərɪ] n victoria

video ['vɪdɪəu] n vídeo ▷ vt grabar (en vídeo); **video call** n videollamada; **video camera** n videocámara, cámara de vídeo; **video cassette recorder** n = **video recorder**; **video**

game n videojuego; **videophone** n videoteléfono, videófono; **video recorder** n vídeo; **video tape** n cinta de vídeo

vie [vaɪ] vi: **to ~ with** competir con

Vienna [vɪˈɛnə] n Viena

Vietnam [vjɛtˈnæm] n Vietnam m; **Vietnamese** [vjɛtnəˈmiːz] adj vietnamita ▷ n (pl inv) vietnamita mf

view [vjuː] n vista; (opinion) opinión f, criterio ▷ vt (look at) mirar; **on ~** (in museum etc) expuesto; **in full ~ of sb** a la vista de algn; **in ~ of the fact that** en vista de que; **viewer** n (TV) telespectador(a) m/f; **viewpoint** n punto de vista

vigilant [ˈvɪdʒɪlənt] adj vigilante

vigorous [ˈvɪɡərəs] adj enérgico, vigoroso

vile [vaɪl] adj (action) vil, infame; (smell) repugnante; (temper) endemoniado

villa [ˈvɪlə] n (country house) casa de campo; (suburban house) chalet m

village [ˈvɪlɪdʒ] n aldea; **villager** n aldeano/a

villain [ˈvɪlən] n (scoundrel) malvado/a; (criminal) maleante mf

vinaigrette [vɪneɪˈɡrɛt] n vinagreta

vine [vaɪn] n vid f

vinegar [ˈvɪnɪɡəʳ] n vinagre m

vineyard [ˈvɪnjɑːd] n viña, viñedo

vintage [ˈvɪntɪdʒ] n (year) vendimia, cosecha

vinyl [ˈvaɪnl] n vinilo

viola [vɪˈəʊlə] n (Mus) viola

violate [ˈvaɪəleɪt] vt violar

violation [vaɪəˈleɪʃən] n violación f; **in ~ of sth** en violación de algo

violence [ˈvaɪələns] n violencia

violent [ˈvaɪələnt] adj violento; (pain) intenso

violet [ˈvaɪələt] adj violado, violeta inv ▷ n (plant) violeta

violin [vaɪəˈlɪn] n violín m

VIP n abbr (= very important person) VIP m

viral adj (Med) vírico; (Comput) viral

virgin [ˈvəːdʒɪn] n virgen mf

Virgo [ˈvəːɡəʊ] n Virgo

virtual [ˈvəːtjuəl] adj virtual; **virtually** adv prácticamente, virtualmente; **virtual reality** n (Comput) realidad f virtual

virtue [ˈvəːtjuː] n virtud f; **by ~ of** en virtud de

virus [ˈvaɪərəs] n virus m inv

visa [ˈviːzə] n visado, visa (LAM)

vise [vaɪs] n (US Tech); = **vice**

visibility [vɪzɪˈbɪlɪtɪ] n visibilidad f

visible [ˈvɪzəbl] adj visible

vision [ˈvɪʒən] n (sight) vista; (foresight, in dream) visión f

visit [ˈvɪzɪt] n visita ▷ vt (person) visitar, hacer una visita a; (place) ir a, (ir a) conocer; **visiting hours** npl (in hospital etc) horas fpl de visita; **visitor** n visitante mf; (to one's house) visita; (tourist) turista mf; **visitor centre, (US) visitor center** n centro m de información

visual [ˈvɪzjuəl] adj visual; **visualize** vt imaginarse

vital [ˈvaɪtl] adj (essential) esencial, imprescindible; (organ) vital

vitality [vaɪˈtælɪtɪ] n energía, vitalidad f

vitamin [ˈvɪtəmɪn] n vitamina

vivid [ˈvɪvɪd] adj (account) gráfico; (light) intenso; (imagination) vivo

V-neck [ˈviːnɛk] n cuello de pico

vocabulary [vəʊˈkæbjʊlərɪ] n vocabulario

vocal [ˈvəʊkl] adj vocal; (articulate) elocuente

vocational [vəʊˈkeɪʃənl] adj profesional

vodka [ˈvɒdkə] n vodka m

vogue [vəʊɡ] n: **to be in ~** estar de moda or en boga

voice [vɔɪs] n voz f; **voice mail** n fonobuzón m

void [vɔɪd] n vacío; (hole) hueco ▷ adj (invalid) nulo, inválido; (empty): **~ of** carente or desprovisto de

volatile [ˈvɒlətaɪl] adj (situation) inestable; (person) voluble; (liquid) volátil

volcano [vɔl'keɪnəu] (pl **volcanoes**)
n volcán m
volleyball ['vɔlɪbɔːl] n voleibol m
volt [vəult] n voltio; **voltage** n
voltaje m
volume ['vɔljuːm] n (of tank) volumen
m; (book) tomo
voluntarily ['vɔləntrɪlɪ] adv
libremente, voluntariamente
voluntary ['vɔləntərɪ] adj voluntario
volunteer [vɔlən'tɪər] n voluntario/a
▷ vt (information) ofrecer ▷ vi ofrecerse
(de voluntario); **to ~ to do** ofrecerse
a hacer
vomit ['vɔmɪt] n vómito ▷ vt, vi
vomitar
vote [vəut] n voto; (votes cast)
votación f; (right to vote) derecho
a votar; (franchise) sufragio ▷ vt
(chairman) elegir ▷ vi votar, ir a votar;
~ of thanks voto de gracias; **voter** n
votante mf; **voting** n votación f
voucher ['vautʃər] n (for meal, petrol)
vale m
vow [vau] n voto ▷ vi hacer voto ▷ vt:
to ~ to do/that jurar hacer/que
vowel ['vauəl] n vocal f
voyage ['vɔɪɪdʒ] n viaje m
vulgar ['vʌlgər] adj (rude) ordinario,
grosero; (in bad taste) de mal gusto
vulnerable ['vʌlnərəbl] adj
vulnerable
vulture ['vʌltʃər] n buitre m

waddle ['wɔdl] vi andar como un
pato
wade [weɪd] vi (fig: a book) leer con
dificultad; **to ~ through the water**
caminar por el agua
wafer ['weɪfər] n (biscuit) barquillo
waffle ['wɔfl] n (Culin) gofre m ▷ vi
meter el rollo
wag [wæg] vt menear, agitar ▷ vi
moverse, menearse
wage [weɪdʒ] n (also: **~s**) sueldo,
salario ▷ vt: **to ~ war** hacer la guerra
wag(g)on ['wægən] n (horse-drawn)
carro; (BRIT Rail) vagón m
wail [weɪl] n gemido ▷ vi gemir
waist [weɪst] n cintura, talle m;
waistcoat n (BRIT) chaleco
wait [weɪt] n (interval) pausa ▷ vi
esperar; **to lie in ~ for** acechar a; **I
can't ~ to** (fig) estoy deseando; **to ~
for** esperar (a); **wait on** vt fus servir
a; **waiter** n camarero; **waiting list**
n lista de espera; **waiting room** n

sala de espera; **waitress** ['weɪtrɪs]
n camarera

waive [weɪv] vt suspender

wake [weɪk] (pt **woke** or **waked**,
pp **woken** or **waked**) vt (also: **~ up**)
despertar ▷ vi (also: **~ up**) despertarse
▷ n (for dead person) velatorio; (Naut)
estela

Wales [weɪlz] n País m de Gales

walk [wɔːk] n (stroll) paseo; (hike)
excursión f a pie, caminata; (gait)
paso, andar m; (in park etc) paseo ▷ vi
andar, caminar; (for pleasure, exercise)
pasearse ▷ vt (distance) recorrer a
pie, andar; (dog) (sacar a) pasear; **10
minutes' ~ from here** a 10 minutos
de aquí andando; **people from all ~s
of life** gente de todas las esferas; **walk
out** vi (go out) salir; (as protest) salirse;
(strike) declararse en huelga; **walker**
n (person) paseante mf, caminante
mf; **walkie-talkie** ['wɔːkɪ'tɔːkɪ] n
walkie-talkie m; **walking** n (el) andar;
walking shoes npl zapatos mpl
para andar; **walking stick** n bastón
m; **Walkman®** n walkman® m;
walkway n paseo

wall [wɔːl] n pared f; (exterior) muro;
(city wall etc) muralla

wallet ['wɒlɪt] n cartera

wallpaper ['wɔːlpeɪpər] n papel m
pintado ▷ vt empapelar

walnut ['wɔːlnʌt] n nuez f; (tree)
nogal m

walrus ['wɔːlrəs] (pl **walrus** or
walruses) n morsa

waltz [wɔːlts] n vals m ▷ vi bailar
el vals

wand [wɒnd] n (also: **magic ~**) varita
(mágica)

wander ['wɒndər] vi (person) vagar,
deambular; (thoughts) divagar ▷ vt
recorrer, vagar por

want [wɒnt] vt querer, desear; (need)
necesitar ▷ n: **for ~ of** por falta de;
wanted adj (criminal) buscado;
"wanted" (in advertisements) "se
busca"

war [wɔːr] n guerra; **to make ~** hacer
la guerra

ward [wɔːd] n (in hospital) sala; (Pol)
distrito electoral; (Law: child: also: **~ of
court**) pupilo/a

warden ['wɔːdn] n (BRIT: of institution)
director(a) m/f; (of park, game reserve)
guardián/ana m/f; (BRIT: also:
traffic ~) guardia mf

wardrobe ['wɔːdrəub] n armario,
ropero

warehouse ['wɛəhaus] n almacén
m, depósito

warfare ['wɔːfɛər] n guerra

warhead ['wɔːhɛd] n cabeza armada

warm [wɔːm] adj caliente; (thanks,
congratulations, apologies) efusivo;
(clothes etc) que abriga; (welcome,
day) caluroso; **it's ~** hace calor;
I'm ~ tengo calor; **warm up** vi
(room) calentarse; (person) entrar en
calor; (athlete) hacer ejercicios de
calentamiento ▷ vt calentar; **warmly**
adv afectuosamente; **warmth** n
calor m

warn [wɔːn] vt avisar, advertir;
warning n aviso, advertencia;
warning light n luz f de advertencia

warrant ['wɔrnt] n (Law: to arrest)
orden f de detención; (: to search)
mandamiento de registro

warranty ['wɔrənti] n garantía

warrior ['wɔrɪər] n guerrero/a

Warsaw ['wɔːsɔː] n Varsovia

warship ['wɔːʃɪp] n buque m or barco
de guerra

wart [wɔːt] n verruga

wartime ['wɔːtaɪm] n: **in ~** en
tiempos de guerra, en la guerra

wary ['wɛərɪ] adj cauteloso

was [wɒz] pt of **be**

wash [wɒʃ] vt lavar; (sweep, carry: sea
etc) llevar ▷ vi lavarse ▷ n (clothes etc)
lavado; (of ship) estela; **to have a ~**
lavarse; **wash up** vi (BRIT) fregar los
platos; (US) lavarse; **washbasin** n
lavabo; **washcloth** n (US) manopla;
washer n (Tech) arandela; **washing**

n (*dirty*) ropa sucia; (*clean*) colada;
washing line *n* cuerda de (colgar) la
ropa; **washing machine** *n* lavadora;
washing powder *n* (BRIT) detergente
m (en polvo)
Washington ['wɔʃɪŋtən] *n*
Washington *m*
wash: washing-up *n* fregado; (*dishes*)
platos *mpl* (para fregar); **washing-up
liquid** *n* lavavajillas *m inv*; **washroom**
n servicios *mpl*
wasn't ['wɔznt] = **was not**
wasp [wɔsp] *n* avispa
waste [weɪst] *n* derroche *m*,
despilfarro; (*of time*) pérdida;
(*food*) sobras *fpl*; (*rubbish*) basura,
desperdicios *mpl* ▷ *adj* (*material*)
de desecho; (*left over*) sobrante;
(*land, ground*) baldío ▷ *vt* malgastar,
derrochar; (*time*) perder; (*opportunity*)
desperdiciar; **waste ground** *n* (BRIT)
terreno baldío; **wastepaper basket**
n papelera
watch [wɔtʃ] *n* reloj *m*; (*vigilance*)
vigilancia; (*Mil: guard*) centinela
m; (*Naut: spell of duty*) guardia ▷ *vt*
(*look at*) mirar, observar; (: *match,
programme*) ver; (*spy on, guard*) vigilar;
(*be careful of*) cuidar, tener cuidado
de ▷ *vi* ver, mirar; (*keep guard*) montar
guardia; **watch out** *vi* cuidarse, tener
cuidado; **watchdog** *n* perro guardián;
(*fig*) organismo de control; **watch
strap** *n* pulsera (de reloj)
water ['wɔːtər] *n* agua ▷ *vt* (*plant*)
regar ▷ *vi* (*eyes*) llorar; **his mouth
~ed** se le hizo la boca agua; **water
down** *vt* (*milk etc*) aguar; (*fig: story*)
dulcificar, diluir; **watercolour,** (US)
watercolor *n* acuarela; **watercress**
n berro; **waterfall** *n* cascada, salto
de agua; **watering can** *n* regadera;
watermelon *n* sandía; **waterproof**
adj impermeable; **water-skiing** *n*
esquí *m* acuático
watt [wɔt] *n* vatio
wave [weɪv] *n* ola; (*of hand*) señal *f* con
la mano; (*Radio*) onda; (*in hair*) onda;

(*fig*) oleada ▷ *vi* agitar la mano; (*flag*)
ondear ▷ *vt* (*handkerchief, gun*) agitar;
wavelength *n* longitud *f* de onda
waver ['weɪvər] *vi* (*faith*) flaquear
wavy ['weɪvɪ] *adj* ondulado
wax [wæks] *n* cera ▷ *vt* encerar ▷ *vi*
(*moon*) crecer
way [weɪ] *n* camino; (*distance*)
trayecto, recorrido; (*direction*)
dirección *f*, sentido; (*manner*) modo,
manera; (*habit*) costumbre *f*; **which
~? — this** ~ ¿por dónde? *or* ¿en qué
dirección? — por aquí; **on the ~**
(*en route*) en (el) camino; **to be on
one's ~** estar en camino; **to be
in the ~** bloquear el camino; (*fig*)
estorbar; **to go out of one's ~ to
do sth** desvivirse por hacer algo; **to
lose one's ~** extraviarse; **in a ~** en
cierto modo *or* sentido; **by the ~** a
propósito; **"~ in"** (BRIT) "entrada";
"~ out" (BRIT) "salida"; **the ~ back**
el camino de vuelta; **"give ~"** (BRIT
Aut) "ceda el paso"; **no ~!** (*inf*) ¡ni
pensarlo!
WC ['dʌblju'siː] *n abbr* (BRIT: = *water
closet*) wáter *m*
we [wiː] *pron pl* nosotros/as
weak [wiːk] *adj* débil, flojo; (*tea, coffee*)
flojo, aguado; **weaken** *vi* debilitarse;
(*give way*) ceder ▷ *vt* debilitar;
weakness *n* debilidad *f*; (*fault*) punto
débil; **to have a weakness for** tener
debilidad por
wealth [wɛlθ] *n* riqueza; (*of details*)
abundancia; **wealthy** *adj* rico
weapon ['wɛpən] *n* arma; **~s of mass
destruction** armas de destrucción
masiva
wear [wɛər] (*pt* **wore**, *pp* **worn**) *n*
(*use*) uso; (*deterioration through use*)
desgaste *m* ▷ *vt* (*clothes, beard*) llevar;
(*shoes*) calzar; (*damage: through use*)
gastar, usar ▷ *vi* (*last*) durar; (*rub
through etc*) desgastarse; **evening ~**
(*man's*) traje *m* de etiqueta; (*woman's*)
traje *m* de noche; **wear off** *vi* (*pain,
excitement etc*) pasar, desaparecer;

wear out vt desgastar; (person, strength) agotar

weary ['wɪərɪ] adj cansado; (dispirited) abatido ▷ vi: **to ~ of** cansarse de

weasel ['wiːzl] n (Zool) comadreja

weather ['wɛðər] n tiempo ▷ vt (storm, crisis) hacer frente a; **under the ~** (fig: ill) mal, pachucho; **weather forecast** n boletín m meteorológico

weave (pt **wove**, pp **woven**) [wiːv, wəʊv, 'wəʊvn] vt (cloth) tejer; (fig) entretejer

web [wɛb] n (of spider) telaraña; (on foot) membrana; (network) red f; **the W~** la Red; **web address** n dirección f de página web; **webcam** n webcam f; **web page** n página web; **website** n sitio web

wed [wɛd] (pt, pp **wedded**) vt casar ▷ vi casarse

Wed. abbr (= Wednesday) miérc.

we'd [wiːd] = **we had; we would**

wedding ['wɛdɪŋ] n boda, casamiento; **wedding anniversary** n aniversario de boda; **silver/golden wedding anniversary** bodas fpl de plata/de oro; **wedding day** n día m de la boda; **wedding dress** n traje m de novia; **wedding ring** n alianza

wedge [wɛdʒ] n (of wood etc) cuña; (of cake) trozo ▷ vt acuñar; (push) apretar

Wednesday ['wɛnzdɪ] n miércoles m inv

wee [wiː] adj (SCOTTISH) pequeñito

weed [wiːd] n mala hierba, maleza ▷ vt escardar, desherbar; **weedkiller** n herbicida m

week [wiːk] n semana; **a ~ today** de hoy en ocho días; **a ~ on Tuesday** del martes en una semana; **weekday** n día m laborable; **weekend** n fin m de semana; **weekly** adv semanalmente, cada semana ▷ adj semanal ▷ n semanario

weep (pt, pp **wept**) [wiːp, wɛpt] vi, vt llorar

weigh [weɪ] vt, vi pesar; **to ~ anchor** levar anclas; **weigh up** vt sopesar

weight [weɪt] n peso; (on scale) pesa; **to lose/put on ~** adelgazar/engordar; **weightlifting** n levantamiento de pesas

weir [wɪər] n presa

weird [wɪəd] adj raro, extraño

welcome ['wɛlkəm] adj bienvenido ▷ n bienvenida ▷ vt dar la bienvenida a; (be glad of) alegrarse de; **thank you — you're ~** gracias — de nada

weld [wɛld] n soldadura ▷ vt soldar

welfare ['wɛlfɛər] n bienestar m; (social aid) asistencia social; **welfare state** n estado del bienestar

well [wɛl] n pozo ▷ adv bien ▷ adj: **to be ~** estar bien (de salud) ▷ excl ¡vaya!, ¡bueno!; **as ~** también; **as ~ as** además de; **~ done!** ¡bien hecho!; **get ~ soon!** ¡que te mejores pronto!; **to do ~** (business) ir bien; **I did ~ in my exams** me han salido bien los exámenes

we'll [wiːl] = **we will; we shall**

well: well-behaved adj: **to be well-behaved** portarse bien; **well-built** adj (person) fornido; **well-dressed** adj bien vestido

wellies ['welɪz] npl (BRIT inf) botas de goma

well: well-known adj (person) conocido; **well-off** adj acomodado; **well-paid** [wel'peɪd] adj bien pagado, bien retribuido

Welsh [wɛlʃ] adj galés/esa ▷ n (Ling) galés m; **Welshman** n galés m; **Welshwoman** n galesa

went [wɛnt] pt of **go**

wept [wɛpt] pt, pp of **weep**

were [wəːr] pt of **be**

we're [wɪər] = **we are**

weren't [wəːnt] = **were not**

west [wɛst] n oeste m ▷ adj occidental, del oeste ▷ adv al or hacia el oeste; **the W~** Occidente m; **westbound** ['wɛstbaʊnd] adj (traffic, carriageway) con rumbo al oeste; **western** adj occidental ▷ n (Cine) película del oeste; **West Indian** adj, n antillano/a

wet [wɛt] adj (damp) húmedo; (wet through) mojado; (rainy) lluvioso; **to get ~** mojarse; **"~ paint"** "recién pintado"; **wetsuit** n traje m de buzo

we've [wiːv] = **we have**

whack [wæk] vt dar un buen golpe a

whale [weɪl] n (Zool) ballena

wharf (pl **wharves**) [wɔːf, wɔːvz] n muelle m

○ **KEYWORD**

what [wɔt] adj **1** (in direct/indirect questions) qué; **what size is he?** ¿qué talla usa?; **what colour/shape is it?** ¿de qué color/forma es?
2 (in exclamations): **what a mess!** ¡qué desastre!; **what a fool I am!** ¡qué tonto soy!
▸ pron **1** (interrogative) qué; **what are you doing?** ¿qué haces or estás haciendo?; **what is happening?** ¿qué pasa or está pasando?; **what is it called?** ¿cómo se llama?; **what about me?** ¿y yo qué?; **what about doing …?** ¿qué tal si hacemos …?
2 (relative) lo que; **I saw what you did/was on the table** vi lo que hiciste/había en la mesa
▸ excl (disbelieving) ¡cómo!; **what, no coffee!** ¡que no hay café!

whatever [wɔt'ɛvəʳ] adj: **~ book you choose** cualquier libro que elijas
▸ pron: **do ~ is necessary** haga lo que sea necesario; **no reason ~** ninguna razón en absoluto; **nothing ~** nada en absoluto; **~ it costs** cueste lo que cueste

whatsoever [wɔtsəu'ɛvəʳ] adj see **whatever**

wheat [wiːt] n trigo

wheel [wiːl] n rueda; (Aut: also: **steering ~**) volante m; (Naut) timón m ▸ vt (pram etc) empujar ▸ vi (also: **~ round**) dar la vuelta, girar; **wheelbarrow** n carretilla; **wheelchair** n silla de ruedas; **wheel clamp** n (Aut) cepo

wheeze [wiːz] vi resollar

○ **KEYWORD**

when [wɛn] adv cuando; **when did it happen?** ¿cuándo ocurrió?; **I know when it happened** sé cuándo ocurrió
▸ conj **1** (at, during, after the time that) cuando; **be careful when you cross the road** ten cuidado al cruzar la calle; **that was when I needed you** entonces era cuando te necesitaba
2 (on, at which): **on the day when I met him** el día en qué le conocí
3 (whereas) cuando

whenever [wɛn'ɛvəʳ] conj cuando; (every time) cada vez que

where [wɛəʳ] adv dónde ▸ conj donde; **this is ~** aquí es donde; **whereabouts** adv dónde ▸ n: **nobody knows his whereabouts** nadie conoce su paradero; **whereas** conj mientras; **whereby** adv mediante el/la cual etc, por lo/la cual etc; **wherever** [wɛər'ɛvəʳ] adv dondequiera que; (interrogative) dónde

whether ['wɛðəʳ] conj si; **I don't know ~ to accept or not** no sé si aceptar o no; **~ you go or not** vayas o no vayas

○ **KEYWORD**

which [wɪtʃ] adj **1** (interrogative, direct, indirect) qué; **which picture(s) do you want?** ¿qué cuadro(s) quieres?; **which one?** ¿cuál?
2: **in which case** en cuyo caso; **we got there at eight pm, by which time the cinema was full** llegamos allí a las ocho, cuando el cine estaba lleno
▸ pron **1** (interrogative) cuál; **I don't mind which** el/la que sea
2 (relative, replacing noun) que; (: replacing clause) lo que; (: after preposition) (el/la) que, el/la cual; **the**

apple which you ate/which is on the table la manzana que comiste/que está en la mesa; **the chair on which you are sitting** la silla en la que estás sentado; **he didn't believe it, which upset me** no se lo creyó, lo cual or lo que me disgustó

whichever [wɪtʃˈɛvəʳ] *adj*: **take ~ book you prefer** coja el libro que prefiera; **~ book you take** cualquier libro que coja

while [waɪl] *n* rato, momento ▷ *conj* mientras; (*although*) aunque; **for a ~** durante algún tiempo

whilst [waɪlst] *conj* = **while**

whim [wɪm] *n* capricho

whine [waɪn] *n* (*of pain*) gemido; (*of engine*) zumbido ▷ *vi* gemir; zumbar; (*fig*: *complain*) gimotear

whip [wɪp] *n* látigo; (*BRIT Pol*) diputado encargado de la disciplina del partido en el parlamento ▷ *vt* azotar; (*Culin*) batir; **whipped cream** *n* nata montada

whirl [wəːl] *vt* hacer girar, dar vueltas a ▷ *vi* girar, dar vueltas; (*leaves, dust, water etc*) arremolinarse

whisk [wɪsk] *n* (*BRIT Culin*) batidor *m* ▷ *vt* (*BRIT Culin*) batir; **to ~ sb away** or **off** llevarse volando a algn

whiskers [wɪskəz] *npl* (*of animal*) bigotes *mpl*; (*of man*) patillas *fpl*

whisky, (*US, IRELAND*) **whiskey** [wɪskɪ] *n* whisky *m*

whisper [wɪspəʳ] *n* susurro ▷ *vi* susurrar ▷ *vt* susurrar

whistle [wɪsl] *n* (*sound*) silbido; (*object*) silbato ▷ *vi* silbar

white [waɪt] *adj* blanco; (*pale*) pálido ▷ *n* blanco; (*of egg*) clara; **whiteboard** *n* pizarra blanca; **interactive whiteboard** pizarra interactiva; **White House** *n* (*US*) Casa Blanca; **whitewash** *n* (*paint*) cal *f*, jalbegue *m* ▷ *vt* blanquear

whiting [waɪtɪŋ] *n* (*pl inv*: *fish*) pescadilla

Whitsun [wɪtsn] *n* (*BRIT*) Pentecostés *m*

whittle [wɪtl] *vt*: **to ~ away, ~ down** ir reduciendo

whizz [wɪz] *vi*: **to ~ past** or **by** pasar a toda velocidad

 KEYWORD

who [huː] *pron* **1** (*interrogative*) quién; **who is it?, who's there?** ¿quién es?; **who are you looking for?** ¿a quién buscas?; **I told her who I was** le dije quién era yo
2 (*relative*) que; **the man/woman who spoke to me** el hombre/la mujer que habló conmigo; **those who can swim** los que saben or sepan nadar

whoever [huːˈɛvəʳ] *pron*: **~ finds it** cualquiera or quienquiera que lo encuentre; **ask ~ you like** pregunta a quien quieras; **~ he marries** se case con quien se case

whole [həʊl] *adj* (*complete*) todo, entero; (*not broken*) intacto ▷ *n* (*total*) total *m*; (*sum*) conjunto; **the ~ of the town** toda la ciudad, la ciudad entera; **on the ~, as a ~** en general; **wholefood(s)** *n*(*pl*) alimento(s) *m*(*pl*) integral(es); **wholeheartedly** [həʊlˈhɑːtɪdlɪ] *adv* con entusiasmo; **wholemeal** *adj* (*BRIT*: *flour, bread*) integral; **wholesale** *n* venta al por mayor ▷ *adj* al por mayor; (*destruction*) sistemático; **wholewheat** *adj* = **wholemeal**; **wholly** *adv* totalmente, enteramente

KEYWORD

whom [huːm] *pron* **1** (*interrogative*): **whom did you see?** ¿a quién viste?; **to whom did you give it?** ¿a quién se lo diste?; **tell me from whom you received it** dígame de quién lo recibiste
2 (*relative*) que; **to whom** a quien(es);

of whom de quien(es), del/de la que; **the man whom I saw** el hombre que vi; **the lady about whom I was talking** la señora de (la) que hablaba; **the lady with whom I was talking** la señora con quien or (la) que hablaba

whore [hɔːʳ] n (inf, pej) puta

KEYWORD

whose [huːz] adj **1** (possessive, interrogative); **whose book is this?, whose is this book?** ¿de quién es este libro?; **whose pencil have you taken?** ¿de quién es el lápiz que has cogido?; **whose daughter are you?** ¿de quién eres hija?
2 (possessive, relative) cuyo/a, cuyos/as m/f pl; **the man whose son they rescued** el hombre cuyo hijo rescataron; **those whose passports I have** aquellas personas cuyos pasaportes tengo; **the woman whose car was stolen** la mujer a quien le robaron el coche
▶ pron de quién; **whose is this?** ¿de quién es esto?; **I know whose it is** sé de quién es

KEYWORD

why [waɪ] adv por qué; **why not?** ¿por qué no?; **why not do it now?** ¿por qué no lo haces or hacemos ahora?
▶ conj: **I wonder why he said that** me pregunto por qué dijo eso; **that's not why I'm here** no es por eso (por lo) que estoy aquí; **the reason why** la razón por la que
▶ excl (expressing surprise, shock, annoyance) ¡hombre!, ¡vaya!; (explaining): **why, it's you!** ¡hombre, eres tú!; **why, that's impossible** ¡pero si eso es imposible!

wicked [ˈwɪkɪd] adj malvado, cruel

wicket [ˈwɪkɪt] n (Cricket) palos mpl
wide [waɪd] adj ancho; (area, knowledge) vasto, grande; (choice) amplio ▷ adv: **to open ~** abrir de par en par; **to shoot ~** errar el tiro; **widely** adv (differing) muy; **it is widely believed that ...** existe la creencia generalizada de que ...; **widen** vt ensanchar; (experience) ampliar ▷ vi ensancharse; **wide open** adj abierto de par en par; **widespread** adj extendido, general
widow [ˈwɪdəu] n viuda; **widower** n viudo
width [wɪdθ] n anchura; (of cloth) ancho
wield [wiːld] vt (sword) blandir; (power) ejercer
wife (pl **wives**) [waɪf, waɪvz] n mujer f, esposa
Wi-Fi [ˈwaɪfaɪ] n abbr (= wireless fidelity) wi-fi m
wig [wɪg] n peluca
wild [waɪld] adj (animal) salvaje; (plant) silvestre; (idea) descabellado; (rough: sea) bravo; (: land) agreste; (: weather) muy revuelto; (inf: angry) furioso; **wilderness** [ˈwɪldənɪs] n desierto; **wildlife** n fauna; **wildly** adv (roughly) violentamente; (foolishly) locamente; (rashly) descabelladamente; (lash out) a diestro y siniestro; (guess) a lo loco; (happy) a más no poder

KEYWORD

will [wɪl] aux vb **1** (forming future tense): **I will finish it tomorrow** lo terminaré or voy a terminar mañana; **I will have finished it by tomorrow** lo habré terminado para mañana; **will you do it? — yes I will/no I won't** ¿lo harás? — sí/no
2 (in conjectures, predictions): **he will** or **he'll be there by now** ya habrá llegado, ya debe (de) haber llegado; **that will be the postman** será el cartero, debe ser el cartero

3 (*in commands, requests, offers*): **will you be quiet!** ¿quieres callarte?; **will you help me?** ¿quieres ayudarme?; **will you have a cup of tea?** ¿te apetece un té?; **I won't put up with it!** ¡no lo soporto!
▶ *vt*: **to will sb to do sth** desear que algn haga algo; **he willed himself to go on** con gran fuerza de voluntad, continuó
▶ *n* **1** voluntad *f*
2 (*Law*) testamento

willing ['wɪlɪŋ] *adj* (*with goodwill*) de buena voluntad; (*enthusiastic*) entusiasta; **he's ~ to do it** está dispuesto a hacerlo; **willingly** *adv* con mucho gusto
willow ['wɪləʊ] *n* sauce *m*
willpower ['wɪlpaʊəʳ] *n* fuerza de voluntad
wilt [wɪlt] *vi* marchitarse
win [wɪn] (*pt, pp* **won**) *n* victoria, triunfo ▶ *vt* ganar; (*obtain*) conseguir, lograr ▶ *vi* ganar; **win over** *vt* convencer a
wince [wɪns] *vi* encogerse
wind¹ [wɪnd] *n* viento; (*Med*) gases *mpl* ▶ *vt* (*take breath away from*) dejar sin aliento a; **into** *or* **against the ~** contra el viento; **to get ~ of sth** enterarse de algo; **to break ~** ventosear
wind² [waɪnd] (*pt, pp* **wound**) *vt* enrollar; (*wrap*) envolver; (*clock, toy*) dar cuerda a ▶ *vi* (*road, river*) serpentear; **wind down** *vt* (*car window*) bajar; (*fig: production, business*) disminuir; **wind up** *vt* (*clock*) dar cuerda a; (*debate*) concluir, terminar
windfall ['wɪndfɔːl] *n* golpe *m* de suerte
wind farm *n* parque *m* eólico
winding ['waɪndɪŋ] *adj* (*road*) tortuoso
windmill ['wɪndmɪl] *n* molino de viento

window ['wɪndəʊ] *n* ventana; (*in car, train*) ventana; (*in shop etc*) escaparate *m*, vidriera (*LAM*); **window box** *n* jardinera (de ventana); **window cleaner** *n* (*person*) limpiacristales *m inv*; **window pane** *n* cristal *m*; **window seat** *n* asiento junto a la ventana; **windowsill** *n* alféizar *m*, repisa
wind: windscreen, (*US*) **windshield** *n* parabrisas *m inv*; **windscreen wiper,** (*US*) **windshield wiper** *n* limpiaparabrisas *m inv*; **windsurfing** *n* windsurf *m*; **wind turbine** *n m* aerogenerador *m*; **windy** *adj* de mucho viento; **it's windy** hace viento
wine [waɪn] *n* vino; **wine bar** *n* bar especializado en vinos; **wine glass** *n* copa (de *or* para vino); **wine list** *n* lista de vinos; **wine tasting** *n* degustación *f* de vinos
wing [wɪŋ] *n* ala; (*Aut*) aleta; **wing mirror** *n* (espejo) retrovisor *m*
wink [wɪŋk] *n* guiño; (*blink*) pestañeo ▶ *vi* guiñar; (*blink*) pestañear
winner ['wɪnəʳ] *n* ganador(a) *m/f*
winning ['wɪnɪŋ] *adj* (*team*) ganador(a); (*goal*) decisivo; (*charming*) encantador(a)
winter ['wɪntəʳ] *n* invierno ▶ *vi* invernar; **winter sports** *npl* deportes *mpl* de invierno; **wintertime** *n* invierno
wipe [waɪp] *n*: **to give sth a ~** pasar un trapo sobre algo ▶ *vt* limpiar; (*tape*) borrar; **wipe out** *vt* (*debt*) liquidar; (*memory*) borrar; (*destroy*) destruir; **wipe up** *vt* limpiar
wire ['waɪəʳ] *n* alambre *m*; (*Elec*) cable *m* (eléctrico); (*Tel*) telegrama *m* ▶ *vt* (*house*) poner la instalación eléctrica en; (*also:* **~ up**) conectar
wireless ['waɪəlɪs] *adj* inalámbrico; **wireless technology** *n* tecnología inalámbrica
wiring ['waɪərɪŋ] *n* instalación *f* eléctrica

wisdom ['wɪzdəm] n sabiduría, saber m; (*good sense*) cordura; **wisdom tooth** n muela del juicio

wise [waɪz] adj sabio; (*sensible*) juicioso

wish [wɪʃ] n deseo ▷ vt querer; **best ~es** (*on birthday etc*) felicidades fpl; **with best ~es** (*in letter*) saludos mpl, recuerdos mpl; **he ~ed me well** me deseó mucha suerte; **to ~ to do/sb to do sth** querer hacer/que algn haga algo; **to ~ for** desear

wistful ['wɪstful] adj pensativo

wit [wɪt] n ingenio, gracia; (*also:* **~s**) inteligencia; (*person*) chistoso/a

witch [wɪtʃ] n bruja

KEYWORD

with [wɪð, wɪθ] prep **1** (*accompanying, in the company of*) con (*con* +*mí, ti, sí* = *conmigo, contigo, consigo*); **I was with him** estaba con él; **we stayed with friends** nos quedamos en casa de unos amigos

2 (*descriptive, indicating manner etc*) con; de; **a room with a view** una habitación con vistas; **the man with the grey hat/blue eyes** el hombre del sombrero gris/de los ojos azules; **red with anger** rojo de ira; **to shake with fear** temblar de miedo; **to fill sth with water** llenar algo de agua

3: **I'm with you/I'm not with you** (*understand*) ya te entiendo/no te entiendo; **to be with it** (*inf: person: up-to-date*) estar al tanto; (*alert*) ser despabilado

withdraw [wɪθ'drɔː] vt (*irreg: like* **draw**) retirar ▷ vi retirarse; **to ~ money (from the bank)** retirar fondos (del banco); **withdrawal** n retirada; (*of money*) reintegro; **withdrawn** adj (*person*) reservado, introvertido ▷ pp of **withdraw**

withdrew [wɪθ'druː] pt of **withdraw**

wither ['wɪðə'] vi marchitarse

withhold [wɪθ'həʊld] vt (*irreg: like* **hold**: *money*) retener; (*decision*) aplazar; (*permission*) negar; (*information*) ocultar

within [wɪð'ɪn] prep dentro de ▷ adv dentro; **~ reach** al alcance de la mano; **~ sight of** a la vista de; **~ the week** antes de que acabe la semana; **~ a mile (of)** a menos de una milla (de)

without [wɪð'aut] prep sin; **to go** or **do ~ sth** prescindir de algo

withstand [wɪθ'stænd] vt (*irreg: like* **stand**) resistir a

witness ['wɪtnɪs] n testigo mf ▷ vt (*event*) presenciar; (*document*) atestiguar la veracidad de; **to bear ~ to** (*fig*) ser testimonio de

witty ['wɪtɪ] adj ingenioso

wives [waɪvz] npl of **wife**

wizard ['wɪzəd] n hechicero

wk abbr = **week**

wobble ['wɔbl] vi tambalearse

woe [wəu] n desgracia

woke [wəuk] pt of **wake**

woken ['wəukn] pp of **wake**

wolf (pl **wolves**) [wulf, wulvz] n lobo

woman (pl **women**) ['wumən, 'wɪmɪn] n mujer f

womb [wuːm] n matriz f, útero

women ['wɪmɪn] npl of **woman**

won [wʌn] pt, pp of **win**

wonder ['wʌndə'] n maravilla, prodigio; (*feeling*) asombro ▷ vi: **to ~ whether** preguntarse si; **to ~ at** asombrarse de; **to ~ about** pensar sobre or en; **it's no ~ that** no es de extrañar que; **wonderful** adj maravilloso

won't [wəunt] = **will not**

wood [wud] n (*timber*) madera; (*forest*) bosque m; **wooden** adj de madera; (*fig*) inexpresivo; **woodwind** n (*Mus*) instrumentos mpl de viento de madera; **woodwork** n carpintería

wool [wul] n lana; **to pull the ~ over sb's eyes** (*fig*) dar a algn gato por liebre; **woollen,** (*us*) **woolen** adj de

w

lana; **woolly**, (US) **wooly** adj de lana; (fig: ideas) confuso

word [wəːd] n palabra; (news) noticia; (promise) palabra (de honor) ▷ vt redactar; **in other ~s** en otras palabras; **to break/keep one's ~** faltar a la palabra/cumplir la promesa; **to have ~s with sb** discutir or reñir con algn; **wording** n redacción f; **word processing** n procesamiento or tratamiento de textos; **word processor** [-'prəusesəʳ] n procesador m de textos

wore [wɔːʳ] pt of **wear**

work [wəːk] n trabajo; (job) empleo, trabajo; (Art, Lit) obra ▷ vi trabajar; (mechanism) funcionar, marchar; (medicine) ser eficaz, surtir efecto ▷ vt (shape) trabajar; (stone etc) tallar; (mine etc) explotar; (machine) manejar, hacer funcionar; **to be out of ~** estar parado, no tener trabajo; **to ~ loose** (part) desprenderse; (knot) aflojarse; see also **works**; **work out** vi (plans etc) salir bien, funcionar ▷ vt (problem) resolver; (plan) elaborar; **it ~s out at £100** asciende a 100 libras; **worker** n trabajador(a) m/f, obrero/a; **work experience** n: **I'm going to do my work experience in a factory** voy a hacer las prácticas en una fábrica; **work force** n mano f de obra; **working class** n clase f obrera ▷ adj: **working-class** obrero; **working week** n semana laboral; **workman** n obrero; **work of art** n obra de arte; **workout** n (Sport) sesión f de ejercicios; **work permit** n permiso de trabajo; **workplace** n lugar m de trabajo; **works** nsg (BRIT: factory) fábrica ▷ npl (of clock, machine) mecanismo; **worksheet** n hoja de ejercicios; **workshop** n taller m; **work station** n estación f de trabajo; **work surface** n encimera; **worktop** n encimera

world [wəːld] n mundo ▷ cpd (champion) del mundo; (power, war) mundial; **to think the ~ of sb** (fig) tener un concepto muy alto de algn; **World Cup** n (Football): **the World Cup** el Mundial, los Mundiales; **world-wide** adj mundial, universal; **World-Wide Web** n: **the World-Wide Web** el World Wide Web

worm [wəːm] n (earthworm) lombriz f

worn [wɔːn] pp of **wear** ▷ adj usado; **worn-out** adj (object) gastado; (person) rendido, agotado

worried ['wʌrɪd] adj preocupado

worry ['wʌrɪ] n preocupación f ▷ vt preocupar, inquietar ▷ vi preocuparse; **to ~ about** or **over sth/sb** preocuparse por algo/algn; **worrying** adj inquietante

worse [wəːs] adj, adv peor ▷ n lo peor; **a change for the ~** un empeoramiento; **worsen** vt, vi empeorar; **worse off** adj (financially): **to be worse off** tener menos dinero; (fig): **you'll be worse off this way** de esta forma estarás peor que antes

worship ['wəːʃɪp] n adoración f ▷ vt adorar; **Your W~** (BRIT: to mayor) su Ilustrísima; (: to judge) su señoría

worst [wəːst] adj (el/la) peor ▷ adv peor ▷ n lo peor; **at ~** en el peor de los casos

worth [wəːθ] n valor m ▷ adj: **to be ~** valer; **it's ~ it** vale or merece la pena; **to be ~ one's while (to do)** merecer la pena (hacer); **worthless** adj sin valor; (useless) inútil; **worthwhile** adj (activity) que merece la pena; (cause) loable

worthy adj (person) respetable; (motive) honesto; **~ of** digno de

 KEYWORD

would [wud] aux vb **1** (conditional tense): **if you asked him he would do it** si se lo pidieras, lo haría; **if you had asked him he would have done it** si se lo hubieras pedido, lo habría or hubiera hecho

2 (*in offers, invitations, requests*): **would you like a biscuit?** ¿quieres una galleta?; (*formal*) ¿querría una galleta?; **would you ask him to come in?** ¿quiere hacerle pasar?; **would you open the window please?** ¿quiere *or* podría abrir la ventana, por favor?
3 (*in indirect speech*): **I said I would do it** dije que lo haría
4 (*emphatic*): **it WOULD have to snow today!** ¡tenía que nevar precisamente hoy!
5 (*insistence*): **she wouldn't behave** no quiso comportarse bien
6 (*conjecture*): **it would have been midnight** sería medianoche; **it would seem so** parece ser que sí
7 (*indicating habit*): **he would go there on Mondays** iba allí los lunes

wouldn't ['wʊdnt] = **would not**
wound¹ [wuːnd] *n* herida ▷ *vt* herir
wound² [waʊnd] *pt, pp of* **wind²**
wove [waʊv] *pt of* **weave**
woven ['waʊvən] *pp of* **weave**
wrap [ræp] (*also:* **~ up**) *vt* envolver; (*gift*) envolver, abrigar ▷ *vi* (*dress warmly*) abrigarse; **wrapper** *n* (*of book*) sobrecubierta; (*on chocolate etc*) envoltura; **wrapping paper** *n* papel *m* de envolver
wreath (*pl* **wreaths**) [riːθ, riːðz] *n* (*also:* **funeral ~**) corona
wreck [rɛk] *n* (*ship: destruction*) naufragio; (*: remains*) restos *mpl* del barco; (*pej: person*) ruina ▷ *vt* destrozar; (*chances*) arruinar; **wreckage** *n* restos *mpl*; (*of building*) escombros *mpl*
wren [rɛn] *n* (*Zool*) reyezuelo
wrench [rɛntʃ] *n* (*Tech*) llave f inglesa; (*tug*) tirón *m* ▷ *vt* arrancar; **to ~ sth from sb** arrebatar algo violentamente a algn
wrestle ['rɛsl] *vi*: **to ~ (with sb)** luchar (con *or* contra algn); **wrestler** ['rɛslə'] *n* luchador(a) *m/f* (de lucha libre); **wrestling** *n* lucha libre

wretched ['rɛtʃɪd] *adj* miserable
wriggle ['rɪgl] *vi* serpentear; (*also:* **~ about**) menearse, retorcerse
wring (*pt, pp* **wrung**) [rɪŋ, rʌŋ] *vt* torcer, retorcer; (*wet clothes*) escurrir; (*fig*): **to ~ sth out of sb** sacar algo por la fuerza a algn
wrinkle ['rɪŋkl] *n* arruga ▷ *vt* arrugar ▷ *vi* arrugarse
wrist [rɪst] *n* muñeca
writable ['raɪtəbl] *adj* (*CD, DVD*) escribible
write (*pt* **wrote**, *pp* **written**) [raɪt, rəʊt, 'rɪtn] *vt* escribir; (*cheque*) extender ▷ *vi* escribir; **write down** *vt* escribir; (*note*) apuntar; **write off** *vt* (*debt*) borrar (como incobrable); (*fig*) desechar por inútil; **write out** *vt* escribir; **write up** *vt* redactar; **write-off** *n* siniestro total; **writer** *n* escritor(a) *m/f*
writing ['raɪtɪŋ] *n* escritura; (*handwriting*) letra; (*of author*) obras *fpl*; **in ~** por escrito; **writing paper** *n* papel *m* de escribir
written ['rɪtn] *pp of* **write**
wrong [rɔŋ] *adj* (*wicked*) malo; (*unfair*) injusto; (*incorrect*) equivocado, incorrecto; (*not suitable*) inoportuno, inconveniente ▷ *adv* mal ▷ *n* injusticia ▷ *vt* ser injusto con; **you are ~ to do it** haces mal en hacerlo; **you are ~ about that, you've got it ~** en eso estás equivocado; **to be in the ~** no tener razón; tener la culpa; **what's ~?** ¿qué pasa?; **to go ~** (*person*) equivocarse; (*plan*) salir mal; (*machine*) estropearse; **wrongly** *adv* incorrectamente; **wrong number** *n* (*Tel*): **you've got the wrong number** se ha equivocado de número
wrote [rəʊt] *pt of* **write**
wrung [rʌŋ] *pt, pp of* **wring**
WWW *n abbr* (= *World Wide Web*) WWW *m or f*

w

X x / Y y

XL *abbr* = **extra large**
Xmas ['ɛksməs] *n abbr* = **Christmas**
X-ray [ɛks'reɪ] *n* radiografía ▷ *vt*
radiografiar
xylophone ['zaɪləfəun] *n* xilófono

yacht [jɔt] *n* yate *m*; **yachting** *n*
(*sport*) balandrismo
yakka ['jækə] *n* (*AUST, NZ: inf*) curro
yard [jɑːd] *n* patio; (*measure*) yarda;
yard sale *n* (*US*) venta de objetos
usados (*en el jardín de una casa
particular*)
yarn [jɑːn] *n* hilo; (*tale*) cuento (chino),
historia
yawn [jɔːn] *n* bostezo ▷ *vi* bostezar
yd. *abbr* (= *yard*) yda
yeah [jɛə] *adv* (*inf*) sí
year [jɪəʳ] *n* año; **to be eight ~s old**
tener ocho años; **an eight-~-old
child** un niño de ocho años (de edad);
yearly *adj* anual ▷ *adv* anualmente,
cada año
yearn [jəːn] *vi*: **to ~ for sth** añorar
algo, suspirar por algo
yeast [jiːst] *n* levadura
yell [jɛl] *n* grito, alarido ▷ *vi* gritar
yellow ['jɛləu] *adj* amarillo; **Yellow
Pages**® *npl* páginas *fpl* amarillas

yes [jɛs] *adv*, *n* sí *m*; **to say/answer ~** decir/contestar que sí

yesterday ['jɛstədɪ] *adv*, *n* ayer *m*; **~ morning/evening** ayer por la mañana/tarde; **all day ~** todo el día de ayer

yet [jɛt] *adv* todavía ▷ *conj* sin embargo, a pesar de todo; **it is not finished ~** todavía no está acabado; **the best ~** el/la mejor hasta ahora; **as ~** hasta ahora, todavía

yew [ju:] *n* tejo

Yiddish ['jɪdɪʃ] *n* yiddish *m*

yield [ji:ld] *n* (*Agr*) cosecha; (*Comm*) rendimiento ▷ *vt* producir, dar; (*profit*) rendir ▷ *vi* rendirse, ceder; (*US Aut*) ceder el paso

yob(bo) ['jɔb(bəu)] *n* (*BRIT inf*) gamberro

yoga ['jəugə] *n* yoga *m*

yog(h)urt ['jəugət] *n* yogur *m*

yolk [jəuk] *n* yema (de huevo)

⬤   **KEYWORD**

you [ju:] *pron* **1** (*subject, familiar, singular*) tú; (: *plural*) vosotros/as (SP), ustedes (LAM); (: *polite*) usted, ustedes *pl*; **you are very kind** eres/es *etc* muy amable; **you French enjoy your food** a vosotros (*or* ustedes) los franceses (*or* les) gusta la comida; **you and I will go** iremos tú y yo
2 (*object, direct, familiar, singular*) te; (: *plural*) os (SP), les (LAM); (: *polite, singular masc*) lo *or* le; (: *plural masc*) los *or* les; (: *singular fem*) la; (: *plural fem*) las; **I know you** te/le *etc* conozco
3 (*object, indirect, familiar, singular*) te; (: *plural*) os (SP), les (LAM); (: *polite*) le, les *pl*; **I gave the letter to you yesterday** te/os *etc* di la carta ayer
4 (*stressed*): **I told YOU to do it** te dije a ti que lo hicieras, es a ti a quien dije que lo hicieras; *see also* **you**
5 (*after prep, NB: con + ti = contigo, familiar, singular*) ti; (: *plural*) vosotros/as (SP), ustedes (LAM); (: *polite*) usted, ustedes *pl*; **it's for you** es para ti/vosotros *etc*
6 (*comparisons, familiar, singular*) tú; (: *plural*) vosotros/as (SP), ustedes (LAM); (: *polite*) usted, ustedes *pl*; **she's younger than you** es más joven que tú/vosotros *etc*
7 (*impersonal: one*): **fresh air does you good** el aire puro (te) hace bien; **you never know** nunca se sabe; **you can't do that!** ¡eso no se hace!

you'd [ju:d] = **you had; you would**

you'll [ju:l] = **you will; you shall**

young [jʌŋ] *adj* joven ▷ *npl* (*of animal*) cría; (*people*): **the ~** los jóvenes, la juventud; **youngster** *n* joven *mf*

your [jɔ:ʳ] *adj* tu, vuestro *pl*; (*formal*) su; *see also* **my**

you're [juəʳ] = **you are**

yours [jɔ:z] *pron* tuyo, vuestro *pl*; (*formal*) suyo; *see also* **faithfully; mine; sincerely**

yourself [jɔ:'sɛlf] *pron* tú mismo; (*complement*) te; (*after prep*) ti (mismo); (*formal*) usted mismo; (: *complement*) se; (: *after prep*) sí (mismo); **yourselves** *pron pl* vosotros mismos; (*after prep*) vosotros (mismos); (*formal*) ustedes (mismos); (: *complement*) se; (: *after prep*) sí mismos

youth [ju:θ] *n* juventud *f*; (*young man*) joven *m*; **youth club** *n* club *m* juvenil; **youthful** *adj* juvenil; **youth hostel** *n* albergue *m* juvenil

you've [ju:v] = **you have**

zoom [zu:m] *vi*: **to ~ past** pasar zumbando; **zoom lens** *n* zoom *m*
zucchini [zu:ˈki:nɪ] *n(pl)* (*US*) calabacín(ines) *m(pl)*

Z

zeal [zi:l] *n* celo, entusiasmo
zebra [ˈzi:brə] *n* cebra; **zebra crossing** *n* (*BRIT*) paso de peatones
zero [ˈzɪərəu] *n* cero
zest [zɛst] *n* ánimo, vivacidad *f*; (*of orange*) piel *f*
zigzag [ˈzɪgzæg] *n* zigzag *m* ▷ *vi* zigzaguear
Zimbabwe [zɪmˈbɑ:bwɪ] *n* Zimbabwe *m*
zinc [zɪŋk] *n* cinc *m*, zinc *m*
zip [zɪp] *n* (*also*: **~ fastener**, (*US*) **zipper**) cremallera, cierre *m* relámpago (*LAM*) ▷ *vt* (*Comput*) comprimir; (*also*: **~ up**) cerrar la cremallera de; **zip code** *n* (*US*) código postal; **zip file** *n* (*Comput*) archivo *m* comprimido; **zipper** *n* (*US*) cremallera
zit [zɪt] *n* grano
zodiac [ˈzəudɪæk] *n* zodíaco
zone [zəun] *n* zona
zoo [zu:] *n* zoo, (parque *m*) zoológico
zoology [zu:ˈɔlədʒɪ] *n* zoología

Introduction

The **Verb Tables** in the following section contain 31 tables of the most common Spanish verbs (some regular, some irregular and some which change their stems) in alphabetical order. Each table shows you the following tenses and forms: **Present**, **Preterite**, **Future**, **Present Subjunctive**, **Imperfect**, **Conditional**, **Imperative**, **Past Participle** and **Gerund**.

In order to help you use the verbs shown in the Verb Tables correctly, there are also a number of example phrases at the bottom of each page to show the verb as it is used in context.

In Spanish there are **regular** verbs (their forms follow the normal rules); **irregular** verbs (their forms do not follow the normal rules); and verbs which change a vowel in their stem (the part that is left when you take off the ending) in fairly predictable ways. The regular verbs in these tables are:

hablar (regular -**ar** verb, Verb Table 12)
comer (regular -**er** verb, Verb Table 3)
vivir (regular -**ir** verb, Verb Table 31)
lavarse (regular -**ar** reflexive verb, Verb Table 15)

▶ **coger** (to take, to catch)

PRESENT		**PRESENT SUBJUNCTIVE**	
(yo)	cojo	(yo)	coja
(tú)	coges	(tú)	cojas
(él/ella/usted)	coge	(él/ella/usted)	coja
(nosotros/as)	cogemos	(nosotros/as)	cojamos
(vosotros/as)	cogéis	(vosotros/as)	cojáis
(ellos/ellas/ustedes)	cogen	(ellos/ellas/ustedes)	cojan

PRETERITE		**IMPERFECT**	
(yo)	cogí	(yo)	cogía
(tú)	cogiste	(tú)	cogías
(él/ella/usted)	cogió	(él/ella/usted)	cogía
(nosotros/as)	cogimos	(nosotros/as)	cogíamos
(vosotros/as)	cogisteis	(vosotros/as)	cogíais
(ellos/ellas/ustedes)	cogieron	(ellos/ellas/ustedes)	cogían

FUTURE		**CONDITIONAL**	
(yo)	cogeré	(yo)	cogería
(tú)	cogerás	(tú)	cogerías
(él/ella/usted)	cogerá	(él/ella/usted)	cogería
(nosotros/as)	cogeremos	(nosotros/as)	cogeríamos
(vosotros/as)	cogeréis	(vosotros/as)	cogeríais
(ellos/ellas/ustedes)	cogerán	(ellos/ellas/ustedes)	cogerían

IMPERATIVE

coge / coged

PAST PARTICIPLE

cogido

GERUND

cogiendo

EXAMPLE PHRASES

La **cogí** *entre mis brazos.* I took her in my arms.
Estuvimos cogiendo *setas.* We were picking mushrooms.
¿Por qué no **coges** *el tren de las seis?* Why don't you get the six o'clock train?

Remember that subject pronouns are not used very often in Spanish.

▶ **comer** (to eat)

PRESENT

(yo)	como
(tú)	comes
(él/ella/usted)	come
(nosotros/as)	comemos
(vosotros/as)	coméis
(ellos/ellas/ustedes)	comen

PRESENT SUBJUNCTIVE

(yo)	coma
(tú)	comas
(él/ella/usted)	coma
(nosotros/as)	comamos
(vosotros/as)	comáis
(ellos/ellas/ustedes)	coman

PRETERITE

(yo)	comí
(tú)	comiste
(él/ella/usted)	comió
(nosotros/as)	comimos
(vosotros/as)	comisteis
(ellos/ellas/ustedes)	comieron

IMPERFECT

(yo)	comía
(tú)	comías
(él/ella/usted)	comía
(nosotros/as)	comíamos
(vosotros/as)	comíais
(ellos/ellas/ustedes)	comían

FUTURE

(yo)	comeré
(tú)	comerás
(él/ella/usted)	comerá
(nosotros/as)	comeremos
(vosotros/as)	comeréis
(ellos/ellas/ustedes)	comerán

CONDITIONAL

(yo)	comería
(tú)	comerías
(él/ella/usted)	comería
(nosotros/as)	comeríamos
(vosotros/as)	comeríais
(ellos/ellas/ustedes)	comerían

IMPERATIVE

come / comed

PAST PARTICIPLE

comido

GERUND

comiendo

EXAMPLE PHRASES

*No **come** carne.* He doesn't eat meat.
*No **comas** tan deprisa.* Don't eat so fast.
***Se ha comido** todo.* He's eaten it all.

Remember that subject pronouns are not used very often in Spanish.

▶ **dar** (to give)

PRESENT

(yo)	doy
(tú)	das
(él/ella/usted)	da
(nosotros/as)	damos
(vosotros/as)	dais
(ellos/ellas/ustedes)	dan

PRESENT SUBJUNCTIVE

(yo)	dé
(tú)	des
(él/ella/usted)	dé
(nosotros/as)	demos
(vosotros/as)	deis
(ellos/ellas/ustedes)	den

PRETERITE

(yo)	di
(tú)	diste
(él/ella/usted)	dio
(nosotros/as)	dimos
(vosotros/as)	disteis
(ellos/ellas/ustedes)	dieron

IMPERFECT

(yo)	daba
(tú)	dabas
(él/ella/usted)	daba
(nosotros/as)	dábamos
(vosotros/as)	dabais
(ellos/ellas/ustedes)	daban

FUTURE

(yo)	daré
(tú)	darás
(él/ella/usted)	dará
(nosotros/as)	daremos
(vosotros/as)	daréis
(ellos/ellas/ustedes)	darán

CONDITIONAL

(yo)	daría
(tú)	darías
(él/ella/usted)	daría
(nosotros/as)	daríamos
(vosotros/as)	daríais
(ellos/ellas/ustedes)	darían

IMPERATIVE

da / dad

PAST PARTICIPLE

dado

GERUND

dando

EXAMPLE PHRASES

Me **da** miedo la oscuridad. I'm scared of the dark.

Nos **dieron** un par de entradas gratis. They gave us a couple of free tickets.

Te **daré** el número de mi móvil. I'll give you my mobile-phone number.

Remember that subject pronouns are not used very often in Spanish.

▶ **decir** (to say, to tell)

PRESENT

(yo)	digo
(tú)	dices
(él/ella/usted)	dice
(nosotros/as)	decimos
(vosotros/as)	decís
(ellos/ellas/ustedes)	dicen

PRESENT SUBJUNCTIVE

(yo)	diga
(tú)	digas
(él/ella/usted)	diga
(nosotros/as)	digamos
(vosotros/as)	digáis
(ellos/ellas/ustedes)	digan

PRETERITE

(yo)	dije
(tú)	dijiste
(él/ella/usted)	dijo
(nosotros/as)	dijimos
(vosotros/as)	dijisteis
(ellos/ellas/ustedes)	dijeron

IMPERFECT

(yo)	decía
(tú)	decías
(él/ella/usted)	decía
(nosotros/as)	decíamos
(vosotros/as)	decíais
(ellos/ellas/ustedes)	decían

FUTURE

(yo)	diré
(tú)	dirás
(él/ella/usted)	dirá
(nosotros/as)	diremos
(vosotros/as)	diréis
(ellos/ellas/ustedes)	dirán

CONDITIONAL

(yo)	diría
(tú)	dirías
(él/ella/usted)	diría
(nosotros/as)	diríamos
(vosotros/as)	diríais
(ellos/ellas/ustedes)	dirían

IMPERATIVE

di / decid

PAST PARTICIPLE

dicho

GERUND

diciendo

EXAMPLE PHRASES

¿Qué **dices**? What are you saying?
Me lo **dijo** ayer. He told me yesterday.
¿Te **ha dicho** lo de la boda? Has he told you about the wedding?

Remember that subject pronouns are not used very often in Spanish.

▶ **dormir** (to sleep)

PRESENT

(yo)	duermo
(tú)	duermes
(él/ella/usted)	duerme
(nosotros/as)	dormimos
(vosotros/as)	dormís
(ellos/ellas/ustedes)	duermen

PRESENT SUBJUNCTIVE

(yo)	duerma
(tú)	duermas
(él/ella/usted)	duerma
(nosotros/as)	durmamos
(vosotros/as)	durmáis
(ellos/ellas/ustedes)	duerman

PRETERITE

(yo)	dormí
(tú)	dormiste
(él/ella/usted)	durmió
(nosotros/as)	dormimos
(vosotros/as)	dormisteis
(ellos/ellas/ustedes)	durmieron

IMPERFECT

(yo)	dormía
(tú)	dormías
(él/ella/usted)	dormía
(nosotros/as)	dormíamos
(vosotros/as)	dormíais
(ellos/ellas/ustedes)	dormían

FUTURE

(yo)	dormiré
(tú)	dormirás
(él/ella/usted)	dormirá
(nosotros/as)	dormiremos
(vosotros/as)	dormiréis
(ellos/ellas/ustedes)	dormirán

CONDITIONAL

(yo)	dormiría
(tú)	dormirías
(él/ella/usted)	dormiría
(nosotros/as)	dormiríamos
(vosotros/as)	dormiríais
(ellos/ellas/ustedes)	dormirían

IMPERATIVE

duerme / dormid

PAST PARTICIPLE

dormido

GERUND

durmiendo

EXAMPLE PHRASES

*No **duermo** muy bien.* I don't sleep very well.
***Nos dormimos** en el cine.* We fell asleep at the cinema.
***Durmió** durante doce horas.* He slept for twelve hours.

Remember that subject pronouns are not used very often in Spanish.

▶ **empezar** (to begin, to start)

PRESENT

(yo)	empiezo
(tú)	empiezas
(él/ella/usted)	empieza
(nosotros/as)	empezamos
(vosotros/as)	empezáis
(ellos/ellas/ustedes)	empiezan

PRESENT SUBJUNCTIVE

(yo)	empiece
(tú)	empieces
(él/ella/usted)	empiece
(nosotros/as)	empecemos
(vosotros/as)	empecéis
(ellos/ellas/ustedes)	empiecen

PRETERITE

(yo)	empecé
(tú)	empezaste
(él/ella/usted)	empezó
(nosotros/as)	empezamos
(vosotros/as)	empezasteis
(ellos/ellas/ustedes)	empezaron

IMPERFECT

(yo)	empezaba
(tú)	empezabas
(él/ella/usted)	empezaba
(nosotros/as)	empezábamos
(vosotros/as)	empezabais
(ellos/ellas/ustedes)	empezaban

FUTURE

(yo)	empezaré
(tú)	empezarás
(él/ella/usted)	empezará
(nosotros/as)	empezaremos
(vosotros/as)	empezaréis
(ellos/ellas/ustedes)	empezarán

CONDITIONAL

(yo)	empezaría
(tú)	empezarías
(él/ella/usted)	empezaría
(nosotros/as)	empezaríamos
(vosotros/as)	empezaríais
(ellos/ellas/ustedes)	empezarían

IMPERATIVE

empieza / empezad

PAST PARTICIPLE

empezado

GERUND

empezando

EXAMPLE PHRASES

Empieza por aquí. Start here.
¿Cuándo **empiezas** a trabajar en el sitio nuevo? When do you start work at the new place?
La semana que viene **empezaremos** un curso nuevo. We'll start a new course next week.

Remember that subject pronouns are not used very often in Spanish.

▶ **entender** (to understand)

PRESENT

(yo)	entiendo
(tú)	entiendes
(él/ella/usted)	entiende
(nosotros/as)	entendemos
(vosotros/as)	entendéis
(ellos/ellas/ustedes)	entienden

PRESENT SUBJUNCTIVE

(yo)	entienda
(tú)	entiendas
(él/ella/usted)	entienda
(nosotros/as)	entendamos
(vosotros/as)	entendáis
(ellos/ellas/ustedes)	entiendan

PRETERITE

(yo)	entendí
(tú)	entendiste
(él/ella/usted)	entendió
(nosotros/as)	entendimos
(vosotros/as)	entendisteis
(ellos/ellas/ustedes)	entendieron

IMPERFECT

(yo)	entendía
(tú)	entendías
(él/ella/usted)	entendía
(nosotros/as)	entendíamos
(vosotros/as)	entendíais
(ellos/ellas/ustedes)	entendían

FUTURE

(yo)	entenderé
(tú)	entenderás
(él/ella/usted)	entenderá
(nosotros/as)	entenderemos
(vosotros/as)	entenderéis
(ellos/ellas/ustedes)	entenderán

CONDITIONAL

(yo)	entendería
(tú)	entenderías
(él/ella/usted)	entendería
(nosotros/as)	entenderíamos
(vosotros/as)	entenderíais
(ellos/ellas/ustedes)	entenderían

IMPERATIVE

entiende / entended

PAST PARTICIPLE

entendido

GERUND

entendiendo

EXAMPLE PHRASES

*No lo **entiendo**.* I don't understand.
*¿**Entendiste** lo que dijo?* Did you understand what she said?
*Con el tiempo lo **entenderás**.* You'll understand one day.

Remember that subject pronouns are not used very often in Spanish.

▶ **enviar** (to send)

PRESENT

(yo)	envío
(tú)	envías
(él/ella/usted)	envía
(nosotros/as)	enviamos
(vosotros/as)	enviáis
(ellos/ellas/ustedes)	envían

PRESENT SUBJUNCTIVE

(yo)	envíe
(tú)	envíes
(él/ella/usted)	envíe
(nosotros/as)	enviemos
(vosotros/as)	enviéis
(ellos/ellas/ustedes)	envíen

PRETERITE

(yo)	envié
(tú)	enviaste
(él/ella/usted)	envió
(nosotros/as)	enviamos
(vosotros/as)	enviasteis
(ellos/ellas/ustedes)	enviaron

IMPERFECT

(yo)	enviaba
(tú)	enviabas
(él/ella/usted)	enviaba
(nosotros/as)	enviábamos
(vosotros/as)	enviabais
(ellos/ellas/ustedes)	enviaban

FUTURE

(yo)	enviaré
(tú)	enviarás
(él/ella/usted)	enviará
(nosotros/as)	enviaremos
(vosotros/as)	enviaréis
(ellos/ellas/ustedes)	enviarán

CONDITIONAL

(yo)	enviaría
(tú)	enviarías
(él/ella/usted)	enviaría
(nosotros/as)	enviaríamos
(vosotros/as)	enviaríais
(ellos/ellas/ustedes)	enviarían

IMPERATIVE

envía / enviad

PAST PARTICIPLE

enviado

GERUND

enviando

EXAMPLE PHRASES

Envíe *todos sus datos personales.* Send all your personal details.
La han **enviado** *a Guatemala.* They've sent her to Guatemala.
Nos **enviarán** *más información.* They'll send us further information.

Remember that subject pronouns are not used very often in Spanish.

▶ **estar** (to be)

PRESENT

(yo)	estoy
(tú)	estás
(él/ella/usted)	está
(nosotros/as)	estamos
(vosotros/as)	estáis
(ellos/ellas/ustedes)	están

PRESENT SUBJUNCTIVE

(yo)	esté
(tú)	estés
(él/ella/usted)	esté
(nosotros/as)	estemos
(vosotros/as)	estéis
(ellos/ellas/ustedes)	estén

PRETERITE

(yo)	estuve
(tú)	estuviste
(él/ella/usted)	estuvo
(nosotros/as)	estuvimos
(vosotros/as)	estuvisteis
(ellos/ellas/ustedes)	estuvieron

IMPERFECT

(yo)	estaba
(tú)	estabas
(él/ella/usted)	estaba
(nosotros/as)	estábamos
(vosotros/as)	estabais
(ellos/ellas/ustedes)	estaban

FUTURE

(yo)	estaré
(tú)	estarás
(él/ella/usted)	estará
(nosotros/as)	estaremos
(vosotros/as)	estaréis
(ellos/ellas/ustedes)	estarán

CONDITIONAL

(yo)	estaría
(tú)	estarías
(él/ella/usted)	estaría
(nosotros/as)	estaríamos
(vosotros/as)	estaríais
(ellos/ellas/ustedes)	estarían

IMPERATIVE

está / estad

PAST PARTICIPLE

estado

GERUND

estando

EXAMPLE PHRASES

Estoy cansado. I'm tired.
Estuvimos en casa de mis padres. We were at my parents' place.
¿A qué hora **estarás** en casa? What time will you be home?

Remember that subject pronouns are not used very often in Spanish.

▶ **haber** (to have (auxiliary))

PRESENT

(yo)	he
(tú)	has
(él/ella/usted)	ha
(nosotros/as)	hemos
(vosotros/as)	habéis
(ellos/ellas/ustedes)	han

PRESENT SUBJUNCTIVE

(yo)	haya
(tú)	hayas
(él/ella/usted)	haya
(nosotros/as)	hayamos
(vosotros/as)	hayáis
(ellos/ellas/ustedes)	hayan

PRETERITE

(yo)	hube
(tú)	hubiste
(él/ella/usted)	hubo
(nosotros/as)	hubimos
(vosotros/as)	hubisteis
(ellos/ellas/ustedes)	hubieron

IMPERFECT

(yo)	había
(tú)	habías
(él/ella/usted)	había
(nosotros/as)	habíamos
(vosotros/as)	habíais
(ellos/ellas/ustedes)	habían

FUTURE

(yo)	habré
(tú)	habrás
(él/ella/usted)	habrá
(nosotros/as)	habremos
(vosotros/as)	habréis
(ellos/ellas/ustedes)	habrán

CONDITIONAL

(yo)	habría
(tú)	habrías
(él/ella/usted)	habría
(nosotros/as)	habríamos
(vosotros/as)	habríais
(ellos/ellas/ustedes)	habrían

IMPERATIVE

not used

PAST PARTICIPLE

habido

GERUND

habiendo

EXAMPLE PHRASES

¿**Has visto** eso? Did you see that?
Ya **hemos ido** a ver esa película. We've already been to see that film.
Eso nunca **había pasado** antes. That had never happened before.

Remember that subject pronouns are not used very often in Spanish.

▶ **hablar** (to speak, to talk)

PRESENT		PRESENT SUBJUNCTIVE	
(yo)	hablo	(yo)	hable
(tú)	hablas	(tú)	hables
(él/ella/usted)	habla	(él/ella/usted)	hable
(nosotros/as)	hablamos	(nosotros/as)	hablemos
(vosotros/as)	habláis	(vosotros/as)	habléis
(ellos/ellas/ustedes)	hablan	(ellos/ellas/ustedes)	hablen

PRETERITE		IMPERFECT	
(yo)	hablé	(yo)	hablaba
(tú)	hablaste	(tú)	hablabas
(él/ella/usted)	habló	(él/ella/usted)	hablaba
(nosotros/as)	hablamos	(nosotros/as)	hablábamos
(vosotros/as)	hablasteis	(vosotros/as)	hablabais
(ellos/ellas/ustedes)	hablaron	(ellos/ellas/ustedes)	hablaban

FUTURE		CONDITIONAL	
(yo)	hablaré	(yo)	hablaría
(tú)	hablarás	(tú)	hablarías
(él/ella/usted)	hablará	(él/ella/usted)	hablaría
(nosotros/as)	hablaremos	(nosotros/as)	hablaríamos
(vosotros/as)	hablaréis	(vosotros/as)	hablaríais
(ellos/ellas/ustedes)	hablarán	(ellos/ellas/ustedes)	hablarían

IMPERATIVE

habla / hablad

PAST PARTICIPLE

hablado

GERUND

hablando

EXAMPLE PHRASES

Hoy **he hablado** con mi hermana. I've spoken to my sister today.
No **hables** tan alto. Don't talk so loud.
No **se hablan**. They don't talk to each other.

Remember that subject pronouns are not used very often in Spanish.

▶ **hacer** (to do, to make)

PRESENT		PRESENT SUBJUNCTIVE	
(yo)	hago	(yo)	haga
(tú)	haces	(tú)	hagas
(él/ella/usted)	hace	(él/ella/usted)	haga
(nosotros/as)	hacemos	(nosotros/as)	hagamos
(vosotros/as)	hacéis	(vosotros/as)	hagáis
(ellos/ellas/ustedes)	hacen	(ellos/ellas/ustedes)	hagan

PRETERITE		IMPERFECT	
(yo)	hice	(yo)	hacía
(tú)	hiciste	(tú)	hacías
(él/ella/usted)	hizo	(él/ella/usted)	hacía
(nosotros/as)	hicimos	(nosotros/as)	hacíamos
(vosotros/as)	hicisteis	(vosotros/as)	hacíais
(ellos/ellas/ustedes)	hicieron	(ellos/ellas/ustedes)	hacían

FUTURE		CONDITIONAL	
(yo)	haré	(yo)	haría
(tú)	harás	(tú)	harías
(él/ella/usted)	hará	(él/ella/usted)	haría
(nosotros/as)	haremos	(nosotros/as)	haríamos
(vosotros/as)	haréis	(vosotros/as)	haríais
(ellos/ellas/ustedes)	harán	(ellos/ellas/ustedes)	harían

IMPERATIVE

haz / haced

PAST PARTICIPLE

hecho

GERUND

haciendo

EXAMPLE PHRASES

Lo **haré** yo mismo. *I'll do it myself.*
¿Quién **hizo** eso? *Who did that?*
Quieres que **haga** las camas? *Do you want me to make the beds?*

Remember that subject pronouns are not used very often in Spanish.

▶ **ir** (to go)

PRESENT

(yo)	voy
(tú)	vas
(él/ella/usted)	va
(nosotros/as)	vamos
(vosotros/as)	vais
(ellos/ellas/ustedes)	van

PRESENT SUBJUNCTIVE

(yo)	vaya
(tú)	vayas
(él/ella/usted)	vaya
(nosotros/as)	vayamos
(vosotros/as)	vayáis
(ellos/ellas/ustedes)	vayan

PRETERITE

(yo)	fui
(tú)	fuiste
(él/ella/usted)	fue
(nosotros/as)	fuimos
(vosotros/as)	fuisteis
(ellos/ellas/ustedes)	fueron

IMPERFECT

(yo)	iba
(tú)	ibas
(él/ella/usted)	iba
(nosotros/as)	íbamos
(vosotros/as)	ibais
(ellos/ellas/ustedes)	iban

FUTURE

(yo)	iré
(tú)	irás
(él/ella/usted)	irá
(nosotros/as)	iremos
(vosotros/as)	iréis
(ellos/ellas/ustedes)	irán

CONDITIONAL

(yo)	iría
(tú)	irías
(él/ella/usted)	iría
(nosotros/as)	iríamos
(vosotros/as)	iríais
(ellos/ellas/ustedes)	irían

IMPERATIVE

ve / id

PAST PARTICIPLE

ido

GERUND

yendo

EXAMPLE PHRASES

¿**Vamos** a comer al campo? Shall we have a picnic in the country?
El domingo **iré** a Edimburgo. I'll go to Edinburgh on Sunday.
Yo no **voy** con ellos. I'm not going with them.

Remember that subject pronouns are not used very often in Spanish.

▶ **lavarse** (to wash oneself)

PRESENT

(yo)	me lavo
(tú)	te lavas
(él/ella/usted)	se lava
(nosotros/as)	nos lavamos
(vosotros/as)	os laváis
(ellos/ellas/ustedes)	se lavan

PRESENT SUBJUNCTIVE

(yo)	me lave
(tú)	te laves
(él/ella/usted)	se lave
(nosotros/as)	nos lavemos
(vosotros/as)	os lavéis
(ellos/ellas/ustedes)	se laven

PRETERITE

(yo)	me lavé
(tú)	te lavaste
(él/ella/usted)	se lavó
(nosotros/as)	nos lavamos
(vosotros/as)	os lavasteis
(ellos/ellas/ustedes)	se lavaron

IMPERFECT

(yo)	me lavaba
(tú)	te lavabas
(él/ella/usted)	se lavaba
(nosotros/as)	nos lavábamos
(vosotros/as)	os lavabais
(ellos/ellas/ustedes)	se lavaban

FUTURE

(yo)	me lavaré
(tú)	te lavarás
(él/ella/usted)	se lavará
(nosotros/as)	nos lavaremos
(vosotros/as)	os lavaréis
(ellos/ellas/ustedes)	se lavarán

CONDITIONAL

(yo)	me lavaría
(tú)	te lavarías
(él/ella/usted)	se lavaría
(nosotros/as)	nos lavaríamos
(vosotros/as)	os lavaríais
(ellos/ellas/ustedes)	se lavarían

IMPERATIVE

lávate / lavaos

PAST PARTICIPLE

lavado

GERUND

lavándose

EXAMPLE PHRASES

Se lava todos los días. He washes every day.
Ayer **me lavé** el pelo. I washed my hair yesterday.
Nos lavaremos con agua fría. We'll wash in cold water.

Remember that subject pronouns are not used very often in Spanish.

▶ **leer** (to read)

PRESENT

(yo)	leo
(tú)	lees
(él/ella/usted)	lee
(nosotros/as)	leemos
(vosotros/as)	leéis
(ellos/ellas/ustedes)	leen

PRESENT SUBJUNCTIVE

(yo)	lea
(tú)	leas
(él/ella/usted)	lea
(nosotros/as)	leamos
(vosotros/as)	leáis
(ellos/ellas/ustedes)	lean

PRETERITE

(yo)	leí
(tú)	leíste
(él/ella/usted)	leyó
(nosotros/as)	leímos
(vosotros/as)	leísteis
(ellos/ellas/ustedes)	leyeron

IMPERFECT

(yo)	leía
(tú)	leías
(él/ella/usted)	leía
(nosotros/as)	leíamos
(vosotros/as)	leíais
(ellos/ellas/ustedes)	leían

FUTURE

(yo)	leeré
(tú)	leerás
(él/ella/usted)	leerá
(nosotros/as)	leeremos
(vosotros/as)	leeréis
(ellos/ellas/ustedes)	leerán

CONDITIONAL

(yo)	leería
(tú)	leerías
(él/ella/usted)	leería
(nosotros/as)	leeríamos
(vosotros/as)	leeríais
(ellos/ellas/ustedes)	leerían

IMPERATIVE

lee / leed

PAST PARTICIPLE

leído

GERUND

leyendo

EXAMPLE PHRASES

*Hace mucho tiempo que no **leo**.* I haven't read anything for ages.
*¿**Has leído** esta novela?* Have you read this novel?
*Lo **leí** hace tiempo.* I read it a while ago.

Remember that subject pronouns are not used very often in Spanish.

▶ **oír** (to hear)

PRESENT

(yo)	oigo
(tú)	oyes
(él/ella/usted)	oye
(nosotros/as)	oímos
(vosotros/as)	oís
(ellos/ellas/ustedes)	oyen

PRESENT SUBJUNCTIVE

(yo)	oiga
(tú)	oigas
(él/ella/usted)	oiga
(nosotros/as)	oigamos
(vosotros/as)	oigáis
(ellos/ellas/ustedes)	oigan

PRETERITE

(yo)	oí
(tú)	oíste
(él/ella/usted)	oyó
(nosotros/as)	oímos
(vosotros/as)	oísteis
(ellos/ellas/ustedes)	oyeron

IMPERFECT

(yo)	oía
(tú)	oías
(él/ella/usted)	oía
(nosotros/as)	oíamos
(vosotros/as)	oíais
(ellos/ellas/ustedes)	oían

FUTURE

(yo)	oiré
(tú)	oirás
(él/ella/usted)	oirá
(nosotros/as)	oiremos
(vosotros/as)	oiréis
(ellos/ellas/ustedes)	oirán

CONDITIONAL

(yo)	oiría
(tú)	oirías
(él/ella/usted)	oiría
(nosotros/as)	oiríamos
(vosotros/as)	oiríais
(ellos/ellas/ustedes)	oirían

IMPERATIVE

oye / oíd

PAST PARTICIPLE

oído

GERUND

oyendo

EXAMPLE PHRASES

*No **oigo** nada.* I can't hear anything.
*Si no **oyes** bien, ve al médico.* If you can't hear properly, go and see the doctor.
*¿**Has oído** eso?* Did you hear that?

Remember that subject pronouns are not used very often in Spanish.

▶ **pedir** (to ask for)

PRESENT	
(yo)	pido
(tú)	pides
(él/ella/usted)	pide
(nosotros/as)	pedimos
(vosotros/as)	pedís
(ellos/ellas/ustedes)	piden

PRESENT SUBJUNCTIVE	
(yo)	pida
(tú)	pidas
(él/ella/usted)	pida
(nosotros/as)	pidamos
(vosotros/as)	pidáis
(ellos/ellas/ustedes)	pidan

PRETERITE	
(yo)	pedí
(tú)	pediste
(él/ella/usted)	pidió
(nosotros/as)	pedimos
(vosotros/as)	pedisteis
(ellos/ellas/ustedes)	pidieron

IMPERFECT	
(yo)	pedía
(tú)	pedías
(él/ella/usted)	pedía
(nosotros/as)	pedíamos
(vosotros/as)	pedíais
(ellos/ellas/ustedes)	pedían

FUTURE	
(yo)	pediré
(tú)	pedirás
(él/ella/usted)	pedirá
(nosotros/as)	pediremos
(vosotros/as)	pediréis
(ellos/ellas/ustedes)	pedirán

CONDITIONAL	
(yo)	pediría
(tú)	pedirías
(él/ella/usted)	pediría
(nosotros/as)	pediríamos
(vosotros/as)	pediríais
(ellos/ellas/ustedes)	pedirían

IMPERATIVE

pide / pedid

PAST PARTICIPLE

pedido

GERUND

pidiendo

EXAMPLE PHRASES

*No nos **pidieron** el pasaporte*. They didn't ask us for our passports.
***Hemos pedido** dos cervezas*. We've ordered two beers.
***Pídele** el teléfono*. Ask her for her telephone number.

Remember that subject pronouns are not used very often in Spanish.

▶ **pensar** (to think)

PRESENT

(yo)	pienso
(tú)	piensas
(él/ella/usted)	piensa
(nosotros/as)	pensamos
(vosotros/as)	pensáis
(ellos/ellas/ustedes)	piensan

PRESENT SUBJUNCTIVE

(yo)	piense
(tú)	pienses
(él/ella/usted)	piense
(nosotros/as)	pensemos
(vosotros/as)	penséis
(ellos/ellas/ustedes)	piensen

PRETERITE

(yo)	pensé
(tú)	pensaste
(él/ella/usted)	pensó
(nosotros/as)	pensamos
(vosotros/as)	pensasteis
(ellos/ellas/ustedes)	pensaron

IMPERFECT

(yo)	pensaba
(tú)	pensabas
(él/ella/usted)	pensaba
(nosotros/as)	pensábamos
(vosotros/as)	pensabais
(ellos/ellas/ustedes)	pensaban

FUTURE

(yo)	pensaré
(tú)	pensarás
(él/ella/usted)	pensará
(nosotros/as)	pensaremos
(vosotros/as)	pensaréis
(ellos/ellas/ustedes)	pensarán

CONDITIONAL

(yo)	pensaría
(tú)	pensarías
(él/ella/usted)	pensaría
(nosotros/as)	pensaríamos
(vosotros/as)	pensaríais
(ellos/ellas/ustedes)	pensarían

IMPERATIVE

piensa / pensad

PAST PARTICIPLE

pensado

GERUND

pensando

EXAMPLE PHRASES

*No lo **pienses** más*. Don't think any more about it.
***Está pensando** en comprarse un piso*. He's thinking of buying a flat.
***Pensaba** que vendrías*. I thought you'd come.

Remember that subject pronouns are not used very often in Spanish.

▶ **poder** (to be able to)

PRESENT		PRESENT SUBJUNCTIVE	
(yo)	puedo	(yo)	pueda
(tú)	puedes	(tú)	puedas
(él/ella/usted)	puede	(él/ella/usted)	pueda
(nosotros/as)	podemos	(nosotros/as)	podamos
(vosotros/as)	podéis	(vosotros/as)	podáis
(ellos/ellas/ustedes)	pueden	(ellos/ellas/ustedes)	puedan

PRETERITE		IMPERFECT	
(yo)	pude	(yo)	podía
(tú)	pudiste	(tú)	podías
(él/ella/usted)	pudo	(él/ella/usted)	podía
(nosotros/as)	pudimos	(nosotros/as)	podíamos
(vosotros/as)	pudisteis	(vosotros/as)	podíais
(ellos/ellas/ustedes)	pudieron	(ellos/ellas/ustedes)	podían

FUTURE		CONDITIONAL	
(yo)	podré	(yo)	podría
(tú)	podrás	(tú)	podrías
(él/ella/usted)	podrá	(él/ella/usted)	podría
(nosotros/as)	podremos	(nosotros/as)	podríamos
(vosotros/as)	podréis	(vosotros/as)	podríais
(ellos/ellas/ustedes)	podrán	(ellos/ellas/ustedes)	podrían

IMPERATIVE	PAST PARTICIPLE
puede / poded	podido

GERUND

pudiendo

EXAMPLE PHRASES

¿*Puedo* entrar? Can I come in?
Puedes venir cuando quieras. You can come when you like.
¿*Podrías* ayudarme? Could you help me?

Remember that subject pronouns are not used very often in Spanish.

▶ **poner** (to put)

PRESENT

(yo)	pongo
(tú)	pones
(él/ella/usted)	pone
(nosotros/as)	ponemos
(vosotros/as)	ponéis
(ellos/ellas/ustedes)	ponen

PRESENT SUBJUNCTIVE

(yo)	ponga
(tú)	pongas
(él/ella/usted)	ponga
(nosotros/as)	pongamos
(vosotros/as)	pongáis
(ellos/ellas/ustedes)	pongan

PRETERITE

(yo)	puse
(tú)	pusiste
(él/ella/usted)	puso
(nosotros/as)	pusimos
(vosotros/as)	pusisteis
(ellos/ellas/ustedes)	pusieron

IMPERFECT

(yo)	ponía
(tú)	ponías
(él/ella/usted)	ponía
(nosotros/as)	poníamos
(vosotros/as)	poníais
(ellos/ellas/ustedes)	ponían

FUTURE

(yo)	pondré
(tú)	pondrás
(él/ella/usted)	pondrá
(nosotros/as)	pondremos
(vosotros/as)	pondréis
(ellos/ellas/ustedes)	pondrán

CONDITIONAL

(yo)	pondría
(tú)	pondrías
(él/ella/usted)	pondría
(nosotros/as)	pondríamos
(vosotros/as)	pondríais
(ellos/ellas/ustedes)	pondrían

IMPERATIVE

pon / poned

PAST PARTICIPLE

puesto

GERUND

poniendo

EXAMPLE PHRASES

Ponlo ahí encima. Put it on there.
Lo pondré aquí. I'll put it here.
Todos nos pusimos de acuerdo. We all agreed.

Remember that subject pronouns are not used very often in Spanish.

▶ **querer** (to want, to love)

PRESENT		PRESENT SUBJUNCTIVE	
(yo)	quiero	(yo)	quiera
(tú)	quieres	(tú)	quieras
(él/ella/usted)	quiere	(él/ella/usted)	quiera
(nosotros/as)	queremos	(nosotros/as)	queramos
(vosotros/as)	queréis	(vosotros/as)	queráis
(ellos/ellas/ustedes)	quieren	(ellos/ellas/ustedes)	quieran

PRETERITE		IMPERFECT	
(yo)	quise	(yo)	quería
(tú)	quisiste	(tú)	querías
(él/ella/usted)	quiso	(él/ella/usted)	quería
(nosotros/as)	quisimos	(nosotros/as)	queríamos
(vosotros/as)	quisisteis	(vosotros/as)	queríais
(ellos/ellas/ustedes)	quisieron	(ellos/ellas/ustedes)	querían

FUTURE		CONDITIONAL	
(yo)	querré	(yo)	querría
(tú)	querrás	(tú)	querrías
(él/ella/usted)	querrá	(él/ella/usted)	querría
(nosotros/as)	querremos	(nosotros/as)	querríamos
(vosotros/as)	querréis	(vosotros/as)	querríais
(ellos/ellas/ustedes)	querrán	(ellos/ellas/ustedes)	querrían

IMPERATIVE

quiere / quered

PAST PARTICIPLE

querido

GERUND

queriendo

EXAMPLE PHRASES

Te **quiero**. I love you.
Quisiera preguntar una cosa. I'd like to ask something.
No **quería** decírmelo. She didn't want to tell me.

Remember that subject pronouns are not used very often in Spanish.

▶ **saber** (to know)

		PRESENT
PRESENT		
(yo)	sé	
(tú)	sabes	
(él/ella/usted)	sabe	
(nosotros/as)	sabemos	
(vosotros/as)	sabéis	
(ellos/ellas/ustedes)	saben	

PRESENT

PRESENT

(yo)	sé
(tú)	sabes
(él/ella/usted)	sabe
(nosotros/as)	sabemos
(vosotros/as)	sabéis
(ellos/ellas/ustedes)	saben

PRESENT SUBJUNCTIVE

(yo)	sepa
(tú)	sepas
(él/ella/usted)	sepa
(nosotros/as)	sepamos
(vosotros/as)	sepáis
(ellos/ellas/ustedes)	sepan

PRETERITE

(yo)	supe
(tú)	supiste
(él/ella/usted)	supo
(nosotros/as)	supimos
(vosotros/as)	supisteis
(ellos/ellas/ustedes)	supieron

IMPERFECT

(yo)	sabía
(tú)	sabías
(él/ella/usted)	sabía
(nosotros/as)	sabíamos
(vosotros/as)	sabíais
(ellos/ellas/ustedes)	sabían

FUTURE

(yo)	sabré
(tú)	sabrás
(él/ella/usted)	sabrá
(nosotros/as)	sabremos
(vosotros/as)	sabréis
(ellos/ellas/ustedes)	sabrán

CONDITIONAL

(yo)	sabría
(tú)	sabrías
(él/ella/usted)	sabría
(nosotros/as)	sabríamos
(vosotros/as)	sabríais
(ellos/ellas/ustedes)	sabrían

IMPERATIVE

sabe / sabed

PAST PARTICIPLE

sabido

GERUND

sabiendo

EXAMPLE PHRASES

*No lo **sé**.* I don't know.
*¿**Sabes** una cosa?* Do you know what?
*Pensaba que lo **sabías**.* I thought you knew.

Remember that subject pronouns are not used very often in Spanish.

▶ **seguir** (to follow)

PRESENT

(yo)	sigo
(tú)	sigues
(él/ella/usted)	sigue
(nosotros/as)	seguimos
(vosotros/as)	seguís
(ellos/ellas/ustedes)	siguen

PRESENT SUBJUNCTIVE

(yo)	siga
(tú)	sigas
(él/ella/usted)	siga
(nosotros/as)	sigamos
(vosotros/as)	sigáis
(ellos/ellas/ustedes)	sigan

PRETERITE

(yo)	seguí
(tú)	seguiste
(él/ella/usted)	siguió
(nosotros/as)	seguimos
(vosotros/as)	seguisteis
(ellos/ellas/ustedes)	siguieron

IMPERFECT

(yo)	seguía
(tú)	seguías
(él/ella/usted)	seguía
(nosotros/as)	seguíamos
(vosotros/as)	seguíais
(ellos/ellas/ustedes)	seguían

FUTURE

(yo)	seguiré
(tú)	seguirás
(él/ella/usted)	seguirá
(nosotros/as)	seguiremos
(vosotros/as)	seguiréis
(ellos/ellas/ustedes)	seguirán

CONDITIONAL

(yo)	seguiría
(tú)	seguirías
(él/ella/usted)	seguiría
(nosotros/as)	seguiríamos
(vosotros/as)	seguiríais
(ellos/ellas/ustedes)	seguirían

IMPERATIVE

sigue / seguid

PAST PARTICIPLE

seguido

GERUND

siguiendo

EXAMPLE PHRASES

Siga por esta calle hasta el final. Go on till you get to the end of the street.
Nos seguiremos viendo. We will go on seeing each other.
Nos siguió todo el camino. He followed us all the way.

Remember that subject pronouns are not used very often in Spanish.

▶ **sentir** (to feel)

PRESENT

(yo)	siento
(tú)	sientes
(él/ella/usted)	siente
(nosotros/as)	sentimos
(vosotros/as)	sentís
(ellos/ellas/ustedes)	sienten

PRESENT SUBJUNCTIVE

(yo)	sienta
(tú)	sientas
(él/ella/usted)	sienta
(nosotros/as)	sintamos
(vosotros/as)	sintáis
(ellos/ellas/ustedes)	sientan

PRETERITE

(yo)	sentí
(tú)	sentiste
(él/ella/usted)	sintió
(nosotros/as)	sentimos
(vosotros/as)	sentisteis
(ellos/ellas/ustedes)	sintieron

IMPERFECT

(yo)	sentía
(tú)	sentías
(él/ella/usted)	sentía
(nosotros/as)	sentíamos
(vosotros/as)	sentíais
(ellos/ellas/ustedes)	sentían

FUTURE

(yo)	sentiré
(tú)	sentirás
(él/ella/usted)	sentirá
(nosotros/as)	sentiremos
(vosotros/as)	sentiréis
(ellos/ellas/ustedes)	sentirán

CONDITIONAL

(yo)	sentiría
(tú)	sentirías
(él/ella/usted)	sentiría
(nosotros/as)	sentiríamos
(vosotros/as)	sentiríais
(ellos/ellas/ustedes)	sentirían

IMPERATIVE

siente / sentid

PAST PARTICIPLE

sentido

GERUND

sintiendo

EXAMPLE PHRASES

Siento mucho lo que pasó. I'm really sorry about what happened.
Sentí un pinchazo en la pierna. I felt a sharp pain in my leg.
No creo que lo **sienta**. I don't think she's sorry.

Remember that subject pronouns are not used very often in Spanish.

▶ **ser** (to be)

PRESENT

(yo)	soy
(tú)	eres
(él/ella/usted)	es
(nosotros/as)	somos
(vosotros/as)	sois
(ellos/ellas/ustedes)	son

PRESENT SUBJUNCTIVE

(yo)	sea
(tú)	seas
(él/ella/usted)	sea
(nosotros/as)	seamos
(vosotros/as)	seáis
(ellos/ellas/ustedes)	sean

PRETERITE

(yo)	fui
(tú)	fuiste
(él/ella/usted)	fue
(nosotros/as)	fuimos
(vosotros/as)	fuisteis
(ellos/ellas/ustedes)	fueron

IMPERFECT

(yo)	era
(tú)	eras
(él/ella/usted)	era
(nosotros/as)	éramos
(vosotros/as)	erais
(ellos/ellas/ustedes)	eran

FUTURE

(yo)	seré
(tú)	serás
(él/ella/usted)	será
(nosotros/as)	seremos
(vosotros/as)	seréis
(ellos/ellas/ustedes)	serán

CONDITIONAL

(yo)	sería
(tú)	serías
(él/ella/usted)	sería
(nosotros/as)	seríamos
(vosotros/as)	seríais
(ellos/ellas/ustedes)	serían

IMPERATIVE

sé / sed

PAST PARTICIPLE

sido

GERUND

siendo

EXAMPLE PHRASES

Soy español. I'm Spanish.
¿**Fuiste** tú el que llamó? Was it you who phoned?
Era de noche. It was dark.

Remember that subject pronouns are not used very often in Spanish.

▶ **tener** (to have)

PRESENT

(yo)	tengo
(tú)	tienes
(él/ella/usted)	tiene
(nosotros/as)	tenemos
(vosotros/as)	tenéis
(ellos/ellas/ustedes)	tienen

PRESENT SUBJUNCTIVE

(yo)	tenga
(tú)	tengas
(él/ella/usted)	tenga
(nosotros/as)	tengamos
(vosotros/as)	tengáis
(ellos/ellas/ustedes)	tengan

PRETERITE

(yo)	tuve
(tú)	tuviste
(él/ella/usted)	tuvo
(nosotros/as)	tuvimos
(vosotros/as)	tuvisteis
(ellos/ellas/ustedes)	tuvieron

IMPERFECT

(yo)	tenía
(tú)	tenías
(él/ella/usted)	tenía
(nosotros/as)	teníamos
(vosotros/as)	teníais
(ellos/ellas/ustedes)	tenían

FUTURE

(yo)	tendré
(tú)	tendrás
(él/ella/usted)	tendrá
(nosotros/as)	tendremos
(vosotros/as)	tendréis
(ellos/ellas/ustedes)	tendrán

CONDITIONAL

(yo)	tendría
(tú)	tendrías
(él/ella/usted)	tendría
(nosotros/as)	tendríamos
(vosotros/as)	tendríais
(ellos/ellas/ustedes)	tendrían

IMPERATIVE

ten / tened

PAST PARTICIPLE

tenido

GERUND

teniendo

EXAMPLE PHRASES

Tengo sed. I'm thirsty.
No **tenía** suficiente dinero. She didn't have enough money.
Tuvimos que irnos. We had to leave.

Remember that subject pronouns are not used very often in Spanish.

▶ **traer** (to bring)

PRESENT		**PRESENT SUBJUNCTIVE**	
(yo)	traigo	(yo)	traiga
(tú)	traes	(tú)	traigas
(él/ella/usted)	trae	(él/ella/usted)	traiga
(nosotros/as)	traemos	(nosotros/as)	traigamos
(vosotros/as)	traéis	(vosotros/as)	traigáis
(ellos/ellas/ustedes)	traen	(ellos/ellas/ustedes)	traigan

PRETERITE		**IMPERFECT**	
(yo)	traje	(yo)	traía
(tú)	trajiste	(tú)	traías
(él/ella/usted)	trajo	(él/ella/usted)	traía
(nosotros/as)	trajimos	(nosotros/as)	traíamos
(vosotros/as)	trajisteis	(vosotros/as)	traíais
(ellos/ellas/ustedes)	trajeron	(ellos/ellas/ustedes)	traían

FUTURE		**CONDITIONAL**	
(yo)	traeré	(yo)	traería
(tú)	traerás	(tú)	traerías
(él/ella/usted)	traerá	(él/ella/usted)	traería
(nosotros/as)	traeremos	(nosotros/as)	traeríamos
(vosotros/as)	traeréis	(vosotros/as)	traeríais
(ellos/ellas/ustedes)	traerán	(ellos/ellas/ustedes)	traerían

IMPERATIVE	**PAST PARTICIPLE**
trae / traed	traído

GERUND

trayendo

EXAMPLE PHRASES

*¿Has **traído** lo que te pedí?* Did you bring what I asked you to?

*No **trajo** el dinero.* He didn't bring the money.

***Trae** eso.* Give that here.

Remember that subject pronouns are not used very often in Spanish.

▶ **venir** (to come)

PRESENT

(yo)	vengo
(tú)	vienes
(él/ella/usted)	viene
(nosotros/as)	venimos
(vosotros/as)	venís
(ellos/ellas/ustedes)	vienen

PRESENT SUBJUNCTIVE

(yo)	venga
(tú)	vengas
(él/ella/usted)	venga
(nosotros/as)	vengamos
(vosotros/as)	vengáis
(ellos/ellas/ustedes)	vengan

PRETERITE

(yo)	vine
(tú)	viniste
(él/ella/usted)	vino
(nosotros/as)	vinimos
(vosotros/as)	vinisteis
(ellos/ellas/ustedes)	vinieron

IMPERFECT

(yo)	venía
(tú)	venías
(él/ella/usted)	venía
(nosotros/as)	veníamos
(vosotros/as)	veníais
(ellos/ellas/ustedes)	venían

FUTURE

(yo)	vendré
(tú)	vendrás
(él/ella/usted)	vendrá
(nosotros/as)	vendremos
(vosotros/as)	vendréis
(ellos/ellas/ustedes)	vendrán

CONDITIONAL

(yo)	vendría
(tú)	vendrías
(él/ella/usted)	vendría
(nosotros/as)	vendríamos
(vosotros/as)	vendríais
(ellos/ellas/ustedes)	vendrían

IMPERATIVE

ven / venid

PAST PARTICIPLE

venido

GERUND

viniendo

EXAMPLE PHRASES

Vengo *andando desde la playa.* I've walked all the way from the beach.
*¿***Vendrás** *conmigo al cine?* Will you come to the cinema with me?
Prefiero que no **venga**. I'd rather he didn't come.

Remember that subject pronouns are not used very often in Spanish.

▶ **ver** (to see)

PRESENT

(yo)	veo
(tú)	ves
(él/ella/usted)	ve
(nosotros/as)	vemos
(vosotros/as)	veis
(ellos/ellas/ustedes)	ven

PRESENT SUBJUNCTIVE

(yo)	vea
(tú)	veas
(él/ella/usted)	vea
(nosotros/as)	veamos
(vosotros/as)	veáis
(ellos/ellas/ustedes)	vean

PRETERITE

(yo)	vi
(tú)	viste
(él/ella/usted)	vio
(nosotros/as)	vimos
(vosotros/as)	visteis
(ellos/ellas/ustedes)	vieron

IMPERFECT

(yo)	veía
(tú)	veías
(él/ella/usted)	veía
(nosotros/as)	veíamos
(vosotros/as)	veíais
(ellos/ellas/ustedes)	veían

FUTURE

(yo)	veré
(tú)	verás
(él/ella/usted)	verá
(nosotros/as)	veremos
(vosotros/as)	veréis
(ellos/ellas/ustedes)	verán

CONDITIONAL

(yo)	vería
(tú)	verías
(él/ella/usted)	vería
(nosotros/as)	veríamos
(vosotros/as)	veríais
(ellos/ellas/ustedes)	verían

IMPERATIVE

ve / ved

PAST PARTICIPLE

visto

GERUND

viendo

EXAMPLE PHRASES

No **veo** muy bien. I can't see very well.
Los **veía** a todos desde la ventana. I could see them all from the window.
¿**Viste** lo que pasó? Did you see what happened?

Remember that subject pronouns are not used very often in Spanish.

▶ **vivir** (to live)

PRESENT

(yo)	vivo
(tú)	vives
(él/ella/usted)	vive
(nosotros/as)	vivimos
(vosotros/as)	vivís
(ellos/ellas/ustedes)	viven

PRESENT SUBJUNCTIVE

(yo)	viva
(tú)	vivas
(él/ella/usted)	viva
(nosotros/as)	vivamos
(vosotros/as)	viváis
(ellos/ellas/ustedes)	vivan

PRETERITE

(yo)	viví
(tú)	viviste
(él/ella/usted)	vivió
(nosotros/as)	vivimos
(vosotros/as)	vivisteis
(ellos/ellas/ustedes)	vivieron

IMPERFECT

(yo)	vivía
(tú)	vivías
(él/ella/usted)	vivía
(nosotros/as)	vivíamos
(vosotros/as)	vivíais
(ellos/ellas/ustedes)	vivían

FUTURE

(yo)	viviré
(tú)	vivirás
(él/ella/usted)	vivirá
(nosotros/as)	viviremos
(vosotros/as)	viviréis
(ellos/ellas/ustedes)	vivirán

CONDITIONAL

(yo)	viviría
(tú)	vivirías
(él/ella/usted)	viviría
(nosotros/as)	viviríamos
(vosotros/as)	viviríais
(ellos/ellas/ustedes)	vivirían

IMPERATIVE

vive / vivid

PAST PARTICIPLE

vivido

GERUND

viviendo

EXAMPLE PHRASES

Vivo en Valencia. I live in Valencia.
Vivieron juntos dos años. They lived together for two years.
Hemos vivido momentos difíciles. We've had some difficult times.

Remember that subject pronouns are not used very often in Spanish.

▶ **volver** (to return)

PRESENT

(yo)	vuelvo
(tú)	vuelves
(él/ella/usted)	vuelve
(nosotros/as)	volvemos
(vosotros/as)	volvéis
(ellos/ellas/ustedes)	vuelven

PRESENT SUBJUNCTIVE

(yo)	vuelva
(tú)	vuelvas
(él/ella/usted)	vuelva
(nosotros/as)	volvamos
(vosotros/as)	volváis
(ellos/ellas/ustedes)	vuelvan

PRETERITE

(yo)	volví
(tú)	volviste
(él/ella/usted)	volvió
(nosotros/as)	volvimos
(vosotros/as)	volvisteis
(ellos/ellas/ustedes)	volvieron

IMPERFECT

(yo)	volvía
(tú)	volvías
(él/ella/usted)	volvía
(nosotros/as)	volvíamos
(vosotros/as)	volvíais
(ellos/ellas/ustedes)	volvían

FUTURE

(yo)	volveré
(tú)	volverás
(él/ella/usted)	volverá
(nosotros/as)	volveremos
(vosotros/as)	volveréis
(ellos/ellas/ustedes)	volverán

CONDITIONAL

(yo)	volvería
(tú)	volverías
(él/ella/usted)	volvería
(nosotros/as)	volveríamos
(vosotros/as)	volveríais
(ellos/ellas/ustedes)	volverían

IMPERATIVE

vuelve / volved

PAST PARTICIPLE

vuelto

GERUND

volviendo

EXAMPLE PHRASES

*Mi padre **vuelve** mañana.* My father's coming back tomorrow.
*No **vuelvas** por aquí.* Don't come back here.
*Ha **vuelto** a casa.* He's gone back home.

Remember that subject pronouns are not used very often in Spanish.